THE 116TH CONGRESS, January 3, 2019–January 3, 2021

UNITED STATES HOUSE OF REPRESENTATIVES

2018 Election Results: Democrats gained control of the House*

Democrats: 233 | Republicans: 200 | Undecided: 2

Democrat

Republican

Undecided

UNITED STATES SENATE

2018 Election Results: Republicans retained control of the Senate*

Democrats: 45 | Republicans: 52 | Independents: 2

2 Democrats
2 Republicans
1 Democrat and 1 Republican
1 Independent and 1 Democrat
1 Independent and 1 Republican
1 Republican and 1 Undecided

*Data are based on election results as of November 26, 2018. Several races remained undecided pending recounts and runoff elections.

THIS REGISTRATION CODE GIVES YOU ACCESS TO

Ebook | InQuizitive

FOR *American Politics Today*, Sixth Edition

ACTIVATE YOUR REGISTRATION CODE!

1) Scratch the foil to view your code

2) Go to digital.wwnorton.com/amerpoltoday6
3) Follow the instructions to register your code

A code can be registered to only one user. Used codes are nontransferable and nonrefundable.

For more help, see the back of this card.

What if my code is scratched off?

You can purchase access at
digital.wwnorton.com/amerpoltoday6

What if I need more help?

For additional support, visit **support.wwnorton.com**

ISBN 978-0-393-67985-4

9 780393 679854

90000

American Politics Today

Sixth Edition

Sixth Edition

American Politics Today

William T. Bianco
Indiana University, Bloomington

David T. Canon
University of Wisconsin, Madison

W. W. NORTON & COMPANY • NEW YORK • LONDON

W. W. Norton & Company has been independent since its founding in 1923, when William Warder Norton and Mary D. Herter Norton first published lectures delivered at the People's Institute, the adult education division of New York City's Cooper Union. The firm soon expanded its program beyond the Institute, publishing books by celebrated academics from America and abroad. By midcentury, the two major pillars of Norton's publishing program—trade books and college texts—were firmly established. In the 1950s, the Norton family transferred control of the company to its employees, and today—with a staff of four hundred and a comparable number of trade, college, and professional titles published each year—W. W. Norton & Company stands as the largest and oldest publishing house owned wholly by its employees.

Editor: Laura Wilk
Project Editor: Linda Feldman
Associate Editor: Samantha Held
Assistant Editor: Anna Olcott
Editorial Assistant: Chris Howard-Woods
Managing Editor, College: Marian Johnson
Managing Editor, College Digital Media: Kim Yi
Production Manager: Ashley Horna
Media Editor: Spencer Richardson-Jones
Associate Media Editor: Michael Jaoui
Media Project Editor: Marcus Van Harpen
Media Editorial Assistant: Tricia Vuong
Marketing Manager, Political Science: Erin Brown
Design Director: Jillian Burr
Text Designer: Open, NY
Photo Editor: Catherine Abelman
Photo Researcher: Julie Tesser
Director of College Permissions: Megan Schindel
Permissions Associate: Elizabeth Trammell
Composition: Cenveo® Publisher Services
Manufacturing: Transcontinental Publishing
Permission to use copyrighted material is included on p. A57

Library of Congress Cataloging-in-Publication Data

Names: Bianco, William T., 1960- author. | Canon, David T., author.
Title: American politics today / William T. Bianco, Indiana University, Bloomington, David T. Canon, University of Wisconsin, Madison.
Description: Sixth Edition. | New York : W.W. Norton & Company, [2018] | Includes bibliographical references and index.
Identifiers: LCCN 2018046035 | **ISBN 9780393644319 (hardcover)**
Subjects: LCSH: United States-Politics and government-Textbooks.
Classification: LCC JK275 .B54 2018 | DDC 320.473-dc23 LC record available at https://lccn.loc.gov/2018046035

W. W. Norton & Company, Inc., 500 Fifth Avenue, New York, NY 10110
wwnorton.com
W. W. Norton & Company Ltd., 15 Carlisle Street, London W1D 3BS
234567890

For our families,
Regina, Anna, and Catherine,
Sarah, Neal, Katherine, and Sophia,
who encouraged, empathized, and
helped, with patience,
grace, and love.

About the Authors

William T. Bianco

is professor of political science at Indiana University, Bloomington. His research focuses on congressional institutions, representation, and science policy. He received his undergraduate degree from SUNY Stony Brook and his MA and PhD from the University of Rochester. He is the author of *Trust: Representatives and Constituents; American Politics: Strategy and Choice*; and numerous articles on American politics. His research and graduate students have received funding from the National Science Foundation and the National Council for Eurasian and East European Research. He has also served as a consultant to congressional candidates and party campaign committees, as well as to the U.S. Department of Energy, the U.S. Department of Health and Human Services, and other state and local government agencies. He was also a Fulbright Senior Scholar in Moscow, Russia, during 2011-12.

David T. Canon

is professor of political science at the University of Wisconsin, Madison. His teaching and research interests focus on American political institutions, especially Congress, and racial representation. He is the author of *Actors, Athletes, and Astronauts: Political Amateurs in the U.S. Congress; Race, Redistricting, and Representation: The Unintended Consequences of Black Majority Districts* (winner of the Richard F. Fenno Prize); *The Dysfunctional Congress?* (with Kenneth Mayer); and various articles and book chapters. He is the editor of the *Election Law Journal* and previously served as the Congress editor of *Legislative Studies Quarterly*. He is an AP consultant and has taught in the University of Wisconsin Summer AP Institute for U.S. Government & Politics since 1997. Professor Canon is the recipient of a University of Wisconsin Chancellor's Distinguished Teaching Award.

Contents in Brief

Contents

3. Federalism 70

4. Civil Liberties   102

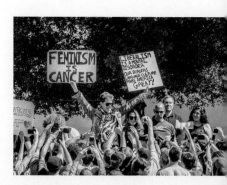

5. Civil Rights   148

Part II: Politics

6. Public Opinion   198

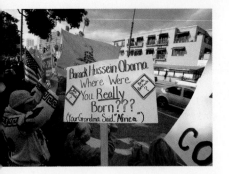

7. The Media   232

8. Political Parties 262

9. Elections 296

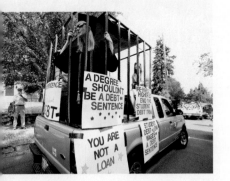

10. Interest Groups   340

Part III: Institutions

11. Congress   374

12. The Presidency   418

Part IV: Policy

15. Economic Policy 530

16. Social Policy 572

17. Foreign Policy 614

Appendix

Preface

This book is based on three simple premises: politics is conflictual, political process matters, and politics is everywhere. It reflects our belief that politics is explainable, that political outcomes can be understood in terms of decisions made by individuals—and that the average college undergraduate can make sense of the political world in these terms. It focuses on contemporary American politics, the events and outcomes that our students have lived through and know something about. The result, we believe, is a book that provides an accessible but rigorous account of the American political system.

American Politics Today is also the product of our dissatisfaction. Thirty years ago we were assistant professors together at the same university, assigned to teach the introductory class in alternate semesters. Though our graduate training was quite different, we found that we shared a deep disappointment with available texts. Their wholesale focus on grand normative concepts such as civic responsibility or their use of advanced analytic themes left students with little idea of how American politics really works, how events in Washington, D.C., affect their everyday lives, and how to piece together all the facts about American politics into a coherent explanation of why things happen as they do. These texts did not engender excitement, fascination, or even passing interest. What they did was put students to sleep.

As with previous editions, the overarching goal of the Sixth Edition is to describe what happens in American politics, but also to explain behavior and outcomes. In part we wish to counter the widespread belief among students that politics is too complicated, too chaotic, or too secretive to make sense of. More than that, we want to empower our students, to demonstrate that everyday American politics is relevant to their lives. This emphasis is also a response to the typical complaint about American government textbooks—that they are full of facts but devoid of useful information, and that after students finish reading, they are no better able to answer "why" questions than they were before they cracked the book.

In this edition, we maintain our focus on conflict and compromise in American politics—identifying what Americans agree and disagree about and assessing how conflict shapes American politics, from campaign platforms to policy outcomes. Though this emphasis seems especially timely given recent elections and the prospect of continued deadlock in Washington under a Trump presidency, our aim is to go beyond these events to identify a fundamental constant in American politics: the reality that much of politics is driven by disagreements over the scope and form of government policy, and that compromise is an essential component of virtually all significant changes in government policy. Indeed, it is impossible to imagine politics without conflict. Conflict was embedded in the American political system by the Founders, who set up a system of checks and balances to make sure that no single group could dominate. The Constitution's division of power guarantees that enacting and implementing laws will involve conflict and compromise. Furthermore, the Constitution itself was constructed as one long series of compromises. Accordingly, despite the general dislike people have for conflict, our students must recognize that conflict and compromise lie at the heart of politics.

Throughout the text, we emphasize common sense, showing students that politics inside the Beltway is often strikingly similar to the students' own everyday interactions. For example, what sustains policy compromises made by members of Congress?

The fact that the members typically have long careers, that they interact frequently with each other, and that they only deal with colleagues who have kept their word in the past. These strategies are not unique to the political world. Rather, they embody rules of thumb that most people follow (or are at least aware of) in their everyday interactions. In short, we try to help students understand American politics by emphasizing how it is not all that different from the world they know.

This focus on common sense is coupled with many references to the political science literature. We believe that contemporary research has something to say about prediction and explanation of events that students care about—and that these insights can be taught without turning students into game theorists or statisticians. Our text presents the essential insights of contemporary research, motivated by real-world political phenomena and explained using text or simple diagrams. This approach gives students a set of tools for understanding politics, provides an introduction to the political science literature, and matches up well with students' common-sense intuitions about everyday life. Moreover, by showing that academic scholarship is not a blind alley or irrelevant, this approach helps to bridge the gap between an instructor's teaching and his or her research.

The Sixth Edition builds on these strengths. We've continued to streamline and improve the presentation of text and graphics, and enhanced our "How It Works" sections. New chapter openers use contemporary stories and examples and offer quotations from people on both sides of the debate (from student loans to marijuana legalization) to highlight the conflict and compromise theme. We refer to these openers throughout the chapters to illustrate and extend our discussion. The "Take a Stand" sections now explicitly argue both sides of policy questions. We have also worked to place the Trump presidency in context, acknowledging the differences between Trump and other presidents, but also explaining how Trump's successes and failures, both in public opinion and in policy terms, can be explained using the same logic we have applied to previous presidents.

The text continues to be ruthlessly contemporary, but also places recent events in context. Although we do not ignore American history, our stress is on contemporary politics—on the debates, actions, and outcomes that most college students are aware of. Focusing on recent events emphasizes the utility of the concepts and insights that we develop in the text. It also goes a long way toward establishing the relevance of the intro class. The new edition discusses the acceptance of same-sex marriage, the debate over immigration reform, and debates over income inequality—all issues that Americans care about. We have also devoted considerable space to describing the 2016 and 2018 campaigns, working to show how recent contests at the presidential and congressional levels fit into a broader theory of how candidates campaign and how voters decide.

Finally, our book offers an individual-level perspective on America's government. The essential message is that politics—elections, legislative proceedings, regulatory choices, and everything else we see—is a product of the decisions made by real flesh-and-blood people. This approach grounds our discussion of politics in the real world. Many texts focus on abstractions such as "the eternal debate," "the great questions," or "the pulse of democracy." We believe that these constructs don't explain where the debate, the questions, or even democracy come from. Nor do they help students understand what's going on in Washington, D.C., and elsewhere, as it's not obvious that the participants themselves care much about these sorts of abstractions—quite the opposite, in fact.

We replace these constructs with a focus on real people and actual choices. The primary goal is to make sense of American politics by understanding why politicians, bureaucrats, judges, and citizens act as they do. That is, we are grounding our description of American politics at the most fundamental level—an individual facing a decision. How, for example, does a voter choose among candidates? Stated that way, it is reasonably easy to talk about where the choice came from, how the individual might evaluate different options, and why one choice might look better than the others. Voters' decisions may be understood by examining the different feasible strategies they employ (issue voting, retrospective evaluations, stereotyping, etc.) and by asking why some voters use one strategy while others use a different one.

By focusing on individuals and choices, we can place students in the shoes of the decision makers, and in so doing, give them insight into why people act as they do. We can discuss, for example, why a House member might favor enacting wasteful pork-barrel spending, even though a proposal full of such projects will make his constituents economically worse off—and why constituents might reward such behavior, even if they suspect the truth. By taking this approach, we are not trying to let legislators off the hook. Rather, we believe that any real understanding of the political process must begin with a sense of the decisions the participants make and why they make them. Focusing on individuals also segues naturally into a discussion of consequences, allowing us to move from examining decisions to describing and evaluating outcomes. In this way, we can show students how large-scale outcomes in politics, such as inefficient programs, don't happen by accident or because of malfeasance. Rather, they are the predictable results of choices made by individuals (here, politicians and voters).

The policy chapters in the Full and Essentials Editions also represent a distinctive feature of this book. The discussion of policy at the end of an intro class often fits awkwardly with the material covered earlier. It is supposed to be a culmination of the semester-long discussion of institutions, politicians, and political behavior, but instead it often becomes an afterthought that gets discarded when time runs out in the last few weeks of class. Our policy chapters explicitly draw on previous chapters' discussions of the actors that shape policy: the president, Congress, the courts, interest groups, and parties. By doing so, these chapters show how all the pieces of the puzzle fit together.

Finally, this book reflects our experience as practicing scholars and teachers, as well as interactions with more than twenty thousand students in introductory classes at several universities. Rather than thinking of the intro class as a service obligation, we believe it offers a unique opportunity for faculty to develop a broader sense of American politics and American political science, while at the same time giving students the tools they need to behave as knowledgeable citizens or enthusiastic political science majors. We hope that it works for you as well as it does for us.

Features of the Text and Media Package

The book's "three key ideas"

are fully integrated throughout the text.

- **Politics Is Conflictual** and conflict and compromise are a normal, healthy part of politics. The questions debated in elections and the policy options considered by people in government are generally marked by disagreement at all levels. Making policy typically involves important issues on which people disagree, sometimes strongly; so compromise, bargaining, and tough choices about trade-offs are often necessary.
- **Political Process Matters** because it is the mechanism we have established to resolve conflicts and achieve compromise. Governmental actions result from conscious choices made by voters, elected officials, and bureaucrats. The media often cover political issues in the same way they do sporting events, and though this makes for entertaining news, it also leads citizens to overlook the institutions, rules, and procedures that have a decisive influence on American life. Politics really is not just a game.
- **Politics Is Everywhere** in that the results of the political process affect all aspects of Americans' everyday lives. Politics governs what people can and cannot do, their quality of life, and how they think about events, other people, and situations.

New chapter openers and conclusions

present two sides of a controversy that has dominated media headlines—and about which people have passionate, emotion-driven opinions from both points of view—framed by quotes from politicians, pundits, and everyday people who hold these views. These include sanctuary cities (Federalism), free speech on college campuses (Civil Liberties), and the Deferred Action for Childhood Arrivals (DACA) program (Congress). The "Unpacking the Conflict" sections at the end of each chapter show how the nuts and bolts of the chapter topic can be applied to help students understand both sides of these debates.

New coverage of 2018 elections and Trump presidency

provides more than 20 pages and numerous graphics analyzing the 2016 and 2018 elections and the first two years of the Trump presidency, including coverage of current issues, such as the failure to pass "Trumpcare," executive actions around immigration, border security and international travel (and judicial responses), tax reform, marijuana policy, North Korea, and President Trump's use of social media.

Organization around chapter goals

stresses learning objectives and mastery of core material.

- **Chapter Goals** appear at the beginning of the chapter and then recur at the start of the relevant sections throughout the chapter to create a more active reading experience that emphasizes important learning objectives.

- **Extensive end-of-chapter review sections organized around the Chapter Goals** include section summaries, practice quiz questions, key terms, and suggested reading lists. Students have everything they need to master the material in each section of the chapter.

Special features for critical thinking

reinforce the three key ideas while introducing other important ways to think about American politics.

- **"How It Works: In Theory/How It Works: In Practice" graphics,** many new to this edition, highlight key political processes and structures and build graphical literacy. New discussions include the Supreme Court's decision on the Masterpiece Cakeshop (Civil Liberties) and passing the Tax Cuts and Jobs Act (Congress).
- **"What Do the Facts Say?" features** develop quantitative reasoning skills by teaching students to read and interpret data on important political issues and current events.
- **"Why Should I Care?" sections** draw explicit connections between the chapter material and students' lives.
- **"Did you know?" features and pull quotes** give students tidbits of information that may induce questions, anger, and may even inspire students to get involved.
- **"Take a Stand" features** address contemporary issues in a pro/con format and invite students to consider how they would argue their own position on the topic. Each feature concludes with two critical-thinking questions.
- **"Nuts & Bolts" features provide students with concise explanations of key concepts,** like the difference between civil liberties and civil rights, different kinds of gerrymanders, and brief summaries of campaign finance rules. These features provide an easy way for quick study and review.

Tools for a dynamic classroom

- **InQuizitive, Norton's adaptive learning tool,** accompanies the Sixth Edition of *American Politics Today* and reinforces reading comprehension with a focus on the foundations of government and major political science concepts. Guiding feedback helps students understand why their answers were right or wrong and steers them back to the text. Norton recently conducted a within-subjects efficacy study in American government, and among the students who did not earn a perfect score on the pre-test, we saw an average InQuizitive Effect of 17 percentage points. To try it out, go to https://digital.wwnorton.com/amerpoltoday6.
- **Features for your Learning Management System (LMS)** allow you to easily bring Norton's high-quality digital content into your existing LMS. The content is fully editable and adaptable to your course needs. The Norton Coursepack for *American Politics Today,* Sixth Edition, contains the following activities and quizzes:
    - **"How to Read Charts and Graphs" tutorial** that provides students with extra practice and guidance interpreting common representations of data that they will encounter in this textbook and in the world,
    - **Chapter quizzes** that assess student knowledge of each chapter's core concepts,
    - **Video exercises** that engage students and help them retain and apply information through real-world events,
    - **"How It Works: In Theory/How It Works: In Practice" animated graphics,** with assessment, that guide students through understanding political processes and institutions,

- **Simulations** that show students how concepts work in the real world,
- **"What Do the Facts Say?" activities** that give students more practice with quantitative skills and more familiarity with how political scientists know what they know, and
- **"Take a Stand" exercises** that present students with multiple sides of contemporary debates and ask them to consider and refine their own views based on what they've learned.
- **Test bank** contains more than 1,800 questions tagged to chapter-learning objectives and keyed to Bloom's taxonomy.
- **An Interactive Instructor Guide (IIG)** includes chapter outlines, class activities, and discussion questions, and suggestions for additional resources to engage students.
- **Instructor PowerPoints** contains fully customizable lecture slides with clicker questions and "How It Works: In Theory" and "How It Works: In Practice" animated PowerPoint slides for optimal classroom presentation.

Acknowledgments

This edition of *American Politics Today* is again dedicated to our families. Our wives, Regina and Sarah, have continued to accommodate our deadlines and schedules and have again served as our most accurate critics and sources of insight and inspiration. Our children have again been forced to contend with politics and textbook writing as a perennial topic of conversation in their visits home, and have responded with critiques and ideas of their own, which appear throughout the text.

Our colleagues at Indiana University and the University of Wisconsin (and before that, Duke University for both of us) provided many opportunities to talk about American politics and teaching this course.

Bill thanks his colleagues at Indiana University and elsewhere, including Christine Barbour, John Brehm, Ted Carmines, Chris DeSante, Mike Ensley, Bernard Fraga, Russ Hansen, Matthew Hayes, Yanna Krupnikov, Lin Ostrom, Regina Smyth, Will Winecoff, and Jerry Wright, for sharp insights and encouragement at crucial moments. He is also grateful to many teaching assistants who have helped him organize and teach the intro class at three universities. Finally, he thanks the students at the Higher School of Economics in Moscow, Russia, where he taught the introductory class as a Fulbright Scholar in 2012.

David gives special thanks to Ken Mayer, whose daily "reality checks" and consistently thoughtful professional and personal advice are greatly appreciated. Barry Burden, Ben Marquez, Don Moynihan, Ryan Owens, Ellie Powell, Howard Schweber, Byron Shafer, Alex Tahk, Dave Weimer, Kathy Cramer, Susan Yackee, and all the great people at Wisconsin have provided a wonderful community within which to teach and research American politics. John Coleman, who has moved on to become a dean at the University of Minnesota, also deserves special thanks as a former member of the intro American team and good friend and colleague. David would also like to thank the students at the University of Debrecen in Hungary, where he taught American politics as a Fulbright Scholar in 2003–2004, and the Eberhard Karls University of Tübingen, Germany, where he taught as a Fulbright Scholar in 2011–2012. The Hungarian students' unique perspective on democracy, civil liberties, and the role of government required David to think about American politics in a different way. The German students' views on the role of political parties, campaigns, and the social welfare state also provided a strong contrast to the views of his American students.

Both of us are grateful to the political science faculty at Duke University, who, in addition to giving us our first academic jobs, worked to construct a hospitable and invigorating place to research and to teach. In particular, Rom Coles, Ruth Grant, John Aldrich, Tom Spragens, Taylor Cole, and David Barber were model teachers, colleagues, and scholars. We both learned to teach by watching them, and we are better instructors and scholars for it.

We are indebted to the outstanding people at W. W. Norton who have been our full partners through all six editions. Peter Lesser's relentless combination of wit, insight, and expertise is evident throughout the book, as are the talents of our new editor, Laura Wilk. The organization and prose of the book has been improved immeasurably by Sam Held's editing. Steve Dunn was responsible for getting the process started and providing good counsel from beginning to end.

Roby Harrington has been a source of constant encouragement and feedback. Linda Feldman has been a superb project editor, bringing to the project her talent for clarity of words and visuals. Cat Abelman put together an excellent photo program. Elizabeth Trammell cleared permissions for the figures and tables. Ashley Horna handled production with efficiency and good humor. Jillian Burr and Open design studio created a beautiful design for the book's interior and cover. Spencer Richardson-Jones and Michael Jaoui's clear vision for the ever-more-complex and rich digital media package has been a major help. We also would like to thank Aaron Javsicas and Ann Shin for their outstanding work on earlier editions. The entire crew at Norton has been incredibly professional and supportive in ways we never knew when we started writing this book. Signing with them fifteen years ago was an eyes-shut home run.

We are also indebted to the many reviewers who have commented on the text.

First Edition Reviewers

Dave Adler, *Idaho State University*

Rick Almeida, *Francis Marion University*

Jim Bailey, *Arkansas State University-Mountain Home*

Todd Belt, *University of Hawaii at Hilo*

Scott Buchanan, *Columbus State University*

Randy Burnside, *Southern Illinois University, Carbondale*

Carolyn Cocca, *SUNY College at Old Westbury*

Tom Dolan, *Columbus State University*

Dave Dulio, *Oakland University*

Matt Eshbaugh-Soha, *University of North Texas*

Kevin Esterling, *University of California, Riverside*

Peter Francia, *East Carolina University*

Scott Frisch, *California State University, Channel Islands*

Sarah Fulton, *Texas A&M University*

Keith Gaddie, *University of Oklahoma*

Joe Giammo, *University of Arkansas at Little Rock*

Kate Greene, *University of Southern Mississippi*

Steven Greene, *North Carolina State University*

Phil Habel, *Southern Illinois University, Carbondale*

Charles Hartwig, *Arkansas State University, Jonesboro*

Ted Jelen, *University of Nevada, Las Vegas*

Jennifer Jensen, *Binghamton University, SUNY*

Terri Johnson, *University of Wisconsin-Green Bay*

Luke Keele, *Ohio State University*

Linda Keith, *The University of Texas at Dallas*

Chris Kelley, *Miami University*

Jason Kirksey, *Oklahoma State University*

Jeffrey Kraus, *Wagner College*

Chris Kukk, *Western Connecticut State University*

Mel Kulbicki, *York College*

Joel Lieske, *Cleveland State University*

Steve Light, *University of North Dakota*

Baodong (Paul) Liu, *University of Utah*

Ken Long, *University of Saint Joseph, Connecticut*

Michael Lynch, *University of Kansas*

Cherie Maestas, *Florida State University*

Tom Marshall, *The University of Texas at Arlington*

Scott McClurg, *Southern Illinois University, Carbondale*

Jonathan Morris, *East Carolina University*

Jason Mycoff, *University of Delaware*

Sean Nicholson-Crotty, *University of Missouri, Columbia*

Timothy Nokken, *Texas Tech University*

Sandra O'Brien, *Florida Gulf Coast University*

John Orman, *Fairfield University*

L. Marvin Overby, *University of Missouri, Columbia*

Catherine Paden, *Simmons College*

Dan Ponder, *Drury University*

Paul Posner, *George Mason University*

David Redlawsk, *University of Iowa*

Russell Renka, *Southeast Missouri State University*

Travis Ridout, *Washington State University*

Andy Rudalevige, *Dickinson College*

Denise Scheberle, *University of Wisconsin-Green Bay*

Tom Schmeling, *Rhode Island College*

Pat Sellers, *Davidson College*

Dan Smith, *Northwest Missouri State University*

Dale Story, *The University of Texas at Arlington*

John Vile, *Middle Tennessee State University*

Mike Wagner, *University of Nebraska*

Dave Wigg, *St. Louis Community College*

Maggie Zetts, *Purdue University*

Second Edition Reviewers

Danny Adkison, *Oklahoma State University*

Hunter Bacot, *Elon College*

Tim Barnett, *Jacksonville State University*

Robert Bruhl, *University of Illinois at Chicago*

Daniel Butler, *Yale University*

Jennifer Byrne, *James Madison University*

Jason Casellas, *The University of Texas at Austin*

Jeffrey Christiansen, *Seminole State College*

Richard Conley, *University of Florida*

Michael Crespin, *University of Georgia*

Brian DiSarro, *California State University, Sacramento*

Ryan Emenaker, *College of the Redwoods*

John Evans, *California State University, Northridge*

John Fliter, *Kansas State University*

Jimmy Gleason, *Purdue University*

Dana Glencross, *Oklahoma City Community College*

Jeannie Grussendorf, *Georgia State University*

Phil Habel, *Southern Illinois University, Carbondale*

Lori Han, *Chapman University*

Katy Harriger, *Wake Forest University*

Richard Himelfarb, *Hofstra University*

Doug Imig, *University of Memphis*

Daniel Klinghard, *College of the Holy Cross*

Eddie Meaders, *University of North Texas*

Kristy Michaud, *California State University, Northridge*

Kris Miler, *University of Illinois at Urbana-Champaign*

Melinda Mueller, *Eastern Illinois University*

Michael Mundt, *Oakton Community College*

Emily Neff-Sharum, *The University of North Carolina at Pembroke*

David Nice, *Washington State University*

Tim Nokken, *Texas Tech University*

Stephen Nuño, *Northern Arizona University*

Richard Powell, *University of Maine, Orono*

Travis Ridout, *Washington State University*

Sara Rinfret, *University of Wisconsin-Green Bay*

Martin Saiz, *California State University, Northridge*

Gabriel Ramon Sanchez, *University of New Mexico*

Charles Shipan, *University of Michigan*

Dan Smith, *Northwest Missouri State University*

Rachel Sondheimer, *United States Military Academy*

Chris Soper, *Pepperdine University*

Walt Stone, *University of California, Davis*

Greg Streich, *University of Central Missouri*

Charles Walcott, *Virginia Tech*

Rick Waterman, *University of Kentucky*

Edward Weber, *Washington State University*

Jack Wright, *Ohio State University*

Third Edition Reviewers

Steve Anthony, *Georgia State University*

Marcos Arandia, *North Lake College*

Richard Barberio, *SUNY Oneonta*

Jody Baumgartner, *East Carolina University*

Brian Berry, *The University of Texas at Dallas*

David Birch, *Lone Star College-Tomball*

Eileen Burgin, *University of Vermont*

Randolph Burnside, *Southern Illinois University, Carbondale*

Kim Casey, *Northwest Missouri State University*

Christopher Chapp, *University of Wisconsin-Whitewater*

Daniel Coffey, *University of Akron*

William Corbett, *The University of Texas at El Paso*

Jonathan Day, *Western Illinois University*

Rebecca Deen, *The University of Texas at Arlington*

Brian DiSarro, *California State University, Sacramento*

Nelson Dometrius, *Texas Tech University*

Stan Dupree, *College of the Desert*

David Edwards, *The University of Texas at Austin*

Ryan Emenaker, *College of the Redwoods*

John Evans, *University of Wisconsin-Eau Claire*

Brandon Franke, *Blinn College, Bryan*

Rodd Freitag, *University of Wisconsin-Eau Claire*

Donna Godwin, *Trinity Valley Community College*

Craig Goodman, *Texas Tech University*

Amy Gossett, *Lincoln University*

Tobin Grant, *Southern Illinois University*

Stephanie Hallock, *Harford Community College*

Alexander Hogan, *Lone Star College-CyFair*

Marvin King, *University of Mississippi*

Timothy LaPira, *James Madison University*

Mary Linder, *Grayson University*

Christine Lipsmeyer, *Texas A&M University*

Michael Lyons, *Utah State University*

Jill Marshall, *The University of Texas at Arlington*

Thomas Masterson, *Butte College*
Daniel Matisoff, *Georgia Institute of Technology*
Jason McDaniel, *San Francisco State University*
Mark McKenzie, *Texas Tech University*
Leonard McNeil, *Contra Costa College*
Melissa Merry, *University of Louisville*
Ann Mezzell, *Lincoln University*
Eric Miller, *Blinn College, Bryan*
Jonathan Morris, *East Carolina University*
Leah Murray, *Weber State University*
Farzeen Nasri, *Ventura College*
Brian Newman, *Pepperdine University*
David Nice, *Washington State University*
Stephen Nichols, *California State University San Marcos*

Tim Nokken, *Texas Tech University*
Barbara Norrander, *University of Arizona*
Andrew Reeves, *Boston University*
Michelle Rodriguez, *San Diego Mesa College*
Dan Smith, *Northwest Missouri State University*
Christopher Soper, *Pepperdine University*
Jim Startin, *The University of Texas at San Antonio*
Jeffrey Stonecash, *Syracuse University*
Linda Trautman, *Ohio University*
Kevin Unter, *University of Louisiana Monroe*
Michelle Wade, *Northwest Missouri State University*
Michael Wagner, *University of Nebraska-Lincoln*
Adam Warber, *Clemson University*
Wayne Wolf, *South Suburban College*

Fourth Edition Reviewers

Rickert Althaus, *Southeast Missouri State University*
Eric K. Austin, *Montana State University*
Evelyn Ballard, *Houston Community College Southeast*
Jim Battista, *University at Buffalo, SUNY*
Kenneth C. Blanchard Jr., *Northern State University*
Heidi Brockmann, *United States Military Academy*
Adriana Buliga-Stoian, *Mount Mercy University*
Abbe Allen DeBolt, *Sandhills Community College*
John C. Evans, *University of Wisconsin-Eau Claire*
Babette Faehmel, *Schenectady County Community College*
Daniel Fuerstman, *State College of Florida*
Stephanie Hallock, *Harford Community College*
John Hitt, *North Lake College*
Debra Jenke, *Angelina College*
Ronald A. Kuykendall, *Trident Technical College*
Paul Lewis, *Arizona State University*
Mary Linder, *Grayson College*
Michael Lyons, *Utah State University*

Wendy Martinek, *Binghamton University, SUNY*
Melissa Merry, *University of Louisville*
Javan "J. D." Mesnard, *Mesa Community College*
Monique Mironesco, *University of Hawai'i-West O'ahu*
Tim Nokken, *Texas Tech University*
David Parker, *Montana State University*
Sylvia Peregrino, *El Paso Community College*
Blayne Primozich, *El Paso Community College*
Bryan Rasmussen, *Collin College*
Suzanne M. Robbins, *George Mason University*
Susan Roomberg, *The University of Texas at San Antonio*
Michael Shamgochian, *Worcester State University*
Geoffrey Shine, *Wharton County Junior College*
Rachel Milstein Sondheimer, *United States Military Academy*
Gregory Streich, *University of Central Missouri*
Jeremy Teigen, *Ramapo College*
Dave Wells, *Arizona State University*

Fifth Edition Reviewers

Leslie Baker, *Mississippi State University*
Evelyn Ballard, *Houston Community College*
Jim Battista, *University at Buffalo, SUNY*
Nathaniel A. Birkhead, *Kansas State University*
William Blake, *Indiana University, Purdue University Indianapolis*

Kenneth C. Blanchard Jr., *Northern State University*
Michael P. Bobic, *Glenville State College*
Ben Christ, *Harrisburg Area Community College*
Rosalyn Crain, *Houston Community College, Northwest College*
Brian Cravens, *Blinn College-Schulenburg*

Stephanie R. Davis, *University of South Carolina*
Christi Dayley, *Weatherford College*
Justin B. Dyer, *University of Missouri*
Jonathan P. Euchner, *Missouri Western State University*
John W. Eyster, *University of Wisconsin-Whitewater*
Eddie Feng, *Weatherford College*
John P. Flanagan, *Weatherford College*
Peter L. Francia, *East Carolina University*
Daniel Fuerstman, *State College of Florida*
Willie Hamilton, *Mt. Jacinto College*
David Huseman, *Butler County Community College*
Debra Jenke, *Angelina College*
Catherine Johnson, *Weatherford College*
Joshua Kaplan, *University of Notre Dame*
Tim LaPira, *James Madison University*
Alan Lehmann, *Blinn College*

Morris Levy, *University of Southern California*
Michael S. Lynch, *University of Georgia*
Rob Mellen Jr., *Mississippi State University*
Timothy Nokken, *Texas Tech University*
Anthony O'Kegan, *Los Angeles Valley College*
Hyung Lae Park, *El Paso Community College*
Donna Rhea, *Houston Community College*
Joseph Romance, *Fort Hays State University*
Sam Scinta, *Viterbo University*
Michael Shamgochian, *Worcester State University*
Lenore VanderZee, *SUNY Canton*
Abram J. Trosky, *United States Coast Guard Academy*
Ronald W. Vardy, *Wharton County Community College; University of Houston*
Gordan Vurusic, *Grand Rapids Community College*
Jeremy Walling, *Southeast Missouri State University*

Sixth Edition Reviewers

Brent Andersen, *University of Maine at Presque Isle*
Nick Anspach, *York College of Pennsylvania*
Nick Beatty, *Missouri State University*
Todd Belt, *University of Hawaii*
Mark Brewer, *University of Maine*
Mark Checchia, *Old Dominion University*
Tom Copeland, *Biola University*
Todd Curry, *The University of Texas at El Paso*
Erin Engels, *Indiana University School of Liberal Arts at IUPUI*
Greg Granger, *Northwestern State University of Louisiana*
Jeanette Harvie, *California State University, Los Angeles*
Susan Haynes, *Lipscomb University*
Carol Jasieniecki, *Santiago Canyon College*
Alana Jeydel, *American River College*
Travis Johnston, *University of Massachusetts Boston*
Jesse Kapenga, *The University of Texas at El Paso*
Cassandra Khatri, *Lone Star College—University Park*
David Kimball, *University of Missouri—St. Louis*

Keith Knutson, *Viterbo University*
Julie Lane, *University of North Carolina Wilmington*
Tim LaPira, *James Madison University*
Beth Leech, *Rutgers University*
Eric Loepp, *University of Wisconsin—Whitewater*
Darrell Lovell, *Lone Star College—University Park*
Drew McMurray, *Wabash Valley College*
Melissa Merry, *University of Louisville*
Akira Ruddle Miyamoto, *University of Hawaii*
James Newman, *Southeastern Missouri State University*
Timothy Nokken, *Texas Tech University*
Stephen Northam, *University of North Georgia*
Hyung Park, *El Paso Community College*
Yuhua Qiao, *Missouri State University*
Jason Sides, *Southeastern Missouri State University*
Anand Edward Sokhey, *University of Colorado Boulder*
Herschel Thomas, *The University of Texas at Arlington*
Paul Weizer, *Fitchburg State University*
Maryann Zihala, *Ozarks Technical Community College*

It is a humbling experience to have so many smart people involved in the process of writing and revising this book. Their reviews were often critical, but always insightful, and you the reader are the beneficiaries of their efforts. In many cases, the improvements in this edition are the direct result of their suggestions. They have our profound thanks.

William T. Bianco
David T. Canon
November 2018

American Politics Today

Sixth Edition

In a democracy, oftentimes other people win.

— C. J. Cregg, *The West Wing*

1

Understanding American Politics

How does politics work and why does politics matter?

» **"The values of free expression and a reverence for the free press have been our global hallmark, for it is our ability to freely air the truth that keeps our government honest and keeps a people free."**
Senator Jeff Flake

« **"The Fake News is working overtime. Just reported that, despite the tremendous success we are having with the economy & all things else, 91% of the Network News about me is negative (Fake). Why do we work so hard in working with the media when it is corrupt? Take away credentials?"**
President Donald Trump

In October 2017, social media companies testified before the Senate Judiciary Committee on the spread of fake news through their platforms during the 2016 election. Fake advertisements like this one, in which a Twitter user encourages people to vote via text, were thought to have a detrimental effect on democratic processes in 2016. (Of course, you *can't* cast a vote by sending a text message.)

Early in 2018, Senator Jeff Flake, a Republican from Arizona, took to the floor of the Senate to make an impassioned defense of the freedom of the press in response to President Donald Trump's criticisms of the "Fake News" media.[1] He called out President Trump for labeling the media the "enemy of the people," noting that Joseph Stalin had used the phrase to silence dissent in the Soviet Union. He continued, "And, of course, the president has it precisely backward—despotism is the enemy of the people. The free press is the despot's enemy, which makes the free press the guardian of democracy. When a figure in power reflexively calls any press that doesn't suit him 'fake news,' it is that person who should be the figure of suspicion, not the press."[2] From this perspective, critical and even negative news coverage of political leaders is an essential part of democratic accountability—it is not fake news.

However, large majorities of the American public share the president's view on fake news. The conventional definition of fake news is the intentional portrayal of false information as

CHAPTER GOALS

Describe the basic functions of government.
pages 4–8

Define *politics* **and identify three key ideas that help explain politics.** pages 8–14

Identify major sources of conflict in American politics. pages 15–20

Explain how the American values of democracy, liberty, and equality work to resolve political conflict. pages 20–24

Understand how to interpret, evaluate, and use political information. pages 24–25 the truth. Ninety-four percent of Americans agree that this is fake news (48 percent say this is "always" fake news and 46 percent say it is "sometimes"). But 79 percent of Americans also believe fake news is an "accurate news story casting a politician or political group in a negative light," and 92 percent say that a story with inaccurate information based on sloppy fact-checking is also fake news. There are also significant partisan differences of opinion, with 17 percent of Democrats and 42 percent of Republicans thinking that accurate but negative stories about a politician are always fake news.[3]

Real fake news is simply deliberately made up, either as "click bait" to make money for the outlet that posted it or as an attempt to influence the outcome of an election. In the three months before the 2016 presidential election, BuzzFeed found that there were more total Facebook engagements (sharing, comments, and so on) with fake news (8.7 million) than with mainstream news (7.3 million). Top stories included "Pope Francis shocks world, endorses Donald Trump for president," and "WikiLeaks confirms Hillary sold weapons to ISIS ... Then drops another bombshell." Another story popularly known as "Pizzagate" alleged that Hillary Clinton was connected to a child sex ring being run out of a pizzeria in Washington, D.C. A few weeks after the election, a poll found that 9 percent of Americans believed the story and 19 percent were not sure if it was true (14 percent of Trump voters believed the story and 32 percent were not sure).[4]

Fake news and sloppy journalism are only two examples of the array of political information that Americans confront every day: from conflicting opinions of friends and family members, to partisan pundits arguing on cable news and Twitter, to official statements from the White House or Congress. The quandaries posed by fake news represent only a fraction of the decisions we must make regarding how to make sense of the political noise around us. In terms of fake news, the danger in confusing completely bogus stories with legitimate journalism that has factual errors or depicts a politician in a negative light is that it makes it much more difficult to sort out real news and objective information from news that is truly fake. Attacks on the media by politicians further undermine confidence in the news and polarize public opinion. It is difficult for the typical American to know if Jeff Flake or President Trump is right. If Americans can't even agree on which news is "fake," how can we know what to trust? How can we meaningfully understand, evaluate, and act on the political information that we encounter? A central goal of this book is to provide the tools you need to answer these questions.

DESCRIBE THE BASIC FUNCTIONS OF GOVERNMENT

Making sense of American government and politics

The premise of this book is simple: *American politics makes sense*. What happens in elections, in Washington, D.C., and everywhere else—even the Trump presidency—has a logical and often simple explanation; we just have to know how to look for it. By the end of this book, we hope you get really good at analyzing the politics you see everywhere—in the news and in your own life.

This claim may seem unrealistic or even naive. On the surface, American politics often makes no sense. Polls show strong support for extreme, unconstitutional, or downright silly proposals. Candidates put more time into insulting their opponents than making credible campaign promises. Members of Congress seem more interested in beating their political opponents than getting something done. Election outcomes look random or even chaotic. As we've just described, information from historically trusted national sources is labeled "fake news." And many policy issues, from reforming immigration policy to deciding what to do about climate change, seem hopelessly intractable.

Many people, we believe, are hostile toward American politics because they don't understand the political process, feel helpless to influence election outcomes or policy making, and believe that politics is irrelevant to their lives. Many people disliked both of the presidential candidates running in 2016 and saw this as more evidence that American politics does not work well. Since you are taking a class on American politics, we hope you have not given up on politics entirely. It is *not* our goal to turn you into a political junkie or a policy expert. You don't need to like politics to make sense of it, but we hope that after finishing this book you will have a basic understanding of the political process and why it matters.

One goal of this book is to help you take an active role in the political process. A functioning democracy allows citizens to defer complicated policy decisions to their elected leaders, but it also requires citizens to monitor what politicians do and to hold them accountable at the voting booth. This book will help you be an effective participant by providing the analytical skills you need to make sense of politics, even when it initially appears to make no sense at all.

We are not going to spend time talking about how American politics should be. Rather, our focus will be on explaining American politics as it is. Here are some other questions we will examine:

- Why don't people vote? Why *do* people vote? How do they decide who to vote for?
- Why do so many people mistrust politicians and the political system?
- Why can't Congress get things done?
- Why is the Supreme Court so political?
- Can presidents do whatever they want? Why can't they do more?
- How much power do bureaucrats have?
- Is the media biased?

We will answer these questions and many others by applying three key ideas about the nature of politics: politics is conflictual, political process matters, and politics is everywhere. But first, we begin with an even more basic question: Why do we have a government?

Why do we have a government?

As we prepare to address this question, let's agree on a definition: **government** is the system for implementing decisions made through the political process. All countries have some form of government, which in general serves two broad purposes: to provide order and to promote the general welfare.

government
The system for implementing decisions made through the political process.

To Provide Order At a basic level, the answer to the question "Why do we have a government?" seems obvious: without government there would be chaos. As the seventeenth-century British philosopher Thomas Hobbes said, life in the "state of nature" (that is, without government) would be "solitary, poor, nasty, brutish, and short."[5] Without government there would be no laws—people could do whatever they wanted. Even if people tried to develop informal rules, there would be no way to guarantee enforcement of those rules. Accordingly, some of the most important roles of government are policing and providing national security.

The Founders of the United States noted this crucial role in the Constitution's preamble: two of the central goals of government are to "provide for the common defense" and to "insure domestic Tranquility." The former refers to military protection against foreign invasion and the defense of our nation's common security interests. The latter refers to policing and law enforcement within the nation, which today includes the National Guard, the Federal Bureau of Investigation (FBI), the Department of Homeland Security, state and local police, and the courts. So at a minimal level, government is necessary to provide security.

However, there's more to it than that. The Founders cited the desire to "establish Justice . . . and secure the Blessings of Liberty to ourselves and our Posterity." But do we need government to do these things? It may be obvious that the police power of the nation is required to prevent anarchy, but can't people have justice and liberty without government? In a perfect world, maybe, but the Founders had a more realistic view of human nature. As James Madison, one of the founding fathers (and the fourth president of the United States), said, "But what is government itself, but the greatest of all reflections on human nature? If men were angels, no government would be necessary. If angels were to govern men, neither external nor internal controls on government would be necessary."[6] Furthermore, Madison continued, people have a variety of interests that have "divided mankind into parties, inflamed them with mutual animosity, and rendered them much more disposed to vex and oppress each other than to co-operate for their common good."[7] That is, without government, we would quickly be headed toward Hobbes's nasty and brutish state of nature because of differences in opinion about what society should look like. Having a government means that people cannot act unilaterally against each other, but it also creates a new problem: people will try to use the government and its powers to impose their views on the rest of society.

Madison's view of human nature might sound pessimistic, but it was also realistic. He assumed that people were self-interested: we want what is best for ourselves and for our families, and to satisfy those interests we tend to form groups with like-minded people. Madison saw these groups, which he called **factions**, as being opposed to the public good, and his greatest fear was of tyranny by a faction imposing its will on the rest of the nation. For example, if one group took power and established an official state religion, that faction would be tyrannizing people who practiced a different religion. This type of oppression is precisely why many of the early American colonists fled Europe in the first place.

As we will discuss in Chapters 2 and 3, America's government seeks to control the effects of factions by dividing government power in three main ways. First, the **separation of powers** divides the government into three branches—judicial, executive, and legislative—and assigns distinct duties to each branch. Second, the system of **checks and balances** gives each branch some power over the other two. (For example, the president can veto legislation passed by Congress; Congress can impeach the president; and the Supreme Court has the power to interpret laws written by Congress to determine whether they are constitutional.) Third, **federalism** divides power yet again by allotting different responsibilities to local, state, and national government. With power divided in this fashion, Madison reasoned, no single faction could dominate the government.

factions
Groups of like-minded people who try to influence the government. American government is set up to avoid domination by any one of these groups.

separation of powers
The division of government power across the judicial, executive, and legislative branches.

checks and balances
A system in which each branch of government has some power over the others.

federalism
The division of power across the local, state, and national levels of government.

To Promote the General Welfare The preamble to the Constitution also states that the federal government exists to "promote the general Welfare." This means tackling the hard problems that Americans cannot solve on their own, such as taking care of the poor, the sick, and the aged and dealing with global issues like climate change, terrorist threats, and poverty in other countries. However, government intervention is not inevitable—people can decide that these problems aren't worth solving. But if people *do* want to address these large problems, government action is necessary because **public goods** such as environmental protection or national defense are not efficiently provided by the free market, either because of **collective action problems** or for other reasons.

It is easy for two people or even a small group to tackle a common problem without the help of government, but 1,000 people (to say nothing of the more than 320 million in the United States today) would have a very difficult time. They would suffer from the **free rider problem**—that is, because it is in everyone's own interest to let someone else do the work, the danger is that no one will contribute, even though everyone wants the outcome that collective contributions would create. A government representing more than 320 million people can provide public goods that all those people acting on their own would be unable to provide, so people elect leaders and pay taxes to provide those public goods.

Collective action problems are common in modern society. Education provides a great example. You benefit personally from your primary, secondary, and college education in terms of the knowledge and experience you gain, and from the higher salary and better job you will earn because of your college degree. However, society also benefits from your education. Your employer will benefit from your knowledge and skills, as will people you interact with. If education were provided solely by the free market, those who could afford schooling would be educated, but the rest would not, leaving a large segment of society with little or no education and therefore unemployable. So public education, like many important services, benefits all levels of society and must be provided by the government for the general welfare.

Now that we understand *why* we have a government, the next question is: *What does the government do to "insure domestic Tranquility" and "promote the general Welfare"?* Many visible components of the government promote these goals, from the police and armed services to the Internal Revenue Service, Federal Reserve, Postal Service, Social Security Administration, National Aeronautics and Space Administration, Department of Education, and Food and Drug Administration. In fact, it is hard to find an aspect of everyday life that does not involve the government in some way, either as a provider of public goods, as a protector of civil liberties, as

public goods
Services or actions (such as protecting the environment) that, once provided to one person, become available to everyone. Government is typically needed to provide public goods because they will be under-provided by the free market.

collective action problems
Situations in which the members of a group would benefit by working together to produce some outcome, but each individual is better off refusing to cooperate and reaping benefits from those who do the work.

free rider problem
The incentive to benefit from others' work without making a contribution, which leads individuals in a collective action situation to refuse to work together.

Two important government functions described in the Constitution are to "provide for the common defense" and "insure domestic Tranquility." The military and local police are two of the most commonly used forces the government maintains to fulfill those roles.

an enforcer of laws and property rights, or as a regulator of individual or corporate behavior. What makes politics both interesting and important is that in most of these cases, Americans disagree on what kinds of public goods the government should provide, or whether government should be involved at all.

Forms of government

While all governments must provide order and promote the general welfare, different types of governments accomplish this in various ways. Greek political philosopher Aristotle, writing in the fourth century BC, developed a classification scheme for governments that is still surprisingly useful. Aristotle distinguished three pure types of government based on the number of rulers versus the number of people ruled: monarchy (rule by one), aristocracy (rule by the few), and polity (rule by the many, such as the general population).

Additional distinctions can be made within Aristotle's third type—constitutional republican governments—based on how they allocate power among the executive, legislative, and judicial branches. Presidential systems such as we have in the United States tend to follow a separation of power among the three branches, while parliamentary systems such as the one in the United Kingdom elect the chief executive from the legislature, resulting in much closer coordination between those two branches.

We can further refine Aristotle's third type by considering the relationships among different levels of government. In a federal system (such as the United States), power is shared among the local, state, and national levels of government. In a unitary system (such as France or Japan), all power is held at the national level, and local governments must comply with orders from the central government. A confederation (like Switzerland) is a less common form of government in which states retain their sovereignty and autonomy but form a loose association at the national level.

What is politics?

We define **politics** as the process that determines what government does—whether and how it provides different public and private goods. You may consider politics the same thing as government, but we view politics as being much broader; it includes ways of behaving and making decisions that are common in everyday life. Many aspects of our discussion of politics will probably sound familiar because your life involves politics on a regular basis. This may sound a little abstract, but it should become clear in light of the three key ideas of this book (see the How It Works graphic in this chapter).

First, *politics is conflictual*. The questions debated in election campaigns and in Washington and the options considered by policy makers generally involve disagreement at all levels. The federal government does not spend much time resolving questions that everyone agrees on the answers to. Rather, making government policy involves issues on which people disagree, sometimes strongly, which makes compromise difficult—and this is a normal, healthy part of politics. Although compromise may be difficult to achieve, it is often necessary to produce outcomes that can be enacted and implemented.

Second, *political process matters*. Governmental actions don't happen by accident—they result from conscious choices made by elected officials and bureaucrats. Politics

DEFINE *POLITICS* AND IDENTIFY THREE KEY IDEAS THAT HELP EXPLAIN POLITICS

politics
The process that determines what government does.

Three Key Ideas for Understanding Politics

Politics Is Conflictual

Conflict and compromise are natural parts of politics. Political conflict over issues like the national debt, abortion, and health care **reflects disagreements among the American people** and often requires compromises within government.

Political Process Matters

How political conflicts are resolved is important. Elections determine who represents citizens in government. **Rules and procedures determine who has power** in Congress and other branches of government.

Politics Is Everywhere

What happens in government affects our lives in countless ways. Policies related to jobs and the economy, food safety and nutrition, student loans, and many other areas shape **our everyday lives**. We see political information in the news and encounter political situations in many areas of our lives.

? Critical Thinking

1. **One implication of the idea that politics is conflictual is that politicians** may not want to negotiate compromises on important policy questions. Why do you think politicians sometimes refuse to compromise rather than work together to get things done?

2. **Think back to the discussion** of fake news at the beginning of this chapter. In what ways do disagreements over what constitutes "fake" news illustrate the three key ideas described here?

puts certain individuals into positions of power and makes the rules that structure their choices. The media often cover political campaigns the way they would report on a boxing match or the Super Bowl, focusing on the competition, rivalries, and entertaining stories, which can lead people to overlook the institutions, rules, and procedures that have a decisive influence on politics. Indeed, the political process is the mechanism for resolving conflict. The most obvious example of the political process at work is elections, which democracies use to resolve a fundamental conflict in society: deciding who should lead the country.

Third, *politics is everywhere*. Decisions about what government should do or who should be in charge are integral to society, and they influence the everyday lives of all Americans. Politics helps determine what people can and cannot do, their quality of life, and how they think about events, people, and situations. Moreover, people's political thought and behavior are driven by the same types of calculations and decision-making rules that shape beliefs and actions in other parts of life. For example, deciding which presidential candidate to vote for is similar to deciding which college to attend. For candidates, you might consider issue positions, character, and leadership ability, while for college you would weigh which school fits your academic goals, how much tuition you can afford, and where different schools are located. In both cases you are making a decision that will satisfy the criteria most important to you.

Politics is conflictual

Political scientists have long recognized the central role of conflict in politics. In fact, one prominent theory in the mid-twentieth century saw conflict between interest groups as explaining most outcomes in American politics. The political scientist E. E. Schattschneider argued that the scope of political conflict—that is, how many people are involved in the fight—determines who wins in politics.[8] Others have argued that some conflict is helpful for group decision making: if nobody challenges a widely shared but flawed view, people may convince themselves that the obvious flaws are not

Conflict is inherent in American politics. Here, supporters and opponents of same-sex marriage argue in front of the Supreme Court building in Washington on the day the Court heard arguments in *Obergefell v. Hodges*, the 2015 case that legalized same-sex marriage throughout the nation.

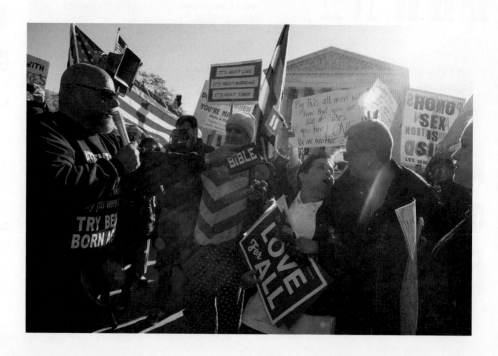

a problem.[9] Bureaucratic politics, congressional politics, elections, and even Supreme Court decision making have all been studied through the lens of political conflict.[10]

Despite the consensus that conflict in politics is inevitable, most people do not like conflict, either in their personal lives or in politics. You probably have heard people say that the three topics one should not discuss in polite company are money, religion, and politics. Indeed, political scientists have found strong evidence that people avoid discussing politics in order to maintain social harmony.[11]

Many people apply their disdain for conflict to politicians as well. "Why is there so much partisan bickering?" our students frequently ask. "Why can't they just get along?" This dislike of conflict, and of politics more generally, produces a desire for what political scientists John R. Hibbing and Elizabeth Theiss-Morse call "stealth democracy"—that is, nondemocratic practices such as running government like a business or taking action without political debate. In essence, this idea reflects the hope that everything would be better if we could just take the politics out of politics. Hibbing and Theiss-Morse argue that, to combat this belief, we need to do a better job of educating people about conflict and policy differences and that the failure to do so "is encouraging students to conclude that real democracy is unnecessary and stealth democracy will do just fine."[12] Conflict cannot be avoided in politics; ignoring fundamental disagreements will not make conflict go away.

The argument over abortion is a good example. Abortion rights have been a perennial topic of debate since a 1973 Supreme Court decision held that state laws banning abortion were unconstitutional. Surveys about abortion rights show that public opinion spans a wide range of policy options, with little agreement about which policy is best. (In Chapter 6, we will examine the political implications of this kind of broad disagreement.) Such conflicts reflect intense differences of opinion that are rooted in self-interest, ideology, and personal beliefs. Moreover, in such situations, no matter what Congress does, many people will be unhappy with the result. You might expect that politicians will ultimately find a compromise that satisfies everyone, but this is not always true. In many cases, no single policy choice satisfies even a slight majority of elected officials or citizens.

The idea that conflict is nearly always a part of politics should be no surprise. Situations in which everyone (or almost everyone) agrees about what government should be doing are easy to resolve: either a popular new policy is enacted or an unpopular issue is avoided, and the debate moves off the political agenda. Although issues where there is consensus resolve quickly and disappear, conflictual issues remain on the agenda as the winners try to extend their gains and the losers work to roll back policies. Thus, one reason that abortion rights is a perennial issue in campaigns and congressional debates is that there is no national consensus on when to allow abortions, no indication that the issue is becoming less important to citizens or elected officials, and no sign of a compromise policy that would attract widespread support.

An important consequence of the inevitable conflicts in American politics is that compromise and bargaining are essential to getting things done. Politicians who bargain with opponents are not necessarily abandoning their principles; striking a deal may be the only way to make some of the policy changes they want. Moreover, agreement sometimes exists even in the midst of controversy. For example, surveys that measure attitudes about abortion find widespread support for measures such as prohibiting government funding for abortions, requiring parental notification when a minor has an abortion, or requiring doctors who perform the procedure to present their patients with information on alternatives such as adoption, while only 15–25 percent (depending on the survey) think that abortion should always be illegal.[13]

Another consequence of conflict is that it is almost impossible to get exactly what you want from the political process. Even when a significant percentage of the

One consequence of political conflict is that one party's policy victories last only until the other party wins control of government. Here, President Trump signs a law repealing most of Dodd-Frank, an Obama-era measure that imposed new regulations on the banking industry in the wake of the 2008 financial crisis.

As long as the reason of man continues fallible, and he is at liberty to exercise it, different opinions will be formed.

—James Madison

population is united behind common goals—such as supporters of Donald Trump after the 2016 election, who demanded repeal of Obamacare—these individuals almost always find that translating these demands into policy change requires them to accept something short of their ideal. Hard-core Trump supporters, and Trump himself, for example, had to accept that there was not enough consensus in Congress (or support from American citizens) for an outright appeal of Obamacare. The need for compromise does not mean that change is impossible, but rather means that what is achievable often falls short of individuals' demands.

Political process matters

The political process is often described like a sporting event, with a focus on strategies and ultimately on "winning." In fact, the *National Journal* magazine regularly publishes a segment titled "Play of the Day" on its online site. This focus overlooks an important point: politics is the process that determines what government does, none of which is inevitable. Public policy—everything from defending the nation to spending on Medicare—is up for grabs. It is not just a game.

Elections are an excellent example of the importance of the political process. Elections allow voters to give fellow citizens the power to enact laws, write budgets, and appoint senior bureaucrats and federal judges. It matters who gets elected. After the 2016 election, which produced unified Republican control of the presidency and Congress, many Obama-era environmental and employment regulations were repealed, conservatives were appointed to the Supreme Court and other federal courts, corporate tax rates were cut, and the United States withdrew from the Paris Agreement on climate change. Clearly, political process matters: if the 2016 election had gone the other way, outcomes in all these important areas would have been significantly different.

Yet politics is more than elections. As you will see, many unelected members of the federal bureaucracy have influence over what government does by virtue of their roles in developing and implementing government policies. The same is true for federal judges, who review government actions to see if they are consistent with the Constitution and other federal laws. These individuals' decisions are part of the political process, even though they are not elected to their positions.

Ordinary citizens are also part of politics. They can vote; donate time or money to interest groups, party organizations, or individual candidates; or demand action from these groups or individuals. Such actions can influence government policy, either by

The political process mattered in the 2016 election, from determining who the candidates were, to affecting which states received the most attention from campaigns. Both Donald Trump and Hillary Clinton spent a lot of time campaigning in Pennsylvania in a bid to win the state's electoral college votes.

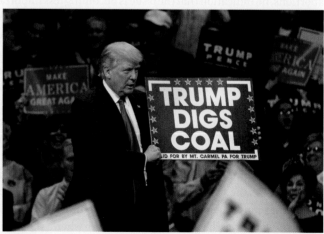

determining who holds the power to change policy directly or by signaling to policy makers which options have public support.

Another important element of politics is the web of rules and procedures that determines who has the power to make choices about government policy. These rules range from the requirement that the president must be born a U.S. citizen, to the rules that structure debates and voting in the House and the Senate, to the procedures for approving new federal regulations. Seemingly innocuous rules can have an enormous impact on what can or does happen, which means that choices about these rules are actually choices about outcomes. The ability to determine political rules empowers the people who make those choices.

I'll let you write the substance, you let me write the procedure, and I'll screw you every time.

—John Dingell

Politics is everywhere

Even though most Americans have little interest in politics, most of us encounter it every day. When you read the newspaper, watch television, go online, or listen to the radio, you'll almost surely encounter a political story. When you are walking down the street, you may see billboards, bumper stickers, or T-shirts advertising a candidate, a political party, an interest group, or an issue position. Someone may ask you to sign a petition. You may walk past a homeless person and wonder whether a winning candidate followed through on her promise to help. You may glance at a headline about violence in the Middle East and wonder if America should be sending in troops.

Many people have an interest in putting politics in front of us on a daily basis. Interest groups, political parties, and candidates work to raise public awareness of the political process and to shape what people know and want. Moreover, the news media offer extensive coverage of elections, governing, and how government policies affect ordinary Americans. Through efforts like these, politics really is everywhere.

Politics is also a fundamental part of how Americans think about themselves. Virtually all of us can name our party identification (Democrat, Republican, or Independent)[14] and can place our views on a continuum between liberal and conservative.[15]

Politics is everywhere in another important way, too: actions by the federal government touch virtually every aspect of your life. Figure 1.1 shows a time line for a typical college student on a typical day. As you can see, from the moment this

7:30	Wake up in dorm funded by federal program.
8:00	Eat cereal regulated by Food and Drug Administration.
8:15	Get dressed in clothing subject to import tariffs and regulations.
8:30	Read weather reports that use data from the National Weather Service.
9:00	Check e-mail using Internet developed with federal funding.
10:00	Drive to school in car whose design is shaped by federal regulations.
10:30	Drive past post office, military recruitment office, and environmental cleanup site.
11:00	Attend lecture by professor whose research receives federal funding.
4:00	Ride home from school on federally subsidized mass transit.
7:30	Pay bursar bill using federally funded student loan.
8:00	Call friend on cellular network regulated by the Federal Communications Commission.
10:00	Watch TV program on station that has federal license.

FIGURE 1.1

Government in a Student's Daily Life

On a typical day, the government plays a critical role in a student's daily life through federal programs, regulation, and spending. In addition to what is listed here, in what other aspects of your life does government play a part?

The idea that "politics is everywhere" means that government actions touch virtually all aspects of our lives, from regulating the business of Internet service providers to maintain net neutrality to mandating equal funding for men's and women's sports in high schools and colleges. Moreover, everyday life often helps us make sense of politics and politicians; for example, 2016 Republican presidential candidate and U.S. senator Ted Cruz's claim that *Star Trek*'s Captain Picard was a Democrat while Captain Kirk was a Republican gives nuance to who we understand Democrats and Republicans to be.

Just because you do not take an interest in politics does not mean that politics will not take an interest in you.

—Pericles (attributed)

student wakes up until the end of the day, his or her actions are influenced by federal programs, spending, and regulations. Moreover, this chart omits actions by state and local governments, which are very active in areas such as education policy and law enforcement. As you will see in later chapters, it's not surprising that the federal government touches your everyday life in many ways. The federal government is extraordinarily large regardless of whether you measure it in terms of spending (more than $4 trillion a year), number of employees (over 2 million, not including contract workers and Postal Service employees), or regulations (over 180,000 pages in the *Code of Federal Regulations*).[16]

Moreover, the idea that politics is everywhere has a deeper meaning: people's political behavior is similar to their behavior in the rest of their lives. For example, collective action problems occur when you live with roommates and need to keep common areas neat and clean. Everyone has an interest in a clean area, but each person is inclined to let someone else do the work. The same principles help us understand campus protests over tuition hikes, alcohol bans, or changes in graduation requirements in terms of which kinds of issues and circumstances foster cooperation. In each case, individual free riders acting in their own self-interest may undermine the outcome that most people prefer.

Similarly, convincing like-minded individuals to contribute to a political group's lobbying efforts is no easy task. Each would-be contributor of time or money also has the opportunity to be a free rider who refuses to participate yet reaps the benefits of others' participation. Because of these difficulties, some groups of people with common goals remain unorganized. College students are a good example: many want more student aid and lower interest rates on government-subsidized student loans, but they fail to organize politically toward those ends.

This similarity between behavior in political situations and in the rest of life is no surprise; everything that happens in politics is the result of individuals' choices. And the connections between politics and everyday life mean you already know more about politics than you realize.

"Why Should I Care?"

When you are trying to make sense of a political situation, think first of the three key ideas that we have just discussed. Focusing on conflict helps you understand what is at stake. Focusing on rules helps explain the strategies that participants use to achieve their goals. And the idea that politics is everywhere is there to remind you that conflicts over government policy are not things that happen only to other people—for better or worse, the outcome of political conflicts can touch virtually all aspects of our lives.

Sources of conflict in American politics

Where does political conflict come from? The reality is that conflict must be addressed in order to find compromise and enact policy. Sometimes, however, disagreements resist resolution because of inherent differences among people and their opinions about government and politics.

Economic interests

People's economic interests today vary widely, and they constitute a source of conflict in politics. In contrast, relative economic equality was a defining characteristic of our nation's early history—at least among white men—since small landowners, businessmen, craftsmen, and their families constituted a large majority of the nation's population. Compared with our European counterparts, the United States has, historically, been relatively free from class-based politics. Over time, our nation has become more stratified by class, to the point that the United States now has one of the highest levels of income inequality among developed nations. Nonetheless, a broad commitment to the **free market** (an economic system based on competition among businesses without government interference) and to *economic individualism* (the autonomy of individuals to manage their own financial decisions without government interference) remains central to our national identity.

Despite this basic consensus on economic principles and a history relatively free of class-based politics, there are important differences among American citizens, interest groups, and political parties in terms of their economic interests and favored economic policies. Democratic politicians and activists tend to favor more **redistributive tax policies** (that is, tax policies that attempt to create greater social equality, such as taxing the rich at higher percentages than the middle class or the poor) and social spending on programs for the poor. Democrats are also more inclined to regulate industry to protect the environment and ensure worker and product safety, but they tend to favor fewer restrictions on the personal behavior of individuals. Republicans favor lower taxes and less spending on social policies. They are also more supportive than Democrats of the free market and less inclined to interfere with business interests, although many Republicans favor regulation of individual behaviors, such as abortion, same-sex marriage, and marijuana consumption.

Cultural values

Another source of conflict in American politics is differing cultural values. For example, political analysts often focus attention on the **culture wars** in the United States between "red-state" Americans, who tend to have strong religious beliefs, and "blue-state" Americans, who tend to be more secular. (The color coding of the states comes from the election-night maps on television that show the states carried by Republican candidates in red and those won by Democrats in blue—but see the What Do the Facts Say? feature for a more nuanced take on this.)

free market
An economic system based on competition among businesses without government interference.

redistributive tax policies
Policies, generally favored by Democratic politicians, that use taxation to attempt to create social equality (for example, higher taxation of the rich to provide programs for the poor).

culture wars
Political conflict in the United States between "red-state" Americans, who tend to have strong religious beliefs, and "blue-state" Americans, who tend to be more secular.

Purple America: The 2016 Presidential Election

The media create maps of the country on election night with red states indicating where Republicans win and blue states where Democrats win, like the top map here. But what do we see if we look beyond the state level to the county level? And what if we look not just at who won and who lost, but which party was stronger relative to the other? This is what the bottom map, created by Robert Vanderbei at Princeton University, shows. The simple view of two Americas—Republican versus Democrat, red versus blue—starts to look a lot more purple.

Source: Provided by Robert J. Vanderbei, Princeton University, "2016 Presidential Election, Purple America," www.princeton.edu/~rvdb/JAVA/election2016 (accessed 11/14/16).

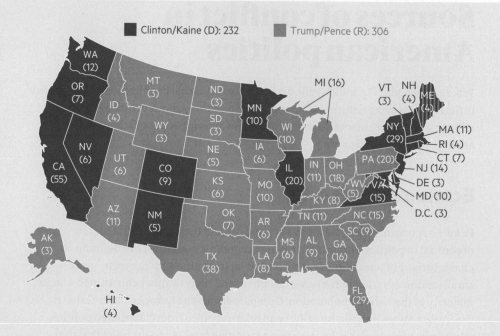

Clinton/Kaine (D): 232   Trump/Pence (R): 306

WA (12)
OR (7)
MT (3)
ND (3)
MN (10)
MI (16)
VT (3)
NH (4)
ME (4)
ID (4)
WY (3)
SD (3)
WI (10)
NY (29)
MA (11)
RI (4)
CT (7)
NV (6)
UT (6)
NE (5)
IA (6)
IL (20)
IN (11)
OH (18)
PA (20)
NJ (14)
DE (3)
MD (10)
CA (55)
CO (9)
KS (6)
MO (10)
KY (8)
WV (5)
VA (15)
D.C. (3)
AZ (11)
NM (5)
OK (7)
AR (6)
TN (11)
NC (15)
SC (9)
AK (3)
MS (6)
AL (9)
GA (16)
TX (38)
LA (8)
FL (29)
HI (4)

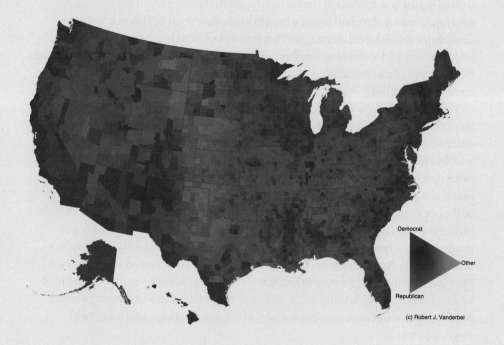

Democrat
Other
Republican
(c) Robert J. Vanderbei

Think about it

- **Which sections of the country were the strongest for Clinton, and which were strongest for Trump?**
- **In the bottom map, which areas are the most mixed (purple)?**
- **Over the next 20 years, the nation will become more racially and ethnically diverse. How do you think these maps will change in light of this growing diversity?**

The Supreme Court weighed in on a divisive cultural issue for Americans when it ruled that lower courts had to rehear a case involving a Colorado baker refusing to sell a wedding cake to a same-sex couple.

Although the precise makeup and impact of "values voters" is still debated, there is no doubt that many Americans disagree on cultural and moral issues. These include the broad category of "family values" (such as whether and how to regulate pornography, gambling, and media obscenity and violence); whether to supplement the teaching of evolution in public schools with intelligent design and creationism; same-sex marriage; abortion; school prayer; legalization of drugs; gun control; school vouchers; immigration policy, including allowing political refugees to enter the country; the federal Common Core curriculum for K–12 schools; and religious displays in public places. These are all hot-button issues that interest groups and activists on all sides attempt to keep at the top of the policy agenda.

Identity politics: racial, gender, and ethnic differences

Many political differences are correlated with racial, gender, and ethnic differences. For example, over the last generation about 90 percent of African Americans have been strong supporters of Democratic candidates. Other racial and ethnic groups have been less cohesive in their voting, with their support for a particular party ranging from 55 to 70 percent. Whites tend to vote Republican; Latinos tend to vote Democratic, with the exception of Cuban Americans, who tend to vote Republican; and Asian Americans tend to support Democrats with about 70 percent of the vote. A gender gap in national politics has also been evident in recent elections, with women being more likely to vote for Democrats and men for Republicans. Because these tendencies are not fixed, however, the political implications of racial, gender, and ethnic differences can change over time.

One of the enduring debates in American politics concerns whether ethnic and racial differences *should* be tied to political interests. One perspective reflects the melting pot image of America, which holds that as different racial and ethnic groups

Civil and voting rights contributed to the realignment of the South in the second half of the twentieth century, as more whites began supporting the Republican Party, and the Democratic Party came to be seen as the champion of minority rights. Here, blacks and whites in Alabama wait in line together to vote at a city hall after the enactment of the 1965 Voting Rights Act.

FIGURE 1.2

The Racial Composition of the United States

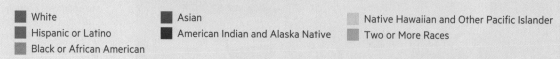

Only about 62 percent of Americans describe themselves as white. Moreover, the proportion of Hispanics and Latinos in the population is about 18 percent and rising, although this category contains many distinct subgroups. What changes would you expect in American politics and federal policy if the actual population in 2060 matches the projections?

- White
- Hispanic or Latino
- Black or African American
- Asian
- American Indian and Alaska Native
- Native Hawaiian and Other Pacific Islander
- Two or More Races

% of population

2015: 61.7 | 17.7 | 12.4 | 5.3 | 0.7 | 0.2 | 2.1

2060: 43.6 | 28.6 | 13.0 | 9.1 | 0.6 | 0.2 | 4.9

Source: Census data aggregated by author. Raw data available at www.census.gov/projections (accessed 6/21/16).

DID YOU KNOW?

One year after graduation, college-educated women working full time earn on average

7%

less than their male peers, even after controlling for differences in major, training, parenthood, hours worked, and other factors.
Source: American Association of University Women

come to this country, they should mostly leave their native languages and customs behind. This perspective focuses on assimilation into American culture, with the belief that while immigrant groups will maintain some traditions from their native country, our common bonds as Americans are more important. Supporters of this view usually advocate making English the country's official language, oppose bilingual public education, and, if they favor immigration at all, prefer that it be restricted to well-off people from English-speaking countries.

However, there are varied alternatives to the melting pot view. These range from racial separatists such as the Nation of Islam, whose members see white-dominated society as oppressive and discriminatory, to multiculturalists, who argue that there is strength in diversity and embrace a "tossed salad" version of assimilation (that is, each ingredient remains distinct but contributes to the overall quality of the salad).[17] In general, people holding this viewpoint favor less restrictive immigration laws and oppose policies that encourage immigrants to assimilate.

This debate over culture is one reason why recent discussions about immigration law have been so conflictual—the two sides start from very different premises about the value of diversity. But regardless of how this debate is resolved, our multiracial makeup is clear, as Figure 1.2 shows. In fact, trends in population growth suggest that by 2060 or so, whites will no longer constitute a majority of the U.S. population. The extent to which this diversity continues to be a source of political conflict depends on the broader role of race in our society. As long as there are racial differences in employment, education, health, housing, and crime and as long as racial discrimination is present in our society, race will continue to be a source of political conflict.

Many of the same observations apply to gender and politics. The women's movement is usually viewed as beginning in 1848 at the first Women's Rights Convention in Seneca Falls, New York. The fight for women's suffrage and legal rights dominated the movement through the late nineteenth and early twentieth centuries. Beginning in the 1960s and 1970s, feminism and the women's liberation movement highlighted a broad range of issues: workplace issues such as maternity leave, equal pay, and sexual harassment; reproductive rights and abortion; domestic violence; and sexual violence.

While progress has occurred on many fronts, including electing women to political office, gender remains an important source of political disagreement and identity politics. Though Hillary Clinton lost in 2016, the 116th Congress has more than 100 female House members and more than 20 female senators. Even so, these percentages are far lower than in the general population, and many other nations have a higher percentage of women in elected office. Gender politics became even more central in the first two years of President Trump's presidency, starting with the January 2017 Women's March, which drew between 3.3 and 4.6 million people in more than 500 U.S. cities, and continuing with the #MeToo movement that has drawn attention to sexual assault (see Chapter 5 for additional details on contemporary civil rights politics).

Ideology

Another source of differences in interests is **ideology**: a cohesive set of ideas and beliefs that allows an individual to organize and evaluate the political world. Ideology may seem most obviously related to political interests through political parties, since Republicans tend to be **conservative** and Democrats tend to be **liberal**. While this is true in a relative sense (most Republicans are more conservative than most Democrats), few Americans consider their own views ideologically extreme.[18]

Ideology shapes specific beliefs. Conservatives promote traditional social practices and favor lower taxes, a free market, and a more limited government, whereas liberals support social tolerance, stronger government programs, and more market regulation. However, the picture gets cloudy if we look more closely. **Libertarians**, for example, prefer very limited government—they believe government should provide for the national defense and should only have a few other narrowly defined responsibilities. Because they are at the extreme end of the ideological continuum on

ideology
A cohesive set of ideas and beliefs used to organize and evaluate the political world.

conservative
The side of the ideological spectrum defined by support for lower taxes, a free market, and a more limited government; generally associated with Republicans.

liberal
The side of the ideological spectrum defined by support for stronger government programs and more market regulation; generally associated with Democrats.

libertarians
Those who prefer very limited government and therefore tend to be conservative on issues such as social welfare policy, environmental policy, and government funding for education but liberal on issues involving personal liberty such as free speech, abortion, and the legalization of drugs.

Libertarians, including some of the very conservative members of the House Freedom Caucus, believe in very limited government. Representative Mark Meadows (R-NC, center), the chairman of the caucus, and other members of the caucus led the charge for an outright repeal of the Affordable Care Act.

this issue, libertarians are generally conservative in areas such as social welfare policy, environmental policy, and government funding for education and generally liberal on issues involving personal liberty such as free speech, abortion, and the legalization of drugs. For libertarians, the consistent ideological theme is limiting the role of government in our lives.

Personal ideologies are not always consistent. Someone can be both a fiscal conservative (favoring balanced budgets) and a social liberal (favoring the pro-choice position on abortion and marital rights for gay men and lesbians), or a liberal on foreign policy issues (supporting humanitarian aid and opposing military intervention overseas) and a conservative on moral issues (being pro-life on abortion and opposing stem-cell research). Ideology is a significant source of conflict in politics, and it does not always operate in a straightforward manner. In Chapter 6, we explore whether America is becoming more ideological and polarized, deepening our conflicts and making compromise more difficult.

Even so, there are clear areas of agreement in American politics, even on issues that once divided us. For example, while there is still considerable disagreement over same-sex marriage, public opinion has clearly shifted toward accepting these unions. Along the same lines, two generations ago Americans were divided on the legality of mixed-race marriage, while today very few people would object. Thus, even though conflict is a constant in American politics, it is wrong to say that we are divided into two groups, red and blue, that oppose each other on all issues of significance.

"Why Should I Care?"

The first step in understanding any political conflict is to determine who wants what. Who is involved? What do they, or their side, want? In modern American politics, citizens' demands are often connected to their economic interests, values, race, gender, ethnicity, and ideology. As a result, the group affiliations of individuals often tell us a lot about what they want from candidates and the government, and why they want it.

EXPLAIN HOW THE AMERICAN VALUES OF DEMOCRACY, LIBERTY, AND EQUALITY WORK TO RESOLVE POLITICAL CONFLICT

Resolving conflict: democracy and American political values

When we say that rules shape how conflicts are worked out in American politics, most of the time we are referring to formal (written-down) constraints that describe how the actions taken by each participant shape the ultimate outcome. For example, most American House and Senate elections are decided using plurality rule (whichever candidate gets the most votes wins), while a few states require winners to receive an absolute majority (50 percent + 1) of votes cast. However, some of the most important rules are not written down—these **norms** constitute America's political culture, or a collective idea of how a government and society should operate, including democracy, equality, and liberty.[19]

norms
Unwritten rules and informal agreements among citizens and elected officials about how government and society should operate.

Democracy

The idea of democracy means that policy disagreements are ultimately resolved through decisions made by citizens, such as their votes in elections. In the simplest terms, "**democracy**" means government by the people. As put into practice, this typically means representative democracy rather than direct democracy—that is, the people elect representatives who decide policies and pass laws rather than determining those things directly. There are some examples of direct democracy in the United States, such as the New England town meeting and the referendum process, through which people in a state directly determine policy.[20] But for the most part, Americans elect politicians to represent us, from school board and city council members at the local level, to state legislators and governors at the state level, to U.S. House members, senators, and the president at the national level.

democracy
Government by the people. In most contexts, this means representative democracy in which the people elect leaders to enact policies. Democracies must have fair elections with at least two options.

Democracy is not the only way to resolve conflict, nor do all societies have as strong a belief in democracy as in America. One mechanism used by authoritarian governments is to suppress conflict though violence and limitations on freedom. Some governments, such as those of China and Russia, control political outcomes while allowing relatively free markets. The Iranian government is a theocracy, in which religious leaders have a veto over the government's policy choices. Part of the reason why these governments have remained in place over time is that their citizens have less of a preference for democracy—given their experience with corrupt, incompetent legislatures and bureaucracies, they favor, for example, a strong leader who can implement policy change without needing consent from elected officials and civil servants. However, authoritarian leaders stay in power through violence and suppressing freedom.

In contrast, democracies resolve conflict through voting and elections rather than through violence or coercion. When the second president of the United States, John Adams, turned over power to his bitter rival, Thomas Jefferson, after losing a hotly contested election in 1800, it demonstrated that democratic government by the people had real meaning. Democracy depends on the consent of the governed: if the views of the people change, then the government must eventually be responsive to those views or the people will choose new leaders. It also means that citizens must accept election results as authoritative—you have to obey the laws passed by a new Congress, even if you voted for the other party's candidates.

Liberty

To the Founders, **liberty** was a central principle for their new government: they believed that people must have the freedom to express their political views, with the understanding that conflict may arise between different views expressed by different people. The Bill of Rights of the Constitution, discussed in Chapter 4, outlines the nature of those liberties: the freedom of speech, press, assembly, and religion, as well as many legal and due process rights protecting individuals from government control.

liberty
Political freedom, such as the freedom of speech, press, assembly, and religion. These and other legal and due process rights protecting individuals from government control are outlined in the Bill of Rights of the U.S. Constitution.

Liberty also means that within broad limits, people are free to determine what they want from government and to organize themselves to demand their preferred policies from elected officials. Thus, in the case of immigration policy, it is acceptable to hold the view that America should have open borders, and it is also acceptable to demand (and lobby Congress to enact) a complete ban on immigration—or to hold any view in between these extremes.

A system in which individuals are free to form their own views about what government should do virtually guarantees conflict over government policy. James Madison recognized this essential trade-off between liberty and conflict. He argued that suppressing conflict by limiting freedom was "worse than the disease" (worse than conflict). To put it another way, any political system that prioritizes liberty will have conflict.

Another consequence of valuing liberty (and the inevitable conflict over policy that results) is the need for compromise in the policy-making process. In most policy areas, Americans and their elected officials hold a wide range of views, with no consensus on what government should do. Getting something done requires fashioning an agreement that gives no one what he or she really wants, but is nevertheless better than nothing. Standing on principle and refusing to compromise may sound like a noble strategy, but it often results in getting none of what you want, as other individuals or groups work to change policy without your involvement.

Equality

equality
In the context of American politics, "equality" means equality before the law, political equality (one person, one vote), and equality of opportunity (the equal chance for everyone to realize his or her potential), but not material equality (equal income or wealth).

Another principle of democracy is **equality**. Even though the Declaration of Independence boldly declared that "all men are created equal," this did not mean that all people were entitled to the same income or even the same social status (and the Founders obviously ignored slavery, as well). Instead, the most widely embraced notion of equality in the United States today is the equality of opportunity—that is, everyone should have the same chance to realize his or her potential. Political equality also means that people are treated the same in the political system. Everyone has one vote in an election, and everyone is equal in the eyes of the law—that is, we are all subject to the same rules that limit how we can lobby, contribute, work for a candidate, or express our opinions. In practice, political equality has not always existed in America. In our early history, only white men could vote and in many states those men needed to be property owners in order to vote. Slowly, political equality expanded as property requirements were dropped; black men (in 1870, but restrictions persisted into the 1960s), women (in 1919), and 18- to 20-year-olds (in 1971) got the right to vote. (For more on the expansion of the right to vote, see Chapter 5.) Today, although wealthy people clearly can have their voices heard more easily than poor people (through campaign contributions or independent expenditures on political ads), the notion of political equality is central to our democracy.

Like democracy, political equality also contributes to resolving conflict. First, if people know that they will be treated equally by the political system, they are more likely to respect the system. Indeed, one of the triggers for revolutions around the world is reaction against rigged elections or policies that benefit only the supporters of winning candidates. Political equality also gives us cues about how to get involved in politics. Most fundamentally, it suggests that the way to change policy is to elect candidates who share your views, rather than appealing to a friend or relative who works in the government or offering a bribe to a bureaucrat.

While America's political culture has many other aspects, the concepts of democracy, liberty, and equality are central to understanding how American politics works. Agreement on these principles helps lessen conflicts and limit their scope. For example, when Democratic senators lost the battle to prevent Trump's Supreme Court nominee Neil Gorsuch from being appointed, they didn't have to worry that Trump would remove them from office or throw them in jail for opposing Gorsuch. (Indeed, this equality norm is one reason why Trump's threat during the campaign to jail Clinton if he won the presidency was so controversial.) Moreover, Democrats have a clear path to preventing Trump from appointing more justices like Gorsuch: attract enough supporters to regain control of the Senate in the 2018 elections, or find a candidate who can defeat Trump in 2020. Americans and their elected officials have been willing to grant one another political equality and to take political defeats in stride because there is agreement on the basic boundaries of political debate. Again, this consensus does not imply there is no conflict—quite the contrary. However, conflict is easier to resolve if it is over a narrower range of options.

Not surprisingly, many aspects of America's political culture will come up throughout this book. You also might want to look out for them when you are watching the news or reading about national politics. When Democrats in Congress talk about the need to provide health insurance for all Americans, they are emphasizing equality—and when President Trump and his Republican allies argue that minimizing government involvement and allowing people more choice (even if it means some people cannot afford insurance) will lead to a better system, they are emphasizing liberty. Moreover, as this example suggests, part of the conflict in

American politics is over which aspect of political culture should carry the day. The fact that issues such as health care have been central in recent elections is a reminder of the importance of elections in a democracy, and our belief that elections are one venue where conflicts are debated and resolved.

"Why Should I Care?"

To truly understand American politics, you must understand America's core values: democracy, liberty, and equality. These values set broad limits on how political conflicts will be resolved. Democracy implies that the people are the ultimate authority over political outcomes. Liberty implies that people are able to express whatever demands they want and to choose among a wide range of strategies in trying to shape the outcomes of political decisions. And equality means that everyone has an equal share of decision-making power. Despite conflicts over their interpretations, most Americans believe in these core values, and reminding ourselves of this can help us work toward resolving political conflicts.

★

UNDERSTAND HOW TO INTERPRET, EVALUATE, AND USE POLITICAL INFORMATION

How to be a critical consumer of politics

One of the biggest problems in understanding American politics today is deciding whom you should believe. If you want to justify a particular policy solution or point of view on any political issue, you can find a source that will help you do just that. Would free college tuition for all create a well-informed American citizenry? There are people who think so—and who have spent a great deal of time making this argument on free and paid media. On the other hand, would making college free do nothing except increase enrollments? There are plenty of easily accessible arguments for this position as well.

In one sense, the mountain of available information is an amazing asset. If you want to learn about politics, there are many more sources and much more content available now compared to generations ago. But if sources disagree, who should you believe? One source may be as objective as possible, offering information without trying to shape the conclusions its audience might draw. But another may be providing information that is clearly trying to push you in one direction. In such a case, it is better to trust the more objective source. But if you can't be sure about the motivations of a source's creator, what should you do?

One answer is to focus on sources that provide evidence to back up their claims. Anyone can say that free tuition will create a well-informed citizenry. However, this argument is more credible if it comes with supporting data, such as a study showing that college graduates are better informed than people who never attended. As engineer David Akin once put it, "Analysis without numbers is only an opinion."

It also helps to gather information from multiple sources, especially if the sources have different ideological or other biases. For example, on June 16, 2017, Trump tweeted about a Rasmussen Reports poll that showed his approval at 50 percent. However, the Rasmussen poll was an outlier; all the other polls taken at the same time showed Trump's approval rating to be significantly lower. In fact, FiveThirtyEight's

The further a society drifts from the truth, the more it will hate those who speak it.

—George Orwell

aggregated estimate that same day was 38.7 percent. Moreover, past Rasmussen polls had also showed higher approval ratings for Trump. We'll talk more about polling and how to interpret poll results—in Chapter 6. For now, these numbers illustrate the dangers of relying on a single information source to make sense of American politics.

Some sources are also better than others. For example, even though pollsters cannot measure public opinion with perfect certainty, they know some techniques are better than others. Accordingly, most public opinion scholars criticize the polling techniques used by Rasmussen Reports, on the grounds that they produce less accurate (and more pro-Republican) findings than the techniques used by other pollsters. Of course, pollsters don't know which techniques are the best in all circumstances—but they can still distinguish better from worse.

You should also be skeptical about simple explanations for political outcomes. For example, one explanation for Hillary Clinton's defeat in 2016 was that Americans were not ready to elect a female president. However, this account ignores the fact that throughout America, women are routinely elected as mayors, governors, and members of Congress. This is not to say that attitudes about gender did not play a role in Clinton's defeat, but rather to note that this outcome was the result of many factors working together. Complex outcomes are rarely explained by a single factor.

Finally, you might ask, If I'm supposed to be skeptical, why should I believe anything in this book? The answer is that throughout this book, we've strived to follow all of the rules presented here. Our aim is to describe how American politics works, rather than to make an argument about how it *should* work. Rather than shaping your preferences, our goal is to give you the tools to understand, evaluate, and interpret political information and to help you be an informed, effective participant in the political process. As we always tell our students, "My goal is not to tell you *what* to think, but to help you learn *how* to think about politics." We emphasize facts and data (often from multiple sources) because the first step in understanding why things happen is to learn the details of actual events. And while we believe that American politics makes sense and that you can learn to make sense of it, we avoid simple explanations, as these generally do not provide much insight into political behavior or policy outcomes.

Unpacking the Conflict

As we consider the three key ideas about politics that we've discussed in this chapter, let's return to the problem of defining "fake news" discussed at the beginning of the chapter. If Americans can't even agree on which news is "fake," how can we know what to trust?

By understanding that politics is conflictual, that it is rooted in process, and that it is everywhere, you will see that modern American political life, with all its apparent contradictions, makes more sense than you might have thought. As you read this book, we hope you will learn important "nuts and bolts" of the American political process as well as some political history that will help you gauge the likely accuracy of what you learn from news reports and will help you determine if there might be more to the story than the narratives that are being presented. In general, your reading in this book will focus on contemporary questions, debates, and examples—the kinds of stories that constitute a lot of political news coverage—to illustrate broader points about our nation's political system.

While you may not always be able to tell if a news story is entirely accurate at first glance, by the end of the semester you will know how to find out. We also hope you will be able to tell the difference between truly fake news such as "Pizzagate" or the Pope endorsing Donald Trump and the negative (and sometimes inaccurate) stories about our political leaders that result from the conflictual world of politics.

Although you will no doubt disagree with—or even be angry about—some aspects of American politics and some media coverage, our goal in this book is to provide you with the tools to understand *why* government operates as it does. We are not arguing that the federal government is perfect or that imperfect responses to policy problems are inevitable. Rather, we believe that any attempt to explain these outcomes, or to devise ways to prevent similar problems, requires an understanding of why they happened in the first place. After reading this book, you will have a better sense of how American politics really works, and why it matters.

What's Your Take?

Is the media the "watchdog" that protects democracy, or is it an out-of-control, self-serving, biased group of partisans?

And if Americans can't even agree on which news is "fake," how can we know what to trust?

STUDY GUIDE

Making sense of American government and politics

Describe the basic functions of government. (Pages 4–8)

Summary

Forms of government can be characterized by the number of people who hold power (many versus few) and the number of levels over which power is distributed (national versus state versus local). Government exists primarily to provide order, although it must do so while avoiding oppression by the rulers. Government also needs to provide public goods because they will be under-provided by the free market.

Key terms

government (p. 5)
factions (p. 6)
separation of powers (p. 6)
checks and balances (p. 6)
federalism (p. 6)
public goods (p. 7)
collective action problems (p. 7)
free rider problem (p. 7)

Practice Quiz Questions

1. **What did Aristotle call a government ruled by the many?**

   a   monarchy

   b   aristocracy

   c   polity

   d   unitary system

   e   democracy

2. **Which term describes giving each branch of government power over the other two?**

   a   separation of powers

   b   checks and balances

   c   federalism

   d   plutocracy

   e   unitary system

3. **Which term describes the inability to get individuals to cooperate to achieve a common goal?**

   a   positive externality

   b   the Samaritan's dilemma

   c   collective action problem

   d   principal-agent problem

   e   public goods

What is politics?

Define *politics* and identify three key ideas that help explain politics. (Pages 8–14)

Summary

Conflict in politics cannot be avoided: the American people disagree on nearly every issue on which politicians make policy decisions. Compromise and bargaining are essential to enacting policy, but this means that it is almost impossible to get exactly what you want from the political process. Policy outcomes are also influenced by the policy process itself—different procedures of making policy can lead to different outcomes. Whether it is on the news or influencing most aspects of your life, politics is all around us.

Key term

politics (p. 8)

Practice Quiz Questions

4. **What is the main reason why politicians have a hard time resolving the issue of abortion?**

   a   Politicians don't listen to the people.

   b   The parties are divided on what abortion policy should look like.

   c   Politicians don't know what their constituents' views are.

   d   The country is closely divided on what abortion policy should look like.

   e   Abortion is a relatively new issue.

5. **Which concept describes the idea that actions by the government touch most aspects of your life?**

   a   Politics is understandable.

   b   Politics is conflictual.

   c   Political process matters.

   d   Politics is everywhere.

   e   People have different interests.

6. **Rules, such as those regulating debate in the Senate or limiting who can vote in elections, serve as evidence that _____.**

   a   politics is understandable

   b   politics is conflictual

   c   political process matters

   d   politics is everywhere

   e   people have different interests

Sources of conflict in American politics

Identify major sources of conflict in American politics. (Pages 15–20)

Summary

Although Americans generally agree on a free market system, there is considerable conflict over how much the government should support tax policies that redistribute wealth. Conflict also arises on cultural grounds, pitting religious "red-state" Americans against the more secular "blue-state" Americans. There is also disagreement on the extent to which racial, gender, and ethnic diversity should be celebrated or minimized.

Key terms

free market (p. 15)
redistributive tax policies (p. 15)
culture wars (p. 15)
ideology (p. 19)

conservative (p. 19)
liberal (p. 19)
libertarians (p. 19)

Practice Quiz Questions

7. **Democrats tend to favor _____ tax policies and are _____ inclined to regulate industry.**

a redistributive; more

b conservative; more

c redistributive; less

d conservative; less

e regressive; less

8. **Which issue is commonly associated with the culture wars?**

a the national debt

b environmental regulation

c affirmative action

d the tax code

e same-sex marriage

9. **An individual who opposes government social welfare policy and supports the legalization of drugs is most likely a _____ .**

a libertarian

b socialist

c Democrat

d Republican

e centrist

Resolving conflict: democracy and American political values

Explain how the American values of democracy, liberty, and equality work to resolve political conflict. (Pages 20–24)

Summary

Democracy, liberty, and equality are American political values that are essential for understanding how conflict is resolved. Representative democracies resolve conflict through elections rather than through violence. Although liberty ensures that people will have the freedom to express differing views, democracy is the best system for resolving those conflicts. Political equality ensures that everyone is treated the same before the law and that all votes are equal, and the equality of opportunity means that every person has an equal chance to realize his or her potential.

Key terms

norms (p. 21)
democracy (p. 21)

liberty (p. 21)
equality (p. 22)

Practice Quiz Questions

10. **Which type of equality is _not_ typically agreed upon in American politics?**

a equality of opportunity

b equality before the law

c political equality

d one person, one vote

e material equality (such as equal income)

11. **What did James Madison argue was "worse than the disease"?**

a giving too much power to state legislatures

b allowing people to have too much freedom, which would lead to chaos

c giving up liberty to get rid of conflict

d allowing politicians to exercise their judgment rather than listen to the people

e taking cod liver oil to treat various ailments

How to be a critical consumer of politics

Understand how to interpret, evaluate, and use political information. (Pages 24–25)

Summary

One of the biggest problems in understanding American politics today is deciding whom you should believe. In one sense, the mountain of available information is an amazing asset. If you want to learn about politics, there are many more sources and much more content available now compared to generations ago. But if sources disagree, who should you believe? One answer is to focus on sources that provide evidence to back up their claims. It also helps to gather information from multiple sources, especially if the sources have different ideological or other biases. You should also be skeptical about simple explanations for political outcomes. Complex outcomes are rarely explained by a single factor.

Suggested Reading

Bartels, Larry M. *Unequal Democracy: The Political Economy of the New Gilded Age,* 2nd ed. Princeton, NJ: Princeton University Press, 2016.

Dahl, Robert. *A Preface to Democratic Theory,* expanded ed. Chicago: University of Chicago Press, 2013.

Dalton, Russell J. *Citizen Politics: Public Opinion and Political Parties in Advanced Industrial Democracies,* 6th ed. Los Angeles: CQ Press, 2014.

Fiorina, Morris P., with Samuel J. Abrams and Jeremy C. Pope. *Culture War? The Myth of a Polarized America,* 3rd ed. New York: Pearson, Longman, 2010.

Gelman, Andrew, David Park, Boris Shor, Joseph Bafumi, and Jeronimo Cortina. *Red State, Blue State, Rich State, Poor State: Why Americans Vote the Way They Do.* Princeton, NJ: Princeton University Press, 2008.

Lupia, Arthur. *Uninformed: Why People Know So Little about Politics and What We Can Do about It.* New York: Oxford University Press, 2016.

Norris, Pippa. *Democratic Deficit: Critical Citizens Revisited.* New York: Cambridge University Press, 2011.

Putnam, Robert D. *Bowling Alone: The Collapse and Revival of American Community.* New York: Simon and Schuster, 2000.

Schattschneider, E. E. *The Semisovereign People: A Realist's View of Democracy in America.* New York: Holt, Rinehart, and Winston, 1960.

2

The Constitution and the Founding

What are the rules of the political game?

 "For Mr. Trump this could be about one of the boldest and most historic moves a U.S. leader has made in foreign relations."
Laura Bicker, BBC News

 "This madman is still the single most powerful person on the planet, with the ability to order the destruction of the world in just over four minutes."
Robert Reich, scholar and former secretary of labor

Almost immediately after Donald Trump was elected in 2016, dozens of articles and think pieces anxiously questioned whether American democracy would survive a Trump presidency. One called Trump "the greatest threat to American democracy in our lifetime." Another asked, "Are we witnessing the end of democracy?"[1] These critics pointed out that as a candidate Trump questioned judicial independence, called the media the "enemy of the people," advocated violating Muslims' equal protection under the law, seemed to be unconcerned about foreign interference in our elections, promised the use of torture against suspected terrorists and their families, and showed little understanding of the Constitution (he vowed to protect "Article XII," which doesn't exist). Indeed, during his first year in office the pundits on the left contended that our democracy was in grave danger.

Perhaps no area generated more angst than war powers, specifically the prospects for nuclear war with North Korea and its leader, Kim Jong-un. Late in the summer of 2017, mainstream media outlets such as *Newsweek* wondered, "Will Trump and Kim's Game of Nuclear Chicken Blow Up the World?"[2] Those concerns intensified after a speech in September to the United Nations in which Trump dismissed Kim as "Rocket Man" and said that if the United States is forced to defend itself or its allies, "we will have no choice but to totally destroy North Korea."[3] While Trump's supporters hailed it as "his finest speech as president,"[4] others were convinced that the United States was on the brink of war. Early in 2018 when Trump agreed to direct talks with Kim, some

In 2018, President Trump and North Korean leader Kim Jong-un met in Singapore. Though Trump's strong language and threat of war was praised by his supporters, others feared it was evidence of presidential overreach.

CHAPTER GOALS

Describe the historical circumstances that led to the Constitutional Convention of 1787. pages 32–39

Analyze the major issues debated by the framers of the Constitution. pages 39–48

Contrast the arguments of the Federalists with those of the Antifederalists. pages 48–51

Outline the major provisions of the Constitution. pages 51–58

Explore how the meaning of the Constitution has evolved. pages 59–65 praised it as a brilliant gamble, while some fretted that he still had the power to blow up the world in four minutes.[5] Could the president start a war with North Korea or launch a nuclear strike on his own? The historic summit between Trump and Kim in June 2018 was similarly met with praise and skepticism. Is this concern warranted?

Trump has indeed raised serious questions and disagreements about the appropriate scope of a president's power (some of which will be discussed later in this chapter, including the war powers). And one thing is for certain: the early years of Trump's presidency have put the Founders' recognition that self-interest and conflict are inherent parts of human nature on full display. The Constitution represents the Founders' attempt to reckon with this propensity for conflict by dispersing power across different parts of government. This means that parts of the political system are always competing with one another in pursuit of various interests: for example, Republicans in Congress may want to cut spending to balance the budget, whereas a Democratic president may want to achieve that goal by using a mix of spending cuts and tax increases. This creates a conflictual process that is often criticized as being mired in "gridlock" and "partisan bickering," but that is exactly the system our Founders sought to create. Think about it this way: dictatorships do not have political conflict because dissenters are sent to jail or shot. We experience political conflict, including the criticisms that some have levied against Trump, because there is free and open competition between different interests and ideas.

But if the critique from the left is correct and President Trump is operating outside of normal political bounds, is American democracy in danger? Do we really need to be afraid of nuclear war? Does the American political system as laid out in the Constitution work to keep conflicts between politicians and branches of government in check, or does it allow space for these conflicts to spiral out of control?

DESCRIBE THE HISTORICAL CIRCUMSTANCES THAT LED TO THE CONSTITUTIONAL CONVENTION OF 1787

The historical context of the Constitution

The Constitution was created through conflict and compromise, and understanding its historical context can help clarify *why* the framers made the specific choices they did and how those choices influence our understanding of the Constitution today. The first event that led many American colonists to question the fairness of British rule and shape their ideas about self-governance was the Stamp Act of 1765, which imposed a tax on many publications and legal documents in the colonies. The British Parliament enacted the tax to help pay for the French and Indian War (1754–1763), which those lawmakers thought was only reasonable because the American colonies had benefited from the protection of British troops during the war. However, many colonists saw this as unfair "taxation without representation," because they had no representation in British Parliament and thus had no say in the passage of the act. A series of escalating events moved the colonies closer to their inevitable break with Great Britain. These included the British-imposed Tea Act (1773) and the resulting Boston Tea Party later that year, in which colonists dumped tea from the British East India Company into the harbor rather than pay the new tax on tea. The British Parliament responded to the Tea Party with the Coercive Acts (or Intolerable Acts) of 1774 in a series of moves aimed at making sure the colonists paid for the tea they had destroyed, and designed to break the pattern of the colonists' resistance to British rule. Attempts at a political solution failed, so the Continental Congress declared independence from Britain on July 4, 1776.[6]

The Articles of Confederation: the first attempt at government

Throughout the Revolutionary and early post-Revolutionary era, the future of the American colonies was very much in doubt. While many Americans were eager to sever ties with the oppressive British government and establish a new nation that rejected the trappings of royalty, there was still a large contingent of Tories (supporters of the British monarchy) and probably an even larger group of Americans who wished the conflict would just go away. Although public opinion on the matter is impossible to know, John Adams, the second president of the United States, estimated that the Second Continental Congress was about equally divided between Tories, "true blue" revolutionaries, and "those too cautious or timid to take a position one way or the other."[7] This context of uncertainty and conflict made the Founders' task of creating a lasting republic extremely difficult.

The first attempt to structure an American government, the **Articles of Confederation**, swung too far in the direction of decentralized and **limited government**. The Articles were written in the summer of 1776 during the Second Continental Congress, which had also authorized and approved the Declaration of Independence. They were submitted to all 13 states in 1777 for approval, but they did not take effect until the last state ratified them in 1781. However, in the absence of any alternative, the Articles of Confederation served as the basis for organizing the government during the Revolutionary War (see Figure 2.1).

In their zeal to reject **monarchy**, the authors of the Articles did not even include provisions for a president or any other executive leader. Instead, they assigned all national power to a Congress in which each state had a single vote. Members of Congress were elected by state legislatures rather than directly by the people. There was no judicial branch; all legal matters were left to the states, with the exception of disputes among the states, which would be resolved by special panels of judges appointed on an as-needed basis by Congress. To limit the power of government, the authors of the Articles gave each state veto power over any changes to the Articles and required approval from 9 of the 13 states on any legislation. Even more important, the states maintained autonomy and did not sacrifice any significant power to the national government; thus, government power was decentralized in the states, rather than centralized in the national government. For example, both the national government and the states could make treaties and coin money.

Articles of Confederation
Sent to the states for ratification in 1777, these were the first attempt at a new American government. It was later decided that the Articles restricted national government too much, and they were replaced by the Constitution.

limited government
A political system in which the powers of the government are restricted to prevent tyranny by protecting property and individual rights.

monarchy
A form of government in which power is held by a single person, or monarch, who comes to power through inheritance rather than election.

FIGURE 2.1

Constitutional Time Line

The sequence of important events leading to independence and the writing and ratification of the Constitution.

January
First publication of Thomas Paine's *Common Sense*

November 15
Articles of Confederation adopted by Congress, sent to the states for ratification

October 19
Cornwallis surrenders the British army at Yorktown

March 1
Articles of Confederation are ratified by the requisite number of states

September
First Continental Congress

May
Second Continental Congress

July
Congress adopts the Declaration of Independence

February 6
Treaty of Alliance with France

1774   1775   1776   1777   1778   1779   1780   1781

1775–1783 Revolutionary War

Congress also lacked any real authority over the states. For example, Congress could suggest the amount of money each state owed to support the Revolutionary army but could not enforce payment. This meant that General George Washington's troops were in dire straits, lacking basic food and clothing—to say nothing about the arms and munitions they needed to defeat the British. At first, Congress tried to compel the states to support their own troops, but this appeal failed. Desperate for funds, Congress tried in 1781 to give itself the power to raise taxes, but the measure was vetoed by Rhode Island, which represented less than 2 percent of the nation's population! If France had not come to the aid of the American army with much-needed funds and troops, the weakness of the national government could have led to defeat.[8]

After the Revolutionary War ended with the Treaty of Paris in September 1783, the inability to raise revenue through taxes continued to plague Congress. The new government owed millions of dollars in war debts to foreign governments and domestic creditors. Because it had no way to make the states pay their share, Congress proposed an amendment to the Articles that would allow the national government to collect import duties to put toward paying off the debt. However, New York, the busiest seaport in the nation, did not want to share its revenue and vetoed the amendment. Foreign trade also suffered because of the weak national government. If a foreign government negotiated a trade arrangement with Congress, it could be vetoed or amended by a state government, so a foreign country wanting to conduct business with the United States might have to negotiate separate agreements with Congress and each state legislature. Even trade among the states was complicated and inefficient: each state could make its own currency, exchange rates varied, and

October 27
Federalist Papers
begin appearing
in New York
newspapers

September 14
Annapolis
delegates
decide that
Articles need
to be fixed

September 17
Constitution
signed

June 21
Constitution
ratified when
New Hampshire
is the ninth
state to ratify

March 4
Constitution
takes effect

September 3
Treaty of Paris signed,
ending the Revolutionary War

**August 1786–
January 1787**
Shays's Rebellion

May 25
Constitutional
Convention
begins in
Philadelphia

| 2 | 1783 | 1784 | 1785 | 1786 | 1787 | 1788 | 1789 |

1–1789 Articles of Confederation period

many states charged tolls and fees to export goods across state lines. (Just imagine how difficult interstate commerce would be today if you had to exchange currency at every state line and if the value of your currency varied depending on which state you were in.)

A small group of leaders decided that something had to be done. A group from Virginia urged state legislatures to send delegates to a convention on interstate commerce in Annapolis, Maryland, in September 1786. Only five states sent delegates. However, Alexander Hamilton and James Madison salvaged success from the convention by getting those delegates to agree to convene again in Philadelphia the following May. Delegates to the Annapolis Convention also agreed that the next convention would examine the defects of the current government and "devise such further provisions as shall appear to them necessary to render the Constitution of the Federal Government adequate to the exigencies of the Union."[9]

The issues that motivated the Annapolis Convention gained new urgency as events unfolded over the next several months. Economic chaos and depression in the years after the war had caused many farmers to lose their land because they could not pay their debts or state taxes. Frustration mounted throughout the latter half of 1786, and early in 1787 a former captain in the Revolutionary army, Daniel Shays, led a force of 1,500 men in an attempt to take over the Massachusetts state government arsenal in Springfield. Their goal was to force the state courts to stop prosecuting debtors and taking their land, but the rebels were repelled by a state militia. Similar protests on a smaller scale took place in Pennsylvania and Virginia. Some state legislatures gave in to the debtors' demands, causing national leaders to fear that Shays's Rebellion had exposed fundamental discontent with the new government. The very future of the fledgling nation was at risk.

Shays's Rebellion
An uprising of about 1,500 men in Massachusetts in 1786 and 1787 to protest oppressive laws and gain payment of war debts. The unrest prompted calls for a new constitution.

The Founders wanted to create a constitution that was general enough to stand the test of time. Their approach succeeded, and the U.S. Constitution is the oldest written constitution still in use today. However, by leaving some passages open to interpretation, they also set the stage for conflict over the meaning of the Constitution. This painting depicts the signing of the document at the Constitutional Convention of 1787.

Political theories of the framers

Although the leaders who gathered in Philadelphia in the summer of 1787 to write the Constitution were chastened by the failure of the Articles of Confederation, these men still shared many of the principles that had motivated the Revolution. There continued to be broad consensus on three key principles: (1) popular control of government through a republican democracy, (2) a rejection of monarchy, and (3) limitations on government power that would protect individual rights and personal property (that is, protect against tyranny).

Republicanism First among these principles was rejection of monarchy in favor of a form of government based on self-rule. Republicanism as understood by the framers is a government in which elected leaders represent the views of the people. Thomas Paine, an influential political writer of the Revolutionary era, wrote a pamphlet titled *Common Sense* in 1776 that was a widely read[10] indictment of monarchy and an endorsement of the principles that fueled the Revolution and underpinned the framers' thinking. Paine wrote that monarchy was the "most bare-faced falsity ever imposed on mankind" and that the common interests of the community should be served by elected representatives.

The Founders' views of republicanism, together with liberal principles of liberty and individual rights, shaped their vision of the proper form of government. The best expression of these principles is found in the Declaration of Independence:

We hold these truths to be self-evident, that all men are created equal, that they are endowed by their Creator with certain unalienable Rights, that among these are Life, Liberty, and the pursuit of Happiness. That to secure these rights, Governments are instituted among Men, deriving their just powers from the consent of the governed. That whenever any Form of Government becomes destructive of these ends, it is the Right of the People to alter or to abolish it, and to institute new Government.

Three crucial ideas are packed into this passage: equality, self-rule, and natural rights. Equality was not given much attention in the Constitution (later in this

republicanism
As understood by James Madison and the framers, the belief that a form of government in which the interests of the people are represented through elected leaders is the best form of government. Our form of government is known as a republican democracy.

chapter we discuss how the problem of slavery was handled), but the notion that a government gains its legitimacy from the **"consent of the governed"** and that its central purpose is to uphold the "unalienable" or **natural rights** of the people was central to the framers. The "right of the people to alter or abolish" a government that did not protect these rights served both to justify the revolt against the British and to remind the framers of their continuing obligation to make sure that those rights were maintained. The leaders who met in Philadelphia thought the Articles of Confederation had become "destructive to those ends" and therefore needed to be altered.

Paine, Jefferson, Madison, and other political thinkers of the American Founding broke new ground in laying out the principles of republican democracy, but they also built on the ideas of political philosophers of their era. As mentioned in Chapter 1, Thomas Hobbes argued that government was necessary to prevent people from living in an anarchic "state of nature" in which life would be "nasty, brutish, and short." However, Hobbes's central conclusion was undemocratic: he believed that a single king must rule because any other form of government would produce warring factions. Another influential seventeenth-century philosopher, John Locke, took the notion of the consent of the governed in determining a government's legitimacy in a more democratic direction. He discussed many of the ideas that later appeared in the Declaration of Independence and the Constitution, including natural rights, property rights, the need for a vigorous executive branch that would be checked by a legislative branch, and self-rule through elections.[11] Baron de Montesquieu, an eighteenth-century political thinker, also influenced the framers. Although he did not use the term "separation of powers," Montesquieu argued in *The Spirit of the Laws* (1748) that no two, let alone three, functions of government (judicial, legislative, and executive) should be controlled by one branch. He also argued that in order to preserve liberty, one branch of government should be able to check the excesses of the other branches.

Human Nature and Its Implications for Democracy

The most comprehensive statement of the framers' political philosophy and democratic theory was a series of essays written by James Madison, Alexander Hamilton, and John Jay titled the *Federalist Papers*. These essays explained and justified the framework of government created by the Constitution; they also revealed the framers' view of human nature and its implications for democracy. The framers' view of human nature as basically being driven by self-interest led to Madison's assessment that "[i]n framing a government which is to be administered by men over men, the great difficulty lies in this: you must first enable the government to control the governed; and in the next place oblige it to control itself." This analysis, which comes from *Federalist 51*, is often considered the clearest articulation of the need for republican government and a system of separated powers.

In *Federalist 10*, Madison described the central problem for government as the need to control factions. He argued that governments cannot control the causes of factions because differences of opinion—based on the fallibility of reason; differences in wealth, property, and native abilities; and attachments to different leaders—are part of human nature. The only way to eliminate factions would be to either curtail liberty or try to make everyone the same. The first remedy Madison called "worse than the disease" of factions themselves, and the second he found "as impracticable as the first would be unwise." Because people are driven by self-interest, which sometimes conflicts with the common good, government must, however, try to control the effects of factions. This was the task facing the framers at the Constitutional Convention.

Seventeenth-century political philosopher John Locke greatly influenced the Founders. Many ideas discussed in Locke's writing appear in the Declaration of Independence and the Constitution.

Economic interests

Political ideas were central to the framers' thinking at the Constitutional Convention, but economic context and interests were equally important. First, while there were certainly class differences among Americans in the late eighteenth century, they were insignificant compared with the inequalities found in Europe. America did not have the history of feudalism that had created tremendous inequality in Europe between landowners and propertyless serfs who worked the land. In contrast, most Americans owned small farms or worked as middle-class artisans and craftsmen. Thus, while political equality did not figure prominently in the Constitution, citizens' relative economic equality did influence the context of debates at the Constitutional Convention.

Second, despite Americans' general economic equality, there were significant regional economic differences. The South was largely agricultural, with cotton and tobacco plantations that depended on slave labor. The region favored free trade because of its export-based economy (bolstered by westward expansion) and the slave trade. The middle Atlantic and northern states, however, had smaller farms and a broad economic base of manufacturing, fishing, and trade. These states favored government-managed trade and commercial development.

Despite these different interests, people in many sectors of the economy favored a stronger national government and reform of the Articles of Confederation (see Nuts & Bolts 2.1). Creditors wanted a government that could pay off its debts to them, southern farmers wanted free trade that could only be efficiently promoted by a central government, and manufacturers and traders wanted a single national currency and uniform interstate commerce regulations. However, there was a deep division between those who supported empowering the national government and those who still favored strong state governments and a weak national government. These two groups became known as the **Federalists** and the **Antifederalists**. Now the stage was set for a productive but contentious convention.

Federalists
Those at the Constitutional Convention who favored a strong national government and a system of separated powers.

Antifederalists
Those at the Constitutional Convention who favored strong state governments and feared that a strong national government would be a threat to individual rights.

The economic context of the American Founding had an important impact on the framing of the Constitution. Most Americans worked on small farms or as artisans or business owners, which meant that economic power was broadly distributed. This woodcut shows New York City around the time the Constitution was written, viewed from upper Manhattan.

Comparing the Articles of Confederation and the Constitution

Issue	Articles of Confederation	Constitution
Legislature	Unicameral Congress	Bicameral Congress divided into the House of Representatives and the Senate
Members of Congress	Between two and seven per state (the number was determined by each state)	Two senators per state; representatives apportioned according to population of each state
Voting in Congress	One vote per state	One vote per representative or senator
Selection of members	Appointed by state legislatures	Representatives elected by popular vote; senators appointed by state legislatures
Chief executive	None (there was an Executive Council within Congress, but it had limited executive power)	President
National judiciary	No general federal courts	Supreme Court; Congress authorized to establish national judiciary
Amendments to the document	When approved by all states	When approved by two-thirds of each house of Congress and three-fourths of the states
Power to coin money	Federal government and the states	Federal government only
Taxes	Apportioned by Congress, collected by the states	Apportioned and collected by Congress
Ratification	Unanimous consent required	Consent of nine states required

The politics of compromise at the Constitutional Convention

ANALYZE THE MAJOR ISSUES DEBATED BY THE FRAMERS OF THE CONSTITUTION

The central players at the Constitutional Convention were James Madison, Gouverneur Morris, Edmund Randolph, James Wilson, Benjamin Franklin, and George Washington, who was the unanimous choice to preside over the convention (despite his initial decision not to attend). Several of the important leaders of the Revolution were not present. Patrick "Give me Liberty, or give me Death!" Henry was selected to attend but declined to do so, as he opposed any changes in the Articles, saying he "smelled a rat." Indeed, those who were opposed to a stronger national government largely avoided the convention. Other prominent leaders who did not attend included Thomas Jefferson and John Adams, who were working overseas as U.S. diplomats, and Thomas Paine, who was back in England. Moreover, John Hancock and Samuel Adams were not selected to attend. The delegates met in secret to encourage open, uncensored debate.

Although there was broad consensus among the delegates that the Articles of Confederation needed to be changed, there were many tensions over the issues

DID YOU KNOW?

The average age of the delegates to the Constitutional Convention was

42

Four of the delegates were in their 20s, and 14 were in their 30s.

Source: teachingamericanhistory.org

that required political compromise (see Nuts & Bolts 2.2). Among them were the following:

- majority rule versus minority rights
- large states versus small states
- legislative power versus executive power (and how to elect the executive)
- national power versus state and local power
- slave states versus nonslave states

These complex competing interests meant that the delegates had to focus on pragmatic, achievable solutions rather than on proposals that represented particular groups' ideals but that could not gain majority support. Robert A. Dahl, a leading democratic theorist of the twentieth century, argues that it was impossible for the Constitution to "reflect a coherent, unified theory of government" because so much compromising and vote trading was required to find common ground.[12] The delegates tackled the problems one at a time, holding lengthy debates and multiple votes on most issues. The most important initial decision they made was to give up on the original plan to revise the Articles of Confederation; instead, they decided to start from scratch with a new blueprint for government.

NUTS & BOLTS 2.2

Major Compromises at the Constitutional Convention

Conflict	Position of the Large States	Position of the Small States	Compromise
Apportionment in Congress	By population	State equality	Great Compromise created the Senate and House
Method of election to Congress	By the people	By the states	House elected by the people; Senate elected by the state legislatures
Electing the executive (president)	By Congress	By the states	By the electoral college
Who decides federal–state conflicts?	Some federal authority	State courts	State courts to decide*
	Position of the Slave States	**Position of the Nonslave States**	**Compromise**
Control over commerce	By the states	By Congress	By Congress, but with 20-year exemption for the importation of slaves
Counting slaves toward apportionment	Counted 1:1 like citizens	Not counted	Three-Fifths Compromise
	Position of the Federalists	**Position of the Antifederalists**	**Compromise**
Protection for individual rights†	Secured by state constitutions; national Bill of Rights not needed	National Bill of Rights needed	Bill of Rights passed by the 1st Congress; ratified by all states as of December 1791

*This was changed by the Judiciary Act of 1789, which provided for appeals from state to federal courts.

†This issue was raised but not resolved until after the convention.

Majority rule versus minority rights

A central problem for any representative democracy is protecting minority rights within a system ruled by the majority. The framers thought of this issue not in terms of racial and ethnic minorities (as we might today), but in terms of regional and economic minorities. How could the framers be sure that small landowners and poorer people would not impose onerous taxes on the wealthier minority? How could they guarantee that dominant agricultural interests would not impose punitive tariffs on manufacturing while allowing free export of farmed commodities? The answers to these questions can be found in Madison's writings on the problem of factions.

Madison defined a "faction" as a group motivated by selfish interests against the common good. If these interests prevailed, it could produce the very kind of tyranny that the Americans had fought to escape during the Revolutionary War. Madison was especially concerned about tyranny by majority factions because, in a democracy, minority tyranny would be controlled by the republican principle: the majority could simply vote out the minority faction. If, however, the majority always rules, majority tyranny could be a real problem. Given the understanding of selfish human nature that Madison so clearly outlined, a populist, majoritarian democracy would not necessarily promote the common good. However, if too many protections were provided to minority and regional interests, the collective interest would not be served because constructive changes could be vetoed too easily, as under the Articles of Confederation.

Madison's solution to this problem provided the justification for our form of government. He argued that to control majority tyranny, factions must be set against one another to counter each other's ambitions and prevent the tyranny of any single majority faction. This was to be accomplished through the "double protection" of the separation of powers within the national government in the form of checks and balances, and by further dividing power across the levels of state and local governments.

Madison also argued that additional protection against majority tyranny would come from the "size principle." That is, the new nation would be a large and diverse republic in which majority interests would be less likely to organize and therefore less able to dominate. According to Madison, "Extend the sphere, and you take in a greater variety of parties and interests; you make it less probable that a majority of the whole will have a common motive to invade the rights of other citizens; or if such a common motive exists, it will be more difficult for all who feel it to discover their own strength, and to act in unison with each other."[13] This insight provides the basis for modern **pluralism**, a political theory that makes the same argument about the crosscutting interests of groups today.

The precise contours of Madison's solution still had to be hammered out at the convention, but the general principle pleased both the Antifederalists and the Federalists. State governments would maintain some autonomy, but the national government would become stronger than it had been under the Articles. The issue was striking the appropriate balance: none of the framers favored a pure populist majoritarian democracy, and few wanted to protect minority rights to the extent that the Articles had.

Small states versus large states

The question of the appropriate balance came to an immediate head in a debate between small-population and large-population states over representation in the national legislature. Under the Articles, every state had a single vote,

pluralism
The idea that having a variety of parties and interests within a government will strengthen the system, ensuring that no group possesses total control.

James Madison argued that it is beneficial to put the interests of one group in competition with the interests of other groups, so that no one group can dominate government. He hoped to achieve this through the separation of powers across different branches of the national government and across the national, state, and local levels.

Virginia Plan

A plan proposed by the larger states during the Constitutional Convention that based representation in the national legislature on population. The plan also included a variety of other proposals to strengthen the national government.

New Jersey Plan

A plan that was suggested in response to the Virginia Plan; smaller states at the Constitutional Convention proposed that each state should receive equal representation in the national legislature, regardless of size.

Great Compromise

A compromise between the large and small states, proposed by Connecticut, in which Congress would have two houses: a Senate with two legislators per state and a House of Representatives in which each state's representation would be based on population (also known as the Connecticut Compromise).

but this did not seem fair to large states. They pushed for representation based on population. This proposal, along with others that would strengthen the national government, was the **Virginia Plan**. The small states countered with the **New Jersey Plan**, which proposed maintaining equal representation for every state. Rhode Island, the smallest state, was so concerned about small-state power that it boycotted the convention. Tensions were running high; this issue appeared to have all the elements of a deal breaker, and there seemed to be no way to resolve the impasse.

Just as it appeared that the convention might grind to a halt before it really got started, Connecticut proposed what became known as the **Great Compromise**, or Connecticut Compromise. The plan suggested establishing a Congress with two houses: the Senate would have two senators from each state, and in the House of Representatives each state's number of representatives would be based on its population. At first glance, the Connecticut Compromise seems to make perfect sense: as the seventh of 13 states in terms of population, Connecticut was positioned to offer a compromise that would appeal to both large and small states. But the situation was actually much more complicated. First, Rhode Island did not attend the convention, so there was no true median state (with only 12 states at the convention, no one stood alone at the center). Second, given that each state had one vote at the convention, the smallest states could have easily outvoted the biggest ones and insisted on equal representation for each state.

Why didn't the smaller states impose their view? Two of the smaller states, Georgia and South Carolina, focused on their future growth, so they supported representation based on population, the Virginia Plan. But when other smaller states balked at their loss of power, the Connecticut Compromise was able to win the support of North Carolina (and Massachusetts's delegates were divided), so the compromise passed 5-4-1.

Despite this more complex picture, an analysis of all 569 votes at the Constitutional Convention clearly shows that Connecticut occupied a pivotal place at the convention (see Figure 2.2). Connecticut was in the middle in terms of desire for representation based on population and in terms of desire for more state power. Connecticut is right in the center of these graphs—no wonder it could broker a compromise!

Legislative power versus executive power

An equally difficult challenge was how to divide power at the national level. Here the central issues revolved around the executive: the president. How much power should the president have relative to the legislative branch? (The courts also figured here, but they were less central to the discussions.) And how would the president be elected?

Limiting Presidential Power The delegates knew what they did not want: the king of England and his colonial governors were viewed as tramplers of liberty. But many delegates rejected outright the idea of a single executive because they believed it was impossible to have an executive who would not be oppressive. Edmund Randolph proposed a three-person executive for this reason, arguing that a single executive would be the "fetus of monarchy." The Virginia Plan envisioned a single executive who would share some legislative power with federal judges in a Council of Revision with the power to veto legislation passed by Congress (however, the veto could be overridden by a simple majority vote in Congress). The delegates finally agreed on the single executive because he would have the most "energy, dispatch, and responsibility for the office," but they constrained the president's power through the system of checks and balances. One significant power they granted to the executive was the veto. It could be overridden by Congress, but only with the support of

**FIGURE
2.2**

Connecticut's Pivotal Place at the Constitutional Convention

Though there were many disagreements over the details of America's new constitution, one of the most intense focused on how states would be represented in Congress, either allocating representatives equally or based on population. After other plans were considered and rejected, the Connecticut Compromise won out. Why do you think Connecticut was well positioned to find a compromise? How do these graphs help us understand why the Virginia and New Jersey Plans were in conflict and ultimately rejected?

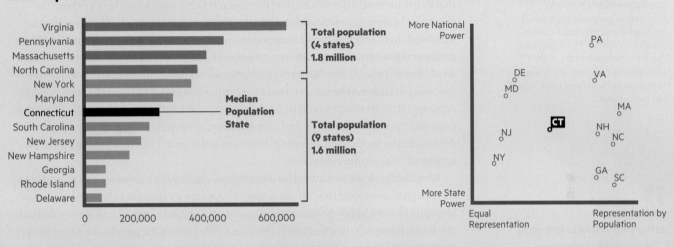

State Populations at the Time of the Constitutional Convention

Virginia
Pennsylvania
Massachusetts
North Carolina

**Total population
(4 states)
1.8 million**

New York
Maryland
Connecticut — **Median Population State**
South Carolina
New Jersey
New Hampshire
Georgia
Rhode Island
Delaware

**Total population
(9 states)
1.6 million**

0   200,000   400,000   600,000

Votes at the Constitutional Convention

More National Power

PA
DE   VA
MD   MA
CT
NJ   NH NC
NY
GA SC

More State Power

Equal Representation   Representation by Population

Source: Keith L. Dougherty and Jac C. Heckelman, "A Pivotal Voter from a Pivotal State: Roger Sherman at the Constitutional Convention," *American Political Science Review* 100:2 (May 2006): 298.

two-thirds of both chambers. This requirement gave the president a significant role in the legislative process.

Hamilton and the other New Yorkers favored a strong executive. This was probably because the governorship of New York closely resembled the type of executive that the Constitution envisioned. The governor of New York was elected by the people rather than by the legislature, served for three years, and was eligible for reelection. The office also had a legislative veto power and considerable control over appointments to politically controlled jobs. The arguments the New Yorkers made on behalf of the strong executive relied heavily on the philosophy of John Locke. Locke saw the general superiority of a government of laws created by legislatures, but he also saw the need for an executive with more flexible leadership powers, or what he called "prerogative powers." Legislatures are unable, Locke wrote, "to foresee, and so by laws to provide for all accidents and necessities." They also are, by virtue of their size and unwieldiness, too slow to alter and adapt the law in times of crisis, when the executive could step in to pursue policies in the public's interest.

Although there was support for this view, the Antifederalists were concerned that if such powers were viewed as open-ended they could give rise to the type of oppressive leader the framers were trying to avoid. Madison attempted to reassure the opponents of executive power, arguing that any prerogative powers would have to be clearly enumerated in the Constitution. In fact, the Constitution explicitly provides only one extraordinary executive power: the right to grant reprieves and pardons, which means that the president can forgive any crimes against the federal government.

Selecting the President Another contentious issue concerning the executive was the method of selecting a president. The way the president was elected involved the issues of majority rule and minority rights, state versus national power, and the nature of executive power itself. Would the president be elected by the nation as a whole, by the states, or by coalitions within Congress? If the state-level governments played a central role, would this mean that the president could not speak for national interests? If Congress elected the president, could the executive still provide a check on the legislative branch?

Most Americans do not realize that (1) our presidential system is unique and (2) we came close to having a parliamentary system, which is the form of government that exists in most other established democracies. In a **parliamentary system**, the executive branch depends on the support of the legislative branch. The Virginia Plan proposed that Congress elect the president, just as Parliament elects the British prime minister. However, facing lingering concerns that a congressionally elected president would be too beholden to that body, a committee of framers subsequently made the following recommendations: (1) that the president be selected by an electoral college, representation in which would be based on the number of representatives and senators each state has in Congress, (2) and that members of each state's legislature would determine the method for choosing their state's electors.[14] The delegates ultimately approved this recommendation.

Why did the delegates favor this complicated, indirect way of electing the president? As with good compromises, all sides could claim victory to some extent. Advocates of state power were happy because state legislatures played a central role in presidential elections; those who worried about the direct influence of the people liked the indirect manner of election; and proponents of strong executive power were satisfied that the president would not simply be an agent of Congress.

However, the solution had its flaws and did not work out the way the framers intended. First, if the electoral college was supposed to provide an independent check on the voters, it never played this role because of the quick emergence of political parties (which the framers did not anticipate). Electors became agents of the parties, as they remain today, rather than independent actors who would use their judgment to pick the most qualified candidate for president. Second, the emergence of parties created a serious technical error in the Constitution: the provision that gave each elector two votes and elected the candidate with the most votes as president and the second-place finisher as vice president. With electors acting as agents of parties, they ended up casting one vote each for the presidential and vice-presidential candidate of their own party. This created a tie in the 1800 presidential election when Thomas Jefferson and Aaron Burr each received 73 electoral votes. The problem was fixed by the Twelfth Amendment, which required that electors cast separate ballots for president and vice president.

National power versus state and local power

Tensions over the balance of power cut across virtually every debate at the convention. The issues included presidential versus legislative power, whether the national government could supersede state laws, apportionment in the legislature, slavery, regulation of commerce and taxation, and the amendment process. The overall compromise that addressed these tensions was the second of Madison's "double protections," the system of federalism, which divided power between autonomous levels of government that controlled different areas of policy.

Federalism is such an important topic that we devote the entire next chapter to it, but two brief points about it are important here. First, the Tenth Amendment, which

---

parliamentary system
A system of government in which legislative and executive power are closely joined. The legislature (parliament) selects the chief executive (prime minister), who forms the cabinet from members of the parliament.

Jefferson: You hear this guy? Man openly campaigns against me, talking 'bout "I look forward to our partnership!"

Madison: It is crazy that the guy who comes in second gets to be vice president.

Jefferson: OOOH! Y'know what, we can change that! Y'know why?

Madison: Why?

Jefferson: 'Cause I'm the president!

—*Hamilton,* the musical

was added as part of the Bill of Rights shortly after ratification, was a concession to the Antifederalists, who were concerned that the national government would gain too much power in the new political system. The Tenth Amendment says: "The powers not delegated to the United States by the Constitution, nor prohibited by it to the States, are reserved to the States respectively, or to the people." This definition of **reserved powers** was viewed as setting outer limits on the reach of national power.

Between 1918 and 1937 and then again starting in the 1990s, the Supreme Court has frequently invoked the Tenth Amendment to nullify various laws passed by Congress as unconstitutional intrusions on the reserved powers of the states (see the discussion in Chapter 3 of the Supreme Court's recent preference for state-centered federalism). The Tenth Amendment continues to play an important role in current debates about the proper level of national power. For example, conservative Republicans argue that the states and the private sector, not the national government, should have the primary responsibility for health care policy, while Democrats in state and local government have served as a check on President Trump's policy agenda concerning immigration and climate change (among other issues).

Second, the **national supremacy clause** of the Constitution (Article VI) says that any national law is the supreme law of the land and takes precedence over any state law that conflicts with it. This is especially important in areas where the national and state governments have overlapping responsibilities for policy.

Slave states versus nonslave states

Slavery was another nearly insurmountable issue for the delegates. Southern states would not agree to any provisions limiting slavery. Although the nonslave states opposed the practice, they were not willing to scuttle the entire Constitution by

reserved powers
As defined in the Tenth Amendment, powers that are not given to the national government by the Constitution, or not prohibited to the states, are reserved by the states or the people.

national supremacy clause
Part of Article VI, Section 2, of the Constitution stating that the Constitution and the laws and treaties of the United States are the "supreme Law of the Land," meaning national laws take precedence over state laws if the two conflict.

This advertisement from a slave-trading company appeared in a Richmond, Virginia, newspaper shortly after the Constitution was signed. Slavery is often referred to as the "original sin" of our nation and proved to be very problematic at the Constitutional Convention: Would there be limits on the importation of slaves? How would runaway slaves be dealt with by nonslave states? And how would slaves be counted for the purposes of congressional representation?

taking a principled stand. Even after these basic positions had been recognized, many unresolved issues remained. Could the importation of slaves be restricted in the future? How would northern states deal with runaway slaves? Most important in terms of the politics of the issue, how would the slave population be counted for the purpose of slave states' representation in Congress? The deals that the convention delegates cut on the issue of slavery illustrate the two most common forms of compromise: splitting the difference and logrolling (trading votes). Splitting the difference is familiar to anyone who has haggled over the price of a car or bargained for something at a flea market; you end up meeting halfway, or splitting the difference. Logrolling occurs when politicians trade votes for one another's pet projects, for example, support for dairy subsidies in one district in exchange for opening up more federal lands for mining in another.

The delegates went through similar negotiations over how slaves would be counted for purposes of states' congressional representation. The states had been through this debate once before, when they addressed the issue of taxation under the Articles of Confederation. At that point, the slave states had argued that slaves should not be counted because they did not receive the same benefits as citizens and were not the same burden to the government. Nonslave states had countered that slaves should be counted the same way as citizens when determining a state's fair share of the tax burden. The sides had reached a compromise by agreeing that each slave would count as three-fifths of a person for purposes of taxation. The arguments over the issue of representation became even more contentious at the Constitutional Convention, where the positions were reversed, with slave states arguing that slaves should be counted like everyone else for the purposes of determining the number of House representatives for each state. Once again, both sides managed to agree on the **Three-Fifths Compromise** (see What Do the Facts Say?).

The other two issues, the importation of slaves and dealing with runaway slaves, were handled by logrolling combined with an element of splitting the difference. Logrolling is more likely to occur than splitting the difference when the issue cannot be neatly divided. For example, northern states either would be obligated to return runaway slaves to their southern owners or would not; there was no way to split the difference. On issues like this with no clear middle ground, opposing sides will look for other issues on which they can trade votes. In this case, the nonslave states saw an opportunity to push for more national government control over commerce and trade than was provided under the Articles, a change that the slave states opposed. A logroll—or vote trade—developed as a way to compromise the competing regional interests of slavery and regulation of commerce. Northern states agreed to return runaway slaves (the Fugitive Slave Clause), and southern states agreed to allow Congress to pass laws regulating commerce and taxing imports with a simple majority vote (rather than the supermajority required under the Articles).

The importation of slaves was included as part of this logroll, along with some split-the-difference negotiating. Northern states wanted to allow future Congresses to ban the importation of slaves; southern states wanted to allow the importation of slaves to continue indefinitely, arguing that slavery was essential to produce their labor-intensive crops. After much negotiation among the states, the final language of the Article resulting from this part of the logroll prevented a constitutional amendment from banning the slave trade until 1808.[15]

From a modern perspective, it is difficult to understand how the framers could have taken such a purely political approach to the moral issue of slavery. Many of the delegates believed slavery was immoral, yet they were willing to negotiate for the

Three-Fifths Compromise
The states' decision during the Constitutional Convention to count each slave as three-fifths of a person in a state's population for the purposes of determining the number of House members and the distribution of taxes.

DID YOU KNOW?

At only about

8,700

words, the U.S. Constitution is much shorter than the average state constitution (39,604 words).
Source: PARCA, Tableau Public

The Three-Fifths Compromise

The Three-Fifths Compromise is often described as the "original sin" of the Constitution, but less recognized is the impact that it had on the electoral college. The figure shows the number of each state's House members in the 1790s based on the Three-Fifths Compromise, and then how many representatives they would have had if only the free population had been counted or if the total population, including slaves, had been counted.

Number of House Members

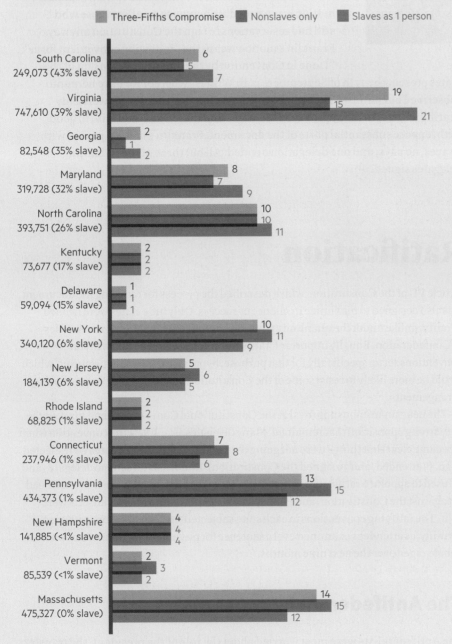

Legend: Three-Fifths Compromise · Nonslaves only · Slaves as 1 person

State	Three-Fifths Compromise	Nonslaves only	Slaves as 1 person
South Carolina 249,073 (43% slave)	6	5	7
Virginia 747,610 (39% slave)	19	15	21
Georgia 82,548 (35% slave)	2	1	2
Maryland 319,728 (32% slave)	8	7	9
North Carolina 393,751 (26% slave)	10	10	11
Kentucky 73,677 (17% slave)	2	2	2
Delaware 59,094 (15% slave)	1	1	1
New York 340,120 (6% slave)	10	11	9
New Jersey 184,139 (6% slave)	5	6	5
Rhode Island 68,825 (1% slave)	2	2	2
Connecticut 237,946 (1% slave)	7	8	6
Pennsylvania 434,373 (1% slave)	13	15	12
New Hampshire 141,885 (<1% slave)	4	4	4
Vermont 85,539 (<1% slave)	2	3	2
Massachusetts 475,327 (0% slave)	14	15	12

Note: These numbers reflect total populations according to the 1790 census.

Source: U.S. Census Bureau, www.census.gov

Think about it

- How many additional seats in the House did southern states get as a result of the Three-Fifths Compromise, relative to the number of seats they would have had if slaves had not been counted at all?
- How many additional seats in the House would southern states have gotten if slaves had been counted as full members of the population?
- How did the Three-Fifths Compromise have an impact on the electoral college? (Remember: each state's number of electors is equal in number to its combined total of representatives in the House and senators.)

Union and Confederate troops clash in close combat in the Battle of Cold Harbor, Virginia, in June 1864. The inability of the framers to resolve the issue of slavery allowed tensions over the issue to grow throughout the early nineteenth century, culminating in the Civil War.

CONTRAST THE ARGUMENTS OF THE FEDERALISTS WITH THOSE OF THE ANTIFEDERALISTS

southern states' support of the Constitution. Some southern delegates were apologetic about slavery, even as they argued for protecting their interests. Many constitutional scholars view the convention's treatment of slavery as its central failure. In fairness to the delegates, the issue of slavery could not be settled since the goal was to create a document that all states would support. However, the delegates' inability to resolve this issue meant that it would simmer below the surface for the next 70 years, finally boiling over into the bloodiest of all American wars: the Civil War.

The convention ended on a relatively harmonious note with Benjamin Franklin moving for adoption. Franklin's motion was worded ambiguously to allow those who still had reservations to sign the Constitution anyway. Franklin's motion was in the "following convenient form": "Done in Convention by the unanimous consent of the States present the 17th of September. . . . In Witness whereof we have hereunto subscribed our names." His clever wording meant that the signers were only bearing witness to the approval by the states and therefore could still, in good faith, oppose substantial parts of the document. Franklin's motion passed with 10 ayes, no nays, and one delegation divided. All but three of the remaining delegates signed.

Ratification

Article VII of the Constitution, which described the process for ratifying the document, was also designed to maximize its chance of success. Only nine states were needed to ratify, unlike under the unanimity rule that had applied to changing the Articles of Confederation. Equally important, ratification votes would be taken in state conventions set up specifically for that purpose, bypassing the state legislatures, which would be more likely to resist some of the Constitution's state–federal power-sharing arrangements.

The near-unanimous approval at the Constitutional Convention's end masked the very strong opposition that remained. Many delegates simply left the convention when it became clear that things were not going their way (overall, 74 delegates were elected to go, 55 attended, and 39 signed the Constitution). Rhode Island sent no delegates and refused to appoint a ratification convention. More ominously, New York seemed dead set against the Constitution, and Pennsylvania, Virginia, and Massachusetts were split. The ratifying conventions in each state subjected the Constitution to intense scrutiny, as attendees examined every sentence for possible objections. A national debate raged over the next nine months.

The Antifederalists' concerns

The Antifederalists were most worried about the role of the president, the transfer of power from the states to the national government, and the lack of specific guarantees of civil liberties. In short, they feared that the national government would become tyrannical. This concern was summarized in Brutus 1, an Anitifederalist paper believed to have been written by Robert Yates, a New York judge and delegate to the Constitutional Convention: the Constitution would create a federal government that will "possess absolute and uncontrollable power. . . "[16] The doubts about the single central executive were expressed by Patrick Henry, a leading Antifederalist. Speaking to the Virginia ratifying convention, Henry was mocking in his indictment: "Your president may easily become a king. . . . There will be no checks, no real balances in this government."[17] Even Thomas Jefferson complained that the president would control the armed forces and could be reelected indefinitely.[18] State power and the ability to regulate commerce were also central concerns. States such as New York would lose substantial revenue if they could no longer charge tariffs on goods that came into their ports. Other states were concerned that they would pay a disproportionate share of national taxes.

The Antifederalists' foremost objection was to the lack of protections for civil liberties in the new political system. During the last week of the convention, Elbridge Gerry and George Mason offered a resolution "to prepare a Bill of Rights." However, the resolution was unanimously defeated by the state delegations. Some believed that the national government posed no threat to liberties, such as freedom of the press, because it did not have the power to restrict them in the first place. Others thought that because it would be impossible to enumerate all rights, it was better to list none at all. Federalists such as Roger Sherman argued that state constitutions, most of which protected freedom of speech, freedom of the press, right to a trial by jury, and other civil liberties, would be sufficient to protect liberty. However, many Antifederalists still wanted assurances that the *national* government would not trample their rights.

A lady asked Dr. [Benjamin] Franklin, "Well, Doctor, what have we got—a republic or a monarchy?"
"A republic," replied the Doctor, "if you can keep it."

—**James McHenry,** *The Records of the Federal Convention of 1787*

This engraving by Amos Doolittle titled *The Looking Glass for 1787* satirizes some of the issues raised in the debate over the ratification of the Constitution. The wagon in the center is carrying Connecticut and sinking into the mud under the weight of debts and paper money as "Federalists" and "Antifederalists" try to pull it out.

The Federalists' strategies

The Federalists counterattacked on several fronts. First, supporters of the Constitution gained the upper hand in the debate by claiming the term "federalist." It is a common tactic in debates to co-opt a strong point of the opposing side as a positive for your side. The opponents of the Constitution probably had a stronger claim than its supporters to being federalists—that is, those who favor and emphasize the autonomous power of the state governments. Today, for example, the Federalist Society is a conservative group organized around the principles of states' rights and limited government. By calling themselves Federalists, the supporters of the Constitution asserted that they were the true protectors of states' interests, which irritated the Antifederalists to no end. The Antifederalists also had the rhetorical disadvantage of having "anti" attached to their name, thereby being defined in terms of their opponents' position rather than their own. But the problem was more than just rhetorical: the Federalists pointed out that the Antifederalists did not have their own plan to solve the problems created by the Articles and therefore were cast as defenders of the status quo, which the Federalists viewed as unsustainable.

Second, as we mentioned earlier, the Federalists published the *Federalist Papers*. Although originally published in New York newspapers, they were widely read throughout the nation. The *Federalist Papers* were essentially one-sided arguments aimed at changing public opinion. The authors downplayed potentially unpopular aspects of the new system, such as the power of the president, while emphasizing points they knew would appeal to the opposition. Despite the authors' biased arguments, the *Federalist Papers* are considered the best comprehensive discussion of the political theory underlying the Constitution, such as the framers' views of self-interested human nature and the dangers of factions, and their interpretations of many of the document's key provisions.

Third, the Federalists agreed that the new Congress's first order of business would be to add a **Bill of Rights** to the Constitution to protect individual rights and liberties. This promise was essential for securing the support of New York, Massachusetts, and Virginia. The ninth state, New Hampshire, ratified the Constitution on June 21, 1788, but New York and Virginia were still dragging their heels, and their support was viewed as necessary for the legitimacy of the United States, even if it technically was not needed. By the end of the summer, both Virginia and New York finally voted for ratification. Rhode Island and North Carolina refused to ratify until Congress made good on its promise of a Bill of Rights (our civil liberties, which are guaranteed in the Bill of Rights, will be examined in Chapter 4). The 1st Congress submitted 12 amendments to the states, and 10 were ratified by all the states as of December 15, 1791.

Alexander Hamilton authored a majority of the *Federalist Papers* and was a strong advocate for ratification of the Constitution.

Bill of Rights
The first 10 amendments to the Constitution; they protect individual rights and liberties.

"Why Should I Care?"

Politicians today have a very difficult time compromising on issues like gun control, abortion rights, and even the proper levels of taxation and spending. At the Constitutional Convention, the framers had to struggle with fundamental issues such as executive power and state versus national power as well as incredibly divisive issues like slavery. The framers were facing uncertainty about the very survival of their new nation and the nearly impossible task of creating a new framework that would allow our nation to not only survive but also flourish. Yet the framers were able to arrive at workable compromises on all of these issues. Without compromise, our nation would not exist. When you hear a politician today say, "I am going to stick to my principles; I am not going to compromise," reflect on the fact that governing is not possible without compromise. "Compromise" is not a dirty word; it is an essential feature of politics.

This political cartoon from 1788 depicts the erection of the "eleventh pillar of the great national dome" when New York became the eleventh state to ratify the Constitution, leaving only North Carolina and Rhode Island (shown as still wobbling in this cartoon) to ratify the document.

The Constitution: a framework for government

OUTLINE THE MAJOR PROVISIONS OF THE CONSTITUTION

The Constitution certainly has its flaws (some of which have been corrected through amendments), primarily its undemocratic qualities: the indirect election of senators and the president, the compromises that suppressed the issue of slavery (indeed, the words "slave" and "slavery" do not appear in the Constitution), and the absence of any general statement about citizens' right to vote. However, given the delegates' political context and the various factions that had to be satisfied, the Constitution's accomplishments are substantial.

The document's longevity is testimony to the framers' foresight in crafting a flexible framework for government. Perhaps its most important feature is the system of separation of powers and checks and balances that prevents majority tyranny while maintaining sufficient flexibility for decisive leadership during times of crisis (such as the Civil War, the Great Depression, and World War II). The system of checks and balances means that each branch of national government has certain exclusive powers, some shared powers, and the ability to check the other two branches (see How It Works: Checks and Balances).

> **The Constitution is the guide which I never will abandon.**
>
> **—George Washington**

Exclusive powers

The framers viewed Congress as the "first branch" of government and granted it significant exclusive powers. With the popularly elected House of Representatives and the Senate indirectly elected by state legislatures, Congress was designed to be both the voice of the people and an institution more removed from the people, with an important role in domestic and foreign policy. Congress was given the specific **enumerated power** to raise revenue for the federal government through taxes and borrowing, regulate interstate and foreign commerce, coin money, establish post offices and roads, grant patents and copyrights, create the system of federal courts,

enumerated powers
Powers explicitly granted to Congress, the president, or the Supreme Court in the first three articles of the Constitution. Examples include Congress's power to "raise and support armies" and the president's power as commander in chief.

Checks and Balances

The Constitution stipulates that if one branch tries to assert too much power, the other branches have certain key powers that allow them to fight back and restore the balance. (In addition to the powers noted in the diagram, Congress can impeach the president and remove him or her from office.)

The president nominates judges.

The president can veto congressional legislation.

The Senate confirms the president's judicial nominations. Congress can impeach and remove judges from office.

Executive

Legislative

Judicial

The Senate approves presidential nominations, and Congress can override the president's veto and pass laws.

The Court interprets the laws passed by Congress.

The Court interprets actions by the executive branch.

Checks and Balances in the War on Terror

Shortly after the attacks of September 11, 2001, President George W. Bush, acting on his power as commander in chief, authorized the Guantánamo Bay detention center in Cuba to be used as a place to detain, interrogate, and try prisoners related to the War on Terror. President Obama tried to close the facility, but President Trump has advocated keeping it open. At the same time, Trump called for a broad ban restricting travel to the United States from six Muslim countries. The controversies and policies surrounding these efforts in the war on terror show how checks and balances work in practice.

He said...

First prisoners are taken to Guantánamo on January 11, 2002. President George W. Bush asserts that Guantánamo is outside legal U.S. jurisdiction and that prisoners held there do not have protections guaranteed to prisoners of war under the Geneva Convention.

But then...

The Supreme Court disagrees in *Hamdan v. Rumsfeld* on June 29, 2006, ruling that the detainees were entitled to basic legal rights and that the Geneva Convention did apply.

Shut it down?

The detention center is increasingly controversial. Two days after taking office, President Obama **signs an order to close the center** by the end of the year and to suspend all Guantánamo military commission hearings for 120 days.

Nope.

A week later, a military court judge **overturns the order** to suspend hearings at Guantánamo.

Another plan.

President Obama **wants to move Guantánamo prisoners** to a federal prison in Illinois.

Plan blocked.

A few months later, **Congress votes to block funds** needed for the transfer or release of prisoners held at the facility.

Sigh.

By the end of Obama's presidency, **41 prisoners remained**. President Trump vows to keep the facility open.

New strategy.

In 2017, President Trump tries a new approach by **issuing a ban on travel** from six mostly Muslim countries.

Is this okay?

Several district courts **strike down the ban as religious profiling,** but the Supreme Court reinstates a more limited version of the ban, citing the president's powers over national security and immigration policy.

? Critical Thinking

1. **Why do you think it has been so difficult for presidents to have their way in fighting terrorism, with regard to the travel ban and Guantánamo?** Is it because of the issue of terrorism and national security? Or is it because of our system of checks and balances? Why?

2. **Do you think our system of checks and balances creates** too much gridlock, or is it an essential check on potential tyranny?

power of the purse
The constitutional power of Congress to raise and spend money. Congress can use this as a negative or checking power over the other branches by freezing or cutting their funding.

necessary and proper clause
Part of Article I, Section 8, of the Constitution that grants Congress the power to pass all laws related to its expressed powers; also known as the elastic clause.

Congress alone has "the power of the purse" to fund government programs. Although President Obama ordered the "troop surge" in Afghanistan, Congress had to continue appropriating money to pay for the war.

declare war, "raise and support armies," make rules for the military, and create and maintain a navy. Most important is the so-called **power of the purse**—control over taxation and spending—given to Congress in Article I, Section 8, of the Constitution: "No money shall be drawn from the Treasury, but in consequence of appropriations made by law." Or, as Madison put it, "the legislative department alone has access to the pockets of the people." One other exclusive congressional power that has received new attention during the first years of the Trump presidency is the "emoluments clause," which gives Congress the sole power to consent to any government official's receipt of anything of value from a foreign state. Lawsuits filed in federal court contend that the Trump family's ownership of hotels that are frequented by foreign officials in business with the federal government constitutes a violation of the emoluments clause. Two of these cases, brought by Maryland and Washington, D.C., and by 200 members of Congress, have been permitted to proceed.

Congress's exclusive powers take on additional significance through the **necessary and proper clause**, also known as the elastic clause. It gives Congress the flexibility to "make all Laws which shall be necessary and proper for carrying into Execution the foregoing Powers, and all other Powers vested by this Constitution in the Government of the United States, or in any Department or Officer thereof." This broad grant of power meant that Congress could pass laws related to any of its exclusive powers. For example, although the Constitution did not explicitly mention Congress's right to compel people to serve in the military, its power to enact a draft was clearly given by the necessary and proper clause, in conjunction with its power to "raise and support armies."

In contrast to Congress's numerous and specific exclusive powers the Constitution grants very limited exclusive powers to the president. The president is the commander in chief of the armed forces, has power to receive ambassadors and foreign ministers, and may issue pardons. While these powers are fewer in number than those of Congress, they are consequential. In addition to the concern about possible war with North Korea discussed at the beginning of the chapter, President Trump also created a stir in 2017 when he explored the possibility of preemptively granting pardons to everyone, including himself, targeted by the Justice Department's Russia investigation.[19] He also thrilled supporters and angered opponents when he granted a pardon to Joe Arpaio, the controversial sheriff from Arizona who had been convicted of criminal contempt of court for ignoring a federal judge's injunction concerning his implementation of immigration law.[20] The president's most important powers are contained in the executive powers clause that says: "The executive power shall be vested in a President of the United States of America" and in the directive to ensure "that the laws are faithfully executed." As we see later in the chapter, these Article II clauses impart most of the president's power.

The courts did not receive nearly as much attention in the Constitution as either Congress or the president. Alexander Hamilton argued in *Federalist 78* that the Supreme Court would be the "least dangerous branch," because it had "neither the power of the purse nor the sword." The most important positive powers that the framers gave the Supreme Court were lifetime tenure for justices "during good behaviour" and relative independence from the other two branches. The critical negative power of judicial review, the ability to strike down the laws and actions of other branches, will be discussed later.

Shared powers

Along with dividing the exclusive powers between branches, the Constitution's system of checks and balances designates some

The president and the Senate share the appointment power to many federal offices: the president makes the nominations, and the Senate provides its "advice and consent." The nomination of Neil Gorsuch (pictured here at left) to the Supreme Court was contentious, but Gorsuch was ultimately confirmed by a 54–45 vote in the Senate.

shared powers. These are areas where no branch has exclusive control. For example, the president has the power to negotiate treaties and make appointments to the federal courts and other government offices, but these executive actions are to be undertaken with the "advice and consent" of the Senate, which means they were intended to be shared powers. In the twentieth century, these particular powers became executive centered, with the Senate providing almost no advice to the president and routinely giving its consent (often disapprovingly called rubber-stamping). However, the Senate can assert its shared power, as shown by the Senate's blocking of several of President George W. Bush's and President Barack Obama's lower-court nominees and Obama's nomination of Merrick Garland to the Supreme Court in 2016.

The war powers, which include decisions about when and how to use military force, were also intended to be shared. After serious disagreements, the ultimate compromise that the framers reached shows checks and balances at work, with the president serving as the commander in chief of the armed forces and Congress having the power to declare war and to appropriate the funds to conduct a war. One other goal of the Founders in making the war powers a shared power was to ensure civilian control of the military. By providing a role for both Congress and the president, the Constitution made it more likely that this important democratic principle would be maintained. George Washington set a critical precedent for this before the Constitution was written when he resigned his commission as commander in chief of the Continental Army. Congress had given Washington complete authority over conduct of the Revolutionary War, and many in Congress wanted him to continue to rule, almost as a king. Washington knew that it was essential for the new nation to have democratically elected leaders control the military. By resigning his commission, he made it clear that any future leadership role he would play (and it was widely assumed by the Founders that he would be the first president) would be as a civilian rather than a general.

Since very early in our nation's history, the president has taken a lead role in the war powers, often making the decision to use military force. Presidents have authorized the use of American troops on hundreds of occasions, but Congress has declared war only five times. Of these, Congress debated the merits of entering only one war, the War

This painting, which hangs in the Capitol rotunda, shows General George Washington resigning his commission as commander in chief of the Continental Army. This set the precedent that democratically elected officials would control the U.S. military.

of 1812. The other "declarations" recognized a state of war that already existed. (For example, after Japan bombed Pearl Harbor, Hawaii, in 1941, Congress's subsequent declaration of war formally recognized what everyone already knew.) As the 2003 invasion of Iraq demonstrated, if a president is intent on going to war, Congress must go along or get out of the way.

However, the president's war powers are not unlimited. If President Trump really wanted to start a nuclear war in North Korea (rather than simply using strong rhetoric as a bargaining tool), it is likely that cooler heads would prevail. Also, since the Vietnam War, Congress has tried to redress the imbalance in the war powers in a variety of ways. In 1970, during the Vietnam War, Congress passed a resolution that prevented any funds from supporting ground troops in Laos or Cambodia (nations that bordered Vietnam). Congress passed the War Powers Resolution in 1973 to further limit the president's war powers (this will be discussed in more detail in Chapter 17). In 2013, Congress was strongly opposed to a military strike against Syria in response to its use of chemical weapons against its own people. A showdown with President Obama, who favored a strike, was averted when Syria agreed to allow weapons inspectors to destroy its chemical weapons stockpile. These examples show that although the president continues to dominate the war powers, Congress can assert its power when it has the will—just as it can by advising the president in treaty negotiations or by withholding approval of the president's nominees for appointed positions.

Negative or checking powers

The last part of the system of checks and balances is the negative power that the branches have over one another. These powers are especially important to ensure that no single branch dominates the national government.

Congressional Checks Congress has two important negative checks on the other branches: impeachment and the power of the purse. The **impeachment** power allows

impeachment
A negative or checking power over the other branches that allows Congress to remove the president, the vice president, or other "officers of the United States" (including federal judges) for abuses of power.

Congress to remove the president, vice president, or other "officers of the United States" (including federal judges) for abuses of power—specifically, "Treason, Bribery, or other High Crimes or Misdemeanors." The framers placed this central check with Congress as part of the overall system of checks and balances.

Through the power of the purse, Congress can punish executive agencies by freezing or cutting their funding or holding hearings on, investigations of, or audits of their operations to make sure money is being spent properly. Congress can also freeze judges' salaries to show displeasure with court decisions, and it has the power to limit the issues that federal courts can consider. Congress can also limit the discretion of judges in other ways, such as by setting federal sentencing guidelines that recommend a range of years in prison that should be served for various crimes. Even today, the system of checks and balances is not fixed in stone but evolves according to the changing political climate.

In addition to these two formal constitutional checks, Congress may limit presidential power through its legislative powers of lawmaking and oversight. When Congress is controlled by a different party than the president, such checking is common; for example, in the last six years of Obama's presidency, Republicans in Congress tried to stop much of his agenda. But even under unified government, as in the first two years of Trump's presidency, Congress can check presidential power. Republicans passed stronger sanctions against Russia, investigated Russian interference in our elections, failed to provide full funding for the wall at the U.S.-Mexico border, and failed to "repeal and replace" the Affordable Care Act (Obamacare), all in the face of Trump's opposition.

Presidential Checks The framers placed important checks on congressional power as well, and the president's most important check on Congress is the veto. Again, there was very little agreement on this topic. The Antifederalists argued that it was "a political error of the greatest magnitude, to allow the executive power a negative, or in fact any kind of control over the proceedings of the legislature." But the Federalists worried that Congress would slowly strip away presidential powers and leave the president too weak. In the end, the Federalist view that the president needed some protections against the "depredations" of the legislature won the day. However, the veto has developed into a major policy-making tool for the president, which is probably broader than the check against "depredations" envisioned by the framers.

The president does not have any formal check on the courts other than the power to appoint judges. However, presidents have, at various times, found unconventional ways to try to influence the courts. For example, Franklin Delano Roosevelt tried to "pack the Court" by expanding the size of the Supreme Court with justices who would be sympathetic to his New Deal policies. More recently, George W. Bush attempted to expand the reach of executive power in the War on Terror by taking over some functions within the executive branch that the courts had previously performed, such as defining which suspected terrorists would have legal rights. However, the Supreme Court struck down some of these policies as unconstitutional violations of defendants' due process rights. President Obama changed many of Bush's policies, such as harsh interrogation methods and excessive secrecy. But other Bush-era policies were either more difficult to change than Obama anticipated, such as the detainment of enemy combatants in the prison at Guantánamo Bay, or deemed necessary to fight terrorism, such as indefinite detention without trial for suspected terrorists who were arrested outside combat areas.[21] President Trump has continued these policies and created other new ones, such as the travel ban aimed at specific countries that are viewed as terrorist threats (see the How It Works graphic in this chapter). Critics claim that the expansion of executive power in order to fight terrorism has threatened the institutional balance of power by giving the president too much control over functions previously carried out by the courts.[22]

Judicial Review The Constitution did not provide the Supreme Court with any negative checks on the other two branches. Instead, the Court itself (in the landmark decision of *Marbury v. Madison* in 1803) established the practice of **judicial review**, the ability of the Supreme Court to strike down a law or an executive branch action as unconstitutional. For example, early in Trump's first year, federal courts struck down the initial versions of his travel ban because they were viewed as discriminatory against Muslims. According to Madison's notes, nine of the eleven framers who spoke on the topic clearly favored explicitly granting the Supreme Court the power of judicial review, but the issue was not resolved at the convention. In several states assertive courts had struck down state laws, and delegates from those states resisted giving an unelected national court similar power over the entire country.

Although judicial review is not explicitly mentioned in the Constitution, supporters of the practice justify it by pointing to the supremacy clause, which states that the "Constitution, and the Laws of the United States which shall be made in Pursuance thereof . . . shall be the supreme Law of the Land." As Chief Justice John Marshall argued in *Marbury v. Madison,* to enforce the Constitution as the supreme law of the land, the Court must determine which laws are "in pursuance thereof." Critics of judicial review argue that the Constitution is supreme because it gains its legitimacy from the people and that therefore elected officials—Congress and the president—should be the primary interpreters of the Constitution rather than the courts. This dispute may never be fully resolved, but Marshall's bold assertion of judicial review made the Supreme Court an equal partner in the system of separate powers and checks and balances rather than "the least dangerous branch" that the framers described.

The Constitution attempts to strike a balance between protecting our civil liberties from government intrusion and providing for a government strong enough to protect our national security. The protesters pictured here were responding to news that the FBI was urging Apple to unlock an iPhone during the investigation into a terrorist attack in San Bernardino, California. Apple has since announced a new secure system that prevents phones from being unlocked.

judicial review
The Supreme Court's power to strike down a law or executive branch action that it finds unconstitutional.

"Why Should I Care?"

If you remember anything from your elementary civics class, it is probably some foggy notion of the system of checks and balances and separation of powers. But why is this system so important? This institutional framework provides the basis for our government and explains the nature of political conflict and outcomes. When the government shuts down because of a dispute over spending or the Senate blocks the president's court nominees, this is because the president and Congress have different roles but can check each other's powers. Understanding checks and balances and separation of powers helps us be realistic about what government can do and shows us that all parts of the government are critical, but none are dominant, in making policy and enforcing laws.

Is the Constitution a "living" document?

Polls suggest that many Americans are unfamiliar with the Constitution's basic provisions. Indeed, a national poll found that only 26 percent could name all three branches of the U.S. government, while 31 percent could not identify even one; 12 percent believed there was a constitutional right to own a pet, and 34 percent thought there was a right to own a home.[23] Even more disconcerting, another poll showed that 52 percent could name at least two members of Bart Simpson's family, while only 28 percent could list more than one of their five First Amendment rights.[24] In the face of such public ignorance, can the Constitution provide the blueprint for modern democratic governance? If so, how has it remained relevant after more than 200 years? The answer to the first question, in our opinion, is clearly yes. Although the United States falls short on many measures of an ideal democracy, the Constitution remains relevant in part because it embodies many of the central values of American citizens: liberty and freedom, majority rule and minority rights, equal protection for all citizens under the laws, and a division of power across and within levels of government. The Constitution presents a list of substantive values, largely within the Bill of Rights, aimed at legally protecting certain individual rights that we still consider basic and necessary. The Constitution also sets out the institutional framework within which the government operates.

But these observations beg the question of *why* the Constitution remains relevant today. Why does this framework of government still work? How can the framers' values still be meaningful to us? There are at least three components of the Constitution that allow it to continue as a "living" document: the ambiguity in central passages that permits flexible interpretation, the amending process, and the document's own designation of multiple interpreters of the Constitution. These factors have allowed the Constitution to evolve with the changing values and norms of the nation (see the Take a Stand feature).

The people made the Constitution, and the people can unmake it. It is the creature of their will, and lives only by their will.

—Justice John Marshall

Ambiguity

The Constitution's inherent ambiguity is a characteristic that has kept the document relevant to this day. Key passages were written in very general language, which has allowed the Constitution to evolve along with changing norms, values, and political contexts. This ambiguity was a political necessity: not only were the framers aware that the document would need to survive for generations, but in many instances the language that they chose was simply the only wording that all the framers could agree on.

Three of the most important parts of the Constitution are also among its most ambiguous: the necessary and proper (or elastic) clause, the **executive powers clause**, and the **commerce clause**. As discussed earlier, the necessary and proper clause gives Congress the power to enact laws that are related to its enumerated powers, or those that are explicitly granted. But what does "necessary and proper" mean? For the most part, Congress gets to answer that question.

The executive powers clause is even more vague: Article II begins with the words "The executive Power shall be vested in a President of the United States of America." This sentence has served to justify a broad range of presidential actions because it does not define any boundaries for the "executive powers" it grants. The vague wording was necessary because the Constitutional Convention delegates could not agree on

executive powers clause
The part of Article II, Section 1, of the Constitution that states: "The executive Power shall be vested in a President of the United States of America." This broad statement has been used to justify many assertions of presidential power.

commerce clause
The part of Article I, Section 8, of the Constitution that gives Congress "the power to regulate Commerce … among the several States." The Supreme Court's interpretation of this clause has varied, but today it serves as the basis for much of Congress's legislation.

A Living Constitution?

Should the Constitution be viewed as a flexible framework or a document that has fixed meaning? The public is evenly split on this issue, with 49 percent saying that constitutional interpretation should be based on "what it means in current time" (the living Constitution approach) and 46 percent saying that it should be based on "what it originally meant" (originalism). However, there is a deep partisan divide on this issue, with 70 percent of Democrats taking the living Constitution approach and 69 percent of Republicans supporting originalism.[a]

 There is a vigorous debate among justices of the Supreme Court as to whether the Constitution is a living document or should be interpreted more strictly according to the original intent of the framers.

The meaning of the Constitution doesn't change.
Justice Clarence Thomas is perhaps the strongest advocate of the originalist view. He wrote: "Let me put it this way; there are really only two ways to interpret the Constitution—try to discern as best we can what the framers intended or make it up."[b] Former chief justice William Rehnquist, although generally adhering to the originalist view, took a more nuanced approach. He favorably cites a 1920 Supreme Court opinion by Oliver Wendell Holmes: "When we are dealing with words that also are a constituent act, like the Constitution of the United States, we must realize that they have called into life a being the development of which could not have been foreseen completely by the most gifted of its begetters."[c] John Marshall in *McCulloch v. Maryland* also endorses this view, saying the Constitution was "intended to endure for ages to come, and consequently to be adapted to the various crises of human affairs." Rehnquist says that "scarcely anyone would disagree" with the idea that the Constitution was written broadly enough to allow principles such as the prohibition against illegal searches and seizures to apply to technologies, such as the telephone or the Internet, that could not have been envisioned by the framers.[d]

However, according to this view, the *meaning* of the Constitution cannot change with the times. Rehnquist writes that "mere change in public opinion since the adoption of the Constitution, unaccompanied by a constitutional amendment, should not change the meaning of the Constitution. A merely temporary majoritarian groundswell should not abrogate some individual liberty truly protected by the Constitution."[e] Therefore, recent rulings restricting the death penalty (which is clearly endorsed by the Constitution), expanding gay rights, or allowing children to testify remotely against their sexual abusers rather than having to confront them directly in court (as guaranteed by the Sixth Amendment) would all be inconsistent with the originalist view. This view would also hold that anything other than relying on the meaning of the words of the Constitution allows justices to "legislate from the bench," which is undemocratic given that the judges are not elected.

The meaning of the Constitution changes with the times. Proponents of a living Constitution argue for a more flexible view. Justice Thurgood Marshall advocated a living Constitution, noting that the framers "could not have imagined, nor would they have accepted, that the document they were drafting would one day be construed by a Supreme Court to which had been appointed a woman and the descendent of an African slave."[f] If the meaning of the Constitution is fixed, then the Court would have to uphold a state law allowing the death penalty for horse stealing, which was common during the Founding era. Executing horse thieves, or, more realistically, children and the mentally impaired (which was allowed in many states until 2005), is unacceptable in a modern society, even if it would be allowed by a strict reading of the Constitution.

Answering the question about how justices should interpret the Constitution ultimately depends on one's broader views of the proper role of the Court within a representative democracy. Should justices be constrained by the original meaning of the Constitution, or should that meaning evolve over time?

take a stand

1. If you were on the Supreme Court, would you adopt an originalist or a living Constitution approach? Justify your position.

2. Based on the originalist view, should a state be allowed to execute whomever it wants to, including minors (or horse thieves)? Based on the living Constitution approach, should limits be placed on justices to prevent them from "legislating from the bench"?

a definition of executive power. The wording also had the desirable consequence of making the clause flexible enough to serve the country both in times that require strong presidential action (such as the Civil War, the Great Depression, or World War II) and in times when the president was not as central (such as the "golden age of Congress" in the late nineteenth century).

Perhaps the best illustration of the importance of ambiguity in the Constitution is the commerce clause, which gives Congress "the power to regulate commerce . . . among the several States." What is "commerce" and what exactly does "among the states" mean? Different interpretations have reflected prevailing norms of the time. In the nineteenth century, when the national government was relatively weak and more power was held at the state level, the Supreme Court interpreted the clause to mean that Congress could not regulate commerce that was entirely within the boundaries of a single state (*intra*state, as opposed to *inter*state, commerce). Because manufacturing typically occurred within the boundaries of a given state, this ruling led to a distinction between manufacturing and commerce, which had significant implications. For example, Congress could not regulate working hours, worker safety, or child labor given that these were defined as part of manufacturing rather than commerce. In the New Deal era of the mid-1930s, the Court adopted a more expansive interpretation of the commerce clause that largely obliterated the distinction between intrastate and interstate commerce. This view was strengthened in the 1960s when the Supreme Court upheld a civil rights law that, among other things, prevented owners of hotels and restaurants from discriminating against African Americans. For nearly 60 years this interpretation held. More recently the Supreme Court has tightened the scope of Congress's powers to regulate commerce, but the clause still serves as the basis for most important national legislation. The commerce clause has been unchanged since 1789, but its ambiguous wording has been used to justify or restrict a varying array of legislation.

One consequence of this ambiguity is that both sides of every major political debate in our history have claimed to ground their views in the Constitution. Proslavery and antislavery factions during the pre–Civil War period, New Deal supporters and opponents during the Great Depression, and civil rights activists and segregationists all claimed to have the Constitution on their side, whether the dispute was over a broad or narrow interpretation of the commerce clause, the Fourteenth Amendment, or the Tenth Amendment. Today's vigorous debate about the proper scope of the national government's powers on issues such as health care, immigration, and economic policy is only the most recent chapter in this perpetual conflict.

Changing the Constitution

The most obvious way that the Constitution keeps up with the times is by allowing for changes to its language. The framers broadly supported the idea behind Article V, which lays out the formal process for amending the Constitution: the people must control their own political system, which includes the ability to change it through a regular, nonviolent process. George Washington called constitutional amendments "explicit and authentic acts," and Thomas Jefferson was adamant that each generation needed to have the power to change the Constitution. Toward the end of his life, he wrote in a letter to James Madison:

Some men look at constitutions with sanctimonious reverence, and deem them like the ark of the covenant, too sacred to be touched. They ascribe to the men of the preceding age a wisdom more than human, and suppose what they did to be beyond amendment. I knew that age well; I belonged to it and labored with it.... It was very like the present.... Let us not weakly believe that one generation is not as capable as another of taking care of itself.[25]

Proposal and Ratification Although there was strong consensus on including in the Constitution a set of provisions for amending it, there was no agreement on how this should be done. The Virginia Plan envisioned a relatively easy process of changing the Constitution "whensoever it shall seem necessary" by means of ratification by the people, whereas the New Jersey Plan proposed a central role for state governments. Madison suggested the plan that was eventually adopted, which once again accommodated both those who wanted a stronger national government and those who favored the states.

Article V describes the two steps necessary to change the Constitution: proposal and ratification. Congress may *propose* an amendment that has the approval of two-thirds of the members in both houses, or an amendment may be proposed by a national convention that has been called by two-thirds of the states' legislatures. In either case, the amendment must be *ratified* by three-fourths of the states' legislatures or state conventions (see Nuts & Bolts 2.3). A national convention has never been used to propose an amendment, and every amendment except for the Twenty-First, which repealed Prohibition, has been ratified by state legislatures rather than state conventions.

A Range of Amendments Amendments have ranged from fairly narrow, technical corrections of errors in the original document (Eleventh and Twelfth Amendments) to important topics such as abolishing slavery (Thirteenth Amendment), mandating equal protection of the laws for all citizens (Fourteenth Amendment), providing for the popular election of senators (Seventeenth Amendment), giving black men and then women the right to vote (Fifteenth and Nineteenth Amendments), and allowing a national income tax (Sixteenth Amendment). Potential constitutional amendments have addressed many other issues, with more than 10,000 proposed; of those, 33 were sent to the states and 27 have made it through the amending process (the first 10 came at once in the Bill of Rights). Table 2.1 shows several amendments that were introduced but not ratified.

Amending the Constitution is difficult and can be controversial. Some amendments that are widely accepted today, like the Nineteenth Amendment giving women the right to vote, were intensely debated prior to their ratification.

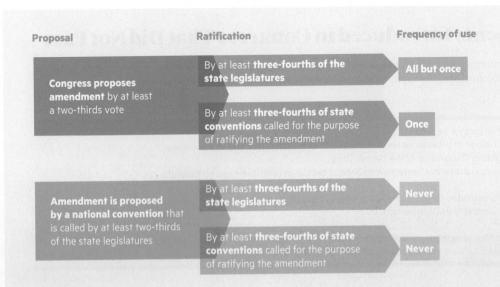

Amending the Constitution

This flowchart shows how amendments to the Constitution can be proposed and ratified and the frequency with which each method has been used. Interestingly, the president is not a part of the formal process of amending the Constitution.

Proposal	Ratification	Frequency of use
Congress proposes amendment by at least a two-thirds vote	By at least **three-fourths of the state legislatures**	All but once
	By at least **three-fourths of state conventions** called for the purpose of ratifying the amendment	Once
Amendment is proposed by a national convention that is called by at least two-thirds of the state legislatures	By at least **three-fourths of the state legislatures**	Never
	By at least **three-fourths of state conventions** called for the purpose of ratifying the amendment	Never

Multiple interpreters

The final way that the Constitution maintains its relevance is through changing views of the document by multiple interpreters. As we pointed out in the previous discussion of the commerce clause, there have been significant changes in the way the Constitution structures the policy-making process, even though the pertinent text of the Constitution has not changed.[26] This point is best understood by examining the concept of **implied powers**—that is, powers that are not explicitly stated in the Constitution but can be inferred from an enumerated power. The Supreme Court often defines the boundaries of implied powers, but Congress, the president, and the public can also play key roles.

Three of the earliest examples of implied powers show the president, the Supreme Court, and Congress each interpreting the Constitution and contributing to its evolving meaning. The first involved the question of how active the president should be in stating national foreign policy principles. In issuing his famous proclamation of neutrality in 1793, George Washington unilaterally set forth a national foreign policy, even though the president's power to do so is not explicitly stated in the Constitution. Alexander Hamilton defended the presidential power to make such a proclamation as implied in both the executive powers clause and the president's explicitly granted powers in the area of foreign policy (receiving ambassadors, negotiating treaties, and serving as commander in chief). Thomas Jefferson, in contrast, thought it was a terrible idea for presidents to have that kind of power. He preferred that such general policy statements be left to Congress.

The Supreme Court first made its mark on the notion of implied powers in a landmark case involving the creation of a national bank. In *McCulloch v. Maryland* (1819), the Court ruled that the federal government had the power to create a national bank and denied the state of Maryland the right to tax a branch of that bank. The Court said it was not necessary for the Constitution to expressly grant Congress the power to create the bank; rather, it was implied in Congress's power over financial matters and from the necessary and proper clause of the Constitution.

Congress got into the act with an early debate over the president's implied power to remove appointed officials. The Constitution clearly gives the president the power to make appointments to cabinet positions and other top executive branch offices, but it is silent on how these people can be removed. This was one of the most difficult issues

implied powers
Powers supported by the Constitution that are not expressly stated in it.

TABLE 2.1

Amendments Introduced in Congress That Did Not Pass

Many proposed constitutional amendments have almost no chance of passing. Indeed, most of those listed here did not even make it to the floor of the House or Senate for a vote. Why do you think a member of Congress would propose an amendment that he or she knew would fail?

115th Congress (2017–2018)	Require that the federal budget be balanced. Abolish the electoral college to provide for the direct election of the president and vice president. Protect the voting rights of the citizens of the United States. Amend the First Amendment to allow limitations on federal campaign contributions and expenditures.
114th Congress (2015–2016)	Require that the rights extended by the Constitution be granted only to natural persons (not corporations). Repeal the Sixteenth Amendment (income tax).
113th Congress (2013–2014)	No treaty, executive order, or agreement with another nation can diminish the rights of U.S. citizens. All laws that apply to U.S. citizens must apply equally to U.S. senators and representatives.

Source: http://thomas.loc.gov (accessed 7/14/17).

The Eighth Amendment's ban on "cruel and unusual punishments" is generally viewed as excluding capital punishment, but the execution of juveniles and the mentally impaired has been found unconstitutional. This picture shows the electric chair in the Southern Ohio Correctional Facility in Lucasville.

that faced the 1st Congress, and members spent more than a month debating the topic. The record of the debate is the most thorough examination of implied powers ever conducted in Congress. However, Congress ended up not taking any action on the issue, which left the president's removal power implicit in the Constitution.

Issues concerning implied powers continue to surface. The president's appointment powers have recently evolved as the Senate has played a much more aggressive role in providing its "advice and consent" on presidential nominations to the federal courts. As we explore in Chapter 14, in the past 20 years the Senate has blocked court appointments at a significantly higher rate than it did in the first half of the twentieth century. The relevant language in the Constitution is the same, yet the Senate's understanding of its role in this important process has changed. The president's power to remove appointees also recently came into play when President Trump fired FBI Director James Comey, who was investigating the Trump campaign's connections to Russia. This situation raised the constitutional question of when (or whether) the president's removal of one of his or her appointees constitutes an obstruction of justice. Presidential use of executive powers to go around Congress when it declines to act on issues the president deems important also demonstrates the ambiguous nature of constitutional powers. For example, Obama's executive actions on immigration policy and EPA rules concerning carbon emissions and Trump's use of executive orders to impose a travel ban on specific countries to limit the threat of terrorism were viewed as either appropriate and necessary executive action or "constitutional overreach," depending on who you ask.

Public opinion and social norms also influence the prevailing interpretation of the Constitution, as is evident in the evolving meanings of capital punishment (the death penalty) and freedom of speech. When the Constitution was written, capital punishment was broadly accepted, even for horse thieves. The framers were concerned only that people not be "deprived of life, liberty, or property without the due process of law." Therefore, the prohibition in the Eighth Amendment against "cruel and unusual punishments" certainly did not mean to the framers that the death penalty was unconstitutional. However, in 1972 the Supreme Court struck down capital punishment as unconstitutional because it was being applied arbitrarily.[27]

Subsequently, after procedural changes were made, the Court once again upheld the practice. However, the Court has since decided that capital punishment for minors and mentally impaired people constitutes cruel and unusual punishment—decisions that reflect modern sensibilities but not the thinking of the framers.[28] Similarly, the text of the First Amendment protections for freedom of speech has never changed, but the Supreme Court has been willing to uphold significant limitations on free speech, especially in wartime. When external threats are less severe, the Court has been more tolerant of controversial speech.

The line between a new interpretation of the Constitution and constitutional change is difficult to define. Clearly, not every new direction taken by the Supreme Court or new interpretation of the constitutional roles of the president or Congress is comparable to a constitutional amendment. In one respect, a constitutional amendment is much more permanent than a new interpretation by the Court. For example, the Court could not unilaterally decide that 18- to 20-year-olds, women, and African Americans no longer have the right to vote. Constitutional amendments expanded the right to vote to include these groups, and only further amendments could either expand or restrict the right to vote. However, gradual changes in constitutional interpretation are probably just as important as the amending process in explaining the Constitution's ability to keep pace with the times. For example, although the Civil War amendments produced lasting and significant changes in the Constitution, during the New Deal shifts in constitutional interpretation helped establish a huge growth in national power without changing a single word of the document.

One of the most remarkable things about the Constitution is its longevity. While there are intense debates about whether a "living Constitution" is a good thing, there is no doubt that its ability to change with the times, whether because of its amending process, multiple interpreters, or ambiguity, has helped make it the oldest constitution in the world. People may joke that the Constitution isn't relevant anymore, but it shapes the boundaries for all of today's policy debates and institutional struggles.

"Why Should I Care?"

Unpacking the Conflict

As we discussed at the beginning of this chapter, the presidency of Donald Trump raises many questions about the strength and resilience of our Constitution. Considering all that we know about how the Constitution works, Is American democracy in danger? Do we really need to be afraid of nuclear war?

While this presidency has raised other new, important constitutional questions such as "Can the president pardon himself?" and "How does the emoluments clause apply to the complex real estate holdings of the Trump family?" a look at the facts indicates that the Constitution is working just as the Founders intended. The first two years of the Trump presidency illustrate many of the themes of this chapter: the conflictual nature of politics established by the Constitution (there has been plenty of conflict!) and the fact that multiple interpreters and ambiguous language provide the flexibility for our political system to respond to challenging times.

To protect against majority tyranny, the separation of powers and the system of checks and balances in our political system divide power by giving each branch

What's Your Take?

Have Trump's actions as president threatened democracy? Or has our system of government as laid out in the Constitution worked to keep conflicts over Trump's policies in check?

of government the power to check the others (and the additional check of divided power across levels of government). Therefore, when the presidency starts to drift out of the mainstream of American politics, Congress, the courts, and state governments can reel it back in. We've seen throughout the chapter how our constitutional system has allowed the courts and Congress to effectively check the more extreme aspects of Trump's agenda that have alarmed pundits on the left, from Trump's proposed immigration and environmental policies, to the failure to "repeal and replace" Obamacare, to the early versions of his travel bans, to his relationship with Russia. Even the military stood up to their commander in chief, both when President Trump tweeted that transgender people would be banned from the military (they said that a tweet is not a policy, so the president should get back to them if he had an actual policy) and in their strong rebuke of Trump's equivocal response to a white supremacist's running down a woman in Charlottesville. And perhaps most significantly, our government has not allowed a Twitter war between President Trump and North Korea's leader, Kim Jong-un, to escalate into a nuclear war. This self-corrective feature of our constitutional system means that no branch of government will attain disproportionate power for very long, it and has kept the political system stable.

Even more fundamentally, the Constitution promotes long-term stability by providing the basis for resolving conflict through elections and representative government rather than by taking up arms. Losers of one round of elections know that they have an opportunity to compete in the next election and that their voices can be heard in another part of the government. Indeed, after heavy losses in 2016, Democrats were especially energized for the competitive 2018 midterms.

Congress, the president, and the Supreme Court all must interpret the Constitution in the normal course of fulfilling their institutional roles, which also helps preserve an institutional balance of power. Having multiple interpreters of the Constitution is built into our system. The Trump presidency has also compelled the general public to become more interested in the Constitution.[29] Maybe with enough attention, those public-opinion polls showing that Americans are more familiar with *The Simpsons* than with the three branches of government can be reversed. If Americans are more informed about the Constitution, they can become even more significant interpreters of the Constitution.

Finally, the general and ambiguous language of the Constitution means that both supporters and opponents of the president can find evidence for their views. It is impossible to know exactly how the emoluments clause should apply to foreign officials staying in a Trump-owned property or whether the president can pardon himself, because these constitutional questions have never come up before. Therefore, answers to these questions, and the broader health of our American democracy, will continue to be determined by the outcome of the political process and democratic elections as established by the Constitution. While there is no guarantee that our nation will be around for another 230 years, these past two years have demonstrated the Constitution's resilience and strength once again.

A leading constitutional scholar, Walter Murphy, addressed the relevance of the Constitution this way: "The ideals it enshrines, the processes it prescribes, and the actions it legitimizes must either help to change its citizenry or at a minimum reflect their current values. If a constitution does not articulate, at least in general terms, the ideals that form or will re-form its people and express the political character they have ..., it will soon be replaced or atrophy."[30] The Constitution's ability to change with the times and reflect its citizens' values has enabled it to remain relevant and important today. Its flexibility and general language mean that there will never be definitive answers to the conflict over its meaning, but they ensure that these debates will be enduring and meaningful.

STUDY GUIDE

The historical context of the Constitution

Describe the historical circumstances that led to the Constitutional Convention of 1787. (Pages 32–39)

Summary

The U.S. Constitution was shaped by historical events preceding its creation, particularly the period of British rule over the colonies, the Revolutionary War, and the states' experience under the Articles of Confederation. Under British rule, the colonies were relatively independent of one another, and the framers sought to create a strong nation while still maintaining the autonomy of the states in the system. The framers based the Constitution on three key principles: the rejection of a monarchy, popular control of the government, and a limited government that protected against tyranny.

Key terms

Articles of Confederation (p. 33)
limited government (p. 33)
monarchy (p. 33)
Shays's Rebellion (p. 35)
republicanism (p. 36)
"consent of the governed" (p. 37)
natural rights (p. 37)
Federalists (p. 38)
Antifederalists (p. 38)

Practice Quiz Questions

1. **How were members of Congress selected under the Articles of Confederation?**

   a   by the state governor

   b   by the state legislature

   c   by the state supreme court

   d   by popular election

   e   by random lot

2. **What power did the president have under the Articles of Confederation?**

   a   power to raise an army

   b   power to veto congressional legislation

   c   power to negotiate foreign agreements

   d   power to nominate federal judges

   e   There was no president under the Articles of Confederation.

3. **Who is the philosopher who argued that without government, life would be "nasty, brutish, and short"?**

   a   Thomas Hobbes

   b   John Locke

   c   Baron de Montesquieu

   d   Thomas Paine

   e   Thomas Jefferson

4. **At the American Founding, what is the best way to describe the economic inequality among classes and the economic diversity among regions?**

   a   high inequality / high diversity

   b   high inequality / low diversity

   c   low inequality / high diversity

   d   low inequality / low diversity

The politics of compromise at the Constitutional Convention

Analyze the major issues debated by the framers of the Constitution. (Pages 39–48)

Summary

Although the framers of the Constitution agreed that the Articles of Confederation needed to be changed, there was little consensus otherwise. The Federalists and Antifederalists clashed on several issues, though the most important were (1) balancing majority rule with minority rights, (2) allocating power between large and small states, (3) allocating power between the legislature and executive, (4) allocating power between the national government and the states, and (5) determining how to handle slavery.

Key terms

pluralism (p. 41)
Virginia Plan (p. 42)
New Jersey Plan (p. 42)
Great Compromise (p. 42)
parliamentary system (p. 44)
reserved powers (p. 45)
national supremacy clause (p. 45)
Three-Fifths Compromise (p. 46)

5. Madison argued that the best way to prevent the tyranny of factions was to _____.

a outlaw political parties

b establish a strong national government

c have various groups compete against one another in the government

d establish strong local governments

e try to ensure that all people were equal

6. The Great Compromise provided solutions to which issue?

a balancing majority rule with minority rights

b allocating power between big and small states

c allocating power between the legislature and executive

d allocating power between national and state governments

e determining how to handle slavery

7. How are executives chosen in most other established democracies?

a by popular election

b by electoral college

c through selection by the judiciary

d through selection by the legislature

e by the United Nations

8. The outcome of the Three-Fifths Compromise was that each slave counted for three-fifths of a person for the purposes of _____ and _____.

a voting; taxation

b congressional representation; taxation

c voting; congressional representation

d taxation; congressional appropriations

e congressional representation; agricultural subsidies

Ratification

Contrast the arguments of the Federalists with those of the Antifederalists. (Pages 48–51)

Summary

After the Constitution was written and approved at the Constitutional Convention, it still needed to be ratified by nine states. The Constitution was primarily criticized by the Antifederalists, which gave way to a lengthy public debate over the merits of the proposed framework. Ultimately, to win over the necessary support in the states, the framers had to include the Bill of Rights, which was tailored to protect the rights of states and individuals from the national government.

Key term
Bill of Rights (p. 50)

Practice Quiz Questions

9. What group was concerned about the Constitution's provisions for the strength of the president and the lack of specific guarantees of civil liberties?

a Tories

b Unionists

c Federalists

d Antifederalists

e Free Soilers

10. A series of arguments originally published in New York newspapers supported the Constitution and outlined the political theory behind it. What are these assembled works called?

a *Pickwick Papers*

b *Federalist Papers*

c *Antifederalist Papers*

d *Common Sense*

e *The Second Treatise of Government*

The Constitution: a framework for government

Outline the major provisions of the Constitution. (Pages 51–58)

Summary

The defining feature of the Constitution is its separation of powers while still maintaining flexibility for leadership in times of crisis. The system of checks and balances gives each branch of the federal government some explicit powers, some shared powers, and some ability to limit the power of the other two branches of government.

Key terms
enumerated powers (p. 51)   **impeachment** (p. 56)

power of the purse (p. 54)   **judicial review** (p. 58)

necessary and proper clause (p. 54)

Practice Quiz Questions

11. The "necessary and proper" clause gives flexibility to which part of government?

a the president

b the Supreme Court

c the bureaucracy

d the Congress

e interest groups

12. Which branch has the fewest explicit powers?

a   the president

b   the Supreme Court

c   the bureaucracy

d   the Congress

e   the people

13. Which of the following negative powers does the president enjoy?

a   the power to veto legislation

b   the power to freeze judicial salaries

c   the power to review the constitutionality of a law

d   the power to impeach federal justices

e   the power to dissolve Congress and call new elections

Is the Constitution a "living" document?

Explore how the meaning of the Constitution has evolved. (Pages 59–65)

Summary

The Constitution is more than 200 years old, yet it still provides a blueprint for modern governance. It has maintained its relevance due to its ambiguity on several key passages, its ability to be amended rather than entirely rewritten, and its designation of multiple interpreters of the Constitution.

Key terms

executive powers clause (p. 59)   implied powers (p. 63)

commerce clause (p. 59)

Practice Quiz Questions

14. Which of the following clauses, central to congressional activity, has been interpreted differently over time though the wording has stayed the same?

a   establishment clause

b   commerce clause

c   enumerated powers clause

d   executive powers clause

e   prerogative powers clause

15. Which part of government often defines the boundaries of implied powers?

a   the president

b   the Supreme Court

c   the bureaucracy

d   the Congress

e   the people

Suggested Reading

Allen, Danielle. *Our Declaration: A Reading of the Declaration of Independence in Defense of Equality*. New York: W. W. Norton, 2014.

Amar, Akhil Reed. *The Constitution Today: Timeless Lessons for the Issues of Our Era*. New York: Basic Books, 2016.

Currie, David P. *The Constitution of the United States: A Primer for the People*, 2nd ed. Chicago: University of Chicago Press, 2000.

Dahl, Robert A. *How Democratic Is the American Constitution?* New Haven, CT: Yale University Press, 2001.

Davis, Sue. *Corwin and Peltason's Understanding the Constitution*, 17th ed. Boston: Wadsworth, 2008.

Hamilton, Alexander, James Madison, and John Jay. *The Federalist Papers*. 1788. Reprint, 2nd ed., edited by Roy P. Fairfield. Baltimore, MD: Johns Hopkins University Press, 1981.

Ketcham, Ralph. *The Anti-Federalist Papers and the Constitutional Convention Debates*. New York: Signet Classics, 2003.

Rossiter, Clinton. *1787: The Grand Convention*. New York: Macmillan, 1966.

Strauss, David. *The Living Constitution*. New York: Oxford University Press, 2010.

Sunstein, Cass R. *Designing Democracy: What Constitutions Do*. New York: Oxford University Press, 2001.

West, Thomas G. *The Political Theory of the American Founding: Natural Rights, Public Policy, and the Moral Conditions of Freedom*. New York: Cambridge University Press, 2017.

Wood, Gordon S. *The Creation of the American Republic*. New York: W. W. Norton, 1969.

3

Federalism

States or the federal government: who's got the power?

 "We don't go after people who don't pay their taxes on time, and we don't enforce EPA regulations, so it's the same thing with immigration. Immigration has always been a federal responsibility, and we don't have the expertise or resources for that."

Lieutenant Peter Davidov, Montgomery County, Maryland, Police

"So-called sanctuary policies make all of us less safe because they intentionally undermine our laws and protect illegal aliens who have committed crimes."

Attorney General Jeff Sessions

Should the government seek out and deport otherwise law-abiding illegal residents? While individual Americans disagree about this question, the states and the federal government also disagree about the states' role in implementing federal immigration policies. In December 2017, protesters in New York City called on state officials to prohibit ICE agents from entering state courthouses.

A few days after assuming office in January 2017, President Trump signed an executive order that threatened to withhold federal funds and grants from so-called sanctuary cities: generally speaking, cities with policies that limit the cooperation that may take place between local law-enforcement officials and the federal agency for Immigration and Customs Enforcement (ICE) as it works to seek out and deport undocumented immigrants. The Justice Department criticized Chicago, New York, and other cities for these policies, which it argued are "putting the well-being of criminal aliens before the safety of our citizens."[1]

In response, police chiefs and mayors of sanctuary cities argued that they were simply enforcing local laws and that the president did not have the authority to force them to comply. The Trump administration wanted localities to undertake aggressive campaigns to find and deport their undocumented residents, even though many local governments believed such efforts were a waste of scarce resources. Sam Liccardo, mayor of San Jose, California, claimed, "[O]ur police chief is the best person to decide how to use the scarce resources we have.... Our police department, like most, doesn't engage in federal tax laws, federal environmental laws or federal immigration laws." New York City mayor Bill de Blasio maintained that complying with Trump's order may

compromise the local police force's relationship with immigrants, on whom the force relies to report crimes in their communities.[2]

This conflict over sanctuary cities is the result of one of the fundamental features of America's government: federalism. In areas such as education and law enforcement, the federal government has only limited power to affect policy choices made at the state and local level. Because of federalism, your experiences with government, including the services you receive, the laws you are supposed to obey, and the regulations that constrain your actions, are different depending on where you live.

As we discussed in Chapter 2, one of the reasons we have a federal system is the desire to limit the power of the national government. Federalism also enables state and local governments to take account of citizens' demands or local conditions—information that might not be available to decision makers in Washington. By giving power to state and local governments, federalism can increase citizen satisfaction and governmental efficiency.

However, as the fight over sanctuary cities suggests, federalism is more than a way to increase responsiveness and efficiency. In many policy areas, federalism sets up conflicts between different levels of government over who gets to make policy choices. In the case of sanctuary cities, while city-level immigration enforcement policies may be designed to make sure that their police forces function as efficiently as possible, the cities' approaches conflict with the federal government's interest in deporting undocumented immigrants who have committed crimes. The conflict triggered by the sanctuary cities is a great example of the tensions created by a federal system. When local and federal officials disagree about sanctuary city policies, who wins? More generally, what are the responsibilities of the states and what is the domain of the national government? What happens when levels of government disagree? How have the answers to these questions changed over the course of American history—and how does federalism work today?

DEFINE *FEDERALISM* **AND EXPLAIN ITS SIGNIFICANCE**

federalism
The division of power across the local, state, and national governments.

sovereign power
The supreme power of an independent state to regulate its internal affairs without foreign interference.

What is federalism and why does it matter?

Federalism is a form of government that divides sovereign power across at least two political units. Dividing **sovereign power** simply means that each unit of government (in the United States, national, state, and local governments) has some degree of authority and autonomy. As discussed in Chapter 2, this division of power across levels of government is central to the system of separated powers in the United States. Dividing power across levels of government seems a simple concept, but as we will see later in this chapter, the political battles over *how* that power is divided have been intense.

In practical terms, federalism is about intergovernmental relations: How do the different levels of government interact and how is power divided? But even that may seem a little abstract. Why does federalism matter? On a broad range of issues, the level of government that dictates policy can make a real difference, simply because preferences vary across these levels. Sometimes these disagreements reflect different beliefs about what citizens want from government. But more commonly, conflicts result from differences of opinion about what government should be doing. In the case of immigration policy, for example, the national government, represented by President Trump and the Justice Department, supports aggressive policies to find and deport illegal residents. While some state and local politicians (as well as their supporters) hold similar feelings, others disagree. This divergence between the policies desired by politicians at different levels of government means that decisions about federalism (which level of government does what) affect how immigration law is ultimately interpreted and enforced.

Levels of government and their degrees of autonomy

A distinguishing feature of federalism is that each level of government has some degree of autonomy from the other levels—that is, each level can carry out some policies without interference from the others. In the United States, this means that the national and state governments have distinct powers and responsibilities (see Nuts & Bolts 3.1). The national government, for example, is responsible for national defense and foreign policy. State and local governments have primary responsibility for conducting elections and promoting public safety, or **police powers**. In other areas, such as transportation, the different levels of government have **concurrent powers**—that is, they share responsibilities. The national government has also taken on additional responsibilities through implied powers that are inferred from the powers explicitly granted in the Constitution (see Chapter 2 and the later discussion in this chapter).

Local governments—cities, towns, school districts, and counties—are not autonomous units of government: they are creatures of state governments. State governments create local governments and control the types of activities they can engage in by specifying in the state charter what local governments can do and cannot do.

police powers
The power to enforce laws and provide for public safety.

concurrent powers
Responsibilities for particular policy areas, such as transportation, that are shared by federal, state, and local governments.

A comparative perspective

It is useful to compare U.S. federalism with forms of government in other countries. Just because a nation is composed of states does not mean that it is a federal system: the key factor in determining whether a system is federal or not is the autonomy of the

The relationship between the national government and the states also involves cooperation. After Hurricane Harvey devastated Houston, Texas, in August 2017, FEMA partnered with state officials, including a task force from Nebraska, to provide relief to residents affected by the storm.

National and State Responsibilities

National Government Powers	State Government Powers	Concurrent Powers
Print money	Issue licenses	Collect taxes
Regulate interstate commerce and international trade	Regulate intrastate (within the state) Businesses	Build roads
Make treaties and conduct foreign policy	Conduct elections	Borrow money
Declare war	Establish local governments	Establish courts
Provide an army and navy	Ratify amendments to the Constitution	Make and enforce laws
Establish post offices	Promote public health and safety	Charter banks and corporations
Make laws necessary and proper to carry out these powers	May exert powers the Constitution does not delegate to the national government or does not prohibit the states from using	Spend money for the general welfare; take private property for public purposes, with just compensation

Powers Denied to the National Government	Powers Denied to State Governments
May not violate the Bill of Rights	May not enter into treaties with other countries
May not impose export taxes among states	May not print money
May not use money from the Treasury without an appropriation from Congress	May not tax imports or exports
May not change state boundaries	May not interfere with contracts
	May not suspend a person's rights without due process

unitary government
A system in which the national, centralized government holds ultimate authority. It is the most common form of government in the world.

confederal government
A form of government in which states hold power over a limited national government.

political subunits. The United Kingdom, for example, is made up of England, Scotland, Wales, and Northern Ireland. In 1998, the British Parliament created a new Scottish government and gave it authority in a broad range of areas. However, Parliament retained the right to unilaterally dissolve the Scottish government; therefore, the subunit (Scotland) is not fully autonomous. This type of government, in which power is centralized at the national level, is a **unitary government**. Unitary governments are the most common in the modern world (about 80 percent); other examples include Israel, Italy, France, Japan, and Sweden. Although U.S.-style federalism is not as common, Australia, Austria, Canada, and Germany, among others, share this form of government.

At the opposite end of the spectrum is a **confederal government**, in which the states have most of the power. This was the first type of government in the United States under the Articles of Confederation, but there are few modern examples. One is Switzerland, where 26 cantons (state-level governments) exercise largely independent policy-making powers except in the areas of foreign policy and control of the armed forces.

Balancing national and state power in the Constitution

Although the Founders wanted a national government that was stronger than it had been under the Articles of Confederation, they also wanted to preserve states' autonomy. These goals are reflected in different parts of the Constitution, which provides ample support for advocates of both state-centered and nation-centered federalism. The nation-centered position has its roots in the document's preamble, which begins: "We the People of the United States." The Articles of Confederation, by contrast, began with the words: "We the undersigned delegates of the States." The Constitution's phrasing emphasizes the nation as a whole over the separate states.

A strong national government

Most of the Founders wanted a strong national government to provide national security and a healthy and efficient economy, so they included various powers in the Constitution that supported the nation-centered perspective. In terms of national security, as we saw in Chapter 2, Congress was granted the power to raise and support armies, declare war, and "suppress Insurrections and repel Invasion," while the president, as commander in chief of the armed forces, would oversee the conduct of war. Congress's power to regulate interstate commerce promoted economic efficiency and centralized an important economic power at the national level. The Constitution outlines restrictions on state power that contribute to the centralization of national military and economic power: states were *prohibited* from entering into "any Treaty, Alliance, or Confederation" or keeping troops or "Ships of War" during peacetime. They also could not coin money or impose duties on imports or exports (see Article I, Section 10).

The necessary and proper clause (Article I, Section 8) was another broad grant of power to the national government: it gave Congress the power "[t]o make all Laws which shall be necessary and proper for carrying into Execution the foregoing Powers." Similarly, the national supremacy clause (Article VI) says that the Constitution and all laws and treaties that are made under the Constitution shall be the "supreme Law of the Land" and that "the Judges in every State shall be bound thereby, any Thing in the Constitution or Laws of any State to the Contrary notwithstanding." This is perhaps the clearest statement of the nation-centered focus of the Constitution. If any state law or constitution conflicts with national law or the Constitution, the national perspective wins. Thus, in the case of same-sex marriages, once the Supreme Court ruled that all laws prohibiting same-sex marriage were unconstitutional, elected officials at all levels knew that if they enacted new prohibitions, the laws would be immediately invalidated by the courts.

You might be thinking, "Wait a minute, if the Constitution and the federal government always win, how can local governments act as sanctuary cities even though the Trump administration opposes them?" The answer is that there is no constitutional provision or law that gives the federal government control over local law enforcement. The same is true in many other policy areas. As we will see, when conflicts between the federal and local governments arise, the federal government can try to persuade local governments by offering grants or other forms of aid to induce cooperation, but it cannot simply order local governments to comply with its wishes.

DID YOU KNOW?

Under the Articles of Confederation, all

13

states had their own militia and navy.

Jim Obergefell, the plaintiff in the *Obergefell v. Hodges* Supreme Court case that legalized same-sex marriage nationwide, is backed by supporters of the ruling on the steps of the Texas capitol during a rally on June 29, 2015, in Austin. This ruling shows the power of the supremacy clause, as it struck down laws in 14 states.

State powers and limits on national power

Despite the Founders' nation-centered bias, many parts of the Constitution also address state powers and set limits on national power. Article II gives the states the power to choose electors for the electoral college, and Article V grants the states a central role in the process of amending the Constitution. Three-fourths of the states must ratify any constitutional amendment (either through conventions or their state legislatures, as specified by Congress), but the states can also bypass Congress in proposing amendments if two-thirds of the states call for a Constitutional Convention (this route to amending the Constitution has never been used).

There are also limitations on Congress's authority over the states. For example, although Congress was given the power to regulate interstate commerce (commercial activity that crosses state lines), it cannot regulate commerce that occurs entirely within a state. Moreover, Congress cannot favor one state over another in regulating commerce, and it cannot impose a tax on any good that is shipped from one state to another.

While Article I of the Constitution enumerates many specific powers for Congress, the list of state powers is much shorter. One could interpret this as more evidence for the nation-centered perspective, but at the time of the Founding the expectation was that most power would be exercised at the state level. Therefore, the federal powers that were exceptions to this rule had to be clearly specified, and state governments received authority over all other matters. The Tenth Amendment supports this view: "The powers not delegated to the United States by the Constitution, nor prohibited by it to the states, are reserved to the states respectively, or to the people."

Clauses that favor both perspectives

Article IV of the Constitution includes provisions that favor both the state-centered and the nation-centered perspectives. For example, its **full faith and credit clause** specifies that states must respect one another's laws, granting citizens the "Full Faith and Credit" of their home state's laws if they go to another state. At the same time, however, the article's **privileges and immunities clause** says that citizens of each state are "entitled to all Privileges and Immunities" of citizens in the other states, which means that states must treat visitors from other states the same as their own residents.

full faith and credit clause
The part of Article IV of the Constitution requiring that each state's laws be honored by the other states. For example, a legal marriage in one state must be recognized across state lines.

privileges and immunities clause
The part of Article IV of the Constitution requiring that states must treat nonstate residents within their borders as they would treat their own residents. This was meant to promote commerce and travel between states.

There are many examples of the full faith and credit clause and privileges and immunities clause at work today. If you have a New York driver's license and are traveling to California, you do not need to stop at every state line to get a new license; each state will honor your New York license. Similarly, a legal marriage in one state (even a same-sex marriage) must be honored by another state. But not all state licenses are subject to full faith and credit: if you have an open or concealed-carry gun permit in one state, that does not automatically give you the right to carry a firearm in another state. Similarly, states do not have to permit nonresidents to vote in state elections, and public colleges and universities may charge out-of-state residents higher tuition than in-state residents. Therefore, the privileges and immunities clause cuts both ways on the question of the balance of power: it allows the states to determine and uphold their own laws autonomously, but it also emphasizes that national citizenship is more important than state citizenship.

The evolving concept of federalism

TRACE THE MAJOR SHIFTS IN STATE AND FEDERAL GOVERNMENT POWER OVER TIME

The nature of federalism has changed as the size and functions of the national and state governments have evolved. In the first century of our nation's history, the national government played a relatively limited role and the boundaries between the levels of government were distinct. As the national government took on more power in the twentieth century, intergovernmental relations became more cooperative and the boundaries less distinct. Even within this more cooperative framework, federalism remains a source of conflict within our political system, both because the levels of government share lawmaking authority and because they may disagree over the details of government policy.

The early years

As the United States gained its footing, clashes between the advocates of state-centered and nation-centered federalism turned into a partisan struggle. The Federalists—the party of George Washington, John Adams, and Alexander Hamilton—controlled the new government for its first 12 years and favored strong national power. One of their strongest allies was Chief Justice John Marshall, who wrote several landmark Supreme Court decisions that enhanced the power of the national government. The Federalists' opponents, the Democratic-Republicans, led by Thomas Jefferson and James Madison, favored state power, or, as it came to be known, **dual federalism**. Dual federalism, as we will discuss, was the guiding principle of Marshall's successor as chief justice, Roger Taney. Table 3.1 highlights several important decisions resolved during Marshall's and Taney's tenures on the Court.

dual federalism
The form of federalism favored by Chief Justice Roger Taney, in which national and state governments are seen as distinct entities providing separate services. This model limits the power of the national government.

Establishing National Supremacy The first confrontation came when the Federalists established a national bank in 1791, followed by a second national bank in 1816. At that time, the state of Maryland, which was controlled by the Democratic-Republicans, tried to tax the National Bank's Baltimore branch out of existence. However, the head cashier of the bank refused to pay the tax, creating a conflict that sent the case to the Supreme Court. In the landmark decision *McCulloch v. Maryland* (1819), Marshall's Court held that even though the word "bank" does not appear in the Constitution, Congress's power to create one is implied through its relevant enumerated powers—such as the power to coin money, levy taxes, and borrow money. The Court also ruled that Maryland did not have the right to tax the bank because of the Constitution's national supremacy clause.

A few years later, Marshall's Court held in *Gibbons v. Ogden* (1824) that Congress has broad power to regulate interstate commerce. The ruling struck down a New York law that had granted a monopoly to a private company operating steamboats on the Hudson River between New York and New Jersey. By granting this monopoly, New York was interfering with interstate commerce, a power reserved to the Congress by the Constitution. Even in the modern era, this ruling underlies many of the federal government's regulations on businesses, which are based on the expectation that virtually any commercial activity will involve buying and selling across state lines.

TABLE 3.1	**Early Landmark Supreme Court Decisions on Federalism**	

Case	Holding and Significance for States' Rights	Direction of the Decision
Chisholm v. Georgia (1793)	Held that citizens of one state could sue another state; led to the Eleventh Amendment, which prohibited such lawsuits.	Less state power
McCulloch v. Maryland (1819)	Upheld the national government's right to create a bank and reaffirmed the idea of "national supremacy."	Less state power
Gibbons v. Ogden (1824)	Held that Congress, rather than the states, has broad power to regulate interstate commerce.	Less state power
Barron v. Baltimore (1833)	Endorsed a notion of "dual federalism" in which the rights of a U.S. citizen under the Bill of Rights did not apply to that same person under state law.	More state power
Dred Scott v. Sandford (1857)	Sided with southern states' view that slaves were property and ruled that the Missouri Compromise violated the Fifth Amendment, because making slavery illegal in some states deprived slave owners of property. Contributed to the start of the Civil War.	More state power

In the early 1800s, the Supreme Court confirmed the national government's right to regulate commerce between the states. The state of New York granted a monopoly to a ferry company serving ports in New York and New Jersey, but this was found to interfere with interstate commerce and was therefore subject to federal intervention.

The emergence of states' rights and dual federalism

Under Marshall's successor, Chief Justice Roger Taney, Court decisions involving federalism shifted to reflect a new concept: dual federalism. According to the system of dual federalism, the national and state governments are considered distinct, with little overlap in their activities or the services they provide. In this view, the national government's activities are confined to powers strictly enumerated in the Constitution.

Dual federalism was expressed most consequentially in the *Dred Scott v. Sandford* decision of 1857. Dred Scott was a slave who had lived for many years with his owner in the free state of Illinois and the free Wisconsin Territory but was living in Missouri, a slave state, when his master died. Scott petitioned for his freedom under the Missouri Compromise, which had made slavery illegal in any free state. The Court did not grant Scott his freedom. Its majority decision held that slaves were not citizens but private property; therefore, the Missouri Compromise's ban on slavery in certain territories violated the Fifth Amendment because it deprived people (slave owners) of their property without the due process of law. Put another way, the *Dred Scott* decision said that state law, not federal, determined the legal status of slaves.

Contrasting Marshall's decisions in favor of national power with Taney's decisions in favor of state power highlights the policy significance of judicial decisions. While we can't be sure whether Marshall and Taney based their decisions on their interpretations of the Constitution or their views on concrete policy questions (for example, whether or not slavery was moral), the fact is that their decisions had strong policy consequences. The Taney Court's decision that the Missouri Compromise was unconstitutional is consistent with a dual federalism interpretation of the Constitution—but it also sustained the legality of slavery in southern states and halted attempts by representatives from the North to limit the spread of slavery into

The *Dred Scott* decision, covered here in *Frank Leslie's Illustrated Newspaper*, was the subject of much public interest when it was handed down in 1857. The decision inflamed tensions between slave states and nonslave states and vindicated those who saw state law as superior to federal law.

states' rights
The idea that states are entitled to a certain amount of self-government, free of federal government intervention. This became a central issue in the period leading up to the Civil War.

the western territories. In this sense, debates about dual federalism during this time were really about the legality of slavery, its expansion into new states, and the rights of former slaves in free states.

Arguments about dual federalism are sometimes framed using the concept of **states' rights**: the idea that states retain some powers under the Constitution (specifically those reserved by the Tenth Amendment) and can ignore federal policies that encroach on these powers. The key question is, where does federal authority end and state authority begin? As this chapter demonstrates, the lines are not always easy to define and are still being debated today. Some people argue that southern states fought the Civil War to preserve the concept of states' rights, but this argument doesn't tell the whole story. Southern secessionists were not interested in states' rights per se; what they wanted was to continue slavery without federal intervention. States' rights was a convenient rationale for their proslavery position.

After the Civil War, constitutional amendments banned slavery (Thirteenth Amendment), prohibited states from denying citizens due process or the equal protection of the laws (Fourteenth Amendment), and gave newly freed male slaves the right to vote (Fifteenth Amendment). Congress also passed the 1875 Civil Rights Act (although it was later overturned by the Supreme Court). The Fourteenth Amendment was the most important in terms of federalism because it was the constitutional basis for many of the civil rights laws passed by the federal government during Reconstruction. The Civil War fundamentally changed the way Americans thought about the relationship between the national government and the states: before the war people said "the United States *are* . . . ," but after the war they said "the United States *is* . . ." The United States now felt like a unified nation, not merely a loose collection of states.

The Supreme Court and Limited National Government The assertion of power by Congress during Reconstruction was short-lived, as the Supreme Court soon stepped in again to limit the power of the national government. In 1873, the Court reinforced the notion of dual federalism, ruling that the Fourteenth Amendment did not change the balance of power between the national and state governments. Specifically, the Court ruled that the Fourteenth Amendment right to due process and equal treatment under the law applied to individuals' rights only as citizens of the United States, not to their state citizenship.[3] By extension, freedom of speech, freedom of the press, and the other liberties protected in the Bill of Rights applied only to laws passed by Congress, not to state laws. Here again, these decisions can be read as an articulation of a theoretical interpretation of the Constitution, but they are also part of a broader, more concrete debate over how much the government should regulate interactions between individuals, or between individuals and corporations.

In 1883, the Court overturned the 1875 Civil Rights Act, which had guaranteed equal treatment in public accommodations. The Court argued that the Fourteenth Amendment did not give Congress the power to regulate private conduct, such as whether a white restaurant owner had to serve a black customer; it affected only the conduct of state governments, not individuals in these states.[4] This narrow view of the Fourteenth Amendment left the national government powerless to prevent southern states from implementing state and local laws that led to complete segregation of blacks and whites in the South (called Jim Crow laws) and the denial of many basic rights to blacks after northern troops left the South at the end of Reconstruction.

The Supreme Court also limited the reach of the national government by curtailing Congress's authority to regulate the economy through its commerce

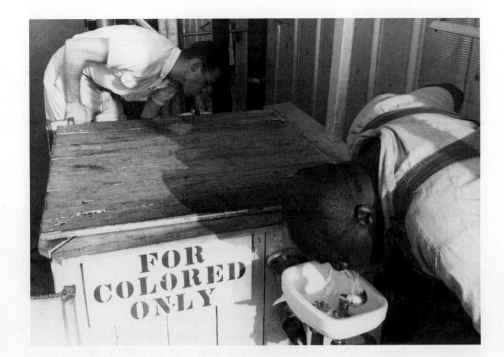

After the Supreme Court struck down the 1875 Civil Rights Act, southern states were free to impose Jim Crow laws. These state and local laws led to complete racial segregation, even for public drinking fountains.

clause powers. In a series of cases in the late nineteenth and early twentieth centuries, the Supreme Court endorsed a view of laissez-faire—French for "leave alone"—capitalism aimed at protecting business from regulation by the national government. To this end, the Court defined clear boundaries between *inter*state and *intra*state commerce, ruling that Congress could not regulate any economic activity that occurred *within* a state (intrastate). The Supreme Court let some national legislation that was connected to interstate commerce stand, such as the Sherman Antitrust Act (1890), which placed limits on monopolies. However, when the national government tried to use this act to break up a cartel of four sugar companies that controlled 98 percent of the nation's sugar production, the Court ruled that Congress did not have this power. The Court's decision argued that the commerce clause allowed Congress to regulate the transportation of goods, not their manufacture, and the sugar in question was made within a single state. Even if the sugar was sold throughout the country, this was "incidental" to its manufacture.[5] On the same grounds, the Court struck down attempts by Congress to regulate child labor.[6]

Cooperative federalism

From the early years of the twentieth century through the 1930s, a new era of American federalism emerged in which the national government became much more involved in activities that were formerly reserved for the states, such as transportation, civil rights, agriculture, social welfare, and management–labor relations. At first, the Supreme Court resisted this broader reach of national power, clinging to its nineteenth-century conception of dual federalism.[7] But as commerce became more national, the distinctions between interstate and intrastate commerce, and between manufacture and transportation, became increasingly difficult to sustain. Starting in 1937 with the landmark ruling *National Labor Relations Board*

cooperative federalism
A form of federalism in which national and state governments work together to provide services efficiently. This form emerged in the late 1930s, representing a profound shift toward less concrete boundaries of responsibility in national–state relations.

picket fence federalism
A more refined and realistic form of cooperative federalism in which policy makers within a particular policy area work together across the levels of government.

Franklin Delano Roosevelt's New Deal shifted more power than ever to the national government. Through major new programs to address the Great Depression, such as the Works Progress Administration construction projects pictured here, the federal government expanded its reach into areas that had been primarily the responsibility of state and local governments.

v. Jones and Laughlin Steel Corporation, the Supreme Court largely discarded these distinctions and gave Congress far more latitude to shape economic and social policy for the nation.[8]

Shifting National–State Relations The type of federalism that emerged in this era is called **cooperative federalism**, or "marble cake" federalism, as opposed to the "layer cake" model of dual federalism.[9] As the image of a marble cake suggests, the boundaries of state and national responsibilities are less well defined than they are under dual federalism. With the increasing industrialization and urbanization of the late 1930s and 1940s, along with the Great Depression, more complex problems arose that could not be solved at one level of government. Cooperative federalism adopted a more practical focus on intergovernmental relations and the efficient delivery of services. State and local governments maintained a level of influence as the implementers of national programs, but the national government played an enhanced role as the initiator, director, and funder of key policies.

"Cooperative federalism" accurately describes this important shift in national–state relations in the first half of the twentieth century, but it only partially captures the complexity of modern federalism. The marble cake metaphor falls short in one important way: the lines of authority and patterns of cooperation are not as messy as implied by the gooey flow of chocolate through white cake. Instead, the 1960s metaphor of **picket fence federalism** is a better description of cooperative federalism in action. As the How It Works graphic shows (p. 84), each picket of the fence represents a different policy area and the horizontal boards that hold the pickets together represent the different levels of government. This is a much more orderly image than the marble cake provides, and it illustrates important implications about how policy is made across levels of government.

The most important point to be drawn from this analogy is that activity in the cooperative federal system occurs *within* pickets of the fence—that is, within policy areas. Policy makers within a given policy area will have more in common with others in that area (even if they are at different levels of government) than they do with people who work in different areas (even if they are at the same level of government). For example, someone working in a state's Department of Natural Resources will have more contact with people working in local park programs and the national Department of the Interior than with people who also work at the state level but who focus on, say, law enforcement.

Cooperative federalism, then, is likely to emerge within policy areas rather than across them. This may create problems for the chief executives who are trying to run the show (mayors, governors, the president), as rivalries develop among policy agencies competing for funds. Also, contact within policy areas is not always cooperative. (Think of detective shows in which the FBI arrives to investigate a local crime and pulls rank on the town sheriff, provoking resentment from local law-enforcement officials.) This is the inefficient side of picket fence federalism in action.

"Why Should I Care?"

Why is it important to understand the history of federalism? You might think that the Civil War ended the debates over nation-centered versus state-centered federalism (in favor of the national government), but disputes today over immigration, health care, welfare, and education policy all revolve around the balance of power between the levels of government. State legislatures that talk about ignoring federal criticisms of their sanctuary policies are invoking the same arguments used by advocates of states' rights in the 1830s and 1840s concerning tariffs and slavery.

Federalism today

Federalism today is a complex mix of all the types of federalism that our nation's political system has experienced in the past. Our current system is predominantly characterized by cooperative federalism, but it has retained strong elements of national supremacy, dual federalism, and states' rights (see Nuts & Bolts 3.2).

Cooperative federalism lives on: fiscal federalism

By cooperative federalism, as we have noted, we mean a system in which federal and state governments share responsibility for delivering a policy. In the case of the Medicaid program that provides health coverage for low-income adults, for example, programs in each state are administered by state agencies operating under federal guidelines. In the modern era, the federal government has also become involved in funding and setting requirements for K–12 education, which was long considered a local responsibility.

Most examples of cooperative federalism involve some element of **fiscal federalism**, a system whereby the federal government provides some of the funds needed to sustain the state programs that deliver services to citizens. For example, the federal government pays a large share of state Medicaid costs and a portion of the funding for local school districts. At one level, fiscal federalism is a way for the federal government to help states deal with responsibilities that outstrip their financial resources. However, fiscal federalism also gives the federal government a way to

fiscal federalism
A form of federalism in which federal funds are allocated to the lower levels of government through transfer payments or grants.

NUTS & BOLTS 3.2

The Evolution of Federalism

Type of Federalism	Period	Characteristics
Dual federalism (layer cake)	1789–1937	The national and state governments were viewed as very distinct with little overlap in their activities or the services they provided. Within this period, federalism could have been state centered or nation centered, but relations between levels of government were limited.
Cooperative federalism (marble cake)	1937–present	This indicates greater cooperation and collaboration between the levels of government.
Fiscal federalism	1937–present	This system of transfer payments or grants from the national government to lower-level governments involves varying degrees of national control over how the money is spent: categorical grants give the national government a great deal of control whereas block grants involve less national control.
Picket fence federalism	1961–present	This version of cooperative federalism emphasizes that policy makers within a given policy area have more in common with others in their area at different levels of government than with people at the same level of government who work on different issues.
Coercive federalism	1970s–present	This involves federal preemptions of state and local authority and unfunded mandates on state and local governments to force the states to change their policies to match national goals or policies established by Congress.

Versions of Federalism

Version 1:
Layer Cake Federalism

1789–1937
No interactions between the levels of government.

National

State

Local

Version 2:
Marble Cake Federalism

1937–today
Interactions between the levels of government are common.

Version 3:
Picket Fence Federalism

1960s–today
Horizontal boards represent different levels of government, and the pickets are policy areas within which coordination happens across those levels.

National

State

Local

Agriculture

Environment

Highways

Housing

Education

Medical Care

Tax Policy

Version 4:
Coercive Federalism

1970s–today
National government uses regulations, mandates, and conditions to pressure states to fall into line with national policy goals.

National

Regulations
National government provides new policy goals.

State

Local

Incentives
National government pressures or incentivizes state and local governments to act according to new goals.

Federalism and Environmental Policy

This is who carries out environmental policy in...

The National Government:
Environmental Protection Agency (EPA), Department of the Interior, Department of Energy

The State Government:
State Department of Natural Resources, State Park Service, State Environmental Protection Agencies

The Local Government:
City park system, city and county oversight boards for land use policy and zoning

Environmental policy shows contemporary federalism in action. As you can see on the right, all levels of government combine to effect environmental policy (exemplifying picket fence federalism). Also, the national government provides both rules and incentives for state and local governments to change their environmental policies (exemplifying coercive federalism).

Congress passed new acts.

Over the last few decades, Congress has passed the **Coastal Zone Management Act**, the **Clean Water Act**, the **Endangered Species Act**, and the **Clean Air Act**.

What does that mean?

This legislation has provided states and localities with **federal regulations and mandates.**

Stricter rules.

In 2015, the EPA set **new tougher standards** for ozone and proposed stricter limits on greenhouse gases.

Also...

The national government **provides many incentives designed to preserve the environment**, including tax credits for electric cars and home improvements that increase energy efficiency.

Good deal.

In 2015, the EPA introduced a Clean Energy Incentive Program to promote expansion of renewable energy and energy efficiency. **States receive emission credits** for the clean energy they produce.

Change happens.

The Trump administration **repealed many EPA regulations**, but has left tax credits for individuals largely intact.

❓ Critical Thinking

1. **Which do you think is a more effective tool** to change environmental policy—the "stick" of regulation or the "carrot" of incentives? Why?

2. **Should the government provide tax credits and other incentives** for things like electric cars and alternative energy, or leave such things up to the free market?

In short:

The national government **imposes new rules** on **state** and **local governments** and **provides incentives** to follow these new rules and goals. However, the content of these rules, as well as whether they stay in place over time, **depends on who is elected to federal office.**

influence the kinds of policies implemented at the state level. In theory, states have large amounts of discretion in terms of determining who is eligible for Medicaid or the fees paid to doctors. However, the promise of federal Medicaid funds comes with program requirements that state agencies must meet in order to receive these funds. This type of relationship may sound familiar. When your parents let you use the car or lent you $50, was it "no strings attached"? Or did they expect something in return—such as help with yard work or other chores? Fiscal federalism works the same way, as the federal government tries to use its resources to gain control over state policies.

An extreme version of fiscal federalism is **coercive federalism**, which is the use of federal mandates or conditions to force or entice the states to change their policies to match national goals or policies established by Congress. A related concept, **federal preemption**, occurs when the federal government passes a law that overrides state law or which makes it impossible for a state to enact its own statute. The Clean Air and Clean Water Acts, the Americans with Disabilities Act (ADA) (which promotes making public buildings and commercial facilities more accessible to those with disabilities), and the Motor Voter Act (which requires states to provide voter registration services at motor vehicle departments) are all laws that forced states to change their policies. The laws most objectionable to the states are **unfunded mandates**, which require states to do certain things but carry no federal money to pay for them. Republican criticism of unfunded mandates in the 1990s led to passage of the Unfunded Mandate Reform Act of 1995. This act made it more difficult for Congress to impose these mandates on the states; it required a separate vote on mandates that imposed costs of more than $50 million, and it required a Congressional Budget Office estimate of exactly how much such mandates would cost the states. Although this law could not prevent unfunded mandates, Republicans hoped that bringing more attention to the practice would create political pressure against such policies.

Types of Federal Aid to States The method used to transfer resources from the federal government to states and localities often determines the effectiveness of fiscal federalism. Today, most federal aid comes in two forms. **Categorical grants** are for specific purposes—they have strings attached. Funds that help states run their Medicaid programs, for example, are delivered as categorical grants. **Block grants** are financial aid to states for use within a specific policy area, but within that area the states have discretion on how to spend the money. An example of a block grant is TANF (Temporary Assistance for Needy Families), which is federal money given to states to help fund their welfare programs. However, in contrast to Medicaid, federal welfare funds are given without restrictions about how the states determine benefits or the eligibility of welfare recipients. As a result, both of these factors vary across states. Since the 1970s, grants to the states as a proportion of the size of the national economy (gross domestic product, or GDP) have been relatively constant, whereas the rate of state and local spending has continued to inch up (see the What Do the Facts Say? feature).

Advocates of cooperative federalism often promote block grants as the best way for the levels of government to work together to solve problems: the national government identifies problem areas and then provides money to the states to help solve them. The problem is that state governments may disagree with the president or Congress on how these programs should be implemented, which creates a temptation for the federal government to move to categorical grants as a way to shape state policy.

A separate argument for block grants is made by people who believe that state governments are more efficient at implementing policies—as well as people who

---

coercive federalism
A form of federalism in which the federal government pressures the states to change their policies by using regulations, mandates, or conditions (often involving threats to withdraw federal funding).

federal preemption
Imposition of national priorities on the states through national legislation that is based on the Constitution's supremacy clause.

unfunded mandates
Federal laws that require the states to do certain things but do not provide state governments with funding to implement these policies.

categorical grants
Federal aid to state or local governments that is provided for a specific purpose, such as a mass-transit program within the transportation budget or a school lunch program within the education budget.

block grants
Federal aid provided to a state government to be spent within a certain policy area, but the state can decide how to spend the money within that area.

Is Federal Spending Out of Control?

Advocates for smaller government often make the argument that spending in Washington is out of control and that state and local governments should have more power. What do the numbers say? What are the trends in state and local spending as a share of the total economy compared to federal spending?

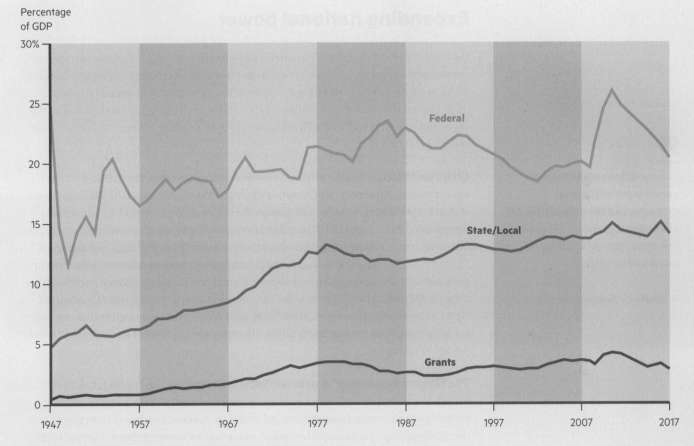

Source: St. Louis Federal Reserve Bank, fred.stlouisfed.org (accessed 9/30/18).

Think about it

- How much is the federal government helping the states in terms of grants? Has this greatly increased? What does this say about the debates between nation-centered and state-centered federalism?
- Should the national government provide more grants to state and local governments to help even out inequalities and address national problems, or leave decisions about funding up to the states?
- What determines whether the local, state, or federal government should be responsible for spending on a given policy?

prefer the results of state-led policies to a situation wherein states must obey federal directives. For example, many Republican attempts to repeal and replace the Affordable Care Act (the ACA, or "Obamacare") have proposed shifting federal Medicaid funds to the states in the form of a block grant. In theory, this block grant would allow states to design health care programs tailored to their specific populations. However, over time, the amount of funds in these block grants would be less than planned spending for Medicaid under Obamacare, meaning that federal spending on health care for the poor would decrease—presumably leading to cuts in the services available to these individuals.

Expanding national power

Despite the overall shift toward cooperative federalism, strong overtones of national government supremacy remain. Three important characteristics of American politics in the past 60 years have reinforced the role of the national government: (1) reliance on the national government in times of crisis and war; (2) the "rights revolution" of the 1950s and 1960s, as well as the Great Society programs of the 1960s; and (3) the rise of coercive federalism.

Crisis and War Reliance on the national government in times of crisis and war has always been a characteristic of American politics. Even in the 1800s, during the period of dual federalism and strong state power, the national government's strong actions were needed during the Civil War to hold the nation together. More recently, after Hurricanes Harvey and Irma devastated coastal communities in Florida, Louisiana, and Texas in 2017, most people looked to the federal government to deliver emergency supplies, aid in rescue operations, and allocate funds for rebuilding affected communities. Policy responses to the major crises of the twentieth century (the Great Depression's New Deal policies, the massive mobilization for World War II), as well as the response to the banking meltdown of 2008–2009, also dramatically shifted the balance of power toward Washington.

The "Rights Revolution" and Great Society Programs The "rights revolution" initiated by the Supreme Court, as well as Lyndon Johnson's Great Society programs, contributed to increased national control over state policies. Landmark Court decisions thrust the national government into policy areas that had typically been reserved to the states. In the school desegregation and busing cases of the 1950s and 1960s, for example, the Court upheld the national goal of promoting racial equality and fighting discrimination over the earlier norm of local control of school districts.[10] The "one person, one vote" decisions, which required that the populations of legislative districts be equalized when district lines were redrawn, put the federal courts at the center of another policy area that had always been left to the states.[11] The rights revolution also applied to police powers, another area of traditional state control, including protection against self-incrimination and preventing illegally obtained evidence from being used in a criminal trial.[12]

These Court actions were paralleled by a burst of legislation that tackled civil rights, education, the environment, medical care for the poor, and housing. These so-called Great Society policies made the national government much more active in policy areas previously controlled by state and local governments. For example, after passage of the 1965 Voting Rights Act, federal marshals were sent to the South to make sure that African Americans were allowed to vote.

In the 1960s, the national government also expanded its reach through a large increase in categorical grants, which the states sorely needed even though the

> The operations of the federal government will be most extensive and important in times of war and danger; those of the State governments, in times of peace and security.
>
> — **James Madison,** *Federalist 45*

In response to the Bush and Obama administrations' perceived overreach into education policy, current secretary of education Betsy DeVos has led the Trump administration's efforts to roll back the federal government's power over education.

funds came with strings attached. For example, the 1964 Civil Rights Act required nondiscrimination as a condition for receiving any kind of federal grants. The Elementary and Secondary Education Act of 1965 gave the federal government heightened control over public education by attaching conditions to federal grant money.

More Unfunded Mandates Despite the legislation enacted by Congress designed to curb unfunded mandates, the practice has continued. President George W. Bush imposed significant mandates related to education testing, sales tax collection, emergency management, infrastructure, and election administration. President Barack Obama's administration required state governments to adopt policies preventing discrimination against the disabled and mandated reforms to local school lunch menus. And the conflict over sanctuary cities discussed in the chapter opener is partly about an unfunded mandate: local communities are expected to keep suspected illegal residents in jail until federal authorities can arrange for a transfer, even though the federal government does not reimburse them for the cost of the detention.

The fact that members of Congress enact unfunded mandates makes sense given the themes of this textbook. First, politics is about conflict, and when there is disagreement between the federal and state government over what policies should look like, we should expect each side to do whatever it can to advance its own priorities. Second, the rules matter. The fact that the Constitution prioritizes federal law over state law, coupled with increased federal aid to state and local governments, gives the federal government considerable leverage to get its way when conflicts arise.

The states fight back

Most Americans support some of the policies that have been imposed on the states: racial equality, clean air and water, a fair legal process, safer highways, and equal access to the voting booth. At the same time, there has always been considerable opposition in some states to federal mandates, whether unfunded or otherwise. For example, over 20 states have refused to accept federal funds to expand Medicaid as outlined in the Affordable Care Act. While the law initially did not give states the flexibility to opt out of the expansion, the Supreme Court found that mandating that states expand their Medicaid programs to receive these funds was unconstitutional.

State governments, led prominently by then–California governor Jerry Brown, have taken up the mantle of meeting the United States' commitments to the climate goals set by the Paris Agreement. Brown addressed the international community during the UN Climate Change Conference in Germany in 2017.

competitive federalism
A form of federalism in which states compete to attract businesses and jobs through the policies they adopt.

Crucial to understanding federalism in modern day America is the concept of mobility, or "the ability to vote with your feet." If you don't support the death penalty and citizens packing a pistol—don't come to Texas. If you don't like medicinal marijuana and gay marriage, don't move to California.

—**Rick Perry,** former Texas governor

States appear to be reversing their traditional role of resisting change and protecting the status quo. In recent years, states have taken the lead on environmental policy, refusing to accept national pollution standards that are too lenient or the lack of national action on issues such as global warming. Many policies to address climate change—including the development of renewable energy sources, carbon emissions limits, and carbon cap and trade programs—have been advocated at the state level, and some governors have announced that their states will comply with the Paris Agreement on climate change regardless of what the federal government does. States have been out in front on fighting electronic waste, mercury emissions, and air pollution more generally.[13] To take another example, Kansas and Montana passed laws holding that federal gun laws do not apply to guns manufactured in their states (and making it a felony to try to enforce those laws).[14] Many such state laws will not stand up in federal court; the Montana gun law has already been struck down. But the laws are clearly a reflection of state frustration with assertions of federal power and with the policy goals that underlie these assertions. Simply put, local elected officials and their constituents often disagree with federal directives. From this perspective, federalism provides a way for state and local officials to shape public policy in ways that favor their own policy goals.

States have one important advantage over the national government when it comes to experimenting with new policies: their numbers. There are 50 states potentially trying a mix of different policies—another reason that advocates of state-centered federalism see the states as the proper repository of government power. In this view, such a mix of policies produces **competitive federalism**—competition among states to provide the best policies to attract businesses, create jobs, and maintain a healthy social fabric.[15] For example, one of the arguments in favor of repealing Obamacare and giving the program's funds to states as a block grant was that state governments might develop better, more efficient ways to deliver health care without having to meet federal requirements.

Fighting for states' rights: the role of the modern Supreme Court

Just as the Supreme Court played a central role in defining dual federalism in the nineteenth and early twentieth centuries and in opening the door to a more nation-centered cooperative federalism in the late 1930s, today's Court is once again reshaping federalism. But this time the move is decidedly in the direction of state power (see Table 3.2).

The Tenth Amendment On paper, it seems that the Tenth Amendment would be at the center of any resurgence of state power because it ensures that all powers not delegated to the national government are reserved to the states or to the people. Until recent years, this amendment had been overshadowed by federal supremacy—state laws contradicting the Constitution or federal laws and regulations were generally found to be unconstitutional. For example, state laws enforcing racial segregation were deemed unconstitutional because they conflicted with the equal protection clause of the Fourteenth Amendment. Similarly, a state law concerning public education, traditionally a state power, is void if it conflicts with the Constitution or with a national law that is based on an enumerated power. For example, a state could not compel an 18-year-old to attend school if the student had been drafted to serve in the army. Under the Tenth Amendment, the constitutionally enumerated national power to "raise and support armies" would trump the reserved state power to support public education.

Recent Important Supreme Court Decisions on Federalism

TABLE
3.2

Case	Holding and Significance for States' Rights	Direction of the Decision
Gregory v. Ashcroft (1991)	The Missouri constitution's requirement that state judges retire by age 70 did not violate the Age Discrimination in Employment Act.	More state power
United States v. Lopez (1995)	Carrying a gun in a school did not fall within "interstate commerce"; thus, Congress could not prohibit the possession of guns on school property.	More state power
Seminole Tribe v. Florida (1996)	The Court used the Eleventh Amendment to strengthen states' sovereign immunity, ruling that Congress could not compel a state to negotiate with Native American tribes about gaming and casinos.	More state power
City of Boerne v. Flores (1997)	The Court struck down the Religious Freedom Restoration Act as an overly broad attempt to curtail the state-sponsored harassment of religion, saying that national legislation aimed at remedying states' discrimination must be "congruent and proportional" to the harm.	More state power
United States v. Morrison (2000)	The Court struck down part of the Violence Against Women Act, saying that Congress did not have the power under the commerce clause to provide a national remedy for gender-based crimes.	More state power
Alabama v. Garrett (2001)	The Court struck down the portion of the ADA that applied to the states, saying that state governments are not required to make special accommodations for the disabled.	More state power
Nevada Department of Human Resources v. Hibbs (2003)	The Court upheld Congress's power to apply the 1993 Family Leave Act to state employees as "appropriate legislation" under Section 5 of the Fourteenth Amendment.	Less state power
United States v. Bond (2011)	The Court upheld an individual's right to challenge the constitutionality of a federal law under the Tenth Amendment.	More state power
National Federation of Independent Business v. Sebelius (2012)	The Court upheld most provisions of the ACA but struck down the expansion of Medicaid as an unconstitutional use of coercive federalism (states could voluntarily take the additional funding to cover the expansion, but they would not lose existing funds if they opted out).	Mixed
United States v. Windsor (2013)	The Court held that Section 3 of DOMA was unconstitutional because it denied federal benefits to same-sex couples who were legally married under state law.	More state power
Shelby County v. Holder (2013)	The Court struck down Section 4 of the Voting Rights Act on the grounds that it violated the "equal sovereignty" of the states.	More state power

However, with the appointment of three conservative justices between 1986 and 1991 who favored a stronger role for the states, the Court started to limit Congress's reach. One of its techniques was to require that Congress provide an unambiguous statement of its intent for a particular law to overrule state authority. For example, the Court ruled that the Missouri constitution, which requires state judges to retire by age 70, did not violate the Age Discrimination in Employment Act because Congress did not make its intentions "unmistakably clear in the language of the statute."[16]

The Fourteenth Amendment The Supreme Court has also empowered states by limiting the applicability of the Constitution's Fourteenth Amendment to state laws. The Fourteenth Amendment was intended to give the national government broad control over the potentially discriminatory laws of southern states after the Civil War. Section 1 guarantees that no state shall make or enforce any law depriving any person of

The immense size and power of the Government of the United States ought not obscure its fundamental character. It remains a Government of enumerated powers.

—Justice Sandra Day O'Connor

remedial legislation
National laws that address discriminatory state laws. Authority for such legislation comes from Section 5 of the Fourteenth Amendment.

states' sovereign immunity
Based on the Eleventh Amendment, immunity that prevents state governments from being sued by private parties in federal court unless the state consents to the suit.

"life, liberty, or property, without due process of law" or denying any person the "equal protection of the laws," and Section 5 empowers Congress "to enforce" those guarantees by "appropriate legislation." Throughout most of the twentieth century, the Court interpreted Section 5 to give Congress broad discretion to pass legislation to remedy bad state laws. For example, discriminatory application of literacy tests prevented millions of African Americans from voting in the South before the Voting Rights Act was passed in 1965.

As part of the federalism revolution of the 1990s, the Court started to chip away at Congress's Fourteenth Amendment powers. In one important case in 1997, the Supreme Court struck down the Religious Freedom Restoration Act as an overly broad attempt to curtail state-sponsored harassment based on religion. This case established a new standard to justify remedial legislation—that is, national legislation that fixes discriminatory state law—under Section 5, saying: "There must be a congruence and proportionality between the injury to be prevented or remedied and the means adopted to that end."[17] In one application of the new standard for remedial legislation, the Court ruled that the Age Discrimination in Employment Act of 1967 could not be applied to state employees because it was not "appropriate legislation."[18] Two applications of this logic also applied to the Eleventh Amendment, which originally was interpreted to mean that residents of any state could not sue other (non-home-state) state governments. More recently, the Supreme Court has expanded the reach of the Eleventh Amendment through the concept of states' sovereign immunity. States are now immune from a much broader range of lawsuits in state and federal court.

The Commerce Clause Another category of cases that have been decided in favor of more state power concerns the commerce clause of the Constitution. The first Court case to limit Congress's commerce powers since the New Deal of the 1930s came in 1995. The case involved the Gun-Free School Zones Act of 1990, which Congress passed in response to the increase in school shootings around the nation. The law made it a federal offense to have a gun within 1,000 feet of a school. Congress assumed that it had the power to pass this legislation, given the Court's expansive interpretation of the commerce clause over the previous 55 years, even though it concerned a traditional area of state power. Although it was a stretch to claim that carrying a gun in or around a school was related to interstate commerce, Congress might have been able to demonstrate the point by showing that most guns are made in one state and sold in another (thus commercially crossing state lines), that crime affects the economy and commerce, and that the quality of education, which is also crucial to the economy, is harmed if students and teachers are worrying about guns in their schools. However, members of Congress did not present this evidence because they did not think it was necessary.

Alfonso Lopez, a senior at Edison High School in San Antonio, Texas, was arrested for carrying a concealed .38-caliber handgun with five bullets in it, in violation of the Gun-Free School Zone Act. Attorneys for Lopez moved to dismiss the charges, arguing that the law was unconstitutional because carrying a gun in a school could not be regulated as "interstate commerce." The Court agreed in *United States v. Lopez*,[19] and the ruling was widely viewed as a warning shot over Congress's bow. If Congress wanted to encroach on the states' turf in the future, it would have to demonstrate that the law in question was a legitimate exercise of the commerce clause powers.

Congress learned its lesson. The next time it passed legislation that affected law enforcement at the state level, it was careful to document the impact on interstate commerce. The Violence Against Women Act was passed in 1994 with strong bipartisan support after weeks of testimony and thousands of pages of evidence were entered into the record showing the links between violence against women and commerce. Despite the evidence Congress presented, the Supreme Court ruled that

The *Lopez* decision struck down the 1990 Gun-Free School Zones Act, ruling that Congress did not have the power to forbid people to carry guns near schools. After the shooting of 34 people at Marjory Stoneman Douglas High School in Parkland, Florida, on February 14, 2018, students led renewed calls nationwide for strengthening gun control laws.

Congress did not have the power under the commerce clause to make a national law that gave victims of gender-motivated violence the right to sue their attackers in federal court (the Court struck down only that part of the law, however; the program funding remained unaffected and was reauthorized in 2013).[20]

The impact of these cases goes well beyond setting limits on the federal government's ability to regulate commerce. Not only has the Supreme Court set new limits on Congress's ability to address national problems, but it has also clearly stated that the Court alone will determine which rights warrant protection by Congress. However, it is important to recognize that the Court does not consistently rule against Congress; it often rules against the states because of broader constitutional principles or general public consensus behind a specific issue. For example, the Court has struck down state laws limiting gay rights as a violation of the equal protection clause of the Fourteenth Amendment.[21] And although the Court rejected the commerce clause as the constitutional justification for national health care reform, it did uphold the ACA based on Congress's taxing power.[22]

Even so, it's important to keep in mind that the national government still has the upper hand in the balance of power and has many tools at its disposal to blunt the impact of any Court decision. First, Congress can pass new laws to clarify its legislative intent and overturn any of the Court cases that involved statutory interpretation. Second, Congress can use its financial power to impose its will on the states. However, the Court has limited Congress's powers of budgetary coercion. For example, in a 2012 case dealing with Obamacare's requirement that states expand Medicaid coverage in order to receive federal subsidies for the program, the Court ruled that the threat embodied in this requirement was a "gun to the head,"[23] meaning states did not have a real choice: without the subsidies, no state could afford to provide Medicaid coverage on its own, even without the expansion in coverage. This was the first time the Court limited Congress's coercive budgetary power over the states, and the boundaries of the new limits will have to be decided in future cases.

Why is it important to understand federalism today? More than at any time in U.S. history, the question of which branch of government has power over a particular policy is up for grabs. This change gives elected officials new opportunities to influence policy—rather than changing the policy itself, they can influence decisions about which level of government implements the policy.

"Why Should I Care?"

[A] state may, if its citizens choose, serve as a laboratory; and try novel social and economic experiments without risk to the rest of the country.

—Justice Louis Brandeis, 1932

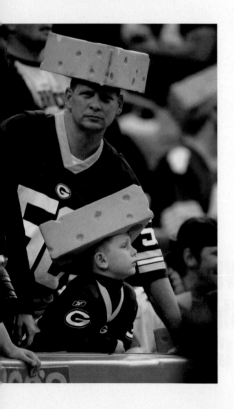

One of the strengths of federalism is that it allows regional diversity to flourish. Green Bay Packers fans proudly wear their cheesehead hats at Lambeau Field, showing that what passes for normal behavior in one part of the country would be viewed differently in other areas.

Assessing federalism

There is much to recommend federalism as a cornerstone of our political system. However, there are disadvantages as well, such as inefficiency in the policy process and inequality in policy outcomes. This section will assess the advantages, disadvantages, and ideological complexities of federalism.

Policy preferences

Issues concerning federalism often seem to break down along traditional liberal and conservative lines. Liberals generally favor strong national power to fight discrimination against women, minorities, disabled people, gay men and lesbians, and the elderly, and they push for progressive national policies on issues such as protecting the environment, providing national health care, and supporting the poor. Conservatives, in contrast, tend to favor limited intrusion from the national government and allowing the states to decide their own mix of social welfare and regulatory policies, including how aggressively they will protect various groups from discrimination. In this way, individuals' feelings about federalism are connected to their policy preferences and their judgments about what kinds of policies should emerge from different levels of government.

However, assessing the implications of having policies carried out by one level of government or another is not always so simple. In recent years the tables have turned, and in many cases liberals are suddenly arguing for states' rights while conservatives are advocating the virtues of uniform national laws. On a broad range of new issues, such as gay rights, aid in dying, and the recreational use of marijuana (see the Take a Stand feature), some state governments are passing socially liberal legislation.[24] Thus, liberals who might have favored a strong national government as a way of implementing their policy goals might find themselves arguing for states' rights, and conservatives might find themselves arguing for the virtues of centralizing power.

Advantages of a strong role for the states

In addition to pointing out the policy implications of federalism, any assessment of federalism today must consider the advantages and disadvantages for our political system. The advantages of a strong role for the states can be summarized in four main points: (1) states can be laboratories of democracy, (2) state and local government is closer to the people, (3) states provide more access to the political system, and (4) states provide an important check on national power.

The first point refers to the role that states can play as the source of policy diversity and innovation. If many states are trying to solve problems creatively, their efforts can complement those of the national government. Successful policies first adopted at the state level often percolate up to the national level. Consider health care. Many provisions of Obamacare were taken from the highly successful state-level program in Massachusetts. Similarly, climate change initiatives emerging in California and other states may provide templates for federal action in the future.

Second, government that is closer to the people can encourage participation in the political process and may be more responsive to local needs. Local politicians know

Recreational Marijuana and Federalism

Should the federal government be able to tell a state that it cannot allow the recreational use of marijuana? While the use and possession of marijuana is illegal under federal law, ten states (Alaska, California, Colorado, Maine, Massachusetts, Michigan, Nevada, Oregon, Vermont, and Washington) have legalized nonmedical use. In most of these states, commercial activity (growing and sales) has also been legalized. Several other states have legalized marijuana use for medical purposes. And in most other states, possession of small amounts of marijuana is no longer treated as a crime. In the coming years, several other states are likely to move toward partial or complete legalization.

The federal government should be "hands off."

Up until recently, the federal government responded to these changes in state law by adopting a "hands off" policy. The so-called Cole Memo (named after Associate Attorney General James Cole, who served during the Obama administration) stated that the federal government would not prosecute marijuana cases unless there had been a violation of both state and federal law. This policy reflected an attitude within the Obama Justice Department that prosecution of marijuana cases was not a high priority. Moreover, some Justice Department staff members (and perhaps President Obama) probably favored federal legalization. However, this step would have required congressional approval, which would have been unlikely during Obama's administration given the Republican majority in the House (and, after January 2015, in the Senate). Thus, deferring to state law helped move parts of the country toward decriminalization without requiring additional legislative action and allowed public support for legalization to build. Opponents of marijuana legalization in Congress may eventually be forced to reconsider their position based on the tides of public opinion.

The federal government should be "hands on."

The situation changed after the election of Donald Trump. Throughout 2017, Attorney General Jeff Sessions argued that the federal government needed to be more aggressive in its enforcement of marijuana laws as a means of reducing drug abuse, fighting criminal organizations, and decreasing violent crime. In January 2018, Sessions

Federal drug enforcement agents raid a medical marijuana club.

formally rescinded the Cole Memo, although his new guidelines did not order U.S. attorneys to give marijuana prosecutions a higher priority, distinguish between medical or recreational use, or provide additional resources for anti-marijuana efforts. Moreover, Sessions did not (and has no power to) order states to change their laws or compel local law-enforcement agencies to change their policies regarding marijuana.

Sessions and the Trump administration do have the option of proposing new federal legislation to increase the penalties for possession or sale of marijuana or to provide local governments with funds or other assistance in enforcing anti-marijuana laws. However, many Republican legislators, particularly from states that have relaxed marijuana laws, might oppose higher penalties. Similarly, law-enforcement agencies in communities that have decriminalized marijuana would likely decline federal help in prosecuting activities that they no longer consider a crime. On the other hand, insofar as Sessions's responsibility to enforce the laws as written, these steps are reasonable options for increased federal involvement in deterring marijuana production, sale, and consumption.

take a stand

1. As a matter of policy, should marijuana be legalized in all cases or just some cases—ranging from complete legalization to legalization only for medical use when prescribed by a doctor? If some possession is legal, what should policies be for growth and sale?

2. Do you tend to support a state-centered or a nation-centered perspective on federalism? Now revisit your answers to question 1. Are your positions more consistent with your views on federalism or with your policy concerns?

Government that is closer to the people can encourage participation in the political process and may be more responsive to local needs. These protesters in New York, for example, are letting their local politicians know their feelings on immigration policy.

DID YOU KNOW?

Owing to a state program that is similar to Obamacare, only

2.5%

of people in Massachusetts don't have health insurance. In Texas, 16.6 percent of people do not have health insurance—the highest percentage in the nation.

Source: Census.gov

better what their constituents want than further-removed national politicians do. If the voters want higher taxes to pay for more public benefits, such as public parks and better schools, they can enact these changes at the state and local levels. On the other hand, if they prefer lower taxes and fewer services, local politicians can be responsive to those desires. In addition, local government provides a broad range of opportunities for direct involvement in politics, from working on local political campaigns to attending school board or city council meetings, which may increase the input that citizens have in the establishment of new policies.

Third, our federalist system provides more potential paths to address problems. For example, the court system allows citizens to pursue complaints under state or federal law. Likewise, cooperative federalism can draw on the strengths of different levels of government to solve problems. A local government may recognize a need and respond to it more quickly than the national government, but if additional resources are needed to address the problem, the municipality may be able to turn to the state or national government for help—as in the cases of Hurricanes Harvey, Irma, and Maria, when local governments were assisted by the U.S. military and FEMA (Federal Emergency Management Agency) and received supplemental federal aid for rebuilding efforts.

Finally, federalism can provide a check on national tyranny. Competitive federalism ensures that Americans have a broad range of social policies, levels of taxation and regulation, and public services to choose from (see Figure 3.1). When people "vote with their feet" by deciding whether to move and where to live, they encourage healthy competition among states that would be impossible under a unitary government.

Disadvantages of too much state power

A balanced assessment of federalism must acknowledge that there are problems with a system that gives too much power to the states. The disadvantages include unequal distribution of resources across the states, unequal protection for civil rights, and competition that produces a "race to the bottom." Also, one puzzle (which we will explore in other chapters) is that more people vote in national elections than in state

**FIGURE
3.1**

State Spending per Person

Spending per person varies dramatically by state. What are some of the advantages and disadvantages of living in a low-spending state or in a high-spending state? What type of state would you rather live in? Why?

Source: State and Local Government Finance Data Query System, http://slfdqs. taxpolicycenter.org (accessed 3/19/18).

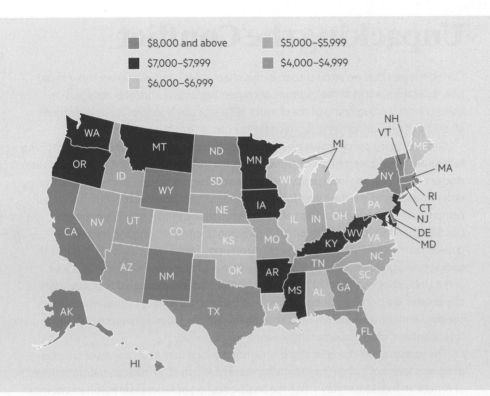

Legend:
- $8,000 and above
- $7,000–$7,999
- $6,000–$6,999
- $5,000–$5,999
- $4,000–$4,999

and local elections. Turnout at the local level is often ridiculously low. If people support local government so strongly, why aren't they more interested?

The resource problem becomes more acute when dealing with national-level problems that affect different areas differently. For example, pollution spills across state lines, and the deteriorating public infrastructure, like the highway system, crosses state boundaries. In fact, one study estimated that 26 percent of U.S. bridges are structurally deficient or obsolete, 15 percent of highways are in need of repair, and 25 percent of mass transit needs to be updated. Solving these and other infrastructure problems will cost $2.2 trillion, vastly outstripping the resources of state and local governments, particularly a small number of localities that have a disproportionate number of bridges and roads needing repairs.

Another problem, unequal civil rights protection, is evident in various federalism cases that have passed before the Supreme Court. These clearly show that states are not uniformly willing to protect the civil liberties and civil rights of their citizens. This was critically important during the 1950s and 1960s when the national government forced southern states to end segregation and passed laws outlawing discrimination in housing, employment, transportation, and voting. The Supreme Court recently stepped in to provide equal rights to marry, but states still vary a great deal in terms of antidiscrimination laws based on sexual orientation. Without national laws, there will be large differences in the levels of protection against discrimination based on age, disability, and sexual orientation.

And last, competitive federalism can create a "race to the bottom" as states attempt to lure businesses by keeping taxes and social spending low. This can place an unfair burden on states that take a more generous position toward the poor or provide services (low college tuition, for example) that others do not. Thus, overall, there is no clear "winner" in determining the appropriate balance of national and state power. The advantages and disadvantages of our federal system ensure that federalism will always remain a central source of conflict in the policy-making process as the various levels of government fight it out.

Unpacking the Conflict

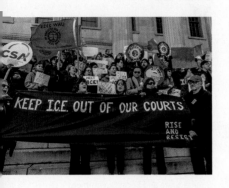

Considering all that we've discussed in this chapter, let's apply what we know about how federalism works to the example of competing federal and local immigration policies from the beginning of the chapter. When local and federal officials disagree about sanctuary city policies, who wins? How can we explain this conflict?

Sanctuary city policies have been so contentious because they involve overlapping federal and local government responsibilities that underpin the principle of federalism. And often, federal and local policy makers want different things. Trump's executive order threatens to interfere with local governments' police power or their traditional responsibility to promote public safety in their communities. Local governments' policies of limited cooperation with ICE threaten to interfere with the federal government's traditional national security responsibilities; the Justice Department sees keeping undocumented immigrants who have committed violent crimes out of the United States as part of this responsibility. Some have argued that sanctuary city policies are unconstitutional under the national supremacy clause, while others cite the Tenth Amendment in their arguments that the federal government cannot "commandeer" state governments to enforce federal law.[25]

The immigration example also highlights the idea that Americans are citizens of several levels of government simultaneously. Martha Derthick, a leading scholar of American federalism, says that the basic question of federalism involves choices about how many communities we will be.[26] If you asked most people in our nation about their primary geopolitical community, they would probably not say, "I am a Montanan" or "I am an Arizonan." Most people would likely say, "I am an American." Yet we have strong attachments to our local communities and state identities. Most Texans would not be caught dead wearing a Styrofoam cheesehead hat, but thousands of football fans in Green Bay, Wisconsin, regularly don the funny-looking things to watch their beloved Packers. We are members of multiple communities, a fact that has had an indelible impact on our political system and the policy choices that affect our everyday life.

What's Your Take?

Should the federal government be able to force states to comply with the country's immigration policy?

Or should state and local officials be able to conduct their business without federal interference?

STUDY GUIDE

What is federalism and why does it matter?

Define *federalism* and explain its significance.
(Pages 72–74)

Summary

A federal system simultaneously allocates power to both the state and federal government, whereas a confederal system gives power only to the states, and a unitary government gives power only to the federal government.

Key terms

federalism (p. 72)   concurrent powers (p. 73)

sovereign power (p. 72)   unitary government (p. 74)

police powers (p. 73)   confederal government (p. 74)

Practice Quiz Questions

1. **What system of government did the Articles of Confederation establish?**

   a   unitary

   b   federal

   c   confederal

   d   monarchy

   e   dictatorship

2. **Which is an example of a concurrent power?**

   a   printing money

   b   building roads

   c   conducting elections

   d   declaring war

   e   establishing post offices

Balancing national and state power in the Constitution

Explain what the Constitution says about federalism.
(Pages 75–77)

Summary

Although the state governments have considerable power in our system, the Founders disproportionately favored the federal government in the Constitution so that the federal government's interests superseded those of the states in the event of a conflict.

Key terms

full faith and credit   privileges and immunities
   clause (p. 76)   clause (p. 76)

Practice Quiz Questions

3. **States' rights are protected in which of the following constitutional provisions?**

   a   the Ninth Amendment

   b   the Tenth Amendment

   c   Article I of the Constitution

   d   Article III of the Constitution

   e   the First Amendment

4. **Which of the following would be best explained by the Tenth Amendment?**

   a   Congress increasing the minimum wage to $10 an hour

   b   the California state legislature declaring it was going to create its own navy

   c   state and local control over education policy

   d   the Supreme Court's recent decisions in same-sex marriage cases

   e   the Environmental Protection Agency passing a new regulation on carbon emissions that applies to all 50 states

The evolving concept of federalism

Trace the major shifts in state and federal government power over time. (Pages 77–82)

Summary

The relationship between the state and federal governments has changed dramatically over time. Whereas the federal and state governments traditionally operated with little interaction under the era of dual federalism, the trend over the past 80 years has been one of increasing federal interaction with state governments to address particular policy areas.

Key terms

dual federalism (p. 78)   **cooperative federalism** (p. 82)

states' rights (p. 80)   **picket fence federalism** (p. 82)

Practice Quiz Questions

5. **Which analogy best describes the federalism arrangement today?**

   a   layer cake federalism

   b   marble cake federalism

   c   picket fence federalism

   d   gumbo federalism

   e   dual federalism

6. **Which case bolstered the federal government's power over the states?**

   a   *Barron v. Baltimore*

   b   *McCulloch v. Maryland*

   c   *Dred Scott v. Sandford*

   d   *Mapp v. Ohio*

   e   *Shelby County v. Holder*

7. **When did the federal government begin cooperating with the states on policy goals?**

   a   1890s

   b   1930s

   c   1950s

   d   1970s

   e   1990s

Federalism today

Describe the major trends and debates in federalism today. (Pages 83–93)

Summary

Today's federal structure offers a complex mix of all previous components of federalism: some elements of national supremacy combine with states' rights for a varied federal landscape. Although the federal and state governments still exercise cooperative federalism to achieve joint policy goals, the federal government has also utilized coercive federalism to impose federal priorities on the states without offering compensation.

Key terms

fiscal federalism (p. 83)   **block grants** (p. 86)

coercive federalism (p. 86)   **competitive federalism** (p. 90)

federal preemption (p. 86)   **remedial legislation** (p. 92)

unfunded mandates (p. 86)   **states' sovereign**

categorical grants (p. 86)   **immunity** (p. 92)

Practice Quiz Questions

8. **Which form of grants are given to the states by the federal government with explicit conditions on how funds are to be allocated?**

   a   block grants

   b   categorical grants

   c   general revenue sharing

   d   federal mandates

   e   tax refunds

9. **Recent moves in Congress to increase state power over public policy generally increase usage of _____.**

   a   block grants

   b   categorical grants

   c   federal taxes

   d   federal mandates

   e   state taxes

10. **The imposition of national priorities on the states through congressional legislation and imposition of the national supremacy clause is called _____.**

    a   cooperative federalism

    b   dual federalism

    c   competitive federalism

    d   federal preemption

    e   remedial legislation

11. **A state would usually challenge the constitutionality of a federal law under which of the following amendments?**

    a   Eighth Amendment

    b   Tenth Amendment

    c   Thirteenth Amendment

    d   Fourteenth Amendment

    e   First Amendment

12. **The Eleventh Amendment's protections of state sovereign immunity guarantee that _____.**

    a   residents of one state cannot sue the government of another state

    b   state governments cannot commit a legal wrong

    c   ambassadors from foreign countries cannot be detained by state governments

    d   state governments can sue the federal government

    e   state governments cannot be sued by anybody

13. The Court has recently overturned a number of congressional laws rooted in the _____.

- a national supremacy clause
- b reserve clause
- c establishment clause
- d commerce clause
- e free exercise clause

Assessing federalism

Analyze the arguments for and against a strong federal government. (Pages 94–97)

Summary

Although conservatives have traditionally advocated for states' rights and liberals generally prefer a stronger national government, contemporary issues do not always fit neatly in this scheme. There are several reasons that strong state governments are beneficial for our country, such as the proximity of state and local governments to the citizens; however, there are also some drawbacks to the federal system, such as the vastly disproportionate distribution of resources across states.

Practice Quiz Questions

14. Conservatives favor strong _____ rights on same-sex marriage and strong _____ rights on providing health care.

- a states'; states'
- b states'; federal government
- c federal government; states'
- d federal government; federal government
- e individual; federal government

15. Which of the following is a drawback to strong state power?

- a State governments are often innovators on policy solutions.
- b State governments give citizens more access to politicians than does the national government.
- c State governments give citizens several paths to pursue policy reform.
- d State governments give different civil rights protections to their citizens.
- e States have an equal distribution of resources.

Suggested Reading

Banks, Christopher P., and John C. Blakeman. *The U.S. Supreme Court and New Federalism: From the Rehnquist to the Roberts Court*. Lanhan, MD: Rowman & Littlefield, 2012.

Beer, Samuel. *To Make a Nation: The Rediscovery of American Federalism*. Cambridge, MA: Harvard University Press, 1993.

Chomsky, Aviva. *Undocumented: How Immigration Became Illegal*. New York: Beacon Press, 2014.

Conlan, Timothy. *From New Federalism to Devolution: Twenty-Five Years of Intergovernmental Reform*. Washington, DC: Brookings Institution, 1998.

Derthick, Martha. *Keeping the Compound Republic: Essays on American Federalism*. Washington, DC: Brookings Institution, 2001.

Elkins, Stanley, and Eric McKitrick. *The Age of Federalism: The Early American Republic, 1788–1800*. New York: Oxford University Press, 1993.

LaCroix, Alison L. *The Ideological Origins of American Federalism*. Cambridge, MA: Harvard University Press, 2010.

Manna, Paul. *School's In: Federalism and the National Education Agenda*. Washington, DC: Georgetown University Press, 2006.

Nagel, Robert F. *The Implosion of American Federalism*. New York: Oxford University Press, 2001.

Ostrom, Elinor. *Governing the Commons: The Evolution of Institutions for Collective Action*, 2nd ed. New York: Cambridge University Press, 2015.

Peterson, Paul E. *The Price of Federalism*. Washington, DC: Brookings Institution, 1995.

Posner, Paul L. *The Politics of Unfunded Mandates: Whither Federalism?* Washington, DC: Georgetown University Press, 1998.

Scheberle, Denise. *Federalism and Environmental Policy: Trust and the Politics of Implementation*, 2nd ed. Washington, DC: Georgetown University Press, 2004.

4

Civil Liberties
It's a free country ... right?

"Feel free to disagree with somebody, but don't try to shut them up."
President Barack Obama

"If I were president of a university and I had some hate speech person coming, I wouldn't let them come. I just wouldn't."
John Kasich, Ohio governor

The constitutional protection for speech is clear and strong: "Congress shall make no law ... abridging the freedom of speech." However, recent protests against controversial speakers booked to speak on college campuses are calling into question the scope of those protections. Must college campuses allow talks by right-wing provocateur Milo Yiannopoulos, who has said child sexual abuse "really is not that big of a deal," or white nationalist Richard Spencer, who has called for a white ethno-state?[1] Must they embrace conservative speakers like political commentator Ann Coulter and economist Charles Murray? All of these speakers met strong and sometimes violent protests at campuses around the country.[2] A CNN headline described the situation as "War on Campus."[3] A speech by Richard Spencer at the University of Florida caused Governor Rick Scott to declare a state of emergency, and the university had to spend nearly $600,000 to provide security for the event. Despite these efforts, three men shouting "Heil Hitler" fired a shot at students demonstrating against Spencer's speech (but nobody was hurt).[4]

Many are calling for limits on the kind of hate speech that some claim speakers like Yiannopoulos and Spencer promote and for the creation of "safe spaces" on campus where students would be protected from hurtful speech within a broader effort to promote social justice. Others see such efforts as "political correctness" run amok and are concerned that free speech is under attack as conservative speakers are prevented from talking. Attorney General Jeff Sessions summarized this view, saying, "A national recommitment to free speech on campus and to ensuring First Amendment rights is long overdue. Protesters are now routinely shutting down speeches and debates across the country in an effort to silence voices that insufficiently conform with their views."[5] While strongly disagreeing with the conservative speakers' views, President Obama weighed in on this issue largely on the free speech side, saying college students shouldn't be "coddled and protected from different points of view."[6] The left-leaning American Civil Liberties Union has also defended free speech on campus, arguing, "Speech that deeply offends our morality or is hostile to our way of life warrants the

Should controversial figures like Milo Yiannopoulos, seen here on the University of California, Berkeley, campus, be allowed to speak on public college campuses in the face of popular opposition to their views? In February 2017, Berkeley students organized protests in response to a planned appearance by Yiannopoulos, and his speech was canceled.

CHAPTER GOALS

same constitutional protection as other speech because the right of free speech is indivisible: when we grant the government the power to suppress controversial ideas, we are all subject to censorship by the state."[7]

Defining the boundaries of our liberties and freedoms, like freedom of speech, is messy and complicated. Can controversial speech on college campuses be limited? When we say America is a free country, what does this really mean? Are there limits to those freedoms? If so, how should political actors draw the lines between protected behavior and actions that may be regulated?

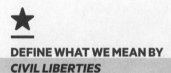

DEFINE WHAT WE MEAN BY *CIVIL LIBERTIES*

civil liberties
Basic political freedoms that protect citizens from governmental abuses of power.

Defining civil liberties

The terms "civil rights" and "civil liberties" are often used interchangeably, but there are important differences (see Nuts & Bolts 4.1). To oversimplify a bit, **civil liberties** are about freedom and civil rights are about equality. Given that civil liberties are rooted in the Bill of Rights, it might have been less confusing if it had been called the "Bill of Liberties." (This distinction is discussed further in Chapter 5.)

Civil liberties are deeply rooted in our key idea that politics is conflictual and involves trade-offs. When the Supreme Court rules on civil liberties cases, it must balance an individual's freedom with government interests and the public good. In some cases, the Court must not only balance these interests but also "draw a line" between permissible and illegal conduct concerning a specific liberty.

Balancing interests

Civil liberties must be balanced against competing interests, because when it comes to our freedoms there are no absolutes. The trade-off between civil liberties and national security in the "war on terrorism" illustrates this point. Many Americans were concerned that civil liberties were being eroded upon discovering that the government was arresting suspected terrorists in the United States and taking them to foreign countries that are less protective of civil liberties—Egypt, Syria, Jordan, and Morocco—to

NUTS & BOLTS 4.1

Distinguishing Civil Liberties from Civil Rights

Civil Liberties	Civil Rights
Basic freedoms and liberties	Protection from discrimination
Rooted in the Bill of Rights and the "due process" protection of the Fourteenth Amendment	Rooted in laws and the "equal protection" clause of the Fourteenth Amendment
Primarily restrict what the government can do to you ("*Congress* shall make no law . . . abridging the freedom of speech")	Protect you from discrimination both by the government and by individuals

be interrogated through torture.[8] Despite these concerns, even the strongest critic of state-sponsored torture would have to admit that, in some instances, it might be justified. For example, if a nuclear device were set to detonate in Manhattan in three hours, few would insist on protecting the civil liberties of someone who knew where the bomb was hidden. Once we recognize that our freedoms are not absolute, it becomes a question of how they are balanced against other interests, such as national security.

Other interests that compete with civil liberties include public safety and public health. For example, members of some Christian fundamentalist churches regularly handle dangerous snakes in their services, but many states and cities have laws prohibiting the practice. The courts have upheld those laws, saying that "public safety is superior to religious practice."[9] Despite the laws, snake handling in churches continues to be a problem. In 2013, Tennessee Wildlife Resource Agency officials cited Reverend Andrew Hamblin, co-star of the National Geographic Channel reality show *Snake Salvation*, for keeping 53 poisonous snakes and using them in services (an estimated 125 churches still handle snakes). Hamblin was eventually acquitted by a grand jury. A couple of months later, his co-star Reverend Jamie Coots died after being bitten by a rattlesnake in his church and refusing treatment.[10] Similarly, in some states the Amish are forced to place reflective "slow-moving vehicle" triangles on their horse-drawn carriages, even if it violates their religious beliefs, because of the paramount concern for public safety (see the How It Works graphic in this chapter).[11] Yet the Amish are not forced to send their children to public schools despite a state law requiring all children to attend school through age 16. In *Wisconsin v. Yoder* (1972), the Court said this law presented "a very real threat of undermining the Amish community and religious practice as it exists today."[12]

These decisions show that balancing interests is never a simple process and involves deciding whether a specific civil liberty or some competing public interest is more compelling in a specific case.

Drawing lines

Along with balancing competing interests, court rulings draw the lines defining the limits of permissible conduct by the government or an individual in the context of a specific civil liberty. For example, despite the First Amendment protection of

How can conflicts be resolved between civil liberties and other legitimate interests, such as public safety and public health? Sometimes freedom is forced to give way. Courts have upheld bans on the religious practice of snake handling and laws requiring the Amish to display reflective triangles when driving slow-moving buggies on public roads, despite religious objections to doing so.

freedom of speech, it is obvious that some speech cannot be permitted. The classic example is falsely yelling "fire!" in a crowded theater. Therefore, the courts must interpret the law to draw the line between protected speech and impermissible speech.

The same applies to other civil liberties, such as the establishment of religion, freedom of the press, freedom from illegal searches, or other due process rights. For example, the First Amendment prohibits the government from establishing an official religion, which the Court has carefully interpreted over the years to avoid "excessive entanglement" between any religion and the government. On these grounds, government-sponsored prayer in public schools has been banned since the early 1960s. But sometimes it is difficult to draw the line between acceptable and impermissible government involvement concerning religion in schools. One such ruling allowed taxpayer subsidies to fund parochial schools for buying books but not maps. (This odd hairsplitting led the late senator Daniel Patrick Moynihan to quip, "What about atlases?"[13]) Another difficult issue is the Fourth Amendment prohibition against "unreasonable searches and seizures" and the role of drug-sniffing dogs. Here the line drawing involves deciding whether a sniff is a search and, if so, under what circumstances it is reasonable (see the Take a Stand feature in this chapter). Search and seizure cases also involve balancing interests: in this case, the individual freedoms of the target of police action and the broader interests in public order and security.

EXPLAIN WHY THE BILL OF RIGHTS WAS ADDED TO THE CONSTITUTION AND HOW IT CAME TO APPLY TO THE STATES

The origins of civil liberties

Courts define the boundaries of civil liberties, but the other branches of government and the public often get involved as well. The earliest debates during the American Founding illustrate the broad public involvement concerning the basic questions of how our civil liberties would be defined: Should government be limited by an explicit statement of individual liberties? Would these limitations apply to the state governments or just the national government? How should these freedoms evolve as our society changes?

Origins of the Bill of Rights

The original Constitution provided only limited protection of civil liberties: it guaranteed habeas corpus rights (a protection against illegal incarceration) and prohibited bills of attainder (legislation punishing someone for a crime without the benefit of a trial) and ex post facto laws (laws that retroactively change the legal consequences of some behavior). Delegates to the Constitutional Convention made a few attempts to include a broader statement of civil liberties, including one by George Mason and Elbridge Gerry five days before the convention adjourned. But their motion to appoint a committee to draft a bill of rights was rejected. Charles Pinckney and Gerry also tried to add a provision to protect the freedom of the press, but that too was rejected.[14]

Mason and Gerry opposed ratification of the Constitution, partly because it did not include a bill of rights, and many Antifederalists echoed this view. In a letter to James Madison, Thomas Jefferson predicted that four states would withhold ratification until a bill of rights was added.[15] Some states ratified the Constitution but urged

Drug-Sniffing Dogs: An Illegal Search?

In 2013, the Supreme Court was presented with the case of Joelis Jardines, whom police suspected of growing marijuana inside his Miami home based on an anonymous tip. Police went to the home with a trained drug-detection dog. On the front porch, the dog gave a positive signal indicating the presence of drugs. The police returned with a search warrant, found a marijuana-growing operation, and arrested Jardines. However, the Florida Supreme Court threw out the evidence, arguing it was an illegal search. The case then made its way to the U.S. Supreme Court, which was faced with this question: Should drug-sniffing dogs be allowed outside a home without a warrant? More broadly, in the context of rapidly changing technology, what is the public's "reasonable expectation" for privacy?

A drug-sniffing dog is no more invasive than the surveillance technologies we encounter every day. The Court has ruled that police do not need a search warrant to have drug-sniffing dogs search luggage at an airport or a car that has been stopped for a traffic violation unrelated to drugs. Lower courts have also ruled that sniffs are not considered searches in a hotel hallway, at a school locker, outside a passenger train's sleeper compartments, or outside an apartment door. Is a sniff outside someone's home any more invasive?

It might not seem that way, especially when you consider the reach of new surveillance methods that are on the horizon. Other technologies that are becoming more common or will be used soon include RFIDs (radio frequency identifications), which are the size of a grain of rice and transmit information wirelessly through radio waves; facial recognition software and iris scanners; "smart dust devices"—tiny wireless micromechanical sensors—that can detect light and movement; and drones, which have primarily been used for military purposes but also have vast potential for tracking suspects in any situation.

Warrantless surveillance of somebody's home crosses a line. Lower courts have been split on whether drug-sniffing dogs may be used outside a home without a warrant, due, in part, to a Supreme Court precedent giving homes stronger Fourth Amendment protection than cars, lockers, or other areas. For example, in 2001 the Court ruled that police needed a warrant to use a thermal-imaging device

outside a home when trying to detect marijuana that was believed to be growing under heat lamps inside.

The U.S. Supreme Court ultimately agreed in the Jardines case, saying that there is a general expectation that anyone may come onto a front porch as long as the uninvited person simply knocks and then leaves if there is no answer. The majority opinion wryly noted: "Complying with the terms of that traditional invitation does not require fine-grained legal knowledge; it is generally managed without incident by the Nation's Girl Scouts and trick-or-treaters." But, they continued, "introducing a trained police dog to explore the area around the home in hopes of discovering incriminating evidence is something else. There is no customary invitation to do *that*."[a]

 Federal agents use a drug-sniffing dog to inspect a car.

New and future technologies continue to complicate the question of just what is "reasonable." Justice Alito raised this question in oral arguments in a Supreme Court case involving a GPS tracking device. He said, "Technology is changing people's expectations of privacy. . . . Maybe 10 years from now 90 percent of the population will be using social networking sites and they will have on average 500 friends and they will have allowed their friends to monitor their location 24 hours a day, 365 days a year, through the use of their cell phones. Then—what would the expectation of privacy be then?"[b]

take a stand

1. If you had to decide the case of the drug-sniffing dog, how would you have ruled? Do you think that homes should have stronger privacy expectations than cars or school lockers? Even when it concerns illegal drugs?

2. How would you answer Justice Alito's question about the expectation of privacy in an era of rapidly changing technology? When should law-enforcement officials have to get a warrant to monitor our behavior?

Congress to draft specific protections for individuals' and states' rights from federal action (they believed protection of civil liberties from state actions should reside in state constitutions). In other states, the Antifederalists who lost the ratification battle continued making their case to the public and Congress. One of the most famous arguments came from the Antifederalists of Pennsylvania, who claimed that a bill of rights was needed to "fundamentally establish those unalienable and personal rights of men, without the full, free, and secure enjoyment of which there can be no liberty, and over which it is not necessary for a good government to have the control."[16] Their statement went on to outline many of those civil liberties that ultimately became the basis for the Bill of Rights.

Madison and other supporters of the Constitution agreed that the first Congress would take up the issue, despite their reservations that a Bill of Rights could lead the people into falsely believing that it was an exhaustive list of all of their rights. State conventions submitted 124 amendments for consideration. That list was whittled down to 17 by the House and then to 12 by the Senate. This even dozen was approved by the House and sent to the states, which in 1791 ratified the 10 amendments that became the Bill of Rights (see Nuts & Bolts 4.2).[17]

Despite the profound significance of the Bill of Rights, one point limited its reach: it applied only to the laws and actions of the national government and not to those of the states. For example, the First Amendment says that "*Congress* shall make no law" infringing on freedom of religion, speech, and the press, among others. Madison submitted another amendment, which he characterized as "the

NUTS & BOLTS 4.2

The Bill of Rights: A Statement of Our Civil Liberties

First Amendment	Freedom of religion, speech, press, and assembly; the separation of church and state; and the right to petition the government.
Second Amendment	Right to bear arms.
Third Amendment	Protection against the forced quartering of troops in one's home.
Fourth Amendment	Protection from unreasonable searches and seizures; "probable cause" is required for search warrants, which must specifically describe the "place to be searched, and the persons or things to be seized."
Fifth Amendment	Protection from forced self-incrimination or double jeopardy (being tried twice for the same crime); no person can be deprived of life, liberty, or property without due process of law; private property cannot be taken for public use without just compensation; and no person can be tried for a serious crime without the indictment of a grand jury.
Sixth Amendment	Right of the accused to a speedy and public trial by an impartial jury, to an attorney, to confront witnesses, to a compulsory process for obtaining witnesses in his or her favor, and to counsel in all felony cases.
Seventh Amendment	Right to a trial by jury in civil cases involving common law.
Eighth Amendment	Protection from excessive bail, excessive fines, and cruel and unusual punishment.
Ninth Amendment	The enumeration of specific rights in the Constitution shall not be construed to deny other rights retained by the people. This has been interpreted to include a general right to privacy and other fundamental rights.
Tenth Amendment	Powers not delegated by the Constitution to the national government, nor prohibited by it to the states, are reserved to the states or to the people.

most valuable of the whole list," requiring states to protect some civil liberties: "The equal rights of conscience, the freedom of speech or of the press, and the right of trial by jury in criminal cases shall not be infringed by any State."[18] But Antifederalists feared another power grab by the Federalists in limiting states' rights, so the proposed amendment was voted down in Congress. This decision proved consequential, because the national government was quite weak for the first half of our nation's history. Because states exercised as much power over people's lives as the national government did, if not more, it would have been more important for the Bill of Rights to limit the reach of the state governments than to limit that of the federal government. Thus, the Bill of Rights played a surprisingly small role for more than a century. The Supreme Court used it only once before 1866 to invalidate a federal action—in the infamous *Dred Scott* case that contributed to the Civil War.

Selective incorporation and the Fourteenth Amendment

The significance of the Bill of Rights increased somewhat with the ratification of the Fourteenth Amendment in 1868. It was one of the three **Civil War amendments** that attempted to guarantee equal rights to the newly freed slaves. (The other two Civil War amendments were the Thirteenth, which abolished slavery, and the Fifteenth, which gave male former slaves the right to vote.) Northern politicians were concerned that southerners would deny basic rights to the former slaves, so the sweeping language of the Fourteenth Amendment was adopted. Section 1 of the Fourteenth Amendment says:

All persons born or naturalized in the United States, and subject to the jurisdiction thereof, are citizens of the United States and of the State wherein they reside. No State shall make or enforce any law which shall abridge the privileges or immunities of citizens of the United States; nor shall any State deprive any person of life, liberty, or property, without due process of law; nor deny to any person within its jurisdiction the equal protection of the laws.

This language was intended to make sure that states would not deny newly freed slaves the full protection of the law.[19] The **due process clause**, which forbids any state from denying "life, liberty, or property, without due process of law," led to an especially important expansion of civil liberties because the similar clause in the Fifth Amendment had previously been interpreted by the Court to apply only to the federal government.

Evolving Interpretations by the Supreme Court Despite the clear language of the amendment saying that "no State shall make or enforce any law," in the Supreme Court's first opportunity to interpret the Fourteenth Amendment in 1873 it continued to rule in favor of protecting states from national government actions only, embracing the "dual citizenship" idea set forth in *Barron v. Baltimore* (the 1833 case ruling that the Fifth Amendment's protection of property from being taken by the government without compensation only applied to the federal government, not to state governments; see Chapter 3).[20] Over the next 50 years, a minority of justices tried mightily to strengthen the power of the Fourteenth Amendment and use it to protect civil liberties against state government action. In two early cases involving property

Civil War amendments
The Thirteenth, Fourteenth, and Fifteenth Amendments to the Constitution, which abolished slavery and granted civil liberties and voting rights to freed slaves after the Civil War.

due process clause
Part of the Fourteenth Amendment that forbids states from denying "life, liberty, or property" to any person without due process of law. (A nearly identical clause in the Fifth Amendment applies only to the national government.)

How it works: in theory
The First Amendment

The First Amendment states:
"Congress shall make no law respecting an establishment of religion, or prohibiting the free exercise thereof; or abridging the freedom of speech, or of the press; or the right of the people peaceably to assemble, and to petition the government for a redress of grievances."

Freedom of Expression

Freedom of Religion

Freedom of Assembly

Freedom to Petition the Government

Freedom of the Press

Freedom of Speech

@user
!!!!!!
Less-protected forms of speech

Political speech and symbolic speech

Establishment
The government cannot establish an official state religion or favor one religion over others.

Free Exercise
The government cannot prevent people from practicing their religion.

Balancing Interests and Drawing Lines: Government and Religion

While the different branches of the First Amendment on the opposite page are an accurate representation of the various aspects of our religious and expressive freedoms, in practice, the implementation of these civil liberties is more complicated.

Free Exercise:

When they refused...

When Masterpiece Cakeshop **refused to make a wedding cake** for a same-sex couple,

They said...

The baker didn't have to bake the cake ... for now (postponing a decision on the broader question).

Here's why.

In cases like these, **courts must balance religious freedom against other state interests,** such as freedom from discrimination.

Establishment Clause:

Banned.

Since 1962 the Supreme Court has **banned school prayer as a violation of the establishment clause.**

What about...?

But does the separation of church and state also apply to town board members who **start their meetings with a prayer?** In 2014, the Court decided by a 5–4 vote that it did not.

It's tough.

The establishment clause often asks courts to **draw lines between what type of religious conduct is allowed** and what would be considered an "excessive entanglement" between church and state.

❓ Critical Thinking

1. **Balancing interests can be tricky. Consider these two scenarios** in which competing interests are in play: Company policy restricts employees from wearing political T-shirts or buttons at work. A pharmacist denies birth control pills to a customer for religious reasons. Which (if either) do you think should be allowed? Why did you select the one(s) you did?

2. **Drawing lines for a given civil liberty** can also be difficult. What if a high school football coach knelt in a private prayer on the field after a game? Should that be allowed? Or, consider a different scenario: Should Congress be able to start its sessions with a prayer? Reference the First Amendment and its interpretations in your answer.

In some cases, the free exercise and establishment clauses are in tension with one another. For example, while the establishment clause prohibits school-sponsored prayer, the free exercise clause guarantees that any student can pray at any time in school on their own, **as long as they are not bothering others.**

rights and self-incrimination, the Supreme Court started to use the Fourteenth Amendment to prohibit state governments from violating individual rights—but stopped short of invoking amendments in the Bill of Rights itself to support their decisions.[21]

This progression culminated in the 1925 case *Gitlow v. New York*. Here the Court said for the first time that the Fourteenth Amendment incorporated one of the amendments in the Bill of Rights (provisions protecting freedom of speech and freedom of the press) and applied it to the states. The case involved Benjamin Gitlow, a radical socialist convicted under New York's Criminal Anarchy Act of 1902 for advocating the overthrow of the government. The Court upheld his conviction, arguing that his writings were the "language of direct incitement," but also warned state governments that there were limits on such suppression of speech. This decision marked the first time that the Court ruled that a state law could be challenged because it violated an amendment in the Bill of Rights.[22]

Applying Civil Liberties to the States Slowly over the next 50 years, most civil liberties covered in the Bill of Rights were applied to the states on a right-by-right, case-by-case basis through the Fourteenth Amendment. However, this process of **selective incorporation** was not smooth and incremental. Rather, it progressed in surges with flurries of activity in the 1930s and the 1960s (see Table 4.1). As a result, the Bill of Rights has evolved from a narrow range of protections for people from national government actions during the early nineteenth century to a robust set of protections for freedom and liberty that limit national, state, and local government actions today.

selective incorporation
The process through which most of the civil liberties granted in the Bill of Rights were applied to the states on a case-by-case basis through the Fourteenth Amendment.

"Why Should I Care?"

Today the Bill of Rights is one of the most revered and important parts of the Constitution. But it didn't start out that way. Initially, the Bill of Rights applied to only the national government, not the states. But through the Fourteenth Amendment and the process of selective incorporation, the Supreme Court has gradually applied most of the Bill of Rights to the states. While all levels of government must respect our civil liberties today, there are many unresolved areas in terms of balancing interests and drawing lines. The next time you feel strongly about an issue concerning civil liberties, take some time to consider the other side—these questions are often not as black-and-white as they seem. Should speakers who hold extreme, even racist, views be allowed to speak on campus? How do we balance our freedom of speech or freedom from illegal searches with the need for national security?

DESCRIBE THE FIRST AMENDMENT RIGHTS RELATED TO FREEDOM OF RELIGION

Freedom of religion

The First Amendment's ringing words are the most famous statement of personal freedoms in the Constitution: "Congress shall make no law respecting an establishment of religion, or prohibiting the free exercise thereof; or abridging the freedom of speech, or of the press; or the right of the people peaceably to assemble, and to petition the Government for a redress of grievances." (The How It Works graphic illustrates how much is packed into this one amendment.)

Selective Incorporation

TABLE
4.1

The process of applying most of the Bill of Rights to the states progressed in two stages. The first, coming in the 1920s and 1930s, applied the First Amendment to the states; the second came a few decades later and involved criminal defendants' rights.

Amendment	Issue	Case
First Amendment	Freedom of speech	*Gitlow v. New York* (1925)
	Freedom of the press	*Near v. Minnesota* (1931)
	Freedom of assembly	*De Jonge v. Oregon* (1937)
	Right to petition the government	*Hague v. CIO* (1939)
	Free exercise of religion	*Hamilton v. Regents of the University of California* (1934); *Cantwell v. Connecticut* (1940)
	Separation of church and state	*Everson v. Board of Education of Ewing Township* (1947)
Second Amendment	Right to bear arms	*McDonald v. Chicago* (2010)
Fourth Amendment	Protection from unreasonable search and seizure	*Wolf v. Colorado* (1949); *Mapp v. Ohio* (1961)*
Fifth Amendment	Protection from forced self-incrimination	*Malloy v. Hogan* (1964)
	Protection from double jeopardy	*Benton v. Maryland* (1969)
Sixth Amendment	Right to a public trial	*In re Oliver* 333 U.S. 257 (1948)
	Right to a fair trial and an attorney in death-penalty cases	*Powell v. Alabama* (1932)
	Right to an attorney in all felony cases	*Gideon v. Wainwright* (1963)
	Right to an attorney in cases involving jail time	*Argersinger v. Hamlin* (1972)
	Right to a jury trial in a criminal case	*Duncan v. Louisiana* (1968)
	Right to cross-examine a witness	*Pointer v. Texas* (1965)
	Right to compel the testimony of witnesses who are vital for the defendant's case	*Washington v. Texas* (1967)
Eighth Amendment	Protection from cruel and unusual punishment	*Robinson v. California* (1962)[†]
	Protection from excessive bail	*Schilb v. Kuebel* (1971)[‡]
Ninth Amendment	Right to privacy and other nonenumerated, fundamental rights	*Griswold v. Connecticut* (1965)[§]

Not Incorporated		
Third Amendment	Prohibition against the quartering of troops in private homes	
Fifth Amendment	Right to indictment by a grand jury	
Seventh Amendment	Right to a jury trial in a civil case	
Eighth Amendment	Prohibition against excessive fines	

* *Wolf v. Colorado* applied the Fourth Amendment to the states (which meant that states could not engage in unreasonable searches and seizures); *Mapp v. Ohio* applied the exclusionary rule to the states (which excludes the use in a trial of illegally obtained evidence).

[†] Some sources list *Louisiana ex rel. Francis v. Resweber* (1947) as the first case that incorporated the Eighth Amendment. While the decision mentioned the Fifth and Eighth Amendments in the context of the due process clause of the Fourteenth Amendment, this argument was not included in the majority opinion that upheld as constitutional the bizarre double electrocution of prisoner Willie Francis (the electric chair malfunctioned on the first attempt but was successful on the second attempt; see Henry J. Abraham and Barbara A. Perry, *Freedom and the Court: Civil Rights and Civil Liberties in the United States*, 8th ed. [Lawrence: University Press of Kansas, 2003], pp. 71–72).

[‡] Justice Blackmun "assumed" in this case that "the Eighth Amendment's proscription of excessive bail [applies] to the states through the Fourteenth Amendment," but later decisions did not seem to share this view. However, Justices Stevens and O'Connor agreed with Blackmun's view in *Browning-Ferris v. Kelco Disposal* (1989). Some sources argue that the excessive bail clause of the Eighth Amendment is unincorporated.

[§] Justice Goldberg argued for explicit incorporation of the Ninth Amendment in a concurring opinion joined by Justices Warren and Brennan. The opinion of the Court referred more generally to a privacy right rooted in five amendments, including the Ninth, but did not explicitly argue for incorporation.

establishment clause
Part of the First Amendment that states "Congress shall make no law respecting an establishment of religion," which has been interpreted to mean that Congress cannot sponsor or favor any religion.

free exercise clause
Part of the First Amendment that states that Congress cannot prohibit or interfere with the practice of religion unless there are important secular reasons for doing so.

The number, the industry, and the morality of the Priesthood, & the devotion of the people have been manifestly increased by the total separation of the Church from the State.

— James Madison

Can a cross be displayed on federal land? The Supreme Court has ruled that religious displays on government property must be part of larger, secular displays. This cross on federal land in the Mojave Desert was covered up after it became controversial. Now it looks like a sign.

The First Amendment has two parts that deal with religion: the **establishment clause**, which has been interpreted to mean that Congress cannot sponsor or endorse any particular religion, and the **free exercise clause**, which has been interpreted to mean that Congress cannot interfere with the practice of religion unless there are important secular reasons for doing so. To simplify only slightly, the former says that Congress should not help religion and the latter that it should not hurt religion. The establishment clause is primarily concerned with drawing lines. For example, does a prayer at a public high school football game or a Nativity scene on government property constitute state sponsorship of religion? The free exercise clause has more to do with balancing interests. Recall the earlier examples of balancing public safety concerns against snake handling in religious services and the use of Amish buggies on highways.

The combination of the establishment and free exercise clauses results in a general policy of noninterference and government neutrality toward religion. As Thomas Jefferson put it in 1802, the First Amendment provides a "wall of eternal separation between church and state." This language continues to be cited in Court cases in which religion and politics intersect.[23] Since both areas carry great moral weight and emotional charge, it's no wonder that vehement debates continue over the appropriateness of the saying "In God We Trust" on our currency, the White House Christmas tree, and whether evolution and "intelligent design" should be taught in public schools. The boundaries of religious expression remain difficult to draw.

The establishment clause and separation of church and state

Determining the boundaries between church and state—the central issue of the establishment clause—is very difficult. As a leading text on civil liberties puts it, the words of the establishment clause—"Congress shall make no law respecting an establishment of religion"—are commanding and clear, but their meaning is entirely unclear. What does the clause allow or forbid?[24] We know that the Founders did not want an official state religion and did not want the government to favor one religion over another, but beyond that it's hard to say. Jefferson's "wall of eternal separation" comment has been used in Court decisions that prohibit state aid for religious activities, but lately the Court has been moving toward a more "accommodationist" perspective that sometimes allows religious activity in public institutions.

Public Prayer The prohibition of prayer in public schools has become the most controversial establishment clause issue. It exploded onto the political scene in 1962 when the Court ruled in *Engel v. Vitale*[25] that the following prayer, written by the New York State Board of Regents and read every day in the state's public schools, violated the separation of church and state: "Almighty God, we acknowledge our dependence upon Thee, and we beg Thy blessing upon us, our parents, our teachers, and our country." Banning the prayer caused a huge public outcry protesting the perceived attack on religion.

Over the next 50 years, Congress repeatedly tried, unsuccessfully, to amend the Constitution to allow school prayer. Meanwhile, the Court continued to take a hard line on school-sponsored prayer. In 1985, the Court struck down the practice of observing a one-minute moment of silence for "meditation or voluntary prayer" in the Alabama public schools, showing that it isn't the *words* of the prayer that are the problem, but the idea of prayer itself.[26] More recently, the Court said that benedictions or prayers at public school graduations and a school policy that allowed an elected student representative to lead a prayer at a high school football game also violated the establishment clause. The former established a strong "coercion test" that prohibited prayers that may appear to be voluntary (students are not required to attend their high school graduation) but in effect are compulsory.[27] Yet the Court has upheld the practice of opening every session of Congress with a prayer, has let stand without comment a lower-court ruling that allowed a prayer that was planned and led by students (rather than recited as school policy) at a high school graduation, and most recently in 2014 upheld prayers by voluntary chaplains for town board meetings in Greece, New York.[28] The latter case was especially significant because the legislative prayers were offered at town meetings that included residents, unlike the previously approved prayers that were intended for the elected leaders only.

Aid to Religious Organizations The Court has had an even more difficult time coming up with principles to govern government aid to religious organizations, either directly, through tax dollars, or indirectly, through the use of public space. One early attempt was known as the **Lemon test**, after one of the parties in a 1971 case involving government support for religious schools (*Lemon v. Kurtzman*). This case said that a practice violated the establishment clause if it (1) did not have a "secular legislative purpose," (2) either advanced or inhibited religion, or (3) fostered "an excessive government entanglement with religion."[29] The third part of the test was later found open to interpretation by lower courts and therefore led to conflicting rulings.

The Court started to move away from the Lemon test in a 1984 case involving a crèche owned by the city of Pawtucket, Rhode Island, and displayed in a park owned by a nonprofit corporation. The Court allowed the Nativity display, saying: "The Constitution does not require complete separation of church and state; it affirmatively mandates accommodation, not merely tolerance, of all religions, and forbids hostility toward any."[30] This "endorsement test" simply says that government action is unconstitutional if a "reasonable observer" would think that the action either endorses or disapproves of religion. Later rulings upheld similar religious displays, especially if they conformed to what observers have labeled the "three plastic animals rule"—if the baby Jesus is surrounded by Rudolph the red-nosed reindeer and other secular symbols, the overall display is considered sufficiently nonreligious to pass constitutional muster.[31]

The Court has also applied the accommodationist perspective to funding for religious schools by looking more favorably on providing tax dollars to students' families to subsidize tuition costs rather than funding parochial schools directly. For example, the Court upheld an Ohio school voucher program that distributed scholarships to needy students so they could attend the Cleveland school of their choice, including private religious schools. The Court said the program did not violate the establishment clause because it allowed students and their families "to exercise genuine choice among options public and private, secular and religious."[32] Critics of the decision pointed out that 96 percent of the students participating in the scholarship program were enrolled in religiously affiliated schools, which amounted to state sponsorship of religious education, something that the Court had not previously allowed. In 2011, the Court expanded taxpayer support for religious education when it upheld an Arizona law that provides state tax credits for contributions to organizations that provide tuition for religious schools.[33] The Court has also ruled that it is acceptable to use federal funds to buy computers and other educational equipment to be used in public and private schools for "secular, neutral, and nonideological programs"[34] and tax dollars for a sign language interpreter for a deaf student who attended a parochial school.[35]

The free exercise clause

While the freedom of belief is absolute, freedom of religious conduct cannot be unrestricted. That is, you can believe whatever you want without government

Lemon test
The Supreme Court uses this test, established in *Lemon v. Kurtzman*, to determine whether a practice violates the First Amendment's establishment clause.

Cake shop owner Jack Phillips did not want to bake a wedding cake for Charlie Craig and David Mullins because it would violate his religious beliefs. In a narrow ruling that did not settle the broader free exercise question, the Court sided with the baker because he had not been treated fairly by the commission that heard his case.

interference, but if you *act* on those beliefs the government may regulate your behavior. And while the government has restricted religious conduct in dozens of cases, the freedom of religion has been among the most consistently protected civil liberties.

Hundreds of cases have come before the Court in the area of the free exercise of religion.[36] Here are some examples of the questions they addressed: May Amish parents be forced to send their children to schools beyond the eighth grade? (No.) May religion serve as the basis for attaining "conscientious objector" status and avoiding the draft? (Generally yes, but with many qualifications.) Is animal sacrifice as part of a religious ceremony protected by the First Amendment? (Generally yes.) May Mormons have multiple wives? (No.) May people be forced to work on Friday night and Saturday if those are their days of worship? (No.) Does the First Amendment protect distribution of religious leaflets on public streets? And religious meetings in public parks? (Yes, for both, but the latter is subject to "time, manner, and place" restrictions.) May religious dress be regulated? (Generally not, but in some contexts, such as the military, yes.) Are all prison inmates entitled to hold religious services (apparently yes, but this is still an open question) and grow short beards? (Yes.) Are religious organizations subject to child labor laws? (Yes.) Whew! Keep in mind that this list is by no means exhaustive.

One particular case, brought by plaintiffs who had been fired for using peyote as part of a religious ceremony and then denied unemployment benefits because they had broken the law, had broad implications that defined the general basis for government restrictions of religious expression. The Court ultimately ruled that the state of Oregon had not violated the free exercise clause in denying the plaintiffs unemployment benefits. More significantly, with this ruling the Court announced a new interpretation of the free exercise clause: the government does not need a "compelling interest" in regulating a particular behavior to justify a law that limits a religious practice; it only needs a demonstration that the law in question was a "neutral law of general applicability."[37] In other words, after this decision it would be easier for the government to limit the exercise of religion because the Court would no longer require a "compelling" reason for the restrictions.

Congress responded by passing the Religious Freedom Restoration Act (RFRA) in 1993, reinstating the need to demonstrate a "compelling state interest" before limiting religious freedoms; the act also specified exceptions to the Controlled Substances Act to allow the use of peyote in religious ceremonies. After several cases and congressional actions, the Court made it clear that it would have the final word in deciding when a compelling interest is required in order to limit religious practice.[38] The Court relied on this standard in the controversial 2014 case involving the family-owned Hobby Lobby stores, ruling that a "closely held" private corporation could not be forced to provide contraception to women under the Affordable Care Act if there was a "less restrictive" means available to have the insurance provide it.[39] This was the first time that a corporation was given First Amendment protections based on the religious beliefs of the owners of the corporation.

The Court also expanded religious freedom when it approved, for the first time in 2017, direct government payments to a church in support of a secular purpose (in this case, funds for a playground in a church-run day care center). The Court ruled that churches should have equal access to state grants made available to fund neutral, secular programs.[40]

In a highly anticipated case, the Court was faced with a difficult question concerning the civil rights of a same-sex couple and the religious beliefs of a cake shop owner. The baker had refused to bake a cake for the couple, saying that it would violate his religious beliefs. The Court avoided ruling on this central question because the Colorado Civil Rights Commission, which initially heard the case, did not treat religion in a neutral manner and did not give the baker a fair hearing. While concluding that the baker did not have to bake the cake because of the Commission's biased behavior, the Court affirmed that LGBTQ people have "equal access to goods and services under a neutral and generally applicable public accommodations law."[41]

Being familiar with these freedoms and the controversies around them is important because they concern the most deeply personal freedoms debated today. Would you, or do you, send your children to religious schools? Should the government pay for it? If you attend a public college or university, should it be allowed to organize a prayer before a football or basketball game? Should business owners be able to deny equal access to a service (baking a wedding cake) or a public program (health insurance) because of their religious beliefs?

"Why Should I Care?"

DESCRIBE THE MAJOR FIRST AMENDMENT RIGHTS RELATED TO FREEDOM OF SPEECH

Freedom of speech, assembly, and the press

As we noted earlier, defining the scope of our civil liberties depends on balancing interests and drawing lines. This is especially true of the First Amendment's freedom of speech, which can be envisioned on a continuum from most to least protected types of speech based on the Supreme Court cases that have tested their limits.

Generally protected expression

Any time you attend a religious service or a political rally, post a Tweet, write a blog post or letter to the editor, or express a political idea, you are protected by the First Amendment. However, the nature of this protection is continually evolving due to political forces and shifting constitutional interpretations. For much of our nation's history, freedom of speech and freedom of the press were not strongly protected. Only recently have the courts developed a complex continuum ranging from strongly protected political speech to less protected speech.

Standards for Protection The basis for the continuum of protected speech is rooted in the content of the speech. The Supreme Court has interpreted the law to mean that content-based regulation of speech is not permissible (unless it falls into one of the categories of exceptions we outline later). For example, the Court struck down a local ordinance that banned picketing outside of schools except for labor picketing.[42] This ordinance was content-based regulation because it favored one form of speech (from labor unions) over others. Such regulation is subject to the **strict scrutiny** standard of judicial review, which means the regulation must be narrowly tailored so that it is the least restrictive on an individual's fundamental right to free speech and the government must demonstrate a compelling state interest to curtail the speech. In most cases, such strict scrutiny by the courts means that the speech will be protected and the regulation will be struck down. If a regulation is content neutral and does not favor any given viewpoint over another, then it is subject to the less demanding **intermediate scrutiny** standard. This means that the government must only demonstrate a substantial interest in curtailing the speech, the interest must be unrelated to the content of the speech, and there must be alternative opportunities for communication.[43]

Political Speech Freedom of speech got off to a rocky start when Congress passed the Alien and Sedition Acts in 1798. The controversial Sedition Act made it a crime to "write, print, utter or publish . . . any false, scandalous and malicious writing or writings against the government of the United States." Supporters of the acts claimed they were necessary to strengthen the national government in response to the French Revolution, but in reality they were an attempt by the governing Federalist Party to neutralize the opposition—the Democratic-Republican Party. As many as 25 people, mostly newspaper editors, were tried under the law and 10 were jailed, including Benjamin Franklin's grandson. The outcry against the laws helped Thomas Jefferson win the presidential election in 1800. Jefferson pardoned the convicted editors, Congress repealed one of the acts in 1802, and the other acts were allowed to expire before the Supreme Court had a chance to rule that they were unconstitutional.

World War I prompted the harshest crackdowns on free speech since the Sedition Act of 1798. The most important case from this period involved the general secretary of the Socialist Party, Charles Schenck, who opposed U.S. involvement in the war. He had printed a leaflet urging young men to resist the draft. Schenck was arrested under the Espionage Act of 1917, which prohibited "interfering with military or naval operations," including the draft. He appealed all the way to the Supreme Court, arguing that the First Amendment permitted him to protest the war and to urge others to resist the draft, but the Court sustained his conviction, noting that free speech is not an absolute right:

The most stringent protection of free speech would not protect a man in falsely shouting fire in a theatre and causing a panic. . . . The question in every case is whether the words used are used in such circumstances and are of such a nature as to create a clear and present danger that they will bring about the substantive evils that Congress has a right to prevent.[44]

This **clear and present danger test** meant that the government could suppress speech it deemed dangerous (in this instance, preventing the government from fighting the war). However, critics of the decision argue that Schenck's actions were not dangerous for the country and should have been allowed.[45]

Justice Oliver Wendell Holmes, author of the *Schenck* decision and the clear and present danger test, had a change of heart and dissented in a case later that year that

---

strict scrutiny
The highest level of scrutiny the courts can use when determining whether a law is constitutional. To meet this standard, the law or policy must be shown to serve a "compelling state interest" or goal, it must be narrowly tailored to achieve that goal, and it must be the least restrictive means of achieving that goal.

intermediate scrutiny
The middle level of scrutiny the courts can use when determining whether a law is constitutional. To meet this standard, the law or policy must be "content neutral," must further an important government interest in a way that is "substantially related" to that interest, and must use means that are a close fit to the government's goal and not substantially broader than is necessary to accomplish that goal.

clear and present danger test
Established in *Schenck v. United States*, this test allowed the government to restrict certain types of speech deemed dangerous.

upheld the conviction of six anarchists who supported the cause of the Bolsheviks in Russia. In one of the most famous statements of the importance of the freedom of speech, he touted the "free trade in ideas," saying, "The best test of truth is the power of the thought to get itself accepted in the competition of the market. . . . [W]e should be eternally vigilant against attempts to check the expression of opinion that we loathe and believe to be fraught with death."[46] This notion of the marketplace of ideas in which good ideas triumph over bad is still central to modern defenses of the First Amendment.

Over the next several decades, the Court struggled to draw the line between dangerous speech and words that were simply unpopular. During the Red Scare of the late 1940s and early 1950s the hunt for communists in government was led by Senator Joe McCarthy, and the Court had many opportunities to defend unpopular speech, but for the most part it declined to do so. For example, in 1951 the Court upheld the conviction of 11 members of the Communist Party under the Smith Act, which banned the advocacy of force or violence against the United States.[47]

Then, in 1969, the Court established a strong protection for free speech, superseding the clear and present danger test, that still holds today. This case involved a leader of the Ku Klux Klan who made a threatening speech at a cross-burning rally that was subsequently shown on television. Twelve hooded figures were shown, many with weapons. The speech said that "revengence [*sic*]" might be taken if "our president, our Congress, our Supreme Court continues to suppress the white, Caucasian race." It continued, "We are marching on Congress July the Fourth, four hundred thousand strong." The Klan leader was convicted under the Ohio law banning "sabotage, violence, or unlawful methods of terrorism as a means of accomplishing industrial or political reform," but the Court unanimously reversed his conviction, arguing that threatening speech could not be suppressed just because it sounded dangerous. Specifically, the **direct incitement test** holds that speech is protected "except where such advocacy is directed to inciting or producing imminent lawless action and is likely to incite or produce such action."[48] Under this standard, most, if not all, of the sedition convictions during World War I and the Red Scare would have been overturned.

Perhaps the strongest example of protecting unpopular speech comes from the case of the Westboro Baptist Church (WBC). Since 2005, members of the WBC have protested at hundreds of funerals of members of the armed services who were killed in Iraq and Afghanistan. However, these are not typical antiwar protests. Instead, the protesters

Restriction of free thought and free speech is the most dangerous of all subversions. It is the one un-American act that could most easily defeat us.

— Justice William O. Douglas, 1952

direct incitement test
Established in *Brandenburg v. Ohio*, this test protects threatening speech under the First Amendment unless that speech aims to and is likely to cause imminent "lawless action."

Should free speech be protected even when the ideas are offensive? The Supreme Court ruled that the Westboro Baptist Church had a right to protest at military funerals, even though many Americans found the arguments and approach of the church members deeply offensive.

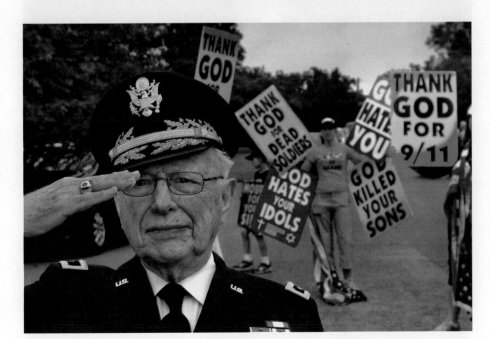

claim that the troops' deaths were God's punishment for "the homosexual lifestyle of soul-damning, nation-destroying filth." The church and its members have drawn strong reactions and counterprotests for their confrontational approach at the military funerals, including their use of signs that say "God Hates Fags," "Thank God for Dead Soldiers," "God Killed Your Sons," and "God Hates America." Critics, including many veterans groups and attorneys general from 48 states, argue that the protests should not be considered protected speech under the First Amendment. The Veterans of Foreign Wars issued a statement saying: "In a time of profound grief and emotional vulnerability, these personal attacks are an affront of the most egregious kind." However, in 2011 the Supreme Court ruled 8–1 that the WBC's protests were protected speech.[49]

Symbolic Speech The use of signs, symbols, or other unspoken acts or methods to communicate in a political manner—symbolic speech—enjoys many of the same protections as regular speech. For example, during the Vietnam War the Court protected the right of a war protester to wear an American flag patch sewn on the seat of his pants,[50] high school students' right to wear an armband to protest the war,[51] and an individual's right to tape a peace symbol on the flag and fly it upside down outside an apartment window.[52] Lower courts had convicted these protesters under state laws that protected the American flag or under a school policy that prohibited wearing armbands to protest the Vietnam War. In the flag desecration case involving the peace symbol, the Court stated that protected "speech" need not be verbal: "there can be little doubt that appellant communicated through the use of symbols."[53]

A 1989 case provided the strongest protection for symbolic speech yet. The case involved a man who burned a flag outside the 1984 Republican National Convention in Texas, chanting along with other protesters, "America the red, white, and blue, we spit on you. You stand for plunder, you will go under." The Court refrained from critiquing the jingle, but its 5–4 decision overturned the man's conviction under Texas's flag desecration law on the grounds that symbolic political speech is protected by the First Amendment.[54] In response to this unpopular decision, Congress passed the Flag Protection Act of 1989, which the Court also struck down as an unconstitutional infringement on political expression.[55] Congress then attempted to pass a constitutional amendment to overturn the Court decision; the House passed

symbolic speech
Nonverbal expression, such as the use of signs or symbols. It benefits from many of the same constitutional protections as verbal speech because of its expressive value.

DID YOU KNOW?

63%

of black Americans and 31 percent of white Americans view the Confederate battle flag primarily as a symbol of racism.
Source: *The Economist*/YouGov poll

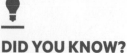

The American flag is a popular target for protesters: it has been spat upon, shredded, turned into underwear, and burned. Here, protesters burn a U.S. flag as they march through downtown Washington, D.C., following the Ferguson, Missouri, grand jury's decision not to indict Officer Darren Wilson for the shooting death of Michael Brown.

the amendment six times between 1995 and 2005 with the necessary two-thirds vote, but each time the measure failed by a narrow margin in the Senate (by just one vote in 2006). President Trump reignited this debate shortly after he was elected, tweeting, "Nobody should be allowed to burn the American flag—if they do, there must be consequences—perhaps loss of citizenship or year in jail!" However, Republican leaders in Congress have not been interested in revisiting this fight.[56]

Although the Court has protected flag burning and other forms of symbolic speech, there are limits, especially when the symbolic speech conflicts with another substantial governmental interest. Here the critical test is whether the action can be regulated for important reasons unrelated to ideas. If so, then the "intermediate scrutiny" standard will apply. For example, Vietnam War protesters who burned their draft cards were not protected by the First Amendment because their actions interfered with Congress's constitutional authority to "raise and support" armies, and the purpose of the draft was not to suppress speech.[57] The Court also ruled in 2015 that states may ban the use of the Confederate battle flag on state vanity plates. The Sons of Confederate Veterans argued that the battle flag honored their southern heritage, but the state of Texas said it was offensive.[58] The debate over the flag intensified after a "Unite the Right" rally in Charlottesville, Virginia, in which a white supremacist killed a woman and injured 19 others, and demonstrators prominently displayed the Confederate battle flag. At least 30 communities around the country took down statues and memorials to Confederate leaders in response to the violence in Charlottesville.[59]

Money as Speech Spending money in political campaigns may also be protected by the First Amendment since it provides the means for more conventional types of political speech. Here the central question is whether the government can control campaign contributions and spending for a broader public purpose such as lessening the potential for corruption, or whether such laws violate the First Amendment rights of candidates or their supporters. You probably have heard the old saying "Money talks," which implies that money is speech. Given the importance of advertising in modern campaigns, limitations on raising and spending money could limit the ability of candidates and groups to reach voters with their message. The Court has walked a tightrope on this one, balancing the public interest in honest and ethical elections and the First Amendment rights of candidates and their advocates. The Court has upheld individual candidates' right to spend their own money in federal elections, but presidential candidates give up that right if they accept federal campaign funds (taxpayers' money) in a presidential election. Also, candidates in federal elections are subject to limits on the types and size of contributions they can receive, and they must report all contributions and spending to the Federal Election Commission.[60]

The Bipartisan Campaign Reform Act, which went into effect for the 2004 elections, included a "Millionaires' Amendment" that lifted restrictions on campaign contributions for candidates whose opponents spent more than $350,000 of their own money in the election. This attempt to level the campaign finance playing field was struck down by the Supreme Court in 2008 as a violation of wealthy candidates' First Amendment rights.[61] In 2010 the Court also extended First Amendment rights to corporations and labor unions that want to spend money on campaign ads, and in 2014 it struck down the aggregate (collective) limits placed on individual contributions to candidates and parties (these cases are discussed in more detail in Chapter 9).[62] However, the Court upheld a ban on unlimited "soft money" contributions because they were seen by the Court as the type of contribution with the most potential for corruption.[63]

Student fees as a form of symbolic speech came up in a case in 2000 involving student activity fees at the University of Wisconsin. A group of students argued that they should not have to pay fees to fund groups whose activities they opposed, including a student environmental group, a gay and bisexual student center, a community legal office, an AIDS support network, a campus women's center, and the Wisconsin Student Public Interest Research Group. The Court ruled that mandatory student fees could continue to support the full range of groups as long as the process for allocating money was "viewpoint neutral." The Court also said that student referendums that could add or cut money for specific groups violated viewpoint neutrality. The potential for the majority to censor unpopular views was unacceptable to the Court, since "the whole theory of viewpoint neutrality is that minority views are treated with the same respect as are majority views."[64]

Hate Speech Whether or not freedom of speech should apply to **hate speech** has been a controversial issue both on college campuses and in society generally. Do people have a right to say things that are offensive or abusive, especially in terms of race, gender, and sexual orientation? By the mid-1990s, more than 350 public colleges and universities said no by regulating some forms of hate speech.[65]

Many of these speech codes were struck down in federal court, but in the last few years the issue has resurfaced on many college campuses. In addition to the controversial speakers discussed in the chapter opener, a variety of "campus climate" issues consumed dozens of schools. At Yale University in 2015, controversy erupted over the response of a residential college faculty administrator, Erika Christakis, to an e-mail students received cautioning them not to wear Halloween costumes that could be racially or culturally insensitive. Christakis wrote that universities no longer allowed students to be "a little bit inappropriate or provocative or, yes, offensive."[66] She resigned a few weeks later, saying, " [T]he current climate at Yale is not, in my view, conducive to the civil dialogue and open inquiry required to solve our urgent societal problems."[67] The president of the University of Missouri also resigned in 2015 after students, including the football team, said that he was racially insensitive and not open to their demands for a more inclusive and supportive environment on campus. In 2017, Indiana University students petitioned to remove part of a mural that depicts the history of the state using imagery of a burning cross and white-hooded Klansmen. University leaders compromised by leaving the artwork but saying that classes would no longer be held in the lecture hall with the mural.[68]

Another significant issue combines the topics of symbolic speech and hate speech. Can a person who burned a cross on a black family's lawn be convicted under a city ordinance that prohibits conduct in St. Paul, Minnesota, that "arouses anger, alarm,

hate speech
Expression that is offensive or abusive, particularly in terms of race, gender, or sexual orientation. It is currently protected under the First Amendment.

A historic mural illustrating a member of the Ku Klux Klan provoked controversy at Indiana University in 2017, with many students calling for the removal of the offensive imagery.

or resentment in others on the basis of race, color, creed, religion, or gender"? Or is the ordinance an unconstitutional limit on First Amendment rights? The Court said the cross burner could be punished for arson, terrorism, trespassing, or other violations of the law, but he could not be convicted under this ordinance because it was overly broad and vague. The Court said: "Let there be no mistake about our belief that burning a cross in someone's front yard is reprehensible. But St. Paul has sufficient means at its disposal to prevent such behavior without adding the First Amendment to the fire."[69] The city ordinance was unconstitutional because it took selective aim at a disfavored message; it constituted "viewpoint discrimination." However, the Court has since upheld more carefully worded bans of cross burning. Eleven years after the St. Paul case, the Court ruled that Virginia could prohibit cross burning if there was intent to intimidate. The Court also noted that the law was content neutral because it did not engage in viewpoint discrimination: any burning of a cross in a threatening context was illegal.[70]

Speech on the Internet Internet hate speech has become increasingly controversial in recent years. Cyberbullying through social media like Myspace, Twitter, Facebook, and Reddit precipitated several suicides. In 2013, Facebook cracked down on offensive content that glorified violence against women, such as pages with headlines like "Violently Raping Your Friend Just for Laughs."[71] Facebook's "community standards" have a more restrictive definition of hate speech than is allowed by the direct incitement test. While Facebook makes a distinction between humor and serious speech, it "do[es] not permit individuals or groups to attack others based on their race, ethnicity, national origin, religion, sex, gender, sexual orientation, disability or medical condition."[72] This led law professor Jeff Rosen to conclude that "today, lawyers at Google, YouTube, Facebook, and Twitter have more power over who can speak and who can be heard than any president, judge, or monarch."[73] This may sound like hyperbole, but he is right: corporations are not restricted by the First Amendment (which, after all, says "*Congress* shall make no law . . ."). So if Facebook and other social media want to restrict hate speech, they can. Although free speech advocates are concerned about restrictions on Internet hate speech, civil rights groups such as the Anti-Defamation League, the Leadership Conference on Civil and Human Rights, and the National Organization for Women all support the move.

While social media companies have great latitude in what they permit online, the government has limited power to regulate access to social media. In 2017, the Court struck down a North Carolina law that prohibited sex offenders from accessing or using social media sites, saying that these sites are the "principal sources for knowing current events, checking ads for employment, speaking and listening in the modern public square, and otherwise exploring the vast realms of human thought and knowledge." Therefore, limiting access to social media would prevent the "legitimate exercise of First Amendment rights."[74]

Freedom of Assembly The right to assemble peaceably has been consistently protected by the Supreme Court.[75] Perhaps the most famous freedom of assembly case involved a neo-Nazi group that wanted to march in Skokie, a suburb of Chicago that had 70,000 residents, nearly 60 percent of whom were Jewish, including many Holocaust survivors. The village passed ordinances that effectively banned the group from marching, arguing that residents would be so upset by the Nazi marchers that they might become violent. But the lower courts did not accept this argument, ruling that if "the audience is so offended by the ideas being expressed that it becomes disorderly and attempts to silence the speaker, it is the duty of the police to attempt to protect the speaker, not to silence his speech."[76] Otherwise, the right to assemble would be restricted by a "heckler's veto." The Court elaborated on this responsibility to protect expressions of unpopular views by striking down another town's ordinance that allowed it to charge a higher permit fee to groups whose march would likely require more police protection.[77] But in many cases, permit fees do not come close to covering the actual costs of security. When white supremacist Richard Spencer came to speak at the University of Florida, as noted in the chapter opener, his group, the National Policy Institute, was only charged $10,564 while the actual costs for security paid by the university and the state were estimated at nearly $600,000.[78]

The August 2017 "Unite the Right" rally in Charlottesville, Virginia—initially organized in opposition to the removal of a statue of Confederate general Robert E. Lee from a public park—raised issues of symbolic speech and freedom of assembly. Can the use of symbols that some deem offensive, such as the Confederate battle flag, be regulated by the government? Should groups promoting hate speech be permitted to peaceably assemble in public areas?

While broad protection is provided for peaceable assemblies, governments may regulate the time, manner, and place of expression as long as these regulations do not favor certain groups or messages over others. For example, the Court ruled that anti-abortion protesters were not allowed to picket a doctor's home in Brookfield, Wisconsin, on the grounds that the ordinance banning all residential picketing was content neutral; there was a government interest in preserving the "sanctity of the home, the one retreat to which men and women can repair to escape from the tribulations of their daily pursuits."[79] "Time, manner, and place" restrictions also may be invoked for practical reasons. For instance, if the Ku Klux Klan planned to hold a march around a football stadium on the day of a game, the city council could deny it a permit and could suggest that it choose another day that would not interfere with game day activities. In the case of Spencer's speech at the University of Florida, the school initially turned down Spencer's request to speak on campus just a month after the tragic events in Charlottesville, saying that it would not have time to provide adequate security for the event. However, it approved the talk for a date a month later.[80]

The legal standard for "time, manner, and place" regulations is that they must be "reasonable." This standard came into play in a 2014 case in which the Court ruled that a Massachusetts state law creating a 35-foot buffer zone around entrances to abortion clinics violated the First Amendment. While the buffer zone was content neutral, it was unreasonable because it was more restrictive than necessary to allow access to the clinics.[81] While the "reasonableness" standard is vague, it allows the courts to balance the right to assemble against other practical considerations.

Freedom of the Press The task of balancing interests is central to many First Amendment cases involving freedom of the press. Which is more important, the First Amendment freedom of the press to disclose details about current events or the Sixth Amendment right to a fair trial, which may require keeping important information out of the public eye? When do national security concerns prevail over journalists' right to keep citizens informed? The general issue here is **prior restraint**, the government's right to prevent the media from publishing something.

Prior restraint has never been clearly defined by the Court, but several landmark cases have set a very high bar for applying it. In 1971, the Pentagon Papers case involved disclosure of parts of the top-secret report on internal planning for the Vietnam War. This incredibly divided case had nine separate written opinions! In a 6–3 decision the Court said that the government could not prevent the publication of the Pentagon Papers, but at least five justices supported the view that, under some circumstances, the government could use prior restraint—although they could not agree on the standard.[82] For some of the justices, a crucial consideration was the Pentagon Papers' revelation that the U.S. government had lied about its involvement in and the progress of the Vietnam War. Justice Hugo Black noted the importance of this point, saying, "Only a free and unrestrained press can effectively expose deception in government."[83]

The debate over restraining the media heated up in 2010, when WikiLeaks released a classified video of an air strike in Baghdad showing U.S. pilots mistakenly firing on two Reuters reporters and more than 91,000 classified battlefield incident reports from Iraq and Afghanistan and U.S. State Department cables. All of these documents had been leaked by U.S. Army Private First Class Bradley (now Chelsea) Manning. This sensational leaking ratcheted up the stakes, and some members of Congress called the leaks treason and urged for prosecution (Manning was tried and convicted in a military court for violations of the Espionage Act and for copying and releasing classified information; he served seven years in prison before President Obama pardoned him, commuting the rest of Manning's 35-year sentence). President Trump has frequently expressed frustration about leaks to the media, and in August 2017 Attorney General Jeff Sessions declared that the "culture of leaking must stop" and threatened that the Department of Justice would subpoena media outlets that publish leaked information.[84]

prior restraint
A limit on freedom of the press that allows the government to prohibit the media from publishing certain materials.

Bradley (now Chelsea) Manning (center), whose job in the U.S. military gave him access to classified information, downloaded thousands of classified videos, diplomatic cables, reports, and other information and gave them to the website WikiLeaks.

The forms of expression discussed in this section—speech, assembly, and press—all have strong protections based on the First Amendment. The strongest protections are for content-based expression—that is, if a regulation is trying to limit *what* can be said, the Court applies the strict scrutiny standard and usually strikes down the regulation. However, there are exceptions, such as speech that directly incites an imminent danger. If the regulation is content neutral and does not favor one viewpoint over another, then it is easier to uphold. But even then, the government must have a substantial reason for limiting expression.

Less protected speech and publications

Some forms of speech do not warrant the same level of protection as political speech because they do not contribute to public debate or express ideas that have important social value. Four categories of speech may be more easily regulated by the government than political speech: fighting words, slander and libel, commercial speech, and obscenity. The first two categories may be prevented by the state if certain conditions are met, and the latter two receive some protection, but not as much as political speech.

Fighting Words Governments may regulate **fighting words**, "which by their very utterance inflict injury or tend to incite an immediate breach of the peace."[85] Such laws must be narrowly written; it is not acceptable to ban all foul language, and the prohibited speech must target a single person rather than a group. Moreover, the question of whether certain words provoke a backlash depends on the reaction of the targeted person. Inflammatory words directed at Pope Francis would not be fighting words because he would turn the other cheek, whereas the same words yelled at musician Kanye West or actor Alec Baldwin *would* be fighting words because he would probably deck you. The Court clarified the test based on "what persons of common intelligence would understand to be words likely to cause an average addressee to fight."[86] While this provides a somewhat objective test, the fighting words doctrine has still been difficult to apply.

Slander and Libel A more extensive line of cases prohibiting speech concerns **slander**, spoken false statements that damage someone's reputation (defamation), and **libel**, written statements that do the same thing. As in many areas of First Amendment law, it is difficult to draw the line between permissible speech and slander or libel. The current legal standard distinguishes between speech about a public figure, such as a politician or celebrity, and about a regular person. In short, it is much more difficult for public figures to prove libel. A public figure has to demonstrate that the defamatory statement was made with "actual malice" and "with knowledge that it was false or with reckless disregard of whether it was false or not."[87]

One of the most famous libel cases was brought against *Hustler* magazine by the Reverend Jerry Falwell, a famous televangelist and political activist. Falwell sued *Hustler* for libel and emotional distress after the magazine published a parody of a liquor advertisement depicting him in a "drunken incestuous rendezvous with his mother in an outhouse" (this quote is from the Supreme Court case).[88] The lower court said that the parody wasn't believable, so *Hustler* couldn't be sued for libel, but they awarded Falwell damages for emotional distress. The Court overturned the damages, saying that public figures and public officials must put up with such things, comparing the parody to outrageous political cartoons, which have always been protected by the First Amendment.

fighting words
Forms of expression that "by their very utterance" can incite violence. These can be regulated by the government but are often difficult to define.

slander
Spoken false statements that damage a person's reputation. They can be regulated by the government but are often difficult to distinguish from permissible speech.

libel
Written false statements that damage a person's reputation. They can be regulated by the government but are often difficult to distinguish from permissible speech.

While it is extremely difficult to win a slander or libel case, Hulk Hogan's 2016 case against the website Gawker shows that it is not impossible. Hogan sued Gawker—and won a $140 million verdict—for posting a sex tape of him with his friend's wife, Heather Clem, that had been recorded without his knowledge. He ultimately settled with Gawker for $31 million, and the website declared bankruptcy because of the case. The case has broader political implications because it shows that public figures may be able to win damages even when the defamatory content is *true*.[89] Melania Trump also reached a settlement with the *Daily Mail*, a British tabloid, for articles that the outlet published in 2016 falsely claiming that she had once worked for an escort service (the paper printed a retraction, apologized, and paid damages).[90] President Trump has vowed to "open up our libel laws" to deter what he claimed were false "fake news" stories. Libel law, however, is controlled by the states, subject to limits from the U.S. Supreme Court, so it is not something that the president can change.[91] Trump is also facing a lawsuit in New York state court from "Apprentice" contestant Summer Zervos, who alleges that he groped her. Her suit claims that Trump slandered her by calling her a liar. In June 2018, a New York state judge ruled that Trump has to testify and that his deposition could last up to seven hours.

Hulk Hogan testifies in court against Gawker Media, which he sued on charges of defamation and emotional distress. In a rare victory against the press, Hogan won his case.

Commercial Speech

Commercial Speech Commercial speech, which mostly refers to advertising, has evolved from having almost no protection under the First Amendment to enjoying quite strong protection. One early case involved a business owner who distributed leaflets to advertise rides on his submarine, which was docked in New York City. Under city ordinances, leafleting was permitted only if it was devoted to "information or a public protest," but not for a commercial purpose. The plaintiff changed the leaflet to have his advertisement on one side and a statement protesting a city policy on the other side (clever guy!). He was arrested anyway, and the Supreme Court upheld his conviction, saying that the city council had the right to regulate the distribution of leaflets.[92]

The Court became much more sympathetic to commercial speech in the 1970s when it struck down a law against advertising prescription drug prices and a law

commercial speech
Public expression with the aim of making a profit. It has received greater protection under the First Amendment in recent years but remains less protected than political speech.

Commercial speech may be protected even if some consider its content offensive. The rock band the Slants won the right to trademark their band name even though it refers to a racial slur against the Asian-American community.

Miller test
Established in *Miller v. California*, this three-part test is used by the Supreme Court to determine whether speech meets the criteria for obscenity. If so, it can be restricted by the government.

prohibiting placing newspaper racks on city streets to distribute commercial publications such as real estate guides.[93] The key decision in 1980 established a test that is still central today: the government may regulate commercial speech if it concerns an illegal activity, if the advertisement is misleading, or if regulating speech directly advances a substantial government interest and the regulation is not excessive. In practice, this test means that commercial speech can be regulated, but the government must have a very good reason to do it.

Commercial speech is even protected when it could be considered offensive. In 2017, the Court sided with the Slants, an Asian-American rock band, in overturning a provision of U.S. patent and trademark law that prohibited the registration of trademarks that "disparage" or "bring . . . into contempt or disrepute" any "persons, living or dead." The Slants, whose application to trademark their band name had been denied, argued that their goal was to reclaim the racial slur against Asian Americans, in the same way that the LGBTQ community over time redefined the use of "queer." The Court agreed, saying, "A law that can be directed against speech found offensive to some portion of the public can be turned against minority and dissenting views to the detriment of all." This ruling also means that the Washington Redskins football team will be able to keep its nickname, despite the fact that many find it offensive.[94]

Obscenity One area in which the press has never experienced complete freedom involves the publication of pornography and material considered obscene. The difficulty arises in deciding where to draw the line. Nearly everyone would agree that child pornography should not be published[95] and that pornography should not be available to minors. However, beyond these points there is not much consensus. For example, some people are offended by nude paintings in art museums, while others enjoy watching hard-core X-rated movies.

Defining obscenity has proven difficult for the courts. In an often-quoted moment of frustration, Justice Potter Stewart wrote that he could not define obscenity, but "I know it when I see it."[96] In its first attempt, the Court ruled that a particular publication could be banned if an "average person, applying contemporary community standards," would find that the material appeals to prurient interests and is "utterly without redeeming social importance."[97] This standard proved unworkable because lower courts differed in their interpretation. The Court took another stab at it in 1973 in a case that gave rise to the **Miller test**, which is still applied today.[98] The test has three standards that must all be met in order for material to be banned as obscene: (1) it appeals to prurient interests, (2) it is "patently offensive," and (3) the work as a whole lacks serious literary, artistic, political, or scientific value. The Court also clarified that *local* community standards were to apply rather than a single national standard, reasoning that what passes for obscenity in Sioux City, Iowa, probably would be considered pretty tame in Las Vegas.

In 2009, the Supreme Court addressed an area of the law that it had not touched for more than 30 years: regulating vulgar language that does not rise to the level of obscenity on broadcast television and radio (but not on cable or other paid-subscription services, which are not regulated as to language). In 1978, the Court ruled that the Federal Communications Commission (FCC) had the power to regulate indecent language, but the FCC had always interpreted that power to only cover repeated use of vulgar words.[99] However, after the use of vulgar words by Bono during the 2003 Golden Globe Awards and by Cher and Nicole Richie during the 2002 and 2003 Billboard Music Awards, the FCC announced that it would no longer tolerate even "isolated uses of sexual and excretory words."

Fox Television challenged this new rule, but in 2009 the Supreme Court upheld the FCC's ban on "fleeting expletives" as "entirely rational" under existing law. (Its opinion also took a swipe at the "foul-mouthed glitteratae from Hollywood.")[100] The Court also ruled the following week that the FCC had not acted capriciously in fining CBS $550,000 for Janet Jackson's infamous "wardrobe malfunction" at the 2004 Super Bowl.[101] However, after sending the cases back to the lower courts and another round of appeals, the Supreme Court ruled that the regulations were unconstitutionally vague and the networks could not be fined. The Court also let stand a lower-court ruling that voided the fine against CBS on similar grounds.[102] But the Court did not address the broader constitutional questions, so the regulation still stands; stronger First Amendment protections for broadcast radio and television will have to come from future cases.

Two more recent cases made clear that violence in published material cannot be regulated in the same way as sexual content. In 2010, the Court struck down a federal law that criminalized depictions "in which a living animal is intentionally maimed, mutilated, tortured, wounded, or killed." The law focused on "crush videos," which show the torture and killing of helpless animals, but also included dog fighting and other forms of animal cruelty. In striking down the law, the Court said the First Amendment protected such depictions, even if the underlying behavior itself could be illegal.[103] In 2011, the Court struck down a California law that banned the sale of violent video games to children, saying: "Like the protected books, plays and movies that preceded them, video games communicate ideas—and even social messages—through many familiar literary devices (such as characters, dialogue, plot and music) and through features distinctive to the medium (such as the player's interaction with the virtual world). That suffices to confer First Amendment protection."[104]

Even if you are not a journalist, do not engage in political protest, or do not contribute to political campaigns, the freedom of speech, the press, and assembly still shapes the world around you. The "marketplace of ideas" ensures that policies are debated and a range of voices can be heard. Our political leaders are held accountable by the free exchange of ideas and a strong independent media that can criticize their actions. Also, other areas of your everyday life that you may not consider to be "speech," such as video games, are protected by the First Amendment. Having an understanding of the law is especially important when the freedom of the press and free speech are regularly challenged in the political world.

"Why Should I Care?"

★

EXPLORE WHY THE SECOND
AMENDMENT'S MEANING
ON GUN RIGHTS IS OFTEN
DEBATED

The right to bear arms

Until recently, the right to bear arms was the only civil liberty that the Supreme Court had played a relatively minor role in defining. Between 1791 and 2007, the Court issued only four rulings directly pertaining to the Second Amendment. The federal courts had always interpreted the Second Amendment's awkward phrasing—"A well regulated Militia, being necessary to the security of a free State, the right of the people to keep and bear Arms, shall not be infringed"—as a right to bear arms within the context of serving in a militia, rather than as an individual right to own a gun.

Although legal conflict over gun ownership has intensified only recently, battles over guns have always been intense in the broader political realm. Interest groups such as the National Rifle Association have long asserted that the Second Amendment guarantees an individual right to bear arms.[105] Critics of this view emphasize the first clause of the amendment and point to the frequent mention of state militias in congressional debates at the time the Bill of Rights was adopted.[106] They argue that the Second Amendment was adopted to reassure Antifederalist advocates of states' rights that state militias, not a national standing army, would provide national security. In this view, the national armed forces and the National Guard have made the Second Amendment obsolete.

Before the Court's recent entry into this debate, Congress and state and local lawmakers had largely defined gun ownership and gun carrying rights, creating significant variation among the states. Wyoming and Montana have virtually no restrictions on gun ownership, for example, whereas California and Connecticut have many. At the national level, Congress tends to respond to crime waves or high-profile assassinations by passing new gun control laws. The broadest one, the Gun Control Act of 1968, was passed in the wake of the assassinations of Robert F. Kennedy and Martin Luther King Jr. The law sets standards for gun dealers, bans the sale of weapons through the mail, and restricts the sale of new machine guns, among other provisions.

Following the assassination attempt on President Reagan in 1981, the push for stronger gun control laws intensified. Spearheading this effort was Sarah Brady, whose husband, James Brady (Reagan's press secretary), was shot and disabled in the assassination attempt. It took nearly 13 years for the campaign to bear fruit, but in 1993 Congress passed and President Clinton signed the Brady Bill, which mandates a background check and a five-day waiting period for any handgun purchase.

While the Constitution guarantees the individual right to bear arms (as illustrated here by the woman taking target practice), the shootings at Marjory Stoneman Douglas High School in Parkland, Florida, shocked the nation. In response, students from the school organized the national March for Our Lives in effort to urge the government to pass gun reform.

But not all gun tragedies lead to more gun control. In 2016 and 2017, there were 729 mass shootings, defined as incidents in which at least four people were killed or injured, not counting the shooter.[107] By the FBI's definition of an "active shooter" there were 220 incidents from 2000 to 2016, including those in Orlando, Florida; San Bernardino, California; Charleston, South Carolina; and Roseburg, Oregon.[108] In the deadliest mass shooting by a single gunman, 58 people were killed and 546 injured in October 2017 at a country music festival in Las Vegas. While 45 states have passed new gun safety laws since 2013 including "smart gun" laws, laws concerning mental health and gun ownership, laws restricting ownership of assault weapons, and stronger background checks, 30 states now make it relatively easy to get a permit to carry a concealed weapon and 12 more states do not require a permit. Many states have also expanded the places in which guns may be carried, including college campuses, and have passed "stand your ground" laws, which allow gun owners to shoot first if they feel threatened.[109]

In 2008, a landmark Supreme Court ruling recognized for the first time an individual right to bear arms for self-defense and hunting.[110] The decision struck down the District of Columbia's ban on handguns, while noting that state and local governments could enforce ownership restrictions, such as preventing felons or the mentally impaired from buying guns. The Court did not apply the Second Amendment to the states in this decision, but it did so two years later in striking down a gun control ordinance in Chicago and reaffirming the ownership restrictions noted in the Washington, D.C., case.[111] The dissenters in both strongly divided 5–4 decisions lamented the Court's activism in reopening a legal question considered settled for 70 years (in 32 instances since a 1939 Court ruling, appeals courts had affirmed the focus on a collective right—in the context of a militia—rather than an individual right to bear arms, and recognized an individual right only twice between 1939 and 2007).[112]

Given the strong public support for gun ownership—there are about 300 million privately owned guns in the United States—and the Supreme Court's endorsement of an individual right to bear arms, stronger gun control at the national level is highly unlikely (especially given the unsuccessful pushes after the shootings at Sandy Hook Elementary School in 2012 and in Orlando, Florida, in 2016 and Las Vegas in 2017; however, the president and Congress have taken some limited steps in recent years). Early in 2016, President Obama issued an executive order requiring most gun sales to be through federally licensed dealers who would conduct background checks. The order also required the Social Security Administration to release information about mentally ill recipients of Social Security benefits, which would be considered as part of the background checks. This provision essentially prohibited people with mental illnesses from buying guns.[113] The second part of the order was overturned by Congress early in 2017. After a mass shooting at a Parkland, Florida, high school that killed 17 students in 2018, high school students organized the March for Our Lives, which had 1.2 to 2 million participants in more than 800 cities around the world. In Florida, gun control laws were strengthened by raising the age to buy a gun to 18, banning bump stocks that allow bullets to be fired more rapidly, and introducing a three-day waiting period before buying a long rifle. Congress passed legislation strengthening the National Instant Criminal Background Check System and providing $1 billion to fund initiatives intended to enhance school safety, such as the addition of metal detectors. President Trump also signed an executive order banning bump stocks. In addition to this limited legislative and executive action, extensive litigation will be necessary to define the acceptable boundaries of gun control and to identify which state and local restrictions will be allowed to stand. Up to this point, the verdicts have been mixed, with some lower courts upholding limitations on gun ownership (such as laws prohibiting felons from owning guns) and other lower courts striking them down. However, 93 percent of challenges to gun control laws have failed and almost all challenges to gun laws in criminal cases have been unsuccessful.[114]

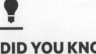

DID YOU KNOW?

37,613

people were killed by guns in the United States in 2017. About 58.5 percent of these deaths were from suicides.

Source: www.gunviolencearchive.org

due process rights
The idea that laws and legal proceedings must be fair. The Constitution guarantees that the government cannot take away a person's "life, liberty, or property, without due process of law." Other specific due process rights are found in the Fourth, Fifth, Sixth, and Eighth Amendments, such as protection from self-incrimination and freedom from illegal searches.

The question of whether the government can compel companies like Apple to assist them in unlocking phones so they can conduct a search remains contentious. This issue became especially prominent after the 2015 shooting in San Bernardino, California, when the FBI ordered Apple to unlock the suspect's phone. The FBI dropped the lawsuit once they unlocked the phone without Apple's help. But in 2018, Apple announced it had changed the iPhone so it couldn't be unlocked.

Law, order, and the rights of criminal defendants

Every advanced democracy protects the rights of people who have been accused of a crime. In the United States, the **due process rights** of the Fourth, Fifth, Sixth, and Eighth Amendments include the right to a fair trial, the right to consult a lawyer, freedom from self-incrimination, the right to know what crime you are accused of, the right to confront the accuser in court, and freedom from unreasonable police searches.

It is difficult to apply the abstract principles of due process to concrete situations in a way that protects civil liberties without jeopardizing order. The Fifth and Fourteenth Amendments specify that life, liberty, and property may not be denied "without due process of law." In general, this language refers to *procedural* restrictions on what government can do and is based on the idea of fairness and justice. The difficulty comes in defining what is fair or just.

The difference between abstract principles of due process and their specific application also raises difficult *political* questions. Most people endorse the principle of "due process of law" and general ideas such as requiring that police legally obtain any evidence used in court. However, when the Supreme Court applies these principles to protect the rights of criminal defendants, there is a public outcry that too many suspects are going free on "legal technicalities," such as having to inform a suspect of his or her right to talk to an attorney before being questioned by the police. Elected politicians are very vulnerable to such public pressure and have a strong incentive to be "tough on crime," while the courts are left to decide whether a specific case involves a legal technicality or a fundamental civil liberty.

The Fourth Amendment: unreasonable searches and seizures

The Fourth Amendment says: "The right of the people to be secure in their persons, houses, papers, and effects, against unreasonable searches and seizures, shall not be violated." Defining "unreasonable" puts us back in the familiar position of drawing lines and balancing interests.

Over the years, the Supreme Court has provided strong protections against searches within a person's physical space, typically defined as his or her home. With the introduction of new technology—first telephones and wiretapping, then more sophisticated listening and searching devices—the Court has had to confront a broad array of complicated questions. It has attempted to achieve a balance between privacy and security by requiring the courts to approve search warrants, yet continuing to carve out limited exceptions to this general rule.

Searches and Warrants Under most circumstances, a law-enforcement official seeking a search warrant must provide the court with "personal knowledge" of a "probable cause" of specific criminal activity and must outline the evidence that is the target of the search. Broad, general "fishing expeditions" for evidence are not allowed.

School officials must also balance the constitutional rights of students against the need to maintain discipline. But school searches may be permitted with a weaker "reasonable suspicion"; this is because the courts have viewed the schools as "in loco parentis" (that is, as playing the role of surrogate parents for the students). In 1985, the Court ruled in favor of a school official who discovered two girls smoking in a school bathroom and, in searching the purse of one of the girls for cigarettes, found marijuana, a pipe, rolling papers, plastic bags, and enough cash to suggest that the girl was selling marijuana. Yet, in other cases, the Court ruled that there are limits to searches by school officials and that students have the right to privacy. For example, in 2003 school administrators in Safford, Arizona, responding to a tip that a student was in possession of prescription-strength ibuprofen pills, subjected 13-year-old Savana Redding to a strip search. After searching her backpack and outer clothing and finding nothing, the police told Savana "to pull her bra out and to the side and shake it, and to pull out the elastic on her underpants, thus exposing her breasts and pelvic area to some degree." The Court ruled that this search violated her Fourth Amendment rights because "the content of the suspicion failed to match the degree of intrusion."[115]

Police searches inherently involve a clash between public safety and an individual's private freedom from government intrusions. These issues came to the fore with the passage of the Patriot Act of 2001 after the terrorist attacks of September 11. (The official name of this law is the USA PATRIOT Act, which is an acronym for the "Uniting and Strengthening America by Providing Appropriate Tools Required to Intercept and Obstruct Terrorism Act.") Several of the most controversial parts of the act strengthen police surveillance powers; make it easier to conduct "sneak and peek" searches (the police enter a home with a warrant, look for evidence, and do not inform the suspect that they searched his or her home until months later); broaden Internet surveillance; increase the government's access to individuals' library, banking, and medical records; and permit roving wiretaps for suspected terrorists.

Most police searches conducted without warrants occur because suspects consent to being searched. Officers are not required to tell a suspect that he or she may say no or request a warrant. Here are examples of other instances in which the Court will allow a warrantless search:

- Conducting a search at the time of a legal arrest that "is confined to the immediate vicinity of the arrest."
- Collecting evidence that was not included in the search warrant but is out in the open and in plain view.
- Using a police roadblock to search for information about a crime, to check for illegal immigrants or contraband at borders, or to conduct sobriety checks (but not for random drug searches or license checks), as long as the roadblock stops all drivers.
- Searching containers in cars if the officer has probable cause to suspect criminal activity.
- Searching passengers and the passenger area of a car if the driver has been stopped for a traffic offense (because people in automobiles do not have the same Fourth Amendment protections as people do in their homes).
- Searching an area where the officer thinks there is either a crime in progress or an "armed and dangerous" suspect.
- Searching school lockers, with probable cause.
- Searching for weapons and/or to prevent the destruction of evidence.[116]

Strip searches after an arrest and before the suspect is put in jail were upheld in 2012 by the Supreme Court even when there was no suspicion of illegal substances. The dissenting justices argued that "the humiliation of a visual strip-search" after being "arrested for driving with a noisy muffler, failing to use a turn signal and riding a bicycle without an audible bell" should not be allowed under the Fourth Amendment.[117]

In 2013, the Court ruled that a DNA swab of an arrested suspect is simply for identification and therefore is no more intrusive than a photograph or fingerprint. The late Justice Scalia, a strong defender of privacy rights, wrote in his dissent: "I doubt that the proud men who wrote the charter of our liberties would have been so eager to open their mouths for royal inspection."[118] Scalia argued that DNA evidence could be used to identify the arrestee as a suspect in an unrelated crime and therefore a swab should be taken only if there is probable cause that another crime has also been committed.

The Court has generally made it easier for law-enforcement officials to conduct searches without warrants, but two important decisions in the other direction were a 2014 case that required a warrant to search cell phones of people who had been arrested[119] and a 2012 case that required a warrant to place a GPS tracking device on a vehicle. In the latter case, the FBI suspected Antoine Jones of selling cocaine, so agents placed a tracking device on his vehicle without a warrant, monitored his movements for four weeks, and then used the evidence to convict him. Jones was sentenced to life in prison. While the Court required a warrant in this specific case, the basis for the majority's decision was fairly narrow: the placement of the device was a "physical trespass," and the lengthy monitoring of his movement constituted an illegal search.[120] The Court provided additional protection for privacy in 2018 when it ruled that a search warrant is required to access cell phone location records. While the ruling made exceptions for emergencies such as "bomb threats, active shootings, and child abductions," the four dissenting justices feared that law-enforcement officials were losing an important tool in fighting crime.[121]

The Exclusionary Rule Another important concern related to the Fourth Amendment is what to do if the police obtain evidence illegally. Here the need to balance security and privacy becomes concrete. Either the evidence is excluded from a criminal trial to protect privacy rights or it is allowed to support the conviction of the suspect. In 1961, the Fourth Amendment was incorporated (applied to the states through the Fourteenth Amendment) in a case, *Mapp v. Ohio*. This case established for all courts the **exclusionary rule**, which says that illegally or unconstitutionally obtained evidence cannot be used in a criminal trial. Previously, the rule had applied only at the national level.[122]

In the landmark case, police broke into Dollree Mapp's residence without a warrant, looking for a suspect thought to be hiding in the house. The officers did not find him, but they did find illegal pornographic material, and Mapp was convicted of possessing it. Mapp's lawyer tried to defend her on First Amendment grounds, claiming she had the right to own the pornography, but instead the Court used the opportunity to apply the Fourth Amendment to the states. The Court threw out Mapp's conviction because the police did not have a search warrant, arguing that applying the Fourth Amendment only to the national government and not to the states didn't make any sense: Why should a state's attorney be able to use illegally obtained evidence while a federal prosecutor could not? The justices ruled that for the exclusionary rule to deter illegal searches and seizures, it must apply to law enforcement at both state and national levels.

Subsequently, the Supreme Court began weakening the exclusionary rule. For example, the Court established a "good faith exception" to the exclusionary rule, allowing evidence to be used as long as the officer believed that he or she had conducted a legal search. In this specific case, the officer had a warrant with the wrong address.[123] Yet another case established an "independent source" exception allowing the use of evidence that was initially obtained in an illegal search but subsequently acquired with a valid warrant. A major new exception was established in 2016 when the Court ruled that drugs found during a search in which an officer stopped a person with no probable cause are admissible as evidence if there was an outstanding arrest warrant for the suspect (in this case for a traffic offense) at the time of the search. Justice Sotomayor pointed out in her dissent that there are 7.8 million outstanding warrants, mostly for traffic and parking violations, which means that this new exception has far-reaching consequences: "The mere existence of a warrant not only gives an officer legal cause to arrest and search a person, it also forgives an officer who, with no knowledge of the warrant at all, unlawfully stops that person on a whim or hunch."[124] The bottom line is

exclusionary rule
The principle that illegally or unconstitutionally acquired evidence cannot be used in a criminal trial.

Can the police search your home without a warrant? After Dollree Mapp was arrested for possession of pornographic material, the case made its way to the Supreme Court and the search was ruled unconstitutional. This case established the exclusionary rule for evidence that is obtained without a warrant.

that the exclusionary rule remains in effect, but in the last several decades the courts have eased the conditions in which prosecutors can use evidence obtained under questionable circumstances.

Drug Testing Another area of Fourth Amendment law concerns drug testing. The clause granting people the right "to be secure in their persons" certainly seems to cover drug testing. However, the courts have long recognized the right of private companies to test their employees for illegal drugs. Moreover, in professional sports testing for performance-enhancing drugs is increasingly common. Lance Armstrong was stripped of his seven Tour de France titles after admitting in 2013 to doping, and Major League Baseball has struggled to rein in steroid and human growth hormone use by many of its players, including stars such as Ryan Braun, Miguel Tejada, and Alex Rodriguez, who was banned from the entire 2014 season for his use of performance-enhancing drugs.

What about drug testing by the state? The Court has upheld random drug testing for high school athletes and mandatory drug testing for any junior high or high school students involved in extracurricular activities.[125] In the case of athletes, proponents of the policy asserted that safety concerns should preclude a 260-pound lineman or a pitcher with a 90-mile-per-hour fastball from using drugs. However, the same arguments could not be made for members of the choir, band, debate club, social dance club, or chess club, so this decision to include all extracurricular activities was a particularly strong endorsement of schools' antidrug policies.

The Court has also upheld drug testing of public employees, with one exception. It struck down a Georgia law that would have required all candidates for state office to pass a drug test within 30 days of announcing a run for office, because candidates are not public employees.[126] Rather than appealing to the courts, former senator Ernest Hollings of South Carolina had a different approach to avoid drug testing. When his opponent challenged him to take a drug test, the senator shot back, "I'll take a drug test if you take an IQ test."

The Post–September 11 Politics of Domestic Surveillance The debate over the trade-off between civil liberties and security intensified in 2005 when a White House–approved domestic surveillance program was revealed. At the center of this controversy is the National Security Agency (NSA), which was created during the Korean War in 1952 by President Harry Truman. The agency was initially kept so secret that for many years the government even denied its existence. Insiders joked that the "NSA" stood for "No Such Agency." Today the NSA is responsible for surveillance to protect national security, whereas the FBI is in charge of spying related to criminal activity and the Central Intelligence Agency (CIA) oversees foreign intelligence gathering. Since the terrorist attacks of September 11, 2001, the NSA has been monitoring the phone calls and Internet usage of many U.S. citizens who have had contact with suspected terrorists overseas. These calls were intercepted without the approval of the Foreign Intelligence Surveillance Court (FISC), which was created by Congress in 1978 under the Foreign Intelligence Surveillance Act (FISA) specifically for approving requests for the interception of calls. The NSA was also found to be creating a database of every phone call made within the borders of the United States. Phone companies AT&T, Verizon, and BellSouth reportedly turned over records of millions of customers' phone calls to the government.[127] In 2013, classified information revealed by Edward Snowden showed that the NSA had been monitoring the phone calls of German chancellor Angela Merkel and other leaders of allied countries, in addition to collecting e-mail traffic in the United States that contained the e-mail address or phone number of a foreign target. In April 2017, the NSA announced that it would no longer collect information on communications that simply mentioned someone rather than being sent to or from that person (so-called "about searches"). It also would discontinue "backdoor" searches in which conversations and Internet data from Americans get swooped up in the course of monitoring foreign targets. However, early in 2018, when Congress reauthorized the foreign surveillance for an additional six years, it opened the door to allowing "about" collection and "backdoor" searches to start up again.[128]

Critics warn that phone surveillance may be the tip of the iceberg, because the government may be monitoring travel, credit card, and banking records more widely than we think. Government agencies have previously skirted the restrictions in the Privacy Act of 1974 and the Fourth Amendment by purchasing this information from businesses, since the Privacy Act requires disclosure of how the government is using personal information only when the government itself collects the data. The Justice Department spent $19 million in 2005 to purchase commercially gathered data about American citizens, according to a report by the Government Accountability Office. These data are then used to search for suspicious patterns of behavior in a process known as data mining.[129] In 2016, a massive data collection program by AT&T called Project Atmosphere was used by law-enforcement agencies investigating everything from murder to medical fraud.[130]

The debate over domestic surveillance has generated intense disagreement. At one extreme, critics conjure up images of George Orwell's classic novel *1984*, in which Big Brother, a reclusive totalitarian ruler, watches the characters' every move. Critics see the surveillance as a threat to civil liberties and to our system of checks and balances and separation of powers. They believe that when the executive branch refuses to obtain warrants through the FISA court to conduct surveillance, it is taking on too much power without consulting the other branches of government. But supporters of the program argue that getting a court order may take too long, jeopardizing the surveillance necessary to protect the country. Congress tried to strike a balance between these two positions when it enacted the FISA Amendments Act of 2008. This law continued the ban on monitoring the purely domestic communications of Americans without a court order, gave the government authority to intercept international communications, and provided legal immunity to the telecommunications companies that had cooperated in the original wiretapping program. However, the *New York Times* revealed that the NSA had still been engaged in "overcollection" of domestic communication between Americans under the new law, including an attempt to wiretap a member of Congress without a court order. Although the NSA vowed to stop purely domestic surveillance without a court order, technical problems make it difficult to distinguish between communications made within the United States and overseas.[131]

The Director of National Intelligence testified at a congressional hearing on possible changes to the FISA as protesters in the background called for an end to government surveillance.

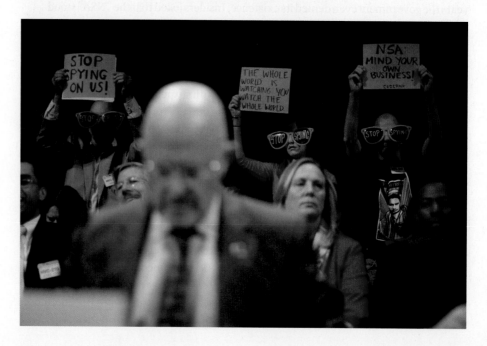

The Fifth Amendment

Miranda Rights and Self-Incrimination The familiar phrase "I plead the Fifth" has been part of our criminal justice system since the Bill of Rights was ratified, ensuring that a suspect cannot be compelled to provide court testimony that would cause him or her to be prosecuted for a crime. However, what about outside a court of law? If a police officer coerces a confession out of a suspect, does that amount to self-incrimination?

Coercive police interrogations were allowed until a landmark case in 1966. Ernesto Miranda had been convicted in an Arizona court of kidnapping and rape, on the basis of a confession extracted after two hours of questioning in which he was not read his rights. The Court overturned the conviction, saying that a police interrogation "is inherently intimidating" and in these circumstances "no statement obtained from the defendant can truly be the product of his free choice."[132] To ensure that a confession is truly a free choice, the Court came up with the well-known **Miranda rights**. If police do not read a suspect these rights, nothing the suspect says can be used in court.

Miranda rights
The list of civil liberties described in the Fifth Amendment that must be read to a suspect before anything the suspect says can be used in a trial.

DEFENDANT		LOCATION	

SPECIFIC WARNING REGARDING INTERROGATIONS

1. YOU HAVE THE RIGHT TO REMAIN SILENT.

2. ANYTHING YOU SAY CAN AND WILL BE USED AGAINST YOU IN A COURT OF LAW.

3. YOU HAVE THE RIGHT TO TALK TO A LAWYER AND HAVE HIM PRESENT WITH YOU WHILE YOU ARE BEING QUESTIONED.

4. IF YOU CANNOT AFFORD TO HIRE A LAWYER ONE WILL BE APPOINTED TO REPRESENT YOU BEFORE ANY QUESTIONING, IF YOU WISH ONE.

SIGNATURE OF DEFENDANT	DATE
WITNESS	TIME

☐ REFUSED SIGNATURE   SAN FRANCISCO POLICE DEPARTMENT   PR.9.1.4

This is a typical example of the Miranda warning card that police officers carry with them and read to every suspect after an arrest.

The Court has carved out exceptions to the Miranda rights requirement because the public has viewed the practice as "coddling criminals" and letting too many people go free on legal technicalities. In one case, police failed to read a suspect his Miranda rights until after they had frisked him, found an empty holster, and asked him where his gun was. The suspect led police to a gun. The lower court dismissed the charges because the gun had been used as incriminating evidence in the trial, but the Supreme Court reinstated the conviction because "concern for public safety must be paramount to adherence to the literal language of the *Miranda* rule."[133]

Although the Court has been willing to carve out limited exceptions to the Miranda rule, in 2000 the Court rejected Congress's attempt to overturn *Miranda* by designating all voluntary confessions as legally admissible evidence. The Court ruled that it, and not Congress, has the power to determine constitutional protections for criminal defendants. The justices also affirmed their intent to protect the Miranda rule, saying: "*Miranda* has become embedded in routine police practice to the point where the warnings have become part of our national culture."[134]

Double Jeopardy Another Fifth Amendment right for defendants is protection against being tried more than once for a particular crime. This is known as **double jeopardy** because the suspect is "twice put in jeopardy of life or limb" for a single offense. This prohibition was extended to the states in 1969.[135] But prosecutors can exploit two loopholes in this civil liberty: (1) a suspect may be tried in federal court and state court for the same crime, and (2) if a suspect is found innocent of one set of *criminal* charges brought by the state, he or she may still be found guilty of the same or closely related offenses based on *civil* charges brought by a private individual.

Usually these loopholes are exploited only in high-profile cases in which there is public or political pressure to get a conviction. For example, in 1992 four Los Angeles police officers were acquitted of beating Rodney King, a driver they had chased for speeding. Before the trial, a bystander's video of the beating had been widely broadcast; subsequently, when people heard the news of the police officers' acquittal, massive and destructive riots broke out that lasted three days. Responding to political pressure, President George H. W. Bush urged federal prosecutors to retry the officers not for the *criminal* use of excessive force but for violating Rodney King's *civil* rights. (Two were ultimately found guilty, and two were acquitted.)

Property Rights The final part of the Fifth Amendment is at the heart of a hot legal debate over property rights. The clause says, "nor shall private property be taken for public use, without just compensation." For most of American history, this civil liberty has been noncontroversial. When the government needs private property for a public use such as building a highway or a park, it may force a property owner to sell at a fair market value in a practice known as eminent domain.

A new, controversial interpretation of the Fifth Amendment's "takings" clause, however, has attempted to expand the principle of just compensation to cover not only "physical takings" but also "regulatory takings." For example, if the Endangered Species Act protects an animal whose habitat is on your land, you would not be able to develop that property. Thus, its market value would probably be lower than if the endangered species did not live on your land. Therefore, the argument goes, because of this law the government has "taken" some of the value of your land by legally protecting the species, so it should compensate you for your loss.

This issue became even more controversial after a case involving a development project in New London, Connecticut. A working-class neighborhood was sold to a private developer to build a waterfront hotel, office space, and higher-end housing, but a homeowner sued the city to stop the development. The Court supported the local government, saying that "promoting economic development is a traditional and long accepted function of government," so a "plausible public use" is satisfied. Justice O'Connor wrote a strong dissent, saying that the "specter of condemnation hangs over all property. Nothing is to prevent the State from replacing any Motel 6 with a Ritz-Carlton, any home with a shopping mall, or any farm with a factory."[136] In reaction to this decision, legislation or constitutional amendments have been passed in 42 states restricting the use of eminent domain for economic development.[137] This is an evolving area of the law, with several recent cases restoring property rights and an important 2017 case providing another setback for property owners.[138]

The Sixth Amendment: the right to legal counsel and a jury trial

The right to an attorney is one of the civil liberties key to criminal law, because the legal system is too complicated for a layperson to navigate. However, at one time, poor people accused of a state felony were forced to defend themselves in court if they could not afford a lawyer (except in cases involving the death penalty, for which the state would provide a lawyer).[139] This changed in 1963 with the celebrated case of *Gideon v. Wainwright*. Clarence Gideon was accused of breaking into a pool hall and stealing beer, wine, and money. He could not afford an attorney, so he tried to defend himself. He did a pretty good job—calling witnesses, cross-examining the prosecutor's witnesses, and providing a good summary argument. However, he was convicted and sentenced to five years in jail, based largely on the testimony of the person who turned out to be the guilty party. The Court unanimously overturned Gideon's conviction, saying: "In our adversary system of criminal justice, any person hauled into court who is too poor to hire a lawyer cannot be assured a fair trial unless counsel is provided for him."[140]

Unlike the exclusionary rule and the protection against self-incrimination, the right to an attorney has been strengthened over time, through both legislation and subsequent Court rulings. One year after *Gideon*, Congress passed the Criminal Justice Act, which provided better legal representation for criminal defendants in federal court; within two years, 23 states had taken similar action. The Court has defined a general right to *effective* counsel (although the bar is set considerably low in terms of defining "effective") and more recently mandated that defense attorneys must conduct any reasonable investigation into possible lines of defense when presenting evidence that could help the defendant.[141]

The Sixth Amendment also protects an individual's right to a speedy and public trial by an impartial jury in criminal cases. The Court affirmed the right to a speedy trial in 1967,[142] and today under the Federal Speedy Trial Act a trial must begin within 70 days of the defendant's arrest or first appearance in court. This law was strengthened by a 2006 Court decision stating that a defendant may not waive the right to a speedy trial.[143]

The most important legal disputes over the "impartial jury" issue concern the process of jury selection and peremptory challenges, in which lawyers from each side may eliminate certain people from the jury pool without providing any reason. The Court has ruled that race and gender may not be the basis for a peremptory challenge.[144] The Court has also made clear that racial bias during jury deliberation is not allowed. Although jury deliberations are normally secret, in a 2017 case in which Miguel Peña-Rodriguez was convicted of misdemeanor sexual assault, two jurors told the judge that one of the jurors had demonstrated a bias against Mexican Americans, saying things like "nine times out of ten Mexican men [are] guilty of being aggressive toward women and young girls." In the majority opinion Justice Kennedy argued that "racial bias in the justice system must be addressed—including, in some instances, after the verdict has been entered" in order to "prevent a systemic loss of confidence in jury verdicts, a confidence that is a central premise of the Sixth Amendment trial right."[145]

The Eighth Amendment: cruel and unusual punishment

The Founders would be surprised by the intense debates over whether the Eighth Amendment prohibition against "cruel and unusual punishments" applies to the death penalty. Clearly, the death penalty was accepted in their time (even stealing a horse was a capital offense!), and the language of the Constitution reflects that. Both the Fifth and Fourteenth Amendments say that a person may not be deprived of "life, liberty, or property, without due process of law," which implies that someone *could* be deprived of life as long as the state followed due process. The death penalty continues to be supported by many people in the United States, with 31 states allowing capital punishment. However, there is a clear overall trend away from the death penalty. Seven U.S. states have abolished the death penalty since 2007 (and four more states have moratoriums on the death penalty imposed by their governors, although Nebraska

The fight against terrorism has raised controversial questions about due process rights. After the United States killed Anwar al-Awlaki—an Al Qaeda leader living in Yemen, and a U.S. citizen—critics argued that his due process rights, such as the right to a fair trial, had been violated.

reinstated the death penalty by state referendum in 2016), and dozens of other countries have done so in recent years. There were 23 executions in the United States in 2017, which is the third-lowest number since 1991 and well below the peak of 98 in 1999.[146] A botched execution in Oklahoma in 2014, in which Clayton Lockett writhed and gasped for nearly 30 minutes when one of the lines filled with the lethal drugs failed, led to renewed calls for abolishing the death penalty.[147]

Supreme Court Rulings on the Death Penalty The Supreme Court remained silent on the issue of the death penalty for nearly two centuries. But in 1972 the Court ruled that the death penalty was unconstitutional because the process of applying it was too inconsistent. Congress and 35 states rushed to make their laws compliant with the Court decision. The typical fix was to say more explicitly which crimes were punishable by death and to make capital sentencing a two-step process: first, the determination of guilt or innocence, and second, a sentencing phase if the suspect is found guilty. Four years later, the Court approved these changes and allowed states to bring back the death penalty.[148]

While never again challenging the constitutionality of the death penalty, the Supreme Court has been chipping away at its edges for two decades. The Court has struck down state laws that mandated the death penalty in murder cases and a law requiring a death sentence for rape. It has also prohibited the execution of insane prisoners and abolished the death penalty for the "mentally retarded"—although the Court left it to the states to define who is "mentally retarded," it has since struck down standards in Florida and Texas that it found to be inappropriate indicators of intellectual capacity.[149] The Court has also prohibited the death penalty for juveniles under the age of 18 and for child rapists.[150]

These death-penalty cases have shown that the Court responds to public opinion and political change. (This is sometimes called the living Constitution perspective, as discussed in Chapters 2 and 14.) In his opinion in the juvenile death-penalty case, Justice Anthony Kennedy noted that 30 states forbid the death penalty for offenders younger than age 18, which was an increase of 5 states from 1989, when the Court had upheld the juvenile death penalty. Similarly, the number of states banning the death penalty for the mentally impaired grew from 14 in 1989 (when the practice was upheld) to 25 in 2002 (when it was struck down).

Privacy rights

You may be surprised to learn that the word "privacy" does not appear in the Constitution. **Privacy rights** were first developed in a 1965 case that questioned the constitutionality of an 1879 Connecticut law against using birth control. Estelle Griswold, the director of Planned Parenthood in Connecticut, was arrested nine days after opening a clinic that dispensed contraceptives. She was fined $100 and appealed her conviction. Although she lost in state court, she appealed all the way to the Supreme Court, which overturned her conviction.[151]

In a very fractured decision (there were six different opinions), the Court agreed that the law was outdated, but the justices agreed on little else. Even the justices who based their opinions on an implied constitutional right to privacy cited various constitutional roots. Justice William O. Douglas found privacy implicit in the First Amendment right of association, the Third Amendment's protection against the quartering of troops, the Fourth Amendment's prohibition against unreasonable searches and seizures, the Fifth Amendment's protection against self-incrimination,

DID YOU KNOW?

351

people have been exonerated post-conviction in the United States based on DNA evidence, out of 1,700 total exonerations. Twenty of those served time on death row and 16 more had been convicted of capital offenses.

Source: The Innocence Project

EXPLAIN WHY THE RIGHTS ASSOCIATED WITH PRIVACY ARE OFTEN CONTROVERSIAL

privacy rights
Liberties protected by several amendments in the Bill of Rights that shield certain personal aspects of citizens' lives from governmental interference, such as the Fourth Amendment's protection against unreasonable searches and seizures.

and the Ninth Amendment's catchall statement "The enumeration in the Constitution, of certain rights, shall not be construed to deny or disparage others retained by the people." These all seem like reasonable grounds for implicit privacy rights except the First Amendment right of association—since the Founders clearly meant political association, not an association with your spouse in bed.

The *Griswold v. Connecticut* case was significant for establishing the constitutional basis for a right to privacy, but the dissenters in the case were concerned about where this right would lead. Justice Black warned that privacy "is a broad, abstract and ambiguous concept" that can be shrunk or expanded in subsequent decisions. He said that Douglas's argument "require[d] judges to determine what is or is not constitutional on the basis of their own appraisal of what laws are unwise or unnecessary. The power to make such decisions is of course that of a legislative body. Surely it has to be admitted that no provision of the Constitution specifically gives such blanket power to courts to exercise such a supervisory veto over the wisdom and value of legislative policies and to hold unconstitutional those laws which they believe to be unwise or dangerous."[152]

Abortion rights

Justice Black's prediction came true eight years later in *Roe v. Wade*, the landmark ruling that struck down laws in 46 states that limited abortion. Twelve of those states allowed abortions for pregnancies due to rape or incest, to protect the life of the mother, and in cases of severe fetal handicap. The much-criticized trimester analysis in the *Roe* ruling said that in the first trimester, states could not limit abortions; in the second trimester, states could regulate abortions in the interests of the health of the mother; and in the third trimester, states could forbid all abortions except those necessary to protect the health or life of the mother. The justices cited a constitutional basis for abortion rights in the general right to privacy outlined in *Griswold*; the concept of "personal liberty" in the Fourteenth Amendment's due process clause; and the "rights reserved to the people" in the Ninth Amendment.[153]

Subsequent decisions have upheld *Roe* but endorsed state restrictions on abortion, such as requiring parental consent, a waiting period, or counseling sessions aimed at convincing the woman not to have an abortion (see the What Do the Facts Say? feature for more on restrictions currently in effect). Most significantly, *Roe*'s trimester analysis has been replaced by a focus on the viability of the fetus. When the fetus would be viable (generally at 22 or 23 weeks), states can ban abortions "except where it is necessary, in appropriate medical judgment, for the preservation of the life or health of the mother."[154] Laws passed in 2013 by Arkansas and North Dakota limiting abortions as soon as a fetal heartbeat can be detected (as early as 6 weeks) were struck down by federal courts, but laws in 19 states now ban abortions at 20 weeks, in apparent contradiction with *Roe v. Wade*.

Since *Roe*, most political action concerning abortion has been in the courts, but that could change if the Supreme Court overturns the decision. Opponents of abortion are hoping that *Roe* will be overturned, which would shift the politics of abortion back to state legislatures and make it an even more contested political issue. One effort to challenge *Roe* was a "personhood amendment" to the Mississippi constitution that defined life as beginning at conception. But the amendment was soundly defeated in a statewide vote in 2011.[155] The pace of state restrictions on abortions accelerated from 2011 to 2013, with more than 200 limitations on abortion services. In 2013, 22 states enacted 70 new restrictions, including a requirement that abortion doctors have admitting privileges at local hospitals—which would close up to one-third of abortion clinics in affected states.[156] In 2016, the Supreme Court struck down the latter as an "undue burden" on the right to an abortion.[157]

WHAT DO THE FACTS SAY?

Abortion Rights Today

The Court's 1973 decision in *Roe v. Wade* made abortion legal throughout the United States. How do abortion rights look today? What do the numbers say?

Source: Guttmacher Institute, *State Policies in Brief,* "An Overview of Abortion Laws," July 1, 2018, www.guttmacher.org (accessed 7/18/18).

Think about it

- **Which states have the most restrictive policies concerning access to abortions?**
- **How do you think waiting periods and parental notification affect the number of abortions in a state? What about the number of abortions nationwide?**

Parental Consent Laws for Abortions for Minors

- No parental notification or consent laws
- One or both parents must consent
- One or both parents must be informed
- Both parental consent and notification required
- Parental consent or notification laws blocked

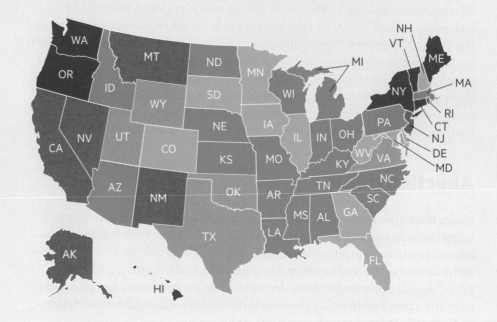

Pre-Abortion Mandatory Waiting Period Laws

- No mandatory waiting period
- Waiting period of less than 24 hours
- Waiting period of 24 hours or more
- Waiting period law blocked

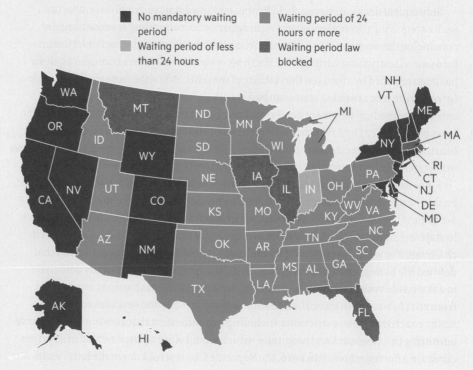

Gay rights

Gay rights have typically been thought of more as a civil right (that is, freedom from discrimination) than a civil liberty, so these issues will be discussed in the next chapter. However, several important cases involving sexual relations are rooted in privacy rights. In 1986, the Court had ruled in *Bowers v. Hardwick* that there was no privacy protection or fundamental right for consenting adults to engage in homosexual sodomy.[158] But in 2003, in *Lawrence v. Texas*, the Court established very broad privacy rights for sexual behavior. The case involved two Houston men, John Geddes Lawrence and Tyron Garner, who were prosecuted for same-sex sodomy after police entered Lawrence's apartment—upon receiving a false tip about an armed man—and found the two having sex. Under Texas law, sodomy was illegal for gays but not for heterosexuals. In a landmark 6–3 ruling, the Supreme Court said that the liberty guaranteed by the Fourteenth Amendment's due process clause allows homosexuals to have sexual relations: "Freedom presumes an autonomy of self that includes freedom of thought, belief, expression, and certain intimate conduct."[159] The decision explicitly overturned *Bowers v. Hardwick* and five members of the majority signed onto the broad "due process" reasoning of the decision, while Justice O'Connor wrote a concurring opinion in which she agreed that the Texas law was unconstitutional but on narrower grounds. With the broader due process logic, a total of 13 state laws that banned sodomy were struck down.

Tyron Garner and John Geddes Lawrence after the Supreme Court decision in *Lawrence v. Texas* in 2003 established broad privacy rights for sexual behavior (including homosexual behavior).

"Why Should I Care?"

Privacy might not seem important. You may think you'll never be accused of a crime or have your privacy invaded or questioned by the government. Indeed, many people think, "I have nothing to hide, so it is fine if the NSA monitors e-mail and Internet traffic to keep tabs on suspected terrorists." What if your e-mail revealed that you had a serious medical or mental health condition? What if the NSA paid special attention to you because of tweets you posted criticizing a government policy? Knowing your rights and how those rights apply to everyone—both criminals and innocent people—will help you make informed decisions about which policies to support.

Unpacking the Conflict

Considering all that we've discussed in this chapter, let's apply what we know about how civil liberties work to the example of free speech on college campuses introduced at the beginning of this chapter. Can controversial speech on college campuses be limited? How can we explain this conflict?

The question of free speech on campus raises difficult questions of balancing interests and drawing lines. Speakers' interests in making their voices and opinions heard must be balanced against the universities' interest in public safety and students' interest in protecting other students from hate speech. The First Amendment is applicable in these instances because the speakers in question are lecturing at public— that is, state government—institutions.

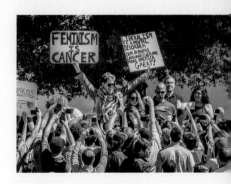

This puts many universities in a difficult spot—they would rather not allow these controversial speakers, especially because of the high cost of providing security. However, the First Amendment protects political speech, and the Supreme Court has established that it cannot be prevented unless there is a direct incitement to imminent violence. Even association with previous acts of violence, as in the case of Richard Spencer, is not sufficient grounds to prevent speech.

You exercise your civil liberties every day, whether speaking in public, going to church, being searched at an airport, participating in a political demonstration, writing or reading an article in your school newspaper, or being free from illegal police searches in your home. Because civil liberties are defined as those things the government *cannot* do to you, defining civil liberties is a political process. Often this process is confined to the courts, but for many issues—including free speech, freedom of the press, pornography, criminal rights, abortion, and gun control—it takes place in the broader political world, where defining civil liberties involves balancing competing ideals and interests and drawing lines by interpreting and applying the law. For example, debates over how to balance national security and civil liberties—whether newspapers should publish stories about classified government programs that may threaten civil liberties, or whether government surveillance powers should be strengthened to fight terrorism—will rage for years.

Other cases, such as the protests at military funerals or the protection of the due process rights of suspected criminals and terrorists, illustrate how difficult and politically unpopular it can be to protect our freedoms and liberty. Nearly everyone would agree that the behavior of the members of Westboro Baptist Church is completely outrageous. But protecting the freedom of speech is easy if you agree with what is being spoken. It becomes much more difficult if the freedom protects the rights of Nazis to march in Skokie, defends a person accused of a heinous crime, or gives a white supremacist like Richard Spencer a platform.

What's Your Take?

Should speakers with controversial, sometimes hateful opinions be allowed to speak on college campuses?

Or do universities' and students' interests outweigh their right to free speech?

STUDY GUIDE

The origins of civil liberties

Explain why the Bill of Rights was added to the Constitution and how it came to apply to the states. (Pages 106–112)

Summary

The Bill of Rights, which lists individual protections from the federal government, was included in the Constitution in response to demands from the Antifederalists, who feared a strong national government. For most of the nineteenth century, these individual freedoms were only guaranteed from the *federal* government and did not extend to protections from *state* governments. With the ratification of the Fourteenth Amendment and the process of selective incorporation, federal freedoms have been gradually extended to the state level.

Key terms

Civil War amendments (p. 109)   **selective incorporation**
due process clause (p. 109)   (p. 112)

Defining civil liberties

Define what we mean by *civil liberties*. (Pages 104–106)

Summary

Civil liberties are the protections that individuals receive from the government. These are not absolute rights, however, as individual freedoms can become at odds with the public good and government interests. The courts often play the deciding role in determining where to draw the line between individual rights and public safety.

Key term

civil liberties (p. 104)

Practice Quiz Questions

1. **Civil liberties are rooted in what document?**

a   the Declaration of Independence

b   the *Federalist Papers*

c   the Magna Carta

d   the Bill of Rights

e   Article I of the Constitution

2. **Why are civil liberties not absolute?**

a   Equality for a group under the law is hard to define.

b   Individual freedoms may conflict with the public good.

c   Laws are often outdated and don't characterize modern society.

d   The Bill of Rights protections were intentionally weakened by Antifederalists.

e   The Supreme Court generally decides not to hear cases concerning civil liberties.

Practice Quiz Questions

3. **The inclusion of the Bill of Rights in the Constitution reflects the _____ concerns that the federal government would be too _____ .**

a   Antifederalists'; strong

b   Antifederalists'; weak

c   Federalists'; strong

d   Federalists'; weak

e   president's; strong

4. **The Bill of Rights originally protected individuals from which level of government?**

a   all levels of American government

b   state governments

c   local governments

d   federal government

e   the bureaucracy

5. **Which amendment has been used as the basis for selective incorporation?**

a   the Eighth Amendment

b   the Fourteenth Amendment

c   the Tenth Amendment

d   the Nineteenth Amendment

e   the Fifth Amendment

Freedom of religion

Describe the First Amendment rights related to freedom of religion. (Pages 112–117)

Summary

Religious freedoms are defined by two clauses in the First Amendment: the establishment clause and the free exercise clause. Together, they do not allow the government to do anything to benefit any particular religion, nor do they allow the government to hinder religious practice without adequate justification. As is often the case, the Court has struggled to define exactly what constitutes "excessive government entanglement" in religion.

Key terms

establishment clause (p. 114)   Lemon test (p. 115)
free exercise clause (p. 114)

Practice Quiz Questions

6. The establishment clause is invoked under which of the following circumstances?

a allowing "conscientious objectors" to avoid the military draft

b outlawing polygamy

c prohibiting prayer in public schools

d allowing the Amish to keep children home from school after the eighth grade

e banning the handling of snakes in church services

7. Which test does the Supreme Court use to establish whether there has been "excessive government entanglement with religion"?

a Lemon test

b Kreutz test

c Miller test

d Meyer test

e Brandenburg test

Freedom of speech, assembly, and the press

Describe the major First Amendment rights related to freedom of speech. (Pages 117–129)

Summary

The Supreme Court's attempt to balance individual freedoms and public good is reflected in the scope of protections guaranteed by the First Amendment. The Court generally prioritizes protecting individual rights to political speech, hate speech, symbolic speech, the freedom to assemble, and the freedom of the press except under extreme circumstances (such as speech that directly incites violence). By contrast, the Court regularly places a lower priority on, and affords less protection to, fighting words, slander, libel, and commercial speech.

Key terms

strict scrutiny (p. 118)   prior restraint (p. 125)
intermediate scrutiny (p. 118)   fighting words (p. 126)
clear and present danger test   slander (p. 126)
  (p. 118)   libel (p. 126)
direct incitement test (p. 119)   commercial speech (p. 127)
symbolic speech (p. 120)   Miller test (p. 128)
hate speech (p. 122)

Practice Quiz Questions

8. Which test does the Court use to determine if speech is considered dangerous and should not be legally protected?

a Lemon test

b clear and present danger test

c Miller test

d direct incitement test

e balancing test

9. Flag burning is an example of _____ that is currently _____ under the First Amendment.

a symbolic speech; protected

b symbolic speech; not protected

c hate speech; protected

d hate speech; not protected

e offensive slander; not protected

The right to bear arms

Explore why the Second Amendment's meaning on gun rights is often debated. (Pages 130–131)

Summary

The Supreme Court has done little to define what freedoms are established in the Second Amendment, largely preferring to allow the national, state, and local governments to make their own laws. The majority of public sentiment appears in favor of continued gun ownership, and limitations on Second Amendment rights appear unlikely.

Practice Quiz Question

10. What is the best summary of the current position of the Supreme Court on the Second Amendment?

a The Court has upheld most gun control laws, both at the state and national level, arguing that there is no individual right to own guns.

b The Court has upheld most gun control laws at the state level but struck down federal gun control laws, arguing that the Second Amendment only applies to Congress.

c The Court has struck down some state and national limitations on gun ownership, arguing that the Second Amendment protects an individual right to bear arms.

d The Court has struck down all state and national limitations on gun ownership, arguing that the Second Amendment protects an individual right to bear arms.

e The Court has refused to take a general position on the individual right to bear arms.

Law, order, and the rights of criminal defendants

Describe the protections provided for people accused of a crime. (Pages 132–140)

Summary

The Fourth, Fifth, Sixth, and Eighth Amendments provide protections to individuals accused of a crime, known as due process rights. Interpreting these general due process rights in specific cases is difficult, however, because specific standards of fairness and justice are very hard to define.

Key terms

due process rights (p. 132) **Miranda rights** (p. 137)
exclusionary rule (p. 134) **double jeopardy** (p. 138)

Practice Quiz Questions

11. Protections from unreasonable searches and seizures are guaranteed by which constitutional amendment?

a the Third Amendment

b the Fourth Amendment

c the Fifth Amendment

d the Seventh Amendment

e the Eighth Amendment

12. The Miranda rights are protections that primarily fall under which constitutional amendment?

a the Third Amendment

b the Fourth Amendment

c the Fifth Amendment

d the Seventh Amendment

e the Eighth Amendment

13. In 1972, the Supreme Court banned the death penalty for what reason?

a It deprived individuals of their rights to "life, liberty, or property."

b It was cruel and unusual.

c It was being inconsistently applied and violated the due process of law.

d It was racially biased.

e It was inconsistent with international law.

Privacy rights

Explain why the rights associated with privacy are often controversial. (Pages 140–143)

Summary

The term "privacy rights" is not found in the Constitution—rather, it was established in a 1965 Supreme Court case—but it may be implied in several amendments in the Bill of Rights. The right to privacy is controversial because of the lack of explicit language in the Constitution and the lack of consensus on exactly what the right to privacy means. It has remained a hot-button issue because recognition of the right to privacy is an important facet of the contemporary debate on abortion.

Key term

privacy rights (p. 140)

Practice Quiz Questions

14. Which of the following freedoms guaranteed in the Bill of Rights is thought to imply a right to privacy?

a right to bear arms

b right to refuse to quarter soldiers

c right to secure legal counsel

d right to request a jury trial

e freedom of speech

15. In what case did the Supreme Court first establish the right to privacy?

a *Roe v. Wade*

b *Lawrence v. Texas*

c *Griswold v. Connecticut*

d *Gonzales v. Oregon*

e *Lemon v. Kurtzman*

Suggested Reading

Abraham, Henry J., and Barbara A. Perry. *Freedom and the Court: Civil Rights and Liberties in the United States*, 8th ed. Lawrence: University Press of Kansas, 2003.

Abrams, Floyd. *The Soul of the First Amendment*. New Haven, CT: Yale University Press, 2017.

Amar, Akhil Reed. *The Bill of Rights*. New Haven, CT: Yale University Press, 1998.

Chemerinsky, Erwin, and Howard Gillman. *Free Speech on Campus*. New Haven, CT: Yale University Press, 2017.

Lewis, Anthony. *Gideon's Trumpet*. New York: Random House, 1964.

Posner, Richard A. *Not a Suicide Pact: The Constitution in a Time of National Emergency*. New York: Oxford University Press, 2006.

Pritchett, C. Herman. *Constitutional Civil Liberties*. Englewood Cliffs, NJ: Prentice Hall, 1984.

Schweber, Howard. *Speech, Conduct, and the First Amendment*. New York: Peter Lang, 2003.

Walker, Samuel. *Presidents and Civil Liberties from Wilson to Obama: A Story of Poor Custodians*. New York: Cambridge University Press, 2014.

5

Civil Rights

You can't discriminate against me . . . right?

>> **"No one should live in fear of being stopped whenever he leaves his home to go about the activities of daily life."**
Shira A. Scheindlin, federal judge

<< **"Well, I think profiling is something that we're going to have to start thinking about as a country. And other countries do it. . . . And they do it successfully. And I hate the concept of profiling. But we have to start using common sense, and we have to use our heads."**
President Donald Trump

>> **"I don't even talk about whether or not racial profiling is legal. I just don't think racial profiling is a particularly good law enforcement tool."**
Eric Holder, former attorney general

Our civil rights protect us from discrimination by the government and our fellow Americans. Most everyone would agree that selective enforcement of laws depending on the color of one's skin constitutes discrimination—and is unacceptable. However, opinions on discrimination become less clear-cut in the realm of law enforcement, particularly when it comes to strategies that involve racial profiling. Not surprisingly, racial profiling is illegal as a general tool for screening suspects. As Shira Scheindlin, the federal judge who struck down New York City's controversial "stop-and-frisk" policy has made clear, Americans should not be singled out for scrutiny by law-enforcement officers just because of the color of their skin.[1] Under this policy, police officers stopped people based on the "reasonable suspicion" that they were engaged in criminal activity. At its peak in 2011, more than 685,000 New Yorkers were stopped by police; 88 percent were entirely innocent, just over half were between 14 and 24 years old, and 87 percent were African American or Latino. In 2017, fewer than 11,000 people were questioned and frisked by police in New York.[2]

However, President Donald Trump and others have called for a "commonsense" approach to profiling when it comes to both matters of local and national security, which would include more intense scrutiny of people who fit a certain profile imagined

Opponents of "stop-and-frisk" policing tactics have argued that the practice encourages illegal racial profiling. Others say that profiling may be necessary in certain circumstances to ensure public safety or advance other goals.

to be more likely to commit crimes .[3] People who take this position argue that it may be necessary to sacrifice some of our civil rights to more effectively keep neighborhoods safe from crime or secure our borders against terrorism. Many, including former attorney general Eric Holder, disagree with this perspective on purely practical grounds and say that racial profiling is simply not an effective tool of law enforcement.[4]

You probably have experience with questions of profiling and discrimination in your own life, beyond the realm of law enforcement. In fact, civil rights are one of the best examples of the idea that politics is everywhere: policies concerning discrimination in the workplace and in housing and against women, minorities, gays, and the disabled affect millions of Americans every day. Consider the following scenarios:

- Scenario 1: You are driving home one night with a few of your friends after a party. It is late at night, but you have not had anything to drink and you are following all traffic laws. Your heart sinks as you see the flashing lights of a squad car signaling you to pull over. As the police officer approaches your car, you wonder if you have been pulled over because you and your friends are African Americans driving in an all-white neighborhood. Have your civil rights been violated? Change the scene to a car full of white teenagers with all the other facts the same. Can an officer pull them over just because he or she thinks that teenagers are more likely than older people to be engaging in criminal activity?
- Scenario 2: You are a 21-year-old Asian-American woman applying for your first job out of college. After being turned down for a job at an engineering firm, you suspect that you didn't get the job because you are a woman and because management thought that you would not fit in with the "good ol' boy" atmosphere of the firm. Have your civil rights been violated?
- Scenario 3: You and your gay partner are told that "your kind" are not welcome in the apartment complex that you want to live in. Should you call a lawyer?
- Scenario 4: You are a white male graduating from high school. You have just received a letter of rejection from the college that was first on your list. You are very disappointed, but then you get angry when a friend tells you that one of your class-mates got into the same school even though he had virtually the same grades as you and his SAT scores were a bit lower. Your friend says that it is probably because of the school's affirmative action policy—the classmate who was accepted is Latino. Are you a victim of "reverse discrimination"? Have your civil rights been violated?

All of these scenarios would seem to be civil rights violations. However, some are, some are not, and some depend on additional considerations (we will return to these examples in the chapter's conclusion). Is it ever acceptable to treat people differently based on the color of their skin, their ethnic status, their gender, or their sexual orientation, in a situation of racial profiling or otherwise? More broadly, when is discrimination legal, and when isn't it? How are civil rights in the United States defined today?

civil rights
Rights that guarantee individuals freedom from discrimination. These rights are generally grounded in the equal protection clause of the Fourteenth Amendment and more specifically laid out in laws passed by Congress, such as the 1964 Civil Rights Act.

DESCRIBE THE HISTORICAL STRUGGLES GROUPS HAVE FACED IN WINNING CIVIL RIGHTS

The context of civil rights

In general, **civil rights** are rights that guarantee individuals freedom from discrimination. In the United States, individuals' civil rights are monitored by the U.S. Commission on Civil Rights, a bipartisan, independent federal commission that was established by the 1957 Civil Rights Act.[5] The commission's mission is to "appraise federal laws and policies," investigate complaints, and collect information regarding citizens who are "being deprived of their right to vote" or who are being discriminated against or denied the "equal protection of the laws under the Constitution because of race, color, religion, sex, age, disability, or national origin." It investigates government actions, such as allegations of racial discrimination in elections, and discriminatory actions of individuals in the workplace, commerce, housing, and education.

This definition seems straightforward enough, but confusion may arise when comparing the terms "civil rights" and "civil liberties." They are often used interchangeably, but there are important differences. "Civil liberties" refers to the freedoms guaranteed in the Bill of Rights, such as the freedom of speech, religious expression, and the press, as well as the due process protection of the Fourteenth Amendment. In contrast, civil rights protect all persons from discrimination and are rooted in laws and the equal protection clause of the Fourteenth Amendment. Moreover, civil liberties primarily limit what the government can do to you ("*Congress* shall make no law . . . abridging the freedom of speech," for example), whereas civil rights protect you from discrimination both by the government and by individuals. As noted in the previous chapter, to oversimplify, civil liberties are about freedom and civil rights are about equality.

Neither civil liberties nor civil rights figured prominently at the Constitutional Convention. Equality is not even mentioned in the Constitution or the Bill of Rights. However, equality was very much on the Founders' minds, as is evident in this ringing passage from the Declaration of Independence: "We hold these truths to be self evident, that all men are created equal, that they are endowed by their Creator with certain unalienable rights, that among these are life, liberty, and the pursuit of happiness." Despite the broad language, this was a limited conception of equality. The reference to "men" was intentional: women had no political or economic rights in the late eighteenth century. Similarly, equality did not apply to slaves or to Native Americans. Even propertyless white men did not have full political rights until several decades after the Constitution was ratified. Equality and civil rights in the United States have been a continually evolving work in progress.

African Americans

From the early nineteenth century and the movement for the abolition of slavery until the mid-twentieth century and the civil rights movement, the central focus of civil rights was on the experiences of African Americans. Other groups received attention more gradually. Starting in the mid-nineteenth century women began their fight for equal rights, and over the next century the civil rights movement expanded to include other groups such as Native Americans, Latinos, and Asian Americans. Most recently, attention has turned to the elderly, the disabled, and LGBTQ people (lesbian, gay, bisexual, transgender, queer/questioning people). The most divisive civil rights issue with the greatest long-term impact, however, has been slavery and its legacy.

Slavery and Its Impact Slavery was part of the American economy from nearly the beginning of the nation's history. Dutch traders brought 20 slaves to Jamestown, Virginia, in 1619, a year before the Puritans landed at Plymouth Rock. It is impossible to overstate the importance of slaves to the southern economy. The 1860 census shows that there were 2.3 million slaves in the Deep South (including Georgia, Alabama, South Carolina, Mississippi, and Louisiana), constituting 47 percent of its population, and there were nearly 4 million slaves in the South overall. The economic benefits for slave owners were clear. By 1860, the per capita income for whites in the South was

Slavery was part of the American economy from the 1600s until it was abolished by the Thirteenth Amendment in 1865. The system of slavery in the South created a highly unequal society in which African Americans were denied virtually all rights. Abolitionists worked to undermine and abolish slavery. Harriet Tubman was instrumental in the success of the Underground Railroad, which brought countless slaves to freedom.

A house divided against itself cannot stand. I believe this government cannot endure permanently half-slave and half-free.

— President Abraham Lincoln

$3,978; in the North, it was $2,040. The South had only 30 percent of the nation's free population, but it had 60 percent of the wealthiest men.[6]

Abolitionists worked to rid the nation of slavery as its importance to the South grew, setting the nation on a collision course that would not be resolved until the Civil War. Despite the work of some early abolitionists, the Founders largely ducked the issue (see Chapter 2), and subsequent legislatures and courts did not come any closer to resolving the impasse between the North and South over slavery. The Missouri Compromise of 1820, which limited the expansion of slavery and kept the overall balance between slave states and free states, eased tensions for a while, but the issue persisted. By the 1830s, the abolitionist movement gained considerable strength. Slave owners became increasingly frustrated with the success of the Underground Railroad, which helped some slaves escape to freedom in the North. In 1850, the debate over admitting California as a free state or a slave state (or making it half-free and half-slave) threatened to split the nation once again. As part of the Compromise of 1850, southern states agreed to admit California as a free state, but only if Congress passed the Fugitive Slave Act, which required northern states to treat escaped slaves as property and return them to their owners. The Compromise also overturned the Missouri Compromise and allowed each new state to decide for itself whether to be a slave state or a free state.[7]

All possibility of further compromise on the issue ended with the misguided *Dred Scott v. Sandford* decision in 1857. The Supreme Court ruled that states could not be prevented from allowing slavery. It also held that slaves were property rather than citizens and, as such, had no legal rights. But, in 1860, believing that slavery was in jeopardy after Abraham Lincoln won the presidency, the southern states seceded from the Union and formed the Confederacy.

The outcome of the Civil War restored national unity and ended slavery, but the price was very high. About 528,000 Americans died in the war, with an astonishingly high casualty rate (25 percent).[8] After the war, Republicans moved quickly to ensure that the changes accomplished by the war could not easily be undone: they promptly adopted the Civil War amendments to the Constitution. The Thirteenth Amendment banned slavery, the Fourteenth guaranteed that states could not deny newly freed slaves the equal protection of the laws and provided citizenship to anyone born in the

United States, and the Fifteenth gave African-American men the right to vote. These amendments were ratified within five years of the war, although southern states resisted giving freed slaves and their descendants "equal protection of the laws" over the next 100 years.

Voting Rights During Reconstruction (1866–1877), blacks in the South gained political power through institutions such as the Freedmen's Bureau and the Union League. With the protection of the occupying northern army, blacks were able to vote and even hold public office. When federal troops withdrew and the Republican Party abandoned the South, however, blacks were almost completely **disenfranchised** (denied the right to vote) through the imposition of residency requirements, poll taxes, literacy tests, physical intimidation, and other forms of disqualification. Later the practice known as the "white primary" allowed only whites to vote in Democratic primary elections and, given that the Republican Party did not exist in most southern states, blacks were effectively disenfranchised. Although most of these provisions were claimed to be race neutral, their impact fell disproportionately on black voters. For example, the **grandfather clause,** which permitted those who had voted before the war and their descendants to vote even if they did not meet current voting requirements, enabled illiterate whites (but not illiterate blacks) to avoid the literacy test.[9] Many states also had "understanding" or "good character" exceptions to the literacy tests, which gave election officials substantial discretion over who would be allowed to vote.

The collective impact of these obstacles virtually eliminated black voting. For example, only 6 percent of blacks were registered to vote in Mississippi in 1890 and only 2 percent were registered in Alabama in 1906. After the last post-Reconstruction black congressman left the House in 1901, 72 years passed before another African American represented a southern district in Congress. In one Mississippi county in 1947, only 6 out of 13,000 eligible blacks were actually registered to vote. Despite the constitutional guarantees of the Fourteenth and Fifteenth Amendments, blacks had little access to the political system in the South and they had little success in winning office at any level in the rest of the nation.[10]

Jim Crow The social and economic position of blacks in the South followed a path similar to their political fortunes. Soon after the Civil War ended, sympathetic Republicans passed the Civil Rights Acts of 1866 and 1875, which aimed to outlaw segregation and provide equal opportunity for blacks. However, there were no enforcement provisions, and when Reconstruction ended in 1877 the southern states enacted "black codes," or **Jim Crow laws,** that led to complete segregation of the races. Then, in 1883, the Supreme Court ruled that the 1875 Civil Rights Act was unconstitutional because Congress did not have the power to forbid racial discrimination in private businesses. Southern states interpreted this decision as a signal that the national government was unconcerned about protecting the rights of blacks.

Jim Crow laws forbade interracial marriage and mandated the complete separation of the races in neighborhoods, hotels, apartments, hospitals, schools, and restrooms, at drinking fountains, and in restaurants, elevators, and even cemetery plots. In cases where it would have been inconvenient to completely separate the races, as in public transportation, blacks had to sit in the back of the bus or in separate cars on the train and give up their seats to whites if asked. The Supreme Court validated these practices in *Plessy v. Ferguson* (1896) by establishing the **"separate but equal" doctrine**, officially permitting segregation as long as blacks had facilities equal to those of whites.

In the first several decades after Reconstruction, the rest of the nation mostly ignored the status of blacks, because 90 percent of all African Americans lived

disenfranchised
To have been denied the ability to exercise a right, such as the right to vote.

grandfather clause
A type of law enacted in several southern states to allow those who were permitted to vote before the Civil War, and their descendants, to bypass literacy tests and other obstacles to voting, thereby exempting whites from these tests while continuing to disenfranchise African Americans and other people of color.

Senator Hiram Revels, the first African American to serve in the U.S. Congress, represented Mississippi in 1870 and 1871.

Jim Crow laws
State and local laws that mandated racial segregation in all public facilities in the South, many border states, and some northern communities between 1876 and 1964.

"separate but equal" doctrine
The idea that racial segregation was acceptable as long as the separate facilities were of equal quality; supported by *Plessy v. Ferguson* and struck down by *Brown v. Board of Education*.

in the South. But blacks' northward migration to urban areas throughout the first half of the twentieth century transformed the nation's demographic profile and its racial politics. America's "race problem" was no longer just a southern problem. Although conditions for blacks were generally better outside the South, they still faced discrimination and lived largely segregated lives throughout the nation. In World Wars I and II, black soldiers fought and died for their country in segregated units. Professional sports teams were segregated, and black musicians and artists could not perform in many of the nation's leading theaters. Moreover, blacks largely were hired for the lowest-paying menial jobs.

Progress began in the 1940s. The Supreme Court struck down the white primary in 1944, Jackie Robinson broke the color line in Major League Baseball in 1947, and President Harry Truman issued an executive order integrating the U.S. armed services in 1948. Then came the landmark decision *Brown v. Board of Education* (1954), which rejected the "separate but equal" doctrine, followed by *Brown II* (1955), which ordered that public schools be desegregated "with all deliberate speed." These events set the stage for the growing success of the civil rights movement, discussed later in this chapter.

Native Americans, Latinos, and Asian Americans

The legacy of slavery and racial segregation in the South has been the dominant focus of U.S. civil rights policies, but many other groups have also fought for equal rights. Native Americans were the first group to come in contact with the European immigrants. Although initial relations between the Native Americans and the European settlers were good in many places, the settlers' appetite for more land and their insensitivity to Native-American culture soon led to a state of continual conflict. Native Americans were systematically pushed from their land and placed on reservations. The most infamous example was the removal of 46,000 members of the "Five Civilized Tribes" from the southeastern United States following the enactment of the Indian Removal Act in 1830. Thousands of Native Americans died on the Trail of Tears on their way to reservations in Oklahoma.[11] Native Americans had no political rights; indeed, through much of the nineteenth century the U.S. government considered them "savages" to be eliminated. They did not gain the universal right to vote until 1924, just after women and well after black men. Although the U.S. government signed treaties with Native-American tribes that recognized them as sovereign nations (not as foreign nations but as "domestic dependent nations"),[12] in practice the government ignored most of the agreements. Only in recent decades has the government started to uphold its obligations, although compliance remains spotty. Native Americans have struggled to maintain their cultural history and autonomy in the face of widespread poverty and unemployment.

Latinos have also struggled for political and economic equality. The early history of Latinos in the United States is rooted in the Mexican-American War (1846–1848) and the conquest by the United States of the territory that today makes up most of the southwestern states. Since that time, Mexicans have resided in large numbers in the Southwest. Although Latinos had long experienced prejudice and discrimination, one of their first major political successes was Cesar Chavez's effort to organize farmworkers in the 1960s and 1970s. He established the United Farm Workers Union and forced growers to bargain with 50,000 mostly Mexican-American fieldworkers in California and Florida.

Native Americans' struggles to maintain the security of their cultural lands were at the forefront of controversy over the construction of the Dakota Access Pipeline. In 2016 and 2017, the Standing Rock Sioux tribe led protests against the oil pipeline and its proposed route, which threatened their ancestral lands and clean water supply.

Although many Mexican Americans have roots that go back hundreds of years, a majority of Latinos have been in the United States for less than two generations. Consequently, they have become a political force only recently, although they are now the nation's largest minority. Latinos' relative lack of political clout when compared with that of African Americans can be explained by two factors. First, Latinos vote at a much lower rate than African Americans, in part because many have language barriers. In addition, about one-third of Latinos cannot vote in national elections because they are not U.S. citizens. Second, unlike African Americans, Latinos are a relatively diverse group politically, composed of people from many Latin American nations. Most Latino voters are loyal to the Democratic Party, but a majority of Cuban Americans are Republicans. Although this diversity means that Latino voters do not speak with one voice, it brings opportunity for increased political clout in the future. The diversity of partisan attachments among Latinos and their relatively low levels of political involvement mean that both parties are eager to attract them as new voters. In 2016, Donald Trump surprised many experts by winning a higher percentage of the Latino vote (29 percent) than Mitt Romney did in 2012 (27 percent).

Asian Americans experienced discrimination beginning with their arrival in the United States in the nineteenth century. The first wave of Chinese immigrants came with the 1848 California gold rush. Initially, foreign miners, including the Chinese, were able to stake out their claims along with Americans. But by 1850, when the easy-to-find gold was gone, Americans tried to drive out the Chinese through violence and the Foreign Miners Tax. Subsequently, Chinese immigrants played a crucial role in building the intercontinental railroad between 1865 and 1869. Yet, because they were given the most dangerous jobs, many lost their lives. After the railroad was completed, Chinese workers returned to the West Coast, where they experienced increasing discrimination and violence. Following several race riots, Congress passed the Chinese Exclusion Act of 1882, which prevented Chinese already in the United States from becoming U.S. citizens—although the Supreme Court later granted their American-born children automatic citizenship under the Fourteenth Amendment.[13] The Chinese Exclusion Act also barred virtually all immigration from China—the first time in U.S. history that a specific ethnic group was singled out in this way. During World War II, more than 110,000 Japanese were placed in internment camps. Despite the internment being upheld by the Supreme Court at the time, a 1980 congressional commission determined that it was a "grave injustice" motivated by "racial prejudice, war hysteria and the failure of political leadership." Eight years later, President Ronald

During World War II, tens of thousands of Japanese Americans were forced to relocate to internment camps. Nearly two-thirds were American citizens, and most lost their homes and jobs.

Reagan signed into law the Civil Liberties Act, which paid more than $1.6 billion in reparations to the survivors of the camps and their heirs.[14] In 2018, the Court explicitly overturned the 1944 decision that approved the internment, saying, "The forcible relocation of U.S. citizens to concentration camps, solely and explicitly on the basis of race, is objectively unlawful and outside the scope of presidential authority."[15] In recent decades, a much broader range of Asians have emigrated to the United States, including Koreans, Filipinos, Hmong, Vietnamese, and Asian Indians. This variation in national heritage, culture, and language means that Asian Americans are quite diverse in their political views, partisan affiliation, and voting patterns.

Women and civil rights

On the eve of the United States' declaration of independence in 1776, John Adams's wife, Abigail, advised him not to "put such unlimited power in the hands of the husbands. Remember, all men would be tyrants if they could. . . . If particular care and attention is not paid to the ladies, we . . . will not hold ourselves bound by any laws in which we have no voice or representation."[16] John Adams did not listen to his wife. The Constitution did not give women the right to vote, and they were not guaranteed that civil right until the Nineteenth Amendment was ratified in 1920—although 16 states had allowed women to vote before then. Until the early twentieth century, women in most parts of the country could not hold office, serve on juries, bring lawsuits in their own name, own property, or serve as legal guardians for their children. A woman's identity was so closely tied to her husband that if she married a noncitizen she automatically gave up her citizenship!

The rationale for these policies was called **protectionism**. The argument was that women were too frail to compete in the business world and needed to be protected by men. This reasoning served in many court cases to deny women equal rights. For example, in 1869 Myra Bradwell requested admission to the Illinois bar to practice law. She was the first woman to graduate from law school in Illinois and the editor of *Chicago Legal News,* and she held all the qualifications to be a lawyer in the state except

protectionism
The idea under which some people have tried to rationalize discriminatory policies by claiming that some groups, like women or African Americans, should be denied certain rights for their own safety or well-being.

for one—she was a woman. Her request was denied, and she sued all the way to the Supreme Court. In 1873, the Court ruled that the prohibition against women lawyers did not violate the Fourteenth Amendment's privileges and immunities clause because there was no constitutional right to be an attorney. If the Court had stopped there, the decision would have been unremarkable for its time. But Justice Joseph Bradley went on to provide a classic example of protectionism:

> *The civil law as well as nature itself has always recognized a wide difference in the respective spheres and destinies to man and woman. Man is, or should be, woman's protector and defender. The natural and proper timidity and delicacy which belongs to the female sex evidently unfits it for many of the occupations of civil life. The constitution of the family organization which is founded in the divine ordinance, as well as the nature of things, indicates the domestic sphere as that which properly belongs to the domains and functions of womanhood.*[17]

While protectionist sentiment on the Court had waned by the mid-twentieth century, as recently as 1961 the Court upheld a Florida law that automatically exempted women but not men from compulsory jury duty. The case involved a woman who killed her husband with a baseball bat after he admitted that he was having an affair and wanted to end the marriage. The woman argued that her conviction by an all-male jury violated her Fourteenth Amendment guarantee of "equal protection of the laws" and that a jury panel containing some women would have been more sympathetic to her "temporary insanity" defense. The Court rejected this argument, ruling that the Florida law excluding women from jury duty was reasonable because "despite the enlightened emancipation of women from the restrictions and protections of bygone years, and their entry into many parts of community life formerly considered to be reserved to men, woman still is regarded as the center of home and family life."[18] Apparently, it was unthinkable to the all-male Court that a man might have to stay home from work and take care of the kids while his wife served on a jury. Later in this chapter, we will describe how the Supreme Court has moved away from this discriminatory position and rejected protectionist thinking.

The LGBTQ community

The most recent group to engage in the struggle for civil rights is the LGBTQ community. For most of American history, gays and lesbians lived secret lives and were subject to abuse and discrimination if they openly acknowledged their sexual orientation. The critical moment that spurred the gay rights movement occurred on June 28, 1969, during a routine police raid on the Stonewall Inn in New York City.[19] (Police often raided gay bars to harass patrons and selectively enforce liquor laws.) This time, rather than submitting to the arrests, the customers fought back, throwing stones and beer bottles, breaking windows, and starting small fires. A crowd of several hundred people gathered, and the fighting raged for three nights. The Stonewall rebellion galvanized the gay community by demonstrating the power of collective action.

Since Stonewall, the gay rights movement has made steady progress through a combination of political mobilization and protest, legislative action, and legal action. Public support for gay rights has increased dramatically in recent years. Between two-thirds and three-fourths of Americans (depending on the poll) agree with the national policy established in 2011 that gays may openly serve in the military, whereas

In 2016, President Obama designated the historic site of the Stonewall uprising in New York City as a national monument to honor the LGBTQ equality movement.

a majority of Americans opposed this policy when it was first proposed by President Clinton in 1993. Between 60 and 64 percent of Americans support same-sex marriage according to recent polls, whereas only 35 to 40 percent held that view in 2009. More than 60 percent believe that same-sex couples should be able to adopt children, 89 percent think that businesses should not be able to discriminate against gays and lesbians, and 63 percent believe that same-sex couples should be entitled to the same benefits as heterosexual couples (whereas only 32 percent think they should not).[20] In May 2012, President Obama endorsed same-sex marriage for the first time (and was the first president to take that position), completing his gradual evolution on the issue. In 2015, the Supreme Court ruled that same-sex marriage is legal in all 50 states (we will discuss this and other issues concerning gay and lesbian rights later in the chapter).[21] In the 2016 presidential campaign Donald Trump said, "I will do everything in my power to protect our LGBTQ citizens from the violence and oppression of a hateful foreign ideology. Believe me." But his record on LGBTQ issues has been criticized by civil rights supporters.[22]

"Why Should I Care?"

Why does this history matter for politics today? First, the effects of slavery and Jim Crow laws are still quite evident: legal racial segregation ended 50 years ago, but its legacy—especially evident in the difference that exists in the relative quality of education available to most whites and blacks—remains. Second, knowing about this history helps us understand where the inequalities (that we discuss in the next section) in our society come from. Finally, active discrimination based on race, gender, and sexual orientation is still evident in our society. Given the importance of race in the everyday lives of millions of Americans and in gaining an understanding of American politics, a grasp of the history that got us to where we are today is an important starting point.

The racial divide today

The racial divide today begins with the unequal treatment of racial minorities, women, gays, and lesbians and is rooted in the gulf that remains between minorities and whites, in terms of their objective condition as well as their political views. Although substantial progress has been made in bridging that gulf, political, social, and economic inequalities remain.

Discriminatory treatment

Discrimination is much more common today than many people realize. The Equal Employment Opportunity Commission (EEOC) filed an average of 90,000 charges of employment discrimination each year in the past five years,[23] while the National Fair Housing Alliance reports an average of 28,000 cases of housing discrimination a year.[24] The Justice Department has won dozens of lawsuits against banks and mortgage lenders who engage in discriminatory practices, winning settlements totaling several hundred million dollars in the past three years.[25]

The experience of a former graduate student in our department who is white and whose wife is black puts a human face on these statistics. The couple wanted to rent a bigger apartment, so they searched the want ads and made appointments to see some apartments. One landlord told them to meet him in front of the apartment at a specific time. They waited where they were told, but the landlord didn't show up. Later they remembered seeing a car that slowed down and almost stopped but then sped away. They wondered if this was a case of a "drive-by landlord"—one who checks out potential tenants' race from a distance; if they are not white, he or she skips the appointment and tells them it is rented if they ask. This is exactly what happened. This couple called the landlord, asked what had happened, and were told that the apartment was already rented. To check their suspicions, they had some friends ask about the apartment, and the friends were told it was available. Their friends (both white) made an appointment to meet the landlord, and this time the same car pulled up and stopped. The landlord showed them the apartment and was very friendly. The next day, the graduate student filed a racial discrimination lawsuit.

These types of stories, ranging from irritating and demeaning to serious violations of the law, are familiar to nearly every racial minority, woman, and LGBTQ person in the United States. Consider the well-dressed businessman who cannot get a cab in a major city because he is black, the woman who is sexually harassed by her boss but hesitates to say anything for fear of losing her job, the teenage Latino who is shadowed in the music store by a clerk, the Arab American who endures taunts about her head covering, or the lesbian couple who cannot find an apartment. Such anecdotal evidence, as well as extensive government data and academic research, indicates continuing discrimination in our society, despite significant progress in the past generation.

Differences in voting access

The United States has a long history of discriminating against racial and ethnic minorities in the election process. Although African Americans voted at a rate that was quite similar to that of whites in presidential elections from 2008 to 2016, their turnout in midterm elections has been somewhat lower than that of whites, and other

DID YOU KNOW?

Bank of America paid

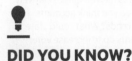

$335 million

in 2011 to settle the largest mortgage discrimination case of its kind.
Source: *New York Times*

> There are very few African-American men in this country who haven't had the experience of being followed when they were shopping in a department store. That includes me.
>
> —President Barack Obama

FIGURE 5.1

Turnout in Presidential Elections by Race

Turnout among African Americans has risen steadily over the last 20 years (with a dip in 2016), while turnout of other groups has remained relatively flat. What do you think accounts for these trends? What could state governments do to increase voter turnout?

Source: United States Elections Project, "Voter Turnout Demographics," www.electproject.org/home/voter-turnout/demographics (accessed 10/26/17).

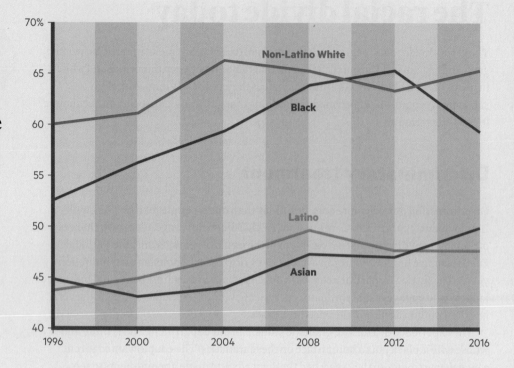

racial and ethnic minorities have generally lower turnouts (see Figure 5.1). Much of the difference in voter turnout can be accounted for by education and income, but there still are practices and institutions that specifically depress minority-voter turnout. And many of these deterrents are intentional. The National Association for the Advancement of Colored People (NAACP), the U.S. Commission on Civil Rights, and the Brennan Center for Justice have all documented such practices in elections going back to 2000, including moving and reducing the number of polling places in areas with predominantly minority voters, changing from district-based to at-large elections (citywide or countywide elections in which there is often a mix of minority and white voters), using voter challenges to target minority voters, redistricting to dilute minority voting power, withholding information about registration and voting procedures from blacks, and "causing or taking advantage of Election Day irregularities."[26]

There are other state practices that are not specifically aimed at minority voters but that have a disproportionate impact on them. Examples have included removing voters' names from the voting rolls if there wasn't an identical match between the name the voter used when registering to vote and the name as it appeared in another state database (often the database of driver's license information); purging the names of people who had committed felonies from the voting registration lists, which often produced false matches to people with the same names who had not committed a crime; and engaging in voter intimidation and deceptive practices. Moreover, several states use technical barriers to voter registration and voting, limit access to voter registration services at social services offices (even though such access is required by federal law), and use poorly designed ballots that are especially confusing to less educated or older voters.[27]

In 2016 and 2017, there were 24 changes in state laws that restricted access to voting, including requiring a photo ID to vote (which has a disproportionate impact on minorities because they are less likely to have a photo ID), requiring proof of citizenship before being allowed to vote, cutting back on early voting days and times, and making it more difficult to register people to vote.[28] In addition, as we will discuss later, in

2013 the Supreme Court struck down an important part of the Voting Rights Act, making it easier for the nine states that had been covered by this provision of the law to implement discriminatory practices. Also, in 2018 the Court upheld a voter purge law in Ohio, despite evidence that the law had a disproportionate impact on minority voters. However, legal challenges in many states pushed back against these changes in voting laws. Those supporting voting rights won at least partial victories in eight states against voter ID laws and restrictions on early voting that had a racial impact. Also, several states passed laws to automatically register voters and restore the right to vote for those with past criminal convictions.[29]

Socioeconomic indicators

The racial divide is also evident in social and economic terms. Nearly three times as many black families are below the poverty line as white families: 21.2 percent compared with 8.7 percent in 2017. The poverty rate of 18.3 percent for Latino families in 2017 was similar to that of black families. While white median household income (that is, income from wages, salaries, interest, and disability and unemployment payments) was $68,145 in 2017, black median household income was $40,258 (59.1 percent of white family income) and Latino median household income was $50,486 (74.1 percent of white family income).[30] Moreover, the gap in overall wealth is much more dramatic. The average white household has more than six times the assets of the typical nonwhite family. In 2016, the median household net worth (that is, the sum of all assets, including houses, cars, and stock) was $171,000 for whites and $17,600 for African Americans, and $20,700 for Latinos.[31] Poverty is not distributed equally throughout the United States but rather is concentrated in areas where the minority population is the highest (see Figure 5.2).

Other indicators show similar patterns. The rate of black adult male unemployment has been about twice as high as that of white adult male unemployment for the past 45 years. In August 2018, the unemployment rate among blacks was 6.3 percent, compared with 3.4 percent for whites and 4.7 percent for Latinos.[32] Moreover, 36.1 percent of black children lived in two-parent households in 2017, compared with 73.6 percent of white children and 61.2 percent of Latino children.[33] Also, blacks are significantly

**FIGURE
5.2**

Poverty and Race, 2016

Carefully examine these maps. What is the relationship between poverty and the minority population? How do you think these patterns might affect the politics of civil rights policies aimed at reducing discrimination in the workplace or housing?

Sources: Poverty data from U.S. Census Bureau, 2016 American Community Survey, www.census.gov/acs; race data from U.S. Census Bureau, Quickfacts, www.census. gov/quickfacts/fact/map (accessed 9/27/18).

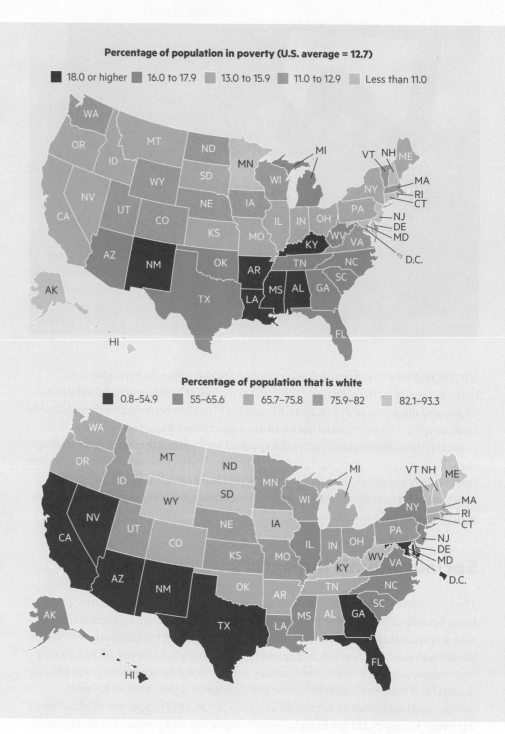

Percentage of population in poverty (U.S. average = 12.7)

| 18.0 or higher | 16.0 to 17.9 | 13.0 to 15.9 | 11.0 to 12.9 | Less than 11.0 |

Percentage of population that is white

| 0.8–54.9 | 55–65.6 | 65.7–75.8 | 75.9–82 | 82.1–93.3 |

more likely than whites to be victimized by crime. African Americans are nearly seven times as likely to be murdered as whites.[34]

On every measure of health—life expectancy, infectious diseases, infant mortality, cancer rates, heart disease, and strokes—the gaps between whites and blacks are large and, in some cases, increasing. For example, life expectancy for blacks is three and a half years shorter than for whites (75.5 years for blacks compared with 79 years for whites), the infant mortality rate is more than double for blacks (11.1 deaths per 1,000 live births compared with 4.95 deaths per 1,000 live births for whites and 4.99 for Latinas), and maternal mortality is more than triple (43.5 deaths per 100,000 births for black women compared with 12.7 deaths per 100,000 births for white women). Similar gaps also exist for incidences of cancer, diabetes, strokes, and heart attacks in blacks and whites.[35]

While social scientists continue to debate the causes of the racial disparities in health outcomes, an increasing body of evidence indicates that at least some of the gap is caused by government policies and business-related decisions. Broadly labeled "environmental racism," these practices mean that minority groups are much more likely to live in areas affected by pollution, toxic waste, and hazardous chemical sites.[36] One of the most extreme examples of this, uncovered in late 2015 and early 2016, involved the public water supply in Flint, Michigan. In 2014, to save money, the city switched its water supply from Lake Huron to the Flint River. Residents of the poor, majority-black city soon reported discolored, foul-looking water, but their complaints were ignored by city and state officials. Researchers demonstrated that levels of lead in the water far exceeded safe levels, and 6,000 to 12,000 residents experiencing serious health issues were found to have elevated levels of lead in their blood. President Obama declared the city a disaster area and aid was provided in early 2016, but permanent damage had already been done.[37] Four officials were charged with felonies for their role in the crisis, and in 2017 a $722 million class-action lawsuit was filed against the Environmental Protection Agency. Early in 2018 the Supreme Court allowed that case to move forward. [38]

Criminal justice and hate crimes

The greatest disparity between racial minorities and whites may be in the criminal justice system. Racial profiling subjects many innocent blacks to intrusive searches.[39] Tim Scott, a Republican African-American senator from South Carolina, said in a speech on the Senate floor that he was pulled over by police officers seven times in one year "for nothing more than driving a new car in the wrong neighborhood." He continued, "I do not know many African-American men who do not have a very similar story to tell—no matter their profession, no matter their income, no matter their disposition in life."[40] As noted in the introduction, early in 2014, Bill de Blasio, the newly elected mayor, said he would change the New York's policing practices to comply with a federal court ruling concerning the city's aggressive "stop-and-frisk" policy.[41] Racial bias is also evident in the criminal system after the initial arrest. Studies have shown that blacks are more likely than whites to be convicted for the same crimes and are also more likely to serve longer sentences.[42]

Recently, tensions have been high between minority communities and the police in the wake of dozens of cases of police shooting unarmed black men. In 2017, police killed

There have been dozens of high-profile cases in recent years of police shooting unarmed black men. Walter Scott was killed by North Charleston, South Carolina, police officer Michael Slager following a traffic stop for a broken brake light, inspiring protests throughout the city.

Mourners outside the Emanuel AME Church in Charleston, South Carolina, pray at the memorial for the nine people shot and killed by white supremacist Dylann Roof during a prayer service.

1,147 people in the United States; of those, 149 were unarmed and 49 were African Americans (see What Do the Facts Say?).[43] Most of these involved tragic circumstances in which police were acting appropriately given existing protocol. But several highly publicized cases reveal negligent and, in some cases, criminal behavior by police officers. In 2013, following the acquittal of a neighborhood watch member, George Zimmerman, for shooting an unarmed 17-year-old African American, Trayvon Martin, the group Black Lives Matter was formed.[44] The next year in Ferguson, Missouri, thousands of protesters gathered to call attention to the killing of an unarmed man, Michael Brown, by a police officer. The officer was acquitted, but an investigation by the Department of Justice found patterns of discriminatory behavior by the Ferguson Police Department. From 2015 to 2018, other high-profile cases of unarmed African Americans being killed by officers happened in Cleveland, Baltimore, Chicago, Staten Island, Baton Rouge, Minneapolis–St. Paul, and Sacramento. One case in North Charleston, South Carolina, led to a murder charge for the officer. Following a daytime traffic stop for a broken taillight, Officer Michael Slager shot Walter Scott in the back eight times from 15 to 20 feet away as Scott was running away, and lied about what happened to cover up his crime. A bystander's video showed the murder and led to Slager's arrest. State first-degree murder charges were dismissed, however, as part of a plea deal. Slager ultimately plead guilty to a federal civil rights charge of using excessive force and was sentenced to 20 years in prison.[45] Overall, convictions in these cases are rare. One study found that of the roughly 12,000 police shootings from 2005 to 2017, there were 80 officers arrested for murder or manslaughter and just over one-third were convicted.[46]

African Americans and other minorities are also subjected to hate crimes much more frequently than whites.[47] According to FBI statistics, in 2016 half of race-related hate crimes in the United States were "anti-black," while only 21 percent were "anti-white" (58 percent of all hate crimes are race based). This means that the rate of anti-black hate crimes is nearly four times what would be expected based on the percentage of African Americans in the United States, while the rate of anti-white hate crimes is less than one-third as high as would be expected. One of the most extreme hate crimes in recent years happened in 2015 when Dylann Roof, a 21-year-old white supremacist, shot and killed nine people at a Bible study in the historic Emanuel African Methodist

Racial Inequality in Law Enforcement

Recent events in Ferguson, Missouri, Baltimore, Maryland, and Staten Island, New York, among other places, have touched off a nationwide debate about fairness in law enforcement. These graphs show both the total number and the relative number (expressed as the number per million), by race, of people killed by police. Do racial inequalities exist in law enforcement? What do the facts say?

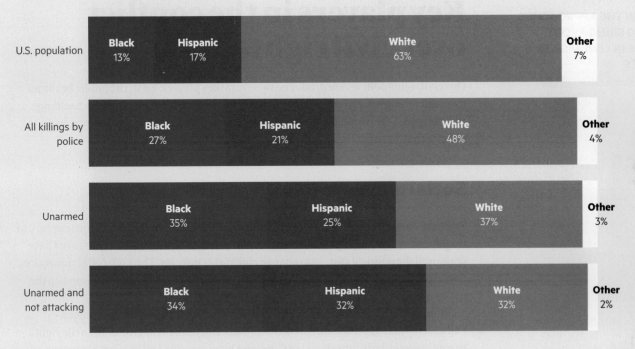

U.S. population
- Black 13%
- Hispanic 17%
- White 63%
- Other 7%

All killings by police
- Black 27%
- Hispanic 21%
- White 48%
- Other 4%

Unarmed
- Black 35%
- Hispanic 25%
- White 37%
- Other 3%

Unarmed and not attacking
- Black 34%
- Hispanic 32%
- White 32%
- Other 2%

Source: "2017 Police Violence Report," Mapping Police Violence, https://policeviolencereport.org (accessed 4/17/18).

Think about it

- For all victims (total and unarmed), what racial category had the highest percentage of deaths? What racial category had the highest percentage of victims unarmed and not attacking? What do you think accounts for this difference?
- Is there a greater racial disparity in the second chart (which shows all people killed by police) or the third chart (which shows unarmed people)?
- What, if anything, surprises you about these numbers? Why?

Episcopal Church in Charleston, South Carolina. Roof later confessed that he was trying to ignite a race war.

This backdrop of racial inequality, discrimination, and violence drives civil rights activists to push their agenda in the three branches of government: legislative, executive, and judicial. In some instances, activists work in several arenas simultaneously; in others, they seek redress in one arena after exhausting alternatives in the others. The civil rights movement, which was crucial in early policy successes, also continues to mobilize from the grass roots.

EXPLAIN THE APPROACHES USED TO BRING ABOUT CHANGE IN CIVIL RIGHTS POLICIES

Key players in the conflict over civil rights

Our civil rights policies are produced by several key players. First, the public becomes involved through social movements to put pressure on the political system to change. But Congress, the president, and the courts all also exert their own influence on policies that define civil rights.

Social movements

From the early women's rights movement and abolitionists of the nineteenth century to the gay rights and civil rights movements of the mid-twentieth century, activists have pressured the political system to change civil rights policies. Through collective action, these social movements have made sure that protecting equal rights remained on the policy agenda.

Women started to push for the right to vote at a convention in 1848 in Seneca Falls, New York. Subsequently, a constitutional amendment to give women the right to vote was regularly introduced in Congress between 1878 and 1913 but never was passed, despite the efforts of women such as Susan B. Anthony and Elizabeth Cady Stanton. After a parallel movement at the state level had some success, the Nineteenth Amendment, giving women the right to vote, was finally passed in 1919 and ratified in 1920 (see Figure 5.3).

FIGURE 5.3 **Women's Rights Time Line**

First women's rights convention held in Seneca Falls, New York.	Territory of Wyoming gives women the right to vote.	Congress requires equal pay for equal work for federal employees (but not for private sector workers).	The Nineteenth Amendment gives women the right to vote.	Equal Pay Act requires equal pay for equal work.	Title VII of the Civil Rights Act bars employment discrimination based on race, sex, and other grounds.
1848	1869	1872	**1920**	1963	1964

The civil rights movement of the 1950s and 1960s, aimed at ending segregation and guaranteeing equal political and social rights for blacks, is the most famous example of a successful social movement (see Figure 5.4). Although the *Brown v. Board of Education* decision, which struck down segregation in public schools, gave the movement a boost, most southern blacks saw little change in their daily lives. As white school boards and local governments resisted integration, black leaders became convinced that the courts would not effect change because of resistance to their decisions. The only way to change the laws was to get the public, both black and white, to demand change.

The spark came on December 1, 1955, in Montgomery, Alabama, when a woman named Rosa Parks refused to give up her seat on a bus to a white person, as she was required to do by law. Parks is often described as a seamstress who was tired after a long day's work and simply did not want to give up her seat. That is true, but there is more to the story. Local civil rights leaders had been waiting for years for an opportunity to boycott the local bus company because of its segregation policy. They needed a perfect test case—someone who would help draw attention to the cause.

Rosa Parks was just that person. She was a well-educated, law-abiding citizen who had been active in local civil rights organizations. In her book, *My Story*, Parks says: "I was . . . no more tired than I usually was at the end of a working day. . . . No, the only tired I was, was tired of giving in."[48] When she was arrested for refusing to give up her seat, local civil rights leaders organized a boycott of the bus company that lasted more than a year. Whites in Montgomery tried to stop the boycott. The police arrested and fined blacks who had arranged a car pool system to get to work: people waiting for a car to pick them up were arrested for loitering, and car pool drivers were arrested for lacking appropriate insurance or having too many people in their car. Martin Luther King Jr. was elected leader of the bus boycott, and he was subjected to harassment and violence—his house was firebombed, and he was arrested several times. Finally, a federal district court ruled that Montgomery's segregation policy was unconstitutional and the Supreme Court upheld the ruling.

Nonviolent Protest On February 1, 1960, four black students in Greensboro, North Carolina, went to a segregated lunch counter at a local Woolworth's and asked to be served. They sat there for an hour without being served and had to leave when the store closed. When 20 students returned the next day, national wire services picked up the story. Within two weeks, the sit-ins had spread to 11 cities. In some cases, the students were met with violence; in others, they were simply arrested. However, the students

Griswold v. Connecticut legalizes the use of contraceptives by married couples.	Federal affirmative action policies are extended to women by an executive order.	Title IX of the Education Amendments of 1972 requires equal access to programs for men and women in higher education.	*Roe v. Wade* establishes a constitutional right to abortion.	Thirty-five states ratify the Equal Rights Amendment, passed by Congress in 1971–1972, falling three states short of the number needed to add the amendment to the Constitution.	Lilly Ledbetter Fair Pay Act makes it easier to sue for gender-based pay discrimination.	The social media campaign #MeToo calls attention to sexual violence against women.
1965	**1967**	**1972**	**1973**	**1982**	**2009**	**2017**

FIGURE 5.4

African-American Civil Rights Time Line

Government Action

May 17
U.S. Supreme Court rules segregated schools are unconstitutional in the *Brown v. Board of Education* decision.

September 9
The Federal Civil Rights Act prohibits discrimination.

September 23
President Eisenhower sends troops to escort black students into a white high school in Little Rock, Arkansas.

1954   1957

Social Movement

December 1
Rosa Parks is arrested for refusing to move to the back of a bus in Montgomery, Alabama.

February 1
Black college students, refused service at a lunch counter in Greensboro, North Carolina, launch a sit-in.

May 4
Freedom Riders test a Supreme Court decision that integrated interstate bus travel, sparking violence.

1955   1960   1961

Source: Adapted from "Civil Rights Movement Timeline," History.com, www.history.com/topics/civil-rights-movement-timeline (accessed 4/18/18).

As part of the Montgomery Bus Boycott, many African Americans organized car pools or walked to work.

continued to respond with passive resistance, and new waves of protesters replaced those who had been arrested. The Student Nonviolent Coordinating Committee (SNCC) was created to coordinate the protests. The Greensboro Woolworth's was integrated on July 26, 1961, but the protests continued in other cities. By August 1961, the sit-ins had 70,000 participants and there had been 3,000 arrests.[49] The sit-ins marked an important shift in the tactics of the civil rights movement: away from the court-based approach, exemplified by the fight against the "separate but equal" doctrine (as we will discuss next), and toward the nonviolent civil disobedience approach that had been successful in Montgomery.

Also during this period, the Freedom Riders were working to get President Kennedy to enforce two Supreme Court decisions that banned segregation in interstate travel, including at bus terminals, in waiting rooms, in restaurants, and in other public facilities related to interstate travel.[50] On May 4, 1961, a group of whites and blacks boarded two buses in Washington, D.C., headed for New Orleans. The whites and blacks sat together and went into segregated areas of bus stations together. The trip was uneventful until Rock Hill, South Carolina, where several Freedom Riders were beaten. Then, in Anniston, Alabama, one bus had its tires slashed and was firebombed. The Freedom Riders were beaten as they fled

July 2
President Johnson signs the Civil Rights Act.

August 6
The Federal Voting Rights Act prohibits denying anyone the vote on the basis of color or race.

April 11
Fair Housing Act protects against discrimination in housing.

1964   1965   1968

April 16
Martin Luther King Jr. writes his "Letter from the Birmingham Jail," defending nonviolent civil disobedience against unjust laws.

February 21
Malcolm X is shot and killed in New York.

March 7
Six hundred voting rights marchers are attacked by police with clubs and whips on the Edmund Pettus Bridge outside Selma, Alabama. On March 21, about 3,200 marchers head out again on a four-day march to Montgomery in support of voting rights.

August 28
Martin Luther King Jr. delivers his "I Have a Dream" speech at the March on Washington.

September 15
Four girls are killed when a Baptist church in Birmingham, Alabama, is bombed.

June 21
Three civil rights workers are murdered outside Philadelphia, Mississippi.

April 4
Martin Luther King Jr. is slain in Memphis, Tennessee.

1963   1964   1965   1968

the burning bus. A second group encountered an angry mob at the bus station in Birmingham and was severely beaten with baseball bats and iron pipes. When it became clear that police protection would not be forthcoming, the Freedom Riders abandoned the trip and regrouped in Nashville. After much internal debate, they decided to continue the rides.

Following more violence in Montgomery, President Kennedy intervened and his brother Robert Kennedy, the attorney general, worked out a deal: the Freedom Riders would receive police protection, federal troops would not intervene, and they would face the local courts upon their arrest for "disturbing the peace." The Freedom Rides continued throughout the summer. Their actions successfully drew national attention to the continuing resistance in the South to desegregation rulings, forced the Kennedy administration to take a stand on this issue, and led to a stronger Interstate Commerce Commission ruling banning segregation in interstate travel.[51]

The next significant events occurred in Birmingham, Alabama, in 1963. Birmingham had more racial violence than any southern city, with 18 unsolved bombings of black churches and homes in a six-year period. The city had closed its parks and golf courses rather than integrate them, and there was no progress on

Left, a 15-year-old civil rights demonstrator, defying an anti-parade ordinance, is attacked by a police dog in Birmingham, Alabama, on May 3, 1963. Reactions against this police brutality helped spur Congress and the president to enact civil rights legislation. Three months later, civil rights leader Martin Luther King Jr. (right) waves to supporters from the steps of the Lincoln Memorial in Washington, D.C. The March on Washington drew an estimated 250,000 people, who heard King deliver his famous "I Have a Dream" speech.

integrating the local schools. A leading supporter of integration had been castrated to intimidate other blacks who might advocate integration. The city's police chief, "Bull" Connor, was a strong segregationist who had allowed the attacks on the Freedom Riders. During a peaceful protest in April 1963, Martin Luther King Jr. and many others were arrested. While in solitary confinement, King wrote his now-famous "Letter from Birmingham Jail," an eloquent statement of the principles of nonviolent civil disobedience.

The letter was a response to white religious leaders who had told King in a newspaper ad that his actions were "unwise and untimely" and that "when rights are consistently denied, a cause should be pressed in the courts and in negotiations among local leaders, and not in the streets." King responded with a justification for civil disobedience, writing that everyone had an obligation to follow just laws but an equal obligation to break unjust laws.

King also laid out the four steps of nonviolent campaigns: (1) collection of the facts to determine whether injustices are alive; (2) negotiation with white leaders to change the injustices; (3) self-purification, which involved training to make sure that the civil rights protesters would be able to endure the abuse that they would receive; and (4) direct action (for example, sit-ins and marches) to create the environment in which change could occur, but always in a nonviolent manner. By following these steps, civil rights protesters ensured that their social movement would draw attention to their cause while turning public opinion against their opponents' violent tactics.

Following King's release from jail, the situation escalated. The protest leaders decided to use children in the next round of demonstrations. After more than 1,000 children were arrested and the jails were overflowing, the police turned fire hoses and police dogs on children who were trying to continue their march. Media coverage of the incident turned the tide of public opinion in favor of the marchers as the country expressed outrage over the violence in Birmingham. Similar protests occurred throughout the South, with more than 1,000 actions in over 100 different southern cities and more than 20,000 people arrested throughout the summer. The demonstration culminated in August 1963, when 250,000 people participated in the March on Washington. King delivered his famous "I Have a Dream" speech and civil rights leaders pressured congressional leaders to pass civil rights legislation.

Protest Today After King's and others' nonviolent protests produced significant successes, mass protest became the preferred tool of many social movements for civil rights and other causes. Vietnam War protesters marched on Washington by the hundreds of thousands in the late 1960s and early 1970s. The women's rights, gay rights, and environmental movements have staged many mass demonstrations in Washington and other major cities. The largest single day of protest in the United States was the Women's March on January 21, 2017, which drew an estimated 4.2 million people in 654 American cities and another 300,000 in 261 cities around the world to protest the election of Donald Trump and call attention to issues concerning women's rights, health care, and immigration reform.[52]

Social movements may also use direct action, rather than mass protests, to advance their causes, as was the case with the protests against the Dakota Access Pipeline in 2016–2017. When an oil pipeline was approved stretching from North Dakota to southern Illinois, Native Americans from the nearby Standing Rock Indian Reservation objected on the grounds that the pipeline's route under the Missouri River posed a threat to their sources of clean water and to their ancient burial grounds. Thousands of protesters occupied the construction site for months in an effort to stop the pipeline, but ultimately law-enforcement officers cleared the protesters with water cannons, tear gas, and rubber bullets. In December 2016, President Obama issued an executive order requiring an environmental impact statement for the part of the pipeline that was to go under the river. However, President Trump overturned that order, and the pipeline was completed in May 2017.[53]

The tools of social movements have evolved in recent years to combine the power of social media with mass protest. #BlackLivesMatter started in 2013 on social media but has since expanded to organize mass protests against police killings in many cities across the country. Black Lives Matter is a large, decentralized movement that is not organized under a traditional hierarchy or national leadership. Black Lives Matter activists have thus used a broad range of tactics to raise awareness and put pressure on police departments to change their policies, including marches, "die-ins" (protests in which participants block traffic by lying in the street), and social media campaigns. Many police departments have responded to the organization's concerns about excessive police violence and a lack of accountability by adopting new policies, such as requiring police officers to wear body cameras.[54] The cause received a boost in 2017 when many NFL players kneeled during the playing of the national anthem before games to call attention to racially biased policing and police violence. President Trump pressured NFL owners to force the players to stand, saying that

After King's and others' nonviolent protests produced significant successes, mass protests became the preferred tool of many social movements, such as the Women's March on Washington (left) and Black Lives Matter (right).

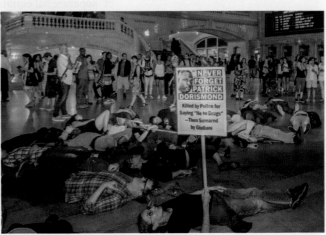

their actions disrespected the flag and the military personnel who serve the country. However, some players continued their protest throughout the season.[55] For the 2018 season, NFL owners required that protesting players remain in the locker room for the national anthem.

The legacy of the civil rights movement has been not only to help change unjust laws but also to provide a new tool for political action across a broad range of policy areas. By putting pressure on political leaders through direct, nonviolent protest, millions of Americans have had their voices heard.

The courts

The Supreme Court has played an important role in defining civil rights, including those pushed for by the social movements just discussed. In the mid-twentieth century, the justices moved away from the "separate but equal" doctrine, required the desegregation of public schools, and upheld landmark civil rights legislation passed by Congress. More recently, they have expanded civil rights for women and the LGBTQ community, but they also have endorsed a color-blind position that some see as a movement away from protecting civil rights.

Challenging "Separate but Equal" in Education In the 1930s, the NAACP, which was established to fight for equal rights for black people, started a concerted effort to nibble away at the "separate but equal" doctrine. Rather than tackling segregation head-on, the NAACP first challenged an aspect of segregation that would be familiar to the Supreme Court justices: the ways in which states kept blacks out of all-white law schools. Another strategy was to challenge admissions practices in law schools outside the Deep South to demonstrate that segregation was not just a "southern problem" and to raise the chances for compliance with favorable Court decisions. A young NAACP attorney named Thurgood Marshall (who later became the first African-American Supreme Court justice) argued that the University of Maryland's practice of sending black students to out-of-state law schools rather than admitting them to the university's all-white law school violated the black students' civil rights. (The state gave black students a $200 scholarship, which did not cover the costs of tuition and travel and was not available to all black students who wanted to attend law school.) In 1936, the circuit court and subsequently the Maryland appeals court rejected this arrangement and ordered that black students be admitted to the University of Maryland law school.[56]

Over the next 15 years, a series of successful lawsuits slowly chipped away at the idea of "separate but equal." After these victories, there was a debate within the NAACP over whether to continue the case-by-case approach against the "separate but equal" doctrine or to directly challenge the principle itself. The latter approach was risky because it was unclear if the Court was ready to take this bold step, and defeat in the Court would set back the movement. However, the signals increasingly indicated that the Supreme Court was ready to strike down the "separate but equal" doctrine. In addition to the law school cases, in 1948 the Court ruled that "restrictive covenants"— clauses in real estate contracts that prevented a property owner from selling to an African American—could not be enforced by state or local courts because the Fourteenth Amendment prohibited the states from denying blacks the "equal protection of the laws."[57]

This application of the Fourteenth Amendment was expanded in the landmark ruling *Brown v. Board of Education*. The case arrived on the Court's docket in 1951, was postponed for argument until after the 1952 election, and then was re-argued in

December 1953. The ruling was postponed for so long because the Court was keenly aware of the firestorm that would ensue. In its unanimous decision, the Court ruled: "In the field of public education, the doctrine of separate but equal has no place. Separate educational facilities are inherently unequal, depriving the plaintiffs of the equal protection of the laws. Segregated facilities may generate in black children a feeling of inferiority that may affect their hearts and minds in a way unlikely ever to be undone."[58] The case was significant not only because it required all public schools in the United States to desegregate but also because it used the equal protection clause of the Fourteenth Amendment in a way that had potentially far-reaching consequences.

Nonetheless, the decision was limited because it focused on segregation in schools rather than segregation more generally and it focused on the psychological damage done to black schoolchildren through segregation rather than on the broader claim that racial classification itself was not allowed by the Constitution. Chief Justice Earl Warren wanted a unanimous vote and knew that two justices would not support a broader ruling that would overturn *Plessy v. Ferguson* and rule segregation unconstitutional in all contexts. Even if segregation in other public places still was legal, the *Brown* ruling provided an important boost to the civil rights movement.

The Push to Desegregate Schools In 1955, *Brown v. Board of Education II* addressed the implementation of desegregation and required the states to "desegregate with all deliberate speed."[59] The odd choice of words, "all deliberate speed," was read as a signal by southerners that they could take their time with desegregation. The phrase does seem to be contradictory: being deliberate does not usually involve being speedy. Southern states engaged in "massive resistance" to the desegregation order, as articulated by Harry F. Byrd, the segregationist senator from Virginia. In some cases, they even closed public schools rather than integrate them—and then reopened the schools as "private" segregated schools for which the white students received government vouchers. However, Maryland, Kentucky, Tennessee, Missouri, and the District of Columbia desegregated their schools within two years.

Eight years after *Brown I*, little had changed in the Deep South: fewer than 1 percent of black children attended school with white children.[60] Through the 1960s, the courts had to battle against continued resistance to integration. In 1971, the Court shifted its focus from **de jure** segregation (segregation mandated by law) to **de facto** segregation (segregation that existed because of segregated housing patterns) and approved school busing as a tool to integrate schools.[61] This approach was extremely controversial. The Court almost immediately limited the application of busing by ruling in a Detroit case that busing could not go beyond the boundaries of a city's school district—that is, students did not have to be bused from suburbs to cities—unless it could be shown that the school district's lines were drawn in an intentionally discriminatory way.[62] This rule encouraged "white flight" from the cities to the suburbs in response to court-ordered busing.

In 2007, in perhaps the most important decision on race in education since *Brown*, the Court invalidated voluntary desegregation plans implemented by public school districts in Seattle and Louisville. Both districts set goals for racial diversity and denied school assignment requests if they tipped the racial balance above or below certain thresholds. In a ringing endorsement of the color-blind approach, the majority opinion said: "The way to stop discrimination on the basis of race is to stop discriminating on the basis of race." In this case, the discrimination was against white students who wanted to be in schools with few minority students, rather than black students who wanted to be in integrated schools.[63]

de jure
Relating to actions or circumstances that occur "by law," such as the legally enforced segregation of schools in the American South before the 1960s.

de facto
Relating to actions or circumstances that occur outside the law or "by fact," such as the segregation of schools that resulted from housing patterns and other factors rather than from laws.

Busing students from one school district to another has been controversial since the 1960s. In Boston in the 1970s, many black students who were bused into white districts needed police protection against protests.

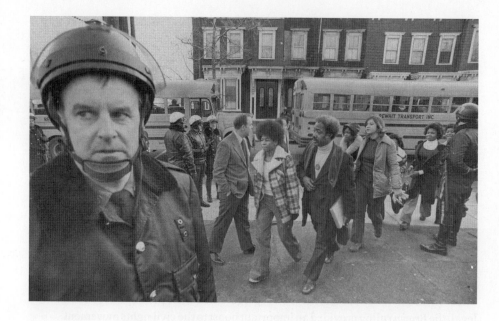

disparate impact standard
The idea that discrimination exists if a practice has a negative effect on a specific group, whether or not this effect was intentional.

Expanding Civil Rights for African Americans Other significant rulings in the 1960s struck down state laws that forbade interracial marriages (16 states had such laws), upheld all significant parts of the Civil Rights Act, and upheld and expanded the scope of the Voting Rights Act (VRA; these important laws will be discussed in the next section). In central cases, the justices ruled that Congress had the power to eliminate segregation in public places, such as restaurants and hotels, under the commerce clause of the Constitution.

The first case involved a hotel in Atlanta that was close to an interstate highway, advertised extensively on the highway, and had a clientele that was about 75 percent from out of state. The Court ruled that this establishment was clearly engaging in interstate commerce, so Congress had the right to regulate it.[64] In the second case, "almost all, if not all," of the patrons of Ollie's Barbecue in Birmingham, Alabama, were local. However, the Court pointed out that meat purchased for the restaurant came from out of state and this constituted 46 percent of the total amount spent on supplies. Therefore, the practice of segregation would place significant burdens on "the interstate flow of food and upon the movement of products generally."[65]

The next important area of cases was in employment law. In 1971, the Court ruled that employment tests, such as written exams or general aptitude tests, that are not related to job performance and that discriminate against blacks violate the 1964 Civil Rights Act.[66] This **disparate impact standard** of discrimination means that if the employment practice has a bad *effect* on a racial group, it doesn't matter whether or not the discrimination is *intended*. The Supreme Court and Congress have gone back and forth in defining this concept, but it is still important in workplace discrimination suits. (See Nuts & Bolts 5.1 for the legal definition of race-based workplace discrimination.)

The Color-Blind Court and Judicial Activism Recently, the Supreme Court has been gradually imposing a "color-blind jurisprudence" over a range of issues—that is, the Court has reasoned that race should not be considered in determining the outcome of certain kinds of cases. One significant area was the 1992 racial redistricting in which 15 new U.S. House districts were drawn to help elect African Americans and 10 new districts were drawn to help elect Latino members. The resulting dramatic change in

Race-Related Discrimination as Defined by the Equal Employment Opportunity Commission

Race/Color Discrimination

Race discrimination involves treating someone (an applicant or employee) unfavorably because he/she is of a certain race or because of personal characteristics associated with race (such as hair texture, skin color, or certain facial features). Color discrimination involves treating someone unfavorably because of skin color complexion. . . . Discrimination can occur when the victim and the person who inflicted the discrimination are the same race or color.

Race/Color Discrimination and Work Situations

The law forbids discrimination when it comes to any aspect of employment, including hiring, firing, pay, job assignments, promotions, layoff, training, fringe benefits, and any other term or condition of employment.

Race/Color Discrimination and Harassment

It is unlawful to harass a person because of that person's race or color. Harassment can include, for example, racial slurs, offensive or derogatory remarks about a person's race or color, or the display of racially offensive symbols. Although the law doesn't prohibit simple teasing, offhand comments, or isolated incidents that are not very serious, harassment is illegal when it is so frequent or severe that it creates a hostile or offensive work environment or when it results in an adverse employment decision (such as the victim being fired or demoted). The harasser can be the victim's supervisor, a supervisor in another area, a coworker, or someone who is not an employee of the employer, such as a client or customer.

Race/Color Discrimination and Employment Policies/Practices

An employment policy or practice that applies to everyone, regardless of race or color, can be illegal if it has a negative impact on the employment of people of a particular race or color and is not job-related and necessary to the operation of the business.

Source: U.S. Equal Employment Opportunity Commission, "Race/Color Discrimination," www.eeoc.gov (accessed 10/4/12).

the number of minorities in Congress (an increase greater than 50 percent) was rooted in the 1982 amendments to the VRA. Instead of mandating a fair *process*, this law and subsequent interpretation by the Supreme Court mandated that minorities have an "equal opportunity" to "elect representatives of their choice" when their numbers and configuration permit. As a result, the legislative redistricting process now had to avoid discriminatory *results* rather than being concerned only with discriminatory *intent*.

However, in a series of decisions starting with the 1993 landmark case *Shaw v. Reno*, the Supreme Court's adherence to a color-blind jurisprudence has thrown the constitutionality of black-majority districts into doubt. The Court has ruled that black-majority districts are legal as long as they are "done right."[67] However, it has consistently held that if race is the predominant factor in drawing district lines, the districts are unconstitutional because they violate the equal protection clause of the Fourteenth Amendment for the white plaintiffs in these cases. Based on this reasoning, black-majority districts in North Carolina, Georgia, Louisiana, Virginia, Texas, and Florida have been found to be unconstitutional. In 2001, the Court upheld the re-drawn 12th District in North Carolina, which no longer was a black-majority district, arguing that when race and partisanship are so intertwined—as they are when 90 percent of African Americans vote for a Democratic candidate—plaintiffs cannot assume that

African Americans were placed together for racial reasons. This ruling opens the door for a greater consideration of race than had been allowed in the previous cases.[68] In 2017, the Court struck down districting plans in North Carolina and Virginia for packing African Americans into districts, thus diluting their ability to have an equal opportunity to elect candidates of their choice.[69] However, racial redistricting remains an unsettled area of the law. The Court also struck down an important part of the 1965 VRA in a 2013 ruling. This case concerned the "coverage formula" that determines which states have to get approval from the Justice Department before implementing changes in an election law or practice (such as redistricting or moving the location of a polling place). This "preclearance" provision of the law was viewed as one of the best ways to stop discriminatory voting practices because it could prevent them before they were implemented, rather than having to wait until they went into effect to challenge them. The Court ruled that the coverage formula was an unconstitutional burden on the covered states and was a violation of the Tenth Amendment.[70]

The racial redistricting and voting rights cases illustrate that the Supreme Court is increasingly activist in issues involving civil rights: it is generally unwilling to defer to the other branches of government, and will assert its view of discrimination and equal protection regardless of what the other branches think (see Chapter 14 for a broader discussion of judicial activism). In some periods, like the 1950s and 1960s, judicial activism has served to further civil rights. More recently, it has served to limit them.

Women's Rights The Supreme Court has also been central in shaping women's civil rights. Until relatively recently, the Court did not apply the Constitution to protect women's rights, despite the Fourteenth Amendment's language that states may not deny any *person* the equal protection of the laws. Apparently, women were not regarded as people when it came to political and economic rights in the nineteenth and early twentieth centuries. These protectionist notions were finally rejected in three cases between 1971 and 1976, when the Court made it much more difficult for states to treat men and women differently.

The first case involved an Idaho state law that gave a man priority over a woman when they were otherwise equally entitled to execute a person's estate. This law was justified on the "reasonable" grounds that it reduced the state courts' workload by having an automatic rule that would limit challenges. But the Court ruled that the law was arbitrary, did not meet the "reasonableness" test, and therefore violated the woman's equal protection rights under the Fourteenth Amendment.[71] The second case involved a female air force officer who wanted to count her husband as a dependent for purposes of health and housing benefits. Under the law at the time, a military man could automatically count his wife as a dependent, but a woman could claim her husband only if she brought in more than half the family income. The Court struck down this practice, saying protectionist laws, "in practical effect, put women not on a pedestal, but in a cage."[72]

rational basis test
The use of evidence to suggest that differences in the behavior of two groups can rationalize unequal treatment of these groups.

These two cases relied on the **rational basis test** for discrimination between men and women (which evolved from the reasonableness test). Along with the strict scrutiny test (see Chapter 4), it allows the Fourteenth Amendment to be applied differently to particular categories of people. Under the rational basis test, states can discriminate against a group of people as long as there is a "rational basis" for the state law in question. Today, for example, states can pass drinking laws that allow only those who are 21 and older to drink on the grounds that traffic fatalities will be lower with that drinking age rather than under a law that allows 18-year-olds to drink.

The strict scrutiny test gives racial minorities the strongest protection as the "suspect classification" under the Fourteenth Amendment, but it has not been applied to women. This test stipulates that there must be a "compelling state interest" to discriminate among people if race is involved. The idea of a suspect classification was first used in a case involving the internment of Japanese Americans during World War II. In a controversial ruling, the Court said that the internment camps were justified on national security grounds, making it one of the few instances in which racial classification has survived strict scrutiny.[73] However, as noted earlier, the Supreme Court overturned this ruling in a 2018 case involving President Trump's travel ban.[74]

In 1976, the Court established a third test, the intermediate scrutiny test (see Chapter 4), in a case involving the drinking age. In the early 1970s, some states had a lower drinking age for women than for men on the "rational basis" that 18- to 20-year-old women are more mature than men of that age. (States argued that women were less likely to be drunk drivers and less likely to abuse alcohol than men are.) The new intermediate scrutiny standard meant that the government's policy must be "substantially related" to an "important government objective" to justify the unequal treatment of men and women, so the law was struck down.[75]

The intermediate scrutiny test gives women stronger protections than the rational basis test, but it is not as strong as strict scrutiny (see How It Works: Civil Rights). To use the legal jargon, the gender distinction would have to serve an "important government objective," but not a "compelling state interest," in order to withstand intermediate scrutiny.

In many instances, as with the Idaho case, the rights of women were strengthened by this new standard of equal protection. However, in other instances women may actually be more restricted by being treated the same as men. For example, in the drinking age case, instead of dropping the drinking age for men to 18, states raised the age for women to 21. Similarly, the Court struck down an Alabama divorce law in which husbands but not wives could be ordered to pay alimony.[76] Arguably, women would have been better off in these two specific instances under the old discriminatory laws (because they could drink at 18 instead of 21 and did not have to pay alimony in some states). However, the more aggressive application of the Fourteenth Amendment for women was an important step in providing them with the equal protection of the laws, as clearly shown in a Court decision that struck down the Virginia Military Institute's (VMI's) male-only admission policy. The majority opinion stated that VMI violated the Fourteenth Amendment's equal protection clause because it failed to show an "exceedingly persuasive justification" for its sex-biased admissions policy.[77]

An important gender-equality case in 2017 concerned the law for determining the citizenship of children born overseas to an unmarried couple when one parent is a citizen and the other is not. Federal law requires a single father to have resided in the United States for five years prior to his child's birth in order for that child to have U.S. citizenship, while a child born overseas to a single American mother would be granted U.S. citizenship if the mother had lived continuously in the United States for just one year prior to the child's birth. The Court ruled that this gender-based distinction was unconstitutional. As with earlier cases involving the drinking age and alimony, the remedy in this case was to make things worse for women in the short term—that is, rather than reducing the residency requirement for men from five years to one, the Court increased it for women to match the longer period for men. However, supporters of women's rights applauded the decision for what it means for gender equality in the long term. One expert on women's rights noted that the gender difference in this law was rooted in outdated notions of parental responsibilities, and argued, "Romantic ideals about the uniqueness of motherhood perpetuate the notion that women, rather than men, should assume responsibility for children. They also contribute to negative stereotypes that diminish women as workers, wage earners, and participants in public life."[78]

Civil Rights

Cases Involving "Suspect Classification" (race, ethnicity, creed, or national origin)	**Cases Involving Sex or Gender Equality**	**Cases Involving Age, Economic Status, or Other Criteria**

Strict Scrutiny Test ## Intermediate Scrutiny Test ## Rational Basis Test

1. Is unequal treatment justified by a **"compelling state interest"**?

1. Is the discriminatory policy **"substantially related"** to an **"important government objective"**?

1. Is the law **rationally related to furthering** a legitimate government interest?

yes **no** → **discrimination is illegal**

yes **no** → **discrimination is illegal**

yes **no** → **discrimination is illegal**

2. Is unequal treatment the **"least restrictive"** option?

2. Is the discrimination **not substantially broader** than it needs to be to protect the important government interest?

2. Does the policy avoid **"arbitrary, capricious, or deliberate"** discrimination?

yes **no** → **discrimination is illegal**

yes **no** → **discrimination is illegal**

yes **no** → **discrimination is illegal**

Some discrimination based on gender is permitted, but this test is harder to pass than the rational basis test applied to gender cases in the past.

This is the easiest hurdle for a law or policy to pass.

Very few cases meet this standard.

→ **discrimination is legal** ←

Evaluating Discrimination Cases

 ## Strict Scrutiny Test

Case 1:

The University of Michigan Law School's "holistic" race-conscious admissions policy is designed to promote diversity.

Case 2:

The University of Michigan's more rigid race-conscious undergraduate admissions policy was designed to promote diversity.

The Court asked...

1. Is unequal treatment justified by a "compelling state interest"?
2. Is unequal treatment the "least restrictive" option?

The Court said...

In Case 1, **discrimination is OK.** In *Grutter v. Bollinger* (2003), the Court ruled that the state's interest in **racial diversity in higher education was compelling,** and that this specific admissions policy was narrowly tailored. This was affirmed in *Fisher v. Univ. of Texas* (2016).

In Case 2, **discrimination is not OK.** In *Gratz v. Bollinger* (2003), the Court **struck down Michigan's undergraduate admissions policy** for not being narrowly tailored.

Intermediate Scrutiny Test

Case 1:

A California state law says that men—but not women—can be guilty of statutory rape.

Case 2:

The Virginia Military Institute maintained a male-only admissions policy.

The Court asked...

1. Is the discriminatory policy "substantially related" to an "important government objective"?
2. Is the discrimination not substantially broader than it needs to be to to protect the important government interest?

The Court said...

In Case 1, **discrimination is OK.** In *Michael M. v. Superior Court* (1981), the Court found that the state had a **strong interest in preventing illegitimate pregnancy** and in punishing only the participant who, by nature, suffers few of the consequences of his conduct.

In Case 2, **discrimination is not OK.** In *United States v. Virginia* (1996), the Court **struck down the Virginia Military Institute's policy** as a violation of the equal protection clause of the Fourteenth Amendment.

Rational Basis Test

Case 1:

States have a 21-year-old drinking age that applies equally to men and women.

Case 2:

An Oklahoma law allowed 18- to 20-year-old women—but not men—to buy 3.2% beer.

The Court asked...

1. Is the law rationally related to furthering a legitimate government interest?
2. Does the policy avoid "arbitrary, capricious, or deliberate" discrimination?

The Court said...

In Case 1, **discrimination is OK.** Various state supreme courts have upheld these laws on the rational basis that **the laws may prevent drunk driving among 18- to 20-year-olds.**

In Case 2, **discrimination is not OK.** In *Craig v. Boren* (1976), the Court **struck down this law,** rejecting the rational basis that Oklahoma had claimed and instead applying intermediate scrutiny.

 ## Critical Thinking

1. **Is it easier for the government to discriminate against** someone based on age or race? Why?

2. **What is the standard used by the Court if the state wants** to make distinctions between people based on race? Under what circumstances and in what scenarios is discrimination based on race legal?

Two other areas where the Supreme Court has helped advance women's rights are affirmative action and protection against sexual harassment. In 1987, the Court approved affirmative action in a case involving a woman who was promoted over a man despite the fact that he had scored slightly higher than she did on a test. The Court ruled that the promotion was acceptable to make up for past discrimination.[79] And in 1993 the Court made it easier to sue employers for sexual harassment, saying that a woman did not have to reach the point of a nervous breakdown before claiming that she was being harassed; it was enough to demonstrate a pattern of "repeated and unwanted" behavior that created a "hostile workplace environment."[80] Later rulings stated that if a single act is flagrant, the conduct does not have to be repeated to create a hostile environment.

The issues of sexual harassment exploded on the national scene in October 2017 when Ashley Judd, Angelina Jolie, Gwyneth Paltrow, and Rose McGowan alleged that Hollywood mogul Harvey Weinstein sexually assaulted them. Ten days later, actress Alyssa Milano encouraged other women to share their stories with the hashtag #MeToo. Within 24 hours, the messages had been retweeted 500,000 times and shared in 12 million posts on Facebook. Allegations of sexual harassment or assault have ended the careers of Fox News anchor Bill O'Reilly, Senator Al Franken, comedian Bill Cosby, Representative John Conyers, Alabama Senate nominee Roy Moore, morning show anchors Matt Lauer and Charlie Rose, Olympic gymnast doctor Lawrence G. Nassar, public radio star Garrison Keillor, celebrity chef Mario Batali, conductor James Levine, actor Kevin Spacey, and many more. *Time* magazine named "The Silence Breakers" their "person of the year" for 2017 for their courage in bringing attention to this problem.[81]

While the court of public opinion and the actual courts have played a central role in bringing justice to the victims of sexual assault and harassment, the Supreme Court has been less sympathetic to plaintiffs in cases involving pay discrimination. Lilly Ledbetter sued Goodyear Tire & Rubber Company because she had received lower pay than men doing the same work over a 20-year period, which she claimed was gender discrimination. The Court rejected her claim, saying that she did not meet the time limit required by law, as the discrimination must have occurred within 180 days of the claim. (This overturned the long-standing policy of the EEOC, which held that each new paycheck restarted the 180-day clock as a new act of discrimination.)[82] Dissenters pointed out that pay discrimination usually occurs in small increments over long periods, so it would be impossible to recognize unequal pay within 180 days of an initial paycheck. Furthermore, workers do not have access to information about fellow workers' pay, so it would be almost impossible to meet the standard set by the Court. Congress restored the old standard in January 2009 by passing the Lilly Ledbetter Fair Pay Act. But as Figure 5.5 shows, significant pay disparities between men and women remain throughout much of the United States. Early in 2016, President Obama issued an executive order requiring companies to report to the federal government what they pay employees by race, gender, and ethnicity. He said, "Women are not getting the fair shot that we believe every single American deserves."[83]

The largest sexual discrimination lawsuit in the nation's history was filed in 2001 against Walmart on behalf of 1.5 million women who had worked at Walmart since 1998. Among other things, the plaintiffs alleged the following:

- Over objections from a female executive, senior management regularly referred to female store employees as "little Janie Qs" and "girls."
- A Sam's Club (Walmart's warehouse retail chain) manager in California told another woman that she should "doll up" to get promoted.
- Managers have repeatedly told female employees that men "need to be paid more than women because they have families to support."
- A male manager in South Carolina told a female employee that "God made Adam first, so women would always be second to men."

DID YOU KNOW?

Women working full-time earn

$0.78

compared to every dollar earned by men.
Source: WhiteHouse.gov

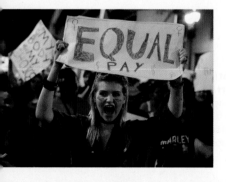

On International Women's Day 2017, demonstrations brought attention to the pay disparity between men and women.

FIGURE 5.5

Lifetime Wage Gap for Women as Compared to Men

There is a substantial difference between women's and men's earnings in the United States. What could account for this variation? How much do you think it has to do with levels of discrimination, and how much with differences in the nature of the jobs that men and women hold?

Sources: "The Lifetime Wage Gap, State by State," National Women's Law Center, based on U.S. Census 2016 American Community Survey Data, https://nwlc.org/resources/the-lifetime-wage-gap-state-by-state (accessed 6/15/18).

Lifetime wage gap is

- Less than $250,000
- Between $250,000 and $350,000
- Between $350,000 and $425,000
- Between $425,000 and $500,000
- Greater than $500,000

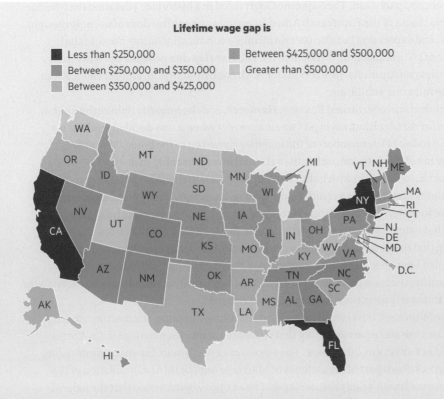

- A female personnel manager in Florida was told by her manager that men were paid more than women because "men are here to make a career and women aren't. Retail is for housewives who just need to earn extra money."[84]

But in 2011 the Court ruled that the class-action lawsuit was not valid because there was no "convincing proof of a companywide discriminatory pay and promotion policy." That is, women would have to prove discrimination individually, not as a group. Civil rights experts said this was the "death knell" for class-action lawsuits seeking monetary damages for discrimination.[85]

Gay Rights The Supreme Court has a similarly mixed record on gay rights. The Court's decisions in early cases were not supportive of gay rights. One of the first cases concerned Georgia's law banning sodomy. As we discussed in Chapter 4, the Supreme Court ruled in *Bowers v. Hardwick* (1986) that homosexual behavior was not protected by the Constitution and that state laws banning it could be justified under the most lenient rational basis test.[86]

After cases where it sidestepped the issue, the Court first endorsed civil rights for gays in 1996. Here the Court struck down an amendment to the Colorado state constitution that would have prevented gays from suing for discrimination in employment or housing. The Court said that the state amendment violated gays' equal protection rights because it "withdrew from homosexuals, but no others, specific legal protection from the injuries caused by discrimination."[87] The Court rejected the state's "rational basis" arguments and came close to putting gays in the "suspect classification" that had been reserved for racial and ethnic minorities.

An important ruling came in 2003 in a case involving two Houston men. As we discussed in Chapter 4, John Geddes Lawrence and Tyron Garner were prosecuted for same-sex sodomy (which was illegal in Texas) after police found them having sex in

The Constitution promises liberty to all within its reach ... [and] extend[s] to certain personal choices central to individual dignity and autonomy, including intimate choices that define personal identity and beliefs.

—Supreme Court's majority opinion in *Obergefell v. Hodges*

Lawrence's apartment. The Supreme Court ruled in a historic 6–3 decision that the due process clause of the Fourteenth Amendment guarantees freedom of not only thought, belief, and expression but also certain intimate conduct (including homosexual relations). This reasoning is rooted in the **substantive due process doctrine** that underlies constitutional protections for birth control, abortion, and decisions about how to raise one's children.

The decision overturned *Bowers v. Hardwick*, and the majority opinion had harsh words for that decision, saying it "was not correct when it was decided, and it is not correct today." Five members of the majority signed on to the broad "due process" reasoning of the decision, rather than the narrower reasoning in Justice O'Connor's concurring opinion, in which she said that the decision should apply only to the four states that treated gays differently (that is, banning sodomy for homosexuals but not for heterosexuals). With the broader due process logic, a total of 13 state laws that banned sodomy were struck down. Justice Scalia wrote a strong dissent, saying that the decision was "the product of a court that has largely signed on to the so-called homosexual agenda" and warned that the ruling "will have far-reaching implications beyond this case." He predicted that the ruling would serve as the basis for constitutional protections for same-sex marriage.[88]

The Supreme Court issued two important rulings on same-sex marriage in 2013. The first case was a narrow ruling that reinstated same-sex marriage in California but did not affect any other state. The second case was a more far-reaching decision that struck down part of the Defense of Marriage Act (DOMA) as a violation of the Fifth Amendment's due process clause. The majority opinion said that the federal government cannot deny benefits to same-sex couples who are legally married under state law. The gradual movement toward endorsing same-sex marriage culminated in 2015 in the landmark ruling *Obergefell v. Hodges*, which legalized same-sex marriage in all 50 states.[89] (For more on the Supreme Court's ruling in this case, see How It Works: The Court System in Chapter 14.) The 5–4 ruling said that the fundamental right to marry is guaranteed by both the due process clause and the equal protection clause of the Fourteenth Amendment.

This section demonstrates that the courts can be both a strong advocate of and an impediment to civil rights. In general, however, the courts have a limited *independent* impact on policy. That is, as the school desegregation cases clearly demonstrate, the courts must rely on the other branches of government to carry out their decisions.

Congress

Congress has provided the basis for today's protection of civil rights through a series of laws that were enacted starting in the 1960s. Applying to racial and ethnic minorities and to women, these laws attempted to ensure that there is a "level playing field" of equal opportunity.

Key Early Legislation The bedrock of equal protection that exists today stems from landmark legislation passed by Congress in the 1960s—the 1964 Civil Rights Act, the 1965 VRA, and the 1968 Fair Housing Act. President Kennedy was slow to seek civil rights legislation for fear of alienating southern Democrats. The events in Birmingham prompted him to act, but he was assassinated before the legislation was passed. President Lyndon Johnson, a former segregationist, helped push through the Civil Rights Act when he became president. The act barred discrimination in employment based on race, sex, religion, or national origin; banned segregation in public places; and established the EEOC as the enforcement agency for the legislation.

DID YOU KNOW?

66.2%
of African Americans voted in 2012 compared with 64.1 percent of whites (but African-American turnout was slightly lower than whites' turnout in 2016).
Source: Pew Research Center

One of the southern opponents of the legislation inserted the language referring to sex, thinking that it would defeat the bill (assuming, perhaps, that there would be a majority coalition of male chauvinists and segregationists), but it became law anyway.

The VRA of 1965 eliminated direct obstacles to minority voting in the South, such as discriminatory literacy tests and other voter registration tests, and also provided the means to enforce the law: federal marshals were charged with overseeing elections in the South. After its passage, President Johnson hailed the VRA as a "triumph for freedom as huge as any ever won on any battlefield."[90] The VRA, which is often cited as one of the most significant pieces of civil rights legislation in our nation's history,[91] precipitated an explosion in black political participation in the South. The most dramatic gains came in Mississippi, where black registration increased from 6.7 percent before the VRA to 59.8 percent in 1967. As one political scientist noted, "The act simply overwhelmed the major bulwarks of the disenfranchising system. In the seven states originally covered, black registration increased from 29.3 percent in March 1965, to 56.6 percent in 1971–1972; the gap between black and white registration rates narrowed from 44.1 percentage points to 11.2."[92]

The last piece of landmark legislation, the Fair Housing Act of 1968, barred discrimination in the rental or sale of a home based on race, sex, religion, and national origin. Important amendments to the law enacted in 1988 added disability and familial status (having children under age 18) to the list of protected categories, provided new administrative enforcement mechanisms, and expanded Justice Department jurisdiction to bring suit on behalf of victims in federal district courts.[93]

There have been many other important amendments to civil rights laws since the 1960s. The 1975 amendments to the VRA extended coverage of many of the law's provisions to language minorities, guaranteeing that registration and voting materials are made available to voters in their native language in certain districts with large numbers of citizens who are not proficient in English. The 1982 VRA amendments extended important provisions of the law for 25 years and made it easier to bring a lawsuit under the act. The 1991 Civil Rights Act overruled or altered parts of 12 Supreme Court decisions that had eroded the initial intent of the 1964 civil rights legislation. It also expanded earlier legislation and increased the costs to employers for intentional, illegal discrimination. In 2006, Congress voted to extend the VRA for another 25 years.

Protections for Women Women have also received extensive protection through legislation. As noted, the section of the Civil Rights Act that bars discrimination based on gender, Title VII, was almost an accidental part of the bill (it was included by an opponent to the legislation). Indeed, the first executive director of the EEOC would not enforce the gender part of the law because it was a "fluke." In 1966, the National Organization for Women (NOW) was formed to push for enforcement of the law. Its members convinced President Johnson to sign an executive order that eliminated sex discrimination in federal agencies and among federal contractors, but the order was difficult to enforce. Finally, in 1970, the EEOC started enforcing the law. Before long, one-third of all civil rights cases involved sex discrimination, and those numbers have remained high in recent years (see Figure 5.6).

Congress passed the next piece of important legislation for women in 1972: Title IX of the Education Amendments, which prohibits sex discrimination in institutions that receive federal funds. The law has had the greatest impact in women's sports. In the 1960s and 1970s, opportunities for women to play sports in college or high school were extremely limited. Very few women's scholarships were available at the college level, and budgets for women's sports were tiny compared with the budgets for men's sports. Although it took nearly 30 years to reach parity between men and women, most universities are now in compliance with Title IX. Nonetheless, the law has its critics.

> No person in the United States shall, on the basis of sex, be excluded from participation in, be denied the benefits of, or be subjected to discrimination under any educational program or activity receiving Federal financial assistance.
>
> —Full text of Title IX

Many men's sports, such as baseball, tennis, wrestling, and gymnastics, were cut at universities that had to bring the number of male and female student athletes into rough parity. Critics argued that such cuts were unfair, especially given that the interest in women's sports was not as high. Defenders of the law argue that the gap in interest in women's and men's sports will not change until there is equal opportunity. There is some evidence to support that claim, as interest is increasing in professional women's soccer with the NWSL (National Women's Soccer League) and professional women's basketball with the WNBA (Women's National Basketball Association), as well as in well-established women's professional sports such as golf and tennis.

Another significant legislative effort during this period was the failed Equal Rights Amendment. The amendment was approved by Congress in 1972 and sent to the states for ratification. Its wording was simple: "Equality of rights under the law shall not be denied or abridged by the United States or any state on account of sex." Many states passed it within months, but the process lost momentum and after seven years (the deadline set by Congress for ratification by the states) the amendment fell 3 states short of the 38 states required for adoption. The amendment received a three-year extension from Congress, but it still did not get the additional three states.

In 1994, Congress passed the Violence against Women Act, which allowed women who were the victims of physical abuse and violence to sue in federal court and provided funding for investigating and prosecuting violent crimes against women, for helping the victims of such crimes, and for prevention programs. In 2000, part of the law was overturned by the Supreme Court, which ruled that Congress had exceeded its powers under the commerce clause.[94] Nonetheless, the funding provisions of the act were reauthorized and expanded by Congress in 2000, 2005, and 2013.

FIGURE 5.6

Discrimination Cases Filed with the Equal Employment Opportunity Commission, 2017

Discrimination based on race and color, and discrimination based on sex, are the two types most frequently reported, but there is a significant amount of discrimination based on age and disability as well. What types of discrimination do you think would be most likely to go unreported?

Note: Percentages do not sum to 100 because complaints may be filed in more than one category.

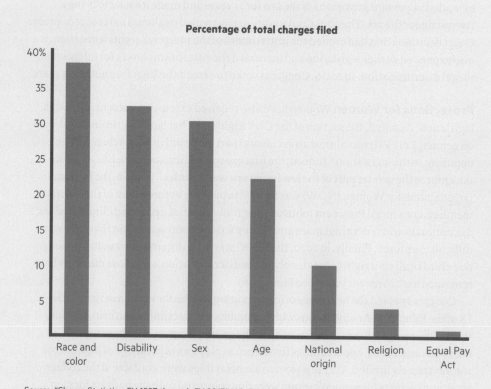

Percentage of total charges filed

Source: "Charge Statistics, FY 1997 through FY 2017," U.S. Equal Employment Opportunity Commission, www.eeoc.gov/eeoc/statistics/enforcement/charges.cfm (accessed 4/13/18).

While many people imagine Title IX as primarily affecting equal funding for college women's sports teams, it also provides important protections for survivors of sexual violence on college campuses. Here, students protest the Education Department's efforts to revise these provisions in February 2017.

Protections for the Disabled and for Gay Rights Yet another important piece of civil rights legislation was the 1990 Americans with Disabilities Act, which provided strong federal protections for the 45 million disabled Americans to prevent workplace discrimination and to provide access to public facilities. This law produced curb cuts in sidewalks, access for wheelchairs on public buses and trains, special seating in sports stadiums, and many other changes that make the daily lives of the disabled a little easier and that provide them with an equal opportunity to participate more fully in society.[95]

Congress's track record in protecting gay rights has not been as strong. In fact, most of the steps taken by Congress have been to restrict rather than expand gay rights. In 1996, Congress passed DOMA to avert the possibility that some liberal states such as Hawaii would allow gay marriage. This act defined marriage as only between a man and woman and barred couples in same-sex marriages from receiving federal insurance or Social Security spousal benefits and from filing joint federal tax returns. Nonetheless, as we have noted, the part of the law depriving same-sex spouses of federal benefits was struck down by the Supreme Court in 2013 and the entire law was overturned in 2015.

In what may represent a change of course, in October 2009 Congress passed the Matthew Shepard and James Byrd Jr. Hate Crimes Prevention Act. This legislation expanded the previous hate-crime laws based on race, color, religion, or national origin to include attacks based on a victim's sexual orientation, gender identity, or mental or physical disability. The law also lifted a requirement that a victim had to be attacked while engaged in a federally protected activity, such as attending school, for it to be a federal hate crime. In signing the bill, President Obama said, "After more than a decade of opposition and delay, we've passed inclusive hate-crimes legislation to help protect our citizens from violence based on what they look like, who they love, how they pray or who they are."[96] The law commemorates the horrific murders of James Byrd Jr., who in 1998 was dragged behind a pickup truck by white supremacists for three miles until his head and right arm were severed, and Matthew Shepard, a gay teenager who in 1998 was beaten by two men, tied to a fence, and left to die. Also, the Employment Non-Discrimination Act, which would prohibit discrimination in employment based on sexual orientation, has been proposed in nearly every Congress since 1994. A version of the bill passed the House in 2007 but died in the Senate.

The president

The mid-century civil rights movement benefited greatly from presidential action. President Truman integrated the armed services in 1948, and President Eisenhower used the National Guard to enforce a court order to integrate Central High School in Little Rock, Arkansas, in 1957. Executive orders by President Kennedy in 1961 and President Johnson in 1965 established affirmative action, and in 1969 Richard Nixon expanded the "goals and numerical ranges" for hiring minorities in the federal government.

The most significant unilateral action taken by a president in the area of civil rights for gays and lesbians was President Clinton's effort to end the ban on gays in the military. Clinton was surprised by the strength of the opposition to his plan, so he ended up crafting a compromise policy of "don't ask, don't tell," which pleased no one. Under this policy, the military would stop actively searching for and discharging gays from the military ranks, and recruits would not need to reveal their sexual orientation. But if the military did find out (without conducting an investigation) that a person was gay, he or she still could be disciplined or discharged.

During the 2008 campaign, President Obama promised to repeal "don't ask, don't tell." Republican filibusters stopped several attempts to change the policy in 2010, but Congress finally passed the Don't Ask, Don't Tell Repeal Act in December 2010 and it went into effect on September 20, 2011. Minutes after the new policy was in place, navy lieutenant Gary Ross and his longtime partner were married in Vermont and Ross became the first openly gay married person in the military.[97] President Obama extended the policy to include transgender service members, but President Trump reversed that policy, tweeting that "the United States Government will not accept or allow transgender individuals to serve in any capacity in the U.S. Military." However, an injunction against the ban was ordered by a federal judge, who said that lawsuits against the ban have a strong chance of prevailing and that the ban "does not appear to be supported by any facts."[98] In March 2018, Trump issued a new executive order with essentially the same ban (but with a version of "don't ask, don't tell"), but that order was also struck down by a federal judge, pending a full trial.[99]

Recent presidential candidates have generally made civil rights policy a low priority, which means that it is less likely that significant and dramatic change will come from unilateral action by the president. Instead, attention to civil rights concerns in the executive branch has primarily been in two areas since 1993: racial diversity in presidential appointments and use of the bully pulpit to promote racial concerns and interests.

President Bill Clinton was active in both areas. In 1992, as a candidate, Clinton promised a government that "looks like America." His cabinet, subcabinet, and judicial appointments achieved the greatest gender and racial balance of any in history. Fourteen percent of Clinton's first-year presidential appointments were African American (compared with 12 percent of the country's population in 1992), 6 percent were Latino (compared with 9.5 percent of the country's population), and the percentages of Asian Americans and Native Americans who were appointed were identical to their proportions in the population. Clinton delivered an administration that "looked like us." And even though the proportion of women appointees—27 percent—was well short of the proportion of women in the population, it still was a record high. Clinton also used the bully pulpit to advocate a civil rights agenda. Most significant was his effort to promote a "National Conversation on Race," which helped focus national attention on many of the problems faced by minorities.

President George W. Bush did not achieve the same level of diversity in his appointments as Clinton did, but his administration was more

President Trump reversed the Obama-era policy of allowing transgender people to serve in the military, but this ban is currently being challenged in court. Here, transgender naval officer Taryn McLean accepts a Military Outstanding Volunteer Service Medal.

diverse than those of other Republican presidents. His initial 19 cabinet and cabinet-rank appointments included 15 men and 4 women, of whom 6 were members of racial minorities. The rhetoric that surrounded these appointments, however, was couched not in terms of affirmative action but rather in terms of merit. Critics argued that gender and race played a central role in Bush's decisions, just as they had with Clinton, even if the rhetoric had a different tone. Despite the different approach, Bush made serious overtures to minorities, especially Latinos, in his effort to expand the Republican Party base.

While the long-term impact of the Obama presidency on the civil rights movement remains to be seen, the historical significance of his successful campaign as a minority candidate is clear. At the 2008 Democratic National Convention, some African-American delegates openly wept as Obama accepted the party's nomination. Many delegates had not expected that they would live to see an African American become a strong contender for the presidency. Obama's nominations for his cabinet and cabinet-level offices consisted of a diverse group of 14 men and 7 women, with 7 of them members of racial minorities. Eric Holder was the first African American to serve as attorney general, and Sonia Sotomayor is the first Latina on the Supreme Court. Obama also nominated Elena Kagan to the Supreme Court, putting three women on the Court for the first time. Obama's second-term team was similar, consisting of 14 men and 8 women, 6 of them racial minorities.

In his first term, Obama tried to downplay race and diversity concerns. Indeed, some observers argue that Obama's presidency signaled the beginning of a "post-racial politics" that places less emphasis on race and devotes more attention to issues that concern all Americans, such as the economy, education, and health care. However, Obama himself rejected this view. In Obama's second term, he used the bully pulpit to draw more attention to women's issues, such as rape on college campuses and equal pay; used executive action on immigration policy to limit deportations of young adults who were brought to the United States as children; called attention to racial disparities in the criminal justice system; and saw the Supreme Court recognize same-sex marriage as a fundamental right.

Donald Trump was elected with racially divisive positions, such as his promises to build a wall between the United States and Mexico and deport 12 million illegal residents. In his election-night victory speech, he emphasized the importance of representing all Americans and uniting the country. As president, Trump has tended to express polarizing opinions on civil rights issues, rather than unifying themes. He failed to condemn the attacks by white supremacists on counterprotesters in Charlottesville, Virginia, instead blaming "both sides" for the violence and saying that some of the white supremacists were "very fine people." He also said that any NFL player who knelt during the national anthem in protest of racial bias in policing was a "son-of-a-bitch," attempted to ban immigration to the United States from several dominantly Muslim countries, and attempted to ban transgender service members from the military.

"Why Should I Care?"

Why is it important for us to know about who the key players are in civil rights? At various times in our history, different branches of government took the lead in promoting civil rights: Congress in the 1960s with the Civil Rights Act and the VRA, Presidents Clinton and Obama with promoting diversity in presidential appointments, and the Supreme Court in endorsing same-sex marriage. But in recent years, both the Supreme Court and President Trump have moved some civil rights policies in the other direction. If we want to see policies on these kinds of issues change, knowing who is involved, and what impact these policies can have, is critical.

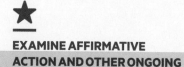
Civil rights issues today

Today, there is vigorous debate among proponents of three main perspectives over the likely direction of the civil rights movement in the twenty-first century. The first group, whose views are articulated by such scholars as Stephan Thernstrom of Harvard University and Abigail Thernstrom of the Manhattan Institute, has suggested that our nation must "move beyond race." This group argues that on many social and economic indicators the gap between blacks and whites has narrowed and that public opposition to race-based policies indicates the need for a new approach. The Supreme Court has largely endorsed this view by implementing a color-blind jurisprudence over a broad range of issues. The second group is represented by traditional civil rights activists and groups such as the Congressional Black Caucus and the NAACP; it argues that the civil rights movement must continue to fight for equal opportunity by enforcing existing law and pushing for equality of outcomes through protecting and expanding affirmative action programs and other policies that address racial inequality. Black Lives Matter, while not a traditional civil rights organization because of its decentralized structure, fits into this category with its fight for racial equality in the criminal justice system. These first two groups share the goal of racial equality and integration but differ on how much progress we have made and how to make further progress. The third group does not support the goal of integration; instead, activists such as Louis Farrakhan and the Nation of Islam argue for African-American self-sufficiency and separation. They believe that African Americans can never gain equality within what they see as the repressive, white-dominated economic and political system.

Most civil rights advocates endorse the second view. They argue that it would be a mistake to conclude that the work of the civil rights movement is complete. They point to the resegregation of public schools, persistent gaps between whites and racial minorities in health and economic status, racial profiling, hate crimes, a backlash against immigrant groups, and continuing discrimination in employment and housing. At the same time, this group rejects calls for racial separation as shortsighted and self-defeating.

The other two groups would argue that although the traditional civil rights agenda made important contributions to racial equality, further progress will require a different approach. Advocates of the color-blind approach prefer to stop making distinctions between people based on race. They want to use government policies to make sure there is no overt discrimination and to provide equal opportunity for all, and then let merit decide outcomes. The segregationists have given up on the civil rights agenda and believe that minorities can achieve success only on their own. Debates among advocates of these three views play out over a broad range of issues, several of which are outlined in the last section of this chapter.

Affirmative action

The Civil Rights Act of 1964 ensured that, at least on paper, all Americans would enjoy equality of opportunity. But even after the act was passed, blacks continued to lag behind whites in socioeconomic status; there was still a substantial gap between the equality of opportunity and the equality of outcomes. In an important speech at Howard University in 1965, President Johnson outlined his argument for affirmative action, saying, "This is the next and the more profound stage of the battle for civil rights.... We seek not just legal equity but human ability, not just equality as a right and a theory but equality as a fact and equality as a result.... To this end equal opportunity is essential, but not enough, not enough."[100] Later that year, Johnson attempted to move closer to equality of outcomes by issuing an executive order requiring all federal agencies and government contractors to submit written proposals to provide an equal opportunity for employment of blacks, women, Asian Americans, and Native Americans within various job categories and to outline programs to achieve those goals. The policy was expanded under President Nixon, and throughout the 1970s and 1980s affirmative action programs grew in the private sector, higher education, and government contracting. Through such programs, employers and universities gave special opportunities to minorities and women, either to make up for past discrimination or to pursue the general goals of diversity.

Affirmative action takes many forms. The most passive type involves extra effort to recruit women and minorities for employment or college admission by placing ads in newspapers and magazines, visiting inner-city schools, or sending out targeted mailings. A more active form involves including race or gender as a "plus factor" in admissions or hiring decisions. That is, from a pool of qualified candidates a minority applicant may receive an advantage over white applicants. Women generally do not receive special consideration in admissions decisions, but gender may be a "plus factor" in some employment decisions, especially in professions in which women are underrepresented, such as engineering, architecture, the building trades, and computer programming. (In fact, many selective schools have been quietly applying affirmative action for men because more highly qualified women apply than men.) The strongest form of affirmative action is the use of quotas—strict numerical targets to hire or admit a specific number of applicants from underrepresented groups.

Affirmative action has been a controversial policy. Polls indicate that minorities are much more supportive of the practice than whites are. Many whites view it as "preferential treatment" and "reverse discrimination." Two-thirds of whites support affirmative action in general terms to "increase the number of black and minority students on college campuses," but when asked specifically about race-based admissions or merit-based admissions, only 22 percent said that college admissions should "take race/ethnicity into account" while 76 percent said that admissions should be based "solely on merit" (the comparable numbers for black respondents were 44 percent and 50 percent).[101] This backlash has spilled over into state politics. California passed Proposition 209 in 1996, which banned the consideration of "race, sex, color, ethnicity or national origin" in public employment, public education, or public contracting.[102] Nine other states have similar laws.

The Supreme Court has helped define the boundaries of this policy debate. The earliest cases concerning affirmative action in employment upheld preferential treatment and rigid quotas when the policies were necessary to make up for past discrimination. The cases involved a worker training program that set aside 50 percent of the positions for blacks, a labor union that was required to hire enough minorities to get its nonwhite membership to 29.23 percent, and a state police force that was required to promote one black officer for every white even if there was a smaller pool of blacks who were eligible for promotion.[103] In each instance, there had been a previous pattern of discrimination and exclusion.

The Court moved in a more color-blind direction in an important reverse-discrimination employment case in 2009. In that case, 17 white firefighters and 1 Latino firefighter sued the city of New Haven, Connecticut, for throwing out the results of a test that would have been used to promote them. The city tried to ignore the results of the test because no African-American firefighters would have qualified for promotion and the city feared a "disparate impact" lawsuit. However, the Court ruled that the exam did appear to be "job related and consistent with business necessity" (as required by Section VII of the Civil Rights Act) and that unless the city could provide a "strong basis in evidence" that it would have been sued, it had to consider the results of the exam.[104]

The landmark decision for affirmative action in higher education was *Regents of the University of California v. Bakke* (1978).[105] Allan Bakke, a white student, sued when he was denied admission to medical school at the University of California, Davis, in successive years. Bakke's test scores and GPA were significantly higher than those of some minority students who were admitted under the school's affirmative action program. Under that program, 16 of the 100 slots in the entering class were reserved for minority or disadvantaged students. The Supreme Court agreed with Bakke that rigid racial quotas were unconstitutional but allowed race to be used in admissions decisions as a "plus factor" to promote diversity in the student body. This standard was largely unquestioned until 1996, when the Fifth Circuit Court of Appeals held that it was unconstitutional to consider race in law school admissions at the University of Texas. In 2000, the Ninth Circuit Court of Appeals in Seattle, however, reached the opposite conclusion and ruled that race could be considered in admissions to promote educational diversity.[106]

In 2003, the Court affirmed *Bakke*, saying that the University of Michigan law school's "holistic approach," which considered race as one of the factors in the admission decision, was acceptable. However, the more rigid approach for undergraduate admissions at Michigan, which automatically gave minority students 20 of the 100 points needed to guarantee admission, was unacceptable.[107] This was the first time that a majority of the Court clearly stated that "student body diversity is a compelling state interest that can justify the use of race in university admissions."[108] In 2006, voters in Michigan passed Proposal 2, an initiative to make it illegal for state bodies to consider race in admissions and hiring decisions; this policy was upheld by the Supreme Court in 2014.[109] This means that states will be able to decide on an individual basis whether to consider affirmative action in higher education, because the policy is neither prohibited nor required by the Constitution.

In 2008, a white student, Abigail Fisher, claimed she was a victim of reverse discrimination and sued the University of Texas at Austin. Texas had achieved a racially diverse student body by extending offers of admission to the top 10 percent of every graduating high school class in the state (in recent years, this policy was changed to the top 7 percent). This approach worked because most high schools in Texas were still segregated. In June 2016, the Court upheld Texas's affirmative action policy by a 4–3 vote.[110] Despite this ruling, documents leaked in August 2017 revealed that the Justice Department was going to "investigate, and potentially sue, colleges and universities over admissions decisions that are perceived as discriminating against white applicants."[111] For more on affirmative action in college admissions, see the Take a Stand feature.

Multicultural and immigration issues

A host of issues involving the multicultural, multiracial nature of American society will become more important as whites cease to constitute the majority of the population by mid-century. At its core, these issues are rooted in the fact that the United States is a nation of immigrants. Will that history continue, and if so, what shape will it take? Is our country a "melting pot," focused on the assimilation of new groups, or is it more like a "tossed salad," in which each immigrant group maintains its cultural identity but creates a new, better collective whole? Groups who favor one or the other of these conceptions of American society often clash over issues such as whether English should be our official language (31 states have such laws) and whether bilingual education should be offered in public schools. But the biggest area for debate on this topic in recent years concerns immigration reform and border security.

Abigail Fisher sued the University of Texas over its affirmative action policy. She is shown talking to reporters outside the Supreme Court after the case was heard in 2016.

Affirmative Action in College Admissions

Since 1978, the Supreme Court has endorsed the idea of race as a "plus factor" in college admissions while rejecting the idea of strict quotas or point systems. This approach was affirmed in a 2003 case involving the University of Michigan's law school, but many Court-watchers believed that affirmative action would be struck down in the 2016 case *Fisher v. University of Texas, Austin.*[a] Instead, swing vote Justice Kennedy sided with the liberal justices, and the Court upheld the practice.

UT Austin's college admissions process has two parts. First, anyone in the top 10 percent of a Texas public high school is guaranteed admission to UT (in recent years this has been closer to the top 7 percent). Because most high schools in Texas are somewhat segregated by race, the 10 percent plan automatically creates diversity for the entering class. Seventy-five percent of in-state students are admitted via the 10 percent plan. Second, the remaining 25 percent of in-state students are admitted by a "holistic" program that evaluates their entire record and includes race as a "plus factor." It was this second part that Abigail Fisher challenged after being denied admission to UT. The legal question that the Court had to decide was whether the university's affirmative action program violated the equal protection clause of the Fourteenth Amendment and civil rights laws barring discrimination on the basis of race, or whether the program could be justified as serving a "compelling state interest" under the strict scrutiny standard.

Diversity deserves consideration. Advocates of affirmative action argue that a diverse student body promotes viewpoint diversity that is essential to learning. Having racial diversity in the student body is likely to produce more viewpoint diversity in classroom discussions than would occur with a mostly white student body. The majority opinion in the Texas case also argued that a more diverse student body leads to "the destruction of stereotypes," promotes "cross-racial understanding," and prepares students "for an increasingly diverse work force and society." Furthermore, proponents argue, the courts are not the proper place to decide these issues. Instead, as with the complex and highly charged topic of racial redistricting, the political branches of government are where these decisions should be made. The Court endorsed this position of judicial restraint in a 2014 case involving a ban on affirmative action in Michigan.[b]

The Court argued that the Texas approach was "narrowly tailored" to serve the compelling state interest of viewpoint diversity because the 10 percent plan, by itself, did not produce the desired level of diversity and would create perverse incentives. Justice Kennedy wrote, "Percentage plans encourage parents to keep their children in low-performing segregated schools, and discourage students from taking challenging classes that might lower their grade point averages."

Affirmative action is just another kind of discrimination. Opponents reply that supporters of affirmative action have not provided convincing evidence that racial diversity in colleges has any beneficial effects. They also argue that "viewpoint diversity" arguments assume that members of all racial minorities think alike, drawing a comparison to racial profiling in law enforcement. It is just as offensive, they say, that an admissions committee thinks that one black student has the same views as another black student as it is that a police officer may pull over a black teenage male just because he fits a certain criminal profile.

Opponents also argue that affirmative action amounts to "reverse discrimination" and that any racial classification is harmful. Justice Alito's scathing dissent in the Texas case said, "U.T. has never provided any coherent explanation for its asserted need to discriminate on the basis of race, and … U.T.'s position relies on a series of unsupported and noxious racial assumptions." Alito also argued that concepts such as viewpoint diversity and "cross-cultural understanding" are "slippery" and difficult to analyze systematically.

The Texas case will not be the end of the debate concerning affirmative action in higher education. A pending suit challenges Harvard University's affirmative action program as discriminating against Asian Americans. If you had to rule on the Texas case, how would you have decided? Take a stand.

 Students protest outside the Supreme Court in support of diversity at the University of Texas.

take a stand

1. To what extent should race be used as a "plus factor" to promote racial diversity and viewpoint diversity, if at all? Is the "top 10 percent" plan a better approach?

2. Think of your own experiences in high school and college. Has racial diversity contributed to viewpoint diversity?

Following the September 11 terrorist attacks, some people saw immigration as a threat that must be curtailed. The government made it clear that it would not engage in racial profiling of Arab Americans—for example, subjecting them to stricter screening at airports—but many commentators argued that such profiling would be justified, and there was at least anecdotal evidence of an increase in discrimination against people of Middle Eastern descent. After the terrorist attacks in Paris and San Bernardino, California, in 2016 the debate in the presidential campaign shifted to a strongly anti-immigrant tone. Donald Trump proposed preventing all Muslims from entering the United States until the government could make sure they did not pose a terrorist threat. He quickly followed through on that pledge, but his original travel ban and a subsequent version that did not narrowly target Muslim countries were also struck down. Federal judges cited Trump's campaign promise as evidence of the ban's true intent. However, in 2018 the Supreme Court upheld the third version of the travel ban, saying that the president's power over immigration policy was not undermined by his political comments about the possible intent of the travel ban.[112]

Over the past two decades, immigration has been central in many political debates. The intensity of that debate increased in 2010 when Arizona enacted an anti-immigration law that requires local law-enforcement officials to check the immigration status of a person in a "lawful stop, detention, or arrest" if there is a "reasonable suspicion" that the person is an illegal alien. The law also requires immigrants to always carry papers verifying their immigration status and bans people without proper documents from seeking work in public places. Many civil rights violations occurred when local law-enforcement officials started enforcing this law. States with similar laws include South Carolina, Alabama, Utah, Georgia, and Indiana. Arizona governor Jan Brewer said, "Decades of federal inaction and misguided policy have created a dangerous and unacceptable situation, and states deserve clarity from the Court in terms of what role they have in fighting illegal immigration."[113] Opponents of the law argue that it requires illegal racial profiling and that the federal government has the sole responsibility for deciding immigration law.

The Supreme Court struck down three of the four main provisions of the law, citing the supremacy clause of the Constitution. This decision meant that Congress, not the states, determines immigration law when the two laws conflict. The Court upheld the controversial "show me your papers" part of the law, saying that the state was simply enforcing the federal law. However, the Court indicated that the law must be applied in a race-neutral way and could be struck down if there was clear evidence of racial profiling.[114] Several months later, a federal district court judge cleared the way for implementation of the "show me your papers" law, saying that the Supreme Court

When President Trump announced his original travel ban preventing individuals from select Muslim-majority countries from entering the United States, people flooded airports across the country in protest.

wanted to see actual evidence of discrimination rather than speculation that the law could have a discriminatory effect.[115]

The immigration system is widely viewed as broken and in need of reform, but neither President Bush nor President Obama was able to get Congress to approve his proposal to provide a "path to citizenship" for undocumented immigrants. Americans are in favor of reform, but their level of support varies depending on the wording of the question. In 2015, a Gallup poll showed that 65 percent of those surveyed said that the government should "allow illegal immigrants to remain in the United States and become U.S. citizens but only if they meet certain requirements"; another 14 percent said illegal immigrants should be able to stay without applying for citizenship, while only 19 percent said they should have to leave the United States. A Pew poll also taken in 2015 showed that 51 percent of Americans think "immigrants today strengthen our country because of their hard work and talents" while 14 percent believe "immigrants today are a burden on our country because they take our jobs, housing and health care."[116] In 2015, President Obama used executive orders to implement part of his immigration policy (concerning the deportation of young adults who were brought to the United States illegally by their parents and the deportation of the parents of children who are citizens). The Supreme Court deadlocked 4-4 in a June 2016 case, upholding the lower court's ruling that struck down the executive order. More than 4 million immigrants had to await the results of the election. President Trump revoked Obama's executive order and, while Congress deadlocked on the issue, the courts allowed the program to continue for those already enrolled. President Trump also instituted a "zero tolerance" policy that led to the separation of thousands of children and parents at the border. The policy violated a federal court order and was reversed, though about 500 children remained in detention centers in late 2018.[117]

The debates over affirmative action, English as the country's official language, and immigration reform clearly illustrate the conflictual nature of civil rights policy. However, history has shown that when public opinion strongly supports a given application of civil rights—for example, the integration of African Americans in the South in the 1960s and, more recently, allowing gays to openly serve in the military and recognizing same-sex marriage—public policy soon reflects those views. Although it is impossible to say when there will be comprehensive immigration reform that includes a path to citizenship, it is likely to eventually happen given the trends in public opinion. However, the Trump administration's efforts to move immigration policy in the opposite direction mean that comprehensive immigration reform is probably off the table until at least 2021.

Despite President Trump's threats of deportation, hundreds of thousands of undocumented immigrants continue to cross into the United States each year. They come seeking better economic opportunities, or fleeing crime, war, or other life-threatening situations in their native country. Here, border control agents detain migrants from Central America seeking asylum.

Unpacking the Conflict

Considering all that we've discussed in this chapter, let's apply what we know about how civil rights work to the examples of profiling introduced at the beginning of this chapter. Is it ever acceptable to treat people differently based on the color of their skin, their ethnic status, their gender, or their sexual orientation, in a situation of racial profiling or otherwise?

Enforcing civil rights means providing equal protection of the law to individuals and groups that are discriminated against, which may include noncitizens and illegal immigrants. Figuring out exactly when an individual's civil rights have been violated can be tricky. When does a routine traffic stop by a police officer turn into racial profiling?

To help figure that out, we now can answer the questions about possible civil rights violations that introduced this chapter:

- Scenario 1: On the one hand, the African-American teenagers who were pulled over by the police may or may not have had their civil rights violated, depending on the laws in their state. In Massachusetts, for example, it is prohibited to consider the "race, gender, national or ethnic origin of members of the public in deciding to detain a person or stop a motor vehicle" except in "suspect specific incidents."[118] On the other hand, in the scenario in which the police pulled over white teenagers, the traffic stop would have been acceptable as long as there had been "probable cause" to justify the stop.
- Scenario 2: The Asian-American woman who did not get the job could certainly talk to a lawyer about filing a "disparate impact" discrimination suit. Under the 1991 Civil Rights Act, the employer would have the burden of proof to show that she was not a victim of the good ol' boy network.
- Scenario 3: The gay couple who could not rent the apartment because of their sexual orientation might have a basis for a civil rights lawsuit based on the Fourteenth Amendment. But this would depend on where they lived, given that there is no federal protection against discrimination against gay men and lesbians (and the Supreme Court has not applied the Fourteenth Amendment in this context).
- Scenario 4: Court decisions concerning affirmative action at the University of Michigan and the University of Texas show that the white student who was not admitted to the university of his choice would just have to take his lumps, as long as the affirmative action program considered race as a general "plus factor" rather than assigning more or fewer points for it (and the practice was allowed by his state).

This review of civil rights in the United States has highlighted only some of the most important issues, but a significant agenda remains. The civil rights movement will continue to use the multiple avenues of the legislative, executive, and judicial branches to secure equal rights for all Americans. Although this process may take many years, history demonstrates that when public opinion becomes more supportive of diversity and stronger civil rights, our political institutions support the views of the people.

What's Your Take?

Should distinctions between people based on race, ethnic status, gender, or sexual orientation be uniformly prohibited? Or are they OK under some circumstances?

STUDY GUIDE

The context of civil rights

Describe the historical struggles groups have faced in winning civil rights. (Pages 150–158)

Summary

Civil rights are protections from discrimination both by the government and by individuals and are rooted in laws and the equal protection clause of the Fourteenth Amendment. The concept of equality has evolved over time, with protections now for the LGBTQ community, women, African Americans, Native Americans, Asian Americans, and Latinos. Despite our attempts to live in a color-blind society, awareness of race still influences many people's opinions and behavior.

Key terms

civil rights (p. 150)
disenfranchised (p. 153)
grandfather clause (p. 153)
Jim Crow laws (p. 153)

"separate but equal"
doctrine (p. 153)
protectionism (p. 156)

Practice Quiz Questions

1. **The distinction between civil rights and civil liberties is that civil rights _____ while civil liberties _____.**

   a protect against discrimination; are guaranteed in the Bill of Rights

   b are guaranteed in the Bill of Rights; protect against discrimination

   c are guaranteed in the Bill of Rights; limit what the government can do to you

   d limit what the government can do to you; protect against discrimination

   e limit what the government can do to you; are guaranteed in the Bill of Rights

2. **The Missouri Compromise _____.**

   a ruled that people held as slaves are not protected by the Constitution

   b established that three-fifths of the slaves could count in a state's population

   c limited the expansion of slavery while maintaining the balance of slave states

   d gave slaves the right to vote

   e ended slavery in the South

3. ***Plessy v. Ferguson* established _____.**

   a the legitimacy of poll taxes

   b the "separate but equal" doctrine

   c that Jim Crow laws were illegal

   d the process of desegregation in the South

   e the legality of slavery

4. **The principle of _____ was used in many court cases to deny women equal rights.**

   a matriarchy

   b "separate but equal"

   c sectionalism

   d misandry

   e protectionism

5. **Early in the nation's history, civil rights activism was focused on _____.**

   a women

   b gays and lesbians

   c African Americans

   d Latinos

   e Native Americans

The racial divide today

Analyze inequality among racial, ethnic, and social groups today. (Pages 159–166)

Summary

Beyond the unequal treatment of racial minorities, women, and LGBTQ individuals, inequalities in political, social, and economic conditions also persist. Whites are able to participate in politics at a higher rate, enjoy a better standard of living, and avoid prejudice in the criminal justice system.

Practice Quiz Questions

6. ***Most* of the differences in voter turnout among whites relative to racial minorities can be accounted for by _____.**

   a contemporary Jim Crow laws

   b voter purge lists

   c voter ID laws

   d poll taxes

   e education and income

7. **The gaps between whites and blacks on health measures are _____ and in many cases _____.**

   a large; decreasing

   b large; increasing

   c small; decreasing

   d small; increasing

   e small; staying the same

8. **In economic terms, the average Latino family is _____ .**

a better off than the average white family from the same area

b likely to have more assets than the average white family

c roughly equal with the average white family

d worse off than the average white family

e more likely than any other group to be poor

Key players in the conflict over civil rights

Explain the approaches used to bring about change in civil rights policies. (Pages 166–187)

Summary

Depending on the political context, each branch of government has played a role in the expansion of civil rights. Moreover, federalism has played a role in this process. Although the state governments often lagged behind the federal government in African Americans' civil rights, they have been on the forefront in protecting the rights of gays and lesbians.

Key terms

de jure (p. 173)

de facto (p. 173)

disparate impact standard (p. 174)

rational basis test (p. 176)

substantive due process doctrine (p. 182)

Practice Quiz Questions

9. **Early in the civil rights movement (before the 1960s), which branch provided most of the successes?**

a state governments

b Congress

c the presidency

d the bureaucracy

e the Supreme Court

10. **The difference between de facto segregation and de jure segregation is that de facto segregation _____ , while de jure segregation _____ .**

a is the result of circumstances; is mandated by law

b is mandated by law; is the result of circumstances

c applies to racial minorities; applies to women

d applies to women; applies to racial minorities

e applies to all groups; applies to racial minorities

11. **The strongest protection as the "suspect classification" applies which test?**

a rational basis

b strict scrutiny

c intermediate scrutiny

d privileged interest

e disparate impact

12. **The VRA _____ .**

a established "majority-minority" districts

b established compulsory voter registration for African Americans

c eliminated direct obstacles to minority voting in the South

d barred discrimination in the rental or sale of a home

e reduced participation by African Americans in the South

13. **Relative to the protection of individuals with disabilities, Congress's track record in protecting gay rights is _____ .**

a stronger

b about the same

c weaker

d nonexistent

e more focused on job discrimination

Civil rights issues today

Examine affirmative action and other ongoing civil rights issues. (Pages 188–193)

Summary

The public is divided on the appropriateness of civil rights policies, with some groups preferring a "color-blind" approach and some groups preferring a "color-conscious" approach. Furthermore, the debates over issues such as affirmative action, immigration reform, and establishing English as the official language in many states indicate the level of conflict over civil rights policy. Nonetheless, when public opinion does strongly support the application of civil rights in a particular arena, policy makers generally respond to these views.

Practice Quiz Questions

14. **The Supreme Court's implementation of "color-blind jurisprudence" fits the agenda of those who argue _____ .**

a that the gap between blacks and whites has narrowed

b that the civil rights movement needs to continue to fight for equal opportunity

c that African Americans need to be separate and fully self-sufficient

d that equality of outcomes is important

e that the gap between blacks and whites has widened

15. **What did the case *Regents of the University of California v. Bakke* establish?**

a that race could play no role in the college admissions process

b that gender could play no role in the college admissions process

c that strict racial quotas in the admissions process were legal

d that race could be used as a "plus factor" in the admissions process

e that gender could be used as a "plus factor" in the admissions process

Suggested Reading

For various websites devoted to civil rights see https://www.justice .gov/crt, https://blacklivesmatter.com, www.womensmarch.com, https://metoomvmt.org, http://nationalfairhousing.org.

Berman, Ari. *Give Us the Ballot: The Modern Struggle for Voting Rights in America*. New York: Farrar, Straus and Giroux, 2015.

Canon, David T. *Race, Redistricting, and Representation: The Unintended Consequences of Black-Majority Districts*. Chicago: University of Chicago Press, 1999.

Dawson, Michael C. *Behind the Mule: Race and Class in African-American Politics*. Princeton, NJ: Princeton University Press, 1994.

Hochschild, Jennifer L., Vesla M. Weaver, and Traci R. Burch. *Creating a New Racial Order: How Immigration, Multiracialism, Genomics, and the Young Can Remake Race in America*. Princeton, NJ: Princeton University Press, 2012.

Katznelson, Ira. *When Affirmative Action Was White: An Untold History of Racial Inequality in Twentieth-Century America*. New York: W. W. Norton, 2005.

Kennedy, Randall. *For Discrimination: Race, Affirmative Action, and the Law*. New York: Vintage Books, 2015.

Kousser, J. Morgan. *Colorblind Injustice: Minority Voting Rights and the Undoing of the Second Reconstruction*. Chapel Hill: University of North Carolina Press, 1999.

Tate, Katherine. *Black Lawmaking in the U.S. Congress from Carter to Obama*. Ann Arbor: University of Michigan Press, 2014.

Thernstrom, Stephan, and Abigail Thernstrom. *America in Black and White: One Nation, Indivisible—Race in Modern America*. New York: Simon and Schuster, 1997.

6
Public Opinion
What do the people want? How should we measure opinion?

 "To all Americans, in every city near and far, small and large, from mountain to mountain, and from ocean to ocean, hear these words: You will never be ignored again. Your voice, your hopes, and your dreams, will define our American destiny."
President Donald Trump

 "You have to remember one thing about the will of the people: it wasn't that long ago that we were swept away by the Macarena."
Jon Stewart, comedian

One of the foundations of democracy is the belief that public opinion matters: while in office, elected officials act in accordance with their constituents' demands or else face the possibility of being defeated in the next election. Every election season, candidates, political parties, journalists, and political scientists take thousands of polls in an attempt to determine who is likely to vote and what sorts of arguments, slogans, and platforms will appeal to these voters.

According to political scientist V. O. Key, basing policy and election strategy on public opinion makes sense because "[i]n the large, the electorate behaves about as rationally and responsibly as we should expect, given the clarity and the alternatives presented to it and the character of the information available to it."[1] The expectation is that citizens' evaluations of what government is doing, their ideas of what they would like done differently, and their thoughts about what they like and don't like more broadly all have some basis in reality. And there is an upside to the information that polls provide. The only way to assess whether government follows the wishes of the people is to have some idea of what people really want—to actually develop surveys, measure public opinion, and compare it to the policy choices made in Washington.

However, a look at the results of some mass surveys might lead you to comedian and political commentator Jon Stewart's concern that public opinion is fickle and only loosely connected to reality. For example, a 2017 study found that a significant percentage of Republican voters believed that Barack Obama was a Muslim—and a significant percentage of Democrats believed that the government had advance

Significant percentages of Americans hold politically consequential beliefs that are factually untrue. For example, large numbers of people believe that Barack Obama is not a U.S. citizen, and therefore was not eligible to be president. Can we trust public opinion?

CHAPTER GOALS

Define *public opinion* and explain why it matters in American politics. pages 200–202

Explain how people form political attitudes and opinions. pages 203–211

Describe basic survey methods and potential issues affecting accuracy. pages 211–220

Present findings on what Americans think about government and why it matters. pages 220–227 knowledge of the attacks on September 11, 2001. (Needless to say, both claims are false.)[2] Statistics like these lead some politicians to take little stock in polls: for example, Donald Trump's 2016 campaign allegedly did very little polling. Was Trump smart to save money on useless polls, or was he just lucky?

Before we blame Americans for believing in conspiracy theories—or take pollsters to task for mismeasuring public opinion—we need to determine how opinions are formed and how they are expressed. What does it mean when someone reveals an opinion, such as a statement about electoral fraud, a desire for change in some policy, or support for a president? Answering this question requires an understanding of how opinions are formed and what goes into them. We also need to determine whether opinions are real, in the sense that they are considered judgments that shape behavior, and what problems arise when we ask people what they think about politics. Do Americans really hold the bizarre beliefs that are sometimes expressed in polling results? Can we take polls seriously, if they produce results like these? Where does public opinion come from? Can politicians trust it?

Are Americans poorly informed about politics? One survey found that more Americans could identify characters on *The Simpsons* than could list which liberties the Bill of Rights guarantees, and another found most respondents unable to name any Supreme Court justices.

DEFINE *PUBLIC OPINION* AND EXPLAIN WHY IT MATTERS IN AMERICAN POLITICS

public opinion
Citizens' views on politics and government actions.

What is public opinion?

Public opinion describes what the population thinks about politics and government— what government should be doing, evaluations of what government *is* doing, and judgments about elected officials and others who participate in the political process, as well as the wider set of beliefs that shape these opinions.

Public opinion matters for three reasons. First, citizens' political actions—including voting, contributing to campaigns, writing letters to senators, and other kinds of activism—are driven by their opinions.[3] For example, as we discuss in more detail in Chapter 8, party identification shapes voting decisions. A voter who thinks of himself or herself as a Democrat is more likely to vote for Democratic candidates than a voter who identifies as a Republican.[4] Therefore, if we want to understand an individual's behavior or analyze broader political outcomes, such as who wins an election or the fate of a legislative proposal, we need good data on public opinion.

Second, examining public opinion helps explain the behavior of candidates, political parties, and other political actors. Later chapters (particularly Chapter 9 and Chapter 11) show a strong link between citizens' opinions and candidates'

HERE'S THE LATEST POLL ON YOUR PERFORMANCE AS DAD. YOUR APPROVAL RATING IS PRETTY LOW, I'M AFRAID.

THAT'S BECAUSE THERE'S NOT NECESSARILY ANY CONNECTION BETWEEN WHAT'S GOOD AND WHAT'S POPULAR. I DO WHAT'S RIGHT, NOT WHAT GETS APPROVAL.

YOU'LL NEVER KEEP THE JOB WITH *THAT* ATTITUDE.

IF SOMEONE ELSE OFFERS TO DO IT, LET ME KNOW.

© 1994 Watterson/Dist. by Universal Press Syndicate

Politicians read public-opinion polls closely to gauge whether their behavior will anger or please constituents. Few politicians always follow survey results—but virtually none would agree with Calvin's father that polls should be ignored entirely.

campaign strategies and their actions in office. Politicians look to public opinion to determine what citizens want them to do and how satisfied citizens are with their behavior in office. For example, in Chapter 11 we see how congressional representatives are reluctant to cast votes that are inconsistent with their constituents' preferences, especially on issues that constituents consider important. Therefore, to explain a legislator's votes you need to begin with his or her constituents' opinions.

Third, because public opinion is a key to understanding what motivates both citizens and political officials, it can shed light on the reasons for specific policy outcomes. For example, changes in the policy mood—the public's demand for new policies—are linked to changes in government spending.[5] When people want government to do more, spending increases more rapidly; when people want government to do less, spending goes down (or increases more slowly).

Different kinds of opinion

Modern theories of public opinion distinguish between two types of opinions: opinions that are preformed and opinions that are formed on the spot as needed. The first kind of opinions are broad expressions, such as how a person thinks about politics, what a citizen wants from government, or principles that apply across a range of issues. These kinds of beliefs typically form early in life and remain stable over time. Some of these beliefs are obviously political, such as party identification, **liberal or conservative ideology**, and judgments about whether elected officials lose touch with citizens. Liberal or conservative ideology is a good example of a stable opinion: the best way to predict an American's ideology at age 40 is to assume it will match his or her ideology at age 20. The same is true for party identification.

The most important thing to understand about public opinion is that although ideology and party identification are largely consistent over time, these particular kinds of opinions are exceptions to the rule.[6] The average person does not maintain a set of fully formed opinions on all political topics, such as evaluations of all the candidates for state or local office or assessments of the entire range of government programs. Instead, most Americans' political judgments are **latent opinions**: they are constructed only as needed, such as when answering a survey question or deciding on Election Day how to vote. For example, when most people are asked about climate change, they probably do not have a specific response in mind simply because they have not thought much about the question. They might have, at best, some vague ideas about whether climate change is a problem and what should be done about it. Their opinions become concrete only when they are asked about them.

People who follow politics closely have more preformed opinions than the average American, whose interest in politics is relatively low. But very few people are so

> **Whoever can change public opinion can change the government.**
>
> **—President Abraham Lincoln**

liberal or conservative ideology
A way of describing political beliefs in terms of a position on the spectrum running from liberal to moderate to conservative.

latent opinion
An opinion formed on the spot, when it is needed (as distinct from a deeply held opinion that is stable over time).

A person's ideological perspective is relatively stable over time. People who subscribe to a conservative ideology generally support small government and decreased spending.

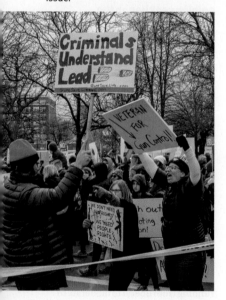

Images of confrontation between pro-gun control and anti-gun control protesters may conceal the more nuanced considerations that underlie most Americans' opinions about the issue.

well informed that they have ready opinions on a wide range of political and policy questions. Moreover, even when people do form opinions in advance, they may not remember every factor that influenced their opinions. Thus, an individual may identify as a liberal or a conservative or as a supporter of a particular party but may be unable to explain the reasons behind these ideological leanings.[7]

Opinions also vary in intensity. For example, one individual might strongly favor policies that allow handgun ownership and open carry in public, while another might oppose both policies but with less intensity. Intensity matters because it shapes whether and how people act on their opinions. The strongly pro-gun individual would be more likely to consider a candidate's gun rights policy when deciding how to vote, while the individual who opposes gun ownership (but less intensely) would likely base his or her vote on other issues. Variation in intensity is one reason why government policies sometimes reflect minority opinions. In the case of gun rights, members of Congress are well aware of polls showing that a majority of people support restrictions on gun ownership. However, polls also show that most supporters of restrictions do not feel strongly about this issue, while people who oppose restrictions are more likely to be intense in their opposition. Thus, when responding to public opinion about gun control, members of Congress reflect the intense minority opinion, not the weaker opinions held by the majority.

"Why Should I Care?"

In a democracy, elected officials stay in office by keeping their constituents happy. As a result, knowing what public opinion looks like—what citizens believe, what they want government to do—helps us understand the choices elected officials make. New policy initiatives such as stricter gun control laws are unlikely to be enacted in the absence of strong, sustained public support. Conversely, even controversial proposals such as Obamacare can be enacted over strong opposition, as long as there are enough enthusiastic supporters. In both ways, public opinion both motivates and constrains elected officials.

Where do opinions come from?

This section describes the sources that people draw from to inform their opinions, and the ways that these different sources interact to determine both individual opinions and collective public opinions. Some opinions are influenced by early life experiences, such as exposure to the beliefs of parents, relatives, or teachers; others result from later life events or from informal conversations with friends. Politicians also play a critical role in the opinion-formation process.

Socialization: families, communities, and networks

Theories of **political socialization** show that children develop a liberal or conservative ideology; a level of trust in others; their own class, racial, and ethnic identity; and other political opinions based on what they learn from their parents.[8] For example, one of the best predictors of a college student's party identification is the party ID of their parents. Opinions formed through socialization are not necessarily permanent; in fact, people often respond to events by modifying their opinions, even those developed early in life. Thus, an individual who originally identified as a Democrat because their parents were Democrats might move away from the party later in life because she did not like the party's candidates, because she thought Democrats did a poor job running the country, or because she disagreed with the party's platform. Even so, for many people, ideas learned during childhood continue to shape their political opinions throughout their lives.[9]

Beyond these influences, research finds broader aspects of socialization that shape political opinions. People are socialized by their communities, the people they interact with while growing up, such as neighbors, teachers, clergy, and others.[10] Support for democracy as a system of government and for American political institutions is higher for individuals who take a civics class in high school.[11] Growing up in a homogeneous community, one where many people share the same cultural, ethnic, or political beliefs, increases adults' sense of civic duty—their belief that voting or other forms of political participation are important social obligations.[12] Volunteering in community organizations as a child also shapes political beliefs and participation in later life.[13] Engaging in political activity as a teenager, such as volunteering in a presidential campaign, generates higher levels of political interest as an adult; it also strengthens the belief that people should care about politics and participate in political activities.[14]

Individuals' opinions are also shaped by their network: the people they interact with on a regular basis. For many people, these interactions are an important source of information about political events as well as how these events should be interpreted. Put another way, you might not think that meeting for coffee with a friend would affect your opinions about climate change, but suppose during the conversation your friend mentioned how much hotter this year had been compared to last year. While such casual conversations are unlikely to have a permanent impact, they might well influence your thinking in the short run—for example, if a week after having coffee, you have to decide how to vote in an election where climate change is an issue.

political socialization
The process by which an individual's political opinions are shaped by other people and the surrounding culture.

Events

Although socialization often influences individuals' fairly stable core beliefs, this does not mean that these beliefs or opinions are fixed. All kinds of events—from everyday interactions to traumatic, life-changing disasters—can capture people's attention and force them to revise their understanding of politics and the role of government.

Some events that shape beliefs are specific, individual experiences. For example, someone who believes that he or she managed to get a college degree only because of government grants and guaranteed student loans might favor a large, activist government that provides a range of benefits to its citizens. And individuals' support for same-sex marriage is strongly influenced by the number of people they know who are gay or lesbian.[15] Major national or world events may also shape beliefs. For example, after the September 11 terrorist attacks, many citizens became more willing to restrict civil liberties to reduce the chances of future attacks.[16]

Some events have a greater impact on public opinion than others, and some people are more likely than others to change their views. Political scientist John Zaller has shown that opinion changes generated by an event or some other new information are more likely when an individual is unfamiliar with the event or information yet considers it to be important. In such cases, the individual does not have a set of preexisting principles or other considerations with which to interpret the event or information. People who do not have strong beliefs are also more likely to change their opinions than are people who hold strong opinions.[17]

Group identity

Individuals' opinions are also influenced by their social categories or groups, such as gender, race, income, and education level. People learn about politics from the people around them. Therefore, those who live in the same region or who were born in the same era might have common beliefs because they experienced the same historical events at similar points in their lives or learned political viewpoints from one another. In the United States, opinions on many issues are correlated with the state or region where a person grew up. For example, until the 1970s relatively few native white southerners identified with the Republican Party.[18] Even today, native white southerners tend to have distinctly different attitudes (such as less support for affirmative action policies and lower support for government involvement in creating racial equality) compared to similar people from other regions of the country.[19]

In some cases, group identity is a function of age. Changes in attitudes about same-sex marriage over the last decade illustrate this phenomenon (see Figure 6.1). The figure shows that overall support for allowing gay and lesbian couples to marry (or allowing civil unions) has more than doubled in the last 15 years. Moreover, while opinions have shifted in all age cohorts, younger Americans are much more likely to express support than are older Americans—in part because they are much more likely to know someone who is gay or a lesbian and in part because they are likely to have other characteristics that predispose them to favor same-sex marriage, such as not being regular churchgoers.

Individuals also may rely on others who "look like" them as a source of opinions. Political scientists Donald Green, Bradley Palmquist, and Eric Schickler, for example,

DID YOU KNOW?

The probability that you will be contacted to participate in a typical national poll is

.001%

Source: General Social Survey Data Archive

argue that group identities shape partisanship: when people are trying to decide between being a Republican or a Democrat, they think about which demographic groups are associated with each party and pick the party that has more members from the groups they identify with.[20]

It is important to examine group variations in public opinion because candidates and political consultants often formulate their campaign strategies in terms of groups. For example, analyses of the three previous presidential elections show that Obama's and Hillary Clinton's electoral strategies were shaped by the goal of attracting support from young Americans, African Americans, Latinos, and women.[21] In contrast, Republican presidential candidates targeted regular churchgoers, as well as older voters and people living in rural areas.

Although events such as wars, economic upheavals, and major policy changes certainly influence public opinion, research shows that most Americans acquire some political opinions early in life from parents, friends, teachers, and others in their community.

Attitudes about Same-Sex Marriage

FIGURE 6.1

Over the last fifteen years, support for same-sex marriage has grown. What do these graphs tell us about the influence of group identity on public opinion? Is support for same-sex marriage likely to increase or decrease in the future? Why?

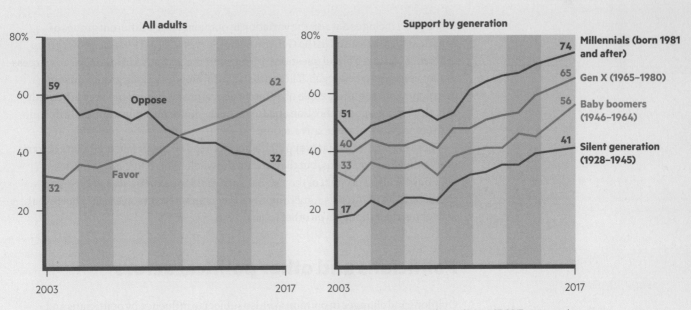

All adults

- Oppose: 59 → 62
- Favor: 32 → 32

Support by generation

- Millennials (born 1981 and after): 51 → 74
- Gen X (1965–1980): 40 → 65
- Baby boomers (1946–1964): 33 → 56
- Silent generation (1928–1945): 17 → 41

Years: 2003 to 2017

Source: Pew Research Center, "Support for Same-Sex Marriage Grows, Even Among Groups That Had Been Skeptical," June 27, 2017, www.people-press.org (accessed 2/7/18).

TABLE
6.1

The Importance of Groups

The General Social Survey (GSS) has been conducted since 1972 to assess the opinions of Americans on certain key issues. Those who take the surveys are asked to indicate if they agree or disagree with statements such as those shown in the table. The percentages indicate those who agree with the statements. Group differences based on such factors as gender, age, race, and family income have been shown to affect the answers given by the respondents.

Source: 2016 Data from General Social Survey 1972–2016, Cumulative Datafile, Survey Documentation and Analysis (SDA) at UC Berkeley, http://sda.berkeley.edu (accessed 11/7/17).

		"Favor preferences in hiring blacks" (percentage who strongly support or support)	"Abortions OK if woman wants one for any reason" (percentage who agree)	"OK to allow anti-American Muslim cleric to speak" (percentage who agree)
Gender	Male	16.8%	41.3%	48.8%
	Female	18.8	39.8	38.4
Age	18–30	20.4	42.1	42.9
	31–40	16.7	44.1	42.8
	41–55	17.9	42.4	46.0
	56–89	16.4	34.5	41.2
Education	Less than high school	28.0	26.2	21.5
	High school	16.1	39.4	37.6
	Bachelor's degree	14.3	53.1	57.0
	Advanced degree	25.1	61.1	63.0
Race	White	12.6	43.6	49.2
	African-American	42.8	40.8	35.1
	Latino	22.6	30.7	26.7
	Other	26.1	47.7	33.4
Family Income	Low	23.1	34.5	32.8
	Lower middle	17.4	37.1	42.5
	Higher middle	14.0	37.8	44.9
	High	15.0	41.3	56.1

Table 6.1 includes data on the variation in opinions across different groups of Americans, as measured in the General Social Survey (GSS). The table shows group differences on three broad questions: hiring preferences for African Americans, access to abortions, and free speech. There are sharp differences among groups on some questions. For example, people of different education levels respond very differently to both questions about abortion and free speech—however, education has little to do with opinions about affirmative action.

These data indicate that group characteristics can be important predictors of some of an individual's opinions, but they are not the whole story.[22] Because Americans' opinions are also a product of their socialization and life experiences, their group characteristics may tell us something about their opinions on some issues but reveal little about their thoughts on other issues.

Politicians and other political actors

Opinions and changes in opinion are also subject to influence by politicians and other political actors, including political parties and party leaders; interest groups; and leaders of religious, civic, and other large organizations. In part, this link exists because Americans look to these individuals for information based on their presumed expertise. For example, if you do not know what to think about immigration reform or gun control, you might seek out someone who appears to know more about the issues than you do. Insofar as the person's opinions seem reasonable, you might adopt them as your own.[23] Of course, people do not search haphazardly for advice; they only take account of an expert's opinions when they generally agree with the expert, perhaps because they are both conservatives or Democrats or because the individual has some other basis for thinking their preferences are alike. For example, during the 2016 general election, Donald Trump's claims that the electoral process was rigged against him reinforced his supporters' high levels of distrust of government.

Politicians on both sides of the debate tried to influence public opinion about health care reform. While Democrats sought to convince Americans that maintaining Obamacare was necessary, opponents played up the possible disadvantages, with references to costs and bureaucratic incompetence.

Politicians and other political actors also actively work to shape public opinion. Political scientists Lawrence R. Jacobs and Robert Y. Shapiro argue that politicians describe proposals through arguments and images designed to tap the public's strong opinions, with the goal of winning support for these proposals.[24] That said, because politicians are generally seen as advocates for a particular point of view, it is relatively difficult for them to convert people to their point of view. For example, although President Trump and his supporters in Congress expended much time and effort in 2017 to promote the repeal of Obamacare, giving dozens of public speeches, holding rallies, and briefing legislators, their efforts had little impact on public opinion. If anything, support for Obamacare increased during this time, perhaps because Trump's efforts made some people consider how they would be affected by repeal of the program.

Considerations: the process of forming opinions

When people form opinions on the spot (which is true for most opinions), they are based on *considerations*: pieces of relevant information from sources like the ones we've just discussed—such as ideology, party identification, the influence of family and community members, personal and national events, group identification, or opinions and actions of politicians—that come to mind when the opinion is requested.[25] The process of forming an opinion usually is not thorough or systematic, since most people don't take into account everything they know about the issue in question.[26]

Rather, they use only considerations that come to mind immediately.[27] Highly informed people who follow politics use this process, as do those with low levels of political interest and knowledge.[28]

In most cases, there are strong commonalities among the considerations that different people use to form opinions about the same topic. For example, in addition to the types of considerations we've already identified, many people use the state of the economy as a consideration. Economic conditions often factor into how people decide whether they approve of the job the president is doing; people are more likely to approve of the president when economic conditions are good compared to when conditions are bad.

However, many other considerations that vary from person to person can enter into the calculation. If you're asked about your approval or disapproval of Donald Trump, the question might call to mind his party (Republican), his personal life (divorced twice), his business experience (a wealthy developer), a picture in today's newspaper of Trump meeting with a foreign leader, a scandal involving one of Trump's appointees— or even what Trump tweeted in the past day. Your opinions might reflect things that have no connection to Trump, such as whether you just received a pay raise, whether you recently watched a video of politicians arguing with each other, or even whether you were just having a bad day. Clearly, you'd reach different conclusions about Trump's performance in office depending on which of these pieces of information went into forming your opinion. Thus, two different people may form evaluations in completely different ways, using very different kinds of information. If we ask about approval of Trump, a substantial percentage of respondents will consider economic conditions and partisanship. But for some people, approval or disapproval of Trump may be based on other factors, from his wealth to his preference for well-done steak. So, if we look at individuals, opinions can be hard to predict or understand, as we don't know which considerations will come to mind when we ask them what they think.

Individual Considerations and Mass Public Opinion While public opinion may be difficult to predict on a person-to-person basis, at the aggregate level (where opinions are averaged across the population of a community, state, or nation) opinions are easier to predict. Over a large group of people, unique differences in how individuals form beliefs largely cancel each other out, leaving common factors that are important for most people, such as (in the case of presidential approval) economic conditions and party identification.

As an example of how considerations work on an aggregate level, consider Figure 6.2, which shows the trend in presidential approval during the first two years in office for Donald Trump, and during the first four years of his two predecessors, Barack Obama and George W. Bush. The first thing to notice is that after a few months in office, presidential approval settles at a relatively stable level. The lack of an identifiable trend makes sense given the role of partisanship in shaping both perceptions of the economy and approval itself. In the main, an individual's partisan identification stays the same over time, so his or her evaluations of the economy and of the president stay the same as well. Of course, some individuals change their opinion from approval to disapproval over time because of something a president says or does—but across the whole country, these movements average out.

The only evidence of a large change in presidential approval in Figure 6.2 is in the plot for George W. Bush, whose ratings spiked after the September 11 attacks in 2001 and after the invasion of Iraq in 2003. These sharp changes in approval suggest that a high percentage of Americans responded to these events by expressing support for the president. However, within a relatively short period of time, the impact of these events (or considerations) faded, and Bush's approval fell back to its previous level. A large, lasting change in overall approval would require significant shifts in partisanship or a lasting movement in economic conditions, which did not occur during the first terms of any of these presidents.

FIGURE 6.2

First-term Presidential Approval Ratings

Compared to President Bush's approval ratings, which moved up and down over time, both President Obama's and President Trump's approval ratings have been relatively stable. What factors account for the differences in these plots?

Source: FiveThirtyEight, "How Popular Is Donald Trump?," https://projects. fivethirtyeight.com/trump-approval-ratings (accessed 10/1/18).

George W. Bush 2001–04

Barack Obama 2009–12

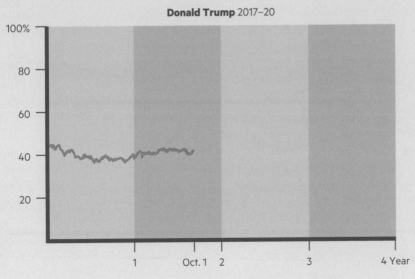

Donald Trump 2017–20

How Considerations Interact Considerations can also interact with each other in the opinion-formation process. One of the most common and important interactions is the impact of partisanship, which acts as a kind of filter that shapes how people assess other events and information. For example, judgments about presidential performance, as well as perceptions of the economy, are often influenced by an individual's party affiliation. That is, if you share the president's party affiliation, you are more likely to think that economic conditions are good and (assuming your judgments about the economy are constant) more likely to approve of the president's performance.

Opinions are often influenced by considerations that compete or contradict. In the case of abortion laws, many people believe in protecting human life but also in allowing women to make their own medical decisions.[29] When a survey asks people who hold both beliefs for their opinion about abortion laws, their response will depend on which consideration comes to mind and seems most relevant when they are answering the question.

When considerations compete, opinions can change rapidly for seemingly unrelated reasons. Consider Figure 6.3, which charts respondents' evaluations of the U.S. military campaign against ISIL. In 2014 through 2016, the percentage of people who said the campaign was going well or fairly well was reasonably constant, with the percentage of Democrats giving a favorable response higher than the percentage of Republicans. However, the Republican percentage sharply increased from October 2016 (when it was just 20 percent) to October 2017 (when it hit 67 percent), while the Democratic percentage changed only modestly. In part, these shifts in opinion reflected victories by the U.S-aided coalition against ISIL. However, the differences between Republicans and Democrats highlight the impact of partisanship on opinions and the impact of the change from Democratic president Barack Obama to Republican president Donald Trump. Republicans became significantly more optimistic not because of facts on the ground in Syria but because a member of their party was now the

FIGURE 6.3

Evaluations of the Campaign against ISIL before and after Trump's Election

The figure shows how Republican evaluations of the campaign against ISIL changed after Donald Trump became president. What would have to happen to shift Republican opinions back to the levels seen during the Obama presidency?

Source: Pew Research Center, "Partisans Have Starkly Different Opinions about How the World Views the U.S.," November 9, 2017, www.people-press.org (accessed 11/9/17).

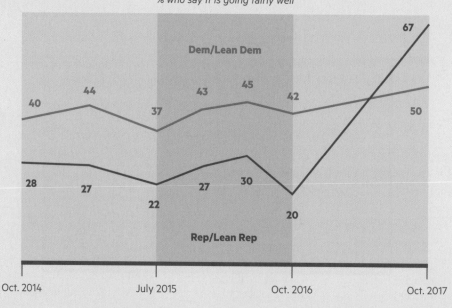

Evaluations of the campaign against ISIL before and after Trump's election
% who say it is going fairly well

Dem/Lean Dem: 40, 44, 37, 43, 45, 42, 50
Rep/Lean Rep: 28, 27, 22, 27, 30, 20, 67

Oct. 2014 · July 2015 · Oct. 2016 · Oct. 2017

president. The shift in Democrats' opinions was much smaller because their opinions were driven by competing considerations: the changes in Syria (positive) and the move to a Republican president (negative).

Studies of public opinion confirm the opinion-formation strategies that we've just discussed: most people form the bulk of their opinions on the spot using a wide range of considerations. Consider the following findings: Attitudes about immigration are shaped by evaluations of the state of the economy.[30] People judge government spending proposals differently depending on whether a Republican or a Democrat made the proposal, using their own party identification as a consideration.[31] Evaluations of affirmative action programs vary depending on whether the survey question reminds respondents that their own personal economic well-being may be hurt by these programs.[32] Voters' party identification and ideology influence their evaluations of candidates.[33] Individuals' willingness to allow protests and other expressions of opinions they disagree with depends on their belief in tolerance.[34] And if people feel obligated to help others in need, they are more likely to support government programs that benefit the poor.[35]

In sum, public opinion at the individual level is driven by many considerations. In the case of gun control, for example, beliefs are likely to depend on individuals' backgrounds—whether they own a gun, hunt, or know someone who does; their political beliefs, including their tolerance for government regulation of individual behavior and even their partisanship; and horrific events involving guns. Thus, although public opinion may shift somewhat in response to events such as a mass shooting or domestic terror attack, such events are only one factor that shapes opinion. As a result, even if an event is momentous, the shift in opinion may be quite small and transitory.

mass survey
A way to measure public opinion by interviewing a relatively small sample of a large population.

population
The group of people whom a researcher or pollster wants to study, such as evangelicals, senior citizens, or Americans.

How people form opinions matters because understanding what people say about politics on the news, or in the classroom, or around the dinner table depends on where they are coming from. Perhaps an important event has shaped their opinion, maybe their parents or connection to a social or generational group has influenced them, or maybe a combination of all of these and more has affected them. Knowing what's behind someone's opinions and arguments on an issue can help you decide how you feel about that issue and whether or not the other person's argument carries weight.

"Why Should I Care?"

Measuring public opinion

DESCRIBE BASIC SURVEY METHODS AND POTENTIAL ISSUES AFFECTING ACCURACY

For the most part, information about public opinion comes from **mass surveys**— in-person or phone interviews with a relatively small number of individuals that aim to measure the attitudes of a large **population** or group of people, such as the residents of a particular congressional district, evangelicals, senior citizens, or even the entire adult population in America (see How It Works: Measuring What a Nation of 330 Million Thinks: A Checklist). For large groups such as these, it would be impossible to survey everyone. So surveys typically involve **samples** of between a few hundred and several thousand individuals. One of the principal attractions of mass surveys is that they can, in theory, provide very accurate estimates of public opinion for a large population (such as a state or even the entire United States) using relatively small samples. This property of surveys is detailed in Nuts & Bolts 6.1. For example,

sample
Within a population, the group of people surveyed in order to gauge the whole population's opinion. Researchers use samples because it would be impossible to interview the entire population.

Measuring What a Nation of 330 Million Thinks: A Checklist

✓ **A Random Sample:**
Were the people who participated in the survey selected randomly, such that any member of the population had an equal chance of being selected?

✓ **Sample Size:**
How many people do researchers need to survey to know what 330 million Americans think? Major national surveys usually use a sample of 1,000–2,000 respondents.

± 2%

✓ **Sampling Error:**
For a group of any size (even 330 million), 95 percent of the time a survey of 1,000 randomly selected respondents will measure the average opinion in a population within 2 percentage points. Reputable surveys will usually give the sampling error (sometimes also called "margin of error").

✓ **Question Wording:**
Did the way the question was worded influence the results? Scientific surveys try to phrase questions in a neutral way, but even in reputable polls, differences in question wording can influence answers.

✓ **Reliable Respondents:** Respondents often give socially acceptable answers rather than truthful ones—or invent opinions on the spot. Is there a reason to think people may not have answered a survey honestly and thoughtfully?

Surveying the 2016 Elections: Two Approaches

To illustrate how these requirements for good survey design play out in real life, we examine how two well-known polling organizations, the Pew Research Center and Rasmussen Reports, designed polls to measure presidential preference during the 2016 campaign.

Rasmussen Reports

Land-line only.

A random sample: Use a **land-line-only sample.**

Sample size: Survey the **first person who answers the phone.**

Adjust results.

Sampling error: If there are more Democrats in your sample than you expect, **adjust your results** to reduce support for Clinton.

Use a script to call.

Reliable respondents: Use a computer script, and only call once. Do the survey in a **short time period (hours).**

Pew Research Center

Include cell phones.

A random sample: Generate a **random sample of Americans,** including people who only have cell phones.

Sample size: When you call a residence, only **talk to the person who's in your sample.**

Don't adjust results.

Sampling error: If the partisan divide in the sample is not what you expect, **treat it as a finding**—people may be changing their party ID.

Use a person to call.

Reliable respondents: Use a live interviewer, and call back people you miss the first time. **Implement the survey over several days.**

Outcome

Rasmussen data are incomplete . . .

A random sample: Rasmussen misses **people who only use cell phones** (many of whom are younger and are Democrats).

Sample size: Rasmussen is **biased toward people likely to answer the phone.** These people tend to be older and include more men than average.

and assume nothing has changed.

Sampling error: Adjusting for partisanship **assumes that no changes in party ID have occurred** since the last election.

Reliable respondents: Rasmussen tactic **lowers response rate.** Rasmussen tactic makes poll results sensitive to short-term events.

Pew is more reliable.

Pew's results were generally regarded as more reliable than Rasmussen's—and ultimately **made more accurate predictions about the 2016 results.** Furthermore, Rasmussen kept its data largely private, while Pew released its questionnaire. This made Pew's survey verifiable and provided an opportunity for further analysis.

---

⑦ Critical Thinking

1. **When evaluating these two polling organizations, how would you respond to someone who said he still** preferred Rasmussen's polls because they correctly predicted the outcome of a Senate race in his state in 2014?

2. **Which kinds of respondents are likely to be put off by polls** that the computer scripts? How might this affect the findings of the survey?

Sampling Error in Mass Surveys

The **sampling error** in a survey (the predicted difference between the average opinion expressed by survey respondents and the average opinion in the population, sometimes called the *margin of error*) using a random sample depends on the sample size. Sampling error is large for small samples of around 200 or fewer but decreases rapidly as sample size increases.

The graph shows how the sampling error for a random sample decreases as sample size increases. For example, in surveys with 1,000 respondents the sampling error is 3 percent, meaning that 95 percent of the time the results of a 1,000-person survey will fall within the range of 3 percentage points above or below the actual percentage of the population who hold a particular opinion. If the sample size was increased to 5,000 people, the sampling error would decline to 1.4 percent. Mass surveys typically interview around 1,000 people. As the figure shows, this is the point where adding interviewees provides relatively little improvement in accuracy.

Sampling errors need to be taken into account when interpreting what a poll says about public opinion. For example, suppose a poll of 1,300 Americans found that 66 percent gave an unfavorable rating of Donald Trump's performance in office, and 33 percent rated him favorably. Because the difference between the percentages (33 points) exceeds the sampling error (about 2.5 points), it is reasonable to conclude that, at the time the poll was conducted, more Americans saw Trump unfavorably than favorably.

In contrast, suppose the poll found a narrow 51 to 49 percent split slightly favoring approval. Because the difference in support is smaller than the sampling error, it would be a mistake to conclude that the majority of Americans have a favorable opinion of Trump. Even though more people in the sample express this opinion, there is a good chance that the opposite is true in the overall population.

You don't need to calculate sampling errors to make sense of political polls—just keep two things in mind. First, large samples (1,000 or more) are much more likely to provide accurate information about population opinions than small ones (fewer than 500). Second, be cautious when you read about small differences in survey responses, as these patterns are unlikely to hold true in the entire population.

sampling error
The predicted difference between the average opinion expressed by survey respondents and the average opinion in the population, sometimes called the *margin of error*. Increasing the number of respondents lowers the sampling error.

DID YOU KNOW?

45

state- and national-level polls of the presidential race were released in the last two weeks of the 2016 campaign.
Source: Pollster.com

although polls taken early in a presidential campaign (such as a year in advance of the election) are poor predictors of the ultimate outcome on Election Day, polls taken at the beginning of the official presidential race, when both parties' nominees are known, can provide very good predictions of who will win the election and how many votes he or she will receive.[36]

An alternate technique for measuring public opinion uses focus groups, which are small groups of people interviewed in a group setting. Because focus groups allow respondents to answer questions in their own words rather than being restricted to a few options in a survey question, they can provide deep insights into why people hold the opinions they do. Candidates sometimes use focus groups to test campaign appeals or fine-tune their messages. However, because of their small size, focus groups cannot be used to draw conclusions about public opinion across the entire country.

Large-scale surveys such as the American National Election Study (ANES), which is conducted every election year (typically both before and after the general election), use various types of questions to measure citizens' opinions. In presidential election years, participants in the ANES are first asked whether they voted for president. If they say they did, they are asked which candidate they voted for: a major-party candidate (for example, Hillary Clinton or Donald Trump in 2016), an independent candidate, or some other candidate.

Another kind of survey question measures people's preferences using an *issue scale*. For a range of topics, two opposing statements are given and respondents are asked to pick the statement, or one of the choices between the two extremes, that comes closest to their views. As we discuss later, on questions such as these, most Americans pick positions in the middle of these scales.

A typical survey like the GSS or the ANES will ask several hundred questions related to issues and candidates, along with additional questions that elicit personal information such as a respondent's age, education, marital status, and other factors. Some surveys conducted by media sources, candidates, or political parties are shorter, focusing on voter evaluations of the candidates and the reasons for these evaluations. In the main, the length of a survey reflects the fact that people have limited attention spans, so there is a trade-off between learning more about each respondent's opinions and getting him or her to agree to be surveyed in the first place. Shorter surveys are also less expensive.

An important development in recent years is the use of techniques to combine different surveys into a more powerful measure of public opinion. These techniques weigh data from different polls based on their accuracy in previous elections and combine state- and national-level results to generate predictions—thus, if a poll finds that candidate A is ahead in state 1 and polls have found that the winner in state 1 will also win state 2, then the results from state 1 will be used to predict the result in state 2. These techniques generate powerful predictions of election returns—for example, Nate Silver of FiveThirtyEight.com was able to correctly predict the winner of 49 out of 50 states in the 2008 and 2012 presidential elections and came the closest of all political analysts in predicting Trump's upset victory in 2016.

Problems in measuring public opinion

Although Nate Silver came close, virtually all major political pollsters failed to predict Trump's 2016 victory. While this result is exceptional—most of the time, polls are extremely accurate predictors of election outcomes—it highlights the difficulty of measuring public opinion. The problems begin with determining and gathering an appropriate, representative sample of subjects. These difficulties are compounded by issues pertaining to the wording of the questions and further complicated by the very nature of public opinion itself. Consequently, survey results must be read carefully, taking into account who is being surveyed, when they are being surveyed, what opinions people are being asked about, and what mechanism is used to ask survey questions.

Issues with Survey Methods Building a **random sample** of individuals is not an easy task. One tactic is to choose households at random from census data and send interviewers out for face-to-face meetings. Another is to contact people by telephone using random digit dialing, which allows surveyors to find people who have unlisted phone numbers or who only use a cell phone. In theory, each of these techniques produces a random sample, but in practice, they both may deviate from this ideal. Face-to-face interviews of people in their homes during work hours won't include adults who work during the day and are not home, and is very expensive. Even with phone surveys, many people refuse to participate. Pollsters must adjust their survey results to account for these and other potential biases. Sometimes these adjustments successfully predict results, and sometimes they don't. For example, in the 2016 presidential race, pollsters did a relatively poor job (compared to recent elections) of predicting who was likely to vote. Most used a technique that relied on respondents' past turnout decisions to predict their behavior in 2016. Usually this technique works very well, but in 2016 it overestimated turnout by African Americans based on their high turnout rates in 2008 and 2012. The 2008 and 2012 numbers most likely were

DID YOU KNOW?

90% of people contacted by phone to participate in a political survey either don't answer or refuse to participate.
Source: Pew Research Center

random sample
A subsection of a population chosen to participate in a survey through a selection process in which every member of the population has an equal chance of being chosen. This kind of sampling improves the accuracy of public-opinion data.

especially high because these elections featured the first African-American major party nominee, Barack Obama. As a result of this error, polls taken close to the election predicted Clinton victories in Wisconsin, Michigan, and Pennsylvania—states that were actually won by Trump.

To keep costs down, many organizations use Internet polling, in which volunteer respondents log on to a website to participate in a survey, or robo-polls, in which a computer program phones people and interviews them. Although these techniques are less expensive, there are often doubts about the quality of the samples they produce. (*Push polls*, in which a campaign uses biased survey questions as a way of driving support away from an opponent, are not legitimate polls because they are not designed to measure opinion—they are designed to shape it and are a form of negative campaigning; see Chapter 9.)

The wording of questions can also influence survey results. Table 6.2 shows different questions asked to measure opinions about providing citizenship to undocumented immigrants. As you can see, support depends on the requirements that people would need to fulfill in order to become citizens. As a result, support for immigration reform is much higher in the top three polls than in the bottom three. These issues shouldn't

TABLE 6.2

The Impact of Question Wording on Opinions

How questions are worded can affect survey results. These surveys all ask about immigration reform but differ in the number of requirements that noncitizens would have to satisfy. In light of how the responses to survey questions are shaped by the precise wording of these questions, what sort of question would you ask if your goal was to show that Americans favored immigration reform? What if you wanted to show high levels of opposition?

% Support or Favor	Question	Pollster	Poll Date
81	Here are some questions about how the U.S. government should treat illegal immigrants who have **been in the country for a number of years, hold a job, speak English and are willing to pay any back taxes they owe.** Would you favor or oppose a bill that allowed immigrants to stay in this country rather than being deported and eventually allow them to apply for U.S. citizenship?	CNN/ORC	2/2/2014
78	Do you favor or oppose allowing illegal immigrants to remain in the country and eventually qualify for U.S. citizenship, **as long as they meet certain requirements like paying back taxes, learning English, and passing a background check**?	Fox News	4/22/2013
77	Would you favor or oppose providing a path to citizenship for illegal immigrants in the United States if they met certain requirements including a **waiting period, paying fines and back taxes, passing criminal background checks, and learning English**?	CBS News	10/21/2013
51	The U.S. Senate is considering an immigration bill that would attempt to **increase border security and create a path to citizenship for many immigrants who are in this country without permission** from the U.S. government. Based on what you have read or heard about this bill, do you favor or oppose it?	CNN/ORC	6/13/2013
46	As you may know, the U.S. Senate passed an immigration law that includes **a path to citizenship for undocumented immigrants now living in the United States and stricter border control at a cost of $46 billion.** Do you support or oppose this proposal?	Post/ABC	7/21/2013
46	Congress is debating changing immigration laws. Do you support or oppose a revision of immigration policies that would provide a **path to citizenship for 11 million undocumented immigrants in the United States**?	Bloomberg	6/3/2013

Source: Scott Clemet, "Immigration Reform Is Super Popular. Here's Why Congress Isn't Listening," *Washington Post*, July 2, 2014 (accessed 11/2/15).

make you suspicious that pollsters are trying to skew their findings—rather, they show just how hard it is to accurately measure opinions. (See Take a Stand for more on public opinion on immigration.)

Unreliable Respondents Another problem with surveys is that people are sometimes reluctant to reveal their opinions. Rather than speaking truthfully, they often give socially acceptable answers or answers that they believe the interviewers want to hear. In the case of voter turnout in elections, up to one-fourth of respondents who say they voted when surveyed actually did not vote at all. Political scientists refer to this behavior as the social desirability bias, meaning that people answering survey questions are less willing to admit to actions or express opinions, such as racial prejudice, that they believe their neighbors or society at large would disapprove of.[37]

Pollsters use various techniques to address this problem. One approach is to ask questions in multiple ways; another is to verify answers whenever possible, such as checking with county boards of elections to see if respondents who said they voted actually went to the polls. When there is concern that respondents will try to hide their prejudices, pollsters sometimes frame a question in terms of the entire country rather than the respondent's own beliefs. For example, during the 2008 and 2016 presidential primaries, rather than asking respondents whether they were willing to vote for a woman candidate (such as Democrat Hillary Clinton), some pollsters posed the question indirectly, asking whether a respondent believed that the country was ready for a woman president. Another tactic is to ask respondents for a different kind of evaluation—rather than asking whether they like or dislike candidates, pollsters ask whether they would sit down for a beer (or coffee) with them.

Of course, attempts to account for the social desirability bias by rephrasing a question can introduce new biases. For example, a survey question designed to ask about a sensitive topic might begin with "Some people have argued that . . ." However, in some cases adding this phrase to a question can produce higher levels of respondent agreement regardless of what is being asked. Again, the problem is not that pollsters are dishonest or inept—the problem is that public opinion is often difficult to measure.

The Accuracy of Public Opinion Because poll results play such an important role in media coverage and public discussions about politics, questions are often raised about the assumptions and corrections that pollsters use to account for the inevitable ambiguities related to poll results. During the 2016 presidential campaign, many Republican politicians and observers argued that polls showing a narrow but significant lead for Democrat Hillary Clinton over Republican Donald Trump were the product of inaccurate assumptions about turnout. Some even argued that pollsters were deliberately skewing their findings so as to bolster support for Clinton. Of course, Trump won the election, and it appears that pollsters did misestimate turnout of some groups. However, this outcome does not imply that pollsters altered their surveys to hurt Trump's chances. The same models that mispredicted turnout in 2016 have proved reliable in many other elections; that's why pollsters used them in 2016. Their mistake highlights the difficulty of accurately surveying the American people and shows why we should be reluctant to overinterpret survey results.

In some cases, inaccurate or outlandish survey results are generated because some respondents don't take surveys seriously. They agree to participate but are not interested in explaining their beliefs to a stranger. Faced with a long list of questions, they give quick, thoughtless responses so as to end the interview as quickly as possible. Misperceptions may also result when respondents form opinions on the basis of whatever considerations come to mind. And most importantly, people may reach for considerations that are easy to use but not very informative. Consider claims about Obamacare. A 2015 poll asked people whether health care spending by the federal government was higher or lower than estimates made at the time the program was enacted in 2010. Forty-two percent said spending was higher, 40 percent did not know—and only 5 percent of respondents gave the correct answer, that spending was less than expected.[38]

How can these findings be squared with our earlier statement that Americans generally hold opinions that have some basis in reality? For one thing, many respondents probably had not thought about these questions in detail—and it's likely that only very few knew anything about health care costs in the first place. When asked for an opinion as part of a survey, respondents had no time to do research or think things through. One possibility is that people used partisan considerations: Obama supporters (Democrats) said they didn't know, while Obama opponents (Republicans) said costs were higher than expected. If so, the responses say more about partisanship and attitudes toward President Obama than about the cost of Obamacare.

Misinformation may also result from politicians making polarizing or extreme statements about an issue. Over the last seven years, Republicans have tried to repeal Obamacare nearly 50 times and Republican pundits have described the program in highly negative terms. Donald Trump made repeal of Obamacare a central plank in his campaign platform, and attempts to repeal the program occupied Congress for much of 2016. It's no wonder, then, that Republican survey respondents select negative responses when asked about Obamacare—after all, that's all they've been hearing from the political figures they listen to and trust.

Finally, many supposed facts are actually "contested truths," meaning that even if people move beyond considerations and take into account multiple, nuanced sources of information, they may nevertheless arrive at different conclusions about complex questions.[39] For example, it is a fact that the unemployment rate fell by over a third during President Obama's years in office and has stayed roughly stable during the first two years of Donald Trump's presidency.[40] Do these changes mean that Obama was a better steward of the economy than Trump? Obama took office during the most severe economic downturn since the Great Depression, while Trump has inherited a stable economy. People can easily arrive at different evaluations of Trump and Obama depending on how they account for these starting points.

Such problems do not arise in all areas of public opinion. Studies show that respondents' ability to express specific opinions, as well as the accuracy of their opinions, rises if the survey questions have something to do with their everyday life.[41] Thus, average Americans would be more likely to have an accurate sense of the state of the economy or their personal economic condition than of the military situation in Syria. Everyday life gives us information about the economy; we learn about Syria only if we take time to gather information. These effects are magnified insofar as the respondent considers the economy the more salient issue of the two.

How useful are surveys?

By now, CNN's disclaimer about the limits of mass surveys should not be much of a surprise. Survey results are most likely to be accurate when they are based on a simple, easily understood question about a topic familiar to the people being surveyed—such as the choice between two candidates, measured close to an election—and when the survey designers have worked to account for all the problems discussed here. Under these conditions, with samples of 1,000 voters or more, poll results are generally within 3 or 4 percentage points of the true population values.[42] You can be even more confident if multiple surveys addressing the same topic in different ways and at different times produce similar findings. However, if a single survey asks about a complex, unfamiliar topic—replacing the income tax with a national sales tax or determining whom to blame for a policy failure—then the results may not provide much insight into public opinion.

Should Politicians Follow the Polls?

Elected officials in America work hard to cast votes and take other actions that their constituents will like. At first glance, this behavior seems easy. All a politician needs to do is take a poll, measure public opinion in his or her state or district, and comply with the demands expressed in the survey responses. The problem is, poll results need interpretation. As we saw in Table 6.2, small differences in question wording can produce very different responses, or public opinion can remain vague, despite the polls. As a result, even if representatives want to follow constituent opinion, they may decide that they don't really know enough about these opinions to decide what they should do.

Imagine that a survey on immigration was conducted in your congressional district, asking voters if they favored allowing illegal immigrants to stay in the country or if people here illegally should be deported as soon as possible. Suppose that the poll results indicate strong support for one of the two options and that you yourself have no strong feelings about illegal immigrants. The decision you face is: Should you demand that Congress enact immigration reform consistent with the poll results, or should you quietly ask that immigration reform be kept off the agenda?

Follow the poll. Elected officials often have strong incentives to do what constituents demand—in this case, to push for immigration reform measures that are consistent with the demands expressed in the poll. As we discuss in Chapter 10, one of a representative's jobs is to act in line with the opinions held by his or her constituents. By this logic, if most constituents want immigrants to gain legal status, then you'd ask for a reform proposal that made legal status possible. Conversely, if the poll indicated that most constituents favored deportation, you would push for legislation that funded a program to achieve this goal. Doing so would allow you to claim some credit for the specifics of the bill, as well as for your vote, which in theory would please most of your constituents and increase your chances of reelection.

Stay quiet. As we discuss throughout the chapter, poll results are highly sensitive to question wording, timing, and other factors, making it hard to interpret even seemingly clear findings. Suppose, for example, the poll indicates support for allowing illegal immigrants to gain legal status. However, the survey did not ask about any of the conditions described in Table 6.2: whether legal status would require learning English, holding a stable job, paying back taxes, or other conditions. Even though none of these conditions were in the question, most of your constituents probably had some of them in mind when they thought about how they wanted to answer the question. In other words, your constituents' support of immigration reform depends on what the reforms look like. Even if you want to act in accordance with their demands, the survey may not tell you much about what exactly they want.

The situation is no easier if your poll indicates support for deportation. Would the government search for illegals to deport or just deport people they happen to find? What would happen to children whose parents entered the country illegally but who were born in the United States and are therefore citizens? For some respondents, the solution is a nationwide house-to-house search, with children deported with their parents. But others would reject a deportation process that did either of these things. So here again, the poll results, one-sided as they are, don't provide you with foolproof guidance about how to vote.

 Americans in both parties agree on the need for immigration reform but differ as to what they think the new immigration policies should be.

take a stand

1. Suppose you are a politician who feels that changes in immigration policy are needed but is faced with the quandary described above. Would you do nothing, so as to avoid alienating your constituency, or would you force a policy change and accept the political consequence—possible removal from office?

2. What poll questions would you use to get a clearer picture of public opinion on immigration?

The timing of surveys may also affect how useful the results are. Surveys taken immediately after an event—for example, a survey on gun control taken immediately after a school shooting—are generally not good guides to public opinion. The problem is not that people are being insincere or thoughtless. Rather, it is that respondents' opinions are colored by the recent tragedy—but only in the short term. Over the next days, weeks, or months, opinions are likely to return to what they were before the event. Thus, polls taken in the wake of a powerful event may not be a good guide to what people might demand from government in light of what has happened, nor may they reflect how people might react a year later given government inaction. The same is true of polls taken well in advance of the time when the public actually has to act on their preferences—for example, a poll about the 2020 presidential election taken two years before the election, when most people know almost nothing about the candidates and have not even begun to think about their choice. Under these conditions, poll results tell us almost nothing about what people will ultimately do.

PRESENT FINDINGS ON WHAT AMERICANS THINK ABOUT GOVERNMENT AND WHY IT MATTERS

What Americans think about politics

In this section, we describe American public opinion, including people's ideological beliefs and what they think of the federal government. These opinions drive overall support for government action and serve as the basis for opinions on more specific policy questions. To understand what America's national government does and why, we have to determine what Americans ask of it.

Ideological polarization

ideological polarization
Sharp differences in Americans' overall ideas of the size and scope of government.

We begin by examining liberal and conservative ideology and party identification to see whether historical data show evidence of **ideological polarization**: sharp differences in Americans' overall ideas of the size and scope of government. Many commentators argue that government's inaction on issues like gun control or immigration reform, as well as continued conflict over issues like Obamacare, reflects increased polarization among the American public. The What Do the Facts Say? feature shows two kinds of survey data that can help us evaluate levels of polarization: responses to a question measuring ideology (liberal-moderate-conservative) and a question that taps a respondent's party identification (Republican-Independent-Democrat). The ideological data show no evidence of increased polarization; in the case of partisanship, a substantial percentage of Americans in 2016 described themselves as independents. (For more details on partisanship, see Chapter 8.)

Looking more closely at opinion polarization, the third part of the What Do the Facts Say? feature divides the electorate into nine groups based on answers to questions that tap

Liberal or Conservative Ideology in America

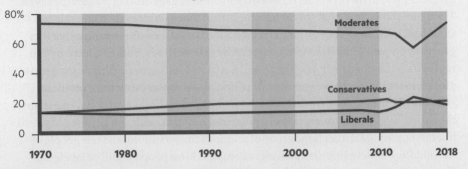

Moderates

Conservatives

Liberals

1970   1980   1990   2000   2010   2018

Party Identification in America

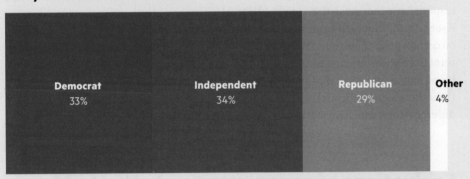

Democrat
33%

Independent
34%

Republican
29%

Other
4%

Political Typology

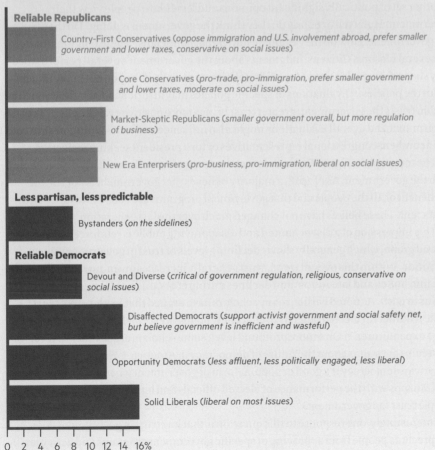

Reliable Republicans

Country-First Conservatives (*oppose immigration and U.S. involvement abroad, prefer smaller government and lower taxes, conservative on social issues*)

Core Conservatives (*pro-trade, pro-immigration, prefer smaller government and lower taxes, moderate on social issues*)

Market-Skeptic Republicans (*smaller government overall, but more regulation of business*)

New Era Enterprisers (*pro-business, pro-immigration, liberal on social issues*)

Less partisan, less predictable

Bystanders (*on the sidelines*)

Reliable Democrats

Devout and Diverse (*critical of government regulation, religious, conservative on social issues*)

Disaffected Democrats (*support activist government and social safety net, but believe government is inefficient and wasteful*)

Opportunity Democrats (*less affluent, less politically engaged, less liberal*)

Solid Liberals (*liberal on most issues*)

0   2   4   6   8   10   12   14   16%

WHAT DO THE FACTS SAY?

Are the American People Polarized?

Many commentators describe politics in America as highly conflictual, with most Americans holding either liberal or conservative points of view and identifying with one of the two major parties. Is polarization as strong as these commentators think?

Sources: Data from General Social Survey 1972–2016, Cumulative Datafile, Survey Documentation and Analysis (SDA) at UC Berkeley, http://sda.berkeley.edu (accessed 11/0/17); Pew Research Center, "Trends in Party Identification, 1939–2016," September 6, 2016, www.people-press.org (accessed 11/7/17); Pew Research Center, "Political Typology Reveals Deep Fissures on the Right and Left," October 26, 2017, www.people-press.org (accessed 11/7/17).

Think about it

- According to the top figure, how have levels of polarization changed since the 1970s?
- What does the political typology reveal about divisions within each political party?

important principles, from foreign policy to domestic issues, civil liberties, and morality. Principles such as these are a kind of consideration—they form the basis for opinions that people express in surveys or act on when they vote or engage in other political behavior. The figure shows, first, that only about one-fifth of the electorate (Solid Liberals and Country-First Conservatives) hold consistent ideological beliefs—meaning that they generally give one kind of answer (conservative or liberal) when asked questions that tap their underlying principles. Moreover, most people fall into one of the intermediate groups, meaning that they express a mix of liberal and conservative issue positions.

While these data confirm that Americans disagree on important policy questions, they argue against the conception of a polarized America, with a large group of secular liberals opposing another large group of religious conservatives, and few people in the middle. Public opinion is much more complex. Most people could be labeled as liberals or as conservatives, secular or religious, depending on which issues they are asked about. Thus, even though people say they are liberals (or conservatives), this response does not mean that they hold liberal (or conservative) preferences on all issues. In addition, self-professed moderates may hold relatively extreme preferences on certain policy questions. Thus, understanding what Americans think and what they want from government often requires data on specific policy questions rather than broad judgments about the liberal or conservative nature of American public opinion. (Whether elected officials themselves are more polarized than their constituents is a different story, which we will discuss in Chapter 11.)

Evaluations of government and officeholders

Another set of politically significant opinions addresses how people view their government: How well or poorly do they think the government is doing? Do they trust the government? How do they evaluate individual politicians? These opinions matter for several reasons. Citizens' judgments about the government's overall performance may shape their evaluations of specific policies, especially if they do not know much about the policies.[43] Evaluations of specific policies may also be shaped by how much a citizen trusts the government; greater trust brings more positive evaluations.[44] Trust in government and overall evaluations might also influence a citizen's willingness to vote for incumbent congressional representatives or for a president seeking reelection.[45]

The top graph in Figure 6.4 reveals that the average American is fairly disenchanted with the government. As of 2018, a majority believes that government is not run for the benefit of all the people and that government programs are usually wasteful and inefficient. These beliefs have not changed much over the last generation.

This impression of a disenchanted and disapproving public is reinforced by the second graph, which generally shows declining levels of trust in government since the 1960s. Within this overall trend, trust generally increases given a strong economy (the mid-1980s and late 1990s) and declines during economic hard times (the mid-2000s to now). As noted earlier, many scholars have argued that low levels of trust make it harder for elected officials to enact new policies, especially those that require large expenditures.[46] On a more profound level, some scholars argue that low levels of trust raise questions about the future of democracy in America.[47] How can we say that American democracy is a good or popular form of government when so many people are unhappy with the performance of elected officials and bureaucrats and so few people trust the government?

Interestingly, one response to this question is that low trust in government does not preclude people from approving of specific government programs and activities.

Trust in government reached a low point during the mid-1970s. The decline partly reflected the economic downturn and conflict over the Vietnam War, but opinions were also shaped by the discovery that President Richard Nixon had lied about the Watergate scandal. Here, Nixon resigns from office to avoid impeachment.

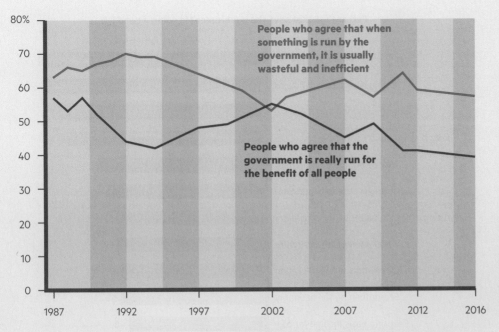

People who agree that when something is run by the government, it is usually wasteful and inefficient

People who agree that the government is really run for the benefit of all people

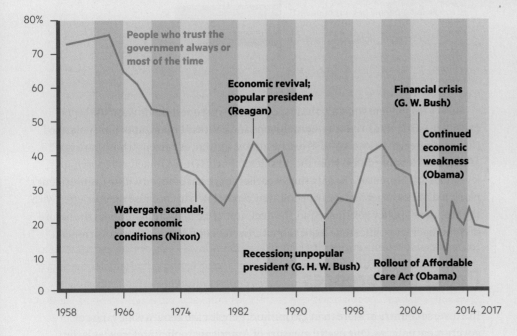

People who trust the government always or most of the time

Watergate scandal; poor economic conditions (Nixon)

Economic revival; popular president (Reagan)

Recession; unpopular president (G. H. W. Bush)

Financial crisis (G. W. Bush)

Continued economic weakness (Obama)

Rollout of Affordable Care Act (Obama)

FIGURE 6.4

What Do Americans Think about Government?

A significant percentage of Americans have always been distrustful and disparaging of the federal government—and the percentage of people holding such views has increased markedly in the last generation. Does the perception that government is wasteful and inefficient make it easier or harder to enact new policies? How might the decline in trust explain the rise of the Tea Party organization and candidates like Donald Trump and Bernie Sanders?

Source: Pew Research Center, "Public Trust in Government, 1958–2017," May 5, 2015, www.people-press.org (accessed 11/8/17).

Figure 6.5 shows that a majority of Americans give positive evaluations of a wide range of government programs, suggesting that the downward trend in trust is not the result of people being increasingly unhappy with what government actually does.

A second response is that although Americans don't like the government in general, they tend to be far more satisfied with their own representatives in Washington (see Chapter 11). One possibility is that putting a human face on government by asking about specific individuals in office improves respondents' opinions because it calls to mind different considerations. Asking about "the government" may call to mind a vast room of bureaucrats pushing paperwork from one desk to another, whereas asking about "your representative" may lead people to think of someone working on their behalf.

FIGURE 6.5

Measuring American Public Opinion: Is the Government Doing a Good Job?

How is it that Americans disapprove of government overall but give relatively high ratings in many specific areas?

Source: Pew Research Center, "Beyond Distrust: How Americans View Their Government," November 23, 2015, www. people-press.org (accessed 12/5/15).

Percentage that says the government is doing a good job . . .

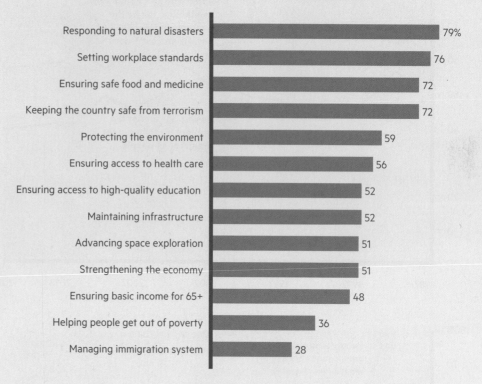

Responding to natural disasters	79%
Setting workplace standards	76
Ensuring safe food and medicine	72
Keeping the country safe from terrorism	72
Protecting the environment	59
Ensuring access to health care	56
Ensuring access to high-quality education	52
Maintaining infrastructure	52
Advancing space exploration	51
Strengthening the economy	51
Ensuring basic income for 65+	48
Helping people get out of poverty	36
Managing immigration system	28

Survey respondents may also be responding to trust questions in ways we do not expect. In particular, in an era where citizens and political organizations are polarized to some degree, high levels of distrust are almost a given, as citizens whose partisan affiliation or leaning differs from the president's party ID are unlikely to report high levels of trust. Moreover, the data shown earlier suggests that even within the president's party, a significant percentage of people may report low trust because they disagree with the president's policy positions. If so, the decline in trust may say more about the nature of contemporary politics than it does about citizens' confidence in their government.

Policy preferences

In a diverse country of more than 330 million, people care about a wide range of government policies. One useful measure of Americans' policy preferences is the **policy mood**, mentioned earlier, which captures the public's collective demands for government action on domestic policies.[48] Policy mood measures are constructed from surveys that ask about opinions on a wide range of policy questions.[49]

Changes in the policy mood in America have led to changes in defense spending, environmental policy, and civil rights policies, among others—and have influenced elections (see Figure 6.6).[50] When the policy mood leans in an activist direction (Americans want government to do more, corresponding to lower values on the vertical axis), such as in the early 1960s, conditions are ripe for an expansion of the federal government involving more spending and new programs. In contrast, when the policy mood leans in the opposite direction (Americans want a smaller, less-active government, corresponding to higher values on the vertical axis), elected officials are likely to enact smaller increases in government spending and fewer new programs—or, as in recent elections, candidates

policy mood
The level of public support for expanding the government's role in society; whether the public wants government action on a specific issue.

Policy Mood

FIGURE 6.6

Surveys assess the public's policy mood by asking questions about specific policy questions such as levels of taxation and government spending and the role of government. The level of conservatism (for example, support for smaller, less-active government) was at a high in 1952 and 1980. Could you have used the policy mood prior to the election to predict the outcomes of the 2018 congressional elections?

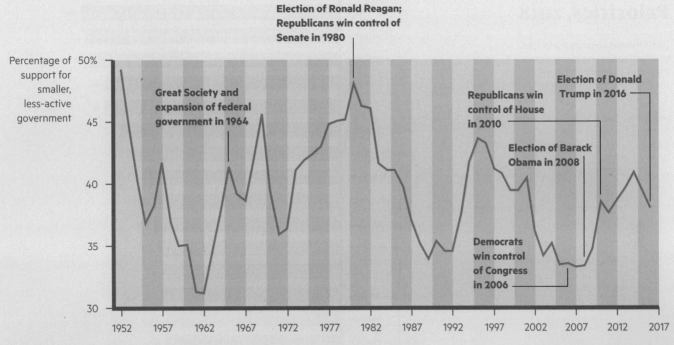

Source: Policy mood data available at http://stimson.web.unc.edu/data (accessed 10/1/18).

who are in favor of a more active government are more likely to be defeated. At present, opposition to government action is at nearly its highest level since the late 1980s. Given these opinions, we should not expect a major expansion in the size and scope of government, at least not until the public policy mood moves in a more activist direction.

Regarding more specific policy preferences, everything we have said in this chapter reinforces the idea that public opinion is often a moving target. While some beliefs and preferences are stable over time, opinions about specific policies can change from year to year, month to month, or even day to day. One of the best ways to take a snapshot of these beliefs is to ask citizens what they see as the top policy priorities facing the nation. Figure 6.7 shows responses to a 2017 survey.

The top priorities—terrorism, the economy, education, Social Security, and health care—have not changed very much over the last several decades. The only difference is that terrorism appeared on the list only after the September 11 attacks in 2001. It is no exaggeration to say that Americans are always worried about the economy. Even when other pressing issues, such as terrorism, surpass the economy as the most important problem to Americans, the economy is typically listed second or third. In general, as the state of the economy declines, more and more people rate the economy as their greatest concern. Moreover, the percentage of people who make reference to their personal economic concerns—for example, unemployment or worries about retirement—also increases.

These policy priorities frame contemporary political debates and divide the political parties. Think about what Republicans and Democrats in Washington argue about:

FIGURE
6.7

The American Public's Policy Priorities, 2018

Given this data on policy priorities, what legislation would you expect President Trump to propose during the final two years of his term?

Source: Pew Research Center, "Economic Issues Decline among Public's Policy Priorities," www.people-press.org (accessed 7/31/18).

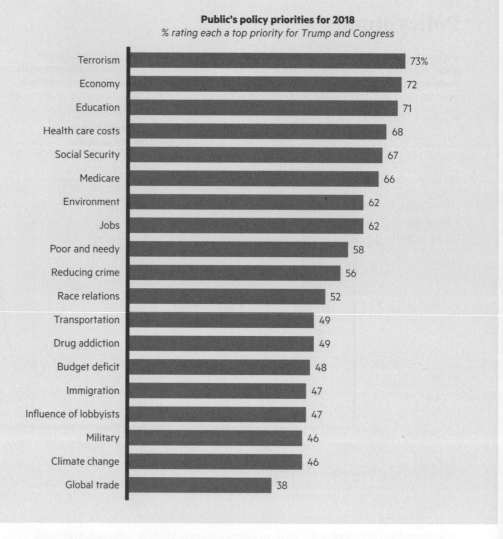

Public's policy priorities for 2018
% rating each a top priority for Trump and Congress

Terrorism	73%
Economy	72
Education	71
Health care costs	68
Social Security	67
Medicare	66
Environment	62
Jobs	62
Poor and needy	58
Reducing crime	56
Race relations	52
Transportation	49
Drug addiction	49
Budget deficit	48
Immigration	47
Influence of lobbyists	47
Military	46
Climate change	46
Global trade	38

how best to fight terrorism and secure the United States from attack, how to increase economic growth and reduce the unemployment rate, and what the government's role should be in providing health care and making sure that Americans have secure retirements. In a very fundamental way, then, this list confirms that American politicians are intimately connected to their constituents—the issues that politicians debate and legislate on are the ones that many people care about.

The list of policy priorities also explains government inaction on some issues. For example, only 46 percent of Americans see climate change as a top policy priority—and gun control doesn't even appear on the list. Thus, the fact that Congress has not legislated on either of these issues in recent years is actually consistent with public opinion. For better or worse, the average American has other priorities for government action.

Does public opinion matter?

We can say with confidence that public opinion remains highly relevant in American politics today. One key piece of evidence is the amount of time and effort politicians, journalists, and political scientists spend trying to find out what Americans think. Of course, it is easy to find examples like gun control in which policy has stayed the same despite a majority supporting change. In other cases, such as the enactment of Obamacare, new policies have been passed even though a majority preferred the status quo at the time of enactment. But these examples do not mean that public opinion is irrelevant—just that the policy-making process is complex. It is not always possible to please a majority of citizens. Politicians' willingness to do so depends on whether the majority is organized into interest groups, how much they care about the issue (and the intensity of the opposition), and, most important, the details of their preferences.

More broadly, public opinion exerts a conspicuous influence in widespread areas of government. We mention this broad influence repeatedly throughout this book. In Chapter 11, we describe how legislators endeavor to determine what their constituents want and how their constituents will respond to different actions. In Chapter 9, we see how voters use retrospective evaluations to form opinions about whom to vote for and how candidates incorporate the public's views into campaign platforms that will attract widespread support. And in Chapter 8, we discuss how voters use candidates' party affiliations like brand names to determine how candidates will behave if elected. Scholars have found that congressional actions on a wide range of issues, from votes on defense policy to the confirmation of Supreme Court nominees, are shaped by constituent opinion.[51] Moreover, careful analysis of the connection between opinions and actions shows that this linkage does not exist because politicians are able to shape public opinion in line with what they want to do; rather, politicians behave in line with their constituents' opinions because to do otherwise would place the politicians in jeopardy of losing the next election.[52]

Public opinion influences government at election time, when voters' opinions about incumbent politicians and the party in power affect their decisions at the polls. In 2018, voters' evaluations of President Trump were an important factor in the election outcome.

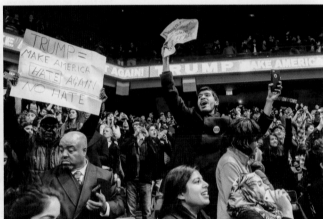

Recent events also speak to the influence of public opinion. Think about the failure of elected officials over the last few years to repeal Obamacare, enact immigration reform, or pass new limits on the ownership of handguns and assault rifles. In all of these cases, a significant portion of Americans wanted policy change, but a substantial percentage were opposed, and even the supporters disagreed on what kinds of changes were best. Congressional inaction on these measures does not reflect a willful ignorance of public opinion. Rather, it reflects the lack of a public consensus about what government should do. Inaction on these issues is exactly what we should expect if public opinion is real and relevant to what happens in politics.

Political scientists and pollsters spend so much time trying to measure public opinion because it shapes election outcomes and policy changes in Washington. If you want to know what the federal government is going to do (or why it's not doing what you think it should be doing), spend some time trying to determine where your own policy opinions fit in with the policy opinions of the country as a whole.

"Why Should I Care?"

Unpacking the Conflict

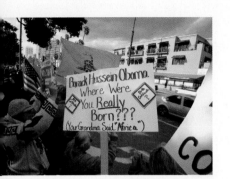

Considering all that we've discussed in this chapter, let's apply what we know about how public opinion works to the examples from the beginning of the chapter. Do Americans really hold the bizarre beliefs that are sometimes expressed in polling results? Can we take polls seriously, if they produce results like these?

Given how people form opinions, it's easy to see what Jon Stewart was talking about: at least some of the time, public opinion will be incomplete at best and wildly inaccurate at worst. But that's not surprising. For most people, politics is not the most important thing in their lives, and they don't spend much time worrying about it, learning the details, or forming judgments until they need to.

When we ask how "good" opinions are, or whether the electorate acts "rationally and responsibly," as V. O. Key argued, the most important thing to remember is that there is no absolute standard of accuracy. One of the fundamental tenets of a democracy is that people are free to hold whatever opinions they want, and to base these opinions on whatever factors they want to consider. If someone says she approves of Trump's performance in office, and we determine that her judgment is based on Trump's being a Republican, this opinion is as legitimate as that of someone whose evaluation is based on a detailed study of multiple factors. Moreover, making sense of politics requires people to make some pretty sophisticated judgments, and it would be no surprise to find that they make mistakes some of the time, particularly given the shortcuts they use to form their opinions. Nevertheless, the model of opinion formation described in this chapter provides observers of American politics with a guide for interpreting public opinion, including how opinions will change given events.

Should we take polls seriously? Yes, but not too much. Given all the potential problems with mass surveys, we should be suspicious about surprising results such as the support for conspiracy theories cited at the beginning of this chapter. Respondents may have not taken the question seriously, they may have focused on subtle details of the question—or their reply may have been driven by considerations that have nothing to do with the question at hand. Republican suspicions about Barack Obama's citizenship probably reflected the fact that their party's presidential candidate, Donald Trump, had repeatedly voiced his suspicions during the campaign. And Democratic concerns about the government's foreknowledge of the September 11 attacks were colored by the identity of the president at the time, Republican George W. Bush. More generally, we should take poll results seriously to the extent that they are based on multiple surveys, with differently worded questions; are conducted by reputable pollsters; and are conducted at a time when respondents are aware of the issues they are being asked about. One poll on its own doesn't tell us very much.

In sum, while you can't take every poll result you see at face value, public opinion is real, and it matters. Americans have ideas about what they want government to do, and they use these ideas to guide their political choices. Polls showing deep disagreement between Americans on some issues describe the policy landscape on which elections will be contested and the subsequent debates in Washington. While very few Americans are policy experts, their views on policy are the ultimate driver of our government's policy choices.

What's Your Take?

Is public opinion important enough that politicians should follow it? Or is public opinion too unreliable and unpredictable to trust? And if public opinion cannot be trusted, whose wishes should government follow, if not the people's?

STUDY GUIDE

and our social groups influence our perspectives later in life. Personal events such as attending college or moving to a new city may also influence how we think about politics, as do national events such as the attacks on September 11, 2001. Even debates among political elites and party leaders shape our political attitudes.

Key term
political socialization (p. 203)

What is public opinion?

Define *public opinion* and explain why it matters in American politics. (Pages 200–202)

Summary

What the population thinks about politics and government matters for three reasons: people's political actions are driven by their opinions; there is a strong linkage between people's opinions and political actors' behavior; and public opinion helps us understand how specific policy outcomes are achieved. Although early research was skeptical that people held meaningful opinions, current research shows that people do have real and meaningful policy positions.

Key terms

public opinion (p. 200)   latent opinion (p. 201)
liberal or conservative ideology
   (p. 201)

Practice Quiz Question

1. **What does it mean that most political judgments are latent opinions?**

   a   Most Americans have preformed opinions.

   b   Most Americans have well-thought-out reasons for preferring a policy.

   c   Most Americans do not have any meaningful political attitudes.

   d   Most Americans form their opinions only as needed.

   e   Most opinions are not accurate.

Where do opinions come from?

Explain how people form political attitudes and opinions. (Pages 203–211)

Summary

Political opinions are influenced by a number of factors. The belief systems of parents and relatives influence our opinions early on,

Practice Quiz Questions

2. **Which of the following is *not* true regarding considerations?**

   a   Well-informed and poorly informed people use them in forming opinions.

   b   Opinions on morally complex issues do not involve considerations.

   c   Political events can become considerations.

   d   They may be contradictory.

   e   Party identification is often used in considerations.

3. **The theory of political socialization says that people's opinions are influenced first by _____.**

   a   what they learned from their parents

   b   the way political parties change over time

   c   genetic and biological factors

   d   their personality traits

   e   politicians

4. **An event or some other new information is most likely to change an individual's opinion when _____.**

   a   the individual is highly informed about the issue

   b   the individual holds strong opinions

   c   the individual is strongly partisan

   d   the individual does not have a set of preexisting principles with which to interpret the event

   e   the individual does not watch the news

5. **The idea that individuals will rely on others who "look like" them for opinions relates to _____.**

   a   party identification

   b   political socialization

   c   group identity

   d   political events

   e   generational effects

6. **Which phrase best completes the following statement regarding the sources of public opinion? "Politicians and other political actors work to _____ public opinion."**

   a   respond to

   b   ignore

   c   disregard

   d   stabilize

   e   shape

Measuring public opinion

Describe basic survey methods and potential issues affecting accuracy. (Pages 211–220)

Summary

While most information on public opinion comes from mass surveys where thousands of people respond, some information comes from focus groups where small groups of people are interviewed together. Despite a number of limitations, most research on public opinion focuses on mass surveys, as they can be used to draw broad conclusions about the country.

Key terms

mass survey (p. 211)   **sampling error** (p. 214)
population (p. 211)   **random sample** (p. 215)
sample (p. 211)

Practice Quiz Questions

7. Why are focus groups helpful in understanding public opinion?

a   They provide deep insights into why people hold the views that they do.

b   They provide a representative sample of the population.

c   They use a small number of respondents to draw conclusions about the country.

d   It is impossible to understand someone's partisanship based on a survey.

e   They restrict respondents to a few answer choices.

8. Which of the following is *not* a random sampling technique?

a   random digit dialing

b   face-to-face interviewing

c   Internet polling

d   push polls

e   robo-polling

9. Why is it important to get a large random survey sample?

a   to keep costs down

b   to provide deep insights into why people hold their opinions

c   to help candidates fine-tune their campaign messages

d   to be able to generalize about the broad population

e   to prevent question wording from biasing survey results

10. Suppose a survey of Americans' attitudes about NSA surveillance of cell phone records reveals that the level of opposition to surveillance varies with how the question is phrased. What is the best explanation for this variation?

a   People don't take surveys seriously.

b   People are afraid to express truthful opinions on surveys.

c   Changes in the wording of questions call to mind different considerations.

d   Changes in the wording of questions make people suspicious.

e   Few people can respond in a rational way to survey questions.

What Americans think about politics

Present findings on what Americans think about government and why it matters. (Pages 220–227)

Summary

As a whole, the American electorate is ideologically moderate, with relatively little ideological polarization. Paradoxically, although trust in the government has declined steadily since the 1960s, people are still generally happy with their own representatives in Washington, D.C., and low trust in government does not preclude Americans from approving of specific government programs and activities. While it can be difficult to determine exactly what the American public wants, public opinion is still quite relevant in American politics. Government policy and congressional outcomes are responsive to changes in public mood, and most policy decisions (and arguments) reflect the priorities of a majority of Americans.

Key terms

ideological polarization (p. 220)   **policy mood** (p. 224)

Practice Quiz Questions

11. In the 1970s, the majority of Americans identified themselves as ideologically _____; in the 2000s, most Americans identified themselves as _____.

a   moderate; conservative

b   moderate; moderate

c   moderate; liberal

d   conservative; moderate

e   conservative; conservative

12. What is policy mood?

a   public support for Congress

b   presidential approval rating

c   trust in government

d   public demand for government action on domestic policies

e   public demand for government action on international policies

13. Which policy area is always near the top of Americans' concerns?

a   economic conditions

b   health care

c   same-sex marriage

d   immigration

e   the environment

14. Americans generally _____ of the government and generally _____ of their own representatives.

a   approve; approve

b   approve; disapprove

c   disapprove; approve

d   disapprove; disapprove

15. When the government enacts policies even though a majority of Americans prefer the status quo, it serves as evidence that _____.

a public opinion is irrelevant

b the policy-making process is complex

c politicians don't listen to what their constituents want

d the government is not trustworthy

e public opinion is stable

_____

Suggested Reading

Achen, Christopher H., and Larry M. Bartels. *Democracy for Realists: Why Elections Do Not Produce Responsive Government*. Princeton, NJ: Princeton University Press, 2016.

Alvarez, R. Michael, and John Brehm. *Hard Choices, Easy Answers*. Princeton, NJ: Princeton University Press, 2002.

Campbell, David. *Why We Vote: How Schools and Communities Shape Our Civic Life*. Princeton, NJ: Princeton University Press, 2006.

Carmines, Edward G., and James A. Stimson. *Issue Evolution: Race and the Transformation of American Politics*. Princeton, NJ: Princeton University Press, 1990.

Delli Carpini, Michael X., and Scott Keeter. *What Americans Know about Politics and Why It Matters*. New Haven, CT: Yale University Press, 1997.

Druckman, James N., and Lawrence P. Jacobs. *Who Governs? Presidents, Public Opinion, and Manipulation*. Chicago: University of Chicago Press, 2015.

Green, Donald P., Bradley Palmquist, and Eric Schickler. *Partisan Hearts and Minds*. New Haven, CT: Yale University Press, 2002.

Hetherington, Mark, and Thomas Rudolph. *Why Washington Won't Work: Polarization, Political Trust, and the Governing Crisis*. Chicago: University of Chicago Press, 2015.

Hibbing, John R., and Elizabeth Theiss-Morse. *Congress as Public Enemy: Public Attitudes toward American Political Institutions*. New York: Cambridge University Press, 1995.

Jacobs, Lawrence R., and Robert Y. Shapiro. *Politicians Don't Pander: Political Manipulation and the Loss of Democratic Responsiveness*. Chicago: University of Chicago Press, 2000.

Lodge, Milton, and Charles Taber. *The Rationalizing Voter*. New York: Cambridge University Press, 2013.

Marcus, George E., John L. Sullivan, Elizabeth Theiss-Morse, and Sandra L. Wood. *With Malice toward Some: How People Make Civil Liberties Judgments*. New York: Cambridge University Press, 1995.

Peffley, Mark, and Jon Hurwitz. *Justice in America: The Separate Realities of Blacks and Whites*. New York: Cambridge University Press, 2010.

Zaller, John. *The Nature and Origins of Mass Opinion*. New York: Cambridge University Press, 1992.

7

The Media

Do the media make us more informed?

» **"Social media [will] spark a revelation that we, the people, have a voice, and through the democratization of content and ideas we can once again unite around common passions, inspire movements, and ignite change."**
Brian Solis, business analyst

« **"If there's one fundamental truth about social media's impact on democracy it's that it amplifies human intent—both good and bad. At its best, it allows us to express ourselves and take action. At its worst, it allows people to spread misinformation and corrode democracy. I wish I could guarantee that the positives are destined to outweigh the negatives, but I can't."**
Samidh Chakrabarti, project manager, Facebook

Social media has transformed virtually all aspects of our everyday lives, including the ways we engage with politics. Many hoped that social media would increase citizens' ability to shape government policies in line with their interests, including business analyst Brian Solis, who touts social media's powers of "democratization."[1]

At one level, Solis is right on the mark: the rise of social media has radically increased the amount of information available to the average citizen. For example, social media makes it easier to research colleges and identify the one that best fits your needs and constraints, particularly by talking directly with people who have firsthand knowledge of different options. Social media does the same in politics: you can use it to find more information in any number of ways, from identifying candidates who share your views to learning about the details of policy proposals. Solis's and others' grand expectations for social media assume that people want to be well informed and are willing to invest time and effort to seek out multiple information sources and weigh differing viewpoints to arrive at detailed judgments about the merits of different candidates and the policies they espouse.

At the same time, there is little evidence that the rise of social media and other changes in media coverage of politics have produced a better-informed or more politically active citizenry. As Samidh Chakrabarti of Facebook acknowledges, along

Immigration activists staged a sit-in in Senator Michael Bennet's office (D-CO) to demand that he act in favor of DREAM legislation. They broadcast the sit-in on Facebook Live to raise awareness of their protest. Social media can be used as a tool for citizens to effect positive political change, but it also has its downsides.

CHAPTER GOALS

Describe the role of the media in American politics and how people get political information. pages 234–241

Explain how politicians use the media to achieve their goals. pages 241–245

Explain how the media influence how people think about politics. pages 245–253

Assess whether the media fulfill their role in American democracy. pages 253–257 with the good that social media facilitates comes the bad.[2] If anything, citizens are more polarized and more suspicious of media coverage than they were even 10 or 20 years ago, in part because of social media. Average citizens do not take the time to conscientiously consult different information presented by social media: as we saw in Chapter 6, they form beliefs only when necessary, and on the basis of relatively little information. The idea that social media would make our politics better also assumed that the producers of media content, from mainstream sources like the *New York Times* to anonymous Twitter users who post insider information about government agency decisions, would all work toward the goal of empowering the American public. The reality is that the media is a business, in which the goal of attracting an audience often conflicts with more idealistic goals of telling people what they need to know to make good decisions and acting as a watchdog to monitor government actions. President Trump's tweets about "fake news" are a symptom rather than a cause of this transformation.

The disconnect between expectations about social media and the actual effects that social media has had on American politics highlights a larger question about the role of the media in American politics. For democracy to work well, citizens need information about what government is doing or could do: they need the media to function as a watchdog, keeping track of politicians and public policy, deconstructing complex issues, and helping to inform the citizenry. However, many Americans are uninformed or misinformed about many aspects of politics and are highly suspicious of both mainstream and social media, the principle mechanism by which they might learn what they need to know. Social media was supposed to inform us and bring us together—what went wrong? Why don't Americans trust the media as a watchdog?

DESCRIBE THE ROLE OF THE MEDIA IN AMERICAN POLITICS AND HOW PEOPLE GET POLITICAL INFORMATION

mass media
Sources that provide information to the average citizen, such as newspapers, television networks, radio stations, podcasts, and websites.

Political media today

This section describes the **mass media**, the many sources of political information available to Americans, and how people use (or don't use) this information. The development of the Internet and the expansion of social media over the last generation has dramatically increased the number of media sources and the range of information available to the average American. This changing media landscape means that it is less important to describe each media source and what kinds of information it can (and cannot) provide. In contemporary America, there are so many sources and so much information that Americans can become experts on virtually any aspect of politics or public policy—if they are willing to search for information and put together what they find.

Historical overview: how did we get here?

The role of the media as an information source and the controversy over how the media report about politics are nothing new. Since the Founding, politicians have understood that Americans learn about politics largely from the media, have complained about coverage, and have sought to influence both the stories the media selects and the way they report on them.

The Media as Watchdog and Business From the beginnings of the United States, mass media has served as a reporter of political events and as a watchdog: keeping track of what politicians are doing and offering insight about their policy successes and failures. Many newspapers chronicled the conflicts of the Revolutionary War; after the war, while politicians negotiated over the size and scope of the new federal government, newspapers became a venue for debates over different plans.[3] While the media cover politics, politicians have always tried to shape this coverage to their advantage. During the ratification of the Constitution, for instance, Alexander Hamilton, John Jay, and James Madison supported pro-ratification forces in New York by publishing (under a pseudonym) a series of articles that came to be known as the *Federalist Papers* in local newspapers.[4] And in 1798 Congress and President John Adams enacted the Alien and Sedition Acts, which made it a crime to publish articles that criticized the president or Congress.[5] While these press restrictions were later repealed or allowed to expire, they serve as a reminder that the American media have never been free of government regulation or of the conflictual relationship between politicians and reporters.

Long before the Internet, changes in technology expanded the media's role as information provider, entertainment, and watchdog. In 1833, the *New York Sun* began selling papers for a penny a copy rather than the standard price of six cents. The price reduction, which was facilitated by cheaper, faster printing presses, made the newspaper available to the mass public for the first time, and this increase in circulation made it possible, even with the lower price, to hire larger staffs of reporters.[6] The development of the telegraph also aided newspapers by enabling reporters on assignment throughout the country to quickly send stories back home for publication. Many of the new publications were unabashedly partisan. For example, the *New York Tribune* was strongly antislavery. By 1860, the *Tribune*'s circulation was larger than that of any other newspaper in the world and its articles "helped to add fuel to the fires of slavery and sectionalism that divided North and South."[7] At the other extreme, the *New York Times* was transformed in the 1800s into a nonpartisan paper with the goals of journalistic impartiality, accuracy, and complete coverage of events—its motto to the present day is "All the News That's Fit to Print."[8]

The media's role as a watchdog has always been constrained by the need to attract a paying audience in order to stay in business and turn a profit. The period after the Civil War saw the beginning of **yellow journalism**, reporting that drew in customers by using bold headlines, illustrations, and sensational stories (the name came from the yellow paper these newspapers were printed on). And during the 1920s hundreds of small, local radio stations appeared, along with some larger stations that could broadcast nationwide. The proliferation of stations eventually led to the development of networks, that is, groups of local radio (and, later, television) stations owned by one company that broadcast a common set of programs. While these new electronic sources made more information available to Americans, many of them were developed not as watchdogs but as highly profitable enterprises that delivered entertainment as well as news to citizens and monetized their audience by selling radio or television time to advertisers.[9]

Regulating the Media Until 1930 or so, there was only minimal federal regulation of the media, reflecting the Constitution's guarantee of freedom of the press—and the fact that newspapers were the only media source that existed. With the rise of the **broadcast media**, including radio and television, and the formation of the **Federal Communications Commission (FCC)** to allocate broadcast frequencies, a new position emerged: if broadcasters were going to make money off their use of a scarce resource, the government could place conditions on how this business operated. In recent years, new technologies (cable TV, the Internet) have changed the calculation; the emphasis is now on encouraging competition among media sources rather than regulating a few providers.

Yellow journalism emphasized sensational stories and bold headlines, but also made information about contemporary politics available to a wider audience.

yellow journalism
A style of newspaper reporting popular in the late 1800s that featured sensationalized stories, bold headlines, and illustrations to increase readership.

broadcast media
Communications technologies, such as television and radio, that transmit information over airwaves.

Federal Communications Commission (FCC)
A government agency created in 1934 to regulate American radio stations and later expanded to regulate television, wireless communications technologies, and other broadcast media.

President Trump has argued that he should receive "equal time" under the FCC's equal time regulations due to the negative coverage he often receives from late-night television hosts like Jimmy Kimmel and Trevor Noah. Trump tweeted: "Late Night host are dealing with the Democrats for their very 'unfunny' & repetitive material, always anti-Trump! Should we get Equal Time?"

equal time provision
An FCC regulation requiring broadcast media to provide equal air time on any non-news programming to all candidates running for an office.

media conglomerates
Companies that control a large number of media sources across several types of media outlets.

Federal regulation of broadcast media was driven by the concern that one company or organization might buy enough stations to dominate the airwaves in a given area and become a monopoly, offering only one set of programs or point of view. For many years, FCC regulations limited the number of radio and television stations a company could own in a community and the total nationwide audience that a company's television stations could reach. The FCC also created the **equal time provision**, which says that if a radio or television station gives air time to a candidate outside of its routine news coverage—such as during an entertainment show or a cooking program—it has to give an equivalent amount of time to other candidates running for the same office. For example, when then–presidential candidate Donald Trump hosted *Saturday Night Live* in November 2015, the television network (NBC) that broadcast the program had to give free television time (in the form of free advertising slots) to other presidential candidates. The FCC also established a fairness doctrine, whereby broadcasters had to present opposing points of view as part of their coverage of important events; usually this was done by broadcasting editorials during news programs that presented both sides of an issue.

Deregulation The FCC's limits on ownership and content as well as the fairness doctrine have been eliminated because of the development of new communications technologies. The logic is that with so many sources of information, if one broadcaster ignores a candidate, an issue, or a viewpoint, citizens can still find out what they want to know from another source. Pressure for deregulation also came from the owners of media companies, who wanted to buy more television, radio, and cable stations, as well as from book and magazine publishers, Internet service providers, and newspapers.[10]

These regulatory changes have shaped the current media landscape in two ways. First, they have allowed for concentration: many media companies own multiple media sources in a town or community. For example, iHeartMedia owns over 850 AM and FM radio stations, including multiple stations in more than 30 cities. The second trend is cross-ownership, in which one company owns several different kinds of media outlets, often in the same community. For example, the Tribune Company in Chicago owns the WGN radio station, the WGN television station, and the *Chicago Tribune* daily newspaper. These trends have given rise to **media conglomerates**, companies that control a wide range of news sources.[11] Nuts & Bolts 7.1 shows the diverse holdings of one such company, News Corp/21st Century Fox.

Media sources in the twenty-first century

Over the last two decades, the Internet has become a major and often dominant information source for information about American politics. Virtually all U.S. newspapers, magazines, television networks, radio stations, and cable stations offer free or (increasingly) paid access to all their content via websites and mobile apps. Many Internet-only sites offer a combination of rumor, inside information, and deep analysis of American politics. Some, such as Politico, Vox, and FiveThirtyEight, have paid staff and report on a wide range of topics. Others have a narrower focus: the Monkey Cage (now affiliated with the *Washington Post*) and the Mischiefs of Faction (now part of Vox) use political science research to explain contemporary American

Holdings of News Corp/21st Century Fox

News Corp/21st Century Fox* is an example of a media conglomerate, a company that controls a variety of media outlets throughout the world. It owns cable television networks, television and radio stations, newspapers, movie-production companies, magazines, and even sports teams. This structure allows the company to rebroadcast or reprint stories in different outlets and thus operate more efficiently, but opponents are concerned that conglomerates might expand to control most—or even all—of the sources that are available to the average citizen, making it impossible to access alternate points of view.

Fox Television Stations	Film Companies	Books and Magazines
32 U.S. stations	21st Century Fox Fox Searchlight Pictures Fox Television Studios Blue Sky Studios 11 other film companies	45 book publishers (including HarperCollins) worldwide 3 magazines

Satellite and Cable Holdings	Newspapers	Other Holdings
Fox News Channel Fox Sports More than 60 other cable channels in and outside the United States 6 satellite television channels	*New York Post* *Wall Street Journal* *Barron's* 4 UK newspapers 19 Australian newspapers 30 local U.S. newspapers	Over 50 news and entertainment websites Many other businesses

*These two companies were created in 2013 by dividing the operations of the News Corporation. However, the founder of the News Corporation, Rupert Murdoch, is the chairman and CEO of 21st Century Fox and the executive chairman of News Corp, and his family trust still holds a controlling interest in both corporations.

politics.[12] And many websites, some run by ordinary citizens, provide their own insights and information about American politics. Finally, Facebook, Twitter, and other social media sites provide users with links to coverage written by others; people also use these sites to report and comment on political events themselves.

These changes have dramatically increased the amount of information about politics that is available to the average American. Imagine yourself in the late 1940s. Suppose you wanted to learn about President Truman's State of the Union address. If you couldn't go to Washington to hear it in person, where could you have gotten information about the speech? If you lived in a big city, the speech would probably be covered in the next day's newspaper. If you lived in a small town, your local paper might or might not run the story. If it didn't, you would need a subscription to either a big-city paper (which would arrive a week after the fact) or a weekly or monthly news magazine, or you would need to have access to a radio that could pick up a station broadcasting the speech.

Now consider the modern era, in which major political events saturate the media and a virtually unlimited amount of information is available on the Internet. Suppose you want to know about President Trump's State of the Union. You can tune in to one of the four major television networks, numerous cable news channels, public television stations, or radio stations. Most television stations will feature pundits' commentaries on the speech and will interview prominent politicians and commentators. Jimmy Fallon and other late-night hosts will probably make jokes about Trump on television,

DID YOU KNOW?

67%

of American adults report they get at least some of their news from social media.
Source: Pew Research Center

DID YOU KNOW?

Newspaper circulation per capita has declined

66%

since 1970.
Source: Pew Research Center

and John Oliver will skewer the speech on his Sunday show. Tomorrow it will be front-page news and larger papers will publish the full text of Trump's speech online. Countless websites will offer analyses. And you will be able to watch a video of the speech on YouTube and many other sites. Some of your friends (perhaps even you) might offer commentary on social media. The point is, there are many places to get information; you would have to work to avoid them.

The Internet has also made new kinds of political information available to the average citizen. For example, the Center for Responsive Politics offers a searchable database of contributions to candidates and political organizations. Many sites, including FiveThirtyEight and Pollster, collect and analyze public opinion surveys, including presidential election polls. Increasingly, podcasts such as the left-leaning *Pod Save America* or the right-leaning *Federalist Radio Hour* are used to deliver analysis and interviews. The Internet also creates new opportunities for interaction between citizens, reporters, and government officials. Many reporters host live online chat sessions, allowing people to ask follow-up questions about published stories, or interact with their audience through a variety of social media sites.

The Internet has also facilitated some entirely new kinds of media sources. People who know something about political events (or think they do) now have a variety of ways, from blogs to Twitter, to contribute to the commentary on political news stories and put information before a wide audience. In 2018, the *New York Post* published an article detailing how "blue-collar voters" in Pittsburgh reacted to President Trump's State of the Union speech—until some individuals with Twitter accounts did some searching and posted that one of the parents was chief of surgery at a local hospital (not exactly "blue-collar"). The *Post* then updated its story to reflect this information.[13] Other sources publish inside information about agency decisions, such as the revelations in late 2017 by the website NASA Watch about software problems in NASA's new rocket, the Space Launch System.

At the same time, the rise of the Internet has exacerbated the trend toward shorter stories in major news sources, with fewer details and less background information. In theory, the elimination of space limitations should have produced longer, more in-depth reporting on the Internet, but in fact the opposite has occurred. Many popular Internet sources, such as Twitter and Axios, are designed to present information in short, easy-to-digest form. Similarly, news accounts that individuals may post on social media sites are often light on details. There is also some evidence that major news sources such as the *New York Times* and the *Washington Post* are shifting both what they report and how they report in favor of stories that can gain the attention of an easily distracted public.

From coverage of protests to refugees filming their journeys, the Internet makes it easy for ordinary citizens to share political information and report on political events as they happen.

While there is much more information available today than there was a generation ago, media sources are constantly in flux. Websites and Web pages come and go. Individuals who post detailed analyses of one political event may be too busy to comment on another. Even well-established media sources can quickly change. For example, in recent years companies that once owned newspapers in Chicago, Philadelphia, and Minneapolis have gone bankrupt, whereas several major U.S. cities, including Seattle, Birmingham, and New Orleans, have a hometown daily newspaper that appears only in digital form. Other newspapers have cut foreign bureaus, reduced their staff, and thinned the amount of news in every edition. At the same time, the major television networks and cable television sources have seen declines in budgets and viewership. At one level, these declines do not present a fundamental barrier to viewers and readers who seek to become well informed about major events, since there are so many alternative news sources to consult. However, information about past events is often difficult to find because it is not archived or because the source of the information goes out of business (this is particularly true for Internet-only sources such as podcasts). And as the budgets for media sources become tighter and tighter, stories that require extensive research (particularly investigative journalism) are less likely to be reported in the first place.

Moreover, as we discussed earlier, the quality of information available on the Internet varies considerably—probably more than it did for the relatively small number of media sources that were available a generation ago. For example, it is easy to find fake photographs of all kinds on the Internet, such as George W. Bush talking into an upside-down phone, Hillary Clinton posing in front of a bookshelf that displays the Confederate flag, Barack Obama shaking hands with Osama bin Laden, or Donald Trump carrying two cats to safety during relief operations for Hurricane Harvey in 2017. As you have no doubt heard your professors say, just because a website publishes a report or news item doesn't mean it's true. The problem is, in a world where websites come and go and where citizens often do not take the time to investigate what they see or read, false information may easily be accepted as true.

A related problem is that the Internet has made it easier for partisan groups to publish biased or inaccurate information under the guise of investigative journalism, with the supposed goal of informing the public. For example, the conservative group Project Veritas recorded undercover encounters with employees of organizations from Planned Parenthood to the *Washington Post*, using leading questions, hidden video cameras, and selective editing to portray these individuals in politically embarrassing situations. These efforts can backfire: during the 2017 Alabama Senate special election, in which Republican candidate Roy Moore was accused by multiple women of past sexual harassment, a Project Veritas worker tried to convince a *Washington Post* reporter that she had had an affair with Moore. Rather than exposing the *Post*'s supposed bias and corrupt motives in reporting on the Moore story (which was Project Veritas' goal), the operation ended when the *Post* investigated her claim, discovered her link to Project Veritas, and published several stories on the organization's attempt to deceive and entrap the *Post*.

Where do people get political information?

While there is a vast amount of information available about politics, very few Americans make it a priority to be well informed about politics—which would require them to systematically consult, evaluate, and integrate information from a range of different sources. Rather, most Americans acquire political information accidentally through a process known as the **by-product theory**.[14] As an example, you may log in to Facebook or some other social media site to see what your friends are doing, and happen to take a look

Doctored photos of elected officials, such as this image of President Trump assisting rescuers after Hurricane Harvey, are widely available on the Internet. Such images highlight the danger of depending on unreliable websites as primary sources of political information.

by-product theory
The idea that many Americans acquire political information unintentionally rather than by seeking it out.

All I know is just what I read in the papers, and that's an alibi for my ignorance.

— Will Rogers

at a political story or video that appears in your news feed. Perhaps the story is a profile of Senator Jeff Flake, who might challenge President Donald Trump in the 2020 elections. Though you didn't plan to read about Jeff Flake, you wind up doing so just because the story comes up in your feed. However, when people receive information as a by-product, they don't evaluate it in the same way that they evaluate information gained through a careful search, such as if you decided on your own to investigate Flake's background and issue positions. Suppose the story criticizes Flake's position on immigration. If you came upon this information after searching on your own, you would probably think about whether the source was credible or whether you cared about immigration policy in the first place. Because you are not consciously searching for information, you are much less likely to be skeptical when you acquire information as a by-product.[15]

Whether people seek out political information deliberately or acquire it as a by-product, there are some systematic differences in media use depending on their ideological beliefs. Table 7.1 shows the main campaign news source for Trump and Clinton voters in the 2016 election.

Clearly, there are some sharp differences between Trump voters and Clinton voters: by a large margin, the most important source for Trump voters was Fox News, while only 3 percent of Clinton voters relied on Fox News for information. Some sources, such as local radio (probably talk radio), local newspapers, the *New York Times*, MSNBC, or NPR, appear on only one list or the other. However, there is also some overlap: both Trump and Clinton voters used the major networks, ABC, NBC, and CBS, as well as local TV. It's important to note that these data are based on a survey question that asked respondents for their main source of information, and it is likely that most voters got information from more than one source. The survey also did not address information gained as a by-product.

The question raised by Table 7.1 is whether the differences in issue positions and policy demands of Trump and Clinton voters are driven by the differences in the media sources they consume. Do some people demand liberal policies because they listen to CNN, while others demand conservative policies because they listen to Fox News? The answer is almost surely no. As we discussed in Chapter 6, people aren't liberal or conservative because of the stories they listen to, watch, or read—their beliefs run much

TABLE 7.1

Main Campaign News Source for Trump and Clinton Voters in 2016

Trump Voters	Clinton Voters
Fox News (40%)	CNN (18%)
CNN (8%)	MSNBC (9%)
Facebook (7%)	Facebook (8%)
NBC (6%)	Local TV (8%)
Local TV (5%)	NPR (7%)
ABC (3%)	ABC (6%)
CBS (3%)	*New York Times* (5%)
Local radio (3%)	CBS (5%)
	NBC (4%)
	Local newspapers (4%)
	Fox News (3%)

Source: Pew Research Center, "Trump, Clinton Voters Divided in Their Main Source for Election News," January 18, 2018, www.journalism.org (accessed 2/1/2018).

deeper than that. It's probably more accurate to say that ideological beliefs drive the selection of media sources, rather than media sources driving ideological beliefs. Even so, insofar as different sources report different information, the choice of which media to consume will shape what a person knows about politics—about the candidates, their policy proposals, and the government's performance overall.

It's important to have a clear and accurate understanding of today's media sources. If you're looking for someone to blame for Americans' lack of knowledge about politics, the mass media is not a good candidate. While most sources fall short in one way or another, there is a wealth of information available, most of it for free. But most people never search for political information and ignore much of what they encounter. Journalists can do the most effective reporting possible—providing in-depth, balanced coverage of critical events—but unless people take time to read or view that coverage, their knowledge of politics will be incomplete and possibly biased.

"Why Should I Care?"

How do politicians use the media? How do the media use politicians?

EXPLAIN HOW POLITICIANS USE THE MEDIA TO ACHIEVE THEIR GOALS

While the media and politicians are often thought of as adversaries, with a watchdog press working to make sure the public knows what politicians are doing, the fact is that each side has something to offer the other. Reporters want to write stories that attract public attention, so they need information from politicians on what is happening inside the government, preferably information that is given only to them. Politicians in turn want media coverage that highlights their achievements, which ideally will build public support and secure their election (or reelection). Bureaucrats want favorable attention for their programs, and interest groups want publicity to further their causes. Thus, coverage of American politics reflects trade-offs between reporters who want complete, accurate information and sources who want favorable coverage.

Politicians' media strategies

Politicians and others in government try to influence coverage by providing select information to reporters. Sometimes they hold press conferences where they take questions from the media. Other times they speak to single reporters or to a group **on background** or **off the record**, meaning that reporters can use the information but cannot attribute it to the politician by name. These efforts are sometimes trial balloons, where politicians release details of a new proposal to gauge public reaction without committing themselves to any particular policy. Other times politicians might reveal some details of a negotiation or conflict with the hope of producing media coverage that puts their contributions in a favorable light.

Some scholars argue that elected officials try to use the media to shape public opinion in their favor by doling out information to reward reporters who write stories that support the officials' points of view.[16] To some extent this argument is true: much

on background or **off the record**
Describes comments a politician makes to the press on the condition that they can be reported only if they are not attributed to that politician.

Information and coverage of important events become instantaneously available through Internet sources like Twitter feeds and blogs. For instance, President Trump has relied on Twitter to communicate his foreign policy and economic policy priorities.

of the information reporters use to write their stories comes from political appointees, bureaucrats, elected officials, and party leaders.[17] Reporters who are known to be writing stories that are critical of a government program or a political leader may find that some people refuse to talk to them. However, while there is no doubt that elected officials would like to receive sympathetic media coverage and are sometimes successful, news reports on American politics reflect a multitude of sources and information. One politician's attempt to shape coverage by talking or remaining silent may be negated by another's efforts to promote a different point of view, with the same reporter or a different one.

President Trump's behavior is mostly consistent with this strategy. Trump's staff has invited the media to events that place Trump in a favorable light (such as Trump's visit to Houston in 2017 to see the damage caused by Hurricane Harvey). And like most other politicians, Trump has selectively released information to reporters whom he believes will write favorable coverage. The difference is that Trump has used Twitter to speak directly to his supporters and the public at large—with a guarantee that the press will report on his tweets, simply because Trump is president. In this way, Trump's tweeting serves as free advertising, as well as a way for Trump to shape press coverage.

Besides talking with the media, politicians also hold events specifically designed to secure favorable press coverage, or appear at an event that the press is likely to cover. This strategy is particularly common among candidates campaigning for office. For example, during the summer of 2015, six months before the Iowa Caucuses met to begin selecting presidential nominees, all the Republican and Democratic candidates for president in 2016 made a point of visiting the Iowa State Fair, where they shook hands, ate some local specialties (from pork chops to fried Snickers bars), and in general tried to attract as much media attention as they could. (Trump even used his private helicopter to give rides to fair attendees.) By attending the fair, candidates were trying to get their names and their pictures in local newspapers and on local television and thereby increase their name recognition. Such coverage might have also helped persuade Iowa voters that a candidate shared their views on the issues.

Another way politicians, especially candidates, try to shape citizen perceptions is to run campaign ads on television, in newspapers, and on websites. As we discuss in Chapter 9, candidates running for federal office generally spend about 80 to 90 percent of their budget on advertising. Candidates target these ads to reach groups of likely supporters. A conservative Republican might try to buy advertising slots during a broadcast of a NASCAR event, knowing that people who are interested in NASCAR tend to vote Republican. These ads are an example of the by-product theory in action; people don't watch NASCAR to learn about politicians, but watching the broadcast means they will be exposed to the candidate's messages.

Potential presidential candidates also often appear on television talk shows as a way of increasing name recognition and gaining some free advertising. Studies have shown that viewing a candidate in such a relaxed, nonconfrontational setting can help persuade opponents that a candidate is worth a second look.[18] Like all campaign strategies, however, candidates' attempts to shape media coverage work only some of the time. For example, a poll in late 2017 by *The Economist* found that only 26 percent of Americans saw Trump's use of Twitter as "appropriate"—and 50 percent did not.

Candidate strategies can also backfire, such as when the campaign of 2018 Republican Senate incumbent Ted Cruz released a radio ad that argued his opponent, Beto O'Rourke, had started using a nickname rather than his first name (Robert) in order to appeal to Hispanic Texas voters.[19] The O'Rourke campaign responded by releasing a childhood photo of the candidate that showed him wearing a shirt with the nickname printed on it.[20] At other points in the campaign, the Cruz organization released a 20-year old photo of O'Rourke playing in a punk rock band, and argued that if elected, O'Rourke would try to ban consumption of barbecue (for the record, the candidate had not mentioned doing so). In all three cases, press coverage benefitted O'Rourke, who narrowly lost to Cruz in the general election.

The pressures and legal limits on reporters

The proliferation of media sources has increased competition among reporters to find and report on interesting stories. Reporters who refuse to use information that a politician has provided may find that the politician refuses to talk with them in the future, so reporters must carefully consider whether they want to use information provided to keep their channel of communication with the politician open. Moreover, the Internet has increased the demand for new stories and updates of old ones. Even if reporters covering Congress think that nothing important is happening on a given day, they may be forced to write a story just to have something new on their newspaper's website. Similarly, an up-and-coming news or commentary site might use a politician's offerings as a way of building its audience.

Because of these demands, reporters rely heavily on their sources—people inside government who provide them with documents, inside information, and the details of negotiations—to supply them with material for new stories. When sources reveal information that is not supposed to be public knowledge, it is often referred to as **leaking**. Reporters covering important or controversial stories often promise their sources that

leaking
The practice in which someone in government provides nonpublic information to a reporter, with the aim of generating press coverage favorable to the leaker's aims.

Leaks coming out of the Trump administration have raised questions about what the role of the press should be in holding government accountable. Reality Winner, an NSA contractor accused of leaking a report on Russian interference in the 2016 election to news organization *The Intercept*, pled guilty to releasing classified information.

they will remain anonymous in any coverage based on the information they provide. These assurances are an important factor in the decision to leak information, especially classified information. However, these assurances are not absolute. Reporters and their editors can, under certain circumstances, be compelled by a court to reveal the sources for their stories. Although some states have shield laws that allow reporters to refuse to name their sources, there is no such law at the federal level. As a result, federal prosecutors can ask a judge to force journalists to name their sources, on the grounds that the source's identity is fundamental to the prosecutor's case. If the judge agrees, reporters can be jailed for contempt indefinitely unless they name their sources.

To be clear, leaking or the publication of leaked information is not illegal as long as the information is not classified. For example, many press stories have reported on things that President Trump has said or threatened to do in private conversations with his senior advisers. Notably, reports surfaced that Trump had threatened to fire Robert Mueller, special prosecutor in charge of the investigation into links between the Trump campaign and Russian intelligence services. While these revelations were certainly embarrassing to Trump, whoever leaked the information did not break the law (although that person may have put his or her job at risk). In another example, Senator Dianne Feinstein released a transcript of a Senate committee's interview with a firm that had investigated a Trump–Russia connection. Trump condemned her in a tweet as "Sneaky Dianne Feinstein," who "releas[ed] testimony in such an underhanded and possible illegal way," but, as a ranking member of the committee, Feinstein was not acting illegally when she gave the transcript of the meeting to the media.

Notwithstanding the freedom of the press guaranteed in the Bill of Rights, reporters are subject to legal limitations that present hurdles as they research stories. If the government can convince a judge that publication of a particular story would lead to immediate harm to a person or persons, a judge can halt publication. But this test sets the bar extremely high for stopping publication of a story. As we discussed in Chapter 4, most attempts to prevent publication have been unsuccessful. In addition, it is not clear as a practical matter how the legal system could control the release of information via social media.

To appreciate the issues surrounding classified information and prior restraint, consider the case of Edward Snowden. While working as a contractor for the U.S. National Security Agency (NSA), Snowden downloaded a number of files that documented the NSA's surveillance activities, including the collection of data on Americans' phone calls overseas and the monitoring of foreign politicians' cell phones. In 2012, Snowden approached several major publications across the world, including the *Washington Post*, to offer access to these documents. After several months of negotiation, the *Post* would not agree to all of Snowden's conditions—among other things, he wanted certain documents to be published in their entirety, while the *Post* wanted to hold back some classified information.[21] Snowden then came to an agreement with a British newspaper, the *Guardian*, which has gradually made the documents public, although he also allowed the *Post* to publish some of the documents.

The *Post*'s refusal to accept Snowden's demands was the product of several months of discussions with the U.S. government over what information could be released without harming national security or placing confidential sources in jeopardy. Although some government officials mentioned the possibility of invoking the prior restraint prohibition, no attempts were made to do so. In any case, even if the *Post* could have been deterred from publication, the information would have soon appeared in stories published by other outlets.

The Snowden episode illustrates how government officials work to deter leaks or influence the media's coverage of a story without resorting to prior restraint. Laws prohibit government officials' disclosure of classified information in the first place, and recent administrations have been very aggressive about prosecuting leakers.

Newspapers can also face prosecution for publishing classified information. In the case of the Snowden documents, the *Post* published its story only when it was rumored that the *Guardian* planned to release its own story. Even then, *Post* reporters and editors agreed to keep certain information out of their stories.

Why do reporters and publishers restrain their stories? Sometimes they agree with the government that keeping secrets is in the national interest. For example, for several years mainstream media voluntarily decided not to run stories about secret American bases in Saudi Arabia from which drone missions were being flown over Iran and other countries. (Ultimately the information was revealed in a *Wired* magazine story.[22]) Other times reporters are rewarded for cooperating—they may get information about another government policy or be promised future access to officials. Alternatively, reporters may be coerced to back down from a story through the threat of losing future access to people in government or even going to jail.

In the main, these constraints apply only to mainstream organizations and their reporters. Groups that are anonymous or that operate outside the United States can violate these laws and norms with impunity. For example, when the international WikiLeaks group released e-mails and documents they had obtained from the Democratic National Committee, the Clinton campaign, and the Gmail account of Clinton campaign chair John Podesta, there was no way for the affected groups (or the government) to initiate legal action or otherwise prevent publication.

Thus, both legal constraints and government officials' efforts to shape the news can affect the way that the media report about politics. Politicians will try to depict their opponents as ill-advised and scandal ridden and to shape media coverage in ways that show them winning and their opponents losing. Given the multitude of media sources, it is not hard for a politician to find a reporter who is willing to write exactly what that politician wants. And that reporter may file a story whether or not he or she believes that the information the politician provides is true or important—the reporter may be motivated by other factors, like attracting an audience, gaining the politician's trust, or hitting a deadline.

"Why Should I Care?"

Understanding the relationship between politicians and the media is critical for evaluating the quality and accuracy of the political news you see and read. Because journalists are constrained in what they can learn about and what they can report, and because politicians may try to influence what reporters say, there is no guarantee that any one media source will be able to publish a full and complete account of a political event or outcome. Under these conditions, the only way to be well informed about politics is to consult multiple sources and remember that politicians and media members both have agendas. Sometimes those agendas are similar, but often politicians and the media want different things.

How do the media influence their audience?

EXPLAIN HOW THE MEDIA INFLUENCE HOW PEOPLE THINK ABOUT POLITICS

The study of media effects explores whether exposure to media coverage of politics changes what people think or do. There is considerable evidence that media coverage influences its audience—in simple terms, much of what Americans know about politics

How News Makes It to the Public

Editor assigns reporter to cover a particular story or event.

Filtering
Editor decides which stories are important and will attract an audience.

Reporter gathers information and prepares a story.

Framing
Reporter's story includes the overall argument and other information that shapes what the audience learns.

Priming
By describing events using some words or phrases and omitting others, the reporter has additional influence over what the audience learns.

The people have a point!

Chaos in the streets!

Editor revises story, decides on length, content, and placement.

Filtering, Framing, and Priming
Decision about where, when, and how to carry the story gives an additional opportunity for filtering. In addition, the editor can make changes to a story that involve framing, and priming.

The Media's Coverage of Off-cycle Elections

The media devoted much attention to a small number of state-level and special congressional elections in 2017, such as the race for governor of Virginia and the special election to fill the Senate seat in Alabama previously held by Jeff Sessions, who had been appointed attorney general. Media narratives tended to view these elections as bellwethers for Republicans' chances of holding on to House and Senate majorities and majorities in state legislatures in 2018. Their coverage shows filtering, framing, and priming in action.

❓

Critical Thinking

1. **Of the three media effects** (filtering, framing, and priming), which is the easiest one for citizens to detect? Which one is the hardest?

2. **Do a Web search for** "special elections." In the first two articles you see, find all the instances of filtering, framing, and priming. Do you think these articles provide a balanced picture of the events? Why or why not?

Filtering
It's a story...

Some news stories argued that the elections in 2017 **allowed observers to see how voters were reacting** to events in the Trump administration.

Or is it?

Others pointed out that off-cycle elections are typically low-turnout events, and so **provide limited insight** into the behavior of the much larger general-election electorate.

Framing
Democrats are challenging!

Some outlets interpreted the fact that Democratic challengers ran strong campaigns in Republican districts, raised lots of campaign cash, and attracted media attention as a **reflection of public dissatisfaction** with President Trump.

Not really.

Other sources framed the outsized contributions and coverage as a result of the fact that **the special elections were the only elections** happening at that time.

Priming
Republicans (mostly) won!

Republican candidates **held most of the Republican seats** contested in 2017 off-cycle elections.

But Democrats looked good.

Democrats won a handful of races, and news coverage pointed out that, although some candidates lost, the percentage of the vote they received was substantially higher than in previous elections.

Filtering, Framing, and Priming
More trouble? No, in the clear!

Subsequent press coverage focused on the high number of Republican retirements from Congress leading up to the 2018 election; the large number of politically experienced, well-funded Democratic challengers; and low public approval of President Trump in suburban congressional districts to predict (correctly) that Democrats would regain majority control of the House in 2018.

media effects
The influence of media coverage on average citizens' opinions and actions.

comes from stories they read, watch, or listen to. In part, **media effects** arise because people exposed to stories that describe a particular event learn new facts as a result of their exposure. However, some of the impact of media coverage stems not from what such stories contain but from how they present information or even whether a story is reported at all (see How It Works: How News Makes It to the Public).[23]

Media bias and partisanship

Many studies have found that exposure to political coverage changes what citizens know: at the most basic level, people who watch, read, or listen to more coverage about politics know more than people who are exposed to less of this coverage.[24] What people learn from the media, in turn, can shape the demands they place on politicians.[25] However, at least part of the media's effect on people's knowledge level arises because of underlying interest: people who are interested in politics know more in the first place and, because of their interest, watch more media coverage of events as they happen. Moreover, because people can pick and choose which coverage to watch, read, or listen to, what they learn from the media tends to reinforce their preexisting beliefs. That is, a conservative might listen to Sean Hannity, while a liberal would opt for watching MSNBC. Both people may learn something from the coverage, but the most likely result is that they will only grow more certain in the opinions that they already have.[26] Finally, changes in opinion caused by media coverage are usually (but not always) short-lived, which is consistent with our discussion in Chapter 6.

Given this evidence on media effects, one of the central questions is whether reporters and editors have a discernable bias: That is, do their decisions about which events to report on and how they report on them reflect a conscious effort to shape public opinion in a liberal, conservative, or other direction? Surveys of the American electorate have found a **hostile media effect**: regardless of respondents' partisan leanings, they believe that the media favor candidates and ideas from the other party.[27] Conservative critics of the media point to surveys that show that most reporters identify themselves as liberals. Liberal critics respond that most pundits, especially on talk radio, offer conservative points of view—and many media sources are owned by large corporations, which could lead to underreporting of some stories, such as those offering a favorable portrayal of labor unions.[28]

Questions about media bias have become more urgent since the election of Donald Trump, who has criticized the media for reporting what he terms "fake news." Trump even claimed, in a February 2017 tweet, that the press is "the enemy of the American people." Sometimes Trump uses the "fake news" label for stories he finds misleading or inaccurate, such as polls during the 2016 campaign that showed him behind Hillary Clinton. The deeper message of the "fake news" label is that Trump believes that media coverage of his presidency cannot be trusted because reporters and their editors simply dislike him and his supporters.

It is easy to find examples of outright mistakes by reporters and their editors that suggest some sort of overt bias in coverage. For example, in December 2017 the *Washington Post* reporter Dave Weigel posted pictures on Twitter showing large numbers of empty seats at a Trump rally. However, the pictures were taken before the start of the rally; by the time it actually began, the stadium was full. After Trump complained on Twitter, Weigel apologized and published pictures showing that all the seats were taken. Similarly, as we describe in Chapter 9 most polls taken during the 2016 campaign failed to predict Donald Trump's victory. However, while Trump and others may have seen this as evidence of a bias against him, the polls were actually largely accurate. These same polls accurately predicted the popular vote totals; where

hostile media effect
The tendency of people to see neutral media coverage of an event as biased against their point of view.

Republican presidential candidate Donald Trump being interviewed by George Stephanopoulos, a so-called liberal media person. Some critics of media coverage claim that a liberal interviewer would not be able to do an impartial interview of a conservative candidate (or vice versa).

they went wrong was in predicting turnout in a small number of rural counties in Wisconsin, Michigan, and Pennsylvania—minor differences that were enough to produce an electoral college victory for Trump. There is no evidence that pollsters were biasing their results to hurt Trump. If anything, each pollster had a strong interest in making correct predictions—any pollster would have been gratified to have been the only one to predict that Trump would win.

Many journalists and commentators admit that they take an ideological or partisan perspective. Talk show hosts Sean Hannity and Rush Limbaugh, for example, describe themselves as strong conservatives. And many commentators on the Fox News Channel make no secret of their conservative viewpoint—just as commentators on MSNBC make no secret of their liberal leanings. Similarly, the political news magazine *The Nation* describes itself as "a weekly journal of left/liberal opinion, covering national and international affairs as well as the arts."[29] These journalists' and organizations' points of view are well known and easy to identify. Some people might even find the bias useful. A liberal, for example, could use *The Nation*'s endorsements as a guide for which candidates to support, and a conservative might listen to Rush Limbaugh to get similar information.

It is also no surprise that politicians complain that media coverage is biased against them: the stakes for them are very high. For example, during the final weeks of the 2016 election, Donald Trump's campaign wanted more coverage of its stance on trade reform and its claims that Hillary Clinton was a corrupt politician, and less attention paid to harassment claims against Trump and his poor performance in the presidential debates. Clinton's campaign in turn complained that the media was focusing too much on rumors of Clinton's health problems or the FBI investigation into her use of an unsecure e-mail server and not enough on Trump's missteps. Thus, while both campaigns complained about bias, the simple explanation for their complaints is that they wanted to win the election and therefore wanted media coverage that exposed their opponent's flaws rather than the flaws of their candidate.

In fact, while it is easy to find media coverage of politics that is incomplete or sloppily reported, cases in which reporters made predictions that later turned out to be false, or stories that candidates wish had not been reported, it is hard to find cases of systematic bias in media coverage. For example, in the fall of 2015 Republican candidate Ben Carson complained that reporters were spending too much time searching for inconsistencies and exaggerations in his autobiography, arguing that they had not scrutinized President Obama or Democratic candidate Hillary Clinton in the same way.[30] Yet it is easy to find exhaustive media coverage of similar issues in Obama's and Clinton's autobiographies. You may think that the media were making too much of Carson's past—but it is hard to say that they gave a free pass to Obama, Clinton, or other candidates.

Moreover, while some academic studies have found evidence of press coverage favoring one type of candidate or issue position over another, an equally large body of work has produced important critiques of these studies. For one thing, a finding that most reporters are liberal (or Democrats) and few are conservative (Republicans) does not imply that political coverage must necessarily favor liberal positions or Democratic candidates. Reporters may prioritize being as objective as possible, fear that favoring one side would cause their audience to decline, or be subject to review by editors who are on guard against bias. Similarly, the fact that a reporter criticizes a politician or party is not evidence of his or her lack of objectivity. Critiques do not by themselves suggest that a reporter is being unfair—the question is, what would a fair analysis look like? Many analyses of President Trump's first year in office acknowledged the strong American economy but gave little credit to Trump for this outcome. Were these reporters biased against Trump, or had they read the literature on political control of the economy, which shows that presidential actions have little impact on economic conditions, particularly in the short run? Untangling these effects is difficult, and if media bias were as pronounced as some critics claim, it would likely be easier to measure.

Filtering and framing

Compared with overt bias, filtering and framing may produce subtler but stronger impacts on public opinion. **Filtering** (also called *agenda-setting*) refers to the ways in which journalists' and editors' decisions about which stories to report influence which stories people think about. **Framing** refers to how the description or presentation of a story, including the details, explanations, and context, changes the ways people react to and interpret the information. Space and time limitations mean that some filtering is inevitable as reporters and editors decide which of many potential news stories to cover. Similar decisions about what to report and how to present the information lead to framing effects. Even if everyone in the political media adhered to the highest standards of accuracy, these influences would still exist.

The concept of filtering is illustrated by Project Censored's annual list of Top Censored Stories.[31] The group's list for 2017 included stories about the risk of personal information being shared on social media, antibiotic-resistant superbugs, and the prevalence of lead in water supplies throughout the nation. The group's point is not that the government forces reporters to keep quiet; rather, it claims that reporters and their editors decide against covering these stories, sometimes for self-serving reasons, such as beliefs about what their audience wants to see or read.

The impact of filtering is also apparent in cases of government inaction. Figure 7.1 shows media coverage (number of stories) of gun control legislation following the mass shooting at Sandy Hook Elementary School in Newtown, Connecticut, in December 2013. The pattern in the graph is typical for mass shootings: after sharp spikes in the number of stories following the shooting, the topic gradually disappeared from coverage, with smaller, temporary spikes after the failure of a Senate gun control bill and a subsequent shooting at the Washington Navy Yard. To a large extent, the drop in media coverage mirrors public opinion—as Americans move on from thinking about a mass shooting, media attention shifts with them. Whether sustained media attention

filtering
The influence on public opinion that results from journalists' and editors' decisions about which of many potential news stories to report.

framing
The influence on public opinion caused by the way a story is presented or covered, including the details, explanations, and context offered in the report.

FIGURE 7.1

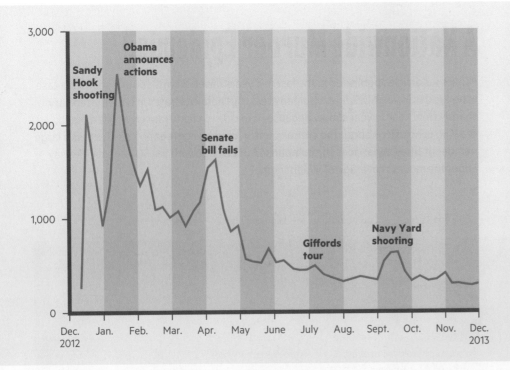

Gun Control Stories per Week, December 2012 to December 2013

Press attention to gun control spikes upward after a mass shooting, then fades as reporters move on to other stories. How does this pattern help opponents of gun control legislation preserve the status quo?

Source: Danny Hayes, "Why It's So Hard to Pass Gun Control Laws (in One Graph)," *Washington Post*, August 26, 2015, www. washingtonpost.com/blogs/monkey-cage (accessed 11/21/15).

would have galvanized public opinion behind stricter gun control laws is an open question. But if one effect of media coverage is to raise public awareness of an issue, people are not going to be aware of an issue the media ignore.

Reporting on violent crime in America shows clear framing effects. Over the last few years, many stories in major publications have reported sharp increases in homicide rates in cities such as Chicago, St. Louis, and Baltimore, suggesting a nationwide problem.[32] However, other cities saw homicide rates decline—in fact, the average murder rate for the top 50 cities has risen only slightly in the last few years and is far below the peak that it reached in the 1990s (see the What Do the Facts Say? feature). Adding data on nationwide crime rates to a story on murders in three cities doesn't change the facts of what's happening there, but it does suggest that these events are not proof of a larger national trend.

The way a story is reported—which information is included in an article or which images are used—makes a big difference in what people learn from it. Stories that focus on cases of violent crime suggest an epidemic of murders, rapes, and assault, but actual data on crime rates paint a very different picture.

A Nationwide Murder Epidemic?

Numerous articles published in the last few years raised alarms about a sharp increase in homicides in large U.S. metropolitan areas. But homicide rates in any city can vary sharply from year to year simply because homicide is a fairly rare crime. As a result, drawing conclusions about the entire country requires aggregating data across a large number of cities. What does the comparison of Chicago with the 50 largest cities say about the media's coverage of violent crime?

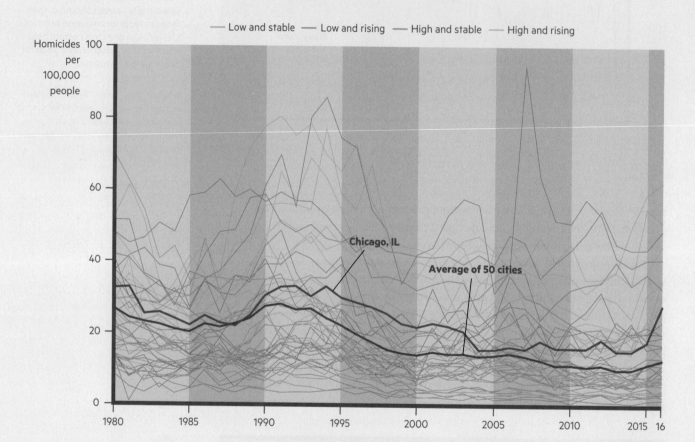

Low and stable — Low and rising — High and stable — High and rising

Homicides per 100,000 people

Chicago, IL

Average of 50 cities

Source: "Daily Chart: Murder Rates in 50 American Cities," *The Economist*, February 7, 2017, www.economist.com/blogs/graphicdetail/2017/02/daily-chart-3 (accessed 2/3/18).

Think about it

- Does the data on homicide rates across the 50 largest U.S. cities confirm or dispute the conclusion of a sharp increase in homicides in recent years?
- One of the principle arguments in this chapter about media coverage is that there is a tendency to describe everything as a major crisis—in this case, to focus on increased homicide rates in a small number of cities, but ignore the fact that homicide rates have been stable or declining in most cities. Why is it so hard for reporters to provide the whole picture to their audiences?

In sum, reporting on politics requires reporters to move beyond "just the facts." They must choose what to report on, how to describe the news, whether to reveal secrets, and which sources to rely on. Moreover, events do not always speak for themselves—they require interpretation. The fact that conservatives and liberals consult very different media sources (as shown in Table 7.1 on page 240) suggests that conservatives and liberals see different media sources as trustworthy, and that they are well aware of framing, filtering, and potential bias and choose their media sources accordingly. Given the vast array of political coverage in modern America, even if we take potential biases as well as filtering and framing into account, virtually all of us can find several sources that we consider reliable, if we take the time to search for those sources.[33]

Americans often demand that journalists give "just the facts and all the facts" about politics and public policy. Most of the time, however, what looks like biased reporting is a journalist trying to make sense of a complex world. The act of reporting requires decisions on which stories matter, which facts deserve mention, and how events should be interpreted. To say that you don't like how a journalist resolves these decisions doesn't mean that he or she is pushing a particular political agenda.

"Why Should I Care?"

Do the media work?

In a democracy, the media's role is to provide citizens with information about politicians, government actions, and policy debates. It is easy to argue that the media are falling down on the job: surveys taken in recent years show that substantial percentages of Americans believe that voter fraud is a major problem, that a third of the federal budget is spent on foreign aid, that America is no longer the preeminent military power, and that undocumented immigration is on the rise. In fact, all of these statements are false (in fact, foreign aid spending is only about 2 percent of the federal budget).

Claims of ideological bias do not explain these shortcomings. The central finding of the political science literature on media effects is that systematic bias is hard to find. In the 2016 election, for example, the press gave considerable attention to vulgar comments about women that Donald Trump made in an *Access Hollywood* tape. But these stories did not appear because reporters and editors are hard-core liberals (or Democrats) who wanted to destroy Trump's chances of getting elected. Rather, coverage was driven by public attention to the scandal and by reporters' belief that the comments were an important signal of how Trump would behave as president. Moreover, the same reporters and editors also gave considerable attention to Hillary Clinton's use of a private e-mail server while she was secretary of state, and to her taking time off during the campaign because of pneumonia. Thus, insofar as the public is misinformed, the reason is not a lack of coverage or biased coverage of events.

Lack of citizen interest

In part, the media's apparent failure to create a well-informed citizenry is driven by a lack of citizen interest. As we discussed in Chapter 6, the average American has a fairly low interest in politics, and only a small percentage of Americans care enough to take

ASSESS WHETHER THE MEDIA FULFILL THEIR ROLE IN AMERICAN DEMOCRACY

the time and effort to become well informed. Everyone else learns about politics as a by-product of other things he or she does throughout the day.

The lack of citizen interest is one reason why the increased amount of information available on the Internet has not produced a better-informed citizenry: while information is available, average Americans make little attempt to find and understand it. Even if they try, finding information, sifting through conflicting sources, and assessing the credibility of different accounts is a difficult task, even for experts. For example, suppose you want to learn more about the conflict in Syria. A Google search in late 2018 of the terms "America," "Syria," and "war" returned over 100 million Web pages, ranging from reports on America's military strategy to pictures of Syrian refugees. Thus, the problem is not in finding information but in deciding which of the millions of pages available will help you learn about the conflict.

In short, despite the Internet's wealth of information, there is no guarantee that people will sit down, search for what they want or need to know, distinguish truth from falsehood, and assemble their findings into coherent conclusions. In fact, rather than creating a uniformly well-informed citizenry, the availability of information on the Internet may exacerbate the pattern we saw in Chapter 6, where a small percentage of Americans are extremely well informed about politics, whereas the vast majority of the public may simply throw up their hands and make no attempt to become better informed.[34]

Market forces

Another influence on media coverage is competition for an audience. Mass media sources have always tried to get as large an audience as possible in order to generate profits and stay in business, but the expansion of the Internet and the increased availability of free information have increased competitive pressures.[35] In part, these pressures have had positive effects for consumers: newspapers, for example, have put their content online and moved from publishing once per day to continually producing new stories and updates. Television stations have placed their video

Many Americans, attracted by clickbait headlines and dramatic storylines, now get the bulk of their political news from nontraditional online sources like BuzzFeed.

content online as well, including footage that was never used in broadcasts, so that people can watch at any time.

One downside of audience pressures is that they lead reporters to search for stories—any stories—to have something new to offer their audience, who otherwise might get its news from somewhere else. For example, although most theories of elections show that polls taken during the early days of a political campaign are almost irrelevant, the media still cover poll results. Early on most people know very little about the candidates, so a well-known figure such as Donald Trump may attract support simply because people know his name. Because reporters need something to write about, they may focus on a new poll even though they are well aware that the poll's findings are almost meaningless. The mere fact that reporters focus so much on each new poll may lead some readers to pay more attention to the findings than they actually deserve.

More generally, audience pressures lead reporters to focus on making their stories simple and dramatic in order to catch the attention of a distracted audience. Stories that say "nothing much happened today in the presidential campaign" or "today's events are hard to explain but almost surely will not affect who wins the election" will lose out to reports that cast events in simple, life-and-death terms. Consider media coverage of special congressional elections in 2017 and 2018. Each election was framed in a way that made it seem significant, and thus more interesting to media audiences, as though it would provide deep insights about Democratic prospects in the 2018 midterms. This coverage often ignored important facts, such as the facts that most of the elections were in strongly Republican districts, most of the candidates received much higher contributions than they would have received in a normal election, and turnout in the elections was much lower than normal. All of these factors should have suggested to reporters that these elections were so atypical that they would not, in fact, be useful in predicting midterm election outcomes. For example, the 2017 Alabama special Senate election was held in one of the most Republican states in the country and featured a Republican candidate, Roy Moore, whose campaign was based on strong religious themes (and who was accused of sexual harassment by multiple women during the campaign), and a Democratic challenger, Doug Jones, who was much more moderate than Democrats serving in the House and Senate. While Doug Jones ultimately won, his victory said little about how other Democrats, running in different districts and facing different challengers, would fare in 2018. (See the How It Works feature earlier in this chapter.)

The media's efforts to spin a story to attract an audience are nothing new.[36] For decades, scholars have documented the rise of **attack journalism**, in which journalists focus on scandal, government failures, and politicians' personal failings.[37] Other researchers have argued that campaign coverage overemphasizes the **horse race** aspects, such as which candidates are ahead and which are falling behind, rather than offering a complete description of each candidate's promises and an analysis of how he or she is likely to behave in office.[38] Similarly, coverage of debates over public policy often focuses on personalities and predictions about who is likely to achieve his or her goals, not the details of what the policies include. Media coverage of politics also emphasizes **soft news** (stories that are sensational or entertaining) over **hard news** (stories that focus on important issues and emphasize facts and figures).[39] The media also often give disproportionate coverage to events that are more likely to be recognized by the average American. For example, media coverage of Hurricane Harvey, which hit land in Texas, was much more extensive than coverage of Hurricane Maria, which devastated Puerto Rico only a month later—and both of these disasters were covered far more aggressively than the far more deadly monsoon storms in Bangladesh.[40]

The bias of the mainstream media is toward sensationalism, conflict, and laziness.

— Jon Stewart

attack journalism
A type of increasingly popular media coverage focused on political scandals and controversies, which causes a negative public opinion of political figures.

horse race
A description of the type of election coverage that focuses more on poll results and speculation about a likely winner than on substantive differences between the candidates.

soft news
Media coverage that aims to entertain or shock, often through sensationalized reporting or by focusing on a candidate or politician's personality.

hard news
Media coverage focused on facts and important issues surrounding a campaign.

TAKE A STAND

Should Facebook Grade the News?

As we have discussed in this chapter, most Americans are exposed to only a small fraction of the media's coverage of American politics. Because people read or watch only a limited number of stories, it is especially important for them to judge the reliability of the sources they consult. Do the stories include the right facts? Are the facts being presented fairly? Is the coverage shaped by the authors' conscious or unconscious biases? These are not easy questions to resolve, especially for the typical American who is not highly interested in politics and who has other demands on his or her time.

Facebook, one of the most common channels through which people get their news, has suggested a solution to this problem. It proposes to ask a sample of Facebook users two questions: Do you recognize a particular media source, and how trustworthy do you rate that source? Facebook would use the results of the survey to determine which stories are promoted in News Feeds. Users looking at their News Feeds would then be able to focus on stories from sources that were rated as highly trustworthy and would not be exposed to stories from sources that received low trust scores. Facebook hopes that by filtering the news stories it promotes in this way, it can help users become more informed about politics.

It's a great idea. By asking a random sample of users, Facebook is letting the mass public express its feelings about which information sources it would like to see. While some people might be biased in favor of one source or another, the hope is that these biases will average out over a large sample, ultimately highlighting more neutral sources. Presumably, the survey results would also favor sources that produce simple, easy-to-understand stories. Conversely, if a panel of experts were consulted to pick the "best" sources for news, it might choose sources that generate overly complicated political analyses that the average Facebook user might ignore entirely or misinterpret. Thus, the mass survey is more likely to identify a set of sources that people will actually use if put in front of them. Of course, it would be great if seeing a political story on Facebook prompted a user to investigate further by going to other sites that offer more details and deeper analysis. But Facebook's trustworthiness surveys will increase the

Many people have blamed Facebook for facilitating the circulation of "fake news" from untrustworthy sources.

chances that people receive accurate information about politics, even if the amount is relatively small.

It could make things worse. Facebook's survey strategy assumes that the biggest problem with individuals' assessments of media sources is that they favor sources that support their preferred candidates or policy proposals. Its hope is that these biases will cancel each other out in a large survey. However, the average American's media consumption is shaped by a variety of conscious and unconscious biases. People tend to trust the sources they regularly consult and distrust sources they have never heard of or have only seen a few times. They favor sources that simplify complex stories and deliver information in easy-to-read graphics. And most fundamentally, people like sources that reinforce their beliefs and dislike sources that challenge what they think or force them to learn new ways of thinking about an issue. Facebook's solution may not account for all of these additional biases. Rating sources by their perceived trustworthiness might well lead to a situation in which people think they are better informed, when in fact they are just as uninformed as they were before Facebook's efforts.

take a stand

1. Why do you think Americans are uninformed about political events? Will Facebook's trustworthiness ratings address this problem?

2. Suppose Facebook chose you to participate in its survey. Which media sources would you rate as trustworthy? Which would you rate as untrustworthy? How many would you have no opinion about?

3. What do you think motivated Facebook to begin its media evaluation initiative? Do you think Facebook is likely to succeed?

Why do journalists ignore details and emphasize scandal? Describing the media as an information source for citizens makes sense in terms of how American politics works, but this description does not capture the sometimes contradictory incentives that journalists face. They may feel the need to demonstrate their independence from politicians and government interests and perhaps counter or prevent claims of media bias. And this may lead to aggressive questioning of elected officials and cynical stories about the political process.[41] But again, reporters and their editors are in a competitive business to attract a paying audience.[42] Most American media outlets are for-profit enterprises. Because they need to produce coverage that attracts an audience, they often seek to create stories that consumers want. So if the media focus on something that seems frivolous like Donald Trump's hair or the outfits worn by his press secretary, Sarah Huckabee Sanders, it is because these stories find a ready audience.

Even if reporters for major news outlets tried to explain how our democratic government works or the complexity of most policy questions, it is unlikely that citizens would respond favorably. There are sources available that work this way. The nightly television program *PBS NewsHour* has a reputation for producing thoughtful, in-depth stories about politics and policy. The same is true for the magazine *National Journal*. But the audience for these sources is minuscule, confirming that most people would prefer soft news, cynicism, and scandals to hard news, policy details, and sober analysis.

Thus, complaints about how the media cover American politics are to a large extent misdirected. The media give Americans the coverage they want. If the average citizen wants to become an expert on politics and public policy, the necessary information is surely available. But few people are interested in seeking that degree of understanding. For most Americans, the media's coverage of politics as a sports event is enough to keep them satisfied, even as they complain about a lack of details and an emphasis on scandal.

Reporters compete for an audience—that's how they stay in business. That means that stories you consider important (or that really are important) may not get media attention because they're too hard to explain or because people aren't interested. The only way to get more detailed, thoughtful political coverage is for Americans to start demanding it.

"Why Should I Care?"

Unpacking the Conflict

Considering all that we've discussed in this chapter, let's apply what we know about the media to understanding why social media has not transformed American politics. Social media was supposed to inform us and bring us together—what went wrong?

News media are the primary source of public information about American politics and policy. The considerable controversy about how well the media fulfill their information-providing role reflects both the importance of the task and the interest many people have in how political coverage is shaped. As we have shown, while the rise of social media has transformed the media as an industry and as an information provider, it has not changed how Americans form opinions as people a generation ago hoped it would.

Social media advocates got the ways the media would change right—but they were wrong about how citizens would react. Even now, most Americans behave as they always have, consulting a few trusted sources for information about politics. The fact that much more information is available now has not changed our consumption habits. The value of gathering additional information is simply not worth the trouble, especially given the need to reconcile what a variety of sources are telling you.

Taking stock of how people use the media also explains increasing distrust of the media and concerns about fake news. There are so many more sources to consult, and there is much better information about how different sources report the news differently. As a result, people have a better sense of which sources they should trust and a much better sense that there are many other sources whose reporting might be suspect. Taken as a group, the media are no less trustworthy than they were a generation ago—but the average American has a much better idea of why he or she should be suspicious of some media coverage.

Social media advocates also had unrealistic expectations about how the media would react to technological change. Even now, content producers must attract an audience to survive. Americans might be better informed if the media ignored sensational stories and focused on the details of public policy, but lurid stories help attract and keep the audience that media companies need to stay in business. Americans will get different media coverage only if they value sources that emphasize details and complexity over scandals and drama.

For all of these reasons, America's news media often falls short of the goal of acting as a watchdog, making sure people have the information they need to bring government policy in line with their interests. Though social media has changed many aspects of our lives, it has not changed this fundamental truth about American politics: we cannot blame people for refusing to take advantage of what the media offers them, but at the same time we cannot blame the media for citizens' ignorance and misinformation.

What's Your Take?

Should social media be judged based on the wealth of information it provides or on its failure to increase citizens' political knowledge? Should Americans put more trust in the media?

STUDY GUIDE

Political media today

Describe the role of the media in American politics and how people get political information. (Pages 234–241)

Summary

The media have been the primary sources of political information in America since the Founding, though the forms of media have changed considerably over time. While the term "media" traditionally referred only to print sources, technological advances have allowed political information to be spread through radio, television, and the Internet. The creation of the Internet and the proliferation of media sources more generally have drastically increased the amount of information about politics that is available to the average American.

Key terms

mass media (p. 234)

yellow journalism (p. 235)

broadcast media (p. 235)

Federal Communications
  Commission (FCC) (p. 235)

equal time provision (p. 236)

media conglomerates
  (p. 236)

by-product theory (p. 239)

Practice Quiz Questions

1. **The deregulation of the media has resulted in _____.**

a increasing enforcement of the equal time provision

b increasing enforcement of the fairness doctrine

c increasing use of the Internet

d increasing scrutiny of media concentration

e increasing frequency of cross-ownership

2. **Which is the result of the decreased barriers to publication on the Internet?**

a Few opportunities exist for citizens to interact with reporters or government officials.

b People with no official connection to politics can contribute to the commentary and reach a wide audience.

c The accuracy of political information has improved.

d Few average citizens report on events as they happen.

e Like-minded political supporters have difficulty organizing and staying informed on issues.

3. **Why hasn't the Internet increased citizens' political knowledge?**

a It can be hard to find political news on the Internet.

b Most people do not have access to the Internet.

c Most people read content from a wide range of balanced media sources.

d Most people fail to systematically search for information about politics.

e Search engines don't include political topics.

4. **What is the by-product theory of political information?**

a Local media sources often rely on major sources for their national news coverage.

b Most Americans learn about politics accidentally.

c Reporters often learn about a political story while working on a different story.

d Bloggers typically do not produce news; rather, they comment on news gathered secondhand.

e News coverage often influences policy decisions.

How do politicians use the media? How do the media use politicians?

Explain how politicians use the media to achieve their goals. (Pages 241–245)

Summary

Coverage of politics requires that the reporter, on the one hand, make a trade-off between cultivating sources with favorable stories and providing complete and accurate information. Politicians, on the other hand, want favorable media coverage that highlights their achievements. One of the best ways reporters can cover political events is to get information "off the record." To maintain this information resource, the confidentiality of sources must be protected, although reporters can be compelled to reveal them in court.

Key terms

on background or off the
  record (p. 241)

leaking (p. 243)

Practice Quiz Questions

5. **Shield laws _____.**

a allow editors to protect their reporters from vengeful politicians

b allow politicians to protect reporters who provide favorable coverage

c protect politicians from slander

d allow reporters to protect confidential sources

e protect reporters from being sued for slander

6. **Why are elected officials often able to successfully demand that journalists give favorable coverage of events and actions?**

a   Elected officials can throw the journalists in jail.

b   The fairness doctrine requires that journalists publish what elected officials tell them.

c   Journalists defer to elected officials because they need the information that elected officials can provide.

d   Journalists are constrained by the equal time provision included in federal law.

e   Media consolidation has increased the power of elected officials.

7. **Prior restraint of reporting on government policy is _____ .**

a   relatively rare because the constitutional guarantees of a free press are very strong

b   relatively rare because reporters are afraid of having to pay large fines

c   common because of media consolidation

d   common in the post–September 11 era

e   ruled as illegal by the Supreme Court

How do the media influence their audience?

Explain how the media influence how people think about politics. (Pages 245–253)

Summary

Much of what Americans know about politics comes not only from the stories that they are exposed to in the news but also from the way these stories are presented (or if stories are reported at all). Potential media bias, filtering, and framing all may influence the type and scope of information that reporters choose to disseminate. In particular, the effects of filtering and framing are simply unavoidable given limited resources.

Key terms

media effects (p. 248)   **filtering** (p. 250)

hostile media effect (p. 248)   **framing** (p. 250)

Practice Quiz Questions

8. **"Filtering" the news refers to _____ .**

a   the media's attempts to frame public opinion

b   sources' attempts to remain confidential

c   newspaper editors determining which stories to report

d   politicians attempting to influence coverage by providing select information

e   reporters' choices to delay a story

9. **Space and time limitations mean that some _____ is inevitable.**

a   filtering

b   slant

c   priming

d   framing

e   soft news

10. **Why do reporters move beyond "just the facts" reporting?**

a   Politicians are corrupt, and people need to know about it.

b   Americans don't realize the media are not always objective.

c   Readers have already interpreted the news themselves.

d   Politics is complicated and often requires some interpretation.

e   Reporters have a strong personal bias and can't write strictly factual stories.

11. **What is one problem with research on media bias?**

a   Few scholars are interested in studying media bias.

b   It is difficult to measure bias.

c   No journalist will admit that bias exists.

d   There's little chance that media sources are biased.

e   There are not enough media sources to create a sample.

Do the media work?

Assess whether the media fulfill their role in American democracy. (Pages 253–257)

Summary

In a democracy, the media's job is to provide citizens with information about politicians, government action, and policy debates. Although the media often fall short of this ideal, there are many reasons for this failure, including market forces and lack of citizen interest.

Key terms

attack journalism (p. 255)   **soft news** (p. 255)

horse race (p. 255)   **hard news** (p. 255)

Practice Quiz Questions

12. **Which is an example of "soft news"?**

a   CNN's coverage of a White House press conference

b   ABC's coverage of the president's State of the Union address

c   NPR's report on the details of the debt-ceiling debate

d   CBS's coverage of election results

e   MSNBC's story about a member of Congress posting risqué photos of himself to his Twitter account

13. Which of the following statements best characterizes soft news?

a   Soft news stories sell far better than hard news stories.

b   Journalists aren't interested in writing hard news and would prefer to write soft news pieces.

c   Hard news and policy analysis articles tend to sell better than soft news.

d   Most citizens have several sources of hard news and they have to search to find soft news stories.

e   Soft news was popular in the past but is now declining.

14. Which of the following would increase the amount of hard news reporting on politics and public policy?

a   Mandating that reporters covering American politics have degrees in political science

b   The rise of new publications that focus on scandals, electoral horse races, and human interest stories

c   Changes in the kinds of stories demanded by the electorate

d   Repeal of the fairness doctrine

e   Increased media concentration and consolidation

Suggested Reading

Baum, Matthew A. *Soft News Goes to War: Public Opinion and American Foreign Policy in the New Media Age.* Princeton, NJ: Princeton University Press, 2003.

Bennett, W. Lance, and Shanto Iyengar. "A New Era of Minimal Effects? The Changing Foundations of Political Communication," *Journal of Communication* 58 (2008): 707–31.

Brader, Ted. *Campaigning for Hearts and Minds: How Emotional Appeals in Political Ads Work.* Chicago: University of Chicago Press, 2006.

Davenport, Christian. *Media Bias, Perspective, and State Repression: The Black Panther Party.* New York: Cambridge University Press, 2010.

Druckman, Jamie. "Media Effects in Politics." In *Oxford Bibliographies Online: Political Science*, ed. Rick Valelly. New York: Oxford University Press, 2012.

Iyengar, Shanto. *Media Politics: A Citizen's Guide.* New York: W. W. Norton, 2016.

Ladd, Jonathan M. *Why Americans Hate the Media and How It Matters.* Princeton, NJ: Princeton University Press, 2012.

Mutz, Diana. "Effects of 'in Your Face' Television Discourse on Perceptions of a Legitimate Opposition." *American Political Science Review* 101 (2007): 621–36.

Norris, Pippa. *A Virtuous Circle? Political Communications in Post-Industrial Democracies.* New York: Cambridge University Press, 2000.

Prior, Markus. *Post-Broadcast Democracy: How Media Choice Increases Inequality in Political Involvement and Polarizes Elections.* New York: Cambridge University Press, 2007.

8

Political Parties
How do political parties organize American politics?

» **"Look at the potential for our country. Look at the direction we've been going. Look at the direction we need to go. And look at what a unified Republican government can get you."**
Paul Ryan, Speaker of the House

« **"The GOP is running as smoothly as a dry Slip 'N Slide made from sandpaper. . . . The Democratic party, meanwhile, has gotten drunk on the spectacle. And as with many a drunk, it's grown oblivious to its own decrepitude."**
Jonah Goldberg, the American Enterprise Institute

In many ways, political parties are at the center of modern American politics. Decades of public opinion research have confirmed that most people have a long-term attachment to one of the major parties and that this attachment shapes the way they think about candidates, policies, and vote decisions. Parties also organize the choices we have in elections: for example, although President Trump campaigned as a political outsider, he won the presidency running as the candidate of the Republican Party. Republican and Democratic party organizations play important roles in recruiting and training candidates and raising money for their campaigns. And once candidates are elected to office, parties are also key players in the legislative process—building majorities in the House and Senate, using legislative rules to secure enactment of policy compromises, and bridging differences with the president. Congressional party leaders such as Senate Majority Leader Mitch McConnell or House Minority Leader Nancy Pelosi are important spokespeople and dealmakers. By providing these services and playing these roles, parties unify and mobilize disparate groups, simplify the choices that voters face, and bring efficiency and coherence to government policy making.

However, to many Americans, American political parties are unpopular, ineffectual, or even irrelevant. Even though Republicans controlled the presidency and both houses of Congress after the 2016 election, their party was unable to follow through on its promises to fully repeal Obamacare, build a wall at the Mexican border, and reform federal welfare programs. Many Republican candidates in 2018 downplayed their party

Though many people describe themselves as either Republicans or Democrats, Americans' dissatisfaction with the governance of both major parties has led to major conflicts within each of them. Outside the Democratic National Convention in 2016, supporters of Democrats Jill Stein and Bernie Sanders protested against the nomination of Hillary Clinton as the party's candidate for president.

CHAPTER GOALS

Define *political parties* **and show how American political parties and party systems have evolved over time.** pages 264–268

Describe the main characteristics of American parties as organizations, in the government, and in the electorate. pages 268–277

Explain the important functions that parties perform in the political system. pages 278–288

Evaluate whether the American party system enhances or hinders democracy. pages 289–291 affiliation, running instead as loyal servants of district interests. And most Americans complain about both political parties' dysfunction and demand the formation of new, more responsive organizations. Research on American political parties confirms that they are often beset by internal conflicts and are thus unable to control who runs under the party banner, what issue positions their candidates take during the campaign, or how the winners behave in office. Moreover, parties often fail at persuading their supporters to get out to the polls and support the party's nominees on Election Day. In other words, the same organizations that are extremely influential in some situations are virtually powerless in others.

Our task in this chapter is to explain this variation. While American political parties are intended to resolve disagreements about what government should do, these differences can sometimes split politicians and activists within an established party organization—making it all but impossible for these individuals to work together. If political parties are so important and powerful, why do they often fail at the very things they are supposed to do? Why do Americans dislike the parties they are so strongly attached to? Why—and when—do parties matter?

DEFINE *POLITICAL PARTIES* AND SHOW HOW AMERICAN POLITICAL PARTIES AND PARTY SYSTEMS HAVE EVOLVED OVER TIME

What are political parties and where did today's parties come from?

Political parties are organizations that run candidates for political office and coordinate the actions of officials elected under the party banner. Looking around the world, we find many different kinds of parties. In many western European countries, the major political parties have millions of dues-paying members and party leaders control what their elected officials do. In contrast, candidates in many new democracies run as representatives of a party, but party leaders have no control over what candidates say during the campaign or how they act in office.

America's major political parties, the Republican Party and the Democratic Party, lie somewhere between these extremes. Rather than being unified organizations with party leaders at the top, candidates and party workers in the middle, and citizen-members at the bottom, American political parties are decentralized, each one a loose network of organizations, groups, and individuals who share a party label but are under no obligation to work together.[1] The **party organization** is the structure of national, state, and local parties, including party leaders and workers. The **party in government** is made up of the politicians who are elected as candidates of the party. And the **party in the electorate** includes all the citizens who identify with the party. For example, the Republican Party's national organization, the RNC, functions independently of Republican leaders in government like Senate Majority Leader Mitch McConnell; neither one is in charge of the other. In fact, McConnell waited only until just before the Republican National Convention to endorse the party's nominee for president, Donald Trump, and often avoids criticizing Trump, even when the president takes positions that are contrary to McConnell's. Similarly, while McConnell is the leader of Republican senators, he cannot tell them what to do. Although McConnell's colleagues may be somewhat sympathetic to his arguments, there is no political compulsion to do what he asks. For example, McConnell was unable to prevent Republican defections on several of President Trump's

party organization
A specific political party's leaders and workers at the national, state, and local levels.

party in government
The group of officeholders who belong to a specific political party and were elected as candidates of that party.

party in the electorate
The group of citizens who identify with a specific political party.

Cabinet nominations and on multiple Obamacare repeals—although McConnell did assemble a Republican majority to approve Trump's controversial Supreme Court nominee, Brett Kavanaugh. Moreover, while many Americans think of themselves as members of a political party, someone who identifies with the Republican Party is not obligated to work for or give money to the party or to vote for its candidates. As you will see, organization matters: the fact that American political parties are split into three parts has important implications for what they do and for their impact on the nation's politics.

History of American political parties

The Republican and Democratic parties have existed for a long time—the Republicans since 1854 and the Democrats since the early 1800s. This section shows that at different points in history American political parties have looked and acted very differently from the way they do today. These differences help explain the structure and behavior of modern parties.

Political scientists use the term **party system** to describe periods of time when the major parties' names, their groups of supporters, and the issues dividing them have all been constant (the beginning and end years that we use throughout this section are approximate). As Table 8.1 shows, there have been six party systems in America.[2] For

American political parties have three largely separate components: the party organization, represented here by Tom Perez, chair of the DNC; the party in government, represented here by House Minority Leader Nancy Pelosi and Senate Minority Leader Chuck Schumer; and the party in the electorate, exemplified here by the crowd at a rally for Alexandria Ocasio-Cortez, who ran for Congress in New York City.

party system
Periods in which the names of the major political parties, their supporters, and the issues dividing them have remained relatively stable.

American Party Systems

TABLE
8.1

There have been six party systems in the United States since 1789.

Party System	Major Parties (dominant party in boldface)	Key Issues
First (1789–1828)	Federalists, Democratic-Republicans (neither party was dominant)	Location of the capital, financial issues (e.g., national bank)
Second (1829–1856)	**Democrats**, Whigs	Tariffs (farmers vs. merchants), slavery
Third (1857–1896)	Democrats, **Republicans**	Slavery (pre–Civil War), Reconstruction (post–Civil War), industrialization
Fourth (1897–1932)	Democrats, **Republicans**	Industrialization, immigration
Fifth (1933–1968)	**Democrats**, Republicans	Size and scope of the federal government
Sixth (1969–present)	Democrats, Republicans (neither party is dominant)	Size and scope of the federal government, civil rights, social issues, foreign policy

party principle
The idea that a political party exists as an organization distinct from its elected officials or party leaders.

spoils system
The practice of rewarding party supporters with benefits like federal government positions.

There's no evidence from decades of Pew Research surveys that public opinion, in the aggregate, is more extreme now than in the past. But what has changed—and pretty dramatically—is the growing tendency of people to sort themselves into political parties based on their ideological differences.

— Pew Research Center

The Tammany Hall political machine, depicted here as a rotund version of one of its leaders, William "Boss" Tweed, controlled New York City politics for most of the nineteenth and early twentieth centuries. Its strategy was "honest graft," rewarding party workers, contributors, and voters for their efforts to keep the machine's candidates in office.

"THAT'S WHAT'S THE MATTER."
Boss Tweed. "As long as I count the Votes, what are you going to do about it? say?"

each party system, the table gives the names of the two major parties, indicates which party dominated (won the most presidential elections or controlled Congress), and describes the principal issues dividing the parties.

The Evolution of American Political Parties While most of the Founding Fathers held a dim view of political parties, many of them participated in the formation of such parties soon after the Founding of the United States. The Federalists and the Democratic-Republicans were primarily parties in government that consisted of like-minded legislators: Federalists wanted a strong central government and a national bank; Democratic-Republicans took the opposite positions. These political parties were quite different from their modern counterparts. In particular, there were no national party organizations, few citizens thought of themselves as party members, and candidates for office did not campaign as representatives of a party. Even so, the goals of those who developed these parties were similar to the goals of party leaders today: like-minded individuals banded together to help enact their preferred policies and defeat their opponents.

For two decades, the two parties were more or less evenly matched in Congress, although the Federalists did not win a presidential contest after 1800. However, in the 1814 elections Federalist legislators, who had opposed the War of 1812 and supported a politically unpopular pay raise for members of Congress, lost most of their congressional seats.[3] These defeats led to the demise of the Federalist Party and the start of the Era of Good Feelings, when there was only one political party: the Democratic-Republican Party. Following the election of President Andrew Jackson in 1828, this party became known as the Democratic Party. At the same time, another new party, the Whig Party, was formed and the second party system began.

The new Democratic Party cultivated electoral support by building organizations to mobilize citizens and bind them to the party. The operations of the party reflected two new concepts: the **party principle**, the idea that a party is not just a group of elected officials but an organization that exists apart from its candidates, and the **spoils system**, whereby party workers were rewarded with benefits such as federal jobs.[4]

In the 1840s, the issue of slavery split the second party system. Most Democratic politicians either supported slavery outright or wanted to avoid debating the issue.[5] The Whig Party was split between abolitionists, who wanted to end slavery, and politicians who agreed with the Democrats. Ultimately, antislavery Whigs left the party and formed the Republican Party, which also attracted antislavery Democrats, and the Whig Party soon ceased to exist. These changes initiated the third party system, in which the country was divided into a largely Republican Northeast, a largely Democratic South, and politically split Midwestern and border states.[6] These developments illustrate that political parties exist not because the Constitution or laws say they must, but because elites, politicians, party leaders, and activists want them to. The Republican Party was created by people who wanted to abolish slavery, and many other politicians subsequently joined the party because of their ambition: these politicians believed that their chances of winning political office were higher as Republicans than as Whigs or Democrats.

After the Civil War, the Republicans and Democrats remained the two prominent national parties. They were divided over whether the federal government should help farmers and rural residents or inhabitants of rapidly expanding cities and whether it should regulate America's rapidly growing industrial base. Democrats built a coalition of rural and urban voters by proposing a larger, more active federal government, as well as other policies that would help both groups. This strategy is one example of how American political parties have adapted their issue positions to societal changes and consequently reflect the basic political divisions between Americans. A similar shift occurred during the transition to the fourth party system, in which the parties were divided on the government's response to industrialization and restrictions on immigration.

The fifth party system was born out of the Great Depression: the worldwide economic collapse that led to the unemployment of millions of people. Many Republicans argued that conditions would improve over time and that government intervention would do little good, whereas Democrats proposed new programs that would help people in need and spur economic growth. The Democratic landslide in the 1932 election led to the New Deal, a series of federal programs proposed by President Franklin Delano Roosevelt and enacted by Congress to stimulate the national economy, help needy people, and impose a variety of new regulations. Debate over the New Deal brought together the New Deal coalition of African Americans, Catholics, Jews, union members, and white southerners, who became strong supporters of Democratic candidates over the next generation.[7] This transformation established the basic division between the parties that exists to the present day: Democrats generally favor a large federal government that takes an active role in managing the economy and regulating behavior, and Republicans generally believe that many such programs should be provided by state and local governments or not provided at all.

The move from the fifth to the sixth party system was marked by the introduction of new political questions and debates that divided the parties.[8] Beginning in the late 1940s, many Democratic candidates and party leaders, particularly outside the South, came out against the "separate but equal" system of racial discrimination in southern states and in favor of programs designed to ensure equal opportunity for minority citizens. Then, during the 1960s, many Democratic politicians argued for expanding the role of the federal government in health care, antipoverty programs, and education. Most Republicans opposed such initiatives, although a significant portion did not.

At the same time, these new issues also began to divide American citizens and organized groups, leading to a gradual but significant shift in the groups that identified with each party.[9] White southerners and some Catholics moved to the Republican Party, and minorities, particularly African Americans, started identifying more strongly as Democrats. Democrats also gained supporters in New England and West Coast states. By the late 1980s, all three elements of the Republican and Democratic parties (organization, government, and electorate) were much more like-minded than they had been a generation earlier.

The sixth party system also brought changes in party organizations. Both the Republican and Democratic parties increased their involvement in recruiting, training, conducting fund-raising, and campaigning for their party's congressional and presidential candidates in an effort to elect like-minded colleagues who would vote with them to enact their preferred policies.[10] At the same time, disagreements between congressional Republicans and Democrats increased, making it harder to find common ground in many policy areas.

Realignments Each party system is separated from the next by a **realignment,** a change in one or more of the factors that define a party system, including the issues that divide the parties, the nature and function of the party organizations, the composition of the party coalitions, and the specifics of government policy. In most cases, a realignment begins with the emergence of a new question or issue debate that captures the attention of large numbers of ordinary citizens, activists, and politicians.[11] To spur a realignment, the issue has to be *crosscutting,* meaning that within each party coalition there are people who disagree on what government should do.

A realignment between the fifth party system (1933–1968) and the sixth (1969–present) produced the division between modern-day Republicans and Democrats.[12] Parties in the fifth party system were primarily divided by their positions on the

Debate over Roosevelt's New Deal programs established the basic divide between Democrats and Republicans that continues to this day: in the main, Democrats favor a larger federal government that takes an active role in managing the economy; Republicans prefer a smaller federal government and fewer programs and regulations.

THIS IS ONE RABBIT THAT NEVER FAILED ME!

SPENDING

OLD RELIABLE!

realignment
A change in the size or composition of the party coalitions or in the nature of the issues that divide the parties. Realignments typically occur within an election cycle or two, but they can also occur gradually over the course of a decade or longer.

appropriate size of the federal government. In the sixth party system, new issues such as civil rights became more important markers of division between the parties and their supporters. By the 1980s, the changes in party coalitions and election outcomes were apparent. Republicans gained House and Senate seats in southern states, and Democrats gained seats in the Northeast, West, and Southwest.[13] After the 2018 elections, Republicans controlled only one Senate seat in New England, while there were only three Democratic senators in the South (two in Virginia).

"Why Should I Care?"

Looking at American political parties today, you might think that Democratic and Republican parties have been around forever, that they are evenly split in party identifiers and officeholders, and that their main disagreement has always concerned the size and scope of government. None of these ideas is true. Moreover, the changes over time in the Republican and Democratic parties illustrate how these organizations adapt to shifts in public opinion. Thus, American political parties may look very different 10 years from now than they do today.

DESCRIBE THE MAIN CHARACTERISTICS OF AMERICAN PARTIES AS ORGANIZATIONS, IN THE GOVERNMENT, AND IN THE ELECTORATE

American political parties today

We've seen that, from the beginning, political parties have been a central feature of American politics. The next steps are to examine the different aspects (the party organization, the party in government, and the party in the electorate) of American political parties, describe the role they play in elections and in government, and understand how their organization and operations shape American democracy.

The party organization

national committee
An American political party's principal organization, comprising party representatives from each state.

The principal body in each party organization is the **national committee** (the Democratic National Committee or the Republican National Committee), which consists of representatives from state party organizations, usually one man and one woman per state. The state party organizations in turn are made up of professional staff plus thousands of party organizations at the county, city, and town levels. The job of these organizations is to run the party's day-to-day operations, recruit candidates and supporters, raise money for future campaigns, and work to build a consensus on major issues. (Of course, other groups in the party, as well as individual politicians, carry out similar tasks at the same time and not always in agreement with the national or state committees.)

Both national party committees also include a number of *constituency groups* (the Democrats' term) or *teams* (the Republicans' term). These organizations within the party work to attract the support of demographic groups—such as African Americans, Latinos, people with strong religious beliefs, senior citizens, women, and many others—who are considered likely to share the party's issue concerns and to assist in fund-raising. In some cases, these organizations also attempt to win over groups typically identified with the other party. For example, African Americans have long been strong supporters of Democratic candidates. Accordingly, the Democratic Party has a constituency group that informs African Americans about the party's candidates and works to convince these citizens to vote on Election Day. The Republican Party's corresponding constituency team works toward the opposite goal, trying to convince African Americans that Republican policies and candidates would better serve their interests.

Each party organization also includes groups designed to build support for, or coordinate the efforts of, particular individuals or politicians. These groups include the Democratic and the Republican Governors' Associations, the Young Democrats, the Young Republicans, and more specialized groups such as the Republican Lawyers' Organization or the Democratic Leadership Council (DLC), an organization of moderate Democratic politicians.[14] The parties use their college and youth organizations to motivate politically minded students to work for the party and its candidates. Groups such as the Governors' Associations and the DLC hold meetings where elected officials discuss solutions to common problems and try to formulate joint strategies. People who work for a party organization perform a wide range of tasks, from recruiting candidates and formulating political strategies to mobilizing citizens, conducting fund-raising, filling out campaign finance reports, researching opposing candidates and parties, and developing websites for the party and its candidates.

Other Allied Groups Many other groups, such as **political action committees (PACs)** or **527 organizations**, labor unions, and other interest groups and organizations, are loosely affiliated with one of the major parties. For example, the organization MoveOn.org typically supports Democratic candidates. Similar organizations on the Republican side include the Club for Growth, Americans for Prosperity, Crossroads GPS, and many evangelical groups. Many of these organizations take advantage of a loophole in a provision of the IRS code to legally solicit large, anonymous donations from corporate and individual contributors. Although these groups often favor one party over the other, they are not part of the party organization and do not always agree with the party's positions or support its candidates—in fact, many have to operate independently of the parties and their candidates to preserve their tax-exempt status. (For more details on campaign finance, see Chapter 9 and Chapter 10.)

political action committee (PAC)
An interest group or a division of an interest group that can raise money to contribute to campaigns or to spend on ads in support of candidates. The amount a PAC can receive from each of its donors and the amount it can spend on federal electioneering are strictly limited.

527 organization
A tax-exempt group formed primarily to influence elections through voter mobilization efforts and to issue ads that do not directly endorse or oppose a candidate. Unlike PACs, 527 organizations are not subject to contribution limits and spending caps.

Both parties include internal organizations that attempt to attract the support of certain demographic groups, even ones that are typically identified with the opposite party. Women, for example, tend to vote more for Democrats on average.

Party organizations at the local level, such as the Ohio county Democratic Party meeting shown here, coordinate support for the party's candidates, but they don't necessarily have to follow the lead of the national party organization.

issue ownership
The theory that voters associate certain issues or issue positions with certain parties (like Democrats and support for government-provided health insurance).

"

I am not a member of an organized political party. I am a Democrat.

— Will Rogers

As this description suggests, the party organization has a fluid structure rather than a rigid hierarchy.[15] Individuals and groups work with a party's leaders and candidates when they share the same goals, but unless they are paid party employees, they are under no obligation to do so. (Even paid party workers can, of course, quit rather than work for a candidate or a cause they oppose.)

Party Brand Names The Republican and Democratic party organizations have well-established "brand names." Because the parties stand for different things, in terms of both their preferred government policies and their ideological leanings, the party names themselves become a shorthand way of providing information to voters about the parties' candidates.[16] Hearing the term "Democrat" or "Republican" calls to mind ideas about what kinds of positions the members of each party support, what kinds of candidates each party runs, and how these candidates will probably vote if they are elected to office. Citizens can use these brand names as a cue to decide whom to vote for in an election. (See Chapter 9 for more information on voting cues.)

Differences in the details of party brand names also create opportunities for **issue ownership**: candidates from a party tend to concentrate their campaigns on issues that are part of their party's brand name and ignore issues that belong to the other party. Figure 8.1 shows one way to measure issue ownership: by surveying citizens who identify with each party about their policy priorities.

Limits of the Party Organization The critical thing to understand about the Democratic and Republican party organizations is that they are not hierarchies. No one person or group in charge determines what either organization does—which often makes them look disorganized. Because the RNC and DNC are organized in the same way, we can consider the example of Tom Perez, the chair of the DNC. He has some influence over who works at the DNC. However, the party organization's issue positions are set not by Perez's employees but by DNC members from all 50 states. The individual committee members are appointed by their state party organizations, so they do not owe their jobs to Perez—in fact, they can remove *him* from office if they like. If Perez and the committee disagree, he can't force the committee members to do what he wants.

The national party organization is also unable to force state and local parties to share its positions on issues or comply with other requests. State and local parties make their own decisions about state- and local-level candidates and issue positions. The national committee can ask nicely, cajole, or even threaten to withhold funds. But if a state party organization, an independent group, or even an individual candidate disagrees with the national committee, there's little the national committee can do to force compliance. For example, Republican leaders could not discourage challengers from running in primaries against their preferred Senate candidates in 2018. Nor could they stop Donald Trump from winning the presidential nomination in 2016—much less control his behavior in office.

The party in government

The party in government consists of elected officials holding national, state, and local offices who took office as candidates of a particular party. They are the public face of the party, somewhat like the players on a sports team. Although players are only one part of a sports franchise—along with owners, coaches, trainers, and support

FIGURE
8.1

Democrats' and Republicans' Top Priorities

The Republican and Democratic party coalitions have different priorities on many issues, ranging from environmental protection to deficit reduction—and their differences are small on a few issues, such as reforming the tax system and reducing the influence of lobbyists. Do these differences make sense in light of each party's "brand name"?

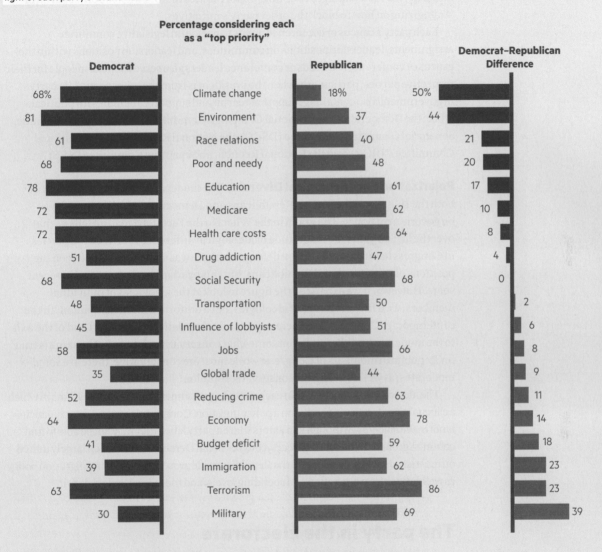

Percentage considering each as a "top priority"

	Democrat	Republican	Democrat–Republican Difference
Climate change	68%	18%	50%
Environment	81	37	44
Race relations	61	40	21
Poor and needy	68	48	20
Education	78	61	17
Medicare	72	62	10
Health care costs	72	64	8
Drug addiction	51	47	4
Social Security	68	68	0
Transportation	48	50	2
Influence of lobbyists	45	51	6
Jobs	58	66	8
Global trade	35	44	9
Reducing crime	52	63	11
Economy	64	78	14
Budget deficit	41	59	18
Immigration	39	62	23
Terrorism	63	86	23
Military	30	69	39

Source: Pew Research Center, "Economic Issues Decline among Public's Policy Priorities," January 25, 2018, www.people-press.org (accessed 2/16/18).

staff—the players' identities are what most people call to mind when they think of the team. Because the party in government is made up of officeholders, it has a direct impact on government policy. Members of the party organization can recruit candidates, write platforms, and pay for campaign ads, but only those who win elections—the party in government—serve as members of Congress or as executive officials and actually propose, debate, vote on, and sign the legislation that determines what government does.

Caucuses and Conferences In the House and Senate, the Democratic and Republican parties are organized around working groups called a **caucus** (Democrats)

caucus (congressional)
The organization of Democrats within the House and Senate that meets to discuss and debate the party's positions on various issues in order to reach a consensus and to assign leadership positions.

or a **conference** (Republicans). The party caucus or conference serves as a forum for debate, compromise, and strategizing among a party's elected officials. Under unified government (when the same party controls Congress and the presidency) these discussions focus on finding common ground within the party—such as the negotiations that led to the Republican tax cut legislation in 2016, which was enacted without Democratic support. Under divided government or when a party is in the minority, the focus changes to finding opportunities to work with the other party, or strategizing on how to block the other party's initiatives.

Each party's caucus or conference meets to decide on legislative committee assignments, leadership positions on committees, and leadership positions within the caucus or conference.[17] Caucus or conference leaders also serve as spokespeople for their respective parties, particularly when the president is from the other party. The party in government also contains groups that recruit and support candidates for political office: the Democratic Congressional Campaign Committee (DCCC), the Democratic Senatorial Campaign Committee (DSCC), the National Republican Congressional Committee (NRCC), and the National Republican Senatorial Committee (NRSC).

Polarization and Ideological Diversity The modern Congress is polarized: in both the House and the Senate, Republicans and Democrats hold different views on government policy. The graph in the What Do the Facts Say? feature tells us that over the last 60 years the magnitude of ideological differences between the parties in Congress has increased. Up until the 1980s there was some overlap between the positions of Democrats and Republicans, but this overlap has disappeared in recent years. However, if we expanded the figure to look at the ideologies of individual members, we'd find a mixture of ideologies, not a uniform consensus opinion. In the contemporary Congress, Democrats vary from the relatively liberal left end of the axis to the moderate (middle) and even somewhat conservative right end. The same is true for Republican members of Congress: while most are conservative, there are some moderates, as well as a range of conservative opinion.

The ideological diversity within each party in government can create situations in which a caucus or conference is divided on a policy question. Compromise within a party caucus is not inevitable—even though legislators share a party label, they may not be able to find common ground. In the last few years, congressional Democrats have been largely united on most issues, while divisions on the Republican side arose on issues of immigration policy as well as health care, taxation and spending levels, and the federal budget deficit.[18]

The party in the electorate

The party in the electorate consists of citizens who identify with a particular political party. Most Americans say they are either Democrats or Republicans, although the percentage has declined slightly over the last two generations. **Party identification (party ID)** is a critical variable in understanding votes and other forms of political participation.

Party Id To say you identify with a party is a personal orientation or decision that does not commit you to anything, nor does it give you any control over a party's actions. Although the Republicans and the Democrats have websites where people can sign up to receive e-mail alerts and to contribute online to party causes, joining a party does not give a citizen any direct influence over what the party does. Rather, the party leaders and the candidates themselves make the day-to-day decisions. These individuals often heed citizens' demands, but there is no requirement that they do so.

Are the Parties More Polarized than Ever?

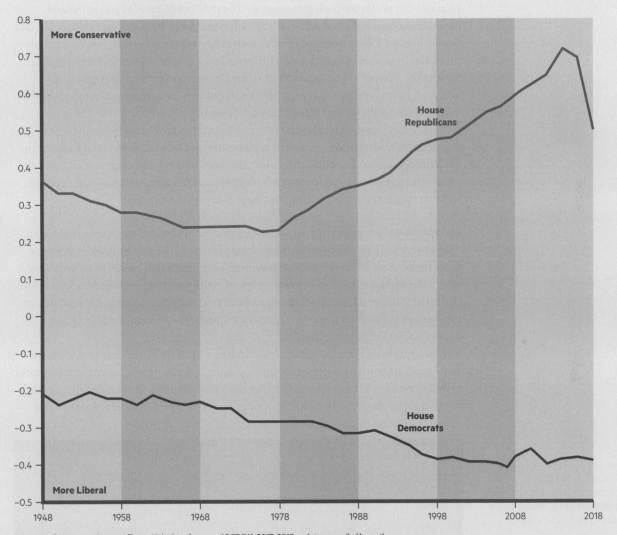
For the last 20 years, it seems as though all the news about political parties has been about conflict and stalemate. It seems like political campaigns are increasingly negative, compromise on issues is rare, and Republicans and Democrats have divided into camps that are never likely to agree on anything. Is this trend new? What do the facts say?

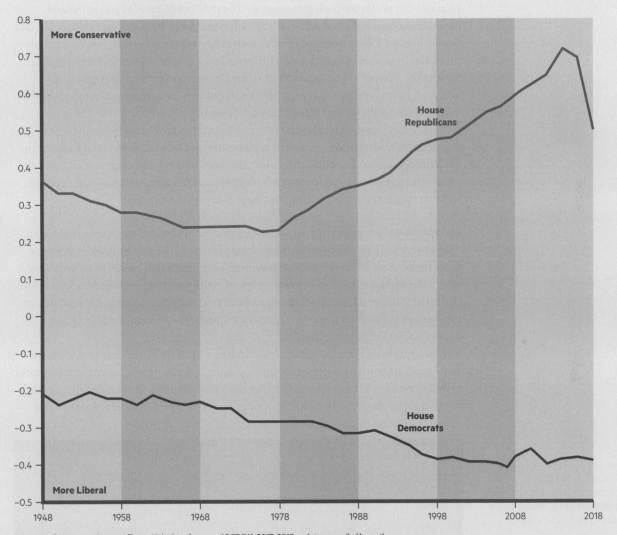

Source: Voteview, voteview.com/Party_Unity.htm (accessed 8/15/16). 2017–2018 updates compiled by author.

Think about it

- **This graph uses voting behavior to measure the average ideology (liberal–conservative) of House Democrats and Republicans. Since the 1980s, have Republicans gotten more conservative, have Democrats become more liberal, or both?**
- **How might these changes make it harder for members of the contemporary Congress to enact major changes in government policy? What is more likely: compromise or gridlock?**

Real participation in party operations is open to citizens who become activists by working for a party organization or one of its candidates. Activists' contributions vary widely and may include stuffing envelopes, helping out with a phone bank, being a delegate to a party convention, attending campaign rallies, or campaigning door-to-door.

Early theories of party ID described it as a deep attachment to a party that was acquired early in life from parents, friends, and political events and was generally unaffected by subsequent events.[19] Further work showed that party ID does not necessarily remain the same but rather involves continuing evaluation that takes account of new information.[20] Thus, when people say they identify with the Republican Party, they are saying that, based on what they have seen in American politics, they prefer the positions suggested by the Republicans' brand name and how Republicans behave in office. At the same time, work by political scientists Donald Green, Bradley Palmquist, and Eric Schickler shows that party ID shapes how people think about politics and react to new information. Thus, when Republicans argue for sending troops to fight ISIL in Syria while Democrats focus on aiding Syrian refugees, the difference is not what they know but how they react to the same pieces of information—a response that is shaped by their party affiliation.

Figure 8.2 gives data on party ID in America from 1992 to 2016, measured when respondents were given the option to say whether they were a Democrat, a Republican, or an Independent. Over this time period, the parties have been nearly evenly split. At various times in the past, one party has opened some advantage over the other (as the Democrats did in the early 2000s), but there is no consistent trend.

Independents Some early analyses concluded that Independents were unaffiliated with a party because they were in the process of shifting their identification from one party to the other.[21] Others saw Independents as evidence that more and more people regard the parties as irrelevant to their view of politics and their voting decisions.[22] The rise in the number of Independents was also seen as an indication that Americans were becoming more politically savvy—learning more about candidates and not always blindly voting for the same party.[23]

More-recent work has modified these findings. Most Independents actually have some weak attachment to one of the major political parties—in fact, some scholars refer to Independents as "closet partisans:" people who have party ties but who simply don't admit that they do.[24] In Figure 8.2, for example, about a third of the electorate says it

Activist volunteers, such as these two students canvassing in the crucial swing state of Ohio, undertake most of the one-on-one efforts to mobilize support for a party and its candidates.

FIGURE 8.2

Party ID Trends among American Voters

In terms of party ID, the parties have moved from rough parity in the 1990s to a slight Democratic advantage in the 2000s, although this change has eroded in recent years. What events might have caused these changes in party ID?

Source: Pew Research Center, "Party Identification Trends, 1992–2016," www.people-press.org (accessed 2/18/18).

does not identify with a party. However, the percentage of true Independents is much smaller: if we asked these so-called Independents if they leaned toward one party or the other, about two-thirds would claim this level of affiliation, and they would be split evenly between Republicans and Democrats. Independents are not necessarily better informed about candidates, parties, or government policy than are party identifiers. However, they are much less likely to get involved in political activity beyond voting, such as contributing to or working for a candidate or party.[25]

With a closer look at voting decisions, Figure 8.3 shows how Democrats, Republicans, and Independents voted in the 2016 presidential election ("closet partisan" Independents

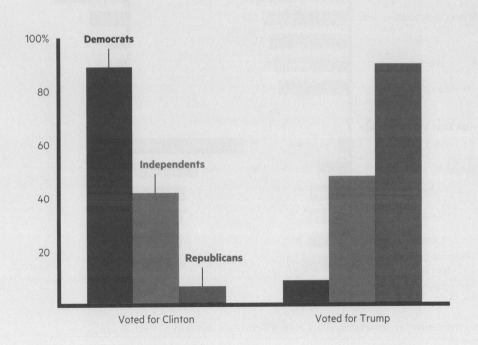

FIGURE 8.3

The Impact of Party ID on Voting Decisions in the 2016 Presidential Election

Americans are much more likely to vote for candidates who share their party affiliation. What does this relationship tell us about the impact of campaign events (including speeches, debates, and gaffes) on voting decisions?

Source: Data compiled from CNN Exit Poll, www.cnn.com/election/results/exit-polls/national/president (accessed 11/9/16).

are grouped with the party they actually affiliate with). This figure shows that if you are trying to predict how someone will vote, the most important thing to know is his or her party ID.[26] Almost 90 percent of Democrats voted for Hillary Clinton, the Democratic nominee, and about the same percentage of Republicans voted for Donald Trump.

party coalitions
The groups that identify with a political party, usually described in demographic terms such as African-American Democrats or evangelical Republicans.

Party Coalitions Data on party ID enable scholars to study **party coalitions**—that is, groups of citizens who identify with each party. Figure 8.4 shows the contemporary Democratic and Republican party coalitions. As you can see, some groups are disproportionately likely to identify as Democrats (African Americans), some are disproportionately likely to identify as Republicans (white evangelicals), and other groups have no clear party favorite (women born in 1945 and earlier). Again, these coalitions have shifted over time, often evolving during periods of realignment and changing from one party system to the next. For example, the Republican advantage among white southerners and white evangelical Protestants has existed only since the 1980s.[27]

The Republican and Democratic party coalitions differ systematically in terms of their policy preferences—what they want government to do—as shown in Figure 8.1. This indicates the extent to which they disagree about the relative importance of issues

FIGURE 8.4

The Party Coalitions

Many groups, such as African Americans and white evangelicals, are much more likely to affiliate with one party than the other. What are the implications of these differences for the positions taken by each party's candidates?

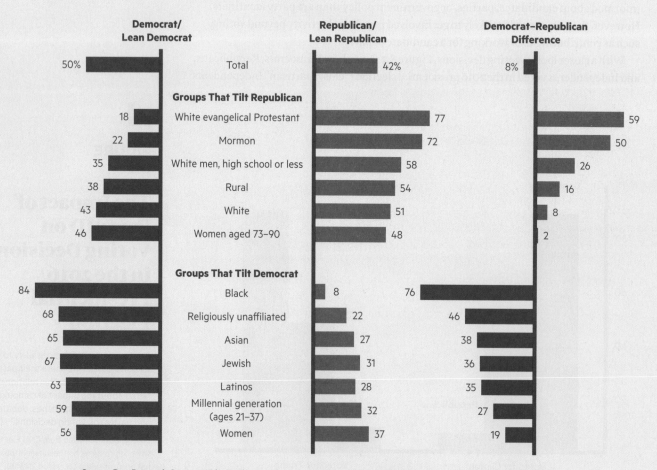

	Democrat/ Lean Democrat	Republican/ Lean Republican	Democrat–Republican Difference
Total	50%	42%	8%
Groups That Tilt Republican			
White evangelical Protestant	18	77	59
Mormon	22	72	50
White men, high school or less	35	58	26
Rural	38	54	16
White	43	51	8
Women aged 73–90	46	48	2
Groups That Tilt Democrat			
Black	84	8	76
Religiously unaffiliated	68	22	46
Asian	65	27	38
Jewish	67	31	36
Latinos	63	28	35
Millennial generation (ages 21–37)	59	32	27
Women	56	37	19

Source: Pew Research Center, "Wide Gender Gap, Growing Educational Divide in Voters' Party Identification," March 20, 2018, www.people-press.org (accessed 8/1/18).

**FIGURE
8.5**

The Parties in the Electorate

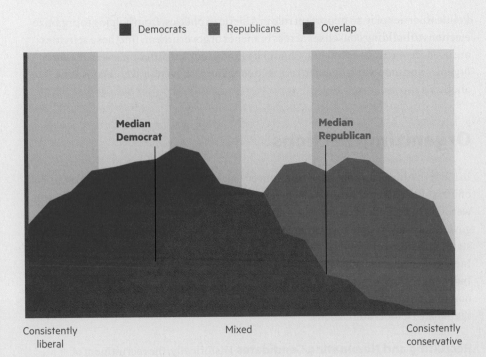

Democrats Republicans Overlap

**Median
Democrat**

**Median
Republican**

Consistently
liberal

Mixed

Consistently
conservative

This graph shows the ideological differences between Democratic and Republican identifiers. The blue area shows the distribution of Democrats, and the red plot shows the distribution of Republicans. This confirms that modern American political parties are ideologically polarized (the median Democrat is a liberal, while the median Republican is a conservative) and homogeneous (most Democrats are liberal or liberal-leaning, while most Republicans are conservative or conservative-leaning). How might these differences affect the kinds of candidates who compete for each party's nomination and the positions they take during campaigns?

Source: Pew Research Center, "Ideological Polarization in the American Public," June 12, 2014, www.people-press.org (accessed 12/20/15).

like providing health insurance to the uninsured, dealing with global warming, and strengthening the military. On only a few issues—for example, fighting drug addiction or dealing with lobbyists—are the percentages of those in both parties who consider the matter a priority nearly the same. These data demonstrate that party labels are meaningful: if you know someone is a Republican (or a Democrat), this information tells you something about what that person probably wants government to do, and how he or she will likely vote in the next election.

Figure 8.5 shows the most fundamental difference in Democratic and Republican identifiers: consistent with the party's brand names and their positions on specific issues, Democrats are the more liberal party in America, while Republicans are more conservative. As you can see, the Democratic Party distribution is dominated by liberal identifiers, while the Republican distribution is dominated by conservatives—although there is still some overlap in the middle, meaning that both parties claim some moderates. Moreover, the current parties are much more homogeneous than a generation ago, with liberals much more likely to be Democrats and conservatives more likely to be Republicans.

Knowing that someone is a Democrat or a Republican tells you a lot about the issues he or she cares about, whether he or she will like or dislike different candidates, and whom he or she will vote for in an election. Taken together, information about the kinds of people who identify with each party tells you a lot about the kinds of candidates who will run under the party banner and the platforms they will campaign on.

"Why Should I Care?"

The role of political parties in American politics

Political parties play an important role in American politics, from helping to organize elections to building consensus across branches of government. But these activities are not necessarily coordinated. Candidates and groups at different levels of a party organization may work together, refuse to cooperate, or even actively oppose one another's efforts.

Organizing elections

In modern American politics, virtually everyone elected to a state or national political office is either a Republican or a Democrat. In the 116th Congress, elected in 2018, there were two Independent senators and no Independent House members. Similarly, the governors of all 50 states are either Democrats or Republicans, and of more than 7,300 state legislators very few are Independents or minor-party candidates. Even then, most Independent elected officials are associated with one of the major parties—one of the Independent U.S. senators, Bernie Sanders, ran for the Democratic Party presidential nomination in 2016, and the other, Angus King, gets his committee assignments from the Senate Democratic Caucus.

Recruiting and Nominating Candidates Historically, the recruitment of candidates was left up to local party organizations. But the process has become much more systematic, with state and national party leaders playing a central role in recruiting, endorsing, and funding candidates—and often promising those candidates help in assembling a staff, organizing a campaign, and raising more money.[28] Actions like these can have a profound impact on congressional elections; years in which one party gains significant congressional seats (such as Democrats in 2006 or Republicans in 2010) are in part the result of one party's disproportionate success in its recruiting efforts.

In fact, one of the most well-known theories of presidential nomination contests argues that endorsements by party leaders and elected officials play a key role in determining which candidate emerges as the nominee.[29] Endorsements enhance a candidate's name recognition and help persuade undecided voters and contributors about candidates' electability and their ability to deliver on campaign promises. In all recent presidential nomination contests except 2016, the winning candidate was the one who gathered the most endorsements from party leaders, elected officials, and other notables. This theory was one of the main reasons why most political scientists thought that Donald Trump was unlikely to be the Republican nominee in 2016. While he led in the polls for several months, he received almost no endorsements from party leaders or elected officials. Conversely, one reason why Hillary Clinton was seen as the inevitable Democratic nominee was the large number of endorsements she garnered from Democratic Party leaders.[30]

Party leaders also play an active role in recruiting candidates for House and Senate seats. When a Senate seat opened up in Utah in 2018 because of Senator Orrin Hatch's retirement, many Republican national and state leaders encouraged former Republican presidential nominee Mitt Romney to enter the race and discouraged other potential candidates. These decisions reflected a simple political logic: party leaders believed that Romney would have a good chance of winning the general election given his reputation (including running the 2002 Winter Olympics in Utah) and Utah's large Mormon population. In addition, party leaders, many of whom opposed President Trump in the 2016 election, wanted to discourage the election of a pro-Trump candidate, such as State Auditor John Dougall.

Despite all of these efforts, however, parties and their leaders do not control who runs in House, Senate, or presidential races (see the Take a Stand feature). In most states, candidates for these offices are selected in a **primary election** or a **caucus**, in which they compete for a particular party's spot on the ballot. About two-thirds of the states use some type of primary election, while the rest use caucuses to select candidates (see Nuts & Bolts 8.1). Most notably, Donald Trump won the 2016 Republican presidential nomination by virtue of his victories in the party's primaries and caucuses over the objections of many party leaders. Trump's victory demonstrates that party endorsements, while significant, are not the only factor in shaping nomination contests.

Running as a major party's nominee, as opposed to running as an Independent, is almost always the easiest way to get on the general-election ballot. Some states give the Republican and Democratic nominees an automatic spot on the ballot. Even in states that don't automatically allocate ballot slots this way, the requirements for the major parties to get a candidate on the ballot are much less onerous than those for minor parties and Independents. For example, in California a party and its candidates automatically qualify for a position on the ballot if any of the party's candidates for statewide office received more than 2 percent of the vote in the previous election. In contrast, Independent candidates need to file petitions with more than 150,000 signatures to get on the ballot without a major-party label—an expensive, time-consuming task.[31] These advantages help explain why virtually all prominent candidates for Congress and the presidency run as Democrats or Republicans.

National parties also manage the nomination process for presidential candidates. This process involves a series of primaries and caucuses held over a six-month period

primary election
A ballot vote in which citizens select a party's nominee for the general election.

caucus (electoral)
A local meeting in which party members select a party's nominee for the general election.

Types of Primaries and Caucuses

NUTS & BOLTS 8.1

Primary Election	An election in which voters choose the major-party nominees for political office, who subsequently compete in a general election.
Closed primary	A primary election system in which only registered party members can vote in their party's primary.
Nonpartisan primary	A primary election system in which candidates from both parties are listed on the same primary ballot. Following a nonpartisan primary, the two candidates who receive the most votes in the primary compete in the general election, even if they are from the same party.
Open primary	A primary election system in which any registered voter can participate in either party's primary, regardless of the voter's party affiliation.
Semi-closed primary	A primary election system in which voters registered as party members must vote in their party's primary, but registered Independents can vote in either party's primary.
Caucus Election	A series of local meetings at which registered voters select a particular candidate's supporters as delegates who will vote for the candidate in a later, state-level convention. (In national elections, the state-convention delegates select delegates to the national convention.) Caucuses are used in some states to select delegates to the major parties' presidential nominating conventions. Some states' caucuses are open to members of any party, while others are closed.

Should Parties Choose Their Candidates?

One of the facts of life for the leaders of the Democratic and Republican parties is that they cannot determine who runs as their party's candidate for political office. They can encourage some candidates to run and attempt to discourage others by endorsing their favorites and funneling money, staff support, and other forms of assistance to the candidates they prefer. But in the end, congressional candidates get on the ballot by winning a primary or a vote at a state party convention; presidential candidates compete in a series of primaries and caucuses. Is this system a good one?

Let the party decide. Many scholars have argued that letting parties choose their candidates increases the chances of getting experienced, talented candidates on the ballot.[a] After all, party leaders probably know more than the average voter about who would make a good candidate or elected official. Plus, party leaders have a strong incentive to find good candidates and convince them to run: their party's influence over government policy increases with the number of people they can elect to political office. And finally, in states that have no party registration or day-of-election registration, giving the nomination power to party leaders would ensure that a group of outsiders could not hijack a party primary to nominate a candidate who disagreed with a party's platform or who was unqualified to serve in office.

While cases of outright hijacking of party nominations are fairly rare, political parties don't always get the nominees their leaders want and party leaders cannot force candidates out of a race. In the 2016 election cycle, for example, many Republican Party leaders believed that Donald Trump was not the party's strongest nominee. Trump gained the nomination over their objections by winning the party's caucus and primary contests.

Let the people decide. One argument in favor of giving the nomination power to the people is that party leaders have not always shown good judgment in picking either electable or qualified candidates. Many of the same Republican leaders who opposed Trump had supported party nominees John McCain in 2008 and Mitt Romney in 2012, both of whom went on to lose in the general-election contest. This track record suggests that party leaders are far from infallible.

The second argument for letting the people decide hinges on a judgment about whose wishes should prevail in nomination contests: the people who make up the party in the electorate or the people in the party organization. What right does the party organization have to select nominees, given that support for the party from the electorate (its contributions and votes in elections) is essential for electoral success? Moreover, shouldn't voters have a say in determining what their electoral choices look like? If party leaders choose, voters may not like any of the options put before them.

Why, then, do voters in America get to pick party nominees in primaries? Direct primaries were introduced in American politics during the late 1800s and early 1900s.[b] The goal was explicit: reform-minded party activists wanted to take the choice of nominees out of the hands of party leaders and give it to the electorate, with the assumption that voters should be able to influence the choice of candidates for the general election. Moreover, reformers believed that this goal outweighed the expertise held by party leaders.

Here is the trade-off: If party leaders select nominees, they will likely choose electable candidates who share the policy goals held by party leaders. If voters choose nominees, they can pick whomever they want, using whatever criteria they like—but there is no guarantee that these candidates will be skilled general-election campaigners or effective in office.

In the end, some groups must be given control over the selection of a party's nominees. Should this power be given to party leaders or to the people?

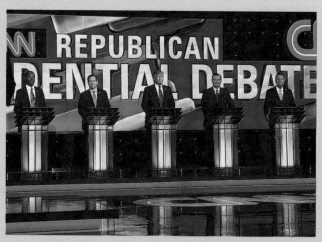

Both political parties organize a series of candidate debates during their presidential nomination contests, giving candidates a chance to present themselves before a national audience.

take a stand

1. One reform proposal would increase the importance of the parties as sources of campaign funds. Would this change have made much of a difference in the 2016 Republican presidential contest?

2. What kind of nomination procedure would be favored by insurgent groups such as the various Tea Party organizations?

beginning in January of a presidential election year. The type of election (primary or caucus) and its date are determined by state legislatures, although national party committees can limit the allowable dates, using their control over seating delegates at the party conventions to motivate compliance. Voters in these primaries and caucuses don't directly select the parties' nominees. Instead, citizens' votes are used to determine how many of each candidate's supporters become delegates to the party's national **nominating convention**, where delegates vote to choose the party's presidential and vice-presidential nominees. The national party organizations determine how many delegates each state sends to the convention based on factors such as state population, the number of votes the party's candidate received in each state in the last presidential election, and the number of House members and senators from the party that each state elected (see How It Works: Nominating Presidential Candidates).

Campaign Assistance One of the most visible ways that the political parties support candidates is by contributing to and spending money on campaign activities. By and large, federal law mandates that these funds be spent by the organization that raised them—the national party, for example, is limited in the amount of money it can directly contribute to congressional and presidential candidates or to state party organizations. As we will discuss in Chapter 10, however, party organizations can use the campaign funds they raise to help candidates in other ways, for example, through independent expenditures—running their own ads in a candidate's district or state.

Figure 8.6 shows the amount of money raised by the top groups within the Republican and Democratic parties for the 2018 election (through October 30). The final figures show that the parties and their various committees raised over a billion dollars. The DNC and RNC raised the most money, but the congressional campaign committees also raised significant sums. Congressional Democratic committees

nominating convention
A meeting held by each party every four years at which states' delegates select the party's presidential and vice-presidential nominees and approve the party platform.

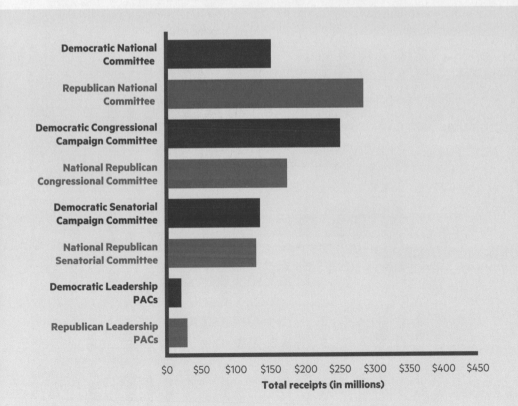

FIGURE 8.6

Democratic and Republican Fund-Raising in the 2017–2018 Election Cycle

In the 2017–2018 election cycle, party and leadership committees raised more than one billion dollars in campaign funds. Although most of this money was raised by the national committees, the state, local, and candidate committees also raised significant sums. To what extent might these funds allow the national committees to force candidates to run on the party platform?

Source: The Center for Responsive Politics, www.opensecrets.org (accessed 10/30/18).

Nominating Presidential Candidates

Primaries and caucuses ...

Closed Primaries
Only voters registered with party vote

Open Primaries
Open to voters from any political party and Independents

Caucus or Local Convention
Party members meet in groups to select delegates

are used to select delegates ...

Republican Party
States can award all delegates to the winning candidate

or award delegates proportionally.

Democratic Party
The state's delegates are divided proportionally.

who attend national nominating conventions.

Delegates from all states attend the national convention, where they vote for the party's presidential and vice-presidential nominees based on the primary and caucus results. Superdelegates—important party leaders—also vote at the convention.

The Nomination of Donald Trump for President, 2016

While Donald Trump was the clear winner in the 2016 Republican presidential nomination contest, his campaign benefited from the rules used in some of the early contests, particularly the use of primary elections rather than caucuses and the use of winner-take-all rules for delegate allocation.

☐ Winner-take-all delegate allocation
☐ Proportional delegate allocation
% Percentage of popular vote won
Ɪ Delegates allocated

		Trump	Rubio	Cruz	Kasich	Caucus/ Primary	Winner Take All?
Feb. 1	Iowa	24%	23%	28%	2%	Caucus	NO
Feb. 9	New Hampshire	35%	12%	11%	16%	Primary	NO
Feb. 20	South Carolina	33%	23%	23%	8%	Primary	YES
Feb. 23	Nevada	46%	24%	21%	4%	Caucus	NO
Mar. 1	Alabama	43%	19%	21%	4%	Primary	NO
	Alaska	34%	15%	36%	4%	Caucus	NO
	Arkansas	33%	25%	31%	4%	Primary	NO
	Georgia	39%	24%	24%	6%	Primary	NO
	Massachusetts	49%	18%	10%	18%	Primary	NO
	Minnesota	21%	37%	29%	6%	Caucus	NO
	Oklahoma	28%	26%	34%	4%	Primary	NO
	Tennessee	39%	21%	24%	5%	Primary	NO
	Texas	27%	19%	44%	4%	Primary	NO
	Vermont	33%	19%	10%	30%	Primary	NO
	Virginia	35%	32%	17%	9%	Primary	NO
Total delegates		**340**	**116**	**230**	**27**		

Note: Colorado has been omitted because its caucus did not allocate delegates.
Source: Data compiled by the authors.

❓ Critical Thinking

1. **Which states used winner-take-all rules in 2016?** How much did Trump benefit from this rule in the early primaries? If there were more winner-take-all states, which candidate(s) would have done better? Which would have done worse?

2. **One argument about caucuses is that they allow** lesser-known candidates (such as John Kasich) to build support. Did this rule hold for Kasich in 2016?

outraised their Republican counterparts. And congressional leaders raised almost $50 million for the campaigns of their colleagues.[32]

Along with supplying campaign funds, party organizations give candidates other assistance, ranging from offering campaign advice (including which issues to emphasize, how to deal with the press, and the like) to conducting polls. Party organizations at all levels also undertake get-out-the-vote activities, encouraging supporters to get to the polls. In the 2016 election, Republican candidate Donald Trump's campaign was almost completely reliant on the Republican Party's mobilization efforts, while Democrat Hillary Clinton's campaign used a combination of campaign and party resources. In the end, however, the Democrats failed to mobilize key groups—like African Americans and Latinos—as successfully as they had in 2012.

party platform
A set of objectives outlining the party's issue positions and priorities. Candidates are not required to support their party's platform.

Party Platforms The **party platform** is a set of promises explaining what candidates from the party will do if elected. The most visible party platform is the one approved at each party's presidential nominating convention, but the party organizations in the House and Senate also release platforms, as do other major-party groups. Party platforms generally reflect the brand name differences between the parties. For example, in the case of abortion rights, the 2016 Republican presidential platform favored a total ban on abortions, while the Democratic presidential platform expressed support for a woman's right to choose, meaning that abortion would be legal under a wider range of conditions.

In theory, party platforms describe differences between the major parties, capture each party's diagnosis of the problems facing the country, and give the party's plan for solving those problems. In this way, party platforms give citizens an easy way to evaluate candidates. However, candidates are not obligated to support their party's platform and many take divergent stances on some issues. For example, notwithstanding the consistently strong pro-choice position on abortion in the Democratic Party's presidential platforms over the last generation, some Democratic members of Congress, such as Illinois representative Dan Lipinski, have promised to vote to restrict abortions—a position closer to the Republican platform.[33] For some of these candidates, their position reflects personal or religious beliefs; for others, it is driven by the desire to reflect the opinion of voters in their district or state.

Despite these exceptions, party platforms are important documents. Political scientist John Gerring's research shows that platforms provide a general guide for voters about the issues and issue positions that separate the major parties. Platforms indicate what sorts of policies winning candidates are likely to vote for if elected. While some candidates may ignore or run against their party's platform, most candidates will support the platform because they agree with it or because they believe it is popular with their constituents.[34]

One of the most important ways parties help candidates is by raising funds. Here, volunteers work the phones in a National Republican Congressional Committee field office in California ahead of midterm elections.

Cooperation in government

As Republicans and Democrats in Congress have become more polarized, particularly in recent years, the majority- and minority-party legislative caucuses have taken on larger roles in efforts to set legislative priorities, formulate compromise proposals, and work to enact these proposals on the floor of the House and Senate.

Agenda-Setting Throughout the year, the parties in government meet to devise strategies for legislative action—that is, to set agendas. What proposals should they offer, and in what order should these proposals be considered? Should the parties try to make a deal with the president or with legislators from the other party? For example, after the 2016 election Republican congressional leaders met with President-elect Donald Trump and his staff to discuss priorities for the 2017–2018 legislative term, including the repeal of Obamacare, tax cuts, changes to immigration law and border security, and increased funding for infrastructure projects. Some of these efforts were successful: late in 2017, Congress enacted tax reform legislation that reduced corporate and individual tax rates.

Yet the party in government can act collectively this way only when its members can agree on what they want. Such agreement is not always possible or may require extensive negotiation and compromise. Even with unified Republican control of Congress, legislators were unable to agree on immigration reform, Obamacare repeal, or infrastructure spending. Part of the problem was the narrow Republican majority in the Senate, yet the deeper issue was splits in Republican ranks that would have made compromise difficult even if Republicans had held a larger majority.

Coordination Political parties play an important role in coordinating the actions taken in different branches of government. Such coordination is extremely important for enacting new laws, because, unless supporters in Congress can amass a two-thirds majority to override a veto, they need the president's support. Similarly, the president needs congressional support to enact the proposals he or she favors. To these ends, the president routinely meets with congressional leaders from his or her party and occasionally meets with the entire caucus or conference. Various members of the president's staff also meet with House and Senate members to present the president's proposals and to hear what members of Congress from both parties want to enact.

During 2017 and 2018, President Trump held many meetings with Republican members of Congress to lobby them to support his proposals for tax cuts and immigration reform. Trump was successful on tax reform, although the final package was modified to gain the last few Republican votes in the Senate. On immigration

Parties don't exert total control over their members. Republican Party leaders could not stop then–freshman senator Ted Cruz (R-TX) from filibustering for 23 hours in an attempt to stop a budget compromise.

unified government
A situation in which one party holds a majority of seats in the House and Senate and the president is a member of that same party.

divided government
A situation in which the House, Senate, and presidency are not controlled by the same party—for example, when Democrats hold the majority of House and Senate seats and the president is a Republican.

reform, however, Trump was unable to persuade Republicans to support his plans to enact substantial reductions in legal immigration into the United States. In fact, when the Senate voted on several proposals in February 2017, Trump's proposal received the lowest number of Republican votes. These two examples illustrate the limits of presidential persuasion: presidential victories have more to do with proposing something that members of Congress already like than with pressuring them to support a proposal they oppose.

Coordination can also occur between caucuses or conferences in the House and Senate. At the same time that President Trump and Republicans in Congress were negotiating over tax reform, congressional Democrats were devising strategies for delaying and defeating these proposals. Although Democratic efforts did not prevent the enactment of tax legislation, the strong opposition of the Democrats required the president and congressional leaders to accept many changes favored by moderate and conservative Republicans in order to enact the legislation without Democratic support.

Such coordination efforts require real work and compromise since party leaders in the House and the Senate do not have authority over each other or over the elected members of their party. Nor can the president order a House member or senator to do anything, even if the legislator is from the president's own party. In 2017, for example, President Trump and congressional leaders needed the votes of several moderate Republicans, including Senator Susan Collins, to pass tax cut legislation through the Senate. The congressional leaders and the president held repeated meetings with Collins and her allies, offering various promises and enticements to secure their votes. Ultimately, these legislators voted for the proposal, but neither the president nor party leaders could have forced them to support it.

Accountability One of the most important functions political parties play in a democracy is to give citizens identifiable groups to reward or punish for government action or inaction. Using the ballot box, voters will reward and punish elected officials, often based on their party affiliation and on the behavior of that party's members in office. In this way, the party system gives the electorate a mechanism that can be used to hold officials accountable for outcomes such as the state of the economy or America's relations with other nations. This mechanism is most clear during periods of **unified government**, when one party holds majorities in both the House and the Senate *and* controls the presidency, meaning that party has enough votes to enact policies in Congress and a good chance of having them signed into law by the president. Arguments along these lines were one of the central themes of the Democratic campaigns during the 2018 midterms—that majority control of the House or Senate would enable Democratic legislators to limit the regulatory changes, judicial appointments, and budget cuts favored by congressional Republicans and the Trump administration.

In contrast, during times of **divided government**, when one party controls Congress but not the presidency or when different parties control the House and Senate (such as during most of Obama's presidency), it is not clear which party should be held accountable for the state of the nation. While Republicans argued in 2012 that Democrats and Obama should be punished for the relatively poor state of the American economy, these arguments did not resonate with the electorate, who believed, at least in part, that Republican majorities in the House and Senate bore some responsibility as well, and reelected Obama to a second term.

Focusing on parties makes it easy for citizens to issue rewards and punishments. For example, if the economy is doing well, people can reward the party in power by voting for its candidates. But if the economy is doing poorly, or if people feel that government is wasting tax money or enacting bad policies, voters can punish the party in power by supporting candidates from the party that is currently out of power. When citizens behave this way, they strengthen the incentive for elected officials from the party in power to work together to develop policies that address voters' concerns—on the premise that if they do, voters will reward them with another term in office. Consider the 2018 midterm elections. Although Republicans lost seats in the House of Representatives, most Republican incumbents were reelected. Why? Some were elected from states or districts dominated by Republican identifiers. But many others were reelected because they campaigned on a platform of changing policy or because of their efforts to help local businesses; in effect, these candidates said, "Instead of punishing me for my party affiliation, reward me for working on your behalf."

In the end, reelecting members of the party in power despite a poor economy or other troubles makes sense given how American political parties are organized and their lack of control over individual officeholders. Of course, insofar as incumbent members of the party in power present themselves as loyal party members and cast votes in accordance with the wishes of party leaders, they will increase the chances that their constituents will take account of their party label when casting their votes—which will help them get reelected in good times but will increase their chances of defeat when conditions turn against their party.

Minor parties

So far, this chapter has focused on the major American political parties, the Republicans and the Democrats, and paid less attention to other party organizations. The reason is that minor political parties in America are *so* minor that they are generally not significant players on the political stage. Many such parties exist, but few run candidates in more than a handful of races and very few minor-party candidates win political office. Few Americans identify with minor parties, and most of these parties exist for only a relatively short period.

Even so, you may think we are giving minor parties too little attention. Consider Jill Stein and Gary Johnson, who ran as the Green and Libertarian party candidates for president in 2016, winning, respectively, 1.1 percent and 3.3 percent of the popular vote. If the votes received by these two candidates had gone to Democrat Hillary Clinton instead, Clinton would have won Wisconsin, Michigan, Pennsylvania, and Florida—and the presidency.

However, the size of the minor-party vote in 2016 doesn't so much highlight the importance of minor parties as it illustrates the closeness of the 2016 presidential election. If Stein and Johnson had not run, Clinton might have received enough additional support to win. But given that Trump's margin of victory in the states listed above was so small, any number of seemingly minor events (rain in some areas and sunshine in others, or some small number of additional pro-Clinton ads) could have had the same effect.

Even in terms of lower offices, minor-party candidates typically attract only meager support. While the Libertarian Party claims to have over 150 officeholders, many of these officials hold unelected positions such as seats on county planning boards or ran unopposed for relatively minor offices.[35]

Looking back in history, some minor-party candidates for president have attracted a substantial percentage of citizens' votes. George Wallace ran as the candidate of the American Independent Party in 1968, receiving about 13 percent of the popular vote nationwide. Ross Perot, the Reform Party candidate for president in

Minor-party presidential candidates, such as Libertarian Gary Johnson in 2016, sometimes attract considerable press attention because of their distinctive policy preferences, but they rarely effect election outcomes.

Duverger's Law
The principle that in a democracy with single-member districts and plurality voting, only two parties' candidates will have a realistic chance of winning political office, as in the United States.

single-member district
An electoral system in which every elected official represents a geographically defined area, such as a state or congressional district, and each area elects one representative.

plurality voting
A voting system in which the candidate who receives the most votes within a geographic area wins the election, regardless of whether that candidate wins a majority (more than half) of the votes.

1996, won 8.4 percent of the popular vote. Perot also ran as an Independent in 1992, winning 18.2 percent of the popular vote. And Ralph Nader received about 5 percent of the popular vote in 2000.

Unique Issues Facing Minor Parties The differences between major and minor political parties in contemporary American politics grow even more substantial when considered in terms other than election outcomes. For most minor parties, the party in government does not exist, as few of their candidates win office. Many minor parties have virtually no organization beyond a small party headquarters and a website. Some minor parties, such as the Green Party, the Libertarian Party, and the Reform Party, have local chapters that meet on a regular basis. But these modest efforts pale in comparison with the nationwide network of offices, thousands of workers, and hundreds of millions of dollars deployed by Republican and Democratic party organizations.

The most significant factor working against minor parties is the basic structure of the American political system. This principle is summed up by **Duverger's Law**, which states that in a democracy that has **single-member districts** and **plurality voting**, there will be only two political parties that are able to elect a significant number of candidates to political office, which is the case in contemporary America. Given these electoral institutions (see Chapter 9), many people consider a vote for a minor-party candidate to be a wasted vote, as there is no chance that the candidate will win office. As a result, well-qualified candidates are driven to affiliate with one of the major political parties because they know that running as a minor-party nominee will put them at a considerable disadvantage. These decisions reinforce citizens' expectations that minor-party candidates have no chance of winning elections and that a vote for them is a wasted vote. Although there is no evidence that the Founders wanted to choose electoral institutions that made it hard for minor parties and their candidates, there is no doubt that the rules of the American electoral game have these effects.

A second problem is that the issues and issue positions taken by minor parties and their candidates are almost always very different from those espoused by the major parties. The Constitution Party, for example, advocates ending government civil service regulations; banning compulsory school attendance laws; withdrawing from the UN and all international trade agreements; abolishing foreign aid, the income tax, the Internal Revenue Service, and all federal welfare programs; and repealing all campaign finance legislation, the Endangered Species Act, and federal firearms regulations. These positions are extreme, not in the sense of being silly or dangerous but in the sense that relatively few Americans agree with them. Even in the 2016 presidential contest, Libertarian Gary Johnson proposed major cuts in defense spending and domestic programs—positions that attract support from only a relatively small minority of Americans.

"Why Should I Care?"

You may dislike political parties or party leaders in Congress, but the fact is, the parties are key players in congressional policy making and in negotiations between Congress and the president. If you are trying to decide whether a new program (or nominee) has a chance of being approved, one of the first things you need to consider is whether the party caucuses in the House and Senate (particularly the majority-party caucuses) are in favor or opposed.

How well do parties operate?

We have argued throughout this chapter that political parties can make democracy operate more smoothly by simplifying and improving the choices that citizens face in elections, and by providing mechanisms that make it easier for elected officials to formulate and enact compromise proposals. However, these arguments are about what parties *can* do, not what they *actually* do. There is no assurance that party leaders, activists, candidates, and citizens who identify with parties will take the actions needed to turn these possibilities into reality. The problem is that the people who make up American political parties are not primarily interested in democracy; they are interested in their own careers, policy goals, and winning political office. These goals often lead them away from actions that would improve American democracy. In this section, we consider when and why American political parties might fall short of our highest expectations for them.

Recruiting good candidates

One of the most important things that American political parties can do for democracy is to recruit candidates who can run effective campaigns and uphold their elected positions. After all, a voter's choices are limited to the people on the ballot. If good candidates decide against running or are prevented from doing so, citizens will be dissatisfied no matter who wins the election.

However, parties have limited influence over candidacy decisions: the potential candidates have to decide for themselves whether their chances of winning justify the enormous investment of time and money needed to run a campaign. When a party is unpopular, the best potential candidates may decide to wait until the next election to run, leaving the already disadvantaged party with a less competitive set of candidates.[36] Even when recruitment is not a problem, party leaders have only limited control over the nomination process—in some states, they cannot even restrict voting in primaries to citizens who are registered with the party. As Donald Trump's candidacy illustrates, party leaders could not prevent Trump from running, from dominating press coverage at the expense of other, more viable candidates, and from saying things that drove some important groups away from the party and its candidates. Of course, Trump won the election, indicating that party leaders underestimated his electability. Even so, insofar as party leaders are experienced politicians with deep knowledge of public opinion and political institutions, their lack of control over the nomination process can lead to unfavorable outcomes.

Working together in campaigns

Parties can improve the working of democracy by simplifying the choices voters face, most notably by getting their candidates to emphasize the same issues or to take similar issue positions. That way, citizens know that when they vote for, say, a Democrat, they are getting someone whose policy positions are likely to differ from those held by a Republican. As we've noted, however, even in modern America, where the differences between the parties are quite large, there are often disagreements within the party, among elected officials or in the party organization. Suppose, for example, you want to vote in an election for the candidate who comes closest to your position on immigration policy. It's relatively easy to place Democratic candidates on the spectrum of positions on immigration, as most favor current limits on legal immigration and some form of legal status for undocumented individuals in the United States. It's much harder to determine a Republican candidate's position, as candidates from that party have a wide range of opinions and preferred immigration policies. Some favor policies close to the Democratic Party norm, while others advocate sharply reducing legal immigration and aggressive deportation efforts against the undocumented. Moreover, immigration is not the exception. The simple fact is that on most issues, political parties in America speak with many voices, not one.

Why don't party leaders simply order their candidates to support the party platform or to work together in campaigns? As we have discussed, party leaders actually have very little power over candidates.[37] They can't kick a candidate off the ballot, because candidates win the nomination in a primary election or caucus, not through party appointment. Even though parties have a lot of campaign money to dispense, their contributions typically make up only a fraction of what a candidate spends on a campaign. And incumbent candidates, who generally hold an advantage over challengers when seeking reelection, are even less beholden to party leaders. Even if party leaders could somehow prevent an incumbent from running for reelection, they would have to find another candidate to take the incumbent's place, which would mean losing the incumbent's popularity and reputation and reducing the party's chances of holding the seat.

Working together in office

After the election, political parties can improve democracy by helping officeholders to find compromise policy proposals that attract broad support, and to select debate and voting procedures that speed enactment of these proposals. Sometimes, finding consensus both within and between parties is easy: for example, congressional Republicans and Democrats united in August 2017 to enact an expansion of educational benefits for military veterans. However, there are also many examples of issues that can split a party wide open, such as immigration reform for Republicans. Sometimes party members can compromise on their differences, as Republicans did to enact tax reform in 2017, but on other issues compromise is all but impossible, as in the case of Republicans' immigration proposals. And of course, even if the members of a party can find common ground, they may fail at building the bipartisan coalitions that are often necessary to enact major legislation, as was the case for many proposals considered during Donald Trump's first two years in office, including immigration reform, infrastructure funding, and cuts to entitlement programs. Even when compromise is reached, the time spent negotiating means that members have less time to scrutinize the details of budgets and policy proposals. For this reason, one recent study argued that the party caucuses are "too weak to govern."[38] Party leaders may do a good job in determining what their colleagues want but be unable to persuade them to support a proposal that they are inclined to oppose.

The fact that American political parties are ideologically diverse means that elected members of the party may not agree on spending, policy, or anything else. And even when senators and House members from a party find a way to bridge their differences, there is no guarantee that the president, even if he or she is from the same party, will agree to the compromise. In that sense, voters can't expect that putting one party in power will result in specific policy changes. Instead, policy outcomes depend on how (and whether) individual officeholders from the party can resolve their differences. Institutions such as the party caucuses or conferences provide a forum in which elected officials can meet and seek common ground, but there is no guarantee that they will find acceptable compromises.

The most important part of a Senate majority leader's education is over by the third grade, when he has learned to count.

—Howard Baker, former Senate Majority Leader

Moreover, concerted action by members of a party in government may be aimed at political rather than policy goals. In recent years, both Democrats and Republicans have decided against bipartisan compromises, believing that standing their ground would help them gain seats in the next elections. This strategy helped Republicans gain seats in 2010 and 2014 and was one factor behind the Democratic resurgence in the 2018 midterms. In this way, the electoral imperatives faced by American political parties can work against the enactment of effective responses to public problems and increase, rather than decrease, the amount of conflict in American politics.

Providing accountability

Finally, parties can improve American democracy by acting as an accountability mechanism that gives citizens an identifiable group to reward when policies work well and to punish when policies fail. However, while individual legislators are happy to take advantage of party labels when being held accountable works in their favor, they will do everything they can to avoid being tied to an unpopular party. Republican legislators, for example, highlighted their party label in the 2010 election, as the party was much more popular than the Democratic Party at that time.[39] But in 2018, when the party brand was much less popular, many Republican incumbents emphasized their work as individual members of Congress on behalf of constituents and tried to stay as far away as possible from their party's unpopular image.

When politicians work to secure their own political future by deemphasizing their party affiliation, they make it harder for voters to use party labels to decide who should be rewarded and who should be punished for government performance. The result is that legislators are held accountable for their own performance in office, such as how they voted—but no one in Congress is accountable for large-scale outcomes such as the state of the economy or for foreign policy. Of course, attempts by officeholders to disassociate themselves from their party are not always successful, which is why Republicans lost their House majority in 2018. Even so, most Republicans and Democrats in Congress managed to survive these elections, suggesting that party-based accountability is rather weak in contemporary American politics.

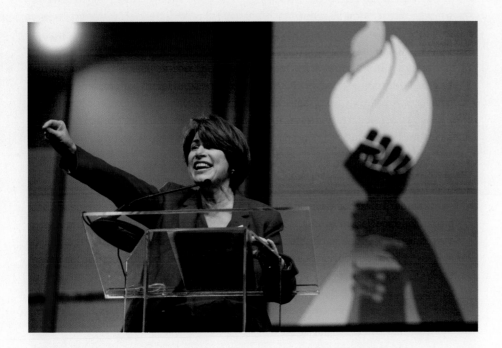

The 2018 midterm elections were described by experts as a referendum on President Trump's agenda. After two years in office, it was the first opportunity for voters to hold the administration accountable. In this divisive political environment, many Democrats ran campaigns emphasizing their opposition to the president. Incumbent senator Amy Klobuchar (D-MN), who had taken a leadership role in opposing President Trump's Supreme Court nominee Brett Kavanaugh, among his other policies, won reelection by 24 points.

Unpacking the Conflict

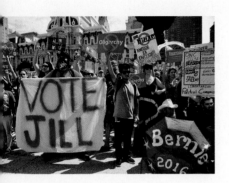

Considering all that we've discussed in this chapter, let's apply what we know about how political parties work to the examples of party dysfunction from the beginning of this chapter. If political parties are so important and powerful, why do they often fail at the very things they are supposed to do? Why do Americans dislike the parties they are so strongly attached to?

America's political system gives enormous opportunities to political parties. Parties can shape election outcomes by formulating campaign platforms, encouraging good candidates to run for office, and mobilizing supporters. After the election, the winners can work inside Congress to build coalitions behind policy proposals and use procedural powers to help enact these proposals—and to work against similar efforts by their opponents in the other party.

However, the fact that these opportunities exist does not ensure that political parties will be able to follow through on them. As we have seen, American political parties are often beset by internal conflicts over who should run for office and what their campaign platforms should look like. The party organization has little control over the party in government (or vice versa). And neither group can order party members in the electorate to work for the party, support its candidates, or do anything they don't want to do.

As a result of these organizational features, there is no guarantee that officeholders and election winners of the same party affiliation will have the same policy priorities or be able to compromise over their differences. This has been true even in recent years, when differences between Republicans and Democrats have been as large as ever. In this sense, the Republicans' failure to capitalize on their capture of both Congress and the presidency in 2016 is not surprising at all. Democrats will likely have similar problems if they win the presidency and gain congressional majorities in a future election. At the same time, while Americans may not approve of these outcomes, they show no signs of totally abandoning the Republicans or the Democrats in favor of new party organizations.

What's Your Take?

Are American political parties too dysfunctional to be useful?

Or do the benefits they provide outweigh their drawbacks?

STUDY GUIDE

What are political parties and where did today's parties come from?

Define *political parties* and show how American political parties and party systems have evolved over time. (Pages 264–268)

Summary

Political parties are organizations that run candidates for political office and coordinate the actions of officials elected under the party banner. Here in the United States, parties are relatively decentralized, putting forth a loose configuration of candidates who share a party label but don't necessarily work together. The parties are composed of three semiautonomous units: the party organization, the party in government, and the party in the electorate. Political parties are a central feature of American politics, although they look and act very differently today than they have in the past. Political scientists use the term "party system" to refer to a period of party stability; in all, there have been six different party systems in the country's history. Party systems are broken up by realignments, which occur when some of the defining factors of the party system are changed or specified and rifts in the group develop because of these changes.

Key terms

party organization (p. 264)
party in government (p. 264)
party in the electorate (p. 264)
party system (p. 265)
party principle (p. 266)
spoils system (p. 266)
realignment (p. 267)

Practice Quiz Questions

1. **Which statement best characterizes the American political parties?**

   a   Parties in the electorate pay dues to the party organization; leaders in the party organization tell elected officials what to do.

   b   Candidates run as representatives of the party; leaders have no influence on how candidates campaign or govern.

   c   Candidates are generally autonomous of the party organization, although they do receive support from the party organization.

   d   Parties help candidates only after they are elected.

   e   Parties handle 90 percent of fund-raising for candidates.

2. **Which were the first well-known parties in the United States?**

   a   Federalists and Democratic-Republicans

   b   Democrats and Republicans

   c   Whigs and Federalists

   d   Democrats and Whigs

   e   Whigs and Republicans

3. **The idea that a party is not just a group but an organization that exists apart from its candidate is called the _____ .**

   a   party system

   b   spoils system

   c   conditional party government

   d   party ID

   e   party principle

American political parties today

Describe the main characteristics of American parties as organizations, in the government, and in the electorate. (Pages 268–277)

Summary

The modern party is composed of three parts. The party organization is a loosely defined group of individuals and organizations that are focused on supporting political candidates when they share the same policy goals. The party in government consists of elected officials who are the members of a particular party. The party in the electorate consists of citizens who identify with a particular political party.

Key terms

national committee (p. 268)
political action committee (PAC) (p. 269)
527 organization (p. 269)
issue ownership (p. 270)
caucus (congressional) (p. 271)
conference (p. 272)
party identification (party ID) (p. 272)
party coalitions (p. 276)

Practice Quiz Questions

4. **The Democratic and Republican party organizations _____ hierarchical; they are _____ to force state and local parties to share their positions on issues.**

   a   are not; able

   b   are not; unable

   c   are; able

   d   are; unable

   e   are; sometimes able

5. A group of elected officials of the same party who come together to organize and strategize is called a _____.

a cabal

b conditional party government

c primary

d PAC

e caucus

6. The modern Congress is _____; the distance between the parties has _____ over the past 60 years.

a polarized; increased

b polarized; stayed the same

c not polarized; decreased

d not polarized; stayed the same

e not polarized; increased

7. What has recent analysis of political Independents concluded?

a They are in the process of changing parties.

b More and more people regard parties as irrelevant.

c Americans are politically savvy and do not blindly follow party lines.

d The number of Independents has grown substantially in the past 20 years.

e Independents are not better informed on candidates, parties, or policy.

The role of political parties in American politics

Explain the important functions that parties perform in the political system. (Pages 278–288)

Summary

Political parties serve two major roles in the political system. First, they compete in elections by recruiting and nominating candidates and supporting candidate campaigns. Second, they facilitate cooperation in government by providing a framework for agenda-setting, coordination, and accountability among members of the same party. There are many different minor political parties, and while they rarely make a significant impact on the political stage, they do occasionally influence election outcomes. The two big issues facing minor parties are that their platforms do not appeal to a large portion of Americans and that the electoral system makes it hard for minor parties to win elections.

Key terms

primary election (p. 279)

caucus (electoral) (p. 279)

nominating convention (p. 281)

party platform (p. 284)

unified government (p. 286)

divided government (p. 286)

Duverger's Law (p. 288)

single-member district (p. 288)

plurality voting (p. 288)

Practice Quiz Questions

8. Which is *not* one of the ways political party organizations support candidates?

a by controlling who runs in House and Senate races

b by contributing money to campaign activities

c by offering advice on how to deal with the press

d by organizing get-out-the-vote activities

e by offering advice on which issues to emphasize

9. Why do most candidates support their party platforms?

a because candidates are required to support the platforms

b because all candidates vote on the platforms that are written

c because candidates get kicked out of the party for not doing so

d because both major parties' platforms are essentially the same

e because most candidates and their constituents generally agree with the platform

10. When the president, House, and Senate are controlled by the same party, this is called _____.

a party in government

b responsible party government

c unified government

d divided government

e conditional party government

11. The principle that single-member districts and plurality voting will support only two political parties is _____.

a Condorcet's theorem

b Pascal's paradox

c Duverger's Law

d Fermat's theorem

e conditional party government

How well do parties operate?

Evaluate whether the American party system enhances or hinders democracy. (Pages 289–291)

Summary

Political parties do a number of things that are important to facilitate good democracy: they generally recruit good candidates, simplify voters' choices, encourage candidates to work together in office, and provide a mechanism for holding politicians accountable. Nonetheless, there are limits to the extent to which parties are able to achieve these goals, partially due to the fact that the people who make up the parties are primarily interested in their own careers.

Practice Quiz Questions

12. Which feature of political parties is undermined by legislators who build a reputation with voters independent of the party label?

a   the recruitment of good candidates

b   the provision of ballot access

c   the simplification of voter choices

d   the encouragement of policy cooperation

e   the provision of electoral accountability

13. Which of the following is *not* a reason why members of a party in government might find it difficult to work together to enact new government programs?

a   Constituents from different districts might demand different policies.

b   Members might disagree about the desirability of different policy changes.

c   The party's national committee might fail to write an acceptable party platform.

d   Enacting legislation might require votes from members of the other party.

e   Members might be focused on getting reelected.

Suggested Reading

Aldrich, John. *Why Parties?*, 2nd ed. Chicago: University of Chicago Press, 2014.

Bartels, Larry M. *Unequal Democracy: The Political Economy of the New Gilded Age*. New York: Russell Sage Foundation, 2008.

Carmines, Edward G., and James A. Stimson. *Issue Evolution: Race and the Transformation of American Politics*. Princeton, NJ: Princeton University Press, 1989.

Cohen, Marty, David Karol, Hans Noel, and John Zaller. *The Party Decides: Presidential Nominations before and after Reform*. Chicago: University of Chicago Press, 2008.

Cox, Gary, and Mathew McCubbins. *Setting the Agenda: Party Government in the U.S. House of Representatives*. New York: Cambridge University Press, 2005.

Fiorina, Morris. *Retrospective Voting in American National Elections*. New Haven, CT: Yale University Press, 1981.

Green, Donald, Bradley Palmquist, and Eric Schickler. *Partisan Hearts and Minds*. New Haven, CT: Yale University Press, 2004.

Noel, Hans. *Political Ideologies and Political Parties in America*. New York: Cambridge University Press, 2014.

Polsby, Nelson. *Consequences of Party Reform*. New York: Oxford University Press, 1983.

Rohde, David. *Parties and Leaders in the Post-reform House*. Chicago: University of Chicago Press, 1991.

Schattschneider, E. E. *Party Government*. New York: McGraw-Hill, 1942.

9

Elections

Who gets to represent the people?

 "We are winning on just about every front and for that reason there will not be a Blue Wave, but there might be a Red Wave!"
President Trump, August 8, 2018

 "The blue wave is not a weather event. . . . It's made. You have to go out and knock on doors and make phone calls and do the work. That's how it happens—you've got to make the wave happen."
Jason Kander, Let America Vote

Every two years, Americans elect 435 House members and 33 or so senators; every four years, we elect a president. The outcomes of these elections are scrutinized because they provide insights into what voters are thinking, because they reveal the usefulness of different campaign strategies, or simply because of what's at stake.

Occasionally, federal elections occur outside the normal election cycle to fill vacancies in the House or Senate. Though these special elections don't always attract the same level of attention that on-cycle elections do, the late-2017 election for an Alabama Senate seat, pitting Democrat Doug Jones against Republican Roy Moore, captured the public's attention for a number of reasons. For one, a Jones victory would affect the narrow 2-vote Republican majority in the Senate. For another, President Trump expressed strong support for Moore, a staunch social conservative who had been accused of sexually harassing young women during the 1990s.

Ultimately, Jones won the seat—somewhat of a surprise in traditionally Republican Alabama. The question is why. Did Jones and his team run a better campaign, successfully mobilizing African Americans? Was Moore too conservative for Alabama, or were voters repelled by his past behavior? Did the outcome reflect dissatisfaction with the Trump presidency or the policy priorities of congressional Republicans? Ultimately, many 2018 Democratic congressional candidates, particularly those running in moderate to conservative suburban districts, used Jones's campaign as a template for their own efforts, which was one factor behind Democratic House gains in 2018.

The 2017 special election between Democrat Doug Jones and Republican Roy Moore captured the country's attention. Was Jones's surprise victory a result of smart campaigning, widespread dissatisfaction with the Republican Party, or something else?

CHAPTER GOALS

Present the major rules and procedures of American elections. pages 298–309

Describe the features, strategies, and funding of campaigns for federal office. pages 309–325

Explain the key factors that influence voters' choices. pages 326–330

Analyze the issues and outcomes in the 2016 and 2018 elections. pages 331–336

The 2017 special election in Alabama is also a good example of the central themes of this text. Elections matter: no one watching the Alabama race would think that Jones and Moore would support the same policies if elected. Candidates competing for political office offer the people distinct, competing visions of what the federal government should do—from what the tax code should look like, to what regulations the government should impose on individuals and corporations. In a very real sense, elections are how Americans resolve conflict over whose vision of government policy should prevail—at least until the next election.

American elections are also about rules. The reason that the 2017 Alabama special election happened at all lies in the rules surrounding a chain of events after Trump's election. Trump's appointment of then-senator Jeff Sessions to the post of attorney general left a Senate seat open in Alabama because of the Constitution's stipulation that cabinet members cannot simultaneously serve in Congress. The special election then took place according to Alabama's rules about replacing members of Congress between regular elections.

More generally, candidates in American elections are elected for different periods of time to represent districts, states, or the entire nation—places that vary tremendously in terms of what constituents want from government and the logistical requirements for running a credible campaign. A variety of rules determine who runs, who votes, and how money is raised and spent. Even ballot layouts and how votes are cast and counted vary across states. All these aspects of the election process—who runs, how candidates campaign, and how voters respond—shape who wins and who loses, what happens in Washington, and ultimately the policies that affect people's everyday lives. Ultimately, how meaningful was Doug Jones's victory in Alabama—or the combination of Democratic House victories and Senate defeats in 2018? What can it tell us about why some candidates win and others lose? Why do these outcomes matter in American politics?

DID YOU KNOW?

510,000

The total number of federal, state, and local elected offices in the United States.
Source: Jennifer Lawless, *Becoming a Candidate*

incumbent
A politician running for reelection to the office he or she currently holds.

How do American elections work?

The American political system is a representative democracy: Americans do not make policy choices themselves, but they vote for individuals who make these choices on their behalf. This section describes the rules and procedures that define American national elections.

Functions of elections

Our working assumption for explaining the rules and processes of elections as well as the behavior of candidates and voters is that they are tied directly to what elections do: select representatives, give citizens the ability to influence the direction of government policy, and provide citizens with the opportunity to reward and punish officeholders seeking reelection.

Selecting Representatives The most visible function of American elections is the selection of officeholders, including, at the national level, members of the House and Senate and the president and vice president. Candidates can be **incumbents,**

running for reelection to their current office, or challengers, running for the office for the first time. Because America is a representative democracy, by voting in elections, Americans have an indirect effect on government policy. Although citizens do not make policy choices themselves, they determine which individuals get to make these choices. In this way, elections are supposed to connect citizen preferences and government actions.

Shaping Policy Although the fundamental choice in an election is between two or more candidates running for some political office, elections also involve a choice between candidates' policy platforms: the set of things they promise to do if elected. By investigating candidates' platforms, citizens learn about the range of options for government policy. Moreover, their voting decisions determine who gets to make choices about future government policy, and thereby shape government policy itself. For example, Republicans' unified control of Congress and the presidency was at stake in the 2018 elections—the fact that the election gave Democrats majority control of the House of Representatives means that they can block Republican policy initiatives and begin investigations of the Trump administration's decisions.

Promoting Accountability The election process also creates a way to hold incumbents accountable. When citizens choose between voting for an incumbent or a challenger, they can make a retrospective evaluation. They consider the incumbent's performance over his or her previous terms in office and ask, "Has he [or she] done a good job on the issues I care about?"[1] Citizens who answer yes typically vote for the incumbent, and those who answer no typically vote for the challenger.

Retrospective evaluations are significant because they make incumbents responsive to their constituents' demands.[2] If elected officials anticipate that some constituents will make retrospective evaluations, they will try to take actions that these constituents will look back upon favorably when they're in the voting booth. If incumbents ignore the possibility of voters' retrospective evaluations, they run the risk of being voted out of office in the next election. Retrospective evaluations can also form the basis for prospective judgments: voters' beliefs about how the country will fare if different candidates win. This provides an additional reason for incumbents to be responsive to citizens' demands.

Two stages of elections

Candidates running for federal office (House, Senate, or president) face a two-step procedure. First, if the prospective candidates want to run on behalf of a political party, they must win the party's nomination in a **primary** election. If the would-be candidates want to run as Independents, they need to gather signatures on a petition to secure a spot on the ballot. Different states hold either **open primaries**, **semi-closed primaries**, or **closed primaries**, and state law sets the timing of these elections. For House and Senate seats, a few states hold single primaries, in which there is one election involving candidates from both parties, with the top two finalists (regardless of party) receiving nominations to the general election.

The second step in the election process is the **general election**, which is held throughout the nation on the first Tuesday after the first Monday in November. Federal law designates this day as Election Day. General elections determine who wins elected positions in government. The offices at stake vary depending on the year. Presidential elections occur every four years (2008, 2012, 2016, . . .). In a presidential election year,

Though incumbents fared well in the 2018 congressional elections, some, such as Representative Joe Crowley (D-NY), lost in the primaries.

primary
A ballot vote in which citizens select a party's nominee for the general election.

open primary
A primary election in which any registered voter can participate in the contest, regardless of party affiliation.

semi-closed primary
A primary in which anyone who is a registered member of the party or registered as an Independent can vote.

closed primary
A primary election in which only registered members of a particular political party can vote.

general election
The election in which voters cast ballots for House members, senators, and (every four years) a president and vice president.

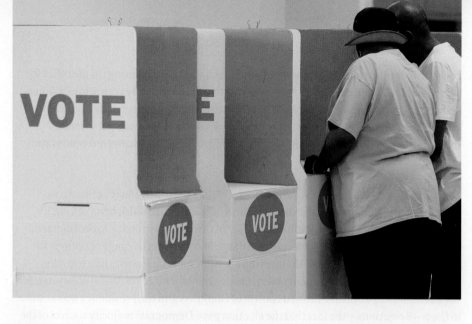

Americans vote in all sorts of places, including libraries, fire stations, schools, and private homes. Here, people vote at the Oklahoma County Board of Elections in Oklahoma City for the 2018 primaries.

Americans elect the entire House of Representatives, one-third of the Senate, and a president and vice president. During midterm elections (2010, 2014, 2018, . . .), there is no presidential contest, but the entire House and a third of the Senate are up for election.

One implication of this two-step process of primary and general elections is that sometimes the winner of a primary is not a party's best candidate for the general election. For example, in the 2016 presidential race, one of the principal arguments for choosing someone other than Hillary Clinton as the Democratic nominee (such as Senator Bernie Sanders, Vice President Joe Biden, or some other Democratic senator or governor) was that these candidates would have had a better chance of winning the general election. While Clinton had many enthusiastic volunteers, a first-rate campaign organization, and considerable Washington experience as First Lady, senator, and secretary of state, she was also strongly disliked by a sizable fraction of the American electorate—partly because of her status as a Washington insider, and partly because of issues such as her use of a private e-mail server while secretary of state. In the end, despite beating Sanders in the primaries and discouraging other Democrats from entering the nomination contest, Clinton lost the general election to Donald Trump. Given the closeness of the 2016 election, another Democrat, someone who did not have Clinton's disadvantages, might well have gone on to defeat Trump.

After Hillary Clinton lost her campaign for president, many Democrats wondered if Senator Bernie Sanders (I-VT) would have been a stronger general-election candidate.

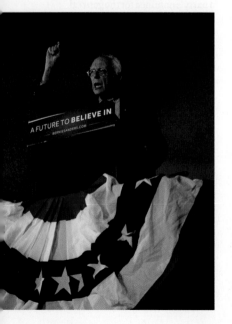

Mechanics of elections

The Constitution limits voting rights to American citizens who are at least 18 years old. There are also numerous restrictions on voter eligibility that vary across states, including residency requirements (usually 30 days) and prohibitions for people convicted of a major crime. A recent development in American elections is an increase in the practice of no-excuse absentee voting as well as early voting, or casting a general-election vote prior to Election Day.[3] Voters in Oregon vote entirely by mail, and almost all votes in Washington State are cast by mail. Across the nation in 2018, more than a third of votes were cast before Election Day and many campaigns distributed absentee ballots to would-be supporters. These changes have had only a modest impact on voter turnout, perhaps because efforts by candidates and parties to encourage early voting have reduced resources allocated to mobilization efforts on Election Day.[4]

The most fundamental feature of American elections is that officeholders are elected in single-member districts in which only the winner of the most votes takes office. (Although both of each state's senators represent the whole state, they are elected separately, usually in different years.) Senate candidates compete throughout the state; House candidates compete in congressional districts. In most states, congressional district lines are drawn by state legislatures. In a few states, nonpartisan commissions perform this function. Redistricting can happen at any time, but in general, district lines are revised after each census to make sure the boundary lines reflect shifts in population across and within states. (For details on redistricting, see Chapter 11.)

Because members of the House and Senate are elected from specific geographic areas, they often represent very different kinds of people. Their constituents differ in terms of age, race, income level, occupation, and political leaning, including party affiliation and ideology. Therefore, legislators from different areas of the country face highly diverse demands from their constituents, which often leads them to pursue very dissimilar kinds of policies.

For example, Democratic senator Charles Schumer, one of the senators from New York, represents a fairly liberal state, where most people take some sort of pro-choice position on abortion rights, while Republican senator Richard Shelby is one of the senators from the conservative state of Alabama, where most voters have long been opposed to abortions. Suppose the Senate votes on a proposal to ban all abortions after the twelfth week of pregnancy. Shelby knows that most of his constituents would probably want him to vote for the proposal, and Schumer knows that most of his constituents would probably want him to vote against it. This example illustrates that congressional conflicts over policy often reflect differences in constituents' demands. Schumer and Shelby themselves may hold different views on abortion rights, but even if they agreed, their constituents' distinct demands would make it likely that as legislators they would vote differently.

Most House and Senate contests involve **plurality voting**: the candidate who gets the most votes wins. However, some states use **majority voting**, meaning that a candidate needs a majority (more than 50 percent of the vote) to win. If no candidate has a majority, a **runoff election** takes place between the top two finishers. Some candidates have lost runoff elections even though they received the most votes in the first contest.

Ballots and Vote Counting Americans vote using a variety of machines and ballot structures based on where they live. States either use electronic touch screen voting machines, usually with some sort of paper receipt to allow manual recounts, or have voters fill out paper ballots that are then scanned and recorded. When the polls close, workers transcribe vote totals from the various machines, then hand-carry the totals and individual ballots or receipts to county boards of election, where totals are aggregated and sent to state agencies, which certify the results. The process is largely run by volunteers, with both major parties having participants or observers at all stages.

plurality voting
A voting system in which the candidate who receives the most votes within a geographic area wins the election, regardless of whether that candidate wins a majority (more than half) of the votes.

majority voting
A voting system in which a candidate must win more than 50 percent of votes to win the election. If no candidate wins enough votes to take office, a runoff election is held between the top two vote-getters.

runoff election
Under a majority voting system, a second election is held only if no candidate wins a majority of the votes in the first general election. Only the top two vote-getters in the first election compete in the runoff.

Many different mechanisms are used to record votes in American elections, including paper keypunch ballots and touch screens (left). The design of the infamous butterfly ballot (right), which was used in the 2000 presidential election to vote in Palm Beach County, Florida, inadvertently led some people who intended to vote for Democrat Al Gore to select Reform Party candidate Patrick Buchanan.

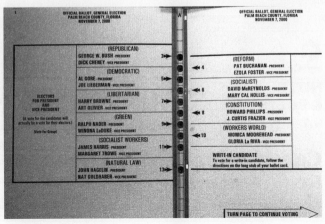

Most states have laws that allow vote recounts if a race is sufficiently close (typically within 1 percent or less). Even when a recount occurs, it may be impossible to definitively determine who won a particular election, as the rules that determine which ballots are valid are often open to interpretation. More significant is that when an election is close the question of which candidate wins may depend on how ballots are structured and votes are counted. The problem is not that election officials are dishonest; rather, close elections inherently tend to produce ambiguous outcomes.

Claims are often made that officials manipulate election rules to guarantee wins for their favored candidates. In some states, Republican state and local officials have enacted laws that require voters to verify their identity by showing polling officials an official form of identification such as a driver's license or a passport. The purported goal of these laws is to prevent voter fraud—one person voting under another's name, casting multiple votes for the same candidate, voting in more than one election, or voting as a noncitizen. However, no reputable study has found evidence of significant voter fraud in American elections. Moreover, voter ID laws create barriers to voting for individuals who lack an official ID—these individuals are generally poor and nonwhite and disproportionately vote Democratic. While some supporters of voter ID laws may be sincerely concerned about preventing fraud, research shows that enacting these laws hurts Democratic candidates by lowering turnout from groups that are likely to support them.[5]

Presidential elections

Many of the rules governing elections, such as who is eligible to vote, are the same for both presidential and congressional elections. But presidential contests have several unique rules regarding how nominees are determined and how votes are counted. Moreover, the constitutional requirements for presidential candidates are also somewhat stricter than those for congressional candidates (see Nuts & Bolts 9.1).

The Nomination: Primaries and Caucuses Presidential nominees from the Democratic and Republican parties are determined by the outcomes of state-level primaries and caucuses held over a five-month period beginning in January of an election year.[6] Primary and caucus voters select a candidate, but their votes do not count directly toward the election of that candidate; their votes instead count toward the selection of delegates who have pledged to support the candidate, who then go on to attend the party nominating conventions. There, the delegates cast votes that determine their party's presidential and vice-presidential nominees. The format of these elections, including their timing and the number of delegates selected per state,

caucus
A local meeting in which party members select a party's nominee for the general election.

NUTS & BOLTS 9.1

Constitutional Requirements for Candidates

Office	Minimum Age	Residency Requirement
President	35	Natural-born citizen (born in the United States or on U.S. territory, or child of citizen parent)
Senator	30	Resident of state; U.S. citizen for at least nine years
Representative	25	Resident of state; U.S. citizen for at least seven years

is determined on a state-by-state basis by the state and national party organizations.[7] In some states, each candidate preselects a list of delegates who will attend the convention if the candidate wins sufficient votes in the primary or caucus. In other states, delegates are chosen by party leaders after the actual primary or caucus takes place. In both cases, a candidate's principal goal is to win as many delegates as possible—and to select delegates who will be reliable supporters at the convention. Some states require delegates to vote for the candidate they are pledged to—at least for the first ballot at the party nominating convention. However, these laws have never been tested and it is not clear that they are enforceable.

The details of translating primary and caucus votes into convention delegates vary from state to state, but some general rules apply. All Democratic primaries and caucuses use **proportional allocation** to divide each state's delegate seats among the candidates; thus, if a candidate receives 40 percent of the votes in a state's primary, the candidate gets roughly 40 percent of the convention delegates from that state. Some Republican contests use proportional allocation, but others use a **winner-take-all** system. In these states, the candidate who receives the most votes gets all the convention delegates. These rules can have a significant effect on candidates' campaign strategies and the outcome of the nomination process (see How It Works: Nominating Presidential Candidates in Chapter 8).

The order in which the primaries and caucuses in different states take place is important because many candidacies do not survive beyond the early contests.[8] Most presidential candidates pour everything they have into the first few elections. Candidates who do well attract financial contributions, campaign workers, endorsements, and additional media coverage, all of which enable them to move on to subsequent primaries or caucuses. Candidates who do poorly in the first contests face the problem identified by former congressman and presidential candidate Richard Gephardt: contributions and coverage dry up, leaving these candidates with no alternative but to drop out of the race. For example, a total of 17 candidates entered the race for the 2016 Republican presidential nomination. Five withdrew before any convention delegates were selected. By mid-March, two months into the process and six months before the convention where the nominee was actually selected, the race was down to only three candidates. Thus, the candidate who leads after the first several primaries and caucuses generally wins the nomination—as was the case for both Donald Trump and Hillary Clinton in 2016.[9] However, when the first few contests do not yield a clear favorite, the race can continue until the last states have voted or even until the convention.

If a sitting president runs for reelection, as Barack Obama did in 2012, he typically faces little opposition for his party's general-election nomination—not because challengers defer to the president but because most presidents are popular enough among their own party's faithful supporters that they can win the nomination without too much trouble. Only presidents with particularly low approval ratings have faced serious opposition in their nomination bids.

Among the states, the presidential nomination process is always changing.[10] In 2016, many southern states held their primaries on the same day in early March (Super Tuesday). Others moved the date of their primary (Florida), moved from a primary to a caucus (Kentucky), or, on the Republican side, added a minimum number of votes a candidate needed to win any delegates. For many years, Iowa and New Hampshire have held the first presidential nomination contests, with the Iowa Caucuses held a week before the New Hampshire primary. These states' position at the beginning of the process is largely a historical accident, but it is controversial. State party officials from other states often complain about the media attention given to these contests and their disproportionate influence in winnowing the candidate pool, but there is no consensus on an alternate schedule. As a result, the 2016 nomination process was roughly the

proportional allocation
During the presidential primaries, the practice of determining the number of convention delegates allotted to each candidate based on the percentage of the popular vote cast for each candidate. All Democratic primaries and caucuses use this system, as do some states' Republican primaries and caucuses.

winner-take-all
During the presidential primaries, the practice of assigning all of a given state's delegates to the candidate who receives the most popular votes. Some states' Republican primaries and caucuses use this system.

Campaigns don't end—they run out of money.

— **Richard Gephardt,** former Speaker of the House and presidential candidate

Senate campaign appearances almost always involve extensive print and electronic media coverage. Here, Arizona Republican and 2018 candidate Dr. Kelli Ward speaks to the media as she prepares to file her nominating petitions. Although she lost the primary, the media helped get out her message and policy agenda.

You win some, you lose some. And then there's that little-known third category.

— Al Gore, who lost the 2000 presidential vote in the electoral college despite winning the most votes on Election Day

popular vote
The votes cast by citizens in an election.

electoral college
The body that votes to select America's president and vice president based on the popular vote in each state. Each candidate nominates a slate of electors who are selected to attend the meeting of the college if their candidate wins the most votes in a state or district.

electoral votes
Votes cast by members of the electoral college; after a presidential candidate wins the popular vote in a given state, that candidate's slate of electors casts electoral votes for the candidate on behalf of that state.

same as in previous years, with Iowa and New Hampshire holding the initial contests in early February 2016, followed by a primary in South Carolina and a caucus in Nevada later in the month and the remaining contests beginning in March and continuing to June. One recent trend is regional primaries, in which all the states in a given area (such as southern states) hold their primaries or caucuses on the same date.

One rule that distinguishes the parties' candidate selection processes is that about one-fifth of the delegates to the Democratic convention are not supporters of a particular candidate, nor have they been chosen to attend the convention based on primary and caucus results. Rather, they are elected officials and party officials whom their colleagues select to serve as superdelegates. Most are automatically seated at the convention regardless of primary and caucus results, and they are free to support any candidate for the nomination. By forcing candidates to court support from superdelegates, the party aims to ensure that the nominee is someone who these officials believe can win the general election and whom they can work with if he or she is elected.[11] Republicans give state party leaders automatic delegate slots at their convention, but the number of such delegates is a much smaller percentage than for Democrats.

The National Convention Presidential nominating conventions happen late in the summer of an election year. Their main task is to select the party's presidential nominee, although usually the vote at the convention is a formality; in most recent presidential contests, one candidate has emerged from the nomination process going into the convention with a clear majority of delegates and has been able to win the nomination on the first ballot. To get the nomination, a candidate needs the support of a majority of the delegates. If no candidate receives a majority after the first round of voting at the convention, the voting continues until someone does.

After the convention delegates nominate a presidential candidate, they nominate a vice-presidential candidate. The presidential nominee gets to choose his or her running mate (generally before the convention), and the delegates almost always ratify this choice without much debate. Delegates also vote on the party platform, which describes what the party stands for and what kinds of policies its candidates will supposedly seek to enact if they are elected.

The final purpose of a convention is to attract public attention to the party and its nominees. Public figures give speeches during the evening sessions when all major television networks have live coverage. At some recent conventions, both parties have drawn press attention by recruiting speakers who support their political goals despite being associated with the opposing party.

Once presidential candidates are nominated, the general-election campaign officially begins—although it often unofficially starts much earlier, as soon as the presumptive nominees are known. We will say more about presidential campaigns in a later section.

Counting Presidential Votes Let's assume for a moment that the campaigning is over and that Election Day has arrived. Even though in the voting booth people choose between the candidates by name, a choice that constitutes the **popular vote**, this vote is not directly for a presidential candidate. Rather, when you select your preferred candidate's name, you are choosing that person's slate of pledged supporters from your state to serve as electors, who will then vote to elect the president.

The number of electors for each state equals the state's number of House members (which varies by state population) plus the state's number of senators (two per state). Altogether, the electors chosen by the citizens of each state constitute the **electoral college**, the body that casts **electoral votes** to formally select the president. Small-population states, therefore, have few electoral votes—Delaware and Montana, for example, each have only 3—while the highest-population state, California, has 55 (see How It Works: The Electoral College). In most states, electoral votes are allocated on a winner-take-all basis: the candidate who receives the most votes from a given state's citizens gets all of that state's electoral votes. But two states, Maine and Nebraska, allocate most of their electoral votes at the congressional district level: in those states, the candidate who wins the most votes in each congressional district wins that district's single electoral vote. Then the remaining 2 electoral votes go to the candidate who gets the most votes statewide.[12]

The winner-take-all method of allocating most states' electoral votes makes candidates focus their attention on two kinds of states: high-population states with lots of electoral votes and so-called swing states where the contest is relatively close. It's better for a candidate to spend a day campaigning in California (55 electoral votes) than in Montana (3 electoral votes). However, if one candidate is sure to win a particular state, both candidates will direct their efforts elsewhere. For example, during the final week of the 2016 campaign, both campaigns focused on states still in play: Trump's campaign followed the strategy described in the How It Works feature, focusing on Florida, North Carolina, and key Rust Belt states, including Pennsylvania, Michigan, and Wisconsin, and the Clinton campaign responded with increased advertising and rallies in Pennsylvania, North Carolina, and Florida.

Nuts & Bolts 9.2 divides states based on their electoral vote and whether they are swing states—defined as states that each party won at least once from 2004 to 2016. The table explains why both campaigns in 2016 spent so much time and campaign funds on states such as Ohio and Florida (swing states with a large number of electoral votes)—and why they largely ignored states such as Delaware (small state, one-party-dominates category).

After citizens' votes are counted, each state's slate of electors meets in December in the state capitals. At their meetings, the electors almost always vote for the presidential candidate they have pledged to support. After the votes are certified by a joint session of Congress, the candidate who wins a majority of the nation's electoral votes (at least 270) is the new president. One peculiarity of the electoral college is that in most states it is legal for an elector to either (1) vote for a candidate he or she is not pledged to support or (2) abstain from voting.[13] Such events are uncommon for the simple reason that electors are selected by the presidential candidates with an eye toward reliable support.

After the 2016 presidential election, the close popular vote tally plus fears of outside interference in electronic vote counting systems led to calls for recounts in several key states. Petitions to conduct recounts were filed in Nevada, Wisconsin, Pennsylvania, Florida, and Michigan (shown here), though several of these recounts were halted by court orders.

**NUTS
& BOLTS
9.2**

Electoral Votes and Swing States

Presidential campaigns focus their attention on states with high electoral votes and swing states where each candidate has a good chance of winning. In this box, we group states into categories based on their number of electoral votes and on whether one party always won the state in recent presidential elections.

| | One Party Dominates in Recent Elections? | |
Number of Electoral Votes	Yes (Not a Swing State)	No (Swing State)
3–5	D.C., Delaware, Alaska, Montana, North Dakota, South Dakota, Vermont, Wyoming, Hawaii, Maine, Rhode Island, Idaho, Nebraska, West Virginia	New Hampshire, New Mexico
6–10	Arkansas, Kansas, Utah, Connecticut, Oregon, Oklahoma, Kentucky, Louisiana, Alabama, South Carolina, Maryland, Mississippi, Missouri, Minnesota	Iowa, Nevada, Colorado, Wisconsin
More than 10	Massachusetts, Arizona, Tennessee, Washington, New Jersey, Georgia, Illinois, New York, Texas, California	Indiana, Virginia, North Carolina, Ohio, Florida, Michigan, Pennsylvania

The Electoral College

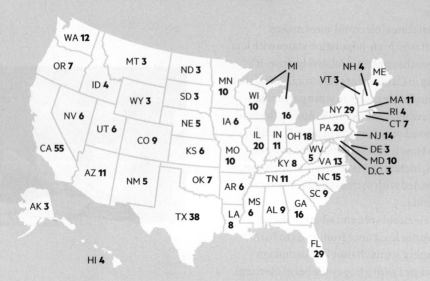

Electoral Votes per State

The number of electors from each state equals the state's number of House members (which varies based on state population) plus the number of senators (two per state). Each elector has one vote in the electoral college.

Who Are the Electors?

Candidates to be electors are nominated by their political parties. They pledge to support a certain candidate if they are elected to the electoral college. When you cast your vote for a presidential candidate, you are in fact voting for the slate of potential electors who support that candidate.

Delaware

Idaho

Nebraska

South Dakota

Washington

West Virginia

California Popular Vote

40%

60%

California Electoral Votes (55)

100%

Winning a State

Most states give all of their electoral college votes to the candidate who wins the most votes in that state. So, even if a candidate only gets 51 percent of the vote in the state, his or her entire slate of electors is elected, and he or she gets all of the state's votes in the electoral college.

100%
of electoral votes
go to winner

How it works: in practice

Donald Trump's Electoral College Strategy, 2016

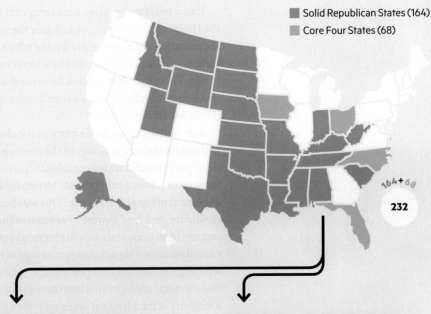

Solid Republican States (164)
Core Four States (68)

164 + 68

232

Trump's campaign started by identifying "solid Republican" states—ones with a history of strong Republican support—which gave them a start of 164 electoral votes. Then, they focused on what campaign manager Kellyanne Conway called their "core four" states—ones they knew they needed in order to have a chance at victory: Florida, North Carolina, Ohio, and Iowa. This would bring them to 232 electoral votes. Where would they go to get the additional 38 electoral votes needed for victory?

Target the Rust Belt: *Michigan, Minnesota, Pennsylvania, and Wisconsin* These states have relatively weak economies and few minority voters.

MN **10**
WI **10**
MI **16**
PA **20**

164 + 68 + 56

288

Hold off Growing Minority Populations: *Arizona, Georgia, Nevada, Colorado* Though Democrats hoped to win all these states because of their high minority populations, only Nevada and Colorado have been swing states in recent elections, and many people felt that Georgia and Arizona had been trending toward Democrats.

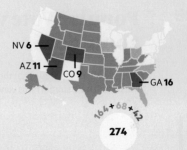

NV **6**
AZ **11**
CO **9**
GA **16**

164 + 68 + 42

274

1

Total Votes

306

2016 Results

Ultimately, Trump used **a combination of these strategies** to win 306 electoral votes, and the presidency.

Trump's Final Winning Electoral College Map

AL **9**	IN **11**	MS **6**	OK **7**	WV **5**
AK **3**	IA **6**	MO **10**	PA **20**	WI **10**
AZ **11**	KS **6**	MT **3**	SC **9**	WY **3**
AR **6**	KY **8**	NE **5**	SD **3**	
FL **29**	LA **8**	NC **15**	TN **11**	
GA **16**	ME **1***	ND **3**	TX **38**	
ID **4**	MI **16**	OH **18**	UT **6**	

❓

Critical Thinking

1. **Why didn't the Trump campaign** focus on some delegate-rich states like California and New York?

2. **In what state do you think the Trump campaign** spent the most money? Where do you think Trump made the most personal appearances? Why?

* Maine splits its electoral votes; Trump received 1, Clinton 3.

If no candidate receives a majority of the electoral college votes, the members of the House of Representatives choose the winner. They follow a procedure in which the members from each state decide which candidate to support and then cast one collective vote per state, with the winner needing a majority of these state-level votes to win. This procedure has not been used since 1824, although it might be required if a third-party candidate wins a significant number of electoral votes or if a state's electors refuse to cast their votes.[14]

A presidential candidate can win the electoral college vote, and thus the election, without receiving a majority of the votes cast by citizens. One way this can happen is if a third-party candidate for president receives a substantial number of votes. Bill Clinton, for example, won a substantial electoral college majority in 1992 while receiving only 43 percent of the popular vote. This was because Ross Perot, running as a third-party candidate, received almost 19 percent of the national popular vote but not enough support in any one state to win electoral votes. Even in a race where no third-party candidate wins a significant percentage of the vote, the electoral college magnifies the winning candidate's vote percentage. Yet because of the way popular votes translate into electoral votes, even when there are only two candidates, one candidate can receive a majority of the electoral votes even though another candidate wins more popular votes (see Figure 9.1). As this figure shows, this outcome occurred in 2016 and 2000. Other presidents who won the electoral college vote but lost the popular vote were John Quincy Adams in 1824, Rutherford B. Hayes in 1876, and Benjamin Harrison in 1888.

FIGURE 9.1

Popular Vote versus Electoral Vote Percentages, 2000–2016

Political scientists argue that the electoral college system tends to magnify the winning candidate's margin of victory. Do the data presented here support this view?

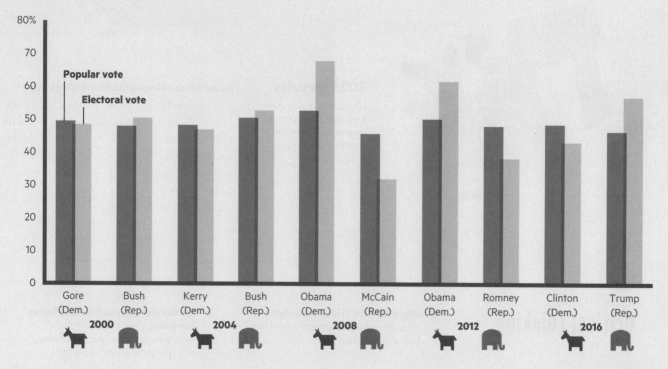

Sources: U.S. National Archives and Records Administration, www.archives.gov/federal-register/electoral-college/historical.html (accessed 5/11/18).

American elections incorporate a complex set of laws, rules, and procedures. And these rules matter—the candidates who win under current rules might lose given other reasonable ways to conduct elections. For example, in 2016, Democrat Hillary Clinton won the popular vote but lost the electoral vote (and the election) due to close losses in Florida, Michigan, Pennsylvania, and Wisconsin. Even small changes in voter registration, voter ID regulations, and other laws in these states might have given Clinton victories in these states—and the presidency.

"Why Should I Care?"

DESCRIBE THE FEATURES, STRATEGIES, AND FUNDING OF CAMPAIGNS FOR FEDERAL OFFICE

election cycle
The two-year period between general elections.

Electoral campaigns

This section explores the campaign process and what candidates do to convince people to vote for them on Election Day. Our emphasis is on things that candidates do, regardless of the office they are running for, across the entire **election cycle**: the two-year period between general elections.

The "fundamentals"

Before talking about all the things candidates and their supporters do to shape election outcomes, it is crucial to understand that many important factors are beyond their control. Political scientists call these factors the *fundamentals*. In part, the fundamentals include the rules that govern elections. Photo ID requirements for voting, which shape voter turnout in ways that hurt some candidates (usually Democrats) and help others, are one good example of electoral rules that affect outcomes. Another fundamental is how many people in a candidate's district share his or her party ID. As we showed in Chapter 8, an individual's party ID is a strong influence on his or her voting decisions. Particularly in presidential elections, economic conditions also have a strong effect on who wins. As you can see in the What Do the Facts Say? feature, a stronger economy benefits incumbent presidents running for reelection (for example, Obama in 2012), while a weak economy hurts incumbents (Jimmy Carter in 1980) and their successors (John McCain in 2008).

Candidates might like to think that they can convince people to vote for them regardless of circumstances. But the fundamentals like party ID and economic conditions tell us which candidates face an uphill fight or an easy ride—either because voters are well aware of these factors before the campaign begins or because campaigns are mechanisms by which voters become informed about them.[15] It may not be fair to reward or blame candidates for the state of the economy, as even presidents have only limited control over economic growth or unemployment levels. For better or worse, however, a significant fraction of American voters behave this way.[16]

It's important to remember, though, that the fundamentals are not the final word in an election. The backgrounds of the candidates, their qualifications for office, and the decisions they make about their campaigns sometimes have significant, even decisive effects. For example, Democrat Conor Lamb won a 2018 special election in a strongly Republican Pennsylvania congressional district—President Trump won there in 2016 by a 20-point margin. At least part of Lamb's victory was due to a decline in Trump's popularity and the resignation of the district's Republican incumbent due

"The Fundamentals" and Presidential Elections

Political scientists argue that "the fundamentals" play a key role in American elections. For example, the state of the economy is thought to influence vote decisions in presidential elections—a strong economy benefits incumbent presidents or their successors. However, most candidates (and journalists) argue that the things candidates say and do during the campaign determine who wins and who loses. What do the facts say?

To answer this question, let's examine this figure, which shows the relationship between presidential election outcomes (vote share for the incumbent president or the candidate from the president's party) and economic conditions (the growth in real personal income in the year before the election). The blue line gives the predicted relationship between economic conditions and the popular vote, showing that on average, as economic conditions improve, the president or candidate from the president's party receives more votes.

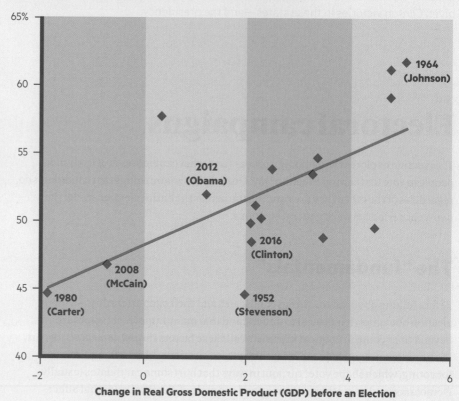

Vote Share for President's Party vs. Economic Growth

Think about it

- Why do incumbent presidents do better when the economy is strong than when it is weak?
- Candidates who lose, such as Clinton in 2016 or Romney in 2012, are criticized for running poor campaigns. Look at the data points that describe economic conditions in these elections and the percentage of the popular vote received by Obama in 2012 and Clinton in 2016. Given the state of the economy in these years, is there any evidence that Romney or Clinton did worse than you would expect?
- What signs are there in the chart that other factors besides "the fundamentals" might influence presidential election outcomes?

to scandal. But Lamb, who took moderate positions on issues such as gun control, was widely regarded as the stronger, more energetic candidate. Under these conditions, Republican voters might well have seen Lamb as someone who would do a better job protecting their district's interests, and supported him on that basis.

Setting the stage

On the day after an election, candidates, party officials, and interest groups all start thinking about the next election cycle. They consider who won and who lost the election, which incumbents look like safe bets for reelection and which ones might be vulnerable, who might retire soon or run for another office in the next election, and whether the election returns reveal new information about what kinds of campaigns or issues might increase voter turnout or support.

These calculations reflect the costs of running for office. Challengers for House and Senate seats know that a campaign will consume at least a year of their time and deplete their financial resources. Presidential campaigns require even more money and effort. If a potential challenger already holds elected office, such as a state legislator running for the House or a House member running for the Senate, that person may have to give up his or her current office to run for a new one.[17]

Party organizations and interest groups also face time and money constraints both in recruiting candidates and in discouraging some people from running. They do not have the funds to offer significant support to candidates in all 435 congressional districts, in 33 or 34 Senate races, and in a presidential contest.[18] So which races draw their attention? The answer depends on many factors, including how well incumbents did in the last election, how much money those who won have available for the next election, whether party affiliation in the state or district favors Republicans or Democrats (and by how much), and whether the newly elected officeholders are likely to run for reelection.

Party committees and candidates also consider the likelihood that incumbents might retire, thereby creating an **open seat**. In the run-up to the 2018 election, some senior citizen legislators such as Senator Orrin Hatch (R-UT, 84 years old) announced their retirement, as did younger incumbents who planned to run for another office, became embroiled in a scandal, or decided to retire from politics. Open seats are of special interest to potential candidates and other political actors because incumbents generally hold an election advantage.[19] When a seat opens up, candidates from the party that does not control the seat know that they may have a better chance to win because they will not have to run against an incumbent. The incumbent's party leaders, in turn, have to recruit an especially strong candidate in order to hold the seat. Thus, in an election in which a relatively large number of members of Congress choose to retire (as did Republicans in 2018), the party with fewer retirements is in the better position because it has fewer open seats to defend.

Presidential campaigns also take incumbency into account. Virtually all first-term presidents run for reelection. Potential challengers in the opposing party study the results of the last election to see how many votes the president received and how this support was distributed across the states to determine their own chances of winning against the incumbent. Candidates in the president's party make the same calculations, although no sitting president in the twentieth century was denied renomination. Nonetheless, some presidents (Harry Truman in 1952, Lyndon Johnson in 1968) retired because their chances of being renominated were not good, while others (Gerald Ford in 1976, Jimmy Carter in 1980) faced tough primary contests.[20]

open seat
An elected position for which there is no incumbent.

Before the campaign

While in Office Most sitting House members, senators, and presidents work throughout the election cycle to secure their reelection. Political scientists describe this activity as the permanent campaign.[21] To stay in office, incumbents have to do two things: keep their constituents happy and raise money for their campaign. As we will see in Chapter 11, congressional incumbents pursue the first goal by taking actions that reflect the demands of their constituents. This, in turn, boosts voters' retrospective evaluations of the incumbents at election time.[22] Incumbent presidents make the same kinds of calculations. For example, during Barack Obama's first months in office, many of his advisers argued that he had to offer an economic stimulus plan in light of polls showing the economy was an overriding concern to most Americans. Obama did so—a decision driven not only by policy concerns but also by the desire to enact legislation that voters would remember in a positive way when they returned to the polls to elect him for another term. Of course, many presidential actions are taken in response to events rather than initiated to gain voter support. Particularly in the case of wars and other conflicts, it is far-fetched to say that presidents take hostile actions for political gain. Even so, presidents, just like other politicians, are keenly aware of the political consequences of their actions and the need to build a record they can run on in the next election.

Presidents can also use the federal bureaucracy both to their own advantage and to help members of their party. For example, some scholars have argued that presidents take measures to try to increase economic growth in the months prior to elections, with the aim of increasing support for their own candidacies (if they are eligible to run for reelection) and for their party's candidates.[23] Given the size and complexity of the U.S. economy and the fact that the independent Federal Reserve System controls monetary policy, it is unlikely that such efforts could have much success. Even so, it seems clear that out of a desire to stay in office and help their party's candidates, presidents would want to be seen as having a positive impact on the economy.

Fund-Raising Candidates for all offices, incumbents and challengers alike, also devote considerable time before the campaign to raising campaign funds. Fund-raising helps an incumbent in two ways.[24] First, it ensures that if the incumbent faces

American presidential campaigns depend on thousands of paid and volunteer staff. Here, volunteers for Democratic candidate Hillary Clinton make phone calls to potential supporters from a Clinton campaign office in Newark, Ohio.

a strong opponent, he or she will have enough money to run an aggressive campaign. Second, successful fund-raising deters opposition. Potential challengers are less likely to run against an incumbent if that individual is well funded with a sizable campaign war chest.[25] We'll discuss campaign fund-raising in more detail later in the chapter.

Promises and Party Positions Candidates also spend time before (and sometimes during) a campaign developing or refining their campaign platform, which includes stances on issues and promises about how the candidate will act in office. Given that few voters are well informed about public policy or inclined to learn, candidates do not win elections by trying to educate the electorate or making complex promises. What works is making promises and taking positions that are simple and consistent with what the average voter believes, even if these beliefs are inconsistent with reality. For example, many people believe that interest groups have too much power in Washington, although their influence is far less powerful than most Americans think (see Chapter 10). Even so, many candidates accuse their opponents of being beholden to interest groups. These claims may be far-fetched, but they work well politically because they play in to citizens' perceptions.

In writing their platforms, candidates may be constrained by positions they have taken in the past or by their party affiliation. For one thing, candidates whose positions vary from one election to another or between the primary and general elections often lose support from voters who see the changes as a sign of manipulation.[26] Also, as we saw in Chapter 8, the parties have strong brand identities that lead many citizens to associate Democrats with liberal policies and Republicans with conservative ones. As a result, candidates often find it difficult to make campaign promises that contradict these perceptions. For example, during the 2016 presidential campaign, Donald Trump pledged to expand Medicare and Social Security benefits. However, in light of past attempts by Republican officeholders to cut these programs, voters might be suspicious that Trump—the Republican nominee—would carry out this pledge if elected. Indeed, two years into Trump's term, there is no sign that he is planning to carry out this change. A candidate's positions are also influenced by demands from potential supporters. In a state or district with many conservative or Republican voters, opposition to Obamacare or to amnesty for undocumented immigrants might be a winning electoral strategy—just as support for these proposals would generally be helpful for candidates running in states or districts where most voters are moderate to liberal or Democrats.

The two-step electoral process in American elections also influences candidate positions. To win office, candidates have to campaign three times: first to build a staff and gain contributors and volunteers (the so-called silent primary or money primary), then in a primary to get on the ballot, and then in a general election. This process gives candidates an incentive to take relatively extreme policy positions—and encourages the entry of relatively extreme candidates—because party activists, contributors, and primary voters (the people whose support candidates need to attract in the first two steps) hold more extreme positions than voters in the general election. Thus, in the typical congressional district, Republican candidates win primaries by taking conservative positions, while Democratic candidates win primaries by upholding liberal views.

However, a position or promise that attracts votes in a primary election might not work so well in the general election, or vice versa. For example, during the 2016 Democratic presidential nomination campaign, challenger Bernie Sanders attracted support by promising to expand government health insurance programs. While this promise was popular among Democratic activists, contributors, and primary voters and helped Sanders compete in a close race against Hillary Clinton for the nomination, it would likely have cost Sanders considerable support in the general election.

Table 9.1 lists part of the campaign platforms of the 2016 presidential candidates and shows their similarities and differences in eight issue areas that received considerable attention during the campaign. In all of these areas, Clinton and Trump offered sharply different ideas of what government should do, although in some cases (for example, the ISIL terrorist organization), one or both platforms did not offer policy details. The sharp differences between the platforms on most of the issues are somewhat uncommon—in most elections, there are a few areas where parties offer similar proposals, differing only in details.

TABLE 9.1

Presidential Candidates' Issue Positions (Selected), 2016

The table indicates where Hillary Clinton and Donald Trump stood on eight key issues in 2016 as the presidential election approached in November: immigration, health care, gun control, trade, climate change, Iran, fighting ISIL, and LGBTQ rights.

Source: Compiled by authors from news coverage and candidate websites.

Issue	Hillary Clinton	Donald Trump
Immigration	Comprehensive reform with path to citizenship for undocumented aliens	Build wall between United States and Mexico, increase deportations, ban refugees
Health care	Improve Obamacare	Repeal Obamacare
Gun control	Expand background check system	Repeal limits on gun ownership and carry
Trade	Generally supportive of free trade	Renegotiate agreements, limit trade
Climate change	Address climate change, stress renewable energy	No action on climate change, withdraw from the Paris Climate Accord
Iran	Support Iran nuclear agreement	Repudiate Iran nuclear agreement
Fighting ISIL	Continue existing U.S. effort against ISIL	Expand effort against ISIL
LGBTQ rights	End discrimination against LGBTQ individuals	Support law giving businesses right to refuse service to LGBTQ individuals

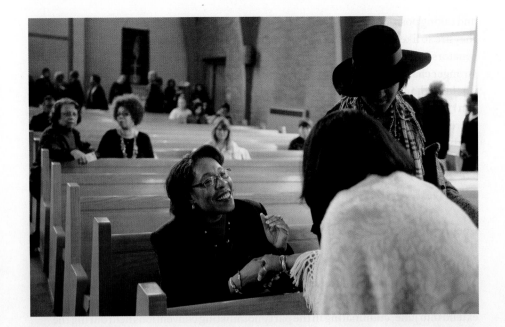

A candidate's issue positions as described in his or her platform help mobilize supporters and attract volunteers, activists, interest-group endorsements, and contributions. Issue positions also define what government will do differently depending on who gets elected. And as we will see later in this chapter, some people vote based on candidates' issue positions. Even so, there is considerable evidence that many voters do not know much about candidates' issue positions, particularly in House and Senate races. As a result, when a candidate wins a race or a party wins seats across the country, it is risky to read the outcome as a sign that the winners had the most popular set of issue positions.

Campaign Staff Finally, candidates spend time before the campaign building their organization.[27] Just like fund-raising, the success or failure of these efforts is a signal of a candidate's prospects. If experienced, well-respected people agree to work in a candidate's campaign, observers conclude that the candidate's prospects for being elected are probably good.

Skilled campaign consultants are among the most sought-after campaign staff. These consultants plan strategies, run public-opinion polls, assemble ads and buy television time, and talk with members of the media on the candidate's behalf, among other things. For many consultants, electioneering is a full-time, year-round position. Many concentrate on electing candidates from one party, although some work for whoever will hire them.

Almost all campaigns have paid and volunteer staff, ranging from the dozen or so people who work for a typical House candidate to the thousands needed to run a major-party candidate's presidential campaign. Some campaign staff work full-time for an incumbent's campaign committee or are on the incumbent's congressional or presidential staff. With some exceptions for senior presidential staff, federal law prohibits government employees from engaging in campaign activities during work hours or with congressional resources.[28] As a result, many congressional or presidential staffers take a leave of absence from their government jobs to work on their bosses' reelection campaigns during the last few months of the election cycle, then return to working for the government after the election—assuming the incumbent is reelected.

It's hard to separate what candidates do at election time from what they do between elections—incumbents are *always* campaigning, always making promises and taking positions, and always raising campaign funds—which is part of the reason they are so likely to win reelection. In many cases, incumbent House members and senators wind up running against poorly funded, inexperienced candidates because stronger challengers—seeing that the incumbent has been working hard to solidify a hold on the constituency—decide to wait until the incumbent retires, when they can run for the open seat. Thus, though incumbents are not automatically favored for reelection, they often win by large margins because of all the things they do while holding office in between elections.[29]

Primaries and the general election

Congressional primary elections occur throughout the spring and summer. For congressional candidates, winning the primary allows them to plan for the general election in November and gives them access to party resources including contributions, workers, and assistance with polling and other logistics. As we discussed earlier, presidential primaries and caucuses begin in early January and extend into June, culminating in the party nominating conventions held during the summer. Officially, the general-election campaigns begin in early September. By then, both parties have chosen their presidential nominees and their congressional candidates. Interest groups, candidates, and party committees have raised most of the funds they will use or donate in the campaign. The race is on.

For presidential candidates, the move from primaries to the general election involves a sharp shift in campaign strategies. Unlike in the early primary states, where candidates engage in "retail politics" by meeting more directly with voters on a small, individual scale, the presidential general-election campaigns emphasize "wholesale politics," a style of campaigning in which candidates contact voters indirectly, such as through media coverage and campaign advertising. At this point, presidential campaign events generally involve large numbers of citizens, and if they are smaller events or one-on-one encounters, they are designed to generate media coverage and thereby reach a larger audience.

In contrast, some general-election campaigns for the House and even a few Senate races are more likely to practice retail politics, stressing direct contact with voters. Even so, the start of these general-election campaigns is usually when congressional candidates and groups supporting and opposing them go "on the air" with campaign advertising. (In contrast, all presidential campaigns run ads throughout the primary and general-election campaigns.)

Name Recognition One of the most fundamental campaign strategies, particularly in congressional campaigns, is to build name recognition. Since many citizens tend not to be well informed about congressional candidates, efforts to increase a candidate's name recognition in these races can deliver a few extra percentage points of support— enough to turn a close defeat into a victory. If the only thing a citizen knows is the name of one of the candidates, that citizen will almost surely vote for that candidate on Election Day. The importance of name recognition is one reason why campaigns invest in buttons, bumper stickers, and yard signs—all of which help ensure that voters know a candidate's name.

Getting Out the Vote A second basic strategy is mobilization. Turnout is not automatic: just because a citizen supports a candidate does not mean that he or she will actually vote. Candidates have to make sure that their supporters go to the polls on Election Day. Moreover, focusing on getting supporters to the polls (or making sure

Candidates may gain media attention and name recognition by hosting campaign events alongside well-known "surrogates." Here, senator and former presidential candidate Ted Cruz (R-TX) stands with now-elected congressman Ron Estes (R-KS) in Wichita, Kansas.

they have an absentee ballot) is a relatively efficient use of candidates' resources. Given that most people don't pay much attention to politics, it's much easier to get a supporter to go to the polls than it is to convert an opponent into a supporter.

Campaign professionals refer to voter mobilization efforts as **GOTV ("get out the vote")** or the **ground game**.[30] Most campaigns for Congress or the presidency use extensive door-to-door canvassing, in which volunteers knock on doors and present their candidate's message to voters one at a time. Campaigns also commonly use phone banks, e-mail campaigns, and social media to reach out to potential supporters. To determine how best to contact these people and convince them to vote, both Republican and Democratic campaigns use sophisticated databases, combining voter registration data with demographics.[31] Sometimes these contacts are made through social media, but many campaigns still use volunteers to knock on doors and present their candidate's message to voters one at a time.

Sometimes candidates also try to decrease support and turnout for their opponent. One tactic is push polling, in which a candidate or a group that supports a candidate conducts a voter "survey," typically by phone, that isn't actually designed to measure opinions so much as to influence them. Campaigns use these so-called polls to spread false or misleading information about another candidate by including this (mis) information in questions posed to large numbers of citizens.[32]

Going Positive or Negative? Candidates and other organizations also need to determine the tenor of their campaign—whether they emphasize their own (or their preferred candidates') qualifications and platform and refrain from critiquing their opponents (positive campaigning), or focus on criticizing their opponent's positions, experience, and lack of qualifications (negative campaigning). For example, when Senator Elizabeth Warren talks about her life growing up or her work on reforming bankruptcy law, that is positive campaigning. But when Warren attacked President Trump for not releasing his tax returns or mentioned allegations of sexual harassment against Trump, that was negative campaigning. Candidates and their supporters often try to raise doubts about their opponents by citing politically damaging statements or unpopular past behavior. In conducting opposition research, candidates and interest groups dig into an opponent's past for embarrassing incidents or personal indiscretions, either by the candidate or by a member of the candidate's family or staff.

The positive or negative tone of a campaign may not be driven completely by the candidates themselves. The Internet, for example, facilitates efforts to popularize damaging information. For example, in early October 2016, various media organizations released video of Donald Trump describing his pursuit of women in vulgar, disturbing terms—ending with the phrase "and when you're a star, they let you do it." While Trump later apologized and tried to explain his comments as "locker room talk," the availability of the video made it difficult for Trump to put the issue to rest. Trump's victory was even more notable in light of the negative publicity generated by media coverage of the video and its aftermath.

Candidates who are behind in the polls (or the organizations that support them) sometimes resort to attack ads: campaign ads that criticize the opponent. While all critical ads are labeled as negative campaigning, campaign experts distinguish between ads that criticize a candidate but at the same time accurately describe the action or position that they are attacking, from ads that stretch the truth (or break it outright). In this sense, Warren's criticisms of Trump were negative but factually correct; Trump has not released his taxes, and there were multiple harassment allegations made against Trump. On the other hand, an ad run during the 2017 special House election in Georgia falsely suggested that the Democratic candidate had ties to terrorist organizations, simply because the Middle Eastern news service Al Jazeera had

GOTV ("get out the vote") or the **ground game**
A campaign's efforts to "get out the vote" or make sure its supporters vote on Election Day.

run a story about the candidate and the race. Of course, attack ads often fail because they are too outlandish. However, some succeed in changing votes, while others force the opposing candidate to spend time and money denying the ads' claims.

Debates Candidates often contrast their own records or positions with those of opposing candidates or make claims designed to lower citizens' opinions of their opponents. Sometimes these interactions occur during a formal debate. Most congressional campaigns involve debates in front of an audience of likely voters, a group of reporters, or the editorial board of a local newspaper. Typically candidates take questions from reporters or a debate moderator, although sometimes candidates question each other or answer questions from the audience.

Presidential campaigns involve multiple debates during the primary and caucus season. During the months before the first primaries and caucuses, each party's candidates gather for many single-party debates using a variety of formats. During the general election, the Republican and Democratic nominees meet for several debates. The number and format are negotiated by the campaigns and the Commission on Presidential Debates, a nonpartisan organization that coordinates the debates.[33] The 2016 presidential campaign featured three debates between the presidential nominees and one between the vice-presidential nominees. The debates not only give candidates a chance to present themselves to the electorate but also offer valuable free exposure. Given a relatively uninterested electorate, candidates must figure out how to present themselves to voters in a way that captures their attention and gains their support. Thus, during the 2016 presidential election debates Republican Donald Trump positioned himself as a successful businessman who could manage the economy and as an agent of change in Washington—a good fit to Trump's status as a political outsider, a good match to voters' concerns about the economy, and a good way to turn his personal wealth into a campaign asset.

Campaign advertising: getting the word out

One of the realities of modern American electoral campaigns is that they are, for the most part, conducted indirectly—through social media, through news coverage of events, and (most important) through paid campaign advertising. Candidates, party committees, and interest groups spend more than several billion dollars during each election cycle on campaign-related activities by all candidates for federal office. Most of that money is spent on 30-second television spots. Campaign advertising is critical because, as we discussed in Chapter 7, candidates cannot assume that citizens will take the time to learn from other sources about the candidates, their qualifications, and their issue positions.

What Do the Ads Involve? Campaign advertising has evolved considerably over the last generation.[34] During the early years of television, many campaign ads consisted of speeches by candidates or endorsements from supporters and they ran several minutes in length. In the 1964 presidential race, Lyndon Johnson's campaign ran a five-minute ad titled "Confessions of a Republican" that featured an actor talking about why he didn't want to vote for Republican presidential candidate Barry Goldwater.[35] Johnson's campaign also ran a one-minute ad titled "Peace Little Girl" (nicknamed "Daisy"), which featured a child holding a daisy and pulling its petals off as she counted them aloud one by one. In the background, a voice provided a parallel countdown to the detonation of a nuclear bomb. The ad ended as the television screen filled with the image of the mushroom cloud produced by the nuclear explosion.[36] The implication was that electing Goldwater would increase the chances of a future conflict involving nuclear weapons. The ad remains one of the most iconic pieces of campaign advertising.

Much like the "Daisy" ad, modern campaign ads are short, with arresting images that often use photomontages and bold text to engage a distracted citizenry. Content varies depending on who is running the ads. Table 9.2 gives data from campaign ads in the 2016 presidential general-election campaign from candidates, parties, and interest groups (the top three from each side are listed). These data show that the Trump campaign spent significantly less than the Clinton campaign. The table also shows a striking difference in ad content: while the candidates ran a mix of positive and negative ads, ads run by political parties and interest groups were uniformly negative.

The "Daisy" ad from the 1964 presidential campaign interspersed images of a child in a field of flowers and footage of a nuclear detonation. It was broadcast only once but caused much controversy—and helped to crystallize doubts about Republican candidate Barry Goldwater.

TABLE 9.2

Campaign Advertising by Major Spenders in the 2016 Presidential Election

The table shows total spending and the total number of ads, as well as the percentage of positive ads, as paid for directly by the candidates, their parties, and Republican PACs and Democratic PACs.

	Organization	Spending (Millions)	Number of Ads	Positive Ads (%)
Candidates	Clinton campaign	$219	231,241	36
	Trump campaign	77	68,805	57
Parties	Republican National Committee	8.3	30,636	Mostly negative
	Democratic National Committee	1.8	475	Mostly negative
Republican Groups	National Rifle Association	9.4	9,236	Mostly negative
	Reform America	1.4	2,051	Mostly negative
	45 Committee	2.1	2,022	Mostly negative
Democratic Groups	Priorities USA Action	75	76,965	Mostly negative
	Next Gen	11	10,437	Mostly negative
	Service Employees Union	1	590	Mostly negative

Source: Calculated by authors from data available at Wesleyan Media Project, mediaproject.wesleyan.edu (accessed 11/7/16).

Do Campaign Ads Work? One critical question about campaign advertising is whether the ads work—whether they shape what people know or influence their voting decisions or other forms of participation. Some observers have complained that campaign ads (particularly negative ads) depress voter turnout and reinforce citizens' negative perceptions of government.[37] Many of these arguments focus on attack ads or negative campaigning. Ads have portrayed candidates as evil blimps hovering over Washington, D.C., or even "demon sheep."[38]

Whether positive or negative, and regardless of whether they feature evil blimps or something else, campaign ads seek to catch voters' attention, to get them to focus on a race long enough to consider the candidates and their real messages. Studies of campaign advertising have shown that most of the time, campaign ads fail at this task. Most citizens ignore the ads or remain unconvinced of their messages. For example, during the 2016 presidential nomination campaign Republican Jeb Bush and groups supporting him spent millions on campaign ads, only to find that citizens simply did not want to vote for Bush regardless of how many ads his campaign ran. In the general election, Hillary Clinton lost despite vastly outspending Donald Trump on campaign ads. And Carly Fiorina, who ran for a California Senate seat using the demon sheep ad, lost her race.

Insofar as ads matter and Americans pay attention to politics, studies of campaign advertising suggest that Americans are reasonably thoughtful when assessing campaign ads. Evidence suggests that campaign advertising has several beneficial effects. Researchers have found that people who are exposed to campaign ads tend to be more interested in the campaign and to know more about the candidates.[39] Moreover, many campaign ads highlight real differences between the candidates and the parties.[40] Nonetheless, average citizens know that they cannot believe everything they see on television, so campaign advertising, if it does anything at all, captures their attention without necessarily changing their minds.[41]

With regard to negative campaigning, evidence suggests that attack ads often do not help the candidates who run them.[42] In fact, negative ads run by a candidate's campaign can backfire, driving away supporters and depressing turnout. As a result, candidates often rely on party committees and interest groups to run negative ads. Then the candidates themselves can run more positive ads (recall Table 9.2) and can try to disassociate themselves from the negative ads run by others.

In the end, despite all the money and effort poured into campaign advertising, these messages must be designed to capture the attention of citizens whose interest in politics is minimal, delivering a message that can be understood without too much interpretation. In this way, campaign advertising reflects an old political belief, that most things candidates do in campaigns are wasted efforts that have little impact on the election. The problem is that candidates don't know which of their actions will amount to wasted efforts and which will help them win, so they try everything they can.

Campaign finance

"Campaign finance" refers to money collected for and spent on campaigns and elections by candidates, political parties, and other organizations and individuals. The **Federal Election Commission** is in charge of administering election laws, including the complex regulations pertaining to how campaigns can spend money. Changes in campaign finance rules, which were passed as the Bipartisan Campaign Reform Act (BCRA), took effect after the 2002 elections and have been modified by subsequent Supreme Court decisions, most notably *Citizens United v. Federal Election Commission* (2010) and *McCutcheon v. Federal Election Commission* (2014), which we describe later.

In the 2016 presidential race, many of the ads aired by the Trump campaign and Republican groups criticized Hillary Clinton, focusing on what they deemed to be her corrupt political associations.

Federal Election Commission
The government agency that enforces and regulates election laws; made up of six presidential appointees, of whom no more than three can be members of the same party.

While campaign finance law is complex, most Americans believe the effects of campaign finance are simple: candidates cannot win without spending money, victory goes to the candidate with the larger budget, and, as a result, candidates listen to large donors and ignore average citizens. They also believe that elections cost too much. The reality is much more complex. Candidates need money to run effective campaigns (and particularly to pay for campaign advertising), but spending does not guarantee victory. And while candidates court large donors, they are even more obsessed with winning the support of ordinary citizens, because in the end elections are about votes, not money.

Types of Contributions and Funding Organizations The limits on campaign contributions in the BCRA—also known as the McCain-Feingold Act—vary depending on whether contributions are made by an individual or a group and by the type of group, as shown in Table 9.3. These limits were modified in April 2014 by a 5–4 ruling in *McCutcheon v. Federal Election Commission*, in which the Supreme Court struck down limits on overall campaign contributions to candidates and PACs. A second Supreme Court decision, *Citizens United v. Federal Election Commission*, also eliminated restrictions on campaign advertising by corporations, organizations, and labor unions within 30 days of a primary or 60 days of a general election.

Current law distinguishes between independent expenditures, in which a party or group spends money to advocate for a candidate but the candidate or the campaign does not control, direct, or approve the activity, and coordinated expenditures, in which the candidate has some control. Independent expenditures are not limited, but coordinated expenditures are. For example, in Senate races, there is a cap on coordinated expenditures by political parties, ranging from several hundred thousand dollars in small states like Delaware to several million dollars in California.

Contribution Limits in the 2018 Elections

TABLE 9.3

The BCRA of 2002 put into effect limits on how much individuals, organizations, and corporations could contribute to candidates' primary and general-election campaigns. The limits were changed based on Supreme Court decisions in 2010 and 2014. At present, although there are still limits on contributions that individuals and PACs can make to each individual candidate, there are no limits on total overall contributions to multiple candidates by individuals and PACs.

	Individual Candidates	National Party Committees	State, District, and Local Parties	PACs	Limit on Total Contributions
Individuals	$2,700	$33,900	$10,000 (combined limit)	$5,000	No limit
PACs	$5,000	$15,000	$5,000 (combined limit)	$5,000	No limit
National Party Committees	$5,000	No limit	No limit	$5,000	$45,400 to Senate candidate per campaign
State, District, and Local Party Committees	$5,000 (combined limit)	No limit	No limit	$5,000 (combined limit)	No limit

Source: Federal Election Commission, "Contribution Limits for 2017–2018," www.fec.gov (accessed 3/11/18).

DID YOU KNOW?

Candidates, parties, and organizations spent a total of

$5.2 billion

during the 2017–2018 election cycle.
Source: Opensecrets.org

Political action committees spend millions on campaign advertising. Often, their ads are highly negative. This one attacks Donald Trump for being homophobic in his rhetoric.

A second distinction in campaign finance laws is between **hard money**, meaning contributions to a candidate, party organization, or other group that are intended to help elect or defeat a specific candidate, and **soft money**, meaning funds that are used for other activities and are not subject to the limits imposed on hard money. Groups defined by IRS regulations as 527 organizations, for example, can raise unlimited soft money from individuals or corporations for voter mobilization and for issue advocacy, but these expenditures must not be coordinated with a candidate or a party. Ads by 527s cannot advocate the election or defeat of a particular candidate or political party.[43] Another type of organization, again described using the IRS code, is the 501(c)(4), which often collects and spends soft money. The principal difference between 527s and 501(c)(4)s is that the latter type of organization does not have to disclose the names of its contributors.

A third type of organization, the political action committee (PAC), is a group that aims to elect or defeat particular candidates or a particular political party. A company or an organization can form a PAC and solicit contributions from employees or group members. As Table 9.3 shows, the amount PACs can give to each candidate in an election is limited, but these limits pertain only to hard money. PACs can also form 527s, which can then accept unlimited amounts of soft money. So-called Super PACs are PACs that do not donate to candidates but use soft money to make unlimited independent expenditures in campaigns. Chapter 10 looks more closely at PACs, 527s, and 501(c)(4)s.

As discussed in Chapter 8, political party committees are entities within the Republican and Democratic parties. Both major parties have a national committee and a campaign committee in each house of Congress. Party committees are limited in the amount of hard money they can give to any given candidate's campaign and in the amount they can spend on behalf of the candidate as a coordinated expenditure. But a party committee (and, after *Citizens United*, corporations and labor unions) can spend an unlimited amount in independent expenditures to elect a candidate or candidates.

Current law gives presidential candidates the ability to receive federal campaign funding for the primary and general-election campaign (in the primary, these are matching funds; in the general, they are a block grant). These federal funds are generated, in part, by money that taxpayers voluntarily allocate out of the taxes they pay to the federal government by checking off a particular box on their federal tax return form. Funds are also given to minor political parties if their candidate received more than 5 percent of the vote in the previous election. However, in order to accept federal funds, presidential candidates must abide by overall spending limits (and, during the nomination process, by state-by-state spending caps). During the last two presidential campaigns, all the major candidates decided against accepting these funds during the nomination and general-election campaign, which meant that they were not bound by the spending caps (although individual contributors were still limited to the amounts shown in Table 9.3).

The Effects of Money in Politics Campaign finance regulations reflect two simple truths. First, any limits on campaign activities involve balancing the right to free speech about candidates and issues with the idea that rich people or well-funded organizations should not be allowed to dominate what voters hear during the campaign. Second, an enormous amount of money is spent on American elections. Table 9.4 shows the amount raised by candidates, political parties, and others in 2016

TABLE
9.4

Candidate, Party, and Interest-Group Election Fund-Raising, 2016–2018

	2016	2018
Presidential Candidates		
Republican	$333,127,164	—
Democrat	$563,756,928	—
Congressional Candidates		
House incumbents	$664,873,622	$711,117,909
House challengers	$149,000,679	$438,927,947
House open-seat candidates	$214,460,277	$384,890,754
Senate incumbents	$368,532,005	$539,389,767
Senate challengers	$203,163,709	$350,187,926
Senate open-seat candidates	$114,716,739	$82,890,927
Political Parties		
Republicans	$969,156,764	$859,438,792
Democrats	$1,279,204,717	$802,172,215
Independent Expenditures	$1,687,082,953	$1,110,325,920
Totals	$6,113,385,432	$5,279,342,217

Source: Calculated by authors from data at www.opensecrets.org (accessed 11/6/18).

Candidates and political parties raise and spend a great deal of money in their campaigns. Do these numbers help explain the high reelection rates for members of Congress?

and 2018. More than $6 billion was raised during 2016, a presidential election year, and $5 billion for the 2018 midterms. Moreover, campaign spending is concentrated among a relatively small number of organizations with sizable electioneering budgets. In each of the last several election cycles, the largest organizations have spent hundreds of millions of dollars on contesting the election.

The principal concern about all this campaign cash is that the amount of money spent on candidates' campaigns might matter more than the candidates' qualifications or issue positions. That is, candidates—in particular, wealthy candidates who could self-fund their campaigns—could get elected regardless of how good a job they would do, simply because they had more money than competing candidates to pay for campaign ads, polls, a large staff, and mobilization efforts. Another concern is that individuals and organizations or corporations that can afford to make large contributions (or to fund their own electioneering efforts) might be able to dictate election outcomes or, by funding campaigns, garner a disproportionate amount of influence over the subsequent behavior of elected officials. In the main, these concerns affect soft money contributions and independent expenditures because the current law places no limits on how much soft money a party can collect, or on the size of a group's independent expenditures (see the Take a Stand feature).

When you look at campaign finance data, the first thing you will see is that it is easy to find which individuals or organizations gave money to a candidate, political party, or other organization.[44] Thus, if you are worried that a particular organization is using campaign contributions to influence elected officials, you can learn which officeholders have received the group's donations. In fact, campaign finance records are so readily available that it is generally easy to identify fraudulent organizations.

However, the raw data do not always tell the whole story. For example, while total spending is often quite high, it is important to remember that a large percentage of campaign expenditures are for advertising. A 30-second ad on a major television network can cost tens or hundreds of thousands of dollars.[45] Given that even House campaigns may run hundreds of ads and presidential campaigns generally run tens of thousands of ads, it is easy to see why campaign costs pile up so quickly.

There is little evidence that campaign contributions alter legislators' behavior or that contributors are rewarded with votes supporting their causes or favorable policies. Research suggests that most contributions are intended to help elect politicians whom contributors already like, with no expectation that these officials will do anything differently because they received a contribution.[46] On the other hand, contributions may help with access, getting the donor an appointment to present arguments to a politician or his or her staff.[47] And yet people and organizations that generally contribute are already friendly with the politicians they support, and so the politicians would likely hear their arguments in any case.

It's also clear that having a lot of campaign cash doesn't make a candidate a winner—and winners don't always outspend their opponents. Consider the 2016 Republican presidential primaries: the campaigns of Jeb Bush, Chris Christie, and Marco Rubio had large budgets and the support of outside groups with deep pockets. Even so, they all lost. The winner of the election, Donald Trump, spent substantially less than his opponents in both the nomination and general-election campaigns. In the general election, for example, Hillary Clinton's campaign outspent Trump's by nearly $200 million. The Democratic Party and allied outside groups also outspent the Republican Party and its groups by a similar amount. Even so, Trump won. Of course, Trump entered the campaign with high levels of name recognition and his campaign message resonated with Republican primary voters. But that is exactly the point: victories aren't bought with campaign cash. Candidates need a base level of funding to hire staff, travel, and run some campaign ads. Beyond that point, success is a function of what candidates say and do, not the amount of contributions they receive or ads run on their behalf.[48]

"Why Should I Care?"

When you follow the news about political campaigns, pay attention to the money candidates raise (and spend), where they campaign (and to whom they appeal), the tone and message of their campaigns, and larger fundamentals, such as the strength of the economy. These factors can provide strong clues about who is likely to win (or lose). Remember, though, that politicians don't win elections just by spending a lot of money. Sometimes candidates win despite lower budgets. The other factors listed here and examined in this chapter often have stronger effects on the outcome than money alone.

Is There Too Much Money in Politics?

Campaign finance regulations place restrictions on what Americans can do to influence election outcomes—but should they? Suppose you are a wealthy person or the head of a corporation with deep pockets. Under current law, you and your corporation can only donate about $15,000 to a candidate's campaign; corporations have to form a PAC to do so and cannot pay for the contribution with business revenues. You can also form one of several types of organizations that can spend unlimited money to run campaign ads designed to help elect your preferred candidates, or you can donate to an existing organization. Clearly, having money gives you options for participation in American elections that are not open to the average citizen. Is that a good thing?

It's a free country, and spending money on politics is part of that freedom. Limits on campaign spending conflict with fundamental tenets of American democracy. The Bill of Rights states that Congress cannot abridge "freedom of speech, or of the press; or the right of the people peaceably to assemble, and to petition the Government for a redress of grievances." One interpretation of the First Amendment that has shaped recent Supreme Court decisions on campaign finance is that people should be free to spend whatever they want on contesting elections—excluding bribes, threats, and other illegal actions, of course.

Another argument for eliminating limits on political activities is that with one exception (donations to 501[c][4] organizations), donors and political activists are required to file quarterly reports on their campaign activities. Therefore, other activists and even ordinary citizens would quickly learn of any large-scale attempts to manipulate election outcomes and could decide to work for the other side or simply vote against a big donor's preferred candidates.

And ultimately, given that campaign spending is no guarantee of electoral success, it is not clear that eliminating spending limits would give big donors control over election outcomes.

Campaign contributions need to be constrained. Even if there's no evidence that money buys elections, there is also no guarantee that under the right circumstances a big donation or ad campaign would not make the difference for one or more candidates. Because money for ads is a necessary component of a political campaign, the possibility remains that a rich donor could change election outcomes by giving large sums to challengers in congressional elections. And in close races, giving a candidate extra funds to increase his or her GOTV efforts or to run additional campaign ads might be enough to change the outcome.

With this possibility in mind, it makes sense to place broad limits on campaign contributions and independent expenditures to level the playing field between ordinary citizens and political activists with deep pockets. Just because someone is rich shouldn't give him or her additional ways to influence election outcomes.

Moreover, while it is true that limiting campaign activities requires imposing limits on speech rights, limitations on civil liberties are nothing new. All the individual rights set out in the Bill of Rights are limited in one way or the other. Even freedom of speech is limited in areas such as hate speech and statements that pose a clear and present danger. Imposing limits on campaign activities could be justified on the grounds that maintaining free and fair elections is important enough to justify a modest limitation on what individuals and organizations can do to influence election outcomes.

 Does money equal speech or should campaign contributions be limited?

Does the risk of allowing rich donors disproportionate power over elections outweigh the dangers associated with restricting their speech rights?

take a stand

1. Limits on individual campaign contributions guard against allowing wealthy people to dominate elections. What are some of the possible drawbacks of such regulations?

2. Under current law, corporations and unions (not just individuals) are allowed unlimited political expenditures as long as they are independent of a candidate's campaign organization. Why do you think independent expenditures are less regulated than direct contributions to campaigns?

Voting is costly in terms of time and effort. After registering and informing themselves about the election, voters have to take the time to go to the polls and possibly wait in line.

paradox of voting
The question of why citizens vote even though their individual votes stand little chance of changing the election outcome.

How do voters decide?

All the electoral activities we have considered so far are directed at citizens: making sure they are registered to vote, influencing their voting decisions, and getting them to the polls. In this section, we examine how citizens respond to these influences. The first thing to understand is that the high level of attention, commitment, and energy exhibited by candidates and other campaign actors is not matched by ordinary citizens. We have seen throughout this chapter and others that although politics is everywhere and elections are the primary mechanism citizens have to control the federal government, only a minority of citizens report high levels of interest in campaigns, many people know little about the candidates or the issues, and many people do not vote.[49]

Who votes, and why?

Politics is everywhere, but getting involved is your choice. Voting and other forms of political participation are optional. Surprisingly, even a strong preference between two candidates may not drive citizens to the polls. They may not be motivated to vote because they feel that their vote is just one of many.[50] And it's true that the only time a vote "counts," in the sense that it changes the outcome, is when the other votes are split evenly so that one vote breaks the tie. Moreover, voting involves costs. Even if citizens don't learn about the candidates but want to vote anyway, they still have to get to the polls on Election Day. Thus, the **paradox of voting** is this: Why does anyone vote, given that voting is costly and the chances of affecting the outcome are small?

Figure 9.2 shows that among Americans the percentage of registered voters who actually voted in recent presidential elections has been around 60 percent, although

FIGURE 9.2

Turnout in Presidential and Midterm Elections, 1992–2018

The figure shows how turnout of registered voters varies both over time and between presidential and midterm elections. Why don't more people vote in midterm election years? Why don't more people vote in any given year?

Source: United States Election Project, www.election-project.org (accessed 11/7/18).

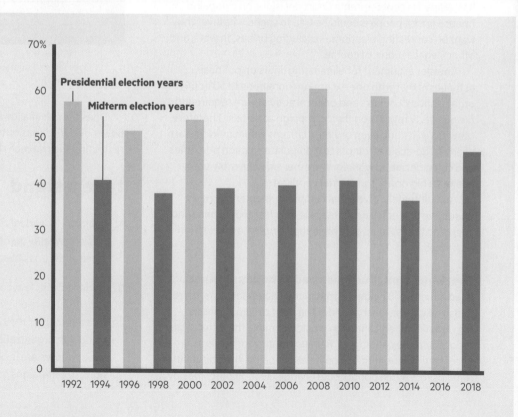

actual turnout (votes as a percentage of the total adult population) has been closer to 50 percent.[51] As the figure shows, turnout is significantly higher in presidential elections than in midterms—although in 2018 turnout was higher than in previous midterms. Turnout is much lower in primaries and caucuses: in the 2016 presidential primaries, some states reported unusually high turnout exceeding 30 percent. Because caucuses can take several hours, turnout is generally only a few percentage points.

In the main, turnout is higher for whites than for nonwhites (African Americans have been an exception in recent elections), for older Americans than for younger Americans, and for college graduates than for people with a high school education or less. Men and women, however, say they vote at roughly the same rate. Many factors explain variation in turnout.

Turnout is affected by structural factors, such as state laws that prohibit convicted felons from voting, laws that require citizens to be registered to vote a set number of days before an election, variation in early voting and voting by mail laws, laws requiring a photo ID to vote, and laws that make it easier or harder to obtain an absentee ballot.

However, turnout is far below 100 percent, even in areas of the country where all of these factors are set to make it easy for people to vote. Analysis shows that turnout is much higher among people who consider going to the polls as an obligation of citizenship, feel guilty when they do not vote, and think that the elections matter. Turnout is much lower among those who are angry with the government, think that government actions do not affect them, or think that voting will have no impact on government policy. Citizens who hold these beliefs are unlikely to care about the outcome of the election, are unlikely to feel guilty for abstaining, and are unlikely to see voting as an obligation.[52] Thus, while it is possible to increase turnout somewhat by changing laws, the biggest gains come from convincing individual Americans that voting is something they should feel obligated to do.

These findings demonstrate the importance of mobilization in elections. As we discussed earlier, many candidates for political office spend at least as much time trying to convince their supporters to vote as they do attempting to persuade others to become supporters in the first place. Because many Americans either do not vote or vote only sporadically, mobilization is a vital strategy for winning elections.

How do people vote?

Some people are highly interested in politics, collect all the information they can about the candidates, and vote based on this information; they are known as **issue voters**.[53] But most citizens are not interested enough in politics to spend their time that way, and they don't care enough about the details of politics to find out which candidates come closest to their preferences. Reliable information about candidates is also often difficult to find. Although candidates, parties, and other organizations produce a blizzard of endorsements, reports, and press releases throughout the campaign, much of this information may be difficult to interpret. It is a daunting task, even for the rare, highly motivated voter.

Voting Cues This combination of a lack of interest and the relatively complex task of seeking information leads the majority of American voters to base their voting decision on easily interpretable pieces of information, or **voting cues**.[54] Voters in American national elections use many kinds of cues, such as party ID (voting for the candidate who shares your party identification, as we discussed in Chapter 8), the personal vote (voting for a candidate who has helped you get assistance from a government agency

DID YOU KNOW?

61.2%

Voter turnout for African Americans in the 2016 presidential election.
Source: Calculated by author from exit polls and historical data.

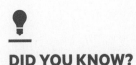

During campaigns, candidates often seek to strengthen the perception that they share (or at least are sympathetic to) average Americans' beliefs and interests. Here, Senator Bill Nelson (D-FL) talks to Hispanic voters in the Little Havana neighborhood in Miami.

issue voters
People who are well informed about their own policy preferences and knowledgeable about the candidates, and who use all of this information when they decide how to vote.

voting cues
Pieces of information about a candidate that are readily available, easy to interpret, and lead a citizen to decide to vote for a particular candidate.

or has helped your community benefit from desirable government projects), personal characteristics (voting for the candidate whose personal characteristics such as age, race, gender, ethnicity, religious beliefs, or background match your own), or pocketbook voting (voting for the incumbent if the economy is strong and for the challenger otherwise). Voters can also use multiple cues. Cues give people a low-cost way to cast what political scientist and campaign consultant Samuel Popkin called a reasonable vote—a vote that, more likely than not, is consistent with the voter's true preference among candidates.[55] Studies have found that citizens who use cues and are politically well informed are more likely to cast a reasonable vote than those who use cues but are otherwise relatively politically ignorant. In essence, knowing something about the candidates and the issues at stake in an election helps people select the right cue on which to base their vote.[56]

On the one hand, the role that cues play in voting decisions is one reason why "the fundamentals matter" in American elections. Because some people vote based on the state of the economy, incumbent presidents are good bets to win reelection when economic conditions are good and poor bets when the economy is in trouble. Similarly, because party ID is often used as a cue, candidates are more likely to win if their party affiliation is shared by the bulk of voters in their state or district. On the other hand, the use of cues also implies that candidates (and campaigns) matter. For example, citizens may use a candidate's record in office to guide their vote decision, especially if the candidate makes this record a central theme in his or her campaign speeches and advertising. In fact, many campaign events and communications are designed to reinforce the impression that candidates share voters' concerns and values. For example, at several points during the 2016 campaign, Donald Trump tweeted pictures of his fast-food dinner on the campaign plane.

Moreover, because personal characteristics are used as a cue, some candidates have a better chance of winning than others, because they have one or more cues that citizens see as desirable. For example, some people voted for Hillary Clinton because she was a woman; because of her political experience as First Lady, senator, and secretary of state; or simply because she was a Democrat. Equally, some people voted for Donald Trump because of his career as a businessman or because he was the Republican nominee. Table 9.5 offers some details on what kind of candidate characteristics attract voter support. On the one hand, many voters consider a candidate's military service as an asset. On the other hand, Americans tend not to vote for a candidate who is a known atheist, has had an extramarital affair, or is gay or lesbian. Of course, candidate information is only one of the things a voter considers and some cues override others—businessman Donald Trump won the presidency despite having never been elected to political office, being 70 years old, and admitting to past extramarital affairs.

Who (usually) wins

All the strategies discussed so far are used to some extent in every election. In normal elections, when congressional reelection rates are high, voters generally use cues that focus on the candidates themselves, such as incumbency, partisanship, a personal connection to a candidate, the candidate's personal characteristics, or retrospective evaluations. This behavior is consistent with what Tip O'Neill, Speaker of the House from 1977 to 1987, meant when he said that "all politics is local": many congressional elections are independent, local contests in which a candidate's chances of winning depend on what voters think of the candidate in particular—not the president, Congress, or national issues. It also explains why electoral **coattails** are typically very weak in American elections and why so many Americans cast **split tickets** rather than **straight tickets**. In the main, voting decisions in presidential and congressional elections are made independently of each other.

coattails
The ability of a popular president to generate additional support for candidates affiliated with his or her party. Coattails are weak or nonexistent in most American elections.

split ticket
A ballot on which a voter selects candidates from more than one political party.

straight ticket
A ballot on which a voter selects candidates from only one political party.

TABLE
9.5

Likelihood of Supporting a Candidate Who . . .	More Likely	Less Likely	Wouldn't Matter
Has served in the military	50%	4%	45%
Attended a prestigious university	20	6	74
Is Catholic	16	8	75
Has Washington experience	22	31	46
Is an Evangelical Christian	22	20	55
Is Mormon	5	23	69
Has used marijuana in the past	6	20	74
Had personal financial troubles	8	41	49
Is an atheist	6	51	41
Is gay or lesbian	4	26	69
Had an extramarital affair in the past	3	37	58

Candidate Traits and Voter Choice

Many Americans cast votes based on candidates' personal characteristics and background. What sorts of candidates are advantaged by this practice—and what sorts are disadvantaged?

Source: Pew Research Center, "Faith and the 2016 Campaign," www.pewforum.org, (accessed 3/18/18).

"Wave" elections generally occur when a large number of voters vote against incumbents because of poor economic conditions, political scandal, or a costly, unpopular war. In 2010, many Americans were concerned about the state of the economy, the size of corporate bailouts, the apparent ineffectiveness of economic stimulus legislation, and the enactment of health care reform, and they blamed the party in power (Democrats) for all of these outcomes. As a result, a significant percentage of Americans voted against Democratic congressional candidates, either as a protest vote, because they disapproved of their performance, or as an effort to put different individuals in charge in the hope that new members would bring about improved conditions. Ultimately, Republicans gained several seats in the Senate and regained majority control of the House with a nearly 80-seat gain. In contrast, 2018 was not a wave election: while Democrats won additional House seats and majority control, their gains were comparable to historical averages. Moreover, Democrats also lost several Senate seats in 2018.

Even in wave elections, reelection rates for members of Congress (the percentage of incumbents who successfully run for reelection) are generally high, as Figure 9.3 shows. Over the last generation, neither party has had a House reelection rate less than 80 percent; even in 2006, when 100 percent of Democratic House incumbents running for reelection won, the reelection rate for House Republican incumbents was almost 90 percent. In wave elections such as the one in 2010, one party's House reelection rate is significantly higher than that of the other party's; in normal elections such as the one in 2014, the House reelection rates are similar and approach 100 percent. Reelection rates for Senate incumbents are somewhat lower but show the same patterns.

Reelection rates for members of Congress are so high because the members work to insulate themselves from electoral challenges through tactics we discussed in this chapter and will discuss further in Chapter 11. They raise large sums of campaign cash well in advance of upcoming elections, use redistricting to give themselves a safe district populated by supporters, and enact pork-barrel legislation that provides government

FIGURE
9.3

Percentage of House Incumbents Reelected

The figure shows that, despite public dissatisfaction with Congress, incumbents still tend to be reelected in their respective districts. According to the chart, which congressional elections were wave elections? Which were normal elections?

Source: Calculated by the authors from election results.

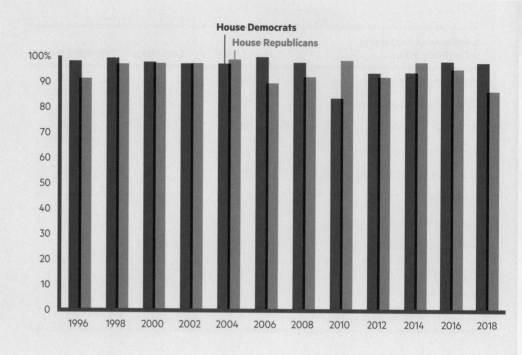

benefits and programs to their constituents. Even so, congressional incumbents are not necessarily safe from electoral defeat. Rather, their high reelection rates result from the actions they take every day, which are calculated to win favor with their constituents. In normal elections, these strategies are generally enough to ensure reelection. In nationalized elections, however, they are not enough to guarantee reelection for some legislators from the disadvantaged party, such as Democrats in 2010.

Wave elections are relatively rare. Most of the time, not many citizens are highly concerned about national issues or hold strong opinions about the president, Congress, or the overall state of the nation. Congressional incumbents also work hard to focus attention during their campaigns on the good things they have done for their constituents. And it is important to remember that even in wave elections some voters still use the incumbent-centered cues described earlier. In a wave election, voters don't suddenly become better informed about politics. Rather, some of them just switch to a different set of voting cues depending on the circumstances of the election.

"Why Should I Care?"

After each election, people look at the results and try to figure out what the election was about—why some candidates won and others lost. Before each election, would-be candidates wonder whether this is "the year" to run for office (you may be one of these candidates someday). The most important thing to understand is that there are no easy explanations and no guarantees. The problem is not that voters are fickle or clueless or that the rules are too complex. Rather, elections boil down to voters and the many different ways they decide how to vote. Knowing what is likely to influence voters can help you make predictions about who will win elections and thus what policies and issues government will tackle.

Understanding the 2016 and 2018 elections

In recent years, every election has been described as "the most important election in American history." And in truth, elections always matter because they determine who exercises power in Washington—who sets government policy. During the 2016 campaign, for example, it seemed likely that America's next president would appoint several Supreme Court justices, leading to significant policy changes on issues like abortion and affirmative action. Republican control of the presidency would make it easier to repeal President Obama's health care and financial reforms, as well as his executive orders. As we discuss throughout this book, the election of Donald Trump in 2016 has brought many of these outcomes to pass.

The essential question in 2018 was whether voters would support the Trump-Republican policy agenda of tax cuts, reductions in domestic spending and increases in military spending, loosening of business and environmental regulations, reestablishment of tariffs, further restrictions on immigration, and selection of conservatives to the federal judiciary. For Democrats, 2018 represented an opportunity to block this agenda, along with the possibility of leading investigations into the Trump administration, provided they could regain control of at least one chamber of Congress.

In political terms, the 2018 elections were scrutinized to see if the patterns seen in the 2016 elections would prove lasting or transitory. Would Republicans retain gains in rural and suburban areas, and among less-educated voters? Would the gender gap widen or narrow? Would minority turnout, which dropped in 2016, increase to earlier levels? The answers would determine which party held majorities in the House and Senate, and thereby shape the trajectory of government policy over the next two years.

Elections matter, especially when they determine who controls the congressional agenda. Republican gains in the Senate in 2014 led to Mitch McConnell (R-KY) taking over as Senate Majority Leader.

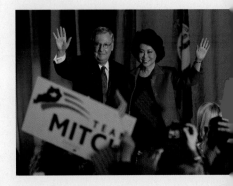

The path to 2018: the 2016 elections

The first thing to understand about the 2016 elections is their uniqueness. For the first time in 50 years, a major party nominated a presidential candidate with no prior political experience, Republican Donald Trump. Trump also ran a unique campaign, with limited advertising, a weak ground game, and a willingness to deviate from the standard Republican platform on issues such as trade, civil liberties, and foreign policy. He was the least popular major-party presidential nominee of all time, and many Republican elected officials and party leaders refused to support Trump in the general election. Democrats in 2016 selected Hillary Clinton, a former First Lady, senator, and secretary of state, as their nominee. This choice was historic: Clinton was the first woman to lead a major-party presidential ticket in America. Even so, Clinton's popularity was only somewhat higher than Trump's.

In retrospect, the conditions of the 2016 Republican nomination were ideal for a candidate like Trump. None of the other Republican candidates had the combination of organization, campaign funds, endorsements, and voter appeal needed to claim the status of frontrunner. Among these candidates, Trump stood out because of his preexisting high name recognition, his popularity among a large group of Republican primary voters, and his ability to largely self-fund his nomination campaign.

In congressional elections, attention focused largely on Senate races, as Democrats needed to gain only five Senate seats to take majority control of the chamber (four if a Democrat won the presidency). In a reversal of 2014, the fundamentals in 2016 favored Democrats, who had only 10 seats to defend. In contrast, 22 Republican senators were

Donald Trump's victory in the 2016 presidential campaign was a shock to many, even his supporters.

up for reelection (plus two open seats). Republican control of the House was thought to be largely secure, given the party's substantial 32-seat majority and a relatively low number of electorally vulnerable members on both sides.

While there were clear differences between the presidential candidates on issues ranging from immigration reform to gun control, there was an even bigger difference in their diagnoses of what was needed to effect policy change in Washington. The message from Clinton's campaign was that partisan conflict reflected sincere differences of opinion, differences that often cannot be compromised. In contrast, Donald Trump argued that his management experience and deal-making talents would give him a unique ability to broker deals. Trump also referred to Clinton as "Crooked Hillary," arguing that, because Clinton had worked as a senator and secretary of state, she was at least partly responsible for policy failures and gridlock in Washington.

By mid-October, Trump had lost significant support from Independents and Republicans due to several allegations of sexual harassment and assault and because of his poor performance during the three debates. In the last two weeks of the campaign, however, the polling gap between Trump and Clinton narrowed considerably, partly driven by a reopening of the FBI investigation into Clinton's use of a private e-mail server. On Election Day, Trump benefited from significantly higher than expected turnout in rural communities, which helped him win the Democratic strongholds of Michigan, Pennsylvania, and Wisconsin. And while Clinton received strong support from African-American, Latino, and younger voters (see Figure 9.4), lower than expected turnout from these groups cost Clinton support. Clinton won more votes overall, but Trump prevailed in the electoral college (see Figure 9.5). Notably, Trump won the election despite receiving fewer votes than losing 2012 Republican candidate, Mitt Romney.

The overriding factor driving the 2016 results was turnout, especially the failure of the Democrats' get-out-the-vote drive compared to the much more modest Republican effort. Trump did not improve on Mitt Romney's poor showing with minority voters in 2012, but lower turnout from these groups was a key factor in Clinton's defeat. Additionally, policy preferences on issues such as immigration reform and the economy were drawn on strongly partisan lines. Vote decisions in 2016 were also highly correlated with evaluations of President Obama (people critical of Obama were more likely to vote for Trump), which makes sense given the importance of party identification in shaping presidential approval.

FIGURE 9.4

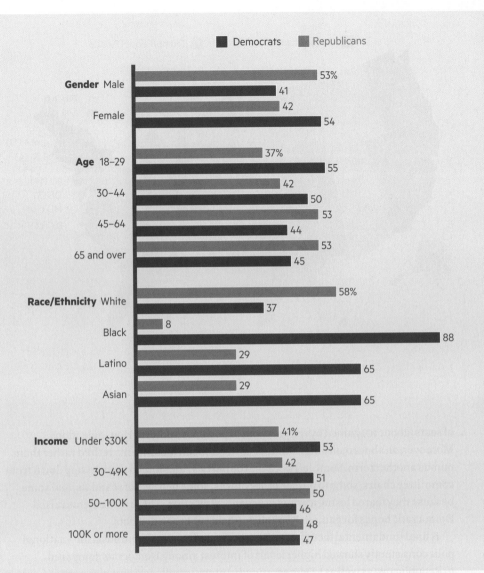

■ Democrats ■ Republicans

Gender		
Male	53%	41
Female	42	54

Age		
18–29	37%	55
30–44	42	50
45–64	53	44
65 and over	53	45

Race/Ethnicity		
White	58%	37
Black	8	88
Latino	29	65
Asian	29	65

Income		
Under $30K	41%	53
30–49K	42	51
50–100K	50	46
100K or more	48	47

Groups and Votes in the 2016 Election

This figure shows variation in group support for Democrats and Republicans in the 2016 elections. How did the positions and issues emphasized by candidates in the two parties create or strengthen these differences?

Source: CNN Exit Poll, www.cnn.com/election/results/exits-polls/national/house (accessed 11/9/16).

The 2018 midterms

The 2018 election involved campaigns for all 435 seats in the House of Representatives, as well as 35 Senate elections. At first glance, electoral forces favored Republicans in 2018, with a strong economy and no major international conflicts. However, sustained partisan polarization meant that economic factors were relatively less important than in previous elections. For many Americans, vote decisions were driven by party identification, and their approval or disapproval of President Trump's performance in office.

The most important structural feature of 2018 was the partisan division of Senate seats: of the 35 seats contested, Democrats controlled 26 and the Republicans only 9. Moreover, of the dozen or so seats that were truly in play, 10 were Democratic, many of them in strongly Republican states such as North Dakota, where President Trump defeated Hillary Clinton in 2016 by more than 35 points. Democrats had to divide campaign resources among a much larger number of seats than Republicans, so the odds favored Republican rather than Democratic gains.

In contrast, Democrats had notable opportunities in House contests. Democrats needed 23 seats to regain majority control—a number smaller than the average number

FIGURE
9.5

The 2016 Presidential Election: State by State

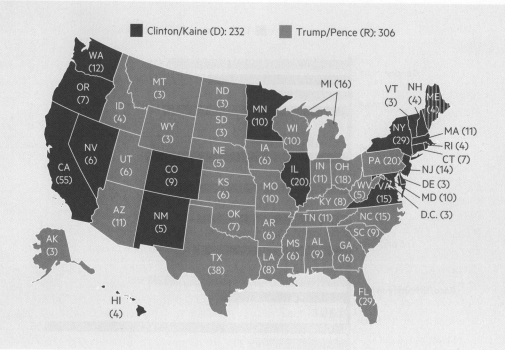

Clinton/Kaine (D): 232   Trump/Pence (R): 306

WA (12) | OR (7) | MT (3) | ND (3) | MN (10) | MI (16) | VT (3) | NH (4) | ME (4)
ID (4) | WY (3) | SD (3) | WI (10) | NY (29) | MA (11)
NV (6) | UT (6) | NE (5) | IA (6) | IL (20) | IN (11) | OH (18) | PA (20) | RI (4) | CT (7)
CA (55) | CO (9) | KS (6) | MO (10) | KY (8) | WV (5) | VA (15) | NJ (14) | DE (3) | MD (10)
AZ (11) | NM (5) | OK (7) | AR (6) | TN (11) | NC (15) | D.C. (3)
AK (3) | TX (38) | LA (8) | MS (6) | AL (9) | GA (16) | SC (9)
HI (4) | FL (29)

of seats (about 30) gained by the party out of power in midterm House elections. Moreover, an abnormally high number of Republican incumbents retired rather than pursue another term. Some left because the party's rules forced them to step down from committee chairs, some to pursue other offices, some because of scandals, and some because they feared losing a primary or general election. These retirements raised Democratic hopes for gains in Republican-held suburban districts.

A final fundamental factor was a Democratic advantage in enthusiasm—national polls consistently showed higher levels of interest among Democrats compared to Republicans, as well as a Democratic advantage in polls asking which party respondents would like to control Congress. Of course, because these polls aggregated results across the entire nation, they did not provide much information about specific races, where voters might favor one party over the other, or where a candidate might run a poor campaign or be beset by scandals. It was also unclear whether these Democratic advantages would translate into higher turnout on Election Day.

The Campaign The early months of the election cycle set the tone for the entire campaign. In House campaigns, Democrats fielded many well-funded, politically experienced candidates, while Republicans struggled to find good replacements for retiring incumbents or as challengers against Democrats. And while Senate Republicans reinforced their structural advantage by nominating a slate of well-qualified candidates (including several House members and governors), Democratic incumbents such as John Tester (D-MT) and Joe Manchin (D-WV) ran effective campaigns that highlighted their attention to local concerns and willingness to vote with President Trump on issues vital to their states. Democrats also outraised their Republican opponents in many races, although this advantage was narrowed by independent groups aligned with Republicans.

In October, public attention to the hearings for Supreme Court nominee Brett Kavanaugh (and accusations of sexual assault against the nominee) appeared to generate slightly increased enthusiasm among Republican voters, but had little impact on most races. In the closing weeks of the campaign, most national-level predictions were close to expectations at the beginning of the election cycle: Democrats were likely to win a House majority, while Republicans would hold the Senate.

Within the parties, however, the campaign revealed important disagreements on policy. In several Democratic primaries, liberal challengers unseated long-time incumbent House members, including Joe Crowley (D-NY), who was Chair of the Democratic Caucus. Many other Democratic challengers refused to commit to voting for Minority Leader Nancy Pelosi as Speaker if Democrats regained the majority. On the Republican side, several incumbents, including senators Jeff Flake (R-AZ) and Bob Corker (R-TN), retired in the face of strong conservative opposition.

The Election During the final weeks of the campaign, polls revealed that many House and Senate seats were still in play, as President Trump also crisscrossed the country, holding rallies in strongly Republican areas. In the end, the 2018 election met expectations: Democrats gained a House majority by capturing Republican suburban districts and capitalizing on Republican open seats. In Senate elections, Democrats captured two seats (Nevada and Arizona) but lost other races, allowing Republicans to retain their Senate majority.

Exit polls that asked respondents about their vote in House elections showed that, for the most part, vote decisions reflected partisanship and opinions about President Trump (see Table 9.6). The 2018 results also showed a strong gender gap, with higher rates of Democratic voting among women, as well as a strong correlation of Democratic voting with race and with education. Moreover, voters who ranked health care

The 2018 midterms favored Republicans in the Senate because they had fewer seats to defend. However, Dean Heller (R-NV), the only Republican senator up for reelection in a state Hillary Clinton won in 2016, lost despite support from President Trump.

TABLE 9.6

Exit Polls in the 2018 Elections

Note: Results data may not always add up to 100 percent due to rounding.

Source: 2018 CNN Exit Poll, www.cnn .com/election/2018/exit-polls (accessed 11/7/18)

		Democrat	Republican
Approval of President Trump	Approve (45%)	11%	88%
	Disapprove (54%)	90	8
Most important issue	Health care (41%)	75	23
	Immigration (23%)	23	75
	Economy (22%)	34	65
	Gun policy (10%)	70	29
Gender	Male (48%)	47	51
	Female (52%)	59	40
Race	White (72%)	44	56
	Non-white (28%)	76	22
Education	College graduate (41%)	59	39
	Not college graduate (59%)	49	49
Partisanship	Democrats (37%)	95	4
	Republicans (33%)	6	94
	Independents (30%)	54	42

and federal gun policy as the most important issues were much more likely to vote Democratic, while voters who saw immigration or the economy as the most important issue showed similarly high rates of voting for Republicans.

Unpacking the Conflict

Considering all that we've discussed in this chapter, let's apply what we know about how elections work to the example of Doug Jones's victory in the 2017 Alabama special election introduced at the beginning of this chapter. Ultimately, how meaningful was Doug Jones's victory in Alabama—or the combination of Democratic House victories and Senate defeats in 2018? What can it tell us about why some candidates win and others lose?

Candidates in American national elections compete for different offices using a variety of rules that determine who can run for office, who can vote, and how ballots are counted and winners determined. Election outcomes are shaped not only by who runs for office and how they campaign, who decides to vote, and how they decide whom to support, but also by the rules that govern electoral competition. By taking these factors into account, we can explain why Doug Jones beat Roy Moore, why Donald Trump defeated Hillary Clinton in 2016—or why Republicans lost the House in 2018 but kept majority control of the Senate.

It is easy to complain about American elections. Citizens are not experts on public policy. They often know little about the candidates running for office. Candidates sensationalize, attack, and dissemble rather than giving details about what they would do if elected. Even so, however candidates campaign and voters vote, elections matter: there are clear, systematic differences between Democratic and Republican candidates that translate into different government policies depending on who holds office. Government policy is different as a result of Trump's victory in 2016, and future policy will reflect the fact that Democrats gained control of the House in 2018.

Campaigns and election outcomes would surely be different if more Americans were well informed about candidates and campaign platforms, if turnout was higher, if campaigns always focused on important issues facing the country, and if attack ads never worked. Even so, despite all their limitations, elections are how we decide who gets to run the government. And as we have discussed, election outcomes are somewhat predictable—they are the product of national and local rules and regulations; the fundamentals of district factors and national forces; candidates' campaign strategies; and citizens' decisions about whether to vote and whom to vote for. The outcome of every election is the result of all these individual-level choices added together. In that sense, election outcomes reflect the preferences of the American people.

What's Your Take?

Do the campaigns that candidates run significantly affect election outcomes, or are the outcomes out of the candidates' control? Are individual election outcomes representative of larger trends?

STUDY GUIDE

How do American elections work?

Present the major rules and procedures of American elections. (Pages 298–309)

Summary

Elections in America generally have two steps. Primary elections select candidates for each party, and general elections determine who wins the office. Some of the rules for presidential elections differ from those for other elections; notably, the electoral college system determines the winner of the general election.

Key terms

incumbent (p. 298)
primary (p. 299)
open primary (p. 299)
semi-closed primary (p. 299)
closed primary (p. 299)
general election (p. 299)
plurality voting (p. 301)
majority voting (p. 301)
runoff election (p. 301)

caucus (p. 302)
proportional allocation (p. 303)
winner-take-all (p. 303)
popular vote (p. 304)
electoral college (p. 304)
electoral votes (p. 304)

Practice Quiz Questions

1. **Runoff elections occur only in states that use _____.**
   a majority voting
   b primary elections
   c plurality voting
   d absentee ballots
   e proportional allocation

2. **The recent trend in the presidential nomination process has been to _____.**
   a schedule primary elections later in the process
   b add so-called regional primaries
   c replace primaries with caucuses
   d break up primaries so that they are not held in the same region at the same time
   e limit the influence of third-party candidates

3. **The winner-take-all method of allocating most states' electoral votes results in candidates focusing on _____ states and _____ states.**
   a low-population; safe
   b high-population; safe
   c low-population; swing
   d high-population; swing
   e safe; swing

Electoral campaigns

Describe the features, strategies, and funding of campaigns for federal office. (Pages 309–325)

Summary

Party organizations and candidates begin preparing for the next election the day after the last election ends. They focus on fund-raising and determining which races are likely to be competitive. Incumbents work throughout the election cycle to maintain their good standing among the voters and secure their reelection bids. During a campaign, candidates work hard, particularly through the use of advertisements, to increase their name recognition and mobilize their supporters.

Key terms

election cycle (p. 309)
open seat (p. 311)
GOTV ("get out the vote") or the **ground game** (p. 317)

Federal Election Commission (p. 320)
hard money (p. 322)
soft money (p. 322)

Practice Quiz Questions

4. **An open-seat election is one in which _____.**
   a there is no challenger in the race
   b there is no incumbent in the race
   c an incumbent loses his or her seat due to redistricting
   d an incumbent faces a challenger in his or her own primary
   e an incumbent faces a challenger in the general election

5. **What effect does fund-raising have for incumbents?**
   a It ensures the potential for an aggressive campaign, but it has no effect on opposition.
   b It ensures the potential for an aggressive campaign, and it deters opposition.
   c It ensures the potential for an aggressive campaign, and it encourages opposition.
   d It has no effect on the potential for an aggressive campaign, but it does deter opposition.
   e It has no effect on the potential for an aggressive campaign, nor does it deter opposition.

6. **"GOTV" and "ground game" refer to a candidate's attempts to _____.**

a   boost name recognition

b   mobilize supporters

c   increase fund-raising

d   deter opposition

e   win endorsements

7. **Research shows that modern campaign ads are likely to _____.**

a   change voters' minds

b   feature speeches by the candidate

c   have beneficial effects, such as informing voters

d   run several minutes in length

e   increase turnout

8. **What is soft money?**

a   money that can be given directly to a candidate

b   money that is given by members of the opposing party

c   money that can be spent to mobilize voters for a specific candidate

d   money that candidates spend to boost the party's reputation

e   money that is not tied to a specific candidate

How do voters decide?

Explain the key factors that influence voters' choices. (Pages 326–330)

Summary

Although politics is everywhere, ordinary voters don't pay much attention to politics. Turnout rates are modest, and people know relatively little about the candidates and their positions. While some voters are highly interested in politics and collect all the information they can about the candidates, most voters make their decision based on voting cues. Most elections are determined by local-level politics, but occasionally national issues come to the fore.

Key terms

paradox of voting (p. 326)   coattails (p. 328)

issue voters (p. 327)   split ticket (p. 328)

voting cues (p. 327)   straight ticket (p. 328)

Practice Quiz Questions

9. **What is the paradox of voting?**

a   Voting is costly, and the chances of affecting the election outcome are small.

b   Voting is costly, and approval for government is high.

c   Voting is easy, and the chances of affecting the election outcome are large.

d   Voting is easy, but informing yourself about the candidates takes time.

e   Approval for government is low, but voter turnout rates are high.

10. **Voters who rely on voting cues to determine their voting choice are _____.**

a   likely to cast a reasonable vote, regardless of their information level

b   unlikely to cast a reasonable vote, regardless of their information level

c   likely to cast a reasonable vote, and more so if they are informed

d   unlikely to cast a reasonable vote, and less so if they are informed

e   neither more nor less likely to cast a reasonable vote than voters who ignore cues

11. **Weak coattails and split tickets serve as indicators that _____.**

a   most voters don't know anything about the candidates

b   most elections are determined by local issues

c   most elections are determined by national issues

d   most voters use political parties as their dominant voting cue

e   most voters use incumbency as their dominant voting cue

Understanding the 2016 and 2018 elections

Analyze the issues and outcomes in the 2016 and 2018 elections. (Pages 331–336)

Summary

Donald Trump's victory in the 2016 elections, along with unified Republican control of Congress, led to significant changes in government policy during the first two years of Trump's presidency. However, Democrats regained control of the House in the 2018 midterms, giving them the power to block many additional changes, as well as the ability to investigate Republican-led agencies and Trump himself. The next two years are likely to continue to demonstrate the conflictual nature of contemporary politics.

Practice Quiz Questions

12. **What is the most accurate statement about the role of presidential approval in the 2018 election?**

a   Looking across the entire nation, presidential approval shifted votes to Trump.

b   Economic factors played a much greater role in vote decisions.

c   Republicans deserted Trump because of their disapproval of his performance in office.

d   Presidential approval did not matter because most Americans based their vote on other issues.

e   Evaluations of Trump played a significant role in vote and turnout decisions.

13. How did the electoral map favor Republican Senate candidates in 2018?

a   Democratic efforts at redistricting gave the Democrats a sharp advantage in Senate contests.

b   Economic growth was uneven across the states, particularly in Senate seats controlled by the Democrats.

c   Democrats had to defend a disproportionate number of Senate seats, and many of these seats were in states where Republicans outnumbered Democrats.

d   Independent candidates drew votes away from Democratic candidates.

e   Republican candidates were more likely to lose in states where a majority of voters supported Donald Trump.

14. Which of the following is the most important factor in explaining Democratic victories in states where Trump won in 2016?

a   the fact that more Americans are Democrats than Republicans

b   perceptions of Trump as trustworthy and honest

c   heightened partisanship and Democratic enthusiasm in suburban areas

d   widespread dislike of Barack Obama and Nancy Pelosi

e   the decision by former senator Hillary Clinton to campaign for Democratic candidates in these states

Suggested Reading

Abramson, Paul, John Aldrich, and David Rohde. *Change and Continuity in the 2012 and 2014 Elections.* Washington, DC: CQ Press, 2015.

Bartels, Larry M., and Christopher H. Achen. *Democracy for Realists: Why Elections Do Not Produce Responsive Government.* Princeton, NJ: Princeton University Press, 2016.

Cramer, Richard Ben. *What It Takes: The Way to the White House.* New York: Vintage Books, 1993.

Fiorina, Morris P. *Retrospective Voting in American National Elections.* New Haven, CT: Yale University Press, 1981.

Grimmer, Justin, Sean J. Westwood, and Solomon Messing. *The Impression of Influence: Legislator Communications, Representation, and Democratic Accountability.* Princeton, NJ: Princeton University Press, 2015.

Halperin, Mark, and John Heilemann. *Double Down: Game Change 2012.* New York: Penguin Books, 2013.

Key, V. O. *The Responsible Electorate.* New York: Vintage Books, 1966.

Popkin, Samuel. *The Reasoning Voter.* Chicago: University of Chicago Press, 1991.

Sides, John, and Lynn Vavreck. *The Gamble: Choice and Chance in the 2012 Presidential Election.* Princeton, NJ: Princeton University Press, 2013.

10

Interest Groups

Do interest groups serve the needs of the many, or the privileged few?

» **"The Democratic majority decided, well look, while we're at it, let's have another Washington takeover. Let's take over the federal student loan program."**
Senator Lamar Alexander (R-TN)

« **"It probably won't surprise you to learn that the big banks and financial institutions hired an army of lobbyists to protect the status quo.... But I didn't stand with the banks and the financial industries in this fight.... We stood with America's students."**
President Barack Obama

There are more than 20 million college students in America today. Many of these students (or their parents) take on large student loans to fund their education. Until recently, banks and other financial institutions provided the money for loans and earned large fees as intermediaries. In 2010, President Obama proposed that the federal government make the loans directly to students and their parents, which would reduce borrowing costs and free up billions of dollars for Pell grants and other programs benefiting college students.

At first glance, reducing the cost of student loans should be an easy sell—who would oppose making college more affordable? The answer is the companies and institutions that make money originating and managing these loans—financial institutions such as Sallie Mae, Citibank, and others. If the government provided direct loans, these financial institutions would lose a lucrative source of income. To stop this legislation, these institutions spent millions of dollars on lobbyists to make their case to the public and Congress, emphasizing that direct loans would put thousands of their employees out of work (and reminding politicians that many of those who work for the financial institutions live and vote in political swing states like Florida). Opponents of the legislation, such as Senator Lamar Alexander (R-TN), lamented that this would be an unnecessary "government takeover" of a privately run program. Supporters pointed to the money that would be shifted from banks to students.

The debate over federal direct student loans pitted well-funded banks and other financial institutions against millions of college students and their parents. Did the banks' ability to lobby members of Congress and bureaucrats translate into a policy victory?

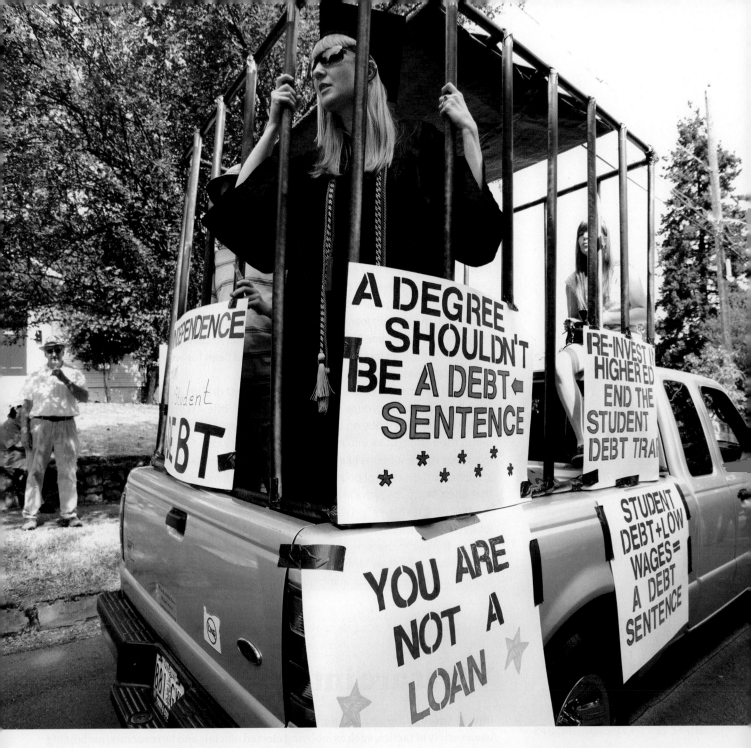

Signs displayed: "INDEPENDENCE", "Student DEBT", "A DEGREE SHOULDN'T BE A DEBT SENTENCE", "RE-INVEST IN HIGHER ED END THE STUDENT DEBT TRAIN", "STUDENT DEBT + LOW WAGES = A DEBT SENTENCE", "YOU ARE NOT A LOAN"

★
―――
**CHAPTER
GOALS**

Define *interest groups* and describe the characteristics of different types of groups. pages 342–352

Explain how successful interest groups overcome collective action problems. pages 352–354

Explore the ways interest groups try to influence government policies. pages 355–364

Evaluate interest group influence. pages 365–369

For most Americans, this story looks all too common: organized, well-funded groups lobbying against changes that would benefit broader segments of the population. How can individuals have a voice in the policy process when they are fighting against organizations that have millions of dollars and extensive connections on their side? Even if individuals try to form new groups to advance their policy goals, their battle against well-entrenched and well-funded groups does not seem like a fair fight.

Surprisingly, the case of student loans is one where David appears to have beaten Goliath. Despite intense, well-funded lobbying against direct loans, legislation implementing this change was enacted in 2010—meaning that you and your parents are now able to get lower-interest loans directly from the federal government. The move was so popular that even when Republicans regained control of Congress and Donald Trump was elected president, they left the program in place. However, Trump's proposed 2018 budget attempted to alter other aspects of the program, such as eliminating the student loan forgiveness program. But Congress expanded the popular program with a one-time $350 million appropriation to cover those who thought they qualified for the loan forgiveness program but had been turned down for various bureaucratic reasons.[1]

This chapter surveys the wide range of interest groups in American politics— from large, powerful groups such as the National Rifle Association (NRA) to small organizations that lobby on issues that concern only a few Americans. Our aim is to get to the bottom of examples where the lobbyists lose, like student loan reform, examples where it seems like the lobbyists always win, like the NRA's apparent influence on gun control policy. Some people, like Senator Alexander, would argue that interest groups provide a necessary check on the federal government's tendency to "take over" private industry. However, many others always root for lobbyists, with their perceived insider connections and undue influence, to lose their battles. Is it fair to characterize all interest groups, like those that worked against student loan reform, as "armies of lobbyists" on self-interested missions? Are interest groups really too-powerful manipulators of the American policy process?

DEFINE *INTEREST GROUPS* AND DESCRIBE THE CHARACTERISTICS OF DIFFERENT TYPES OF GROUPS

interest group
An organization of people who share common political interests and aim to influence public policy by electioneering and lobbying.

lobbying
Efforts to influence public policy through contact with public officials on behalf of an interest group.

What are interest groups?

Interest groups are organizations that seek to influence government policy. They use a variety of tactics, such as lobbying elected officials and bureaucrats, mobilizing group members and the public, and helping to elect candidates who support the organizations' policy goals. In its most basic form, **lobbying** involves persuasion and monitoring policy development by using reports, protests, informal meetings, or other techniques to convince an elected official or bureaucrat to help enact a law, craft a regulation, or do something else that a group wants. The members of an interest group can be individual citizens, local governments, businesses, foundations or nonprofit organizations, churches, or virtually any other entity. An interest group's employees or members may lobby on the group's behalf, or a group may hire a lobbyist or lobbying firm to do the work for it. Groups may lobby on their own or work with other groups to enact compromise proposals. Many organizations also have lobbying operations or hire lobbyists to work on their behalf. (See Nuts & Bolts 10.1 for some examples of the types of interest groups found in contemporary American politics.)

Types of Interest Groups

Scholars often divide interest groups into categories based on who their members are or the number or kinds of things they lobby for.

- *Institutional interest groups* are formed by nonprofits such as universities, think tanks, or museums. For example, the Big Ten Academic Alliance is a group of universities that prepares research to help individual universities make the case for continued federal support.
- *Businesses* are for-profit enterprises that aim to influence policy in ways that will increase profits or satisfy other goals. Many corporations, such as Google, Exxon, Boeing, Facebook, Citibank, and Sallie Mae, have lobbying operations that petition government for contracts or favorable regulations of their firm or industry.
- *Trade or peak associations* are groups of businesses (often in the same industry) that band together to lobby for policies that benefit all of them. For example, the National Beer Wholesalers Association, a nationwide group of local businesses that buy beer from brewers and resell it to stores and restaurants, lobbies to require intermediaries between beer producers and the stores, bars, and restaurants that sell beer to consumers.

- *Professional associations* represent individuals who have a common interest in a profession; for example, the American Society of Civil Engineers, National Education Association, American Medical Association, and American Bar Association.
- *Labor organizations* lobby for regulations that make it easy for workers to form labor unions, as well as for a range of other policies. The largest of these is the American Federation of Labor and Congress of Industrial Organizations (AFL-CIO).
- *Citizen groups* range from those with mass membership (such as the Sierra Club) to those that have no members but claim to speak for particular segments of the population. One such group is the Family Research Council (FRC), which describes itself as "promoting the Judeo-Christian worldview as the basis for a just, free, and stable society." FRC Action (the lobbying arm of the organization) promotes a range of policies, from legislation that defines marriage as between a man and a woman to legislation that would eliminate estate taxes.

Some interest groups have primarily political motives and goals. One such group is Public Citizen, which conducts research projects, lobbies legislators and bureaucrats, and tries to rally public opinion on a range of environmental, health, and energy issues. In other cases, lobbying is only one part of what an organization does. The NRA, for example, endorses candidates, contributes to campaigns, and lobbies elected officials, but it also runs gun safety classes, holds competitions, and sells gun accessories to its members. Interest group activity is almost hidden within other organizations. For example, most drivers know that AAA (formerly the American Automobile Association) provides emergency roadside service and maps, but many people are not aware that AAA is also an interest group that lobbies for policies such as limiting new drivers to daylight-only hours.

As these descriptions suggest, interest groups and lobbying are ubiquitous in American politics. You may think that you don't belong to a group that lobbies the federal government, but the odds are that you do. In fact, one important view of American politics, *pluralism*, identifies interest groups as America's fundamental political actors.[2] Pluralists argue that most Americans participate in politics through their membership in interest groups like Public Citizen, the NRA, or even AAA. These groups lobby, try to elect candidates who share their views, and negotiate among themselves to encourage legislators to pursue policies that benefit their members. Pluralists see interest groups as important and appropriate participants in the democratic process. Others see interest groups in a more negative light, describing America as an **interest group state**, meaning that these groups are involved whenever policy is made, but in a self-interested way that can undermine the collective good.[3] More recent perspectives on interest group pluralism, such as Frank Baumgartner and coauthors' study of lobbying,[4] note that interest groups' influence is contextual and depends on a number of factors, but their importance in the political system is clear.

interest group state
A government in which most policy decisions are determined by the influence of interest groups.

The business of lobbying

Interest group lobbying is regulated.[5] Lobbying firms must file quarterly reports identifying their clients, specifying how much each client paid, and the issues they lobbied on. Similarly, interest groups and corporations must file reports listing staff members who spent more than 20 percent of their time lobbying Congress, and total expenditures to lobbying firms. Also, most executive or legislative branch employees who take lobbying jobs are legally required to refrain from lobbying people in their former office or agency for one year; elected officials who become lobbyists must wait two years.

Today lobbying involves billions of dollars a year. Figure 10.1 (top) presents annual lobbying expenditures for 2000 through 2017. As the figure shows, a total of $3.37 billion

FIGURE 10.1

Growth in Spending on Lobbying and Total Federal Spending, 2000–2017

These data show that in recent years interest groups have spent several billion dollars lobbying the federal government. Does this amount seem surprisingly large or surprisingly small, given what lobbyists do and given the total federal outlays of money?

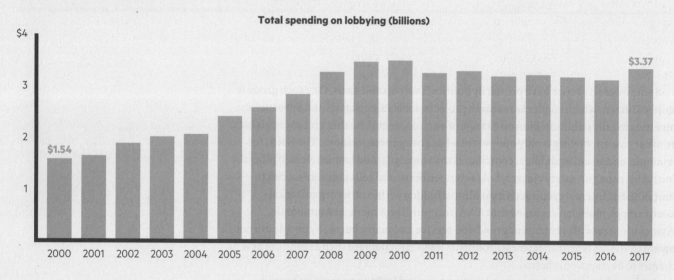

Total spending on lobbying (billions)

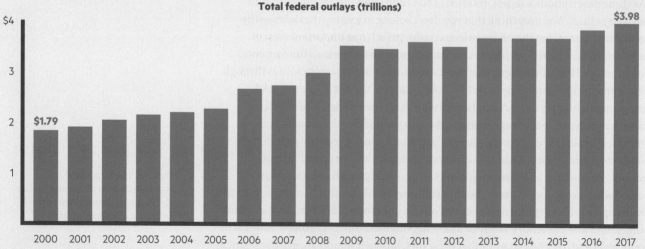

Total federal outlays (trillions)

Sources: Lobbying data available at Center for Responsive Politics, "Lobbying Database," www.opensecrets.org/lobby; Federal spending from Congressional Budget Office, Historical Budget Data, April 2018, www.cbo.gov/about/products/budget-economic-data#2 (both accessed 8/16/18).

was spent on lobbying in 2017. The amount spent as well as the number of groups lobbying government increased significantly from 2000 to 2010 and has held steady since then.

Why are there so many interest groups and registered lobbyists, and why are their numbers increasing? Figure 10.1 (bottom) suggests that this proliferation is related to the large size and widespread influence of the federal government. Simply put, the federal government does so many things and spends so much money that many individuals, organizations, and corporations have strong incentives for lobbying: corporations may lobby for a government contract or for regulations that favor their business sector. Corporations may also lobby to prevent new regulations or reverse existing rules that hurt their profits: in the first two months of the Trump administration, Congress reversed 14 regulations that were passed at the end of Obama's presidency, and 67 environmental rules were overturned in Trump's first year.[6] Energy companies lobbied hard on the Keystone XL pipeline, offshore drilling in the Atlantic and Arctic Oceans, and calculations of the social cost of carbon, and they won. While business dominates lobbying spending, individuals may lobby the government to place limits on what citizens can do or to relax restrictions on behavior—or to change corporate behavior. Trade unions and single-issue groups also spend millions of dollars on lobbying.

Studies of Washington-based lobbying operations confirm this: interest groups are more likely to form around issues that have high levels of government involvement or when new programs or changes in government policy are likely.[7] Moreover, as groups form on one side of a policy question and start to lobby, people who oppose them may form their own interest groups and start lobbying as well, either separately or in concert.[8] The pressure of lobbying is especially strong when new policies are under consideration, such as in the move to direct student loans. Firms such as Sallie Mae had always lobbied elected officials and bureaucrats, but the prospect of losing lucrative student loan operations gave these institutions a strong incentive to increase their efforts. In fact, the data show that over the last 15 years Sallie Mae spent over $40 million on direct lobbying, and even more was spent by associations and other groups that the firm was a member of.

Expenditures on lobbying pay for many things. For example, while engineers at the Lockheed Martin Corporation worked to build the new F-35 fighter-attack plane for the military, Lockheed's lobbyists were working to ensure that the program retained its government funding and that Lockheed had government approval for exporting the plane to other countries. These meetings involved members of Congress, congressional staff, senior members of President Bush's (and later Obama's) staff, and the leaders of labor unions whose members worked for Lockheed.[9] Lockheed also ran ads in newspapers in Washington, D.C., promoting its new warplane. Thus, to support its goal of F-35 sales, Lockheed paid the salaries of its employees who planned and executed the lobbying effort, paid for outside lobbyists and their meetings on Capitol Hill, and spent money on broader publicity efforts.

Figure 10.2 shows lobbying expenditures for several different firms and associations for the last two years with complete data (2016–2017). Four associations were the highest spenders on lobbying during this time. It's not hard to imagine why each group devotes so much effort to lobbying: realtors, for example, might be concerned about maintaining government policies that make it almost essential to hire a realtor to help buy or sell a home. While the $129 million the National Association of Realtors spent on lobbying may sound like a lot, it really isn't that much. After all, over a million people work in real estate, generating billions of dollars in profits every year. The surprise is that real estate brokers are willing to spend only a tiny fraction of their profits to keep their near monopoly in place. The same is true for the large firms listed in Figure 10.2. Apple, for example, is one of the largest firms in the United States, but it spends only about $6 million per year on

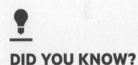

DID YOU KNOW?

38%

The percentage of total lobbying expenditures made by the top 100 interest groups.
Source: Opensecrets.org

FIGURE
10.2

Variation in Lobbying Expenditures, 2016–2017

Lobbying expenditures vary widely. Some influential groups (such as the U.S. Chamber of Commerce) spend hundreds of millions of dollars a year, but many other influential groups (such as NARAL Pro-Choice America and the Family Research Council) spend relatively little. How can groups have influence over government policy despite spending almost nothing on lobbying?

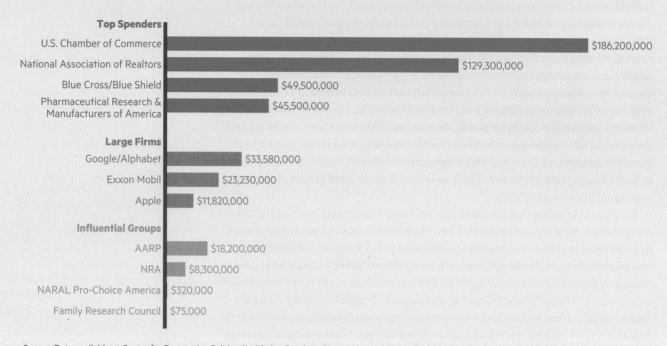

Top Spenders

U.S. Chamber of Commerce	$186,200,000
National Association of Realtors	$129,300,000
Blue Cross/Blue Shield	$49,500,000
Pharmaceutical Research & Manufacturers of America	$45,500,000

Large Firms

Google/Alphabet	$33,580,000
Exxon Mobil	$23,230,000
Apple	$11,820,000

Influential Groups

AARP	$18,200,000
NRA	$8,300,000
NARAL Pro-Choice America	$320,000
Family Research Council	$75,000

Source: Data available at Center for Responsive Politics, "Lobbying Database," www.opensecrets.org/lobby/index.php (accessed 8/21/18).

lobbying ($11.8 million over two years). And only one of the influential interest groups in Figure 10.2 (the AARP) spends more than $10 million per year on lobbying. Clearly, the big spenders on lobbying are exceptions to the rule, and most interest groups and firms spend relatively little on lobbying.[10] For example, the group that sends a turkey to the White House for a ceremonial pardon every year at Thanksgiving, the National Turkey Federation, spends $140,000 a year to lobby the federal government on a relatively small range of issues. Many other groups spend even less, barely scraping together enough cash to send someone to plead their case in Washington. In fact, a few groups account for a substantial fraction of total lobbying expenditures.

That concentration of spending is evident in another way as well: a large proportion of lobbying is done by the business sector and relatively little by political or public interests. All of the top six sectors were business interests (health, finance, miscellaneous business, communication, energy, and transportation), with 76 percent of the total spending on lobbying, while education, nonprofits, and public officials (listed under "Other") and ideological/single-issue political groups came in seventh and eighth, spending 6.6 and 4.4 percent respectively.[11]

Although the amount of money spent on lobbying by interest groups may seem like a lot (and often leads to calls for restrictions on lobbying, as discussed in the Take a Stand feature on page 349), it is small compared with how much is at stake.[12] The federal government now spends more than $4 trillion every year. In recent years, spending by interest groups and by the lobbying arms of organizations and corporations has amounted to $3 billion every year. That's a lot of money, but it's still only about one-tenth of 1 percent of total federal spending. This difference raises a critical question: If interest groups can control policy choices by spending money on lobbying, why aren't they spending more?

Organizational structures

There are two main models of interest group structure. Most large, well-known organizations like the AARP and the NRA are **centralized groups**, which means the organization's leadership is concentrated in its headquarters. These national organizations typically have headquarters in Washington, D.C., field offices in large state capitals, and members nationwide. Their leaders have the responsibility to determine the group's lobbying goals and tactics. The other structural model is a **confederation**, which is composed of largely independent, local organizations. For example, the National Independent Automobile Dealers Association (NIADA) is made up of 50 state-level organizations that provide membership benefits to car dealers who join the organization and that raise much of the money that NIADA contributes to candidates running for political office (several million dollars in recent elections).

Both organizational structures have advantages and disadvantages. A centralized organization controls all of the group's resources and can deploy them efficiently, but it can be challenging for these groups to find out what their members want. Confederations have the advantage of maintaining independent chapters at the state and local levels, so it is easier for the national headquarters to learn what their members want—all they have to do is contact their local groups. But this strength is closely related to a weakness: confederated groups are often beset with conflict. Since state and local chapters attract members and raise money largely on their own, they mostly function independently of the national headquarters. However, the national headquarters depends on the local organizations for funds to pay its staff and make campaign contributions. In return, it allows the locals to direct contributions to their preferred candidates, and different local chapters may disagree over what to lobby for and which candidates to support.

Some organizations are hard to categorize, such as the Indivisible grassroots progressive movement that started in 2016 in reaction to the election of Donald Trump. The organizations that make up this movement are very diverse. Some hold meetings or public protests, some endorse candidates, and some simply consist of a website run by one or two people. The issues that motivate each Indivisible organization also vary widely, from opposition to President Trump's policies to calls for radical changes in government. Virtually all the groups lack formal dues-paying members, a headquarters, and a formal organizational structure, and few engage in the wide range of lobbying activities that we describe later in this chapter. For all these reasons, very few of the organizations that identify themselves as part of Indivisible are interest groups as we describe them here, although some may evolve into formal interest groups in the future.

Staff

Interest group staff fall into two categories: experts on the group's main policy areas and people with useful government connections and knowledge of procedures. The first group includes scientists, engineers, and others with advanced degrees; the second is dominated by people who have worked inside government as elected

centralized groups
Interest groups that have a headquarters, usually in Washington, D.C., as well as members and field offices throughout the country. In general, these groups' lobbying decisions are made at headquarters by the group leaders.

confederations
Interest groups made up of several independent, local organizations that provide much of their funding and hold most of the power.

Centralized interest groups typically have headquarters close to Washington, D.C., such as the NRA's offices shown here in Fairfax, Virginia. These offices serve as a hub for the organization's leadership, and the close proximity to the capitol facilitates their lobbying goals.

revolving door
The movement of individuals from government positions to jobs with interest groups or lobbying firms, and vice versa.

DID YOU KNOW?

429

former members of Congress were registered lobbyists as of 2018.
Source: Opensecrets.org

officials, bureaucrats, or legislative staff.[13] Sometimes these former members of government are also policy experts, but their unique contribution is their knowledge of how government works and their relationships with officeholders and other former coworkers.

The practice of moving from a government position to a job with an interest group or lobbying firm, or of transitioning from a lobbyist job to holding office, is often called the **revolving door**.[14] For example, as of 2018, nearly two-thirds of the members of Congress who retired at the end of the 114th Congress and were employed had moved to lobbying jobs.[15] The percentages are similar for congressional staff and bureaucrats. Many observers view this dynamic as potentially sowing seeds of corruption; they fear that past government employees might capitalize on personal ties with their former colleagues to negotiate favorable deals for their interest groups—or that people working in government may give special treatment to a corporation or interest group that might hire them as a lobbyist in the future. These concerns have led to proposed restrictions on the revolving door, including banning former elected officials, staff, and bureaucrats from working as lobbyists for some time period after they have left government service, as well as banning former lobbyists in government positions from administering programs that they previously lobbied for. President Trump's vow to "drain the swamp" was centered on these proposals to limit the revolving door. Of the five specific promises to tighten restrictions on lobbying that he made during the 2016 campaign, only one has been fulfilled (an executive order that bans executive branch officials from lobbying for foreign governments and overseas political parties after they leave the administration).[16]

Such restrictions have costs as well as benefits. On the one hand, people who have worked in an industry or as lobbyists know a particular field and the relevant laws very well, making them well qualified to work in the corresponding area of the executive branch. Thus, a ban on hiring lobbyists may lead to a shortage of experienced candidates for government positions. Similarly, former officeholders, congressional staff, and bureaucrats are attractive candidates for lobbying jobs because they have firsthand knowledge of how policies are made and enjoy established relationships with people in government. On the other hand, these restrictions would help lower the potential for corruption mentioned earlier. It is very hard to craft restrictions that avoid these problems.

Restrictions on Interest Group Lobbying

Under current rules, members of Congress and their staffs are severely limited in the size of gifts they can receive from lobbyists. These restrictions were tightened in the mid-2000s after it was revealed that former-congressional-staffer-turned-lobbyist Jack Abramoff had used "golf junkets, free meals at the restaurant he owned, seats at sporting events, and, in some cases, old-fashioned cash" to lobby members of Congress.[a] The current restrictions limit members and their staffs to accepting gifts only if they are valued at less than $50—moreover, the total worth of the gifts that any lobbyist can give to a particular member of Congress or staffer is limited to $100 per year. In addition, "cooling off" rules, which prevent staffers and former members of Congress from lobbying for one year after leaving their government job, were instituted in an attempt to limit the revolving door between government and lobbying firms. President Trump vowed to "drain the swamp" of lobbyist influence in Washington, but little progress has been made on strengthening the rules. Are current restrictions fair? Do they help or hurt the political process? Are even stronger limitations needed?

Keep the rules, and maybe tighten them. Supporting this option seems like a no-brainer. These regulations are based on a sensible intuition that laws are needed to prevent well-funded, unscrupulous lobbyists from offering inducements to members of Congress and their staffs in return for policy change. Simply put, groups that can send people to Washington to wine and dine members of Congress, congressional staff, and bureaucrats might gain a significant advantage over those who are unable to do so. Even if a fancy lunch doesn't buy a legislator's vote, it might help with access—that is, give the group a chance to make their arguments and perhaps change some minds. In this way, rules that allow even small gifts create an advantage for interest groups that have a Washington office or hire lobbyists and a disadvantage for those that do not. As a result, many reform proposals should go further, preventing lobbyists from giving anything to a member of Congress, legislative staffer, or bureaucrat—even a cup of coffee.

Relax the rules (a little). Some argue that worries about interest group influence seem a little overstated. Congressional staff and the legislators they work for are going to support a group's proposals only if they help the member's constituents or if they move policy in a way the member favors, not just because of an interest group's free lunch.

When scandals surrounding Jack Abramoff came to light in 2005, many Americans considered him a typical lobbyist. Abramoff's actions were illegal, but the question remains: Are his tactics common in Washington, or was he a rare exception?

There are also downsides to tight controls on these gifts and perks. The current rules on lobbyists' gifts create a lot of paperwork for members and their staffs, who have to file reports on just about anything they receive from a lobbyist, even if that individual is a former colleague, neighbor, or friend. The rules are also extremely complicated—for example, legislators are allowed to eat the hors d'oeuvres provided at a reception, but they cannot sit down to a full meal without violating the gift restrictions. The disclosure requirements are also a burden to smaller interest groups and firms, which have to document everything they do on complex forms. As a result, members of Congress, their staff, interest groups, and lobbying firms spend considerable time and effort on documenting small gifts that are unlikely to have any effect on policy outcomes.

Do both. Another approach would be to relax some of the rules and strengthen others. For example, one suggestion is to get rid of the "cooling off" periods, but have better disclosure of who is lobbying so constituents will be able to hold their elected officials accountable. Many lobbyists skirt current disclosure rules by generously interpreting the 20 percent rule mentioned earlier in the chapter to exclude what most would consider lobbying activity. These "shadow lobbyists" would be exposed by stricter disclosure rules.[b]

take a stand

1. To what extent do you think current congressional rules limiting the size of gifts that members of Congress and their staffers can receive from lobbyists have curbed illegal behavior by interest groups?

2. Are these rules aimed at exceptional cases or average interest groups?

Many interest groups speak for large
numbers of Americans, while others
lobby for changes that would benefit
only a few people. Mass associations,
such as the Sierra Club, have large
numbers of dues-paying members.
Here, members in Michigan promote
biking, hiking, and skating in an annual
parade to raise awareness for muscle-
powered transportation, one of the
environmental issues the organization
promotes.

Membership

Interest groups can be categorized in terms of the size of their membership and the members' role in the group's activities. **Mass associations**, with many dues-paying members, tend to be citizens' groups and labor organizations. One example is the Sierra Club, which has over 3 million members. Besides keeping its members informed about the implementation of environmental policy in Washington, D.C., the Sierra Club endorses judicial nominees and candidates for elected positions, files lawsuits to increase environmental protection on government projects, and works with members of Congress to develop legislative proposals. The group's members elect the organization's board of directors.

Yet not all mass associations give members a say in selecting their leaders or determining their mission. To join the AARP, which has nearly 38 million members, one must be at least 50 years old and pay dues of about $16 per year. Members get discounts on insurance, car rentals, and hotels, as well as driver safety courses and help doing their taxes. The AARP claims to lobby for policies its members favor, but members actually have no control over which legislative causes the group chooses. Moreover, the AARP does not poll members to determine its issue positions, nor do members elect AARP leadership.

The members of **peak associations** are businesses or other organizations rather than individuals.[17] Individuals cannot join peak associations—they may work for member companies or organizations, but they cannot become dues-paying members on their own. The Business–Industry Political Action Committee (BIPAC), an association of several hundred businesses and trade associations that aims to elect "pro-business individuals" to Congress, is a good example of a peak association.[18] The umbrella organization that led efforts to enact direct funding for student loans, the Student Aid Alliance, is another such peak association.

Resources

Interest groups use three key resources to support their lobbying efforts: people, money, and expertise. The resources that a group has at its disposal significantly influence its available lobbying strategies. (We will examine some of these strategies in more detail in a later section.) Some large groups have sufficient funding and staff to pursue a wide range of strategies, whereas some smaller groups with fewer resources have only a few lobbying options.

People A crucial resource for most interest groups is their membership. Group members can write to or meet with elected officials, travel to Washington for demonstrations, and even offer expertise or advice to their leaders. When the "members" of a group are corporations, as is the case with trade associations, CEOs and other corporate staff can help with the group's lobbying efforts.

Many mass organizations try to get their members involved in the lobbying process through links on their website that encourage members to contact their members of Congress. One organization opposed to President Trump's agenda has developed a service, Resistbot, whose *exclusive* purpose is to make it easier for people to have their voices heard. Resistbot allows users to contact their elected officials by texting "RESIST" to the number 50409 (or by messaging the bot on Facebook). The bot asks for information, like name and zip code, so that it can identify the appropriate senators and House member to contact for each person. After getting information about the user's concerns, the bot faxes or e-mails the politician's office with a personalized message from the user. The first version of Resistbot only sent faxes, but the volume (5 million faxes in six months) overwhelmed congressional offices. Now, the bot first

Interest groups use a variety of tactics to draw attention to their concerns, including events designed to generate media coverage. People for the Ethical Treatment of Animals (PETA), known for its bold media campaigns, stationed a life-size mechanical elephant outside the Ringling Bros. circus to protest the company's treatment of its elephants.

tries to communicate with congressional offices electronically, and if that doesn't work, it will send a fax or make a phone call. In its first six months, the bot sent and received 91,421,000 text messages from more than 1.3 million unique users.[19] Use of this technique was widely credited with helping stop the repeal of Obamacare.

Interest groups' ability to use people as a resource faces two major challenges. First, it requires having members in the first place, and recruiting new members can be difficult and expensive. The second challenge is motivating members to participate. As we discuss later, although some interest groups have managed to change government policy by persuading their members to write to and visit elected officials, interest groups more often receive little response when they ask for members' help.[20]

Money Virtually everything interest groups do can be purchased as services: groups can spend money on hiring people to meet with elected officials and to fight for what they want in court. Money can also go toward campaign contributions or developing and running campaign ads. And, of course, money is necessary to fund interest groups' everyday operations. The importance of money for interest group operations is evident in their funding appeals to members. For example, the donations page from the Sierra Club's website shows that supporters can give a membership as a gift, join as a life member, or pay dues monthly. They can make commemorative or memorial gifts, set up a planned giving scheme, or donate stock. The group even offers gift-giving plans for non-U.S. residents and a Spanish-language version of its donations page.

Well-funded interest groups and firms have a considerable advantage in the lobbying process. If they need an expert, a lobbyist, or a lawyer, they can simply hire one or open a Washington office to increase contacts with legislators and bureaucrats. They can pay for campaign ads and make contributions to candidates and parties. Groups with less cash, however, cannot use these strategies. Smaller firms might join a trade association that will lobby for policies that benefit all of the association's members.

Still, groups can be effective without spending much. They can rely on members to lobby for them, hire staff willing to work for low pay because they share the group's goals, or cite published research rather than funding their own studies to bolster their case for policy change. Moreover, the fact that a group has lots of money is no guarantee that its lobbying efforts will succeed. As we discussed earlier, even though Sallie Mae and the other firms that opposed student loan reform spent a considerable sum on lobbying, they were unable to prevent this policy change.

Expertise Expertise takes many forms. Groups can employ staff (or can hire experts) to conduct research or develop policy proposals related to their interests. A firm's in-house lobbyists can provide information about how a change in government policy will affect the firm's profits and employment. Some lobbying firms (especially those that employ former members of Congress or congressional staff) may also have inside information on the kinds of policies that are likely to be enacted in the House or Senate. Interest groups with dues-paying members (such as the Sierra Club) can poll them to find out what they would like government to do. All of this information can be deployed to persuade elected officials or bureaucrats about the merits of a group's or a firm's demands (as well as the political consequences of inaction) and offer ready-made policy solutions to the problems the group has identified.

Consider the AARP, whose website offers a vast array of research and analyses, including information about seniors' part-time employment, how people invest their 401(k) retirement accounts, and a comparison of long-term care policies in Europe and the United States.[21] The AARP's lobbyists use this research when arguing for policy changes in their public testimony and in private meetings with members of Congress and congressional staff. And they hire former members of Congress and bureaucrats so they are well informed about the preferences of those inside government. However, only a few interest groups can match the AARP's wealth of expertise and resources.

Individual lobbyists also vary in what they offer to a group or corporation. Former members of Congress might know a lot about policy options and the preferences of their former colleagues but be less informed about public opinion or the business challenges faced by the firm that hires them to lobby. In-house lobbyists might know a lot about the firm they work for but much less about congressional preferences. And an interest group's policy expert might know everything there is to know about current government policies in some areas but know nothing about how to sell new proposals to a skeptical member of Congress.

"Why Should I Care?"

When you think of a lobbyist, don't imagine a person in an expensive suit carrying a briefcase of cash (or a campaign contribution). More often, people become lobbyists because they believe in the goals of the group they represent. And they generally don't wear expensive suits. Understanding who lobbyists really are, and the boundaries of what they can really do, is key to evaluating whether or not they have too much influence in American politics.

EXPLAIN HOW SUCCESSFUL INTEREST GROUPS OVERCOME COLLECTIVE ACTION PROBLEMS

Getting organized

A new interest group's first priority is to get organized, which involves raising the money needed to hire staff, rent an office, and set up a website, and formulating policy goals and a lobbying strategy. In some cases, a lobbying firm is hired to perform these jobs. Once organized, the group must continue to attract funds for ongoing operations. These tasks are not easy. Even if a group of people (or corporations) shares the same goals, it may be challenging to persuade them to donate time or money to the lobbying operation.

The logic of collective action

collective action problem
A situation in which the members of a group would benefit by working together to produce some outcome, but each individual is better off refusing to cooperate and reaping benefits from those who do the work.

Research has found that **collective action problems** arise when a group of individuals (or corporations) has an opportunity to make itself better off through the cooperative provision of public goods. For interest groups, the public good in question would be

Collective Action Problems

a change in government policy desired by group members. Scholars refer to these situations as involving collective action. Even when all members of a group agree on the desirability of a public good and the costs of producing the good are negligible, cooperation is neither easy nor automatic (see Nuts & Bolts 10.2).

The logic of collective action provides insights into how interest groups are organized and how they make lobbying decisions. First, the logic of collective action tells us that group formation is not automatic. Even when a number of citizens want the same things from government, their common interest may not lead them to organize. Society is full of groups of like-minded people (such as college students) who do not organize to lobby or who choose to engage in **free riding** and thus enjoy the benefits of organizations without participating. This tendency explains why certain debates in Washington feature well-organized groups on one side of the issue but few on the other.

Unless people can easily see benefits from participating, which does not happen often, group leaders must worry about finding the right strategies to get people to join. Thus, given the logic of collective action, motivating people to join and participate is just as important for a group's success as its lobbying strategy. Most organizations develop mechanisms to make cooperation and participation in an interest group's efforts worthwhile. These **selective incentives** fall into three categories: benefits from participation, coercion, and material goods.

Studies of political parties and interest groups find that some individuals volunteer out of a sense of duty or because they enjoy working together toward a common goal. Scholars refer to these benefits of participation as either **solidary benefits**, which come from working with like-minded people, or **purposive benefits**, which come from working to achieve a desired policy goal.[22] If most people were spurred to political action because of participation benefits, the free rider problem wouldn't exist.

When solidary or purposive benefits are not enough to solve the free rider problem, groups may require participation through **coercion**. Consider labor unions. They

free riding
Relying on others to contribute to a collective effort while failing to participate on one's own behalf, yet still benefiting from the group's successes.

selective incentives
Benefits that can motivate participation in a group effort because they are available only to those who participate, such as member services offered by interest groups.

solidary benefits
Satisfaction derived from the experience of working with like-minded people, even if the group's efforts do not achieve the desired impact.

purposive benefits
Satisfaction derived from the experience of working toward a desired policy goal, even if the goal is not achieved.

coercion
A method of eliminating nonparticipation or free riding by potential group members by requiring participation, as in many labor unions.

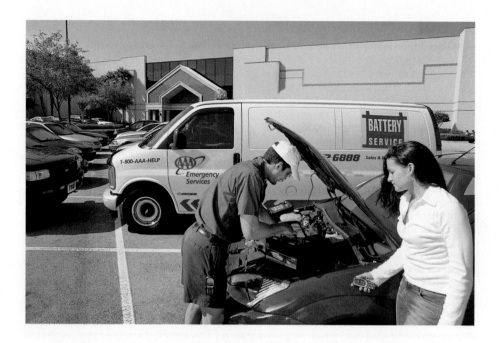

AAA (formerly the American Automobile Association) is a well-known provider of emergency road service, yet few people are aware of its role as an interest group that lobbies for a wide range of policy changes and builds awareness of key transportation issues.

material benefits
Benefits that are provided to individuals for joining a group, such as a coffee mug or a T-shirt, that are distinct from the collective benefits provided by the group.

provide public goods to workers by negotiating with management on behalf of worker-members over pay and work requirements. Why don't union members free ride? Because in many cases they have to join the union: union shop laws require them to pay union dues as a condition of their employment. These laws are critical to unions; states with laws that make union membership optional typically have weak unions—if any.

Finally, **material benefits** are benefits given only to the members of an interest group. These incentives are not public goods; an individual can receive a material benefit only by joining the group. Thus, interest groups offer material benefits in the hope of providing people with new reasons to participate. One of the most interesting cases of material benefits provided by an interest group involves AAA. Members with car trouble can call AAA at any time for emergency service. AAA also provides its members with annotated maps and travel guides, a travel agency, a car-buying service, discounts at hotels and restaurants, and other benefits. These services mask the interest group role of AAA. For example, its Foundation for Traffic Safety delivers research reports to legislators on topics ranging from lowering the blood alcohol level threshold that legally defines drunk driving to increasing the restrictions on driving by senior citizens.[23] It's unlikely that many AAA members—who join for the selective incentives—are aware of the organization's lobbying efforts. The incentives drive membership, which funds the organization's lobbying operation.

"Why Should I Care?"

The logic of collective action says that organization is neither automatic nor easy. Rather than complaining about how many lobbyists there are or how much they spend, we should consider whether some groups in society are ignored because they are never able to organize themselves and lobby for their concerns. Are you free riding off of any groups' efforts right now? What would it take to get you involved?

Interest group strategies

Once a group has organized and determined its goals, the next step is to decide how to lobby. There are two types of possible tactics: **inside strategies**, which are actions taken inside government (whether federal, state, or local), and **outside strategies**, which are actions taken outside government (see How It Works: Lobbying the Federal Government).[24] In general, these strategies are undertaken by a single group working on its own, sometimes in opposition to another group or groups. However, as we discuss later, interest groups sometimes work together toward common legislative goals.

Inside strategies

Inside strategies involve some form of contact with elected officials or bureaucrats. Thus, inside strategies require a group to establish an office in Washington, D.C., or to hire a lobbying firm to act on its behalf.

Direct Lobbying When interest group staff meet with officeholders or bureaucrats, they plead their case through **direct lobbying**, asking government officials to change policy in line with the group's goals.[25] Such contacts are very common—on any given day, each congressional or administrative office gets phone calls, visits, or e-mails from dozens of lobbyists.

Direct lobbying is generally aimed at officials and bureaucrats who are sympathetic to the group's goals.[26] Through these efforts, interest groups and their representatives do not try to convert opponents into supporters; rather, they are a way of helping legislators enact policies that they already prefer—and that the group prefers as well.[27] Groups can assist in a number of ways, from sharing information about proposed changes, to providing lists of other legislators who might be persuadable, to drafting legislative proposals or regulations. These efforts usually do not involve a trade in which the group expects legislative action in return for its help. In fact, legislators and their staff are often happy to meet with a like-minded group's representatives, as the information the group can provide may be vital to the legislators' efforts to enact legislation, manage the bureaucracy, or keep the support of constituents back home in their districts.[28] For example, corporations that stood to lose business if the government moved to direct student loans lobbied legislators whose districts included the companies' call centers and headquarters. For these legislators, helping these companies might have been good public policy, but it was also a way of preserving their constituents' jobs.

Interest groups also contact both legislators who disagree with their goals and "fence-sitters" who neither support nor oppose them, with the goal of converting them into supporters. These efforts are less extensive than the lobbying of supporters, however, because opponents are unlikely to change their minds unless a group can provide new information that causes them to rethink their position. However, lobbying opponents may be useful if it forces opposing interest groups to counterlobby, using their limited resources to make sure that their allied legislators do not change their positions.[29]

As these descriptions indicate, interest groups place a high priority on maintaining access to their lobbying targets and being able to present their arguments, regardless of whether they expect to get what they want. Of course, interest groups want to achieve their policy goals, but access is the necessary first step that makes persuasion possible. Therefore, many interest groups try to keep their efforts low-key, providing information to friends and opponents alike, avoiding threats or harsh words, in the hope that they will leave a favorable impression and be able to gain access the next

EXPLORE THE WAYS INTEREST GROUPS TRY TO INFLUENCE GOVERNMENT POLICIES

inside strategies
The tactics employed within Washington, D.C., by interest groups seeking to achieve their policy goals.

outside strategies
The tactics employed outside Washington, D.C., by interest groups seeking to achieve their policy goals.

direct lobbying
Attempts by interest group staff to influence policy by speaking with elected officials or bureaucrats.

Lobbying the Federal Government: Inside and Outside Strategies

Inside Strategies

Groups **lobby government officials directly** in Washington, D.C.

Examples:

 meeting with lawmakers

 drafting legislation

 providing research and testimony

 taking the government to court

Outside Strategies

Groups use **public pressure, elections, and the media** to influence government.

Examples:

 grassroots e-mail, letter, or phone campaigns

contributing to election campaigns

 getting media coverage of their cause

AIPAC and the Iran Nuclear Deal

Throughout negotiations between Iran and the United States and its allies over limiting Iran's nuclear research program, the American Israel Public Affairs Committee (AIPAC)—an influential pro-Israel interest group—strongly opposed the deal. AIPAC engaged in a diverse set of lobbying activities with the goal of persuading members of Congress to disapprove the deal before a crucial deadline passed and the deal was enacted.

⬤ Inside strategies

⬤ Outside strategies

Critical Thinking

1. **Despite its lobbying efforts, AIPAC's** side initially did not prevail in this situation. It wasn't until they had a more sympathetic ear in the White House that the policy was changed. If you were advising them, what strategy would you suggest they spend time on: inside or outside? Why?

2. **Suppose you are the head of AIPAC.** How could you use the Iran agreement to illustrate AIPAC's power and influence in Washington, despite the fact that the group's position did not prevail in Congress? Given the ultimate outcome, would you change how your group allocates its time and resources?

Do we have a deal?

July 14, 2015
The United States and its negotiation partners announce details of their **nuclear agreement with Iran.**

And they're off!

July 15, 2015
AIPAC announces its opposition to the Iran deal and **forms a new advocacy group to lobby** against the agreement.

Gathering forces.

July 2015
AIPAC organizes a series of **speeches and town hall meetings** in congressional districts and states of undecided legislators.

Making introductions.

July 28–29, 2015
AIPAC arranges a "Washington fly-in"— a series of **meetings between lawmakers and hundreds of constituents** who are opposed to the deal.

Running ads.

August 2015
AIPAC spends over **$20 million running television ads** opposing the deal in 23 states.

Funding trips.

August 2015
AIPAC organizes a **trip to Israel for 58 members of Congress** to meet with Israeli citizens and officials.

Going right to the source.

August 2015
AIPAC representatives **lobby undecided senators** to oppose the agreement.

No luck for AIPAC.

September 2, 2015
Deadline for Congress to disapprove the deal **passes without action.**

But there's a new sheriff in town!

May 8, 2018
Despite initially extending the deal, **President Trump withdraws from the agreement,** saying, "This was a horrible one-sided deal that should have never, ever been made."

While AIPAC's efforts were initially unsuccessful, they illustrate the many ways interest groups can work to influence the policy process.

time they want to lobby their opponents. After all, people who are opposed to a group's current priorities one day may agree with the group on some future issue.

Whom do these groups contact for direct lobbying? Analysis of lobbyists' annual disclosure forms shows that they contact people throughout the federal government, including elected officials, members of the president's staff, and bureaucrats in the executive branch. They seek this wide range of contacts because different officials play distinct roles in the policy-making process and thus have various types of influence. Members of Congress shape legislation and budgets; members of the president's staff influence the formation of new policies and obtain presidential consent for new laws; and executive branch bureaucrats change the ways regulations are written and policies are implemented.

Drafting Legislation and Regulations Interest groups sometimes draft legislative proposals and regulations, which they deliver to legislators and bureaucrats as part of their lobbying efforts.[30] Surveys of interest groups found that more than three-quarters reported drafting proposals for members of Congress.[31] The role of lobbyists in drafting legislation has become more prominent as Congress has less internal capacity to write the laws because of cuts in committee staff.[32] In the case of direct student loans, for example, the antireform forces developed a plan that would cut fees and lower interest rates for student loans but preserve the existing system.

Interest groups do not give proposals to just anyone: they seek out legislators who already support their cause and who have significant influence within Congress. A lobbying effort aimed at cutting interest rates on student loans would target supporters of this change who are also members of the congressional committee with jurisdiction over student loan programs—preferably someone who chairs the committee or one of its subcommittees.[33] Interest groups also lobby bureaucrats to influence the details of new regulations.[34] If the types of regulations involved can go into effect without congressional approval, then lobbying the bureaucracy can result in groups' getting exactly what they want. But even if new regulations require approval by Congress or White House staff, interest groups can increase their chances of success by getting involved in the initial drafting of policy.

Research Interest groups often prepare research reports on topics of interest to the group. For example, Public Citizen featured on its website a series of research reports on topics such as financial reform, climate and energy, health and safety, and regulatory policy.[35] Such reports serve multiple purposes. They may sway public opinion, help persuade elected officials or bureaucrats, or directly influence the industry that is the subject of the report. They also help interest group staff claim expertise on some aspect of public policy. Members of Congress are more likely to accept a group's legislative proposal if they think that the group's staff has research to back up their claims. Journalists are also more likely to respond to an interest group's requests for publicity if they think that the group's staff has supporting evidence.

Hearings Interest group staff often testify before congressional committees. In part, this activity is aimed at informing members of Congress about issues that matter to the interest group. For example, the NRA's website shows that its staff has testified in favor of "right-to-carry" laws as well as laws that would grant immunity to gun manufacturers for harm committed with weapons they produced.[36]

Litigation Another inside strategy involves taking the government to court. In bringing their case, interest groups can argue that the government's actions are not consistent with the Constitution or that the government has misinterpreted existing

The American Civil Liberties Union is an interest group that often uses litigation strategies in its efforts to change government policy. Here, members of the ACLU chapter in Washington State announce their filing of an abortion rights lawsuit against several local hospitals.

law.[37] Interest groups can bring these actions via lawyers on their staff, a hired law firm, or lawyers who will work for no fees. Interest groups can also become involved in an existing case by filing amicus curiae ("friend of the court") briefs, documents that offer judges the group's rationale for how the case should be decided. The drawback of litigation is that it is costly and time-consuming—cases can take years to work through the federal court system. At a minimum, groups that use the litigation strategy generally combine it with direct lobbying or other strategies.

Working Together To increase their chances for success, interest groups can work together in their lobbying efforts, formulating a common strategy and future plans. In general, these coalitions of groups are short-term efforts focused on achieving a specific outcome, like supporting or opposing the confirmation of judicial and cabinet nominees.[38] The fight against direct student loans, for example, involved corporations such as Citibank and Sallie Mae, along with the U.S. Chamber of Commerce. Support for change came from the Student Aid Alliance, a group composed of colleges, think tanks, and associations of law schools and other professional schools. This group had formed in 1999 to lobby for increases in student aid, then stayed together to lobby on other issues.

Why do groups work together? The most obvious reason lies in the power of large numbers: legislators are more likely to respond, or at least provide access, when many groups with large or diverse memberships are all asking for the same thing.[39]

The problem with working together is that groups may agree on general goals but disagree on specifics, thereby requiring negotiation. If differences cannot be bridged, groups may undertake separate and possibly conflicting lobbying efforts or decide against lobbying entirely. For example, although there are many groups pressing for climate change legislation, they have not developed a unified lobbying effort. The problem? The groups disagree on which policies should be implemented, who should pay for them, and whether the government should aid companies that would be forced to purchase new antipollution equipment. In the absence of agreement, working alone seems a better strategy.[40]

Outside strategies

Outside strategies involve things that groups do across the country rather than in Washington. Again, these activities can be orchestrated by the group or be organized by a firm hired by the group.

Grassroots Lobbying Directly involving interest group members in lobbying efforts is called **grassroots lobbying**. Members may send letters, make telephone calls, participate in a protest, or express their demands in other ways. Many groups

grassroots lobbying
A lobbying strategy that relies on participation by group members, such as a protest or a letter-writing campaign.

Mass protests such as the 2017 Women's March, which attracted more than 5 million protesters worldwide, are intended to attract media attention and demonstrate the depth of public support for a group's goals.

Astroturf lobbying
Any lobbying method initiated by an interest group that is designed to look like the spontaneous, independent participation of many individuals.

encourage grassroots lobbying. For example, the AARP's website has a page where members can find contact information for their elected leaders in Washington.[41] Other links allow members to e-mail or to fax their representatives letters that are prewritten by the AARP to express the group's positions on various proposals, such as pension protection legislation and proposals to curb identity theft. The AARP also organizes district meetings with elected officials and encourages its members to attend.

Mass protests are another form of grassroots lobbying. In addition to trying to capture the attention of government officials, mass protests also seek to draw media attention, with the idea of publicizing the group's goals and perhaps gaining new members or financial support. For example, after the election of Donald Trump, hundreds of groups partnered with the organizers of the Women's March on January 21, 2017, in 673 marches on all seven continents (yes, there was one in Antarctica!), including 408 marches in the United States. There were more than 5 million participants worldwide (the estimates for the United States range from 3.3 to 5.2 million).[42] The marches were aimed at drawing attention to a range of progressive issues connected with women's rights. The lead sponsors were Planned Parenthood and the Natural Resources Defense Council; more than 550 organizations were listed as "partners" on the Women's March website.[43]

Grassroots strategies are useful because elected officials are loath to act against a large group of citizens who care enough about an issue to express their position.[44] These officials may not agree with the group's goals, but they are likely to at least arrange a meeting with its staff, so that they appear willing to learn about their constituents' demands.[45] However, these member-based strategies work only for a small set of interest groups. To take advantage of these strategies, groups first need a large number of members. Legislators begin to pay attention to a letter-writing campaign only when they receive several thousand pieces of mail.

In addition, for grassroots lobbying to be effective, the letters or other efforts have to come from a Congress member's own constituents. The effectiveness of grassroots lobbying also depends on perceptions of how much a group has done to motivate participation. Suppose a representative gets 10,000 e-mails demanding an increase in student aid. However, virtually all the messages contain the same appeal because they were generated and sent from a group's website. Congressional staff refer to these efforts as **Astroturf lobbying**.[46] Given the similarity of the letters, the representative may discount the effort, believing that it says more about the group's ability to make campaign participation accessible than it does about the number of district residents who strongly support an increase in student aid. Even so, politicians are sometimes reluctant to completely dismiss Astroturf efforts—the fact that so many people participated, even with facilitation by an interest group, means that their demands must at least be considered.

Mobilizing Public Opinion One strategy related to grassroots lobbying involves trying to change what the public thinks about an issue in the hope that elected officials will see this change and respond by enacting (or opposing) new laws or regulations to keep their constituents happy.

Virtually all groups try to influence opinion. Most maintain a website that presents their message, and they write press releases to get media coverage. Most groups are also very active on social media, using Facebook, Twitter, and Instagram to keep in touch with members and let them know about issues that the group is working on. Any contact with citizens, whether to encourage them to join the group, contribute money, or engage in grassroots lobbying, also involves elements of persuasion—trying to transform citizens into supporters and supporters into true believers and even activists. In the case of gun control, for example, the NRA has an aggressive campaign to encourage members to contact their elected officials and to express their opinions.

A focused mobilization effort involves contacting large numbers of potential supporters (beyond just members) through e-mail, phone calls, direct mail, television advertising, print media, social media, and websites. In order to get legislators to respond, a group has to persuade large numbers of people to get involved. One example of mobilization occurs during congressional hearings on nominees to the Supreme Court or other federal judgeships. One study found that about one-third of the groups that lobbied for or against these nominees also deployed direct mail and leaflets and ran phone banks as a way to influence public opinion.[47]

Electioneering Interest groups get involved in elections by making contributions to candidates, mobilizing people (including their own staff) to help in a campaign, endorsing candidates, funding campaign ads, or mobilizing a candidate's or party's supporters. All these efforts seek to influence who gets elected, with the expectation that changing who gets elected will affect what government does.

Federal laws limit groups' electioneering and lobbying efforts (see Nuts & Bolts 10.3). For example, most private organizations and associations in America are organized as 501(c)(3) organizations, a designation based on their Internal Revenue Service classification, which means that donations to the group are tax deductible. However, 501(c)(3) organizations are not allowed to advocate for or against political candidates, and lobbying must not constitute more than 20 percent of the group's total expenditures (certain public-education programs or voter-registration drives that are conducted in

NUTS & BOLTS 10.3

Interest Groups and Electioneering: Types of Organizations

An interest group's ability to engage in electioneering depends on how it is organized—specifically, what section of the IRS code applies to the organization. The following table gives details on four common organizations: 501(c) organizations, 527 organizations, PACs, and so-called Super PACs. Many individuals choose to contribute money to nonprofits organized as 501(c)(4) groups, which can lobby and engage in electioneering as long as their "primary activity" (at least half of their overall activity) is not political.

Type of Organization	Advantages	Disadvantages
501(c)(3)	Contributions tax deductible	Cannot engage in political activities, and lobbying can be no more than 20 percent of spending (but voter education and mobilization is permitted)
527	Can spend unlimited amounts on issue advocacy and voter mobilization	Cannot make contributions to candidates or coordinate efforts with candidates or parties
501(c)(4)	Can spend unlimited amounts on electioneering; does not have to disclose contributors	At least half of its activities must be nonpolitical; cannot coordinate efforts with candidates or parties
PACs	Can contribute directly to candidates and parties	Strict limits on direct contributions
Super PACs	Can spend unlimited amounts on electioneering; can support or oppose specific candidates	Cannot make contributions to candidates or coordinate efforts with candidates or parties

political action committee (PAC)
An interest group or a division of an interest group that can raise money to contribute to campaigns or to spend on ads in support of candidates. The amount a PAC can receive from each of its donors and the amount it can spend on federal campaigning are strictly limited.

527 organization
A tax-exempt group formed primarily to influence elections through voter mobilization efforts and issue ads that do not directly endorse or oppose a candidate. Unlike PACs, 527s are not subject to contribution limits and spending caps.

a nonpartisan manner do not count toward that 20 percent), although some groups are always looking for loopholes in these restrictions. Groups that want to engage in lobbying or electioneering without looking for exceptions can incorporate under other IRS designations and operate as a **political action committee (PAC)**, a **527 organization**, or a 501(c)(4). Although contributions to these organizations are not tax deductible, such organizations have fewer restrictions on the size of the contributions they can make and on how their money is spent—for example, 527 organizations have no contribution or spending limits. Two new options for electioneering by interest groups emerged in recent elections: "Super PACs" and 501(c)(4) organizations. The former was a consequence of the *Citizens United* Supreme Court decision that authorized unlimited independent spending by corporations and labor unions in federal elections.[48] Many groups set up new PACs to take advantage of these latest rules—the "Super" label reflects the fact that these groups take in and spend much more money than the typical PAC. All the major 2016 presidential candidates had an independent Super PAC running ad campaigns on their behalf.

In 2016, federally focused 527 organizations raised more than $494 million on electioneering, and PACs and Super PACS raised about $1.8 billion on electioneering and contributions to candidates and parties.[49] However, these large numbers mask some important details. To begin with, some of the largest firms in America (Google, Walmart, and Exxon Mobil, for example) have PACs that spend only a million or so on contributions. Another large firm, Apple, has no PAC. The PAC for the Pharmaceutical Research & Manufacturers of America is also small, and the other influential interest groups mentioned earlier in Figure 10.2 (the AARP, NARAL Pro-Choice America, and Family Research Council) spend even less or don't have a PAC or a 527. These numbers suggest that money doesn't buy elections or policy outcomes—if it did, these organizations would probably spend a lot more on campaign donations and television ads.

Spending totals can also be deceptive. The National Association of Realtors, for example, made over $10 million in contributions—but spread out over 500 candidates, with slightly more going to Republicans than Democrats. The PAC for EMILY's List collected over $40 million but spent most of this on a direct mail operation that generated funds, leaving only a fraction left for campaign contributions. The Gay and Lesbian Victory Fund focused on recruiting and endorsing candidates and made no contributions at all. Finally, another large spender in 2016, NextGen Climate Action, was funded largely by a single wealthy donor. Moreover, most of the candidates the organization supported in 2014 and 2016 lost their elections.

Finally, while the $1.8 billion that these groups raised together seems large, only $1.1 billion was spent, and the average amount each group spent was much smaller. Most PACs contributed to only a few candidates. And while more than a thousand Super PACs were active in the 2016 election, most were small, and the average group spent just over $500,000. These data highlight a sharp difference in electioneering strategies between the very few large, well-funded interest groups and everyone else. A few 527s, Super PACs, 501(c)(4)s, and PACs have the money to deploy massive advertising and mobilization efforts for candidates or issues they like or against those they don't like. There are also some very large associations that can persuade large numbers of members to work for and vote for candidates whom the group supports or against candidates that the group wants to defeat. And just a few rich individuals can make outsized contributions to a candidate they favor.

But these strategies are not available to the vast majority of interest groups, which simply don't have the resources. Most interest groups hope to give modest help to a few candidates who are sympathetic to their goals. These contributions are generally made in the hope that, once elected, the officeholder will remember their contribution when their group asks for a meeting. It is important to remember that electioneering is only one strategy available to interest groups. Some groups do not do any electioneering

Conservative Super PACs, such as the Conservative Political Action Committee (CPAC), hold conventions that give candidates a venue to present themselves to conservative activists and donors.

at all, possibly because they lack sufficient funds, because they want to avoid making enemies based on whom they support or don't support, or because other strategies are more promising given the resources that are available to them. Many groups opt for quiet lobbying efforts that use their expertise, or they undertake grassroots efforts to build public support for their policy goals. Massive electioneering operations by interest groups are relatively rare.

Cultivating Media Contacts Media coverage helps a group publicize its concerns without spending any money. Thus, most interest group leaders talk often with journalists to pursue favorable coverage of news stories that pertain to the group's issues. Such attention may mobilize public opinion indirectly, by getting people to join the group, contribute money, or demand that elected officials support the group's agenda. Favorable media coverage also helps a group's leaders assure members that they are actively working on members' concerns.

Journalists listen when interest groups call if they feel that the group's story will catch their readers' attention or address their concerns. Smart interest group leaders make it easy for journalists to cover their cause, holding events that produce intriguing news stories. These stories may not change anyone's mind, but the media coverage provides free publicity for the groups' policy agendas.

Bypassing Government: The Initiative Process A final outside strategy for interest groups bypasses government entirely: a group can work to get its proposed policy change voted on by the public in a general election through an initiative or a referendum. Referenda and initiatives allow citizens to vote on specific proposed changes in policy. The difference between these procedures lies in the source of the proposal. In a **referendum** the legislature or another government body proposes the question that is put to a vote, whereas in an **initiative** citizens put questions on the ballot, typically after gathering signatures of registered voters on a petition.

Initiatives can occur only in states and municipalities that have the appropriate procedures in place; there is no mechanism for a nationwide vote on an interest group's proposal. So if a group wants to use this process to effect national change, it has to get its

referendum
A direct vote by citizens on a policy change proposed by a legislature or another government body. Referenda are common in state and local elections, but there is no mechanism for a national-level referendum.

initiative
A direct vote by citizens on a policy change proposed by fellow citizens or organized groups outside government. Getting a question on the ballot typically requires collecting a set number of signatures from registered voters in support of the proposal. There is no mechanism for a national-level initiative.

measure on the ballot in one state at a time. Moreover, only some states allow initiatives and some permit this kind of vote only on a narrow range of issues. The champion state for initiatives is California, whose citizens often vote on dozens of initiatives in each general election, ranging from funding for stem-cell research to limits on taxation and spending.[50]

There are many examples of groups using the initiative process to change government policy. Most notably, advocates of term limits for state legislators have used the initiative process to establish such limits in 21 states, although the limits in some states have since been overturned by legislative action or subsequent initiatives.[51] Also, twenty-four states have approved legal use of marijuana in some form through statewide ballot measures.[52] There were five states with marijuana initiatives on the ballot in 2018. Research shows that states with more active interest groups have more initiatives on the ballot, so groups are taking advantage of this mechanism for influencing policy.[53]

One of the principal concerns about the initiative process is that it favors well-funded groups that can advertise heavily in support of their proposals and can mobilize their supporters to vote on Election Day.[54] But spending a lot of money often is not enough: even groups with substantial resources have sometimes been unable to reform policy through the initiative process.[55]

Choosing strategies

Most groups give testimony, do research, contact elected officials and bureaucrats, talk with journalists, and develop legislative and regulatory proposals.[56] A particular group's decisions about which strategies to use depend partly on its resources and partly on what approach the group believes will be most effective in promoting its particular issues. Some strategies that work well for one group's agenda might not be appropriate for another's. The Humane Society of the United States is an organization that lobbies to prevent the abuse and neglect of animals. It had a $196 million annual budget in 2016 but only a small Washington office. Its lobbying expenses for 2016 were $390,000. Rather than lobbying members of Congress, the group's focus is on investigations and grassroots organizing, highlighting situations in which corporations and countries are not behaving according to existing laws against animal cruelty.

Other interest groups advance their causes in ways that don't look like lobbying. For example, as NASA begins to formulate plans for sending humans to Mars in the 2030s, the Boeing Company has released a series of films and videos about these plans. At one level, Boeing's efforts are all about highlighting the many important discoveries that a voyage to Mars might generate—but they are also a way to increase the chances that NASA's plans will attract public support and be funded by Congress, which, if it happens, will likely generate a series of very lucrative contracts for Boeing to build and help operate exploration hardware.

"Why Should I Care?"

At first glance, lobbying victories should go to the groups that can spend a lot on contributions to candidates or on direct lobbying. But there are many other ways to succeed in the battle to shape public policy, from organizing American citizens to preparing new proposals or doing background research. Policy influence isn't as much about the size of a group's budget as it is about factors such as the size of the group's membership or the perception of its expertise. Even poorly funded groups can find ways to win. If there's an issue that you believe in, you can find a group that supports it, large or small, and get involved in any number of ways.

How much power do interest groups have?

One 2016 presidential candidate, Democrat Lawrence Lessig, built his entire campaign around a pledge to convince members of Congress to enact campaign-finance reform. This, he argued, is the only way to break the influence of special interests over policy making in Washington. Once reform was enacted, Lessig promised to resign from office. While Lessig's campaign went nowhere, his pledge illustrates a widely held belief about how Washington works: that interest groups have too much power and something drastic must be done to end their domination over policy making in Washington. Donald Trump capitalized on this same sentiment with his pledge to "drain the swamp."

As we discuss in the What Do the Facts Say? feature, some studies of interest group influence support Lessig's claims—but others tell a very different story, one in which a group's chances of getting what it wants depend on whether there is organized opposition to their demand. In other words, as one analysis put it, "the solution to lobbying is more lobbying."[57]

Scholarly research also reveals four reasons why it is so hard to measure interest group influence. First, we know that interest groups usually lobby their friends in government rather than their enemies and moderate their demands in the face of resistance.[58] As a result, what looks like success may in fact be a signal of something else. For example, the NRA leadership would probably favor a new federal law that made it legal to carry a concealed handgun throughout the nation. Why doesn't the NRA demand enactment of this legislation? Because there is no sign that Congress would comply. A more-limited proposal that would force states to honor concealed carry permits issued by other states passed the House late in 2017 with the strong support of the NRA,[59] but has not come up for a vote in the Senate. Thus, the NRA's decision to not push for national concealed carry legislation and its inability to get the more-limited bill through the Senate show the limits of the organization's power.

Second, some complaints about the power of interest groups come from the losing side in the political process. Consider the "net neutrality" rule that was recently overturned by the Federal Communications Commission. The rule "prohibited

> I will Make Our Government Honest Again—believe me. But First, I'm going to have to #DrainTheSwamp in DC.
>
> **— President Donald Trump**

While many observers credit lobbying by the pharmaceutical industry for policies such as the Medicare Prescription Drug Benefit (and its ban on importing medicines), favorable public opinion, the efforts of the AARP, and bureaucrats' independent judgments probably had greater influence on passing the Drug Benefit Act.

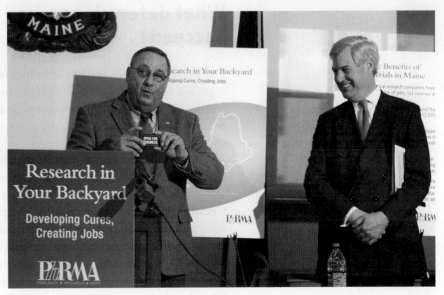

internet service providers (ISPs) from blocking, slowing or speeding up web content or charging customers additional fees to access certain web services," so corporations like AT&T, Verizon, and Comcast were strongly in favor of eliminating the regulation. The losing side of this debate, which included Microsoft, Google, and Netflix, complained that the large ISPs influenced the outcome with tens of millions of dollars in lobbying and contributions. However, lobbying was intense on both sides.[60]

Third, many interest groups claim responsibility for policies and election outcomes regardless of whether their lobbying made the difference. Consider the hotly contested election to fill the Senate seat of Attorney General Jeff Sessions in Alabama. In the campaign for or against the two candidates, 45 outside groups spent about $13.7 million, which surpassed the $13.5 million spent by the candidates themselves. With nearly $10.3 million of the outside money being spent on behalf of the winning Democratic candidate Doug Jones, it is not surprising that interest groups would take some credit for the win. However, Roy Moore was a deeply flawed candidate who was shunned by the Republican leadership in the Senate (but endorsed by Donald Trump). He was accused of sexually assaulting a 14-year-old when he was an attorney in his 30s, said that the United States was better off under slavery, and had been kicked off the state supreme court for refusing to follow the order of a federal court. Clearly these factors were central in Moore's defeat.[61] Yet the leaders of interest groups have a considerable incentive to make strong claims about their group's influence and impact, as these claims help them attract members and keep their jobs.[62]

Fourth, arguments about the impact of interest groups on election outcomes, such as Moore's defeat in 2017, ignore the fact that interest groups are almost always active on both sides of an election campaign. Although Moore was the target of attack ads funded by interest groups and many groups gave contributions to his opponent, he also received support from interest groups in the form of campaign contributions and independent ads. Thus, it doesn't make sense to attribute Moore's defeat to actions taken by one set of groups without asking why similar efforts on his behalf had no effect. You can't conclude that interest groups are all-powerful without explaining why Moore's supporters were unable to help him win the election in an overwhelmingly Republican state.

In sum, dire claims about the overwhelming influence of interest groups and lobbying on Washington policy making are probably wrong. Rather than making a blanket claim about interest group influence, a better response is to ask, What are the conditions that enhance a group's influence over policy, and what are the conditions that reduce it? That is, what determines when interest groups succeed?

What determines when interest groups succeed?

Three factors shape interest group influence. The first is the group's goal: Does it want to change a policy (including enacting a new policy) or to prevent change? The second is salience: How many Americans care about what a group is trying to do? The third is conflict: To what extent do other groups or the public oppose the policy change?

Change versus Preventing Change In general, groups are going to have an easier time preventing a change than working to implement one. As we discuss in Chapter 2, enacting a new policy requires the approval of both houses of Congress, the president's signature (or a veto override), and implementation from the appropriate bureaucratic agency. Each of these steps provides an opportunity for interest groups to lobby members of government to do nothing. So if the groups are successful, change will not occur. Studies show that groups are much more likely to be successful when their goals involve this kind of negative lobbying that seeks to block changes in policy.[63] Most of the NRA's legislative victories in recent years fit this description: the NRA has successfully

Interest Group Power

Conventional wisdom says that business interest groups have too much power over policy outcomes in Washington. But what do the facts say?

To address this question, a group of political scientists tracked a series of issues through years of lobbying, congressional debate, legislative action, and implementation by the bureaucracy. Their goal was to determine whether business groups were successful in getting what they want from Congress, particularly when their efforts were opposed by citizen groups or government officials. This figure shows what they found.

Which Interest Groups Win . . . and When?

After four years ...

■ Business Groups Win   ■ Other Side Wins   ■ Both/Neither Win

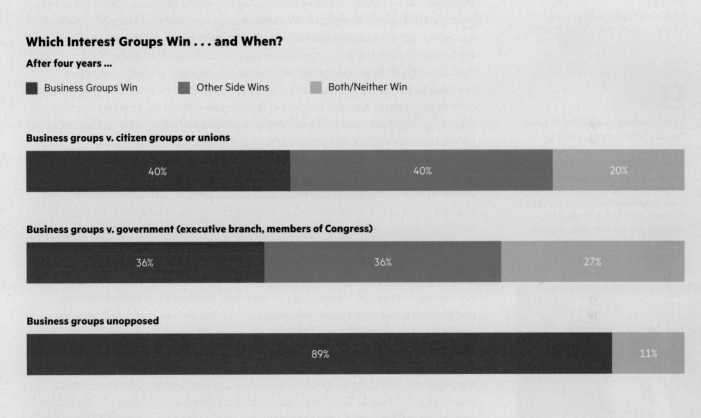

Business groups v. citizen groups or unions

| 40% | 40% | 20% |

Business groups v. government (executive branch, members of Congress)

| 36% | 36% | 27% |

Business groups unopposed

| 89% | 11% |

Think about it

- Many people believe that business groups always succeed in their lobbying efforts. Does this figure confirm or deny these suspicions?
- After looking at these data, do you think business groups have too much power? How do these data help us understand the winners and losers in the student loan reform debate discussed at the beginning of this chapter?

Source: Marie Hojnacki, Kathleen Marchetti, Frank Baumgartner, Jeffrey M. Berry, David C. Kimball, and Beth L. Leech, "Assessing Business Advantage in Washington Lobbying," *Interest Groups and Advocacy* 4 (2015): 206–24.

lobbied against a new ban on assault weapons, against reforms to the system of national background checks for handgun purchases, and against new limits on ownership of guns by mentally ill people.

While the success of the NRA's negative lobbying attracts considerable attention, its failures in lobbying for policy change do not. Consider the NRA's advocacy of concealed carry laws. As noted earlier, there is little doubt that the NRA's leaders and most of its members favor the passage of such laws nationwide, but efforts to lobby Congress in favor of such laws are unlikely to be successful given public opposition and well-funded interest groups that are against concealed carry. These groups could respond with negative lobbying against any effort the NRA might make. As a result, while the NRA lobbies for concealed carry, it has failed to help enact national legislation; the limits on its power over legislation do not get much publicity.

Salience Interest groups are more likely to succeed when their request has low **salience** or attracts little public attention.[64] When the average voter does not know or care about a group's request, legislators and bureaucrats do not have to worry about the political consequences of giving the group what it wants. The only question is whether the officials themselves favor the request or can be convinced that the group's desired change is worthwhile. In contrast, when salience is high, legislators' response to lobbying will hinge on their judgment of constituent opinion: Do voters favor what the group wants? After all, the average legislator has a strong interest in reelection and is unlikely to act against his or her constituents' wishes. As a result, lobbying may count for nothing in the face of public opposition or be superfluous when the group's position already has public support.[65]

While the idea of interest group lobbying probably brings to mind titanic struggles on controversial issues, such as gun control, abortion rights, or judicial nominations, low-salience issues are surprisingly common. Many groups are indeed active for or against these high-profile issues and try to capture public attention as a way of pressuring people in government. However, the typical issue attracts much less activity. One analysis of lobbying disclosure forms found that 5 percent of issues attracted more than 50 percent of lobbying activity and 50 percent of issues attracted less than 3 percent.[66] Thus, the typical issue debated by members of Congress may involve relatively little interest group activity, and a group's request may generate little or no opposition from other groups. Remember the National Turkey Federation—the people who give the president a turkey every Thanksgiving? In the winter of 2014, the federation successfully lobbied federal bureaucrats to increase propane supplies to Midwest states facing record cold temperatures, including areas where the federation's members use propane to heat their barns. The policy change resulting from the federation's lobbying efforts attracted no publicity, which is precisely the point. When few people know or care about a policy change, interest groups are able to dominate the policy-making process.

Conflict Interest group influence is much less apparent on conflictual issues—those over which public opinion is split and groups are typically active on both sides of the question. Consider a high-salience issue such as gun control. The ongoing debate over gun control attracts many well-funded interest groups and coalitions, which support different versions of gun control or want no change to current policy. There is no consensus among members of Congress, interest groups, or the American public about which policy changes are needed. Under these conditions, access doesn't count for very much; legislators have a keen sense of the political costs of accommodating a group's demands. As a result, stalemate is the likely result, which is exactly what has happened over the last few years: gun control laws have not been strengthened, but other than an increase in "concealed carry" laws, there have not been significant changes in the other direction. After the massacre in Las Vegas, in which 58 people were killed and 546 injured, the NRA said it would favor additional regulation of "bump stocks," which allow 90 rounds to be

salience
The level of familiarity with an interest group's goals in the general population

If you have ever heard of the National Turkey Federation, it's probably because of its participation in the annual presidential "pardoning" of a turkey before Thanksgiving. The federation's relative anonymity has been beneficial: its effort to increase the amount of turkey served in federally funded school lunches was aided by most Americans' lack of awareness of the proposal.

fired in 10 seconds. President Trump started the process of banning bump stocks through an executive order in March 2018. If policy change occurs at all, it is likely to reflect a complex process of bargaining and compromise, with no groups getting exactly what they want. In such cases, it is hard to say whether a particular group has won or lost or to attribute any aspect of the final bargain to a particular group's efforts.

The case of gun control illustrates that the fact that a group is large or well funded does not mean government officials will always comply with its requests. As mentioned earlier, many people worry that well-funded interest groups will use their financial resources to dominate the policy-making process, even if public opinion is against them, but these fears are largely unfounded. The conditions that are ripe for well-funded interest groups to become involved in a policy debate typically ensure that there will be well-funded groups on all sides of a question. Under these conditions, no group is likely to get everything it wants and no group's lobbying efforts are likely to be decisive. Some groups may not get anything.

While Congress has considered various forms of gun control legislation in recent years, the NRA has been successful at blocking such measures at the federal level and even liberalizing state-level gun laws. Here, members of the NRA and other gun rights supporters counterprotest during a gun control rally outside of the NRA's headquarters in Fairfax, Virginia.

However, gun control is not a typical case. Most cases of interest group influence look a lot like the Turkey Federation's request for more propane: a group asks for something, there is relatively little opposition, and Congress or the bureaucracy responds with appropriate policy changes. The situation might have been very different if another group had lobbied on the other side against the Turkey Federation. If so, satisfying one group would have required displeasing at least one other group. Faced with this no-win situation, bureaucrats or legislators would be less likely to give the group what it wanted. At a minimum, they would have had to measure the Turkey Federation's arguments against those made by the other groups.

Suppose you want to change some federal government policy—you want more funding for a program or an end to some regulation. Does having enough money guarantee a win? Generally speaking, the answer is no. What matters more is the salience of the policy or regulation you're trying to change and whether there is organized opposition on the other side. If your group is the only one lobbying, chances are good that you'll win. But if the issue is highly salient and you have opposition, your prospects aren't good, regardless of the size of your bankroll.

"Why Should I Care?"

Unpacking the Conflict

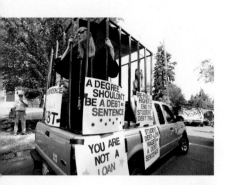

Considering all that we've discussed in this chapter, let's apply what we know about how interest groups work to the example of student loan reform discussed at the beginning of this chapter. Is it fair to characterize all interest groups, like those that worked against student loan reform, as "armies of lobbyists" on self-interested missions? Are interest groups really too-powerful manipulators of the American policy process?

Many Americans think that interest groups are powerful manipulators of the American policy process and that they are able to get what they want regardless of the impact on everyone else. Federal direct student loans are seemingly a perfect example: a small number of well-funded lobbyists worked to defeat a policy change that would lower the cost of attending college for most students.

As you have seen, the truth is much more complex. Interest groups represent many different Americans, many of whom are unaware that lobbying occurs on their behalf. Moreover, for many groups the challenge is to get organized in the first place or to scrape together enough resources to start lobbying. These efforts don't always succeed. Interest groups are more likely to get what they want when their demands attract little public attention and no opposition from other groups. When a group asks for a large or controversial policy change, it stands little chance of success, even if the group has many members, a large lobbying budget, or an influential leader directing its operation.

The debate over direct student loans exemplifies all of these findings. Although the corporations that stood to lose from the direct loan proposal had significant lobbying operations, the proposal had relatively high salience and was controversial. Consequently, legislators' voting decisions were less likely to be affected by lobbying or other interest group strategies such as electioneering. These lobbying efforts may have helped inform members of Congress about the details of the proposal or the impact that the change would have on employment in their districts, but there is no evidence that support for these proposals was shaped by lobbying. And although these lobbying efforts delayed the move to direct loans, they did not prevent it.

In sum, while individual lobbying efforts often reflect the efforts of small groups to achieve favored policy outcomes at the expense of the majority, when we look across the entire range of interest group activities, a different picture emerges: in the main, interest groups reflect the conflictual nature of American politics and the resulting drive of individuals, groups, and corporations to shape American public policy in line with their policy goals. The average citizen benefits as well as loses from lobbying activities.

What's Your Take?

Are interest groups really too-powerful manipulators of the American policy process?

Or do groups play an important role in helping all citizens' voices be heard?

STUDY GUIDE

What are interest groups?

Define *interest groups* and describe the characteristics of different types of groups. (Pages 342–352)

Summary

Interest groups are organizations that seek to influence government policy by helping elect candidates who support their policy goals and by lobbying elected officials and bureaucrats. Although they are generally viewed with disdain, interest groups are ubiquitous—most organizations have lobbyists working on their behalf—and, under the theory of pluralism, are regarded as fundamental actors in American politics.

Key terms

interest group (p. 342)
lobbying (p. 342)
interest group state (p. 343)
centralized groups (p. 347)
confederations (p. 347)
revolving door (p. 348)
mass associations (p. 350)
peak associations (p. 350)

Practice Quiz Questions

1. **In contrast to political parties, interest groups _____.**
   a run candidates for office
   b coordinate the activities of elected officials
   c guarantee that certain candidates appear on electoral ballots
   d directly influence government activity
   e indirectly influence government activity

2. **Why is the number of lobbyists increasing?**
   a The federal government is growing in size and influence.
   b Lobbying is not closely regulated.
   c Citizens are now more supportive of special interests.
   d Politicians can concurrently serve their terms and work as lobbyists.
   e Interest groups have more money to spend.

3. **One of the main advantages of a centralized interest group is that it _____.**
   a maintains lots of independent chapters
   b often has local chapters competing over resources
   c deploys the group's resources more efficiently
   d is able to easily find out what its members want
   e has no weaknesses

4. **The practice of moving from government positions to working for interest groups is called _____.**
   a interest-group capture
   b the revolving door
   c an iron triangle
   d escalator politics
   e the spoils system

Getting organized

Explain how successful interest groups overcome collective action problems. (Pages 352–354)

Summary

A primary challenge in operating an interest group is getting members to coordinate with one another. Interest groups have a number of different ways of overcoming the problem of collective action, with varying degrees of success.

Key terms

collective action problem (p. 352)
free riding (p. 353)
selective incentives (p. 353)
solidary benefits (p. 353)
purposive benefits (p. 353)
coercion (p. 353)
material benefits (p. 354)

Practice Quiz Questions

5. **The logic of collective action says that even when people _____ on policy priorities and the costs are _____, cooperation is not easy.**
   a agree; high
   b agree; covered by one person
   c agree; low
   d disagree; high
   e disagree; low

6. **Purposive benefits come from _____, while solidary benefits come from _____.**
   a working with like-minded people; working to achieve a desired policy goal
   b receiving material goods; working with like-minded people
   c receiving material goods; working to achieve a desired policy goal
   d working to achieve a desired policy goal; receiving material goods
   e working to achieve a desired policy goal; working with like-minded people

7. **Labor unions are generally able to overcome the collective action problem through the use of _____.**
   a solidary benefits
   b purposive benefits
   c coercion
   d selective incentives
   e recruitment

Interest group strategies

Explore the ways interest groups try to influence government policies. (Pages 355–364)

Summary

Interest groups have two types of tactics for lobbying elected officials. They can attempt to influence politics by taking action in Washington or they can take action elsewhere. The decision to pursue an inside or outside strategy comes down to the interest group's resources and which strategy members think will be most effective.

Key terms

inside strategies (p. 355)
outside strategies (p. 355)
direct lobbying (p. 355)
grassroots lobbying (p. 359)
Astroturf lobbying (p. 360)
political action committee (PAC) (p. 362)
527 organization (p. 362)
referendum (p. 363)
initiative (p. 363)

Practice Quiz Questions

8. Asking government officials to change policy in line with the group's goals is _____.

a revolving door lobbying
b Astroturf lobbying
c direct lobbying
d indirect lobbying
e outside lobbying

9. Interest groups generally _____ draft legislation; they generally _____ provide testimony before committees.

a do; do
b do not; do
c do; do not
d do not; do not

10. Directly involving interest group members in lobbying efforts is called _____.

a Astroturf lobbying
b grassroots lobbying
c democratic lobbying
d lobbying through referendum
e inside lobbying

11. For grassroots lobbying to be effective, _____.

a only a few pieces of mail are necessary
b mail must come from all over the country
c all messages have to have exactly the same appeal
d letters have to come from constituents
e letters have to come from prominent officials

12. Interest groups that want to maximize the amount of access they receive in return for a campaign contribution will sometimes _____.

a contribute to weak candidates who need the money
b contribute to candidates who oppose the group's goals
c wait until the general election to make a contribution
d help candidates who support them, even if they are electorally safe
e avoid electioneering efforts altogether

How much power do interest groups have?

Evaluate interest group influence. (Pages 365–369)

Summary

It is commonly argued that elected officials are letting interest groups define their agenda. However, the evidence on interest groups does not support these claims: there is no correlation between the amount of money spent on lobbying and a group's success, nor is there conclusive evidence that group lobbying influences policy. Groups are generally most influential when the issues attract little public attention and when an issue does not have organized opposition.

Key term

salience (p. 368)

Practice Quiz Questions

13. Interest groups generally lobby _____ in government.

a their opponents
b their friends
c the undecided
d the newly elected
e the less informed

14. Interest groups are more likely to succeed when their request has _____ salience and when it has _____ conflict.

a low; little
b high; little
c low; high
d high; high
e high; zero

Suggested Reading

Ainsworth, Scott. *Analyzing Interest Groups: Group Influence on People and Policies*. New York: W. W. Norton, 2002.

Baumgartner, Frank, Jeffrey M. Berry, Marie Hojnacki, David C. Kimball, and Beth L. Leech. *Lobbying and Policy Change: Who Wins, Who Loses, and Why*. Chicago: University of Chicago Press, 2009.

Carpenter, Daniel. *The Forging of Bureaucratic Autonomy: Reputations, Networks, and Policy Innovation in Executive Agencies, 1862–1928*. Princeton, NJ: Princeton University Press, 2002.

Drutman, Lee. *The Business of America Is Lobbying: How Corporations Became Politicized and Politics Became More Corporate*. New York: Oxford University Press, 2015.

Gilens, Martin, and Benjamin Page. "Testing Theories of American Politics: Elites, Interest Groups, and Average Citizens." *Perspectives on Politics* 12:3 (September 2014): 564–81.

Kollman, Kenneth. *Outside Lobbying: Public Opinion and Interest Group Strategies*. Princeton, NJ: Princeton University Press, 1998.

Olson, Mancur. *The Logic of Collective Action*, 2nd ed. Cambridge, MA: Harvard University Press, 1971.

Schattschneider, E. E. *The Semisovereign People*. New York: Harper and Row, 1959.

Schlozman, Kay Lehman, and John Tierney. *Organized Interests and American Democracy*. New York: HarperCollins, 1986.

Schlozman, Kay Lehman, Sidney Verba, and Henry E. Brady. *The Unheavenly Chorus: Unequal Political Voice and the Broken Promise of American Democracy*. Princeton, NJ: Princeton University Press, 2012.

Stigerwalt, Amy. *The Battle over the Bench: Senators, Interest Groups, and Lower Court Confirmations*. Charlottesville: University of Virginia Press, 2010.

11

Congress
Who does Congress represent?

» **"I have offered DACA a wonderful deal, including a doubling in the number of recipients and a twelve year pathway to citizenship."**
President Donald Trump

» **"I do not believe we should be granting a path to citizenship to anybody here illegally."**
Senator Ted Cruz (R-TX)

« **"We want a clean DREAM Act. That is what it's going to take for me and others to sign on."**
Representative Luis Gutiérrez (D-IL)

Representative Lou Correa (D-CA) greets supporters before the start of a press conference with Senate and House Democrats to urge congressional Republicans to stand up to President Trump's decision to terminate the Deferred Action for Childhood Arrivals (DACA) initiative. Although polls showed strong public support for providing Dreamers with a pathway to citizenship, it is not unusual for congressional leaders to use a consensual policy (DACA) to help pass more-controversial legislation (building the wall with Mexico). This issue demonstrates how members of Congress make tough decisions, often involving political trade-offs and compromises.

Late in the first year of his presidency, Donald Trump announced that he would end President Obama's Deferred Action for Childhood Arrivals (DACA) program on March 5, 2018. The program allowed residents who were brought illegally to the United States as children to remain in the country if they had graduated from high school, were currently in school, or had served in the military, and had not committed a felony. President Trump expressed strong support for the program, calling the 700,000 people enrolled "incredible kids." However, Trump believed that President Obama had overstepped his authority by creating the program through executive action, so Trump asked Congress to create a legislative solution.[1] In a meeting with congressional leaders early in 2018, President Trump said that he would sign whatever compromise on DACA that Congress could agree to. Polls showed that between 73 and 87 percent of Americans favored allowing the Dreamers, as program participants are called, to stay and have a path to citizenship.[2]

One would think that enacting a policy that is supported by more than three-fourths of Americans, the president, and both parties in Congress would be a no-brainer. But shortly before the March 5 deadline, the wheels came off. Democrats initially tried to attach the DACA bill to a must-pass budget bill, but this effort failed after a three-day government shutdown. Democrats agreed to a two-year budget bill three weeks later, but without a resolution to the DACA issue. In a reversal of his earlier position that he would sign any DACA bill that Congress put forward, President Trump took a hard line against bills that did not include $25 billion in funding for the border wall with Mexico and that did not

replace the lottery program for legal immigration and family-based immigration with a merit-based system. Trump's proposal would also extend legal status and create a path to citizenship for the 1.8 million Dreamers, including those eligible for the program who did not sign up. Critics on the far right, such as Senator Ted Cruz, called it amnesty for illegal immigrants, while those on the far left called for a "clean bill" that addressed only the Dreamers. The "Common Sense Caucus" offered a bipartisan compromise that provided funding for the wall, the DACA fix, and some changes to family-based immigration, but this was rejected by the president.

On a basic level, this appears to be an example of congressional incompetence and dysfunction. How could a policy with such broad support and positive consequences for the economy not be passed? But it is not unusual for congressional leaders to use a consensual policy (DACA) to help pass more controversial legislation (building the wall with Mexico). Some would argue that it is an essential feature of the legislative process.

The essential nature of conflict and compromise in the legislative process is not very well understood by the general public. Americans often view the type of wheeling and dealing that is necessary to reach compromises as improper and wonder why there is so much conflict. A typical sentiment is, "Why does there have to be so much partisan bickering? Can't they just implement the best solutions to our problems?"

In this chapter, we argue that Congress members' behavior is driven by their desire to respond to constituent interests (and the closely related goal of reelection) and constrained by the institutional structures within which they operate (such as the committee system, parties, and leadership). At the same time, members try to be responsible for broader national interests, which are often at odds with their constituents' interests and, consequently, the goal of reelection.

This tension between being responsible and responsive is a source of conflict and requires members of Congress to make tough decisions, often involving political trade-offs and compromises. Should a House member vote for dairy price supports for her local farmers even if it means higher milk prices for families around the nation? Should a senator vote to subsidize the production of tobacco, the biggest cash crop in his state, despite the tremendous health costs it imposes on millions of Americans? Should a member vote to close a military base, as requested by the Pentagon, even if it means the loss of thousands of jobs back home? These are difficult questions. On a complex issue, such as immigration, there is no obvious "responsible" solution and fair-minded people can disagree. These disagreements take on a partisan edge, as most Republicans favor building a stronger border with more limits on legal immigration while most Democrats do not, which obviously leads to conflict. Why is it so hard for Congress to compromise on issues that appear to be consensual, like protecting the Dreamers? How can members of Congress best serve the collective interests of the nation while also representing their local constituents?

EXPLAIN HOW MEMBERS OF CONGRESS REPRESENT THEIR CONSTITUENTS AND HOW ELECTIONS HOLD MEMBERS ACCOUNTABLE

Congress and the people

Congress and the Constitution

Congress was the "first branch" in the early decades of our nation's history. The Constitution specified for Congress a vast array of enumerated powers, including regulating commerce, coining money, raising and supporting armies, creating the courts, establishing post offices and roads, declaring war, and levying taxes (see Article I,

Section 8, of the Constitution in the appendix). In contrast, the president was given few explicit powers and played a much less prominent role early in our history. Furthermore, much of Congress's authority came from its implicit powers, which were rooted in the elastic clause of Article I of the Constitution, which gives Congress the power "to make all Laws which shall be necessary and proper for carrying into Execution the foregoing Powers."

As noted in Chapter 2, the compromises that gave rise to Congress's initial structure reflected an attempt to reconcile the competing interests of the day (large versus small states, northern versus southern interests, and proponents of strong national power versus state power). These compromises included establishing a system of **bicameralism**, that is, a bicameral (two-chambered) institution made up of a popularly elected House and a Senate chosen by state legislatures; allowing each slave to count as three-fifths of a person for purposes of apportionment for the House; and setting longer terms for senators (six years) than for House members (two years).

But these compromises also laid the foundation for the split loyalties that members of Congress have: they must respond to both their local constituencies and the nation's interests. Although the Founders hoped that Congress would pass legislation that emphasized the national good over local interests, they also recognized the importance of local constituencies. Thus, the relatively short two-year House term was intended to tie legislators to public sentiment.

At the same time, the *Federalist Papers* made it clear that the new government was by no means a direct democracy that would put all policy questions to the public. In *Federalist 57*, Madison asserted that "the aim of every political constitution is, or ought to be, first to obtain for rulers men who possess most wisdom to discern, and most virtue to pursue, the common good of the society." This common good may often conflict with local concerns, such that members are expected to both "refine and enlarge the debate" to encompass the common good *and* represent their local constituents.

In general, the Founders viewed the Senate as the more likely institution to enlarge the debate and speak for the national interests; it was intended to check the more responsive and passionate House. Because senators were indirectly elected and served longer terms than House members, the Senate was more insulated from the people. A famous (although perhaps fictional) story of an argument between George Washington and Thomas Jefferson points out the differences between the House and Senate. Jefferson did not think the Senate was necessary, while Washington supported having two chambers. During the argument, Jefferson poured some coffee he was drinking into his saucer. Washington asked him why he had done so. "To cool it," replied Jefferson. "Even so," said Washington, "we pour legislation into the senatorial saucer to cool it." This idea of a more responsible Senate survived well into the twentieth century, even after the Seventeenth Amendment in 1913 allowed the direct, popular election of senators.

Today the Senate is still more insulated than the House. Because of the six-year terms of senators, only one-third of the 100 Senate seats are contested in each election, while all 435 House members are elected every two years. However, differences between the representational roles of the House and the Senate have become muted as senators seem to campaign for reelection 365 days a year, every year, just like House members.[3] This "permanent campaign" means that senators are now less insulated from electoral forces than they were in the past.

The relationship between the president and Congress has also evolved significantly. In the nineteenth century, Congress's roots in geographic constituencies made it well suited for the politics of the time. Although several great presidents left their mark on national politics early in U.S. history (George Washington, Andrew Jackson,

bicameralism
The system of having two chambers within one legislative body, like the House and Senate in the U.S. Congress.

The Founders viewed the House as more passionate than the Senate, or as the "hot coffee" that needed to be cooled in the "saucer" of the Senate. This perception probably did not include coming to blows over differences in policy as congressmen Albert G. Brown and John A. Wilcox did in 1851 about whether Mississippi should secede from the Union.

and Abraham Lincoln, among others), Congress dominated much of the day-to-day politics, which revolved around issues such as the tariff (taxes on imported or exported goods), slavery, and internal improvements such as building roads and canals. Given the tendency to address these issues with patronage and the pork barrel—that is, jobs and policies targeted to benefit specific constituents—Congress was better suited for the task than the president was.

Beginning around the turn of the twentieth century and accelerating with the New Deal of the 1930s (which established modern social welfare and regulatory policies), the scope of national policy expanded and politics became more centered in Washington. With this nationalization of politics and the increasing importance of national security issues from World War II through the War on Terror, the president has assumed a more central policy-making role. Nonetheless, the central tensions between representing local and national interests remain essential in understanding the legislative process and the relationship between members of Congress and their constituents.

Congress represents the people (or tries to)

Americans have a love-hate relationship with Congress; that is, we love our own member of Congress, but we hate Congress as a whole. Well, "hate" is a strong word, but as we show later in this section, individual members of Congress routinely have approval ratings 30 to 40 points higher than the institution's. One poll found that members of Congress landed third from the bottom in a ranking of 22 professions in terms of perceived honesty and ethical standards, narrowly ahead of car salespeople and lobbyists (nurses and military officers were at the top).[4] A more whimsical poll by Public Policy Polling asked respondents questions such as "What do you have a higher opinion of, Congress or root canals?" Root canals won handily, 56 percent to 32 percent. Congress was also less popular than head lice, traffic jams, and cockroaches, but narrowly beat out Lindsay Lohan and had a comfortable margin over the Ebola virus, the Kardashians, and meth labs.[5] Why is Congress so unpopular? How do members of Congress try to represent their constituents? And how do elections influence this important dynamic?

Types of Representation The relationships between constituents and their member of Congress can be characterized in two basic ways: as both descriptive and substantive. Descriptive representation occurs when members of Congress "look like" their constituents in demographic or socioeconomic terms. For example, are members African American, Latino, or white; male or female; Catholic, Protestant, or some other religion; middle-class or upper-class? Many people believe that this kind of representation is a distinct value in itself. Having positive role models for various demographic groups helps create greater trust in the system. Moreover, constituents benefit from being represented by someone who shares something as basic as their skin color.

Descriptive representation is also related to the perceived responsiveness of a member of Congress. In general, constituents report higher levels of satisfaction with representatives who are of their same racial or ethnic background. Thus, descriptively represented constituents are more likely than those who are not to assume that their interests are being represented.[6] If you doubt that descriptive representation makes a difference, ask yourself whether it would be fair if all 435 House members and 100 senators were white male Protestants. Although the demographics of Congress are considerably more diverse than this, the legislature does not come close to "looking like us" on a nationwide scale (see the What Do the Facts Say? feature). This is especially true in the Senate, where only ten African Americans and nine Latinos have served in the history of the institution (three African Americans and five Latinos currently are in the Senate as of 2017).[7]

Descriptive Representation in the 115th Congress

Compared with a generation ago, the number of women and racial and ethnic minorities in Congress has increased. But on these dimensions, how representative of the people is Congress? How close does Congress come to "looking like us"? What do the facts say?

Gender in Congress

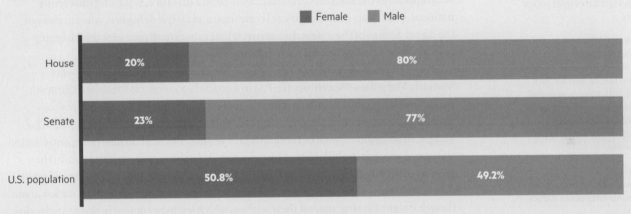

Racial and Ethnic Composition of Congress

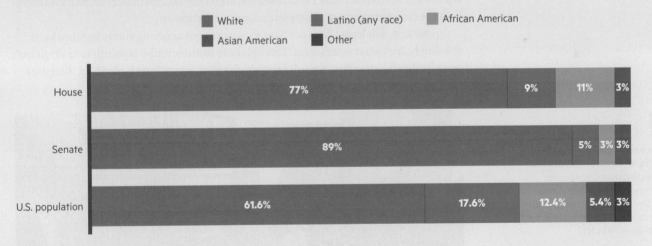

Think about it

- Which comes closer to "looking like us," the House or the Senate?
- How could having more women or racial and ethnic minorities in Congress affect legislation and policy decisions?
- Latinos now make up the largest ethnic minority in the United States, yet they still lag behind African Americans in terms of representation in the House. Why do you think this is?

Source: Jennifer Manning, Congressional Research Service, "Membership of the 115th Congress: A Profile," October 1, 2018, fas.org/sgp/crs/misc/R44762.pdf (accessed 10/17/18).

Although descriptive representation is important, it goes only so far. More important than a member's race, gender, or religion, many argue, is the *substance* of what that person does. The fact that a representative shares some characteristics with you does not necessarily mean that he or she will represent your interests. However, extensive research demonstrates a link between descriptive representation and how our elected leaders represent us: minority members of Congress are more likely to pay attention to racial issues than white members are, and female members are more committed to women's issues than male members are. For example, political scientist Michele Swers finds that women senators are more active than male senators on women's issues, playing a key role on fair pay, abortion, women's rights, and representation on the Supreme Court.[8]

Substantive representation involves *how* the member serves constituents' interests. Two long-standing models of this kind of representation are (1) the **trustee**, who represents the interests of constituents from a distance, weighing numerous national, collective, local, and moral concerns; and (2) the **delegate**, who carries out the direct desires of the voters. In a sense, trustees are more concerned with being responsible and delegates are more interested in being responsive.

One of the most famous examples of a representative acting as a trustee was Marjorie Margolies-Mezvinsky (D-PA) in a crucial 1993 vote on President Clinton's budget, which included controversial tax increases and spending cuts to balance the budget. Hours before the vote, she told reporters that she would vote against the budget, in accordance with her constituents' wishes. But she had also promised Clinton she would support the bill if her vote was needed. As she cast the critical vote in the 218–216 cliff-hanger (in which she fulfilled her promise to the president), she did what she thought was in the best long-term interests of her constituents and the nation, even though it meant voting against their wishes, which led to her defeat in the next election. More recently, in 2008, bipartisan majorities in the House and Senate voted for the hugely unpopular Troubled Asset Relief Program (TARP or, as its critics called it, the Wall Street bailout) because President Bush and congressional leaders convinced them it was necessary to prevent a complete economic meltdown.

In contrast, a delegate does not have to worry about angering voters because he or she simply does what voters want. Examples are so numerous it is pointless to single out one member for attention: when it comes to tax cuts, agricultural subsidies, increases

substantive representation
Representation in which a member of Congress serves constituents' interests and shares their policy concerns.

trustee
A member of Congress who represents constituents' interests while also taking into account national, collective, and moral concerns that sometimes cause the member to vote against the preference of a majority of constituents.

delegate
A member of Congress who loyally represents constituents' direct interests.

Members of Congress spend a good deal of time in their districts, developing relationships with constituents. Here, Representative Elise Stefanik (R-NY) speaks with constituents in a town hall meeting in South Glens Falls, NY.

in Medicare payments, or new highway projects, hundreds of representatives act as delegates for their districts' interests.

Truth be told, nearly all members act like trustees in some circumstances and like delegates in others. The third model of representation captures this reality: the **politico** is more likely to act as a delegate on issues that are highly salient to his or her constituency (such as immigration reform or farm subsidies) but as a trustee on less salient or very complex issues (such as some foreign policies). Therefore, the crucial component of representation is the nature of the constituency and how the member of Congress attempts to balance and represent constituents' conflicting needs and desires.

The Role of the Constituency Most voters do not monitor their representatives' behavior closely. Can representation work if voters are not paying attention?

Members of Congress behave as if voters were paying attention, even when constituents are inattentive. Incumbents know that at election time challengers may raise issues that become salient after the public thinks about them, so they try to deter challengers by anticipating what the constituents would want *if* they were fully informed.[9] For example, the public didn't know much about the FBI's inability to hack into locked phones, but it became an issue in the 2016 elections when the FBI tried to force Apple to allow it to access a phone used by a suspect in the San Bernardino shootings. Savvy incumbents would have tried to stake out a position consistent with what the voters would want *before* a strong challenger raised the issue in a campaign. Richard F. Fenno, one of the leading congressional scholars of the twentieth century, points out that some segments of the constituency are more attentive and more important for a member's reelection than others (see Figure 11.1).[10]

Another way to examine the representative–constituency relationship is to look at differences across districts. How do districts vary? First, they differ in size: Senate "districts" (that is, states) vary in terms of area and population. House districts all have about 755,000 people, but they vary tremendously in geographic size. Second, districts differ in terms of who lives there and what they want from government. Some districts are located in poor city neighborhoods, where voters' concerns are economic development, crime control, antipoverty programs, and looser immigration

politico
A member of Congress who acts as a delegate on issues that constituents care about (such as immigration reform) and as a trustee on more complex or less salient issues (such as some foreign policy or regulatory matters).

FIGURE 11.1

How Do Representatives See Their Constituents?

The concentric circles of a congressional constituency illustrate the various parts of a district that a member represents. Can you think of an issue on which House members would be more responsive to their reelection constituency than to their geographic constituency?

Source: Based on Richard F. Fenno, *Home Style: House Members in Their Districts* (Boston: Little, Brown, 1978).

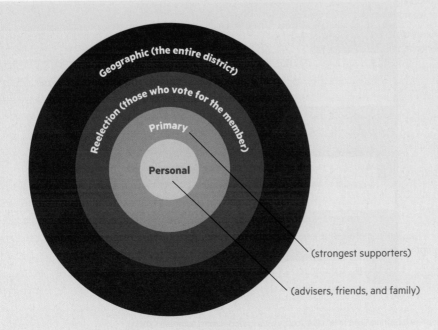

Geographic (the entire district)

Reelection (those who vote for the member)

Primary

Personal

(strongest supporters)

(advisers, friends, and family)

regulations. Some are wealthy and urban, where citizens are more supportive of foreign aid and higher taxes. Some are suburban, where funding for education and transportation is critical. Some are conservative and rural, where agricultural policies, gun rights, and support for tax cuts dominate. Districts vary from the religious to the secular, from domination by one industry to a diversified corporate base to no industry at all. Some consider government a force for good, while others argue that government should get off people's backs. And some districts are a mixture of all these things.

Because districts are so multifaceted, the legislators they elect differ from one another as well. Regardless of the office, most voters want to elect someone whose policy positions are close to theirs. As a result, legislators tend to reflect the central tendencies of their districts. At one level, electing a legislature that "thinks like America" sounds good: if legislators act and think like their districts, then the legislature will contain a good mixture of the interests representing the country or state. But this often makes finding compromise difficult. We elect legislators to get things done, but they may be unable to agree on anything because their disagreements are too fundamental to bridge. Consider abortion rights. The country is sharply divided on this issue, as are the House, the Senate, and most state legislatures. The fact that legislators have not come to a decision on this issue is no surprise: just as citizens disagree, so do their elected representatives.

Despite the vast differences between congressional constituencies, voters want many of the same things: a healthy economy, a safe country (in terms of national defense and local crime), good schools, and effective health care. Figure 11.2 reports responses to a survey about how citizens feel that legislators should do their jobs. The

FIGURE 11.2

What Do People Want from Congress?

Members of Congress are often criticized for being out of touch with their constituents. Based on a *USA Today* poll, Americans seem to want their congressional members to vote in line with their constituents' views, to work across party lines, and to spend more time in the district rather than Washington, D.C. But what happens if these goals conflict? What if the member represents a very partisan district where the majority does not want him or her to work with the other party? Also, is there no room for trustees who follow their conscience and stick to their principles?

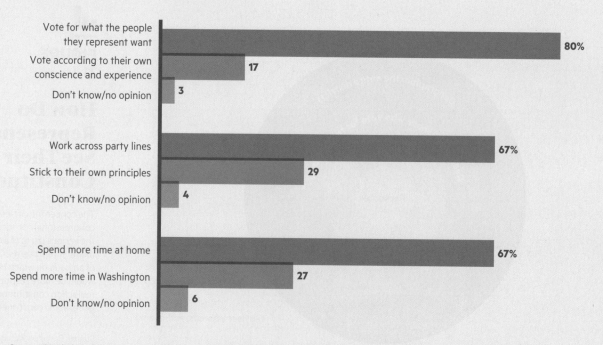

Source: "Divided We Still Stand—and Getting Used to It," *USA Today*, www.usatoday.com (accessed 4/11/14).

survey shows tensions between being a delegate and a trustee. Respondents want their representatives to "vote for what the people they represent want" and "spend more time at home," though they show little interest in having the representatives "spend more time in Washington." Thus, responsibilities for national interests may be more difficult for members of Congress to explain to their constituents.

Members of Congress want to keep their jobs

Members' relationships to their constituents also must be understood within the context of their desire to be reelected. Political scientist David R. Mayhew argues in *Congress: The Electoral Connection* that reelection must come first.[11] Members certainly hold multiple goals, including making good policy, but if they cannot maintain their seats, then they cannot attain other goals in office.

After assuming that reelection is central, Mayhew asks this question: "Members of Congress may be electorally motivated, but are they in a position to do anything about it?"[12] Although individual members of Congress cannot do much to alter national economic or political forces that may affect voters' choices, they can control their own activities in the House or Senate. The importance of the **electoral connection** in explaining the behavior of members of Congress seems especially clear for marginal incumbents who are constantly trying to shore up their electoral base. But for those from safe districts, why should they worry?

electoral connection
The idea that congressional behavior is centrally motivated by members' desire for reelection.

Incumbents Work toward Reelection While objectively it looks as though about 90 percent of House members (and a large proportion of senators) are absolutely safe (see Figure 11.3), incumbents realize that this security is not guaranteed. Even in elections

FIGURE 11.3

House and Senate Reelection Rates

The whole House is up for reelection every two years, so the line showing the reelection of House members in a given election year represents the percentage of the entire House. Since senators are up for reelection every six years, only one-third of the members are seeking reelection every two years. The line for the Senate represents the percentage of those who won who were up for reelection in that election year. Why do you think that House members have an easier time getting reelected than senators?

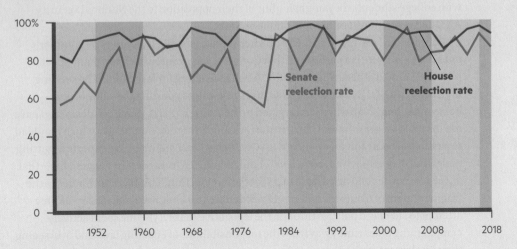

Sources: The 1946–2012 percentages were compiled from Norman J. Ornstein, Thomas E. Mann, Michael J. Malbin, and Andrew Rugg, "Vital Statistics on Congress," www.brookings.edu/vitalstats, pp. 49–50 (accessed 4/18/14); 2014–2018 percentages were calculated from opensecrets.org (accessed 11/7/18).

with relatively low turnover overall, many incumbents are "running scared"; in every election, a few supposedly safe incumbents are unexpectedly defeated, and members tend to think that it could happen to them the next time around. Mayhew warns: "When we say 'Congressman Smith is unbeatable,' we do not mean that there is nothing he could do that would lose him his seat." As we noted in Chapter 9, this actually means: "Congressman Smith is unbeatable as long as he continues to do the things that he is doing."[13] Members recognize that becoming inattentive to their district, being on the wrong side of a key string of votes, or failing to bring home the district's share of federal benefits could cost them their seats. A potential challenger is always waiting in the wings.

Mayhew outlines three ways that members promote their chances for reelection: advertising, credit claiming, and position taking. Each approach shapes the way members relate to their constituents. "Advertising" in this context refers to appeals or appearances without issue content that get the member's name in front of the public in a favorable way. Advertising includes activities associated with "working the district," such as attending town meetings; appearing in a parade; going to a local Rotary Club lunch; or sending letters of congratulation for graduations, birthdays, or anniversaries. Members of Congress also spend a fair amount of time meeting with their constituents in Washington, D.C., including seeing school groups, tourists, and interest groups from their districts.

In "credit claiming," the member of Congress takes credit for something of value to voters—most commonly, pork-barrel policies targeted to benefit specific constituents or the district as a whole. The goods must be specific and small enough in scale that the member of Congress may believably claim credit. In other words, it is far less credible to take credit for a national drop in violent crime or an increase in SAT scores than for the renovations at a local veterans' hospital or a highway improvement grant. The other main source of credit claiming is **casework** for individual constituents who request help with tasks such as tracking down a lost Social Security check or expediting the processing of a passport. This activity, like advertising, has both district-based and Washington-based components.

"Position taking" refers to any public statement—such as a roll call vote, speech, editorial, or position paper—about a topic of interest to constituents or interest groups. This may be the toughest aspect of a member's job, because, on many issues, the member is likely to alienate a certain segment of the population no matter what position he or she takes. Members try to appeal to specific audiences within their district. For example, while speaking to the Veterans of Foreign Wars members might emphasize their support for a particular new weapons program, but in meetings with college students they might highlight their opposition to the National Security Agency's collection of millions of phone records.

Representatives' focus on reelection has some costs. We'll identify five common ones here: (1) There is a perception that Congress has granted itself too many special privileges aimed at securing reelection (such as funding for large staffs and sending mail at no cost). (2) Evidence suggests that some voters question the value of pork-barrel spending, even when it is targeted to their district.[14] (3) Members' desire to please means that Congress has a difficult time refusing any group's demands, which may lead to passage of contradictory policies. (4) Given that most members are experts at getting reelected, they achieve a certain level of independence from the party leadership—that is, they do not depend on party leaders for their reelection. This fact contributes to the fragmentation of Congress and creates difficulties for congressional leaders as they attempt to shepherd policies through the legislative maze. (5) Time spent actively campaigning takes time away from the responsibilities of enacting laws and overseeing their implementation.

The desire to be reelected influences House members' and senators' behavior both in their districts and in Congress. Consider the early career of Senator Tammy

casework
Assistance provided by members of Congress to their constituents in solving problems with the federal bureaucracy or addressing other specific concerns.

Baldwin (D-WI), who served as the representative of Wisconsin's 2nd congressional district from 1999 to 2013. Initially elected in 1998, she was Wisconsin's first female representative and the first openly gay person ever elected to a freshman term in Congress.[15] In her first two elections, she won with the overwhelming support of liberal voters in Madison, but she lost the surrounding rural areas and suburbs, narrowly winning districtwide. Baldwin recognized that she needed to shore up support outside Madison, and she spent time over the next several years meeting with constituents in the rural and suburban parts of her district. She also explored issues important to these voters, such as the dairy price support program and the problem of chronic wasting disease in Wisconsin deer. Having built up her electoral base (and having benefited from favorable redistricting in 2002), she cruised to victories in her next two elections, winning nearly two-thirds of the vote. After winning reelection to the House four more times, she became the first lesbian elected to the Senate in 2012.

The Incumbency Advantage Members' success at pleasing constituents produces large election rewards. As Figure 11.3 shows, very few members are defeated in their reelection races. One way that political scientists have documented the growth of the incumbency advantage is to examine the electoral margins in House elections. If a member is elected with less than 55 percent of the vote, he or she is said to hold a marginal seat. Since the late 1960s, the number of marginal districts has been declining. Having fewer marginal districts does not necessarily translate into fewer incumbent defeats, but in the past two decades incumbent reelection rates have been near record high levels, with 95 to 98 percent of House incumbents winning in many years.[16]

In 2008, in an election that many called transformational, 95 percent of House incumbents were still reelected. Although the Democrats picked up some seats in the Senate, reelection remained the norm there as well. Even in the "tsunami" election of 2010, in which Republicans made the largest gains in the House since 1948, picking up 63 seats, 86 percent of all incumbents were reelected. Why are incumbents so successful? Scholars have offered several reasons for this increase in incumbency advantage.

In the District: Home Style One explanation for increasing incumbency advantage is rooted in the diversity of congressional districts and states. Members typically respond to the diversity in their districts by developing an appropriate home style: a way of relating to the district.[17] A home style shapes the way members allocate resources, the way incumbents present themselves to their district, and the way they explain their policy positions.

Given the variation among districts, members' home styles vary as well. In some rural districts it is important for representatives to have local roots and voters expect extensive contact with members. Urban districts expect a different kind of style. They have a more mobile population, so it is not crucial to be homegrown. Voters expect less direct contact and place more emphasis on how members explain their policy positions. Incumbency advantage may be explained in part by the skill with which members have cultivated their individual home styles in the last two decades. Members are spending more time at home and less time in Washington than was true a generation ago. This familiarity with the voters has helped them remain in office.

Table 11.1 shows how one member, Senator Tammy Baldwin, spent her time in Washington and in her district as a House member. In general, a legislator's workday in the Capitol is split between committee meetings, briefings, staff meetings, meetings with constituents, and various dinners and fund-raisers with interest groups and other organizations, punctuated by dashes to the floor of the House or Senate to vote. Days in the district are spent meeting with constituents to explain what is happening in Washington and to listen to voters' concerns.

incumbency advantage
The relative infrequency with which members of Congress are defeated in their attempts for reelection.

TABLE
11.1

Typical Workdays for a Congressional Representative

Members of Congress are generally busy from morning until late at night, both in Washington, D.C., and in their districts, attending meetings and events. This is the actual schedule for Tammy Baldwin when she represented Wisconsin's 2nd congressional district in the House.

In Washington, D.C. (votes scheduled throughout the day)

9:15–9:45	Office time
9:45–10:00	Caucus, Democratic members, Subcommittee on Energy and Environment on markup legislation
10:00–12:00	Markup H.R. 3276, H.R. 3258, H.R. 2868, Subcommittee on Energy and Environment
11:30–11:45	Step outside markup to meet with constituents on specifics of health care reform legislation
12:00–12:15	Travel to Department of Justice
12:15–1:15	Lunch with Attorney General Eric Holder
1:30–1:45	Meet with health care CEO on specifics of health care reform legislation
2:00–3:00	Meet with members who support single-payer health care amendment
3:00–4:30	Markup H.R. 3792, Subcommittee on Health
4:30–5:30	Office time
5:30–6:00	Caucus, Democratic members, Energy and Commerce Committee on financial services bill
6:00–6:30	Meet with legislative staff
6:30–7:00	Meet with chief of staff
7:00–7:50	Office time
8:00–10:00	Dinner with chief of staff and political adviser

In the District

7:00 ET–8:00 CT	Fly from Washington, D.C., to Madison, WI
8:15–10:30	Free time at home
10:30–10:40	Phone interview with area radio station on constituent survey, health care reform, and upcoming listening session
12:15–12:25	Travel to office
12:25–1:00	Office time, edit/sign correspondence
1:00–1:20	Travel to Madison West High School
1:30–1:55	Remarks at school plaza dedication ceremony
2:00–2:30	Travel to Stoughton, WI
2:45–5:00	Listening session (originally scheduled for one hour but continued until all present could speak)
5:00–5:40	Travel home
5:15–5:20	Phone interview with University of Wisconsin student radio station
6:15–6:45	Travel to Middleton, WI
7:00–8:00	Attend and give brief remarks at NAACP annual banquet
8:05–8:25	Travel home

Note: The authors would like to thank then-Representative Tammy Baldwin and her press secretary, Jerilyn Goodman, for sharing this information. Ms. Goodman emphasized that there really isn't a "typical day" for a member but said that these two days illustrate the workload. Baldwin was elected to the U.S. Senate in 2012.

Campaign Fund-Raising Raising money is also key to staying in office. Incumbents need money to pay for campaign staff, travel, and advertising. It takes at least $1 million to make a credible challenge to an incumbent in most districts, and in many areas with expensive media markets the minimum price tag is $2 million or more. Few challengers can raise that much money. The gap between incumbent and challenger spending has grown dramatically in the past decade, and incumbents now spend about three times as much, on average, as challengers. (For more on campaign finance, see Chapters 9 and 10.)

Money also functions as a deterrent to potential challengers. A sizable reelection fund signals that an incumbent knows how to raise money and will run a strong campaign. The aim is to convince would-be challengers that they have only a slim chance of beating the incumbent—and to convince contributors and party organizations that there's no point in trying to find or support a challenger.

This last point is crucial in explaining incumbency advantage, because it is nearly impossible for a weak challenger to beat an incumbent. Consider that only 10 to 15 percent of challengers in a typical election year have any previous elective experience; when such a high proportion of challengers are amateurs, it is not surprising that so many incumbents win.

Constituency Service Another thing incumbents do to get reelected is "work their districts," taking every opportunity to meet with constituents, listen to their concerns, and perform casework (helping constituents interact with government programs or agencies). Most legislators travel around their districts or states with several staffers whose job is to follow up with people who meet the incumbent, write down their contact information, and note what the incumbent has promised to do for them. High levels of constituency service may help explain why some incumbents have become electorally secure.

DID YOU KNOW?

On average, House incumbents raised

$1,804,091

for their campaigns in 2018. The average Senate incumbent raised $12,773,950. This is compared with $392,259 and $1,882,731 for the average House and Senate challengers.

Source: Opensecrets.org

Tammy Duckworth (D-IL) meets with constituents in her office in Washington, D.C., in 2013.

Members of Congress love doing constituency service because it is an easy way to make voters happy. If a member can help a constituent solve a problem, that person will be more likely to support the member in the future.[18] Many voters might give the incumbent some credit simply for being willing to listen. Therefore, most members devote a significant portion of their staff to constituency service, publish newsletters that tout their good deeds on behalf of constituents, and solicit citizens' requests for help through their newsletters and websites. Most House members have a "How can I help?" type of link on their home page that connects to information on government agencies, grants, internships, service academies, and visiting Washington, D.C.

Most House members work their districts to an extreme; they are said to be in the "Tuesday to Thursday Club," meaning they are in Washington only during the middle of the week and spend the rest of their time at home in their districts. These members go to diners and coffee shops on Saturday mornings to chat, spend the day at public events in their "Meet Your Representative" RV, then hit the bowling alleys at night to meet a few more people. One member has even joked that his wife has given up sending him out for groceries because he spends three hours talking with people while getting a loaf of bread.

This combination of factors gives incumbents substantial advantages over candidates who might run against them. By virtue of their position, they can help constituents who have problems with an agency or a program. They attract media attention because of their actions in office; small local newspapers will even reprint members' press releases verbatim. Members can use the money and other resources associated with their position for casework and contact with voters (trips home to their district and the salaries of their staffers who do constituency service are taxpayer funded). And they use their official position as a platform for raising campaign cash. A contributor who donates as a way to gain access to the policy-making process will be inclined to give to someone already in office. Finally, most incumbents represent states or districts whose partisan balance (the number of likely supporters of their party versus the number likely to prefer the other party) is skewed in their favor—if it weren't, they probably wouldn't have won the seat in the first place.

House reelection rates have gone upwards of 80 percent for decades, but incumbents still campaign vigorously. Congressman Dana Rohrabacher (R-CA) is shown here celebrating his primary win ahead of the general election. He ultimately lost his reelection bid to Democrat Harley Rouda.

National Forces in Congressional Elections There is also another consequence of the electoral connection. Because congressional politics tends to be local, voters generally are not strongly influenced by the president or the national parties. Because most incumbents can insulate themselves from national forces, it is more difficult to hold members of Congress accountable. For example, in the 2016 elections 62 percent of the people believed the nation was "on the wrong track." Yet 97 percent of House incumbents won reelection.

Many House and Senate candidates distance themselves from the national party. For example, in a 2018 House race in suburban Philadelphia, Republican nominee Dan David was asked if he wanted President Trump to campaign for him and he replied, "I would like the president to do his job and I'll do mine."[19] (He lost by nearly 27 points.) However, there are nationalized "wave" elections in which national issues can overwhelm incumbents' attempts to insulate themselves. In 2006, many House Republicans tried to distance themselves from President Bush and the unpopular war in Iraq, but more than 20 Republicans were defeated and Democrats regained control of the House. In the 2010 midterms, the same thing happened to moderate Democrats, who were ousted by voters who believed the government had gone too far in its response to the recession and providing access to health care. These national forces led the Democrats to lose 63 House seats (and 6 Senate seats), with the result that the Republicans regained control of the House.

National forces in congressional elections also may be evident in presidential years. In 2008, Republicans faced a backlash against Bush, whose approval ratings had hit record lows. Republican members of Congress avoided being seen with him, and Democrats highlighted their opponents' earlier support for the president. In 2012, the congressional elections ratified the status quo; despite Obama's solid win, the Republicans retained control of the House and the Democrats increased their majority in the Senate only slightly. The 2016 presidential election featured two nominees, Hillary Clinton and Donald Trump, who had the highest negative ratings of any pair of major-party candidates. Republican congressional candidates were especially likely to distance themselves from their party's nominee. Overall, the localized nature of congressional elections and the incumbency advantage promote congressional stability in the face of presidential change. This dynamic has profound implications for governance because it increases the likelihood that different parties will control the presidency and Congress. Divided government complicates accountability. Because the president and Congress have become adept at blaming each other when things go wrong, voters do not always know who to vote out of office when they're unhappy with the status quo.

Redistricting connects representation and elections

The shape and makeup of congressional districts are critical to understanding representation in Congress and the electoral connection. District boundaries determine who is eligible to vote in any given congressional race, and these boundaries are re-drawn every 10 years, after each national census. **Redistricting** is usually the task of state legislatures. Its official purpose is to ensure that districts are roughly equal in population, which in turn ensures that every vote counts equally in determining the composition of the legislature.

District populations vary over time as people move from state to state or from one part of a state to another. At the national level, states gain or lose legislative seats after each census through **apportionment**, which is the process of dividing the fixed number of House seats (435) among the states based on increases and decreases in state populations. Thus, states growing the fastest gain seats, and states that are not growing as fast or that are losing population lose seats (for example, after the 2010 census Texas gained four seats in Congress while Ohio lost two). The one legislature in America that is not redistricted is the U.S. Senate, which has two legislators elected per state. Voters in small states thus have proportionally more influence than those in large states when it comes to the Senate.

redistricting
Re-drawing the geographic boundaries of legislative districts. This happens every 10 years to ensure that districts remain roughly equal in population.

apportionment
The process of assigning the 435 seats in the House to the states based on increases or decreases in state population.

In theory, redistricting proceeds from a set of principles that define what districts should look like. One criterion is that districts should be roughly equal in population based on the principles of "one-person, one-vote" established by the Supreme Court in the 1960s.[20] They should also reflect "communities of interest," grouping like-minded voters into the same district. There are also technical criteria, including compactness (districts should not have extremely bizarre shapes) and contiguity (one part of a district cannot be completely separated from the rest of the district). Mapmakers also try to respect traditional natural boundaries, avoid splitting municipalities, preserve existing districts, and avoid diluting the voting power of racial minorities.

Partisan Redistricting Although the preceding principles are important, they are not the driving force in the redistricting process. Suppose a Democrat holds a House seat from an urban district populated mainly by citizens with strong Democratic Party ties. After a census, the Republican-dominated state legislature develops a new plan that extends the representative's district into the suburbs, claiming that the change counteracts population declines within the city by adding suburban voters. However, these suburban voters will likely be Republicans, increasing the chance that the Democrat will face strong opposition in future elections and maybe lose his or her seat. Such changes have an important impact on voters as well. Voters who are "shifted" to a new district by a change in boundaries may be unable to vote for the incumbent they have supported for years and may instead get a representative who doesn't share their views.

In congressional redistricting, a reduction in the number of seats allocated to a state can lead to districting plans that put two incumbents in the same district, forcing them to run against each other. Incumbents from one party use these opportunities to defeat incumbents from the other party. Both parties use this technique and other tools of creative cartography to gain partisan advantage.

These attempts to use the redistricting process for political advantage are called **gerrymandering**. The term is named after Elbridge Gerry, a Massachusetts House member and governor, vice president under James Madison, and author of the original partisan redistricting plan in 1812 (including a district with a thin, winding shape resembling a salamander). While partisan motivations have produced some funny-looking districts (see Nuts & Bolts 11.1 for examples of a partisan gerrymander and redistricting strategies), the courts have allowed the practice to continue until recently. More than 30 years ago, the Supreme Court ruled that partisan gerrymandering *may* be unconstitutional, but over the next three decades the Court struggled to find a standard that allowed it to distinguish between partisan bias so extreme that it violated the Constitution and normal partisan politics.[21]

Then, from 2016 through 2018, a flood of litigation in federal and state courts showed judges' increasing willingness to rule that parties had gone too far in their redistricting plans. Increasingly sophisticated mapping programs and access to detailed political data allowed parties to slice and dice districts with increasing precision, yielding partisan maps that were no longer acceptable to the courts. In Wisconsin, North Carolina, Maryland, and Pennsylvania federal and state courts struck down state legislative and congressional maps that they ruled to be unfairly partisan (see the Take a Stand feature for more on the debate on this topic). However, in June 2018, the Supreme Court declined to rule on the constitutionality of partisan gerrymandering, instead referring the Wisconsin and Maryland cases back to the lower courts.[22] Cases from those two states, and probably North Carolina and Michigan, may make their way back to the Supreme Court in time for the 2020 congressional elections.

Racial Redistricting Redistricting may yield boundaries that look highly unusual. During the 1992 redistricting process in North Carolina, the Justice Department told state legislators that they needed to create two districts with majority populations of

gerrymandering
Attempting to use the process of re-drawing district boundaries to benefit a political party, protect incumbents, or change the proportion of minority voters in a district.

Types of Gerrymanders

We have learned that the redistricting process is a powerful tool politicians can use to help their party, or individual members, win and maintain seats in Congress. Let's look at two key types of gerrymandering.

Partisan gerrymanders

Elected officials from one party draw district lines that benefit candidates from their party and hurt candidates from other parties. This usually occurs when one party has majorities in both houses of the state legislature and occupies the governorship and can therefore enact redistricting legislation without input from the minority party.

Redistricting
■ The new 9th district

Previous Districts
■ 10th—Dennis Kucinich
■ 13th—Betty Sutton
■ 9th—Marcy Kaptur

After the 2010 census, Ohio lost two seats in Congress (see our discussion of apportionment on page 389). Republicans controlled the redistricting process and wanted the loss of seats to come from the Democrats. So the Republicans drew a new 9th congressional district that cut across the districts of three existing Democratic members of Congress. Obviously only one could win the Democratic primary—that happened to be Marcy Kaptur. Democrats Kucinich and Sutton had to leave Congress.

Racial gerrymanders

Redistricting is used to help or hurt the chances of minority legislative candidates. The Voting Rights Act (VRA) of 1965 mandated that districting plans for many parts of the South be approved by the U.S. Department of Justice or a Washington, D.C., district court. Subsequent interpretations of the 1982 VRA amendments and Supreme Court decisions led to the creation of districts in which racial minorities are in the majority. The aim of these majority-minority districts was to raise the percentage of African-American and Latino elected officials.

Chicago

■ The new 4th congressional district

Illinois's 4th congressional district is a clear example of racial gerrymandering. The district has a very odd shape, but it incorporates two heavily Latino areas. (The northern part has a high Puerto Rican population and the southern part is largely Mexican; both areas are heavily Democratic.) This district is a stronghold of Democrat Luis Gutiérrez, who is of Puerto Rican descent, and is seen as a safe district for Democrats.

Partisan Redistricting

Partisan redistricting is the redrawing of legislative district lines in a way that gives one party an advantage. As we have noted, until recently the courts allowed the practice as a normal part of politics: of course, the majority party that controls the redistricting process has tried to stack the deck in its favor. When combined with the reluctance of the Supreme Court to address "political questions"—those that are better left to the elected branches—there was a powerful incentive to stay out of the "political thicket."[a] But as mapping software and "big data" political tools became readily available, the extent of partisan bias in redistricting became more pronounced. In Pennsylvania, a Republican gerrymander gave the party 13 of the state's 18 U.S. House seats, despite the Republicans' failure to win a majority of the statewide vote in the House races. In Maryland, a Democratic gerrymander turned a safe Republican House seat into a Democratic seat. Should this practice be reined in by the Court? Is it fair that some votes seem to count more than others?

Redistricting is always partisan. Those who say that the courts should stay out of redistricting argue that the practice is inherently partisan. The majority party will always try to solidify or expand its power when it has the opportunity. This has been true since the earliest years of our nation. Furthermore, those on this side of the argument say that courts are not well suited to draw legislative maps; this responsibility should remain with the state legislatures.

A second line of argument concedes that the process has gotten a little out of hand, but contends that the standard for redistricting should be partisan neutrality rather than partisan fairness. That is, rather than trying to make sure that the votes for candidates of one party have the same collective impact on the outcome of elections as the votes for the other party (fairness), the redistricting process should simply ignore partisanship (neutrality).

Partisan redistricting undermines democracy. The other side of the debate counters that just because we have always had partisan gerrymandering doesn't make it right. Indeed, democracy means that voters should be able to choose their representatives, not the other way around. Because politicians have a self-interest in maintaining their political power and will work to further this self-interest through redistricting, unfairly drawn districts undermine democratic accountability.

The strategy of emphasizing neutrality instead of fairness in redistricting is plausible, but does not convince those who support this side of the argument. While it is true that Republicans would continue to have some advantage in most states if districts were neutrally drawn, it is possible to draw maps that follow traditional districting principles but also promote partisan fairness.

As noted on page 390, the Supreme Court declined to rule on the constitutionality of partisan gerrymandering in 2018 and will probably have to revisit this issue before the 2020 elections.

take a stand

1. If you were a Supreme Court justice, how would you have ruled in the Wisconsin and Maryland cases? Should partisan redistricting be limited?

2. Is the appropriate standard for evaluating a legislative map partisan neutrality or partisan fairness? Or should the courts stay out of redistricting entirely?

Maryland's 6th congressional district.

Pennsylvania's 7th congressional district from 2011 map.

North Carolina Redistricting, 1992

FIGURE
11.4

This set of House districts was the subject of the landmark Supreme Court ruling *Shaw v. Reno* (1993), in which the Court said that "appearances matter" when drawing district lines. Do you agree? Should other factors such as race, party, and competitiveness play a greater role than district shape?

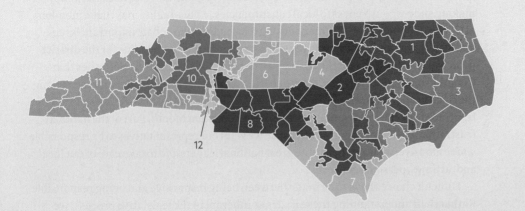

Source: North Carolina General Assembly, 1992 Congressional Base Plan No. 10, http://ncga.state.nc.us (accessed 10/26/12).

minority voters (called majority-minority districts). Figure 11.4 shows the plan the legislature enacted, in which the district boundaries look like a pattern of spiderwebs and ink blots. Moreover, one of the districts had parts that ended up being only as wide as I-85, following the highway off an exit ramp, over a bridge, and down the entrance ramp on the other side. This move prevented the I-85 district from bisecting the district it was traveling through, which would have violated the state law requiring contiguous districts.

The North Carolina example shows how convoluted redistricting plans can become. Part of the complexity is due to the availability of census databases that allow line drawers to divide voters as closely as they want, moving neighborhood by neighborhood, even house by house. Why bother with this level of detail? Because redistricting influences who gets elected; it is active politicking in its most fundamental form. The North Carolina plan was ultimately declared unconstitutional by the U.S. Supreme Court—a ruling that opened the door for dozens of lawsuits about racial redistricting. (See the discussion in Chapter 5 of the Voting Rights Act of 1965 and more recent Supreme Court rulings on racial redistricting, especially the 2013 case in which the Court struck down the part of the law that identified states that needed to have their redistricting plans preapproved by the Justice Department.[23]) The current legal standard is that race cannot be the predominant factor in drawing congressional district lines, but it can be one of the factors. Nonetheless, there is still plenty of room to create districts that will be composed of voters who will vote in ways that will have profound political consequences. The obvious political implications of redistricting often lead to demands that district plans be prepared or approved by nonpartisan committees or by panels of judges who are theoretically immune from political pressure. Such a process, as in Iowa, often produces more competitive districts.

The responsibility–responsiveness dilemma

As mentioned earlier, polls show that despite generally approving of their own member of Congress, people hold Congress itself in very low esteem. This is rooted in the conflicts that arise from Congress's dual roles: responsibility for national policy making and responsiveness to local constituencies.[24] This duality may make members of Congress appear to be simultaneously great leaders who debate important issues and locally oriented representatives who work hard to deliver benefits for the district (which may not be good for the country as a whole). Indeed, the range of issues that Congress must address is vast, from debating tax and health care reform to overseeing the classification of black-eyed peas, from debating the war on terror and expanding free trade to declaring a National Cholesterol Education Month. Part of the national frustration with Congress arises because we want our representatives to be responsible *and* responsive; we want them to be great national leaders *and* to take care of our local and, at times, personal concerns.

Difficult choices have to be made between being responsive and being responsible. Rather than understanding these issues as inherent in the legislative process, we often accuse members of **gridlock** and partisan bickering when our conflicting demands are not met. For example, public-opinion polls routinely show that the public wants lower taxes; more spending on education, the environment, and health care; and balanced budgets. But those three things cannot happen simultaneously. We often expect the impossible from Congress and then are frustrated when it doesn't happen.

gridlock
An inability to enact legislation because of partisan conflict within Congress or between Congress and the president.

Party leadership is central in the legislative process. In 2017 and 2018, Speaker of the House Paul Ryan (R-WI), Senate Majority Leader Mitch McConnell (R-KY), Senate Minority Leader Chuck Schumer (D-NY), and House Minority Leader Nancy Pelosi (D-CA) had to work together and with other members of Congress to pass legislation.

The responsibility–responsiveness dilemma brings us back to the puzzle we posed at the beginning of this section: Why is there a persistent 30 to 40 percent gap between approval ratings for individual members and for the institution? As Richard Fenno put it, "If Congress is the 'broken branch,' how come we love our congressman so much?"[25] The answer may simply be that members of Congress tend to respond more to their constituents' demands than to take on the responsibility of solving national problems. And when Congress becomes embroiled in debates about constituencies' conflicting demands, the institution may appear ineffectual. But as long as members keep the "folks back home" happy, their individual popularity will remain high.

How would you like your member of Congress to represent you? Should members represent the interests of just their district or the broader nation? Should they be responsive or responsible? Constituents have an interest in holding their members accountable, yet most congressional elections are not very competitive. So if you don't like how your member is representing you, what can you do about it? Understanding the nature of representation and the incumbency advantage can help answer these important questions.

"Why Should I Care?"

The structure of Congress

EXAMINE HOW PARTIES, THE COMMITTEE SYSTEM, AND STAFFERS ENABLE CONGRESS TO FUNCTION

As we have seen, the goal of getting reelected greatly influences the behavior of members of Congress. The reelection goal also has a strong influence on the way that Congress is structured, both formally (staff, the committee system, parties, and leadership roles) and informally (norms). Despite the importance of the electoral connection, the goal of being reelected cannot explain everything about members' behavior and the congressional structure. This section examines some other explanations that underlie the informal and formal structures of Congress: the policy motivations of members, the partisan basis for congressional institutions, and the importance of the committee system.

Informal structures

Various norms provide an informal structure for the way Congress works. *Universalism* is the norm that when benefits are divided up, they should be awarded to as many districts and states as possible. Thus, when it comes to handing out federal highway dollars or expenditures for the Pentagon's weapons programs, the benefits are broadly distributed across the entire country, which means that votes in support of these bills tend to be very lopsided. For example, the $305 billion 2015 transportation bill contained some spending in every part of the country and passed by an 83–16 vote in the Senate and a 359–65 margin in the House.[26]

Another norm, **logrolling**, reinforces universalism with the idea that "if you scratch my back, I'll scratch yours." This norm leads members of Congress to support bills that they otherwise might not vote for in exchange for other members' votes on bills that are very important to them. For example, House members from a dairy state might vote for tobacco price supports even if their state has no tobacco farmers, and in return they would expect a member from the tobacco state to vote for the dairy price support bill. This norm can produce wasteful pork-barrel spending. For example, in the 2011 budget a $1.1 trillion omnibus appropriations bill contained more than 6,488 **earmarks** worth $8.3 billion, so nearly everyone gained something by passing it. The 2016 omnibus appropriations bill did not include any traditional earmarks, following the ban on formal earmarks in both the House and Senate in 2011, but there were still billions of dollars in targeted spending

logrolling
A form of reciprocity in which members of Congress support bills that they otherwise might not vote for in exchange for other members' votes on bills that are very important to them.

earmarks
Federally funded local projects attached to bills passed through Congress.

as members of Congress found ways to secure funding for their district or state. The late senator John McCain (R-AZ), Senate Armed Services Committee chairman, called it a last-minute mess full of "wasteful, unnecessary, and inappropriate pork-barrel projects."[27]

Representative Bill Flores (R-TX) poses with Faye, a potbellied pig, after a news conference held by Citizens Against Government Waste at the Phoenix Park Hotel to release the 2017 Congressional Pig Book, which identifies pork-barrel spending in Congress.

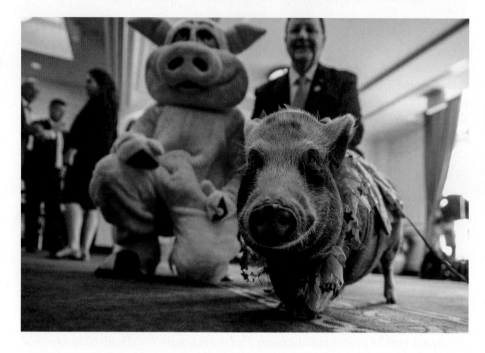

The norm of *specialization* is also important, both for the efficient operation of Congress and for members' reelection. By specializing and becoming an expert on a given issue, members provide valuable information to the institution as a whole and also create a basis for credit claiming. This norm is stronger in the House, where members often develop a few areas of expertise, whereas senators tend to be policy generalists. For example, Representative John Lewis (D-GA) has dedicated much of his decades-long House career to the issue of civil rights, while Senator John McCain (R-AZ) had his hand in a variety of issues, including campaign finance and lobbying reform, tax policy, telecommunications and aviation issues, national defense, foreign policy, and immigration policy.

The **seniority** norm also serves individual and institutional purposes. This norm holds that the member with the longest service on a given committee will chair that committee. Although there have been numerous violations of this norm in the past 30 years, whereby the most senior member has been passed over for someone whom the party leaders favored, the norm benefits the institution by ensuring orderly succession in committee leadership.[28] The norm also benefits members by providing a tangible reason why voters should return them to Congress year after year. Many members of Congress make this point when campaigning, and the issue is more than just posturing. Committee chairs *are* better able to "bring home the bacon" than a junior member who is still learning the ropes.

seniority
The informal congressional norm of choosing the member who has served the longest on a particular committee to be the committee chair.

Formal structures

Formal structures also shape members' behavior in Congress. Political parties, party leadership, the committee system, and staff provide the context within which members of Congress make policy and represent their constituents (see Nuts & Bolts 11.2).

Parties and Party Leaders Political parties are important for allocating power in Congress. Party leaders are always elected on straight party-line votes, with the

Majority-Party Structure in the House of Representatives and the Senate

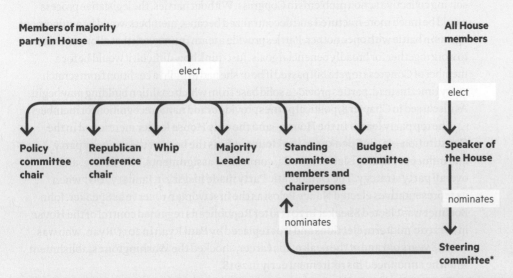

Members of majority party in House — elect

- Policy committee chair
- Republican conference chair
- Whip
- Majority Leader
- Standing committee members and chairpersons
- Budget committee

All House members — elect

- Speaker of the House — nominates — Steering committee*

Steering committee* — nominates → Standing committee members and chairpersons

*Steering committee includes the Speaker, majority leader, and whip, and some members who are appointed by the Speaker and some who are elected by the conference.

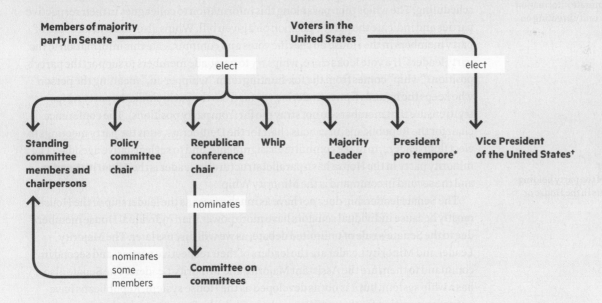

Members of majority party in Senate — elect

Voters in the United States — elect

- Standing committee members and chairpersons
- Policy committee chair
- Republican conference chair
- Whip
- Majority Leader
- President pro tempore*
- Vice President of the United States†

Republican conference chair — nominates → Committee on committees

Committee on committees — nominates some members → Standing committee members and chairpersons

*The president pro tempore is elected by the majority party members, but by custom is the most senior member of the majority party.
†The vice president of the United States is the president of the Senate, but rarely presides over the floor. The vice president's most important role is to break tie votes.

majority party determining committee leadership, the division of seats on committees, and the allocation of committee resources. Parties in Congress also become more important when opposing parties control the two chambers. This was the case from 1981 to 1986 and in 2018, when Republicans controlled the Senate and Democrats controlled the House, and in part of 2001 and 2002 and 2011–2014 when the opposite was true.

A leading theory of congressional organization points to the importance of parties in solving collective action problems in Congress. Without parties, the legislative process would be much more fractured and decentralized because members would be autonomous agents in battle with one another. Parties provide a team framework that allows members to work together for broadly beneficial goals. Just think how difficult it would be for a member of Congress to get a bill passed if he or she had to build a coalition from scratch every time. Instead, parties provide a solid base from which coalition building may begin. As discussed in Chapter 8, political parties provide brand name recognition for members.

The top party leader in the House—and the only House leader mentioned in the Constitution—is the **Speaker of the House**, who is the head of the majority party and influences the legislative agenda, committee assignments, scheduling, and overall party strategy. The Democratic Party made history in January 2007 when its representatives elected Nancy Pelosi as the first woman to serve as Speaker. John Boehner was elected Speaker in 2011 after Republicans regained control of the House in the 2010 midterm elections and was replaced by Paul Ryan in 2015. Ryan, who was only 48 years old and at the peak of his career, shocked the Washington establishment when he announced his retirement early in 2018.

The Speaker is aided by the **Majority Leader**, the Majority Whip, and the conference or caucus chair (in addition to many others in lower-level party positions). The Majority Leader is one of the national spokespersons for the party and also helps with the day-to-day operation of the legislative process. The Majority Whip oversees the extensive **whip system**, which has three functions: information gathering, information dissemination, and coalition building. The whips meet regularly to discuss legislative strategy and scheduling. The whips then pass along this information to colleagues in their respective parties and indicate the party's position on a given bill. Whips also take a head count of party members in the House on specific votes and communicate this information to the party leaders. If a vote looks close, whips try to persuade members to support the party's position ("whip" comes from the fox-hunting term "whipper-in," meaning the person who keeps the hounds from wandering too far from the pack; similarly, party whips try to ensure that members do not stray too far from party positions). The conference chair for the Republicans, or caucus chair for the Democrats, runs the party meetings to elect floor leaders, to make committee assignments, and to set legislative agendas. The minority party in the House has a parallel structure: its leader is the **Minority Leader**, and the second in command is the Minority Whip.

The Senate leadership does not have as much power as the leadership of the House, mostly because individual senators have more power than individual House members due to the Senate's rule of unlimited debate, as we will discuss later. The Majority Leader and Minority Leader are the leaders of their respective parties, and second in command to them are the Assistant Majority and Minority Leaders. The Senate also has a whip system, but it is not as developed as the House system. Republicans have a separate position for the conference chair, while the Democratic leader also serves as the caucus chair. Officially, the country's vice president is also the president of the Senate, but he or she appears in the chamber only when needed to cast a tie-breaking vote. The Constitution also mentions the **president pro tempore** of the Senate, whose formal duties involve presiding over the Senate when the vice president is not there. This is typically the most senior member of the majority party, and the position does not have any real power. In fact, the actual president pro tempore rarely presides over the Senate and the task is typically given to a more junior senator.

Speaker of the House
The elected leader of the House of Representatives.

Majority Leader
The elected head of the party holding the majority of seats in the House or Senate.

whip system
An organization of House leaders who work to disseminate information and promote party unity in voting on legislation.

Minority Leader
The elected head of the party holding the minority of seats in the House or Senate.

president pro tempore
A largely symbolic position usually held by the most senior member of the majority party in the Senate.

The Role of Parties and Conditional Party Government Political parties in Congress also reflect the individualism of the institution. Compared with parliamentary systems, U.S. congressional parties are very weak. They do not impose a party line or penalize members who vote against the party. Indeed, they have virtually no ability to impose electoral restrictions (such as denying the party's nomination) on renegade members.

Although still weaker than their overseas counterparts, parties in Congress have greatly strengthened since the 1960s (see Figure 11.5). Partisanship—evident when party members stick together in opposition to the other party—reached its highest

Party Votes and Unity in Congress, 1962–2017

FIGURE 11.5

(A) Party votes are said to occur when a majority of one party opposes a majority of the other party, and **(B)** party unity refers to the percentage of the party members who vote together on party votes. These two graphs make two important points. First, partisanship has increased in the last two decades, in terms of both the proportion of party votes and the level of party unity. Second, despite these increased levels of partisanship, only about two-thirds of all votes in the House and Senate divide the two parties. Given these potentially conflicting observations, how would you assess the argument that partisanship in Congress is far too intense?

(A) Party votes in Congress

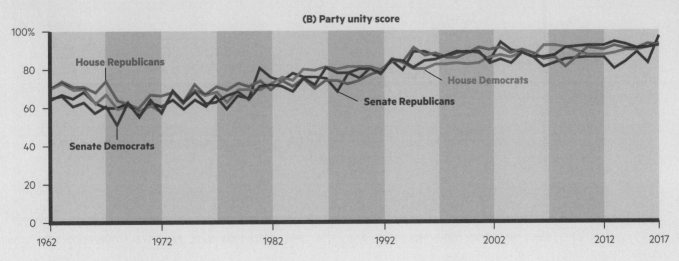

(B) Party unity score

Source: CQ Roll Call, http://cqrollcall.com/cq (accessed 10/1/18).

roll call vote
A recorded vote on legislation; members may vote yes, no, abstain, or present.

party vote
A vote in which the majority of one party opposes the position of the majority of the other party.

party unity
The extent to which members of Congress in the same party vote together on party votes.

levels in the post–World War II era in recent years. About 70 percent of all **roll call votes** were **party votes**, in which a majority of one party opposed a majority of the other party. The proportion of party votes fell to between 50 and 60 percent between 1996 and 2008 but recently has hit new highs. The highest proportions were 72 percent in the Senate in 2009 and 75.8 percent in the House in 2011; the numbers remained at about those levels in the House, but fell in the Senate in 2016. In the last year of Obama's tenure, not much happened in the Senate (former Republican leader Trent Lott called the Senate's output a "nothing burger"). Partisanship returned in 2017 with the Tax Cuts and Jobs Act, which passed with razor-thin margins. **Party unity**, the percentage of party members voting together on party votes, soared during this period as well, especially in the House. Party unity hit an all-time high for House Republicans in 2016, with 93 percent of them voting together on party vote. House Democrats were almost as unified at 91 percent.[29]

Party-line votes have become more common as the Democratic Party has become more cohesive: southern Democrats now vote more like their northern counterparts, partly because of the importance of African-American voters, who tend to vote for Democrats in the South. Moreover, increasing Republican strength in the South means that the remaining Democratic districts are more liberal, because Republicans defeat the more moderate Democrats. Similarly, there are fewer moderates within the Republican Party, as most regions of the country that used to elect moderate Republicans are now electing Democrats.[30]

Another way to examine changes in the composition of the parties is to examine the ideological distribution of members of Congress (see Figure 11.6). The parties in Congress are now more polarized than they have been at any point in U.S. history. In the 1970s, there was considerable overlap between the Democratic and Republican

FIGURE 11.6

Ideological Polarization in Congress, 1879–2017

Although party polarization in Congress has been high in the past, it lessened in the early twentieth century. Polarization has increased steadily in the last 70 years, and today's Congress is more polarized than ever. What do you think causes this extreme polarization?

Source: Polarization in Congress, "Liberal-Conservative Partisan Polarization by Chamber," Jeff Lewis, March 11, 2018, https://voteview.com/articles/party_polarization (accessed 6/7/18).

parties. But in the most recent Congress, the two parties are almost completely separated—that is, only a few Democrats are more conservative than the most liberal Republican. At the same time, the parties are growing farther apart, which makes it even harder for the Republicans and the Democrats to work together and compromise to pass legislation.

This greater cohesiveness within parties and separation across parties means that conditional party government (see Chapter 8) may be in play—that is, strong party leadership is possible in Congress, but it is conditional on the consent of party members.[31] That consent is more likely if there are strong differences between the parties but unity within parties. Leaders' chief responsibility is to get their party's legislative agenda through Congress, but they primarily have to rely on persuasion and control over the timing of when bills come up for a vote rather than telling members what to do. Leaders' success largely depends on personal skills, communicative abilities, and trust. Some of the most successful leaders, such as Lyndon Johnson (D-TX), Majority Leader of the Senate from 1955 to 1961, and Sam Rayburn (D-TX), Speaker of the House for more than 17 years, kept in touch with key members on a daily basis. Another important tool of the leadership is agenda control: both positive (getting bills to the floor that are favored by the party) and negative (preventing votes on bills that would divide the majority party).

Leaders also must have the ability to bargain and compromise. One observer noted, "To Senator Johnson, public policy evidently was an inexhaustibly bargainable product."[32] Such leaders find solutions where none appear possible. Leaders also do favors for members (such as making campaign appearances, helping with fundraising, contributing to campaigns, helping them get desired committee assignments, or guiding pet projects through the legislative process) to engender a feeling of personal obligation to the leadership when it needs a key vote.

The party's most powerful positive incentives are in the area of campaign finance. In recent years the congressional campaign committees of both parties and the national party organizations have been supplying candidates with money and resources in an attempt to gain more influence in the electoral process. Party leaders may also help arrange

If you want to get along, go along.

—**Sam Rayburn,** former Speaker of the House

Senate Majority Leader Mitch McConnell (R-KY) joined Senator John Barrasso (R-WY, left), Senator John Thune (R-SD), and Majority Whip John Cornyn (R-TX) to meet with reporters following a closed-door Republican strategy session on Capitol Hill in Washington, Tuesday, March 20, 2018. Lawmakers had to beat a midnight Friday deadline to avert another federal shutdown.

A sitting president can be a powerful ally in a campaign. Here, President Trump campaigns for Marsha Blackburn (R-TN), who won her bid for Senate in 2018.

a campaign stop or a fund-raiser for a candidate with party leaders or the president. For example, President Obama held dozens of fund-raisers for Democrats in 2014, earning him the label of "Fundraiser-in-Chief" from CNN.[33] Such events typically raise $500,000 to more than $1 million. President Trump campaigned actively for congressional Republicans during the 2018 midterms. Despite headlining a record-breaking fund-raiser, he held fewer for other candidates than any president since Ronald Reagan.[34]

Despite these positive reinforcements, members' desire for reelection always comes before party concerns and leadership rarely tries to force a member to vote against his or her constituents' interests. For example, Democrats from rural areas, where most constituents support gun ownership and many are hunters, would not be expected to vote the party line favoring a gun control bill. But if a member of Congress did something much more extreme that crossed the party's leadership—for example, supporting the opposing party's candidate for Speaker or passing strategic information to the opposition—he or she could expect to be disciplined by the party's leaders.

The most difficult challenge for party leadership in recent years in terms of party cohesion has been the Freedom Caucus within the House Republicans. This group of conservative members forced several government shutdowns during the Obama years over funding for Obamacare and tax increases. Most significantly, they forced John Boehner to resign as Speaker of the House in September 2015 and then rejected the heir apparent, Majority Leader Kevin McCarthy, because he was too moderate. Finally, they agreed to accept Paul Ryan as Speaker, but nine Freedom Caucus members voted against him.[35] When President Trump was elected, many Republicans believed that they would finally be able to enact a conservative policy agenda, but it has been difficult to pass legislation that both the Freedom Caucus in the House and moderate Republicans in the Senate can agree to. The deadlock over DACA, discussed in the chapter opener, is a prime example.

The Committee System The committee system in the House and Senate is another crucial part of the legislative structure. There are four types of committees: standing, select, joint, and conference. **Standing committees**, which have ongoing membership and jurisdictions, are where most of Congress's work gets done. These committees draft legislation and oversee the implementation of the laws they pass. For example, the Agriculture Committees in the House and Senate have jurisdiction over farm programs such as commodity price supports, crop insurance, and soil conservation. But they also create and oversee policy for rural electrification and development; the food stamp and nutrition programs; and the inspection of livestock, poultry, seafood, and meat products. Many committees share jurisdiction on policy—for example, the House Natural Resources Committee oversees the National Forest Service and forests on federally owned lands, and the Agriculture Committee oversees policy for forests on privately owned lands. There are 21 standing committees in the House and 20 in the Senate.

Select committees typically address a specific topic for one or two terms, such as the Select Committee on Energy Independence and Global Warming that operated from 2007 to 2010. These committees do not have the same legislative authority as standing committees; rather, they mostly serve to collect information, provide policy options, and draw attention to a given issue.

There are four **joint committees** made up of members of both the House and the Senate, and they rarely have legislative authority. The Joint Committee on Taxation, for example, does not have authority to send legislation concerning tax policy to the floor of the House or Senate. Instead, it gathers information and provides estimates of the consequences of proposed tax legislation. Joint committees may also be temporary, such as the "Supercommittee" (officially the Joint Select Committee on Deficit Reduction) that was formed in 2011 to try to reach bipartisan agreement on a deficit reduction plan. The committee failed to reach agreement and was disbanded in 2012.

standing committees
Committees that are a permanent part of the House or Senate structure, holding more importance and authority than other committees.

select committees
Committees in the House or Senate created to address a specific issue for one or two terms.

joint committees
Committees that contain members of both the House and Senate but have limited authority.

Conference committees are formed as needed to resolve specific differences between House and Senate versions of legislation that are passed in each chamber. These committees mostly comprise standing committee members from each chamber who worked on the bill in question.

The committee system creates a division of labor that helps members get reelected by facilitating specialization and credit claiming. For example, a chair of the Agriculture Committee or of a key agricultural subcommittee may reasonably take credit for passing an important bill for the farmers back home, such as the Cottonseed Payment Program that provides assistance to cottonseed farmers who lost crops due to hurricanes.[36]

The number of members who could make these credible claims expanded dramatically in the 1970s with the proliferation of subcommittees (there are 100 in the House and 67 in the Senate). Speaking about the House, one observer said, with some exaggeration, that if you ever forget a member's name you can simply refer to him or her as "Mr. or Ms. Chairman" and you will be right about half the time. This view of congressional committees is based on the **distributive theory**, which is rooted in the norm of reciprocity and representatives' incentives to provide benefits for their districts. The theory holds that members will seek committee assignments to best serve their district's interests, the leadership will accommodate those requests, and the floor will respect the views of the committees in a big institution-level logroll— that is, committee members will support one another's legislation. This means that members tend to have an interest in and to support the policies produced by the committees they serve on. For example, members from farm states would want to serve on the Agriculture Committee and members with a lot of military bases or defense contractors in their districts would want to be on the Armed Services Committee.

Nonetheless, the committee system does not exist simply to further members' electoral goals. According to **informational theory**, it also provides collective benefits to the rest of the members through committee members' expertise on policy, which helps reduce uncertainty about policy outcomes.[37] By deferring to expert committees, members are able to achieve beneficial outcomes while using their time more efficiently. This informational theory is also consistent with the argument made by Richard Fenno 45 years ago that members will serve on committees for reasons other than simply trying to achieve reelection (which is implied by the distributive theory). Fenno argued that members also were interested in achieving power within the institution and in making good policy.[38] Others argue that goals vary from bill to bill and all members pursue reelection advantage, institutional power, and effective policy in different circumstances.[39] Thus, the committee system does not exist only to further members' electoral goals, but it often serves that purpose.

Committees also serve the policy needs of the majority party, largely because the party in power controls a majority of seats on every committee. The party ratios on each committee generally reflect the partisan distribution in the overall chamber, but the majority party gives itself somewhat larger majorities on the important committees such as Ways and Means (which controls tax policy), Appropriations, and Rules. This is especially true for the Rules Committee (in which the majority party controls 9 of the 13 seats). The Rules Committee is important to the majority party because it structures the nature of debate in the House: it sets the length of debate and the type and number of amendments to a bill that will be allowed. These decisions are called *rules* and must be approved by a majority of the House members. The Rules Committee has become an arm of the majority-party leadership, and in many instances it provides rules that support the party's policy agenda or that protect its members from having to take controversial positions. For example, the Rules Committee prevented amendments on the 2017 tax bill; if the amendments had come to a vote, they would have divided the Republican Party.[40] Majority members are expected to support their party on votes on rules, even if they end up voting against the related legislation.

conference committees
Temporary committees created to negotiate differences between the House and Senate versions of a piece of legislation that has passed through both chambers.

distributive theory
The idea that members of Congress will join committees that best serve the interests of their district and that committee members will support one another's legislation.

informational theory
The idea that having committees in Congress made up of experts on specific policy areas helps ensure well-informed policy decisions.

Congressional Staff The final component of the formal structure of Congress is congressional staff. The size of personal and committee staff exploded in the 1970s and 1980s but has since leveled off. The total number of congressional staff is more than four times as large as it was 50 years ago. Part of the motivation for this growth was to reduce the gap between the policy-making capability of Congress and the president, especially with regard to fiscal policy. The other primary motivation was electoral. By increasing the size of their personal staff, members were able to open multiple district offices and expand opportunities for helping constituents. When the Republicans took control of Congress in 1994, they vowed to cut the waste in the internal operation of the institution, in part by cutting committee staff. However, although they reduced committee staff by nearly a third, they made no cuts in personal staff.

"Why Should I Care?"

The Constitution says very little about the internal structure of Congress, so the institution is largely the creation of its members. The norms of the institution and its formal structure facilitate members' electoral and policy goals, so if they don't like the way something works, they can change it. While this may sound very self-serving, members of Congress also work to serve broader collective and policy goals—or else they would be booted out of office. Understanding this fundamental point provides great insight into why Congress is structured the way that it is.

★

TRACE THE STEPS IN THE LEGISLATIVE PROCESS

How a bill becomes a law

Every introductory textbook on American politics has an obligatory section including a neat little diagram that describes how a bill becomes a law (see How It Works: Passing Legislation). But we provide an important truth-in-advertising disclosure: many important laws do not follow this orderly path. In fact, Barbara Sinclair's book *Unorthodox Lawmaking* argues that "the legislative process for major legislation is now less likely to conform to the textbook model than to unorthodox lawmaking."[41] After presenting the standard view, we describe the most important deviations from that path.

The conventional process

The details of the legislative process can be incredibly complex, but its basic aspects are fairly simple. The most important thing to understand about the process is that before a piece of legislation can become a law it must be passed *in identical form* by both the House and the Senate and signed by the president. If the president vetoes the bill, it can still be passed with a two-thirds vote in each chamber. Note, however, that all legislation that is signed by the president (or overrides a veto) carries the weight of law; legislation that is not signed by the president has only internal legislative or symbolic purposes (see Nuts & Bolts 11.3 for a description of different types of legislation). Here are the basic steps of the process to pass a bill:

1. A member of Congress introduces the bill.
2. A subcommittee and committee craft the bill.
3. Floor action on the bill takes place in the first chamber (House or Senate).
4. Committee and floor action takes place in the second chamber.

Types of Legislation

- **Bill:** A legislative proposal that becomes law if it is passed by both the House and the Senate in identical form and approved by the president. Each is assigned a bill number, with "H.R." indicating bills that originated in the House and "S.R." denoting bills that originated in the Senate. Private bills are concerned with a specific individual or organization and often address immigration or naturalization issues. Public bills affect the general public if enacted into law.
- **Simple resolution:** Legislation used to express the sense of the House or Senate, designated by "H.Res." or "S.Res." Simple resolutions affect only the chamber passing the resolution, are not signed by the president, and cannot become public law. Resolutions are often used for symbolic legislation, such as congratulating sports teams or naming a post office after a famous person (see Figure 11.7).
- **Concurrent resolution:** Legislation used to express the position of both chambers on a nonlegislative matter to set the annual budget or to fix adjournment dates, designated by "H.Con.Res" or "S.Con.Res." Concurrent resolutions are not signed by the president and therefore do not carry the weight of law.
- **Joint resolution:** Legislation that has few practical differences from a bill (passes both chambers in identical form, signed by the president) unless it proposes a constitutional amendment. In that case, a two-thirds majority of those present and voting in both the House and the Senate, and ratification by three-fourths of the states, are required for the amendment to be adopted and it does not require the president's signature.

5. The conference committee works out any differences between the House and Senate versions of the bill. (If the two chambers pass the same version, steps 5 and 6 are not necessary.)

6. The conference committee version is given final approval on the floor of each chamber.

7. The president either signs or vetoes the final version.

8. If the bill is vetoed, both chambers can attempt to override the veto with a two-thirds vote in both chambers.

The first part of the process, unchanged from the earliest Congresses, is the introduction of the bill. Only members of Congress can introduce the bill, either by dropping it into the "hopper," a wooden box at the front of the chamber in the House, or by presenting it to one of the clerks at the presiding officer's desk in the Senate. Even the president would need to have a House member or senator introduce his or her bill. Each bill has one or more sponsors and often many co-sponsors. Members may introduce bills on any topic they choose, but often the bills are related to a specific constituency interest. For example, Senator Pat Toomey (R-PA) introduced Senate Resolution 399, "Congratulating the Philadelphia Eagles on their triumph in Super Bowl LII" (see Figure 11.7). Obviously, most legislation is more substantive, but members of Congress are always attentive to issues their constituents care about.

The next step is to send the bill to the relevant committee. House and Senate rules specify committee jurisdictions (there are more than 200 categories), and the bill is matched with the committee that best fits its subject matter. In the House, major legislation may be sent to more than one committee in a practice known as multiple referral, but one of the committees is designated the primary committee and the bill is reviewed by the other committees sequentially or in parts. The practice is less common in the Senate, partly because senators have more opportunities to amend legislation on the floor. However, there were three committees in the House and five in the Senate that simultaneously worked on health care reform in 2009.

Once the bill goes to a committee, the chair refers it to the relevant subcommittee, where much of the legislative work is done. One important point: 80 to 90 percent of bills die at this stage of the process; they never make it out of the subcommittee or committee. For bills that see some action, the subcommittee holds hearings, calls witnesses, and

How it works: in theory
Passing Legislation

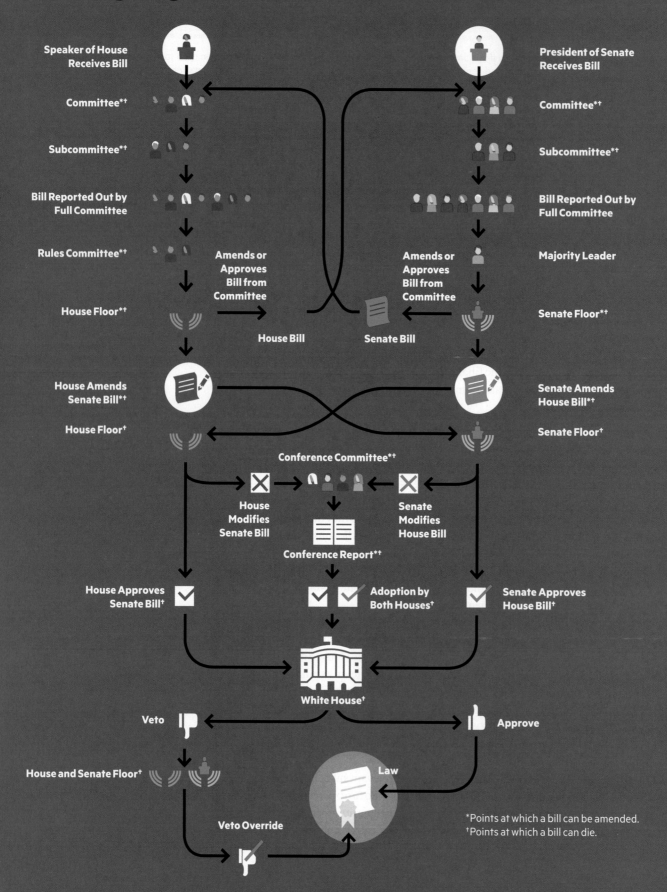

Speaker of House Receives Bill

President of Senate Receives Bill

Committee*†

Committee*†

Subcommittee*†

Subcommittee*†

Bill Reported Out by Full Committee

Bill Reported Out by Full Committee

Rules Committee*†

Amends or Approves Bill from Committee

Amends or Approves Bill from Committee

Majority Leader

House Floor*†

Senate Floor*†

House Bill

Senate Bill

House Amends Senate Bill*†

Senate Amends House Bill*†

House Floor†

Senate Floor†

Conference Committee*†

House Modifies Senate Bill

Senate Modifies House Bill

Conference Report*†

House Approves Senate Bill†

Adoption by Both Houses†

Senate Approves House Bill†

White House†

Veto

Approve

House and Senate Floor†

Law

Veto Override

*Points at which a bill can be amended.
†Points at which a bill can die.

Passing the Tax Cuts and Jobs Act

The 2017 Tax Cuts and Jobs Act provides an example of how passing legislation often deviates from the conventional method.

In the House...

The House Ways and Means Committee crafted H.R. 1, the House version of the Tax Bill. **All tax bills must originate in the House.**

In the Senate...

The Senate Finance Committee **crafted the initial Senate version.**

House passes its version.

Not so fast.

Republicans **cannot pass the Finance Committee's version** without the 60 votes needed to break a filibuster.

So the Budget Committee saves the day.

The Senate Budget Committee packages the Finance Committee's bill with a bill on drilling for oil as a reconciliation bill (which only needs 51 votes, rather than a filibuster-proof 60, to be approved). **It keeps the title of the House bill, H.R. 1, on this new bill to preserve the fiction that it originated in the House** and then submits it in the Senate.

Meanwhile, on the Left...

10 Democratic senators **try to slow the bill down** by sending it to the Finance Committee.

Meanwhile, on the Right...

Several Republican senators say **they will vote against the bill if changes are not made,** so Majority Leader Mitch McConnell cuts some deals.

Vote-a-rama!

After 355 amendments to the reconciliation bill are proposed, key provisions ratifying McConnell's deals are approved and the **Democrats' efforts are defeated** in a marathon of overnight voting.

Senate passes its version.

Conference committee **works out the differences** in the House version of H.R. 1 and the revamped Senate version of H.R. 1.

Passed!

House passes the conference report.

Passed!

Senate passes the conference report—with amendments.

Passed!

House passes the Senate's amendments.

Signed into law.

President Trump signs the **bill into law.**

❓ Critical Thinking

1. **What are the most significant ways in which** the process to pass the 2017 Tax Cuts and Jobs Act deviated from the conventional method?

2. **Do you think the 2017 Tax Cuts and Jobs Act could have been** passed without this unconventional process? Why or why not?

FIGURE 11.7

Taking Care of the Fans

The congratulatory resolution here is symbolic and commends the Philadelphia Eagles for winning the Super Bowl in 2018. Why do you think members of Congress spend time passing seemingly trivial resolutions like this?

S. RES. 399

In the Senate of the United States
February 7, 2018

Congratulating the Philadelphia Eagles on their triumph in Super Bowl LII.

Whereas, on February 4, 2018, the Philadelphia Eagles became champions of the National Football League by defeating the New England Patriots 41–33 in Super Bowl LII;

Whereas, with this victory the Philadelphia Eagles won their first Super Bowl in franchise history and fourth National Football League Championship;

Whereas the Eagles, a franchise born in the depths of the Great Depression, forged in the furnace of South Philadelphia, has come to represent the resiliency, ingenuity, and fortitude of the great people of the "City of Brotherly Love";

Whereas the fans of the Eagles, whose devotion and enthusiasm is renowned throughout sport, have waited for this moment for 58 years;

Whereas this Eagles team, written off by the rest of the world after suffering numerous injuries to key players, took the field in Minneapolis as the underdog, as they had been in every previous playoff game, despite having the best record in the National Football League;

Whereas quarterback Nicholas Edward Foles, stepping in for injured star quarterback Carson James Wentz, commanded the field with an uncanny precision, calmness, and leadership that earned him recognition as the Most Valuable Player of the Super Bowl; ...

Whereas the vaunted Eagles defense ... took charge in the waning moments of the fourth quarter when Brandon Lee Graham forced the opposing quarterback to fumble the football into the waiting hands of rookie Derek Anthony Barnett;

... Now, therefore, be it

Resolved, That the Senate—

(1) congratulates the entire Philadelphia Eagles organization on their triumph in Super Bowl LII;

(2) commends the Philadelphia Eagles fans for their devotion, enthusiasm, and persistence over the past 58 years; ...

Source: Congress.gov, www.congress.gov/bill/115th-congress/senate-resolution/399/text (accessed 2/20/18).

markup
One of the steps through which a bill becomes a law, in which the final wording of the bill is determined.

gathers the information necessary to rewrite, amend, and edit the bill. The final language of the bill is determined in a collaborative process known as the **markup**. During this meeting, members debate aspects of the issue and offer amendments to change the language or content of the bill. After all amendments have been considered, a final vote is taken on whether to send the bill to the full committee. If it is sent, the full committee then considers whether to pass it along to the floor. This committee also has the option of amending the bill, passing it as is, or tabling it (which kills the bill). Every bill sent to the floor by a committee is accompanied by a report and full documentation of all the hearings. These documents constitute the bill's legislative history, which the courts, executive departments, and the public use to determine the purpose and meaning of the law.

When the bill makes it to the floor, it is placed on one of the various legislative calendars. Bills are removed from the calendar to be considered by the floor under a broad range of possible rules. When the bill reaches the floor, the majority party and minority party each designate a bill manager who is responsible for guiding the debate on the floor. In the House, debate proceeds according to tight time limits and rules governing the nature of amendments. Senate debate is much more open and unlimited in most circumstances (unless all the senators agree to a limit). If you have ever watched

C-SPAN, you know that often there are very few people on the floor during debates. Typically only the small number of people who are most interested in the bill (usually members of the committee that produced it) actively participate and offer amendments.

When debate is completed and all amendments have been considered, the presiding officer calls for a voice vote, with those in favor saying "aye" and those opposed "no." If it is unclear which side has won, any member may call for a "division vote," which requires members on each side to stand and be counted. At that point, any member may call for a recorded vote (there is no way of recording members' positions on voice votes and division votes). If at least 25 members agree that a recorded vote is desired, buzzers go off in the office buildings and committee rooms, calling members to the floor for the vote. Once they reach the floor, members vote by an electronic system in which they insert ATM-like cards into slots and each vote is recorded on a big board at the front of the House or Senate chamber.

If the bill passes the House and the Senate in different forms, the discrepancies have to be resolved. On many minor bills, one chamber may simply accept the other chamber's version to solve the problem. On other minor bills and some major bills, differences are resolved through a process known as amendments between the chambers. In this case, one chamber modifies a bill passed by the other chamber and sends it back. These modifications can go back and forth several times before both houses agree on an identical bill. A complicated version of this approach was used to pass health care reform in 2010.

The most common way to resolve differences on major legislation is through a conference committee made up of key players in the House and the Senate. A majority of major bills go to a conference committee, but minor bills rarely do.[42] Sometimes the conferees split the difference between the House and Senate versions, but at other times the House and Senate approaches are so different that one must be chosen—an especially tricky prospect when different parties control the two chambers. Sometimes the conference cannot resolve differences and the bill dies. If the conference committee can agree on changes, each chamber must pass the final version, the conference report, by a majority vote and neither chamber is allowed to amend it.

The bill is then sent to the president. If the president approves and signs the measure within 10 days (not counting Sundays), it becomes law. If he or she objects to the bill, the president may **veto** it within 10 days, sending it back to the chamber where it originated, along with a statement of objections. Unless both the House and the Senate vote to override the veto by a two-thirds majority, the bill dies. If the president does not act within 10 days and Congress is in session, the bill becomes law without the president's approval. If Congress is not in session, the measure dies through what is known as a **pocket veto**.

One final point on how a bill becomes a law is important: any bill that appropriates money must pass through the two-step process of authorization and appropriation. In the authorization process, members debate the merits of the bill, determine its language, and limit the amount that can be spent on the bill. The appropriations process involves the Budget Committees in both the House and the Senate, which set the overall guidelines for the national budget, and the Appropriations Committees in the two chambers, which determine the actual amounts of money that will be spent. In recent years, Congress has been unable to pass its appropriations bills in time for the start of the new fiscal year, so it ends up having to pass "continuing resolutions" that spend money at the last year's levels in order to keep the government open. Congress passed five continuing resolutions for the 2018 fiscal year. That may sound like a lot, but the record is 21 for the 2001 fiscal year.[43]

veto
The president's rejection of a bill that has been passed by Congress. A veto can be overridden by a two-thirds vote in both the House and Senate.

pocket veto
The automatic death of a bill passed by the House and Senate when the president fails to sign the bill in the last 10 days of a legislative session.

Deviations from the conventional process

There are many ways in which legislation may not follow the typical path. First, in some Congresses up to 20 percent of *major* bills bypass the committee system. This may be done by a discharge petition, in which a majority of the members force a bill out of its assigned committee, or by a special rule in the House. In some cases, a bill may go to the relevant committee, but then party leadership may impose its version of the bill later in the process. For example, in the wake of the terrorist attacks of September 11, the House Judiciary Committee after hard bipartisan work quickly approved a version of the Patriot Act to be considered by the full House to give the government stronger surveillance powers. But a few days later, according to committee member Representative Jerrold Nadler (D-NY), "[t]hen the bill just disappeared. And we had a new several hundred-page bill revealed from the Rules Committee" that had to be voted on the next day. Most members of Congress did not have a chance to read it.[44] The Affordable Care Act (ACA) also deviated from the standard path.

Second, about one-third of major bills are adjusted post-committee and before the legislation reaches the floor by supporters of the bills to increase their chances of passage. Sometimes the bill goes back to the committee after these changes, and sometimes it does not. One good example of this approach was the ACA, which was altered by House and Senate leadership after the committees deadlocked on different versions of the bill. The legislation also bypassed the conference committee; party leadership worked out the differences between the House and Senate versions directly. Thus, although most of the legislative work is accomplished in committees, a significant amount of legislation bypasses committee review.

Third, summit meetings between the president and congressional leaders may bypass or jump-start the normal legislative process. For example, rather than going through the Budget Committees to set budgetary targets, the president may meet with top leaders from both parties and hammer out a compromise that is presented to Congress as a done deal. This technique is especially important on delicate budget negotiations or when the president is threatening to use the veto. Often the congressional rank and file go along with the end product of the summit meeting, but occasionally they reject it—as happened in February 2014, when all but 28 House Republicans voted against their leadership on the extension of the debt ceiling that had been agreed to by President Obama and House and Senate leaders.

Fourth, **omnibus legislation**—massive bills that run hundreds of pages long and cover many different subjects and programs—often requires creative approaches by the leadership to guide the bill through the legislative maze. In addition, the massive legislation often carries riders—extraneous legislation attached to the "must pass" bill to secure approval for pet projects that would otherwise fail. This is a form of pork-barrel legislation and another mechanism used in the quest for reelection. One example was the 2,232-page 2018 omnibus spending legislation that combined all 12 appropriation bills and authorized more than $1.3 trillion in spending. Some of the "extras" in the bill included $1.6 billion for the border wall (Trump had asked for $25 billion), $4.65 billion to help address the opioid crisis, and $380 million to the federal Election Assistance Commission to improve election security and technology.[45]

omnibus legislation
Large bills that often cover several topics and may contain extraneous, or pork-barrel, projects.

Differences in the House and Senate legislative processes

There are three central differences in the legislative processes of the House and the Senate: (1) the continuity of the membership and the impact this has on the rules, (2) the way in which bills get to the floor, and (3) the structure of the floor process, including debate and amendments. First, as discussed earlier, the Senate is a continuing body, with two-thirds of its members returning to the next session without facing reelection (because of the six-year term), whereas all House members are up for reelection every two years. This has an important impact on the rules of the two chambers: there has been much greater stability in the rules of the Senate than in those of the House. Whereas the House adopts its rules anew at the start of each new session (sometimes with major changes, sometimes with only minor modifications), the Senate has not had a general reaffirmation of its rules since 1789. However, the Senate rules can be changed at the beginning of a session to meet the needs of the new members.

The floor process is much simpler and less structured in the Senate than in the House. In part, this is due to the relative size of the two chambers: the House with its 435 members needs to have more rules than the Senate with its 100 members. Ironically, however, the floor process is actually much easier to navigate in the House because of its structure. Since the adoption of Reed's Rules in 1890, the House has been a very majoritarian body—that is, a majority of House members can almost always have their way. Named after Speaker Thomas Reed, the rules were an implementation of his view that "the best system is to have one party govern and the other party watch."[46] In contrast, the Senate has always been a much more individualistic body. Former Majority Leader Howard Baker compared leading the Senate to "herding cats," saying it was difficult "trying to make ninety-nine independent souls act in concert under rules that encourage polite anarchy and embolden people who find majority rule a dubious proposition at best."[47]

The Filibuster Part of the challenge in getting the Senate to act collectively is rooted in the Senate's unlimited debate and very open amendment process. Unless restricted by a unanimous consent agreement, senators can speak as long as they want and offer any amendment to a bill, even if it isn't directly related to the underlying bill. Debate may be cut off only if a supermajority of 60 senators agree in a process known as invoking cloture. Therefore, one senator can stop any bill by threatening to talk the bill to death if 40 of his or her colleagues agree. This practice is known as a filibuster. The filibuster strengthens the hand of the minority party in the Senate, giving it veto power over legislation unless the majority party has 60 senators who support a bill.

Before the 1960s, senators really did hold the floor for hours by reading from the phone book or reciting recipes. The late senator Strom Thurmond of South Carolina holds the record of 24 hours and 18 minutes of continuous talking. Today it is rare for a filibuster to tie up Senate business, since a senator's threat to filibuster a bill is usually enough to take the bill off the legislative agenda. If the bill is actually filibustered, it goes on a separate legislative track so that it does not bring the rest of the business of the Senate to a halt. Alternatively, if supporters of the bill think they have enough votes, they can invoke cloture to stop the filibuster and bring the bill to the floor for a vote. Frustrated over repeated Republican filibusters on President Obama's nominations to federal courts and agencies, Senate Democrats in November 2013 removed the filibuster for all presidential nominations, except those to the Supreme Court.[48] When Democrats filibustered Trump's nomination of Neil Gorsuch to the Supreme Court in April 2017, the Senate changed the rules again to allow Supreme Court nominees to be confirmed by a simple majority vote.[49]

Because of the practice of unlimited debate in the Senate, much of its business is conducted under unanimous consent agreements by which senators agree to adhere to time limits on debate and amendments. However, because these are literally *unanimous* agreements, a single senator can obstruct the business of the chamber by issuing a hold on the bill or presidential nomination. This practice is often a bargaining tool to extract concessions from the bill's supporters, but sometimes, especially late in a session when time gets tight, a hold can actually kill a bill by removing it from the active agenda.

One way that the Senate has circumvented the filibuster is through the reconciliation process, which was established in 1974 to make the budget process more efficient. If reconciliation legislation is related to budget matters and does not increase the deficit outside the specified time period (and satisfies several other rules), it may be passed with a simple majority vote in the House and Senate. The process was initially used for budget items, but in recent years it has been used to pass other

cloture
A procedure through which the Senate can limit the amount of time spent debating a bill (cutting off a filibuster) if a supermajority of 60 senators agree.

filibuster
A tactic used by senators to block a bill by continuing to hold the floor and speak—under the Senate rule of unlimited debate—until the bill's supporters back down.

hold
An objection to considering a measure on the Senate floor.

reconciliation
Reconciliation allows for expedited consideration of certain tax, spending, and debt limit legislation. The main advantage of the procedure is that reconciliation legislation is not subject to filibusters in the Senate, and therefore may be passed with simple majorities in the House and Senate.

controversial bills that threatened to be derailed by a filibuster. For example, the ACA was passed in 2010 through reconciliation, and the process was also used for various attempts to repeal the ACA (the most recent attempt, in 2017, failed in the Senate by a single vote). It was also used to pass the 2017 Tax Cuts and Jobs Act.

House Rules In contrast to the Senate, the House is a more orderly, although complex, institution. The Rules Committee exerts great control over the legislative process, especially on major legislation, through special rules that govern the nature of debate on a bill. There are three general types of rules: **closed rules** do not allow any amendments to the bill, **open rules** allow any germane amendments, and **modified rules** allow some specific amendments but not others. Once a special rule is adopted, general debate is tightly controlled by the floor managers. Amendments are considered under a five-minute rule, but this rule is routinely bent as members offer phantom "pro forma" amendments to, for example, "strike the last word" or "strike the requisite number of words." This means that the member is not really offering an amendment but simply going through the formal procedure of offering one in order to get an additional five minutes to talk about the amendment.

These descriptions of the two chambers show that although the Senate is formally committed to unlimited debate, senators often voluntarily place limits on themselves through unanimous consent, which makes the Senate operate much more like the House. Similarly, although the House has very strict rules concerning debate and amendments, there are ways of bending those rules to make the House operate a bit more like the potentially freewheeling Senate.

closed rules
Conditions placed on a legislative debate by the House Rules Committee prohibiting amendments to a bill.

open rules
Conditions placed on a legislative debate by the House Rules Committee allowing relevant amendments to a bill.

modified rules
Conditions placed on a legislative debate by the House Rules Committee allowing certain amendments to a bill while barring others.

"Why Should I Care?"

Otto von Bismarck, the Prussian statesman of the late nineteenth century, famously said, "Laws are like sausages; it is better not to see them being made." Indeed, the legislative process may be messy, but knowledge of how laws are made is important both for being an effective legislator and for being a good democratic citizen. Understanding how a bill becomes a law, seeing the various stages of the process, and recognizing the various veto points at which a bill may die all help put into context the simplistic complaints about gridlock and conflict. Now that you have a better understanding of the legislative process, you should have a stronger basis for evaluating what Congress is doing.

DESCRIBE HOW CONGRESS ENSURES THAT THE BUREAUCRACY IMPLEMENTS POLICIES CORRECTLY

Oversight

Once a bill becomes a law, Congress plays another crucial role by overseeing the implementation of the law to make sure the bureaucracy interprets it as Congress intended. Other motivations drive the oversight process as well, such as the desire to gain publicity that may help in the reelection quest or to embarrass the president if he or she is of the opposite party. For example, in 2015 Republicans used their oversight powers to call attention to Hillary Clinton's use of private servers for her work-related e-mail as secretary of state and the way that she handled the attack on the U.S. embassy in Benghazi. While these hearings were, at least in part, politically motivated (she was no longer secretary of state), the most important motivation for oversight is to ensure that laws are implemented properly.[50]

There are several mechanisms that Congress may use to accomplish this goal (see also Chapter 13). First, the bluntest instrument is the power of the purse. If members of Congress think an agency is not properly implementing their programs, they can simply cut off the funds to that agency. However, this approach to punishment is rarely used because it often eliminates good aspects of the agency along with the bad.

Second, Congress can hold hearings and investigations. By summoning administration officials and agency heads to a public hearing, Congress can use the media spotlight to focus attention on problems within the bureaucracy or on issues that have been overlooked. For example, House Republicans called former Health and Human Services secretary Kathleen Sebelius to testify several times in 2013 and 2014 about the rocky rollout of the healthcare.gov website for Obamacare. Hearings may also be used to support the president, as when the House Intelligence Committee examined alleged bias within the Department of Justice during its investigation of Russian involvement in the 2016 elections.[51] This type of oversight is known as "fire alarm oversight"—that is, members wait until there is a crisis before they spring to action.[52] This is in contrast to "police patrol" oversight, which involves constant vigilance in overseeing the bureaucracy. For example, the House Veterans' Affairs Committee recently investigated extremely long waits for medical appointments at VA hospitals and the falsification of records to cover up how long veterans had to wait to be seen by doctors, which eventually led to General Eric Shinseki's resignation as the secretary of Veterans' Affairs.[53] Of the two, fire alarm oversight is far more common because Congress does not have the resources to constantly monitor the entire bureaucracy.

Finally, the Senate exercises specific control over other executive functions through its constitutional responsibilities to provide "advice and consent" on presidential appointments and approval of treaties. The Senate typically defers to the president on these matters, but it may assert its power, especially when constituent interests are involved. Two current examples would be the Senate's increasing skepticism about free-trade agreements negotiated by the president's trade representatives and the Senate's holds on presidential nominations.

The ultimate in congressional oversight is the process of removing the president, vice president, other civil officers, or federal judges through impeachment. The House and Senate share this power: the House issues articles of impeachment, which outline the charges against the official, and the Senate conducts the trial of the impeached officials. Two presidents have been impeached: Andrew Johnson in the controversy over Reconstruction after the Civil War, and Bill Clinton over the scandal involving White House intern Monica Lewinsky. However, neither president was convicted and removed by the Senate.

Former FBI director James Comey testifies before the Senate Judiciary Committee on Capitol Hill, in Washington, in May 2017. Comey defended his rationale for notifying Congress about new e-mails relevant to the Hillary Clinton e-mail investigation less than two weeks before Election Day.

Unpacking the Conflict

I have seen in the Halls of Congress more idealism, more humanness, more compassion, more profiles of courage than in any other institution that I have ever known.

—**Hubert Humphrey,** former senator and vice president

Considering all that we've learned in this chapter about how Congress works, let's return to our discussion of DACA. Why is it so hard for Congress to compromise on issues that appear to be consensual, like protecting the Dreamers? How can members of Congress best serve the collective interests of the nation while also representing their local constituents?

Although the details of the legislative process and the institutions of Congress can be complicated, the basic explanations for members' behavior are quite straightforward when viewed in terms of the trade-off between responsiveness and responsibility. Members of Congress want to be reelected, so they are generally quite responsive to constituents' interests. They spend considerable time on casework—meeting with people in their district and delivering benefits for their district. At the same time, members are motivated to be responsible—to rise above local interests and attend to the nation's best interests. The conflict between these two impulses can create contradictory policies that contribute to Congress's image problem. For example, the chapter opener discussed the difficulty/inability of reaching a compromise on DACA. Both parties and the president appeared to want to help the Dreamers, but conservatives in the Republican Party were strongly opposed to providing any path to citizenship. Clearly, the country as a whole benefits from the economic and social contributions of the Dreamers, but some members of Congress responded to their political base by opposing a compromise. The tension between responsible lawmaking and responsiveness to constituents is evident on many issues.

Considering members' motivations is crucial to understanding how Congress functions, but their behavior is also constrained by the institutions in which they operate. When moderate House Republicans were on the verge of forcing a vote on the Dreamers, the Senate Republican Leader stood firm in his opposition, saying he would not bring a bill to a vote in the Senate that did not have President Trump's approval. So ultimately, it did not matter that the House was able to find a compromise solution. In this instance, party leadership served as a constraint, but the committee system can provide a positive vehicle for lawmaking as an important source of expertise and information, and it provides a platform from which members can take positions and claim credit. When they aren't obstructing legislation, parties in Congress can provide coherence to the legislative agenda and help structure voting patterns on bills. Rules and norms constrain the nature of debate and the legislative process. Although these institutions shape members' behavior, it is important to remember that members can also change those rules and institutions. Therefore, Congress has the ability to evolve with changing national conditions and demands from voters, groups, and the president.

In this context, much of what Congress does can be understood in terms of the conflicts inherent in politics. As we have seen, even on consensual issues like DACA, conflict and political strategy may doom the common ground that is within reach. The extremes on the right and left did not want to compromise on DACA: the former viewed any path to citizenship as amnesty and the latter wanted a "clean bill" with no money for the wall or other changes to immigration policy. There was a huge majority in the middle that could have passed a DACA bill with some money for border security and the wall, but President Trump and Republicans wanted to leverage the consensual issue of DACA to enact the broader immigration policies they favored. Their approach did not work, and we got deadlock instead. Congress does not always live up to the expectations of being the "first branch" of government, but it tries to do the best it can to balance the conflicting pressures it faces.

What's Your Take?

Does Congress do a reasonable job of representing both national and local interests? If not, how should Congress change?

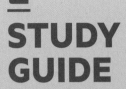

STUDY GUIDE

Congress and the people

Explain how members of Congress represent their constituents and how elections hold members accountable. (Pages 376–395)

Summary

The Constitution gave Congress vast enumerated powers, making it the "first branch" of government. While Congress has long dominated day-to-day politics, the president has become considerably more powerful over time. Despite the low approval ratings for Congress itself, most voters like their members of Congress. Members of Congress work hard to strike a balance between responding to what constituents want, and what is in the constituency's best interest. In the balance, however, they prioritize district interests over national policy.

Key terms

bicameralism (p. 377)
pork barrel (p. 378)
descriptive representation (p. 378)
substantive representation (p. 380)
trustee (p. 380)
delegate (p. 380)
politico (p. 381)

electoral connection (p. 383)
casework (p. 384)
incumbency advantage (p. 385)
redistricting (p. 389)
apportionment (p. 389)
gerrymandering (p. 390)
gridlock (p. 394)

Practice Quiz Questions

1. What did the Seventeenth Amendment do?

a   repeal Prohibition

b   grant women's suffrage

c   give senators six-year terms

d   allow for direct election of senators

e   lower the voting age to 18

2. Why do senators have longer terms than members of the House of Representatives?

a   to reduce the number of candidates in each election

b   to make sure that senators were tied to public sentiment

c   to provide more opportunities for pork-barrel legislation

d   to make elections easier to administer

e   to make sure that senators were somewhat insulated from the people

3. What is the most common style of representation in Congress?

a   trustee

b   politico

c   delegate

d   consulate

e   adviser

4. Most constituents are _____; most members of Congress act as if the constituency _____ paying attention.

a   inattentive; is not

b   inattentive; is

c   attentive; is not

d   attentive; is

e   selectively attentive; is not

5. Members of Congress generally hold multiple goals. Which goal comes first?

a   getting reelected

b   passing good policy

c   serving their political party

d   blocking the opposing party

e   serving special interests

6. What is apportionment?

a   determining presidential primary election winners

b   determining whether the state legislature or courts will re-draw district lines

c   determining which states gain/lose seats in the Senate

d   determining which states gain/lose seats in the House

e   determining how many seats a party has in Congress

7. A home style shapes the way members of Congress _____.

a   work with party leaders

b   vote in Congress

c   write legislation in committees

d   present themselves to their district

e   spend campaign money

8. On average, incumbents spend _____ times as much as challengers.

a   one and one-half

b   three

c   five

d   ten

e   twenty

The structure of Congress

Examine how parties, the committee system, and staffers enable Congress to function. (Pages 395–404)

Summary

Many aspects of Congress are set up to meet the needs of its members. The norms of universalism and reciprocity still dominate, meaning that members of Congress share resources more broadly than partisan politics would dictate.

Key terms

logrolling (p. 395)

earmarks (p. 395)

seniority (p. 396)

Speaker of the House (p. 398)

Majority Leader (p. 398)

whip system (p. 398)

Minority Leader (p. 398)

president pro tempore (p. 398)

roll call vote (p. 400)

party vote (p. 400)

party unity (p. 400)

standing committees (p. 402)

select committees (p. 402)

joint committees (p. 402)

conference committees (p. 403)

distributive theory (p. 403)

informational theory (p. 403)

Practice Quiz Questions

9. **The norm of _____ says that federal highway dollars are likely to be divided up so that many districts benefit.**

a reciprocity

b seniority

c party unity

d universalism

e specialization

10. **Committee leadership, division of seats on committee, and allocation of committee resources are determined by _____.**

a the majority party

b the size of the election margin

c unanimous consent

d seniority

e the president pro tempore

11. **The Senate leadership is _____ the House leadership.**

a more powerful than

b as powerful as

c less powerful than

d irrelevant to

12. **Party leaders have the power to _____.**

a force members of Congress to vote a particular way

b keep a member of Congress off the ballot in the next election

c force their members to share their campaign money

d exclude a member from a roll call vote

e help their members get favorable committee assignments

How a bill becomes a law

Trace the steps in the legislative process. (Pages 404–412)

Summary

Most bills become law in a conventional manner, but major pieces of legislation generally deviate considerably from this path. The legislative process differs for the House and Senate, sometimes making it difficult to reconcile differences between bills.

Key terms

markup (p. 408)

veto (p. 409)

pocket veto (p. 409)

omnibus legislation (p. 410)

cloture (p. 411)

filibuster (p. 411)

hold (p. 411)

reconciliation (p. 411)

closed rules (p. 412)

open rules (p. 412)

modified rules (p. 412)

Practice Quiz Questions

13. **Compared with the Senate, the floor process in the House is very _____ and _____.**

a unstructured; majoritarian

b structured; majoritarian

c unstructured; individualistic

d structured; individualistic

e individualistic; majoritarian

14. **Which of the following is the most important characteristic of how a bill becomes a law?**

a The bill must be passed by a conference committee composed of House and Senate members.

b The bill must be signed by the Speaker of the House.

c A majority of the majority-party members of the House and Senate must support the bill.

d The bill must pass the House and Senate in identical form.

e The bill must be introduced by the president or one of his or her staff members.

Oversight

Describe how Congress ensures that the bureaucracy implements policies correctly. (Pages 412–413)

Summary

After passing bills into law, Congress oversees the bureaucracy in its implementation of the law, making sure it fits Congress's intentions. Although controlling funding is the most powerful mechanism for this, Congress has a number of other mechanisms for achieving bureaucratic fidelity. Generally, Congress does not actively patrol the bureaucracy, but waits until a crisis emerges to act.

Practice Quiz Questions

15. Waiting for a crisis to emerge before taking action is called _____.

a   police patrol oversight

b   fire alarm oversight

c   emergency room oversight

d   reactionary oversight

e   bureaucratic oversight

16. The most important reason for congressional oversight is _____.

a   to try to embarrass political opponents

b   to help raise funds for a political campaign

c   to support the president's policy-making efforts

d   to make sure that laws are implemented properly

e   to amend previously passed legislation

Suggested Reading

Adler, Scott E., and John D. Wilkerson. *Congress and the Politics of Problem Solving*. New York: Cambridge University Press, 2013.

Bianco, William T. *Trust: Representatives and Constituents*. Ann Arbor: University of Michigan Press, 1994.

Canon, David T. *Race, Redistricting, and Representation: The Unintended Consequences of Black Majority Districts*. Chicago: University of Chicago Press, 1999.

Fenno, Richard F. *Congressmen in Committees*. Boston: Little, Brown, 1973.

Hall, Richard L. *Participation in Congress*. New Haven, CT: Yale University Press, 1996.

Jacobson, Gary C. *The Politics of Congressional Elections*, 8th ed. New York: Pearson, 2012.

Lapinski, John S. *The Substance of Representation: Congress, American Political Development, and Lawmaking*. Princeton, NJ: Princeton University Press, 2013.

Mayhew, David R. *Congress: The Electoral Connection*, 2nd ed. New Haven, CT: Yale University Press, 2004.

Theriault, Sean. *Party Polarization in Congress*. New York: Cambridge University Press, 2008.

12

The Presidency
Why can't the president get more done?

 "I've taken this position that I will not be involved with the Justice Department. I'm very disappointed in my Justice Department. I may change my mind at some point because what's going on is a disgrace; it's an absolute disgrace."
President Donald Trump in a FOX News interview

 "Why don't the Democrats give us the votes to fix the world's worst immigration laws? Where is the outcry for the killings and crime being caused by gangs and thugs, including MS-13, coming into our country illegally?"
President Donald Trump via Twitter

Outlining the major achievements of Donald Trump's first two years in office illustrates the immense power of the presidency. Trump commands the most powerful military forces on earth—and has pushed through budget increases that will make them even stronger. Working with Republicans in Congress, Trump enacted the largest tax cut in American history. His directives have transformed federal policy in areas such as immigration and the environment.

A look at the personal style that Trump has brought to the office, too, seems to underline its power. Two years in, there is little doubt that Trump behaves very differently compared to his predecessors. He hires and fires people working at the highest levels of government, seemingly at whim. Anything he says—even an offhand comment or tweet—becomes the focus of public attention. He relies on social media to communicate directly with the American people; responds to criticism with strong, personal attacks; makes abrupt, radical changes in America's domestic and foreign policy; routinely ignores many presidential traditions and norms; and has made personal loyalty a dominant criterion for his appointees.

Yet the two quotes at the beginning of this chapter illustrate the limits of Trump's power. In April 2018, Trump referred to "my Justice Department," claiming he had total authority over the organization, including the ability to direct the investigation into Russian collusion with his campaign—although Trump did not intervene, then or now. And two months later, Trump called on Democrats in Congress to reverse a Justice Department decision to separate children from parents who were apprehended when trying to enter the United States illegally, claiming that he lacked the authority to do so.

More generally, while Trump campaigned on promises to repeal Obamacare and build a wall on the Mexican border, he has been unable to translate these ideas into

The transfer of presidential power pushes us to ask fundamental questions about the tone and policy direction of the country. What will Trump do with the power of the presidency? Will he work with Congress or act more unilaterally? What policies from the past will he keep? What will he abandon? Will President Trump be able to accomplish all he promised?

law. His attempts to force other nations to lower tariffs on American goods have been largely unsuccessful. Trump's approval rating in national polls has remained relatively low despite a strong economy, and, due in part to voters' dissatisfaction with Trump's Republican administration, Republicans lost their majority in the House of Representatives in the 2018 midterms. Perhaps most notably, Trump has not stopped federal and state investigations into his business dealings and Russian tampering in the 2016 elections: investigations that have hurt his popularity, tarnished his reputation, and could lead to his removal from office.

Examining Trump's failures alongside his successes suggests that his presidency may not be transformational or especially unusual. Rather, just like the other 44 individuals who have served as president, Trump is often constrained by factors that are out of his control, from disagreements with other members of the federal government to the sometimes-fickle opinions of the American public. The fact is that the president is but one actor in a complex political system, a truth that has constrained all presidents, not just Trump.

Trump's at times unorthodox approach to the office of the presidency has raised questions about what, exactly, presidential power can achieve. Will Trump and the outcomes of his tenure in office redefine what makes a successful president? What are the factors that enable any president to be successful?

★
TRACE THE EVOLUTION OF PRESIDENTIAL POWER

The development of presidential power

As we consider the history of America's 45 presidents, four facts stand out: (1) Presidents matter. Their actions have had profound consequences for the nation, in both domestic and foreign policy. (2) Presidents get their power from a variety of sources, from provisions of the Constitution to their management of the actions taken by the executive branch of government. (3) Presidential power has increased over time, not because of changes in the Constitution but because of America's growth as a nation, its emergence as a dominant actor in international politics, the expansion of the federal government, and various acts of legislation that have given new authority to the president. (4) There are sharp limits to presidential power. Presidents are often forced to compromise or abandon their plans in the face of public, congressional, or foreign opposition.

These lessons are particularly important as we consider the presidency of Donald Trump. Trump's background and behavior in office are often described as being radically different from those of past presidents. Even so, Trump must contend with the same limits on presidential power faced by his predecessors, including voters' high expectations for presidential performance, conflict within Trump's own Republican Party as well as between Republicans and Democrats in Congress, and differences between Trump's goals and those held by federal bureaucrats who implement his decisions. Understanding how the accomplishments of past presidents were shaped by these constraints gives us some insight into what we can expect from the Trump presidency.

Early years through World War I

Since the early years of the republic, presidents' actions have had profound consequences for the nation. Presidents George Washington, John Adams, and Thomas Jefferson forged compromises on domestic issues such as choosing a permanent location for the nation's capital, establishing the federal courts, and financing the government. Presidents Andrew Jackson and Martin Van Buren were instrumental in forming the Democratic Party and its local party organizations.[1]

In addition, early presidents made important foreign policy decisions. For example, the Monroe Doctrine issued by President James Monroe in 1823 stated that America would remain neutral in wars involving European nations and that these nations must cease attempts to colonize or occupy areas in North and South America.[2] Presidents John Tyler and James Polk oversaw the admission of the huge territory of Texas into the Union following the Mexican-American War, as well as the acquisition of land that later became Oregon, Washington, Idaho, and parts of Montana and Wyoming.[3]

Presidents also played key roles in the conflict over slavery. President Millard Fillmore's support helped enact the Compromise of 1850, which limited slavery in California, and Franklin Pierce supported the Kansas-Nebraska Act, which regulated slavery in those territories. And, of course, Abraham Lincoln, who helped form the Republican Party in the 1850s, played a transformative role during the Civil War. His orders raised the huge Union army, and as commander in chief he directed the conduct of the bloody war that ultimately brought the southern states back into the Union. Moreover, he issued the Emancipation Proclamation, which freed the slaves in the South.[4]

During the late 1800s and early 1900s, presidents were instrumental in federal responses to the nation's rapid expansion and industrialization.[5] The country's growing size and economy generated conflict over which services the federal government should provide to citizens and the extent to which the government should regulate individual and corporate behavior.[6] Various acts of legislation created new federal agencies as well as new presidential powers and responsibilities. For example, Republican president Theodore Roosevelt used the Sherman Antitrust Act to break up the Northern Securities Company, a mammoth nationwide railroad trust. Roosevelt also expanded federal conservation programs and increased the power of the Interstate Commerce Commission to regulate businesses. Democratic president Woodrow Wilson further increased the government's role in managing the economy through his support of the Clayton Antitrust Act, the Federal Reserve Act, the first federal income tax, and legislation banning child labor.[7]

As these examples illustrate, presidential power has grown over time as the federal government has expanded. The president and members of the executive branch have obtained new regulatory powers over corporations and individual Americans. Presidents have also proposed new policies in response to shifts in public opinion. Moreover, the power of the presidency grew around the turn of the century and thereafter due to the actions of presidents, particularly Roosevelt and Wilson, who firmly believed that the presidency was the most important federal office.

Yet the limits of presidential power were also evident during this era—for example, in Wilson's foreign policy initiatives. Although he campaigned in the 1916 election on a promise to keep America out of World War I, Wilson ultimately ordered American troops to fight on the side of the Allies. After the war, Wilson offered a peace plan that proposed reshaping the borders of European countries in order to mitigate future conflicts; creating an international organization, the League of Nations, to prevent future conflicts; and taking other measures to encourage free trade and democracy.[8] However, America's allies rejected most of Wilson's proposals and the Senate refused to allow American participation in the League of Nations.

George Washington remains, for many Americans, the presidential ideal—a leader whose crucial domestic and foreign policy decisions shaped the growth of America's democracy.

The Great Depression through the present

Presidential actions defined the government's response to the Great Depression—the worldwide economic collapse in the late 1920s and 1930s marked by high unemployment, huge stock market declines, and many bank failures. After winning the 1932 presidential election, Democrat Franklin Roosevelt and his staff began reshaping American government in an effort to pull the country out of the Depression. Roosevelt's New Deal reforms created many federal agencies that helped individual Americans and imposed many new corporate regulations.[9] This expansion continued under Roosevelt's successors. Even Republican Dwight Eisenhower, whose party had initially opposed many New Deal reforms, presided over the creation of new agencies and the building of the interstate highway system.[10]

Presidential power also grew as the United States became more involved in the international arena. America was a key player in the Allied coalition against Germany and Japan in World War II, with President Roosevelt leading the negotiation of key agreements with American allies over war aims and the establishment of the United Nations. After the war, through the beginning of the Cold War with the Soviet Union, America's military might, dominant nuclear forces, and overwhelming economic power made it the leader of the free world. Because of this position, postwar presidents such as Harry Truman had enormous influence over the lives of people throughout the world.

Presidents throughout the twentieth century expanded the power of the office in terms of both domestic and foreign policy making. President Franklin Delano Roosevelt (left) called on the public to support his New Deal social programs through his signature "fireside chat" radio broadcasts. President Ronald Reagan (right) was instrumental in negotiating and executing numerous arms reduction agreements with the Soviet Union, then led by Mikhail Gorbachev.

Presidents were instrumental in the civil rights reforms and expansion of the federal government in the 1960s. With congressional approval, President Lyndon Johnson's administration created a wide range of domestic programs, such as the Department of Housing and Urban Development, Medicare, Medicaid, and federal funding for schools. The job of enacting voting rights and civil rights legislation also took place during Johnson's presidency.

Both Johnson and his successor, Richard Nixon, directed America's involvement in the Vietnam War, with the goal of forcing the North Vietnamese to abandon their plans to unify North and South Vietnam. But presidential efforts in Vietnam did not meet with success. Despite enormous deployments of American forces and the deaths of more than 58,000 American soldiers, Nixon eventually signed an agreement that allowed American troops to leave but did not end the conflict, which concluded only after a North Vietnamese victory in 1975.

The two presidents immediately after Nixon, Republican Gerald Ford and Democrat Jimmy Carter, faced the worst economic conditions since the Great Depression, largely due to increased energy prices. Both presidents offered plans to reduce unemployment and inflation, restore economic growth, and enhance domestic energy sources. However, their efforts were largely unsuccessful, which became a critical factor in their failed reelection bids. The experiences of Ford and Carter highlight that presidents often face situations for which there are no good solutions. Given the realities of the American economy in the 1970s, it is hard to imagine policies that would have improved on Ford and Carter's performance.

The political and policy importance of presidential actions continued to increase during the presidency of Republican Ronald Reagan, despite the fact that he ran on a platform of tax cuts, fewer regulations, and smaller government. Reagan and his staff also negotiated important arms control agreements with the Soviet Union. Reagan's successor, Republican George H. W. Bush, led American and international participation in the Persian Gulf War during 1990 and 1991, which succeeded in removing Iraqi forces from Kuwait with minimal American casualties.

Democrat Bill Clinton's presidency was marked by passage of the North American Free Trade Agreement, welfare reform, arms control agreements, and successful peacekeeping efforts by U.S. troops in Haiti and the Balkans. His presidency also was distinguished by having one of the longest periods of economic growth in U.S. history and the first balanced budgets since the 1960s. President George W. Bush won congressional approval of his tax cuts and education reforms, but he is remembered for managing America's response to the September 11 attacks, including the wars in Iraq and Afghanistan.

President Obama secured several notable changes in domestic and foreign policy, including the enactment of health care reform, economic stimulus legislation, new financial regulations, and the appointment of two Supreme Court justices. However, because of strong Republican opposition in Congress after 2010, Obama had to compromise in enacting many of these new policies, and in areas such as immigration reform and gun control he was largely unsuccessful in achieving his policy goals. Obama's experience highlights a fundamental limit on presidential power: in many areas, presidents require congressional support in order to achieve their policy goals.

constitutional authority (presidential)
Powers derived from the provisions of the Constitution that outline the president's role in government.

statutory authority (presidential)
Powers derived from laws enacted by Congress that add to the powers given to the president in the Constitution.

After presidents leave office, their performance is often evaluated as though their powers and foresight during their term had been unlimited. The history of presidential successes and failures reminds us that, in fact, presidents are often constrained by circumstances. Many of the problems past presidents have faced were totally unanticipated or had no good solutions. Other times, attempts to address national needs failed because of congressional resistance. Thus, before we make judgments about presidential performance, we need to understand the president's job and the resources available to accomplish it.

"Why Should I Care?"

The president's job description

DESCRIBE THE CONSTITUTIONAL AND STATUTORY POWERS OF THE PRESIDENT TODAY

This section describes the president's **constitutional authority** (powers derived from the provisions of the Constitution), **statutory authority** (powers that come from laws), and the additional capabilities that presidents derive from their position as the head of the executive branch of government. Nuts & Bolts 12.1 summarizes the president's constitutional and statutory powers. As the box indicates, some presidential

Presidential Powers

Power	Source of Power
Head of government, head of state (vesting clause)	Constitutional authority
Implementation of laws ("faithful execution")	Constitutional and statutory authority
Executive orders and similar directives (rare)	Constitutional and statutory authority
Administration of executive branch	Constitutional authority
Nominations and appointments to executive branch and judiciary	Constitutional and statutory authority
Commander in chief of armed forces	Constitutional authority
Negotiation of treaties and executive agreements	Constitutional and statutory authority
Veto of congressional actions	Constitutional authority
Presidential pardons	Constitutional authority
Other ceremonial powers	Constitutional authority
Executive privilege	Other
Recommendation of spending levels and other legislative initiatives	Other

powers arise from the Constitution only, and others derive from a combination of constitutional and statutory authority. Our aim is to show how the provisions that define presidential authority operate in modern-day American politics: what kinds of opportunities and constraints they create for the current president and future holders of the office.

Head of the executive branch

vesting clause
Article II, Section 1, of the Constitution, which states: "The executive Power shall be vested in a President of the United States of America," making the president both the head of government and the head of state.

head of government
One role of the president, through which he or she has authority over the executive branch.

head of state
One role of the president, through which he or she represents the country symbolically and politically.

A president's responsibilities and the source of presidential power begin with the constitutional responsibilities of the office. The Constitution's **vesting clause**—"The executive Power shall be vested in a President of the United States of America"—makes the president the **head of government**, or the leader of the executive branch, as well as the **head of state**, or the symbolic and political representative of the country. The precise meaning of the vesting clause has been debated for more than 200 years. Presidents and their supporters argue for an expansive meaning, while their opponents counter that the clause is so vague as to be meaningless. These debates are an important clue that presidential power is only partially due to specific constitutional grants of authority—some of it comes from how each president interprets less concrete statements such as the vesting clause.

The Constitution also places the president in charge of the implementation of laws, saying "he shall take Care that the Laws be faithfully executed." Sometimes the implementation of a law is nearly automatic, as was the case with a 2014 law that has raised the cost of federal flood insurance in recent years for homeowners who live in flood-prone areas. The aim of the legislation was to increase insurance rates gradually so that they would eventually be enough to fully fund the program. In this case, all the president needed to do to implement the law was to ask FEMA bureaucrats to devise a multiyear rate increase plan, then order them to collect the higher premiums from policyholders.

More commonly, the president's authority to implement the law requires using judgment to translate legislative goals into programs, budgets, and regulations. For example, over the last 30 years, Congress has enacted a series of laws that give presidents broad authority to raise or lower tariffs—a president's decisions on tariff policy go into effect unless Congress enacts a law reversing any changes. So, when President Trump decided in spring 2018 to impose new tariffs on imports of steel and aluminum, but later exempted some of America's allies from these tariffs, his decisions reflected prior decisions by members of Congress (as expressed in law) to delegate tariff policy to the president.

After Congress failed to pass the DREAM (Development, Relief, and Education for Alien Minors) Act, President Obama issued an executive order to stop the deportation of some young illegal immigrants in 2012—an order reversed by President Trump in 2017. Although the scope of both presidents' orders were constrained by subsequent court decisions, they stand as an example of how presidential power derives from control over how laws are implemented.

Appointments

The president appoints ambassadors, senior bureaucrats, and members of the federal judiciary, including Supreme Court justices.[11] As the head of the executive branch, the president can appoint individuals to about 8,000 positions, ranging from high-profile jobs such as secretary of state to mundane administrative and secretarial positions. About 1,200 of these appointments—generally high-level positions such as cabinet secretaries—require Senate confirmation. These individuals "serve at the pleasure of the president," meaning that the president can remove them from their positions whenever he or she likes. Thus, when Donald Trump fired Secretary of Veterans Affairs David Shulkin in March 2018, this action was a legitimate exercise of presidential authority, as was Trump's nomination of White House Physician Ronny Jackson to succeed Shulkin. (Jackson later withdrew his nomination, and Trump later nominated Robert Wilkie, who was confirmed.)

The president also nominates individuals to fill federal judgeships, including Supreme Court justices, although these nominations require Senate approval in order to take effect. Because these positions are lifetime appointments, they enable the president to put people into positions of power who will remain after he or she leaves office. For example, in the first months of President Trump's first term, he nominated many young conservative justices to federal judgeships, including Supreme Court associate justices Neil Gorsuch and Brett Kavanaugh. The full effects of these and future judicial appointments by Trump will not be completely apparent for years to come.

The need for Senate confirmation of the president's appointments is one of the fundamental limits on presidential power. Historically, the Senate has approved virtually all nominees without much debate or controversy, although in recent years senators (particularly Republicans during Obama's presidency) have blocked votes on judicial and agency nominees. Some of Trump's cabinet appointees, including Secretary of Education Betsy DeVos, were approved only because Vice President Mike Pence (who is the president of the Senate under the Constitution) voted to break a tie. Trump also nominated Andrew Puzder to be secretary of labor, but he was forced to withdraw the nomination when it became clear that a majority of Senators opposed Puzder's candidacy.

If the Senate is in recess (adjourned for more than three days), the president can make a **recess appointment**, whereby an appointee is temporarily given a position without a Senate vote and holds the office until the beginning of the next congressional session. All presidents make recess appointments, but typically for relatively minor offices and for noncontroversial nominees—for example, when the Republican-controlled Senate refused to vote on President Obama's 2016 Supreme Court nominee, Merrick Garland, it would have been highly unusual (and perhaps unconstitutional) for President Obama to appoint Garland to the Supreme Court via a recess appointment. In any case, the Senate can (and sometimes does) eliminate the possibility of recess appointments by holding brief working sessions as often as needed to ensure that no recess lasts more than three days.

Executive orders

Presidents have the power to issue **executive orders**—that is, proclamations that unilaterally change government policy without subsequent congressional consent[12]— as well as other kinds of orders that change policy, such as National Security Presidential Directives and Presidential Findings (see the How It Works feature on page 434). For example, one of President Trump's memos issued in April 2018 ordered National Guard troops to patrol the U.S. border with Mexico. An executive order issued at the same time was designed to end the "catch and release" protocol whereby illegal immigrants detained at the border were immediately sent back to Mexico without detention or legal proceedings.

As the What Do the Facts Say? feature shows, all presidents issue many numbers of executive orders. Most are not consequential, like the annual order that gives federal employees an early dismissal on the last working day before Christmas. But some executive orders implement large changes in federal policy. Lincoln's Emancipation Proclamation was issued as an executive order. Similarly, President Trump issued a series of executive orders in 2017 that were intended to limit the number of refugees admitted to the United States each year.

Executive orders may appear to give the president authority to do whatever he or she wants, even in the face of strong opposition from Congress. However, particularly during the Trump administration, executive orders have been used to signal intentions

recess appointment
Selection by the president of a person to be an ambassador or the head of a department while the Senate is not in session, thereby bypassing Senate approval. Unless approved by a subsequent Senate vote, recess appointees serve only to the end of the congressional term.

executive orders
Proclamations made by the president that change government policy without congressional approval.

The public sees presidents as speechmakers, but it's mostly butt-in-seat work, a continuous cycle of meetings, decisions, and preparation for meetings and decisions. Governing is a lot harder than tweeting.

—**Michael Grunwald,**
Politico reporter

President Trump's Executive Orders

Many critics (including then–presidential candidate Donald Trump) argued that President Obama issued an unprecedented number of executive orders in order to bypass a Republican Congress that was unsympathetic to his policy proposals. Was Obama an outlier? How has Trump behaved in office?

Executive Orders Issued by Recent Presidents

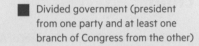

■ Divided government (president from one party and at least one branch of Congress from the other)

■ Unified government (president and both branches of Congress from the same party)

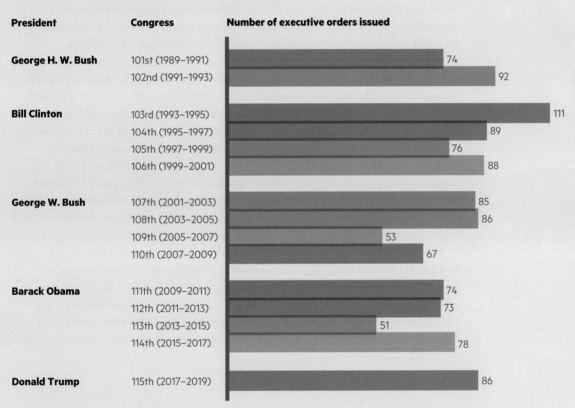

President	Congress	Number of executive orders issued
George H. W. Bush	101st (1989–1991)	74
	102nd (1991–1993)	92
Bill Clinton	103rd (1993–1995)	111
	104th (1995–1997)	89
	105th (1997–1999)	76
	106th (1999–2001)	88
George W. Bush	107th (2001–2003)	85
	108th (2003–2005)	86
	109th (2005–2007)	53
	110th (2007–2009)	67
Barack Obama	111th (2009–2011)	74
	112th (2011–2013)	73
	113th (2013–2015)	51
	114th (2015–2017)	78
Donald Trump	115th (2017–2019)	86

Think about it

- Is there any evidence that Obama issued more executive orders than his predecessors?
- How does Trump's behavior compare to that of Obama and other presidents?

Note: Data current as of November 2018.

Source: "Executive Orders Disposition Tables Index," *Federal Register*, www.archives.gov (accessed 11/8/18).

rather than directly change policy. For example, the "catch and release" order did not command the Border Patrol to hold all illegal immigrants for trial; rather, it instructed the agency to determine what changes would be needed to implement this practice. Moreover, efforts to implement Trump's executive orders on refugees have been overturned or narrowed by the federal courts.

In the main, when the president issues an order that makes real policy changes and Congress does not respond, it means that congressional majorities agree with the president's actions or there is already a law giving the president the authority that he or she is exercising in the order. In the case of the order that sent National Guard troops to the U.S.-Mexico border, for example, Trump has the authority to do this because he is the commander in chief.

Commander in chief

The Constitution makes the president the commander in chief of America's military forces but gives Congress the power to declare war. These provisions are potentially contradictory, and the Constitution leaves open the broader question of who controls the military.[13] In practice, however, the president controls day-to-day military operations through the Department of Defense and has the power to order troops into action without explicit congressional approval. For example, both the Trump and Obama administrations have joined over a dozen other nations to aid rebel forces in the Syrian civil war. They have provided arms and training to rebel fighters and conducted air strikes against ISIL and Syrian government forces, most recently in 2018, with an attack on Syrian chemical weapons production and storage facilities. Similarly, the 2011 attack on Osama bin Laden's compound was carried out without prior congressional approval, although some congressional leaders were notified in advance. In fact, even though the United States has been involved in hundreds of military conflicts, there have been only five declarations of war: the War of 1812, the Mexican-American War (1846), the Spanish-American War (1898), World War I (1917), and World War II (1941).

As a way of restraining presidential war-making power, Congress enacted the War Powers Resolution of 1973 (Nuts & Bolts 12.2 lists the specific provisions of the resolution). However, a 2004 report by the Congressional Research Service found that between 1975 and 2003, despite dozens of U.S. military actions—ranging from embassy evacuations to large-scale operations, including the invasions of Iraq and Afghanistan—the War Powers Resolution has been formally used by Congress to limit

NUTS & BOLTS 12.2

The War Powers Resolution of 1973

1. The president is required to report to Congress any introduction of U.S. forces into hostilities or imminent hostilities.
2. The use of force must be terminated within 60 days unless Congress approves of the deployment. The time limit can be extended to 90 days if the president certifies that additional time is needed to safely withdraw American forces.
3. The president is required whenever possible to consult with Congress before introducing American forces into hostilities or imminent hostilities.
4. Any congressional resolution authorizing the continued deployment of American forces will be considered under expedited procedures.

Source: Richard F. Grimmett, "The War Powers Resolution: After Thirty Years," Congressional Research Service Report RL32267, March 11, 2004, www.hsdl.org/?view&did=446200 (accessed 10/1/18).

presidential authority only once, to limit the duration of a deployment of Marines in Lebanon on a peacekeeping mission.[14] Moreover, although it has been in effect for nearly 40 years, it has never faced Supreme Court review. Some scholars have even argued that the resolution actually expands presidential power because it gives the president essentially unlimited control for the first 90 days of a military operation—and in many cases, 90 days is more than enough time to complete military action without getting Congress involved.[15]

Even with its limitations, the War Powers Resolution has shaped presidential decisions regarding the use of force. Threats by members of Congress to invoke the War Powers Act were one factor in President Obama's 2011 decision to curtail American involvement in the NATO-led mission to end the Libyan civil war. The impact of the War Powers Act is also evident in the fact that presidents often consult with congressional leaders or try to gain congressional approval before committing troops to battle. It is important to remember, too, that the act is not the only tool available to members of Congress who disagree with a president's policy: they can curb a president's war-making powers through budget restrictions, legislative prohibitions, public appeals, and, ultimately, impeachment.[16]

Treaty making and foreign policy

Treaty-making power is shared between Congress and the president: presidents and their staff negotiate treaties, which are then sent to the Senate for approval. (Many need the support of a two-thirds majority of senators to be approved, but some only need a simple majority.) However, the president has a first-mover advantage in the treaty-making process. Congress considers treaties only after negotiations have ended; there is no way for members of Congress to force the president to negotiate a treaty or limit its scope. That said, the need for congressional approval often leads presidents to take account of senators' preferences when negotiating treaties, which often results in significant compromise between the two branches.

Presidents have two strategies for avoiding a congressional treaty vote. One is to announce that the United States will voluntarily abide by a treaty without ratifying it. In the case of the 2015 Paris Climate Accord, one of the reasons why President Obama supported voluntary targets for reductions in greenhouse gases was that such an agreement did not require Senate approval. Of course, this strategy allowed Obama's successor, Donald Trump, to unilaterally withdraw from the accord in 2017.

It is also possible to structure a deal as an **executive agreement** between the executive branch and a foreign government, which does not require Senate approval. This strategy was followed in the case of the deal between the United States, its allies, and the Iranian government to curtail Iran's nuclear weapons research program. In this case, Congress passed (and President Obama signed) a law giving members 30 days to review the deal and the opportunity to pass a resolution rejecting it. The deal ultimately went into effect, although Donald Trump ended U.S. participation in early 2018.

The president also serves as the principal representative of the United States in foreign affairs other than treaty negotiations. Presidential duties include communicating with foreign leaders, nongovernmental organizations, and even ordinary citizens to persuade them to act in ways that the president believes are in the best interest of the United States. For example, in March 2016 President Barack Obama traveled to Cuba, where he toured Cuba's capital, Havana, watched a baseball game between American and Cuban teams, met with Cuban dissidents, and gave a speech on Cuban television that criticized the regime for human rights violations. While speeches and baseball games have no direct effect on policy, they can raise public awareness of their government's shortcomings and perhaps increase pressures for change.

executive agreement
An agreement between the executive branch and a foreign government, which acts as a treaty but does not require Senate approval.

The president often meets with foreign leaders in both formal and informal settings—for example, Barack Obama watched a baseball game in Havana, Cuba, with Cuban leader Raúl Castro in March 2016, and in 2018, President Trump met with Kim Jung-un, the supreme leader of North Korea, in Singapore. Such meetings provide a venue for the president not only to present American views and mediate disagreements but also to act as a visible symbol of America's position as a world superpower.

The amount of time the administration devotes to foreign policy is subject to domestic and world events and therefore not entirely under presidential control. Barack Obama campaigned on a pledge to reduce American military operations abroad, but he expanded drone and Special Forces attacks on members of terrorist organizations, promoted American participation in Libya and Syria, and sent American forces and military aid to eastern Europe in response to Russia's annexation of Crimea. Similarly, while President Trump also promised to limit overseas military operations, he largely continued Obama's policies in Syria and Crimea. In the case of North Korea, Trump's public pressure on the North Korean regime (including threats to respond with "fire and fury" following a North Korean attack on the United States) was a departure from the Obama administration in terms of tone, as was Trump's willingness to hold a one-day meeting with North Korean leader Kim Jong-un. Even so, there are few observable policy differences between Trump's and Obama's policies toward North Korea.

Legislative power

The Constitution establishes lawmaking as a shared power between the president and Congress, and compromise between the two branches is fundamental to passing laws that satisfy both.[17] The president recommends policies and legislative priorities to Congress, notably in the annual **State of the Union** address. Presidents and their legislative staff also work with Congress to develop legislative proposals: they spend considerable time lobbying members of Congress to support their proposals and negotiating with legislative leaders over policy details. Although the president cannot formally introduce legislation, it is typically easy to find a member of Congress willing to sponsor a presidential proposal.[18]

The president's legislative power also stems from the ability to veto legislation (see Nuts & Bolts 12.3). Once both chambers of Congress have passed a bill by simple majority, the president must decide within two weeks of congressional action whether to sign it or issue a veto. Signed bills become law, but vetoed bills return to the House and Senate for a vote to override the veto. If both chambers enact the bill again with at least two-thirds majorities, the bill becomes law; otherwise, it is defeated. If Congress adjourns before the president has made a decision, the president can *pocket veto* the proposal by not responding to it. Pocket vetoes cannot be overridden, but as has happened in recent years, congressional leaders can avoid them by keeping Congress in session for two weeks after a bill is enacted.

State of the Union
An annual speech in which the president addresses Congress to report on the condition of the country and to recommend policies.

The Veto Process

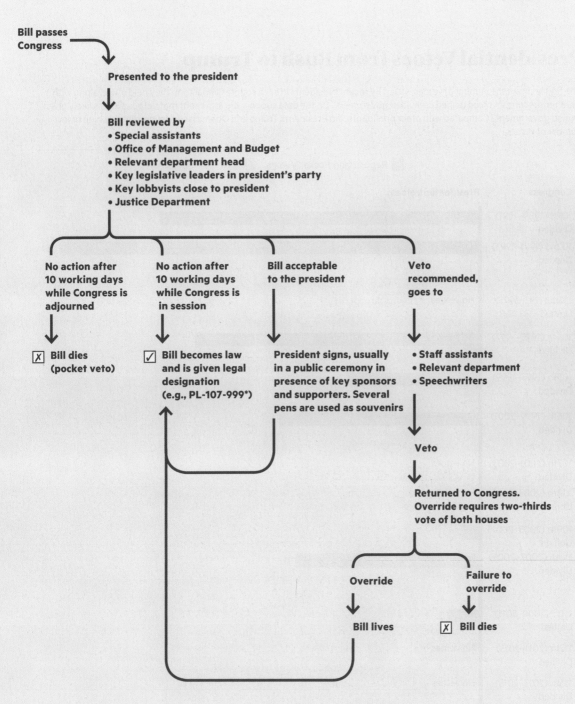

Bill passes Congress

Presented to the president

Bill reviewed by
- **Special assistants**
- **Office of Management and Budget**
- **Relevant department head**
- **Key legislative leaders in president's party**
- **Key lobbyists close to president**
- **Justice Department**

No action after 10 working days while Congress is adjourned

No action after 10 working days while Congress is in session

Bill acceptable to the president

Veto recommended, goes to

☒ **Bill dies (pocket veto)**

☑ **Bill becomes law and is given legal designation (e.g., PL-107-999*)**

President signs, usually in a public ceremony in presence of key sponsors and supporters. Several pens are used as souvenirs

- **Staff assistants**
- **Relevant department**
- **Speechwriters**

Veto

Returned to Congress. Override requires two-thirds vote of both houses

Override

Failure to override

Bill lives

☒ **Bill dies**

*PL = public law; 107 = number of Congress (107th was 2001–2003); 999 = number of the law.

Figure 12.1 shows the number of vetoes issued by recent presidents—and the number overridden by Congress. In general, vetoes are most likely to occur under divided government, when a president from one party faces a House and Senate controlled by the other party (in the case of Obama, the relatively small number of vetoes reflects a

**FIGURE
12.1**

Presidential Vetoes from Bush to Trump

The figure shows the number of vetoes issued by recent presidents in each congressional term they held office, along with whether the term involved unified or divided government. Do the data support the argument that vetoes are less likely given unified government? Compared with other presidents, did Presidents Trump and Obama issue an inordinately high or low number of vetoes?

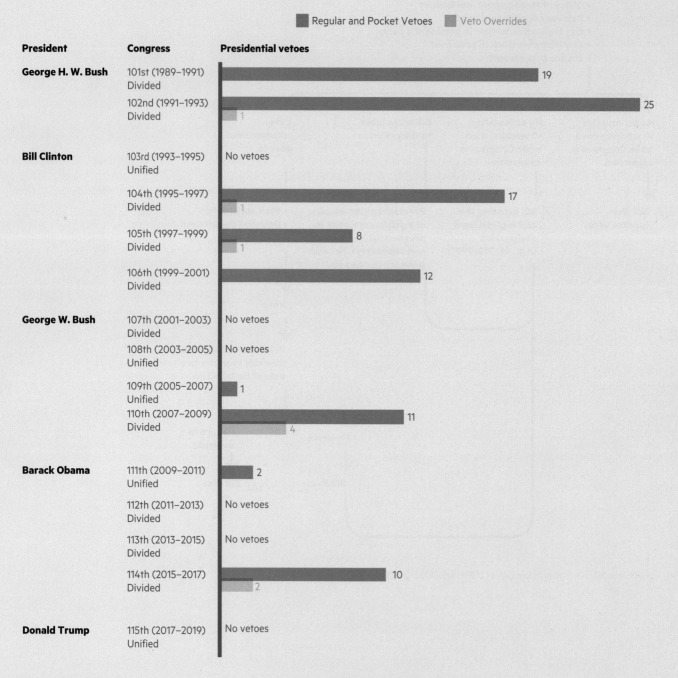

Source: Data aggregated by the author.

sharp reduction in the number of laws enacted by Congress).[19] Vetoes are much less likely under unified government, when one party controls both Congress and the presidency, because the chances are much higher that the president and legislators from his or her party hold similar policy priorities. Thus, in the first two years of the Trump administration, when a Republican president faced a Republican Congress, the president did not veto any legislation. A president's veto threats also allow the president to specify what kinds of proposals he or she is willing or unwilling to accept from Congress. Legislators then know that they need to write a proposal that attracts two-thirds support in both houses or accede to a president's demands.

Pardons and commutations

The Constitution gives the president several additional powers, including the authority to pardon people convicted of federal crimes or to commute (reduce) their sentences. The only limit on this power is that a president cannot pardon anyone who has been impeached and convicted by Congress. (Thus, if a president is removed from office via impeachment, he or she can neither pardon himself or herself nor be pardoned when the vice president assumes the presidency.)

Although most presidential pardons attract little attention, some have been extremely controversial. Many of Obama's pardons involved individuals with no prior criminal record who had been sentenced to long prison terms for nonviolent drug offenses. Obama also pardoned army private Chelsea Manning, who had been convicted of leaking classified information to the WikiLeaks organization. As of late 2018, Donald Trump has issued only a few pardons, although this is not atypical for the first two years of a president's term. Notably, in 2017 President Trump pardoned former Arizona sheriff Joe Arpaio, who had been convicted of contempt of court for refusing a judge's order to stop racial profiling in police traffic stops, and in 2018 pardoned conservative commentator Dinesh D'Souza, who had been convicted of campaign finance law violations.

Executive privilege

Finally, although this power is not formally set out in the Constitution or a statute, all presidents have claimed to hold the power of **executive privilege**. This refers to the ability to shield themselves and their subordinates from revealing White House discussions, decisions, or documents (including e-mails) to members of the legislative or judicial branches of government.[20]

Although claims of executive privilege have been made since the ratification of the Constitution in 1789, it is still not clear exactly what falls under the privilege and what does not. In the 1974 case *United States v. Nixon*, a special prosecutor appointed by the Justice Department to investigate the Watergate scandal challenged President Nixon's claims of executive privilege to force him to hand over tapes of potentially incriminating Oval Office conversations involving Nixon and his senior aides. The Supreme Court ruled unanimously that executive privilege does exist but that the privilege is not absolute. The Court's decision required Nixon to release the tapes, which proved his involvement with attempts to cover up the scandal—but the ruling did not clearly state the conditions under which a future president could withhold such information.[21]

All presidents have claimed executive privilege, although the circumstances have differed. During the congressional investigation of Russian interference in the 2016 election, several of President Trump's appointees, including Attorney General Jeff Sessions, claimed executive privilege in refusing to answer questions about Oval Office

DID YOU KNOW?

Through his two terms in office, President Obama pardoned or commuted the sentences of

1,927

individuals convicted of federal crimes.
Source: U.S. Department of Justice

executive privilege
The right of the president to keep executive branch conversations and correspondence confidential from the legislative and judicial branches.

How Presidents Make Policy Outside the Legislative Process

The Constitution describes the president's influence over new policy initiatives in terms of the power to sign or veto acts of Congress. But what can the president do when Congress fails to act how he or she wants?

President + White House staff develop proposals—they talk to the public, members of Congress, interest groups, union and corporation heads, party leaders, and others. Some of these groups initiate contact and submit their own ideas or even fully drafted plans.

President + Congress sometimes find compromise proposals— but other times negotiations reveal that the president's plans will not receive majority support in the House and Senate.

President + White House staff investigate whether some or all of the president's goals can be achieved through executive order or other means.

President issues appropriate orders and directives.

Congress decides whether to enact legislation reversing the president's actions. They need a two-thirds majority in both houses to override an expected presidential veto.

Presidential appointees, assuming congressional attempts to reverse the new policies are unsuccessful, administer implementation of the new policies.

Presidential Action and the Paris Climate Agreement

The United States' involvement in the Paris Climate Agreement illustrates how a president can bypass Congress and initiate meaningful policy change. Members of President Obama's executive branch participated in the initial talks to develop the accord, and Obama announced that the United States would comply with the agreement in late 2015. However, Donald Trump opposed the agreement during his 2016 campaign, and as president has announced his intention to withdraw from it.

? Critical Thinking

1. **Why do you think President Obama decided to treat the accord as an executive agreement** rather than a treaty? Would the situation be different if Democrats were the majority party in the Senate?

2. **Candidate Trump campaigned against the Paris Agreement—** but President Trump has shown some willingness to remain in a renegotiated accord. Why would it make sense that his position changed once he was in office?

President + staff + other nations:

This is important.

During both of President Obama's campaigns for office, **he argued in favor** of new international agreements to fight climate change.

Let's talk.

Obama, White House staff, and others in the executive branch **discussed policy options** and negotiation strategies. **American diplomats were deeply involved** in negotiating the United Nations Framework Convention on Climate Change.

We have a deal.

Building on the framework convention, representatives from **196 nations developed the Paris Climate Agreement.** U.S. Secretary of State John Kerry signed the accord in November 2015.

President + Congress

We want a say!

Many Republican senators who opposed the accord **demanded that President Obama submit the agreement** for ratification as a treaty.

You don't get one.

The Obama administration announced it would implement the accord as an executive agreement, so a **congressional vote was not required.**

This is a risk.

Although making the accord an executive agreement removed the risk that the Senate would reject the treaty, it also meant that **any future president** could end the United States' participation without further action by Congress.

A new president

We're out!

In August 2017, President Trump announced that the **United States intended to withdraw** from the agreement.

Well, maybe not.

Under the terms of the agreement, a country cannot submit a notice to withdraw **until the agreement has been in effect for four years,** meaning the United States must remain bound by the agreement for Trump's first term.

More negotiation?

In December 2017, Trump said that **he was open to keeping the United States in the accord** if some of its provisions were renegotiated.

The Limits of Executive Privilege

Deciding what information a president can be compelled to release to the public or to other branches of government and what information can be kept confidential requires confronting fundamentally political questions. There are no right answers, and the limits of executive privilege remain unclear. On the one hand, members of Congress need facts, predictions, and estimates from the executive branch to make good public policy. On the other hand, the president and his or her staff have a right to keep their deliberations confidential, as well as a practical need to keep some things secret.

Consider the controversy over the practice (begun during the Bush administration and continued under Presidents Obama and Trump) of targeting terrorists using attacks by unmanned drone aircraft. Compared with deployments of other military forces, on the one hand, drone attacks have the advantages of surprise (drones are small and fly high enough to be invisible), low cost (drones are cheaper than fighters or bombers), and lower risk (the drones can be controlled from anywhere, so there is no risk of American casualties in an attack). On the other hand, drone attacks carry the risk of collateral damage—an attack may also hurt or kill innocent civilians. Moreover, because drone attacks are conducted in secret, there is little to no congressional oversight of who gets targeted by drone strikes or the potential for collateral damage. Should drone attacks fall under executive privilege?

Keep the attacks secret. Clearly, revealing the targets of drone strikes in advance of the actual attacks would destroy the secrecy that makes these strikes so effective— terrorists could stop using cell phones, stay indoors as much as possible, travel only at night, and take other actions to make themselves hard to spot from the air. But there would be danger even in forcing an administration to release information after an attack, as such documents would reveal the criteria used to decide which terrorists to target, the limits of the drone technology, and what factors made it easier to carry out a successful attack. All of this information would help terror targets evade future drone attacks and perhaps require a return to using Special Forces to attack terror targets, which would place American lives at risk.

Reveal the information. The problem with imposing a high level of secrecy on drone attacks is that it is an exception to the rule of keeping Congress informed about the use of military force. In the end, a drone is simply a different way of attacking terrorists or their organization. While the need for secrecy in advance of an attack makes sense, it is not obvious why it should continue after an attack has been carried out. In general, presidents are required to give Congress (in the case of secret operations, the chairs and ranking members of the Intelligence Committees) "prompt notification" of all secret operations. This rule was intended to govern reporting of all covert operations. Should drone attacks be given a higher level of secrecy, or should presidents be forced to keep members of Congress informed?

 The president's role as commander in chief of America's armed forces gives him or her a tremendous amount of power—power that often can be exercised secretly. What should be the limits on presidential secrecy?

take a stand

1. One argument for using drones to attack terrorist targets highlights their greater effectiveness and lower costs than other options. But drone attacks also involve lower political risks to the president. Explain why this is so.

2. Under current law, the president has to inform only a few members of Congress about covert operations and can wait until an operation is in progress before releasing information. Why would members of Congress want expanded notification requirements, such as informing more members or requiring disclosure during the planning of an operation?

conversations with the president. President Obama invoked executive privilege several times, in cases ranging from demands by congressional Republicans for documents related to a Justice Department sting operation, to requests by both Republicans and Democrats for information on drone strikes against terrorist groups (see the Take a Stand feature). In the former case, federal courts rejected Obama's claim, forcing release of the documents; in the latter, members of Congress did not pursue their claims in the courts. The claims made by Trump's appointees have also not been litigated.

Claims of executive privilege present a dilemma. On the one hand, members of Congress need to know what is happening in the executive branch. In the case of President Nixon and the Watergate scandal, claims of executive privilege allowed the Watergate cover-up to continue for more than a year and would have kept this information secret permanently if the Supreme Court had ruled in Nixon's favor.[22] Exercising executive privilege can also weaken accountability to the public, as restricting information may leave the average voter unaware of what an administration is doing. On the other hand, the president and his or her staff need to be able to communicate freely and discuss alternative strategies, hypothetical situations, or national security secrets without fear that they will be forced to reveal conversations that could become politically embarrassing or costly.

Attorney General Jeff Sessions claimed executive privilege in refusing to answer questions about Oval Office conversations with the president in the Russia investigation.

Criticisms of presidents often center on cases of inaction or failure, in which they do nothing to address a national problem or they try to change policy but are unsuccessful. The underlying expectation is that presidents are powerful and can do anything. The reality is that presidents are more powerful in some areas than others—for example, when they negotiate with foreign leaders versus when they propose changes in spending, which require congressional approval. Thus, when we judge presidents' performance, we must consider whether achieving their goals required the assistance of others to make their proposals a reality.

"Why Should I Care?"

The presidency as an institution

As head of the executive branch, the president runs a huge, complex organization with hundreds of thousands of employees. We speak of this organization as an "institution" to emphasize that both the *structure* of the executive branch (the division of responsibilities across different agencies and offices) and the *individuals* who serve in different positions (their experience, skills, and ideological leanings) can have a profound impact on government policies. This section describes the organizations and staff who help the president exercise his or her vast responsibilities, from managing disaster-response efforts to implementing policy changes.[23] Among these employees are appointees who hold senior positions in the government. These individuals serve as the president's eyes and ears in the bureaucracy, making sure that bureaucrats are following presidential directives.

★

EXPLAIN HOW THE EXECUTIVE OFFICE OF THE PRESIDENT, THE VICE PRESIDENT, THE FIRST SPOUSE, AND THE CABINET HELP THE PRESIDENT

The Executive Office of the President

Council of Economic Advisers	Office of National Drug Control Policy
Council on Environmental Quality	Office of Science and Technology Policy
Domestic Policy Council	Office of the First Lady
Homeland Security Council	Office of the United States Trade Representative
National Economic Council	President's Foreign Intelligence Advisory Board
National Security Council	Privacy and Civil Liberties Oversight Board
Office of Administration	USA Freedom Corps
Office of Faith-Based and Community Initiatives	White House Fellows Office
Office of Management and Budget	White House Military Office
Office of National AIDS Policy	White House Office

The Executive Office of the President

Executive Office of the President (EOP)
The group of policy-related offices that serve as support staff to the president.

> **You don't need to know who's playing on the White House tennis court to be a good president.**
>
> —**James Baker,** former White House chief of staff

The executive branch's organizational chart begins with the **Executive Office of the President (EOP)**, which has employed about 1,800 people in recent administrations. About one-third of these employees are concentrated in two offices: the Office of Management and Budget, which develops the president's budget proposals and monitors spending by government agencies, and the Office of the United States Trade Representative, which negotiates trade agreements with other nations. Nuts & Bolts 12.4 lists the organizations that make up the EOP.

One of the most important duties of EOP staff is helping presidents achieve their policy goals and get reelected. In the Trump White House, for example, Senior Adviser Stephen Miller focuses on domestic policy (especially immigration policy) but also helps write Trump's speeches, including the 2018 State of the Union address. Trump's daughter Ivanka and her spouse, Jared Kushner, also play important advisory roles. These three individuals, as well as other influential EOP staff, occupy offices in the West Wing of the White House. The West Wing contains the president's office, known as the Oval Office, and space for the president's chief aide and personal secretary, as well as senior aides such as the vice president, the president's press secretary, and the chief of staff (for Trump, retired general John Kelly), who manages all aspects of White House operations—including, as former Reagan chief of staff James Baker put it, who gets to play tennis on the White House courts. Some recent chiefs of staff have been central in the development of policy proposals and negotiations with members of Congress. However, the chief of staff serves as the agent of the president—what matters is what the president wants, not a chief of staff's policy preferences.

Most EOP staff members are presidential appointees who retain their positions only as long as the president who appointed them remains in office. These individuals are often drawn to government service out of loyalty to the president or because they share the president's policy goals. However, most leave their positions after two or three years to escape the pressures of the job, the long hours, and the relatively low government salaries.[24] Some EOP offices—such as the Office of Management and Budget, the Office of the United States Trade Representative, and the National Security Council (NSC)—also have a significant number of permanent staff analysts and experts.[25] The emphasis on loyalty in presidential appointments has obvious drawbacks: appointees may not know much about the jobs they are given, and they may not be very effective at managing the agencies they are supposed to control. For example, Trump's son-in-law, Jared Kushner, was given responsibility for American efforts to negotiate a peace deal between Israel and the Palestinian Authority, even though his prior experience was as a real estate developer and he had never served in government.

Trump's EOP appointments are a departure from previous practice in several respects. First, while all presidents must balance expertise and loyalty in their appointments, Trump appears to have placed a very high weight on personal loyalty. Second, Trump has appointed significantly fewer individuals to EOP positions, keeping many positions empty even after two years in office. Third, turnover in Trump's EOP has been much higher than in previous administrations. Even so, Trump's emphasis on loyalty in making presidential appointments is similar to that of his predecessors.

The vice president

As set out in the Constitution, the vice president's job is to preside over Senate proceedings. This largely ceremonial job is, in practice, usually delegated to the president pro tempore of the Senate, who in turn typically gives the duty to a more junior member. The vice president also has the power to cast tie-breaking votes in the Senate. Mike Pence, for example, cast such a vote in 2017 to appoint Betsy DeVos as secretary of education. The vice president's other formal responsibility is to become president if the current president dies, becomes incapacitated, resigns, or is impeached. Of the 45 people who have become president, 9 were vice presidents who became president in midterm.

The president's closest advisers are chosen for their loyalty to the president and his or her policy goals. President Trump's closest advisers include his daughter Ivanka Trump and his son-in-law, Jared Kushner (center), who are seen here meeting with Japanese prime minster Shinzō Abe.

While many people perceive the vice president's position to be ceremonial and relatively powerless, recently the vice president's role has expanded significantly. President Trump's vice president, Mike Pence, serves as a trusted policy adviser and directs several initiatives such as the National Space Council.

These rather limited official duties of the vice president pale in comparison with the influential role played by recent vice presidents. Vice President Dick Cheney, who served with President George W. Bush, exerted a significant influence over many policy decisions, including the rights of terror suspects, tax and spending policy, environmental decisions, and the writing of new government regulations.[26] Although Cheney's level of influence was unique, other recent vice presidents have also had real power. Mike Pence, for example, attends most significant meetings in the Oval Office and has considerable private discussion time with President Trump.

The first spouse

Presidential spouses have also played a key but largely informal role in presidential administrations, typically as one of a president's most important advisers. There are examples where they have been an informal conduit for expressing the president's opinions to political appointees, members of Congress, or the media. They also represent America at a wide range of international events, from funerals to conferences. And of course, presidential spouses are a highly visible symbol of the nation, performing a role similar to the president's role as head of state.

Attempts by first spouses to have an official policy-making role in a president's administration are generally limited. For one thing, a first spouse's staff is not set up to assess policy problems or solutions. The commitments of first spouses often keep them out of Washington for substantial periods. Finally, insofar as the first spouse's work is controversial at all, opponents can always argue that the first spouse should not be involved in policy making, as he or she was not elected to do so. During Bill Clinton's presidency, for example, then–first spouse Hillary Clinton was criticized for her leadership role in health care reform efforts.

In light of these constraints, most first spouses pick a largely noncontroversial policy area to focus their official efforts. For example, George W. Bush's spouse, Laura Bush, made numerous public appearances to support education and literacy programs as well as international HIV/AIDS treatment and prevention efforts. Michelle Obama worked to support exercise and healthy eating programs (including changes to federal student lunch guidelines). Donald Trump's spouse, Melania Trump, has kept a low public profile but has made some appearances at events aimed at deterring cyberbullying and supporting her Be Best campaign.

The president's Cabinet

Cabinet
The group of 15 executive department heads who implement the president's agenda in their respective positions.

The president's **Cabinet** is composed of the heads of the 15 executive departments in the federal government, along with other appointees given cabinet rank by the president. Nuts & Bolts 12.5 lists the Cabinet and cabinet-level positions. The cabinet members' principal job is to be the frontline implementers of the president's agenda in their executive departments. As we discuss in Chapter 13, these appointees monitor the actions of the lower-level bureaucrats who retain their jobs regardless of who is president and are not necessarily sympathetic to the president's priorities.

Like other presidential appointees, cabinet members are chosen for a combination of loyalty to the president and expertise. An early supporter of Trump, Attorney General Jeff Sessions is a former senator who served on the Judiciary Committee. Trump's secretary of defense, James Mattis, is a highly respected retired Marine general who commanded troops during Operation Desert Storm in 2001 and during the Iraq War.

Cabinet and Cabinet-Level Positions

NUTS
& BOLTS
12.5

The president's Cabinet is composed of the heads of the 15 executive departments along with other appointees given cabinet rank by the president.

Secretary of Agriculture	Secretary of Transportation
Secretary of Commerce	Secretary of the Treasury
Secretary of Defense	Secretary of Veterans Affairs
Secretary of Education	Vice President
Secretary of Energy	White House Chief of Staff
Secretary of Health and Human Services	Attorney General
Secretary of Homeland Security	Head of the Environmental Protection Agency
Secretary of Housing and Urban Development	Head of the Office of Management and Budget
Secretary of the Interior	Head of the Office of National Drug Control Policy
Secretary of Labor	United States Trade Representative
Secretary of State	

Having read the job description for America's president, you might reasonably ask, How does any one person handle all of these responsibilities? The answer is that presidents have help: trusted advisers and people chosen for policy knowledge, political skills, and loyalty. Put another way, if you want to know whether someone will make a good president, don't look at his or her experience or campaign promises—look at the people he or she picks to help run the government.

Presidential power today

EXPLAIN HOW MODERN PRESIDENTS HAVE BECOME EVEN MORE POWERFUL

As we have discussed, presidential authority comes from two sources, on paper: the limited powers granted by the Constitution, and laws that have expanded the president's power. Even so, assessing presidential power requires expanding our notions of where this power actually comes from. Saying that presidents have become more powerful over time because of the expansion of the United States or the increased size of the federal budget or bureaucracy tells only part of the story. What about these circumstances made presidents more powerful?

One important clue about where presidential power comes from is that, after more than two centuries, many of the limits to these powers are not well defined. It is unclear, for example, which executive actions require congressional approval and which ones can be reversed by Congress. The very ambiguity of the Constitution and most statutes also creates opportunities for the exercise of presidential power. As we have seen, the Constitution makes the president military commander in chief but gives Congress the power to declare war and to raise and support armies, without specifying which branch of government is in charge of the military. Thus, at least part of presidential authority must be derived or assumed from what the Constitution and statutes *do not say*—ways in which they fail to define or delineate presidential power—and how presidents use this ambiguity to pursue their goals.

In addition to these ambiguities, presidents also gain real power from other, more informal aspects of their office. Recall our discussion of the president's ability to influence the legislative process. In the Constitution, the president's powers in this realm are limited to advising Congress on the state of the union and to vetoing legislation (subject to congressional override). But presidents often have very real influence at all points in the legislative process: they can offer a variety of small inducements, such as visits to the Oval Office and campaign assistance, and they can draw on the natural respect that most people (including members of Congress) feel for the presidency regardless of who holds the office, thereby securing compromises that achieve the president's policy goals.[27] Donald Trump, like his predecessors, has used all of these tactics to help enact his policy agenda.

The 2018 debate over U.S. attacks on suspected chemical weapons facilities in Syria provides a good example of how constitutional ambiguities create opportunities for unilateral action. The Trump administration argued that because the operation involved only air strikes, it did not trigger the "hostilities or imminent hostilities" provisions of the War Powers Act.

Presidents, unilateral action, and policy making

unilateral action (presidential)
Any policy decision made and acted upon by the president and presidential staff without the explicit approval or consent of Congress.

Political scientists Terry M. Moe and William G. Howell argue that constitutional and statutory ambiguities in some cases enable presidents to take **unilateral action**, changing policy on their own without consulting Congress or anyone else.[28] Although Congress can, in theory, undo unilateral actions through legislation, court proceedings, or impeachment, Moe and Howell maintain that the costs of doing so, in terms of time, effort, and public perceptions, are often prohibitive. The result is that presidents can take unilateral action despite congressional opposition, knowing that their actions stand little chance of being reversed.

The 2018 debate over U.S. attacks on suspected chemical weapons facilities in Syria provides a good example of how constitutional ambiguities create opportunities for unilateral action. The Trump administration argued that because the operation involved only air strikes, it did not trigger the "hostilities or imminent hostilities" provisions of the War Powers Act. While some in Congress disagreed and wanted to vote on whether to authorize the operation, no such vote was ever taken.

This example is far from the first time that a president has argued that military operations were not subject to congressional review. For example, the arguments advanced by the Trump administration were very similar to those made by the Obama administration when it sent military aid and advisers to Syria in 2011. Even during the Iraq War, when some Democrats in Congress wanted to cut off war funding to force the withdrawal of American forces, supporters of the Bush administration cited the **unitary executive theory** to argue that the Constitution's description of the president as commander in chief of America's armed forces meant that, even if Congress refused to appropriate funds for the war, the president could order American forces to stay in Iraq and order the Department of the Treasury to spend any funds necessary to continue operations. (The unitary executive theory was also cited during the investigation of possible collusion between the Russian government and the 2016 Trump presidential campaign, when President Trump's lawyers used it to justify their claim that, since the Constitution made Trump the head of the executive branch (including the Justice Department), he could not be indicted for committing a crime.)

In both cases, the positions of the Obama and Bush administrations left members of Congress with a single unattractive option: invoking the War Powers Resolution to force the end of combat operations. This option would take time, as it would require building majority support in the House and the Senate for the resolution. It would also trigger Supreme Court review of the War Powers Resolution, which is a significant risk—if the Court were to rule in favor of the president and to hold that the resolution was unconstitutional, it would sharply reduce Congress's control over future military operations.

Presidents act unilaterally to make domestic policy as well. President Trump, for example, has issued orders to limit the admission of refugees into the United States and to move toward adding work requirements for recipients of federal welfare benefits. Similarly, during President Obama's second term in office, Obama gave several directives to the Justice Department that limited deportations of undocumented immigrants. And while President Trump has reversed some of Obama's executive orders (particularly those dealing with deportations), the others will remain in place until a future president, Congress, or federal court acts to rescind them.

It is important to understand that throughout the nation's history, there have been many other examples of unilateral presidential actions, such as the annexation of Texas, the freeing of slaves in the Emancipation Proclamation, the desegregation of the U.S. military, the initiation of affirmative action programs, and the creation of agencies such as the Peace Corps.[29] In part, unilateral actions are the product of the president's constitutional and statutory authority, which gives the president the right to act unilaterally under some circumstances. Additional opportunities are created by the ambiguities in the president's authority that we discussed earlier. Finally, because no one becomes president without a strong, broad vision of what he or she would like government to do, it should be no surprise that presidents are continually testing the bounds of their authority by taking unilateral actions as a way of translating their policy ideas into reality.

unitary executive theory
The idea that the vesting clause of the Constitution gives the president the authority to issue orders and policy directives that cannot be undone by Congress.

Control over the interpretation and implementation of laws

By virtue of their control over the executive branch, presidents are sometimes in a position to shape policy outcomes by influencing how a law is implemented. For example, after Congress passed a law in 2017 that mandated sanctions on Russians who had participated in efforts to interfere in the 2016 American presidential election, the Trump administration took over six months to identify which individuals would be subject to sanctions. Besides missing a deadline laid out in the bill, the administration's actions targeted only a small number of individuals—significantly fewer than supporters of the law had expected. However, because the law did not specify how extensive the sanctions had to be, the administration's actions, while unilateral, were in fact legal.

Other presidents have found and exploited loopholes in laws that were initially designed to restrict presidential power. For example, current law requires the president to give congressional leaders "timely notification" of secret intelligence operations. However, during the Reagan administration, senior officials did not reveal the existence of ongoing operations for several months. When these operations were eventually discovered, officials claimed they were within the letter of the law because it did not specify a time limit within which Congress must be notified.[30]

Most presidents have tried to control the implementation of laws by issuing **signing statements** when signing bills into law. These documents, which explain the president's interpretation of a new law, are issued most often when the president wishes to approve the bill but disagrees with the way that supporters of the bill in Congress interpret the legislation. Presidents issue signing statements so that if the courts have to resolve uncertainties about the bill's intent, judges can take into account not only the views expressed during congressional debates about the bill but also the president's interpretation of it.[31]

signing statement
A document issued by the president when signing a bill into law explaining his or her interpretation of the law, which often differs from the interpretation of Congress, in an attempt to influence how the law will be implemented.

Congressional responses to unilateral action

In theory, members of Congress can undo a president's unilateral action by enacting a law to overturn it, but this is harder than it may sound.[32] Some members of Congress may approve of what the president has done or be indifferent to it, or they may give a higher priority to enacting other laws, making it hard to assemble a majority of legislators who are motivated enough to pass a law overturning the president's action. For example, the Trump administration went far enough on its implementation of the Russia sanctions that only a minority of House members and senators were willing to invest the time to enact a new bill that went farther. Still, reversals do happen: Congress enacted a Russia sanctions bill in the first place in a reversal of the Trump administration's refusal to agree that Russians actually interfered in the 2016 election or that America should impose sanctions as a response.

Members of Congress can also write laws in a way that limits the president's authority over their implementation.[33] However, this strategy has drawbacks. The problem is that members of Congress delegate authority to the president or the executive branch bureaucracy for good reasons—either because it is difficult for legislators to predict how a policy should be implemented or because they cannot agree among themselves on an implementation plan.[34] In the case of Russia sanctions, for example, members of Congress may have been unsure of whom to sanction or what appropriate punishments would look like. Members of Congress from the president's party may also want to grant authority to the president because they hold policy goals similar to the president's and would therefore benefit from the exercise of unilateral power.

Aside from legislation, the only option for members of Congress to overturn a president's unilateral action is to take the president to court (probably all the way to the Supreme Court) to demonstrate that he or she has overstepped his or her authority. In the case of the Trump administration's travel ban barring people from six countries with large Muslim populations from entering the United States, some members of Congress were involved in court cases intended to suspend or reverse the ban. The problem with pursuing this option is the time required for judicial proceedings—and the fact that the courts may uphold the president's right to act unilaterally. A later version of the ban was upheld by the Supreme Court in June 2018. But policies that contradict congressional intent may in fact be completely constitutional.

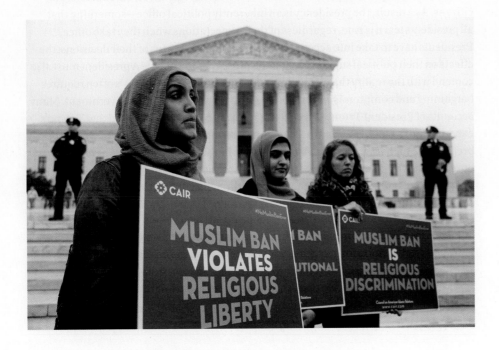

Protesters from the Council on American-Islamic Relations stand outside of the Supreme Court as they hear arguments about whether President Trump's travel ban on travelers from six mostly Muslim countries violates immigration laws or the Constitution.

Congress also has the power to remove the president or vice president from office through the impeachment process. However, removing a president is much more difficult than passing a law to undo a unilateral action. First, House members must impeach (indict) the president by majority vote, which accuses him or her of a crime or breach of his or her sworn duties. Then senators hold a trial, followed by a vote in which a two-thirds majority is required to remove the president from office. Only two presidents have faced an impeachment vote: Andrew Johnson in 1866 and Bill Clinton in 1999 (a third president, Richard Nixon, resigned from office to prevent an impeachment vote). Johnson was involved in a political dispute over administration of the southern states after the Civil War; Clinton was alleged to have lied under oath in a sexual harassment lawsuit. Although both of these presidents were impeached by the House, they were not convicted by the Senate, so they stayed in office. One reason impeachment is difficult is that members of Congress who are upset about certain presidential actions might nevertheless oppose removing the president from office. They might approve of the president's other initiatives, want to prevent the vice president from becoming president, or have concerns about the political backlash that impeachment could generate against them or their party. Thus, even though Democrats took over the House in the 2018 midterms, they still lacked a plurality in the Senate (let alone the 67-vote supermajority) necessary to remove Trump from office.

In sum, ambiguities in the Constitution create opportunities for unilateral presidential action. These actions are subject to reversal through legislation, court decisions, and impeachment, but members of Congress face significant costs if they undertake any of these options. As long as presidents are careful to limit their exercise of unilateral power to actions that do not generate intense opposition in Congress, they can implement a wide range of policy goals without official congressional consent—provided that bureaucrats go along with the president's wishes, a question we take up in the next chapter.

Presidents as politicians

Aside from situations in which the president has (or has been given) the authority to act unilaterally, the reality of presidential power is that much of what presidents do (or want to do) requires support from others, including legislators, bureaucrats, and citizens. As a result, the presidency is an inherently political office—something that all presidents learn is true, regardless of their expectations when they take office.[35] Presidents have to take into account the political consequences of their decisions: the effects on their political support, reelection prospects, and party. A president must also contend with the reality that achieving his or her personal policy goals often requires bargaining and compromising with others, both inside and outside government. Many accounts of President Trump's first two years in office have emphasized that Trump's experience as a CEO, the head of an organization in which his word was law, did not prepare him for being president, a role in which he faces members of Congress and bureaucrats who often have the power to reject presidential initiatives.

In part, presidents must keep their eyes on the political implications of their actions in office because they want to be reelected to a second term. One important indicator of presidential performance is the **presidential approval rating**, the percentage of the public who think the president is doing a good job in office. Figure 12.2, which shows the presidential approval ratings for the last nine presidents who ran for reelection, reveals that first-term presidents with less than 50 percent approval are in real trouble. No recent president has been reelected with less than a 50 percent approval rating.

Of course, it would be wrong to say that presidents are single-mindedly focused on keeping their approval rating as high as possible. For one thing, as we discussed

> He'll sit here, and he'll say, "Do this! Do that!" And nothing will happen. Poor Ike—it won't be a bit like the Army. He'll find it very frustrating.
>
> —**President Harry Truman,** describing incoming president Dwight Eisenhower

presidential approval rating
The percentage of Americans who think that the president is doing a good job in office.

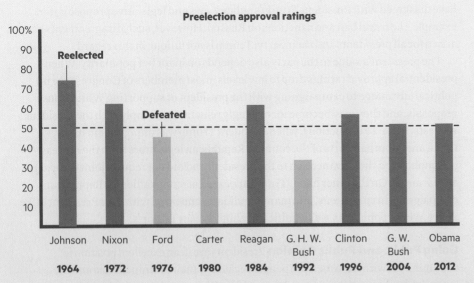

Preelection approval ratings

Reelected

Defeated

	Johnson	Nixon	Ford	Carter	Reagan	G. H. W. Bush	Clinton	G. W. Bush	Obama
	1964	1972	1976	1980	1984	1992	1996	2004	2012

Source: Approval data from the Roper Center for Public Opinion Research, Cornell University, "Presidential Approval," https://presidential.roper.center (accessed 7/30/18).

FIGURE 12.2

Presidential Popularity and Reelection

This figure shows the preelection-year average approval ratings for recent presidents who ran for reelection. It shows that a president's chances of winning reelection are related to his or her popularity. At what level of approval would you say that an incumbent president is likely to be reelected?

in Chapter 6, presidential approval is shaped by factors that they have only limited control over, such as the state of the economy. And all presidents have taken actions that were politically costly because they believed that the policies were worthwhile—for example, many of President Trump's decisions (such as the travel ban) and his legislative initiatives (such as the tax cuts enacted in 2017) were opposed by a majority of Americans. Even so, presidents and their advisers are keenly aware of the political consequences of their actions, and there is no doubt that these consequences shape both their decisions and how they explain these actions to American citizens.

The President as Party Leader The president is the unofficial head of his or her political party and generally picks the party's day-to-day leaders (or at least has considerable influence over their selection). This process begins when a presidential candidate captures the party's nomination and continues through the president's time in office. For example, while many members of the Republican National Committee (RNC) opposed Donald Trump's nomination in 2016, the party organized to help Trump get elected and ran countless campaign ads on his behalf. After the election, Trump supporters, including the current chair of the RNC, Ronna McDaniel, moved into senior positions within the party organization.

The connection between the president and the party reflects their intertwining interests. The president needs support from members of his or her party in Congress to enact legislation, and the party and its candidates need the president to compile a record of policy achievements that reflect well on the organization and to help raise the funds needed for the next election. Therefore, party leaders generally defer to a presidential candidate's (or a president's) staffing requests, and most presidents and presidential candidates take time to meet with national party leaders and the congressional leadership from their party to plan legislative strategies, make joint campaign appearances, and raise funds for the party's candidates. This is not to say that members of the president's party always agree with his or her behavior and issue positions: during the first two years of Trump's term, many Republican legislators, including Senate Majority Leader Mitch McConnell and former House Speaker Paul Ryan, have disagreed with President Trump's policy views and legislative proposals (for example, the travel ban and sanctions on Russia). However, such disagreements have arisen for all presidents and their party; Trump is not unique in this regard.

The president's value to the party also depends on his or her popularity. When presidential approval ratings drop to low levels, most members of Congress see no political advantage to campaigning with the president or supporting White House proposals, and they may become increasingly reluctant to comply with the president's requests. In the 2018 elections, when President Trump was unpopular in many urban and suburban parts of the country, Republican legislators from these areas de-emphasized their connection to the president and did not request joint campaign appearances. On the other hand, Trump appeared at many rallies for Republicans campaigning in rural areas, and many candidates appeared with Vice President Mike Pence, whose popularity was significantly higher than Trump's.

Going Public and Public Opinion Presidents are in an excellent position to communicate with the American people because of their prominent role and the extensive media coverage devoted to anything they say to the nation. Broadcast and cable networks even give the president prime-time slots for the State of the Union speech and other major addresses. The media attention that comes with the presidency provides the president with a unique strategy for shaping government policy: **going public**, that is, appealing directly to American citizens.[36] Presidential appeals are designed partly to persuade and partly to motivate the president's supporters, in the hope that they will pressure members of the House and Senate to support the president's requests.

Going public sometimes works—but more often it is ineffectual or even counterproductive. A president's appeals may energize supporters, but they may also have a similar effect on opponents.[37] Thus, rather than facilitating compromise (or a wholesale presidential victory), publicizing an issue may deepen existing conflicts. More generally, studies suggest that most Americans ignore or reject a president's attempts to go public. As presidency scholar George C. Edwards III notes, people who disapprove of a president's time in office are not going to change their minds just because of a presidential speech.[38] Thus, unless a president is extraordinarily popular, going public is not going to help enact the president's agenda.

President Donald Trump shakes hands with Senate Majority Leader Mitch McConnell of Kentucky, who has been supportive of his agenda, before a meeting with House and Senate leadership at the White House.

Approval ratings

Source: FiveThirtyEight, "How Popular is Donald Trump?," https://projects.fivethirtyeight.com/trump-approval-ratings (accessed 10/1/18).

📊

**FIGURE
12.3**

Presidential Approval Ratings for Donald Trump

Donald Trump's approval ratings were remarkably stable during the first two years of his presidency, which is what we would expect given steady economic growth and high levels of partisan polarization. Many Democrats argued that Trump should be blamed for tax cuts that favored the rich as well as statements and actions that damaged America's relations with other nations. Does the trend in Trump's approval ratings suggest these attacks had much effect?

These findings explain why most recent presidents have had little success with their efforts to go public. President George W. Bush gave many speeches to build support for his Iraq war policies and for his proposal to privatize Social Security. President Barack Obama did the same in an effort to enact gun control legislation. And while President Trump has used a broader range of media outlets compared to his predecessors (most notably, Twitter), his efforts to shape public opinion on issues such as the travel ban, the border wall, or immigration reform have not significantly changed what people think (see Figure 12.3). Thus, while presidents have a unique platform from which to deliver their arguments directly to the American people, in practice they are often frustrated in their ability to shape public opinion.

The difficulty presidents have in shaping public opinion is another reason why some presidents seem to accomplish more than others. Political scientist Stephen Skowronek argues that presidents are constrained by the era in which they govern.[39] Some presidents (such as Ronald Reagan in 1981) take office when public opinion is strongly behind their policy agenda, making it easier for them to persuade Congress and bureaucrats to comply with their requests. Other presidents have the misfortune to hold office when public opinion is not supportive of significant policy change in the form of new laws or changes in regulations. Under these conditions, presidents are limited in what they can do, even with all their powers and capability for unilateral action. Even though President Donald Trump has held office with unified Republican control of the House and Senate, there has been only modest public support for many Republican initiatives, such as repealing Obamacare, cutting entitlement programs, or curtailing government regulations. This political climate has contributed to the difficulties Trump has faced in trying to enact these parts of his agenda.

Unpacking the Conflict

Considering all that we've discussed in this chapter, let's apply what we know about how the office of the president works to the questions we presented at the beginning of this chapter. Will Trump and the outcomes of his tenure in office redefine what makes a successful president? What are the factors that enable *any* presidents to be successful?

President Donald Trump occupies an office whose power is derived from constitutional authority, statutory authority, and ambiguities that enable unilateral action. While he promised during the campaign to transform America, his presidency highlights the difficulties that any president would face in trying to deliver on this promise. Although presidents are given considerable powers, big policy changes generally require congressional consent. And as we have seen, even with unified government, Trump has been no more successful than his predecessors at persuading members of Congress to accept his policy plans such as the building of a border wall. Trump has also faced opposition from within the bureaucracy and from citizens pursuing their claims through the federal judicial system. The fact that Republicans lost their House majority in the 2018 midterms will only magnify these difficulties.

Even so, Trump has had some notable successes, particularly in areas where he can act unilaterally using executive orders, as well as in shaping American foreign policy. Trump's appointees to posts in Cabinet departments and federal agencies have made significant progress in implementing his agenda in the form of regulatory changes and new interpretations of existing laws. Taking together these successes and the failures that we've noted, we should not conclude that Donald Trump has some special powers that his predecessors have lacked or is deficient in some crucial talent. While his day-to-day behavior is sometimes different from what we have come to expect from our presidents, Trump's overall performance is not surprising. Rather, it illustrates both the possibilities and the limitations of the presidency in contemporary American politics.

What's Your Take?

Does Trump's presidency represent a departure from the norm? How do the results he's achieved in office compare with those of previous presidents?

STUDY GUIDE

The development of presidential power

Trace the evolution of presidential power.
(Pages 420–423)

Summary

Presidents get their powers from a variety of sources: some powers are from the Constitution; others have more informal origins. Although the president's constitutional powers have not changed, presidential power has grown substantially over time. Nonetheless, even presidents' power is still limited in a number of contexts.

Practice Quiz Questions

1. **Which of the following is not a reason why presidential power has increased over time?**

   a   changes in the Constitution

   b   America's growth as a nation

   c   America's emergence as a dominant actor in international politics

   d   the expansion of the federal government

   e   acts of legislation passed by Congress

2. **Which of the following events during Donald Trump's presidency best illustrates the limits of presidential power?**

   a   congressional consideration of new gun control laws

   b   the nomination of Neil Gorsuch to the Supreme Court

   c   the use of airstrikes in Syria

   d   the failure to repeal Obamacare

   e   Trump's defeat of Hillary Clinton in 2016

The president's job description

Describe the constitutional and statutory powers of the president today. (Pages 423–437)

Summary

The president's formal powers arise from a combination of constitutional provisions and additional laws that give him or her

increased responsibilities. The president has many duties, but the primary responsibilities of the office are to oversee the executive branch and implement laws passed by Congress. Although some presidents might prefer to focus on either domestic or foreign policy, most find that their priorities are determined by domestic and world events.

Key terms

constitutional authority (p. 423)

statutory authority (presidential) (p. 423)

vesting clause (p. 424)

head of government (p. 424)

head of state (p. 424)

recess appointment (p. 426)

executive orders (p. 426)

executive agreement (p. 429)

State of the Union (p. 430)

executive privilege (p. 433)

Practice Quiz Questions

3. **Presidents use recess appointments when they are trying to _____.**

   a   fill a judicial vacancy outside the scheduled period

   b   fill a vacant seat in Congress

   c   temporarily dodge the need for Senate approval

   d   temporarily dodge the need for House approval

   e   fill vacancies with a permanent replacement

4. **A presidential proclamation that unilaterally changes government policy without congressional consent is called _____.**

   a   an executive privilege

   b   a fast-track authority

   c   an executive agreement

   d   an executive order

   e   statutory authority

5. **Some scholars argue that the War Powers Resolution has effectively expanded the power of _____.**

   a   the president

   b   Congress

   c   the Supreme Court

   d   the Department of Defense

   e   the State Department

6. **The first-mover advantage refers to the president's negotiating advantage over _____.**

   a   foreign leaders

   b   governors

   c   the bureaucracy

   d   Congress

   e   international organizations

The presidency as an institution

Explain how the Executive Office of the President, the vice president, the first spouse, and the Cabinet help the president. (Pages 437–441)

Summary

The executive branch is a huge, complex organization that helps the president exercise vast responsibilities. Appointees to the branch serve as the president's eyes and ears on the bureaucracy. Almost all appointees are replaced when a new administration begins.

Key terms

Executive Office of the President (EOP) (p. 438)   **Cabinet** (p. 440)

Practice Quiz Questions

7. **In most appointments to EOP positions, presidents generally emphasize _____ .**

a   experience

b   expertise

c   effectiveness

d   public opinion

e   loyalty

8. **Recent vice presidents have had _____ official duties and/but _____ been influential in their role.**

a   no; have not

b   limited; have

c   limited; have not

d   extensive; have

e   extensive; have not

9. **The primary job of most of the people who work in the Executive Office of the President is _____ .**

a   to help the president manage the federal bureaucracy

b   to lobby members of Congress to enact the president's program

c   to manage the president's reelection campaign

d   to find ways to build public support for the president

e   to oversee the organization of the president's party

Presidential power today

Explain how modern presidents have become even more powerful. (Pages 441–449)

Summary

While presidents have gained power over time, the Constitution grants the president rather limited powers. The growth of presidential power is closely related to the fact that most limits on it are not well-defined and presidents have succeeded in taking advantage of these ambiguities.

Key terms

unilateral action (presidential) (p. 442)

unitary executive theory (p. 443)

signing statement (p. 444)

presidential approval rating (p. 446)

going public (p. 448)

Practice Quiz Questions

10. **The _____ was used by the George W. Bush administration to argue in favor of the power to station American forces in Iraq.**

a   principal-agent theory

b   unitary executive theory

c   unilateral agreement theory

d   dual presidency theory

e   signing statement power

11. **Most presidents use the _____ to control the interpretation and implementation of laws.**

a   line-item veto

b   recess appointment

c   executive order

d   signing statement

e   pocket veto

12. **Congressional challenges to presidential unilateral action are _____ used and are generally _____ at constraining presidential power.**

a   rarely; successful

b   rarely; unsuccessful

c   commonly; successful

d   commonly; unsuccessful

13. **Presidential reelection is often tied to _____ .**

a   economic conditions

b   policy positions

c   presidential actions

d   presidential appointments

e   an absence of scandals

14. **What is the best explanation for the ability of presidents to act unilaterally in the face of congressional opposition?**

a   Americans' dislike of Congress

b   the perception that presidents only act in the interests of the entire nation

c   the doctrine of executive privilege

d   the difficulty of enacting a law to reverse a president's actions

e   the theory of the unitary executive

15. For most presidents, the problem with going public is that _____.

a   the public is more focused on Congress

b   the president's speeches are not very persuasive

c   they energize their opponents

d   they generally address unimportant issues

e   they do not reach their target audience

Suggested Reading

Alter, Jonathan. *The Promise: President Obama, Year One*. New York: Simon and Schuster, 2010.

Canes-Wrone, Brandice. *Who Leads Whom? Presidents, Policy, and the Public*. Chicago: University of Chicago Press, 2006.

Edwards, George C. III. *Predicting the Presidency: The Potential of Persuasive Leadership*. Princeton, NJ: Princeton University Press, 2015.

Hallett, Brian. *Declaring War: Congress, the President, and What the Constitution Does Not Say*. New York: Cambridge University Press, 2012.

Howell, William G. *Power without Persuasion: The Politics of Direct Presidential Action*. Princeton, NJ: Princeton University Press, 2003.

Katznelson, Ira. *Fear Itself: The New Deal and the Origins of Our Time*. New York: W. W. Norton, 2013.

Lewis, David E. *Presidents and the Politics of Agency Design: Political Insulation in the United States Government Bureaucracy, 1946–1997*. Palo Alto, CA: Stanford University Press, 2003.

Mayer, Kenneth. *With the Stroke of a Pen: Executive Orders and Presidential Power*. Princeton, NJ: Princeton University Press, 2001.

Neustadt, Richard E. *Presidential Power and the Modern Presidents: The Politics of Leadership from Roosevelt to Reagan*. New York: Free Press, 1990.

Rudalevige, Andrew. *Managing the President's Program: Presidential Leadership and Legislative Policy Formation*. Princeton, NJ: Princeton University Press, 2002.

Skowronek, Stephen. *Presidential Leadership in Political Time: Reprise and Reappraisal*, 2nd ed. Lawrence: University of Kansas Press, 2011.

The Bureaucracy
What's with all this red tape?

 "Government! Three fourths parasitic and the other fourth stupid fumbling."
Robert A. Heinlein, American writer

 "Bureaucracy is not an obstacle to democracy but an inevitable complement to it."
Joseph A. Schumpeter, American economist

On Donald Trump's first day in office in 2017, his press secretary announced that the crowd watching him take the oath of office was the largest ever to attend an inauguration. Several hours later, bureaucrats at the National Park Service retweeted photos showing that Trump's crowd was clearly smaller than the crowd at President Obama's inauguration in 2009. White House officials immediately ordered the Park Service to stop issuing tweets, but questions about crowd size at the inauguration (and the subsequent Twitter ban) became a distraction to the new administration during its first weeks in office.

The Park Service's tweets illustrate what has been an often-contentious relationship between President Trump and the federal bureaucracy. During his first two years in office, Trump has often accused the so-called deep state (career members of the bureaucracy) of ignoring his policy agenda—or worse, of fighting to delay or kill Trump's initiatives. Many of these accusations targeted officials in the Justice Department (including the FBI) and their investigation of Russian involvement in the 2016 elections, but Trump has also complained about bureaucrats in the State Department, the Environmental Protection Agency (EPA), and many other government offices.

Evaluating Trump's complaints requires us to move beyond what bureaucrats are doing to assess the reasons for their behavior. After all, as we discussed in Chapter 12, while Trump wields considerable power as president, he cannot simply order bureaucrats to do whatever he wants. Bureaucratic actions that anger Trump may stem from opposition to his agenda, but they may also reflect constitutional or legislative directives that leave bureaucrats with no choice but to pursue policies that are contrary to Trump's wishes.

Trump's description of the bureaucracy as a more or less autonomous "deep state" raises more serious questions about how American politics works. Up to now, we've described the policy-making process in terms of three steps: citizens elect

In response to inaccurate claims by President Trump's press secretary that the crowds at his inauguration surpassed those of any other president, the National Park Service retweeted photos showing that there were clearly fewer attendees at Trump's inauguration than Obama's. In response, the White House ordered the Park Service to stop tweeting, demonstrating the often-contentious relationship between President Trump and the federal bureaucracy.

CHAPTER GOALS

Define *bureaucracy* and explain its major functions. pages 456–465

Trace the expansion of the federal bureaucracy over time. pages 465–469

Describe the size and structure of the executive branch today. pages 469–475

Describe who bureaucrats are and the regulations that govern their employment. pages 475–478

Explain how Congress and the president oversee the executive branch. pages 479–483 representatives, these representatives go to Washington and enact laws, and then bureaucrats are given these laws to implement. The reality in our system is that the responsibility for implementing laws conveys policy-making power. When bureaucrats write regulations, sign contracts with private corporations, or deliver services to citizens, they are translating often-vague statutes into concrete decisions. Moreover, because of their training and experience, bureaucrats are often better informed than elected officials about the details of government policy. As a result, we can't think of bureaucrats as simply doing what they are told. Rather, their jobs involve judgment, initiative, and creativity.

Bureaucratic expertise creates a new problem for elected officials: if they ignore what bureaucrats tell them or force bureaucrats to implement laws and directives as written, the result may be policy failures. However, if elected officials acknowledge that bureaucrats are experts and allow them to make as well as implement government policy, elected officials in effect give up all their power to the bureaucracy—something that the Trump administration is unwilling to risk. Are bureaucrats really obstructing the Trump agenda, or are they just doing their jobs? How do elected officials control a bureaucracy of experts?

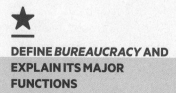

DEFINE *BUREAUCRACY* **AND EXPLAIN ITS MAJOR FUNCTIONS**

bureaucracy
The system of civil servants and political appointees who implement congressional or presidential decisions; also known as the *administrative state*.

civil servants
Employees of bureaucratic agencies within the government.

political appointees
People selected by an elected leader, such as the president, to hold a government position.

What is the federal bureaucracy?

The federal **bureaucracy** is the vast network of agencies that makes up the government's executive branch. It is composed of millions of **civil servants**, who work for the government in permanent positions, and thousands of **political appointees**, who hold short-term, usually senior positions and are appointed by an elected leader such as the president. Another name for the bureaucracy is the *administrative state*, which refers to the role bureaucrats play in administering government policies.[1] Most constitutional scholars agree that the president is nominally in charge of the bureaucracy—although generally the president shares this power with members of Congress.

In general, the job of the federal bureaucracy includes a wide range of tasks, from regulating the behavior of individuals and corporations to buying pencils, jet fighters, and everything in between. At one level, these actions implement policy decisions made by others, including presidential directives or legislation enacted by Congress. But as we will see, implementation often involves giving bureaucrats considerable discretion over the details of policy decisions. Moreover, these activities are inherently political and often conflictual: ordinary citizens, elected officials, and bureaucrats themselves often disagree about aspects of these activities, and they work to influence bureaucratic actions to suit their policy goals.

What do bureaucrats do?

The task of the bureaucracy is to develop and implement policies established by congressional acts or presidential decisions. Sometimes the tasks associated with putting these laws and resolutions into effect are very specific. For example, in the appropriations bill for fiscal year 2019 Congress mandated that the navy purchase 150 F-35 attack jets from defense contractor Lockheed Martin. This provision required no discretion on the part of the bureaucrats tasked to implement it—all they needed to do was sign the contract, make sure the jets were delivered, and pay Lockheed Martin.

More commonly, however, legislation provides only general guidelines for meeting governmental goals. Bureaucrats thus have considerable latitude to develop particular policies and programs. For example, the 1938 Federal Food, Drug, and Cosmetic Act gave the Food and Drug Administration (FDA) the job of determining which drugs are safe and effective, but it allowed FDA bureaucrats to develop their own procedures for making these determinations. Currently, the FDA requires that drug manufacturers first test new drugs for safety and then conduct further trials to determine their effectiveness. An FDA advisory board of scientists and doctors reviews the results of these tests, and FDA bureaucrats decide whether to allow the manufacturer to market the drug. While members of Congress and the president created this procedure, they have no way to intervene in the process except by enacting a new bill that makes an exception to the FDA's normal procedures or revamps these procedures entirely.

Developing Regulations A **regulation** is a rule that allows the government to exercise control over individuals and corporations by allowing or prohibiting behavior, setting out the conditions under which certain behaviors can occur, or assessing costs or granting benefits based on behavior. Bureaucrats gain the authority to write regulations from acts passed by Congress, either through the statute that initially set up their agency or through subsequent laws. Consider the EPA's Clean Power Plan, enacted in 2015, which imposes limits on the amount of carbon dioxide that can be emitted from electrical power plants. The EPA's authority to develop these regulations, as well as limits on other power plant emissions, comes from the Clean Air Act legislation of 1970 (for more details, see How It Works: Bureaucracy and Legislation).

Regulations are developed according to the **notice-and-comment procedure**.[2] Before a proposed regulation can take effect, it must be published in the *Federal Register*, an official journal that includes rules, proposed rules, and other types of government documents. Individuals and companies potentially affected by the regulation can then comment, or respond to the agency that proposed it, either supporting or opposing the regulation or offering different versions for consideration. They can also appeal to members of Congress or to the president's staff for help

regulation
A rule that allows the government to exercise control over individuals and corporations by restricting certain behaviors.

Although the term *bureaucracy* may suggest workers sitting behind desks in offices, the agencies of the federal bureaucracy perform a wide range of tasks. The U.S. Forest Service—a federal agency—helped fight the wildfires that swept through California in 2017.

notice-and-comment procedure
A step in the rule-making process in which proposed rules are published in the *Federal Register* and made available for debate by the general public.

Bureaucracy and Legislation

After Congress passes legislation and the president signs it, the transition from legislation to regulation begins. Input from local government officials, interest groups, and others helps to refine the regulations as they are developed, and has a strong influence on how regulations will affect people "on the ground."

Congress passes legislation.

The president signs the bill into law.

Bureaucrats interpret the law
and design appropriate regulations.

Courts respond to challenges to the law,
and they can provide guidelines for implementation.

Other bureaucrats disseminate regulations to state and local governments, corporations, and individuals, and they monitor compliance.

Citizens and interest groups provide information and proposals to bureaucrats, and they lobby for their preferred implementation of the legislation.

Regulations can be revised
in light of changing circumstances, different political climates, or unanticipated consequences.

Regulating Greenhouse Gas Emissions

In November 2017, the Trump administration announced a plan to repeal and replace the Environmental Protection Agency (EPA)'s Clean Power Plan regulations that limited CO_2 emissions from fossil fuel power plants. This action was only the latest step in a 20-year process of court cases, presidential directives, and actions by EPA bureaucrats.

New Acts!

Congressional Action: Congress enacts two Clean Air Acts, in 1963 and 1970 respectively, with amendments in 1977 and 1990, authorizing the government to monitor and limit emissions of harmful chemicals into the atmosphere.

Although... maybe not?

Bureaucratic Action (2003): The EPA announces that the **Clean Air Act does not give it the authority to regulate CO_2** and other greenhouse gases.

Actually...yes.

Judicial Action (2007): In response to a case brought by 12 states, the Supreme Court rules that **greenhouse gases are covered by the Clean Air Act.**

Obama weighs in.

Presidential Directive, June 2013: President Obama **directs the EPA to develop additional regulations** for limiting CO_2 emissions from new and existing power plants.

Results?

September 2013: The EPA modifies its draft regulations to place **CO_2 standards** on new power plants and issues a revised proposal.

June 2014: The EPA proposes an additional rule that aims to **cut CO_2 emissions from existing power plants.**

Feedback.

September 2013– March 2014: Supporters and opponents of the new rules submit over **6 million comments.**

Third try!

New Regulations Finalized (August 2015): The EPA **announces its Clean Power Plan,** which will regulate CO_2 emissions from both new and existing power plants.

Stand by.

February 2016: The Supreme Court puts implementation of the Clean Power Plan for existing plants on hold, pending litigation. Moreover, these regulations are subject to change by the Trump administration.

Up in the air?

November 2017: Under the Trump administration, **the EPA announces a plan to repeal and replace the Clean Power Plan.** However, the process is subject to additional comments and court challenges, and may not be completed before the 2018 election.

❓ Critical Thinking

1. **Critics of the regulatory process complain that unelected** bureaucrats make most of the decisions while elected officials sit on the sidelines. Is this complaint supported by the case of the Clean Power Plan?

2. **The Clean Power Plan illustrates how acts of legislation are often** reinterpreted years after their passage. Why don't members of Congress write legislation in ways that prevent this from happening?

in lobbying bureaucrats to revise the proposal. The agency then issues a final regulation that incorporates changes based on the comments. This final regulation is also published in the *Federal Register* and then put into effect. The process is time-consuming. The ongoing work of the Federal Aviation Administration (FAA) to develop regulations on the use of drone aircraft began with a congressional mandate issued in 2012. In 2015, the FAA issued a regulation requiring all but the smallest drones to be registered with the agency, but it is still developing rules to govern larger package-delivery drones that must fly over populated areas. Many regulations can take even longer to craft from beginning to end.

This process of devising or modifying regulations is often political. Members of Congress and the president usually have strong opinions about how new regulations should look—and even when they don't, they may still get involved on behalf of a constituent or an interest group. Bureaucrats take account of these pressures from elected officials for two reasons: (1) the bureaucrats' policy-making power may derive from a statute that members of Congress could overturn; and (2) bureaucrats need congressional support to get larger budgets and to expand their agency's mission. Thus, despite bureaucrats' power to develop and implement policies, their agencies' budgets, appointed leaders, and overall missions are subject to elected officials' oversight.

Many regulations are issued each year. In recent years, the *Federal Register* has run to more than 20,000 pages containing thousands of new regulations a year.[3] Although nearly all government agencies issue regulations, most come from a few agencies, including the Federal Trade Commission (FTC), which regulates commerce; the Federal Communications Commission (FCC), which regulates media companies that create content as well as telecommunications companies that transmit information; and the Food and Drug Administration (FDA), which regulates drugs, medical products, food, and cosmetics.

The nine most terrifying words in the English language are: I'm from the government, and I'm here to help.

—President Ronald Reagan

Federal regulations influence many aspects of everyday life that would seem unlikely to be affected by government actions. The increase in the number of women's intercollegiate athletic teams is partly due to regulations that require equal funding for men's and women's teams. Pictured here is Notre Dame University's 2018 NCAA women's basketball championship team.

Federal regulations affect most aspects of everyday life. They influence the gas mileage of cars sold in the United States, the materials used to build roads, and the price of gasoline. They determine the amounts that doctors can charge senior citizens for medical procedures; the hours that medical residents can work; the criteria used to determine who gets a heart, lung, or kidney transplant; and the allowable emissions from power plants. Regulations set the eligibility criteria for student loans, limit how the military can recruit on college campuses, determine who can get a home mortgage and what the interest rate will be, and describe what constitutes equal funding for men's and women's college sports teams. Regulations also shape contribution limits and spending decisions in political campaigns.

Regulations are often controversial because they involve trade-offs between incompatible goals, as well as decisions made under uncertain circumstances. For example, the regulations that guide the FDA drug-approval process prioritize the goal of preventing harmful drugs from coming to market.[4] As a result, patients sometimes cannot get access to experimental treatments because FDA approval has not been granted, even when those treatments are the patients' only remaining option.[5] Advocates for patients have argued that people with dire prognoses should be allowed to use these treatments as a potentially lifesaving last resort.[6] However, current FDA regulations prevent them from doing so except under very special circumstances; the agency argues that unapproved treatments may do more harm than good for these patients and warns that allowing wider access to these drugs may tempt manufacturers to market new drugs without adequate testing.

President Trump campaigned on a platform of reducing government regulations and has issued many directives to bureaucrats to reduce the number and scope of regulations. You may wonder if the number of regulations has, in fact, been reduced during the Trump administration. The short answer is no. Though federal agencies have issued fewer new regulations in the two years since Trump took office, much of this decline can be attributed to the delay or cancellation of proposed rules that Trump inherited from the Obama administration. Congress has also taken advantage of a law that allows the House and Senate to repeal regulations issued during the last months of a presidential term. However, Trump has had only limited success in eliminating regulations that were already in force when he entered office. The problem is that once regulations are in place, changing or repealing them is a lengthy process that often requires Congress to pass new laws. For example, while Trump and his appointees at the EPA have proposed repealing the Clean Power Plan, this process will take at least two years and could be delayed further or even stopped by court challenges. One possible argument is that since the EPA has the authority to regulate air pollution, it cannot simply repeal the regulations without replacing them with something else. Thus, while reducing the number of government regulations was one of the central promises of Trump's campaign, his administration has made very little progress toward this goal.

Bringing Expertise to Policy Making Bureaucrats are also an important source of new government policies. For example, Congress and the president give civilian and military personnel in the Department of Defense the job of revising military doctrines—broad directives on how our armed forces should go about accomplishing specific tasks such as fighting the ISIL terrorist organization in Syria, building civil society in Afghanistan, or running military training operations in Africa. While military doctrines reflect input from members of Congress, the State Department and the president's appointees, and groups outside government (including lobbyists, think tanks, and defense contractors), they also reflect the preferences of the bureaucrats assigned to the task. Thus, as in the case of regulations, when it comes to government policy, bureaucrats are not just implementers: they have a significant influence on what government does and does not do.

Delivering Services Some bureaucrats are the face of the federal government, interacting directly with citizens to provide services and other benefits. People working in the Department of Agriculture assist farmers by processing crop loans and providing advice on new technologies and techniques. Members of the Park Service operate the network of national parks and wilderness areas. And the Transportation Security Administration staffs the security checkpoints at American airports. These and other jobs are a reminder of how intertwined the federal government is with the lives of ordinary Americans. We may like to think of the federal government as something that exists only in Washington, D.C., but the reality is that bureaucrats are spread out across the country and are deeply involved with all elements of American society.

Bureaucratic expertise and its consequences

Bureaucrats are experts. Even compared with most members of Congress or presidential appointees, the average bureaucrat is a specialist in a certain policy area (often holding an advanced degree), with a good grasp of his or her agency's mission. For example, people who hold scientific or management positions in the FDA usually know more about the benefits and risks of new drugs than people outside the agency do. Their decision to deny unapproved drugs to seriously ill patients may seem cruel, but it may also reflect a thoughtful balancing of two incompatible goals: preventing harmful drugs from reaching the market and allowing people who have exhausted all other treatments access to risky, experimental products. A bureaucracy of experts is an important part of what political scientists call **state capacity**—the knowledge, personnel, and institutions needed to effectively implement policies.[7]

While having an expert bureaucracy seems like an obvious good idea, it creates a new problem for elected officials. Bureaucrats can bring expertise to their policy choices only if elected officials stop ordering bureaucrats around and instead allow them to act as they think best. But when elected officials allow such discretion, they risk losing control over the policy-making process and having to live with policy choices that serve bureaucratic interests without satisfying the elected officials or their constituents.

The Problem of Control: Principals and Agents Political scientists refer to the difficulty that elected officials and their staff face when they try to interpret or influence bureaucratic actions as the **problem of control**.[8] A classic example is the **principal–agent game**. The principal–agent game describes an interaction in which an individual or a group (an "agent") acts on behalf of another (the "principal"). In the federal government, the president and Congress are principals and bureaucrats are agents. An agent in the bureaucracy may not want to work (because they are lazy) or may prefer outcomes that the principal does not like. Moreover, because the agent is an expert at the task he or she has been given, he or she has additional knowledge and experience that is inaccessible to the principal. The conundrum for the principal, then, is this: giving the agent very specific orders prevents the agent from acting based on expertise, but if the principal gives the agent the freedom to make decisions based on expertise, the principal has less control over the agent's actions.

For example, suppose Congress and the president directed the FDA to shorten its drug-approval process. FDA officials might have mandated a lengthy process based on their expert assessment of the best way to screen out harmful drugs. By giving orders that superseded the FDA officials' screening process, elected officials would be sacrificing the valuable bureaucratic expertise behind the policy and risking the hasty approval of unsafe drugs. On the other hand, if Congress and the president allowed

DID YOU KNOW?

28%

of federal bureaucrats have an advanced degree (post-bachelor). The corresponding percentage for large private businesses is about 11 percent.
Source: Office of Management and Budget

state capacity
The knowledge, personnel, and institutions that the government requires to effectively implement policies.

problem of control
A difficulty faced by elected officials in ensuring that when bureaucrats implement policies they follow these officials' intentions but still have enough discretion to use their expertise.

principal–agent game
The interaction between a principal (such as the president or Congress), who needs something done, and an agent (such as a bureaucrat), who is responsible for carrying out the principal's orders.

FIGURE 13.1

How Americans View the Federal Bureaucracy

Many Americans believe the bureaucracy is wasteful and inefficient. Note, however, that the magnitude of negative feelings varies over time. Consider the time frame represented on the graph. What happened during these years that might explain the changes in citizens' opinions about the government?

Source: Pew Research Center, "Majority Continue to Say Government Is 'Almost Always Wasteful and Inefficient'," October 4, 2017, www.people-press.org (accessed 8/16/18).

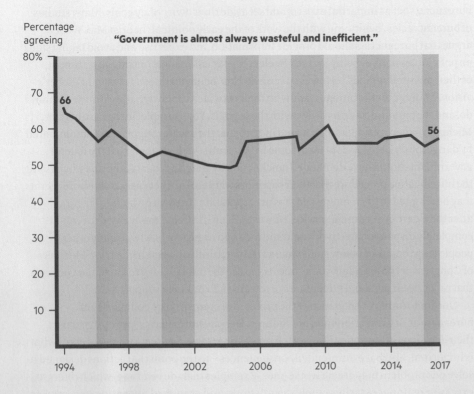

Percentage agreeing

"Government is almost always wasteful and inefficient."

66

56

1994   1998   2002   2006   2010   2014   2017

FDA bureaucrats to devise their own procedures and regulations, there would be a chance that the FDA could use this freedom to pursue goals that have nothing to do with drug safety. For example, critics of the FDA's procedures have asserted that a drawn-out approval process is designed to favor large companies that already have drugs on the market over smaller companies trying to get approval for drugs that would compete with existing products.

The principal-agent game can also be framed in terms of citizens. Figure 13.1 shows that a majority of survey respondents agreed that the federal government is typically inefficient and wasteful—although the percentage agreeing with this assessment declined from its peak in 1994 until more recent years, when it again increased. Such opinions give citizens a strong motivation to demand that elected officials control the bureaucracy—to reduce the waste and inefficiency or, as the earlier quote from Ronald Reagan suggests, to prevent bureaucrats from overly intruding into American society.

Members of Congress and citizens are sometimes right to question the motives of members of the bureaucracy. Sometimes bureaucratic actions are the result of **regulatory capture**, which occurs when bureaucrats cater to a small group of individuals or corporations, regardless of the impact of these actions on public welfare. For example, until very recently the FCC allowed telecommunications companies to charge very high rates for phone calls made by individuals in federal prisons to their families, friends, or legal counsel. The companies have long argued to the FCC that these rates were justified by the cost of special hardware needed to monitor prison calls—but no one was lobbying the FCC in favor of federal prisoners, who have no alternative but to pay what the companies charge.[9]

regulatory capture
A situation in which bureaucrats favor the interests of the groups or corporations they are supposed to regulate at the expense of the general public.

Scott Pruitt, the Environmental Protection Agency administrator, testified on the agency's 2019 budget during a hearing of the House Energy and Commerce subcommittee after concerns about his conduct and spending, which included first-class flights and the installation of a $43,000 soundproof phone booth in his office. Pruitt ultimately resigned in 2018 amid growing concerns about his ethics.

red tape
Excessive or unnecessarily complex regulations imposed by the bureaucracy.

standard operating procedures (SOPs)
Rules that lower-level bureaucrats must follow when implementing policies.

You might think that the problem of control isn't too difficult to solve as long as bureaucrats act as impartial experts and set aside their own policy goals. Many studies of bureaucracies, beginning with the work of the early political theorist Max Weber, argue that bureaucrats should provide information and expertise and avoid taking sides on policy questions or being swayed by elected officials, people outside government, or their own policy goals.[10] However, bureaucrats' behavior doesn't always fit Weber's vision. Many enter the bureaucracy with their own ideas about what government should do, and they make decisions in line with those goals. For example, in the case of Flint, Michigan, where residents discovered in 2016 that their water supply was contaminated by dangerously high levels of lead, some EPA scientists felt strongly that the federal government should have demanded quick action by state and local authorities, bypassing the investigative procedure that their superiors wanted. In other cases, some bureaucrats may be tempted to favor interest groups or corporations to secure a better-paying job after they leave government service. However, even if bureaucrats wanted to remain completely dispassionate, they would still face a government in which many other people with their own policy goals would attempt to influence their behavior. Members of Congress or the president sometimes try to use the bureaucracy to implement policies that reflect their personal preferences or reward their political supporters.[11]

One important consequence of the problem of control is the complexity of bureaucratic organizations and procedures. Despite bureaucrats' policy expertise, their decisions often appear to take too much time, rely on arbitrary judgments of what is important, and have unintended consequences—to the point that actions designed to solve one problem may create worse ones. Examples include **red tape**, which refers to excessive or unnecessarily complex regulations, and **standard operating procedures (SOPs)**, which are the rules that lower-level bureaucrats must follow, regardless of whether they actually apply, when implementing policies.

In part, red tape and SOPs are inevitable given the complexity of the tasks bureaucrats are given to do. For example, the U.S. Tax Code takes up thousands of pages—but in a country as large as the United States, where people have many different sources of income and there are many distinct kinds of corporate activity, a tax code that treats people and companies fairly while raising enough revenue to run the government is inevitably going to be complicated.

However, sometimes red tape and SOPs are the result of elected officials' attempts to mitigate the problem of control. For example, some of the complexity of the American tax code is due to Congressional mandates that create tax breaks for favored corporations and individuals. In the abstract, elected officials might prefer that the tax code be determined by expert bureaucrats. In reality, however, members of Congress want to make sure their state or district is treated fairly—as well as provide tax breaks in order to increase their chances of getting reelected—and are willing to sacrifice expertise in favor of these other benefits, even if it makes the tax code more complex.

In other ways, such as the notice-and-comment procedure described earlier, elected officials require bureaucrats to inform them in advance about proposed policy decisions before they are implemented. Other congressional mandates define who can work in different jobs at an agency, where agency offices are located, and many other specifics of agency structure and process. Very few of these mandates contribute to bureaucratic nimbleness, but that is not their intent. What they are designed to do is give elected officials ways to mitigate the problems of control.

The problem of control has existed throughout the history of the federal government. It affects both the kinds of policies that bureaucrats implement and the structure of the federal bureaucracy, including the number of agencies and their missions, staff, and tasks. Moreover, elected officials use a variety of methods to solve

Despite their policy expertise, bureaucrats still make mistakes. When the Medicare program implemented the Prescription Drug Benefit in 2006, information about the coverage was available on an easy-to-read website, but the agency soon learned that many seniors who needed the information did not own a computer or even know how to use a Web browser.

the problem of control, including making it easier for people outside government to learn about agency actions before they take effect. However, all these tactics are, at best, partial solutions to the problem of control. The trade-off between expertise and control remains.

Bureaucrats aren't mindless paper pushers. Rather, they are experts who have considerable power to shape what government does. The way many elected officials talk, it's easy to think that once they pass a piece of legislation or issue an executive order, government policy automatically changes. In most cases, however, these directives are only the first step. To bring these changes to life, bureaucrats must step in to translate often-vague goals into concrete regulations, budgets, and actions. In other words, while you might not think much about bureaucrats, they can have a profound effect on your daily life.

"Why Should I Care?"

How has the American bureaucracy grown?

TRACE THE EXPANSION OF THE FEDERAL BUREAUCRACY OVER TIME

The evolution of America's federal bureaucracy was not steady or smooth. Most of its important developments occurred during three short periods: the late 1890s and early 1900s, the 1930s, and the 1960s.[12] In all three, the driving force was a combination of citizens' demands for enhanced government services and government officials' desires to either respond to these demands or increase the size and scope of the federal government to be more in line with their own policy goals.

The beginning of America's bureaucracy

From the Founding of the United States until the election of Andrew Jackson in 1828, the staff of the entire federal bureaucracy numbered at most in the low thousands. The small size of the federal government during these years reflected Americans' deep suspicion of government, especially unelected officials. In the Declaration of Independence, in fact, one of the charges against George III was that he had "erected a multitude of new offices and sent hither swarms of officers to harass our people and eat out their substance."[13]

In these early years, there were only three executive departments (State, Treasury, and War), along with a postmaster general,[14] and executive branch offices were formed only when absolutely necessary. This small bureaucracy performed a very narrow range of tasks. It collected taxes on imports and exports and delivered the mail. The national army consisted of a small Corps of Engineers and a few frontier patrols. The attorney general was a private attorney who had the federal government as one of his clients. Members of Congress outnumbered civil servants in Washington, and the president had very little staff at all.[15]

Despite its small size, conflicts soon arose around control of the bureaucracy. The legislation that established the departments of State, Treasury, and War allowed the president to nominate the people in charge of these departments but made these appointments subject to Senate approval. The same is true today for the heads of all executive departments and many other presidential appointments.

The election of Andrew Jackson in 1828 brought the first large-scale use of the spoils system: people who had worked for Jackson's campaign were rewarded with new positions in the federal government (usually as local postmasters).[16] The spoils system was extremely useful to party organizations, as it gave them a powerful incentive with which to convince people to work for the party, and it was a particularly important tool for Jackson. His campaign organization was at that time the largest ever organized.

The challenge facing the spoils system was ensuring that these government employees, who often lacked experience in their new fields, could actually carry out their jobs. The solution was to develop procedures for these employees that guided them on exactly what to do even if they had little or no experience or training.[17] These instructions became one of the earliest uses of standard operating procedures. They ensured that the government could function even if large numbers of employees had been hired in reward for political work rather than because of their qualifications.[18]

As America expanded in size, so did the federal government, which saw an almost eightfold increase in the bureaucracy between 1816 and the beginning of the Civil War in 1861. This growth did not reflect fundamental changes in what the government did; in fact, much of the increase came in areas such as the Post Office, which needed to serve a geographically larger nation—and, of course, to provide "spoils" for party workers in the form of government jobs.[19] Even by the end of the Civil War, the federal government still had very little involvement in the lives of ordinary Americans. State and local governments provided services such as education, public works, and welfare benefits, if they were provided at all. The federal government's role in daily life was limited to mail delivery, the collection of import and export taxes, and work in a few other sectors.

This cartoon of a monument depicting President Andrew Jackson riding a pig decries his involvement in the spoils system, which allowed politicians to dole out government service jobs in return for political support.

Building a new American state: the Progressive Era

Political developments in the second half of the nineteenth century transformed America's bureaucracy.[20] While the transformation began after the Civil War, the most significant changes occurred during the Progressive Era, from 1890 to 1920. Many laws and executive actions increased the government's regulatory power during this period, including the Sherman Antitrust Act of 1890, the Pure Food and Drug Act of 1906, the Federal Meat Inspection Act of 1906, expansion of the Interstate Commerce Commission, and various conservation measures.[21] Now the federal government was no longer simply a deliverer of mail and a defender of borders; rather, it had an indirect impact on several aspects of everyday life. When Americans bought food or other products, went to work, or traveled on vacation, the choices available to them were shaped by the actions of federal bureaucrats in Washington and elsewhere.

These developments were matched by a fundamental change in the federal bureaucracy following passage of the 1883 Pendleton Civil Service Act. This measure created the **federal civil service**, in which the merit system (qualifications, not political connections) would be the basis for hiring and promoting bureaucrats. In other words, when new presidents took office they could not replace government workers with their own campaign workers. Initially, only about 13,000 federal jobs acquired civil service protections, but over the next two decades many additional positions were incorporated into the civil service. In some cases, presidents gave civil service protections to people who had been hired under the spoils system to prevent the next president from replacing these bureaucrats with his or her own loyalists. Over time, these reforms created a bureaucracy in which people were hired for their expertise and allowed to build a career in government without having to fear being fired when a new president or Congress took office.[22] In the modern era, virtually all full-time, permanent government employees have civil service protection.

federal civil service
A system created by the 1883 Pendleton Civil Service Act in which bureaucrats are hired on the basis of merit rather than political connections.

The New Deal, the Great Society, and the Reagan Revolution

Dramatic expansion of the federal bureaucracy occurred during the New Deal period in the 1930s and during the mid-1960s Great Society era. In both cases, the changes were driven by a combination of citizen demands and the preferences of elected officials who favored an increased role of government in society. These expansion trends were only marginally curtailed during the Reagan Revolution of the 1980s.

The New Deal "The New Deal" refers to the government programs implemented during Franklin Roosevelt's first term as president in the 1930s. At one level, these programs were a response to the Great Depression and the inability of local governments and private charities to provide adequate support to Americans during this economic crisis. Many advocates of the New Deal also favored an expanded role for government in American society, regardless of the immediate need for intervention.[23] Roosevelt's programs included reforms to the financial industry as well as efforts to help people directly, including the stimulation of employment and economic growth and the formation of labor unions. The Social Security Act, the first federally funded pension program for all Americans, was also passed as part of the New Deal.[24]

These reforms resulted in a vast increase in the size, responsibilities, and capacity of the bureaucracy, as well as a large transfer of power to bureaucrats and to the president.[25] While the Progressive Era reforms created an independent bureaucracy and increased its state capacity, the New Deal reforms broadened the range of policy

Franklin Roosevelt's New Deal programs greatly expanded the power of the federal government and the bureaucracy. As this cartoon shows, these changes were controversial, with some seeing them as moving too much power from Congress to the president and bureaucracy.

Under President George W. Bush, the federal bureaucracy continued to expand. Programs like No Child Left Behind increased the role of government in society.

areas in which this capacity could be applied. Before the New Deal, the federal government influenced citizens' choices through activities such as regulating industries and workplace conditions. After the New Deal, the federal government took on the role of directly delivering a wide range of benefits and services to its citizens—ranging from jobs to electricity. It also increased regulations on many industries, including those in the banking and financial sectors.

The expansion of the federal government and the subsequent delegation of power to bureaucrats and to the president were controversial changes, both when they were enacted and as they were implemented in subsequent years.[26] Many Republicans opposed New Deal reforms because they believed that the federal government could not deliver services efficiently and that an expanded federal bureaucracy would create a modern spoils system. Many southerners worried that the federal government's increased involvement in everyday life would endanger the system of racial segregation in southern states.[27] Even so, Democratic supporters of the New Deal, aided by public support, carried the day.

The Great Society The Great Society was a series of federal programs enacted during Lyndon Johnson's presidency (1963–1969) that further expanded the size, capacity, and activities of the bureaucracy. During these years, Johnson proposed and Congress passed programs that funded bilingual education, loans and grants for college students, special education, preschools, construction of elementary and secondary schools, mass-transit programs in many cities, health care for seniors and poor people, job training and urban renewal, enhanced voting rights and civil rights for minorities, environmental protection, funding for the arts and cultural activities, and space exploration.[28]

The Great Society programs had mixed success. Voting rights and civil rights reforms ended the "separate but equal" system of social order in southern states and dramatically increased political participation by African Americans.[29] But many of the antipoverty programs were dismal failures. During the 1960s and 1970s, poverty rates among most groups remained relatively constant, and other indicators, such as the rate of teen pregnancy, actually increased.[30] In retrospect, the people who designed and implemented these programs did not realize the complexities of the problems they were trying to address.[31] For example, many antipoverty programs were built on the assumption that most people receiving welfare needed job training programs in order to transition from welfare to permanent, paid employment. However, additional data that became available a decade after these laws were passed showed that most people receiving welfare do so for short periods because of medical or family crises—problems that the Great Society programs did not address.[32] Despite these shortcomings, the expansion of the federal government during the New Deal and Great Society has remained in place well into the twenty-first century.

The Reagan Revolution and Afterward The election of Ronald Reagan to the presidency in 1980, along with a Republican takeover of the Senate and Republican gains in the House of Representatives, created an opportunity for conservatives to roll back the size and scope of the federal government. These efforts were largely unsuccessful. In the years since Reagan, members of Congress and presidents from both parties have fought for large expansions in government policy. For example, while Democrat Barack Obama's administration issued many new environmental regulations and profoundly changed the American health care system, these changes are not too different in magnitude from the reforms championed by Republican

George W. Bush, including education policies that increased federal control over local school districts, new drug financing benefits for seniors, and changes to financial regulations that increased financial reporting requirements for corporations. After two years in office, the Trump administration has had little success in cutting overall federal spending or in reducing the size of specific agencies. For example, the administration initially proposed a one-third cut in the budget of the State Department for fiscal year 2018, only to ultimately accept a congressional budget that kept spending levels constant.

DESCRIBE THE SIZE AND STRUCTURE OF THE EXECUTIVE BRANCH TODAY

The modern federal bureaucracy

The size and scope of the modern federal bureaucracy reflect the expansion of the federal government over the last half century and its increased role in the lives of everyday Americans. The structure of the bureaucracy also reflects ongoing attempts by presidents, members of Congress, and others to control bureaucratic actions in line with their policy goals.

The structure of the federal government

Nuts & Bolts 13.1 shows the structure of the executive branch of the federal government. As discussed in Chapter 12, the Executive Office of the President (EOP) contains organizations that support the president and implement presidential policy initiatives. Individuals working in these organizations aim to ensure that bureaucrats (agents) act appropriately to implement the president's (principal's) policy priorities and preferences.[33] Among its many offices, the EOP contains the **Office of Management and Budget**, which prepares the president's annual budget proposal to Congress and monitors government spending and the development of new regulations. Below the EOP are the 15 executive departments, from the Department of Agriculture to the Department of Veterans Affairs, which constitute the major divisions within the executive branch. The heads of these 15 organizations make up the president's Cabinet.

Office of Management and Budget
An office within the EOP that is responsible for creating the president's annual budget proposal to Congress, reviewing proposed rules, and performing other budget-related tasks.

The Executive Branch of the Federal Government

The executive branch includes the 15 cabinet offices, as well as several independent agencies, commissions, and government corporations.

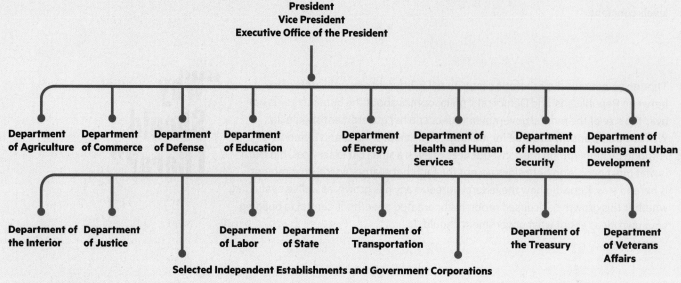

President
Vice President
Executive Office of the President

| Department of Agriculture | Department of Commerce | Department of Defense | Department of Education | Department of Energy | Department of Health and Human Services | Department of Homeland Security | Department of Housing and Urban Development |

| Department of the Interior | Department of Justice | Department of Labor | Department of State | Department of Transportation | Department of the Treasury | Department of Veterans Affairs |

Selected Independent Establishments and Government Corporations

Central Intelligence Agency
Consumer Product Safety Commission
Environmental Protection Agency
Equal Employment Opportunity Commission
Federal Communications Commission
Federal Deposit Insurance Corporation
Federal Election Commission
Federal Reserve System

Federal Trade Commission
General Services Administration
National Aeronautics and Space Administration
National Foundation on the Arts and the Humanities
National Labor Relations Board
National Railroad Passenger Corporation (Amtrak)
National Science Foundation
Occupational Safety and Health Review Commission

Peace Corps
Securities and Exchange Commission
Selective Service System
Small Business Administration
Social Security Administration
U.S. Agency for International Development
U.S. Postal Service

Source: Based on *GPO Access: Guide to the U.S. Government,* http://bensguide.gpo.gov/files/gov_chart.pdf (accessed 9/22/12).

independent agencies
Government offices or organizations that provide government services and are not part of an executive department.

Each executive department contains many smaller, sometimes diverse organizations. Nuts & Bolts 13.2 shows the organizational chart for the Department of Agriculture, for example. As you can see, the Department of Agriculture includes offices that help farmers produce and sell their crops and offices that ensure food safety, but it also houses the Forest Service and offices that manage issues related to housing and utilities in rural areas. The Department of Agriculture also administers the food stamps program, even though the program has no direct connection to farming or food safety.

In addition to executive departments, the government contains a group of agencies, commissions, and government corporations that are called **independent agencies** to highlight that they are not part of an executive department. Most of these agencies carry out specialized functions, such as regulating a particular activity (these are called independent regulatory agencies) or carrying out policy in a narrow area. The Federal Reserve System, for example, manages the money supply, banking system, and interest rates, while the National Aeronautics and Space Administration (NASA) directs aviation research and space exploration. Nuts & Bolts 13.1 includes only some noteworthy or well-known agencies; there are many more.

The Structure of the Department of Agriculture

The Department of Agriculture is headed by the secretary of agriculture and the deputy secretary of agriculture and includes various assistant secretaries and undersecretaries for specific areas, such as natural resources and the environment, farm services, rural development, and food safety.

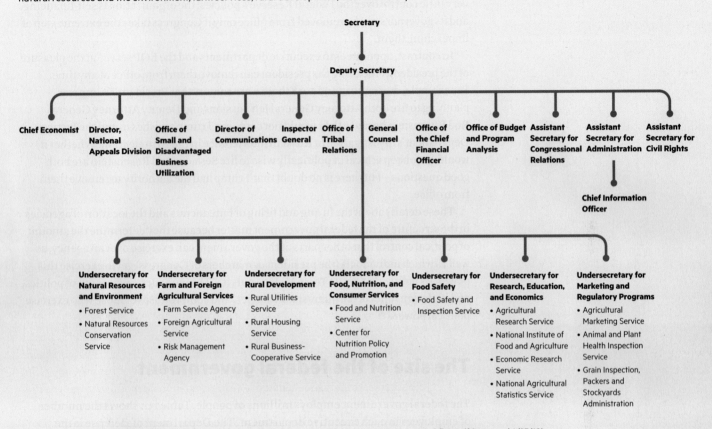

Source: U.S. Department of Agriculture, "USDA Organization Chart," www.usda.gov/documents/AgencyWorkflow.pdf (accessed 4/23/10).

There are two important lessons to draw from these charts. First, the federal government handles an enormous range of functions. Second, the division of activities among executive departments and independent agencies does not always have an obvious logic. Why, for example, does the Department of Agriculture administer rural utilities programs and food stamps? Similarly, it is not always clear why certain tasks are handled by an independent agency whereas others fall within the scope of an executive department.[34] Why is the Food and Drug Administration (FDA) an independent agency rather than part of the Department of Commerce—and why is the Federal Aviation Administration (FAA) located within the Department of Transportation rather than being independent?

Organizational decisions like these often reflect elected officials' attempts to shape agency behavior—and the extent to which political process matters. Part of the difference between independent agencies and the organizations contained within executive departments has to do with the president's ability to control these organizations' activities. Organizations that fall within an executive department, such as the FAA or the Federal Highway Administration (FHA) (both within the Department of Transportation), can be controlled by the president (to some extent) through his or her appointees.[35] In contrast, independent agencies are often designed to have more freedom from oversight and control by the president and Congress. For example, governors of the Federal Reserve, though nominated by the president and confirmed by the Senate, serve for 14 years—outlasting the administration that nominated them. Outside the nomination and confirmation process, the president and Congress have very little control over the Federal Reserve's policies; the organization is self-financing, and its governors can be removed from office only if Congress takes the extreme step of impeaching them.

In contrast, appointees to executive departments and the EOP serve "at the pleasure of the president," meaning the president can remove them from office at any time. For example, during 2017 and 2018 there were rumors that President Trump was planning to fire both Attorney General Jeff Sessions and Deputy Attorney General Rod Rosenstein because they would not carry out Trump's wishes to end the Justice Department's investigation of Russian interference in the 2016 election. Whether it would have been ethical or politically wise to fire Sessions and Rosenstein are both good questions—but there is no doubt that Trump had the authority to remove them from office.

These details about the hiring and firing of bureaucrats and the location of agencies in the structure of the federal government matter because they determine the amount of political control that other parts of the government can exercise over an agency, as well as which individuals (the president or members of Congress) get to exercise this power. As political scientist Terry M. Moe puts it, "The bureaucracy rises out of politics, and its design reflects the interests, strategies, and compromises of those who exercise political power."[36]

The size of the federal government

The federal government employs millions of people. Table 13.1 shows the number of employees in each executive department. The Department of Defense is the largest cabinet department, with more than 700,000 civilian personnel. The Department of Education is the smallest, with only 4,100 employees. Many departments are on the small side: four cabinet departments have fewer than 20,000 employees. The same is true for many independent agencies and organizations within the EOP. The General Services Administration (GSA), for example, has only about 12,000 employees. Millions of additional people work for the government as members of the armed forces, as employees of the Postal Service, as employees of civilian companies that contract with the government, or as recipients of federal grant money.

The What Do the Facts Say? feature in this chapter shows the number of civilian federal employees from 1961 to 2017. Clearly, the federal workforce has steadily increased over time, although it has declined from its peak in the 1990s and remained steady in recent years. Some observers argue that growth in employment was driven by the fact that bureaucrats are **budget maximizers** who never pass up a chance to increase the size of their organization regardless of whether the increase is worthwhile.[37] Of course, the fact that federal employment has remained steady in recent years suggests that something besides budget maximization is at work. The best explanation for overall size of the federal government is the size of America itself—more than 330 million people spread out over an area more than twice the size of the European Union—combined with America's position as the most powerful nation

budget maximizers
Bureaucrats who seek to increase funding for their agency whether or not that additional spending is worthwhile.

Is the Federal Bureaucracy Too Big?

One of the most intense conflicts in American political life is over the size of the federal government. Generally, Republicans say that the size of federal bureaucracy should be reduced, while Democrats tend to favor increasing the size of government programs, including adding more employees if needed. Has the size of government increased over time?

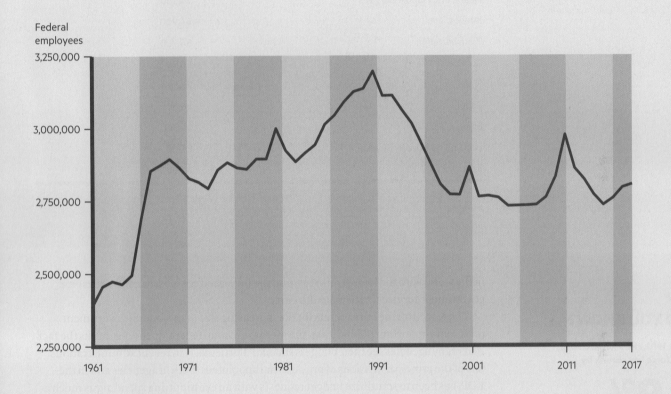

Think about it

- **During the 2016 presidential campaign, candidate Donald Trump claimed that the size of the bureaucracy had significantly increased under President Obama. Does the data support this assertion?**
- **Since 1960, the size of the federal bureaucracy increased significantly during the 1960s and 1970s, then declined after about 1990. What political or historical events explain these changes?**

Source: Based on Federal Reserve Bank, St. Louis, "All Employees: Government: Federal," https://fred.stlouisfed.org/series/CES9091000001#0 (accessed 5/6/18).

TABLE 13.1

Employment in Cabinet Departments

Source: "Budget of the United States Government Fiscal Year 2019," www.whitehouse.gov/wp-content/uploads/2018/02/spec-fy2019.pdf (accessed 5/17/18).

Organization	Total Employees
Defense (civilian only)	726,000
Veterans Affairs	345,100
Homeland Security	182,400
Justice	118,200
Treasury	92,400
Agriculture	87,300
Health and Human Services	74,100
Interior	64,900
Transportation	54,700
Commerce	40,900
State	27,600
Labor	16,500
Energy	14,700
Housing and Urban Development	8,000
Education	4,100

DID YOU KNOW?

Since 1992, the federal civilian workforce has shrunk by

18%

Source: Office of Management and Budget

in the world with the largest military, and the increased costs associated with some government services, such as health care.

Those who blame bureaucrats for the increasing size of the federal government miss some important points. First, the increase in total federal spending masks the fact that many agencies see their budgets shrink.[38] Particularly in recent administrations, one of the principal missions of presidential appointees, both in agencies and in the EOP, has been to scrutinize budget requests with an eye to cutting spending as much as possible.[39] And in most years, some government agencies are eliminated (in fact, most of the executive department head counts in Table 13.1 have grown smaller in recent editions of this text).[40]

Public-opinion data also provide an explanation for the overall growth in government: the American public's demand for services.[41] Despite complaints about the federal bureaucracy, polls find little evidence of demands for less government. When the Pew Research Center asked people in 2017 to name two programs that should have their spending cut as a way of reducing the budget deficit, the only program that was named by more than a quarter of respondents was foreign aid (see Table 13.2). Far fewer people favored cuts in the programs that account for the overwhelming majority of federal spending: defense, health care spending, and Social Security. In other words, while in the abstract Americans might want a smaller government that is less involved in everyday life, they do not support the large-scale budget cuts that would be necessary to achieve this goal. The public's desire for more government services is often encouraged by elected officials, who create new government programs (and expand existing ones in response to constituent demands) as a way of building support and improving their chances of reelection.

**TABLE
13.2**

Public Opinion on Spending Cuts

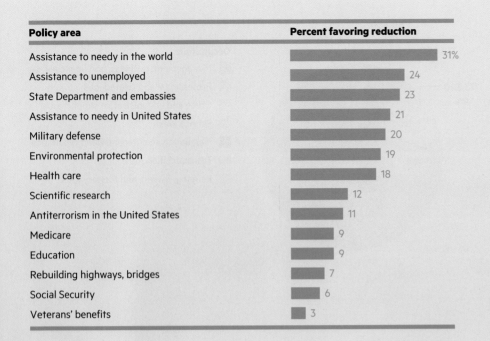

Policy area	Percent favoring reduction
Assistance to needy in the world	31%
Assistance to unemployed	24
State Department and embassies	23
Assistance to needy in United States	21
Military defense	20
Environmental protection	19
Health care	18
Scientific research	12
Antiterrorism in the United States	11
Medicare	9
Education	9
Rebuilding highways, bridges	7
Social Security	6
Veterans' benefits	3

Many Americans complain about the size of the federal government. However, their complaints do not translate into support for reductions in policy areas or cuts in specific programs that could significantly reduce spending. Based on these data, are there any kinds of proposals for significantly reducing the size of the federal government that might attract widespread support?

Source: Pew Research Center, "With Budget Debate Looming, Growing Share of Public Prefers Bigger Government," April 17, 2017, www.people-press.org (accessed 5/17/18).

You might think that the government spends too much and that the bureaucracy is too large. The questions you have to ask yourself are: What am I willing to sacrifice to make government smaller? Am I OK with a smaller military, fewer regulations on banks and credit card companies, less oversight of food and drug safety? And how much money would these changes actually save? We have a large, costly federal government because, in the end, most people want it that way.

"Why Should I Care?"

The human face of the bureaucracy

DESCRIBE WHO BUREAUCRATS ARE AND THE REGULATIONS THAT GOVERN THEIR EMPLOYMENT

The term "bureaucrat" applies to a wide range of people with different qualifications and job descriptions. The federal government includes so many different kinds of jobs because of the vast array of services it provides (see Figure 13.2). This section describes who these people are and the terms of their government employment.

Although citizens and politicians often complain about the efficiency or motivations of federal bureaucrats, surveys show that many employees in these positions have a strong interest in public service or the implementation of good public policy. In fact, these motivations are often strong enough that scholars

FIGURE 13.2

Types of Federal Workers

Source: Bureau of Labor Statistics, "Occupational Employment Statistics," www.bls.gov/oes/current/naics4_999100.htm#00-0000 (accessed 5/18/18).

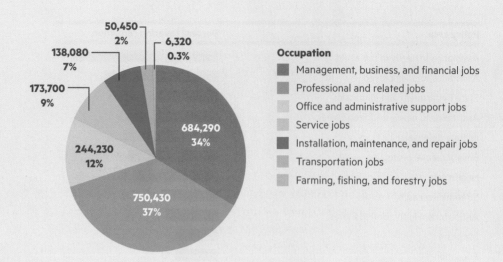

50,450 2%

6,320 0.3%

138,080 7%

173,700 9%

244,230 12%

684,290 34%

750,430 37%

Occupation
- Management, business, and financial jobs
- Professional and related jobs
- Office and administrative support jobs
- Service jobs
- Installation, maintenance, and repair jobs
- Transportation jobs
- Farming, fishing, and forestry jobs

such as James L. Perry have argued against attempts to motivate federal workers with monetary incentives—bureaucrats who work hard because they feel it is the right thing to do may resent incentive schemes that presume they are lazy or only interested in money.[42]

Civil service regulations

Most jobs in the federal bureaucracy are subject to the civil service regulations that we described earlier.[43] The current civil service system sets out job descriptions and pay ranges for all federal jobs. The system also establishes tests that determine who is hired for low-level clerical and secretarial positions. People with less than a college degree are generally eligible for entry-level jobs, and, as in the private sector, a college degree or an advanced degree and work experience qualify an individual for higher-level positions. Federal salaries are supposed to be comparable to what people earn in similar, private-sector positions, and salaries are somewhat higher for federal employees who work in areas with a high cost of living.

Civil service regulations provide job security. After three years of satisfactory performance, employees cannot be fired except "for cause," meaning that the firing agency must cite a reason. Civil service regulations set out a multistep procedure for firing someone, beginning with low performance evaluations, then warning letters given to the employee, followed by a lengthy appeals process before a firing takes place. One study found that only about 11,000 civil servants are fired in a given year—a very small percentage of the total civilian federal workforce of more than 2.5 million people.[44] A subpar performer may be assigned other duties, transferred to another office, or even given nothing to do in the hope that the person will leave voluntarily out of boredom.

If you think civil service regulations sound cumbersome, you're right.[45] The hiring criteria remove a manager's discretion to hire someone who would do an excellent job but lacks the education or work experience that the regulations specify as necessary for the position. The firing requirements make it extremely difficult to remove poor performers. The salary and promotion restrictions create problems with rewarding excellent performance or promoting the best employees rather than those with the most seniority.

Why do these requirements exist? Recall that the aim of civil service regulations was to separate politics from policy. The mechanism for achieving this goal was a set of rules and requirements that made it hard for elected officials to control the hiring and firing of government employees to further their own political goals. In effect, even though civil service regulations have obvious drawbacks, they also provide this less apparent but very important benefit. For example, without civil service protections, members of Congress might pressure employees in the Office of Personnel Management to increase pensions for retiring federal workers in the representatives' constituencies.

Although loyalty to the president is a widely accepted criterion for hiring agency heads and other presidential appointees, professionals with permanent civil service positions are supposed to be hired on the basis of their qualifications, not their political beliefs. In fact, it is illegal to bring politics into these hiring decisions. However, there is no doubt that all presidential administrations worry about the political loyalties of midlevel bureaucrats because of the problem of control, as we discussed earlier.

Limits on political activity

Legislation places limits on the political activities that federal employees can undertake. The Hatch Act, enacted in 1939 and amended in 1940, prohibited federal employees from engaging in organized political activities.[46] Under the act, employees could vote and contribute to candidates but could not work for candidates or for political parties. These restrictions were modified in the 1993 Federal Employees Political Activities Act, which allows federal employees to participate in a wider range of political activities, including fund-raising and serving as an officer of a political party. Senior members of the president's White House staff and political appointees are exempt from most of these restrictions, although they cannot use government resources for political activities.

While the Hatch Act is often invoked when government employees express controversial views, it technically restricts only activities that directly help a particular political candidate, such as a public endorsement at a mass rally. For example, during a television interview in late 2017, Kellyanne Conway, a senior adviser to President Trump, endorsed the Republican Senate candidate in an Alabama special election. The Office of the Special Counsel, a Justice Department agency that enforces the Hatch Act, later found that Conway's endorsement violated the Hatch Act. However, Conway was not penalized. The Hatch Act makes life especially difficult for presidential appointees whose job duties, such as helping the president they work for get reelected, often mix government service with politics. In order to comply with Hatch Act restrictions, these officials need to carry separate cell phones to make calls related to their political activities and maintain separate e-mail accounts—usually provided by the party or campaign committee—for their political communications.

Political appointees and the Senior Executive Service

Not every federal employee is a member of the civil service. Over 7,000 senior positions in the executive branch—such as the leaders of executive departments and independent agencies like NASA, as well as members of the EOP—are not subject to civil service regulations. The president appoints individuals to these positions, and, in

Federal employees must be careful that their comments to the media comply with Hatch Act restrictions. Kellyanne Conway, counselor to President Trump, violated the Hatch Act when she advocated for and against candidates in the Alabama Senate special election on CNN and Fox News programs.

some cases, the Senate must confirm them. The majority of a president's appointees act as the president's eyes, ears, and hands throughout the executive branch. They hold positions of power within government agencies, serving as secretaries of executive departments, agency heads, or senior deputies. Their jobs involve finding out what the president wants from their agency and ordering, persuading, or cajoling their subordinates to implement presidential directives.

Some appointees get their jobs as a reward for working on the president's campaign staff, contributing substantial funds to the campaign, or raising money from other donors. These individuals are not always given positions with real decision-making power. Some government agencies have the reputation of being **turkey farms**, places where campaign stalwarts can be appointed without the risk that their lack of experience will lead to bad policy.[47] In many agencies, people in the top positions are members of the Senior Executive Service (SES), who are also exempt from civil service restrictions.[48] As of 2018, there were a few thousand SES members, most of whom were career government employees who held relatively high-level agency positions before moving to the SES. This change of employment status costs them their civil service protections but allows them to apply for senior leadership positions in the bureaucracy. Some political appointees are also given SES positions, although most do not have the experience or expertise held by career bureaucrats who typically move to the SES.

President Trump's use of political appointments raises a puzzle. At one level, his campaign promises to undertake large-scale changes in government policy suggested that Trump would make appointments as rapidly as possible, so that he would have people in each agency who were loyal to him and would implement his reform efforts. However, the pace of Trump's appointments was slow compared to that of previous presidents, and even after a year in office many senior-level positions in the bureaucracy were vacant.[49] In part, appointments were slowed by Senate Democrats who opposed Trump's nominees. In addition, however, some potential appointees did not want to work in a Trump-led administration. Others were dropped from consideration because they had opposed Trump during the 2016 campaign. Whatever the reason, the slow pace of appointments complicated Trump's reform efforts.

Perhaps because of the difficulties in appointing senior-level officials in the early months of the Trump presidency, junior individuals who had worked for Trump during the campaign were dispatched to various executive departments and independent agencies.[50] These individuals were chosen for their loyalty to Trump rather than their knowledge of the agency they were assigned to. Most of them held advisory positions, so they were not involved with day-to-day agency operations. Their job was to monitor agency operations and to report how agency staff were responding to Trump's directives. However, because these individuals knew little about their agencies, and because they had no authority to issue policy directives on their own, they were relatively ineffective in implementing the Trump agenda.

turkey farms
Agencies to which campaign workers and donors can be appointed in reward for their service because it is unlikely that their lack of qualifications will lead to bad policy.

"Why Should I Care?"

The problem of control shapes the kinds of people who are hired as bureaucrats as well as their job protections. Political appointees and members of the SES are supposed to ride herd on the rest of the bureaucracy. Civil service protections exist to ensure that bureaucrats' decisions reflect expertise rather than political considerations.

Controlling the bureaucracy

As the expert implementers of legislation and presidential directives, bureaucrats hold significant power to influence government policy. This situation creates the problem of control illustrated by the principal–agent game, as we discussed earlier: elected officials must figure out how to reap the benefits of bureaucratic expertise without simply giving bureaucrats free rein to do whatever they want.

One strategy is to take away discretion entirely and give bureaucrats simple, direct orders. For example, from 1996 to 2015 a law passed by Congress forbade the U.S. Centers for Disease Control (CDC) from conducting research that would "advocate or promote gun control"—which was interpreted by the CDC as limiting all gun-related research by agency scientists or by outside researchers who received agency funds.[51] (The ban was repealed after a series of mass shootings in 2013, although to this day the CDC conducts very little gun-related research.) Similarly, the Trump administration banned the use of the words "climate change" and "global warming" from the Environmental Protection Agency's websites and documents and abolished scientific advisory panels dealing with this topic.[52]

The problem with eliminating bureaucrats' discretion in this way is that it limits the positive influence of their expertise. Particularly when new policies are being developed, taking away bureaucratic discretion is costly for legislators or presidential appointees, as it forces them to work out the policy details themselves—and may produce less effective policies than those constructed by bureaucrats with specialized knowledge.[53] Moreover, preventing bureaucrats from using their judgment makes it impossible for them to craft policies that take into account new developments or unforeseen circumstances.[54]

For all these reasons, elected officials must find other ways to reduce or eliminate **bureaucratic drift**—that is, bureaucrats' pursuit of their own goals rather than their assignments from officeholders or appointees—while still reaping the benefits of bureaucratic expertise. This section describes two common strategies: changing the way agencies are organized and staffed and using standardized procedures for monitoring agency actions. In both cases, the aim is to set up agencies so that bureaucrats can use their expertise, while making sure their actions are consistent with elected officials' wishes.[55] These measures mitigate—but do not eliminate—the problem of control (see the Take a Stand feature).

bureaucratic drift
Bureaucrats' tendency to implement policies in a way that favors their own political objectives rather than following the original intentions of the legislation.

Agency organization

Over the last 20 years, political scientists have shown how agencies can be organized to minimize bureaucratic drift.[56] Specifically, when an agency is set up or given new responsibilities, the officials who initiate the change don't simply tell the new agency what to do. To make sure that the agency pursues the policies officials want, they also determine where the agency is located within the federal government structure and who runs it. These efforts may occur solely within Congress, may involve both Congress and the president, or may be arranged by presidential actions.[57]

For example, one of the Obama administration's responses to the 2008 financial crisis was to form a new agency, the Consumer Financial Protection Bureau (CFPB), which would help enforce new bank regulations and investigate consumer complaints about financial firms. However, Republican senators opposed Obama's initial nominee to run the agency, Elizabeth Warren, believing she would encourage her subordinates to be excessively pro-consumer. Similarly, in 2017 President Trump

TAKE A STAND

Is Political Control of the Bureaucracy Beneficial?

When working with bureaucrats, elected officials (the president or members of Congress) face the problem of political control: Should they allow bureaucrats to exercise judgment when implementing policies or give them specific, narrow directives? Compounding this problem is the fact that most bureaucrats are civil service employees, meaning they cannot be fired except under very extreme circumstances. As a result, even when elected officials give very specific directives to an agency, they may find that bureaucrats essentially ignore the directives and that very little can be done to force compliance (after all, regardless of what bureaucrats do or don't do, they will still have a job). Civil service protections also mean that members of Congress or a new presidential administration cannot clean house in an agency, replacing untrustworthy bureaucrats with individuals who will do what they are told. Should civil service protections be abolished?

Get rid of civil service protections. The civil service system began in an era when few government jobs required specialized knowledge, expertise, or an advanced degree.

The modern federal bureaucracy is exactly the opposite: most jobs, particularly those that involve real policy-making power, require expertise to be done effectively. Under these conditions, civil service protections are to some extent unnecessary, as bureaucrats have considerable job security because of their expertise and experience. Getting rid of recalcitrant bureaucrats involves significant costs: by removing their knowledge of the policies being decided and the procedures by which decisions are made, it may become impossible for an agency to function at all. Moreover, a bureaucrat's reluctance to behave as ordered may be a sign that something is wrong—that the directive makes no sense or that there are easier ways of accomplishing the task.

Consider the U.S. Environmental Protection Agency. There is little doubt that most EPA scientists believe that climate change is real and that it is the result of human actions. Both of these views are in opposition to President Trump's stated positions. Are civil service protections the only thing preventing Trump from firing these scientists? Doing so would decimate the EPA and make it impossible for the agency to carry out many of its functions, some of which (like cleaning up Superfund sites) are things Trump favors. Trump may not like having EPA scientists

 Civil service protections help ensure that agency scientists will continue to do cutting-edge research and report their findings, even if their conclusions conflict with the views of their political superiors.

that disagree with him, but he would probably like the consequences of a mass firing even less.

Civil service protections are still needed. The fact that firing bureaucrats costs the government the benefit of their experience and expertise does not mean that elected officials will never threaten to do so, or even carry out their threats. Removing civil service protections—making bureaucrats vulnerable to threats about their future employment—could easily lead to bad policy outcomes. Eliminating civil service protections would also change the kinds of people who undertake careers in government service. Civil service protections enable policy experts to work for the government without fearing that they will be fired for simply voicing their concerns or because a new administration places a high value on loyalty. Without the protections afforded by civil service regulations, these individuals might choose a different career, depriving the federal government (and the American people) of the benefits of their knowledge and training.

In the case of the EPA, civil service protections help ensure that agency scientists will continue to do cutting-edge research and report their findings, even if their conclusions conflict with the views of their political superiors—and that these scientists will work for the agency in the first place.

take a stand

1. In general, contemporary Democratic politicians tend to favor civil service protections, while Republicans want to weaken them. Does this preference make sense in light of what we know about the differences between the parties in their beliefs about the size and scope of government?

2. Not all jobs in the federal bureaucracy require specialized knowledge and expertise. Would it make sense to abandon civil service protections for low-level jobs such as clerical positions? Why or why not?

appointed Michael Mulvaney to run the agency, even though Mulvaney was a long-time opponent of the CFPB who as a member of Congress had sought to abolish the agency. Both Trump and Obama's appointments were intended to shape agency operations by appointing an individual who was expected to act in line with the then-president's preferences.

Monitoring

One of the most important ways elected officials prevent bureaucratic drift is by keeping an eye on what bureaucrats are doing or planning to do. Information gathering by members of Congress about bureaucratic actions is termed **oversight**. Congressional committees often hold hearings to question agency heads, secretaries of executive departments, or senior agency staff. Similarly, one of the primary responsibilities of presidential appointees is to monitor how lower-level bureaucrats are responding to presidential directives. The problem is that appointees may be unable to fulfill this role. Because they are chosen for their loyalty to the president, they may lack the experience needed to fully understand what bureaucrats in their agency are doing (as discussed earlier, this was especially true for some of Trump's lower-level appointees). Moreover, given that appointees typically hold their position for only a year or two, they have little time to learn the details of agency operations.

Advance Warning Members of Congress, the president, and his or her staff gain advance knowledge of planned bureaucratic actions through the notice-and-comment procedure described earlier in the chapter, which requires bureaucrats to disclose proposed regulations before they take effect.[58] This delay gives opponents the opportunity to register complaints with their congressional representatives, and it allows these legislators time either to pressure the agency to revise the regulation or to even enact another law undoing or modifying the agency action. Members of Congress also pressure bureaucrats to release memos, working drafts, and other documents as a way of keeping track of what bureaucrats are doing—for example, in 2018 members of Congress demanded release of travel records and related documents for EPA Administrator Scott Pruitt. In particular, they wanted to know whether Pruitt's decision to fly first-class while on government business was due to security concerns, as Pruitt had claimed.

Investigations: Police Patrols and Fire Alarms Congress, legislative staff, or presidential appointees may initiate investigations of government programs or offices to scrutinize the organization, its expenditures, and its activities. There are two types of investigation: police patrol oversight and fire alarm oversight. Ideally, every agency would be investigated on a consistent basis, with agencies that have large budgets or carry out important functions being investigated more frequently. These investigations may involve fact-finding trips to local offices, interviews with senior personnel, audits of agency accounts, and calls to the agency to see how it responds to citizens' requests. This method of investigation is called **police patrol oversight**.[59] Think of a police officer walking his or her beat, rattling doors to see if they are locked, checking out broken windows, and looking down alleys for suspicious behavior.

The disadvantage of police patrol oversight is that it is costly in terms of money and staff time. Moreover, these investigations often find that agencies are doing what they should be doing. Because of these problems, Congress and the president often follow a different strategy. Rather than undertaking a series of investigations, they wait until

The Senate's power over the confirmation of senior agency officials is often used as a tool to shape agency policy and operations. Richard Cordray, the first head of the Consumer Financial Protection Agency, was nominated after some senators objected to President Obama's first nominee, Elizabeth Warren, who was a Harvard Law professor at the time.

oversight
Congressional efforts to make sure that laws are implemented correctly by the bureaucracy after they have been passed.

police patrol oversight
A method of oversight in which members of Congress constantly monitor the bureaucracy to make sure that laws are implemented correctly.

fire alarm oversight
A method of oversight in which members of Congress respond to complaints about the bureaucracy or problems of implementation only as they arise rather than exercising constant vigilance.

One reason that attempts to pass legislation forcing the FDA to alter its drug-approval process have had little success is that the FDA's process is considered to have worked mostly as intended: approving new drugs that are safe and effective, and keeping ineffective or unsafe drugs off the market.

they receive a complaint about bureaucratic actions, then focus investigative efforts on those cases. This practice is labeled **fire alarm oversight**.[60] The so-called fire alarm that sets off an investigation can take many different forms. Constituents may let their congressional representatives or their staff know of a problem with the bureaucracy. Similarly, lobbyists, corporate executives, and ordinary citizens often contact the president and his or her staff with complaints. Newspaper reporters and Internet bloggers also provide information on what bureaucrats are doing. In addition, some agencies have advisory committees that not only help make agency decisions but also keep Congress and the president informed about their agencies' actions.[61]

The case of the Park Service Twitter account mentioned at the beginning of this chapter is a clear example of fire alarm oversight. After major media outlets reported on the tweet ban, many members of Congress demanded that it be rescinded. Faced with this response, the White House quietly allowed the Park Service to start tweeting again. These fire alarms provide exactly the sort of information that Congress and the president often lack about how bureaucrats are implementing laws and directives, including cases in which bureaucrats are doing (or planning to do) something that contradicts their mandate. Such communications tell Congress and the president where to focus their efforts to monitor the bureaucracy, drawing their attention to agencies or programs in which problems have been reported and removing the need to try to oversee the entire government at once.

Correcting violations

When members of Congress or the president find a case of bureaucratic drift, they can take steps to influence the bureaucrats' actions. Many tactics can be used to bring a wayward agency into line. Legislation or an executive order can send a clear directive to an agency or remove its discretion, tasks and programs can be moved to an agency that is more closely aligned with elected officials' goals, political appointees at an agency can be replaced, and agencies can be reorganized. For example, one consequence of the Trump administration's slow process of making political appointments, particularly for the State Department, was a shift in policy-making power to individuals in the White House.

One of the most significant difficulties in dealing with bureaucratic drift is disagreement between members of Congress and the president about whether an agency is doing the right thing—regardless of whether the agency is following its original orders. Many strategies for influencing an agency's behavior require joint action by the president and congressional majorities. Without presidential support, members of Congress need a two-thirds majority to impose corrections. Without congressional support, the president can only threaten to cut an agency's proposed budget, change its home within the federal bureaucracy, or set up a new agency to do what the errant agency refuses to do. Actually carrying out these threats requires congressional approval. As a result, disagreements between the president and Congress can give an agency significant freedom, as long as it retains the support of at least one branch of government.

An agency may also be able to fend off elected officials' attempts to take political control if it has a reputation for expertise. For example, one reason that attempts to pass legislation forcing the FDA to alter its drug-approval process have had little success is that the FDA's process is thought to have worked mostly as intended, approving new drugs that are safe and effective and keeping ineffective or unsafe drugs off the market. At the same time, the FDA has responded to pressure from Congress and the president to revise some rules on its own.[62]

Finally, agencies can sometimes combat attempts to control their behavior by appealing to groups that benefit from agency actions.[63] For example, since the 1980s the Occupational Safety and Health Administration (OSHA) has resisted attempts by Republican presidents and Republican members of Congress to eliminate the agency or limit its operations.[64] One element of its strategy has been to build strong ties to labor unions. As a result, OSHA is much more likely to receive complaints about workplace safety from companies with strong unions. The second prong of the strategy has involved building cooperative arrangements with large companies to prevent workplace accidents, an approach that not only protects workers but can save companies a lot of money over the long term. Moreover, when OSHA levies fines against companies that violate safety regulations, the fines are generally much less than the maximum fines that would be allowed by law. As a result, when proposals to limit or eliminate OSHA are debated in Congress, members hear from unions as well as many large corporations in support of keeping the agency in place. Over time, this strategy has generated support for the agency from Democrats and Republicans in the House and Senate.

The consequences of control

Elected officials' competing desires to both control what bureaucrats do and tap their expertise explain many of the seemingly dysfunctional aspects of the bureaucracy. Part of the problem is the nature of the tasks given to bureaucrats. Even when members of Congress and the president agree on which problems deserve attention, bureaucrats often face the much harder task of translating these officials' lofty problem-solving goals into concrete policies. Given the magnitude of this job, it is no surprise that even the best efforts of government agencies do not always succeed.

Most important, the use of standard operating procedures is rooted partly in the complexity of bureaucrats' tasks—but also in the desire of agency heads and elected officials to control the actions of lower-level staff. In some disaster relief efforts, government agencies have found that preset plans and procedures worked against the need to respond quickly to alleviate human suffering. And while the FDA's drug-approval process succeeds for the most part at preventing harmful drugs from coming to market, the delays imposed by the process do prevent some patients from receiving lifesaving treatments. However, in all these cases the decisions do not reflect incompetence or malice. Rules and procedures are needed in any organization to ensure that decisions are made fairly and that they reflect the goals of the organization. But it is impossible to find procedures that will work well in all cases, particularly for the kinds of policy decisions made by bureaucrats.

"Why Should I Care?"

Cases of bureaucratic failure (poorly conceived policies or regulations, inaction, red tape) are often cited to "prove" that bureaucrats are incompetent, lazy, or dumb. The real story is that bureaucrats are often given nearly impossible tasks or political mandates that limit their authority. In this sense, complaints about bureaucrats have more to do with what we want them to do than with their unwillingness or inability to execute these missions.

Unpacking the Conflict

Considering all that we've discussed in this chapter, let's return to President Trump's often-contentious relationship with members of the federal bureaucracy. Are bureaucrats really obstructing the Trump agenda, or are they just doing their jobs? How do elected officials control a bureaucracy of experts?

A deeper look shows that some of the time, conflicts between President Trump and bureaucratic officials reflect real disagreements over outcomes. In the case of the Justice Department, for example, there is little doubt that Trump would prefer an investigation of the campaign of his 2016 opponent, Hillary Clinton, rather than the current investigation of his own campaign. However, the fact that many bureaucrats are policy experts suggests a different explanation of alleged resistance to President Trump's initiatives. Rather than stonewalling policy changes they oppose, bureaucrats may be acting from expertise, trying to mitigate unforeseen consequences and ensure the government operates in an efficient, effective manner.

Bureaucratic expertise and the resulting problem of control also explain the cumbersome procedures for hiring, firing, and decision making that are a feature of operations in many government agencies. Sometimes bureaucrats simply make mistakes, choosing the wrong policy because they—and, in some cases, all the people involved—lack information about the tasks they were given. Bureaucrats may drag their feet when they oppose their tasks on policy grounds. But in many cases, cumbersome procedures are the result of a fundamental trade-off faced by elected officials between wanting to exercise control over the bureaucracy and wanting to ensure that changes in policy produce their intended effect. Put another way, conflict over public policy often translates into conflicting ideas about what bureaucrats should do, resulting in complex, often-contradictory mandates and directions imposed on bureaucrats. In this way, politics shapes virtually all aspects of the bureaucracy and of the choices bureaucrats make, even in places where it is hard to discern political motivations.

What's Your Take?

Should elected officials defer to bureaucratic expertise?

Or should the president's agenda override other concerns?

STUDY GUIDE

What is the federal bureaucracy?

Define *bureaucracy* and explain its major functions.
(Pages 456–465)

Summary

The bureaucracy is composed of both civil servants and political appointees and is in charge of interpreting and implementing a wide range of government policies. While bureaucrats are policy experts, most members of Congress are not. Nonetheless, Congress tries to control how the bureaucracy operates, which can result in inefficiencies.

Key terms

bureaucracy (p. 456)

civil servants (p. 456)

political appointees (p. 456)

regulation (p. 457)

notice-and-comment
  procedure (p. 457)

state capacity (p. 462)

problem of control (p. 462)

principal–agent game
  (p. 462)

regulatory capture (p. 463)

red tape (p. 464)

standard operating
  procedures (SOPs) (p. 464)

Practice Quiz Questions

1. **A government rule that affects the choices that individuals or corporations make is called _____.**

   a an initiative

   b a referendum

   c a regulation

   d a procurement

   e an appropriation

2. **One of the reasons bureaucrats respond to pressure from elected officials is that _____.**

   a bureaucrats need congressional support to get larger budgets

   b elected officials are experts

   c bureaucrats are all appointed by members of Congress

   d bureaucrats' offices are housed in the Congress

   e bureaucrats are required by law to do so

3. **In the problem of control, the _____ is the principal and the _____ is the agent.**

   a bureaucracy; president

   b bureaucracy; Congress

   c president; Congress

   d president; bureaucracy

   e Congress; president

4. **_____ occurs when bureaucrats cater to a small group of individuals regardless of the impact of these actions on the public welfare.**

   a Bureaucratic drift

   b Regulatory capture

   c The revolving door

   d An iron triangle

   e Neutral competence

How has the American bureaucracy grown?

Trace the expansion of the federal bureaucracy over time.
(Pages 465–469)

Summary

The bureaucracy has grown substantially since the turn of the twentieth century, largely in response to citizens' demands that the government do more for the people. The federal government had a very limited role in daily life for much of the nineteenth century, but it expanded during the Progressive Era, when regulatory activity increased and the spoils system was replaced by the federal civil service. The bureaucracy expanded again with the New Deal and Great Society programs, which increased the number of services the government provided.

Key term

federal civil service (p. 467)

Practice Quiz Questions

5. **How did the bureaucracy change during the Progressive Era?**

   a It expanded the delivery of government services directly to individuals.

   b The spoils system was first established.

   c It created a number of antipoverty and educational programs.

   d It reduced the government's regulatory activity.

   e It increased the government's regulatory activity.

6. **The civil service reforms of the Progressive Era _____ the spoils system and _____ the power of party organizations.**

   a ended; increased

   b ended; decreased

   c instituted; increased

   d instituted; decreased

   e expanded; increased

7. How has the bureaucracy changed since the Reagan Revolution?

a The government stopped passing regulatory policies.

b The size of the federal government shrank.

c The size of the federal government increased.

d The civil service reforms were weakened.

e The civil service reforms were strengthened.

The modern federal bureaucracy

Describe the size and structure of the executive branch today. (Pages 469–475)

Summary

The modern bureaucracy serves a wide range of functions, but the division of labor within the bureaucracy does not always have an obvious logic. Overlapping or confusing jurisdictions can be the result of elected officials' attempts to shape the agency behavior by assigning a task to an executive department rather than an independent agency. The overall size of the bureaucracy reflects the demands of constituents but also fits the needs of elected officials to improve their chances of reelection.

Key terms

Office of Management and Budget (p. 469)

independent agencies (p. 470)

budget maximizers (p. 472)

Practice Quiz Questions

8. What is the job of the Office of Management and Budget?

a to prepare the president's annual budget proposal for Congress

b to prepare a response to the budget passed by Congress

c to prepare annual budget proposals for the states

d to monitor government spending for the Supreme Court

e to monitor government spending for Congress

9. Independent agencies have _____ freedom from oversight than executive departments do and _____ be controlled by the president through his appointees.

a more; cannot

b more; can

c less; cannot

d less; can

10. The federal budget is growing in size because _____ .

a bureaucrats are budget maximizers

b politicians do not scrutinize budget requests

c government agencies are never eliminated

d the public does not support large-scale budget cuts

e a growing percentage of Americans are going into civil service

The human face of the bureaucracy

Describe who bureaucrats are and the regulations that govern their employment. (Pages 475–478)

Summary

The regulations within the civil service system were established to separate politics from policy. Rather than getting and retaining a job for political reasons, individuals are hired based on merit and are quite difficult to fire. However, the president makes senior-level appointments that are not protected by civil service regulations and are more political in nature. These appointments are instrumental in helping the president control the bureaucracy.

Key term

turkey farms (p. 478)

Practice Quiz Questions

11. Compared with employees in private business, government employees are motivated _____ by salary and benefits than/as by the chance to make a difference.

a more

b just as much

c less

12. The civil service regulations _____ the flexibility that managers have in their hiring decisions and _____ the influence of elected officials.

a decrease; decrease

b increase; increase

c increase; decrease

d decrease; increase

e increase; have no effect on

Controlling the bureaucracy

Explain how Congress and the president oversee the executive branch. (Pages 479–483)

Summary

With their expertise, bureaucrats have the power to significantly influence government policy. This creates a dilemma for elected officials, who want to enjoy the benefits of the expertise while retaining control of the bureaucracy. Lawmakers can generally organize agencies and monitor their behavior to reduce, but not eliminate, bureaucratic drift.

Key terms

bureaucratic drift (p. 479)

oversight (p. 481)

police patrol oversight (p. 481)

fire alarm oversight (p. 482)

Practice Quiz Questions

13. When bureaucrats pursue their own goals rather than their assignments from officeholders, this is called _____ .

a an iron triangle

b regulatory capture

c the problem of control

d turkey farming

e bureaucratic drift

14. Giving direct orders to bureaucrats _____ the influence of their policy expertise and _____ the potential to respond to unforeseen circumstances.

a limits; reduces

b increases; reduces

c limits; increases

d increases; increases

e limits; has no effect on

15. While police patrol oversight has the advantage of being _____ , it has the drawback of being _____ .

a affordable; unresponsive

b responsive; costly

c affordable; generally unnecessary

d responsive; unpopular

e affordable; ineffective

Suggested Reading

Brehm, John, and Scott Gates. *Teaching, Managing Tasks, and Brokering Trust: Functions of the Public Executive.* New York: Russell Sage Foundation, 2008.

Carpenter, Daniel P. *The Forging of Bureaucratic Autonomy: Reputations, Networks, and Policy Innovation in Executive Agencies, 1862–1928.* Princeton, NJ: Princeton University Press, 2001.

Huber, John D., and Charles R. Shipan. *Deliberate Discretion? The Institutional Foundations of Bureaucratic Autonomy.* New York: Cambridge University Press, 2002.

Lewis, David E. *The Politics of Presidential Appointments: Political Control and Bureaucratic Performance.* Princeton, NJ: Princeton University Press, 2010.

Light, Paul. *A Government Well-Executed: Public Service and Public Performance.* Washington, DC: Brookings Institution Press, 2003.

McCubbins, Mathew D., Roger G. Noll, and Barry R. Weingast. "Structure and Process as Solutions to the Politician's Principal-Agency Problem," *Virginia Law Review* 74 (1989): 431–82.

Miller, Gary. *Managerial Dilemmas: The Political Economy of Hierarchy.* New York: Cambridge University Press, 1987.

Moe, Terry M. "Political Control and the Power of the Agent." *Journal of Law, Economics, and Organization* 22 (2006): 1–21.

Nelson, Michael. "A Short, Ironic History of American National Bureaucracy." *Journal of Politics* 44 (1982): 747–78.

Skowronek, Stephen. *Building a New American State: The Expansion of National Administrative Capacities, 1877–1920.* New York: Cambridge University Press, 1982.

Workman, Samuel. *The Dynamics of Bureaucracy in the U.S. Government.* New York: Cambridge University Press, 2015.

14

The Courts

What is the role of courts in our political system?

 "He is a faker. He has no consistency about him. He says whatever comes into his head at the moment."
Justice Ruth Bader Ginsburg, commenting on Donald Trump

"Justice Ginsburg of the U.S. Supreme Court has embarrassed all by making very dumb political statements about me. Her mind is shot—resign!"
Donald Trump

In the heat of the 2016 presidential campaign, Justice Ruth Bader Ginsburg cut loose with a series of comments about a possible Trump presidency. In addition to labeling Trump a "faker" in an interview conducted by CNN,[1] Ginsburg told the *New York Times*, "I can't imagine what this place would be—I can't imagine what the country would be—with Donald Trump as our president."

These comments set off a firestorm, not just from Trump and his supporters but also from left-leaning editorial boards such as that of the *Washington Post*. It called her observations "inappropriate," noting that the Code of Conduct for United States Judges "flatly states" that a "judge should not . . . publicly endorse or oppose a candidate for public office."[2] Under the headline "Donald Trump Is Right about Justice Ruth Bader Ginsburg," the *New York Times* was even more critical, saying, "Justice Ruth Bader Ginsburg needs to drop the political punditry and the name-calling."[3] We have come to expect such personal attacks from politicians, but not from Supreme Court justices, which is why Ginsburg's words were so jarring.

Bowing to the public pressure, Justice Ginsburg backed off, saying, "On reflection, my recent remarks in response to press inquiries were ill-advised and I regret making them. Judges should avoid commenting on a candidate for public office. In the future I will be more circumspect."[4]

Why all the fuss? Why should the political comments of a sitting justice be so controversial? The simple answer is that our political system is strongly committed to the image of the blindfolded Lady Justice, holding the scales, neutrally applying the law. As Chief Justice John G. Roberts Jr. famously said, justices are like baseball umpires, just calling the balls and strikes within the constitutional system. After all, the guiding principles of the "rule of law" in the American political system—embodied in the words carved above the entrance to the Supreme Court ("equal justice under the

Justice Ginsburg broke from the image of the blindfolded Lady Justice when she expressed her opinions on a Trump presidency. Here, Justice Ginsburg (far left), along with other Supreme Court justices, looks on as President Trump makes a speech during the swearing-in ceremony for Judge Neil Gorsuch in the Rose Garden.

law") and the image of Lady Justice—seem to contradict the view of a political Supreme Court. We normally think of the courts as objectively applying the law and interpreting the Constitution for each case. Indeed, there is often consensus among the justices on how to rule in a given case. In the 2017–2018 term, 39 percent of the cases decided were unanimous (28 of 71) and 6 more had only one dissenting vote.[5]

However, a massive body of political science research shows that the Supreme Court can be quite political and divided ideologically. In the most recent term, 26 percent of cases were decided by a 5–4 vote, including controversial cases concerning public employee unions, searches of cell phone records, Internet sales taxes, and President Trump's travel ban for countries suspected of terrorism. As justices interpret the Constitution, they also play one of two roles in our political system: either asserting their own policy-making authority or deferring to the decisions of others (Congress, the president, or the people). The Court's decision about which path to take in a given case is often political, involving conflict, trade-offs, and compromise, much like decision making in Congress.

For those who resist the view that the courts are a policy-making institution, the theme "political process matters" may not seem to apply in this chapter. However, the courts often *do* make policy, and the way they make decisions has an impact on outcomes. To see how political process matters for the courts, it is important to answer the following questions: What are the different roles of the courts and the structure of the judicial system? How do court decisions shape policy? In a nutshell, what is the nature of judicial decision making? With this context in mind, we can reexamine the controversy over Justice Ginsburg's comments. Did Justice Ginsburg overstep her boundaries with her remarks on Donald Trump, or was it appropriate for her to express her opinions? What is the proper place of the courts within our political system? Should judges attempt to neutrally apply the law, or should their political views play a role?

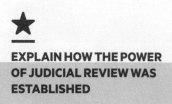

★
EXPLAIN HOW THE POWER OF JUDICIAL REVIEW WAS ESTABLISHED

The development of an independent and powerful federal judiciary

The Constitution did not definitively establish the role of the courts in American politics or the Supreme Court's authority as the ultimate interpreter of the Constitution. The powers of the Supreme Court evolved over time, and debates about its proper role continue to this day.

The Founders' views of the courts: the weakest branch?

The Federalists and Antifederalists did not see eye to eye on much, and the judiciary was no exception. Alexander Hamilton, writing in *Federalist 78*, said that the Supreme Court would be "beyond comparison the weakest of the three departments of power." In contrast, one of the authors of the *Antifederalist Papers* wrote: "The supreme court under this constitution would be exalted above all other power in the government and subject to no control."[6] Hmmm, which is it: weakest or strongest? Although the framers could not agree on how powerful the Court was likely to be relative to the other branches of government, there was surprisingly little debate at the Constitutional Convention about the judiciary. Article III of the Constitution, which concerns the judicial branch of government, created one Supreme Court and gave the courts independence by providing federal judges with lifetime terms (assuming "good behavior").

The main disagreements about the judiciary had to do with how independent the courts should be vis-à-vis the other branches of government and how much power to give to the courts. Some of the framers feared a tyrannical Congress and wanted to create judicial and executive branches that could check this power. Others argued for making the executive and judicial branches more closely related so they would be better able to balance Congress. A central debate was whether to give the judiciary some "revisionary power" over Congress, similar to the president's veto power. This idea of judicial review would have given the Supreme Court the power to strike down laws passed by Congress that violated the Constitution. The framers could not agree on judicial review, so the Constitution remained silent on the matter.

While the Constitution clearly specified the kinds of cases over which the Court would have **original jurisdiction** (see Nuts & Bolts 14.1), many details about the Supreme Court were left up to Congress, including its size, the time and place it would meet, and its internal organization. These details, and the system of lower federal courts, were outlined in the **Judiciary Act of 1789**. This law set the number of justices at six (one chief justice and five associates). The number of justices gradually increased to ten by the end of the Civil War and was then restricted to seven under Reconstruction policies. In 1869 the number was set at nine, where it has remained ever since.[7] The 1789 act also created a system of federal courts, which included 13 **district courts** and 3 circuit courts—the intermediate-level courts with **appellate jurisdiction**. Since the circuit courts hear cases on appeal from lower courts, they are now more commonly called appeals courts. The district courts each had one judge, while the circuit courts were each staffed by two Supreme Court justices and one district judge. This odd arrangement in which Supreme Court justices had to preside over both cases in

original jurisdiction
The authority of a court to handle a case first, as in the Supreme Court's authority to initially hear disputes between two states. However, original jurisdiction for the Supreme Court is not exclusive; it may assign such a case to a lower court.

Judiciary Act of 1789
The law in which Congress laid out the organization of the federal judiciary. The law refined and clarified federal court jurisdiction and set the original number of justices at six. It also created the office of the attorney general and established the lower federal courts.

district courts
Lower-level trial courts of the federal judicial system that handle most U.S. federal cases.

appellate jurisdiction
The authority of a court to hear appeals from lower courts and change or uphold the decision.

NUTS & BOLTS 14.1

Jurisdiction of the Federal Courts as Defined in Article III of the Constitution

Source: Lee Epstein and Thomas G. Walker, *Constitutional Law for a Changing America: Institutional Powers and Constraints*, 5th ed. (Washington, DC: CQ Press, 2004), p. 65.

Jurisdiction of Lower Federal Courts

- Cases involving the U.S. Constitution, federal laws, and treaties.
- Controversies between two or more states. (Congress passed a law giving the Supreme Court exclusive jurisdiction over these cases.)
- Controversies between citizens of different states.
- Controversies between a state and citizens of another state. (The Eleventh Amendment removed federal jurisdiction in these cases.)
- Controversies between a state or its citizens and any foreign states, citizens, or subjects.
- Cases affecting ambassadors, public ministers, and consuls.
- Cases of admiralty and maritime jurisdictions.
- Controversies between citizens of the same state claiming lands under grants of different states.

Jurisdiction of the Supreme Court
Original Jurisdiction*

- Cases involving ambassadors, public ministers, and consuls.
- Cases that involve a state.

Appellate Jurisdiction

- Cases falling under the jurisdiction of the lower federal courts, "with such exceptions, and under such Regulations as the Congress shall make."

*This does not imply exclusive jurisdiction. For example, the Supreme Court may refer to a district court for a case involving an ambassador (the more likely outcome).

The Supreme Court building features the words "Equal Justice Under Law" across the façade, as well as a statue titled "The Contemplation of Justice."

judicial review
The Supreme Court's power to strike down a law or an executive branch action that it finds unconstitutional.

Washington and cases in their assigned circuit remained in place for more than 100 years, over the objections of the justices who resented having to "ride circuit" in difficult traveling conditions.[8] Today separate judges are appointed to fill the circuit courts.

The Supreme Court had a rough start. Indeed, it seemed determined to prove Alexander Hamilton right, that it was the weakest branch. Of the six original justices appointed by George Washington, one declined to serve and another never showed up for a formal session. The Court's first sessions lasted only a few days because it did not have much business. In fact, the Court did not decide a single case in 1791 or 1792. When Justice Rutledge resigned in 1791 to take a state court position, two potential appointees turned down the job in order to keep their positions in their state legislatures! Such career decisions would be unimaginable today, when serving on the Supreme Court is considered the pinnacle of a legal career.[9]

Judicial review and *Marbury v. Madison*

The Court started to gain more power when John Marshall was appointed chief justice in 1801. Marshall single-handedly transformed the Court into an equal partner in the system of checks and balances. The most important step was the decision *Marbury v. Madison* (1803), which gave the Supreme Court the power of **judicial review**. As noted earlier, the framers were split on the wisdom of giving the Court the power to strike down laws passed by Congress, and the Constitution does not explicitly address the issue. However, historians have established that a majority of the framers, including the most influential ones, favored judicial review (Hamilton endorsed it in some detail in *Federalist 78*). Given that the Constitution did not address the issue of judicial review, Marshall simply asserted that the Supreme Court had the power to determine when a law was unconstitutional. As the power of judicial review has evolved, it has become a central part of the system of checks and balances (see Chapter 2).

The facts and legal reasoning behind *Marbury* are worth explaining because it is one of the most important court cases in American history. The Federalists had just lost the election of 1800 to Thomas Jefferson and the Democratic-Republicans. In a last-minute power grab, the Federalist-controlled lame-duck Congress gave outgoing President Adams an opportunity to appoint 42 new justices of the peace for the District of Columbia and Alexandria, Virginia. Adams made the appointments, and the Senate confirmed them, but not before time ran out and the new administration took over. The secretary of state, John Marshall (the same Marshall who had just been confirmed as chief justice before President Adams left office), failed to ensure that all the commissions for the new judges were delivered by midnight. When President Jefferson assumed office, he ordered his new secretary of state, James Madison, not to deliver the remaining commissions that had been issued by the outgoing Federalist administration. William Marbury was one of the people who did not receive his commission, and he asked the Supreme Court to issue an order giving him the position.

As leading figures in opposing parties, Chief Justice Marshall and President Jefferson did not like each other. This put Marshall in a difficult position. He was concerned that if he issued the order that Marbury wanted, giving Marbury his job, Jefferson probably would ignore it. (Though Secretary of State Madison was technically the other party in the lawsuit, Jefferson was calling the shots.) Given the weakness of the Court, having such an order disregarded by the president could have been a final blow to its position in the national government. However, if the Court did not issue the order, it would be giving in to Jefferson despite the merits of Marbury's case—he really had been cheated out of his job. It appeared that the Court would lose whether it issued the order or not.

To get out of the predicament, Marshall applied the idea of judicial review. Although the idea was not original to Marshall, the Court had never before exercised its authority to rule on the constitutionality of a federal law. Marshall's reasoning was quite clever: the Court's opinion said that Marbury was due his commission, but the Court could not give him his job because the part of the Judiciary Act of 1789 that gave it the power to do so was unconstitutional! The portion of the act in question was Section 13, which gave the Court the power to issue orders (writs of mandamus) to anyone holding federal office. Because this section expanded the original jurisdiction of the Supreme Court, Marshall ruled that Congress had overstepped its bounds in passing it. The original jurisdiction of the Court is clearly specified in the Constitution, so any attempt by Congress to change that jurisdiction through legislation would be unconstitutional; the only way to change original jurisdiction would be through a constitutional amendment.[10] Marshall writes: "It is emphatically the province and duty of the judicial department to say what the law is. ...If two laws conflict with each other, the courts must decide on the operation of each. So if a law be in opposition to the Constitution...the court must determine which of these conflicting rules governs the case. This is of the very essence of judicial duty."[11]

Judicial review in practice

Chief Justice Marshall and the Federalists lost the battle—poor Mr. Marbury never did get his job, and Jefferson appointed the people he wanted to be justices of the peace—but the Supreme Court won the war. By asserting its power to review the constitutionality of laws passed by Congress, the Court became an equal partner in the institutional balance of power. Although it would be more than 50 years until the Court would use judicial review again to strike down a law passed by Congress (in the unfortunate 1857 *Dred Scott* case, which concerned slavery and effectively led to the Civil War), the reasoning behind *Marbury* has never been challenged by subsequent presidents or Congresses.[12]

Interpreting federal laws may seem like a logical responsibility for the Supreme Court, but what about state laws? Should the Supreme Court have final say over them as well? The Constitution does not answer this question. But the supremacy clause requires that the Constitution and national laws take precedence over state constitutions and state laws when they conflict. The Judiciary Act of 1789 made it clear that the Supreme Court would rule on these matters.

The contours of the relationship between the national government and the states have been largely defined by the Supreme Court's assertion of judicial review and its willingness to intervene in matters of state law. For much of the nineteenth century, the Court embraced dual federalism, in which the national government and the states operated on two separate levels (see Chapter 3). Later the Court involved itself more in state law as it moved toward a more active role for the national government in regulating interstate commerce and using the Fourteenth Amendment to selectively incorporate the amendments that constitute the Bill of Rights (see Chapter 4).

All in all, the Court has struck down more than 180 acts of Congress (and about 1,400 state laws). This sounds like a lot, but Congress passed more than 60,000 laws in its first 230 years. Over time, the Court has ruled on state laws in many important areas, including civil liberties, desegregation and civil rights, abortion, privacy, redistricting, labor laws, employment and discrimination, and business and environmental regulation.

When the Supreme Court strikes down a congressional or state law, it engages in **constitutional interpretation**—that is, it determines that the law is unconstitutional. But the Supreme Court also engages in **statutory interpretation**—that is, it applies national and state laws to particular cases (statutes are laws that are passed by legislatures). Often the language of a

constitutional interpretation
The process of determining whether a piece of legislation or governmental action is supported by the Constitution.

statutory interpretation
The various methods and tests used by the courts for determining the meaning of a law and applying it to specific situations. Congress may overturn the courts' interpretation by writing a new law; thus, it also engages in statutory interpretation.

Chief Justice John Marshall favored the idea of judicial review and claimed this power for the Court in the *Marbury v. Madison* decision.

statute may be unclear and the Court must interpret how to apply the law. For example, should the protection of endangered species prevent economic development that may destroy the species' habitat? How does one determine if an employer is responsible for punishing sexual harassment in the workplace? How should the voting rights of minorities be protected? In each case, the Court must interpret the relevant statutes to determine what Congress really meant. In addition, in the third main area of the law—administrative law—the Court is sometimes required to assess how federal agencies have interpreted and implemented laws passed by Congress. Often this involves the controversial practice of consulting legislative histories—floor debates, congressional hearings, and so on—to determine how the legislature intended for the laws to be interpreted. But the late justice Antonin Scalia argued that such searches are inherently subjective and that justices should only interpret the actual text of the laws in question.

Although politicians and other political actors accept judicial review as a central part of the political system, critics are concerned about its antidemocratic nature. Why, for example, do we give nine unelected justices such extraordinary power over our elected representatives? Debates about the proper role for the Court will continue as long as it is involved in controversial decisions. We will take up this question later in the chapter when we address the concepts of judicial activism and judicial restraint.

"Why Should I Care?"

Judicial review may seem like "inside baseball" that doesn't really matter for most Americans. However, the power to strike down laws and government actions means that the Court may act against political majorities to strike down unconstitutional actions such as segregating schools by race and discriminating against same-sex marriage. Judicial review may also be used, however, to frustrate popular majorities during times of political change, such as during the New Deal of the 1930s. In the most recent term, the Court did some of both—requiring the government to have a court order to search cell phone records but also deciding that states must collect sales taxes on Internet sales, despite public opposition to the practice. In either case, this is an awesome political power that puts the Supreme Court on an equal institutional footing with Congress and the president.

OUTLINE THE STRUCTURE OF THE COURT SYSTEM

The American legal and judicial system

Two sets of considerations are necessary to understand the overall nature of our judicial system: the fundamentals of the legal system that apply to all courts in the United States, and the structure of the court system within our system of federalism. You may have a pretty good understanding of the legal system from watching *Law and Order,* but a refresher on the basics never hurts.

Court fundamentals

plaintiff
The person or party who brings a case to court.

defendant
The person or party against whom a case is brought.

The general characteristics of the court system begin with the people who are in the courtroom. The **plaintiff** brings the case, and the **defendant** is the person or party who is being sued or charged with a crime. If the case is appealed, the petitioner is the person bringing the appeal and the respondent is on the other side of the case. In a civil case, the plaintiff sues to determine who is right or wrong and to gain something of value, such as monetary damages, the right to vote, or admission to a university. For example, imagine that your neighbor accidentally backs his car into the fence that divides your property, destroying a large section of it. The neighbor does not have adequate insurance to cover the damages and refuses to pay for the repairs. You do not want to pay the $1,000 deductible on your insurance policy, so you (the plaintiff) sue your neighbor (the defendant) to see whether your neighbor has to pay for the repairs. In a criminal case, the plaintiff is the government and the prosecutor attempts to prove the guilt of the defendant (the person accused of the crime).

Many, but not all, civil and criminal cases are heard before a jury that decides the outcome in the case, which is called the verdict. Often cases get settled before they go to trial (or even in the middle of the trial) in a process known as **plea bargaining**. In a civil case, this would mean that the plaintiff and the defendant agree on a monetary settlement and admission of guilt (or not; in some cases the defendant may agree to pay a fine or damages but not to admit guilt). In a criminal case, the defendant may agree to plead guilty in exchange for receiving a shorter sentence or being charged with a lesser crime. More than 95 percent of federal felony cases that result in a conviction are settled in this way.[13] Plea bargaining is an excellent example of how legal conflict between two parties can be resolved through compromise.

Differences between Civil and Criminal Cases There are important differences between civil and criminal cases. One is the standard of proof that serves to determine the outcome of the case. In civil cases, the jury has to determine whether the "preponderance of evidence"—that is, a majority of the evidence—proves that the plaintiff wins. In criminal cases, a much stiffer standard must be met: the defendant must be found guilty "beyond a reasonable doubt."

Another difference is where the burden of proof lies. In criminal cases, there is a presumption of "innocent until proven guilty"—that is, the state must prove the guilt of the defendant. However, in civil cases the burden of proof may be on either the plaintiff or the defendant, depending on the law that governs the case. Even more complicated, in civil cases the plaintiff may have to prove certain points and the defendant other points. For example, in certain race-based voting rights cases plaintiffs would have to prove that race was the predominant motivation for creating a black-majority congressional district to support their complaint that their interests were not being served in the district. If that point is demonstrated, then the burden of proof shifts to the defendants to show that there was some "compelling state interest" to justify the use of race as a predominant factor.

One type of civil suit is the **class-action lawsuit**, a case brought by a group of individuals on behalf of themselves and others in similar circumstances. Their target may be a corporation that produced hazardous or defective products or that harmed a particular group through illegal behavior. For example, 1.5 million current and former female Walmart employees sued the retailing giant for sex discrimination in 2011, claiming that the store had paid women less than men for the same work and had promoted fewer women than men.[14] Suits are often filed on behalf of shareholders of companies that have lost value because of fraud committed by corporate leaders. Cases like these are an important mechanism for providing accountability and justice in our economic system. Federal regulators do not have the ability to ensure the complete safety of food, drugs, and consumer products or to continually monitor all potential business fraud. Therefore, consumers rely on the legal system and class-action lawsuits to ensure that businesses act fairly and produce safe products.

plea bargaining
Negotiating an agreement between a plaintiff and a defendant to settle a case before it goes to trial or the verdict is decided. In a civil case, this usually involves an admission of guilt and an agreement on monetary damages; in a criminal case, this often involves an admission of guilt in return for a reduced charge or sentence.

O. J. Simpson dons a pair of gloves during testimony in his double-murder trial in Los Angeles in June 1995. The jury was not convinced of his guilt "beyond a reasonable doubt" and thus acquitted Simpson in this criminal trial. However, a subsequent civil trial found that a "preponderance of evidence" was against him.

class-action lawsuit
A case brought by a group of individuals on behalf of themselves and others in the general public who are in similar circumstances.

common law
Law based on the precedent of previous court rulings rather than on legislation. It is used in all federal courts and 49 of the 50 state courts.

precedent
A legal norm established in court cases that is then applied to future cases dealing with the same legal questions.

standing
Legitimate justification for bringing a civil case to court.

jurisdiction
The sphere of a court's legal authority to hear and decide cases.

Common Elements of the Judicial System Several characteristics of the judicial system apply to all cases. First, ours is an adversarial system in which lawyers on both sides have an opportunity to present their case, challenge the testimony of the opposing side, and try to convince the court that their version of the events is true. The process of "discovery," in which both sides share the information that will be presented in court before the trial begins, ensures a fair process and few last-minute surprises. Second, 49 of the 50 states and the federal courts operate under a system of **common law**, which means that legal decisions build from precedents established in previous cases and apply commonly throughout the jurisdiction of the court. The alternative, which is practiced only in Louisiana, is the civil law tradition, which is based on a detailed codification of the law that is applied to each specific case.

The notion of **precedent** (or stare decisis: "let the decision stand") deserves special attention. Precedent is a previously decided case or set of cases that serves as a guide for future cases on the same topic. Lower courts are bound by Supreme Court decisions when there is a clear precedent that is relevant for a given case. In many cases, following precedent is not clear-cut because several precedents may seem relevant. The lower courts have considerable discretion in sorting out which precedents are the most important. The Supreme Court tries to follow its own precedents, but in the past 50 years justices have been willing to deviate from earlier decisions when they think that the precedent is flawed. The Court has overruled more than twice as many decisions since 1953 as it overturned in the previous 164 years. Part of this can be explained by the relatively small number of precedents that *could* have been overturned in the first few decades of our nation's history. But even when accounting for the natural accumulation of more precedents to potentially overturn, recent Courts have been much more willing to deviate from precedent than previous Courts. For example, in the case concerning taxes on Internet sales, the Court overturned part of a 26-year-old precedent that said state sales taxes cannot be collected on businesses that do not have a physical presence in a state.[15] As this record indicates, precedent is not a rule the Court must follow but a norm that constrains its behavior.

Another characteristic common to all cases is that the person bringing the case must have **standing** to sue in a civil case, which means that the person has a legitimate basis for bringing the case. This usually means that the individual has suffered some direct and personal harm from the action addressed in the court case. Standing is easy to establish for private parties; in our earlier example, if your neighbor destroys your fence, you have been harmed. However, determining who has standing gets more interesting when the government is the one being sued. For example, when an environmental group challenged the Interior Department's interpretation of the Endangered Species Act, the Supreme Court ruled that the group did not have standing to sue because it had not demonstrated that the government's policy would cause it "imminent" injury.[16] Similarly, federal courts have ruled that 10 members of Congress did not have standing to challenge American bombing in Libya and that taxpayers do not have standing to sue the government if they disagree with a specific policy.[17] Depending on your politics, you may not want your hard-earned cash going to buy school lunches for poor children or to fund various wars. However, your status as a taxpayer does not give you enough of a personal stake in these policies to challenge them in court, and so you do not have standing. Later, in the section discussing how cases get to the Supreme Court, we will see that justices have some leeway in defining standing.

The final general characteristic of the legal system is the **jurisdiction** of the court. When bringing a case before the court, you must choose a court that actually has the power to hear your case. For example, if you wanted to contest a speeding ticket, you would not file your case in the state supreme court or in the federal district court; you would file it in your local traffic court. What if you believed you were the victim of discrimination in the workplace? Would you sue in state or federal court? You probably could do either, but the decision would be based on which set of laws would provide you with more protection from discrimination. This varies by state, so the proper jurisdiction for a given case is often a judgment call based on specific legal questions. (This practice of seeking the best court for your case is called *venue shopping.*)

Structure of the court system and federalism

The structure of the court system is like the rest of the political system: it is divided within and across levels of government. Across the levels of government, the court system operates on two parallel tracks within (1) the state and local courts and (2) the federal courts. Within each level of government, both tracks include courts of original jurisdiction, appeals courts, and courts of special jurisdiction. As shown in the How It Works graphic, the state courts are entirely separate from the federal courts, with the exception of the small proportion of cases that are appealed from a state supreme court to the U.S. Supreme Court. There is much variation between the states in terms of how they structure their court systems. However, they all follow the same general pattern of trial courts with limited and general original jurisdiction and appeals courts (either one or two levels, depending on the state).

District Courts Workhorses of the federal system, the district courts handle more than a quarter of a million filings a year. There are 89 districts in the 50 states, with at least one district court for each state. There are also district courts in Puerto Rico, the Virgin Islands, the District of Columbia, Guam, and the Northern Mariana Islands to bring the total to 94 districts with 677 judges.[18] There are two limited-jurisdiction district courts: the Court of International Trade, which addresses cases involving international trade and customs issues, and the U.S. Court of Federal Claims, which handles most claims for money damages against the United States, disputes over federal contracts, unlawful "takings" of private property by the federal government, and other claims against the United States.

Appeals Courts The **appeals courts** (officially called circuit courts until 1948)[19] are the intermediate courts of appeals, but in practice they are the final court for most federal cases that are appealed from the district courts. The losing side in a federal case can appeal to the Supreme Court, but given that the highest court in the land hears so few cases, the appeals courts usually get the final word. Appeals courts did not always have this much power; in fact, through much of the nineteenth century they had very limited appellate jurisdiction and did not hear many significant cases.

The number of appeals courts in the nation slowly expanded as the workload of these courts grew. Currently, there are 12 regional courts and the Court of Appeals for the Federal Circuit, which handles specialized cases from all over the country. The smallest of the regional appeals courts is the First Circuit, which has 6 judges, and the largest is the Ninth Circuit, which has 29 judges.[20] In 2017, there were 179 appeals court judges and about 85 "senior judges" (these numbers include the appeals court for the federal circuit).[21] Senior judges are semiretired judges who hear certain cases to help out with the overall federal court system workload; they typically handle about 15 percent of the workload for the federal court system.

The Supreme Court The Supreme Court sits at the top of the federal court system. The Supreme Court is the "court of last resort" for cases coming from both the state

appeals courts
The intermediate level of federal courts that hear appeals from district courts. More generally, an appeals court is any court with appellate jurisdiction.

How it works: in theory
The Court System

If federal question →

State Supreme Courts or Courts of Last Resort

52 courts (Texas and Oklahoma each have two courts of last resort)

346 judges; about 75,000 cases per year

Final Appeals Courts

U.S. Supreme Court

Received 6,305 filings in the 2016–2017 term; 71 cases were argued; 68 were disposed of in 61 signed opinions.

Courts of Appeals

94 courts in 41 states

939 judges; about 257,000 cases per year

Intermediate Appeals Courts

U.S. Courts of Appeals

12 regional courts and the U.S. Court of Appeals for the Federal Circuit

50,506 filings in the 2016–2017 term

Trial Courts of Limited and Special Jurisdiction

16,920 judges
About 55 million cases per year

Examples: juvenile court, traffic court, small claims court, justice of the peace, family court

Trial Courts of General and Original Jurisdiction

10,650 judges
About 30 million cases per year

Examples: district courts, county courts, municipal courts

Trial Courts

Trial Courts of General and Original Jurisdiction

94 district courts
267,769 civil cases and 77,018 criminal cases filed in the 2016–2017 term

Trial Courts of Limited and Special Jurisdiction

Examples: federal claims court, tax court, Court of International Trade, Court of Veterans Appeals

State and Local Courts

Federal Courts

Sources: Data on federal courts are from the U.S. Supreme Court, "2017 Year-End Report on the Federal Judiciary," www.supremecourt.gov/publicinfo/year-end/2017year-endreport.pdf (accessed 6/25/18). Data on state courts are from National Center for State Courts, www.ncsc.org (accessed 6/25/18); Ballotpedia.org, "Intermediate Appellate Courts," https://ballotpedia.org/Intermediate_appellate_courts (accessed 6/25/18) and Ron Malega and Thomas H. Cohen, "State Court Organization, 2011," U.S. Department of Justice, Bureau of Justice Statistics, www.bjs.gov/content/pub/pdf/sco11.pdf (accessed 6/25/18).

Same-Sex Marriage through the Court System

Same-sex marriage has been addressed in dozens of state and federal court cases in the past decade. A landmark case decided in June 2015 illustrates how cases make their way through the court system and how the Supreme Court resolves conflicts between the lower courts.

Okay, let's resolve this.

Supreme Court:
The Supreme Court resolved this conflict in a landmark 5–4 decision, *Obergefell v. Hodges* (2015), holding that the fundamental **right to marry is guaranteed to same-sex couples** by both the due process clause and the equal protection clause of the Fourteenth Amendment to the U.S. Constitution.

The conflict between the circuit courts meant that same-sex marriage was legal in some states, but not in others. At the end of June 2015, same-sex couples could marry in 29 states and the District of Columbia, but not in 21 states.

It's constitutional.

It's unconstitutional.

Federal Court of Appeals:
Appeals court rulings from the Fourth, Seventh, Ninth, and Tenth Circuits, representing 23 states, **struck down state-level bans on same-sex marriage** as unconstitutional.

Federal Court of Appeals:
Six federal district court cases from Michigan, Ohio, Kentucky, and Tennessee were appealed to the Sixth Circuit Court, which **upheld the bans on same-sex marriage in these four states.**

Yeah, but...

Eleven federal district court decisions were appealed by states attempting to uphold their bans.

Rights awarded!

State and Federal Trial Courts:
Following the Supreme Court's landmark ruling in 2013 striking down the Defense of Marriage Act, more than **two dozen state courts and federal district courts struck down bans on same-sex marriage.**

? Critical Thinking

1. **What are the advantages and disadvantages** of having such a complex court system?

2. **When does a case that goes through the state courts** end up in the U.S. Supreme Court? Can you think of an issue other than same-sex marriage where this is likely to occur?

and the federal courts. One important function of the Court is to ensure that the application and interpretation of the Constitution are consistent nationwide by resolving conflicts between lower courts, or between state law and federal law, or between laws in different states. A district court or appeals court ruling is applicable only within the specific region of that court, whereas Supreme Court rulings apply to the entire country.

Although the Supreme Court is the most important interpreter of the Constitution, the president and Congress also interpret the Constitution on a regular basis. This means that the Supreme Court does not always have the final say. For example, if the Court strikes down a federal law for being overly vague, Congress can rewrite the law to clarify the offending passage. When this happens, Congress may have the final word. For example, Congress overturned *Ledbetter v. Goodyear Tire & Rubber Co.* (2007) when it passed the Lilly Ledbetter Fair Pay Act in 2009. The law explicitly states that the Supreme Court had misinterpreted the 1964 Civil Rights Act when it ruled that Ledbetter would have had to file her pay discrimination suit within 180 days of being hired.[22]

Even on matters of constitutional interpretation rather than statutory interpretation, Congress can fight back by passing a constitutional amendment. However, this is a difficult and time-consuming process (see Chapter 2). Nevertheless, that option is available as a way of overturning an unpopular Court decision. Perhaps the best example of this is the very first major case ever decided by the Supreme Court—*Chisholm v. Georgia* (1793). This case upheld the right of a citizen of one state to sue another state in federal court. The states were shocked by this challenge to their sovereignty, and a constitutional amendment to overturn the decision quickly made its way through Congress. By 1795, the Eleventh Amendment had been ratified and citizens could no longer sue a state (in federal court) in which they did not live.[23]

How judges are selected

Although the Constitution provides detailed stipulations for serving in Congress and as president, it does not specify requirements for serving on the federal courts. Federal judges don't even have to have a law degree! (This is probably due to the limited number of law schools at the time of the Founding; when the Constitution was written, someone who wanted to be a lawyer generally would serve as an apprentice in a law office to learn the trade.) The president appoints federal judges with the "advice and consent" of the Senate, which in practice means that the Senate must approve the nominees with a majority vote.

Nomination battles for federal judges can be intense, because the stakes are high: the Supreme Court plays a central role in the policy process, and because justices have life tenure, a justice's impact can outlive the president and Senate who put him or her on the Court. Justices often serve for decades, much longer than the people who appoint them.

The Role of the President Given the Constitution's silence on the qualifications of federal judges, presidents have broad discretion over whom to nominate. Presidents have always tried to influence the direction of the federal courts, especially the Supreme Court, by picking people who share their views. Because the Senate often has different ideas about the proper direction for the Court, nomination disputes end up being a combination of debates over the merit of a nominee and partisan battles about the ideological composition of the Court.

DID YOU KNOW?

47

of the 113 people to serve on the Supreme Court have had law degrees. However, all since 1957 have had law degrees, and all of the current Court justices attended either Harvard or Yale law school.

Source: SupremeCourt.gov

Although presidents would *like* to influence the direction of the Court, it is not always possible to predict how judges will behave once they are on the bench. Earl Warren is a good example. He was appointed by Republican president Dwight Eisenhower and had been the Republican governor of California, yet he turned out to be one of the most liberal chief justices of the last century. Eisenhower called Warren's nomination the biggest mistake he ever made.[24]

Nonetheless, the president can make a good guess about how a justice is likely to vote based on the nominee's party affiliation and the nature of his or her legal writings and decisions (if the nominee has prior judicial experience). Not surprisingly, 103 of 113 justices who have served on the Court have shared the nominating president's party (91 percent). Overall, more than 90 percent of the lower-court judges appointed by presidents in the twentieth century have also belonged to the same party as the president.

President Trump, who nominated Judge Neil Gorsuch to the Supreme Court, watches as Supreme Court Justice Anthony Kennedy swears him in during a ceremony in the Rose Garden of the White House.

The most partisan move to influence the Court was President Franklin Delano Roosevelt's infamous plan to pack the Court. FDR was frustrated because the Court had struck down several pieces of important New Deal legislation, so to get a more sympathetic Court, he proposed nominating a new justice for every justice who was over 70 years old. At the time, six justices were over 70, so this would have increased the size of the Court to 15 justices. Roosevelt's effort to disguise the partisan power play as a humanitarian gesture (to help the old-timers with their workload) didn't fool anyone. The plan to pack the Court ran into opposition, but once the Court started ruling in favor of the New Deal legislation, the plan was dropped.

In addition to the ideological considerations about whom to nominate, the president also considers the individual's reputation as a legal scholar and his or her personal relationship to the candidate. Further considerations are the candidate's ethical standards, religion, gender, and race (see Figure 14.1). The religion of justices has undergone a complete transformation: for the nation's first 125 years, nearly all justices were Protestants. Now there are five Catholic justices, three Jewish justices, and one unknown (Gorsuch was raised Catholic but most recently attended an Episcopal church).[25] Over time, the federal courts have steadily become more diverse in terms of race and gender. However, Donald Trump is reversing this trend. Of his first 87

FIGURE
14.1

Race and Gender on Federal Circuit Courts

Since the 1980s, the proportion of women on the federal bench has gone up fivefold while the percentage of white men has plummeted by more than half. Do you think that descriptive representation in the judicial branch is important?

Number and percentage of U.S. Circuit Court nominees by gender in president's first year in office

Number and percentage of U.S. Circuit Court nominees by race in president's first year in office

Source: Barry J. McMillion, "U.S. Circuit and District Court Nominations during President Trump's First Year in Office: Comparative Analysis with Recent Presidents," Congressional Research Service, May 2, 2018, https://fas.org/sgp/crs/misc/R45189.pdf (accessed 10/19/18).

nominees to the federal courts, only one was African American and only one was Latino. Judges' demographic backgrounds also became an issue in the 2016 campaign when Trump said that federal district judge Gonzalo P. Curiel could not be objective in the lawsuit concerning Trump University because Curiel was a Mexican (the judge was born in Indiana and his parents are from Mexico).

The Role of the Senate The Senate is the other half of the equation that determines the composition of the federal courts. The Senate has shifted from a very active role in providing "advice and consent" on court appointments to a passive role and then back to an active role. One constant is that the Senate rarely rejects nominees because of their qualifications; rather, it tends to reject them for political reasons. Of 28 Supreme Court nominees rejected by the Senate in the history of the United States, only 2 were turned down because they were seen as unqualified. Serious questions were also raised about a third justice, Clarence Thomas, who had served for only 18 months as a federal judge before being nominated to the Court. Thomas also was accused of sexual harassment by former colleague Anita Hill. Hill's testimony in 1991 predates the #MeToo movement by 26 years and brought sexual harassment into the public limelight for the first time. There were only two women in the Senate at the time and the unsympathetic hearing she received before the all-male Senate Judiciary Committee helped produce the "Year of the Woman" in House and Senate races the next year (there are now 23 women in the Senate, an all-time high). Nonetheless, Thomas ultimately won confirmation by a 52–48 vote, the second-narrowest successful margin in history. The other 26 nominees were rejected for political reasons. Most commonly, when a president makes a nomination close to an election and the Senate is controlled by the opposing party, the Senate will kill the nomination, hoping that its party will win the presidency and nominate a justice more to its liking.

Throughout the nineteenth century, the Senate was very willing to turn down Court nominations for political reasons. In fact, between 1793 and 1894 the Senate did not confirm 21 nominees to the Court, which was about a third of the total number nominated. In contrast, between 1894 and 1968 the Senate did not even require nominees to testify and during that period only 4 nominees were rejected.

A rethinking of this passive role occurred in the late 1960s. President Nixon vowed to pull the Court back from the "liberal excesses" of the Warren Court, but the Senate stiffened its spine and rejected two conservative nominees in a row: Clement Haynsworth (in 1969) and G. Harrold Carswell (in 1970). With Haynsworth, there were ethical problems involving his participation in cases in which he had a financial interest. Carswell had a mediocre judicial record, and civil rights groups raised questions about his commitment to enforcing antidiscrimination laws. Nixon must have thought that the Senate wouldn't reject his choice twice in a row! The most recent Senate rejection was of Judge Robert Bork, a brilliant, very conservative, and controversial figure. Liberal interest groups mobilized against him, and the Senate rejected him by the widest margin of any nominee since 1846 (the vote was 42 to 58), giving the English language a new verb: to get "borked" means to have your character and record challenged in a very public way. The Senate's unwillingness to even consider President Obama's nomination of Merrick Garland to the Supreme Court to fill the vacancy left by Justice Antonin Scalia's death in February 2016 may signal a return to the more politicized era of Supreme Court nominations in the nineteenth century, especially given that the strategy worked. Garland was picked to appeal to moderates in the Senate, but the Republican leadership decided to leave the seat open for the rest of Obama's presidency in an unprecedented move. The gamble paid off when Trump won the presidency and nominated Neil Gorsuch, who was approved by a 54-45 vote in the Senate.[26] Brett Kavanaugh, whose confirmation was more contentious due to sexual assault allegations, was ultimately confirmed in a 50-48 vote.

Yet not all recent Supreme Court nominations have been controversial. President Bill Clinton's two Supreme Court picks were judicial moderates who were overwhelmingly confirmed—Ruth Bader Ginsburg by a 96-3 vote and Stephen Breyer by an 87-9 vote. George W. Bush's nominees, John G. Roberts Jr. and Samuel Alito Jr., were confirmed by comfortable margins. President Obama appointed the first Latina to serve on the Supreme Court, Sonia Sotomayor, who was confirmed by a 68-31 vote. Elena Kagan's confirmation by a 63-37 vote in 2010 meant that three women were serving on the Court for the first time.

Battles over Lower-Court Judges The contentious battles between the president and the Senate over nominees to the federal bench and the Supreme Court have recently expanded to include nominees to the district and appeals courts. For much of the nation's history, the president did not play a very active role in the nomination process for district courts, instead deferring to the home-state senators of the president's party to suggest candidates—a norm called **senatorial courtesy**. If neither senator from the state was from the president's party, he would consult House members from his party and other high-ranking party members from the state for district court nominees. The president typically has shown more interest in appeals court nominations. The Justice Department plays a key role in screening candidates, but the local senators of the president's party remain active as well through the "blue slip" process: home-state senators record their support or opposition to nominees on blue slips of paper. Some committee chairs have allowed a single home-state senator to use the blue slip to veto a nominee, but others have not followed the process so strictly.

senatorial courtesy
A norm in the nomination of district court judges in which the president consults with his or her party's senators from the relevant state in choosing the nominee.

FIGURE 14.2

Average Confirmation Delay for Uncontroversial Federal Court Nominations, 1981–2012

Since the 1980s, the length of time needed to confirm federal court nominations has increased dramatically. Why do you think this happened? Why does it matter?

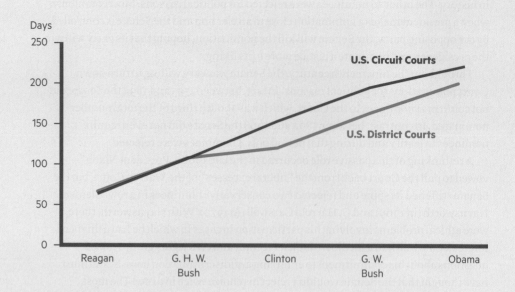

Note: "Uncontroversial" nominees are those who were reported from the Judiciary Committee by a voice vote or a unanimous vote and were confirmed by the Senate with a voice vote or no more than five votes in opposition.

Source: Barry J. McMillion, "Length of Time from Nomination to Confirmation for 'Uncontroversial' U.S. Circuit and District Court Nominees: Detailed Analysis," Congressional Research Service, September 18, 2012, http://fas.org (accessed 6/25/14).

President Obama nominated Judge Merrick Garland (right) to the Supreme Court. Here, the nominee meets with Senator Cory Booker (D-NJ). Judge Garland, however, was not confirmed prior to the end of Obama's term, and in 2017, President Trump nominated Judge Gorsuch to fill the vacancy left by Justice Scalia's death.

Recently the process has become much more contentious. While the confirmation rate for federal judges has been relatively stable in the past 35 years (between 80 and 90 percent), the average time to confirm nominees has increased dramatically. The average length of delay from nomination to confirmation has increased from a little over 50 days in the 1980s to over 200 days in recent years (see Figure 14.2 for data on noncontroversial nominations; when all nominations are included, the waits are even longer, especially for George W. Bush's nominees), and the situation has intensified. Democrats blocked 39 of President Bush's nominees between 2001 and 2009,[27] and Republicans returned the favor during Obama's presidency by blocking dozens of his nominees, which included employing a record number of filibusters of lower-court nominees. After the Senate blocked three nominees to the D.C. Court of Appeals, the second-most-important court in the nation, Democrats responded in November 2013 by eliminating the filibuster on lower-court and executive branch nominations but not Supreme Court nominations.[28] This move was originally labeled the "nuclear option" by Democrats who had threatened to shut down the Senate if the Republican leadership got rid of the filibuster during the George W. Bush presidency. In response to the detonation of the nuclear option, the confirmation process slowed to a trickle in President Obama's last year, which produced a near-record level of vacancies (more than 10 percent of all federal judgeships). With unified control of government for the first time since 2009, Republicans moved quickly to fill many of those vacancies and approve Trump's nominations. To approve Neil Gorsuch's nomination, Senate Republicans eliminated the filibuster on Supreme Court nominations. They also approved a record number of appeals court nominees in Trump's first year (12). However, there are still 95 vacancies on the federal bench without nominees.[29]

Although there is no definitive answer as to how active the Senate should be in giving "advice and consent," it is clear that the Founders intended the Senate to play an active role. The first draft of the Constitution gave the Senate the sole power to appoint Supreme Court justices. However, the final version made appointment a shared power with the president. It was not expected that the Senate would compete with the president over whom to nominate, but it *was* assumed that the Senate would exercise independent judgment as to the suitability of the president's nominees.

"Why Should I Care?"

It is safe to assume that most Americans do not follow the details of battles over court nominations. However, these battles are every bit as important as the elections that *do* capture much attention. Unelected judges often serve for 20 or 30 years, much longer than the average member of Congress, and have the power to strike down laws that Congress passes. Confirmation battles also support our argument that politics is conflictual and that we should expect it to be that way. The Founders certainly did not expect that the process would be free of politics or that the Senate would be an essentially passive and subordinate player in a nominally joint enterprise. Even George Washington had two of his nominations turned down by the Senate for political reasons. Therefore, politics will continue to play an important role in deciding who serves on the federal bench.

Access to the Supreme Court

★

DESCRIBE HOW CASES REACH THE SUPREME COURT

It is extremely difficult to have a case heard by the Supreme Court. Currently the Court hears just over 1 percent of the cases submitted (71 of 6,305 cases in the most recent completed term).[30] This section explains how the Court decides which cases to hear. When a case is submitted, the clerk of the Court assigns it a number and places it on the docket, which is the schedule of cases.

The Court's workload

Statistics on the Supreme Court's workload initially suggest that the size of the docket has increased dramatically since the 1970s (see Figure 14.3). However, a majority of cases are frivolous and are dismissed after limited review. The Court has become increasingly impatient with these frivolous petitions and has moved to prevent "frequent filers" from harassing the Court. One often-cited case involved Michael Sindram, who asked the Court to order the Maryland courts to remove a $35 traffic ticket from his record. Our favorite example concerned a wealthy drug dealer, Frederick W. Bauer, who was convicted on 10 counts of dealing drugs and petitioned the Court 12 times on various issues. The justices finally had enough and directed "the Clerk not to accept any further petitions for certiorari or petitions for extraordinary writs from Bauer in noncriminal matters" unless he paid his docketing fees. They concluded that the order will allow this Court to focus on "petitioners who have not abused our processes."[31]

FIGURE 14.3

The Court Sees More Opportunities ... but Hears Fewer Cases

The Supreme Court's workload appears to be headed in two directions: the Court is receiving more cases but hearing fewer of them. What are the implications of having the Supreme Court hear fewer cases? Should something be done to try to get the Court to hear more cases?

Source: Data compiled from "Chief Justice's Year-End Reports on the Federal Judiciary," www.supremecourt.gov (accessed 3/14/18).

Although the increase in workload is not as significant as it appears due to the high number of frivolous cases, another change is more important: the number of opinions issued by the Court has fallen by more than half in the past 20 years. The Court heard roughly 150 cases a year through the 1980s, but this number has fallen to only 65 to 85 cases in recent years (see Figure 14.3).[32] The change is even more dramatic when one considers that the Court has reduced the number of "summary decisions" it issues (cases that do not receive a full hearing but on which the Court issues a decision anyway) from 150 a year in the 1970s to a handful today. The number of summary judgments declined when Congress gave the Court more control over its docket and dramatically reduced the number of cases that it was *required* to hear on appeal. However, there is no good explanation for why the Court issues half as many opinions as it used to, other than that the chief justices have decided that the Court shouldn't issue so many opinions. The lower number of cases heard in the 2016–2017 term was partly explained by the vacancy created by Justice Scalia's death. Because of the potential 4–4 deadlock, justices were unwilling to take on some cases until they were back to full strength.[33]

Rules of access

With the smaller number of cases being heard, it is even more important to understand how the Court decides which cases to consider. There are four paths that a case may take to get to the Supreme Court. First, Article III of the Constitution specifies that the Court has original jurisdiction in cases involving a foreign ambassador or foreign countries or cases in which a state is a party. As a practical matter, the Court shares jurisdiction with the lower courts on these issues.

In recent years, the Court has invoked original jurisdiction only in cases involving disputes between two or more states over territorial or natural resource issues. For example, New Jersey and New York had a disagreement about which state should control 24 acres of filled land that the federal government had added around Ellis Island. Another case involved a dispute between Kansas and Colorado over which state should have access to water from the Arkansas River (recent disputes often concern water rights).[34] If original jurisdiction is granted and there are factual issues to be resolved, the Court will appoint a "special master" (usually a retired federal judge) to hold a hearing, gather evidence, and make a recommendation to the Court. This process is necessary because the Supreme Court is not a trial court. In the history of our nation, only about 190 cases have made it to the Court through this path, an average of less than 1 per year, and typically these cases do not have any broader significance beyond the parties involved.[35]

The other three routes to the Court are all on appeal: as a matter of right (usually called "on appeal"), through certification (a process that has been used only five times since 1982),[36] or through a writ of *certiorari*. Cases on appeal are those that Congress has determined to be so important that the Supreme Court must hear them. Before 1988, these cases constituted a larger share of the Court's docket and they included (1) cases in which a lower court declared a state or federal law unconstitutional and (2) cases in which a state court upheld a state law that had been challenged as unconstitutional under the U.S. Constitution. The Court currently has much more discretion on these cases, however; the only ones that the Court is still compelled to take on appeal are some voting rights and redistricting cases.

The third path is the most common: at least 95 percent of the cases in most sessions arrive through a **writ of *certiorari*** (from the Latin "to be informed"). In these cases, a litigant who lost in lower court can file a petition to the Supreme Court explaining why the Court should hear the case. If four justices agree, the case will get a full hearing (this

writ of *certiorari*
The most common way for a case to reach the Supreme Court, in which at least four of the nine justices agree to hear a case that has reached them via an appeal from the losing party in a lower court's ruling.

is called, reasonably enough, the Rule of Four). This process may sound simple, but sifting through the 7,000 or so cases that the Court receives every year and deciding which 75 of them will be heard is daunting. Former justice William O. Douglas said that this winnowing process is "in many respects the most important and interesting of all our functions."[37]

The Court's criteria

How does the Court decide which cases to hear? Several factors come into play, including the specific characteristics of the case and the broader politics surrounding it. Although several criteria generally must be met before the Court will hear the case, justices still have leeway in defining the boundaries of these conditions.

Collusion, Standing, and Mootness First, there are the constitutional guidelines, which are sparse. The Constitution limits the Court to hearing actual "cases and controversies," which has been interpreted to mean that the Court cannot offer advisory opinions about hypothetical situations but must deal with actual cases. The term "actual controversy" also includes several other concepts that limit whether a case will be heard: collusion, standing, and mootness. *Collusion* simply means that the litigants in the case cannot want the same outcome and cannot be testing the law without an actual dispute between the two parties.[38]

Standing, as we noted earlier, means that the party bringing the case must have a personal stake in the outcome. The Court has discretion in defining standing: it may hear cases that it thinks are important even when the plaintiff may not have standing as traditionally understood, or it may avoid hearing cases that may be politically sensitive on the grounds that there is no standing. In an example of the former, the Court decided several important racial redistricting cases even when the white plaintiffs had not suffered any personal harm by being in the black-majority districts.[39] In an example of the latter, the Court decided not to hear a politically sensitive case involving the Pledge of Allegiance and the First Amendment, saying that the father of the student who brought the case did not have standing because he did not have sufficient custody over his daughter (he was divorced and the mother had primary custody).[40] Clearly, the Court was more eager to voice its views on redistricting than on the Pledge of Allegiance, because it could have just as easily avoided hearing the former case by saying the plaintiffs did not have standing and taken up the latter case despite the concern over custody (it was his daughter after all, which should have given him some stake!). This is an important point to consider: the Court often avoids hearing a controversial case based on a "threshold" issue like standing and then does not have to decide on the merits of the case.

A controversy must still be relevant when the Court hears the case; **mootness** occurs when a case is irrelevant by the time it is brought before a federal court. Nonetheless, there are exceptions to this principle, because some types of cases are necessarily moot by the time they get to the Supreme Court. For example, exceptions have been made for abortion cases because a pregnancy lasts only nine months, and it always takes longer than that for a case to get from district court to the appeals court to the Supreme Court.

Thousands of cases every year meet these basic criteria. One very simple guideline eliminates the largest number of cases: if a case does not involve a "substantial federal question," it will not be heard. This essentially means that the Court does not have to hear a case if the justices do not think it is important enough. Of course, the "federal" part of this standard is also important: if a case is governed by state law rather than federal law, the Court will decline to hear the case unless there are constitutional

mootness
The irrelevance of a case by the time it is received by a federal court, causing the Supreme Court to decline to hear the case.

Deciding to Hear a Case in the Supreme Court

Rule 10 of the *Rules of the U.S. Supreme Court* says that a case is more likely to be heard when

- there is conflict between appeals court opinions or between a state supreme court opinion and another state supreme court on an important federal question,
- there is conflict between a federal appeals court and a state supreme court on an important federal question,
- a lower-court decision has "departed from the accepted and usual course of judicial proceedings,"
- a state supreme court or appeals court has ruled on a substantial federal question that has not yet been addressed by the Court, or
- a state supreme court or appeals court ruling conflicts with Supreme Court precedent.

Rule 10 also states that *certiorari* is unlikely to be granted when "the asserted error consists of erroneous factual findings or the misapplication of a properly stated rule of law."

Source: U.S. Supreme Court, *Rules of the U.S. Supreme Court*, adopted April 19, 2013, effective July 1, 2013, www.supremecourt.gov/ctrules/2013RulesoftheCourt.pdf (accessed 5/27/16).

implications. The "political question doctrine" is another basis upon which the Court may decide not to hear a case (as we'll discuss in more detail later, these are cases that the Court thinks are better handled by the elected branches of government). After considering all of these criteria, 20 to 30 percent of the cases originally submitted for the Court's consideration are left. These cases are then winnowed to the final list with the more specific guidance of Rule 10 in the Supreme Court rules (see Nuts & Bolts 14.2). Of the criteria listed in Rule 10, conflict between appeals court decisions is most likely to produce a Supreme Court hearing.

Internal politics

Not much is known about the actual discussions that determine which cases will be heard by the Court. The justices meet in conference with no staff or clerks. Leaks are rare, but a few insider accounts and the papers of retired justices provide some insights to the process. First, since the late 1970s most justices have used a **cert pool**, whereby their law clerks take a first cut at the cases. Law clerks to the justices are top graduates of elite law schools who help justices with background research at several stages of the process. Clerks write joint memos about groups of cases, providing their recommendations about which cases should be heard. The ultimate decisions are up to the justices, but clerks have significant power to help shape the agenda.

Second, the chief justice has an important agenda-setting power: he or she decides the "discuss list" for a given day. Any justice can add a case to the list, but there is no systematic evidence on how often this happens. Only 20 to 30 percent of the cases are discussed in conference, which means that about three-quarters of the cases that are submitted to the Supreme Court are never even discussed by the justices. The decision not to discuss certain cases is often justified because of the high proportion of frivolous suits submitted to the Court.[41]

Many factors outside the legal requirements or internal processes of the Court influence access to the Court and which cases will be heard. Cases that have generated a lot of activity from interest groups or other governmental parties, such as the solicitor general, are more likely to be heard. The **solicitor general** is a presidential appointee who works in the Justice Department and supervises the litigation of the executive branch. In cases in which the federal government is a party, the solicitor

cert pool
A system initiated in the Supreme Court in the 1970s in which law clerks screen cases that come to the Supreme Court and recommend to the justices which cases should be heard.

Law clerks, such as those seen here with Justice Clarence Thomas, often take a first cut at the cases and help justices with background research.

solicitor general
A presidential appointee in the Justice Department who conducts all litigation on behalf of the federal government before the Supreme Court and supervises litigation in the federal appellate courts.

general or someone else from that office will represent the government in court. The Court accepts about 70 to 80 percent of cases in which the U.S. government is a party, compared with about 1 percent overall.[42]

Even with these influences, the Court has a great deal of discretion as to which cases it hears. Well-established practices such as standing and mootness may be ignored (or modified) if the Court wants to hear a specific case. However, one final point is important: although the justices may pick and choose their cases, they cannot completely set their own agenda. They can select only from the cases that come to them.

DESCRIBE THE SUPREME COURT'S PROCEDURES FOR HEARING A CASE

Hearing cases before the Supreme Court

A surprisingly small proportion of the Court's time—only about 37 days per term—is actually spent hearing cases. The Court's term extends from the first Monday in October through the end of June. It hears cases on Mondays through Wednesdays in alternating two-week cycles in which it is in session from 10 A.M. to 3 P.M., with a one-hour break for lunch. In the two weeks of the cycle when it is not in session, justices review briefs, write opinions, and sift through the next batch of petitions. On most Fridays during the Court's term, the justices meet in conference to discuss cases that have been argued and decide which cases they will hear. Opinions are released throughout the term, but the bulk of them come in May and June.[43]

The Court is in recess from July through September. Justices may take some vacation, but they mostly use the time for study, reading, writing, and preparing for the next term. During the summer, the Court also considers emergency petitions (such as stays of execution) and occasionally hears important cases. For example, on September 9, 2009 (nearly a month before the fall session started), the Court heard a challenge to the Bipartisan Campaign Reform Act, more commonly known as the McCain–Feingold Act after its two principal sponsors. Congress urged the Court to give the law a speedy review, given its importance for the upcoming 2010 elections. In the blockbuster case *Citizens United v. Federal Election Commission*, the Supreme Court decided that independent spending in campaigns by corporations and labor unions is protected by the First Amendment.

Briefs

During its regular sessions, the Court follows rigidly set routines. The justices prepare for a case by reading the briefs submitted by both parties. Because the Supreme Court hears only appeals, it does not call witnesses or gather new evidence. Instead, in structured briefs of no more than 50 pages the parties present their arguments about why they either support the lower-court decision or believe the case was improperly decided. Interest groups often submit **amicus curiae** ("friend of the court") briefs that convey their opinions to the Court; in fact, 85 percent of cases before the Supreme Court have at least one amicus brief.[44] The federal government also files amicus briefs on important issues such as school busing, school prayer, abortion, reapportionment of legislative districts, job discrimination against women and minorities, and affirmative action in higher education.

It is difficult to determine the impact of amicus briefs on the outcome of a case, but those that are filed early in the process increase the chances that the case will

amicus curiae
Latin for "friend of the court," referring to an interested group or person who shares relevant information about a case to help the Court reach a decision.

be heard.[45] Given the limited information that justices have about any given case, interest group involvement can be a strong signal about the importance of a case. There is also some evidence that briefs from the solicitor general have an impact on the outcome of a case.[46]

Oral argument

Once the briefs are filed and have been reviewed by the justices, cases are scheduled for **oral arguments**. Except in unusual circumstances, each case gets one hour, which is divided evenly between the two parties. In especially important cases, extra time may be granted (for example, the case challenging Obamacare had six hours of oral argument, which was the most since a Voting Rights Act case in 1966).[47] Usually there is only one lawyer for each side who presents the case, but parties who have filed amicus briefs may participate if their arguments "would provide assistance to the Court not otherwise available." Given the tight time pressures, the Court is usually unwilling to extend the allotted time to allow "friends of the court" to testify.[48]

The Court is strict about its time limits and uses a system of three lights to show the lawyers how much of their allotted 30 minutes is left. A green light goes on when the speaker's time begins, a white light provides a five-minute warning, and a red light means to stop. Most textbooks cite well-known examples of justices cutting people off in midsentence or walking out of the courtroom as the lawyer drones on. One source implies that these anecdotes are generally revealing of Court procedure, saying: "Anecdotes probably tell as much about the proceeding of the Court during oral argument as does any careful study of the rules and procedures."[49]

HUSTED V. A. PHILIP RANDOLPH INSTITUTE, Eric E. Murphy, State Solicitor for Ohio at lectern 1-10-18

Cameras are not allowed in the Supreme Court, so artists' sketches are the only available images of oral arguments. Depicted here is the oral argument in a 2018 case on Ohio's voter registration laws.

However, having a preference for "careful study" over anecdotes, we were curious about how common it was for justices to strictly impose the time limits. Initially, we examined 42 cases from the 2004–2005 term, using the online transcripts on the Court's website.[50] We found that most lawyers did not use all their allotted time, with 62 percent of the cases coming in under 60 minutes, 17 percent at exactly an hour, and 21 percent at over an hour. One-sixth of the lawyers still had at least five minutes left on the clock. We found only two instances in which a justice cut someone off in midsentence after the person had gone over the half-hour limit. We updated the analysis for the Roberts Court, examining all 74 cases argued in the 2009 calendar year. Roberts was not much of a stickler for adhering to the time limits: nearly 60 percent of oral arguments went past their allotted time (most by only a minute or two), 13.5 percent were exactly one hour, and 27 percent were under an hour. Again, only 2 of the 74 oral arguments ended with an attorney being cut off in midsentence by the chief justice. Thus, while the Court tries to encourage attorneys to stay within the time limits, it is not as draconian as some anecdotes imply.

Some lawyers may not use all their time because their train of thought is interrupted by aggressive questioning. Transcripts reveal that justices jump in with questions almost immediately and some attorneys never regain their footing. The frequency and pointedness of the questions vary by justice, with Justices Breyer, Roberts, and Sotomayor being the most aggressive on the current Court. Justice Thomas went more than 10 years without asking a single question but broke his streak in 2016, perhaps feeling the need to fill the void created by the death of Justice Scalia.[51] Cameras are not allowed in the courtroom, so most Americans have never seen the Court in action—although a small live audience is admitted every morning the Court is in session. If you are curious about oral arguments, audio recordings of every case since 1995 are available at www.oyez.org.

Conference

After oral arguments, the justices meet in conference to discuss and then vote on the cases. As with the initial conferences, these meetings are conducted in secret. We know, based on notes in the personal papers of retired justices, that the conferences are orderly and structured but can become quite heated. The justices take turns discussing the cases and outlining the reasons for their positions. Justice Thurgood Marshall described the decision-making process in conference and the need for secrecy as

> *a continuing conversation among nine distinct individuals on dozens of issues simultaneously. The exchanges are serious, sometimes scholarly, occasionally brash and personalized, but generally well-reasoned and most often cast in understated, genteel language.... In other cases, a majority of justices start down one path, only to reverse direction.... This is the kind of internal debate that the justices have argued should remain confidential, taking the position that only their final opinions have legal authority. They have expressed concern that premature disclosure of their private debates and doubts may undermine the Court's credibility and inhibit their exchange of ideas.[52]*

Opinion writing

After the justices indicate how they are likely to vote on a case, if the chief justice is in the majority (which is most of the time), the chief justice decides who will write the majority opinion. Otherwise, the most senior justice in the majority assigns the opinion. Several considerations determine how a case will be assigned. First, the chief justice will try to ensure the smooth operation of the Court by trying to equalize the number of cases across the nine justices. John Roberts has been especially careful to spread out the workload evenly.[53] A second factor is the justices' individual areas of expertise. For example, Justice Harry Blackmun had developed expertise in medical law when he was in private practice. This experience played a role in Chief Justice Burger's decision to assign Blackmun the majority opinion in the landmark abortion decision *Roe v. Wade* (1973). Likewise, Justice Sandra Day O'Connor developed expertise in racial redistricting cases and authored most of those decisions in the 1990s, while Justice Samuel Alito has specialized in criminal justice cases in recent years.[54]

Strategy on the Court Other factors in how opinions are assigned are more strategic, taking into account the Court's external relations, internal relations, and the personal policy goals of the opinion assigner. The Court must be sensitive to how others might respond to its decisions because it must rely on the other branches of government to enforce them. One famous example of this consideration in an opinion assignment came in a case from the 1940s that struck down a practice that had prevented African Americans from voting in Democratic primaries.[55] Originally, the opinion was assigned to Justice Felix Frankfurter, but Justice Robert Jackson wrote a memo suggesting that it might be unwise to have a liberal, politically independent Jew from the Northeast write an opinion that was sure to be controversial in the South. Chief Justice Harlan Fiske Stone agreed and reassigned the opinion to Justice Stanley Reed, a Protestant and Democrat from Kentucky.[56] It may not seem that the Court is sensitive to public opinion, but these kinds of considerations happen fairly frequently in important cases. Internal considerations occasionally cause justices to vote strategically—differently from their sincere preferences—so they can put themselves in the majority. If they are the most senior justice in the majority, they then have the power to assign the opinion, and they often assign it to themselves.

Justices may also assign opinions to further their own personal policy goals. The most obvious strategy is for the chief justice to assign opinions to justices who are closest to his or her position. This practice is constrained by the chief justice's responsibility to ensure the smooth operation of the Court. If the chief justice assigned all the opinions to the justices who are closest to him or her ideologically, then justices with other ideological leanings would get a chance to write opinions only in the 15 to 20 percent of cases in which the chief is in the minority. However, Chief Justice Roberts has allocated the most important cases to his ideological allies and has taken about twice as many of the most important cases for himself (compared to what would have been expected by chance).[57] Charles Hughes, chief justice from 1930 to 1941, sometimes assigned opinions on liberal decisions to conservative justices and cases with conservative outcomes to liberal justices in order to downplay the importance of ideology on the Court.[58]

After the opinions are assigned, the justices work on writing a draft opinion. Law clerks typically help with this process. Some justices insist on writing all of their opinions, whereas others allow a clerk to write the first draft. The drafts are circulated to the other justices for comments and reactions. Some bargaining may occur, in which a justice says he or she will withdraw support unless a provision of the opinion is changed. Justices may join the majority opinion, may write a separate concurring opinion, or may dissent (see Nuts & Bolts 14.3 for details on the types of opinions).

Dissents Two final points about the process of writing and issuing opinions are important. First, until 1940, there was a premium placed on unanimous decisions. John Marshall, who was chief justice from 1800 to 1835, started this practice. Through the 1930s, about 80 to 90 percent of decisions were unanimous. This changed dramatically in the 1940s, when most cases had at least one dissent. In recent decades, about two-thirds of cases have had a dissent.[59] However, in the 2013–2014 term two-thirds of the cases were unanimous, the highest proportion since at least 1946. That proportion fell

Chief Justice John Roberts (right) stands with Associate Justices Elena Kagan and Stephen Breyer as they await the arrival of President Trump before his State of the Union address.

So that's the dissenter's hope: that they are writing not for today but for tomorrow.

—Justice Ruth Bader Ginsburg

NUTS & BOLTS 14.3

Types of Supreme Court Decisions

- **Majority opinion:** The core decision of the Court that must be agreed upon by at least five justices. The majority opinion presents the legal reasoning for the Court's decision.

- **Concurring opinion:** Written by a justice who agrees with the outcome of the case but not with part of the legal reasoning. Concurring opinions may be joined by other justices. A justice may sign on to the majority opinion and write a separate concurring opinion.

- **Plurality opinion:** Occurs when a majority cannot agree on the legal reasoning in a case. The plurality opinion is the one that has the most agreement (usually three or four justices). Because of the fractured nature of these opinions, they typically are not viewed as having as much clout as majority opinions.

- **Dissent:** Submitted by a justice who disagrees with the outcome of the case. Other justices can sign on to a dissent or write their own, so there can be as many as four dissents. Justices can also sign on to part of a dissent but not the entire opinion.

- **Per curiam (Latin for "by the court") opinion:** An unsigned opinion of the Court or a decision written by the entire Court. However, this is not the same as a unanimous decision that is signed by the entire Court. Per curiam opinions are usually very short opinions on noncontroversial issues, but not always. For example, *Bush v. Gore*, which decided the outcome of the 2000 presidential election, was a per curiam opinion. Per curiam decisions may also have dissents.

to 39 percent in the 2017–2018 term.[60] Second, dissents serve an important purpose. Not only do they allow the minority view to be expressed, but they also often provide the basis later on for reversing a poorly reasoned case. When justices strongly oppose the majority opinion, they may take the unusual step of reading a portion of the dissent from the bench.

"Why Should I Care?"

The process of hearing cases before the Court, including the written briefs, oral arguments, discussions in conference, and opinion assignment, is a very political one. As discussed in the chapter opener, it may be disturbing to think of the Court as a political institution that bargains and considers external forces like public opinion. Although justices do not have to answer to voters, they are still sensitive to a broad range of considerations in hearing cases.

★

ANALYZE THE FACTORS THAT INFLUENCE SUPREME COURT DECISIONS

Supreme Court decision making

Judicial decision making is influenced by many different factors, but the two main categories are *legal* and *political*. Legal factors include the precedents of earlier cases and the norm that justices must follow the language of the Constitution. Political influences include the justices' preferences or ideologies, their stances on whether the Court should take a restrained or activist role with respect to the elected branches, and external factors such as public opinion and interest group involvement. Most observers of the Court recognize that both legal and political factors are important in explaining judicial decision making, but some stake out a view more strongly on one side or the other. Some scholars argue, for example, that all Court behavior is political and that the use of legal factors is just a smoke screen for hiding personal preferences. The fact that there are differences of opinion as to which factors are most important can often make empirical arguments—those that describe the way decisions are made—evolve into normative arguments—those about the way that justices *should* behave. These different perspectives about how justices make decisions may also lead to arguments about the proper role of the Court within our political system, which we will explore in the next section.

Legal factors

Legal factors embody the image we cited at the beginning of the chapter of Lady Justice neutrally applying the law while fairly balancing various interests. While this ideal image is incomplete, legal factors do independently influence judicial decision making on a broad range of cases.

Precedent The most basic legal factor is precedent, discussed earlier. Precedent does not determine the outcome of any given case, because every case has a range of precedents that can serve to justify a justice's decision. The "easy" cases, in which settled law makes the outcome obvious, are less likely to be heard by the Court because of the justices' desire to focus on the more controversial areas of unsettled law or cases in which there is conflict between lower courts' decisions. However, in some areas of the law—such as free speech, the death penalty, and search and seizure—precedent is an important explanation for how the justices decide a case.

The Language of the Constitution The Constitution is the obvious starting point for any Supreme Court case that involves a Constitutional right.[61] However, there are various perspectives on exactly how, and to what degree, the language of the Constitution can and should influence judicial decision making today.

People in one camp argue that the *language* used in the Constitution is the most important guiding factor. Their perspectives fall under the heading of **strict construction**. The most basic of these is the literalist view of the Constitution. Sometimes this view is called a textualist position because it sees the text of the document as determining the outcome of any given case. Literalists argue that justices need to look no further than the actual words of the Constitution.

Justice Hugo Black was one of the most famous advocates of the literalist position. When the First Amendment says that "Congress shall make no law ... abridging the freedom of speech," that literally means *no* law. Justice Black said, "My view is, without deviation, without exception, without any ifs, buts, or whereases, that freedom of speech means that government shall not do anything to people ... either for the views they have or the views they express or the words they speak or write."[62] While that may be clear enough with regard to political speech, how about pornography, Internet speech, or symbolic speech, such as burning an American flag or wearing an armband to protest the Vietnam War? A literal interpretation of the Constitution does not necessarily help determine whether these forms of speech should be restricted. (Indeed, Black was one of the two dissenters in a case that upheld students' right to wear armbands as a form of symbolic speech. Black believed that school officials should be allowed to decide whether a symbolic protest would be too disruptive in the classroom and argued that only spoken and written speech should be afforded the

strict construction
A way of interpreting the Constitution based on its language alone.

strongest protection of the First Amendment. So much for "without deviation, without exception" concerning restricting expression of the "views … [people] have"!)

Critics of strict construction also point out that the Constitution is silent on many important points (such as a right to privacy) and could not have anticipated the many legal implications of changes in technology in the twentieth and twenty-first centuries, such as eavesdropping devices, cloning, and the Internet. Also, although the language of the First Amendment is relatively clear when it comes to political speech, other equally important words of the Constitution such as "necessary and proper," "executive power," "equal protection," and "due process" are open-ended and vague.

Some strict constructionists respond by arguing that, if the words of the Constitution are not clear, the justices should be guided by what the Founders *intended* by the words, a perspective called the **original intent** or originalist perspective. Clarence Thomas is the current justice who is most influenced by this view, especially on issues of federalism.

original intent
The theory that justices should surmise the intentions of the Founders when the language of the Constitution is unclear.

Mary Beth Tinker and two other students in the Des Moines, Iowa, public schools were suspended for wearing armbands to protest the Vietnam War. The Supreme Court ruled in *Tinker v. Des Moines Independent Community School District* (1969) that the First Amendment protected symbolic political speech, even in public schools. Mary Beth is shown here with her mother and brother.

Justice Antonin Scalia had a similar view, arguing that the text of the Constitution should be closely followed and, if the text is ambiguous, justices should figure out what the words generally meant to people at the time they were written. This view led Scalia to some unpopular positions, such as his view that the Sixth Amendment provision that "in all criminal prosecutions the accused shall enjoy the right … to be confronted with the witnesses against him" applies even in the case of an accused child molester. The majority of the Court disagreed and held that it was acceptable to have the child testify in front of the prosecutor and defense attorney, with the judge, the jury, and the accused viewing from another room over closed-circuit television because of the potential trauma the child would experience by having to confront the defendant face-to-face.[63]

Those in the other camp are often described as supporting a **living Constitution** perspective on the document (see Chapter 2). They argue that originalism or other versions of strict construction can "make a nation the prisoner of its past, and reject any constitutional development save constitutional amendment."[64] If the justices are bound to follow the literal words of the Constitution, *with the meaning they had when*

living Constitution
A way of interpreting the Constitution that takes into account evolving national attitudes and circumstances rather than the text alone.

the document was written, we certainly could be legally frozen in time. The option of amending the Constitution is a long and difficult process, so that is not always a viable way for the Constitution to reflect changing norms and values. Justice William Brennan, a critic of originalism, also argued it was "arrogance cloaked in humility" to presume to know what the framers intended. According to this view, interpreting the Constitution is always somewhat subjective and it is misleading to claim otherwise.[65]

Political factors

The living Constitution perspective points to the second set of influences on Supreme Court decision making: political factors. Indeed, many people are uncomfortable thinking about the Court in political terms and prefer to think of the image of "blind justice," in which constitutional principles are fairly applied. However, political influences are clearly evident in the Court—maybe less than in Congress or the presidency, but they are certainly present. This means that the courts respond to and shape politics in ways that often involve compromise, both within the courts themselves and in the broader political system.

Political Ideology and Attitudes There is evidence that justices' ideology or attitudes about various issues influence their decisions. Those who argue that this is the most important factor in understanding Supreme Court decision making are said to take an **attitudinalist approach**. Liberal judges are strong defenders of individual civil liberties (including defendants' rights), tend to be pro-choice on abortion, support regulatory policy to protect the environment and workers, support national intervention in the states, and favor race-conscious policies such as affirmative action. Conservative judges favor state regulation of private conduct (especially on moral issues), support prosecutors over defendants, tend to be pro-life on abortion, and support the free market and property rights over the environment and workers, states' rights over national intervention, and a color-blind policy on race. See the What Do the Facts Say? feature for more on how the balance between liberal and conservative judges has shifted.

These are, of course, just general tendencies. However, they do provide a strong basis for explaining patterns of decisions, especially on some types of cases. For example, there were dramatic differences in the chief justices' rulings on civil liberties cases from 1953 to 2001: Earl Warren took the liberal position on 79 percent of the 771 cases he participated in, Warren Burger took the liberal position on 30 percent of 1,429 cases, and William Rehnquist took the liberal position on only 22 percent of his 2,127 cases.[66] If justices were neutrally applying the law, there would not be such dramatic differences.

Proponents of the attitudinalist view also argue that justices who *claim* to be strict constructionists or originalists are really driven by ideology because they selectively use the text of the Constitution. For example, Justice Thomas voted against the University of Michigan's affirmative action program without considering whether the authors of the Fourteenth Amendment supported the practice (the historical record shows that they supported similar policies for the newly freed slaves). Therefore, if Justice Thomas had been true to his originalist perspective, he would have supported affirmative action, but his ideology led him to oppose the policy. The example of Hugo Black's contradictory position on free speech rights cited earlier demonstrates that a liberal textualist view may also be inconsistently applied.

Other Justices' and Politicians' Preferences Another approach to understanding Supreme Court decision making, known as the strategic model, focuses on justices'

The words of the Constitution . . . are so unrestricted by their intrinsic meaning or by their history or by tradition or by prior decisions that they leave the individual Justice free, if indeed they do not compel him, to gather meaning not from reading the Constitution but from reading life.

—Justice Felix Frankfurter

attitudinalist approach
A way of understanding decisions of the Supreme Court based on the political ideologies of the justices.

The Shifting Ideological Balance of the Court

After Justice Antonin Scalia died in early 2016, the open seat on the Supreme Court became a major issue in the presidential election. Why? As this figure shows, when justices are replaced, the ideological shifts can be quite large (as when Thurgood Marshall, a very liberal justice, was replaced by a strong conservative, Clarence Thomas) or nonexistent (as when Sonia Sotomayor replaced David Souter—they both were moderate liberals). Many people said that replacing Scalia with Merrick Garland would have drastically altered the ideological makeup of the Court, given the 4–4 split on the Court between liberal and conservative justices. When Scalia was replaced by Neil Gorsuch instead of Garland, what happened to the ideological balance of the Court? Then, when Kennedy retired in 2018, he was replaced by conservative Brett Kavanaugh, whose ideological score has not been caluclated as of November 2018, and the center of the Court was kept in about the same place. What do the facts say?

Arrows represent a shift in ideology when a vacancy is filled on the Court, either to a more conservative or more liberal justice.

Each dot represents the ideology of the incoming and outgoing justice.

Dotted line represents hypothetical shift in ideology.

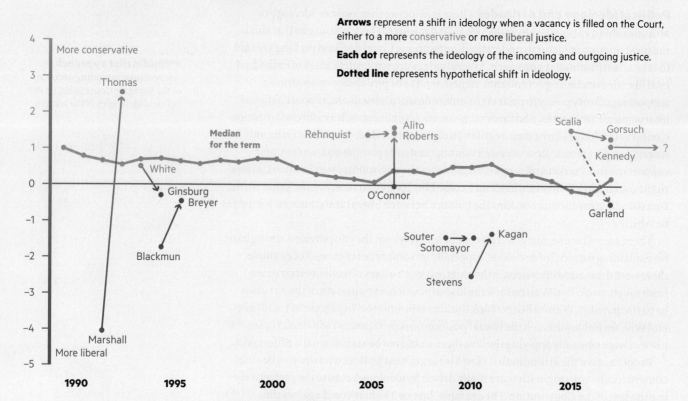

Source: The Upshot, "A Supreme Court with Merrick Garland Would Be the Most Liberal in Decades," www.nytimes.com (accessed 8/16/18); data for Scalia and Gorsuch are from Martin Quinn Scores, Measures, http://mqscores.lsa. umich.edu/measures.php; estimate for Garland from Adam Bonica, et al., "New Data Show How Liberal Merrick Garland Really Is," washingtonpost.com (accessed 8/16/18).

Think about it

- Look at where Scalia is on the ideological scale. If Hillary Clinton had been elected, where would Scalia's dot have likely moved?
- Did the median justice change with the addition of Neil Gorsuch to the Court?
- Merrick Garland probably would have been at about −0.5 on the scale. What would have happened to the median justice if he had been confirmed in 2016?
- What happened when John Roberts replaced Kennedy as the median justice for the 2018 term?

calculations about the preferences of the other justices, the president, and Congress; the choices that other justices are likely to make; and the institutional context within which they operate. After all, justices do not operate alone: at a minimum, they need the votes of four of their colleagues if they want their position to prevail. Therefore, it makes sense to focus on the strategic interactions that take place to build coalitions.

The median voter on the Court—the one in the middle when the justices are arrayed from the most liberal to the most conservative—has an especially influential role in the strategic model. For many years, the median justice was Sandra Day O'Connor; when Samuel Alito replaced her, Anthony M. Kennedy became the new median justice. The four conservatives to his right (Thomas, Scalia, Roberts, and Alito) and the four liberals to his left (Breyer, Ginsburg, Souter, and Stevens) all wanted to attract his vote. When Justice Sotomayor replaced Justice Souter, Justice Kagan replaced Justice Stevens, and Justice Gorsuch replaced Justice Scalia, Kennedy remained the median voter on the Court (because Souter, Sotomayor, Stevens, and Kagan were all to his left and Gorsuch and Scalia were both to his right). When Kennedy retired and Brett Kavanaugh took his place, Roberts became the median and the center of the Court stayed in roughly the same place. Research shows that at least one justice switches his or her vote at some stage in the process (from the initial conference to oral arguments to the final vote) on at least half of the cases, so strategic bargaining appears to be fairly common.[67] Our earlier discussion of opinion assignment and writing opinions to attract the support of a specific justice is more evidence in support of the strategic model.

Separation of Powers Another political influence on justices' decision making is their view of the place of the Court with respect to the democratically elected institutions (Congress and the president). Specifically, do they favor an activist or a restrained role for the Court? Advocates of **judicial restraint** argue that judges should defer to the elected branches and not strike down their laws or other actions. In contrast, advocates of **judicial activism** argue that the Court must play an active role in interpreting the Constitution to protect minority rights even if it means overturning the actions of the elected branches. (We will discuss these views in more detail later in the chapter.)

Outside Influences: Interest Groups and Public Opinion Finally, there are external influences on the Court, such as public opinion and interest groups. We have already talked about the role of interest groups in filing amicus briefs. This is the only avenue of influence open to interest groups; other tactics such as lobbying and fundraising are either inappropriate or irrelevant (because justices are not elected). The role of public opinion is more complex. Obviously, justices do not consult public-opinion polls the way elected officials do. However, the Court expresses the public's preferences in several indirect ways.

The first was most colorfully expressed by Mr. Dooley, a fictional Irish-American bartender whom newspaper satirist Finley Peter Dunne created in 1898. Mr. Dooley offered keen insights on politics and general social criticism, including this gem on the relationship between the Supreme Court and the public: "th' supreme coort always follows th' iliction returns."[68] That is, the public elects the president and the Senate, who nominate and confirm the justices. Therefore, sooner or later, the Court should reflect the views of the public. Subsequent work by political scientists has confirmed this to be largely the case,[69] especially in recent years, when Supreme Court nominations have become more political and more important to the public.[70]

The second mechanism through which public opinion may influence the Court is somewhat more direct: when the public has a clear position on an issue that is before the Court, the Court tends to agree with the public. One study found that the "public

judicial restraint
The idea that the Supreme Court should defer to the democratically elected executive and legislative branches of government rather than contradicting existing laws.

judicial activism
The idea that the Supreme Court should assert its interpretation of the law even if it overrules the elected executive and legislative branches of government.

The Supreme Court, of course, has the responsibility of ensuring that our government never oversteps its proper bounds or violates the rights of individuals. But the Court must also recognize the limits on itself and respect the choices made by the American people.

—Justice Elena Kagan

mood" and Court opinions correlated very highly between 1956 and 1981, but their association was weaker through the rest of the 1980s.[71] One scholar found that three-fifths to two-thirds of Supreme Court decisions are consistent with public opinion when the public has a clear preference on an issue.[72] More recent work demonstrates that the Court is constrained by public opinion, in part because it may fear resistance to implementing an unpopular decision.[73]

Several high-profile examples support the idea that the Court is sensitive to public opinion: the Court switched during the New Deal in the 1930s to support Roosevelt's policy agenda after standing in the way for four years, gave in to wartime opinion to support the internment of Japanese Americans during World War II, limited an accused child molester's right to confront his or her accuser in a courtroom, and supported same-sex marriage. In each of these cases, the justices reflected the current public opinion of the nation rather than a strict reading of the Constitution or the Founders' intent. On the other hand, there are plenty of decisions in which the Court has stood up for unpopular views, such as banning prayer in schools, allowing flag burning, and protecting criminal defendants' rights.

Sometimes the Court may shift its views to reflect *international* opinion. The most recent example struck down the death penalty for minors in 12 states. Ruling by a 5–4 vote that the execution of 16- or 17-year-olds violated the Eighth Amendment's prohibition against "cruel and unusual punishments," the majority opinion overturned a 1989 case and said that the new decision was necessary to reflect the "evolving standards of decency" concerning the definition of "cruel and unusual punishments." Justice Kennedy, who had voted on the other side of this issue 16 years earlier, wrote: "It is fair to say that the United States now stands alone in a world that has turned its face against the juvenile death penalty." Justice Kennedy said that although the Court was not obligated to follow foreign developments, "it is proper that we acknowledge the overwhelming weight of international opinion" for its "respected and significant confirmation for our own conclusions."[74] This explicit recognition of the role of public opinion firmly placed a majority of the Court on the side of the "living Constitution" perspective on this issue, while rejecting the strict constructionist view of the dissenters.

Another way that the Court may consider the public mood is to shift the timing of a decision. The best example here is the landmark school desegregation case, *Brown v. Board of Education* (1954), that the Court sat on for more than two years—until after the 1952 presidential election—because it didn't think the public was ready for its bombshell ruling.[75] Others have argued that the Court rarely *changes* its views to reflect public opinion,[76] but at a minimum the evidence supports the notion that the Court is usually in step with the public.

"Why Should I Care?"

Shouldn't the Court be neutrally applying the words of the Constitution to the cases it hears? While a normatively appealing view, this textualist view ignores many of the realities of how the Court actually operates. Justices often let their own political views shape their decisions, but more neutral forces such as precedent and deferring to the elected branches also play important roles. A realistic perception of the various factors that go into a justice's decision can help you understand why the Court strikes down some laws and upholds others.

The role of the Court in our political system

We conclude with the topic addressed early in the chapter—the place of the Court within the political system. Is the Court the "weakest branch"? As Alexander Hamilton pointed out, the Court has "neither the power of the purse nor the sword." Therefore, it is not clear how it can enforce decisions. In some instances, the Court can force its views on the other branches; in other cases, it needs their support to enforce its decisions.

Compliance and implementation

To gain compliance with its decisions, the Court can rely only on its reputation and on the actions of Congress and the president to back them up. If the other branches don't support the Court, there isn't much it can do. The Court's lack of enforcement power is especially evident when a ruling applies broadly to millions of people who care deeply about the issue. Consider school prayer, which still exists in hundreds of public schools nationwide despite having been ruled unconstitutional more than 50 years ago. It is impossible to enforce the ban unless someone in a school complains and is willing to bring a lawsuit.

In most cases that involve a broad policy, the Court depends on the president for enforcement. After *Brown v. Board of Education* (1954), the landmark school desegregation case, Presidents Eisenhower and Kennedy had to send in federal troops to desegregate public schools and universities. However, presidential foot-dragging can have a big impact on how the law is enforced. President Nixon attempted to lessen the impact of a school busing decision in 1971 that forced the integration of public schools by interpreting it very narrowly. Republican presidents who oppose abortion have limited the scope of *Roe v. Wade*, which legalized abortion in 1973, by denying federal support for abortions for Medicaid recipients, banning abortions on military bases, and preventing doctors from mentioning abortion as an option during pregnancy counseling. The Court must rely on its reputation and prestige to compel the president and Congress not to stray too far from its decisions.

Students at a middle school in Alton, Illinois, gather around a flag pole for prayers before the start of the school day. Unless someone complains, it is difficult to enforce the ban on prayer in public schools.

Relations with the other branches

Relations with the other branches of government may become strained when the Court rules on fundamental questions about institutional power. In some cases, the other branches may fight back; in others, the Court may exercise self-restraint and not get involved.

Judicial Activism and Restraint A central question concerning the role of the Court within our political system revolves around judicial review: Should the Court strike down laws passed by Congress and actions of the executive (activism) or defer to the elected branches (restraint)? Often the answer to this question varies when considered in light of specific lines of cases. A political conservative may favor activist decisions striking down environmental laws or workplace regulations but oppose activist decisions that defend flag burning or defendants' rights. Political liberals may do the opposite—calling for judicial restraint on the first set of cases but for judicial activism to protect civil liberties.

The term "activist judges" often appears in the media. Sometimes the media mistakenly assert that liberal justices are more activist than conservative justices. In fact, though, that is not always the case. The current Court is quite conservative, but it is also activist.[77] Two conservative justices, Kennedy and Thomas, have voted to overturn laws passed by Congress 93 percent and 81 percent of the time, respectively, whereas two of the most liberal justices, Breyer and Ginsburg, have taken the activist position in only 42 percent and 48 percent of the cases.[78] The 1930s Court that struck down much of the New Deal legislation was also conservative and activist, but the Warren Court of the late 1950s and early 1960s was liberal and activist.

In a survey taken about the judicial branch, most respondents were unable to name any Supreme Court justices. Just so you are not in danger of falling into that category, as of the summer of 2018 the justices were (front row, left to right) Ruth Bader Ginsburg, Anthony M. Kennedy (replaced by Brett Kavanaugh after retiring), John G. Roberts Jr. (chief justice), Clarence Thomas, Stephen Breyer, (standing, left to right) Elena Kagan, Samuel Alito Jr., Sonia Sotomayor, and Neil Gorsuch.

A prominent legal journalist observed that the way the popular media describe activism and restraint typically boils down to ideology: if you like a decision, it is restrained; if you do not like a decision, it is activist. For example, *Bush v. Gore*, the decision that decided the outcome of the 2000 presidential election, shows that "most conservatives tie themselves in knots to defend judicial activism when they like the results and to denounce it when they do not. As the reactions to *Lawrence* [the gay sodomy case discussed in Chapter 4] and, earlier, *Roe* [the landmark abortion case] have shown, liberals have been no less selective in their outrage at judicial adventurousness."[79] However, there are instances in which restraint reflects more than ideology and preferences. Justice O'Connor, for example, took restrained positions on abortion and affirmative action, despite her personal views against these policies. Another prominent example of judicial restraint being more important than ideology is Chief Justice Roberts's position in the health care reform case; he said that some decisions "are entrusted to our nation's elected leaders, who can be thrown out of office if the people disagree with them." However, despite providing the pivotal vote to uphold central provisions of the law, he made his personal views against the law clear. "It is not our job," he said, "to protect the people from the consequences of their political choices."[80]

It is important to define activism and restraint in terms of the Court's role in our nation's system of separated powers: Does the Court check the elected branches by overturning their decisions through judicial review? If so, the Court has taken an activist position.

Resistance from the Other Branches The president and Congress often fight back when they think the Court is exerting too much influence, which can limit the Court's power as a policy-making institution. For the president, this can escalate to open conflict. In the Take a Stand feature, we discussed President Obama's criticism of the Court's ruling in *Citizens United v. Federal Election Commission* (2010) in his State of the Union message and President Trump's conflict with the federal courts over his travel ban. Such open conflict with the Court is often criticized as inappropriate. For example, during his confirmation process, Neil Gorsuch told Senator Richard Blumenthal (D-CT) that Trump's criticisms were "disheartening" and "demoralizing" to independent federal courts.[81] The president can counter the Court's influence in a more restrained way by failing to enforce a decision vigorously.

Congress can try to control the Court by blocking appointments it disagrees with (however, this often involves a disagreement with the president more than the Court), limiting the jurisdiction of the federal courts, changing the size of the Court, or even impeaching a judge. The latter three options are rarely used, but Congress often threatens to take these drastic steps. The most common way for Congress to respond to a Court decision that it disagrees with is simply to pass legislation that overturns the decision (if the case concerns the interpretation of a law).

Self-Imposed Restraint In general, the Court avoids stepping on the toes of the other branches unless it is absolutely necessary. The Court often exercises self-imposed restraint and refuses to act on "political questions"—issues that are outside the judicial domain and should be decided by elected officials. The practice dates back to an 1804 dispute over whether a piece of land next to the Mississippi River belonged to Spain or the United States. The Court observed: "A question like this, respecting the boundaries of nations, is . . . more a political than a legal question, and in its discussion, the courts of every country must respect the pronounced will of the legislature."[82]

A more recent application of the doctrine came when the Washington, D.C., district court dismissed a lawsuit from Representative Charles Rangel (D-NY) against former Speaker John A. Boehner (R-OH) concerning the House of Representatives' censure of Rangel for tax evasion and other unethical behavior. The district court dismissed the suit, in part on the grounds that this was a political question that should be decided by Congress, not the Court: "The House has wide discretion to discipline its Members under the Discipline Clause, and this Court may not lightly intrude upon that discretion."[83] The Court is generally reluctant to get involved in internal congressional disputes.

Although this self-imposed limitation on judicial power is important, one must also recognize that the Court reserves the right to decide what a political question is. Therefore, one could argue that this is not much of a limit on judicial power after all. For example, for many decades the Court avoided the topic of legislative redistricting, saying that it did not want to enter that "political thicket." However, it changed its position in the 1960s in a series of cases that imposed the idea of "one person, one vote" on the redistricting process, and it has been intimately involved in redistricting ever since. The Court's ability to define the boundaries of political questions is an important source of its policy-making power.

The Court's Multifaceted Role This "big picture" question about the relationship of the Court to the other branches boils down to this: Does the judiciary constrain the other branches, or does it defer to their wishes? Given the responsiveness of the elected branches to the will of the people, this question can alternatively be stated: Does the Court operate against the political majority to protect minority interests, or does it defer to the popular will? The evidence on this is mixed.

TAKE A STAND

The Independence of the Courts

Many presidents have been frustrated by federal court decisions that they perceived to be unreasonable. Some have responded by lashing out at the courts—an action that never fails to stir controversy. Recently, both Presidents Obama and Trump have criticized high-profile Court decisions. In Obama's 2010 State of the Union address, he noted his disagreement with the Court's ruling in *Citizens United v. Federal Election Commission* (2010) and stated that he believed the decision had opened the floodgates for corporate spending—including by foreign corporations—in elections. Justice Alito was caught on camera mouthing the words "not true" in response. Washington was abuzz for days about whether the president's comment or Alito's response was out of line.[a] President Trump, for his part, was incensed with several lower-court rulings that suspended his travel ban aimed at preventing terrorists from coming into the country, and tweeted, "Just cannot believe a judge would put our country in such peril. If something happens blame him and court system. People pouring in. Bad!"[b] Though it is not very common for presidents to openly criticize the federal courts, they routinely try to influence the courts through nominations to the federal bench. As we discussed earlier, all presidents try to pick justices who share their political views. Is this kind of influence different than that of presidents who directly express their opinions on Court decisions? Is either kind of influence acceptable?

Presidents should be able to influence the courts. Some argue that whether it is President Obama criticizing the Court's ruling on campaign finance or President Trump expressing his views on the lower courts' actions on his travel ban, presidents should be able to express their views on the important issues of the day. Furthermore, presidents are not obligated to nominate centrist judges. If a Republican president can nominate conservative judges, that is certainly his or her right. Trump has exercised this right, to the dismay of some observers who believe that he has picked extremely conservative judges to push his policy agenda.

Trump's appointees, like those of any other president, still need to be confirmed by the Senate. If people don't like the ideological makeup of the judges selected, they can vote out the president and their senator in the next election. Besides, the president speaks for the people who elected him, while the courts are less democratic because they are not elected.

 President Barack Obama was criticized during his 2010 State of the Union address for his comments on *Citizens United v. Federal Election Commission*, a federal court decision that he perceived to be unreasonable.

The independence of the courts is crucial: the president needs to back off. Others argue that, while it is fine for the president to express his policy views on issues that come before the Court, he should refrain from direct criticism of specific cases or judges. Just as it was improper for Justice Ginsburg to criticize Trump during the campaign, presidents should not interject politics into the Court.

And though it is true that all presidents try to influence the Court through their nominations, moderation here would also serve the long-term interests of the country better than wild swings between ideological extremes.

The ballot box is the ultimate recourse for accountability, but even the mighty power of the vote is limited when it comes to holding judges responsible: many judges will serve on the bench for 25 years or more, much longer than the president or most senators.

take a stand

1. Where would you draw the line on presidents' criticizing the courts?

2. Does it bother you that courts are not accountable to the people and yet make important policy decisions? If so, how should presidents be able to influence the courts?

3. Should presidents be able to nominate whomever they want to the courts (subject to Senate approval, of course), or should the process be less partisan and less ideological?

The Court has been an important protector of minority rights, including in the civil rights era. This picture from 1953 shows people waiting in line at the Supreme Court to hear oral arguments in *Brown v. Board of Education*. But at other times, the Court has supported the will of the majority.

The judicial branch as a whole contains a basic paradox: it may be simultaneously seen as the least democratic and most democratic branch.[84] The least democratic part is obvious: federal judges and many state and local judges are unelected and are not accountable to the voters (except indirectly through the elected leaders who appoint them). But the judiciary can also be seen as the most democratic branch. Cases that are brought to the courts come from the people and, as long as the legal criteria for bringing a case are met, the courts must hear those cases. Although people have the right to petition "the government for a redress of grievances," there is no guarantee that Congress or the executive branch will listen to them. Of course, only a small fraction of the cases brought to the Supreme Court are heard, so the antidemocratic charge carries more weight at the top. However, the court system as a whole may be seen as providing an important outlet for participation in our political system.

Whether the Supreme Court goes against our elected leaders—that is, is the Court a countermajoritarian force in our political system?—is also a complicated question to sort out. The Court is activist on many issues, exercising judicial review, but on many other issues it defers to the elected institutions. Sometimes an activist Court defends minority interests on issues such as criminal defendants' rights, school prayer, gay rights, and flag burning, but that is not always the case. Is the Court acting undemocratically when it exercises its power of judicial review (or, as critics would say, "legislates from the bench")? Or is it playing its vital role in our constitutional system as a check on the other branches, as with some of its recent cases concerning the legal rights of enemy combatants in the War on Terror and the early versions of President Trump's travel bans?

The answers depend somewhat on one's political views. Conservatives would generally applaud the activism of the Rehnquist and Roberts Courts, while liberals would see it as an unwarranted check on the elected branches. Moreover, the Court's role has varied throughout history: in some instances, it defended unpopular views and strongly protected minority rights; in other cases, it followed majority opinion and declined to play that important role. But clearly, the Court has the *potential* to play an important policy-making role in our system of checks and balances; whether it actually plays that role depends on the political, personal, and legal factors outlined in this chapter.

Unpacking the Conflict

Considering all that we've discussed in this chapter, let's apply what we know about how the courts work to the story introduced at the beginning of this chapter: Justice Ginsburg's comments about Donald Trump during the 2016 presidential campaign. Did Justice Ginsburg overstep her boundaries with her remarks on Donald Trump, or was it appropriate for her to express her opinions? What does this flap reveal about the broader question of the proper place of the courts within our political system?

The chapter-opening example demonstrates that we often have a difficult time coming to grips with the political nature of the Supreme Court and prefer the comforting image of the neutral and fair Lady Justice: that is why there was such a strong reaction to Justice Ginsburg's comments about Trump. We *want* our courts to be politically neutral, but the reality is very different.

Politics is indeed everywhere, even in the courts, where you would least expect to see it. Politics affects everything from the selection of judges to the decisions they make. Some characteristics of the federal courts (the most important of which is judges' lifetime tenure) insulate the system from politics. However, courts are subject to influence by judges' ideologies, interest groups, and the president and Senate, who try to shape the courts' composition through the nomination process.

While many recoil from a politicized Court, we also value its independence and don't want the president and Congress stepping on its toes. Thus, if the federal courts are allowed to play their proper role, they can serve as a referee between the other branches of government, and between the national and state governments, by defining the boundaries of permissible conduct.

The courts demonstrate that politics is conflictual. And many conflicts demonstrate that the courts are political. Although plenty of unanimous Supreme Court decisions do not involve much conflict among the justices, many landmark cases deeply divide the Court on constitutional interpretation and how to balance those competing interpretations against other values and interests. These conflicts in the Court often reveal deeper fault lines in the broader political system.

What's Your Take?

What should the proper place of the courts be in our political system? How much influence should the executive and legislative branches have over the courts, and vice versa?

STUDY GUIDE

The development of an independent and powerful federal judiciary

Explain how the power of judicial review was established. (Pages 490–494)

Summary

The Constitution offers few specifics on the organization of the judiciary, in contrast to other branches of government. In fact, most of the details on the arrangement of the judiciary do not come from the Constitution at all, but from congressional action. In addition, the Supreme Court's strongest power—judicial review—is not even mentioned in the Constitution but was established in the *Marbury v. Madison* decision.

Key terms

original jurisdiction (p. 491)
Judiciary Act of 1789 (p. 491)
district courts (p. 491)
appellate jurisdiction (p. 491)
judicial review (p. 492)

constitutional interpretation (p. 493)
statutory interpretation (p. 493)

Practice Quiz Questions

1. Most of the details about the Supreme Court were established in _____.

a   the Judiciary Act of 1789
b   Article I of the Constitution
c   Article II of the Constitution
d   the *Federalist Papers*
e   *Marbury v. Madison*

2. *Marbury v. Madison* is significant because it _____.

a   established the Supreme Court
b   introduced the process of selective incorporation
c   changed the manner of judicial selection
d   established judicial review
e   gave Supreme Court justices lifetime appointments

3. Judicial review enables the Supreme Court to _____.

a   submit legislation to Congress
b   strike down laws passed by Congress
c   revise laws passed by Congress
d   oversee presidential appointments to the bureaucracy
e   approve judicial appointments to lower courts

4. The Court's application of national and state laws to particular cases is called _____.

a   constitutional interpretation
b   judicial restraint
c   judicial activism
d   original jurisdiction
e   statutory interpretation

The American legal and judicial system

Outline the structure of the court system. (Pages 494–505)

Summary

All courts within the United States have a similar set of fundamental attributes, such as the distinction between civil and criminal cases and the reliance on legal precedent. The judicial system is divided between state and federal courts, and within each level of government there are courts of original jurisdiction and appeals courts.

Key terms

plaintiff (p. 494)
defendant (p. 494)
plea bargaining (p. 495)
class-action lawsuit (p. 495)
common law (p. 496)

precedent (p. 496)
standing (p. 496)
jurisdiction (p. 496)
appeals courts (p. 497)
senatorial courtesy (p. 503)

Practice Quiz Questions

5. A system of _____ relies on legal decisions that are built from precedent established in previous cases.

a   common law
b   civil law
c   statutory law
d   stare decisis
e   plea bargaining

6. When one has suffered direct and personal harm from the action addressed in a case, it is called _____.

a   precedent
b   appellant
c   plea bargaining
d   jurisdiction
e   standing

7. **The president appoints federal judges with the "advice and consent" of the _____ .**

a   House of Representatives

b   Senate

c   Supreme Court

d   attorney general

e   vice president

Access to the Supreme Court

Describe how cases reach the Supreme Court. (Pages 505–510)

Summary

The Supreme Court hears only about 1 percent of the cases that are brought to it. To help decide which cases to hear, the Court generally uses three factors: collusion, standing, and mootness. Ultimately, the justices have a great deal of discretion in deciding to hear a case, but they can only hear cases that come to them.

Key terms

writ of *certiorari* (p. 507)   **cert pool** (p. 509)

mootness (p. 508)   **solicitor general** (p. 509)

Practice Quiz Questions

8. **When a litigant who lost in a lower court files a petition, the case reaches the Supreme Court _____ .**

a   as a matter of right

b   through a writ of certification

c   through a writ of *certiorari*

d   as a matter of original jurisdiction

e   through senatorial courtesy

9. **_____ means that the controversy is not relevant when the Court hears the case.**

a   Mootness

b   Amicus

c   Collusion

d   Standing

e   Precedent

10. **Most justices _____ in initially deciding which cases should be heard.**

a   personally review all cases

b   personally review a random sample of cases

c   follow the recommendations of the chief justice

d   use a random selection process

e   use a cert pool

Hearing cases before the Supreme Court

Describe the Supreme Court's procedures for hearing a case. (Pages 510–514)

Summary

When hearing a case, the justices prepare by reading briefs before they hear the oral arguments. After oral arguments, the justices meet in conference to discuss and vote on the cases. The majority opinion explains the rationale for how a decision is reached, although justices can also write dissenting and concurring opinions.

Key terms

amicus curiae (p. 510)   **oral arguments** (p. 511)

Practice Quiz Questions

11. **The most important impact of a large number of amicus curiae briefs on a case is _____ .**

a   the decision is more likely to be unanimous

b   the case is more likely to be heard

c   the decision is more likely to go against the government

d   the case is less likely to be heard

e   the decision is more likely to have a liberal outcome

12. **Oral arguments generally last _____ , and justices _____ wait until the end of the arguments to ask questions.**

a   one hour; will

b   one hour; do not

c   one day; will

d   one week; will

e   one week; do not

13. **Generally, the chief justice or the _____ justice decides who writes the majority opinion; justices' individual areas of expertise _____ a factor in making this assignment.**

a   most junior; are not

b   most junior; are

c   most senior; are not

d   most senior; are

e   dissenting; are not

Supreme Court decision making

Analyze the factors that influence Supreme Court decisions. (Pages 514–520)

Summary

The Court makes decisions based on legal factors such as precedent and informal norms, and political factors such as the justices' own ideologies and positions on the role that the Court plays in government. Although the Court does not consider public opinion the way elected officials do, most decisions generally stay in step with the public.

Key terms

strict construction (p. 515)

original intent (p. 516)

living Constitution (p. 516)

attitudinalist approach (p. 517)

judicial restraint (p. 519)

judicial activism (p. 519)

Practice Quiz Questions

14. The perspective that when the Constitution is not clear, the justices should be guided by what the Founders wanted is called _____.

a   judicial activism

b   strict construction

c   original intent

d   the attitudinalist approach

e   the interpretive statute

15. Advocates of _____ argue that the Court must defer to the elected branches and not strike down their laws.

a   judicial restraint

b   judicial activism

c   judicial limitation

d   legal maximization

e   the strategic model

The role of the Court in our political system

Assess the Supreme Court's power in the political system. (Pages 521–526)

Summary

Given the constitutional weakness of the Court, it is unclear how it is able to enforce its decisions. Depending on context, the Court is occasionally able to force its views on the elected branches, although more often it requires their support.

Practice Quiz Question

16. In general, the Court _____ challenges with the elected branches and often _____ to act on "political questions."

a   avoids; agrees

b   avoids; refuses

c   pursues; agrees

d   pursues; refuses

Suggested Reading

Baum, Lawrence. *Judges and Their Audiences: A Perspective on Judicial Behavior.* Princeton, NJ: Princeton University Press, 2006.

Black, Ryan C., and Ryan J. Owens. *The Solicitor General and the United States Supreme Court: Executive Influence and Judicial Decisions.* New York: Cambridge University Press, 2012.

Cornell University Law School, Supreme Court Collection, www.law. cornell.edu/supremecourt/text/home.

Hansford, Thomas G., and James F. Spriggs II. *The Politics of Precedent on the U.S. Supreme Court.* Princeton, NJ: Princeton University Press, 2006.

Northwestern University, Oyez: Supreme Court Multimedia, www.oyez.org.

O'Brien, David M. *Storm Center: The Supreme Court in American Politics,* 11th ed. New York: W. W. Norton, 2017.

Posner, Richard A. *The Federal Judiciary: Strengths and Weaknesses.* Cambridge, MA: Harvard University Press, 2017.

Rosen, Jeffrey. *The Most Democratic Branch: How the Courts Serve America.* New York: Oxford University Press, 2006.

Sunstein, Cass R., David Schkade, Lisa M. Ellman, and Andres Sawicki. *Are Judges Political? An Empirical Analysis of the Federal Judiciary.* Washington, DC: Brookings Institution Press, 2006.

Tushnet, Mark. *A Court Divided: The Rehnquist Court and the Future of Constitutional Law.* New York: W. W. Norton, 2006.

U.S. Supreme Court website, www.supremecourt.gov.

15

Economic Policy

How does the government help promote a strong economy?

 "When a country (USA) is losing many billions of dollars on trade with virtually every country it does business with, trade wars are good, and easy to win."
President Donald Trump

"Hopefully the president is just blowing off steam again but, if he's even half-serious, this is nuts."
Senator Ben Sasse (R-NE)

In the 2016 presidential campaign, Donald Trump made foreign trade one of his central themes. One important way to "Make America Great Again," according to Trump, was to rip up bad trade deals, get foreign countries to start treating the United States fairly, and bring jobs back to the country. In a campaign speech Trump said, "We allowed foreign countries to subsidize their goods, devalue their currencies, violate their agreements and cheat in every way imaginable, and our politicians did nothing about it."[1] This position won him the support of traditionally Democratic states that had lost manufacturing jobs, like Pennsylvania, Michigan, and Wisconsin, and helped propel him to victory.

Shortly after taking office, the president pulled out of the Trans Pacific Partnership (TPP), a pact with 11 nations that was aimed at reducing barriers to trade and improving the members' economic position relative to that of China. In 2018, President Trump imposed tariffs on aluminum and steel on the grounds of national security, started a trade war with China, imposed tariffs on our allies (such as Canada and the European Union), and pressured Mexico and Canada to renegotiate the North American Free Trade Agreement (NAFTA).

The reaction of financial markets, the United States' allies, most economists, and even some Republicans in Congress (as reflected in the quote from Senator Sasse)[2] was very negative. The Republican Party has been a strong supporter of free trade and Democratic leadership supports most free-trade treaties. These critics of

President Trump's position on foreign trade won him support in traditionally Democratic states that had lost manufacturing jobs. However, the financial markets reacted negatively once he started acting on his campaign promise. Though it may seem like tariffs on steel and aluminum will help those industries, the overall impact of the trade barriers is almost certain to cost some factory workers their jobs.

CHAPTER GOALS

Explain the main purposes of government involvement in the economy.
pages 533–539

Describe the roles played by each of the branches of government in shaping economic policy.
pages 539–550

Examine how fiscal, monetary, regulatory, and trade policies influence the economy.
pages 551–567

the president's position tout the value of free trade in increasing wealth, reducing consumer prices, and promoting the efficient allocation of resources. About the only group that is traditionally opposed to free trade is liberal Democrats with ties to organized labor. In fact, in the 2016 presidential campaign Bernie Sanders and Donald Trump sounded almost identical on the topic of trade.[3]

While it may seem like tariffs on steel and aluminum will help those industries, the overall impact of the trade barriers is almost certain to cost jobs. The U.S. steel industry employs about 147,000 people, but manufacturers that need steel employ about 6.5 million people each year and the construction industry employs 6.3 million. For example, the average car has about 1.2 tons of steel, so the tariffs would increase the cost of a car by about $300. This could lead to an estimated loss of 40,000 jobs in the auto industry as consumers buy cheaper imports.[4] The beer industry was also concerned about increased prices due to the higher costs of aluminum cans. MillerCoors, for example, said that it was "disappointed" in the move and that it "is likely to lead to job losses across the beer industry," while the Beer Institute said, "Imported aluminum used to make beer cans is not a threat to national security" (in reference to Trump's rationale for imposing the tariffs).[5] In short, trade policies aimed at helping one segment of the economy come at the expense of another part, which creates political conflict.

Critics of the president's position tout the value of free trade in increasing wealth, reducing consumer prices, and promoting the efficient allocation of resources. While President Trump tried to take steps to actively support American manufacturers, companies like motorcycle manufacturer Harley-Davidson continued with plans to close American plants.

Conflict over economic policy goes beyond trade policy. Many of America's political debates concern economic policy: Should we run deficits or have balanced budgets? Should we have a largely unregulated free market—or regulations for things like pollution and health care? Should we spend more money to create "green jobs" and promote alternative energy, or subsidize more offshore drilling and build pipelines to maximize the extraction of oil and natural gas? Democrats tend to favor a more activist government that supports a broader range of redistributive programs and regulates the economy to ensure a range of public goods, such as rebuilding the infrastructure. Republicans tend to favor a more limited approach to government that promotes lower taxes and less regulation and allows the free market to determine more social and economic decisions, such as allowing greater development of domestic energy sources.

As our political leaders debate how best to support a growing economy, it becomes increasingly important to understand the economic policy-making process. Which side is right about trade policy, and what should the government do, if anything, about trade deficits? More generally, what is the proper role of the government in a free market economy? How do political players deal with the conflict that is inherent in economic policy making?

Goals of economic policy

Public policy is a course of action pursued by government to address a specific problem. Economic policy makers thus attempt to influence the economy with specific goals in mind. This section will examine those goals, and later in the chapter we will look at the tools used to pursue the goals. The most important tools are **fiscal policy**—taxing and spending policy that is created by Congress and the president—and **monetary policy**—control of the money supply and interest rates, which is primarily the domain of the Federal Reserve System, or "the Fed."

Many economic policy goals seem obvious, such as full employment (clearly, it is better to have more people working than not working). However, it may be less obvious why other goals, such as promoting stable prices and market growth, are important for the economy. These varied goals are often difficult for policy makers to pursue simultaneously because there are trade-offs among some of them.

Full employment

Employment seems like a good starting point for a healthy economy. If people have jobs, they pay taxes and do not depend directly on the government for support. Despite this, **full employment** was not an explicit goal of economic policy until 1946, when Congress passed the Employment Act. Leaders were concerned that with millions of World War II veterans returning and the wartime economy gearing down, the nation might slide back into the **economic depression** that had created so much hardship in the 1930s. Although the act was largely symbolic (it did not create a guaranteed right to employment), it did create the **Council of Economic Advisers (CEA)**, which provides the president with economic information and advice. A more concrete effort to ensure that returning veterans could find jobs was the 1944 Servicemen's Readjustment Act (the GI Bill). By the time this law expired in 1956, it had provided low-interest home mortgages for 2.4 million veterans and higher education assistance to 7.8 million veterans. Today the government seeks to support the creation of as many jobs as possible by maintaining a strong economy. By early 2014, the number of American workers finally reached the level of employment before the 2008–2009 recession, but policy makers disagreed over whether more government action was necessary to stimulate more job growth.

On a technical level, "full employment" does not literally mean that everyone is working. Instead, economists consider a 4 to 4.5 percent unemployment rate to be the level of full employment, or the "natural rate of unemployment." This accounts for the substantial portion of potential workers who are not looking for a job, and a certain amount of "frictional unemployment" when people are between jobs.

EXPLAIN THE MAIN PURPOSES OF GOVERNMENT INVOLVEMENT IN THE ECONOMY

public policy
A course of action pursued by government to address a specific problem.

fiscal policy
Government decisions about how to influence the economy by taxing and spending.

monetary policy
Government decisions about how to influence the economy using control of the money supply and interest rates.

full employment
The theoretical point at which all citizens who want to be employed have a job.

economic depression
A deep, widespread downturn in the economy, like the Great Depression of the 1930s.

Council of Economic Advisers (CEA)
A group of economic advisers, created by the Employment Act of 1946, that provides objective data on the state of the economy and makes economic policy recommendations to the president.

It's a recession when your neighbor loses his job; it's a depression when you lose your own.

—President Harry Truman

FIGURE 15.1

Inflation and Unemployment, 1960–2018

The Misery Index is the sum of the unemployment rate and the inflation rate. Which periods have had the highest misery rate since 1960? Were there any external explanations for the high misery rate? How did the government respond to the high levels of unemployment and inflation?

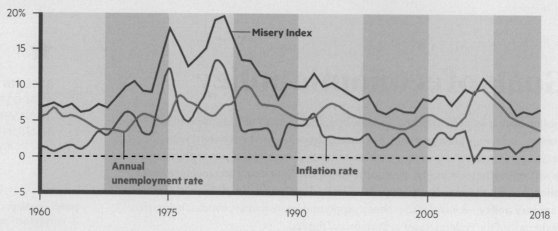

Source: Data from the U.S. Department of Labor, Bureau of Labor Statistics, www.bls.gov (accessed 9/7/18).

Stable prices

inflation
The increase in the price of consumer goods over time.

The importance of having stable prices is not as obvious as the need for jobs. Why are rising prices—**inflation**—a problem? This is a common question during periods of low inflation. Especially for workers who have automatic raises (cost of living adjustments, or COLAs) as part of their basic pay package, moderate inflation isn't much of a problem. For example, if your rent goes up 4 percent, the price of groceries goes up 3 percent, and the cost of entertainment goes up 3 percent, and you get a 4 percent raise, you will likely be at least as well-off as you were in the previous year. However, it's possible for inflation to be much higher: from 1979 to 1980 inflation was running at 12 to 14 percent rather than the 2 to 3 percent that has been typical in recent years (see Figure 15.1).

Double-digit inflation can have serious effects on the economy. First, because the entire economy is not indexed to inflation, some people will experience an erosion of their purchasing power. If your rent goes up 10 percent and groceries go up 15 percent, but your pay goes up by only 4 percent, you are substantially worse off. Second, high inflation penalizes savers as inflation outstrips savings interest rates (so savings are actually worth *less* over time). On the other hand, inflation may benefit debtors, because people can repay their debts with dollars that are worth less in the future. Finally, long-term economic planning by businesses becomes more difficult when inflation is high: investors will demand high interest rates to compensate for the added risk of future inflation, and businesses will be reluctant to accept loans at these rates. In 1979 and 1980, for example, short-term interest rates spiked as high as 18 percent. Very few businesses were willing to take on additional debt at that rate of interest rather than the more typical 5 to 8 percent for long-term loans, so the economy headed into a recession.

deflation
A decrease in the general prices of goods and services.

As counterintuitive as it may sound, *falling* prices, or **deflation**, may be equally as devastating for an economy as prices that are rising too quickly. During the Great Depression, prices fell by 10 percent each year from 1930 to 1933. This trend exacerbated the depression as businesses made less money, wages fell (for those who were still working), production fell, and real debt increased (that is, when wages were falling by 30 percent, it was much harder to pay off debts, because they couldn't be repaid with cheaper dollars). American policy makers were concerned about possible deflation after the Great Recession of 2008–2009, but those fears subsided as inflation remained at a low level.[6]

Typically, unemployment and inflation are not high at the same time. The unusual period of relatively high unemployment and inflation in the 1970s generated two new economic terms to describe this phenomenon: "stagflation" (a stagnant economy with inflation) and the "Misery Index" (the sum of the inflation rate and the unemployment rate). The Misery Index started to creep up in 1970–1971, and policy makers were desperate to do something about it. President Nixon wanted to halt inflation in its tracks, in part to help his reelection chances in 1972. He announced a 90-day wage freeze in 1971, followed by wage and price controls after his reelection. The experiment was abandoned in 1974 when it became obvious that interfering with market forces in these ways was not working.[7] From that point on, fighting inflation has largely been left to the Federal Reserve, which raises interest rates to cool down the economy. We will discuss this process later in the chapter.

Promotion of the free market and growth

The American economy is a capitalist system, which means that most economic decisions are voluntarily made between individuals and firms for their mutual benefit. The government generally stays out of most economic activity, except to regulate the market when it produces too much of something that is not in the public's interest, such as pollution or unsafe products. Economists tout the advantage of the free market as promoting the most efficient use of resources. Economic growth is also a central goal. Growth is seen in an increase in **gross domestic product (GDP)**, a measure of the nation's overall economic output and activity. A growing economy provides a better standard of living for each generation.

gross domestic product (GDP)
The value of a country's economic output taken as a whole.

Though government does not get directly involved in most economic transactions, it can provide the foundation for a strong free market and economic growth. The government protects property rights so that businesses that invest in the growth of their company know that another firm or the government cannot appropriate their property. Property rights also cover intellectual property, which is protected by patent and copyright laws. If entrepreneurs know that they will benefit from their own discoveries and labor, they are more likely to put in the countless hours required for innovative breakthroughs in science, technology, and medicine. The government also guarantees the security and transparency of capital markets through the oversight of the Securities and Exchange Commission and provides a secure banking system through the Federal Deposit Insurance Corporation and the Federal Reserve System.

Critics of the government's focus on the market and growth claim that the free market often produces inequality and that growth doesn't measure well-being. This was a big issue in the 2016 Democratic presidential primaries as Bernie Sanders made income inequality the centerpiece of his campaign. But historically, the United States has not focused as much on this economic policy goal as many other Western nations have. As a consequence, the United States ranks 115th in the world (out of 156 nations in the study) in income equality, just behind nations such as Cameroon, Guyana, Thailand, and Iran, and it has become less equal than Europe in the distribution of wealth (see Figure 15.2).[8] Other critics of the focus on growth include environmentalists who advocate a "small is beautiful"[9] approach and point out the environmental costs of economic growth. In addition, there are economists who question the traditional

FIGURE
15.2

Wealth Inequality across the World

Economic inequality was higher in Europe than in the United States until the late twentieth century. Today the United States has a higher income inequality than Europe and China have. What are the factors that have led to increased economic inequality in the United States?

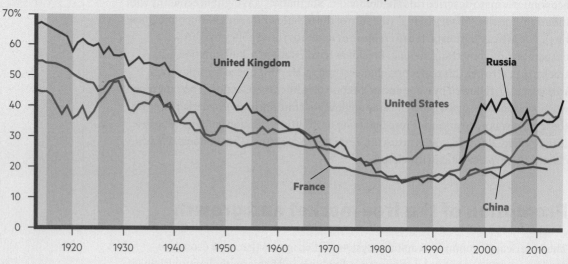

Percentage of national wealth held by top 1%

Sources: World Inequality Database, "Top 1% National Income Share," www.wid.world.com (accessed 6/28/18).

interpretations of economic growth measurements—in particular, the increase in GDP. These critics argue that a significant part of GDP actually captures a decline in well-being. For example, if we have to spend billions of dollars putting alarms in our homes and cars to warn against intruders, this does not signal an improvement in the standard of living from the time when such alarms were unnecessary. Yet the purchase of such crime-fighting tools adds to GDP. An ideal measure of economic growth would distinguish between positive and negative forms of economic activity.[10]

Balanced budgets

balanced budget
A spending plan in which the government's expenditures are equal to its revenue.

budget deficit
The amount by which a government's spending in a given fiscal year exceeds its revenue.

Maintaining a **balanced budget** has been a central economic goal since the 1980s, when **budget deficits** skyrocketed (see Nuts & Bolts 15.1). Large deficits, projected to be $973 billion in 2019, are a concern for several reasons. First, the debt accumulated over years of running budget deficits takes a big bite out of current spending. About $390 billion, or 8.7 percent, of the 2019 fiscal year budget is for financing the federal debt.[11] These dollars went to people and financial institutions that earn interest on the money that they loaned to the federal government; this money did not pay for a single uniform for a soldier, highway exit ramp, or student loan. Second, the total federal debt is a burden on future generations. Each man, woman, and child in the United States in effect carries more than $47,975 of debt (total debt has grown steadily; see What Do the Facts Say?). This means that future generations will either have fewer government services and less generous benefits from programs like Social Security or pay higher taxes (or a mix of the two). Third, borrowing by the government "crowds out" private borrowing in the overall economy, because there is a finite pool of dollars that people can invest. Let's say you have $1,000 to invest. You could invest it privately and buy stocks or

Deficits and Debt

Budget deficits and the federal debt are related concepts that are easily confused.

- A *budget deficit* occurs when tax revenue is not sufficient to cover government spending in a given year. If tax revenue is higher than spending, then there is a budget surplus.
- The *federal debt* is the total accumulation of all outstanding borrowing by the government.
- The concepts of deficit and debt are related because when the government runs a deficit it must borrow money to cover the gap. This borrowing then builds up the federal debt.

   You can think of this in terms of your own spending habits. Any time you spend more money in a given month than you earn, you are running a deficit. You must borrow money to make up that deficit from a bank, from your parents, or by running up the balance on your credit card. The accumulated sum of your monthly deficits is the total debt that you owe. However, there is one obvious point that should be made: you cannot print your own money, unlike the government!

corporate bonds that provide businesses the money they need to expand, or you could invest it publicly and buy government bonds that allow the government to spend your $1,000 with the promise to pay it back later with interest. In the aggregate, this means that if the government is borrowing $981 billion in a given year (like 2019), then that $981 billion is not available for private borrowing that could go directly to creating more jobs and generating economic growth. People may obviously choose to invest in private debt, but U.S. government bonds are a very attractive investment option. They are seen as the most secure investment in the world, so especially during times of economic uncertainty, investors around the world buy U.S. bonds even if they pay a lower interest rate than private debt.

Balance of payments, or the current account

The balance of payments may sound like balanced budgets, but the two are completely different: the latter has to do with the federal budget that we just discussed, while the balance of payments concerns international monetary transactions. The broadest measure of a nation's balance of payments with the rest of the world is the **current account**: the difference between a nation's receipts (exports and money that Americans earn on foreign investments) and its payments (imports and money that foreigners earn on American investments). The aspect of the current account that gets the most political attention is the **trade deficit**, the difference between imports and exports. The American appetite for foreign goods is huge, and in recent years the United States has gone from being the world's largest creditor nation to being the world's largest debtor nation.

   There are differences of opinion over whether the United States' debtor status with respect to other countries is a problem. Most economists agree that if the current account deficit is driven by more foreign investment in America than America has invested overseas, there is no great cause for concern. Although some economists worry about the increasing share of U.S. businesses and real estate owned by foreign investors, overall this is simply evidence of the strength of the U.S. economy—that is, investors think they can get a greater return on their investments in America than in other countries. However, if the current account deficit is driven by the trade deficit, which is based on consumption rather than investment, unsustainable longer-term economic problems may be created. We discuss this topic more in the section on trade policy.[12]

current account
The balance of a country's receipts and its payments in international trade and investment.

trade deficit
A measure of how much more a nation imports than it exports.

Are Deficits and the National Debt out of Control?

Many politicians say that government spending has gotten out of control and that the federal budget deficit (the amount by which the government's spending exceeds its revenue in a given year) and the federal debt (the accumulation of these annual deficits) are too high. Is this true? What do the facts say? Let's look at each in two different ways.

Budget Deficits

Note: Deficits include the Social Security Trust Fund.

Public Debt

Note: This figure shows publicly held debt, excluding intragovernmental holdings.
Source: Congressional Budget Office, Budget Projections, various documents from www.cbo.gov/topics/budget (accessed 6/5/18).

Think about it

- **What is the biggest difference between the figures on the left and right of each chart?**
- **Which data, the left or the right, do you think are a better indication of the size of our budget deficit and debt? Why? Do both sets of numbers reveal something useful?**
- **Economists argue that debt becomes a potentially serious problem when it is as big as the overall economy. Have we ever hit that level since 1940?**
- **After examining these data, do you think the United States' budget deficits and national debt are out of control? Why or why not?**

Trade-offs between economic goals

One challenge facing economic policy makers is that it is difficult to "have it all." Though the United States enjoyed low unemployment, low inflation, economic growth, falling budget deficits (and a surplus by the end of the decade), and a healthy current account throughout most of the 1990s, this was relatively unusual. Typically, at least part of the economy is not performing well and some goals are not being met. For example, if inflation starts to increase, the Federal Reserve will attempt to bring it down by increasing interest rates. When interest rates go up, the economy slows because businesses are less willing to expand when the cost of borrowing increases. As a result, unemployment increases. Therefore, there is a trade-off, at least in the short run, between stable prices and full employment and economic growth.

Steps to address the trade deficit also conflict with other goals. Politicians are often under pressure to protect American jobs and prevent them from going overseas. But if policy makers impose barriers to free trade to protect domestic products and jobs, this action violates the goal of promoting an efficient free market. That is, political goals and economic goals may come into conflict. Another example would be budget deficits: politicians have a strong political incentive to keep budget deficits high (because, even though people don't like paying taxes, they support keeping spending the same or increasing it for most policies), but this may not be the best economic policy in some situations. Policy makers must tread carefully when addressing economic problems to ensure that they are not making some other problem worse. The next section explores who these policy makers are.

Understanding the goals of economic policy is essential for making sense of much of what happens in Washington and in political campaigns. If a presidential candidate promises to cut your taxes and increase spending on education and national defense, without increasing budget deficits, your truth-o-meter should be buzzing. If the president talks about slapping punitive tariffs on China, you should be concerned about the impact of a trade war on the economy. Having a realistic set of goals is an important first step for sound economic policy.

"Why Should I Care?"

The key players in economic policy making

DESCRIBE THE ROLES PLAYED BY EACH OF THE BRANCHES OF GOVERNMENT IN SHAPING ECONOMIC POLICY

Now that we know the goals of economic policy, we need to answer these questions: Who are the key policy makers? What role do they play in shaping American economic policy?

Congress

The Constitution places Congress at the center of economic policy making by giving legislators the "power of the purse"—that is, power over the nation's fiscal policy of taxing and spending. In a way, everything Congress does has an impact on the economy, whether it is providing money for an interstate highway or a student loan, regulating the level of air pollutants, or funding the Social Security system.

Some committees are more directly related than others to economic policy. Budget, appropriations, and tax committees (Ways and Means in the House and Finance in the Senate; see Chapter 11) direct fiscal policy, while the banking committees have a hand in overseeing aspects of monetary policy. The commerce committees, especially in the House, also have their hand in a range of economic policies. Because it is the most important of Congress's economic policy-making responsibilities, we focus our discussion on the budget-making process.

Budget making in Congress was decentralized through much of its history, with no real way to coordinate activity among the various committees and subcommittees involved in the process. The appropriations committees had a difficult time keeping spending requests from other committees in line with overall budgetary expectations because of the two-step process Congress uses to approve any spending: the authorizing committee writes the law that authorizes the spending, and then the appropriations committee approves the level of spending.[13] As a result, budgetary power shifted from Congress to the president, starting with the Budget and Accounting Act of 1921. From that point on, presidents have played a central role in the budget process by submitting their budgets to Congress. The president's budget often serves as the starting point for the congressional budget.

Congress revamped the budget process in 1974 with the Budget and Impoundment Control Act. This law created the Budget Committees in the House and Senate, set up the budget process (see the How It Works graphic), and established the Congressional Budget Office (CBO). This office gave Congress independent expertise and advice on budgetary matters so it did not have to rely on the president's numbers. For the first time, Congress had the institutional capacity on budgetary matters to deal with the president on an equal footing.

However, the new process and institutions did not guarantee smooth sailing. In fact, Congress has continued to have a difficult time meeting the various deadlines, and the process has not helped to eliminate budget deficits. **Budget reconciliation**, a powerful tool in the 1974 Budget Act, was first used in 1980 to bring spending levels into line with the budget resolution. (This obviously requires that there *be* a budget resolution—11 times in the past 17 years Congress has failed to adopt the overall budget blueprint, most recently with the 2019 fiscal year budget).[14] In fact, the budget committees decided to not produce a budget resolution at all for the 2019 budget to protect Republicans from having to vote for a budget with a trillion dollar deficit. As a *Forbes* headline put it, "GOP-Led Budget Committees Have Just One Job . . . and Are Refusing to Do It." A former budget committee staffer observed, "[T]he budget rules that are supposed to guide what the president and Congress do about the budget each year have died an ignominious death because of a combination of abject abuse and atrocious neglect."[15]

Although the budget process is sometimes ignored, committees are supposed to meet specific spending targets laid out in the budget resolution, and then any necessary changes to individual committees' budgets are supposed to be combined into one omnibus reconciliation bill. In terms of adopting budget cuts—which are always difficult to pass because most programs have strong advocates who oppose the cuts—this procedure has two advantages. First, having everything in a single huge bill makes it much more difficult for members to vote against it, because to do so would mean turning down the entire package, including elements of the bill that individual members of Congress like. Depending on the timing, failure to pass an omnibus spending bill may mean shutting down the government. Second, the Senate treats reconciliation bills differently from other bills or amendments. Most important, in the Senate these bills cannot be filibustered—and anything unrelated to deficit reduction can be struck down, which makes reconciliation an important tool in deficit reduction.[16] Overall, reconciliation has been used in about two-thirds of the budgets since 1980 and has been

budget making
The processes carried out in Congress to determine how government money will be spent and revenue will be raised.

budget reconciliation
The process by which congressional committees are held to the spending targets specified in the budget resolution. During this process, the House and Senate Budget Committees combine the budgetary changes from all the legislative committees into an omnibus reconciliation bill to be approved by Congress.

responsible for cutting hundreds of billions of dollars of proposed spending. As we discussed in Chapter 11, reconciliation was crucial in passing the Tax Cuts and Jobs Act in 2017 because it allowed Republicans to avoid a Democratic filibuster.

In response to exploding budget deficits in the early to mid-1980s, which even reconciliation was inadequate to address, an additional mechanism was employed in 1990 to give Congress more traction in managing the deficits: a zero-sum, pay-as-you-go (PAYGO) process whereby any new tax cut or spending increase had to be paid for by raising another tax or cutting spending in some other program. The PAYGO procedure, along with the tax increases in President Clinton's 1993 budget, put the nation on the path for the first budget surpluses since the 1960s. By 1999, the budget was balanced, and in 2000 there was a substantial surplus ($86.3 billion) for the first time in nearly 50 years.[17]

However, the surpluses soon evaporated and massive budget deficits returned in 2002. One major contribution to this explosion in the deficits was that PAYGO was allowed to lapse for the 2002 budget—in part to enable funding the war in Iraq and the war on terrorism but also to make it politically easier to pass additional tax cuts. Congress reinstated the PAYGO rule in 2007 and made it permanent in 2010. However, there are exemptions in the statutory PAYGO rule for Social Security, interest on the debt, and at least 12 other programs.[18] The rule also has been routinely suspended whenever Congress wants to extend a popular tax cut or pay for emergency spending, such as drought relief, extension of unemployment benefits, or expansion of Medicare and the Children's Health Insurance Program (CHIP).[19] Without the need to pay for tax cuts or spending increases, it has proved too tempting to let the deficits increase to unsustainable levels.

Increased partisan polarization in Congress and differences between Democrats and Republicans in their view of taxing and spending policy have made it difficult to pass a budget in a timely fashion. In recent years, Congress has relied on "continuing resolutions," which keep spending at the level of last year's budget, when members cannot agree on a new budget. Even traditionally noncontroversial aspects of fiscal policy, such as increasing the debt ceiling to authorize government borrowing, have become opportunities for partisan politics. And even unified control of government for the first time since 2010 did not make the budget process work more smoothly.

The president

Once they are in office, presidents quickly realize that the public expects them to promote a healthy economy. Indeed, the state of the economy has a big impact on the public's assessment of presidential performance, and it also influences election outcomes. President Obama focused on the economy in his first months in office, pushing through a massive stimulus bill; later, in the face of major unemployment, Obama also signed legislation aimed at creating more jobs. The signature achievement of President Trump's first two years was enacting the $1.5 trillion tax cut, which gave a short-term boost to the economy.[20] The Tax Cuts and Jobs Act of 2017 reduced individual income taxes by more than $1.1 trillion over 10 years, reducing the top marginal rate from 39.6 percent to 37 percent, nearly doubling the standard deduction, and doubling the child tax credit. The law also limited the deductions for state and local income tax, sales tax, and property taxes to $10,000, which could raise taxes for some people in states with high taxes. The corporate tax rate was lowered from 35 percent to 21 percent, and a 20 percent deduction in "pass through income" will benefit many small business owners. The law also doubled the value of assets that would be exempt from the estate tax.

How it works: ~~in theory~~

The Budget Process

First Monday in February:
The president submits budget request to Congress.

February 15:
Congressional Budget Office (CBO) issues budget and economic outlook report.

Within six weeks of president's submission:
Other committees with budgetary responsibilities submit "views and estimates" to budget committees.

Early April:
House Budget Committee creates its budget resolution and the House votes on it.

Early April:
Senate Budget Committee creates its budget resolution and the Senate votes on it.

Early April:
Budget Conference Committee reconciles the House and Senate versions of the budget resolution.

By April 15:
House votes on conference version. Senate votes on conference version.

Appropriations:
After both houses approve the budget resolution, appropriations committees draft legislation authorizing expenditures to the relevant agencies. Each appropriations bill must be passed by both houses and signed into law by the president. If this process is not completed by October 1, and no temporary measure (a "continuing resolution") is in place, the government will shut down.

October 1:
Start of the fiscal year.

The 2018 Budget Process

Although there is a "textbook" path that politicians try to follow when passing a budget, they almost always deviate wildly from it. In fact, it has been 22 years since Congress passed all 12 appropriations bills using the regular process. In 2018, the budget resolution was six months late, so Congress resorted to continuing resolutions, a government shutdown (complicated by negotiations over DACA and the "Dreamers," as we discussed in Chapter 11), and eventually an omnibus bill that combined the 12 appropriations bills.

Cleaning up last year's mess.

May 5, 2017: Congress passes an omnibus spending bill to fund the government through the end of the 2017 fiscal year. **This bill should have been passed by October 1, 2016.**

Starting a little late.

May 23: President Trump submits his budget for the 2018 fiscal year—**106 days late.**

CBO does its thing.

July 13: CBO submits its analysis of the president's budget—**176 days late.** (But who's counting? Oh, I guess we are.)

Whatever...

Over the summer, the budget committees **fail to pass a budget resolution.** This should have been passed by April 15.

Wait, can they do that?

June–July: House and Senate Appropriations Committees **forge ahead without a budget resolution.** (Yes, they can do that.)

Let's make a deal!

September 8: Congress enacts the deal that **Trump strikes with minority leaders Chuck Schumer and Nancy Pelosi** to suspend the debt ceiling and fund the government through December 8.

But...that's backward!

On September 14, the House **passes all 12 appropriations bills;** on October 5, it passes its budget resolution. The Senate passes its own budget resolution on October 19.

Finally.

October 26: The House **passes the Senate's budget resolution** (more than six months behind schedule).

What about the Dreamers?

December–January: Democrats want to attach a solution for the Dreamers to the budget, but cannot make progress. **They agree to three separate continuing resolutions** to keep the government open.

Shut down!

January 19–22, 2018: With no progress on the Dreamers, **Senate Democrats shut down the government for three days** before agreeing to another continuing resolution.

A deal!

February 9: Trump signs **a two-year budget deal with $300 billion in additional spending** and yet another continuing resolution to keep the government open through May 23.

Passed.

May 23: Congress passes an omnibus spending bill authorizing $1.3 trillion in spending and $1.9 billion in tax cuts (over 10 years).

? Critical Thinking

1. **How might the type of "brinkmanship" budgeting** described here—that is, using the threat of a government shutdown to achieve nonbudgetary policy goals—affect the economy?

2. **If you were a businessperson trying to decide** whether or not to expand, would the uncertainty created by a threatened shutdown affect your decision?

As we discussed in Chapter 12, the president is unable to accomplish much single-handedly on the economic front: Congress, the Fed, and broader domestic and international economic forces all exert an equal or greater influence on the health of the economy. However, the executive branch has a large advising structure that helps the president formulate economic policy. The Office of Management and Budget (OMB), the Council of Economic Advisers (CEA), the Office of the **United States Trade Representative (USTR)**, and the **National Economic Council (NEC)** all provide important economic advice.

The department with the longest track record is the OMB. It plays a central role in creating the budget by soliciting spending requests from all federal agencies, suggesting additional cuts, and then coordinating these requests with presidential priorities. It is ultimately responsible for putting together the president's budget, which is then submitted to Congress. The OMB also oversees government reorganization plans and recommends improvements in departmental operations.

The CEA was created by the Employment Act of 1946. Its central function is to provide the president with objective data on the state of the economy and expert advice on economic policy. The agency is responsible for creating the *Annual Economic Report of the President*, which has a wealth of data on various aspects of the economy and an overview of the president's policies. Presidents have varied in how closely they work with the CEA or the other parts of their economic team. Some prominent CEA members have been influential in shaping and promoting the administration's tax policy and jobs program. Others have had a more secondary role.

United States Trade Representative (USTR)
An agency founded in 1962 to negotiate with foreign governments to create trade agreements, resolve disputes, and participate in global trade-policy organizations. Treaties negotiated by the USTR must be ratified by the Senate.

National Economic Council (NEC)
A group of economic advisers created in 1993 to work with the president to coordinate economic policy.

The president and his advisers on trade policy, including the U.S. trade representative (Robert Lighthizer, right) must coordinate with Congress on economic policy making. Here, Lighthizer, Canadian minister of foreign affairs Chrystia Freeland (left), and Mexican economy minister Idelfonso Guajardo (center) address the media during NAFTA talks in Mexico City. President Trump made it a priority to renegotiate this trade agreement.

The USTR is responsible for developing and coordinating U.S. international trade, commodity, and direct investment policy and for overseeing negotiations on trade policy with other countries.[21] With the increasing importance of globalization and international trade, and Congress's deference to the executive branch on trade issues through the fast-track authority, the USTR is an important player in economic policy making. The fast-track process gives the USTR wide latitude to negotiate trade deals that have to be approved by Congress but cannot be amended or filibustered.

The NEC was established in 1993 to fulfill a campaign promise by President Clinton to elevate economic policy to the level of national security and foreign policy. It has four principal functions: "to coordinate policy-making for domestic and international economic issues, to coordinate economic policy advice for the President, to ensure that policy decisions and programs are consistent with the President's economic goals, and to monitor implementation of the President's economic policy agenda."[22] The NEC coordinates policy by bringing together cabinet secretaries who work on economic issues, such as the Treasury secretary, budget director, Commerce secretary, CEA chairman, and Labor secretary. The NEC initially appeared to challenge the CEA's turf, but a division of labor has preserved an important role for each: the NEC is the political arm that coordinates economic policy, and the CEA is the technical arm that provides information about the economy.

Though we have described the roles of Congress and the president separately, understanding the interactions between these government branches is central to understanding economic policy. If the president's party controls Congress, then the president's budget becomes the starting point for congressional negotiations over the budget. If the opposing party controls Congress, then the president's budget is usually considered "dead on arrival" and Congress creates its own document. In 2018, Trump's budget was ignored by congressional leadership, although the president and the leadership belonged to the same party. Of course, the president can use the veto threat to try to move Congress closer to his or her position, but when the budget is contained in one large package that must be signed or vetoed in its entirety, it is difficult to carry out such threats.[23]

The bureaucracy

All the departments explained so far could be considered part of the larger bureaucracy, but they are included within the Executive Office of the President and therefore are usually considered in conjunction with the president. Here, we will focus on two bureaucratic agencies that are key in creating monetary policy: the **Federal Reserve System** (an independent agency) and the **Treasury Department** (a cabinet-level department). While the Fed and the Treasury are the most important agencies for economic policy making, many other agencies are important for both making regulatory policy (which we discuss later) and implementing spending on a broad range of policies, from agricultural subsidies to building highways to defense spending. All of these bureaucratic decisions have an impact on the economy.

The Federal Reserve System The Federal Reserve Act of 1913 established the Federal Reserve System (commonly known as "the Fed") to bring stability and continuity to the nation's banking system. The Federal Reserve Reform Act of 1977 gave the Fed a dual mandate of pursuing stable prices and maximum employment. The chair, vice-chair, and five other governors serve on the **Federal Reserve Board**. The governors have 14-year overlapping terms and are appointed by the president and approved by the Senate. The president selects the chair and vice-chair from the sitting governors for 4-year terms; they may be renominated for additional terms as chair or vice-chair until their terms on the Board of Governors expire. The board is responsible for establishing monetary policy for the nation, which includes influencing interest rates and the money supply, and regulating the lending activity of member banks (discussed in more detail later in the chapter). There are 12 regional Federal Reserve banks and more than 3,000 member banks out of the more than 8,000 banks in the nation.[24] We examine the Fed's operations in the section on monetary policy, but briefly, the regional banks lend money to banks, hold reserves for them, supply currency and coins, buy and sell government securities, and report on the state of the economy in their respective regions.

Federal Reserve System
An independent agency that serves as the central bank of the United States to bring stability to the nation's banking system.

Treasury Department
A cabinet-level agency that is responsible for managing the federal government's revenue. It prints currency, collects taxes, and sells government bonds.

Federal Reserve Board
The group of seven presidential appointees who govern the Federal Reserve System.

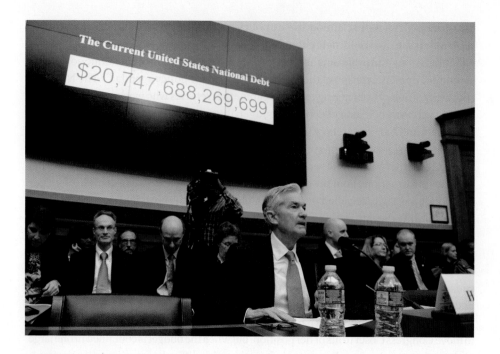

U.S. Federal Reserve chair Jerome Powell sits in front of a national debt sign ahead of his first appearance before a congressional panel to deliver the Fed's semi-annual report on monetary policy.

One crucial characteristic of the Fed is its political independence, which has three primary sources. First, the Fed is an independent agency: though the president and Senate determine who sits on the board of the Fed, its decisions are not subject to presidential or congressional review. Second, the 14-year terms for the governors and the 4-year terms for the chair and vice-chair purposefully do not overlap with the federal election calendar. One strong indication of the Fed's independence is that presidents typically reappoint chairs who were initially appointed by presidents of the other party. For example, Ben Bernanke was nominated by Bush and renominated by Obama for one term.[25] However, Trump broke that tradition by replacing Janet Yellen with Jerome Powell. Unlike other presidential appointees in the bureaucracy, members of the Federal Reserve Board can be removed only "for cause," the precise definition of which has never been tested. This largely insulates the Fed from the political process.

Third, the Fed does not depend on Congress for its operating budget because it can literally create its own money (as we will discuss later). Congress's control of the bureaucracy is rooted in the power of the purse (see Chapter 13), but because Congress does not provide the Fed's budget, Congress has much less leverage over it. The Fed's primary source of income is interest on the Treasury securities it owns. After paying for all its expenses, the Fed returned about $81 billion to the Treasury in 2017. Overall, in 2017 the Fed employed 19,161 people with total salaries of $2.1 billion.[26] The employees are not subject to civil service rules or pay grades; thus, the Fed can offer top salaries and hire some of the best people in finance and economics.

Is the Fed's independence a good thing or a bad thing? Supporters point out that the Fed's central goal is shared by nearly all politicians and Americans: a stable economy and slow, steady growth (as mentioned earlier, the Fed has a dual mandate of pursuing stable prices and maximum employment). Therefore, the argument goes, we should leave the Fed alone, let it do its job, and keep politics out of monetary policy. However, critics argue that the Fed's lack of accountability means that it can do things that hurt the economy—and voters have no recourse. For example, during Jerome Powell's confirmation hearing in 2017 senators grilled the nominee about the impact of the Fed's policies on the economy. Senator Sherrod Brown (D-OH) worried that the Fed would ease up on enforcing regulations on big banks, saying, "Americans are still

Though the Fed's monetary policy is always aimed at stabilizing the economy and fostering steady growth, markets can still have adverse reactions. When the Fed announced that it would raise interest rates in June 2018, the Dow Jones Industrial Average dropped 119 points at the day's close.

struggling because of low wages, underemployment or unemployment and lack of opportunities. And loosening the rules for some of the country's largest banks isn't the way to solve these problems."[27] If the Fed moves in that direction, voters can do nothing about it.

But the Fed is not immune to political influence. In fact, one line of research argues that the Fed tries to help presidents during reelection years by encouraging a pro-growth economy.[28] Evidence on this point is mixed, but at a minimum presidents do have the ability to make it clear when they disagree with the Fed's policies. Presidents also have the opportunity to appoint the chair and vice-chair of the Fed, but presidents usually go for continuity over change because they do not want to upset the financial markets. Other research has shown that the Fed is at least somewhat sensitive to the preferences of the president and Congress, who may publicly criticize the Fed when they disagree with its policies.[29]

The Fed's ultimate accountability is to Congress, because if things really got out of hand—for example, if the Fed decided to increase interest rates to 20 percent without good reason—Congress could amend the Federal Reserve Act and remove the Fed's responsibility or autonomy in specific areas. The Fed must report to Congress annually on its activities and to the banking committees of Congress twice a year on its plans for monetary policy. The Fed's annual report is subject to an outside audit. Fed officials also frequently testify before Congress on a broad range of issues.

The Treasury Department The Treasury Department is another part of the bureaucracy that plays an important role in economic policy making. According to its website, the mission of the Treasury "is to promote the conditions for prosperity and stability in the United States and encourage prosperity and stability in the rest of the world." Specifically, the range of its responsibilities related to economic policy making includes:

- managing federal finances;
- collecting taxes, duties, and monies paid to and due to the United States and paying all bills of the United States;
- producing currency and coinage;

- managing government accounts and the public debt;
- supervising national banks and thrift institutions;
- advising on domestic and international financial, monetary, economic, trade, and tax policy;
- enforcing federal finance and tax laws; and
- investigating and prosecuting tax evaders, counterfeiters, and forgers.[30]

Some of these responsibilities overlap with the Fed's, especially supervising banks and managing the public debt. In most instances the responsibilities are complementary rather than competing, such as the management of currency and coins: the Treasury produces currency at the Bureau of Engraving and Printing (about 25 million bills are printed every day) and coins at the U.S. Mint (which made just over 14 *billion* coins in 2017), and the Fed distributes them to member banks.[31] Financing federal debt is another matter. The Treasury generally prefers lower interest rates to keep down the cost of financing the debt and to promote economic growth, whereas the Fed is concerned about keeping rates high enough to avoid inflation. Therefore, the Fed and Treasury must often coordinate their policies to avoid working at cross-purposes.

How economic policy makers interact: the 2008 economic crisis

A dramatic example of cooperation between the Fed and Treasury is the 2008 economic crisis. Problems in the subprime, or high-risk, mortgage market; the collapse of housing prices; and the tightening of credit markets had been putting pressure on the economy through the spring and summer. The first sign of serious trouble came in March 2008 when the New York Federal Reserve made a loan of $30 billion to JP Morgan Chase to facilitate the buyout of Bear Stearns, an investment

During the financial crisis of 2008–2009, the government had to take unprecedented action to avoid an even deeper crisis. Here, then–Senate Majority Leader Harry Reid (D-NV) speaks to reporters. He was joined by other congressional leaders and Ben Bernanke (far right), who was Federal Reserve chairman at the time.

bank that was going bankrupt because of its exposure to mortgage-backed securities. Over the next six months, "Fannie Mae" and "Freddie Mac," which fund most of the home loans in the nation; investment bank Merrill Lynch; and the world's largest insurance company, American International Group (AIG), had to be bailed out by the federal government. When investment bank Lehman Brothers went bankrupt and Washington Mutual, the nation's sixth-largest bank, failed, the markets panicked.

This series of disasters and near disasters led to around-the-clock meetings of Fed and Treasury leaders, who produced a plan for the government to buy mortgage-related assets from banks and other financial institutions. In a stunning rebuke to party leaders and President Bush, the Senate initially rejected the proposed plan and took the lead on retooling the bill. The Senate passed the bill by a bipartisan 75–24 vote.[32] Two days later the House passed the bill by a 263–171 vote, with strong support from both parties.[33] President Bush signed the Emergency Economic Stabilization Act into law on October 3, 2008. The Troubled Asset Relief Program (TARP) was established under the act to buy up to $700 billion in bad assets to help stabilize the banks.

Despite this significant rescue plan, the crisis spiraled out of control in the following weeks. Stock markets plunged worldwide, with the U.S. stock market shedding 35 percent of its value in the two months after the crisis began. Credit markets remained frozen, and it became clear that an alternative approach was needed. European leaders swiftly agreed to an approach in which governments would directly invest in banks, providing them with desperately needed capital in return for equity stakes in the banks. The United States followed suit with an initial allocation of $250 billion to directly invest in banks, followed by an announcement that the Treasury would abandon its plan to buy toxic debt created by the subprime mortgage mess and use all the funds to directly invest in banks. By mid-November, the economic panic had eased, but the situation remained fragile.

When President Obama took office in 2009, things were still very grim. Stocks finally bottomed in March 2009 (down 56 percent from their October 2007 high), shortly after Treasury Secretary Timothy Geithner announced the administration's Financial Stability Plan. The plan focused on four problems: frozen credit markets, weakened bank capital, a backlog of troubled mortgage assets on bank balance sheets, and falling home prices. Working with the Fed to stabilize the financial markets, the Treasury had largely resolved three of those four problems one year later. Credit markets were operating, and banks were in much better shape, having raised more than $140 billion in capital and $60 billion in unsecured debt. Banks used these funds to repay the Treasury, which as of March 2018 has earned a 10.3 percent profit for the government. The Treasury expects to eventually recover all of the TARP expenditures (with 96.6 percent recovered as of June 2018).[34] The housing market has also stabilized, with sales up and prices slowly rising in most markets. Troubled mortgage assets remain on the balance sheets of many banks, but with their stronger base of capital and the strengthened housing market, these securities were not as great a concern as they had been.[35] In September 2012, the Fed announced a new policy to inject money into the economy, promising to buy $40 billion a month of mortgage-backed securities. Three months later this policy was increased to $85 billion a month. This was an open-ended commitment and was seen as the boldest move yet by the Fed to revive the economy. Overall, the Fed increased its balance sheet from just over $900 billion when the crisis began to just over $4.5 trillion when the balance sheet peaked in October 2015 (see Figure 15.3). Thus, the Fed injected

Protesters at a rally against government bailouts for Wall Street called for the resignation of the chief executive of Goldman Sachs and cancellation of bonuses for all Goldman employees. Huge profits and bonuses on Wall Street in 2009–2010 were very controversial, as the national unemployment rate held at nearly 10 percent.

FIGURE 15.3

The Fed Balance Sheet

The amount of assets held by the Fed in mortgage-backed securities expanded after the 2008 financial crisis. What effect does increasing the balance sheet have on the circulation of the dollar?

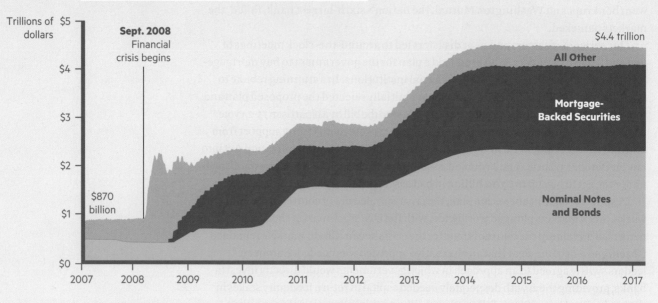

Source: Norbert Michel, "The Crisis Is Over: It Is Time to End Experimental Monetary Policy," The Heritage Foundation, November 9, 2017, www.heritage.org/monetary-policy/report/the-crisis-over-it-time-end-experimental-monetary-policy (accessed 9/18/14).

more than $3.6 trillion into the economy. Late in 2017, the Fed announced it would end this policy and start selling its assets. By July 2018, the Fed had reduced its holdings by about $277 billion.[36]

Despite the broad success of the financial rescue, it remained a political liability. The rescue was widely perceived as a bailout of Wall Street. Many citizens were outraged over corporate salaries and bonuses, the government bailouts, and the perception that not enough was being done to help average Americans. The economy lost 8.4 million jobs in 2008–2009, millions of Americans were losing their homes, and unemployment remained stuck around 9.5 percent through 2010. Discontent with the bailout contributed to the crushing defeat for Democrats in the 2010 midterm elections, despite the fact that it was a bipartisan plan passed at the end of the Bush administration. The issue continued to play a role in the 2018 midterms, with President Trump and some Republicans calling for less regulation of the financial sector and Democrats wanting to continue or strengthen the Obama-era reforms.

"Why Should I Care?"

The president, Congress, and the Fed all play an important role in making economic policy. As a citizen and voter, you have a strong interest in wanting to have our elected leaders be responsive to our preferences. Yet in the area of economic policy, one of the central players—the Fed—is largely independent from political influence. The Fed is designed this way to make sure that it can make unpopular decisions that may be important for the health of the economy, such as helping to bail out Wall Street during an economic crisis. Political goals and economic goals may not always align, so is the Fed necessary to save us from ourselves, or should there be more democratic control of monetary policy?

Tools and theories of economic policy

Now that we know the key players in economic policy and their goals, it is time to examine the tools those policy makers use to accomplish those goals. Policy makers cannot pull levers and push buttons to achieve desired outcomes, nor are they immune from external forces that can sink the economy despite their best efforts. However, there are certain things that leaders can do to move the massive U.S. economy in the right direction.

Fiscal policy

Fiscal policy is the use of the government's taxing and spending power to influence the direction of the economy. Developed by economist John Maynard Keynes in the 1930s, **Keynesian economics** argues that policy makers can soften the effects of a recession by stimulating the economy when overall demand is low—during a recession, when people aren't spending as much—through tax cuts or increased government spending. Tax cuts put more money in people's pockets, allowing them to spend more than they otherwise would. The government can also inject money into the economy by purchasing various goods, such as highways or military equipment, or by issuing direct payments to individuals, such as unemployment compensation. From this perspective, it is acceptable to run budget deficits to increase employment and national income, which in turn gives a short-term boost to the economy. Keynes also pointed out that if overall demand is too high, which might result in inflation, policy makers should cool off the economy by cutting spending or raising taxes.[37]

Perhaps the best example of a Keynesian tax cut used to stimulate the economy was the Revenue Act of 1964. The tax cut, one of the largest in the twentieth century, helped lay the foundation for unprecedented economic expansion in the 1960s.[38]

A competing theory of fiscal policy was the basis for Ronald Reagan's tax cuts in 1981 and has been the centerpiece of economic policy for many Republicans since then. **Supply-side economics** focuses on the effects of tax policy and regulations on the labor supply (how much people work) rather than their effects on overall demand (how much people spend). The idea is based on the relationship between the top **marginal tax rate** and total tax revenue, a measure of how much people are working (as more people work, more tax revenue is generated), as shown in the Laffer curve, named for economist Arthur Laffer (see Figure 15.4). The basic shape of the curve is intuitive, and the end points are noncontroversial: if the tax rate is zero, there will be no tax revenue; if the tax rate is 100 percent, nobody will work because they won't get to keep any of their money, so total tax revenue at that end of the curve is also zero.[39] Laffer argued that if tax rates are too high (to the right of the peak in the graph), people will work less because a large percentage of their income is going to the government. In this situation, the government should cut taxes in order to raise total government revenue—a claim that seems counterintuitive.[40]

In practice, this theory was too good to be true. When the Reagan administration cut taxes in 1981, with the top marginal rate going from 70 to 50 percent, revenue fell and budget deficits exploded. Supporters of the supply-side theory argued that the problem was on the spending side of the equation rather than on the tax revenue side. That is, deficits went up because the Democratic Congress spent too much, not because of Reagan's tax cuts. However, both taxes and government spending as a share of the

Keynesian economics
The theory that governments should use economic policy, like taxing and spending, to maintain stability in the economy.

"

No nation has ever taxed itself into prosperity.

—Rush Limbaugh

supply-side economics
The theory that lower tax rates will stimulate the economy by encouraging people to save, invest, and produce more goods and services.

marginal tax rate
The tax rate paid on income up to some threshold. For example, in 2018 single people paid no income tax on their first $12,000 of income (because of the $12,000 standard deduction). After deductions, they paid 10 percent on the first $9,525 of taxable income; 12 percent on income between $21,526 and $50,700; 22 percent on income between $50,701 and $94,500; and so on, all the way up to 37 percent on income over $512,000.

**FIGURE
15.4**

The Laffer Curve

The Laffer curve shows the theoretical relationship between the tax rate and total tax revenue. How did this curve contribute to the budget deficits of the 1980s?

business cycle
The normal pattern of expansion and contraction of the economy.

overall economy fell during the Reagan presidency, which suggests that spending was not the source of the budget deficits in the 1980s.[41] A similar relationship between a cut in tax rates and a decline in revenue was observed after the Bush tax cuts in 2001.

While it is too early to know how the $1.5 trillion Trump tax cuts will play out, it is clear that they were motivated by this same supply-side thinking. Clearly the tax cut could not be justified on Keynesian grounds, given that the economy was at full employment at the time of the tax cuts.

How Much Can Fiscal Policy Really Affect the Economy? Economists continue to debate the extent to which fiscal policy can influence the economy. Two factors have limited the effectiveness of fiscal policy. First, fiscal policies often cannot be implemented quickly enough to have the intended impact on the **business cycle**— the normal expansion and contraction of the economy. This is especially true when one party controls Congress and the other controls the presidency, but it can also be the case even during unified government.

The $787 billion American Recovery and Reinvestment Act of 2009, designed to stimulate the economy and create jobs after the 2008 economic crisis, ran into problems along these lines. Although the legislation had a limited immediate impact on the economy, it is impossible to spend that much money (or implement tax cuts) without some time lag. Of the $787 billion total, tax cuts comprised $288 billion; contracts, grants, and loans were $275 billion; and one-time payments to Social Security recipients were $224 billion. One year after the recovery bill was enacted, the government reported that nearly 600,000 jobs had been saved, but only 34.6 percent of the money ($272.2 billion) had been spent. Austerity policies at the state level also blunted the impact of the stimulus; that is, at the same time that the national government was trying to stimulate the economy, states were cutting spending and raising taxes to balance their budgets. Republicans criticized the Democrats, who controlled Congress and the presidency at the time, for spending too much money and not enacting policies that would have had a more immediate effect (such as payroll tax cuts). Critics on the left, meanwhile, argued that the stimulus wasn't big enough. A payroll tax cut was implemented for 2011–2012 that reduced the rate from 6.2 to 4.2 percent, putting an additional $1,000 in the pocket of the average American household for each of those years.

Second, on the other side of the Keynesian coin, tax increases or spending cuts during good economic times are much more difficult to implement than tax cuts or spending increases, which are more politically popular. Although the latter are limited by the difficulty of timing these fiscal policies to have a maximum economic impact, the former are limited by politics: politicians do not like to raise taxes or cut spending. Furthermore, even if politicians *wanted* to cut spending to influence the economy or to reduce the federal deficit, it is becoming increasingly difficult to do so because a growing portion of the federal budget is devoted to **mandatory spending**—that is, entitlements such as Social Security, which must be spent by law, and interest on the federal debt, which must be paid (if the United States defaulted on its debt, there would be an international economic meltdown).

With the 2019 deficit projected at $973 billion, Congress would have to eliminate all nondefense **discretionary spending**—spending that can be cut from the budget without changing the underlying law, which is everything other than defense, entitlements, and interest on the debt ($550 billion)—and 59 percent of discretionary defense spending ($423 billion of $716 billion) to balance the budget.[42] This would literally mean shutting down the State Department; Homeland Security; the Justice Department, which includes the FBI and all federal law enforcement; and the Interior Department, which includes the National Park Service and the National Forest Service; and eliminating all spending on science, including the National Science Foundation and NASA; transportation; the arts and public broadcasting; student loans; and the food stamp and child nutrition programs. The share of the budget allotted to discretionary spending is projected to fall from 13 percent of GDP in 1968 to only 5.5 percent by 2028 (see Figure 15.5). This has clear implications for efforts to balance the budget in the future: it cannot be done through cutting discretionary spending alone and will have to include cuts in mandatory spending (such as Social Security and Medicare) and tax increases.

mandatory spending
Expenditures that are required by law, such as the funding for Social Security.

discretionary spending
Expenditures that can be cut from the budget without changing the underlying law, which is everything other than defense, entitlements, and interest on the debt.

**FIGURE
15.5**

Mandatory and Discretionary Spending, 1968–2028

The percentage of the budget allocated for discretionary spending has been shrinking since the 1960s. What implications does this have for members of Congress and the president as they try to reduce the federal deficits?

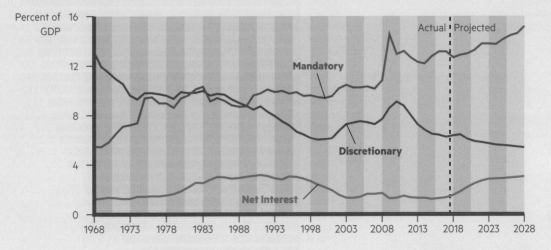

Source: Congressional Budget Office, The Budget and Economic Outlook, 2018–2028, Figure 2-1, p. 45, www.cbo.gov/system/files/115th
-congress-2017-2018/reports/53651-outlook.pdf (accessed 4/24/18).

Given the tenuous relationship between fiscal policy and the state of the economy, critics have suggested an alternative rationale to justify large budget deficits in relatively good economic times. (Recall that a Keynesian perspective says that the government should run surpluses during good times, and supply-siders argue that tax cuts should produce surpluses rather than deficits.) Instead of being primarily an effort to stimulate the economy, large tax cuts and budget deficits like those of the 1980s and early 2000s are the only way to cut down the size of government—they are, as Reagan's budget director David Stockman called them, an attempt to "starve the beast."[43] If there is no money available, liberals will not be able to propose new programs, and conservatives will be more likely to cut existing programs. The only alternative is raising taxes, which is usually politically unpopular, even though our tax bite is relatively small compared with that of other countries, ranking fourth from the bottom of nations belonging to the Organization for Economic Cooperation and Development (OECD) (see Figure 15.6). The other possibility, of course, is to simply accept large budget deficits as a permanent part of the economic landscape. Although that may be politically tempting, it is not a sustainable strategy in the long run.

Redistributive Implications of Fiscal Policy Fiscal policy may have a relatively modest impact on the economy, but it determines how the tax burden is distributed and which parts of the economy and policy areas benefit from federal spending. In other words, fiscal policy has *redistributive* implications. There are two ways of thinking about the characteristics of federal taxes: (1) the different types of taxes

FIGURE 15.6

Comparing Global Tax Rates

Tax rates vary considerably around the world. Given the data below, do you feel that taxes in the United States are too low or too high?

Source: OECD.org, Tax Policy Analysis, Revenue Statistics, http://stats.oecd.org/index.aspx?DataSetCode=REV (accessed 4/24/18).

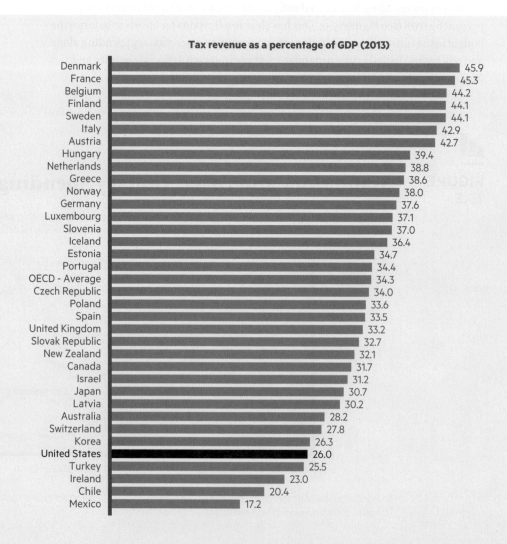

Tax revenue as a percentage of GDP (2013)

Country	%
Denmark	45.9
France	45.3
Belgium	44.2
Finland	44.1
Sweden	44.1
Italy	42.9
Austria	42.7
Hungary	39.4
Netherlands	38.8
Greece	38.6
Norway	38.0
Germany	37.6
Luxembourg	37.1
Slovenia	37.0
Iceland	36.4
Estonia	34.7
Portugal	34.4
OECD - Average	34.3
Czech Republic	34.0
Poland	33.6
Spain	33.5
United Kingdom	33.2
Slovak Republic	32.7
New Zealand	32.1
Canada	31.7
Israel	31.2
Japan	30.7
Latvia	30.2
Australia	28.2
Switzerland	27.8
Korea	26.3
United States	26.0
Turkey	25.5
Ireland	23.0
Chile	20.4
Mexico	17.2

Federal Revenues and Spending, 1962 and 2019

FIGURE
15.7

A much larger share of tax revenue comes from payroll taxes than was true in the 1960s. What implications does this have for the redistributive nature of federal taxes? What have been the biggest changes since the 1960s in the way the federal tax dollar is spent? Are these trends likely to reverse or continue in the next 30 years?

Revenues, 1962

Excise Taxes and all other **16.6%**
Payroll Taxes **17.1%**
Individual income taxes **45.7%**
Corporate Income Taxes **20.6%**

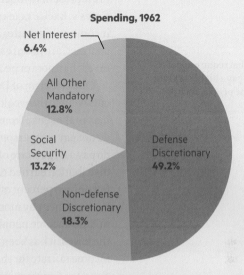

Spending, 1962

Net Interest **6.4%**
All Other Mandatory **12.8%**
Social Security **13.2%**
Non-defense Discretionary **18.3%**
Defense Discretionary **49.2%**

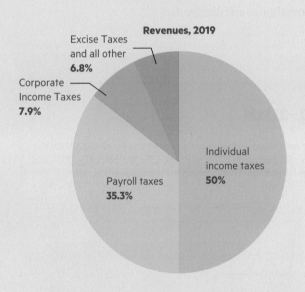

Revenues, 2019

Excise Taxes and all other **6.8%**
Corporate Income Taxes **7.9%**
Payroll taxes **35.3%**
Individual income taxes **50%**

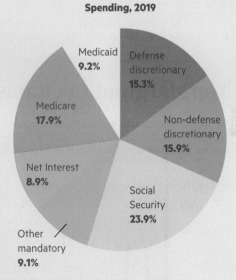

Spending, 2019

Medicaid **9.2%**
Defense discretionary **15.3%**
Medicare **17.9%**
Non-defense discretionary **15.9%**
Net Interest **8.9%**
Other mandatory **9.1%**
Social Security **23.9%**

Sources: Congressional Budget Office, *Updated Budget Projections*, 2016–2026, Table 1, p. 15, and Table 4, pp. 21–22, www.cbo.gov (accessed 6/3/16); numbers for 2019 are from Congressional Budget Office, *The Budget and Economic Outlook*, 2018–2028, Table 2-1, p. 44, Table 3-1, p. 67, www.cbo.gov/system/files/115th-congress-2017-2018/reports/53651-outlook.pdf (accessed 4/24/18).

and (2) their redistributive nature—that is, whether a specific tax is regressive, neutral, or progressive. There are four major types of federal taxes: personal income taxes, corporate taxes, payroll taxes (for Social Security and Medicare), and excise taxes (such as taxes on cigarettes, alcohol, gasoline, air travel, and telephone lines). The pie charts in Figure 15.7 show how the distribution of tax revenue changed between 1962 and 2019. The proportion of personal income taxes held relatively steady, but excise taxes and corporate taxes fell and payroll taxes more than doubled.

DID YOU KNOW?

45%

of Americans pay no income tax.
Source: Tax Policy Center

regressive
Describes taxes that take a larger share of poor people's income than wealthy people's income, such as sales taxes and payroll taxes.

progressive
Describes taxes that require upper-income people to pay a higher tax rate than lower-income people, such as income taxes.

The increasing share of tax revenue that comes from the payroll tax has important implications for the redistributive nature of taxes. Payroll taxes are **regressive** because everyone who works pays the same rate of 6.2 percent, up to a certain income level ($128,400 in 2018; in addition, all workers pay an additional 1.45 percent on all income to support Medicare). Thus, someone who earns $128,400 pays the same *amount* of Social Security tax ($7,961) as a wealthy individual such as Bill Gates does, but the tax represents a much larger share of the lesser-paid person's income than it does of Gates's. Excise taxes are also regressive—poor people spend a larger portion of their income on cigarettes, alcohol, and gas than wealthier people do. Income taxes, in contrast, are **progressive**: upper-income people pay a larger share of their income in taxes than poorer people.

One criticism of Donald Trump's tax cut was that a disproportionate share of the cuts went to the wealthiest people in the country, making taxes less progressive. This may make sense from one perspective, given that the bottom 45 percent of taxpayers do not pay any personal income tax. However, poor and lower-middle-income people do pay a large share of the total payroll tax. Thus, the top quarter of the income distribution earned 69 percent of total income and paid 87 percent of all income taxes but only 50 percent of payroll taxes.[44] So income tax cuts will help wealthier people because they pay most of the income tax, whereas payroll tax cuts will help poor and middle-income people more. At the same time, the top marginal tax rate is close to the lowest it has been since the 1920s (see Figure 15.8). As a result, the overall personal income tax rate for the top fifth of the income distribution dropped from 17.5 percent in 2000 to 16 percent in 2014. This lower overall tax rate for the wealthy is also explained by the lower 15 percent rate for capital gains and dividends.[45]

FIGURE 15.8

Top Marginal Tax Rates, 1913–2018

The top marginal tax rate, which is the tax rate paid by the richest Americans on their income above some threshold ($500,000 in 2018 for a single taxpayer), plummeted from 94 percent in 1945 to 35 percent in 2012, rose back up to 39.6 percent in 2013, and then fell back down to 37 percent in 2018. What are the arguments for and against increasing the top marginal tax rate?

Sources: Data from the Internal Revenue Service, "Internal Revenue Bulletin: 2007-45," November 5, 2007, Rev. Proc. 2007-66, www.irs.gov (accessed 5/12/12); 2008–2018 rates from www.irs.gov (accessed 4/24/18).

Monetary policy

What is money? You probably think that you know what the green stuff in your wallet is. You may wish you had more of it, but you know what it is. But money is much more than bills and coins. You probably pay for more things with plastic (debit and credit cards) than with coins and currency. Are those cards "money" as well? Economists categorize debit cards as money because debit cards represent the money you already have in your checking account—which *is* the same as cash. Credit cards are not considered money because when you use a credit card you are, in essence, getting a short-term loan. Broader definitions of money also include savings accounts and certificates of deposit. So far, so good. The tricky part involves understanding where money comes from. The answer may seem simple: the government prints it. But what about the banking part? If you've never thought this through, it can be confusing or even unsettling.

Consider this example: You have just graduated from college and you want to start your own business as a political consultant. You have volunteered on several campaigns and have even run a few statewide campaigns. Two candidates want to hire you for the next election cycle, but you need to rent an office and buy computers, phones, and other office equipment. This will obviously take some money. So you go to a bank with your business proposal and show them your contracts for the coming election and your plan for repaying the $100,000 loan that you are requesting. To your surprise, the loan officer says yes and you leave the bank with a checkbook and debit card $100,000 strong! The bank just created $100,000, seemingly out of thin air.[46] How can that be? Doesn't money have to be something more tangible? Doesn't it have to be based on gold or other real assets rather than just a contractual promise to repay the money? No—at least not in this country. In 1933, the United States nationalized privately held gold and said that contracts must be paid in dollars, not gold; then in 1971, the country completely abandoned the gold standard. Why doesn't the whole system fall apart? Because it is based on trust and confidence in the banking system. After you receive your loan from the bank, you could go directly to the computer store and purchase $10,000 worth of computers with your new debit card. And because your debit card purchase will be electronically authorized at the cash register, the sales staff will have no reason to ask where your money came from. They would just give you the computers.

Most people rarely think about how the banking system works, simply assuming that their money is safe. But now that we have gotten you thinking about where money comes from, we will provide more details about the banking system by examining the targets and tools of monetary policy.

Targets of Monetary Policy The Fed monitors levels of bank lending, the money supply, and interest rates and tries to meet specific targets in each of these three categories set at its monthly meetings. Bank lending is important to monitor and regulate because it is the source of most new money in the economy. It is crucial for economic growth because businesses borrow money to expand, and as they grow they add jobs. If credit is tight and businesses cannot borrow money, economic growth will suffer, as became painfully evident in late 2008 and 2009. Large public corporations can raise money to expand by selling shares of their company in the stock market, but small businesses do not have this option.

The money supply is also central to economic growth and directly related to levels of lending activity. The Fed can influence the amount of money in the system by making it easier or harder for banks to lend money. According to the **monetarist theory** of macroeconomic policy, the amount of money in circulation is the most important

It is well enough that people of the nation do not understand our banking and monetary system, for if they did, I believe there would be a revolution before tomorrow morning.

—Henry Ford

In the late 1800s, presidential candidate William Jennings Bryan railed against the burdensome "cross of gold" and argued for a silver-backed currency. But since 1971, the value of the U.S. dollar depends not on gold or silver but on the banking system and international currency markets.

monetarist theory
The idea that the amount of money in circulation (the money supply) is the primary influence on economic activity and inflation.

determinant of economic activity and inflation. If there is too much money chasing too few goods, there could be inflationary pressure on the economy and prices might rise too quickly.[47] In contrast, if there isn't enough money available, a recession could occur.

Perhaps the most obvious targets of monetary policy are interest rates. Changing interest rates affects the economy by making borrowing money either cheaper or more expensive. Businesses and consumers are more likely to borrow if the interest rate is 6 percent than if it is 12 percent. Consumer purchases of big-ticket items, those things that are financed by borrowing rather than being purchased with cash, also increase when interest rates are low. These purchases dry up when interest rates are high. That is why so many appliance stores and car dealers advertise: "Zero dollars down, and zero percent interest until next January!" Entire sectors of the economy, such as housing, construction, consumer durables, and cars, are very sensitive to interest rates.

Tools of Monetary Policy What can the Fed do to meet targets it sets on credit availability, the money supply, and interest rates? It uses three central tools of monetary policy. The **reserve requirement** is the most obvious and potentially powerful tool for affecting the availability of credit, but it isn't used as often as the other two tools. Banks are required to have a certain amount of money in reserve to make sure they have cash on hand to cover withdrawals. If everyone decided to take all their money out at once, the banking system would collapse, because banks are required to have only 10 percent of all deposits on reserve.

By simply changing the amount of money that banks are required to hold for every deposit, the Fed can have a big impact on the amount of money that banks can lend. For example, requiring banks to hold 15 percent of all deposits in reserve instead of 10 percent would contract the amount of money those institutions could lend, whereas dropping the requirement to 5 percent would have the opposite effect. However, because changing the reserve requirement has such a powerful impact on the economy, the Fed has rarely used this tool.[48]

The second monetary-policy tool, interest rates, is more difficult to manage than the reserve requirement. With the reserve requirement, the Fed simply announces the change in the rate. With interest rates, there is only one rate—the **discount rate**—that the Fed sets directly. This is the rate that the Fed charges member banks for short-term loans. However, it is far less important as a policy tool than the **federal funds rate (FFR)**, the rate that member banks charge one another on overnight loans, which are short-term loans that banks use to meet their reserve requirements. Beginning in 1995, the FFR has been the central interest rate target for the Fed.[49] The FFR is set by the demand for overnight loans that are necessary to settle accounts, but the Fed greatly affects those rates.

To make this process clearer, let's go back to our example of the enterprising campaign consultant who got the $100,000 loan. If the bank that gave the loan also had some unexpected withdrawals during that business day, its "vault cash" at the end of the day may have been short of the 10 percent reserve requirement. The bank would have to go to the federal funds market and borrow money from a bank that had excess reserves on that given day. This process of borrowing and lending allows money to flow smoothly throughout the banking system. If reserves are tight all around the country, the price of the short-term loans will be bid up and the FFR will rise. If this happens, the Fed can inject more reserves into the system to keep the FFR at its target (we will explain how in the next section). The FFR has a broad impact on the economy because many short-term interest rates track the FFR quite closely. Despite the Fed's ability to influence short-term interest rates, it has only an indirect impact on long-term interest rates, including consumer rates such as mortgages and student loans. Long-term rates are set by the market—specifically by the expectations of the bond market for inflation.

reserve requirement
The minimum amount of money that a bank is required to have on hand to back up its assets.

discount rate
The interest rate that a bank must pay on a short-term loan from the Federal Reserve Bank.

federal funds rate (FFR)
The interest rate that a bank must pay on an overnight loan from another bank.

If an investor thinks that inflation will increase from 3 percent to 6 percent over the next five years, the investor will demand a higher interest rate for lending his or her money to the government or a corporation than if he or she thinks inflation will hold steady at about 3 percent.

The third tool that the Fed uses to meet its monetary targets is **open market operations**—the buying and selling of securities. This is the Fed's most important tool because it influences the FFR and the level of bank reserves and thus the money supply. If the Fed wants to increase the money supply and put downward pressure on the FFR, it will purchase securities such as government bonds from a bank. The bank gives the Fed its bonds, and the Fed deposits the appropriate amount of money into the bank's account at the Fed. The bank can use this money to support new loans.

Where does the Fed get its money to buy the bonds from the bank? Well, the Fed simply creates the money. You probably have heard the claim that if the government wanted to, it could just "print money" to pay for its programs and policies. That claim is literally true, but it would be completely irresponsible. Any government that would run the printing presses to pay for its programs, rather than raising the money through taxes, fees, and borrowing, would soon find itself with hyperinflation as experienced in Germany, Poland, Austria, and Hungary after World War I. (The worst inflation ever recorded was in Hungary after World War II: between July 1945 and August 1946, prices rose by a factor of 30,000,000,000,000,000,000,000,000,000!)[50] Our government prints money only to meet the demand for currency from its member banks. However, the Fed's purchase of a government security is like "printing money" and has the same potential inflationary impact, so this powerful tool must be used only when new money is needed in the system. The tool may also be used to contract the money supply or raise interest rates; if this is the desired outcome, the Fed will sell government securities. The member bank will give the Fed money to cover the cost of the bond and therefore take money out of circulation.

In 2008, the supply of new money in the economy was significantly limited as a result of the subprime mortgage market meltdown and related problems in the bond markets. As we noted above, Fed chair Ben Bernanke responded to this "credit crunch" by "flooding the street with money," just as the famous banker Benjamin Strong had advocated as the appropriate response to the Great Depression.[51] The Fed increased its assets from $927 billion on September 10, 2008, to an eye-popping $2.26 trillion by November 11, 2008. Assets held by the Fed, mostly government securities and mortgage-backed securities, peaked at $4.5 trillion in October 2015 and have fallen since.[52] This unprecedented intervention in the financial sector clearly prevented a serious crisis, but as noted, critics argue that the Fed has become a too powerful, unaccountable player in economic policy making.

Regulatory policy

Government regulation has a huge impact on the economy. For example, the federal government regulates the quality of food and water, the safety of workplaces and airspaces, and the integrity of the banking and finance system. In general, regulations address market failures such as monopolies, imperfect information, and negative externalities (which we'll discuss later in the chapter). There are two main types of regulation: economic and social. Economic regulation sets prices or conditions for entry of firms into an industry, whereas social regulation addresses issues of quality and safety.[53]

Economic and Social Regulation A common type of economic regulation concerns price regulation of monopolies. A monopoly occurs when a single firm controls the

open market operations
The process by which the Federal Reserve System buys and sells securities to influence the money supply.

Hyperinflation in Germany, Hungary, and other parts of Europe between the two world wars was so high that some countries' currency became essentially worthless. In Germany in 1923, it was cheaper to burn money than to buy wood, as this woman demonstrates—using several million deutsche marks as kindling.

DID YOU KNOW?

The Fed owns

$2.54 trillion

in U.S. Treasury securities, which is slightly more than the U.S. debt owned by China and Japan combined.

Source: FederalReserve.gov

entire market for a product and thus is not subject to competition. In this situation, the firm with the monopoly could charge extremely high prices if the government did not regulate it. Sometimes a "natural monopoly" occurs because getting into a specific business is so costly that it only makes sense to have one company. For example, to have more than one water company in a given town or city would not make sense because it costs so much to install water pipes and other necessary infrastructure. Though in this instance there is only one company, the government regulates the prices that the company can charge; alternatively, the water system may be owned by the local government.

When the competitive situation is not a natural monopoly, a large firm may act in a monopolistic way to restrict competition—for example, by slashing prices to drive the competition out of business. As soon as all competitors go out of business, the monopoly is free to raise prices again. Concern about this type of behavior led to the first two significant laws aimed at economic regulation: the Interstate Commerce Act (1887), which created the Interstate Commerce Commission to regulate railroad rates, and the Sherman Antitrust Act (1890), which served to break up Standard Oil in 1910, among other monopolies.

More common than a true monopoly is the situation where a firm that controls most but not all of a market starts acting like a monopoly. For example, in 1998 Microsoft was sued by the Justice Department and 19 states for trying to quash its competition in the rapidly growing area of Internet browsers. Microsoft claimed that Internet Explorer (IE) was an integral part of its Windows operating system, whereas government prosecutors argued that IE was a separate piece of software that was being given away for free, putting competitors like Netscape at a huge disadvantage. The district court judge agreed with the Justice Department and ordered that Microsoft be broken up into a Windows-based company and another company that would sell Internet Explorer and other programs. This ruling was overturned on appeal. In the meantime, George W. Bush was elected to his first term as president, and his Justice Department announced that it would not challenge the appeals court ruling. Instead, it proposed a settlement that required Microsoft to share its application programming interfaces with third-party companies.[54] This settlement was challenged by several states but upheld by an appeals court in 2004. In a more recent similar case, the European Union fined Google a record $2.7 billion for illegally steering users toward its comparative shopping site.[55]

The Microsoft and Google examples offer two lessons. First, regulation affects our daily lives in ways that may not be obvious. The extent to which a company can dominate the software industry is determined, in part, by the extent to which the

Government regulation affects many aspects of our lives. Regulations may be aimed at producing a cleaner environment (left) or preventing monopolies (Microsoft founder Bill Gates testifies about possible antitrust violations, right).

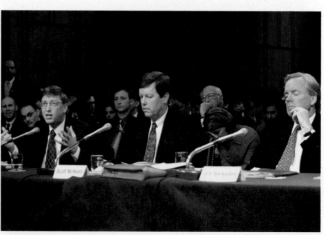

government regulates the company's behavior. Second, politics plays a key role in this process. An important event in the Microsoft case was the election of a president who took a less aggressive stance on regulating potential monopolies than his predecessor had. Recall that Republicans tend to favor a strong role for the free market and advocate a pro-business perspective, which both require a smaller role for government regulation, whereas Democrats generally favor more government regulation to protect the interests of consumers (in the Microsoft case, these interests would have led to a broader range of options for Internet browsers), the environment, and workers.

The most common market failures that lead to social regulation are negative externalities: they occur when the costs of a firm's behavior are not entirely borne by the firm and are passed on to other people. When this happens, the firm produces more of an unwanted good than is socially desirable. The classic example is pollution. In a free market, the owners of a coal-fired power plant do not bear the cost of the pollution spewing out of its smokestacks. The people who live downwind from the plant bear the cost. Therefore, the power plant owners have little incentive to curb pollution unless the government regulates it. Other examples of agencies that set social regulations are those that promote safety, such as the National Highway Traffic Safety Administration, the Consumer Product Safety Commission, and the Occupational Safety and Health Administration. Carbon emissions are another good example of a product (carbon) that would be overproduced by the market if there were no regulations.

Externalities may also be positive. For example, firms invest in research and development, but the knowledge and products that come from that R&D may have broader social benefits (such as developing a new drug that cures a disease). Goods with positive externalities may be *under*-produced by the free market unless firms are given economic incentives to invest in them. One important policy tool to address positive externalities is a patent. Patents are exclusive "property rights" that are given for a specific period of time to an inventor or company that develops a new product. The money to be gained from holding these rights provides an incentive to invest in developing innovative technology and ideas. In 2015, the U.S. Patent Office granted 325,979 patents of the 629,647 applications it received.[56]

The Politics of Regulation Regulatory policy also involves interbranch politics between Congress and the bureaucracy. Even when members of Congress agree on some general policy goal—for example, limiting air pollution—they often cannot agree on the precise mechanisms for achieving that goal, so they delegate authority to a regulatory agency. As discussed in Chapter 13, this produces a "principal–agent problem" in which Congress (the principal) cannot be sure that the bureaucracy (the agent) will implement policy according to its legislative goals. A related concern is that the regulatory agency will not be responsive to the wishes of Congress because it has been "captured" by the interests it is supposed to regulate (see Chapter 13). The Food and Drug Administration, the Federal Aviation Administration, and the U.S. Department of Agriculture, among others, have been accused of serving the very industries they are supposed to regulate, rather than protecting American consumers.[57]

Another area in which regulatory policy has generated some political heat concerns the trade-off between regulation and economic growth. Regulations impose costs on the free market, which may limit job growth. The Trump administration has moved aggressively to limit regulations and allow the free market to make more decisions. Some of the significant actions to reduce regulation include pulling out of the Paris Climate Accord, revising the fuel-efficiency regulations for cars and light trucks (this process is underway), repealing the Clean Power Plan, opening the Arctic Wildlife Refuge for oil production, dismantling parts of the Dodd-Frank law to impose fewer regulations on smaller banks, and dropping the Clinton-era policy of "once in, always in" that aimed to lock in reductions of hazardous air pollution from industrial sources. More than one-third of all rules issued by non-independent agencies were reviewed, even when they did not have an economic impact (which is a significant departure from previous administrations). At least 67 regulations have been eliminated or are in the process of being revised. According to the former head of the Environmental Protection Agency, Scott Pruitt, this has saved businesses over $1 billion, but critics are concerned about the long-term damage to the environment.[58]

Despite these recent moves to tackle the trade-off between regulation and economic growth by favoring free market policies, in recent years another approach to economic policy has attempted to address the trade-off by using the free market to further environmental goals. First, economists have long argued for introducing more market incentives and reducing government regulation to achieve environmental goals. Under cap and trade, the government sets an overall cap on carbon emissions, and then companies buy permits that allow them to emit a certain amount of carbon. Companies that reduce their carbon emissions can sell their permits to companies that want to emit more carbon. The benefit of this approach is that it uses market forces, rather than regulations, to find the best way to reduce carbon emissions. Launched in 2013, California's cap-and-trade program has been called "the best-designed program in the world" and is expected to reduce carbon emissions by more than 16 percent between 2013 and 2020, and by an additional 40 percent by 2030.[59] In cases like this, environmentalists have learned that using market principles can work to their advantage; another example, involving grazing rights in the West, is discussed in the Take a Stand feature.

Second, rather than simply regulating old sources of dirtier energy, an alternative is to promote a clean-energy economy or "green jobs" focused on biofuels, hybrid and electric cars, hydrogen fuel cells, and renewable energy sources such as solar and wind. Barack Obama promised to create 5 million green jobs and laid out a plan to invest $150 billion over 10 years. Those goals were not fully funded, nor was the target reached, but green jobs are a growth area. The Bureau of Labor Statistics (BLS) provided the first count of green jobs in 2009: 2.2 million jobs. By 2011 that had grown to 3.4 million jobs, but the BLS stopped collecting this information because of budget cuts.[60] However, other estimates reveal that green jobs continue to grow. In 2016, the Department of Energy counted 3.4 million people directly employed by clean energy businesses and another 2.2 million jobs related to energy efficiency.[61]

So while political debates over regulatory policy may still be quite intense, common ground may be found in pursuing market solutions to regulatory problems. In general, the public interest is often served by regulations that protect the environment, ensure the safety of the food supply, and regulate the dumping of hazardous chemicals, whether it is through traditional economic regulations or market approaches. In each instance, *politics* ends up defining how the public interest is served through regulation.

Trade policy and the balance of payments

Many of the factors that shape trade policy are beyond policy makers' control. It is extremely difficult for the U.S. government to influence the strength of the dollar relative to other currencies, consumer tastes, the low cost of labor in developing nations (especially China and India), and economic conditions worldwide—all issues that influence the trade balance. As such, strategies aimed at influencing trade can be considered the most difficult area of economic policy making.

Many American consumer products, including cars, clothing, and electronics, are made overseas because labor costs are so much less in developing countries. Even people who want to "buy American" have a difficult time, given the increasing globalization of multinational corporations.

Grazing Rights and Free Market Environmentalism

Grazing rights, environmental policy, and control of western lands have been controversial for decades. The issue received attention in the 2016 presidential campaign when Senator Marco Rubio said that "the federal government controls far too much land in the western parts of the United States," indicating that he favors transferring some federal lands to the states.[a] The federal government owns more than 600 million acres, including 47 percent of the land in western states, and there are intense disagreements between environmentalists and ranchers, loggers, and miners about how those lands should be used.

There are three basic positions on this issue: the pro-business and antiregulation stance (ranchers, loggers), the pro-environment regulatory approach (conservationists and recreational users), and a middle ground called free market environmentalism that attempts to find free market solutions to protect the environment.

The scenario that you have to consider here is an actual case publicized in a *New York Times* op-ed piece.[b] The case involves a fifth-generation rancher in southern Utah named Dell LeFevre. He is no friend of environmentalism, saying, "We've got easterners who don't know the land telling us what to do with it. I am a bitter old cowboy." His bitterness was deepened back in 1991 when he found two dozen of his cows shot to death. He thinks the deed was done by an environmentalist who was trying to get ranchers to leave a scenic part of the Escalante River canyon. So LeFevre seems to be an unlikely candidate to have sat down with an environmentalist named Bill Hedden to accomplish that very goal of ending ranching in the area. Hedden works for a group called the Grand Canyon Trust (GCT) that, as the *New York Times* article explained, "doesn't use lobbyists or lawsuits (or guns) to drive out ranchers. These environmentalists get land the old-fashioned way. They buy it." The GCT spent about $100,000 to buy and retire the grazing rights from LeFevre for this scenic canyon area. The environmentalists are happy because the vegetation is coming back, and LeFevre is happy because he doesn't have to battle the environmentalists anymore and was able to buy grazing rights in a different area that is better for his cattle. Supporters of "free market environmentalism" say this is a perfect example of allowing the market to determine the best use of the land.

The pro-business approach. If the story ended here, there would be no controversy. But local groups, such as the Canyon Country Rural Alliance, which opposed all limitations on ranchers' grazing rights, lobbied Congress and the Interior Department

 Rancher Dell LeFevre and two of his children.

to disallow arrangements that remove grazing rights from some public lands. Bowing to pressure, the Interior Department decided that "only Congress may permanently exclude lands from grazing use," so the GCT had no guarantee that the Bureau of Land Management would not change its mind and allow grazing. The process of resolving this conflict bounced around the Interior Department and the federal courts for nearly 10 years.

The free market environmental compromise. GCT members went to plan B: they decided to become ranchers. If the Interior Department wouldn't grant permanent conservation use permits on land designated for grazing, they would buy some cattle. The GCT is now one of the largest ranchers in the Colorado Plateau, with 1,000 acres of private land and grazing permits that cover 860,000 acres of federal and state lands, including a large part of the Kaibab National Forest adjacent to the North Rim of the Grand Canyon. It is managing the land in an eco-friendly manner with only 800 head of cattle. Though it may seem odd that an environmental group had to take up ranching to get the policy outcome it wanted, this compromise made all sides of the dispute relatively happy. As one opponent of the GCT put it, "We turned them from environmentalists into cowboys. I guess what they can do is get their cows and start losing money like the rest of us."[c]

take a stand

1. Do you favor the regulatory approach of permanently removing grazing rights from land that an environmental group would buy, the business approach of not having any permanent limits on grazing rights, or the free market environmental approach of allowing the environmental groups to buy land and grazing rights and become ranchers to protect the land?

2. Does the compromise position in which the GCT took up ranching strike you as a reasonable middle ground? Why or why not?

Exchange Rates, Consumer Tastes, and Labor Costs The first factor influencing trade and the balance of payment is the relative value of currencies. However, there isn't much the government can do about the value of the dollar because that value is determined by international currency markets. When the dollar is strong, imports are relatively cheap to consumers in the United States and U.S. exports are expensive to consumers in other countries. Therefore, if the United States is running a trade deficit—importing more than it is exporting—it would like the value of the dollar to fall in the hopes that this would increase the sales of U.S. products abroad.

How does the value of the dollar affect the trade deficit? Consider the following example. As of September 2018, a dollar was worth .86 euro. Therefore, a BMW 320i that would sell for 40,000 euros in Germany would go for about $46,512 in the United States, whereas a Cadillac XTS that would retail in America for $46,000 would sell for 39,560 euros in Europe—although this example doesn't factor in shipping costs, dealer incentives, higher taxes in Europe, and so on.

Now see what happens if the dollar falls in value: now you can only get .70 euro for a dollar instead of .86. Now that Cadillac could be purchased in Germany for 32,200 euros and the BMW would still cost 40,000 euros, while the BMW would cost an American consumer $57,143 and the Cadillac would still cost $46,000. Nothing has changed except the value of the dollar, but suddenly the car buyer's choices have changed dramatically. In both countries, the Cadillac has become a much better bargain, and therefore, theoretically, Cadillac sales (and sales of other GM models, as well as those of Chrysler and Ford) should increase and BMW (and Mercedes, Volkswagen, Fiat, MINI Cooper, etc.) sales should fall.

We say "theoretically" because of the second factor that influences trade—consumer tastes. If consumers are willing to pay an increasing premium for foreign goods, then a weaker dollar may not help the trade deficit. There isn't much policy makers can do about consumer tastes, despite the ongoing campaign urging citizens to "buy American." Even with President Trump's campaign pledge to "Make American Great Again" and the focus on restoring American jobs, there is little evidence that this political talk has influenced consumer tastes or broad market forces.

The low cost of labor is a third factor affecting the trade balance that policy makers cannot do much to influence. If a foreign firm pays its workers a daily wage that is equal to what American workers earn in a single hour for the same job, the foreign firm has a huge competitive advantage. Consequently, the United States has been flooded with cheap consumer goods from nations where labor is very cheap. Low prices are good for American consumers, but they come at the price of large trade deficits and lost American jobs. Furthermore, foreign firms sometimes absorb some currency fluctuations and do not raise the price of their goods in the United States as the dollar falls in value relative to their currency. The final factor—the strength of foreign economies—is also outside the control of American policy makers. If foreign economies are weak, consumers abroad do not have the income to purchase U.S. exports.

Trade Policy and Trade Deficits Although it is difficult to control trade outcomes because exchange rates, consumer tastes, and labor costs in other countries are all largely outside the control of policy makers, Congress and the president still try by altering trade policies. The main target of trade policy is the trade balance, which is defined as the difference between the total value of our exports and imports. In recent years, the balances reached record deficits, exceeding $830 billion a year in 2008 before falling back to $491 billion for the 12-month period ending in September 2016 (see Figure 15.9). The current account deficit, the broadest measure of the balance of payments including investments, has also been running at record levels. Economists have warned that deficits of this level are not sustainable. There is increasing consensus that something must change—either we need to stop buying as many imports and sell more exports or the value of the dollar must fall to help make this happen.

DID YOU KNOW?

The United States exported

$341 billion

in goods and services to Canada in 2017 (more than any other country) and imported the most from China ($523 billion, with Mexico second at $345 billion).

Source: Bureau of Economic Analysis

**FIGURE
15.9**

Trade Deficits, 1990–2018

The trade deficit remains high. Which groups are most likely to support policies aimed at reducing the trade deficit, and which groups would oppose these policies?

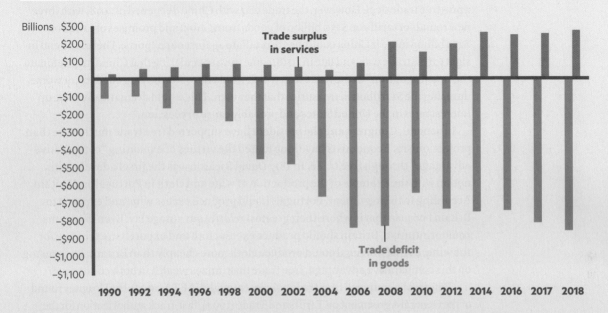

Note: Totals are calculated on a balance of payment basis.

Sources: Data from the U.S. Department of Commerce, Bureau of Economic Analysis, International Economic Accounts: Trade in Goods and Services, www.bea.gov (accessed 9/7/18).

The trade deficits have to be financed with borrowing from overseas. In the past, these loans came largely from foreign investment by private individuals who saw greater returns on their investments in the United States than in other countries. The net international investment position in June 2018 was –$7.8 trillion (that is, the value of foreign investments in the United States exceeded the value of U.S. investments abroad).[62] Foreign investors now own about 42 percent of our publicly owned government debt, with Japan and China owning 35 percent of that foreign debt.[63] Why does this matter? If foreign governments decide to stop investing in treasury securities or to start selling them, interest rates will have to rise, perhaps dramatically, to attract buyers for our debt.

To reduce the trade deficit, people in government may support protectionist policies such as trade sanctions, tariffs, and quotas, or attempt to reduce the value of the dollar. Advocates for protectionist policies argue that "free trade" is a myth and we are being taken advantage of by nations that engage in unfair trade practices while selling goods in our open markets. Former senator Ernest F. Hollings once said, "We hear those in the national Congress running around saying, 'Free trade, free trade, I am for free trade,' when they know free trade is like dry water. There is no such thing."[64] As discussed in the chapter opener, Donald Trump focused on this issue in the 2016 campaign, arguing that the United States is getting "ripped off," "absolutely crushed," and "killed" on trade with China, Japan, and Mexico.[65] It is only fair, protectionist proponents argue, that we set up trade barriers or impose quotas to support our own goods and protect American jobs. Although broadly based protectionist policies have been rare in the past couple of decades, U.S. policy makers have applied protection in selected markets. For example, in September 2009, President Obama imposed a 35 percent tariff on Chinese tires. The chapter opener discussed the steel and aluminum tariffs imposed by President Trump in 2017 and tensions with Mexico and Canada over renegotiating NAFTA. The latter was successfully resolved with a new United States Mexico Canada Agreement (USMCA) that received some concessions from Mexico and Canada (especially for the auto and dairy industries) and was generally viewed as a pro–free trade deal. However, the trade war with China deepened in 2018, with three new rounds of tariffs on $250 billion of goods from China and promises of tariffs on $279 billion more if China continues to retaliate against our exports. There is no end in sight to this trade war, and late in 2018, some were speculating that China may detonate the "nuclear option" in the trade war, which would be to stop buying our debt, or worse, dumping the $1 trillion in treasuries that they own. This would dramatically drive up interest rates in the United States and probably cause a recession.

In general, Congress and the president have supported free trade much more than protectionism. Economists have long touted the virtues of exploiting "comparative advantage" through free trade. In 1817 David Ricardo was the first to develop this notion with the example of the production of wine and cloth in Portugal and Britain.[66] According to the argument, Portugal should produce excess wine and export it to Britain because that is where their greatest *relative* advantage lay. Even if it seems counterintuitive, Britain should produce excess cloth and export it in exchange for the wine, even if Portugal could produce cloth more cheaply than Britain. By focusing on this comparative advantage, free trade maximizes wealth in both countries.[67]

Congress has pursued free-trade policies through NAFTA (1993), the Uruguay round of the General Agreement on Tariffs and Trade (1994), fast-track authorization for the USTR to negotiate trade agreements with minimal congressional interference (2002), most-favored-nation trading status for China (2000), and the Central American Free Trade Agreement (CAFTA, 2005), which reduced barriers and opened markets. The Trans-Pacific Partnership (TPP) with 11 nations in the Asia-Pacific region was signed on February 4, 2016, but President Trump pulled out of TPP early in 2017. As noted in the chapter opener, he also has vowed to renegotiate NAFTA. Critics of the laws say that they do not provide adequate protections for workers and the environment, promoting a "race to the bottom" to cut costs while putting additional pressure on American jobs and wages.

The impact of free-trade agreements on American jobs and wages varies widely, with estimates ranging from 1 to 4 million jobs lost in the past 20 years. Supporters of the law point out that even when some jobs have been lost, the overall economy has benefited; one study found that for every job lost because of NAFTA, $450,000 was added to the economy in the form of higher productivity and lower consumer prices.[68] Also, some of these jobs would have been lost even without the trade agreements, even in areas thought to be the United States' comparative advantage, such as computer programming. When programmers or computer customer support staff in India earn about one-tenth of what they make in the United States, it is difficult for American firms to compete in international markets unless they employ cheaper labor.[69] This downward pressure on wages has contributed to income inequality in the United States, and competitive pressures have led to the virtual extinction of some U.S. industries, such as the manufacturing of consumer electronics, textiles, shoes, and, increasingly, clothing. Thus, while free trade generally enhances worldwide economic growth, there can be significant consequences for specific industries.

The Politics of Trade Policy With stakes this high, it is not surprising that politics often plays a central role in trade policy. There are two main explanations for the nature of political influence on trade policy: constituency and ideology.[70] The constituency explanation sees the two major parties as representing different groups—Democrats representing labor, Republicans representing capital—which tends to make the Democrats more protectionist and the Republicans more supportive of free trade. Though the constituency explanation is generally true, there are divisions within each constituency. For example, autoworkers' and steelworkers' unions are much more protectionist than dockworkers' unions because any industry with strong exports will support free trade, whereas those that have relatively few exports but are vulnerable to cheap imports are more likely to be protectionist. The ideological explanation focuses on the bipartisan consensus on trade that emerged after the Great Depression, which was seen as having been caused in part by the protective tariffs of the 1930 Smoot-Hawley Act.[71] As with the theories of regulation, both perspectives explain part of the truth. Our political leaders largely support a free-trade ideology (with the obvious exception of the Trump presidency), but there are divisions along constituency lines on some legislation.

Unpacking the Conflict

There is a common perception that economic policies would work better if we could just take politics out of the economic policy-making process. But that would be like saying "football would be better if we could eliminate the contact" or "poker would be better if we could take out the element of chance." Economic policy making is inherently political. It isn't possible or desirable to have economic policy produced by economists who would push and pull the levers of growth, productivity, and efficiency, implementing their economic theories without interference from politicians. Politics must enter into this process. Economic policy determines who wins and who loses, and elected leaders must be involved in this process if representative democracy is to have any meaning. This is especially true of the budget process because the redistributive implications of taxing and spending are so clear, but as we have discussed, even monetary policy is not insulated from politics. As discussed in the chapter opener, winners and losers are also very evident in trade policy. Returning to the questions of the opener, which side is right about trade policy, and what should the government do, if anything, about trade deficits? More generally, what is the proper role of the government in a free market economy? How do political players deal with the conflict that is inherent in economic policy making?

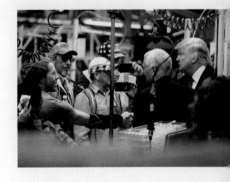

Both economic theory and history tell us that we are better off with free trade than having politicians pick winners and losers in the economy. However, there is still clearly a role for the government in the economy through regulations, taxing and spending policy, and monetary policy. Having the government in the economy means that politics must have a role in economic policy making. In fact, this is guaranteed by our system of checks and balances: Congress, the president, and to some extent the courts all have a hand in shaping economic policy. The clash between politics and economic theory and the conflicted nature of economic policy making can be illustrated with a few examples.

We discussed earlier the limitation of implementing Keynesian economic theories in fiscal policy. Often political considerations make it impossible to implement the swift, targeted action called for in the theory. That is because the budget inherently involves debates over some central political questions: How large should the government be? How progressive should the income tax be? Should we impose tariffs on our trading partners to try to get them to change their trade policies? Should budget deficits be allowed to expand to put pressure on government spending, rather than to stimulate the economy? These are not purely economic questions but also political ones that must be answered through debate and conflict between the opposing parties and branches of government.

These debates have been central in the disputes over trade policy discussed in the chapter opener. There is a strong bipartisan consensus that free trade is generally a good thing for the United States. However, when voters in Rust Belt states rallied to Trump's call to bring back manufacturing jobs by ripping up unfair trade deals, protectionist policies gained political power. When the dust settles in a few years, trade policy may still reflect the old bipartisan consensus, or it may be more U.S. centered and less internationally focused.

These examples are not intended to suggest that politics shouldn't enter into the economic policy-making process. Indeed, just the opposite. They are excellent illustrations of the themes that politics is everywhere and politics is conflictual. It shouldn't be surprising when politics enters the economic policy debate. Elected leaders should be responsive to what their constituents think about the central questions concerning the direction of the economy.

What's Your Take?

How often should the government intervene in the economy, if ever? Do the complexity and fragility of the economy make intervention here and there necessary?

STUDY GUIDE

Goals of economic policy

Explain the main purposes of government involvement in the economy. (Pages 533–539)

Summary

Policy makers' pursuit of economic goals—such as full employment, stable prices, or growth—is a complex process. Not only is the government unable to attain these goals on its own, but the pursuit of one goal often comes at the expense of other economic goals.

Key terms

public policy (p. 533)
fiscal policy (p. 533)
monetary policy (p. 533)
full employment (p. 533)
economic depression (p. 533)
Council of Economic Advisers (CEA) (p. 533)
inflation (p. 534)

deflation (p. 534)
gross domestic product (GDP) (p. 535)
balanced budget (p. 536)
budget deficit (p. 536)
current account (p. 537)
trade deficit (p. 537)

Practice Quiz Questions

1. The difference between fiscal policy and monetary policy is that fiscal policy is concerned with _____, while monetary policy is concerned with _____.

    a   controlling the money supply and spending; taxing and interest rates

    b   taxing and controlling the money supply; spending and interest rates

    c   taxing and spending; controlling the money supply and interest rates

    d   controlling the money supply and interest rates; taxing and spending

    e   taxing and interest rates; spending and controlling the money supply

2. The CEA was established _____.

    a   by the Employment Act of 1946

    b   by the Balanced Budget Amendment

    c   in Article I of the Constitution

    d   in Article III of the Constitution

    e   by the Federal Reserve Board

3. Technically, full employment means an unemployment level of about _____.

    a   0 percent

    b   1–2 percent

    c   4–5 percent

    d   8–9 percent

    e   10 percent

4. The responsibility of fighting inflation largely falls on _____.

    a   the president

    b   the OMB

    c   the Congress

    d   the Federal Reserve

    e   the private sector

5. When the government attempts to reduce inflation, it typically results in _____.

    a   growth for businesses

    b   higher interest rates

    c   lower unemployment

    d   an increase in GDP

    e   lower interest rates

The key players in economic policy making

Describe the roles played by each of the branches of government in shaping economic policy. (Pages 539–550)

Summary

The primary actors in making economic policy are Congress, through the "power of the purse"; the president, in shaping taxing and spending policy; and the bureaucracy, in implementing monetary policy. While they all share the same general goal of a healthy economy, coordinating action across these actors can be difficult.

Key terms

budget making (p. 540)
budget reconciliation (p. 540)
United States Trade Representative (USTR) (p. 544)
National Economic Council (NEC) (p. 544)

Federal Reserve System (p. 545)
Treasury Department (p. 545)
Federal Reserve Board (p. 545)

Practice Quiz Questions

6. Budget reconciliation has the advantages of _____ and _____.

a decreasing bipartisanship; preventing a Senate filibuster

b allowing members to get everything they want; not being subject to a presidential veto

c making it difficult for members to vote against the bill; preventing a Senate filibuster

d not being subject to a presidential veto; decreasing bipartisanship

e making it difficult for members to vote against the bill; not being subject to presidential veto

7. The Federal Reserve Board's actions _____ subject to presidential or congressional review, while the appointment terms of personnel _____ overlap with the federal election calendar.

a are; do

b are; do not

c are sometimes; do

d are not; do

e are not; do not

8. The Treasury generally prefers _____ interest rates; the Federal Reserve Board generally prefers _____ interest rates.

a higher; lower

b higher; higher

c lower; lower

d lower; higher

e stable; lower

Tools and theories of economic policy

Examine how fiscal, monetary, regulatory, and trade policies influence the economy. (Pages 551–567)

Summary

Policy makers have a variety of tools at their disposal to help push the economy in their desired direction. Although there are different theories on the best approach, the use of fiscal policy, monetary policy, and regulation allows the government to influence the country's economic performance.

Key terms

Keynesian economics (p. 551)

supply-side economics (p. 551)

marginal tax rate (p. 551)

business cycle (p. 552)

mandatory spending (p. 553)

discretionary spending (p. 553)

regressive (p. 556)

progressive (p. 556)

monetarist theory (p. 557)

reserve requirement (p. 558)

discount rate (p. 558)

federal funds rate (FFR) (p. 558)

open market operations (p. 559)

9. Keynesian economics argues that the effects of an economic recession can be reduced by _____.

a decreasing government spending

b increasing government spending

c increasing income taxes

d reducing the budget deficit

e discouraging consumer spending

10. Reducing the federal deficit by cutting spending is difficult because _____.

a the interest rates are too high

b a growing portion of the budget is mandatory spending

c a growing portion of the budget is discretionary spending

d members of Congress put too much pork in budgetary bills

e large deficits benefit the economy in the long run

11. Regressive taxes, like the payroll tax, mean that compared with the wealthy, poor people spend _____ of their income on taxes.

a none

b much less

c slightly less

d an equal amount

e more

12. What does the "reserve requirement" refer to?

a the interest rate the Fed charges to member banks

b the rate member banks charge one another on overnight loans

c the minimum activity level of the Fed's open market operations

d the lowest price for government bonds

e the minimum level of money banks must always have on hand

13. When the competitive situation is a natural monopoly, the government generally _____.

a regulates prices

b breaks up the monopoly

c stimulates competition

d works to reduce negative externalities

e does not intervene

14. In general, Congress supports _____; the president supports _____.

a protectionism; free trade

b protectionism; protectionism

c free trade; protectionism

d free trade; free trade

e tariffs; protectionism

Suggested Reading

Conti-Brown, Peter. *The Power and Independence of the Federal Reserve*. Princeton, NJ: Princeton University Press, 2016.

Friedman, Milton. *Capitalism and Freedom*, 40th anniversary ed. Chicago: University of Chicago Press, 2002.

Friedman, Thomas L. *The World Is Flat: A Brief History of the Twenty-First Century*. New York: Farrar, Straus and Giroux, 2005.

Hacker, Jacob S., and Paul Pierson. *Winner-Take-All Politics: How Washington Made the Rich Richer—and Turned Its Back on the Middle Class*. New York: Simon and Schuster, 2011.

Keynes, John Maynard. *The General Theory of Employment, Interest, and Money*. 1936. Reprint, New York: Macmillan, 2007.

King, Mervyn, *The End of Alchemy: Money, Banking, and the Future of the Global Economy*. New York: W. W. Norton, 2016.

Lewis, Michael. *The Big Short: Inside the Doomsday Machine*. New York: W. W. Norton, 2010.

Phillips, Kevin. *Bad Money: Reckless Finance, Failed Politics, and the Global Crisis of American Capitalism*. New York: Viking, 2008.

Piketty, Thomas. *Capital in the Twenty-First Century*. Cambridge, MA: Belknap Press, 2014.

Soros, George. *The New Paradigm for Financial Markets: The Credit Crash of 2008 and What It Means*. New York: PublicAffairs Books, 2008.

Stiglitz, Joseph E. *Globalization and Its Discontents Revisited: Anti-Globalization in the Era of Trump*. New York: W. W. Norton, 2017.

16

Social Policy

What should be the role of the government in providing the social safety net?

▶▶ **"We essentially repealed Obamacare because we got rid of the individual mandate ... and that was a primary source of funding of Obamacare."**
President Donald Trump

◀◀ **"Overall, this change will be disruptive, but not terminal. It certainly does not 'essentially repeal' Obamacare. We rate Trump's claim False."**
PolitiFact

President Obama signed the Patient Protection and Affordable Care Act ("Obamacare") into law on March 30, 2010. This comprehensive and historic health care reform legislation was the culmination of a 15-month partisan struggle in Congress. The $1 trillion law (over 10 years) provides subsidized health insurance to most Americans who don't have insurance, while preventing health insurance companies from dropping sick policy holders or refusing to cover people with preexisting conditions.

Health care reform was controversial from the start. As public opposition grew, it became clear that the votes for health care reform would have to come from within the Democratic Party. Indeed, the final version of the bill passed without any Republican support. Republicans cried foul because Democratic leaders used the reconciliation process in an unorthodox way to avoid a filibuster in the Senate (the process is typically used for budget-related issues, not for passing substantive policy).

The day after the law went into effect, House Republicans introduced a bill to repeal it. After regaining control of the House in the 2010 midterms, House Republicans voted 62 times over the next six years to repeal or change part of Obamacare, including 6 times to repeal the entire law.[1] Of course, Senate Democrats were having none of it and ignored the House's efforts. These conflicting views came to a head in the fall of 2013 when House Republicans tied approval of the annual budget to repealing Obamacare. Democrats viewed this as blackmail and refused to negotiate, while Republicans argued that the public was on their side as polls showed that most

Social policies can be complicated, conflictual, and personal, though few issues have been as contentious as health care reform. The political process used to tackle these conflicts is often tedious, complex, and time-consuming.

CHAPTER GOALS

Explain what we mean by social policy and how the national government's role in social policy has evolved. pages 575–578

Examine the problem of poverty as a target of social policies. pages 579–582

Describe the roles played by each branch of the national government and by the states in making and implementing social policy. pages 583–586

Trace the steps through which problems are addressed by social policies. pages 586–591

Analyze the current major areas of social policy. pages 591–609

The disagreements over social policy run deep. Conflicts over "Trumpcare," the proposed replacement to Obamacare, led to the legislative failure of any repeal or replacement of the ACA.

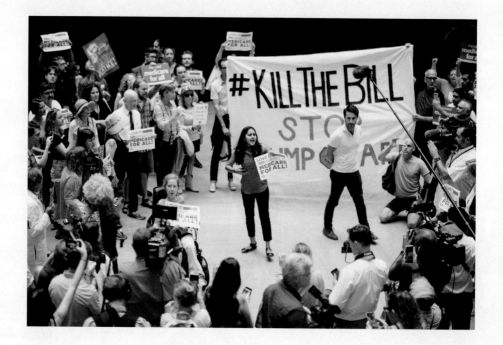

Americans did not approve of Obamacare. This disagreement led to a shutdown of all nonessential federal government services from October 1 to 16, 2013. The White House estimated that the shutdown cost the economy about 120,000 jobs and between $2 and $6 billion.[2] While Obamacare remained unpopular, most Americans rejected the confrontational tactics and blamed House Republicans for the shutdown.[3]

When Donald Trump was elected and Republicans had unified control of the government, they had the opportunity to repeal and replace Obamacare. However, with no agreed-upon plan to replace the law, repeal failed by a single vote in the Senate in 2017. While Republicans were unable to repeal the law, they enacted several measures weakening the law, hoping to slowly kill it off. They eliminated the unpopular individual mandate tax penalty for individuals who do not have health insurance, cut the ACA's advertising budget by 90 percent, shortened the open-enrollment period from three months to six weeks a year, and reduced funds for personal enrollment assistance by 41 percent.[4]

Despite these efforts, and contrary to President Trump's claim that his administration had "essentially repealed" Obamacare, by mid-2018 more than 26 million Americans had gained health insurance coverage because of the law, many for the first time.[5] Perhaps most surprising was the strong enrollment in the health care exchanges, with 11.8 million people signing up during the enrollment period for 2018. This was only a 3.5 percent drop from the previous year despite the 50 percent shorter enrollment period and the lack of advertising promoting the enrollment.[6] The percentage of uninsured had fallen to a record 8.6 percent in early 2016, but by 2018 it had crept back to 15 percent according to one survey.[7] While the ACA is proving to be resilient, its long-term status remains uncertain. President Trump issued an executive order in 2018 allowing small businesses to provide insurance that did not include the 10 basic components required by the ACA and continued a legal challenge to the law in federal courts concerning the insurance subsidies.[8] Is this how social policy works? A contentious battle and a frustrating outcome for most, if not all, involved? Although the level of conflict around Obamacare is unusual in American politics, trade-offs between social policy and other government priorities often produce political conflict. More money for health insurance subsidies, Social Security, Medicare, food stamps, and welfare means less money for highways, the military, or development of alternative energy. These trade-offs become especially acute as the population ages, requiring an increasing share of federal spending to go to Social Security and Medicare. The trade-offs must be resolved through a political process filled with conflict and compromise.

One of the biggest challenges Americans face today is how to make sense of all the claims they hear about public policy. Is Social Security going bankrupt, and will it therefore not pay the current generation of young Americans any benefits when they retire? Does the government spend too much money on food stamps and welfare, or are these important tools for reducing inequality? Has the Trump administration essentially eliminated Obamacare? This chapter will help answer these important questions by discussing the evolution of social policy in the United States, outlining the conditions that create the need for social policies, describing the key players in the social policy-making process, and explaining the status of key social policies today and the efforts to reform them. We begin with the historical background of social policy.

The roots and goals of social policy

Social policy is generally defined in terms of the "social safety net," or welfare, which is financial or other assistance provided to individuals by the government, usually based on need. A broader conception of social policy includes government programs aimed at achieving some general social goal, such as programs that support public education, the income tax deduction for interest paid on home mortgages (to encourage home ownership), or policies designed to promote job creation and growth. This chapter will address both types of social policies and discuss how some traditional social welfare programs, such as Social Security, are not based on need. First, we'll outline the evolution of social policy in the United States and describe various types of social policy (see Nuts & Bolts 16.1).

Early social-policy efforts

Early in our nation's history, the federal government took little responsibility for social welfare. Private charities, churches, and families largely took care of the poor and disadvantaged. The first significant social policy appeared in the nineteenth century in the form of federal financial support for Civil War veterans and their families. Between 1880 and 1910, the national government spent more than a quarter of its budget on Civil War pensions and support for veterans' widows. Other than interest on the debt, this was a larger share of the budget than any other single item and a greater percentage of federal spending than today's expenditure on Social Security.[9] (Today we spend nearly one-fourth of our budget on Social Security, but, of course, the overall budget was much smaller then.) During the recession of the mid-1890s, populist and progressive reformers sought a national system of unemployment compensation, but such broad-scale policies were several decades ahead of their time.

EXPLAIN WHAT WE MEAN BY SOCIAL POLICY AND HOW THE NATIONAL GOVERNMENT'S ROLE IN SOCIAL POLICY HAS EVOLVED

social policy
An area of public policy related to maintaining or enhancing the well-being of individuals.

welfare
Financial or other assistance provided to individuals by the government, usually based on need.

Types of Social Policy

1. **Contributory** (or social insurance) programs include Social Security, Medicare, disability insurance, and unemployment compensation.
   - Programs are similar to insurance programs in that people pay a specified amount of money to cover some future benefit (either expected, as with the programs related to retirement, or unexpected, as with disability and unemployment).
   - Programs are not means-tested; that is, all people may participate in the program regardless of their income

2. **Noncontributory** (or public-assistance) programs include Medicaid, food stamps, housing assistance, welfare, and school lunches.
   - Recipients are not expected to pay for the programs, which are means-tested, meaning that they are aimed at helping poor people

The ACA ("Obamacare") has elements of both contributory and noncontributory programs. People who are required to buy health insurance are "contributing" to their own insurance. However, those who cannot afford to pay for their insurance receive government subsidies (and thus are participating in a noncontributory program).

The test of our progress is not whether we add more to the abundance of those who have much; it is whether we provide enough for those who have too little.

—President Franklin D. Roosevelt

New Deal
The set of policies proposed by President Franklin Roosevelt and enacted by Congress between 1933 and 1935 to promote economic recovery and social welfare during the Great Depression.

The New Deal

The stock market crash in 1929 and the ensuing Great Depression created a desperate economic situation for millions of Americans. The value of the stock market shrank by 80 percent, the gross national product decreased by 25 percent, and unemployment climbed to at least 25 percent in the depth of the depression in 1933. Yet, during the presidential campaign of 1932, the Republican incumbent, Herbert Hoover, upheld the administration's policy of limited government intervention in the economy and in social welfare policies. In contrast, the Democratic candidate, Franklin Delano Roosevelt, pledged "a new deal for the American people" in which the federal government would actively confront the problems of the depression. FDR won a sweeping victory. Democrats also gained control of both houses of Congress, which paved the way for the enactment of FDR's policies.

An immediate concern was to alleviate the suffering caused by unemployment. As FDR argued, "No country, however rich, can afford the waste of its human resources. Demoralization caused by vast unemployment is our greatest extravagance. Morally, it is the greatest menace to our social order."[10] FDR also wanted to implement a broader "preventative social policy" as outlined by social scientists at the University of Wisconsin, including John R. Commons, who was a significant force in the creation of unemployment compensation policies, and Edwin Witte, the architect of Social Security.[11] The **New Deal** included a number of policies enacted between 1933 and 1935:

- The Agricultural Adjustment Administration provided farmers with much-needed assistance. Farmers were hit hard in the depression when plummeting commodity prices forced many family farms into bankruptcy.
- The National Recovery Administration and Public Works Administration reinvigorated the business sector.
- The Federal Emergency Relief Administration provided $500 million in emergency aid for the poor (about $7 billion in today's dollars).
- Jobs programs such as the Civil Works Administration and Civilian Conservation Corps put more than 2 million people to work. Later the Works Progress

Before the New Deal programs in the 1930s, poverty relief was provided mainly by private charities. Here, future First Lady Eleanor Roosevelt serves meals to unemployed women and their children in a New York restaurant.

Administration, a broader program, employed at least one-third of the nation's unemployed.

- Social Security, including the familiar retirement policy, also supported the states with funds to spend on unemployment compensation, disability programs, and support for dependent children of single mothers. This New Deal–era program was the precursor of the central welfare program, Aid to Families with Dependent Children (AFDC), which existed until 1996.
- The National Labor Relations Act guaranteed the right to organize a union and set regulations for collective bargaining between management and labor.[12]

The role of the federal government in social policy was forever changed. Although some aspects of the New Deal, such as the jobs programs, were never repeated on such a broad scale, most of its other programs became the cornerstone of social policy for subsequent generations.

The Great Society

The next major expansion of social policy came during the **Great Society** of President Lyndon Johnson in the mid-1960s. In Chapter 5, we discussed one pillar of this social agenda: the civil rights movement, which culminated with the passage of the Civil Rights Act in 1964 and the Voting Rights Act in 1965. The other important aspect of Johnson's Great Society included the War on Poverty and programs concerning health, education, and housing. Johnson's "unconditional" War on Poverty brought economic development and jobs to depressed areas, especially the inner cities, by creating the Office of Economic Opportunity, the Jobs Corps, the Neighborhood Youth Corps, Volunteers in Service to America (VISTA, a domestic counterpart to the Peace Corps), and the Model Cities program. Other programs focused on helping children, including Head Start, which provided preschool education and enrichment for poor children; the Child Nutrition Act of 1966; and an expanded school lunch program. Johnson's administration also greatly expanded the food stamp program; developed more public housing; created the new cabinet-level department of Housing and Urban Development; and got more involved in an area that typically had been left to the states

Great Society
The wide-ranging social agenda promoted by President Lyndon Johnson in the mid-1960s that aimed to improve Americans' quality of life through governmental social programs.

in the Elementary and Secondary Education Act of 1965. Perhaps the most significant legislation was in health care, with the creation of Medicare, the national program that funds medical care for the elderly, and Medicaid, which funds health care for the poor.[13]

Over the following decades, Johnson's Great Society suffered some setbacks. The mounting costs of the Vietnam War in the late 1960s and early 1970s created a trade-off: it wasn't possible to continue funding both ambitious social programs and the war without causing inflation. In addition, there was some conservative backlash against the "welfare state," especially during the Reagan years (1981–1989), as spending on social programs was cut and some programs were eliminated. However, with some exceptions, the Great Society programs remain core components of today's social safety net.

President George W. Bush maintained most existing programs with some cuts and one major expansion, the addition of a prescription benefit to Medicare. As a "compassionate conservative," Bush attempted to place his stamp on American social policy with the idea of an **ownership society**, in which people take more responsibility for their own social welfare. Bush proposed privatizing part of Social Security and creating private savings accounts to cover more out-of-pocket medical expenses, in combination with more free market forces and a bigger role for private and religious charity. President Obama favored an approach that emphasized the market and community while preserving an important role for government. As the 2008–2009 recession and natural disasters such as Hurricane Sandy have demonstrated, crises may overwhelm even the most aggressive and sustained community responses. Market forces cannot adequately address the needs of the unemployed and very poor, especially in times of economic recession.

President Trump and the Republican Congress have attempted to scale back social policies, most significantly Obamacare, as noted in the chapter introduction. By eliminating the individual mandate, giving employers the freedom to provide policies with less coverage, cutting back on the open enrollment period, and reducing subsidies to buy insurance, the opponents of Obamacare are trying to create a "death spiral" in which the health insurance program will become more expensive and therefore less attractive. Trump is also attempting to reshape welfare programs; he issued an executive order in 2018 directing federal agencies to review their social programs, with the goal of getting more people to work and off of welfare. House Republicans have tried to move policy in this direction, approving a bill by a 213–211 vote in June 2018, that would impose work requirements for 5 to 7 million of the more than 40 million recipients of the Supplemental Nutrition Assistance Program (SNAP), more commonly known as food stamps.[14] At the time of this writing, it appeared unlikely that this bill would pass the Senate.

ownership society
The term used to describe the social-policy vision of President George W. Bush, in which citizens take responsibility for their own social welfare and the free market plays a greater role in social policy.

"

Working for a just distribution of the fruits of the earth and human labor is not mere philanthropy. It is a moral obligation. For Christians, the responsibility is even greater: it is a commandment.

—Pope Francis

"Why Should I Care?"

Historical context is always important for understanding current policy, but this is especially true for social policy. Most of our important social policies today, such as Social Security, Medicare, and Medicaid, date back to the New Deal or Great Society periods. All Americans will be touched by the "social safety net" at some point in their lives. Some of this may seem remote—you may feel that you don't have to think about it until you are closer to retirement. However, most of you will be affected in the next few years by an important change in social policy: the ACA allows you to stay on your parents' health insurance until you are 26 years old.

Poverty and income inequality

The economic dislocation and poverty of the Great Depression and the desire to eliminate poverty in the 1960s were the two central stimuli for social policies. Although these policies had some success in reducing poverty, the persistence of poverty remains the primary motivator for most social policy. In 2017, the poverty line for a family of four was an annual income of $24,858; for a single person it was $12,752.[15] In 2017, official estimates determined 39.7 million Americans were living in poverty—12.3 percent of the population. Even the social programs that do not directly help the poor and disadvantaged, such as Social Security and Medicare, affect poverty. As the What Do the Facts Say? feature shows, the percentage of the elderly population living in poverty plummeted from more than 35 percent in 1959 to 9.2 percent in 2017. Official statistics on poverty were not collected before 1959, but the rate was certainly much higher in the 1930s, before Social Security was established.[16] Given that more than half of the elderly rely on Social Security as their primary income, the poverty rate for the elderly would be much higher if Social Security and Medicare did not exist.

Another source of concern for some policy advocates is the growing income and wealth inequality in the United States. Indeed, people in the top income levels in the nation are benefiting disproportionately from income increases. From 1993 to 2015, the top 1 percent of the income distribution had 52 percent of the net income gains. The real income of the top 1 percent rose 94.5 percent during this period compared to a 14.3 percent gain for the bottom 99 percent. These trends have produced a growing concentration of income at the top. In 2015, the top 10 percent of households—those earning more than $124,810 a year—earned more than half of the income, which is the highest proportion since 1917 (see Figure 16.1); and in 2015, the top 1 percent—those earning more than $443,000—earned 22 percent of the nation's income.[17]

The wealth gap is far greater. The median (meaning that half are above this level and half are below) net worth of U.S. households in 2013 was $177,900, but the median wealth for the top 10 percent was $1.87 million, and this group held 75.3 percent of the nation's wealth. Even within the top 10 percent, the wealth is concentrated at the top. *Forbes* publishes a list of the wealthiest Americans every year. Bill Gates topped the 2017 list for the twenty-fourth year in a row, with a net worth of $89 billion, and the person at the bottom of the "Forbes 400" was worth $2 billion. The collective net worth of the nation's wealthiest 400 people in 2016 was $2.4 trillion, which is a 30-fold increase since 1982, when *Forbes* first calculated their net worth at $93 billion.[18] This is a trillion dollars more than the total wealth held by the bottom 50.

One important point to recognize when considering social policy as a tool to address income inequality is that government policies help middle-income people and even the wealthy, in addition to the poor. Consider federal housing policy: in fiscal year 2019, poor people received $31.8 billion a year from the federal government in direct subsidies for their rent (with another $19 billion spent on all housing programs for the poor). However, this number is dwarfed by the $130 billion spent on tax expenditures for housing in 2017, mostly for the mortgage interest deduction, property tax deduction, and capital gains tax exclusions. Most of this money went to relatively wealthy people; for example, 73 percent of the tax savings from deducting mortgage interest goes to people in the top 20 percent.[19] Other government policies that help the wealthy include patent and copyright law, bankruptcy law, bailouts of the financial sector, immigration policy, enforcement of tax law, and monetary policy.[20]

Government programs that help the wealthy not only target individuals but also benefit corporations. These policies, often called "corporate welfare," are defined by

There's class warfare, all right, but it's my class, the rich class, that's making war, and we're winning.

—**Warren Buffett,** America's third-wealthiest person

FIGURE 16.1

Percentage of All Income Earned by the Wealthiest 10 Percent, 1917–2014*

Income inequality in the United States today is higher than ever. The wealthiest 10 percent of Americans now receive 50.4 percent of all U.S. income. How will this inequality affect the outcomes of social policy?

* Includes capital gains. This figure shows the most recent data available.

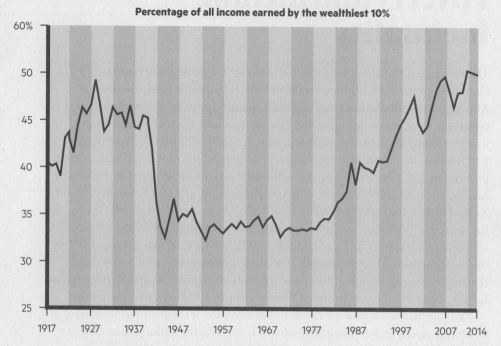

Percentage of all income earned by the wealthiest 10%

Source: Thomas Piketty and Emmanuel Saez, "Income Inequality in the United States, 1913–1998," *Quarterly Journal of Economics*, 118:1 (2003): 1–39. (Longer updated version published in A. B. Atkinson and Thomas Piketty, eds., *Top Incomes over the Twentieth Century: A Contrast between European and English Speaking Countries* [Oxford: Oxford University Press, 2007].) (Tables and figures updated to 2015 in Excel format, June 2016, https://eml.berkeley.edu/~saez/ [accessed 7/3/18].)

the Cato Institute, a libertarian think tank, as "any government spending program that provides unique benefits or advantages to specific companies or industries. That includes programs that provide direct grants to businesses, programs that provide research and other services for industries, and programs that provide subsidized loans or insurance to companies." The Cato Institute estimates that there are more than 100 corporate welfare programs in the federal budget, including crop subsidies to large corporate farmers and tax deductions for oil companies to encourage exploration and drilling, with annual expenditures of more than $100 billion.[21] Liberal groups such as Citizens for Tax Justice estimate levels of corporate welfare at nearly three times that amount. Clearly, there is much more to welfare policies than programs for the poor.

Nonetheless, the social programs described in this chapter are very important for reducing income inequality. The nonpartisan Congressional Budget Office shows that means-tested transfers, such as Medicaid, food stamps, and Supplemental Security Income (SSI), and federal taxes cause household incomes to be more evenly distributed. In 2014, the most recent year included in its 2018 study, transfers and taxes increased average income for the bottom quintile by $12,000 to $31,000, while they decreased the income of the highest quintile by $74,000 to $207,000.[22] Figure 16.2 shows how the income of the bottom quintile, and to some extent the second through fourth quintiles, has increased much more than it would have without our social policies and progressive taxes.

Partisanship and income inequality

These statistics generate different reactions among politicians and are a good reminder that politics is conflictual. Republicans, on the one hand, argue that the best way to address poverty is through supply-side tax cuts that promote the creation of capital,

Poverty Rates by Age

Children today are in poverty at nearly twice the rate of the elderly, whereas 50 years ago the poverty rate among the elderly was twice that of children. What changes in social policies in the past 80 years could help explain this change? What do the facts say?

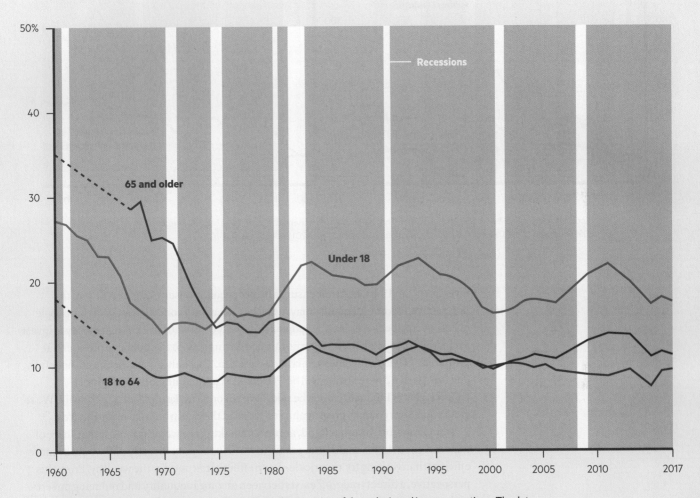

Note: The data for 2013 and beyond reflect the implementation of the redesigned income questions. The data points are placed at the midpoints of the respective years. Data for people aged 18 to 64 and aged 65 and older are not available from 1960 to 1965. For information on recessions, see p. 25 of source. For information on confidentiality protection, sampling error, nonsampling error, and definitions, see www2.census.gov/programs-surveys/cps/techdocs/cpsmar17.pdf.

Think about it

- The white shaded areas show economic recessions, when economic activity shrinks. What do you notice about the poverty rate in those years?
- What are the most important things that the government can do to address poverty?
- Would it be better to leave support for the social safety net up to private charities and more personal funding of health care and retirement benefits? Why or why not?

Source: Jessica L. Semega, Kayla R. Fontenot, and Melissa A. Kollar, "Income and Poverty in the United States: 2017," September 2018, U.S. Census, Figure 6, p. 15.

FIGURE
16.2

Cumulative Growth in Average Income, by Income Group, 1979–2014

Social policies such as Social Security, Medicare, and progressive income taxes have a big impact on reducing income inequality. How much greater would income inequality be today without those transfers and taxes? How much income inequality remains?

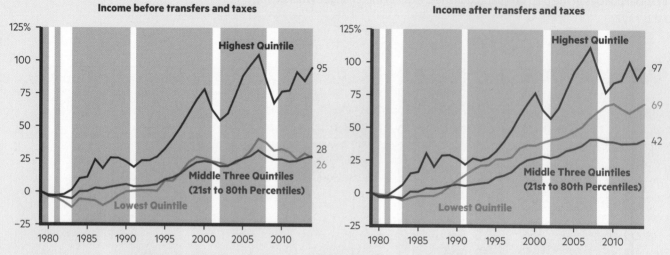

Source: Congressional Budget Office, March 2018, The Distribution of Household Income, 2014, https://www.cbo.gov/system/files?file=115th-congress-2017-2018/reports/53597-distribution-household-income-2014.pdf (accessed 8/7/18).

investment, and jobs, and thus ensure a healthy economy (see Chapter 15). From this perspective, income inequality may in fact be a necessary condition for bringing people out of poverty, because wealthy people are the only ones who have enough money to invest to create jobs. Indeed, Rick Santorum argued during the 2012 Republican presidential primaries, "There is income inequality in America. There always has been and, hopefully, and I do say that, there always will be."[23] Donald Trump came close to this direct endorsement of inequality when he said, "We're gonna make our county rich again. We're gonna make our country great again, and we need the rich in order to make the great."[24]

Democrats, on the other hand, argue that making the wealthy pay a larger share of their income in taxes could fund programs to help the poor directly and would be more efficient than waiting for the trickle-down effect of tax cuts for the wealthy. From this perspective, a direct trade-off exists between income inequality and reducing poverty, and progressive taxes are needed to help the poor.

"Why Should I Care?"

Income inequality is one of the central issues of the past decade. It emerged as an important issue in the 2018 midterm elections. Democrats and Republicans alike agree that steps need to be taken to address inequality, although obviously they differ in their approaches. Democrats emphasize increasing the minimum wage and improving the affordability of health care and housing, while Republicans tout the benefits of the 2017 tax cuts and the low unemployment rate. A recent survey showed that 47 percent of Americans couldn't come up with $400 to pay for a car repair or health care emergency, while one in five say they have more credit card debt than emergency savings.[25] If you were in this category, who would you turn to for help?

The key players in social policy making

★

DESCRIBE THE ROLES
PLAYED BY EACH BRANCH
OF THE NATIONAL
GOVERNMENT AND BY
THE STATES IN MAKING
AND IMPLEMENTING
SOCIAL POLICY

Congress, the president, and the bureaucracy all play key roles in shaping social policy. State governments also play a central role in some policy areas such as education and welfare policy, while interest groups are especially important for policies that affect the elderly.

Congress and the president

Given the differences between how the Democratic and Republican parties approach social policy as a tool for reducing income inequality, it may not be surprising that the poverty rate is more likely to fall during Democratic presidencies than Republican. This is exactly what Figure 16.3 shows. Between 1960 and 2017, Democrats controlled the White House for 28 years and Republicans for 29 years. During Democratic presidencies, the poverty rate fell from the previous year in 22 of those 28 years and for 2 years remained the same as in the previous year. The poverty rate fell during Republican presidencies in only 14 of the 29 years they were in power and remained the same in 3 years. Overall, the mean change in the poverty rate was −0.47 percent in Democratic years and it went up by 0.07 percent in Republican years. These differences may not sound like much, but given that each percentage point change in the poverty rate represents more than 3 million people today, the differences are significant. Political scientist Larry M. Bartels finds that in the past six decades the inflation-adjusted incomes of working poor families increased six times faster under Democratic presidents than under Republican presidents.[26] This makes some sense given the political base of the two parties: Democrats win large percentages of the votes of poor people, and Republicans usually do better among wealthier voters.

Changes in Poverty Rates by Party

**FIGURE
16.3**

The poverty rate tends to decrease under Democratic presidents and to go up by about the same margin under Republican presidents. What could explain this difference?

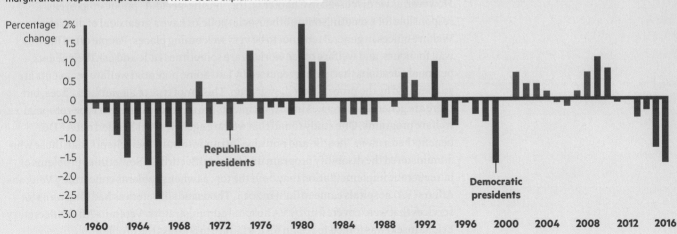

Source: Data from the U.S. Census Bureau, Poverty: Historical Tables, available at www.census.gov (accessed 9/24/16).

The data on changes in the poverty rate during different presidential administrations by party ignored one important point: Democratic presidents were more likely than Republican presidents to have a Congress controlled by their party. From 1961 to 2017, Democrats and Republicans each controlled the presidency for 28 years. But Democrats had unified control of government for 16 years and Republicans had control for only 5 years. This means that Democratic presidents had more opportunity to implement their agendas, whereas Republican presidents had to do more negotiating with the other party. You might argue that this divided control only prevented Republican presidents from making even deeper cuts in social programs, which could have driven the poverty rate even higher, because Democrats in Congress would not have been supporting those cuts. Although this is a possibility, especially during the Reagan years, divided control may also have prevented Republican presidents from implementing their alternative visions of the best way to address poverty.

This discussion underlies the more basic point that Congress and the president both play central roles in shaping social policy. In some instances, the president may take the lead, as with FDR and the New Deal or Lyndon Johnson and the Great Society. In other instances, Congress plays a central role, as with health care reform in 2009–2010. In all cases, the president and Congress must find some common ground. This may be especially difficult under divided government, but even when the president and Congress are of the same party, Congress may be obstructionist: in 2005 a Republican-controlled Congress ignored President Bush's effort to partially privatize Social Security, in 2009–2010 a Democrat-controlled Congress did not follow through on President Obama's comprehensive immigration reform or take action on the administration's initiatives concerning global warming, and in 2017 a Republican-controlled Congress failed to deliver on one of President Trump's key campaign promises to "repeal and replace" Obamacare.

The bureaucracy

You might assume that the bureaucracy itself makes little difference in social policy because it simply implements the policies determined by Congress and the president. For some policies, that is fairly close to what happens. For example, in the case of Social Security and other programs that have levels of benefits determined by law, implementing policy largely involves determining that the proper amount of money is going to the right people and making sure that these people receive the money. However, as we discussed in Chapter 13, the "on-the-ground" public employees responsible for executing many other social policies have a great deal of discretion. Welfare offices in general tend not to be very welcoming places. People often have to wait for hours, and welfare office workers are sometimes rude and ask their clients personal questions that are not required by law. Some potential welfare recipients are so alienated by the process that they give up. This is not true of all welfare offices, but there are general differences in how recipients are treated in different types of social welfare programs. One study found that welfare agencies that handed out AFDC benefits had a more "hostile and punitive" attitude toward their clients than those who administered the disability program under Social Security.[27] Sometimes problems of bureaucratic implementation may be at the top, as when problems concerning Veterans Affairs (VA) hospitals came to light in 2014. Thousands of veterans had long waits for services that were covered up by VA hospital administrators. Veterans Affairs Secretary Eric Shinseki was forced to resign for his failure to address the problem.[28]

Welfare offices can be alienating places in which it is very difficult to navigate through the bureaucracy. Here, dozens of people wait to speak to counselors in this Lawrenceville, Georgia, welfare office.

Bureaucratic discretion may also serve more positive ends. Political scientist Daniel P. Carpenter reported that many bureaucratic agencies in the late nineteenth and early twentieth centuries developed political autonomy and strong reputations that allowed them to analyze and solve problems, create new programs, and plan and administer programs efficiently.[29] Many of the same insights apply to agencies that deliver social policies today, such as the Social Security Administration, which has a very strong base of popular and political support.

The states

Social policy has always been strongly influenced by our system of federalism. As long as welfare has existed in the United States, it has been administered at the state and local levels, with varying degrees of national control. The 1996 welfare reform bill, Temporary Assistance to Needy Families (TANF), gave more power to the states and eliminated all national guarantees. Medicaid is administered at the state level (with federal assistance), and education is almost completely controlled by local and state governments. One sticking point with health care reform in 2009–2010 was the extent to which policy would be centered in the states or have a stronger national component. Many Democrats argued for a national "public option," while Republicans favored a more limited approach in which insurance companies would be allowed to compete across state lines. The stronger national approach failed, but the new law clearly signaled a shift to a more national role in health care. Education policy is another area where the trend has been toward more involvement of the national government rather than more power returning to the states. But even with the national accountability mechanisms and testing requirements established by President Bush's No Child Left Behind Act and the incentives provided by President Obama's Race to the Top program, education policy remains largely a state and local affair. President Trump's education policy has been consistent with maintaining the central role for state and local government, calling for cuts in many federal programs but big increases in spending for public and private school choice programs.[30]

Interest groups

In general, interest groups that advocate for social policy are not as influential as business or labor groups, many other professional associations, or even other public interest groups that focus on specific issues such as gun ownership or protection of the environment. A major exception is AARP, one of the most powerful lobbies in the United States (see Chapter 10). AARP has long had a strong voice on behalf of Social Security and Medicare. For example, when President George W. Bush proposed "personal savings accounts" to replace part of the Social Security system, AARP mobilized its significant political muscle to crush the idea before it could receive serious debate in Congress. Similarly, when Medicaid and Medicare were targeted for deep cuts in the 2019 fiscal year budget, AARP was a powerful voice for protecting those programs (while Medicaid is based on financial need rather than age, many seniors in nursing homes receive assistance from the program).[31]

Many interest groups and think tanks work on behalf of the poor, the homeless, and other disadvantaged people, but decision makers in Washington, D.C., generally are less responsive to their concerns because these groups and the people they are aligned with are not politically powerful. The poor tend not to vote or donate money to political campaigns. Many politicians in Washington care deeply about issues concerning poverty, homelessness, and other social-policy problems, but the interest groups and think tanks that try to focus politicians' attention on these issues face a particularly difficult task because of the relatively disadvantaged position of the people they represent.

TRACE THE STEPS THROUGH WHICH PROBLEMS ARE ADDRESSED BY SOCIAL POLICIES

The policy-making process

Another way to understand the role of key players in making policy is to examine the various stages of the process. The How It Works graphic shows the stages by which Social Security was conceived and enacted, but all policies go through similar steps. The first stage is to define a problem as an issue that requires the federal government's attention. Of the thousands of possible issues, Congress acts on a relatively small number. Consider a social policy such as food stamps. Poor and hungry people have been part of American society since the arrival of the first settlers, but this was not seen as a problem requiring government intervention until the twentieth century. What causes a society to change its assumptions about whether and how government should address social problems?

Sometimes there is a triggering event: the assassination of President John F. Kennedy led to the passage of gun control legislation, the energy crisis of the early 1970s led to the first comprehensive discussions of energy policy, and Hurricane Katrina led to a reexamination of our readiness for emergencies and our social safety net. Sometimes redefining an issue can move the policy to the next step of the process. For example, the estate tax has been part of our tax system since 1917, but when Republican leaders in Congress redefined it as the "death tax" in the late 1990s, they transformed the politics of the debate and made it a problem that needed a solution. After all, who could support a tax on dead people? (Of course, dead people don't pay taxes—the estate's heirs do—but that nuance was lost in the redefinition of the problem.)

Recognizing and defining a problem is just the first step; it still needs to come to the attention of political leaders and then get on the **policy agenda**. The basic idea is that when conditions are right, with the appropriate national political mood and

policy agenda
The set of desired policies that political leaders view as their top priorities.

participation from key interest groups and government actors, an issue can reach the agenda. Once the issue is on the active agenda, alternatives are proposed and debated and the final version of the policy is formulated in Congress (if it is a bill) or the executive branch (if it is an administrative action). Enactment involves a roll call vote in the House and the Senate and then a signature by the president, a regulatory decision or administrative action by the bureaucracy, or unilateral action by the president (such as an executive order or agreement).

Many factors determine whether or not the finalized policy is implemented successfully. First, the problem the policy is designed to fix has to be solvable. Second, the policy must be clear and consistent in its objectives. It wouldn't make sense for Congress to pass a law telling the Department of Health and Human Services to "make sure everyone has health care," because such a law would not indicate how this should be done. Third, the policy must be funded adequately and administered by competent bureaucrats who have the required expertise. Finally, external support from the public and relevant interest groups may be critical to the policy's success. For example, AARP's support is critical for the success of any social policy that affects older people. Its support helped pass the Prescription Drug Benefit that was added to Medicare in 2003 and comprehensive health care reform in 2010.[32]

Implementation of a policy is an ongoing process. To ensure that the desires of Congress and the president are being followed, policy evaluation is a critical stage of the policy-making process. (See Chapter 13 for a discussion of attempts by Congress and the president to control the bureaucracy.) Evaluation has become more visible since passage of the Government Performance and Results Act of 1993. Under the law, agencies are required to publish strategic plans and performance measures. Though these efforts sound impressive, it is incredibly difficult to assess whether a government program is achieving its aims. The law also improved policy implementation by focusing on performance. A review of the effort to "reinvent government" on its 25th anniversary noted improvements in the areas of procurement, acquisition of IT systems, and category management, which involves leveraging government's buying power to get discounts for large volumes. The Trump administration has been enthusiastic in applying and expanding these market-oriented practices through the Office of American Innovation (with leadership from Trump's son-in-law, Jared Kushner).[33]

Political scientist James Q. Wilson explains the difference between measuring success in the private and public sectors—specifically, he compares McDonald's with the Department of Motor Vehicles (DMV).[34] It is relatively easy to know whether McDonald's is doing a good job: simply look at the profits being generated and compare them with those of the previous period. If profits are going up at a reasonable pace, the burger flippers and fry cooks are doing their jobs. The DMV's performance is much more difficult to assess because there is no simple measure, such as profit, to look at. Maybe you could review the number of people served per hour or the average length of time people have to wait to get their driver's license. But that would ignore many other considerations, such as how well the DMV serves disadvantaged populations or people for whom English is a second language. We wouldn't expect a DMV office where 50 percent of its applicants don't speak English to be as efficient as one at which all applicants speak English.

Evaluating a public agency such as the State Department is even more difficult. How do we know if diplomacy is being conducted in a manner consistent with congressional and presidential preferences? Would success be defined as staying out of war? Increasing economic activity or cultural exchanges between countries? Strengthening democratic institutions in emerging democracies? Getting cooperation in the war on terrorism? Measuring the achievement of objectives like these is very difficult even if those goals can be clearly defined.

The Social Policy-Making Process

Problem recognition

Attention is drawn to an existing problem. This can be triggered by an event or disaster, such as the emergency response to Hurricane Sandy, the impact of an economic recession on the jobless and the poor, or global warming.

Agenda setting

Public awareness of the problem increases as the media, relevant interest groups, and political leaders talk about the problem. The problem becomes a priority for the government.

Deliberation and formulation

Different policy proposals are suggested to address the problem, input is provided by interested parties, relevant executive agencies, and congressional committees.

Enactment

Congress passes the legislation and the president signs it into law.

Implementation

The relevant bureaucratic agencies put the law into effect, writing specific regulations when needed, distributing benefits, and handling government contracts and procurement.

Evaluation

Policy analysts, inside and outside government, determine whether the policy is working as intended.

Possible modification, expansion, or termination of policy

Based on the policy evaluations and public reaction to the policy, political leaders tweak the law to improve it, expand the scope of the law if it is working well, or sometimes repeal the law.

The Enactment and Evolution of Social Security

Social Security, the federal government's social insurance program to provide financial support to retired people, provides a good example of the various stages of the policy-making process.

There is a problem.

A large proportion of elderly people were living in poverty.

We need to fix this.

As poverty among the elderly worsened during the Great Depression, **solving the problem became a priority within FDR's New Deal agenda.**

We have an idea.

The proposal for **Social Security came from FDR's President's Committee on Economic Security.**

Signed into law.

Social Security was passed by Congress and **signed into law by the president in 1935.**

Moving forward...

The Social Security Administration **implements the policy.**

Let's look at that again.

Social Security has been **evaluated at various times,** most recently by presidential commissions on reform.

Updated.

Social Security has been modified and expanded several times, most recently in 1983.

? Critical Thinking

1. **Social Security is one of our** most popular social programs. Under what conditions would it be modified or changed?

2. **What groups are most likely to oppose reductions** in Social Security benefits? Which are most likely to support them? Do you think these groups should have influence on Social Security policy? Why or why not?

Despite these limitations, extensive efforts to evaluate policy do provide decision makers with some basis for deciding whether to modify, expand, or terminate a policy. Programs are notoriously difficult to cut or eliminate. Examples abound, such as wool and mohair subsidies implemented after World War II and the Korean War. More than half of the wool needed to make uniforms during these wars was imported, so the Pentagon wanted to increase domestic production of wool. The National Wool Act in 1954 provided direct subsidies to farmers. By 1994 the program was spending nearly $240 million a year, despite the fact that the Pentagon removed wool from its "strategic materials" list in 1960! The subsidies were finally killed in 1994, but the 2002 Farm Act added wool and mohair to the list of commodities eligible for marketing assistance loans and the subsidy persists today.[35] Some policies are like the zombies in *The Walking Dead*—unless you kill them in just the right way, they keep coming back.

Alternative perspectives on the policy-making process

The "stages model" of policy making described earlier is a pretty basic description of the process. Several elaborations and extensions provide a more nuanced understanding of the process.[36] For example, the first two steps, problem recognition and agenda setting, were conceptualized by John Kingdon as multiple streams of problems, politics, and policies. These three streams are independent and may or may not intersect. Objective conditions may or may not turn into problems. For example, the abuse of opioid painkillers has been evident for many years. But the death of the musician Prince called attention to this condition and turned it into a *problem* that policy makers felt more pressure to address. This changed the *politics* of the problem as people were more likely to see the problem as something that required government action. Congress responded in July 2016 by passing the Comprehensive Addiction and Recovery Act (CARA), which changed the government's *policy* related to the opioid problem. With 175 Americans dying every day from opioid overdoses, many politicians recognized it as a crisis that needed further government action.[37]

There typically are various policy options available to address any given problem, but whether or not policy makers act on them depends on either the presence of a policy entrepreneur who pushes for change or, more broadly, the occurrence of a political change that creates a "policy window"—an opportunity to implement the policy. Political change may occur thanks to a change in the national mood, interest group pressure, or an administrative or legislative change in control.[38] All this is to say that agenda setting and eventually passing a law are not as linear and static as implied by the basic stages model.

Frank R. Baumgartner and Bryan D. Jones provide additional insight into *how* policy change happens with their "punctuated equilibrium" model. They argue that the policy process features long periods of incremental change punctuated by brief periods of major policy change. Change comes about when an alternative "policy image" can expand an issue beyond the control of the policy specialists who resist change. For example, the ACA overcame decades of resistance to major change in health insurance by emphasizing a policy image that focused on the millions of Americans who did not have insurance.[39]

One final question about the policy-making process concerns policy diffusion: Why do some policies quickly spread across the country while others are adopted in only a few states? The idea that states are "laboratories of democracy" is an invitation to explore that variation. One comprehensive study took up the challenge and examined

130 policy innovations, explaining the relative rates of diffusion by the type of policy, the involvement of interest groups, and the level of government attention. For example, the "Amber Alert" child abduction notification system that was adopted in more than 30 states in less than six years is an example of a "policy outbreak" that quickly spread across the states.[40] And an analysis of anti-smoking policy found that learning from early adopters, economic competition between proximate cities, imitation of larger cities, and coercion from state governments all explained whether or not a city adopted an anti-smoking policy.[41]

Social policy today

As of the 2019 fiscal year, Social Security, Medicare, and Medicaid make up nearly half of all federal spending ($2.1 trillion out of $4.4 trillion). With an aging population and health care costs that continue to grow as a percentage of the economy, these policies will take an even greater share of the budget in the future. Given other spending priorities, political pressure is mounting to put spending for social programs on a more sustainable path. This section will explain the nature of these important programs and discuss recent efforts to reform them.

ANALYZE THE CURRENT MAJOR AREAS OF SOCIAL POLICY

Social Security

Social Security is the most popular social program in the United States. Consequently, it has developed a reputation as the "third rail" of politics (like the dangerous, power-conducting rail on electrified train tracks) because a politician who dares to touch Social Security risks political death. Despite serious problems concerning its long-term solvency, Social Security has proven remarkably immune to any steps that could be taken to shore up its financial health, such as cutting benefits, raising taxes, or privatizing part of the program. Why is Social Security so popular, what long-term challenges does it face, and what are the possible solutions to ensure the program's long-term viability?

One reason that Social Security is so popular is its universal quality—that is, nearly every working American participates in the program, from Donald Trump to the teenager flipping burgers at McDonald's. Once people reach a certain age, they are all entitled to Social Security checks without regard to how much income they have from other sources, such as dividends, interest, or other pensions. So, unlike many social programs that help only a subset of the population, and thus may foster an "us

Social Security
A federal social insurance program that provides cash benefits to retirees based on payroll taxes they have paid over the course of their careers. It is a "pay as you go" program in which working Americans pay taxes to support today's retirees, with a promise that when today's workers retire their benefits will be paid by the next generation.

against them" mentality (taxpayers may ask, "Why should we have to support other people?"), Social Security does not pit citizens from different classes or ethnic groups against each other. Social Security is also popular because it works. It is more efficient than most privately managed pensions, with about 0.8 percent going to administrative expenses, compared with the average mutual fund that spends more than 1 percent. More important, Social Security has accomplished its central goal of helping most Americans have an adequate retirement income: fewer than 10 percent of the elderly are in poverty today (8.8 percent), which is a lower rate than for the general public (see What Do the Facts Say?) and significantly lower than the 35 percent of the elderly who were in poverty in 1960. Census data also show that 40 percent of the elderly would be in poverty today without their Social Security payments.[42]

How Social Security Works Before we examine the various proposals to change Social Security, it is important to understand how the program works. Social Security is funded by a payroll tax of 6.2 percent on income up to $128,400 (in 2018) with an equal 6.2 percent that is paid by employers. (The self-employed have to pay both halves.) The payroll tax has an additional 1.45 percent on all income for Medicare (which we will discuss later). This is considered a regressive tax because poor and middle-income people put a higher percentage of their income toward the Social Security tax than wealthy people do. The maximum Social Security tax you can pay is $7,961 a year, which is 6.2 percent of $128,400. So a millionaire would pay less than 1 percent of his or her income in the Social Security payroll tax (0.796 percent, to be exact) compared with the 6.2 percent that everyone earning less than $128,400 pays. Although the taxes are regressive, the benefits are progressive; that is, poorer people receive back in benefits a larger share of their lifetime payroll taxes than wealthy people receive (see Nuts & Bolts 16.2).

In 1983 several changes were made to Social Security to strengthen its long-term finances. One significant change was a gradual increase in the retirement age from 65 to 67. People born in 1937 or earlier could retire in 2002 at age 65 and receive full benefits. Between 2003 and 2027 the retirement age increases gradually to 67 for

Social Security

Number of Recipients for Old-Age, Survivors, and Disability Insurance

Old-Age Insurance (the basic retirement program)	46,100,000
Survivors Insurance (retirement program for widows, widowers, and the children of deceased primary wage earners)	6,010,000
Disability Insurance (payments for people and their families who cannot work because of a disability and are not yet retired)	10,345,000

Monthly Retirement Benefits

Individual	Average: $1,372	Maximum: $2,788
Couple	Average: $2,283	Maximum: $4,879

Sources: Figures on the number of recipients are from the U.S. Social Security Administration Office of Policy, "Monthly Statistical Snapshot, May 2018," Table 2, www.ssa.gov/policy/docs/quickfacts/stat_snapshot/index.html; figures on monthly benefits are from Social Security Administration, *2018 OASDI Trustees Report*, June 5, 2018, Table V.C7, p. 150, www.ssa.gov/OACT/TR/2018/tr2018.pdf (both accessed 7/5/18).

full benefits. Early retirement at 62 is an option, if the retiree is willing to accept a permanently reduced benefit level. Delaying retirement until age 70 permanently increases the retiree's Social Security benefits.

Social Security's Long-Term Challenges Despite its successes and overall popularity, Social Security faces long-term problems. Unless certain fundamental issues are tackled, the program will be unable to cover its obligations. The longer we wait to address the shortfall, the more difficult solving the problem will be.

Basic changes in the nation's demographic profile are driving the projected shortfall. The **baby-boom generation**, people born between 1946 and 1964, is starting to retire. Between 2000 and 2030 the number of Americans over the age of 65 will more than double, whereas the number of working-age Americans (20–64) will grow by only 20 percent.[43] This trend means that there will be fewer workers to support the increasing number of retirees. In fact, the number of workers per Social Security recipient fell from 16.5 in 1950 to 2.8 in 2017; by 2035 it will be only 2.2.[44] See Figure 16.4 for evidence of the aging population.

"Wait a minute," you may be saying. "Why does it matter how many workers there are for each retiree? I thought that Social Security was a pension program that you pay into while you're working and then get the benefits when you retire." Not exactly. Social Security is not a self-funded pension but a "pay as you go" system in which today's workers support today's retirees through the payroll tax discussed earlier. Therefore, the huge increase in the number of retirees will strain the system because each worker will have to pay higher taxes to maintain the same level of Social Security benefits. Of course, benefits could be cut, but the third-rail status of the program has prevented that, at least up to now.

Another problem with the pay-as-you-go nature of Social Security is the intergenerational transfer of wealth. The flip side of Social Security's success in reducing the poverty rate for seniors is that more children and working poor are in poverty today (17.5 percent of those under 18 are in poverty, compared with only 9.2 percent of those over 65 and 11.2 percent between 18 and 65).[45] Some critics have wondered if it makes sense, for example, for single mothers working for the minimum

baby-boom generation
Americans born between 1946 and 1964, who are retiring in large numbers over the next 20 years.

DID YOU KNOW?

15.5%
of women and 24 percent of men 65 and older are working full-time.
Source: Bureau of Labor Statistics

FIGURE 16.4

People 65 and Older as a Share of the U.S. Population

Elderly people will constitute a much larger share of the U.S. population in 2060 than they do today. How might the aging population affect social policy—both in terms of the politics of policy making and in terms of the fiscal implications of this trend?

Source: U.S. Census Bureau, 2014 National Population Projections, Table 3, www.census.gov (accessed 6/9/16).

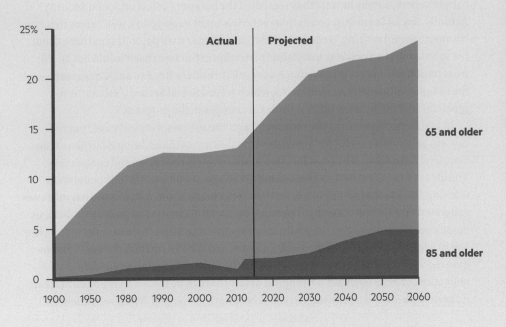

wage or recent college graduates who are starting their careers and paying off student loans to pay 6.2 percent of their income in taxes to support the benefits of some people who are living comfortably in retirement. This critique also points out that current retirees will receive far more in benefits than they paid in Social Security taxes, while many current workers won't get back as much as they paid in (if interest on the taxes paid is considered). For example, the average worker who retired in 1990 got back all of his or her Social Security taxes, plus interest, by 1999. It is difficult to project the rate of return for current workers because we do not know what future benefits or taxes will be.[46] However, it is safe to bet that taxes will be higher and benefits will not maintain the same rate of increase that they have had for the past several decades. Therefore, today's retirees are reaping a windfall that strikes some critics as unfair, especially given that these retirees are better off, on average, than the workers who are currently paying taxes. Now you can start to see why reforming Social Security is so controversial. Debate over Social Security reform exposes highly charged class-based and intergenerational tensions.

The pay-as-you-go nature of Social Security creates intergenerational inequities. Relatively poor young people working for minimum wage help fund the Social Security benefits for retired people who are often reasonably well-off.

Policy makers have known since the early 1960s about the eventual wave of retiring baby boomers, so why haven't they remedied the boomers' effect on Social Security? Actually, Social Security faced its first real crisis in the early 1980s, well before the boomers started retiring. Benefits had increased faster than payroll taxes throughout the 1970s, and the Social Security Administration estimated that it would not be able to meet its obligations as early as 1983. As a result, President Reagan and Congress passed the 1983 Social Security Amendments, which solved Social Security's short-term problems and made many other significant changes in the program.

In addition to increasing the retirement age, the 1983 reforms increased payroll taxes to generate a surplus for a trust fund to take care of the additional burden of the boomers' retirement. The trust fund is a source of great confusion and controversy. The idea behind the trust fund was sound: build up a surplus while the boomers are working and use that money to pay for their retirement. From 1983 to 2008 payroll taxes generated far more revenue than spending on Social Security. The problem is that this money wasn't really saved: the government spent it elsewhere, for example, to fund the war in Afghanistan, food stamps, school loans, and the FBI. In turn, the government gave the Social Security trust fund an IOU in the form of "special public-debt obligation." These IOUs are not tangible assets that can be traded on the open market; rather, they are used like an internal bookkeeping mechanism. The government will pay them off, but the only way it can do so is through increasing taxes, cutting spending in other areas, or additional borrowing.

The best way to understand this is to examine the numbers from the Trustees Report on Social Security. In 2017, Old-Age, Survivors, and Disability Insurance had $997 billion in income ($874 billion from payroll taxes, $85 billion from interest on the trust fund, and $38 billion from taxation of Social Security benefits) and $953 billion in expenditures. But remember, the $85 billion in interest on the trust fund is just IOUs rather than real assets. So taxes fell $41 billion short of covering expenses ([$874 + $38] − $953). This means that the shortfall had to be made up with general tax revenue. As Figure 16.5 shows, the present value of the trust fund peaked at $2.8 trillion in 2017 and will move downward when promised benefits exceed payroll tax revenue. The trust fund runs out in 2034, at which point the Social Security system will be able to fund only about 79 percent of its obligations.[47]

Democrats and Republicans alike have misused this issue for political purposes. Democrats criticize Republicans any time they try to reform Social Security, claiming that the program is on strong fiscal ground—while ignoring that the need for $2.8 trillion from general taxes over a 16-year period will further strain the system and that a huge shortfall remains, even after generating that additional money. Republicans argue that the system is in crisis and that privatization is the only way out. Some Republicans suggest that Social Security will be "bankrupt" in 2034, which is incorrect given that the system would still be able to pay about 75 percent of its obligations. Although both sides have used the issue as demagoguery, both parties do raise important points. Republicans are correct that the sooner we act, the better. The system may not be in crisis today, but it *will* be if we don't do anything about it soon. Democrats are correct that the problems can be solved with relatively small changes to benefits and taxes (the most recent Trustees Report estimates that the 75-year projected shortfall amounts to 2.84 percent of taxable payroll), but the required changes won't be small if we wait much longer.[48]

FIGURE 16.5

Social Security Trust Fund

Since 2010, the cost of the Social Security program has exceeded Social Security payroll taxes, so taxes will need to be raised to cover the trust fund's obligations and the program's ongoing expenses. What do you think are the best solutions to address the long-term future of Social Security? What are the politically viable solutions?

Source: Social Security Administration, June 2018, "The 2018 Annual Report of the Board of Trustees of the Federal Old-Age and Survivors Insurance and Federal Disability Insurance Trust Funds" Figure II.D5.

Social Security Reform So what is to be done? Dozens of plans to reform Social Security and make it fiscally sound for coming generations have been suggested. There is a surprising amount of agreement among all the serious plans that saving Social Security requires a mixture of benefit cuts and tax increases. The calculations get very complicated in terms of the projected fiscal impact of various reforms, but a mixture of these options would take care of the long-term fiscal problems of Social Security:[49]

· Raise payroll taxes by 1 percent and increase the income ceiling that is taxable.
· Lower benefits for nonworking spouses (that is, spouses who did not work during their earning years). Currently, nonworking spouses receive 50 percent of the benefits that their working partners do. Some proposals would cut that benefit to 33 percent.
· Index current and future benefits to inflation instead of wages. Currently benefit increases are linked to national average wage increases. Because inflation does not increase as fast as wages, linking benefit increases to inflation would generate significant savings. Because this would mean a large reduction of benefits over the long run, a less extreme version has been proposed called progressive price indexing. This approach would reduce benefits only for those in the top 50 percent or 70 percent of the income distribution by indexing them to inflation (those in the bottom half of the income distribution would still have benefits indexed to wage increases).
· Gradually raise the retirement age to 70 (by 2030). This proposed change is viewed by many as fair because it adjusts for the fact that people live longer now than they did in the early years of Social Security. Life expectancy of people who turned 65 in 1940 was 77.7 years, so the average Social Security recipient would receive about 13 years of benefits. Those who turned 65 in 2017 could expect to live 19.5 more years, and life expectancy is expected to increase by about six months per decade. Therefore, by 2030 the average life expectancy for those who reach 65 will be 85.3 years (it is 86.5 for women and 84.1 for men). To bring the expected stream of benefits back in line with where it was in 1940, the retirement age would have to be increased to 71.6.[50] Changing the retirement age to 70 would save $620 billion by 2040.

A more controversial proposal is this:

· Lower benefits for wealthier recipients. The strongest argument in favor of this approach is that Bill Gates doesn't need the measly couple of thousand dollars he will receive each month from Social Security. In fact, he wouldn't even notice if that money was used to reduce Social Security's deficit. More broadly, if benefits are phased out for those in the top third of income levels, it will save billions of dollars a year. The main argument against this proposal is that it would end the universal nature of Social Security and possibly turn it into another welfare program.

A bipartisan commission established by President Obama to examine the long-term viability of Social Security favored increasing the retirement age to keep up with longevity, so it would be age 69 by 2075; increasing the amount of income subject to the payroll tax to 90 percent of all income; and making benefits more progressive, which would reduce benefits for wealthier people while increasing them for poorer people. The commission said that these changes would place Social Security on a secure long-term foundation.[51] However, despite the bipartisan nature of the recommendations, Congress ignored the report.

The most controversial plans concern partial or full **privatization** of Social Security. This is the main issue that divides Democrats and Republicans: Democrats favor maintaining the basic structure of Social Security's public social insurance system, and

privatization
The process of transferring the management of a government program (like Social Security) from the public sector to the private sector.

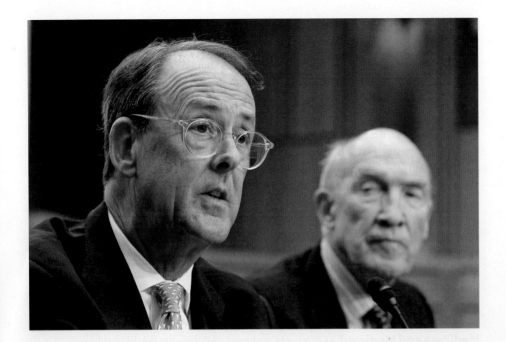

Obama's bipartisan commission, which included the Debt Commission chairmen Erskine Bowles (left) and Alan Simpson, made recommendations to Congress and the president about how to fix Social Security. Despite the bipartisan nature of the commission and its recommendations, no reforms were implemented.

Republicans favor moving part or all of the "pay as you go" system to private accounts. The central argument in favor of private accounts is that over the long term investing in the stock market has historically provided returns higher in value than the Social Security checks that people can expect to receive. Also, with private accounts, all assets in the account are owned by the individual and that person's heirs, whereas with Social Security, when an individual dies that person's heirs do not receive any additional benefits from his or her lifetime contributions to Social Security (but a surviving spouse continues to receive benefits from those contributions that will vary depending on the couple's work histories). Advocates argue that if all workers were able to take their 6.2 percent payroll tax and put that in a retirement account, they would have a modest nest egg by the time they retired.

Democrats point out the problems with this approach—most important, the transition costs. Because the current system is "pay as you go," if we stopped taking payroll taxes and allowed people to put the money into private accounts, there wouldn't be any money to pay for today's retirees and everyone else who has paid into the system for a substantial number of years. These transition costs are estimated to be $7 to $8 *trillion*!

A second criticism of privatization is that Social Security should be a part of everyone's retirement plan that they can count on. Investing in the stock market is fine as a supplement to Social Security, but it is too risky to be counted on as a sole source of retirement income. Although it is true that the stock market outperforms other investments over the long haul, there have been periods as long as 20 years when stock market returns have been flat. So if you happened to retire at the end of one of those slumps, you could find yourself with a much smaller nest egg than you had counted on. Finally, critics point out that the administrative overhead costs of these private accounts would eat up any additional returns that they might earn.

These issues are not likely to be resolved anytime soon, which illustrates that politics is conflictual. Social Security reform can pit one generation against another or wealthy people against poor people. The stakes in Social Security are extremely high because it is the most popular and visible social program, which makes it all the more difficult to handle.

Health care

Health care policy seemed as difficult to reform as Social Security. Every president since Theodore Roosevelt who attempted comprehensive reform failed until President Obama's success in 2010 with the ACA. In order to understand the law, we have to understand how health care is provided in the United States and the factors that the ACA has been designed to address: the nation's aging population, health care costs that are rising faster than inflation, and the lack of health insurance among a significant number of Americans before the implementation of the law. The United States spends more on health care than any other nation in the world—$3.4 trillion, or 17.2 percent of GDP, compared with 8.9 percent for other developed countries (for example, Japan spends 10.7 percent, Germany 11.3 percent, Canada 10.4 percent, and Italy 8.9 percent).[52] All these countries have government-funded universal health care; thus, we spend almost 90 percent more than they do (in relative terms) but leave nearly 30 million people without coverage. This set up a two-tier system in which those who had access to health care got some of the best care in the world and those without access were much less likely to get the health care they need.

Medicare and Medicaid As Figure 16.6 shows, our current system combines government spending (Medicare and Medicaid), private insurance, and out-of-pocket

FIGURE 16.6

The Health Care Dollar: Where It Comes from and Where It Goes

Funding for our current health care system comes from a variety of sources and is spent on many types of care. In an effort to slow the increases in health care costs, which areas should receive the most attention?

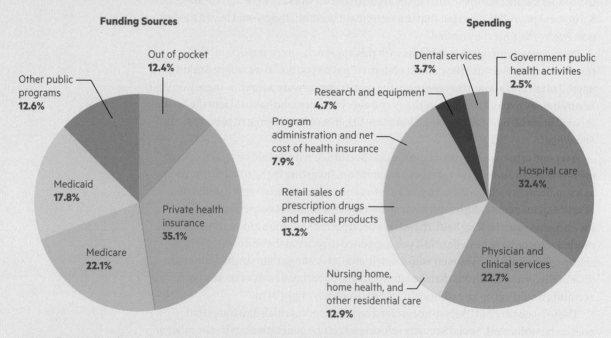

Funding Sources

- Out of pocket 12.4%
- Other public programs 12.6%
- Medicaid 17.8%
- Medicare 22.1%
- Private health insurance 35.1%

Spending

- Dental services 3.7%
- Government public health activities 2.5%
- Research and equipment 4.7%
- Program administration and net cost of health insurance 7.9%
- Retail sales of prescription drugs and medical products 13.2%
- Nursing home, home health, and other residential care 12.9%
- Hospital care 32.4%
- Physician and clinical services 22.7%

Note: Percentages shown may not add up to 100 percent because of rounding.

Source: Centers for Medicare and Medicaid Services, National Health Expenditures data, spending data from Table 2, funding sources from Table 6, www.cms.gov (accessed 7/5/18).

payments. Medicare and Medicaid, the two pillars of federally provided health care that predate the ACA, are administered by the Department of Health and Human Services.

Medicare, the federal health care program for retired people, has three main parts. Part A automatically applies to retirees when they qualify for Social Security; it covers inpatient care in hospitals and skilled nursing facilities, hospice care, and some home health care. Medicare Part B helps cover doctors' services; outpatient hospital care; some other medical services that Part A does not cover, such as some physical and occupational therapy; and other types of home health care. In 2003, Congress passed an important new benefit, the Medicare Prescription Drug, Improvement, and Modernization Act (Part D). The plan covers about 75 percent of the cost of prescription drugs for anyone who is enrolled in Part A or Part B of Medicare, up to a certain level of expenses.

The other government health care program, **Medicaid**, serves poor people who otherwise would have no health care. Medicaid is administered through the states with substantial funding from the federal government. Although Medicaid is an **entitlement**, states have considerable discretion over the program. As the government's website on Medicaid explains, each state

> establishes its own eligibility standards; determines the type, amount, duration, and scope of services; sets the rate of payment for services; and administers its own program. Medicaid policies for eligibility, services, and payment are complex and vary considerably, even among states of similar size or geographic proximity. Thus, a person who is eligible for Medicaid in one state may not be eligible in another state, and the services provided may differ considerably in amount, duration, or scope from services provided in a similar or neighboring State.[53]

This variation in state coverage means that some states cover virtually all poor people and others cover as few as one-third of those in need. Overall, 72.3 million Americans receive health care through Medicaid at a cost of $582 billion. The federal government reimburses the states for 63 percent of the costs ($367 billion in 2017), but this percentage varies by state income level and whether or not a state accepted the expansion of Medicaid under Obamacare, as we will discuss below.[54] The federal government paid all the costs associated with expanding Medicaid for the 12 poorest states in fiscal year 2019 under the enhanced reimbursements from the ACA, and 88 percent of the costs for the 14 wealthiest states, which is the minimum level set by law.[55] Like Medicare, Medicaid faces growing budgetary pressures in the coming years. An increasing share of Medicaid's costs is for long-term nursing home care for the indigent elderly, and the need for this service continues to grow as the population ages. At the other end of the age spectrum, Medicaid was expanded in 1997 to provide health care for children in families that make too much to qualify for Medicaid but not enough to buy private insurance for their children (incomes that are no more than double the poverty level). By 2017, the Children's Health Insurance Program (CHIP) covered 9.46 million children and 36.9 million additional children were covered by Medicaid.[56] This popular program had always received strong bipartisan support until 2017, when House Republicans attempted to tie cuts in Obamacare to reauthorization of CHIP. A deadlock left the program unfunded for nearly four months, until Congress reauthorized it for six more years early in 2018.[57]

Federally Provided Health Care's Long-Term Challenges The long-term fiscal problems of Medicare and Medicaid are severe. In fact, they dwarf Social Security's problems. The *2018 Medicare Trustees Report* estimates that Social Security's unfunded

Medicare
The federal health care plan created in 1965 that provides coverage for retired Americans for hospital care (Part A), medical care (Part B), and prescription drugs (Part D).

Medicaid
An entitlement program funded by the federal and state governments that provides health care coverage for low-income Americans who would otherwise be unable to afford health care.

entitlement
Any federal government program that provides benefits to Americans who meet requirements specified by law.

liabilities through 2093, or the amount of additional money (beyond the current payroll tax) required to fund all the program's commitments, is $16.1 trillion, and Medicare has unfunded liabilities of $37.7 trillion.[58] Even though such projections depend on assumptions about future economic performance, demographic trends, and other uncertain variables, the *relative* difference between the two programs is significant. Medicare's troubles are more than twice as serious as Social Security's! Although the long-term Medicare deficit is huge, the projected unfunded liabilities were cut in half by the ACA. However, the trustees noted that their projections assume that cuts in Medicare reimbursements mandated in the new health care law will stick. The report expressed skepticism that this would happen.[59]

Another study by the nonpartisan CBO shows that federal spending on health care (including Medicare, Medicaid, and subsidies for the new health insurance exchanges) will continue to grow through 2048 (see Figure 16.7). The CBO estimates that by 2046 federal spending on health care, Social Security, and interest on the debt will reach 21.8 percent of GDP. That is, if the size of the federal government stays around its historic average of 20 percent of GDP, the two major social-policy programs will constitute all of noninterest federal spending by 2048. The choices are clear: either everything else must be cut from the budget (defense, education, transportation), health care costs and Social Security must be reined in, or the size of government will grow. Clearly, the current trends are not sustainable.

Health Care Reform Central to President Obama's 2008 campaign platform was reforming America's health care system. Upon election in 2009, he outlined several goals: controlling health care costs, providing health insurance for more Americans (as close to universal coverage as possible), and paying for the program without adding to the deficit. He then urged Congress to hammer out the details.

In formulating the legislation, Congress sifted through hundreds of options that represent three main types of systems: (1) national single-payer plans,

DID YOU KNOW?

Sixty percent of uninsured Americans can get health care coverage for

$100

or less per month and 87 percent of those with a marketplace account get some assistance.

Source: ObamacareFacts.com

FIGURE 16.7

Projected National Spending on Health Care (Percentage of GDP)

If current spending patterns hold, an increasing percentage of federal spending will be devoted to health care, crowding out other programs. Clearly, such trends are not sustainable. What changes do you support to reduce health care spending in the long run?

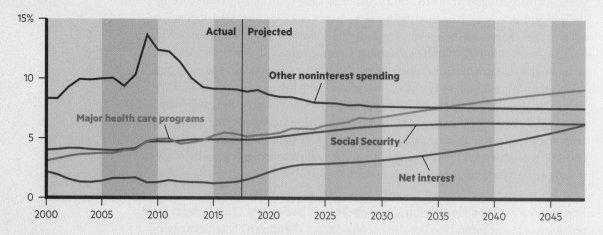

Source: Congressional Budget Office, "The 2018 Long-Term Budget Outlook," Figure 2, p. 7, www.cbo.gov (accessed 7/5/18).

Proposed budgetary solutions to Medicare and Social Security's unfunded liabilities involve politically unpopular benefit cuts and tax increases. To illustrate, Senator Bernie Sanders stands behind 2 million signatures asking Congress to reject proposed cuts in 2013.

(2) state-regulated health insurance networks combined with public subsidies to help pay for insurance for those who cannot afford it, and (3) market-based solutions based on tax credits and flexible spending accounts. The first of these was quickly rejected by Congress and is not likely to be implemented in the United States, despite being the program of choice for nearly all other Western developed nations. Critics dismiss single-payer plans as "socialized medicine" and point to the rationing of care that often occurs under such programs. Similarly, market-based solutions, which most Republicans supported, were rejected by Democratic leaders who believed the approach would leave too many Americans uninsured. This approach has the greatest potential for addressing the inflation of health care costs, but some health care professionals argued that many people would lack the knowledge base necessary to make the appropriate decisions concerning their own health care, because buying health care is much more difficult than shopping for food, clothing, or other consumer goods.

This left the middle ground between a single-payer plan and market-based approaches. In the introduction to this chapter, we discussed the politics of how reform passed. Here we summarize the main provisions, as it is impossible to discuss all the details of the voluminous, more-than-2,000-page law that one reporter described as "twice as long, and half as intelligible, as Tolstoy's masterwork *War and Peace*."[60]

Understanding the ACA ("Obamacare") The president's first goal—comprehensive coverage—was essential. The problem had to be tackled as a whole. If the law were to require insurance companies to cover people with preexisting conditions without mandating that everyone have insurance, people would avoid personal expense and wait until they were seriously ill before they purchased any health insurance. To spread the costs of expensive care needed by those with preexisting conditions and others, the law needed to mandate coverage for all, thus "pooling" healthy people and young people with older and sick people. Comprehensive coverage was achieved by requiring businesses with more than 50 employees to provide coverage and by requiring all individuals without employer coverage to purchase insurance through new state-regulated private health insurance exchanges, which were implemented in 2014. Businesses and individuals who did not comply with the mandate would face government fines. However, individuals who could not afford to purchase their own insurance would receive federal tax credit subsidies on a sliding scale (using a complicated formula that would provide the biggest subsidies to the poorest people and some support to people with incomes all the way up to four times the federal poverty rate). The individual mandate was one of the most controversial parts of the bill, but supporters point out that states already require people to purchase auto insurance if they have a car. During the formulation of the law, it was stated that most people who were pleased with their current health insurance through their employer would not have to change anything. However, people with policies that did not meet the minimum standards of the law would be required to get new insurance policies. This became a sticky issue for President Obama once the ACA was rolled out.

Other features of the law included incentives to computerize medical records, seen as a way to reduce medical mistakes, facilitate medical evaluations, and, as a result, improve the overall quality of care. Integration of technology into medical processes and record keeping was one of the law's central cost-control mechanisms. In addition, a new nonprofit organization, the Patient-Centered Outcomes Research Institute, would be authorized to engage in "comparative effectiveness research" to identify the best practices in health care. It would research such questions as which health care procedures work to make people healthier and which are a waste of money, and why some parts of the country spend more than twice as much on treating the same conditions. The ACA would encourage health care providers to adopt identified best practices. The law was also designed to focus more resources on preventive care to keep people healthy, so that, theoretically, people would be less likely to get sick and need further, expensive treatment.

One other goal was that health care had to pay for itself. Obama vowed that the bill would not "add one dime to the deficit." With a price tag of just under $1 trillion over the first 10 years, paying for the bill was a challenge. However, a combination of higher Medicare taxes, a new investment tax for the wealthy, an excise tax on insurers for expensive "Cadillac" health care plans, new fees for drug companies and health insurers, and cuts in Medicare reimbursement meant that the law would actually reduce the federal deficit by $143 billion over the first decade.[61]

Nonetheless, the political battle over health care reform was not over when Obama signed the bill into law. House Republicans repeatedly attempted to repeal the law. As discussed in the chapter opener, although these efforts were not successful, the rollout of the law was very rocky. The national health care insurance exchange, Healthcare. gov, was supposed to be operational on October 1, 2013, but the system repeatedly crashed during the first several months of operation, leading to substantial delays and great frustration for those Americans attempting to enroll. Millions of poor Americans were not able to get coverage when the states they lived in declined the option to expand Medicaid to cover everyone whose income was 138 percent of the poverty line (see Chapter 3 for a discussion of this conflictual issue). Because of the bumpy start, President Obama granted about a dozen extensions of various deadlines, including enrollment deadlines for the individual mandate, the employer mandate to cover all employees for businesses with between 50 and 100 employees (which was extended until the end of 2016), the high-risk pool that was intended to be temporary, and the requirement that people who had previously been covered by a substandard insurance policy get insurance on the exchange (this, too, was extended until the end of 2016).[62] An additional problem is that not as many young healthy people have signed up on the exchanges as predicted. So some insurance companies, such as Aetna and United Health, have lost significant amounts of money and are pulling out of many states. This means less competition and rising rates.

The Future of "Obamacare" President Trump and the Republican leadership in Congress have vowed to "repeal and replace" Obamacare. However, they will face many challenges. First, more than 26 million more Americans had health insurance in 2018 because of the law: 11.8 million Americans who previously did not have health insurance have successfully used the exchanges to sign up for insurance, and more than 6 million young adults have been able to remain on their parents' health insurance until age 26.[63] Also, 8.8 million new enrollees are covered through the expansion of Medicaid.[64] Second, many popular parts of the law have already been in effect since 2010—and these types of benefits are hard to repeal once the American public recognizes their value. These include a high-risk insurance pool for adults with preexisting conditions (which includes making it against the law for insurers of children under 19 years old with preexisting conditions to be dropped from their parents' policies); a fix for the Medicare prescription drug plan "donut hole" (previously, people who spent above a minimal level on drugs but below a high amount were not covered by the law); and coverage for young adults (up to age 26) on their parents' plans. Other popular parts of the law that went into effect in 2013 prohibit insurers from charging co-payments or deductibles for preventive care on all new insurance plans and prevent insurers from dropping policy holders when they get sick.

However, President Trump and congressional Republicans have tried to keep the popular parts while getting rid of the unpopular parts (such as the individual mandate). It is not clear that this is going to work. If the insurance companies must provide coverage for people with preexisting conditions but people are not required to buy insurance, then people will wait until they have some serious condition before they sign up for insurance, while healthy people will opt out. This means that rates will go up for everyone, making it even more difficult to get coverage. This appears to be happening in some markets: premiums for health insurance on the state exchanges are increasing by double digits, while more than 1 million people have said that they will drop their coverage now that they are no longer required to have it.[65] Although Republicans agree on repealing Obamacare, no single Republican alternative has universal support within the party. Most Republicans have argued for market-based reforms that would introduce more competition into the system to help keep costs down and for health savings accounts that would be tax deductible. But the basic problem of how to maintain coverage for the 26 million people who currently have insurance under Obamacare has not been resolved.

Income support and welfare

When most people think of social policy aimed at helping the poor, they think of welfare. The earlier section on the history of social policy outlined the evolution of welfare from a limited policy aimed at helping dependent children of single mothers to a broader policy directed more generally to households headed by one person. Welfare is usually thought of as cash support for people who cannot support themselves. However, **income support** can take many forms, including food stamps, unemployment insurance, the Earned Income Tax Credit (EITC), and Supplemental Security Income (SSI). We will discuss each and then describe the major reform of welfare in 1996.

The Supplemental Nutrition Assistance Program (SNAP) provides food stamps, which are government-issued coupons that may be used as cash to buy groceries. Anyone who has an income that is less than 130 percent of the poverty level and

income support
Government programs that provide support to low-income Americans, such as welfare, food stamps, unemployment compensation, and the EITC.

has resources that do not exceed specific levels may qualify for food stamps. In 2018, the maximum monthly gross income to qualify for food stamps for a family of four was $2,665. As the effects of the economic crisis lingered through 2013, the number of people using food stamps peaked at a record of nearly 47.8 million in June 2013, with an average monthly benefit of $133 per person. With improvements in the economy, by mid-2018 the numbers had dropped to 39.6 million and $123 per person.[66]

The Federal-State Unemployment Compensation Program was established in 1935 as part of the Social Security Act. The U.S. Department of Labor oversees the program, but it is administered by the states. The program provides temporary and partial wage replacement for people who have been laid off from their jobs and helps stabilize the economy during recessions. States set a broad range in benefit levels, minimum amount of income earned, and hours worked during the period leading up to unemployment. (For example, you do not qualify for unemployment insurance if you have worked only five hours a week in a minimum wage job.) Also, laid-off workers have to make themselves "available for work." About 97 percent of workers are covered by unemployment insurance, but only about half of the eligible unemployed make use of the benefit. The regular state programs provide up to 26 weeks of income support, and the Federal-State Extended Benefits Program temporarily provides up to 20 additional weeks in states with relatively high unemployment rates. In the first quarter of 2018, 3.1 million Americans filed claims (12.4 million filed in the previous 12 months) and the average weekly benefit check was $360, which replaced 33.8 percent of the average worker's previous salary. Workers received benefits for an average of 15.4 weeks in early 2018.[67]

The EITC is one of the most successful programs for providing income support for the working poor. Established in 1975, the program aims to help poor people move from welfare to work: it provides tax credits to people who do not earn enough to pay income taxes and are relatively poor. It is intended to offset the burden of Social Security taxes, which all workers pay as part of payroll taxes. In 2018, you could qualify for an EITC if you had two children and earned less than $45,802, one child and earned less than $40,320, or no children and earned less than $15,270; the figures were about $5,600 higher if you were married and filing jointly.[68] The federal government provided $65 billion in EITCs in 2017 to more than 27 million recipients, with an average annual benefit of $2,445;[69] Figure 16.8 shows average yearly figures for other programs. Clearly, nobody is getting rich from this program, but it provides added assistance for the working poor.

Another source of income support for poor people is SSI, a program for aged, blind, and disabled individuals with limited income. The Social Security Administration runs the SSI program, but it is financed through general tax revenues, not Social Security taxes, and it is a means-tested program rather than a contributory program. Many states supplement the maximum monthly federal benefit of $750 for an individual and $1,125 for a couple (in 2018). More than 8.3 million people received SSI benefits in 2016, and 86 percent of those recipients were disabled or blind.[70]

Welfare is straight cash assistance for people who are not working and do not qualify for unemployment compensation. The primary welfare program for the latter half of the twentieth century was **Aid to Families with Dependent Children (AFDC)**. This program became increasingly unpopular through the 1980s, and in 1992 Bill Clinton was the first Democratic presidential nominee to campaign against welfare, promising to "end welfare as we know it."[71] Clinton got the ball rolling on welfare reform in June 1993 by appointing a task force that submitted its bipartisan plan in January 1994; the president's plan was submitted to Congress in June. When the Republicans took over Congress in 1994, the momentum for reform grew. Clinton and Congress haggled

Aid to Families with Dependent Children (AFDC)
The federal welfare program in place from 1935 until 1996, when it was replaced by TANF under President Clinton.

FIGURE
16.8

Average Yearly Benefits in Means-Tested Programs

Some types of social welfare benefits have increased in the past few decades, whereas others have decreased and some have remained the same. Identify examples from each category and try to provide a political explanation for why those benefits have increased, decreased, or been funded at about the same level.

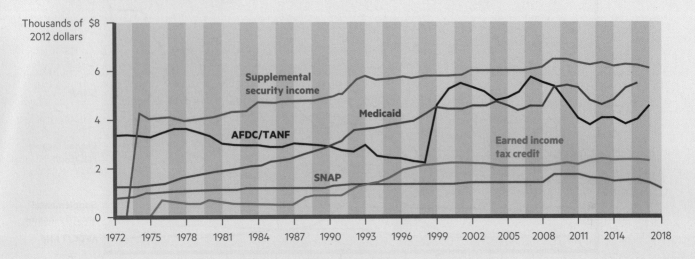

Note: Data from AFDC/TANF and the EITC cover people of all ages, including the elderly.

Source: "Growth in Means-Tested Programs and Tax Credits for Low-Income Households," Congressional Budget Office, February 2013, www.cbo.gov (accessed 6/10/16). Most recent data collected from a variety of sources.

over the issue for two years, with the president vetoing three versions of the bill that he believed were too harsh.

Finally, in 1996 they agreed on a major reform called **Temporary Assistance for Needy Families (TANF)**. The new law set a five-year lifetime limit on welfare benefits, required single mothers with children above the age of five to find work after two years of receiving benefits, required unmarried mothers who were younger than 18 years old to live with an adult and attend school to get full benefits, denied benefits to drug users who were convicted of a felony, and limited people who were not raising children and were between the ages of 18 and 50 to three months of food stamps in any three-year period in which they were not working. Perhaps most important, welfare lost its status as an entitlement and would be administered by the states with the assistance of federal block grants. In 2006, Congress reauthorized TANF and required that half of a state's caseload participate in work activities for at least 30 hours per week. Congress has not reauthorized TANF since 2010 but has extended the program through annual block grants to states. Welfare reform significantly reduced the number of people on welfare, as Figure 16.9 shows, but it has been criticized for being too hard on the people who need government assistance the most. When the policy was enacted in 1996, two-thirds of all families in poverty received TANF assistance; in 2016 the fraction was less than one-quarter (23 percent). Critics also point out that TANF block grants have not been adjusted for inflation in most states since they were first created and were worth 25 percent less in 2018 than in 1996.[72]

Temporary Assistance for Needy Families (TANF)
The welfare program that replaced AFDC in 1996, eliminating the entitlement status of welfare, shifting implementation of the policy to the states, and introducing several new restrictions on receiving aid. These changes led to a significant decrease in the number of welfare recipients.

FIGURE 16.9

Participation in Means-Tested Programs

The social-policy "safety net" is supposed to protect poor Americans during periods of economic recession. A deep recession happened in the early 1980s, and the other recession during the time frame depicted here was in the early 1990s. To what extent did the safety net accomplish the goal for which it was intended?

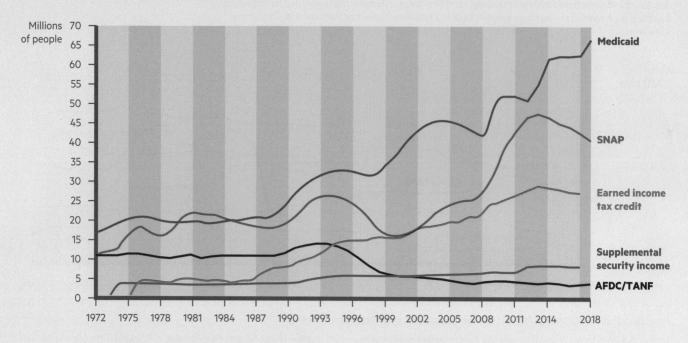

Sources: Data for 1972–2013 from Congressional Research Service, based on data from the U.S. Department of Health and Human Services; and from Congressional Budget Office, "Changes in Participation in Means-Tested Programs," February 2013, www.cbo.gov (both accessed 11/15/16). Most recent data were collected by the author from various sources.

Education

Education policy is largely the domain of state and local governments. For the first century of our nation's history, the national government played virtually no role in education. One important exception was the Morrill Act in 1862, also known as the Land Grant College Act. This law gave land to eligible states to establish colleges that would promote education in the practical professions such as agriculture and mechanical arts. More than 75 colleges and universities today are land grant institutions.

The next major forays by the federal government into education policy came with the GI Bill of Rights in 1944, which provided access to higher education for returning World War II veterans, and the Elementary and Secondary Education Act of 1965, which was part of President Johnson's War on Poverty. The Department of Education was created in 1980, signaling the national government's interest in playing an important role in education policy by:

- establishing and monitoring policies on federal financial aid for education,
- collecting data on America's schools and disseminating research,
- focusing national attention on key educational issues, and
- prohibiting discrimination and ensuring equal access to education.[73]

A more recent debate concerning the national government's role in education policy has focused on standards-based education reform: Should the national government establish standards and impose accountability as a way to improve public schools? The No Child Left Behind Act of 2001 required yearly statewide standardized testing in math and reading. If the test results showed that a school was not meeting annual academic benchmarks, it was labeled a "failing school," which meant that it lost some federal funding and its students could transfer to another public school. Critics argue that standardized test results are a poor measurement of progress because top-down standards incentivize schools to "teach to the test" and manipulate other aspects of the evaluation system. Responding to these concerns that one size does *not* fit all, Congress enacted the Every Student Succeeds Act in 2015. The new law maintains annual testing but gives states more control over setting student performance targets and school ratings.

The latest example of a nationwide, state-based effort to shape education is the Common Core standards that were developed by the National Governors Association in response to concerns that American schools were falling behind. This relatively modest set of standards in math and English was quickly adopted by 46 states between 2010 and 2015 but became a lightning rod for concern about national control of education. Conservative radio host Glenn Beck said that the standards "are breeding an entire new generation of slaves"; then–Louisiana governor Bobby Jindal compared the standards to central planning in the Soviet Union; and Florida state representative Charles Van Zant said the Common Core's goal is to "attract every one of your children to become as homosexual as they possibly can."[74] So far, the backlash has led six states to rescind their adoption of the Common Core standards, and repeal efforts are under way in at least 28 more states.[75]

President Obama's Race to the Top grant program used a "carrot" rather than a "stick" approach to educational innovation, dedicating $4.35 billion to competitive grants from 2010 to 2013 to encourage schools to adopt more challenging standards and better tools of assessment, promote better leadership and methods for assessing and rewarding excellent teaching, create better data systems for tracking students' progress, and obtain stronger commitments for improving the worst-performing schools. These grants were aimed at strengthening the quality of public education while also improving accountability.[76] The emphasis on accountability was criticized

TAKE A STAND

School Vouchers

One of the most controversial areas of education policy over the past 20 years has been school vouchers—the practice of providing taxpayers' money directly to families to allow them to send their children to private schools rather than public schools. The vouchers are similar to a scholarship and are used in 13 states, including Wisconsin, which implemented the first voucher program in 1999 in Milwaukee, and Indiana, which implemented the first statewide program in 2011.[a]

Vouchers establish needed competition between public and private schools. Supporters of the program say that it introduces competition into public education, which suffers from the inefficiencies that are typical of monopolies. They argue that many urban school systems have failed to educate their children and that poor minority students deserve a better education than the one they get in public schools. They say that students who are given the opportunity to leave public schools often improve their academic performance in private schools. Secretary of Education Betsy DeVos recently pushed a proposal that would provide private school vouchers for military families instead of the "impact aid" for public schools that the federal government has always provided for public schools by military bases.

Supporters of school vouchers are an unusual alliance between free market conservatives, who are typically Republicans, and inner-city minorities, who normally are strong Democrats. The former believe that school systems can benefit from introducing competitive market forces, and the latter are desperate for anything that will rescue their children from failing public schools. These supporters of vouchers are opposed by teachers' unions, most Democratic politicians, and those who favor strengthening the public schools by investing more money in them and trying new approaches, such as public magnet schools, charter schools, and public school choice.

Vouchers undermine an already challenged public school system. Opponents say that private schools engage in "cherry picking," choosing the more motivated students and leaving the more difficult to educate in the public school classrooms, contributing to a downward spiral in these institutions. Opponents also argue that standardized test scores do not improve for students who participate in voucher programs. Finally, they claim that voucher programs are an unconstitutional violation of the separation between church and state because an overwhelming proportion of the students in these programs attend Catholic parochial schools.

Most school vouchers go to private Catholic schools, like the one shown here.

Evidence on voucher opponents' first two points is mixed, but the bulk of the evidence supports their views. The most studied voucher program is the Milwaukee program mentioned earlier. In the most systematic analysis of that program, John F. Witte, political scientist and expert on education policy, argues that vouchers should be evaluated on a basic question of values, the clash between freedom of choice and equality of opportunity, rather than specific programmatic outcomes, because the effects are small to nonexistent.[b]

The Supreme Court has upheld voucher programs while asserting that they did not violate the separation of church and state. However, in a case upholding Cleveland's voucher program the Court did not give vouchers a green light beyond the narrow facts of the case. Indeed, that 5–4 decision required a voucher program to, among other things,

- be a part of a much wider program of multiple educational options, such as magnet schools and after-school tutorial assistance;
- offer parents a real choice between religious and nonreligious education, perhaps even providing incentives for nonreligious education; and
- not only address private schools but also ensure that benefits go to schools regardless of whether they are public or private, religious or not.[c]

Meanwhile, the state supreme courts in Arizona and Colorado struck down school voucher programs as a violation of the separation of church and state, but a similar program was upheld in Alabama.

take a stand

1. What do you see as the advantages and disadvantages of providing vouchers to allow students to attend any school they want?

2. Should these programs be expanded, or would they undermine the quality of public schools?

by both the left and the right. The largest teachers' union, the National Education Association, called for Education Secretary Arne Duncan's resignation (he left the administration in early 2016). Many Republicans thought that Duncan was interfering too much in state education policy. There was more bipartisan support behind Obama's effort to expand programs to improve access to higher education, such as increasing the number of Pell Grant recipients to 9.3 million and, in 2016, launching a new online "college scorecard" to provide objective information about college costs and quality.

States and local school districts are also experimenting with various policies aimed at introducing more competition for public schools, including public school choice (allowing students to choose which public school they attend) and publicly funded vouchers for attending private schools. These approaches are strongly favored by the secretary of education, Betsy DeVos (see the Take a Stand feature). Private foundations have also gotten involved in education policy. The Gates Foundation has contributed more than $2.8 billion to create smaller schools, reduce class sizes, provide scholarships for higher education (most significantly, $1.5 billion to the United Negro College Fund), improve the use of data, and provide access to technology.[77]

"Why Should I Care?"

Social Security and Medicare may seem like things you don't have to worry about for at least 40 years. However, 7.65 percent of every dollar you earn goes to pay for these programs. Also, given changes that will almost certainly be made to these programs in the next few years, it is important to understand what is at stake. Education policy is more obviously important for your life. While state and local politics are more central for shaping education policy, federal programs support both higher education and K–12 schools.

Unpacking the Conflict

The varying successes and failures of efforts to reform Social Security and health care reveal a great deal about the role of key players in the policy-making process. The interaction between the president and Congress is central to both stories. With Social Security reform, the president initiated a serious reform agenda, but Congress killed the proposal by failing to act. With health care reform, Congress and the president worked together to pass significant legislation, but now under different party leadership, Congress is working to undo that legislation. In both instances, interest groups played a key role. Doctors, other health care providers, insurance companies, and drug companies largely supported health care reform, which helped Congress pass the historic but controversial legislation. With Social Security reform, opposition from AARP and a tepid response from the public doomed the idea of private savings accounts, at least for now. But the last chapter on reform is yet to be written. Sooner or later, policy makers will have to confront the massive long-term deficits in these programs. Is this how social policy works? A contentious battle and a frustrating outcome for most, if not all, involved?

The experiences with social-policy reform also illustrate the themes of this book. First, health care reform is a perfect example of the conflictual nature of politics. From initial debates over health coverage for illegal immigrants and abortion to repeated efforts to repeal the ACA in the House, health care reform ignited many contentious debates. Substantive disagreements about the scope of coverage and how to pay for it also revealed deep fault lines across and within the parties. Despite this conflict, congressional leaders pieced together compromises that created an imperfect but historic law. However, conflict over social policy is far from resolved as Republicans in Congress work to change Obamacare. The reform of Social Security and Medicare provides fertile ground for intergenerational struggle and class conflict. Clearly, resolving the long-term problems facing social policy in the United States will involve many intense debates.

Social policy, especially the recent legislative struggles over health care reform, demonstrates that political process matters. The filibuster in the Senate played an important role in the first stages of shaping health care reform, and the decision to use the reconciliation process late in the game ensured passage of the law. House Republicans' decision to shut down the government in an effort to repeal the law ended up backfiring, but it is yet another example of how the political process can be used in ways that have substantive impacts: the shutdown cost billions of dollars and slowed economic growth. Politicians' decisions have a key impact on policy outcomes, and the timing and politics of the policy-making process clearly drive the results. Had congressional leaders made different decisions, it is possible that health care reform would have failed. Finally, politics is everywhere. Social policies touch all Americans at some point in their lives, and the struggles over reforming these policies are at the core of contemporary American politics.

What's Your Take?

Has Obamacare been "essentially repealed"? Are Social Security and Medicare going bankrupt?

Should these social programs be strengthened or repealed?

STUDY GUIDE

The roots and goals of social policy

Explain what we mean by social policy and how the national government's role in social policy has evolved. (Pages 575–578)

Summary

"Social policy" is the catchall term for government programs that are designed to achieve a general social goal. While the early federal government took little responsibility for social welfare, the federal government has gradually expanded its role since the late nineteenth century. Today it plays a significant part in ensuring the welfare of its people.

Key terms

social policy (p. 575)   Great Society (p. 577)
welfare (p. 575)   ownership society (p. 578)
New Deal (p. 576)

Practice Quiz Questions

1. **The first significant example of broad federal involvement in social policy is _____.**
a   the New Deal
b   aid to Civil War veterans
c   the Great Society
d   aid to Mexican-American War veterans
e   unemployment compensation in the 1890s

2. **Social Security was established under the _____; Medicare was established under the _____.**
a   New Deal; Great Society
b   New Deal; New Deal
c   Great Society; Great Society
d   Great Society; New Deal
e   New Deal; Opportunity Society

3. **The principle of the "ownership society" is that _____.**
a   the government has responsibility for the people's social welfare
b   the government has responsibility for the poor's social welfare
c   the government has responsibility for health care but not education
d   the rich have responsibility for the poor's social welfare
e   people have responsibility for their own welfare

Poverty and income inequality

Examine the problem of poverty as a target of social policies. (Pages 579–582)

Summary

Most social programs have an impact on poverty, either directly or indirectly. There is a growing gap between the top income levels and the incomes at the bottom. Government policies tend to disproportionately favor the wealthy, largely based on the type of social policies the government chooses to implement.

Practice Quiz Questions

4. **The primary motivator for social policy is _____.**
a   intergenerational equality
b   poverty
c   the deficit
d   care for the elderly
e   gender inequality

5. **Under Democratic presidents, the incomes of working poor families _____ than/as under Republican presidents.**
a   increased faster
b   increased slower
c   stayed the same
d   decreased slower
e   decreased faster

The key players in social policy making

Describe the roles played by each branch of the national government and by the states in making and implementing social policy. (Pages 583–586)

Summary

At the federal level, social policy is shaped by Congress, the president, and the bureaucracy. Other groups play a role in social policy as well: policy concerning the elderly is particularly affected by interest groups, whereas state governments focus on policy concerning welfare and education.

Practice Quiz Questions

6. Bureaucratic discretion _____ agency-to-agency consistency of policy provision; it _____ the ability to administer policies efficiently.

a   increases; increases

b   increases; decreases

c   decreases; increases

d   decreases; decreases

e   decreases; has no effect on

7. States influence policies on _____, but not _____.

a   Social Security; education

b   Social Security; Medicaid

c   education; Medicaid

d   Medicaid; education

e   Medicaid; Social Security

The policy-making process

Trace the steps through which problems are addressed by social policies. (Pages 586–591)

Summary

Once an issue is recognized and defined as a problem and when the conditions are right, the issue reaches the congressional agenda. Once a policy is in place, its effectiveness and implementation are evaluated in an ongoing process, though very few programs are ultimately terminated.

Key term
policy agenda (p. 586)

Practice Quiz Questions

8. What is the policy agenda?

a   the set of desired policies that political leaders view as priorities

b   the set of issues that political leaders view as priorities

c   the set of issues that issue groups view as priorities

d   the set of desired policies that issue groups view as priorities

e   the set of desired policies that issue groups and political leaders view as priorities

9. Relative to the private sector, public-sector programs are _____ to evaluate.

a   easier

b   equally easy

c   harder

d   equally as hard

e   not important

Social policy today

Analyze the current major areas of social policy. (Pages 591–609)

Summary

The aging population and rising health care costs threaten the future of Social Security and Medicare, which currently make up half the federal budget. Despite the importance of reforming these programs, politicians are reluctant to enact serious policy changes for fear of jeopardizing their own political futures.

Key terms
Social Security (p. 591)
baby-boom generation (p. 593)
privatization (p. 596)
Medicare (p. 599)
Medicaid (p. 599)
entitlement (p. 599)
income support (p. 603)

Aid to Families with Dependent Children (AFDC) (p. 604)
Temporary Assistance for Needy Families (TANF) (p. 605)

Practice Quiz Questions

10. Which group of working Americans is eligible to receive Social Security benefits?

a   those whose income is in the bottom 15 percent

b   those whose income is in the bottom 25 percent

c   those whose income is in the bottom 50 percent

d   income is not a criterion for eligibility

e   only the unemployed are eligible

11. The primary reason Social Security will be financially strained in the coming years is that _____.

a   it is a pay-as-you-go program

b   its stipends are indexed to inflation

c   it is transitioning to privately held accounts

d   compensation to nonworking spouses is equal to benefits for the working spouses

e   most Americans don't approve of Social Security

12. State governments _____ have influence on Medicaid; they _____ have influence on Medicare.

a   do; do

b   do; do not

c   do not; do

d   do not; sometimes

e   do not; do not

13. **In President Obama's health care plan, why was it essential to guarantee comprehensive coverage?**

a   to make sure enough people were paying into the system

b   to pool risk between sick and healthy people

c   to reduce the risks of fraud

d   to prevent individuals from having only one price to pay

e   to win broad political support

14. **The major welfare reform of 1996 instituted the _____ program, which _____ welfare spending relative to its predecessor.**

a   Aid for Families with Dependent Children (AFDC); reduced

b   AFDC; increased

c   Temporary Assistance to Needy Families (TANF); reduced

d   TANF; increased

e   Medicaid; reduced

15. **The long-term fiscal problems of _____ are most severe.**

a   Social Security

b   Medicare/Medicaid

c   welfare

d   federally subsidized student loans

e   education

Suggested Reading

Altman, Nancy J. *The Battle for Social Security: From FDR's Vision to Bush's Gamble*. New York: Wiley, 2005.

Bartels, Larry M. *Unequal Democracy: The Political Economy of the New Gilded Age*, 2nd ed. Princeton, NJ: Princeton University Press, 2016.

Jacobs, Lawrence R., and Theda Skocpol. *Health Care Reform and American Politics: What Everyone Needs to Know*, 3rd ed. New York: Oxford University Press, 2016.

King, Ronald F. *Budgeting Entitlements: The Politics of Food Stamps*. Washington, DC: Georgetown University Press, 2000.

Lindert, Peter H., and Jeffrey G. Williamson. *Unequal Gains: American Growth and Inequality since 1700*. Princeton, NJ: Princeton University Press, 2016.

Oberlander, Jonathan. *The Political Life of Medicare*. Chicago: University of Chicago Press, 2003.

Piketty, Thomas. *The Economics of Inequality*. Cambridge, MA: Belknap Press, 2015.

Skocpol, Theda. *Social Policy in the United States: Future Possibilities in Historical Perspective*. Princeton, NJ: Princeton University Press, 1995.

Soss, Joe. *Unwanted Claims: The Politics of Participation in the U.S. Welfare System*. Ann Arbor: University of Michigan Press, 2000.

Weaver, R. Kent. *Ending Welfare as We Know It*. Washington, DC: Brookings Institution Press, 2000.

17

Foreign Policy

What is America's role in the world?

 "American foreign policy must be more than the management of crisis. It must have a great and guiding goal: to turn this time of American influence into generations of democratic peace."
George W. Bush

 "Upon my inauguration, I announced that the United States would return to a simple principle: The first duty of our government is to serve its citizens, many of whom have been forgotten. But they are not forgotten any more. With every decision and every action, we are now putting America first."
Donald Trump

From the first day of the campaign, Donald Trump argued he was a dealmaker, someone who would use insight, brinksmanship, and grit to transform America's relations with the world. He claimed that other countries were taking advantage of America, tapping its open markets while keeping American firms shut out of their own. More than that, Trump argued that this problem could be fixed quickly and easily with a combination of tough talk and an unwillingness to accept the status quo.

In his first two years in office, Trump combined strong rhetoric with concrete policy change. He moved to impose punitive tariffs on America's major trading partners, ordered the renegotiation of long-standing trade agreements, and made it clear that America expects to get more from these agreements than it has in the past. However, other nations did not respond as Trump predicted. Rather, they imposed additional tariffs on American goods and stood firm against Trump's demands for renegotiation, raising the possibility of a global trade war that could reduce economic growth across the entire world.

The case of Donald Trump's attempt to reshape the global economy illustrates the importance of foreign policy in American politics, as well as some common misconceptions about how foreign policy gets made. Take the state of America's economy. As discussed in Chapter 15, over the last generation American politicians have approved a series of treaties that reduced tariffs on imports and exports, generating enormous profits for some American companies. However, trade liberalization has hurt companies that could not respond to increased foreign

Tough talk, including threats of an international trade war, characterized the Trump administration's foreign policy strategy in the first year of his presidency. For example, during the June 2018 G7 summit, President Trump's confrontational attitude toward American allies garnered praise from his supporters, but left fellow world leaders on edge.

competition. Many of their workers have been laid off or have taken incentives to quit their jobs or retire early rather than face an uncertain future of layoffs and wage cuts. At the same time, Americans enjoy cheaper prices for many products that can now be sold in U.S. markets.

Many Americans expect foreign policy to be an area of consensus—believing that as Americans we hold similar ideas of what our country should be doing outside our borders. As a result, many Americans agree with Senator Arthur Vandenberg, who is often credited for the saying "Politics stops at the water's edge." Americans tend to see disagreement over foreign policy as somehow unpatriotic. But as the trade example suggests, foreign policy choices create winners and losers, just as in the domestic arena. Lowering trade barriers made some Americans better off and some worse off. The same is true for Donald Trump's trade policies, and this would be the case even if they worked as advertised.

Foreign policy is political even in the case of national security. Should America intervene in the Syrian civil war, and if so, should its goal be to replace the government, prevent attacks on civilians, or eliminate the terrorist organization ISIL (Islamic State of Iraq and the Levant) that occupied some Syrian territory? Are diplomacy and economic sanctions the right response to North Korea's nuclear weapons program, or is a military attack warranted? And after two decades of combat operations against the Taliban in Afghanistan, is it time for America to withdraw its forces and leave the Afghan population on its own? These examples illustrate that we should expect disagreement over America's foreign policy, including between the political parties, inside the executive branch, and even between civilians and military personnel. Although these debates often have political consequences, with positions sometimes taken for political gain, in the main they reflect sincere differences of opinion. In this way, foreign policy closely resembles domestic policy.

The reality of disagreement about foreign policy options raises the question of how these differences are resolved. Are President Trump's unilateral moves to reshape America's trade policy an exception or the rule? What is the role of Congress, the Courts, and the bureaucracy in the making of foreign policy? Where does public opinion enter into this process? Who gets to decide America's foreign policy? How is foreign policy made?

DESCRIBE THE MAJOR APPROACHES TO UNDERSTANDING FOREIGN POLICY, AND TRACE HOW AMERICA'S ROLE IN THE WORLD HAS EVOLVED

foreign policy
Government actions that affect countries, corporations, groups, or individuals outside America's borders.

What is foreign policy?

"**Foreign policy**" refers to government actions that affect countries, corporations, groups, and individuals that lie outside America's borders. Foreign policy includes military operations, economic interactions, human rights policies, environmental agreements, foreign aid, helping build or sustain democratic systems, interventions in civil wars and other conflicts, and international efforts to limit weapons of mass destruction (WMDs), including nuclear weapons.

Foreign policy principles and perspectives

Foreign policy actions are often rooted in general principles or rules that guide people or nations in their decision making. These principles and rules capture the decision to act, whether America acts alone or with other nations, and the motivations for actions. (See Nuts & Bolts 17.1 for a summary of these guiding principles.)

Theories of Foreign Policy

Realism	Foreign policy is driven by a state's national interest, as defined by its leaders.
Liberalism	Foreign policy reflects the ideals held by a state's leaders, such as protection of human rights.
Internationalism	States should, whenever possible, pursue their foreign policy goals by working together with other nations.
Isolationism	States should, whenever possible, work alone to define and implement their foreign policy, working with other nations only when absolutely necessary.
Constructivism	Foreign policy is determined not by objective factors such as national interest, by ideologies such as liberalism, or by admonitions about working alone or with other nations, but by how a state's leaders define these factors.

Should We Act Alone? There are three important distinctions in foreign policy. The first is between unilateral action and multilateral action. **Unilateral action** occurs when one country does something on its own, without coordinating with other countries. For example, some U.S. antiterrorism operations under recent presidents have been undertaken without any consultation with or notice to U.S. allies, such as the 2017 attack on an Al Qaeda group in Yemen, which was carried out by U.S. forces without any notice to U.S. allies or the Yemeni government. Similarly, some of President Trump's actions during preparations for his June 2018 summit meeting with North Korean leader Kim Jong Un, such as the snap decision in May to cancel the summit entirely (a decision Trump later reversed), were made without first talking with U.S. allies.

American foreign policy more commonly involves **multilateral action** by the United States alongside other countries or international organizations such as the UN. For example, in 2018, after the Syrian government used chemical weapons against civilians, the United States, Great Britain, and France launched a coordinated missile attack to destroy several Syrian chemical weapons manufacture and storage facilities. Along the same lines, the Quartet on the Middle East, a group comprising the United States, Russia, the European Union (EU), and the UN, is working to facilitate peace negotiations between Israel and the Palestinians.

Should We Intervene? A second important distinction in foreign policy is between **isolationism** and **internationalism**. Isolationists believe that the United States should avoid making alliances and agreements with other nations, concentrate on defending America's borders, and let the people in other countries work out their problems for themselves. In the case of the humanitarian crisis in Syria, an isolationist might argue that U.S. intervention would be futile or potentially counterproductive, too costly, or simply inappropriate—that it is not America's problem to solve.[1]

An internationalist, however, would argue that the United States should establish many agreements with other nations and intervene in international crises whenever it may be able to help, both because of possible economic and security gains and because intervening in civil wars and helping solve humanitarian crises is morally right. In the case of ISIL, internationalists would at a minimum support U.S. efforts to help and protect the local population, either in concert with other nations or alone if other nations were unwilling to intervene.[2]

unilateral action (national)
Independent acts of foreign policy undertaken by a nation without the assistance or coordination of other nations.

multilateral action
Foreign policy carried out by a nation in coordination with other nations or international organizations.

isolationism
The idea that a country should refrain from involvement in international affairs.

internationalism
The idea that a country should be involved in the affairs of other nations, out of both self-interest and moral obligation.

realism
The idea that a country's foreign policy decisions are motivated by self-interest and the goal of gaining more power.

liberalism
The idea that foreign policy decisions reflect normative goals such as justice, equality, and human rights.

nation building
The use of a country's resources, including the military, to help nondemocratic nations transform themselves into democracies.

constructivism
The idea that foreign policy is shaped by how a state's leaders define the national interest, ideology, and other factors.

When the United States acts multilaterally in foreign policy, it often works through organizations such as the UN. Here, Donald Trump addresses a session of the UN General Assembly, where he made promises to prioritize American interests in foreign affairs.

Are We Only Out for Ourselves? The third major distinction in foreign policy making is between **realism** and **liberalism**.[3] Realists believe that countries pursue their own interests, seeking to increase their economic and military power and their international influence. In approaching a policy decision, a realist would choose the policy that maximizes American military and economic power relative to other states. Liberals (note: this label means something different than the liberal ideology in domestic politics), in contrast, believe that states' concerns extend beyond increasing their power and should include upholding principles such as freedom or democracy. For example, liberals generally believe in helping nondemocratic nations transform themselves into democracies with strong court systems (also called **nation building**). **Constructivism** offers an alternative to both positions, arguing that state actions are shaped by how leaders interpret events for their citizens and by the overarching ideals that these leaders believe in. For example, a constructivist might argue that America's policies toward North Korea are driven by the underlying belief that North Korea is a rogue state, one that is unwilling to comply with international agreements—and that unless America changes its beliefs, it will be unable to negotiate a denuclearization agreement with North Korea, regardless of what North Korea's leaders want or are willing to agree to.

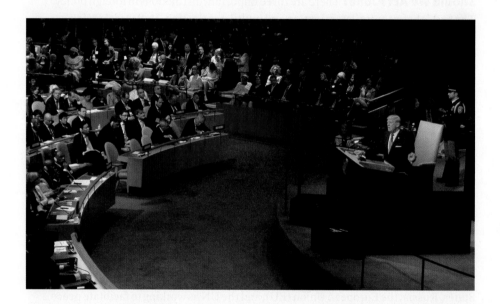

To illustrate the differences between these explanations, consider the cases made by each side regarding intervention in Syria. Realist scholar John Mearsheimer has argued that there was no need to intervene.[4] In his view, America has no compelling interest in the outcome of the civil war in Syria. Moreover, intervention would be costly, would put American lives at risk, and could produce a wider conflict involving America's allies in the Middle East. This position is close to that of President Trump, who has argued that America's interest in the Syrian conflict should be limited to destroying the ISIL terrorist organization that is an active participant in the conflict. In contrast, the idea that America is morally obligated to help Syrian rebels fight against their brutal government—a position held by some Democrats and some Republicans in Congress—is a clear example of liberalism.

These terms are used often in foreign policy debates because they offer convenient ways to summarize the motivations behind policy decisions. That is how we use them in this chapter, but in reality, none of these terms provides a fully accurate definition of what motivates nations or individuals. As the quote from President Barack Obama illustrates, no one is a realist or a liberal all the time. For example, Obama's support for intervention in the Libyan civil war was squarely liberal in its motivation—done with the hope that dissident elements in Libya could unite to build a stable democracy. Conversely, Obama's reluctance to send ground troops to Syria is a classic example of realism: while the situation was a human rights catastrophe, it put no fundamental American interests at stake.

History of American foreign policy

American foreign policy has evolved throughout the country's history. Tracing the course of America's relations with other nations since the Founding allows us to illustrate the types of choices U.S. politicians have faced, how these policy options have changed over time, and the fact that politicians have always disagreed about how to resolve foreign policy issues.

The Founding to World War I Until America's entry into World War I in 1917, American foreign policy was largely isolationist. Most presidents and other elected officials behaved in accordance with George Washington's assertion that the United States should "avoid entangling alliances" with other nations.[5] Isolationism made sense during this period for several reasons. America's distance from Europe reduced the potential for international economic interactions, lowered the level of military

threat, and gave early America room to expand without conflicting with European nations.[6] The **Monroe Doctrine**, established by President James Monroe in 1823, stated that America would remain neutral in wars involving European nations and that the United States expected these nations to stop trying to colonize or occupy areas in North and South America.[7]

America's foreign policy was never completely isolationist, however, even in the early years. The American navy was deployed on many occasions to protect U.S. ships and citizens, and America had several colonies far beyond its borders. Even in the early years, the United States expanded by purchasing land from other countries or from

You take victories where you can. You make things a little bit better rather than a little bit worse. And that's in no way a concession to this idea that America is withdrawing or there's not much we can do. It's just a realistic assessment of how the world works.

—President Barack Obama

Internationalists argue that America is the only nation with the will and the resources needed to address humanitarian crises throughout the world, such as by providing food aid to people in Syrian refugee camps.

Monroe Doctrine
The American policy initiated under President James Monroe in 1823, stating that the United States would remain neutral in conflicts between European nations and that these nations should stop colonizing or occupying areas of North and South America.

Native Americans—adding much of the Midwest through the Louisiana Purchase—and by annexing land after military conflicts, such as the large section of the Southwest acquired from Mexico following the Mexican-American War. Later, America built the Panama Canal, leasing land from Panama in the process, and sent troops into conflicts in Nicaragua and other Central American countries. America also maintained significant trading relationships with nations in Europe and elsewhere.

Still, America's involvement in World War I (1914-1918) marked a sharp departure in foreign policy, both in terms of the country's participation in an international alliance and the president's willingness to continue alliance membership after the conflict.[8] With the war almost over, President Woodrow Wilson offered a peace plan, the Fourteen Points, which proposed reshaping the borders of European countries to mitigate future conflict, creating measures to encourage free trade and democracy, and establishing an international organization that would prevent wars.[9] American diplomats participated in the negotiations that culminated in the Treaty of Versailles, which officially ended the war.[10] The treaty created the League of Nations, an organization similar to the modern UN, but the U.S. Senate rejected the treaty, which meant that the United States never joined the League of Nations.[11]

The Rise of Internationalism World War II (1939-1945) marked a great transition in American foreign policy. The United States became directly involved in the conflict on December 8, 1941, declaring war on Japan the day after the country carried out air attacks on Pearl Harbor in Hawaii and American bases in the Philippines. Germany subsequently declared war on the United States on December 11. However, even before the United States officially became involved, the U.S. military had been supplying Great Britain and its allies with arms, ships, and other supplies in return for payments and long-term leases on British military bases throughout the world—actions that only narrowly escaped a congressional vote to reverse. During the war, the Allied Powers—the United States, Great Britain, the Soviet Union, and other countries—fought as a formal alliance, making joint plans and sharing military hardware and intelligence.

After World War II, American politicians and scholars felt that the United States should be a central actor in world affairs. This new policy was justified by realist arguments, such as the need to deter future conflicts and the desire for economic benefits from trading with other nations.[12] Liberals argued for the same policies on the grounds that America had a moral obligation to preserve world peace.[13] However, this shift toward internationalism only increased the amount of conflict in American foreign policy, as actors disagreed on where the United States should get involved; what its goals should be; whether intervention should involve military force, foreign aid, diplomacy, or some other policy tool; and whether the country should act alone or in concert with other nations.

Cold War
The period of tension and arms competition between the United States and the Soviet Union that lasted from 1945 until 1991.

containment
An important feature of American Cold War policy in which the United States used diplomatic, economic, and military strategies in an effort to prevent the Soviet Union from expanding its influence.

The Cold War Soon after World War II ended, the **Cold War** (1945-1991) began, as the victorious Allies disagreed—with the United States and Great Britain on one side and the Soviet Union on the other—over the reconstruction of Germany and the reformation of Eastern European countries that Germany had occupied during the war. In a 1946 speech, former British prime minister Winston Churchill referred to an "iron curtain" that had split Eastern and Western Europe, leaving the East under Soviet domination with few political freedoms.[14] American diplomat George F. Kennan argued that America should use diplomatic, economic, and military means to prevent the Soviet Union from expanding the set of countries that it controlled or was allied with—a strategy that he deemed "**containment**."[15] This idea served as a guiding principle for American foreign policy over the next generation.[16]

During this period the United States implemented several measures to build and strengthen alliances against the Soviet threat. The first was the Marshall Plan, a series of aid and development programs enacted in the late 1940s to restore the economies of Western European countries devastated during World War II.[17] The United States was also instrumental in the formation of the World Bank and the International Monetary Fund (IMF), as well as international trade agreements such as the General Agreement on Tariffs and Trade (we will discuss these institutions in more detail later in this chapter).

The Marshall Plan, which helped European nations rebuild their economies after World War II, was part of America's strategy to build alliances against the Soviet Union.

The United States also formed alliances with other countries, including the North Atlantic Treaty Organization (NATO) in 1949. The goal of these organizations was the maintenance of collective security, based on the principle that "an attack against one is an attack against all."[18] The aim was to deter Soviet attacks throughout the world by formalizing America's commitment to defend its allies. The Soviets formed their own alliances, most notably the Warsaw Pact, with nations in Eastern Europe.[19]

The United States was also behind the 1945 creation of the UN, an international organization with the aim of preventing wars by facilitating negotiations between combatants and, if necessary, sending military forces from member states to stop conflicts. The UN has also been instrumental in administering relief efforts for refugees, running development efforts, codifying international law, and publicizing and condemning human rights violations.

Clearly, the goal of containment influenced every aspect of American foreign policy after World War II.[20] The Korean War, in which American troops defended South Korea against invasion by North Korea, was motivated largely by containment—North Korea's efforts had the strong support of the Soviet Union and China.[21] America also supported brutal dictators in other countries, such as the Shah of Iran during the 1970s, and overlooked these governments' dismal human rights records on the grounds that their leaders would be valuable allies against the Soviets.[22]

mutually assured destruction
The idea that two nations that possess large stores of nuclear weapons—like the United States and the Soviet Union during the Cold War—would both be annihilated in any nuclear exchange, thus making it unlikely that either country would launch a first attack.

domino theory
An idea held by American foreign policy makers during the Cold War that the creation of one Soviet-backed communist nation would lead to the spread of communism in that nation's region.

détente
An approach to foreign policy in which cultural exchanges and negotiations are used to reduce tensions between rival nations, such as between the United States and the Soviet Union during the 1970s.

America also maintained large military forces, beginning its first peacetime draft in the 1950s and building a large store of nuclear weapons. These weapons were intended to deter war with the Soviet Union through the threat of **mutually assured destruction**: the idea that even if the Soviet Union unleashed an all-out nuclear assault on U.S. forces, enough American weapons would remain intact to deliver a similarly devastating counterattack. The United States stationed hundreds of thousands of troops in Western Europe and elsewhere to deter the Soviet threat. War nearly broke out during the Cuban missile crisis, when the Soviets tried to site nuclear missiles in Cuba—within striking range of the United States. However, the issue was defused once the Soviets withdrew in the face of an American naval blockade of Cuba and a secret American promise to withdraw similar missiles from Turkey in return.

In the early 1960s America became involved in the conflict in Vietnam, believing that North Vietnam's drive to take over South Vietnam was part of the Soviet Union's plan for world domination.[23] The **domino theory** held by many Americans at the time posited that if the United States did not prevent the fall of South Vietnam, the next step would be a Soviet-backed conflict in the Philippines, in Australia, or in the territory of some other American ally. The Vietnam War demonstrated that the domino theory was fundamentally inaccurate; the conflict between North and South Vietnam was a civil war rather than an international event.[24] Though the North Vietnamese accepted Soviet support, they did not take orders from the Soviets.

Beginning in the early 1970s, President Richard Nixon and his National Security Advisor, Henry Kissinger, began a process of **détente** with the Soviet Union, which involved a series of negotiations and cultural exchanges designed to reduce tensions and promote cooperation.[25] These efforts culminated in the 1972 Strategic Arms Limitation Treaty (SALT I), which limited the growth of U.S. and Soviet missile forces.[26]

At the same time, the Arab nations' embargo prohibiting oil shipments to Western countries after the 1973 Arab-Israeli war served as a reminder that containment of the Soviet Union could not be America's only foreign policy priority. Tensions over oil increased again when the Organization of the Petroleum Exporting Countries (OPEC) raised prices in 1979. Both events contributed to a recession in America and the electoral defeats of two incumbent presidents: Gerald Ford in 1976 and Jimmy Carter in 1980. Carter's defeat was also, in part, the result of the Iran hostage crisis, in which Iranian students, with government backing, held American embassy staff hostage for more than 14 months.[27]

Tensions with the Soviets increased again with their support for the Sandinista rebellion in Nicaragua in the late 1970s and then with their invasion of Afghanistan in 1980.[28] In response to Soviet military actions in Afghanistan, President Carter withdrew the U.S. Olympic team from the 1980 games in Moscow, suspended sales of wheat to the Soviets, and increased defense spending. These increases steepened under Ronald Reagan, who vowed to put communism "on the ash heap of history." Notwithstanding this rhetoric, Reagan also worked to negotiate arms control agreements with the Soviet Union.[29]

The real change in U.S.–Soviet relations began with the selection of Mikhail Gorbachev as leader of the Soviet Union in 1985 and his policies of glasnost ("openness") and perestroika ("restructuring"). The Warsaw Pact was dissolved in 1991, and most of its former members became democracies. The Soviet Union splintered into 15 countries in 1991, effectively ending the Cold War. Scholars still debate the reasons for these changes. Some argue that the costs of responding to America's military buildup bankrupted the Soviet state, while others point to disaffection of Soviet citizens with the communist ideology and the inability of the Soviet economy to provide goods and services.[30]

In 1989, the fall of the Berlin Wall, which separated West Berlin from communist East Berlin, provided a powerful symbol of the end of the Cold War. With just one superpower—the United States—left, many predicted that democracy would spread and peace would prevail. However, new foreign policy challenges quickly emerged.

Since the end of the Cold War, the United States and Russia have continued to disagree over many policies, including the enlargement of NATO to include most former Warsaw Pact countries, the deployment of American anti-ballistic missile systems in Eastern Europe, the U.S. invasion of Iraq in 2003, the Russian invasion of Georgia in 2008, Russia's annexation of Crimea in 2013, Russia's intervention on the side of the Syrian government starting in 2015, and Russia's efforts to influence citizen opinions and votes in the 2016 U.S. presidential election. While tensions have increased in recent years as a result of all these conflicts, it is important to remember that only 20 years ago both countries had enough weapons aimed at each other to destroy the entire world. Today, however, there is little chance of direct conflict between the United States and Russia.

After the Cold War: Human Rights, Trade, and Terrorism The end of the Cold War, along with the growing number of democracies worldwide and the development of democratic peace theories (which argue that democracies will not fight other democracies), suggested to some observers that military conflicts would become much rarer and other concerns would emerge to influence America's foreign policy.[31] Events early in the post–Cold War era seemed to support this thesis. Human rights became a more important foreign policy topic.[32] The United States became involved in humanitarian relief and nation-building efforts in Somalia, Bosnia, and Kosovo. A series of agreements, including the North American Free Trade Agreement (NAFTA) in 1994 and the formation of the World Trade Organization (WTO) in 1995, lowered tariffs throughout the world. Technological advances in transportation also lowered the cost of shipping goods worldwide, and the industrialization of many third world countries made them low-cost suppliers of manufactured goods to the United States, causing many domestic factories to close. These developments exemplify the concept of "soft power:" that is, America's exertion of influence over other nations through increased economic interactions and cultural ties rather than the use of military force.[33]

However, it is important to understand that there is considerable disagreement about the usefulness of soft power. Some Republicans, including President Donald Trump, argue that military force remains the dominant factor in shaping international relations, meaning that America must remain the dominant military power in order to maintain its security and strong economy. The resolution of this ongoing debate shapes America's military spending and deployments of armed forces, its decisions about participation in international trade agreements and climate control agreements, its decisions about intervention in internal conflicts such as the Syrian civil war and the Israeli–Palestinian conflict, and many other areas.

The Al Qaeda terrorist organization headed by Osama bin Laden was the driving force behind many terrorist attacks on Americans, including the 2001 attacks on the World Trade Center and the Pentagon. In 2011, American forces killed bin Laden, but the group, along with newer organizations such as ISIL, remains a significant threat.

Bush Doctrine
The foreign policy of President George W. Bush, under which the United States would use military force preemptively against threats to its national security.

However, new security threats emerged in the form of terrorist groups, most notably Al Qaeda, led by Osama bin Laden, who organized the September 11, 2001 attacks on the World Trade Center in New York and the Pentagon in Washington, D.C. Some analysts and politicians, including President George W. Bush, described these attacks as part of a worldwide "clash of civilizations" or a global War on Terror, pitting the secular West against radical Islam.[34] After the attacks, President George W. Bush announced a new U.S. policy, the **Bush Doctrine**, or the doctrine of preemption, whereby the United States would not wait until after an attack to respond but would use military force to eliminate potential threats before they could be put in motion. This policy change was intended to prevent another September 11 attack, as the quote from Bush's National Security Advisor and secretary of state Condoleezza Rice illustrates.

President Obama emphasized improving foreign perceptions of America and Americans, ending the ground war in Iraq, and avoiding unilateral action in favor of multilateral coalitions. However, many of Obama's policies in regard to the War on Terror, such as his emphasis on drone attacks (see the Take a Stand feature in this chapter) and America's limited involvement in the Syrian civil war, were quite similar to those established by the Bush administration.

TAKE A STAND

Should America Carry Out Drone Attacks against Terrorists?

One of the elements of America's strategy to fight terrorist groups is the increased use of drones—small, pilotless aircraft that fly into foreign airspace, monitor the activities of terror suspects on the ground, and launch missiles against these targets. Over the last decade, drone attacks in countries such as Afghanistan, Yemen, and Pakistan have decimated the leadership and infrastructure of terrorist groups and inflicted significant casualties on lower-level fighters. Drones also played a key role in identifying the safe house in Pakistan where Al Qaeda leader Osama bin Laden was located, making possible the attack that resulted in bin Laden's death in 2011. Drone surveillance and attacks have played a key role in the Syrian conflict. However, the use of drones by American forces continues to be highly controversial inside the United States and throughout the world.

Drones are an effective tool. Drone attacks allow the United States to combat terrorists throughout the world without putting American troops at risk. Drone attacks are also less expensive than conventional forces. For example, rather than sending a special operations unit across the world to attack a target in the Middle East, American crews working at a base in Nevada can remotely control drones launched from a secure base in Saudi Arabia. Because drones have no crew, they can be small and quiet and stay in the air for long periods of time, making a surprise attack more feasible. Even if an attack is not being planned, drones allow the United States to monitor suspected terrorists and deter future operations.

Describing drones as a tool also highlights their similarity to other examples of military force. How different is it if a terrorist camp is attacked by a drone rather than U.S. ground troops? Any argument against drones (the danger of civilian casualties or that terrorists can publicize the attack as a way of galvanizing public opposition to the U.S. strategy) can be applied just as well to other ways the United States might attack terrorists.

Drones bring risks and negatively affect decision making. Some people foresee that the very advantages ascribed to drones—that they are relatively inexpensive and require no human pilots—could likely lead decision makers to use drones more quickly than they might use conventional weapons. In a similar vein, there are those who believe that drones remove the personal element from warfare, making it easier to disregard the moral implications of an attack.

Moreover, at least up to now, drone strikes have occurred with little congressional oversight or approval. As we discussed in Chapter 12, Congress has the power to limit military operations—but doing so in the case of drones would be difficult because most of these operations are carried out in secret. How could members stop an operation they didn't know about until after it occurred?

While mistakes are possible in any military operation, drone attacks involve special risks. Because drone operators view their targets through long-range cameras mounted on the drones, the chances of civilian casualties or other collateral damage are probably higher than with Special Forces units who carry out their attacks at short range.

The problem for decision makers is this: prohibiting drone attacks on suspected terrorists does not mean that these individuals and organizations will go scot-free; most of these operations will instead be carried out by American armed forces, with the risk that some of these troops will be wounded, killed, or taken hostage. Should decision makers use drones or send in the troops?

The use of drones is controversial. Here, a protester in Yemen holds a sign denouncing the practice.

take a stand

1. If you were writing a letter to your member of Congress about the use of drones, what position would you take? What arguments would you use to support your position?

2. If you favor the use of drones, are there situations in which we shouldn't use them? If you oppose them, are there situations in which drones have advantages over traditional troops?

On one level, Donald Trump's foreign policy, with its emphasis on "putting America first," is a sharp departure from that of his predecessors, particularly the imposition of trade tariffs on other countries and the withdrawal from trade agreements with other nations, threats to use military force against countries such as North Korea, efforts to reduce admissions of refugees to the United States, and the emphasis on enhanced border security (including a proposal to build a wall between the United States and Mexico). On another level, while all these changes are significant, major portions of America's foreign policy remain unchanged. For example, while Trump's rhetoric has emphasized attacking ISIL forces in Syria rather than helping rebel forces fighting the Syrian government, it appears that America and its allies have continued to give military aid and technical support to rebel forces.

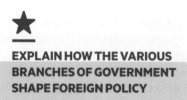

Maybe you don't care about foreign policy—although as we discuss throughout this chapter, you probably should. In the modern era, no nation can separate itself from the rest of the world. The same is true for individual citizens, even you. Your job, cost of living, and even your personal safety are affected by America's foreign policy. Making sense of foreign policy (or deciding where you stand on foreign policy questions) requires you to know some history and some basic terminology. History helps you understand America's place in the world and how different issues came about. Knowing the basic terminology used in foreign affairs helps you understand what politicians and pundits are talking about when they discuss foreign policy issues.

★

EXPLAIN HOW THE VARIOUS BRANCHES OF GOVERNMENT SHAPE FOREIGN POLICY

Foreign policy makers

Who shapes the United States' relations with other nations, and what is the source of their influence? We begin with the president and the executive branch, then consider Congress, the courts, and, finally, other groups and individuals outside the government. Nuts & Bolts 17.2 summarizes the foreign policy powers of the two most important actors: the president and Congress.

NUTS & BOLTS 17.2

Foreign Policy Powers of the President and Congress

President	Congress
Commander in chief of armed forces	Can declare war
Nominates and appoints senior officials in Department of Defense	Senate must approve Defense nominees
Negotiates treaties and executive agreements with other nations	Treaties take effect only if approved by Senate
Changes policy with executive orders and findings	Can overturn orders and findings with legislation
Attempts to mobilize public opinion behind foreign policy goals	Makes policy using "power of the purse" (annual budget)

Our discussion focuses on people and organizations in government whose primary job is foreign policy making, but virtually all executive branch departments and agencies have some responsibility for issues with international reach. For example, the Department of Education administers programs that fund undergraduate, graduate, and scholarly study of the politics, history, and culture of other nations, as well as educational exchanges with universities abroad (in fact, both authors of this text are former Fulbright Scholars). Similarly, the Department of Agriculture oversees programs that encourage food exports to other nations and that protect Americans against unsafe imports.

The president and the executive branch

The president is the dominant actor in American foreign policy.[35] The president can negotiate treaties or executive agreements with other nations, change policy through executive orders or findings, mobilize public opinion to prompt action by Congress, and shape foreign policy by appointing people to agencies and departments that administer these policies (see Chapter 12). The president also serves as commander in chief of America's armed forces.

While the president comes first in our discussion of how foreign policy gets made, presidents do not act on their own. Staff throughout the executive branch play key roles in defining as well as implementing policy options, and representing the United States throughout the world. Moreover, as we discuss here and in Chapter 12, presidential power is limited by the Constitution, by statutes, and by the ability of members of Congress and the courts to set policy or reverse presidential elections. For example, President Trump's executive orders in 2017 to ban travel to the United States from six Muslim-majority nations were reversed or limited by lower federal courts, then ultimately upheld by the Supreme Court. Thus, a full accounting of the policy-making process requires us to go beyond the president to consider all these other actors.

Within the Executive Office of the President (EOP), the principal foreign policy agency is the **National Security Council (NSC)**, which develops foreign policy options and presents them to the president. The EOP also includes the Office of the United States Trade Representative, which focuses on tariffs and trade disputes; the president's Foreign Intelligence Advisory Board, a group of academics, politicians, and former government officials who advise the president; and the Office of Management and Budget, which prepares the president's annual budget proposals for federal agencies and departments, including those with foreign policy responsibilities.

The Department of State The principal foreign policy department in the executive branch is the Department of State. Its head, the secretary of state, acts as the official spokesperson for the United States in foreign relations and is an important adviser to the president. State Department officials operate U.S. embassies abroad and interact extensively with the leaders of other countries; they also offer expertise to elected officials on the politics, economics, and cultures of other nations. Aside from senior staff such as the secretary of state, who is nominated by the president and confirmed by the Senate, State Department personnel are generally career civil servants who remain in their positions even after a new president takes office. There are many different offices and working groups in the State Department, from people who deal with treaties to coordinators of international aid, arms control, or assistance for refugees.

National Security Council (NSC)
An agency within the EOP that advises the president on matters of foreign policy.

Secretary of State Mike Pompeo is the official spokesperson for the United States in foreign relations and is often one of the most powerful and influential members of the president's Cabinet. Pompeo replaced the Trump administration's first secretary of state, Rex Tillerson, who was fired by the president in early 2018.

civilian control
The idea that military leaders do not formulate military policy but rather implement directives from civilian leaders.

The Department of Defense The Department of Defense carries out military actions as ordered by civilian authorities, ranging from large military operations such as those in Afghanistan to smaller operations such as the ongoing drone attacks against Al Qaeda and ISIL forces throughout the Middle East or the deployment of troops, ships, and aircraft for training, humanitarian relief, and other purposes.

The military's role in foreign policy is not limited to uses of force. Military personnel also deliver humanitarian aid or help American citizens evacuate from areas of conflict. For example, U.S. ships and helicopters delivered medical supplies and evacuated patients from hospitals in Puerto Rico after Hurricane Maria in 2017. The American military advises and trains armed forces in other countries, including hot spots such as Syria, Somalia, and Yemen. And military personnel may also play a role in foreign policy making, with senior military officials serving as consultants during policy debates and midlevel officers serving in the NSC and on the staff of some congressional committees. For example, General H. R. McMasters served as one of Donald Trump's National Security Advisors, and former general James Mattis is the secretary of defense.

The overriding principle of America's military is the concept of **civilian control**—the idea that military personnel do not formulate policy but rather implement directives from their civilian leaders in the executive branch (the president and senior leaders in the Defense Department) and Congress. Of course, just as in other areas of the executive branch, members of the military are experts who will often know more than their civilian leaders about the feasibility of goals and the best ways to achieve them.

What should a president do when military leaders disagree with his or her policy goals? Their disagreement may reflect fundamental problems with the president's plans or simply indicate that military leaders would prefer a different policy. As we discussed in Chapter 13, these dilemmas are inevitable in all areas of the bureaucracy, including the military, given the reality of bureaucratic expertise. Most of the time, such disagreements are resolved through dialogue. Other times, the president and other civilian leaders may consult additional sources to either confirm the military's advice or negate it. In general, the norm is that military leaders are free to express their disagreement as long as they do so in private and are willing to carry out the orders they are ultimately given without hesitation.

The Department of Homeland Security The Department of Homeland Security was formed after the September 11 attacks by combining the Coast Guard, the Transportation Security Administration, the Border Patrol, and several other agencies. The department's responsibilities are to secure America's borders, prevent future terrorist attacks, and coordinate intelligence gathering. On the one hand, Homeland Security's record is exemplary: there has not been a major terrorist attack on American soil since September 11, 2001. On the other hand, there is concern that many Homeland Security policies (such as requiring extensive screening for all airline passengers) impose large societal costs while having a marginal impact on safety.[36]

Intelligence Agencies Agencies such as the Central Intelligence Agency (CIA) and National Security Agency (NSA) are primarily responsible for government intelligence gathering. Most of their work consists of collecting information from public or semipublic sources, such as data on industrial outputs. However, these agencies also undertake covert operations to acquire intelligence, use satellites and other technology to monitor communications, or even attack individuals, other nations, or organizations. The Director of National Intelligence in the EOP leads and coordinates the activities of the various intelligence agencies.

How Much Foreign Policy Power Does the President Have? Some people argue that the broad powers of the modern presidency have allowed for "imperial presidents" who can implement their preferred foreign policies without the consent of Congress, the American people, or anyone else.[37] These complaints reflect a simple truth: presidents dominate the making of American foreign policy. Thus, in 2017, when President Trump ordered military strikes in Syria in response to that government's use of chemical weapons against civilians, he did not need congressional approval prior to launching the strike. Similarly, congressional consent was not required when Trump withdrew the United States from the Paris Climate Accord—although if the accord had been initially voted on as a treaty, a two-thirds vote in the Senate would have been required for Trump's decision to take effect.

The explanation for presidents' dominance of foreign policy lies in the ability of presidents to act unilaterally (see Chapter 12).[38] Although the Constitution grants the president only several specific foreign policy powers, it does not set explicit limits on what the chief executive can and cannot do. This ambiguity has given presidents considerable latitude to make foreign policy as they see fit. Members of Congress who disagree with the president must build veto-proof, two-thirds majorities in the House and Senate to overturn presidential foreign policy actions. For example, while some Democrats in Congress criticized Trump's decision to withdraw from the Paris Accord, they could not build the two-thirds majority needed to prevent it.

President Obama's trip to Vietnam in 2016 illustrates that one type of important foreign policy decision involves deciding which countries the president should visit and whom they should shake hands with while there.

Nonetheless, presidents sometimes pull back from a new foreign policy if they believe congressional support will not be forthcoming. For example, President Trump initially decided in 2017 to withdraw U.S. military advisers from Syria, where they were aiding rebel forces, only to reverse the decision after criticism from senior advisers and members of Congress. Similarly, no president has ever submitted the 1996 Nuclear Test Ban Treaty for Senate ratification, although all presidents since Bill Clinton have implemented a voluntary moratorium on tests. And congressional opposition was one argument against sending ground forces to fight ISIL.

Clearly, the president dominates foreign policy—but Congress can reverse or thwart presidential initiatives. Thus, in most cases in which presidents appear to have acted without constraints, the reality is that members of Congress actually approved of the president's action, were unaware of the action, or were unwilling or unable to organize to overturn the president's policy.

Congress

Congress holds three types of influence over foreign policy. The first is the power of the purse. Since members of Congress write annual budgets for every government department and agency, one way for members to shape foreign policy is to forbid expenditures on activities that members want to prevent.

Second, the Senate has the power to approve treaties and confirm the appointments of senior members of the president's foreign policy team, including the secretaries of state and defense, the Director of National Intelligence, and America's ambassador to the UN. Although it is rare for senators to reject a treaty or nominee, sometimes they issue preemptive warnings about what kinds of treaties they will accept (in response, presidents often avoid asking for a vote on treaties they know will be rejected).

Third, the Constitution grants Congress the power to declare war on other nations. However, the Constitution does not say that this declaration must occur before hostilities can begin or whether the declaration is necessary at all. In fact, although the United States has been involved in hundreds of military conflicts since the Founding, there have been only five U.S. declarations of war: the War of 1812, the Mexican-American War (declared in 1846), the Spanish-American War (in 1898), and both world wars (declared in 1917 and 1941, respectively). In an attempt to codify war-making powers, in 1973 Congress adopted the War Powers Resolution. This legislation was designed to limit the president's war-making powers and to give members of Congress a way to reverse a president's decision to deploy American forces. Although the resolution has been in effect for over 30 years, the question of which branch of the government controls America's armed forces remains controversial. (See the How It Works graphic for more details.)

Several groups within Congress participate in making foreign policy. The Committee on Foreign Affairs in the House and the Foreign Relations Committee in the Senate are responsible for writing legislation that deals with foreign policy, including setting the annual budget for agencies that carry out those policies. These committees also hold hearings in which they pose questions to foreign policy experts from inside and outside government. While hearings do not necessarily lead to changes in policy, they can educate members of Congress on foreign policy matters, draw media and public attention to issues important to the committee, and force presidential nominees to make commitments about how they will perform in office. For example, during confirmation hearings in 2018, CIA Director Gina Haspel agreed that CIA operatives would conform to limitations on the use of torture when interrogating suspects.

The House and Senate each have an Intelligence Committee that oversees covert operations and the actions of the CIA, the NSA, and similar agencies. Under current law, the president is supposed to give Congress "timely notification" of covert intelligence operations (although there is some dispute over what "timely" means).[39] These arrangements help to ensure that someone outside the executive branch knows about secret operations and can organize congressional opposition if these actions are deemed illegal, immoral, or unwise.

Of course, members of Congress always have the power to block a president's foreign policy initiatives, but doing so requires enacting a law with enough votes to override a presidential veto, which is often an impossible task. In the debate over funding for the Iraq War, in 2007 the House and Senate passed a funding resolution that included a withdrawal time line for U.S. troops, but it was approved by a margin of only a few votes in each chamber. After President Bush vetoed the resolution, the two houses passed a new funding resolution without these restrictions. In more recent cases, such as during the debate over U.S. participation in the NATO operations in Libya or interventions in Syria, resolutions were offered to cut off funding but did not pass either house of Congress.

The federal courts

The federal courts, including the Supreme Court, weigh in on foreign policy questions through judicial review, determining whether laws, regulations, and presidential actions are consistent with the Constitution. For example, during the War on Terror, a series of lower-court and Supreme Court decisions forced the Bush administration to revise its policy of holding terror suspects indefinitely without charges; the rulings required that the suspects be charged with crimes and tried on those charges. Although this example shows how the courts can reverse presidential actions, two points are key. First, the decisions were not a complete defeat for President Bush. While his policy was overturned, the courts acknowledged that similar policies would be constitutional. Second, court proceedings require time: adjudicating the terror suspect cases required several years, during which the administration's policy remained in place and the defendants were imprisoned without trial or any way to contest their imprisonment.[40]

Groups outside the federal government

A variety of individuals, groups, and forces outside government influence foreign policy. These include interest groups, the media, and public opinion, as well as intergovernmental, nongovernmental, and international organizations.

Interest Groups Interest groups are organizations that work to convince elected officials and bureaucrats to implement policy changes in line with the group's goals. Diverse groups and organizations lobby government over foreign policy.[41] For example, during the congressional debate in the summer of 2015 over the agreement with Iran regarding its nuclear weapons program and President Trump's subsequent decision to withdraw from the deal, the American-Israel Public Affairs Committee (AIPAC), one of the most powerful interest groups in Washington, was a key member of the opposition. A coalition of smaller groups (including J Street, another pro-Israel lobbying organization that often opposes AIPAC, as well as groups of scientists and the left-leaning organization Move On) lobbied in favor of approval.

U.S. politicians and government officials regularly speak at AIPAC events. Vice President Mike Pence is shown here addressing AIPAC's annual convention. However, it would be a mistake to conclude that the attention paid to this or other interest groups automatically translates into U.S. government support for the groups' policy proposals.

War Powers: Who Controls the Armed Forces?

The President

Has the power to deploy troops as commander in chief

Under the War Powers Resolution, has to notify Congress, and the use of force must be terminated within 60 days if Congress does not approve. However, Congress has never voted to terminate military action, and most presidents have argued that the act is unconstitutional.

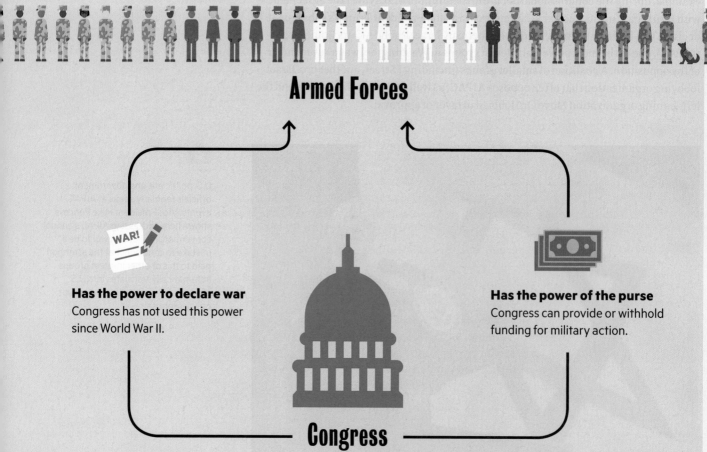

Armed Forces

Has the power to declare war
Congress has not used this power since World War II.

Has the power of the purse
Congress can provide or withhold funding for military action.

Congress

WAR!

America's Role in Syria's Civil War

America's ongoing intervention in the Syrian civil war illustrates how the constitutional allocation of war powers plays out in practice. Although presidents Obama and Trump had the authority to order U.S. forces into combat, their actions were taken after consultation with other nations and debate within the United Nations, and were subject to congressional review and limitations.

Civil war!

March 2011: A civil war begins between the Syrian government and opposition forces.

Taking sides.

Soon after the conflict begins, the United States and its allies **send assistance to opposition** forces, while Russia helps the Syrian government.

Uh oh...

January 2012: ISIL forces move from Iraq to Syria, **capturing territory** from both government and opposition forces.

It gets worse.

2012–14: Reports surface of **Syrian government attacks on civilians** (some using chemical weapons). Civilians fleeing the conflict flood into refugee camps in neighboring countries.

Nope.

September 2013: Attempts by Senate Democrats to authorize intervention in the Syrian civil war are **defeated.**

International agreement.

September 2013: Under pressure from the international community and the United Nations, the Syrian government **agrees to destroy** all of its chemical weapons.

Giving the go-ahead.

September 2014: President Obama requests that Congress appropriate funds to aid Syrian rebels and **orders airstrikes against ISIL forces.** Congress approves both actions, and airstrikes soon begin.

Change, or the same?

Incoming president Trump promises a **more aggressive** U.S. policy in Syria.

Missile attacks.

In April 2017, U.S. cruise missiles are used to **destroy a Syrian air force base** that was used to launch chemical weapons attacks against opposition forces.

❓ Critical Thinking

1. **As you see in this example,** though the president is commander in chief, military action generally follows an extended process of consultation and negotiation with members of Congress and representatives from other nations. What are the benefits and costs of this deliberative process?

2. **At the beginning of this chapter,** we noted that some Americans believe that "politics stops at the water's edge." Does the United States' intervention in the Syrian civil war support or disprove this statement?

Lobbying efforts can even involve foreign governments. In these cases, lobbying efforts center on economic and military aid, trade deals, and more general efforts to improve a country's image among members of Congress and the bureaucracy. In the case of the Iran deal, Israel's ambassador to the United States called many members of Congress to persuade them to oppose the deal when it was negotiated and, later, to support President Trump's withdrawal.

Sometimes interest group lobbying pits business interests against other concerns such as national security. For example, during both the Obama and Trump presidencies, the Chinese government and two of its major telecommunications technology firms, Huawei and ZTE, have complained that the U.S. government has prevented these firms from expanding into U.S. markets. ZTE has also been heavily fined by the United States for violating sanctions against sales to firms in Iran. U.S. technology firms argue that Huawei and ZTE should be kept out of the United States because their equipment might be used for spying or cyberattacks. Although these charges might be true (the evidence is classified), it is also the case that U.S. technology firms have lost market share to Chinese firms in recent years. Raising national security concerns may just be a way to force the federal government to keep Huawei and ZTE out of the lucrative American market.

Finally, some groups focus on publicizing international events in the hope of prompting citizens to demand government action. For example, in 2016 and 2017 religious groups met with elected officials and worked to gain press coverage of the plight of refugees fleeing the civil war in Syria. At the same time, major American media outlets published photos of squalid refugee camps and refugee children who drowned after the boat they were traveling on sank in the Mediterranean.

As mentioned in Chapter 10, the impact of these lobbying efforts is hard to determine. At the same time that groups were lobbying in favor of Syrian refugees, the Obama administration was granting asylum to thousands of refugees each year. However, it is likely that the individuals making these asylum decisions (including, at the top, President Obama) were sympathetic to the refugees and would have admitted them in any case. And in fact, despite the ongoing problems in Syria and other countries, overall refugee admissions to the United States have plunged to near zero under President Trump, highlighting the limits of lobbying efforts.

The Media Television, radio, print media, and the Internet all inform the public about events in America and elsewhere. As discussed in Chapter 7, although media coverage is a prime source of information about domestic and foreign policy for most Americans, one cannot say that evaluations of America's foreign policy are driven solely by the news media's decisions about what to cover and how to report it. The press informs individuals about events and may to some extent frame the criteria people use to judge America's foreign policy and consider alternatives, but as we have seen elsewhere, most of the time, media attention to a foreign policy question or problem has a limited impact on opinions and policy choices.

Public Opinion Foreign policy decisions are also sensitive to public opinion. As with many domestic issues, elected officials are well aware of their constituents' views and are reluctant to support policies that conflict with opinions held by a majority of their constituents. On issues such as lowering tariffs with other countries, congressional voting is highly correlated with constituents' support of or opposition to these measures. However, public opinion is not a decisive influence on foreign policy. For example, in the case of Syrian refugees, American public opinion has consistently been opposed to allowing them to live in the United States. (This finding is not exceptional—in many other cases, Americans have opposed admission of refugees from political crises.[42])

One reason that foreign policy does not always mirror public opinion was discussed in Chapter 11: most politicians have political goals other than winning reelection, including affecting some aspect of American relations with other nations. For example, President Obama favored admission of Syrian refugees and ordered American forces to intervene in the Syrian civil war with air strikes, arms shipments, and military assistance, although a strong majority of the American public favored different policies (some Americans wanted a more aggressive effort, while others favored disengagement). Given the public's opposition, it is hard to square Obama's policy choices with the goal of mirroring public opinion. A better explanation is that Obama acted in accord with his own conception of what America's foreign policy should look like. This is not to say that public opinion was irrelevant to Obama's choices (as in the case of Syrian refugees, for example), but it is not the only (or even the decisive) factor shaping policy choices. The same is true for President Trump. His decision to end admissions of Syrian refugees, as well as the ongoing debate within the executive branch over assistance to Syrian rebel forces, reflects the opinions of Trump and his advisers, not a shift in public opinion.

The final reason that American public opinion is not decisive is that many Americans know little about other countries. A case in point occurred during the 2014 conflict between Russia and the West over Ukraine: a survey asked Americans to locate Ukraine on a map.[43] The results are shown in Figure 17.1. Although two-thirds of respondents said they were following the situation in Ukraine "very closely," only 16 percent of respondents were successful in locating Ukraine. Most people knew Ukraine's location only approximately, and a significant percentage were wildly wrong. More recent surveys confirm this impression—for example, a 2016 survey found that most college-educated adults incorrectly identified China as America's largest trading partner (the correct answer, Canada, was picked by only 10 percent of respondents).[44]

Americans are more likely to pay attention to foreign policy news or concerns following an important event. Thus, six months after the September 11 attacks, one poll found that Americans rated preventing future attacks a higher priority than

FIGURE 17.1

Where's Ukraine?

These data reveal a marked lack of geographic knowledge among Americans. Despite the considerable media attention given to Russia's annexation of a portion of Ukraine, in a 2014 survey only a small fraction could locate Ukraine on a map (more accurate dots are red; less accurate dots are blue). What might explain this lack of geographical knowledge?

Source: Kyle Dropp, Joshua D. Kertzer, and Thomas Zeitzoff, "The Less Americans Know about Ukraine's Location, The More They Want U.S. to Intervene," April 7, 2014, www.washingtonpost.com (accessed 8/5/14).

any particular domestic policy, even though domestic policy as a general category took priority over foreign policy. [45] However, as the attacks receded into the past, the intensity of public concern about preventing future attacks declined somewhat as well, and domestic concerns such as economic growth and unemployment became the paramount concern of most Americans, as noted in Chapter 6. The same pattern is true for more recent terrorist attacks, as well as other major international events, such as the civil war in Syria or the threat of nuclear weapons use by North Korea.

Intergovernmental Organizations, Nongovernmental Organizations, and International Organizations

America's relationship with the rest of the world is not just about government action. Members of **intergovernmental organizations (IGOs)** and **nongovernmental organizations (NGOs)** provide information and humanitarian assistance and carry out other activities that the U.S. government is unable or unwilling to undertake. IGOs are associations of sovereign states, while NGOs are private organizations. Thousands of IGOs and NGOs operate throughout the world. [46]

A primary goal of NGOs and IGOs is promoting global economic development and growth. One of the largest IGOs, the **World Bank**, funds economic development projects throughout the world. Another IGO, the **International Monetary Fund (IMF)**, helps countries manage budget deficits and control the value of their currencies. Many NGOs, such as the Asia Foundation, focus on development in a particular region or on certain activities, such as microlending, in which banks or other institutions provide small loans to citizens in developing nations as a way of stimulating business growth and reducing poverty.

A second role of NGOs is providing humanitarian relief. In the wake of a disaster such as an earthquake or a flood, or during a famine or a war, organizations such as Oxfam International supply populations in crisis with basic necessities. Other groups such as Doctors without Borders provide medical care to populations threatened by violence, epidemics, or natural disasters. These groups played a key role in the response to Ebola outbreaks in Africa. Some NGOs also promote human rights. Amnesty International spotlights international cases of people jailed for their political beliefs or held without trial and the use of cruel punishments such as stoning. Amnesty's campaigns, as well as those of other NGOs, are not always supportive of U.S. policy. In recent years, for example, Amnesty has criticized the rendition of terror suspects by the United States. [47]

Finally, NGOs help build democracies. The Open Society Foundations fund efforts to increase mass political participation, strengthen political organizations, and verify the fairness of elections in new democracies throughout the world. The National Democratic Institute and the International Republican Institute conduct similar activities—both organizations, for example, are working with groups in countries such as Burma, Ukraine, and Pakistan to increase the transparency of electoral institutions, recruit candidates, and help citizens build political organizations.

The United States is also a member of many international organizations. Best known is the **United Nations (UN)**, an assembly of ambassadors representing almost all of the world's nations that addresses issues of worldwide concern. The UN is involved in economic development, environmental protection, humanitarian relief, and peacekeeping efforts. The UN has deployed peacekeeping forces to separate warring parties in Africa, the Middle East, and the former Yugoslavia. As of fall 2018, more than 100,000 UN peacekeeping troops, police, and other personnel were deployed in 19 different areas.

intergovernmental organizations (IGOs)
Organizations that seek to coordinate policy across member nations.

nongovernmental organizations (NGOs)
Groups operated by private institutions (rather than governments) to promote growth, economic development, and other agendas throughout the world.

World Bank
A nongovernmental organization established in 1944 that provides financial support for economic development projects in developing nations.

International Monetary Fund (IMF)
A nongovernmental organization established in 1944 to help stabilize the international monetary system, improve economic growth, and aid developing nations.

United Nations (UN)
An international organization made up of representatives from nearly every nation, with a mission to promote peace and cooperation, uphold international law, and provide humanitarian aid.

Inside the UN, the Security Council, a group of 15 nations (permanent members Britain, China, France, Russia, and the United States, plus 10 rotating nations), makes the most important UN decisions, particularly those involving its military missions. The UN General Assembly, in which each nation has one vote, debates and votes on other concerns.

It may look to you like foreign policy is all about what the president wants. However, for the most part, the same kinds of people (in many cases, the same people) who influence domestic policy choices also shape America's foreign policy—including elected officials, interest groups, and the public at large. The president is a key player in making foreign policy choices, but he or she is far from being the only voice that matters.

"Why Should I Care?"

★ EXAMINE THE WAYS AMERICAN FOREIGN POLICY IS IMPLEMENTED

The tools of foreign policy

Now that we know the key players in foreign policy making, what are the tools and methods these players use to implement policy?

Diplomacy

Diplomacy has often been a limited but useful foreign policy tool. The process of diplomacy involves using personal contact and negotiations with national leaders and representatives to work out international agreements or persuade other nations to change their behavior. Sometimes these efforts involve the threat of military action or economic sanctions, or incentives such as economic assistance or other forms of aid. The United States may participate directly in such efforts or mediate between the parties in a dispute. When two countries refuse to meet face-to-face, U.S. diplomats may take part in shuttle diplomacy, in which they meet separately with each country's representatives to convey the other country's proposals and counterproposals. For example, the efforts of American and Russian diplomats were instrumental in establishing a brief cease-fire in Syria in 2016 and in getting both sides of the conflict to allow convoys carrying relief supplies to enter besieged areas of the country—although this agreement had little impact on the larger conflict.

Diplomacy has its limits. The various parties in a conflict have to be willing to make a deal and to accept American efforts to negotiate. In the case of Syria, attempts to build on the cease-fire deal were stalled by U.S.-Russia conflicts in other areas and by the Syrian government's belief that it could win the conflict on the battlefield. Moreover, diplomatic interventions require political support. In his public statements, President Trump has argued that America's goals in the Syrian conflict are limited to defeating the ISIL terrorist organization, meaning that ending the civil war is not an American goal.

The makers of foreign policy may also simply decide that diplomatic negotiations are not worth the effort. By increasing the defense budget, keeping many senior State Department positions unfilled, pushing career diplomats to retire, and withdrawing from efforts to negotiate international agreements, the Trump administration has signaled that it is less interested than its predecessors in diplomacy as a tool of foreign policy. On the other hand, Trump's willingness to hold a summit meeting with North Korean Leader Kim Jong Un is a clear exception to this trend. Time will confirm which path the administration will follow in its use of diplomacy.

Trade and economic policies

Trade and economic policies can be crucial instruments of foreign policy: they can sustain economic growth in the United States and elsewhere, as well as create foreign markets for the goods produced by America's domestic industries. Figure 17.2 shows total American trade (imports and exports) with other countries over the last 20 years, expressed as a percentage of U.S. gross domestic product (GDP), which measures the size of the U.S. economy. In recent years, imports and exports together have constituted almost 40 percent of GDP. Investment returns (profits from American-owned companies located abroad) are also becoming an ever-larger component of total trade. In dollar terms, the report cited in Figure 17.2 estimated that the total value of U.S. trade with other nations was over $5 trillion per year. Clearly, foreign trade is a critical component of the American economy.

The main tools of trade policy are tariffs and trade agreements. A **tariff** is a tax on the import or export of certain commodities, and a trade agreement sets tariff levels or limits the quantities of particular items that can be imported or exported. The United States International Trade Commission maintains a list of all tariffs in effect.[48] By adjusting tariff rates, the government can help or hurt domestic industries. High tariffs on imports help American producers charge lower prices than foreign competitors, and low tariffs on exports help American producers sell to overseas markets.

Over the last two generations, the United States and most other nations have been lowering tariffs and establishing free-trade zones, agreements to eliminate tariffs on all imports and exports among specific nations. Examples include a long-standing free trade agreement with Canada and Mexico, and the Central American Free Trade Agreement (CAFTA) among the United States, five Central American nations, and the Dominican Republic. Other organizations, such as the **World Trade Organization (WTO)**, facilitate negotiations over tariffs and provide a mechanism for adjudicating cases when one nation believes that another is using tariffs unfairly. Finally, the United

tariff
A tax levied on imported or exported goods.

World Trade Organization (WTO)
An international organization created in 1995 to oversee trade agreements between nations by facilitating negotiations and handling disputes.

FIGURE 17.2

U.S. Imports and Exports as a Percentage of GDP

This figure illustrates the importance of trade to the U.S. economy. In recent years imports and exports have accounted for almost 40 percent of U.S. economic activity, and the percentage is increasing over time. Based on these data, what arguments would you make for lowering or increasing barriers to trade?

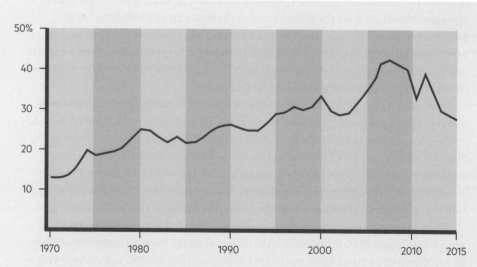

Source: Office of the United States Trade Representative, *2018 Trade Policy Agenda and 2017 Annual Report,* www.ustr.gov (accessed 6/20/18).

Diplomacy often involves protracted negotiations and many participants. The Singapore Summit between North Korea and the United States, which yielded a promise for peaceful relations and denuclearization of the Korean Peninsula, required months of preparation and the cooperation of the Singapore government.

States has granted many other countries **most-favored-nation status**: tariffs on imports to the United States from these nations are set at the lowest rate placed on any other nation.

Donald Trump has overturned many of these policies, claiming that many of these trade deals did not serve U.S. interests. Over the last two years, he has sought to renegotiate trade agreements and has used existing laws to impose punitive tariffs on various countries, including China and members of the European Union, arguing that these countries use regulations and other mechanisms to prevent American companies from selling products to their corporations and citizens. These nations have responded with additional tariffs on American exports. These actions may well lead to reduced economic growth in America and throughout the world, although their effects are not yet clear. While some Republican and Democratic elected officials have protested Trump's actions, there have been no organized attempts in Congress to reverse them.

What is the argument for reversing the move toward free trade? Trade deals are inherently controversial because they almost always involve winners and losers. Even if a deal increases overall economic growth in the United States, some people will be made worse off. For example, if a deal makes it possible for an entrepreneur in a developing nation to sell a product in the United States at a lower price than domestic suppliers of the same product are charging, Americans who buy the imported goods are better off (they pay less for the same product). However, the people who work for the U.S. suppliers are in trouble (their employers may go out of business if they cannot find another market for their products). One reason for Donald Trump's victory in 2016 was high support from rural communities (particularly in the Midwest Rust Belt) that have lost manufacturing jobs because companies responded to lower tariffs by moving factories overseas and because companies face competition from foreign suppliers.

Trade is an important part of foreign policy. The United States has used free-trade agreements and tariffs to bargain with countries for concessions in noneconomic policy areas or to cement international alliances. For example, one of the incentives Trump offered to North Korea as part of a denuclearization deal was to reduce economic sanctions on the country, allowing increased trade and investment. Similarly, one of the reasons why America has played a central role in crafting trade agreements with Asian nations was that the government wanted to strengthen America's political and economic

most-favored-nation status
A standing awarded to countries with which a nation has good trade relations, providing the lowest possible tariff rate. WTO members must give one another this preferred status.

One of the most conflictual issues of the Trump administration's foreign policy strategy is tariffs. Touted initially as a defense of the United States' national security, President Trump's steel tariff had unintended consequences, including the increase of steel prices domestically and the escalation of a trade war abroad.

economic sanctions
Penalties applied by one country or group of countries on another, usually in the form of tariffs or other trade barriers.

ties with these nations, as a counter to the increased regional economic and military power of China. Withdrawing from these agreements, as Trump has decided to do, means that these foreign policy issues will need to be addressed using other means.

Economic policies are also used to threaten or sanction countries as a way of inducing them to change their behavior. Working with the United States and other nations, the UN Security Council authorized **economic sanctions** against Iran aimed at forcing the nation to stop enriching uranium, a first step in the production of nuclear weapons.[49] These sanctions banned arms sales to the country and made it all but impossible for Iranian citizens and corporations to do business outside their nation's borders. The damage caused by sanctions was one important reason why Iran agreed to negotiate a deal with the United States and the European Union, resulting in the 2016 deal in which Iran agreed to curb its nuclear research programs and Western nations agreed to remove economic sanctions. This outcome also explains why President Trump's decision to withdraw from the deal is unlikely to change Iranian behavior: none of the sanctions formerly imposed by EU nations have been reinstated.

Foreign aid

Foreign aid is money, products, or services given to other countries or the citizens of these countries. Sometimes aid reflects the desire to provide basic assistance to satisfy fundamental human needs. For example, American military ships and aircraft are often used to deliver food and medical supplies to the victims of earthquakes and other natural disasters. Foreign aid also serves to stimulate economic growth in other nations. For instance, funding from the United States helps build factories; pays for technical advisers who provide locals training on the construction and operation of water, power, or sewage treatment plants; and buys hardware to support infrastructure such as Internet access or telephone networks. Foreign aid also facilitates international agreements. For example, the peace treaty between Egypt and Israel in 1979 was facilitated by America's agreement to provide substantial military and economic assistance to both countries.[50] Promises of continued American aid to Israel have also been one factor in discouraging Israel from attacking Iranian nuclear facilities in the last several years.

Figure 17.3 shows the level of American nonmilitary foreign aid in 2017 measured as a percentage of gross national income (GNI, which includes GDP as well as accounting

Long after the end of the Cold War, relations between the United States and Russia remain tense. When Russia invaded Crimea in 2014, the United States and NATO allies sent troops to signal support for the Ukrainian government.

FIGURE 17.3

U.S. Foreign Aid in Comparative Perspective

This figure shows foreign aid contributions expressed both in total volume and as a percentage of gross national income (GNI). Do these data imply that America is less generous with aid than other nations are? What other explanations are there for the differences across countries?

Note: Bars represent aid in volume and dots represent aid as percent GNI. Data from 2017.

Source: Organization for Economic Cooperation and Development, "Development Cooperation Report 2018," www.oecd.org (accessed 6/16/18).

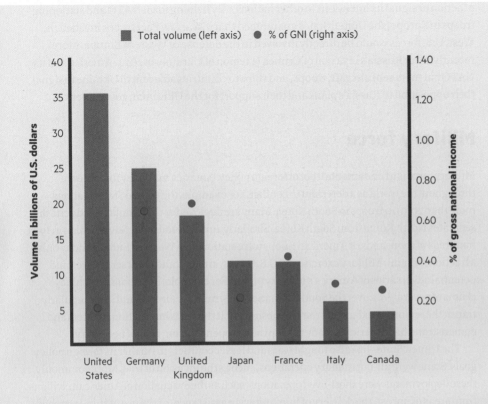

Total volume (left axis) ● % of GNI (right axis)

United States | Germany | United Kingdom | Japan | France | Italy | Canada

for investment income from other countries) and total volume in U.S. dollars, compared with that of the six other countries that are members of the G7 group of major industrialized nations. Compared to these countries, America gives a relatively low percentage of GNI in foreign aid, although part of the explanation lies in the size of the U.S. economy: America's foreign aid contributions are the largest of any country when measured in total dollars, but it also has the largest GNI of any country.

Alliances and treaties

A treaty is an agreement between nations to work together on economic or security issues. An alliance is an agreement that commits nations to security guarantees, which are assurances that one country will help another if it is attacked. America is a member of many international alliances, most notably NATO. This alliance was formed by the North Atlantic Treaty after World War II to provide collective security against the Soviet Union and Warsaw Pact countries. The organization's mission shifted after the Cold War to focus on coordinating military force toward common goals, with the organization's 2011 intervention in the Libyan civil war the first instance of operations outside Europe. Historically, the United States has paid a disproportionate share of the cost of NATO operations and devoted a larger share of GNI to defense spending. In recent years, the United States has successfully pressured its NATO allies to increase their spending on defense. Such demands have continued under President Trump, who made doing so one of the central themes of his presidential campaign.

The United States is a party to treaties with many countries.[51] Several of these treaties implemented significant changes in both U.S. and other military forces, from capping the size of nuclear forces, to restricting the numbers of these forces, to banning some kinds of weapons. These agreements enable the United States to commit itself to a course

DID YOU KNOW?

The United States spends

<1%

of its annual budget on foreign aid. According to one poll, Americans on average think the country spends 28 percent.

Source: Kaiser Family Foundation Poll

of action or signal its intentions to other nations.[52] By helping form NATO and stationing troops in Europe, the United States guaranteed that if Warsaw Pact troops invaded the West, U.S. forces would be directly involved in the defense of Western Europe. More recently, after Russia's invasion of Crimea (a region of Ukraine) in 2014, America and its NATO partners sent aircraft, troops, and ships to countries adjacent to Ukraine to signal their opposition to Russia's plans and their support for the Ukrainian government.

Military force

Military force is a fundamental tool of foreign policy. America's military forces serve throughout the world as a deterrent to conflict. For example, the United States stations more than 20,000 troops in South Korea. Many are deployed at the demilitarized zone that separates North Korea from South Korea. Similarly, until the fall of the Soviet Union in 1991 hundreds of thousands of American troops were stationed in Western Europe (today only a fraction remain). Military exercises by U.S. troops, aircraft, and ships serve to remind potential adversaries of America's military power. For example, in response to Chinese claims of sovereignty over the South China Sea, U.S. military aircraft and ships regularly transit the region to underscore the U.S. position that the sea is international waters and demonstrate that America is ready to keep the sea open by using force if necessary.

The United States has also fought wars and lesser conflicts to further its foreign policy goals. Some were all-out military operations, such as the invasion of Iraq. More commonly, these deployments were short-lived operations, such as the evacuation of American civilians from areas of unrest, the delivery of humanitarian assistance, or the use of ship-launched cruise missiles to attack terrorist camps and similar targets.[53] In the case of fighting ISIL, America has sent military advisers and training personnel to several nations, carried out numerous attacks by Special Forces and drones, and, in the case of Syria and Iraq, conducted many air strikes against ISIL forces and infrastructure as well as Syrian ground forces.

The size and power of America's military provide numerous options for policy makers. For example, after the September 11 attacks, in an attempt to prevent future terror attacks by Al Qaeda, U.S. forces invaded Afghanistan, which had been used as a base of operations for the organization.[54] It is highly unlikely that any other country would have been able to carry out such a large-scale operation so far from home. America's military also provided the majority of international forces in the attacks in Libya and Syria and against ISIL.

Nonetheless, military force is not all-powerful. For example, despite nearly two decades of combat operations in Afghanistan and large amounts of economic and military aid to the Afghan government, the Taliban (a religious–political organization) still controls a significant percentage of the Afghan countryside and the Afghan government's ability to defeat the Taliban without American help is highly questionable. Similarly, while air strikes in Iraq and Syria have significantly reduced ISIL's military might, the organization remains able to plan future terror attacks throughout the world. Moreover, it is not clear whether any level of military force can remove this threat.

"Why Should I Care?"

It's easy to think that America can get what it wants from other nations by making threats involving military force—after all, America's military is the largest in the world by far. However, foreign policy isn't that simple. There are many other ways for America to achieve its foreign policy goals, from diplomacy to economic sanctions or even aid programs. The reason why these strategies are used is that they work—and often work better than force would.

The politics of foreign policy today

The making of foreign policy, like everything else in the federal government, is a political act—a contest involving elected officials, bureaucrats, interest groups, and other actors, all of whom have their own goals. In this sense, there are always conflicts over what America's foreign policy should look like and compromise is fundamental to the making of it. This section describes three of the major foreign policy issues facing America in the contemporary era: trade, terrorism, and nuclear proliferation—and how all these issues raise human rights concerns. These issues demonstrate the complexity of America's foreign policy choices and how these decisions are shaped both by conflicts and by political processes.

In addition, this section argues against claims about the decline of American influence throughout the world. Although it is true that other countries such as China and India are increasing their economic and military power and that the United States faces many new and complex issues, it still continues to be an international power and in many respects is the strongest nation on the globe, with enormous influence over economic, social, and military events worldwide. How the issues described in this section will be resolved remains in question, but there is no doubt that the foreign policy choices of the United States will play a decisive role.

Managing international trade: China

For the United States, trade is a necessity. America imports a wide range of resources and manufactured goods from other countries, and increased trade can enhance the economic growth of the nation overall. Many economic analyses describe trade in terms of the theory of comparative advantage, which holds that nations export items they can produce cheaply, in return for imports that can be produced more efficiently elsewhere. Similarly, outsourcing jobs to foreign countries with lower labor costs makes American companies more efficient, which raises their profits and allows them to expand operations, which may result in new jobs.

These practices are examples of **globalization**: the trend toward increasing interaction and connections among individuals, corporations, and nations (see Chapter 15). New technologies have leveled the global playing field, allowing suppliers of goods and services to sell their products throughout the world. Many American companies and their employees profit from this process. Reflecting this development, the last generation of American politics has been marked by international agreements to reduce or eliminate tariffs among nations, the growth of international organizations such as the WTO to regulate trade and adjudicate trade disputes, and increases in outsourcing of manufacturing jobs and services from developed countries to developing countries.[55] The trade policy of the Trump administration, which emphasizes threats of higher tariffs and withdrawal from trade agreements, is a sharp departure from these trends.

At the same time, even if trade deals increase economic growth in America as a whole, opening America's markets will hurt some individuals—those whose livelihoods are threatened by cheaper foreign imports. For example, in many Midwestern towns, manufacturing plants have been closed because of competition from cheaper foreign imports. In theory, displaced workers could enter retraining programs and move to new jobs with companies who are able to grow because of new opportunities to export to other countries. However, these workers may not be able to find, afford, or complete a retraining program and may not want to move to another state for a new

globalization
The increase over the last generation in trade, travel, and the flow of ideas and beliefs between nations.

job, particularly if it involves a significant pay cut. As a result, while trade deals attract significant political support, they also generate strong opposition from individuals and communities that correctly see the deals as a threat to their way of life. An additional complication is that even if countries reduce or eliminate tariffs, existing regulations create significant barriers to foreign companies that want to sell products there.

America's relations with China are a prime example of these developments. Many American companies have factories in China that produce a variety of products that are sold in America. China is a major producer of rare earth metals that are used to build computer chips. American corporations are also opening stores in China—the coffee chain Starbucks, for example, opens more than one store per day there. In recent years, China has been one of America's largest trading partners, with $711 billion in trade during 2017.

Globalization has transformed economics and society in the United States and abroad. Brands such as Starbucks have spread around the world. Revenue growth for the company in China and Southeast Asia has been substantially higher than in the United States.

Although these moves toward increased trade with China generate significant benefits, the changes do not make everyone better off. American manufacturing jobs have been lost as factories that could not compete with cheaper foreign suppliers have either closed or moved to another country, leaving behind unemployed American workers.[56] Moreover, there have been numerous complaints that Chinese companies have stolen trade secrets from American corporations or violated American copyright laws—in some cases with the apparent support of the Chinese government. In fact, even after an official agreement in 2015 to eliminate industrial espionage, Chinese hackers continue to attempt to infiltrate the computer networks of American tech and pharmaceutical firms.[57] Moreover, China requires technology companies to disclose trade secrets and source codes as a condition of being allowed to sell products there. America has also enacted restrictions, such as the ban on government purchases of telecommunications equipment from Chinese firms discussed earlier.

President Trump has departed from previous administrations in his aggressive use of punitive tariffs to force China and other countries to change their trade practices. The problem is, in a global economy where America is only one potential market, these threats may only lead foreign companies to sell their goods elsewhere, raising the prices paid by American consumers. Trump's tariffs have also triggered increased tariffs on American goods, which reduces American exports and hurts employees of affected companies. Most important, however, even if trade barriers disappear and global markets become completely open, some American communities will still suffer because of increased foreign imports. While there are some federal programs to retrain workers whose jobs are eliminated because of new trade agreements, many workers who have lost their jobs due to globalization are not eligible for these programs, and others are unaware that they exist. Moreover, it is often extremely difficult to retrain people to compete for new jobs that will provide pay and benefits comparable to what they received in their former positions. In addition, there are no systematic American efforts to help citizens of other countries who are hurt by globalization.

One of the effects of globalization is outsourcing—moving jobs to different countries, usually to take advantage of lower wages and looser restrictions on manufacturing practices. Here, workers in China assemble electronic products for a foreign company.

Finally, globalization raises new human rights questions. For example, do U.S. companies such as Apple, which has outsourced the production of iPhones to factories in China, have a responsibility to monitor conditions in these factories and ensure that workers there are paid a fair wage? More generally, should the United States increase its trade with a country such as China that restricts the political, religious, and social freedoms of its citizens in ways that most Americans would find objectionable? Or should it push for as much trade as possible, on the grounds that exposure to American commerce and culture will encourage the other country's citizens to press their government for reforms?

Trade is an example of a more general phenomenon: the state of each national economy is increasingly linked to economic conditions throughout the world. For example, China has an enormous trade surplus with America and holds hundreds of billions of dollars in American government bonds. Some observers believe these assets give the Chinese the ability to severely damage the American economy, either by withholding exports or by selling large quantities of American government bonds on international markets, thus raising the interest rate the United States would have to offer to finance its budget deficit. However, the Chinese economy is equally vulnerable. Eliminating the U.S. market for exports would leave Chinese factories without one of their major buyers. And selling bonds at below-market prices to increase American interest rates would likely damage the Chinese economy even more than the American economy.

One way to respond to these complications is to take a stand along the lines of Donald Trump's punitive tariffs—that the United States should renegotiate trade agreements to protect American workers and increase American exports, with the threat that America will impose high import tariffs on countries that refuse to comply

What I'm saying is this: I'm saying that we do it, but if they [China] don't start treating us fairly and stop devaluing and let their currency rise so that our companies can compete and we don't lose all of these millions of jobs that we're losing I would certainly start taxing goods that come in from China. Who the hell has to lose $505 billion a year?

—**Donald Trump,** Republican debate, January 13, 2016

with these demands. This attitude illustrates a central truth: decisions to encourage trade and globalization are real choices, choices that are sure to generate high levels of conflict in American politics. While U.S. policy can encourage or discourage trade, outsourcing, and other interactions that cross national borders, all these choices will make some people better off and some worse off. As in so many other areas of American politics, because of the wide range of interests that Americans bring to the table, there is no one trade policy that is clearly better than all the others.

Fighting terrorism: ISIL

There have been no major terrorist attacks on the United States since September 11, 2001, and the worldwide Al Qaeda organization that planned the September 11 attacks has been decimated by a decade-long series of U.S. counterattacks using drones, Special Forces troops, air strikes, and operations by ground forces. Nevertheless, the potential for terrorism remains, and groups such as ISIL have continued to carry out smaller operations, such as attacks in various European cities. ISIL has also encouraged individuals to plan and execute their own attacks, such as the attacks in San Bernardino by an American citizen and a permanent resident in December 2015 and the attacks by an American citizen in a Miami nightclub in June 2016.

The fight against global terror is different from a conventional war. In a conventional war, there are clear victory criteria: the losing nation's government capitulates. In contrast, terrorism involves multiple organizations with fluid memberships. Eliminating one individual or group may not reduce the danger of future attacks, because these victories do not address the factors that drive terrorism, including poverty and a deep-set anger that some individuals have against Western interests. For example, while the United States and its allies have recaptured land in Syria and Iraq that was controlled by ISIL and have killed or captured many ISIL fighters, offshoots of the organization still exist throughout the world, as do anti-American, anti-West sentiments among some groups.

The same is true for Al Qaeda. Over the last 17 years, the United States has invaded Afghanistan and removed the Afghan Taliban government that supported Al Qaeda, destroyed many camps and other centers in Afghanistan and elsewhere, and captured or killed many operatives and leaders of the organization. However, while Al Qaeda is far weaker than it was in 2001, the possibility of an attack on Americans in the United States or abroad by the remnants of Al Qaeda remains very real (although, as we discuss in the What Do the Facts Say? feature, many Americans overestimate the threat of terrorist attacks). Moreover, even after over a decade of military action and efforts to build a stable democracy and a growing economy, Afghanistan remains a dangerous, unstable place. Should the United States be responsible for creating a stable, prosperous Afghan nation? What will happen if America withdraws its support? Would the Taliban and Al Qaeda return, or would another equally bad group emerge?

Political scientist John Mueller argues that terrorism is hard to deter because its primary purpose is to frighten people; as a result, the set of possible targets is very large.[58] We typically think of terrorists attacking big, visible targets such as the World Trade Center or the U.S. Capitol, but in fact, there are many public places, from malls to urban centers, where an attack could cause high casualties and public panic. This fact makes the job of preventing attacks virtually impossible. And given that the number of actual terrorists is quite small, they are extremely difficult to find, regardless of whether they are in Syria or in America.

Human rights concerns also shape antiterrorism efforts. American attacks against terror groups have the potential to cause civilian casualties—especially in places such as Afghanistan, where these groups have tried to hide among civilians to discourage such attacks. In addition, investigating terror groups may involve increased surveillance of

The Threat of Terrorism

As the Gallup poll here indicates, a substantial percentage of Americans worry that they or members of their family will be the victims of a terrorist attack—in fact, these concerns even predate the September 11 attacks. Are these fears justified? How great is the risk? What do the facts say?

How Worried Are You That You or Someone in Your Family Will Become a Victim of Terrorism?

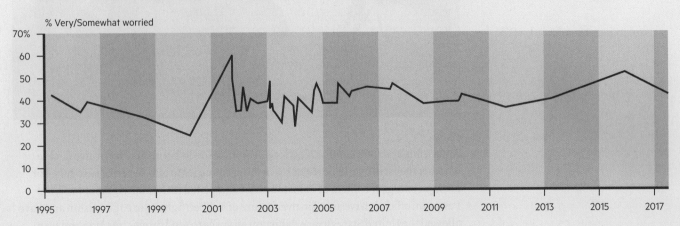

Hazard	Annual Fatality Risk
Traffic accidents	1 in 8,200
Homicide	1 in 22,000
Industrial accidents	1 in 53,000
Natural disasters	1 in 480,000
Drowning in bathtub	1 in 950,000
Home appliances	1 in 1,500,000
Deer accidents	1 in 2,000,000
Commercial aviation	1 in 2,300,000
Peanut allergies	1 in 6,000,000
Lightning	1 in 7,000,000
Terrorist attack	1 in 110,000,000

Sources: Gallup Poll, "Terrorism in the United States," www.gallup.com (accessed 8/16/18); John Mueller and Mark G. Stewart, *Chasing Ghosts: The Policing of Terrorism* (New York: Oxford University Press, 2015).

Think about it

- Is the public's concern over the dangers of terrorist attacks justified by the fatality data?
- Suppose you were a bureaucrat from the Department of Homeland Security who was testifying before Congress on the need to increase funding for antiterrorism programs. One of the members of Congress at the hearing argued that such funding was unnecessary because the likelihood of dying from a terrorist incident was so low. How would you respond?

One of the United States' strategies to increase stability in Afghanistan is to train the Afghan National Army and police in order to provide the Afghan government a greater level of control over the region.

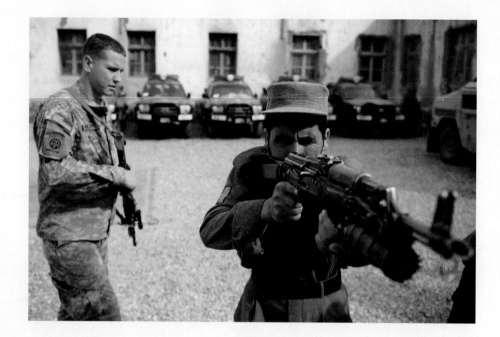

Americans and their communications. American decision makers must also decide whether they will overlook problems in other countries to pursue terror suspects. For example, the government of Pakistan is routinely cited for human rights abuses, but Pakistani officials have aided in the capture of Taliban fighters in Afghanistan and have allowed the United States to use Pakistani airspace to send drones into Iraq and Iran.

In sum, regardless of what happens in Syria, Afghanistan, and other areas where ISIL and other terrorist organizations operate, the fight against global terrorism will continue for the foreseeable future. It is easy to work backward from this conclusion to a critique of past policies—to conclude, for example, that things would be better if the United States had sent more troops or economic aid to Afghanistan, had not invaded Iraq, or had refused to intervene in the Syrian civil war. However, because terror attacks can come from many sources, because the fight against these organizations touches on human rights concerns, and because it is not clear how to eliminate the threat, there is no clear best strategy in the War on Terror. As a result, the threat from terrorism, and the debate over how to respond, will persist.

Preventing the spread of WMDs: North Korea

weapons of mass destruction (WMDs)
Weapons that have the potential to cause large-scale loss of life, such as nuclear bombs and chemical or biological weapons.

The term "**weapons of mass destruction (WMDs)**" refers to nuclear bombs, chemical weapons such as nerve gas, and biological weapons such as anthrax. Given the potential for these weapons to inflict mass casualties, the United States has placed a high priority on (1) limiting the number of nations that have these weapons and (2) preventing terrorist organizations from obtaining or developing them. For example, North Korea's efforts to build and test a nuclear arsenal raise concerns that North Korea might use the weapons against South Korea or even the United States or that terrorist organizations could buy or steal the weapons to use themselves. (Similar concerns arise for other nuclear powers, including Pakistan and other countries with nuclear weapons research programs, such as Iran.)

The enduring problem for the United States is to determine how to respond to North Korea's nuclear capabilities. Military operations are problematic, as North Korea's weapons and the factories that manufacture them are buried deep underground and may not be destroyed even by a massive attack. An unsuccessful attack might goad the

North Korean government to launch its remaining weapons against U.S., Korean, or Japanese targets. Moreover, how should America respond to a nuclear attack against its citizens or its allies, particularly if it is unclear which nation or group is responsible?

Historically, America's policy toward North Korea as well as other near-nuclear powers has emphasized incentives as well as threats. Economic and military sanctions serve to pressure nations that continue to develop weapons, while offers of economic aid and even civilian nuclear reactors serve to persuade nations to give up their weapons programs.[59] Of course, because these agreements are voluntary, nations giving up their nuclear weapons programs get something in return. In the case of the deal with Iran, the United States and its allies made crucial concessions—the lifting of economic sanctions and the return of Iranian assets held after the Iranian Revolution of 1979. These concessions were hugely valuable to the Iranian regime because of their importance in the Iranian economy. While President Trump has moved beyond previous administrations by making threats about the magnitude of the U.S. response to a North Korean attack, as well as by meeting with North Korea's leader, Kim Jong Un, in 2018, in concrete terms his policies are not significantly different from those of his predecessors.

The problem with America's carrots and sticks is that the North Korean economy is already in shambles and the country has relatively little trade with other nations. As a result, economic sanctions are not very threatening. The North Korean government has essentially isolated its citizens from the outside world and carried out a widespread program of indoctrination to reinforce beliefs that building nuclear weapons is an appropriate response to threats from the rest of the world. The government also imprisons dissidents and withholds basic resources from the North Korean people, focusing instead on building a strong military. Under these conditions, the offer to reopen commercial and cultural ties is not very attractive to the North Korean leadership.

The difficulty of the problem does not eliminate conflict in American politics over what policy to follow. The disagreement is in part over the potential for success of different tactics. Some believe that North Korea's weapons could be destroyed by a bombing attack, for example. Despite ongoing missile tests, it is also uncertain whether North Korea has the means to reliably launch nuclear weapons against American targets. Others see a wider range of motivations, agreeing that North Korea's nuclear capability must be eliminated but also arguing that it is America's responsibility to free the North Korean people from an oppressive dictatorship.

North Korea has one of the world's least predictable and most isolated political regimes. Its nuclear capabilities and large military make North Korea a threat to the stability of the region. However, because of the poor state of the country's economy, economic sanctions are unlikely to foster movement toward democracy and openness.

How this conflict is resolved will drive future policy choices. On the one hand, if human rights concerns dominate or if the threat is seen as imminent, it is likely that military operations will proceed. On the other hand, if North Korea is seen as making threats it cannot carry out and if the cost of conflict (including the suffering of the North and South Korean people following an attack) is seen as unacceptably high, then the status quo of diplomacy and the promise of economic aid is likely to continue, even as the threat posed by North Korean weapons remains.

Unpacking the Conflict

Foreign policy matters. National security is a top priority for many Americans. The state of the American economy, from home prices to the unemployment rate, is affected by economic conditions elsewhere. Trade agreements with other nations determine how much American companies are allowed to export and what taxes and fees they must pay to import raw materials and other goods. It is hard to find a domestic issue that does not have a foreign policy component.

Why did President Trump's trade policies fail to work as advertised? As with many other issues in politics, the importance of foreign policy is not matched by the ability of elected officials to manage events and achieve desired outcomes. President Trump and his supporters believed that a combination of punitive tariffs and demands for renegotiation of existing trade agreements would increase U.S. exports and improve the American economy, only to find that foreign leaders responded with their own punishments and demands, leading to an outcome in which everyone was worse off. The problem is not that Trump's desire to reward his supporters by protecting American manufacturers and exporters is bad per se. But in a world where all countries want to maximize exports and protect domestic industries, the United States cannot have it both ways—it cannot demand that other countries open their economies but accept U.S. restrictions.

Who gets to decide America's foreign policy? How is foreign policy made? One significant difference between foreign and domestic policies is the preeminent role played by the president in determining America's relations with other nations and its role in the world. Even so, other actors, especially Congress, can block presidential initiatives or set policy on their own. In fact, many presidential foreign policy powers, such as the ability to change tariffs, have been delegated to the executive branch by Congress.

The most important thing to remember about foreign policy making is that it is conflictual. It is tempting to think that because foreign policy involves dealing with other countries, Americans should hold similar preferences and stand united. The reality is that disagreements among elected officials over what to do against ISIL or over trade agreements or any other question of foreign policy are not just attempts to attract political support or get media attention. These differences of opinion reflect real dilemmas over what government should do and how it should do it.

In all these respects, the issues discussed in this chapter, including the fight against global terrorism, the Middle East, conflicts with China over trade policy, and persuading Iran and North Korea to curb their nuclear ambitions, are not exceptions to the rule; rather, they epitomize just how close to home foreign policy is. Ordinary Americans are finding their lives increasingly affected by actions taken outside U.S. borders—a trend that is likely to continue over the next generation. And the political process will determine how these pressing foreign policy questions will be resolved.

STUDY GUIDE

What is foreign policy?

Describe the major approaches to understanding foreign policy, and trace how America's role in the world has evolved. (Pages 616–626)

Summary

Foreign policy is any government action toward a group outside America's borders. Foreign policy goals are complex, and debates on what America's goals should be are traditionally framed in terms of general principles. The goals of American foreign policy have changed over time and have become increasingly internationalist.

Key terms

foreign policy (p. 616)
unilateral action (national) (p. 617)
multilateral action (p. 617)
isolationism (p. 617)
internationalism (p. 617)
realism (p. 618)
liberalism (p. 618)
nation building (p. 618)

constructivism (p. 618)
Monroe Doctrine (p. 619)
Cold War (p. 620)
containment (p. 620)
mutually assured destruction (p. 622)
domino theory (p. 622)
détente (p. 622)
Bush Doctrine (p. 624)

Practice Quiz Questions

1. **When one country does something on its own without coordinating with other countries, it is _____.**

a isolationist
b internationalist
c acting unilaterally
d acting multilaterally
e nation building

2. **_____ believe that countries pursue their own interests.**

a Realists
b Liberals
c Constructivists
d Internationalists

3. **The Monroe Doctrine stated that in European wars America would _____.**

a support Britain
b support the attacking country
c support the attacked country
d provide arms but not troops
e remain neutral

4. **American foreign policy became increasingly internationalist following _____.**

a the Civil War
b World War I
c World War II
d the Vietnam War
e the Cold War

5. **The goal of containment influenced the _____ and _____.**

a war in Iraq; the war in Afghanistan
b Korean War; the war in Iraq
c Vietnam War; the war in Iraq
d Korean War; the Cuban missile crisis
e Vietnam War; World War II

Foreign policy makers

Explain how the various branches of government shape foreign policy. (Pages 626–637)

Summary

The major actors in foreign policy are the president and Congress, although the Supreme Court, interest groups, and public opinion all influence foreign policy decisions to a degree. The president's advantage over Congress lies in the ambiguity in the Constitution and the unilateral presidential power.

Key terms

National Security Council (NSC) (p. 627)
civilian control (p. 628)
intergovernmental organizations (IGOs) (p. 636)
nongovernmental organizations (NGOs) (p. 636)

World Bank (p. 636)
International Monetary Fund (IMF) (p. 636)
United Nations (UN) (p. 636)

6. The principal foreign policy department in the executive branch is _____.

a   the Department of Defense

b   the Council on Foreign Relations

c   the Department of International Relations

d   the Department of State

e   the Foreign Intelligence Advisory Board

7. The idea that military personnel do not formulate policy but rather implement directives from civilians is _____.

a   military deference

b   civilian control

c   the Geneva system

d   civilian–military alliance

e   the Bush Doctrine

8. Congress holds the _____ and the _____, which both influence foreign policy.

a   power to deploy troops; power of the purse

b   power to approve treaties; power to deploy troops

c   power to declare war; power of the purse

d   power to deploy troops; power to declare war

e   power to approve appointments; power to deploy troops

9. The War Powers Resolution was designed to _____.

a   limit the president's war-making powers

b   limit the Congress's war-making powers

c   limit the Department of Defense's war-making powers

d   limit the Pentagon's war-making powers

e   limit the State Department's war-making powers

The tools of foreign policy

Examine the ways American foreign policy is implemented. (Pages 637–642)

Summary

American foreign policy is implemented using a variety of tools—beyond the use of military force, other tools include the provision of foreign aid or changes to trade policy. Though all tools can be used in pursuit of desired policy outcomes, the specific tool is selected based on careful consideration of context.

Key terms

tariff (p. 638)

World Trade Organization (WTO) (p. 638)

most-favored-nation status (p. 639)

economic sanctions (p. 640)

10. The process of _____ involves using personal contact and negotiations with leaders to work out international agreements.

a   nation building

b   diplomacy

c   unilateralism

d   the Bush Doctrine

e   the use of force

11. When a country is given "most-favored-nation" status, it means that the United States _____ any other nation.

a   gives the country higher levels of foreign aid than

b   gives the country higher levels of military aid than

c   sets tariffs on imports to the United States to the lowest rate given to

d   sets tariffs on exports from the United States to the lowest rate given to

e   sends that country more troops than

12. The World Trade Organization is an example of _____.

a   a bilateral agreement

b   an alliance

c   a tariff

d   a multilateral agreement

e   a sanction

The politics of foreign policy today

Analyze several major areas of foreign policy and why they are often controversial. (Pages 643–650)

Summary

Focusing on three contemporary foreign policy issues—trade, terrorism, and WMDs—reveals a variety of conflicts among citizens and elected officials alike over how America's foreign policy should look. Notwithstanding this conflict, it is clear that America's policy choices on these issues will have enormous consequences both for American citizens and for people throughout the world.

Key terms

globalization (p. 643)

weapons of mass destruction (WMDs) (p. 648)

Practice Quiz Questions

13. What factor limits the American response to potential terrorist threats?

a American public opinion opposes attacks on terrorist organizations.

b The War Powers Resolution limits military actions to those approved by Congress.

c Other nations would impose economic sanctions on American corporations.

d It is difficult to identify terrorists or determine their plans.

e Addressing terrorism requires a multilateral effort, which is difficult to coordinate.

14. The American government hesitates to pressure Pakistan on human rights violations, most likely because _____.

a doing so would threaten economic ties with Pakistan

b attempts to protect human rights may make it harder for the United States to achieve goals in Afghanistan

c evidence of human rights violations in Pakistan is unreliable

d there is little international condemnation for the Pakistani violations of human rights

e Pakistan enforces a Bill of Rights

15. Efforts to eliminate the threat of North Korean WMDs are limited by all of these factors except _____.

a Russian support for the North Korean regime

b the limited impact of economic sanctions

c the possibility that North Korea would respond militarily to an attack

d the isolation of North Korea's population

e the fact that North Korean WMDs are stored in well-protected facilities

Suggested Reading

Auerswald, David P., and Stephen Saideman. *NATO in Afghanistan: Fighting Together, Fighting Alone*. Princeton, NJ: Princeton University Press, 2014.

Bueno de Mesquita, Bruce. *Principles of International Politics*. Washington, DC: CQ Press, 2005.

Fortna, V. Page. *Does Peacekeeping Work?: Shaping Belligerents' Choices after Civil War*. Princeton, NJ: Princeton University Press, 2008.

Enloe, Cynthia. *Bananas, Beaches and Bases: Making Sense of Feminist International Politics*. Chicago: University of Chicago Press, 2014.

Huntington, Samuel P. *The Clash of Civilizations and the Remaking of World Order*. New York: Free Press, 2002.

Jentleson, Bruce. *American Foreign Policy: The Dynamics of Choice in the 21st Century*. 5th Ed. New York: W. W. Norton, 2013.

Mearsheimer, John J. *The Tragedy of Great Power Politics*. New York: W. W. Norton, 2001.

Mueller, John, and Mark G. Stewart. *Chasing Ghosts: The Policing of Terrorism*. New York: Oxford University Press, 2015.

Nye, Joseph. *Soft Power: The Means to Success in World Politics*. New York: Hachette Book Group, 2009.

Sen, Amartya. *Identity and Violence: The Illusion of Destiny*. New York: W. W. Norton, 2007.

Simmons, Beth, Frank Dobbin, and Geoffrey Garrett. *The Global Diffusion of Markets and Democracy*. New York: Cambridge University Press, 2008.

Stiglitz, Joseph E. *Making Globalization Work*. New York: W. W. Norton, 2007.

APPENDIX

The Declaration of Independence

In Congress, July 4, 1776

The unanimous Declaration of the thirteen united States of America,

When in the Course of human events, it becomes necessary for one people to dissolve the political bands which have connected them with another, and to assume among the powers of the earth, the separate and equal station to which the Laws of Nature and of Nature's God entitle them, a decent respect to the opinions of mankind requires that they should declare the causes which impel them to the separation.

We hold these truths to be self-evident, that all men are created equal, that they are endowed by their Creator with certain unalienable Rights, that among these are Life, Liberty and the pursuit of Happiness.—That to secure these rights, Governments are instituted among Men, deriving their just powers from the consent of the governed.—That whenever any Form of Government becomes destructive of these ends, it is the Right of the People to alter or to abolish it, and to institute new Government, laying its foundation on such principles and organizing its powers in such form, as to them shall seem most likely to effect their Safety and Happiness. Prudence, indeed, will dictate that Governments long established should not be changed for light and transient causes; and accordingly all experience hath shewn, that mankind are more disposed to suffer, while evils are sufferable, than to right themselves by abolishing the forms to which they are accustomed. But when a long train of abuses and usurpations, pursuing invariably the same Object evinces a design to reduce them under absolute Despotism, it is their right, it is their duty, to throw off such Government, and to provide new Guards for their future security.—Such has been the patient sufferance of these Colonies; and such is now the necessity which constrains them to alter their former Systems of Government. The history of the present King of Great Britain is a history of repeated injuries and usurpations, all having in direct object the establishment of an absolute Tyranny over these States. To prove this, let Facts be submitted to a candid world.

He has refused his Assent to Laws, the most wholesome and necessary for the public good.

He has forbidden his Governors to pass Laws of immediate and pressing importance, unless suspended in their operation till his Assent should be obtained; and when so suspended, he has utterly neglected to attend to them.

He has refused to pass other Laws for the accommodation of large districts of people, unless those people would relinquish the right of Representation in the Legislature, a right inestimable to them and formidable to tyrants only.

He has called together legislative bodies at places unusual, uncomfortable, and distant from the depository of their public Records, for the sole purpose of fatiguing them into compliance with his measures.

He has dissolved Representative Houses repeatedly, for opposing with manly firmness his invasions on the rights of the people.

He has refused for a long time, after such dissolutions, to cause others to be elected; whereby the Legislative powers, incapable of Annihilation, have returned to the People at large for their exercise; the State remaining in the mean time exposed to all the dangers of invasion from without, and convulsions within.

He has endeavoured to prevent the population of these States; for that purpose obstructing the Laws for Naturalization of Foreigners; refusing to pass others to encourage their migrations hither, and raising the conditions of new Appropriations of Lands.

He has obstructed the Administration of Justice, by refusing his Assent to Laws for establishing Judiciary powers.

He has made Judges dependent on his Will alone, for the tenure of their offices, and the amount and payment of their salaries.

He has erected a multitude of New Offices, and sent hither swarms of Officers to harrass our people, and eat out their substance.

He has kept among us, in times of peace, Standing Armies without the Consent of our legislatures.

He has affected to render the Military independent of and superior to the Civil power.

He has combined with others to subject us to a jurisdiction foreign to our constitution, and unacknowledged by our laws; giving his Assent to their Acts of pretended Legislation:

For Quartering large bodies of armed troops among us:

For protecting them, by a mock Trial, from punishment for any Murders which they should commit on the Inhabitants of these States:

For cutting off our Trade with all parts of the world:

For imposing Taxes on us without our Consent:

For depriving us in many cases, of the benefits of Trial by Jury:

For transporting us beyond Seas to be tried for pretended offences:

For abolishing the free System of English Laws in a neighboring Province, establishing therein an Arbitrary government, and enlarging its Boundaries so as to render it at once an example and fit instrument for introducing the same absolute rule into these Colonies:

For taking away our Charters, abolishing our most valuable Laws, and altering fundamentally the Forms of our Governments:

For suspending our own Legislatures, and declaring themselves invested with power to legislate for us in all cases whatsoever.

He has abdicated Government here, by declaring us out of his Protection and waging War against us.

He has plundered our seas, ravaged our Coasts, burnt our towns, and destroyed the lives of our people.

He is at this time transporting large Armies of foreign Mercenaries to compleat the works of death, desolation and tyranny, already begun with circumstances of Cruelty & perfidy scarcely paralleled in the most barbarous ages, and totally unworthy the Head of a civilized nation.

He has constrained our fellow Citizens taken Captive on the high Seas to bear Arms against their Country, to become the executioners of their friends and Brethren, or to fall themselves by their Hands.

He has excited domestic insurrections amongst us, and has endeavoured to bring on the inhabitants of our frontiers, the merciless Indian Savages, whose known rule of warfare, is an undistinguished destruction of all ages, sexes and conditions.

In every stage of these Oppressions We have Petitioned for Redress in the most humble terms: Our repeated Petitions have been answered only by repeated injury. A Prince whose character is thus marked by every act which may define a Tyrant, is unfit to be the ruler of a free people.

Nor have We been wanting in attentions to our Brittish brethren. We have warned them from time to time of attempts by their legislature to extend an unwarrantable jurisdiction over us. We have reminded them of the circumstances of our emigration and settlement here. We have appealed to their native justice and magnanimity, and we have conjured them by the ties of our common kindred to disavow these usurpations, which, would inevitably interrupt our connections and correspondence. They too have been deaf to the voice of justice and of consanguinity. We must, therefore, acquiesce in the necessity, which denounces our Separation, and hold them, as we hold the rest of mankind, Enemies in War, in Peace Friends.

We, Therefore, the Representatives of the United States of America, in General Congress, Assembled, appealing to the Supreme Judge of the world for the rectitude of our intentions, do, in the Name, and by Authority of the good People of these Colonies, solemnly publish and declare, That these United Colonies are, and of Right ought to be Free and Independent States; that they are Absolved from all Allegiance to the British Crown, and that all political connection between them and the State of Great Britain, is and ought to be totally dissolved; and that as Free and Independent States, they have full Power to levy War, conclude Peace, contract Alliances, establish Commerce, and to do all other Acts and Things which Independent States may of right do. And for the support of this Declaration, with a firm reliance on the protection of divine Providence, we mutually pledge to each other our Lives, our Fortunes and our sacred Honor.

The foregoing Declaration was, by order of Congress, engrossed, and signed by the following members:

John Hancock

New Hampshire
Josiah Bartlett
William Whipple
Matthew Thornton

Massachusetts Bay
Samuel Adams
John Adams
Robert Treat Paine
Elbridge Gerry

Rhode Island
Stephen Hopkins
William Ellery

Connecticut
Roger Sherman
Samuel Huntington
William Williams
Oliver Wolcott

New York
William Floyd
Philip Livingston
Francis Lewis
Lewis Morris

New Jersey
Richard Stockton
John Witherspoon
Francis Hopkinson
John Hart
Abraham Clark

Pennsylvania
Robert Morris
Benjamin Rush
Benjamin Franklin
John Morton
George Clymer
James Smith
George Taylor
James Wilson
George Ross

Delaware
Caesar Rodney
George Read
Thomas M'Kean

Maryland
Samuel Chase
William Paca
Thomas Stone
Charles Carroll, of Carrollton

Virginia
George Wythe
Richard Henry Lee
Thomas Jefferson
Benjamin Harrison
Thomas Nelson, Jr.
Francis Lightfoot Lee
Carter Braxton

North Carolina
William Hooper
Joseph Hewes
John Penn

South Carolina
Edward Rutledge
Thomas Heyward, Jr.
Thomas Lynch, Jr.
Arthur Middleton

Georgia
Button Gwinnett
Lyman Hall
George Walton

Resolved, That copies of the Declaration be sent to the several assemblies, conventions, and committees, or councils of safety, and to the several commanding officers of the continental troops; that it be proclaimed in each of the United States, at the head of the army.

The Articles of Confederation

Agreed to by Congress November 15, 1777;
ratified and in force March 1, 1781

To all whom these Presents shall come, we the undersigned Delegates of the States affixed to our Names, send greeting. Whereas the Delegates of the United States of America, in Congress assembled, did, on the fifteenth day of November, in the Year of Our Lord One thousand Seven Hundred and Seventy seven, and in the Second Year of the Independence of America, agree to certain articles of Confederation and perpetual Union between the States of Newhampshire, Massachusetts-bay, Rhodeisland and Providence Plantations, Connecticut, New-York, New-Jersey, Pennsylvania, Delaware, Maryland, Virginia, North-Carolina, South-Carolina and Georgia in the words following, viz. "Articles of Confederation and perpetual Union between the states of Newhampshire, Massachusettsbay, Rhodeisland and Providence Plantations, Connecticut, New-York, New-Jersey, Pennsylvania, Delaware, Maryland, Virginia, North-Carolina, South-Carolina and Georgia.

Art. I. The Stile of this confederacy shall be "The United States of America."

Art. II. Each state retains its sovereignty, freedom and independence, and every Power, Jurisdiction and right, which is not by this confederation expressly delegated to the United States, in Congress assembled.

Art. III. The said states hereby severally enter into a firm league of friendship with each other, for their common defence, the security of their Liberties, and their mutual and general welfare, binding themselves to assist each other, against all force offered to, or attacks made upon them, or any of them, on account of religion, sovereignty, trade, or any other pretence whatever.

Art. IV. The better to secure and perpetuate mutual friendship and intercourse among the people of the different states in this union, the free inhabitants of each of these states, paupers, vagabonds and fugitives from Justice excepted, shall be entitled to all privileges and immunities of free citizens in the several states; and the people of each state shall have free ingress and regress to and from any other state, and shall enjoy therein all the privileges of trade and commerce, subject to the same duties, impositions and restrictions as the inhabitants thereof respectively, provided that such restriction shall not extend so far as to prevent the removal of property imported into any state, to any other state, of which the Owner is an inhabitant; provided also that no imposition, duties or restriction shall be laid by any state, on the property of the united states, or either of them.

If any Person guilty of, or charged with treason, felony, or other high misdemeanor in any state, shall flee from Justice, and be found in any of the united states, he shall, upon demand of the Governor or executive power, of the state from which he fled, be delivered up and removed to the state having jurisdiction of his offence.

Full faith and credit shall be given in each of these states to the records, acts and judicial proceedings of the courts and magistrates of every other state.

Art. V. For the more convenient management of the general interests of the united states, delegates shall be annually appointed in such manner as the legislature of each state shall direct, to meet in Congress on the first Monday in November, in every year, with a power reserved to each state, to recall its delegates, or any of them, at any time within the year, and to send others in their stead, for the remainder of the Year.

No state shall be represented in Congress by less than two, nor by more than seven Members; and no person shall be capable of being a delegate for more than three years in any term of six years; nor shall any person, being a delegate, be capable of holding any office under the united states, for which he, or another for his benefit receives any salary, fees or emolument of any kind.

Each state shall maintain its own delegates in a meeting of the states, and while they act as members of the committee of the states.

In determining questions in the united states, in Congress assembled, each state shall have one vote.

Freedom of speech and debate in Congress shall not be impeached or questioned in any Court, or place out of Congress, and the members of congress shall be protected in their persons from arrests and imprisonments, during the time of their going to and from, and attendance on congress, except for treason, felony, or breach of the peace.

Art. VI. No state without the Consent of the united states in congress assembled, shall send any embassy to, or receive any embassy from, or enter into any conference, agreement, or alliance or treaty with any King, prince or state; nor shall any person holding any office or profit or trust under the united states, or any of them, accept of any present, emolument, office or title of any kind whatever from any king, prince or foreign state; nor shall the united states in congress assembled, or any of them, grant any title of nobility.

No two or more states shall enter into any treaty, confederation or alliance whatever between them, without the consent of the united states in congress assembled, specifying accurately the purposes for which the same is to be entered into, and how long it shall continue.

No state shall lay any imposts or duties, which may interfere with any stipulations in treaties, entered into by the united states in congress assembled, with any king, prince or state, in pursuance of any treaties already proposed by congress, to the courts of France and Spain.

No vessels of war shall be kept up in time of peace by any state, except such number only, as shall be deemed necessary by the united states in congress assembled, for the defence of such state, or its trade; nor shall any body of forces be kept up by any state, in time of peace, except such number only, as in the judgment of the united states, in congress assembled, shall be deemed requisite to garrison the forts necessary for the defence of such state; but every state shall always keep up a well regulated and disciplined militia, sufficiently armed and accoutred, and shall provide and constantly have ready for use, in public stores, a due number of field pieces and tents, and a proper quantity of arms, ammunition and camp equipage.

No state shall engage in any war without the consent of the united states in congress assembled, unless such state be actually invaded by enemies, or shall have received certain advice of a resolution being formed by some nation of Indians to invade such state, and the danger is so imminent as not to admit of a delay, till the united states in congress asssembled can be consulted; nor shall any state grant commissions to any ships or vessels of war, nor letters of marque or reprisal, except it be after a declaration of war by the united states in congress assembled, and then only against the kingdom or state and the subjects thereof, against which war has been so declared, and under such regulations as shall be established by the united states in congress assembled, unless such state be infested by pirates; in which case vessels of war may be fitted out for that occasion, and kept so long as the danger shall continue, or until the united states in congress assembled shall determine otherwise.

Art. VII. When land-forces are raised by any state for the common defence, all officers of or under the rank of colonel, shall be appointed by the legislature of each state respectively, by whom such forces shall be raised, or in such manner as such state shall direct, and all vacancies shall be filled up by the state which first made the appointment.

Art. VIII. All charges of war, and all other expences that shall be incurred for the common defence or general welfare, and allowed by the united states in congress assembled, shall be defrayed out of a common treasury, which shall be supplied by the several states in proportion to the value of all land within each state, granted to or surveyed for any Person, as such land and the buildings and improvements thereon shall be estimated according to such mode as the united states in congress assembled, shall from time to time direct and appoint.

The taxes for paying that proportion shall be laid and levied by the authority and direction of the legislatures of the several states within the time agreed upon by the united states in congress assembled.

Art. IX. The united states in congress assembled, shall have the sole and exclusive right and power of determining on peace and war, except in the cases mentioned in the sixth article—of sending and receiving ambassadors—entering into treaties and alliances, provided that no treaty of commerce shall be made whereby the legislative power of the respective states shall be restrained from imposing such imposts and duties on foreigners, as their own people are subjected to, or from prohibiting the exportation of any species of goods or commodities whatsoever—of establishing rules for deciding in all cases, what captures on land or water shall be legal, and in what manner prizes taken by land or naval forces in the service of the united states shall be divided or appropriated—of granting letters of marque and reprisal in times of peace—appointing courts for the trial of piracies and felonies committed on the high seas and establishing courts for receiving and determining finally appeals in all cases of captures, provided that no member of congress shall be appointed a judge of any of the said courts.

The united states in congress assembled shall also be the last resort on appeal in all disputes and differences now subsisting or that hereafter may arise between two or more states concerning boundary, jurisdiction or any other cause whatever; which authority shall always be exercised in the manner following. Whenever the legislative or executive authority or lawful agent of any state in controversy with another shall present a petition to congress stating the matter in question and praying for a hearing, notice thereof shall be given by order of congress to the legislative or executive authority of the other state in controversy, and a day assigned for the appearance of the parties by their lawful agents, who shall then be directed to appoint by joint consent, commissioners or judges to constitute a court for hearing and determining the matter in question: but if they cannot agree, congress shall name three persons out of each of the united states, and from the list of such persons each party shall alternately strike out one, the petitioners beginning, until the number shall be reduced to thirteen; and from that number not less than seven, nor more than nine names as congress shall direct, shall in the presence of congress be drawn out by lot, and the persons whose names shall be so drawn or any five of them, shall be commissioners or judges, to hear and finally determine the controversy, so always as a major part of the judges who shall hear the cause shall agree in the determination: and if either party shall neglect to attend at the day appointed, without shewing reasons, which congress shall judge sufficient, or being present shall refuse to strike, the congress shall proceed to nominate three persons out of each state, and the secretary of congress shall strike in behalf of

such party absent or refusing; and the judgment and sentence of the court to be appointed, in the manner before prescribed, shall be final and conclusive; and if any of the parties shall refuse to submit to the authority of such court, or to appear to defend their claim or cause, the court shall nevertheless proceed to pronounce sentence, or judgment, which shall in like manner be final and decisive, the judgment or sentence and other proceedings being in either case transmitted to congress, and lodged among the acts of congress for the security of the parties concerned: provided that every commissioner, before he sits in judgment, shall take an oath to be administered by one of the judges of the supreme or superior court of the state, where the cause shall be tried, "well and truly to hear and determine the matter in question, according to the best of his judgment, without favour, affection or hope of reward:" provided also, that no state shall be deprived of territory for the benefit of the united states.

All controversies concerning the private right of soil claimed under different grants of two or more states, whose jurisdictions as they may respect such lands, and the states which passed such grants are adjusted, the said grants or either of them being at the same time claimed to have originated antecedent to such settlement of jurisdiction, shall on the petition of either party to the congress of the united states, be finally determined as near as may be in the same manner as is before prescribed for deciding disputes respecting territorial jurisdiction between different states.

The united states in congress assembled shall also have the sole and exclusive right and power of regulating the alloy and value of coin struck by their own authority, or by that of the respective states—fixing the standard of weights and measures throughout the united states—regulating the trade and managing all affairs with the Indians, not members of any of the states, provided that the legislative right of any state within its own limits be not infringed or violated—establishing and regulating post-offices from one state to another, throughout all the united states, and exacting such postage on the papers passing thro' the same as may be requisite to defray the expences of the said office—appointing all officers of the land forces, in the service of the united states, excepting regimental officers—appointing all the officers of the naval forces, and commissioning all officers whatever in the service of the united states—making rules for the government and regulation of the said land and naval forces, and directing their operations.

The united states in congress assembled shall have authority to appoint a committee, to sit in the recess of congress, to be denominated "A Committee of the States," and to consist of one delegate from each state; and to appoint such other committees and civil officers as may be necessary for managing the general affairs of the united states under their direction—to appoint one of their number to preside, provided that no person be allowed to serve in the office of president more than one year in any term of three years; to ascertain the necessary sums of Money to be raised for the service of the united states, and to appropriate and apply the same for defraying the public expenses—to borrow money, or emit bills on the credit of the united states, transmitting every half year to the respective states an account of the sums of money so borrowed or emitted,—to build and equip a navy—to agree upon the number of land forces, and to make requisitions from each state for its quota, in proportion to the number of white inhabitants in such state; which requisition shall be binding, and thereupon the legislature of each state shall appoint the regimental officers, raise the men and cloath, arm and equip them in a soldier like manner, at the expense of the united states; and the officers and men so cloathed, armed and equipped shall march to the place appointed, and within the time agreed on by the united states in congress assembled: But if the united states in congress assembled shall, on consideration of circumstances judge proper that any state should not raise men, or should raise a smaller number than its quota, and that any other state should raise a greater number of men than the quota thereof, such extra number shall be raised, officered, cloathed, armed and equipped in the same manner as the quota of such state, unless the legislature of such state shall judge that such extra number cannot be safely spared out of the same, in which case they shall raise officer, cloath, arm and equip as many of such extra number as they judge can be safely spared. And the officers and men so cloathed, armed and equipped, shall march to the place appointed, and within the time agreed on by the united states in congress assembled.

The united states in congress assembled shall never engage in a war, nor grant letters of marque and reprisal in time of peace, nor enter into any treaties or alliances, nor coin money, nor regulate the value thereof, nor ascertain the sums and expenses necessary for the defence and welfare of the united states, or any of them, nor emit bills, nor borrow money on the credit of the united states, nor appropriate money, nor agree upon the number of vessels of war, to be built or purchased, or the number of land or sea forces to be raised, nor appoint a commander in chief of the army or navy, unless nine states assent to the same: nor shall a question on any other point, except for adjourning from day to day be determined, unless by the votes of a majority of the united states in congress assembled.

The congress of the united states shall have power to adjourn to any time within the year, and to any place within the united states, so that no period of adjournment be for a longer duration than the space of six Months, and shall publish the Journal of their proceedings monthly, except such parts thereof relating to treaties, alliances or military operations, as in their judgment require secrecy; and the yeas and nays of the delegates of each state on any question shall be entered on the Journal, when it is desired by any delegate; and the delegates of a state, or any of them, at his or their request shall be furnished with a transcript of the said Journal, except such parts as are above excepted, to lay before the legislatures of the several states.

Art. X. The committee of the states, or any nine of them, shall be authorised to execute, in the recess of congress, such of the powers of congress as the united states in congress assembled, by the consent of nine states, shall from time to time think expedient to vest them with; provided that no power be delegated to the said committee, for the exercise of which, by the articles of confederation, the voice of nine states in the congress of the united states assembled is requisite.

Art. XI. Canada acceding to this confederation, and joining in the measures of the united states, shall be admitted into, and entitled to all the advantages of this union: but no other colony shall be admitted into the same, unless such admission be agreed to by nine states.

Art. XII. All bills of credit emitted, monies borrowed and debts contracted by, or under the authority of congress, before the assembling of the united states, in pursuance of the present confederation, shall be deemed and considered as a charge against the united states, for payment and satisfaction whereof the said united states and the public faith are hereby solemnly pledged.

Art. XIII. Every state shall abide by the determinations of the united states in congress assembled, on all questions which by this confederation are submitted to them. And the Articles of this confederation shall be inviolably observed by every state, and the union shall be perpetual; nor shall any alteration at any time hereafter be made in any of them; unless such alteration be agreed to in a congress of the united states, and be afterwards confirmed by the legislatures of every state.

And Whereas it hath pleased the Great Governor of the World to incline the hearts of the legislatures we respectively represent in congress, to approve of, and to authorize us to ratify the said articles of confederation and perpetual union. Know Ye that we the undersigned delegates, by virtue of the power and authority to us given for that purpose, do by these presents, in the name and in behalf of our respective constituents, fully and entirely ratify and confirm each and every of the said articles of confederation and perpetual union, and all and singular the matters and things therein contained: And we do further solemnly plight and engage the faith of our respective constituents, that they shall abide by the determinations of the united states in congress assembled, on all questions, which by the said confederation are submitted to them. And that the articles thereof shall be inviolably observed by the states we respectively represent, and that the union shall be perpetual. In Witness whereof we have hereunto set our hands in Congress. Done at Philadelphia in the state of Pennsylvania the ninth day of July, in the Year of our Lord one Thousand seven Hundred and Seventy-eight, and in the third year of the independence of America.

The Constitution of the United States of America

[PREAMBLE]

We the People of the United States, in Order to form a more perfect Union, establish Justice, insure domestic Tranquility, provide for the common defence, promote the general Welfare, and secure the Blessings of Liberty to ourselves and our Posterity, do ordain and establish this Constitution for the United States of America.

Article I

SECTION 1
[LEGISLATIVE POWERS]

All legislative Powers herein granted shall be vested in a Congress of the United States, which shall consist of a Senate and House of Representatives.

SECTION 2
[HOUSE OF REPRESENTATIVES, HOW CONSTITUTED, POWER OF IMPEACHMENT]

The House of Representatives shall be composed of Members chosen every second Year by the People of the several States, and the Electors in each State shall have the Qualifications requisite for Electors of the most numerous Branch of the State Legislature.

No Person shall be a Representative who shall not have attained to the Age of twenty five Years, and been seven Years a Citizen of the United States, and who shall not, when elected, be an Inhabitant of that State in which he shall be chosen.

Representatives and *direct Taxes*[1] shall be apportioned among the several States which may be included within this Union, according to their respective Numbers, *which shall be determined by adding to the whole Number of free Persons, including those bound to Service for a Term of Years, and excluding Indians not taxed, three fifths of all other Persons.*[2] The actual Enumeration shall be made within three Years after the first Meeting of the Congress of the United States, and within every subsequent Term of ten Years, in such Manner as they shall by Law direct. The Number of Representatives shall not exceed one for every thirty Thousand, but each State shall have at Least one Representative; *and until such enumeration shall be made, the State of New Hampshire shall be entitled to chuse three, Massachusetts eight, Rhode-Island and Providence Plantations one, Connecticut five, New-York six, New Jersey four, Pennsylvania eight, Delaware one, Maryland six, Virginia ten, North Carolina five, South Carolina five, and Georgia three.*[3]

When vacancies happen in the Representation from any State, the Executive Authority thereof shall issue Writs of Election to fill such Vacancies.

The House of Representatives shall chuse their Speaker and other Officers; and shall have the sole Power of Impeachment.

SECTION 3
[THE SENATE, HOW CONSTITUTED, IMPEACHMENT TRIALS]

The Senate of the United States shall be composed of two Senators from each State, *chosen by the Legislature thereof,*[4] for six Years; and each Senator shall have one Vote.

Immediately after they shall be assembled in Consequence of the first Election, they shall be divided as equally as may be into three Classes. The Seats of the Senators of the first Class shall be vacated at the Expiration of the second Year, of the second Class at the Expiration of the fourth Year, and of the third Class at the Expiration of the sixth Year, so that one third may be chosen every second Year; *and if Vacancies happen by Resignation, or otherwise, during the Recess of the Legislature of any State, the Executive thereof may make temporary Appointments until the next Meeting of the Legislature, which shall then fill such Vacancies.*[5]

No Person shall be a Senator who shall not have attained to the Age of thirty Years, and been nine Years a Citizen of the United States, and who shall not, when elected, be an Inhabitant of that State for which he shall be chosen.

The Vice President of the United States shall be President of the Senate, but shall have no Vote, unless they be equally divided.

The Senate shall chuse their other Officers, and also a President pro tempore, in the Absence of the Vice President, or when he shall exercise the Office of President of the United States.

The Senate shall have the sole Power to try all Impeachments. When sitting for that Purpose, they shall be on Oath or Affirmation. When the President of the United States is tried, the Chief Justice shall preside: And no Person shall be convicted without the Concurrence of two thirds of the Members present.

Judgment in Cases of Impeachment shall not extend further than to removal from Office, and disqualification to hold and enjoy any Office of honor, Trust or Profit under the United States: but the Party convicted shall nevertheless be liable and subject to Indictment, Trial, Judgment and Punishment, according to Law.

SECTION 4
[ELECTION OF SENATORS AND REPRESENTATIVES]

The Times, Places and Manner of holding Elections for Senators and Representatives, shall be prescribed in each State by the Legislature thereof; but the Congress may at any time by Law make or alter such Regulations, except as to the Places of chusing Senators.

The Congress shall assemble at least once in every Year, and such Meeting shall be on the first Monday in December, unless they shall by Law appoint a different Day.[6]

SECTION 5
[QUORUM, JOURNALS, MEETINGS, ADJOURNMENTS]

Each House shall be the Judge of the Elections, Returns and Qualifications of its own Members, and a Majority of each shall constitute a Quorum to do Business; but a smaller Number may adjourn from day to day, and may be authorized to compel the

---

[1] Modified by Sixteenth Amendment.
[2] Modified by Fourteenth Amendment.
[3] Temporary provision.
[4] Modified by Seventeenth Amendment.
[5] Modified by Seventeenth Amendment.
[6] Modified by Twentieth Amendment.

Attendance of absent Members, in such Manner, and under such Penalties as each House may provide.

Each House may determine the Rules of its Proceedings, punish its Members for disorderly Behaviour, and, with the Concurrence of two thirds, expel a Member.

Each House shall keep a Journal of its Proceedings, and from time to time publish the same, excepting such Parts as may in their Judgment require Secrecy; and the Yeas and Nays of the Members of either House on any questions shall, at the Desire of one fifth of those Present, be entered on the Journal.

Neither House, during the Session of Congress, shall, without the Consent of the other, adjourn for more than three days, nor to any other Place than that in which the two Houses shall be sitting.

SECTION 6
[COMPENSATION, PRIVILEGES, DISABILITIES]

The Senators and Representatives shall receive a Compensation for their Services, to be ascertained by Law, and paid out of the Treasury of the United States. They shall in all Cases, except Treason, Felony and Breach of the Peace, be privileged from Arrest during their Attendance at the Session of their respective Houses, and in going to and returning from the same; and for any Speech or Debate in either House, they shall not be questioned in any other Place.

No Senator or Representative shall, during the Time for which he was elected, be appointed to any civil Office under the Authority of the United States, which shall have been created, or the Emoluments whereof shall have been encreased during such time; and no Person holding any Office under the United States, shall be a Member of either House during his Continuance in Office.

SECTION 7
[PROCEDURE IN PASSING BILLS AND RESOLUTIONS]

All Bills for raising Revenue shall originate in the House of Representatives; but the Senate may propose or concur with Amendments as on other Bills.

Every Bill which shall have passed the House of Representatives and the Senate, shall, before it become a Law, be presented to the President of the United States: If he approve he shall sign it, but if not he shall return it, with his Objections to that House in which it shall have originated, who shall enter the Objections at large on their Journal, and proceed to reconsider it. If after such Reconsideration two thirds of that House shall agree to pass the Bill, it shall be sent, together with the Objections, to the other House, by which it shall likewise be reconsidered, and if approved by two thirds of that House, it shall become a Law. But in all such Cases the Votes of both Houses shall be determined by yeas and Nays, and the Names of the Persons voting for and against the Bill shall be entered on the Journal of each House respectively. If any Bill shall not be returned by the President within ten Days (Sundays excepted) after it shall have been presented to him, the Same shall be a Law, in like Manner as if he had signed it, unless the Congress by their Adjournment prevent its Return, in which Case it shall not be a Law.

Every Order, Resolution, or Vote to which the Concurrence of the Senate and House of Representatives may be necessary (except on a question of Adjournment) shall be presented to the President of the United States; and before the Same shall take Effect, shall be approved by him, or being disapproved by him, shall be repassed by two thirds of the Senate and House of Representatives, according to the Rules and Limitations prescribed in the Case of a Bill.

SECTION 8
[POWERS OF CONGRESS]

The Congress shall have Power

To lay and collect Taxes, Duties, Imposts and Excises, to pay the Debts and provide for the common Defence and general Welfare of the United States; but all Duties, Imposts and Excises shall be uniform throughout the United States;

To borrow Money on the credit of the United States;

To regulate Commerce with foreign Nations, and among the several States, and with the Indian Tribes;

To establish an uniform Rule of Naturalization, and uniform Laws on the subject of Bankruptcies throughout the United States;

To coin Money, regulate the Value thereof, and of foreign Coin, and fix the Standard of Weights and Measures;

To provide for the Punishment of counterfeiting the Securities and current Coin of the United States;

To establish Post Offices and post Roads;

To promote the Progress of Science and useful Arts, by securing for limited Times to Authors and Inventors the exclusive Right to their respective Writings and Discoveries;

To constitute Tribunals inferior to the supreme Court;

To define and punish Piracies and Felonies committed on the high Seas, and Offences against the Law of Nations;

To declare War, grant Letters of Marque and Reprisal, and make Rules concerning Captures on Land and Water;

To raise and support Armies, but no Appropriation of Money to that Use shall be for a longer Term than two Years;

To provide and maintain a Navy;

To make Rules for the Government and Regulation of the land and naval Forces;

To provide for calling forth the Militia to execute the Laws of the Union, suppress Insurrections and repel Invasions;

To provide for organizing, arming, and disciplining, the Militia, and for governing such Part of them as may be employed in the Service of the United States, reserving to the States respectively, the Appointment of the Officers, and the Authority of training the Militia according to the discipline prescribed by Congress;

To exercise exclusive Legislation in all Cases whatsoever, over such District (not exceeding ten Miles square) as may, by Cession of particular States, and the Acceptance of Congress, become the Seat of the Government of the United States, and to exercise like Authority over all Places purchased by the Consent of the Legislature of the State in which the Same shall be, for the Erection of Forts, Magazines, Arsenals, dock-Yards, and other needful Buildings;—And

To make all Laws which shall be necessary and proper for carrying into Execution the foregoing Powers, and all other Powers vested by this Constitution in the Government of the United States, or in any Department or Officer thereof.

SECTION 9
[SOME RESTRICTIONS ON FEDERAL POWER]

The Migration or Importation of such Persons as any of the States now existing shall think proper to admit, shall not be prohibited by the Congress prior to the Year one thousand eight hundred and eight, but a Tax or duty may be imposed on such Importation, not exceeding ten dollars for each Person.[7]

---

[7] Temporary provision.

The Privilege of the Writ of Habeas Corpus shall not be suspended, unless when in Cases of Rebellion or Invasion the public Safety may require it.

No Bill of Attainder or ex post facto Law shall be passed.

No Capitation, or other direct, Tax shall be laid, unless in Proportion to the Census or Enumeration herein before directed to be taken.[8]

No Tax or Duty shall be laid on Articles exported from any State.

No Preference shall be given by any Regulation of Commerce or Revenue to the Ports of one State over those of another; nor shall Vessels bound to, or from, one State, be obliged to enter, clear, or pay Duties in another.

No Money shall be drawn from the Treasury, but in Consequence of Appropriations made by Law; and a regular Statement and Account of the Receipts and Expenditures of all public Money shall be published from time to time.

No Title of Nobility shall be granted by the United States: And no Person holding any Office of Profit or Trust under them, shall, without the Consent of the Congress, accept of any present, Emolument, Office, or Title, of any kind whatever, from any King, Prince, or foreign State.

SECTION 10
[RESTRICTIONS UPON POWERS OF STATES]

No State shall enter into any Treaty, Alliance, or Confederation; grant Letters of Marque and Reprisal; coin Money; emit Bills of Credit; make any Thing but gold and silver Coin a Tender in Payment of Debts; pass any Bill of Attainder, ex post facto Law, or Law impairing the Obligation of Contracts, or grant any Title of Nobility.

No State shall, without the Consent of the Congress, lay any Imposts or Duties on Imports or Exports, except what may be absolutely necessary for executing its inspection Laws: and the net Produce of all Duties and Imposts, laid by any State on Imports or Exports, shall be for the Use of the Treasury of the United States; and all such Laws shall be subject to the Revision and Control of the Congress.

No State shall, without the Consent of Congress, lay any Duty of Tonnage, keep Troops, or Ships of War in time of Peace, enter into any Agreement or Compact with another State, or with a foreign Power, or engage in War, unless actually invaded, or in such imminent Danger as will not admit of delay.

Article II

SECTION 1
[EXECUTIVE POWER, ELECTION, QUALIFICATIONS OF THE PRESIDENT]

The executive Power shall be vested in a President of the United States of America. *He shall hold his Office during the Term of four Years, and, together with the Vice President, chosen for the same Term, be elected, as follows*[9]

Each State shall appoint, in such Manner as the Legislature thereof may direct, a Number of Electors, equal to the whole Number of Senators and Representatives to which the State may be entitled in the Congress: but no Senator or Representative, or Person holding an Office of Trust or Profit under the United States, shall be appointed an Elector.

The electors shall meet in their respective States, and vote by ballot for two Persons, of whom one at least shall not be an Inhabitant of the same State with themselves. And they shall make a List of all the Persons voted for, and of the Number of Votes for each; which List they shall sign and certify, and transmit sealed to the Seat of the Government of the United States, directed to the President of the Senate. The President of the Senate shall, in the Presence of the Senate and House of Representatives, open all the Certificates, and the Votes shall then be counted. The Person having the greatest Number of Votes shall be the President, if such Number be a Majority of the whole Number of Electors appointed; and if there be more than one who have such Majority, and have an equal Number of Votes, then the House of Representatives shall immediately chuse by Ballot one of them for President; and if no Person have a Majority, then from the five highest on the List the said House shall in like Manner chuse the President. But in chusing the President, the Votes shall be taken by States, the Representation from each State having one Vote; A quorum for this Purpose shall consist of a Member or Members from two thirds of the States, and a Majority of all the States shall be necessary to a Choice. In every Case, after the Choice of the President, the person having the greatest Number of Votes of the Electors shall be the Vice President. But if there should remain two or more who have equal Votes, the Senate shall chuse from them by Ballot the Vice President.[10]

The Congress may determine the Time of chusing the Electors, and the Day on which they shall give their Votes; which Day shall be the same throughout the United States.

No Person except a natural born Citizen, or a Citizen of the United States, at the time of the Adoption of this Constitution, shall be eligible to the Office of President; neither shall any Person be eligible to that Office who shall not have attained to the Age of thirty five Years, and been fourteen Years a Resident within the United States.

In Case of the Removal of the President from Office, or his Death, Resignation, or Inability to discharge the Powers and Duties of the said Office, the Same shall devolve on the Vice President, and the Congress may by Law provide for the Case of Removal, Death, Resignation or Inability, both of the President and Vice President, declaring what Officer shall then act as President, and such Officer shall act accordingly, until the Disability be removed, or a President shall be elected.

The President shall, at stated Times, receive for his Services, a Compensation, which shall neither be increased nor diminished during the Period for which he shall have been elected, and he shall not receive within that Period any other Emolument from the United States, or any of them.

Before he enter on the Execution of his Office, he shall take the following Oath or Affirmation:—"I do solemnly swear (or affirm) that I will faithfully execute the Office of President of the United States, and will to the best of my Ability, preserve, protect and defend the Constitution of the United States."

SECTION 2
[POWERS OF THE PRESIDENT]

The President shall be Commander in Chief of the Army and Navy of the United States, and of the Militia of the several States, when called into the actual Service of the United States; he may require the Opinion, in writing, of the principal Officer in each of the executive Departments, upon any Subject relating to the Duties of their respective Offices, and he shall have Power to grant Reprieves and Pardons for Offences against the United States, except in Cases of Impeachment.

He shall have Power, by and with the Advice and Consent of the Senate, to make Treaties, provided two thirds of the Senators present concur; and he shall nominate, and by and with the Advice

---

[8] Modified by Sixteenth Amendment.
[9] Number of terms limited to two by Twenty-second Amendment.
[10] Modified by the Twelfth and Twentieth Amendments.

and Consent of the Senate, shall appoint Ambassadors, other public Ministers and Consuls, Judges of the supreme Court, and all other Officers of the United States, whose Appointments are not herein otherwise provided for, and which shall be established by Law: but the Congress may by Law vest the Appointment of such inferior Officers, as they think proper, in the President alone, in the Courts of Law, or in the Heads of Departments.

The President shall have Power to fill up all Vacancies that may happen during the Recess of the Senate, by granting Commissions which shall expire at the End of their next Session.

SECTION 3
[POWERS AND DUTIES OF THE PRESIDENT]

He shall from time to time give to the Congress Information of the State of the Union, and recommend to their Consideration such Measures as he shall judge necessary and expedient; he may, on extraordinary Occasions, convene both Houses, or either of them, and in Case of Disagreement between them, with Respect to the Time of Adjournment, he may adjourn them to such Time as he shall think proper; he shall receive Ambassadors and other public Ministers; he shall take Care that the Laws be faithfully executed, and shall Commission all the Officers of the United States.

SECTION 4
[IMPEACHMENT]

The President, Vice President and all civil Officers of the United States, shall be removed from Office on Impeachment for, and Conviction of, Treason, Bribery, or other high Crimes and Misdemeanors.

Article III

SECTION 1
[JUDICIAL POWER, TENURE OF OFFICE]

The judicial Power of the United States, shall be vested in one supreme Court, and in such inferior Courts as the Congress may from time to time ordain and establish. The Judges, both of the supreme and inferior Courts, shall hold their Offices during good Behaviour, and shall, at stated Times, receive for their Services, a Compensation, which shall not be diminished during their Continuance in Office.

SECTION 2
[JURISDICTION]

The judicial Power shall extend to all Cases, in Law and Equity, arising under this Constitution, the Laws of the United States, and Treaties made, or which shall be made, under their Authority;—to all Cases affecting Ambassadors, other public Ministers and Consuls;—to all Cases of admiralty and maritime Jurisdiction;—to Controversies to which the United States shall be a Party;—to Controversies between two or more States;—*between a State and Citizens of another State;*—between Citizens of different States,—between Citizens of the same State claiming Lands under Grants of different States, *and between a State,* or the Citizens thereof, *and foreign States, Citizens or Subjects.*[11]

In all Cases affecting Ambassadors, other public Ministers and Consuls, and those in which a State shall be Party, the supreme Court shall have original Jurisdiction. In all the other Cases before mentioned, the supreme Court shall have appellate Jurisdiction, both as to Law and Fact, with such Exceptions, and under such Regulations as the Congress shall make.

The Trial of all Crimes, except in Cases of Impeachment, shall be by Jury; and such Trial shall be held in the State where the said Crimes shall have been committed; but when not committed within any State, the Trial shall be at such Place or Places as the Congress may by Law have directed.

SECTION 3
[TREASON, PROOF, AND PUNISHMENT]

Treason against the United States, shall consist only in levying War against them, or in adhering to their Enemies, giving them Aid and Comfort. No Person shall be convicted of Treason unless on the Testimony of two Witnesses to the same overt Act, or on Confession in open Court.

The Congress shall have Power to declare the Punishment of Treason, but no Attainder of Treason shall work Corruption of Blood, or Forfeiture except during the Life of the Person attainted.

Article IV

SECTION 1
[FAITH AND CREDIT AMONG STATES]

Full Faith and Credit shall be given in each State to the public Acts, Records, and judicial Proceedings of every other State. And the Congress may by general Laws prescribe the Manner in which such Acts, Records and Proceedings shall be proved, and the Effect thereof.

SECTION 2
[PRIVILEGES AND IMMUNITIES, FUGITIVES]

The Citizens of each State shall be entitled to all Privileges and Immunities of Citizens in the several States.

A Person charged in any State with Treason, Felony or other Crime, who shall flee from Justice, and be found in another State, shall on Demand of the executive Authority of the State from which he fled, be delivered up, to be removed to the State having Jurisdiction of the Crime.

No person held to Service or Labour in one State, under the Laws thereof, escaping into another, shall, in Consequence of any Law or Regulation therein, be discharged from such Service or Labour, but shall be delivered up on Claim of the Party to whom such Service or Labour may be due.[12]

SECTION 3
[ADMISSION OF NEW STATES]

New States may be admitted by the Congress into this Union; but no new State shall be formed or erected within the Jurisdiction of any other State; nor any State be formed by the Junction of two or more States, or Parts of States, without the Consent of the Legislatures of the States concerned as well as of the Congress.

The Congress shall have Power to dispose of and make all needful Rules and Regulations respecting the Territory or other Property belonging to the United States; and nothing in this Constitution shall be so construed as to Prejudice any Claims of the United States, or of any particular State.

---

[11] Modified by the Eleventh Amendment.

[12] Repealed by the Thirteenth Amendment.

SECTION 4
[GUARANTEE OF REPUBLICAN GOVERNMENT]

The United States shall guarantee to every State in this Union a Republican Form of Government, and shall protect each of them against Invasion; and on Application of the Legislature, or of the Executive (when the Legislature cannot be convened), against domestic Violence.

Article V
[AMENDMENT OF THE CONSTITUTION]

The Congress, whenever two thirds of both Houses shall deem it necessary, shall propose Amendments to this Constitution, or, on the Application of the Legislatures of two thirds of the several States, shall call a Convention for proposing Amendments, which, in either Case, shall be valid to all Intents and Purposes, as Part of this Constitution, when ratified by the Legislatures of three fourths of the several States, or by Conventions in three fourths thereof, as the one or the other Mode of Ratification may be proposed by the Congress; *Provided that no Amendment which may be made prior to the Year One thousand eight hundred and eight shall in any Manner affect the first and fourth Clauses in the Ninth Section of the first Article;* and that no State, without its Consent, shall be deprived of its equal Suffrage in the Senate.

Article VI
[DEBTS, SUPREMACY, OATH]

All Debts contracted and Engagements entered into, before the Adoption of this Constitution, shall be as valid against the United States under this Constitution, as under the Confederation.

This Constitution, and the Laws of the United States which shall be made in Pursuance thereof; and all Treaties made, or which shall be made, under the Authority of the United States, shall be the supreme Law of the Land; and the Judges in every State shall be bound thereby, any Thing in the Constitution or Laws of any State to the Contrary notwithstanding.

The Senators and Representatives before mentioned, and the Members of the several State Legislatures, and all executive and judicial Officers, both of the United States and of the several States, shall be bound by Oath or Affirmation, to support this Constitution; but no religious Test shall be required as a Qualification to any Office or public Trust under the United States.

Article VII
[RATIFICATION AND ESTABLISHMENT]

The Ratification of the Conventions of nine States, shall be sufficient for the Establishment of this Constitution between the States so ratifying the Same.

Done in Convention by the Unanimous Consent of the States present the Seventeenth Day of September in the Year of our Lord one thousand seven hundred and Eighty seven and of the Independence of the United States of America the Twelfth. *In Witness* whereof We have hereunto subscribed our Names,

G:° WASHINGTON—
Presidt. and deputy from Virginia

New Hampshire
John Langdon
Nicholas Gilman

Massachusetts
Nathaniel Gorham
Rufus King

Connecticut
Wm. Saml. Johnson
Roger Sherman

New York
Alexander Hamilton

New Jersey
Wil: Livingston
David Brearley
Wm. Paterson
Jona: Dayton

Pennsylvania
B Franklin
Thomas Mifflin
Robt. Morris
Geo. Clymer
Thos. FitzSimons
Jared Ingersoll
James Wilson
Gouv Morris

Delaware
Geo: Read
Gunning Bedford jun
John Dickinson
Richard Bassett
Jaco: Broom

Maryland
James McHenry
Dan of St Thos. Jenifer
Danl. Carroll

Virginia
John Blair—
James Madison Jr.

North Carolina
Wm. Blount
Richd. Dobbs Spaight
Hu Williamson

South Carolina
J. Rutledge
Charles Cotesworth
Pinckney
Charles Pinckney
Pierce Butler

Georgia
William Few
Abr Baldwin

Amendments to the Constitution

Proposed by Congress and Ratified by the Legislatures of the
Several States, Pursuant to Article V of the Original Constitution.

Amendments I–X, known as the Bill of Rights, were proposed by
Congress on September 25, 1789, and ratified on December 15, 1791.

Amendment I
[FREEDOM OF RELIGION, OF SPEECH, AND OF THE PRESS]

Congress shall make no law respecting an establishment of
religion, or prohibiting the free exercise thereof; or abridging
the freedom of speech, or of the press; or the right of the people
peaceably to assemble, and to petition the Government for a redress
of grievances.

Amendment II
[RIGHT TO KEEP AND BEAR ARMS]

A well regulated Militia, being necessary to the security of a free
State, the right of the people to keep and bear Arms, shall not be
infringed.

Amendment III
[QUARTERING OF SOLDIERS]

No Soldier shall, in time of peace be quartered in any house,
without the consent of the Owner, nor in time of war, but in a manner
to be prescribed by law.

Amendment IV
[SECURITY FROM UNWARRANTABLE SEARCH AND SEIZURE]

The right of the people to be secure in their persons, houses,
papers, and effects, against unreasonable searches and seizures,
shall not be violated, and no Warrants shall issue, but upon probable
cause, supported by Oath or affirmation, and particularly describing
the place to be searched, and the persons or things to be seized.

Amendment V
[RIGHTS OF ACCUSED PERSONS IN CRIMINAL PROCEEDINGS]

No person shall be held to answer for a capital, or otherwise
infamous crime, unless on a presentment or indictment of a Grand
Jury, except in cases arising in the land or naval forces, or in the
Militia, when in actual service in time of War or in public danger;
nor shall any person be subject for the same offence to be twice put
in jeopardy of life or limb; nor shall be compelled in any criminal
case to be a witness against himself, nor be deprived of life, liberty,
or property, without due process of law; nor shall private property be
taken for public use, without just compensation.

Amendment VI
[RIGHT TO SPEEDY TRIAL, WITNESSES, ETC.]

In all criminal prosecutions, the accused shall enjoy the right
to a speedy and public trial, by an impartial jury of the State and
district wherein the crime shall have been committed, which district
shall have been previously ascertained by law, and to be informed
of the nature and cause of the accusation; to be confronted with the
witnesses against him; to have compulsory process for obtaining
witnesses in his favor, and to have the Assistance of Counsel for his
defence.

Amendment VII
[TRIAL BY JURY IN CIVIL CASES]

In suits at common law, where the value in controversy shall
exceed twenty dollars, the right of trial by jury shall be preserved,
and no fact tried by a jury, shall be otherwise reexamined in any
Court of the United States, than according to the rules of the
common law.

Amendment VIII
[BAILS, FINES, PUNISHMENTS]

Excessive bail shall not be required, nor excessive fines imposed,
nor cruel and unusual punishments inflicted.

Amendment IX
[RESERVATION OF RIGHTS OF PEOPLE]

The enumeration in the Constitution, of certain rights, shall not
be construed to deny or disparage others retained by the people.

Amendment X
[POWERS RESERVED TO STATES OR PEOPLE]

The powers not delegated to the United States by the
Constitution, nor prohibited by it to the States, are reserved to the
States respectively, or to the people.

Amendment XI
[*Proposed by Congress on March 4, 1794; declared ratified on January 8, 1798.*]
[RESTRICTION OF JUDICIAL POWER]

The Judicial power of the United States shall not be construed to
extend to any suit in law or equity, commenced or prosecuted against
one of the United States by Citizens of another State, or by Citizens or
Subjects of any Foreign State.

Amendment XII
[*Proposed by Congress on December 9, 1803; declared ratified on September 25, 1804.*]
[ELECTION OF PRESIDENT AND VICE PRESIDENT]

The Electors shall meet in their respective states and vote by
ballot for President and Vice-President, one of whom, at least,

shall not be an inhabitant of the same state with themselves; they shall name in their ballots the person voted for as President, and in distinct ballots the person voted for as Vice-President, and they shall make distinct lists of all persons voted for as President, and of all persons voted for as Vice-President, and of the number of votes for each, which lists they shall sign and certify, and transmit sealed to the seat of the government of the United States, directed to the President of the Senate;—the President of the Senate shall, in presence of the Senate and House of Representatives, open all the certificates and the votes shall then be counted;—The person having the greatest number of votes for President, shall be the President, if such number be a majority of the whole number of Electors appointed; and if no person have such majority, then from the persons having the highest numbers not exceeding three on the list of those voted for as President, the House of Representatives shall choose immediately, by ballot, the President. But in choosing the President, the votes shall be taken by states, the representation from each state having one vote; a quorum for this purpose shall consist of a member or members from two-thirds of the states, and a majority of all the states shall be necessary to a choice. And if the House of Representatives shall not choose a President whenever the right of choice shall devolve upon them, before the fourth day of March next following, then the Vice-President shall act as President, as in the case of the death or other constitutional disability of the President.—The person having the greatest number of votes as Vice-President, shall be the Vice-President, if such number be a majority of the whole number of Electors appointed, and if no person have a majority, then from the two highest numbers on the list, the Senate shall choose the Vice-President; a quorum for the purpose shall consist of two-thirds of the whole number of Senators, and a majority of the whole number shall be necessary to a choice. But no person constitutionally ineligible to the office of President shall be eligible to that of Vice-President of the United States.

Amendment XIII

[*Proposed by Congress on January 31, 1865; declared ratified on December 18, 1865.*]

SECTION 1
[ABOLITION OF SLAVERY]

Neither slavery nor involuntary servitude, except as a punishment for crime whereof the party shall have been duly convicted, shall exist within the United States, or any place subject to their jurisdiction.

SECTION 2
[POWER TO ENFORCE THIS ARTICLE]

Congress shall have power to enforce this article by appropriate legislation.

Amendment XIV

[*Proposed by Congress on June 13, 1866; declared ratified on July 28, 1868.*]

SECTION 1
[CITIZENSHIP RIGHTS NOT TO BE ABRIDGED BY STATES]

All persons born or naturalized in the United States, and subject to the jurisdiction thereof, are citizens of the United States and of the State wherein they reside. No State shall make or enforce any law which shall abridge the privileges or immunities of citizens of the United States; nor shall any State deprive any person of life, liberty, or property, without due process of law; nor deny to any person within its jurisdiction the equal protection of the laws.

SECTION 2
[APPORTIONMENT OF REPRESENTATIVES IN CONGRESS]

Representatives shall be apportioned among the several States according to their respective numbers, counting the whole number of persons in each State, excluding Indians not taxed. But when the right to vote at any election for the choice of electors for President and Vice-President of the United States, Representatives in Congress, the Executive and Judicial officers of a State, or the members of the Legislature thereof, is denied to any of the male inhabitants of such State, being twenty-one years of age, and citizens of the United States, or in any way abridged, except for participation in rebellion, or other crime, the basis of representation therein shall be reduced in the proportion which the number of such male citizens shall bear to the whole number of male citizens twenty-one years of age in such State.

SECTION 3
[PERSONS DISQUALIFIED FROM HOLDING OFFICE]

No person shall be a Senator or Representative in Congress, or elector of President and Vice-President, or hold any office, civil or military, under the United States, or under any State, who, having previously taken an oath, as a member of Congress, or as an officer of the United States, or as a member of any State legislature, or as an executive or judicial officer of any State, to support the Constitution of the United States, shall have engaged in insurrection or rebellion against the same, or given aid or comfort to the enemies thereof. But Congress may by a vote of two-thirds of each House, remove such disability.

SECTION 4
[WHAT PUBLIC DEBTS ARE VALID]

The validity of the public debt of the United States, authorized by law, including debts incurred for payment of pensions and bounties for services in suppressing insurrection or rebellion, shall not be questioned. But neither the United States nor any State shall assume or pay any debt or obligation incurred in aid of insurrection or rebellion against the United States, or any claim for the loss or emancipation of any slave; but all such debts, obligations and claims shall be held illegal and void.

SECTION 5
[POWER TO ENFORCE THIS ARTICLE]

The Congress shall have power to enforce, by appropriate legislation, the provisions of this article.

Amendment XV

[*Proposed by Congress on February 26, 1869; declared ratified on March 30, 1870.*]

SECTION 1
[NEGRO SUFFRAGE]

The right of citizens of the United States to vote shall not be denied or abridged by the United States or by any State on account of race, color, or previous condition of servitude.

SECTION 2
[POWER TO ENFORCE THIS ARTICLE]

The Congress shall have power to enforce this article by appropriate legislation.

Amendment XVI

[Proposed by Congress on July 2, 1909; declared ratified on February 25, 1913.]
[AUTHORIZING INCOME TAXES]

The Congress shall have power to lay and collect taxes on incomes, from whatever source derived, without apportionment among the several States, and without regard to any census or enumeration.

Amendment XVII

[Proposed by Congress on May 13, 1912; declared ratified on May 31, 1913.]
[POPULAR ELECTION OF SENATORS]

The Senate of the United States shall be composed of two Senators from each State, elected by the people thereof, for six years; and each Senator shall have one vote. The electors in each State shall have the qualifications requisite for electors of the most numerous branch of the State legislatures.

When vacancies happen in the representation of any State in the Senate, the executive authority of such State shall issue writs of election to fill such vacancies: *Provided,* That the legislature of any State may empower the executive thereof to make temporary appointments until the people fill the vacancies by election as the legislature may direct.

This amendment shall not be so construed as to affect the election or term of any Senator chosen before it becomes valid as part of the Constitution.

Amendment XVIII

[Proposed by Congress December 18, 1917; declared ratified on January 29, 1919.]

SECTION 1
[NATIONAL LIQUOR PROHIBITION]

After one year from the ratification of this article the manufacture, sale, or transportation of intoxicating liquors within, the importation thereof into, or the exportation thereof from the United States and all territory subject to the jurisdiction thereof for beverage purposes is hereby prohibited.

SECTION 2
[POWER TO ENFORCE THIS ARTICLE]

The Congress and the several States shall have concurrent power to enforce this article by appropriate legislation.

SECTION 3
[RATIFICATION WITHIN SEVEN YEARS]

This article shall be inoperative unless it shall have been ratified as an amendment to the Constitution by the legislatures of the several States, as provided in the Constitution, within seven years from the date of the submission hereof to the States by the Congress.[1]

Amendment XIX

[Proposed by Congress on June 4, 1919; declared ratified on August 26, 1920.]

---

[1] Repealed by the Twenty-first Amendment.

[WOMAN SUFFRAGE]

The right of citizens of the United States to vote shall not be denied or abridged by the United States or by any State on account of sex.

Congress shall have power to enforce this article by appropriate legislation.

Amendment XX

[Proposed by Congress on March 2, 1932; declared ratified on February 6, 1933.]

SECTION 1
[TERMS OF OFFICE]

The terms of the President and Vice President shall end at noon on the 20th day of January, and the terms of Senators and Representatives at noon on the 3d day of January, of the years in which such terms would have ended if this article had not been ratified; and the terms of their successors shall then begin.

SECTION 2
[TIME OF CONVENING CONGRESS]

The Congress shall assemble at least once in every year, and such meeting shall begin at noon on the 3d day of January, unless they shall by law appoint a different day.

SECTION 3
[DEATH OF PRESIDENT-ELECT]

If, at the time fixed for the beginning of the term of the President, the President elect shall have died, the Vice President elect shall become President. If a President shall not have been chosen before the time fixed for the beginning of his term, or if the President elect shall have failed to qualify, then the Vice President elect shall act as President until a President shall have qualified; and the Congress may by law provide for the case wherein neither a President elect nor a Vice President elect shall have qualified, declaring who shall then act as President, or the manner in which one who is to act shall be selected, and such person shall act accordingly until a President or Vice President shall have qualified.

SECTION 4
[ELECTION OF THE PRESIDENT]

The Congress may by law provide for the case of the death of any of the persons from whom the House of Representatives may choose a President whenever the right of choice shall have devolved upon them, and for the case of the death of any of the persons from whom the Senate may choose a Vice President whenever the right of choice shall have devolved upon them.

SECTION 5
[AMENDMENT TAKES EFFECT]

Sections 1 and 2 shall take effect on the 15th day of October following the ratification of this article.

SECTION 6
[RATIFICATION WITHIN SEVEN YEARS]

This article shall be inoperative unless it shall have been ratified as an amendment to the Constitution by the legislatures of three-fourths of the several States within seven years from the date of its submission.

Amendment XXI

[*Proposed by Congress on February 20, 1933; declared ratified on December 5, 1933.*]

SECTION 1
[NATIONAL LIQUOR PROHIBITION REPEALED]

The eighteenth article of amendment to the Constitution of the United States is hereby repealed.

SECTION 2
[TRANSPORTATION OF LIQUOR INTO "DRY" STATES]

The transportation or importation into any State, Territory, or Possession of the United States for delivery or use therein of intoxicating liquors, in violation of the laws thereof, is hereby prohibited.

SECTION 3
[RATIFICATION WITHIN SEVEN YEARS]

This article shall be inoperative unless it shall have been ratified as an amendment to the Constitution by conventions in the several States, as provided in the Constitution, within seven years from the date of the submission hereof to the States by the Congress.

Amendment XXII

[*Proposed by Congress on March 21, 1947; declared ratified on February 27, 1951.*]

SECTION 1
[TENURE OF PRESIDENT LIMITED]

No person shall be elected to the office of President more than twice, and no person who has held the office of President or acted as President, for more than two years of a term to which some other person was elected President shall be elected to the office of the President more than once. But this Article shall not apply to any person holding the office of President when this Article was proposed by the Congress, and shall not prevent any person who may be holding the office of President, or acting as President, during the term within which this Article becomes operative from holding the office of President or acting as President during the remainder of such term.

SECTION 2
[RATIFICATION WITHIN SEVEN YEARS]

This article shall be inoperative unless it shall have been ratified as an amendment to the Constitution by the legislatures of three-fourths of the several States within seven years from the date of its submission to the States by the Congress.

Amendment XXIII

[*Proposed by Congress on June 16, 1960; declared ratified on March 29, 1961.*]

SECTION 1
[ELECTORAL COLLEGE VOTES FOR THE DISTRICT OF COLUMBIA]

The District constituting the seat of Government of the United States shall appoint in such manner as the Congress may direct:

A number of electors of President and Vice President equal to the whole number of Senators and Representatives in Congress to which the District would be entitled if it were a State, but in no event more than the least populous State; they shall be in addition to those appointed by the States, but they shall be considered, for the purposes of the election of President and Vice President, to be electors appointed by a State; and they shall meet in the District and perform such duties as provided by the twelfth article of amendment.

SECTION 2
[POWER TO ENFORCE THIS ARTICLE]

The Congress shall have power to enforce this article by appropriate legislation.

Amendment XXIV

[*Proposed by Congress on August 27, 1962; declared ratified on January 23, 1964.*]

SECTION 1
[ANTI-POLL TAX]

The right of citizens of the United States to vote in any primary or other election for President or Vice President, for electors for President or Vice President, or for Senator or Representative of Congress, shall not be denied or abridged by the United States or any State by reason of failure to pay any poll tax or other tax.

SECTION 2
[POWER TO ENFORCE THIS ARTICLE]

The Congress shall have power to enforce this article by appropriate legislation.

Amendment XXV

[*Proposed by Congress on July 6, 1965; declared ratified on February 10, 1967.*]

SECTION 1
[VICE PRESIDENT TO BECOME PRESIDENT]

In case of the removal of the President from office or his death or resignation, the Vice President shall become President.

SECTION 2
[CHOICE OF A NEW VICE PRESIDENT]

Whenever there is a vacancy in the office of the Vice President, the President shall nominate a Vice President who shall take the office upon confirmation by a majority vote of both houses of Congress.

SECTION 3
[PRESIDENT MAY DECLARE OWN DISABILITY]

Whenever the President transmits to the President pro tempore of the Senate and the Speaker of the House of Representatives his written declaration that he is unable to discharge the powers and duties of his office, and until he transmits to them a written declaration to the contrary, such powers and duties shall be discharged by the Vice President as Acting President.

SECTION 4
[ALTERNATE PROCEDURES TO DECLARE AND TO END PRESIDENTIAL DISABILITY]

Whenever the Vice President and a majority of either the principal officers of the executive departments, or of such other body as Congress may by law provide, transmit to the President pro tempore of the Senate and the Speaker of the House of Representatives their written declaration that the President is unable to discharge the powers and duties of his office, the Vice President shall immediately assume the powers and duties of the office as Acting President.

Thereafter, when the President transmits to the President pro tempore of the Senate and the Speaker of the House of Representatives his written declaration that no inability exists, he shall resume the powers and duties of his office unless the Vice President and a majority of either the principal officers of the executive department, or of such other body as Congress may by law provide, transmit within four days to the President pro tempore of the Senate and the Speaker of the House of Representatives their written declaration that the President is unable to discharge the powers and duties of his office. Thereupon Congress shall decide the issue, assembling within forty eight hours for that purpose if not in session. If the Congress, within twenty one days after receipt of the latter written declaration, or, if Congress is not in session, within twenty one days after Congress is required to assemble, determines by two-thirds vote of both Houses that the President is unable to discharge the powers and duties of his office, the Vice President shall continue to discharge the same as Acting President; otherwise, the President shall resume the powers and duties of his office.

Amendment XXVI

[Proposed by Congress on March 23, 1971; declared ratified on July 1, 1971.]

SECTION 1
[EIGHTEEN-YEAR-OLD VOTE]

The right of citizens of the United States, who are eighteen years of age or older, to vote shall not be denied or abridged by the United States or by any State on account of age.

SECTION 2
[POWER TO ENFORCE THIS ARTICLE]

The Congress shall have power to enforce this article by appropriate legislation.

Amendment XXVII

[Proposed by Congress on September 25, 1789; declared ratified on May 8, 1992.]
[CONGRESS CANNOT RAISE ITS OWN PAY]

No law varying the compensation for the services of the Senators and Representatives, shall take effect, until an election of representatives shall have intervened.

The Federalist Papers

No. 10: Madison

Among the numerous advantages promised by a well constructed Union, none deserves to be more accurately developed than its tendency to break and control the violence of faction. The friend of popular governments never finds himself so much alarmed for their character and fate, as when he contemplates their propensity to this dangerous vice. He will not fail therefore to set a due value on any plan which, without violating the principles to which he is attached, provides a proper cure for it. The instability, injustice, and confusion introduced into the public councils have, in truth, been the mortal diseases under which popular governments have everywhere perished, as they continue to be the favorite and fruitful topics from which the adversaries to liberty derive their most specious declamations. The valuable improvements made by the American constitutions on the popular models, both ancient and modern, cannot certainly be too much admired; but it would be an unwarrantable partiality to contend that they have as effectually obviated the danger on this side, as was wished and expected. Complaints are everywhere heard from our most considerate and virtuous citizens, equally the friends of public and private faith and of public and personal liberty, that our governments are too unstable, that the public good is disregarded in the conflicts of rival parties, and that measures are too often decided, not according to the rules of justice and the rights of the minor party, but by the superior force of an interested and overbearing majority. However anxiously we may wish that these complaints had no foundation, the evidence of known facts will not permit us to deny that they are in some degree true. It will be found, indeed, on a candid review of our situation, that some of the distresses under which we labor have been erroneously charged on the operation of our governments; but it will be found, at the same time, that other causes will not alone account for many of our heaviest misfortunes; and, particularly, for that prevailing and increasing distrust of public engagements and alarm for private rights which are echoed from one end of the continent to the other. These must be chiefly, if not wholly, effects of the unsteadiness and injustice with which a factious spirit has tainted our public administration.

By a faction I understand a number of citizens, whether amounting to a majority or minority of the whole, who are united and actuated by some common impulse of passion, or of interest, adverse to the rights of other citizens, or to the permanent and aggregate interests of the community.

There are two methods of curing the mischiefs of faction: the one, by removing its causes; the other, by controlling its effects.

There are again two methods of removing the causes of faction: the one, by destroying the liberty which is essential to its existence; the other, by giving to every citizen the same opinions, the same passions, and the same interests.

It could never be more truly said than of the first remedy, that it is worse than the disease. Liberty is to faction what air is to fire, an aliment without which it instantly expires. But it could not be a less folly to abolish liberty, which is essential to political life, because it nourishes faction, than it would be to wish the annihilation of air, which is essential to animal life, because it imparts to fire its destructive agency.

The second expedient is as impracticable, as the first would be unwise. As long as the reason of man continues fallible, and he is at liberty to exercise it, different opinions will be formed. As long as the connection subsists between his reason and his self-love, his opinions and his passions will have a reciprocal influence on each other; and the former will be objects to which the latter will attach themselves. The diversity in the faculties of men, from which the rights of property originate, is not less an insuperable obstacle to a uniformity of interests. The protection of these faculties is the first object of Government. From the protection of different and unequal faculties of acquiring property, the possession of different degrees and kinds of property immediately results; and from the influence of these on the sentiments and views of the respective proprietors, ensues a division of the society into different interests and parties.

The latent causes of faction are thus sown in the nature of man; and we see them everywhere brought into different degrees of activity, according to the different circumstances of civil society. A zeal for different opinions concerning religion, concerning Government, and many other points, as well of speculation as of practice; an attachment to different leaders ambitiously contending for pre-eminence and power; or to persons of other descriptions whose fortunes have been interesting to the human passions, have in turn divided mankind into parties, inflamed them with mutual animosity, and rendered them much more disposed to vex and oppress each other, than to co-operate for their common good. So strong is this propensity of mankind to fall into mutual animosities, that where no substantial occasion presents itself, the most frivolous and fanciful distinctions have been sufficient to kindle their unfriendly passions, and excite their most violent conflicts. But the most common and durable source of factions has been the various and unequal distribution of property. Those who hold and those who are without property have ever formed distinct interests in society. Those who are creditors, and those who are debtors, fall under a like discrimination. A landed interest, a manufacturing interest, a mercantile interest, a moneyed interest, with many lesser interests, grow up of necessity in civilized nations, and divide them into different classes, actuated by different sentiments and views. The regulation of these various and interfering interests forms the principal task of modern Legislation, and involves the spirit of party and faction in the necessary and ordinary operations of Government.

No man is allowed to be judge in his own cause, because his interest would certainly bias his judgment and, not improbably, corrupt his integrity. With equal, nay with greater reason, a body of men are unfit to be both judges and parties at the same time; yet what are many of the most important acts of legislation but so many judicial determinations, not indeed concerning the rights of single persons, but concerning the rights of large bodies of citizens; and what are the different classes of legislators but advocates and parties to the causes which they determine? Is a law proposed concerning private debts? It is a question to which the creditors are parties on one side and the debtors on the other. Justice ought to hold the balance between them. Yet the parties are, and must be, themselves the judges; and the most numerous party, or in other words, the most powerful faction must be expected to prevail. Shall domestic manufacturers be encouraged, and in what degree, by restrictions on foreign manufacturers? are questions which would be differently decided by the landed and the manufacturing classes, and probably by neither with a sole regard to justice and the public good. The apportionment of taxes on the various descriptions of property is an act which seems to require the most exact impartiality; yet there is, perhaps, no legislative act in which greater opportunity and temptation are given to a predominant party to trample on the rules of justice. Every shilling with which they overburden the inferior number is a shilling saved to their own pockets.

It is in vain to say that enlightened statesmen will be able to adjust these clashing interests and render them all subservient to the public good. Enlightened statesmen will not always be at the helm. Nor, in many cases, can such an adjustment be made at all without taking into view indirect and remote considerations, which will rarely prevail over the immediate interest which one party may find in disregarding the rights of another or the good of the whole.

The inference to which we are brought is that the *causes* of faction cannot be removed and that relief is only to be sought in the means of controlling its *effects*.

If a faction consists of less than a majority, relief is supplied by the republican principle, which enables the majority to defeat its sinister views by regular vote. It may clog the administration, it may convulse the society; but it will be unable to execute and mask its violence under the forms of the Constitution. When a majority is included in a faction, the form of popular government, on the other hand, enables it to sacrifice to its ruling passion or interest both the public good and the rights of other citizens. To secure the public good and private rights against the danger of such a faction, and at the same time to preserve the spirit and the form of popular government, is then the great object to which our enquiries are directed. Let me add that it is the great desideratum by which alone this form of government can be rescued from the opprobrium under which it has so long labored and be recommended to the esteem and adoption of mankind.

By what means is this object attainable? Evidently by one of two only. Either the existence of the same passion or interest in a majority at the same time must be prevented, or the majority, having such co-existent passion or interest, must be rendered, by their number and local situation, unable to concert and carry into effect schemes of oppression. If the impulse and the opportunity be suffered to coincide, we well know that neither moral nor religious motives can be relied on as an adequate control. They are not found to be such on the injustice and violence of individuals, and lose their efficacy in proportion to the number combined together, that is, in proportion as their efficacy becomes needful.

From this view of the subject it may be concluded that a pure Democracy, by which I mean a Society consisting of a small number of citizens, who assemble and administer the Government in person, can admit of no cure for the mischiefs of faction. A common passion or interest will, in almost every case, be felt by a majority of the whole; a communication and concert results from the form of Government itself; and there is nothing to check the inducements to sacrifice the weaker party or an obnoxious individual. Hence it is that such Democracies have ever been spectacles of turbulence and contention; have ever been found incompatible with personal security or the rights of property; and have in general been as short in their lives as they have been violent in their deaths. Theoretic politicians, who have patronized this species of Government, have erroneously supposed that by reducing mankind to a perfect equality in their political rights, they would at the same time be perfectly equalized and assimilated in their possessions, their opinions, and their passions.

A Republic, by which I mean a Government in which the scheme of representation takes place, opens a different prospect and promises the cure for which we are seeking. Let us examine the points in which it varies from pure Democracy, and we shall comprehend both the nature of the cure and the efficacy which it must derive from the Union.

The two great points of difference between a Democracy and a Republic are: first, the delegation of the Government, in the latter, to a small number of citizens elected by the rest; secondly, the greater number of citizens and greater sphere of country over which the latter may be extended.

The effect of the first difference is, on the one hand, to refine and enlarge the public views by passing them through the medium of a chosen body of citizens, whose wisdom may best discern the true interest of their country and whose patriotism and love of justice will be least likely to sacrifice it to temporary or partial considerations. Under such a regulation it may well happen that the public voice, pronounced by the representatives of the people, will be more consonant to the public good than if pronounced by the people themselves, convened for the purpose. On the other hand, the effect may be inverted. Men of factious tempers, of local prejudices, or of sinister designs, may, by intrigue, by corruption, or by other means, first obtain the suffrages, and then betray the interests of the people. The question resulting is, whether small or extensive Republics are most favorable to the election of proper guardians of the public weal; and it is clearly decided in favor of the latter by two obvious considerations.

In the first place it is to be remarked that however small the Republic may be, the Representatives must be raised to a certain number in order to guard against the cabals of a few; and that however large it may be they must be limited to a certain number in order to guard against the confusion of a multitude. Hence, the number of Representatives in the two cases not being in proportion to that of the Constituents, and being proportionally greatest in the small Republic, it follows that if the proportion of fit characters be not less in the large than in the small Republic, the former will present a greater option, and consequently a greater probability of a fit choice.

In the next place, as each Representative will be chosen by a greater number of citizens in the large than in the small Republic, it will be more difficult for unworthy candidates to practise with success the vicious arts by which elections are too often carried; and the suffrages of the people being more free, will be more likely to centre on men who possess the most attractive merit and the most diffusive and established characters.

It must be confessed that in this, as in most other cases, there is a mean, on both sides of which inconveniencies will be found to lie. By enlarging too much the number of electors, you render the representative too little acquainted with all their local circumstances and lesser interests; as by reducing it too much, you render him unduly attached to these, and too little fit to comprehend and pursue great and national objects. The Federal Constitution forms a happy combination in this respect; the great and aggregate interests being referred to the national, the local and particular to the State legislatures.

The other point of difference is the greater number of citizens and extent of territory which may be brought within the compass of Republican than of Democratic Government; and it is this circumstance principally which renders factious combinations less to be dreaded in the former than in the latter. The smaller the society, the fewer probably will be the distinct parties and interests composing it; the fewer the distinct parties and interests, the more frequently will a majority be found of the same party; and the smaller the number of individuals composing a majority, and the smaller the compass within which they are placed, the more easily will they concert and execute their plans of oppression. Extend the sphere and you take in a greater variety of parties and interests; you make it less probable that a majority of the whole will have a common motive to invade the rights of other citizens; or if such a common motive exists, it will be more difficult for all who feel it to discover their own strength and to act in unison with each other. Besides other impediments, it may be remarked, that where there is a consciousness of unjust or dishonorable purposes, communication is always checked by distrust in proportion to the number whose concurrence is necessary.

Hence, it clearly appears that the same advantage which a Republic has over a Democracy in controlling the effects of faction is enjoyed by a large over a small republic—is enjoyed by the Union over the States composing it. Does this advantage consist in the substitution of representatives whose enlightened views and virtuous sentiments render them superior to local prejudices and to schemes of injustice? It will not be denied that the representation of the Union will be most likely to possess these requisite endowments. Does it consist in the greater security afforded by a greater variety of parties, against the event of any one party being able to outnumber and oppress the rest? In an equal degree does the increased variety of parties comprised within the Union increase this security? Does it, in fine, consist in the greater obstacles opposed to the concert and accomplishment of the secret wishes of an unjust and interested majority? Here again the extent of the Union gives it the most palpable advantage.

The influence of factious leaders may kindle a flame within their particular States but will be unable to spread a general conflagration through the other States: a religious sect may degenerate into a political faction in a part of the Confederacy; but the variety of sects dispersed over the entire face of it must secure the national Councils against any danger from that source: a rage for paper money, for an abolition of debts, for an equal division of property, or for any other improper or wicked project, will be less apt to pervade the whole body of the Union than a particular member of it; in the same proportion as such a malady is more likely to taint a particular county or district than an entire State.

In the extent and proper structure of the Union, therefore, we behold a republican remedy for the diseases most incident to Republican Government. And according to the degree of pleasure and pride we feel in being republicans ought to be our zeal in cherishing the spirit and supporting the character of federalist.

PUBLIUS

No. 51: Madison

To what expedient, then, shall we finally resort, for maintaining in practice the necessary partition of power among the several departments as laid down in the constitution? The only answer that can be given is that as all these exterior provisions are found to be inadequate the defect must be supplied, by so contriving the interior structure of the government as that its several constituent parts may, by their mutual relations, be the means of keeping each other in their proper places. Without presuming to undertake a full development of this important idea I will hazard a few general observations which may perhaps place it in a clearer light, and enable us to form a more correct judgment of the principles and structure of the government planned by the convention.

In order to lay a due foundation for that separate and distinct exercise of the different powers of government, which to a certain extent is admitted on all hands to be essential to the preservation of liberty, it is evident that each department should have a will of its own; and consequently should be so constituted that the members of each should have as little agency as possible in the appointment of the members of the others. Were this principle rigorously adhered to, it would require that all the appointments for the supreme executive, legislative, and judiciary magistracies should be drawn from the same fountain of authority, the people, through channels having no communication whatever with one another. Perhaps such a plan of constructing the several departments would be less difficult in practice than it may in contemplation appear. Some difficulties, however, and some additional expense would attend the execution of it. Some deviations, therefore, from the principle must be admitted. In the constitution of the judiciary department in particular, it might be inexpedient to insist rigorously on the principle: first, because peculiar qualifications being essential in the members, the primary consideration ought to be to select that mode of choice which best secures these qualifications; second, because the permanent tenure by which the appointments are held in that department must soon destroy all sense of dependence on the authority conferring them.

It is equally evident that the members of each department should be as little dependent as possible on those of the others for the emoluments annexed to their offices. Were the executive magistrate, or the judges, not independent of the legislature in this particular, their independence in every other would be merely nominal.

But the great security against a gradual concentration of the several powers in the same department consists in giving to those who administer each department the necessary constitutional means and personal motives to resist encroachments of the others. The provision for defence must in this, as in all other cases, be made commensurate to the danger of attack. Ambition must be made to counteract ambition. The interest of the man must be connected with the constitutional rights of the place. It may be a reflection on human nature that such devices should be necessary to control the abuses of government. But what is government itself but the greatest of all reflections on human nature? If men were angels, no government would be necessary. If angels were to govern men, neither external nor internal controls on government would be necessary. In framing a government which is to be administered by men over men, the great difficulty lies in this: You must first enable the government to control the governed; and in the next place oblige it to control itself. A dependence on the people is, no doubt, the primary control on the government; but experience has taught mankind the necessity of auxiliary precautions.

This policy of supplying, by opposite and rival interests, the defect of better motives, might be traced through the whole system of human affairs, private as well as public. We see it particularly displayed in all the subordinate distributions of power, where the constant aim is to divide and arrange the several offices in such a manner as that each may be a check on the other; that the private interest of every individual may be a sentinel over the public rights. These inventions of prudence cannot be less requisite in the distribution of the supreme powers of the State.

But it is not possible to give to each department an equal power of self-defense. In republican government, the legislative authority necessarily predominates. The remedy for this inconveniency is to divide the legislature into different branches; and to render them, by different modes of election and different principles of action, as little connected with each other as the nature of their common functions and their common dependence on the society will admit. It may even be necessary to guard against dangerous encroachments by still further precautions. As the weight of the legislative authority requires that it should be thus divided, the weakness of the executive may require, on the other hand, that it should be fortified. An absolute negative on the legislature appears, at first view, to be the natural defense with which the executive magistrate should be armed. But perhaps it would be neither altogether safe nor alone sufficient. On ordinary occasions it might not be exerted with the requisite firmness, and on extraordinary occasions it might be perfidiously abused. May not this defect of an absolute negative be supplied by some qualified connection between this weaker branch of the stronger department, by which the latter may be led to support the constitutional rights of the former, without being too much detached from the rights of its own department?

If the principles on which these observations are founded be just, as I persuade myself they are, and they be applied as a criterion to the several State constitutions, and to the federal Constitution, it will be found that if the latter does not perfectly correspond with them, the former are infinitely less able to bear such a test.

There are, moreover, two considerations particularly applicable to the federal system of America, which place that system in a very interesting point of view.

First. In a single republic, all the power surrendered by the people is submitted to the administration of a single government; and usurpations are guarded against by a division of the government into distinct and separate departments. In the compound republic of America, the power surrendered by the people is first divided between two distinct governments, and then the portion allotted to each subdivided among distinct and separate departments. Hence a double security arises to the rights of the people. The different governments will control each other, at the same time that each will be controlled by itself.

Second. It is of great importance in a republic not only to guard the society against the oppression of its rulers, but to guard one part of the society against the injustice of the other part. Different interests necessarily exist in different classes of citizens. If a majority be united by a common interest, the rights of the minority will be insecure. There are but two methods of providing against this evil: The one by creating a will in the community independent of the majority—that is, of the society itself; the other, by comprehending in the society so many separate descriptions of citizens as will render an unjust combination of a majority of the whole very improbable, if not impracticable. The first method prevails in all governments possessing an hereditary or self-appointed authority. This, at best, is but a precarious security; because a power independent of the society may as well espouse the unjust views of the major as the rightful interests of the minor party, and may possibly be turned against both parties. The second method will be exemplified in the federal republic of the United States. Whilst all authority in it will be derived from and dependent on the society, the society itself will be broken into so many parts, interests and classes of citizens, that the rights of individuals, or of the minority, will be in little danger from interested combinations of the majority. In a free government the security for civil rights must be the same as that for religious rights. It consists in the one case in the multiplicity of interests, and in the other in the multiplicity of sects. The degree of security in both cases will depend on the number of interests and sects; and this may be presumed to depend on the extent of country and number of people comprehended under the same government. This view of the subject must particularly recommend a proper federal system to all the sincere and considerate friends of republican government: Since it shows that in exact proportion as the territory of the Union may be formed into more circumscribed Confederacies, or States, oppressive combinations of a majority will be facilitated; the best security, under the republican form, for the rights of every class of citizens, will be diminished; and consequently the stability and independence of some member of the government, the only other security, must be proportionally increased. Justice is the end of government. It is the end of civil society. It ever has been and ever will be pursued until it be obtained, or until liberty be lost in the pursuit. In a society under the forms of which the stronger faction can readily unite and oppress the weaker, anarchy may as truly be said to reign as in a state of nature, where the weaker individual is not secured against the violence of the stronger: And as, in the latter state, even the stronger individuals are prompted, by the uncertainty of their condition, to submit to a government which may protect the weak as well as themselves: So, in the former state, will the more powerful factions or parties be gradually induced, by a like motive, to wish for a government which will protect all parties, the weaker as well as the more powerful. It can be little doubted that if the State of Rhode Island was separated from the Confederacy and left to itself, the insecurity of rights under the popular form of government within such narrow limits would be displayed by such reiterated oppressions of factious majorities that some power altogether independent of the people would soon be called for by the voice of the very factions whose misrule had proved the necessity of it. In the extended republic of the United States, and among the great variety of interests, parties, and sects which it embraces, a coalition of a majority of the whole society could seldom take place on any other principles than those of justice and the general good; and there being thus less danger to a minor from the will of the major party, there must be less pretext, also, to provide for the security of the former, by introducing into the government a will not dependent on the latter, or, in other words, a will independent of the society itself. It is no less certain than it is important, notwithstanding the contrary opinions which have been entertained, that the larger the society, provided it lie within a practicable sphere, the more duly capable it will be of self-government. And happily for the *republican cause,* practicable sphere may be carried to a very great extent by a judicious modification and mixture of the *federal principle.*

PUBLIUS

No. 78: Hamilton

To the People of the State of New York:

we proceed now to an examination of the judiciary department of the proposed government.

In unfolding the defects of the existing Confederation, the utility and necessity of a federal judicature have been clearly pointed out. It is the less necessary to recapitulate the considerations there urged, as the propriety of the institution in the abstract is not disputed; the only questions which have been raised being relative to the manner of constituting it, and to its extent. To these points, therefore, our observations shall be confined.

The manner of constituting it seems to embrace these several objects: 1st. The mode of appointing the judges. 2d. The tenure by which they are to hold their places. 3d. The partition of the judiciary authority between different courts, and their relations to each other.

First. As to the mode of appointing the judges; this is the same with that of appointing the officers of the Union in general, and has been so fully discussed in the two last numbers, that nothing can be said here which would not be useless repetition.

Second. As to the tenure by which the judges are to hold their places; this chiefly concerns their duration in office; the provisions for their support; the precautions for their responsibility.

According to the plan of the convention, all judges who may be appointed by the United States are to hold their offices DURING GOOD BEHAVIOR; which is conformable to the most approved of the State constitutions and among the rest, to that of this State. Its propriety having been drawn into question by the adversaries of that plan, is no light symptom of the rage for objection, which disorders their imaginations and judgments. The standard of good behavior for the continuance in office of the judicial magistracy, is certainly one of the most valuable of the modern improvements in the practice of government. In a monarchy it is an excellent barrier to the despotism of the prince; in a republic it is a no less excellent barrier to the encroachments and oppressions of the representative body. And it is the best expedient which can be devised in any government, to secure a steady, upright, and impartial administration of the laws.

Whoever attentively considers the different departments of power must perceive, that, in a government in which they are separated from each other, the judiciary, from the nature of its functions, will always be the least dangerous to the political rights of the Constitution; because it will be least in a capacity to annoy or injure them. The Executive not only dispenses the honors, but holds the sword of the community. The legislature not only commands the purse, but prescribes the rules by which the duties and rights of every citizen are to be regulated. The judiciary, on the contrary, has no influence over either the sword or the purse; no direction either of the strength or of the wealth of the society; and can take no active resolution whatever. It may truly be said to have neither FORCE nor WILL, but merely judgment; and must ultimately depend upon the aid of the executive arm even for the efficacy of its judgments.

This simple view of the matter suggests several important consequences. It proves incontestably, that the judiciary is beyond comparison the weakest of the three departments of power; that it can never attack with success either of the other two; and that all possible care is requisite to enable it to defend itself against their attacks. It equally proves, that though individual oppression may now and then proceed from the courts of justice, the general liberty of the people can never be endangered from that quarter; I mean so long as the judiciary remains truly distinct from both the legislature and the Executive. For I agree, that "there is no liberty, if the power of judging be not separated from the legislative and executive powers." And it proves, in the last place, that as liberty can have nothing to fear from the judiciary alone, but would have every thing to fear from its union with either of the other departments; that as all the effects of such a union must ensue from a dependence of the former on the latter, notwithstanding a nominal and apparent separation; that as, from the natural feebleness of the judiciary, it is in continual jeopardy of being overpowered, awed, or influenced by its co-ordinate branches; and that as nothing can contribute so much to its firmness and independence as permanency in office, this quality may therefore be justly regarded as an indispensable ingredient in its constitution, and, in a great measure, as the citadel of the public justice and the public security.

The complete independence of the courts of justice is peculiarly essential in a limited Constitution. By a limited Constitution, I understand one which contains certain specified exceptions to the legislative authority; such, for instance, as that it shall pass no bills of attainder, no ex-post-facto laws, and the like. Limitations of this kind can be preserved in practice no other way than through the medium of courts of justice, whose duty it must be to declare all acts contrary to the manifest tenor of the Constitution void. Without this, all the reservations of particular rights or privileges would amount to nothing.

Some perplexity respecting the rights of the courts to pronounce legislative acts void, because contrary to the Constitution, has arisen from an imagination that the doctrine would imply a superiority of the judiciary to the legislative power. It is urged that the authority which can declare the acts of another void, must necessarily be superior to the one whose acts may be declared void. As this doctrine is of great importance in all the American constitutions, a brief discussion of the ground on which it rests cannot be unacceptable.

There is no position which depends on clearer principles, than that every act of a delegated authority, contrary to the tenor of the commission under which it is exercised, is void. No legislative act, therefore, contrary to the Constitution, can be valid. To deny this, would be to affirm, that the deputy is greater than his principal; that the servant is above his master; that the representatives of the people are superior to the people themselves; that men acting by virtue of powers, may do not only what their powers do not authorize, but what they forbid.

If it be said that the legislative body are themselves the constitutional judges of their own powers, and that the construction they put upon them is conclusive upon the other departments, it may be answered, that this cannot be the natural presumption, where it is not to be collected from any particular provisions in the Constitution. It is not otherwise to be supposed, that the Constitution could intend to enable the representatives of the people to substitute their will to that of their constituents. It is far more rational to suppose, that the courts were designed to be an intermediate body between the people and the legislature, in order, among other things, to keep the latter within the limits assigned to their authority. The interpretation of the laws is the proper and peculiar province of the courts. A constitution is, in fact, and must be regarded by the judges, as a fundamental law. It therefore belongs to them to ascertain its meaning, as well as the meaning of any particular act proceeding from the legislative body. If there should happen to be an irreconcilable variance between the two, that which has the superior obligation and validity ought, of course, to be preferred; or, in other words, the Constitution ought to be preferred to the statute, the intention of the people to the intention of their agents.

Nor does this conclusion by any means suppose a superiority of the judicial to the legislative power. It only supposes that the power of the people is superior to both; and that where the will of the legislature, declared in its statutes, stands in opposition to that of the people, declared in the Constitution, the judges ought to be governed by the latter rather than the former. They ought to regulate their decisions by the fundamental laws, rather than by those which are not fundamental.

This exercise of judicial discretion, in determining between two contradictory laws, is exemplified in a familiar instance. It not uncommonly happens, that there are two statutes existing at one time, clashing in whole or in part with each other, and neither of them containing any repealing clause or expression. In such a case, it is the province of the courts to liquidate and fix their meaning and operation. So far as they can, by any fair construction, be reconciled to each other, reason and law conspire to dictate that this should be done; where this is impracticable, it becomes a matter of necessity to give effect to one, in exclusion of the other. The rule which has obtained in the courts for determining their relative validity is, that the last in order of time shall be preferred to the first. But this is a mere rule of construction, not derived from any positive law, but from the nature and reason of the thing. It is a rule not enjoined upon the courts by legislative provision, but adopted by themselves, as consonant to truth and propriety, for the direction of their conduct as interpreters of the law. They thought it reasonable, that between the interfering acts of an equal authority, that which was the last indication of its will should have the preference.

But in regard to the interfering acts of a superior and subordinate authority, of an original and derivative power, the nature and reason of the thing indicate the converse of that rule as proper to be followed. They teach us that the prior act of a superior ought to be preferred to the subsequent act of an inferior and subordinate authority; and that accordingly, whenever a particular statute contravenes the Constitution, it will be the duty of the judicial tribunals to adhere to the latter and disregard the former.

It can be of no weight to say that the courts, on the pretense of a repugnancy, may substitute their own pleasure to the constitutional intentions of the legislature. This might as well happen in the case of two contradictory statutes; or it might as well happen in every adjudication upon any single statute. The courts must declare the sense of the law; and if they should be disposed to exercise WILL instead of judgment, the consequence would equally be the substitution of their pleasure to that of the legislative body. The observation, if it prove any thing, would prove that there ought to be no judges distinct from that body.

If, then, the courts of justice are to be considered as the bulwarks of a limited Constitution against legislative encroachments, this consideration will afford a strong argument for the permanent tenure of judicial offices, since nothing will contribute so much as this to that independent spirit in the judges which must be essential to the faithful performance of so arduous a duty.

This independence of the judges is equally requisite to guard the Constitution and the rights of individuals from the effects of those ill humors, which the arts of designing men, or the influence of particular conjunctures, sometimes disseminate among the people themselves, and which, though they speedily give place to better information, and more deliberate reflection, have a tendency, in the meantime, to occasion dangerous innovations in the government, and serious oppressions of the minor party in the community. Though I trust the friends of the proposed Constitution will never concur with its enemies, in questioning that fundamental principle of republican government, which admits the right of the people to alter or abolish the established Constitution, whenever they find it inconsistent with their happiness, yet it is not to be inferred from this principle, that the representatives of the people, whenever a momentary inclination happens to lay hold of a majority of their constituents, incompatible with the provisions in the existing Constitution, would, on that account, be justifiable in a violation of those provisions; or that the courts would be under a greater obligation to connive at infractions in this shape, than when they had proceeded wholly from the cabals of the representative body. Until the people have, by some solemn and authoritative act, annulled or changed the established form, it is binding upon themselves collectively, as well as individually; and no presumption, or even knowledge, of their sentiments, can warrant their representatives in a departure from it, prior to such an act. But it is easy to see, that it would require an uncommon portion of fortitude in the judges to do their duty as faithful guardians of the Constitution, where legislative invasions of it had been instigated by the major voice of the community.

But it is not with a view to infractions of the Constitution only, that the independence of the judges may be an essential safeguard against the effects of occasional ill humors in the society. These sometimes extend no farther than to the injury of the private rights of particular classes of citizens, by unjust and partial laws. Here also the firmness of the judicial magistracy is of vast importance in mitigating the severity and confining the operation of such laws. It not only serves to moderate the immediate mischiefs of those which may have been passed, but it operates as a check upon the legislative body in passing them; who, perceiving that obstacles to the success of iniquitous intention are to be expected from the scruples of the courts, are in a manner compelled, by the very motives of the injustice they meditate, to qualify their attempts. This is a circumstance calculated to have more influence upon the character of our governments, than but few may be aware of. The benefits of the integrity and moderation of the judiciary have already been felt in more States than one; and though they may have displeased those whose sinister expectations they may have disappointed, they must have commanded the esteem and applause of all the virtuous and disinterested. Considerate men, of every description, ought to prize whatever will tend to beget or fortify that temper in the courts: as no man can be sure that he may not be to-morrow the victim of a spirit of injustice, by which he may be a gainer to-day. And every man must now feel, that the inevitable tendency of such a spirit is to sap the foundations of public and private confidence, and to introduce in its stead universal distrust and distress.

That inflexible and uniform adherence to the rights of the Constitution, and of individuals, which we perceive to be indispensable in the courts of justice, can certainly not be expected from judges who hold their offices by a temporary commission. Periodical appointments, however regulated, or by whomsoever made, would, in some way or other, be fatal to their necessary independence. If the power of making them was committed either to the Executive or legislature, there would be danger of an improper complaisance to the branch which possessed it; if to both, there would be an unwillingness to hazard the displeasure of either; if to the people, or to persons chosen by them for the special purpose, there would be too great a disposition to consult popularity, to justify a reliance that nothing would be consulted but the Constitution and the laws.

There is yet a further and a weightier reason for the permanency of the judicial offices, which is deducible from the nature of the qualifications they require. It has been frequently remarked, with great propriety, that a voluminous code of laws is one of the inconveniences necessarily connected with the advantages of a free government. To avoid an arbitrary discretion in the courts, it is indispensable that they should be bound down by strict rules and precedents, which serve to define and point out their duty in every particular case that comes before them; and it will readily be conceived from the variety of controversies which grow out of the folly and wickedness of mankind, that the records of those precedents must unavoidably swell to a very considerable bulk, and must demand long and laborious study to acquire a competent knowledge of them. Hence it is, that there can be but few men in the society who will have sufficient skill in the laws to qualify them for the stations of judges. And making the proper deductions for the ordinary depravity of human nature, the number must be still smaller of those who unite the requisite integrity with the requisite knowledge. These considerations apprise us, that the government can have no great option between fit character; and that a temporary duration in office, which would naturally discourage such characters from quitting a lucrative line of practice to accept a seat on the bench, would have a tendency to throw the administration of justice into hands less able, and less well qualified, to conduct it with utility and dignity. In the present circumstances of this country, and in those in which it is likely to be for a long time to come, the disadvantages on this score would be greater than they may at first sight appear; but it must be confessed, that they are far inferior to those which present themselves under the other aspects of the subject.

Upon the whole, there can be no room to doubt that the convention acted wisely in copying from the models of those constitutions which have established good behavior as the tenure of their judicial offices, in point of duration; and that so far from being blamable on this account, their plan would have been inexcusably defective, if it had wanted this important feature of good government. The experience of Great Britain affords an illustrious comment on the excellence of the institution.

PUBLIUS

Endnotes

Chapter 1

1. Donald Trump (@realDonaldTrump), Twitter Post, May 9, 2018, 4:38 AM, https://twitter.com/realDonaldTrump/status/994179864436596736 (accessed 5/24/18).

2. Politico Staff, "Full text: Jeff Flake on Trump speech transcript," *Politico*, January 17, 2018, www.politico.com/story/2018/01/17/full-text-jeff-flake-on-trump-speech-transcript-343246 (accessed 5/24/18).

3. Knight Foundation and Gallup, "American Views: Trust, Media and Democracy," January 15, 2018, pp. 27–29, https://knightfoundation.org/reports/american-views-trust-media-and-democracy (accessed 1/22/18). For the negative stories, 28 percent said they are always fake news and 51 percent believed they are sometimes fake news; for the inaccurate stories based on sloppy fact-checking, 35 percent said they are always fake news and 57 percent believed they are sometimes fake news.

4. Public Policy Polling, "Trump Remains Unpopular; Voters Prefer Obama on SCOTUS Pick," December 9, 2016, www.publicpolicypolling.com/wp-content/uploads/2017/09/PPP_Release_National_120916.pdf (accessed 1/23/18).

5. Thomas Hobbes, *Leviathan* (1651; repr., Indianapolis, IN: Bobbs, Merrill, 1958).

6. Alexander Hamilton, James Madison, and John Jay, *The Federalist Papers*, ed. Roy P. Fairfield, 2nd ed. (1788; repr., Baltimore, MD: Johns Hopkins University Press, 1981), p. 160.

7. Hamilton, Madison, and Jay, *The Federalist Papers*, p. 18.

8. E. E. Schattschneider, *The Semisovereign People: A Realist's View of Democracy in America* (New York: Holt, Rinehart, and Winston, 1960).

9. Irving L. Janis, *Victims of Groupthink: A Psychological Study of Foreign-Policy Decisions and Fiascoes* (Boston: Houghton Mifflin, 1972).

10. Larry M. Bartels, *Unequal Democracy: The Political Economy of the New Gilded Age, 2nd ed.* (Princeton, NJ: Princeton University Press, 2016); Lawrence Baum, *Ideology in the Supreme Court* (Princeton, NJ: Princeton University Press, 2017).

11. Robert S. Erikson and Kent L. Tiden, *American Public Opinion*, 9th ed. (New York: Routledge, 2015).

12. John R. Hibbing and Elizabeth Theiss-Morse, *Stealth Democracy: Americans' Beliefs about How Government Should Work* (New York: Cambridge University Press, 2002), p. 147. See Diana E. Hess, *Controversy in the Classroom: The Democratic Power of Discussion* (New York: Routledge, 2009), for evidence that diverse viewpoints in the classroom have important effects on discussion.

13. For various surveys on abortion, see www.pollingreport.com/abortion.htm (accessed 1/16/18).

14. Donald Green, Bradley Palmquist, and Eric Schickler, *Partisan Hearts and Minds* (New Haven, CT: Yale University Press, 2004); Christopher Achen, "Political Socialization and Rational Party Identification," *Political Behavior* 24:2 (2002): 151–70.

15. Robert S. Erikson, Michael B. MacKuen, and James A. Stimson, *The Macro Polity* (New York: Cambridge University Press, 2002); Christopher H. Achen and Larry M. Bartels, *Democracy for Realists: Why Elections Do Not Produce Responsive Government* (Princeton, NJ: Princeton University Press, 2016).

16. Congressional Budget Office, "Budget," www.cbo.gov/topics/budget; The President's Budget for Fiscal Year 2018, "Historical Tables," Table 16.1, www.gpo.gov/fdsys/pkg/BUDGET-2018-TAB/pdf/BUDGET-2018-TAB.pdf; Regulatory Studies Center, George Washington University, "Reg Stats," https://regulatorystudies.columbian.gwu.edu/reg-stats#Pages%20in%20the%20Federal%20Register%20(1936%20-%202016) (all accessed 1/17/18).

17. Andrew Heywood, *Political Theory: An Introduction*, 4th ed. (New York: Macmillan, 2015).

18. Morris P. Fiorina, with Samuel J. Abrams and Jeremy C. Pope, *Culture War: The Myth of a Polarized America*, 3rd ed. (New York: Pearson, Longman, 2010), pp. 46–7.

19. For more on political culture, see Pippa Norris, *Democratic Deficit: Critical Citizens Revisited* (New York: Cambridge University Press, 2011).

20. Frank M. Bryan, *Real Democracy: The New England Town Meeting and How It Works* (Chicago: University of Chicago Press, 2004).

Chapter 2

1. See, for example, Steven Levitsky and Daniel Ziblatt, "Is Donald Trump a Threat to Democracy?," December 16, 2016, www.nytimes.com/2016/12/16/opinion/sunday/is-donald-trump-a-threat-to-democracy.html?_r=0; Ari Berman, "Donald Trump Is the Greatest Threat to American Democracy in Our Lifetime," *The Nation*, November 28, 2016, www.thenation.com/article/donald-trump-is-the-greatest-threat-to-american-democracy-in-our-lifetime/; Neil H. Buchanan, "Are We Witnessing the End of Democracy?," *Newsweek*, November 25, 2016, www.newsweek.com/neil-buchanan-are-we-witnessing-end-democracy-524169; and David Frum, "How to Build an Autocracy," *The Atlantic*, March 2017, www.theatlantic.com/magazine/archive/2017/03/how-to-build-an-autocracy/513872/ (all accessed 8/17/17).

2. Lawrence Wittner, "Will Trump and Kim's Game of Nuclear Chicken Blow Up the World?," Newsweek, August 18, 2017, www.newsweek.com/will-trump-and-kims-game-nuclear-chicken-blow-world-652080 (accessed 9/22/17).

3. Donald Trump, "Remarks by President Trump to the 72nd Session of the United Nations General Assembly United Nations," New York, September 19, 2017, www.whitehouse.gov/the-press-office/2017/09/19/remarks-president-trump-72nd-session-united-nations-general-assembly (accessed 9/28/17).

4. Cal Thomas, "Trump Discovers Once 'Useless' UN is Now Useful," *Wisconsin State Journal*, September 21, 2017, http://host.madison.

com/wsj/opinion/column/cal-thomas-trump-discovers-once-useless-un-is-now-useful/article_55c3ced5-c01f-546b-8fcf-eccec0723964.html (accessed 9/22/17).

5. Laura Bicker, "Trump and North Korea talks: The political gamble of the 21st Century," *BBC News*, March 9, 2018, www.bbc.com/news/world-asia-43334320 (accessed 5/24/18); Robert Reich (RBReich), Twitter Post, January 2, 2018, 6:40 PM, https://twitter.com/rbreich/status/948383424821145600?lang=en (accessed 5/24/18).

6. For a good overview of the political thought of the American Revolution, see Gordon S. Wood, *The Radicalism of the American Revolution* (New York: Vintage Books, 1993). For an excellent summary of the history, see Wood's *The American Revolution: A History* (New York: Modern Library, 2003).

7. David McCullough, *John Adams* (New York: Simon and Schuster, 2001), p. 90.

8. A classic text on the Founding period is Gordon S. Wood, *The Creation of the American Republic* (New York: W. W. Norton, 1969).

9. J. W. Peltason, *Corwin and Peltason's Understanding the Constitution*, 7th ed. (Hinsdale, IL: Dryden Press, 1976), p. 12.

10. The pamphlet sold 120,000 copies within a few months of publication, a figure that would leave the Harry Potter books in the dust in terms of the proportion of the literate public that purchased the book.

11. Thomas Hobbes, *Leviathan* (1651; repr., Indianapolis, IN: Bobbs, Merrill, 1958); John Locke, *Second Treatise of Government* (1690; repr., Indianapolis, IN: Bobbs, Merrill, 1952).

12. Robert A. Dahl, *How Democratic Is the American Constitution?* (New Haven, CT: Yale University Press, 2001), p. 12.

13. Alexander Hamilton, John Jay, and James Madison, *The Federalist Papers*, ed. Roy P. Fairfield, 2nd ed. (1788; repr., Baltimore, MD: Johns Hopkins University Press, 1981), p. 22.

14. Many delegates probably assumed that the electors would reflect the wishes of the voters in their states, but there is no clear indication of this in Madison's notes. (Hamilton makes this argument in the *Federalist Papers*.) Until the 1820s, many electors were directly chosen by state legislatures rather than by the people. In the first presidential election, George Washington won the unanimous support of the electors, but in only five states were the electors chosen by the people.

15. The actual language of the section avoids the term "slavery." Instead, it says: "The Migration or Importation of such Persons as any of the States now existing shall think proper to admit, shall not be prohibited by Congress prior to the Year one thousand eight hundred and eight." The ban on the importation of slaves was implemented on the earliest possible date, January 1, 1808.

16. Brutus 1, October 18, 1787, The Constitution Society, www.constitution.org/afp/brutus01.htm (accessed 6/28/18).

17. Patrick Henry, "Shall Liberty or Empire Be Sought?," in *America, 1761-1837*, vol. 8 of *The World's Famous Orations*, ed. William Jennings Bryan (New York: Funk and Wagnalls, 1906), pp. 73, 76.

18. Thomas Jefferson to John Adams, 1787, in *The Writings of Thomas Jefferson*, Memorial Edition, ed. Andrew A. Lipscomb and Albert Ellery Bergh (Washington, DC: Thomas Jefferson Memorial Association of the United States, 1903), vol. 6, p. 370.

19. Charlie Savage, "Can Trump Pardon Himself? Explaining Presidential Clemency Powers," *New York Times*, July 21, 2017, www.nytimes.com/2017/07/21/us/politics/trump-pardon-himself-presidential-clemency.html (accessed 8/17/17).

20. Julie Hirschfeld Davis and Maggie Haberman, "Trump Pardons Joe Arpaio, Who Became Face of Crackdown on Illegal Immigration," *New York Times*, August 25, 2017, www.nytimes.com/2017/08/25/us/politics/joe-arpaio-trump-pardon-sheriff-arizona.html?_r=0 (accessed 9/28/17).

21. Charlie Savage, "Obama's War on Terror May Resemble Bush's in Some Areas," *New York Times*, February 17, 2009, p. A1.

22. Peter M. Shane, *Madison's Nightmare: How Executive Power Threatens American Democracy* (Chicago: University of Chicago Press, 2009).

23. The responses on the three branches are from "Americans' Knowledge of the Branches of Government Is Declining," Annenberg Public Policy Center, September 13, 2016, www.annenbergpublicpolicycenter.org/americans-knowledge-of-the-branches-of-government-is-declining (accessed 7/14/17); the responses on the right to own a pet or home are from "Is There a Constitutional Right to Own a Home or a Pet?," Annenberg Public Policy Center, September 16, 2015, www.annenbergpublicpolicycenter.org/is-there-a-constitutional-right-to-own-a-home-or-a-pet (accessed 9/30/15).

24. "Characters from 'The Simpsons' More Well Known to Americans than Their First Amendment Freedoms," McCormick Tribune Freedom Museum survey, March 1, 2006, http://documents.mccormickfoundation.org/news/2006/pro30106.aspx (accessed 10/30/15).

25. Thomas Jefferson to James Madison, in *Thomas Jefferson on Democracy*, ed. Saul Padover (New York: Mentor Books, 1953), p. 153.

26. Cass R. Sunstein, "Making Amends," *New Republic*, March 3, 1997, p. 42.

27. *Furman v. Georgia*, 408 U.S. 238 (1972).

28. The case concerning minors was *Roper v. Simmons*, 543 U.S. 551 (2005), and the case concerning the mentally retarded was *Atkins v. Virginia*, 536 U.S. 304 (2002).

29. Valerie Strauss, "In the Age of Trump, a New Surge of Interest in the Constitution," *Washington Post*, August 17, 2017, www.washingtonpost.com/news/answer-sheet/wp/2017/08/17/in-the-age-of-trump-a-new-surge-of-interest-in-the-u-s-constitution/?utm_term=.e3abb53b9976 (accessed 8/18/2017).

30. Walter F. Murphy, "The Nature of the American Constitution," The Edmund Janes James lecture, December 6, 1987 (Department of Political Science, University of Illinois at Urbana-Champaign, 1989), p. 8, http://babel.hathitrust.org/cgi/pt?id=mdp.39015078286518;view=1up;seq=12.

Take a Stand

a. Jocelyn Kiley, "Americans Divided on How the Supreme Court Should Interpret the Constitution," Pew Research Center, July 31, 2014, www.pewresearch.org/fact-tank/2014/07/31/americans-divided-on-how-the-supreme-court-should-interpret-the-constitution (accessed 10/30/15).

b. Clarence Thomas, "How to Read the Constitution," *Wall Street Journal*, October 20, 2008.

c. *State of Missouri v. Holland*, 252 U.S. 416 (1920), 252.

d. William Rehnquist, "The Notion of a Living Constitution," *Harvard Journal of Law and Public Policy* 29 (2006): 402.

e. Rehnquist, "The Notion," p. 405.

f. Thurgood Marshall at the Annual Seminar of the San Francisco Patent and Trademark Law Association, Maui, Hawaii, May 6, 1987, www.thurgoodmarshall.com/speeches/constitutional_speech.htm (accessed 12/20/13).

Chapter 3

1. William Bianco and Edan Gomez, "Forget Trump's Complaints about Sanctuary Cities. Most Communities Are Actually Helping Enforce Immigration Laws," *Washington Post*, June 2, 2017, www.washingtonpost.com/news/monkey-cage/wp/2017/06/02/forget-trumps-complaints-about-sanctuary-cities-most-communities-are-actually-helping-enforce-immigration-laws/?utm_term=.ae02061d4f9a (accessed 2/23/18); Alexia Fernández Campbell, "US police chiefs are fighting the crackdown on 'sanctuary cities'," *Vox*, August 18, 2017, www.vox.com/policy-and-politics/2017/8/18/16130954/police-sanctuary-cities (accessed 5/25/18).

2. Campbell, "US police chiefs are fighting the crackdown on 'sanctuary cities'," Liz Robbins, "'Sanctuary City' Mayors Vow to Defy Trump's Immigration Order," *New York Times*, January 25, 2017, www.nytimes.com/2017/01/25/nyregion/outraged-mayors-vow-to-defy-trumps-immigration-order.html; Eugene Scott, "NYC Mayor: 'We Will Go to Court Immediately' If Funding Halted over 'Sanctuary City' Executive Order," CNN, January 27, 2017, www.cnn.com/2017/01/26/politics/sanctuary-cities-bill-de-blasio-trump-court/index.html (both accessed 2/23/18).

3. Slaughterhouse Cases, 83 U.S. 36 (1873). See Ronald M. Labbe and Jonathan Lurie, *The Slaughterhouse Cases: Regulation, Reconstruction, and the Fourteenth Amendment* (Lawrence: University Press of Kansas, 2003).

4. Civil Rights Cases, 109 U.S. 3 (1883).

5. *United States v. E. C. Knight Co.*, 156 U.S. 1 (1895).

6. *Hammer v. Dagenhart*, 247 U.S. 251 (1918).

7. *Schechter Poultry Corporation v. United States*, 295 U.S. 495 (1935).

8. Four key cases are *West Coast Hotel Company v. Parrish* (1937), *Wright v. Vinton Branch* (1937), *Virginia Railway Company v. System Federation* (1937), and *National Labor Relations Board v. Jones and Laughlin Steel Corporation* (1937).

9. Martin Grodzins, *The American System* (New York: Rand McNally, 1966).

10. *Brown v. Board of Education*, 347 U.S. 483 (1954); *Swann v. Charlotte-Mecklenburg Board of Education*, 402 U.S. 1 (1971).

11. *Baker v. Carr*, 369 U.S. 186 (1962); *Reynolds v. Sims*, 377 U.S. 533 (1964); *Wesberry v. Sanders*, 376 U.S. 1 (1964); Martha Derthick, *Keeping the Compound Republic: Essays in American Federalism* (Washington, DC: Brookings Institution, 2001).

12. *Miranda v. Arizona*, 384 U.S. 436 (1966); *Mapp v. Ohio*, 367 U.S. 643 (1961).

13. Barry Rabe, "Environmental Policy and the Bush Era: The Collision between the Administrative Presidency and State Experimentation," *Publius 37:3 (May 2007)*: 413–31.

14. Lois Beckett, "Nullification: How States Are Making It a Felony to Enforce Federal Gun Laws," *ProPublica*, May 2, 2013, www.propublica.org/article/nullification-how-states-are-making-it-a-felony-to-enforce-federal-gun-laws (accessed 11/15/13).

15. From a review of Michael S. Greve, *Real Federalism: Why It Matters, How It Could Happen* (Washington, DC: American Enterprise Institute Press, 1999), www.federalismproject.org/publications/books (accessed 10/10/07).

16. *Gregory v. Ashcroft*, 501 U.S. 452 (1991).

17. *City of Boerne v. Flores*, 521 U.S. 507 (1997), 520.

18. *Kimel et al. v. Florida Board of Regents*, 528 U.S. 62 (2000).

19. *United States v. Lopez*, 514 U.S. 549 (1995).

20. *United States v. Morrison*, 529 U.S. 598 (2000); Nia-Malika Henderson, "Obama Signs a Strengthened Violence Against Women Act," *Washington Post*, March 7, 2013, www.washingtonpost.com/politics/obama-signs-a-strengthened-violence-against-women-act/2013/03/07/e50d585e-8740-11e2-98a3-b3db6b9ac586_story.html (accessed 3/21/14).

21. *Romer v. Evans*, 517 U.S. 620 (1996).

22. *National Federation of Independent Business v. Sebelius*, 132 S. Ct. 2566 (2012).

23. *National Federation of Independent Business v. Sebelius*, 132 S. Ct. 2566 (2012), p. 51.

24. Jonathan Turley, "It's Not the Cannabis, It's the Constitution," *Los Angeles Times*, August 5, 2002, Metro section, part 2, p. 11.

25. Hans A. von Spakovsky, "Sanctuary Cities? That's a Constitutional 'Hell No,'" The Heritage Foundation, April 18, 2017, www.heritage.org/immigration/commentary/sanctuary-cities-thats-constitutional-hell-no; Ilya Somin, "Federalism, the Constitution, and Sanctuary Cities," *Washington Post*, November 26, 2016, www.washingtonpost.com/news/volokh-conspiracy/wp/2016/11/26/federalism-the-constitution-and-sanctuary-cities/?utm_term=.64a36265e347 (both accessed 2/25/18).

26. Martha Derthick, *Keeping the Compound Republic: Essays on American Federalism* (Washington, DC: Brookings Institution, 2001), pp. 9–32.

Chapter 4

1. Patrick Strudwick, "Milo Yiannopoulos Calls Abuse Victims 'Whinging, Selfish Brats' in a Newly Emerged Video," BuzzFeed, March 11, 2017, www.buzzfeed.com/patrickstrudwick/milo-yiannopoulos-described-sexual-abuse-victims-as-whinging?utm_term=.sgZNwrBGy#.kmGkJoeZd (accessed 4/11/18); Graeme Wood, "His Kampf: Richard Spencer is a Troll and an Icon for White Supremacists," *The Atlantic*, June 2017, www.theatlantic.com/magazine/archive/2017/06/his-kampf/524505 (accessed 4/9/18).

2. A partial list of campuses that have protested conservative speakers includes Middlebury College; University of California, Berkeley; University of Florida; DePaul University; Harvard University; Auburn University; Emory University; and the University of Washington. For an insightful discussion of the broader debate, see Julian E. Zelizer and Morton Keller, "Is Free Speech Really Challenged on Campus?," *The Atlantic*, September 15, 2017, www.theatlantic.com/education/archive/2017/09/students-free-speech-campus-protest/539673/(accessed 10/24/17).

3. Eliott C. McLaughlin, "War on Campus: The Escalating Battle over College Free Speech," CNN, May 1, 2017, www.cnn.com/2017/04/20/us/campus-free-speech-trnd/index.html (accessed 10/24/17).

4. Meghan Keneally and Julia Jacobo, "Police: Suspect Shouted 'Heil Hitler' before Shooting Incident after Spencer Event," ABC News, October 20, 2017, http://abcnews.go.com/US/security-ramped-white-nationalist-richard-spencers-florida-event/story?id=50585570 (accessed 10/24/17).

5. Rebecca R. Ruiz, "Sessions Calls for 'Recommitment' to Free Speech on Campus, Diving into Debate," *New York Times*, September 26, 2017, www.nytimes.com/2017/09/26/us/politics/jeff-sessions-campus-free-speech-georgetown.html?_r=0 (accessed 10/23/17).

6. Yanan Wang, "Obama to Campus Protesters: Don't 'Shut Up' Opposing Viewpoints," *Washington Post*, December 22, 2015, www.washingtonpost.com/news/morning-mix/wp/2015/12/22/obama-to-campus-protesters-dont-shut-up-opposing-viewpoints (accessed 12/30/15).

7. "Speech on Campus," American Civil Liberties Union, www.aclu.org/other/speech-campus (accessed 10/24/17).

8. *Arar v. Ashcroft et al.*, WL 346439 (E.D. N.Y. 2006). The case was also dismissed because Arar, a Canadian citizen, did not have standing to sue the U.S. government. Supporters of this decision (and the practice more generally) say that it is an essential part of the War on Terror and that the enemy combatants who are arrested have no legal rights. Opponents say that the practice violates international law and our own standards of decency; furthermore, torture almost never produces useful information because people will say anything to get the torture to stop.

9. *State v. Massey et al.*, 51 S.E.2d 179 (N.C. 1949). The case was appealed to the Supreme Court, but the Court declined to hear the case, which means that the state decision stands (*Bunn v. North Carolina*, 336 U.S. 942 [1949]).

10. Alan Blinder, "Tennessee Pastor Disputes a Wildlife Possession Charge by State," *New York Times*, November 15, 2013, www.nytimes.com/2013/11/16/us/tennessee-pastor-disputes-wildlife-possession-charge-by-state.html?_r=0 (accessed 1/24/14).

11. *Pennsylvania v. Miller*, Court of Common Pleas, WL 31426193 (Penn. 2002). However, supreme courts in Minnesota, Wisconsin, and several other states have decided that requiring the Amish to use orange SMV triangles violates their free exercise of religion.

12. *Wisconsin v. Yoder*, 403 U.S. 205 (1972).

13. Jeffrey Rosen, "Lemon Law," *New Republic*, March 29, 1993, p. 17.

14. Max Farrand, ed., *The Records of the Federal Convention of 1787*, rev. ed. (New Haven, CT: Yale University Press, 1937), pp. 587–88, 617–18.

15. *The Papers of Thomas Jefferson*, ed. J. Boyd (Princeton, NJ: Princeton University Press, 1958), pp. 557–83, cited in Lester S. Jayson, ed., *The Constitution of the United States of America: Analysis and Interpretation* (Washington, DC: U.S. Government Printing Office, 1973), p. 900.

16. Ralph Ketcham, *The Anti-Federalist Papers and the Constitutional Convention Debates* (New York: Signet Classic, Penguin Putnam, 2003), p. 247.

17. The two that were not ratified by the states were a complicated amendment on congressional apportionment and the pay raise amendment.

18. *Annals of Congress* 755 (August 17, 1789), cited in Lester S. Jayson, ed., *The Constitution of the United States of America* (Washington, DC: U.S. Government Printing Office, 1973), p. 898.

19. There is an intense scholarly debate on whether the authors of the Fourteenth Amendment intended for it to apply the Bill of Rights to the states. The strongest argument against this position is Raoul Berger's *The Fourteenth Amendment and the Bill of Rights* (Norman: University of Oklahoma Press, 1989), and a good book in support is Akhil Reed Amar's *The Bill of Rights* (New Haven, CT: Yale University Press, 1998).

20. *Barron v. Baltimore* 32 U.S. 243 (1833), 250. The 1873 case was *Slaughter-House Cases*, 83 U.S. 36 (1873). The Supreme Court also declined to apply the Bill of Rights to the states in the *Civil Rights Cases*, 109 U.S. 3 (1883), in which the Court ruled that the Fourteenth Amendment did not give Congress the power to regulate the conduct of private business (thus the Civil Rights Act of 1875 was unconstitutional and private businesses could discriminate on the basis of race).

21. *Chicago, Burlington, and Quincy Railroad v. Chicago*, 166 U.S. 226 (1897), *Twining v. New Jersey*, 211 U.S. 78, 98 (1908).

22. *Gitlow v. New York*, 268 U.S. 652 (1925).

23. James Hutson, "'A Wall of Separation,'" *Library of Congress Information Bulletin* 57:6 (June 1998), www.loc.gov/loc/lcib/9806/danbury.html (accessed 3/3/08).

24. Henry J. Abraham and Barbara A. Perry, *Freedom and the Court: Civil Rights and Civil Liberties in the United States*, 8th ed. (Lawrence: University Press of Kansas, 2003), p. 300.

25. *Engel v. Vitale*, 370 U.S. 421 (1962).

26. *Wallace v. Jaffree*, 482 U.S. 38 (1985).

27. *Lee v. Weisman*, 505 U.S. 577 (1992); *Santa Fe Independent School District v. Doe*, 530 U.S. 290 (2000).

28. *Marsh v. Chambers*, 463 U.S. 783 (1983); *Jones v. Clear Creek Independent School*, 61 LW 3819 (1993); *Town of Greece, N.Y. v. Galloway*, 572 U.S. ___ (2014).

29. *Lemon v. Kurtzman*, 403 U.S. 602 (1971).

30. *Lynch v. Donnelly*, 465 U.S. 668 (1984), 672–73.

31. Jeffrey Rosen, "Big Ten," *New Republic*, March 14, 2004, p. 11.

32. *Zelman v. Simmons-Harris*, 536 U.S. 639 (2002).

33. *Arizona Christian School Tuition Organization v. Winn*, U.S. Supreme Court slip. op. 09-987 and 09-991 (2011).

34. *Mitchell v. Helms*, 530 U.S. 793 (2000).

35. *Zobrest v. Catalina School District*, 509 U.S. 1 (1993). A similar decision in 1997 allowed a public school teacher to teach in a special program in a parochial school, *Agostini v. Felton*, 521 U.S. 203 (1997).

36. We will not cite all the cases here. See Abraham and Perry, *Freedom and the Court*, Chapter 6, for a summary of cases on this topic, especially Tables 6.1 and 6.2.

37. *Employment Division, Department of Human Resources of Oregon v. Smith*, 494 U.S. 872 (1990), 878–80. This case is often erroneously reported as having banned the religious use of peyote. In fact, the Court said: "Although it is constitutionally permissible to exempt sacramental peyote use from the operation of drug laws, it is not constitutionally required."

38. *City of Boerne v. Flores*, 521 U.S. 527 (1997); *Cutter v. Wilkinson*, No. 03-9877 (2005); *Gonzales v. O Centro Espirita Beneficente Uniao do Vegetal (UDV) et al.*, 546 U.S. 418 (2006). The Sherbert test requires that whenever the government limits religious expression it must prove a compelling interest that is narrowly tailored to achieve that interest if a person is substantially burdened by the law (*Sherbert v. Verner*, 374 U.S. 398 [1963]).

39. *Burwell v. Hobby Lobby*, 573 U.S. ___ (2014).

40. *Trinity Lutheran Church of Columbia, Inc. v. Comer*, 582 U.S. ___ (2017). This case would appear to be an establishment clause case (can the state provide direct funds to a church?), but it was decided on free exercise grounds. This opens the door to a broader range of protections for religious activity. See Garrett Epps, "A Major Church-State Ruling That Shouldn't Have Happened," *The Atlantic*, June 27, 2017, www.theatlantic.com/politics/archive/2017/06/a-major-church-state-case-that-shouldnt-have-happened/531789 (accessed 10/18/17).

41. *Masterpiece Cakeshop v. Colorado Civil Rights Commission*, 584 U.S. ___ (2018).

42. *Police Department of Chicago v. Mosley*, 408 U.S. 92 (1972).

43. *United States v. O'Brien*, 391 U.S. 367 (1968); *Ladue v. Gilleo*, 512 U.S. 43 (1994).

44. *Schenck v. United States*, 249 U.S. 47 (1919), 52.

45. Alan Dershowitz, *Shouting Fire: Civil Liberties in a Turbulent Age* (New York: Little, Brown, 2002).

46. *Abrams v. United States*, 250 U.S. 616 (1919), 630–31.

47. *Dennis v. United States*, 341 U.S. 494 (1951).

48. *Brandenburg v. Ohio*, 395 U.S. 444 (1969).

49. *Snyder v. Phelps*, 131 S.Ct. 1207 (2011).

50. *Smith v. Goguen*, 415 U.S. 566 (1974).

51. *Tinker v. Des Moines School District*, 393 U.S. 503 (1969).

52. *Spence v. Washington*, 418 U.S. 405 (1974).

53. *Spence v. Washington*, 418 U.S. 409–10 (1974).

54. *Texas v. Johnson*, 491 U.S. 397 (1989).

55. *United States v. Eichman*, 496 U.S. 310 (1990).

56. David Wright, "Trump: Burn the Flag, Go to Jail," CNN, November 29, 2016, www.cnn.com/2016/11/29/politics/donald-trump-flag-burning-penalty-proposal/index.html (accessed 10/18/17).

57. *United States v. O'Brien*, 391 U.S. 367, 376 (1968).

58. *Walker v. Texas Division, Sons of Confederate Veterans*, 576 U.S. ____ (2015).

59. Jess Bidgood et al., "Confederate Monuments Are Coming Down across the United States. Here's a List," *New York Times*, August 28, 2017, www.nytimes.com/interactive/2017/08/16/us/confederate-monuments-removed.html; Christopher Carbone, "Which Confederate Statues Were removed? A Running List," Fox News. October 18, 2017, www.foxnews.com/us/2017/10/18/which-confederate-statues-were-removed-running-list.html (both accessed 10/18/17).

60. *Buckley v. Valeo*, 424 U.S. 1 (1976).

61. *Davis v. Federal Election Commission*, 554 U.S. 724 (2008).

62. *Citizens United v. Federal Election Commission*, 558 U.S. 310 (2010); *McCutcheon v. Federal Election Commission*, 572 U.S. ____ (2014).

63. *McConnell v. Federal Election Commission*, 540 U.S. 93 (2003).

64. *Board of Regents of the University of Wisconsin System et al., Petitioners v. Scott Harold Southworth et al.*, 529 U.S. 217 (2000).

65. One example was a speech code adopted at the University of Michigan that prohibited "any behavior, verbal or physical, that stigmatizes or victimizes an individual on the basis of race, ethnicity, religion, sex, sexual orientation, creed, national origin, ancestry, age, marital status, handicap, or Vietnam veteran status" and "creates an intimidating, hostile, or demeaning environment for educational pursuits, employment or participation in University-sponsored extra-curricular activities." Kermit L. Hall, "Free Speech on Public College Campuses: Overview," www.firstamendmentcenter.org/speech/pubcollege/overview.aspx (accessed 2/10/08).

66. Liam Stack, "Yale's Halloween Advice Stokes a Racially Charged Debate," *New York Times*, November 8, 2015, www.nytimes.com/2015/11/09/nyregion/yale-culturally-insensitive-halloween-costumes-free-speech.html?_r=0 (accessed 12/30/15).

67. Michael D. Regan, "Yale Lecturer Resigns over Halloween Costume Email Controversy," *Christian Science Monitor*, December 8, 2015, www.csmonitor.com/USA/Education/2015/1208/Yale-lecturer-resigns-over-Halloween-costume-email-controversy (accessed 12/30/15).

68. One of the authors of this book took Introduction to American Politics in that lecture hall, and the other has taught many classes in the room. For a description of the controversy, see Dwight Adams and Holly V. Hays, "IU: Room with Mural of KKK Rally Will No Longer Be a Classroom," *Indianapolis Star*, September 29, 2017, www.indystar.com/story/news/2017/09/29/indiana-university-no-longer-use-room-mural-showing-kkk-rally-classroom/717308001 (accessed 10/18/17).

69. *City of St. Paul v. RAV*, 505 U.S. 377 (1992).

70. *Virginia v. Black*, 538 U.S. 343 (2003).

71. The Editorial Board, "Hate Speech on Facebook," *New York Times*, May 30, 2013, www.nytimes.com/2013/05/31/opinion/misogynist-speech-on-facebook.html (accessed 1/28/14).

72. Facebook "community standards" on hate speech, www.facebook.com/communitystandards (accessed 1/28/14).

73. Jeff Rosen, "Who Decides? Civility v. Hate Speech on the Internet," *Insights on Law and Society* 13:2 (Winter 2013), www.americanbar.org/publications/insights_on_law_andsociety/13/winter_2013/who_decides_civilityvhatespeechontheinternet.html (accessed 1/29/14).

74. *Packingham v. North Carolina*, 582 U.S. ____ (2017).

75. *De Jonge v. State of Oregon*, 299 U.S. 353 (1937); *Edwards v. South Carolina*, 372 U.S. 229 (1963).

76. The Supreme Court declined to review the case in *Smith v. Collin*, 439 U.S. 916 (1978), which meant that the lower-court rulings stood (447 F. Supp. 676 [1978], 578 F.2d 1197 [1978]). See Donald A. Downs, *Nazis in Skokie: Freedom, Community and the First Amendment* (Notre Dame, IN: University of Notre Dame Press, 1985), for an excellent analysis of this important case.

77. *Forsyth County v. Nationalist Movement*, 505 U.S. 123 (1992).

78. Keneally and Jacobo, "Police."

79. *Frisby et al. v. Schultz et al.*, 487 U.S. 474 (1988).

80. See https://freespeech.ufl.edu/ for a discussion of all the related issues (accessed 3/7/18).

81. *McCullen v. Coakley*, 573 U.S. ____ (2014).

82. *New York Times Co. v. United States*, 403 U.S. 713 (1971).

83. *New York Times Co. v. United States*, 403 U.S. 713 (1971).

84. Tom Porter, "Trump Administration Threatens Freedom of the Press in New Leaks Crackdown," *Newsweek*, August 5, 2017, www.newsweek.com/trump-administration-goes-after-press-new-leaks-crackdown-646908 (accessed 10/18/17).

85. *Chaplinsky v. State of New Hampshire*, 315 U.S. 568 (1942).

86. *Chaplinsky v. State of New Hampshire*, 315 U.S. 568 (1942).

87. *New York Times v. Sullivan*, 376 U.S. 254 (1964), cited in Abraham and Perry, *Freedom and the Court*, p. 193.

88. *Hustler v. Falwell*, 485 U.S. 46 (1988).

89. Jeffrey Toobin, "Gawker's Demise and the Trump-Era Threat to the First Amendment," *New Yorker*, December 19 and 26, 2016, www.newyorker.com/magazine/2016/12/19/gawkers-demise-and-the-trump-era-threat-to-the-first-amendment (accessed 10/16/2017).

90. "Melania Trump and *Daily Mail* Settle Her Libel Suits," *New York Times*, April 12, 2017, www.nytimes.com/2017/04/12/business/media/melania-trump-daily-mail-libel.html (accessed 10/16/17).

91. Adam Liptak, "Can Trump Change Libel Laws?," *New York Times*, March 30, 2017, www.nytimes.com/2017/03/30/us/politics/can-trump-change-libel-laws.html (accessed 10/16/17).

92. *Valentine v. Chrestensen*, 316 U.S. 52 (1942).

93. *Virginia State Board of Pharmacy v. Virginia Citizens Consumer Council, Inc.*, 425 U.S. 748 (1976); *City of Cincinnati v. Discovery Network, Inc. et al.*, 507 U.S. 410 (1993).

94. *Matal v. Tam*, 582 U.S. ____ (2017).

95. In 1996, Congress passed the Child Pornography Prevention Act. This law makes the possession, production, or distribution of child pornography a criminal offense punishable with up to 15 years in jail and a fine. However, two parts of the law were struck down by the Court for being "overbroad and unconstitutional." *Ashcroft v. Free Speech Coalition*, 353 U.S. 234 (2002).

96. *Jacobellis v. Ohio*, 378 U.S. 184, 197 (1964).

97. *Roth v. United States*, 354 U.S. 476 (1957).

98. *Miller v. California*, 413 U.S. 15 (1973).

99. *Federal Communications Commission v. Pacifica Foundation*, 438 U.S. 726 (1978).

100. *Federal Communications Commission et al. v. Fox Television Stations*, 556 U.S. 502 (2009).

101. *Federal Communications Commission and United States v. CBS Corporation*, 556 U.S. 1218 (2009).

102. *Federal Communications Commission v. Fox Television Stations*, 567 U.S. ____ (2012); *Federal Communications Commission v. CBS Corporation*, no. 11-1240 (2012), writ of certiorari denied.

103. *United States v. Stevens*, 559 U.S. 460 (2010).

104. *Brown v. Entertainment Merchants Association*, 564 U.S. (2011).

105. David French, "Of Course the Second Amendment Protects an Individual Right to Keep and Bear Arms," *National Review*, April 13, 2016, www.nationalreview.com/2016/04/second-amendment-protects-individual-right-keep-bear-arms (accessed 3/29/18).

106. Dorothy Samuels, "The Second Amendment Was Never Meant to Protect an Individual's Right to a Gun," *The Nation*, September 23, 2015, www.thenation.com/article/how-the-roberts-court-undermined-sensible-gun-control/; John Paul Stevens, "Repeal the Second Amendment," *New York Times*, March 27, 2018, www.nytimes.com/2018/03/27/opinion/john-paul-stevens-repeal-second-amendment.html (accessed 3/29/18).

107. Gun Violence Archive, www.gunviolencearchive.org (accessed 4/9/18).

108. The FBI defines an active shooter as "an individual actively engaged in killing or attempting to kill people in a confined and populated area." For data on active shooters see Federal Bureau of Investigation, Office of Partner Engagement, "Quick Look: 220 Active Shooter Incidents in the United States Between 2000–2016," www.fbi.gov/about/partnerships/office-of-partner-engagement/active-shooter-incidents-graphics (accessed 4/9/18).

109. Giffords Law Center, "Gun Law Trend Watch, 2017 Year-End Review," http://lawcenter.giffords.org/wp-content/uploads/2017/12/Trendwatch-2017-Year-End-12.19.17-pages.pdf, and "Concealed Carry," http://lawcenter.giffords.org/gun-laws/policy-areas/guns-in-public/concealed-carry (accessed 4/9/18).

110. *District of Columbia v. Heller*, 554 U.S. 290 (2008).

111. *McDonald v. Chicago*, 08-1521 (2010).

112. Robert J. Spitzer, *The Politics of Gun Control* (Chatham, NJ: Chatham House, 1995). Also see www.bradycampaign.org/reforming-gun-industry-practices for a complete list of the cases (accessed 6/27/18). The two cases recognizing the individual right to bear arms were *United States v. Timothy Joe Emerson*, 46 F. Supp. 2d 598 (1999) and the D.C. Circuit Court case that was appealed in the landmark ruling *Parker v. District of Columbia*, 478 F.3d 370 (D.C. Cir. 2007).

113. Juliet Eilperin and David Nakamura, "An Emotional Obama Flexes His Executive Muscle on Gun Control," *Washington Post*, January 5, 2016, www.washingtonpost.com/politics/obama-moves-on-guns-with-executive-actions-that-circumvent-congress/2016/01/05/97f23336-b3bc-11e5-a76a-0b5145e8679a_story.html?hpid=hp_hp-top-table-main_obamaguns-1215pm%3Ahomepage%2Fstory (accessed 4/9/18).

114. Giffords Law Center, "Post-*Heller* Litigation Summary," December 2017, http://lawcenter.giffords.org/wp-content/uploads/2017/12/PHLS-December-17-Update-Final.pdf (accessed 4/9/18).

115. *New Jersey v. T. L. O.*, 469 U.S. 325 (1985); *Safford United School District No. 1 et al. v. Redding*, 557 U.S. 364 (2009).

116. See Abraham and Perry, *Freedom and the Court*, Chapter 4, for a discussion of these cases. The most recent case is *Kentucky v. King*, 563 U.S. ____ (2011).

117. *Florence v. County of Burlington*, U.S. 10-945 (2012).

118. *Maryland v. King*, 133 S.Ct. 1958 (June 3, 2013).

119. *Riley v. California*, 513 U.S. ____ (2014).

120. *United States v. Jones*, 565 U.S. ____ (2012).

121. *Carpenter v. United States*, 585 U.S. ____ (2018).

122. *Mapp v. Ohio*, 367 U.S. 643 (1961).

123. *Herring v. United States*, 555 U.S. 135 (2009).

124. *Utah v. Strieff*, 579 U.S. ____ (2016).

125. *Vernonia School District v. Acton*, 515 U.S. 646 (1995); *Board of Education of Pottawatomie County v. Earls*, 536 U.S. 832 (2002).

126. *Chandler v. Miller*, 520 U.S. 305 (1997).

127. Leslie Cauley, "NSA Has Massive Database of Americans' Phone Calls," *USA Today*, May 11, 2006, p. 1.

128. Andrew Crocker and David Ruiz, "How Congress's Extension of Section 702 May Expand the NSA's Warrantless Surveillance Authority," Electronic Frontier Foundation, February 1, 2018, www.eff.org/deeplinks/2018/02/how-congresss-extension-section-702-may-expand-nsas-warrantless-surveillance (accessed 6/14/18).

129. Lorraine Woellert and Dawn Kopecki, "The Snooping Goes beyond Phone Calls," *Business Week*, May 29, 2006, p. 38; "Data Mining: Federal Efforts Cover a Wide Range of Uses," GAO Report 04-548, May 2004, www.gao.gov/assets/250/242241.pdf (accessed 5/13/14).

130. Anthony Cuthbertson, "AT&T Spying Program Is 'Worse than Snowden Revelations,'" *Newsweek*, October 26, 2016, www.newsweek.com/att-spying-program-worse-snowden-revelations-513812 (accessed 10/23/17).

131. Eric Lichtblau and James Risen, "Officials Say U.S. Wiretaps Exceeded Law," *New York Times*, April 16, 2009.

132. *Miranda v. Arizona*, 384 U.S. 436 (1966).

133. *New York v. Quarles*, 467 U.S. 649 (1984).

134. *Dickerson v. United States*, 530 U.S. 428 (2000).

135. *Benton v. Maryland*, 395 U.S. 784 (1969).

136. *Kelo v. City of New London*, 545 U.S. 469 (2005).

137. National Conference of State Legislatures, "Eminent Domain Overview," January 1, 2012, www.ncsl.org/research/environment-and-natural-resources/eminent-domain-overview.aspx (accessed 1/31/14).

138. The 2017 case, *Murr v. Wisconsin* 582 US ____ (2017), involved a property owner who tried to sell a lot that was contiguous to another lot that he owned; he did not have to be compensated for the value of that lot when it was rendered worthless by a state regulation. The recent cases that ruled in favor of property owners were *Arkansas Game and Fish Commission v. United States*, 568 U.S. ____ (2012); *Koontz v. St. Johns River Water Management District*, 568 U.S. ____ (2013); and *Horne v. United States Department of Agriculture*, 569 U.S. ____ (2013).

139. *Powell v. Alabama*, 287 U.S. 45 (1932).

140. *Gideon v. Wainwright*, 372 U.S. 335 (1963).

141. *Evitts v. Lucy*, 469 U.S. 387 (1985); *Wiggins v. Smith*, 539 U.S. 510 (2003). See Elizabeth Gable and Tyler Green, "*Wiggins v. Smith*: The Ineffective Assistance of Counsel Standard Applied Twenty Years after *Strickland*," *Georgetown Journal of Legal Ethics* (Summer 2004): 755–71, for a discussion of many of these issues.

142. *Klopfer v. North Carolina*, 386 U.S. 213 (1967).

143. The law is 18 U.S.C. § 3161(c)(1) and the ruling is *Zedner v. United States*, 05-5992 (2006).

144. The case concerning African Americans is *Batson v. Kentucky*, 106 S.Ct. 1712 (1986); the case about Latinos is *Hernandez v. New York*, 500 U.S. 352 (1991); and the gender case is *J. E. B. v. Alabama ex rel. T. B.*, 511 U.S. 127 (1994). Two more-recent cases affirming that peremptory challenges cannot be used in a racially discriminatory fashion are *Miller-El v. Dretke*, 545 U.S. 231 (2005) and *Snyder v. Louisiana*, 552 U.S. 472 (2008).

145. *Peña-Rodriguez v. Colorado*, 580 U.S. ____ (2017).

146. Death Penalty Information Center, "Number of Executions since 1976," www.deathpenaltyinfo.org/executions-year (accessed 4/9/18); *Hall v. Florida*, 572 U.S. ____ (2014).

147. Erik Eckholm, "One Execution Botched, Oklahoma Delays the Next," *New York Times*, April 29, 2014, www.nytimes.com/2014/04/30/us/oklahoma-executions.html (accessed 5/13/14).

148. *Furman v. Georgia*, 408 U.S. 238 (1972); *Gregg v. Georgia*, 428 U.S. 513 (1976).

149. *Moore v. Texas*, 581 U.S. ____ (2017)

150. See Abraham and Perry, *Freedom and the Court*, pp. 72–73, for a discussion of the earlier cases, and Charles Lane, "5–4 Supreme Court Abolishes Juvenile Executions," *Washington Post*, March 2, 2005, p. A1, for a discussion of the 2002 and 2005 cases. The cases were *Atkins v. Virginia*, 536 U.S. 304 (2002); *Roper v. Simmons*, 543 U.S. 551 (2005); and *Kennedy v. Louisiana*, 554 U.S. 407 (2008).

151. *Griswold v. Connecticut*, 381 U.S. 479 (1965), 482–86.

152. *Griswold v. Connecticut*, 381 U.S. 479 (1965), 511–12.

153. *Roe v. Wade*, 410 U.S. 113 (1973), 129.

154. *Planned Parenthood of Southeastern Pennsylvania v. Casey*, 505 U.S. 833 (1992).

155. Katharine Q. Seelye, "Mississippi Voters Reject Anti-Abortion Measure," *New York Times*, November 8, 2011, www.nytimes.com/2011/11/09/us/politics/votes-across-the-nation-could-serve-as-a-political-barometer.html (accessed 12/5/11).

156. Erik Eckholm, "Access to Abortion Falling as States Pass Restrictions," *New York Times*, January 3, 2014, www.nytimes.com/2014/01/04/us/women-losing-access-to-abortion-as-opponents-gain-ground-in-state-legislatures.html (accessed 1/31/14).

157. *Whole Woman's Health v. Hellerstedt*, 579 U.S. ____ (2016).

158. *Bowers v. Hardwick*, 478 U.S. 186 (1986).

159. *Lawrence v. Texas*, 539 U.S. 558 (2003).

Take a Stand

a. *Florida v. Jardines*, 569 U.S. ____ (2013), 6–7.

b. Oral arguments in *U.S. v. Jones* (2012), November 8, 2011, www.supremecourt.gov/oral_arguments/argument_transcripts/2011/10-1259.pdf, p. 44 (accessed 4/9/18).

Chapter 5

1. Joseph Goldstein, "Judge Rejects New York's Stop-and-Frisk Policy, *New York Times*, August 12, 2013, www.nytimes.com/2013/08/13/nyregion/stop-and-frisk-practice-violated-rights-judge-rules.html (accessed 11/7/17).

2. Stop and Frisk Data, New York Civil Liberties Union, April 2, 2018, www.nyclu.org/en/stop-and-frisk-data (accessed 4/13/18).

3. *Face the Nation*, CBS News, June 19, 2016, transcript, www.cbsnews.com/news/face-the-nation-transcripts-june-19-2016-trump-lynch-lapierre-feinstein/ (accessed 11/7/17).

4. *Meet the Press*, NBC News, May 9, 2010, transcript, www.nbcnews.com/id/37024384/ns/meet_the_press/t/meet-press-transcript-may/#.WgIRPXZryiM (accessed 11/7/17).

5. There are eight commissioners on the U.S. Commission on Civil Rights, four appointed by the president and four by Congress. The commissioners serve six-year terms and do not require Senate confirmation, and no more than four members may be of the same political party.

6. Howard Dodson, "How Slavery Helped Build a World Economy," in Schomburg Center for Research in Black Culture of the New York Public Library, *Jubilee: The Emergence of African-American Culture* (Washington, DC: National Geographic Press, 2003).

7. Other provisions of the Compromise of 1850, which was a package of five bills, included creating the current boundaries for Texas as it dropped its claim to land in parts of five current states in exchange for the federal government's assumption of $10 million in debt from the old Texas Republic. Also, slave trade, but not slavery itself, was abolished in the District of Columbia. See "The Compromise of 1850," Primary Documents in American History, Library of Congress, www.loc.gov/rr/program/bib/ourdocs/Compromise1850.html (accessed 10/26/17).

8. John W. Wright, ed., *New York Times 2000 Almanac* (New York: Penguin Reference, 1999), p. 165. Estimates from various online sources are quite a bit higher, averaging about 620,000 deaths.

9. V. O. Key Jr., *Southern Politics in State and Nation* (New York: Knopf, 1949), p. 538. For example, the Louisiana grandfather clause read: "No male person who was on January 1, 1867, or at any date prior thereto, entitled to vote under the Constitution of the United States, wherein he then resided, and no son or grandson of any such person not less than twenty-one years of age at the date of the adoption of this Constitution ... shall be denied the right to register and vote in this State by reason of his failure to possess the educational or property qualifications." Grandfather clauses as they applied to voting were ruled unconstitutional in 1915.

10. Chandler Davidson, "The Voting Rights Act: A Brief History," in *Controversies in Minority Voting: The Voting Rights Act in Perspective*, ed. Bernard Grofman and Chandler Davidson (Washington, DC: Brookings Institution, 1992), p. 21.

11. "Indian Removal: 1814–1848," Public Broadcasting System, www.pbs.org/wgbh/aia/part4/4p2959.html (accessed 1/26/12).

12. *Cherokee Nation v. Georgia*, 30 U.S. 1 (1831).

13. *United States v. Wong Kim Ark*, 169 U.S. 649 (1898).

14. Bilal Qureshi, "From Wrong to Right: A U.S. Apology for Japanese Internment," August 9, 2013, National Public Radio, www.npr.org/sections/codeswitch/2013/08/09/210138278/japanese-internment-redress (accessed 1/29/16).

15. *Trump v. Hawaii*, 585 U.S. ____ (2018).

16. This Day in History, "Abigail Adams Urges Husband to 'Remember the Ladies,'" Abigail Adams to John Adams, March 31, 1776, www.history.com/this-day-in-history/abigail-adams-urges-husband-to-remember-the-ladies (accessed 4/13/18).

17. *Bradwell v. Illinois*, 83 U.S. 130 (1873).

18. *Hoyt v. Florida*, 368 U.S. 57 (1961).

19. Lucian K. Truscott IV, "The Real Mob at Stonewall," *New York Times*, June 25, 2009, p. A19.

20. "LGBT," Pollingreport.com, various surveys, www.pollingreport.com/civil.htm (accessed 10/26/17).

21. *Obergefell v. Hodges*, 576 U.S. ____ (2015).

22. Sean Cahill, "Trump Administration Amasses Striking Anti-LGBT Record in First Year, *The Hill*, January 19, 2018, http://thehill.com/opinion/campaign/369790-trump-administration-amasses-striking-anti-lgbt-record-in-first-year (accessed 4/13/18).

23. "Charge Statistics, FY 1997 through FY 2017," U.S. Equal Employment Opportunity Commission, www.eeoc.gov/eeoc/statistics/enforcement/charges.cfm (accessed 4/13/18).

24. "The Case for Fair Housing: 2017 Fair Housing Trends Report," National Fair Housing Alliance, p. 77, http://nationalfairhousing.org/wp-content/uploads/2017/07/TRENDS-REPORT-2017-FINAL.pdf (accessed 4/13/18).

25. "Recent Accomplishments of the Housing and Civil Enforcement Section," U.S. Department of Justice, April 4, 2018, www.justice.gov/crt/recent-accomplishments-housing-and-civil-enforcement-section (accessed 4/13/18).

26. Davidson, "The Voting Rights Act," p. 22; also see U.S. Department of Justice, Civil Rights Division, "About Section 5 of the Voting Rights Act," www.justice.gov/crt/about-section-5-voting-rights-act (accessed 4/13/18), for a complete list of cases in which the Justice Department has denied "preclearance" of a change in an electoral practice under Section 5 of the Voting Rights Act. Note that in racially homogeneous single-member districts, minority candidates usually win. But in at-large elections, in which representatives are elected citywide or countywide (and which thus may contain a mix of minority and white voters from the districts making up the city or county), the majority-white voters can outvote the minority voters and elect an all-white city council or school board.

27. "The Long Shadow of Jim Crow: Voter Suppression in America," Special Report, People for the American Way Foundation and NAACP, http://archive.fairvote.org/righttovote/PFAW-NAACP.pdf (accessed 4/13/18); "Election 2016: Restrictive Voting Laws by the Numbers," Brennan Center for Justice, September 28, 2016, www.brennancenter.org/analysis/election-2016-restrictive-voting-laws-numbers, (accessed 11/2/17).

28. "New Voting Restrictions in America," Brennan Center for Justice, www.brennancenter.org/new-voting-restrictions-america (accessed 4/13/18).

29. *Husted v. A. Philip Randolph Institute*, 584 U.S. ___ (2018).

30. Kayla Fontenot, Jessica Semega, and Melissa Kollar, "Income and Poverty in the United States: 2017," U.S. Census, Current Population Reports, September 2018, poverty rates from Table 3, p. 12, income from Table 1, p. 2, www.census.gov/content/dam/Census/library/publications/2018/demo/p60-263.pdf (accessed 9/26/18).

31. Jesse Bricker et al., "Changes in U.S. Family Finances from 2013 to 2016: Evidence from the Survey of Consumer Finances," *Federal Reserve Bulletin* 103:3 (September 2017), Table 2, p. 12, https://www.federalreserve.gov/publications/files/scf17.pdf (accessed 4/13/18).

32. Employment Situation Summary, Bureau of Labor Statistics, Tables A2 and A3, September 7, 2018, www.bls.gov/news.release/empsit.nr0.htm (accessed 9/26/18).

33. "America's Families and Living Arrangements: 2017," U.S. Census, Table C3, www.census.gov/data/tables/2017/demo/families/cps-2017.html (accessed 9/26/18).

34. Federal Bureau of Investigation, "Crime in the United States, 2014, Expanded Homicide Data Tables, Table 2," https://ucr.fbi.gov/crime-in-the-u.s/2014/crime-in-the-u.s.-2014/tables/expanded-homicide-data/expanded_homicide_data_table_2_murder_victims_by_age_sex_and_race_2014.xls (accessed 10/17/16).

35. Life expectancy data are from Elizabeth Arias, et al., "United States Life Tables, 2013," *National Vital Statistics Reports*, Centers for Disease Control and Prevention, April 11, 2017, Table A, p. 3, www.cdc.gov/nchs/data/nvsr/nvsr66/nvsr66_03.pdf. Infant mortality numbers are from T. J. Mathews, Danielle M. Ely, and Anne K. Driscoll, "State Variations in Infant Mortality by Race and Hispanic Origin of Mother, 2013-2015," NCHS Data Brief No. 295, Centers for Disease Control and Prevention, January 2018, www.cdc.gov/nchs/products/databriefs/db295.htm. Maternal mortality rates are from "Pregnancy Mortality Surveillance System," November 9, 2017, Centers for Disease Control and Prevention, www.cdc.gov/reproductivehealth/maternalinfanthealth/pmss.html. (All sources accessed 4/13/18.)

36. See the National Resource Defense Council's program on the Environmental Justice, www.nrdc.org/about/environmental-justice, and the Environmental Justice and Health Alliance for Chemical Policy reform's report "Who's in Danger? Race, Poverty, and Chemical Disasters," May 2014, http://comingcleaninc.org/assets/media/images/Reports/Who%27s%20in%20Danger%20Report%20FINAL.pdf (both accessed 4/13/18).

37. Greg Botelho, Sarah Jorgensen, and Joseph Netto, "Water Crisis in Flint, Michigan, Draws Federal Investigation," CNN.com, January 9, 2016, www.cnn.com/2016/01/05/health/flint-michigan-water-investigation (accessed 1/30/16).

38. Lawrence Hurley, "U.S. Supreme Court Allows Flint Water Contamination Lawsuits," *Reuters*, March 19, 2018, www.reuters.com/article/us-usa-court-water/u-s-supreme-court-allows-flint-water-contamination-lawsuits-idUSKBN1GV1RB (accessed 7/24/18).

39. Evelyn Diaz, "Nick Cannon Accuses L.A. Cops of Racial Profiling," BET News, www.bet.com/news/celebrities/2011/11/18/nick-cannon-accuses-la-cops-of-racial-profiling.html (accessed 1/29/12).

40. Cristina Corbin, "Senate's Lone Black GOP Member Says Police Stopped Him 7 Times in a Year," Fox News, July 14, 2016, www.foxnews.com/politics/2016/07/14/senates-lone-black-gop-member-says-police-stopped-him-7-times-in-year.html (accessed 11/2/17).

41. Benjamin Weiser and Joseph Goldstein, "Mayor Says New York City Will Settle Suits on Stop-and-Frisk Tactics," *New York Times*, January 30, 2014, www.nytimes.com/2014/01/31/nyregion/de-blasio-stop-and-frisk.html (accessed 4/6/14).

42. Hundreds of studies have examined these patterns, and, not surprisingly, there are divergent findings. However, most have found differences in sentencing based on race. A 2015 Bureau of Justice Statistics study found that "black men received roughly 5% to 10% longer prison sentences than white men for similar crimes, after accounting for the facts surrounding the case." See "Federal Sentencing Disparity: 2005-2012," Bureau of Justice Statistics, October 2015, www.bjs.gov/content/pub/pdf/fsd0512_sum.pdf. Government statistics on crime may be found on the FBI site at www.fbi.gov. (Both sources accessed 11/2/17.)

43. "2017 Police Violence Report," Mapping Police Violence, https://policeviolencereport.org (accessed 4/17/18).

44. "Herstory," Black Lives Matter, https://blacklivesmatter.com/about/herstory (accessed 4/17/18).

45. Holly Yan, Khushbu Shah, and Emanuella Grinberg," Ex-officer Michael Slager Pleads Guilty in Shooting Death of Walter Scott," CNN, May 2, 2017, www.cnn.com/2017/05/02/us/michael-slager-federal-plea/ (accessed 2/23/18).

46. Madison Park, "Police Shootings: Trials, Convictions Are Rare for Officers," CNN, June 24, 2017, www.cnn.com/2017/05/18/us/police-involved-shooting-cases/index.html (accessed 11/3/17).

47. "2016 Hate Crime Statistics," U.S. Department of Justice, www.fbi.gov/about-us/cjis/ucr/hate-crime/2016/tables/table-1 (accessed 4/17/18).

48. Rosa Parks with James Haskins, *Rosa Parks: My Story* (New York: Dial Books, 1992), p. 116.

49. Clayborne Carson, David J. Garrow, Gerald Gill, Vincent Harding, and Darlene Clark Hine, eds., *The Eyes on the Prize Civil Rights Reader* (New York: Penguin Books, 1997).

50. *Boynton v. Virginia*, 363 U.S. 454 (1960).

51. David Halberstam, *The Children* (New York: Ballantine Books, 1999).

52. Matt Broomfield, "Women's March against Donald Trump Is the Largest Day of Protests in US History, Say Political Scientists," *Independent*, January 23, 2017, www.independent.co.uk/news/world/americas/womens-march-anti-donald-trump-womens-rights-largest-protest-demonstration-us-history-political-a7541081.html (accessed 10/26/17). Jeremy Pressman of the University of Connecticut and Erica Chenoweth of the University of Denver collected data on the Women's March, https://docs.google.com/spreadsheets/d/1xaoiLqYKz8x9Yc_rfhtmSOJQ2EGgeUVjvV4A8LsIaxY/edit#gid=0 (accessed 10/26/17). The low end of their estimate is 3,267,134, the high end is 5,246,670, and their "best guess" is 4,157,894.

53. "Dakota Access Pipeline in Operation after Months of Resistance," *PBS News Hour*, June 3, 2017, www.pbs.org/newshour/nation/dakota-access-pipeline-operation-months-resistance (accessed 10/26/17).

54. See https://blacklivesmatter.com/ for more information about the movement, including the "Black Lives Matter 4-Year Anniversary Report" and news about recent events (accessed 10/26/17).

55. By the end of the regular season, only five teams featured at least one player regularly sitting or kneeling on the sidelines for the anthem: the Seattle Seahawks, the San Francisco 49ers, the Miami Dolphins, the New York Giants, and the Oakland Raiders. Valerie Richardson, "NFL's Kneeling Comes to Abrupt Halt: Protesters Miss Playoffs," *The Washington Times,* January 15, 2018, www.washingtontimes.com/news/2018/jan/15/nfls-kneeling-protesters-miss-playoffs (accessed 4/17/18). Mark Maske, "NFL Owners Approve New National Anthem Policy with Hope of Ending Protests, *Washington Post*, May 23, 2018, www.washingtonpost.com/news/sports/wp/2018/05/23/nfl-owners-leaning-towards-requiring-players-to-stand-for-national-anthem-or-remain-in-locker-room/?utm_term=.71eed9fa2d60 (accessed 6/15/18).

56. *Pearson v. Murray*, 169 Md. 478 (1936).

57. *Shelley v. Kraemer*, 334 U.S. 1 (1948).

58. *Brown v. Board of Education*, 347 U.S. 483 (1954).

59. *Brown v. Board of Education II*, 349 U.S. 294 (1955).

60. Paul Brest and Sanford Levinson, *Process of Constitutional Decision Making: Cases and Material* (Boston: Little, Brown, 1982), pp. 471–80.

61. *Swann v. Charlotte-Mecklenberg Board of Education*, 402 U.S. 1 (1971).

62. *Milliken v. Bradley*, 418 U.S. 717 (1974).

63. *Parents Involved in Community Schools Inc. v. Seattle School District*, 05-98 (2007); *Meredith v. Jefferson County (Ky.) Board of Education*, 551 U.S. 701 (2007).

64. *Heart of Atlanta Motel, Inc. v. United States*, 379 U.S. 241 (1964).

65. *Katzenbach v. McClung*, 379 U.S. 294 (1964).

66. *Griggs v. Duke Power*, 401 U.S. 424 (1971).

67. *Easley v. Cromartie*, 532 U.S. 234 (2001), rehearing denied, 532 U.S. 1076 (2001).

68. *Easley v. Cromartie*, 532 U.S. 1076 (2001).

69. *Bethune-Hill v. Virginia State Board of Elections*, 580 U.S. ____ (2017); *Cooper v. Harris*, 581 U.S. ____ (2017). In *Alabama Legislative Black Caucus v. Alabama* 575 U.S. ____ (2015), the Court also struck down state legislative districts in Alabama as unconstitutional "packing." In January 2017, a three-judge panel also struck down the state's next attempt to draw the districts, and finally, in October 2017, the third attempt was upheld.

70. *Shelby County v. Holder*, 570 U.S. (2013).

71. *Reed v. Reed*, 404 U.S. 71 (1971).

72. *Frontiero v. Richardson*, 411 U.S. 677 (1973).

73. *Koremastu v. United States*, 323 U.S. 214 (1944).

74. *Trump v. Hawaii*, 585 U.S. ____ (2018).

75. *Craig v. Boren*, 429 U.S. 190 (1976).

76. *Orr v. Orr*, 440 U.S. 268 (1979).

77. *United States v. Virginia*, 518 U.S. 515 (1996).

78. Joanna L. Grossman, "Policing Sexism at the Border: The Supreme Court's Decision in *Sessions v. Morales-Santana*," Verdict: Legal Analysis and Commentary from Justia, June 20, 2017, https://verdict.justia.com/2017/06/20/policing-sexism-border-supreme-courts-decision-sessions-v-morales-santana (accessed 11/6/17). The case is *Sessions v. Morales-Santana*, 582 US ____ (2017).

79. *Johnson v. Transportation Agency of Santa Clara*, 480 U.S. 616 (1987).

80. *Harris v. Forklift Systems*, 510 U.S. 17 618 (1993).

81. Stephanie Zacharek, Eliana Dockterman and Haley Sweetland Edwards, "Person of the Year 2017: The Silence Breakers," *Time*, http://time.com/time-person-of-the-year-2017-silence-breakers (accessed 4/18/18).

82. *Ledbetter v. Goodyear Tire & Rubber Co.*, 550 U.S. 618 (2007).

83. Julie Hirschfeld Davis, "Obama Moves to Expand Rules Aimed at Closing Gender Pay Gap," *New York Times*, January 29, 2016, www.nytimes.com/2016/01/29/us/politics/obama-moves-to-expand-rules-aimed-at-closing-gender-pay-gap.html (accessed 1/30/16).

84. "Women Present Widespread Discrimination at Wal-Mart," press release, April 28, 2003, www.walmartclass.com/staticdata/press_releases/wmcc.html (accessed 10/4/12).

85. David Savage, "Supreme Court Blocks Huge Class-Action Suit against Wal-Mart," *Los Angeles Times*, June 21, 2011. The case is *Dukes v. Wal-Mart Stores, Inc.* (2011).

86. *Bowers v. Hardwick*, 478 U.S. 186 (1986), rehearing denied, 478 U.S. 1039 (1986).

87. *Romer v. Evans*, 517 U.S. 620 (1996).

88. *Lawrence v. Texas*, 539 U.S. 558 (2003). Because the basis for the decision was the due process clause of the Fourteenth Amendment and not the equal protection clause, this ruling upheld a civil liberty rather than a civil right. As such, it applied to all laws regarding sodomy, not just those that applied to gays. However, the decision has been widely regarded as a landmark civil rights case because it provided equal rights for gays.

89. The three cases are *Hollingsworth v. Perry*, 570 U.S. (2013), *United States v. Windsor*, 570 U.S. ____ (2013), and *Obergefell v. Hodges*, 576 U.S. ____ (2015).

90. Quoted in Voting Rights Act Extension: Report of the Subcommittee of the Constitution of the Committee on the Judiciary, U.S. Senate, 97th Congress, 2nd session, May 25, 1982, S. Rept. 97-417, 4.

91. Drew S. Days III, "Section 5 Enforcement and the Justice Department," in *Controversies in Minority Voting: The Voting Rights Act in Perspective*, ed. Bernard Grofman and Chandler Davidson (Washington, DC: Brookings Institution Press, 1992), p. 52; Frank R. Parker, *Black Votes Count* (Chapel Hill: University of North Carolina Press, 1990), p. 1.

92. Davidson, "The Voting Rights Act," p. 21.

93. "Fair Housing: It's Your Right." U.S. Department of Housing and Urban Development, www.hud.gov/program_offices/fair_housing_equal_opp/online-complaint (accessed 4/18/18).

94. *United States v. Morrison*, 529 U.S. 598 (2000).

95. *Board of Trustees of the University of Alabama v. Garrett*, 531 U.S. 356 (2001). However, in *State of Tennessee v. George Lane and Beverly Jones*, 541 U.S. 509 (2004), the Court ruled that the disabled must have access to courthouses.

96. The White House, "Remarks by the Reception Commemorating the Enactment of the Matthew Shepard and James Byrd Jr. Hate Crimes Prevention Act," October 28, 2009, https://obamawhitehouse.archives.gov/the-press-office/remarks-president-reception-commemorating-enactment-matthew-shepard-and-james-byrd- (accessed 4/18/18).

97. Tim Mak, "Post-'Don't Ask,' Gay Navy Lt. Marries," *Politico*, September 20, 2011, www.politico.com/news/stories/0911/63909.html (accessed 1/24/12).

98. Justin Jouvenal, "Federal Judge in D.C. Blocks Part of Trump's Transgender Military Ban," *Washington Post*, October 30, 2017, www.washingtonpost.com/local/public-safety/federal-judge-in-dc-blocks-part-of-trumps-transgender-military-ban/2017/10/30/41d41526-bd94-11e7-959c-fe2b598d8c00_story.html?utm_term=.fe88c4776b62 (accessed 11/6/17).

99. On July 18, 2018, the U.S. Court of Appeals for the 9th Circuit upheld a block on the implementation of the ban. See Ellen Mitchell, "Court Rules Against Trump Administration on Transgender Military Ban," *The Hill*, July 18, 2018, www.thehill.com/policy/defense/397702-court-rules-against-trump-admin-on-transgender-military-ban (accessed 7/24/18).

100. *Public Papers of the Presidents of the United States: Lyndon B. Johnson, 1965*, vol. 2, entry 301 (Washington, DC: Government Printing Office, 1966), pp. 635-40.

101. The first poll is from the Pew Research Center, October 4, 2017, www.people-press.org/2017/10/05/4-race-immigration-and-discrimination/4_7-6/ and the second from Gallup, July 8, 2016, news.gallup.com/poll/193508/oppose-colleges-considering-race-admissions.aspx (both accessed 4/18/18).

102. State of California, article 1, section 31.

103. The training program case was *United Steel Workers of America v. Weber*, 443 U.S. 193 (1979); the labor union case was *Sheet Metal Workers v. EEOC*, 478 U.S. 421 (1986); and the Alabama state police case was *U.S. v. Paradise*, 480 U.S. 149 (1987).

104. *Ricci v. DeStefano*, 557 U.S. (2009).

105. *Regents of the University of California v. Bakke*, 438 U.S. 265 (1978).

106. *Smith v. University of Washington*, 233 F3d 1188 (9th Cir. 2000).

107. *Grutter v. Bollinger*, 539 U.S. 306 (2003), was the law school case and *Gratz v. Bollinger*, 539 U.S. 244 (2003), was the undergraduate admissions case.

108. In *Bakke*, Justice Lewis Powell was the only member of the Court who held this position, even if it became the basis for all affirmative action programs over the next 25 years. Four justices in the *Bakke* decision wanted to get rid of race as a factor in admissions, and another four thought that the "strict scrutiny" standard should not even be applied in this instance.

109. *Schuette v. Coalition to Defend Affirmative Action*, 572 U.S. _____ (2014).

110. *Fisher v. University of Texas, Austin*, 579 U.S. _____ (2016).

111. Adam Harris, "In Trump Era, the Use of Race in Admissions Comes under New Scrutiny," *Chronicle of Higher Education*, August 2, 2017, www.chronicle.com/article/In-Trump-Era-the-Use-of-Race/240821?cid=rclink (accessed 11/6/17).

112. *Trump v. Hawaii*, 585 U.S. _____ (2018).

113. James Vicini, "Supreme Court to Decide Arizona Immigration Law," Reuters, December 12, 2011, www.reuters.com/article/2011/12/12/us-usa-immigration-arizona-idUSTRE7BB0XJ20111212 (accessed 2/2/12).

114. *Arizona v. United States*, 567 U.S. _____ (2012).

115. Fernanda Santos, "Arizona Immigration Law Survives Ruling," *New York Times*, September 6, 2012, www.nytimes.com/2012/09/07/us/key-element-of-arizona-immigration-law-survives-ruling.html?r=0 (accessed 10/5/12).

116. Immigration, various polls, www.pollingreport.com/immigration.htm (accessed 1/30/16).

117. Kirk Semple and Miriam Jordan, "For Families Split at Border, an Anguished Wait for Children's Return," *New York Times*, September 1, 2018, www.nytimes.com/2018/09/01/world/americas/immigrant-families-separation-border.html (accessed 9/26/18).

118. "An Act Providing for the Collection of Data Relative to Traffic Stops," Massachusetts state law, Chapter 228 of the Acts of 2000, www.mass.gov/legis/laws/seslaw00/sl000228.htm (accessed 7/22/08).

Take a Stand

a. *Fisher v. University of Texas at Austin*, 579 U.S. _____ (2016).

b. *Schuette v. Coalition to Defend Affirmative Action*, 572 U.S. _____ (2014).

Chapter 6

1. V. O. Key, *The Responsible Electorate*. (Cambridge, MA: Harvard University Press, 1966).

2. Adam Berinsky, "Telling the Truth about Believing the Lies? Evidence for the Limited Prevalence of Expressive Survey Responding," *Journal of Politics* 80:1 (2018): 211-24.

3. For a review, see Arthur Lupia and Mathew D. McCubbins, *The Democratic Dilemma* (New York: Cambridge University Press, 1998).

4. Larry Bartels, "Partisanship and Voting Behavior, 1952-1996," *American Journal of Political Science* 44 (2000): 35-50.

5. Robert S. Erikson, Michael B. Mackuen, and James A. Stimson, *The Macro Polity* (New York: Cambridge University Press, 2002).

6. John Zaller, "Coming to Grips with V. O. Key's Concept of Latent Opinion" (unpublished paper, University of California, Los Angeles, 1998).

7. Morris Fiorina, *Retrospective Voting in American National Elections* (Cambridge, MA: Harvard University Press, 1981).

8. Virginia Sapiro, "Not Your Parents' Political Socialization: Introduction for a New Generation," *Annual Review of Political Science* 7 (2004): 1-23.

9. M. Kent Jennings and Richard G. Niemi, *Generations and Politics: A Panel Study of Young Adults and Their Parents* (Princeton, NJ: Princeton University Press, 1981).

10. Robert Putnam, *Bowling Alone: The Collapse and Revival of American Community* (New York: Simon and Schuster, 2000).

11. Richard G. Niemi and Mary Hepburn, "The Rebirth of Political Socialization," *Perspectives on Politics* 24 (1995): 7-16.

12. David Campbell, *Why We Vote: How Schools and Communities Shape Our Civic Life* (Princeton, NJ: Princeton University Press, 2006).

13. Sidney Verba, Kay Schlozman, and Henry Brady, *Voice and Equality: Civic Volunteerism in American Politics* (Cambridge, MA: Harvard University Press, 1995).

14. Paul Allen Beck and M. Kent Jennings, "Pathways to Participation," *American Political Science Review* 76 (1982): 94-108.

15. Pew Research Center, "In Gay Marriage Debate, Both Supporters and Opponents See Legal Recognition as 'Inevitable,'" June 6, 2013, www.people-press.org/2013/06/06/in-gay-marriage-debate-both-supporters-and-opponents-see-legal-recognition-as-inevitable (accessed 10/30/15).

16. Pew Research Center, "United in Remembrance, Divided over Policies: Ten Years after 9/11," September 1, 2011, www.people-press.org/2011/09/01/united-in-remembrance-divided-over-policies/1 (accessed 9/5/12).

17. John Zaller, *The Nature and Origins of Mass Opinion* (New York: Cambridge University Press, 1992).

18. Richard Nadwau et al., "Class, Party, and South-Nonsouth Differences," *American Politics Research* 32 (2004): 52–67.

19. James H. Kuklinski et al., "Racial Prejudice and Attitudes toward Affirmative Action," *American Journal of Political Science* 41 (1997): 402–19.

20. Donald P. Green, Bradley Palmquist, and Eric Schickler, *Partisan Hearts and Minds* (New Haven, CT: Yale University Press, 2002).

21. Pew Research Center, "Young Voters Supported Obama Less, but May Have Mattered More," November 26, 2012, www.people-press.org/2012/11/26/young-voters-supported-obama-less-but-may-have-mattered-more (accessed 3/17/14).

22. For elaboration on this point, see William T. Bianco, Richard G. Niemi, and Harold W. Stanley, "Partisanship and Group Support over Time: A Multivariate Analysis," *American Political Science Review* 80 (September 1986): 969–76.

23. Lupia and McCubbins, *The Democratic Dilemma*.

24. Lawrence R. Jacobs and Robert Y. Shapiro, *Politicians Don't Pander: Political Manipulation and the Loss of Democratic Responsiveness* (Chicago: University of Chicago Press, 2000).

25. Zaller, *The Nature and Origins of Mass Opinion*.

26. R. Michael Alvarez and John Brehm, *Hard Choices, Easy Answers* (Princeton, NJ: Princeton University Press, 2002).

27. John Zaller and Stanley Feldman, "A Theory of the Survey Response: Revealing Preferences versus Answering Questions," *American Journal of Political Science* 36 (1992): 579–616.

28. Janet M. Box-Steffensmeier and Susan DeBoef, "Macropartisanship and Macroideology in the Sophisticated Electorate," *Journal of Politics* 63:1 (2001): 232–48.

29. R. Michael Alvarez and John Brehm, "American Ambivalence towards Abortion Policy: Development of a Heteroskedastic Probit Model of Competing Values," *American Journal of Political Science* 39:4 (1995): 1055–82.

30. Pew Research Center, "Beyond Red vs. Blue: The Political Typology. Section 6: Foreign Affairs, Terrorism and Privacy," June 26, 2014, www.people-press.org/2014/06/26/section-6-foreign-affairs-terrorism-and-privacy (accessed 3/11/16).

31. Richard Wike and Katie Simmons, "Global Support for Principle of Free Expression, but Opposition to Some Forms of Speech: Americans Especially Likely to Embrace Individual Liberties," Pew Research Center, November 18, 2015, www.pewglobal.org/2015/11/18/global-support-for-principle-of-free-expression-but-opposition-to-some-forms-of-speech (accessed 11/18/15).

32. Milton Lodge and Charles Taber, "Three Steps toward a Theory of Motivated Political Reasoning," in *Elements of Reason: Cognition, Choice, and the Bounds of Rationality*, ed. Arthur Lupia, Mathew D. McCubbins, and Samuel L. Popkin (London: Cambridge University Press, 2000); Marcus, Neuman, and Mackuen, *Affective Intelligence*; David Redlawsk, "Hot Cognition or Cool Consideration? Testing the Effects of Motivated Reasoning on Political Decision Making," *Journal of Politics* 64 (2002): 1021–44; David Redlawsk, Andrew Civettini, and Karen Emmerson, "The Affective Tipping Point: Do Motivated Reasoners Ever 'Get It'?" *Political Psychology* 31, no. 4 (2010): 563–93.

33. Desilver, "5 Facts" (accessed 11/23/15).

34. See Harry Holloway and John George, *Public Opinion* (New York: St. Martin's Press, 1986); Paul R. Abramson, *Political Attitudes in America* (San Francisco: Freeman, 1983).

35. See Paul M. Sniderman and Edward G. Carmines, *Reaching beyond Race* (Cambridge, MA: Harvard University Press, 1997).

36. Christopher Wlezien and Robert S. Erikson, "The Horse Race: What Polls Reveal as the Election Campaign Unfolds," *International Journal of Public Opinion Research* 19:1 (2007): 74–88.

37. Anton J. Nederhof, "Methods of Coping with Social Desirability Bias: A Review," *European Journal of Social Psychology* 15:3 (2006): 263–80.

38. Sarah Kliff, "Obamacare Is 5 Years Old, and Americans Are Still Worried about Death Panels," Vox.com, May 23, 2015, www.vox.com/2015/3/23/8273007/obamacare-poll-death-panels (accessed 11/2/15).

39. Michael X. Delli Carpini and Scott Keeter, *What Americans Know about Politics and Why It Matters* (New Haven, CT: Yale University Press, 1997).

40. Dan Diamond, "The Unemployment Rate Doubled under Bush. It's Fallen by More than One-Third under Obama," Vox.com, November 7, 2015, www.vox.com/2015/11/7/9684780/unemployment-rate-obama (accessed 11/7/15).

41. Delli Carpini and Keeter, *What Americans Know about Politics and Why It Matters*.

42. Nate Silver, "How FiveThirtyEight Calculates Pollster Ratings," September 25, 2014, http://fivethirtyeight.com/features/how-fivethirtyeight-calculates-pollster-ratings (accessed 11/6/15).

43. For a review of the literature on trust in government, see Karen Cook, Russell Hardin, and Margaret Levi, *Cooperation without Trust* (New York: Russell Sage Foundation, 2005), as well as Marc J. Hetherington, *Why Trust Matters: Declining Political Trust and the Demise of American Liberalism* (Princeton, NJ: Princeton University Press, 2004).

44. William T. Bianco, *Trust: Representatives and Constituents* (Ann Arbor: University of Michigan Press, 1994).

45. Sean M. Theriault, *The Power of the People: Congressional Competition, Public Attention, and Voter Retribution* (Columbus: Ohio State University Press, 2005).

46. Thomas Rudolph and Jillian Evans, "Political Trust, Ideology, and Public Support for Government Spending," *American Journal of Political Science* 49 (2005): 660–71.

47. Patricia Moy and Michael Pfau, *With Malice toward All? The Media and Public Confidence in Democratic Institutions* (Boulder, CO: Praeger, 2000).

48. Erikson, Mackuen, and Stimson, *The Macro Polity*.

49. James A. Stimson, *Public Opinion in America: Moods, Swings, and Cycles* (Boulder, CO: Westview Press, 1999).

50. Robert S. Erikson, Michael B. Mackuen, and James A. Stimson, "American Politics: The Model" (unpublished paper, Columbia University, 2000).

51. Larry Bartels, "Constituency Opinion and Congressional Policy Making: The Reagan Defense Buildup," *American Political Science Review* 85 (June 1991): 457–74; Jonathan Kastellec, Jeffrey R. Lax, and Justin H. Phillips, "Public Opinion and Senate Confirmation of Supreme Court Nominees," *Journal of Politics* 72 (2010): 767–84.

52. Jacobs and Shapiro, *Politicians Don't Pander: Political Manipulation and the Loss of Democratic Responsiveness.*

Chapter 7

1. Brian Solis, *Engage! The Complete Guide for Brands and Businesses to Build, Cultivate, and Measure Success in the New Web* (New York: Wiley and Sons, 2010), p. 29.

2. Samidh Chakrabarti, "Hard Questions: What Effect Does Social Media Have on Democracy?" https://newsroom.fb.com/news/2018/01/effect-social-media-democracy/?frame-nonce=bd5e374778 (accessed 5/10/18).

3. William H. Riker, *The Strategy of Rhetoric: Campaigning for the American Constitution* (New Haven, CT: Yale University Press, 1996).

4. Garry Wills, *Explaining America: The Federalist* (New York: Penguin Press, 2001).

5. Geoffrey R. Stone, *Perilous Times: Free Speech in Wartime from the Sedition Act of 1798 to the War on Terrorism* (New York: W. W. Norton, 2004).

6. John D. Stevens, *Sensationalism and the New York Press* (New York: Columbia University Press, 1991).

7. Robert C. Williams, *Horace Greeley: Champion of American Freedom* (New York: New York University Press, 2006).

8. Gay Talese, *The Kingdom and the Power* (New York: Calder and Boyars, 1983).

9. For a detailed history, see United States Early Radio History, www.earlyradiohistory.us (accessed 9/17/12).

10. The Project for Excellence in Journalism, "The State of the News Media. http://www.pewresearch.org/topics/state-of-the-news-media (accessed 5/3/18).

11. The *Columbia Journalism Review* maintains a list of holdings for major media companies at Who Owns What, www.cjr.org/tools/owners (accessed 9/17/12).

12. See www.themonkeycage.org (accessed 1/25/18) and www.vox.com/mischiefs-of-faction (accessed 2/23/18).

13. For the original and revised versions, see "New York Post Goes On Cletus Safari, Finds This Scrappy Blue Collar ... Chief Of Surgery?" https://wonkette.com/629157/new-york-post-goes-on-cletus-safari-finds-this-scrappy-blue-collar-chief-of-surgery (accessed 5/3/2018).

14. Matthew Baum, "Sex, Lies and War: How Soft News Brings Foreign Policy to the Inattentive Public," *American Political Science Review* 96 (2002): 91–109.

15. Patti M. Valkenburg, Jochen Peter, and Joseph B. Walther, "Media effects: Theory and research," *Annual Review of Psychology* 67 (2016): 315–38.

16. Lance Bennett, *News: The Politics of Illusion* (New York: Pearson, 2012).

17. Danny Hayes and Matthew Guardino, *Influence from Abroad: Foreign Voices, the Media, and U.S. Public Opinion* (New York: Cambridge University Press, 2013).

18. Matthew Baum, "Talking the Vote: Why Presidential Candidates Hit the Talk Show Circuit," *American Journal of Political Science* 49 (2005): 213–34.

19. Harriet Sinclair, "Ted Cruz Releases Strange Song about Opponent Beto O'Rourke as Pair Win Primaries," *Newsweek*, March 7, 2018, www.newsweek.com/ted-cruz-beto-orourke-texas-834257 (accessed 10/2/18).

20. Tara Golshan, "The Raging Controversy over Beto O'Rourke's Full Name, Explained," Vox.com, March 8, 2018, www.vox.com/policy-and-politics/2018/3/7/17091094/controversy-beto-orourke-robert-name-ted-cruz (accessed 10/2/18).

21. Barton Gellman, "Code Name 'Verax': Snowden, in Exchanges with *Post* Reporter, Made Clear He Knew Risks," *Washington Post*, June 13, 2012, p. A1.

22. Michael Kelly, "Bing Maps Appear to Show the 'Secret' U.S. Drone Base in Saudi Arabia," February 8, 2013, www.businessinsider.com/wired-finds-americas-drone-base-in-saudi-arabia-2013-2 (accessed 8/30/16).

23. For a discussion of these concepts, see Paul M. Sniderman and Sean M. Theriault, "The Structure of Political Argument and the Logic of Issue Framing," in *Studies in Public Opinion*, ed. William E. Saris and Paul M. Sniderman (Princeton, NJ: Princeton University Press, 2004); and Shanto Iyengar and Donald Kinder, *News That Matters* (Chicago: University of Chicago Press, 1987). See also Maxwell McCombs and Donald L. Shaw, "The Agenda-Setting Functions of Mass Media," *Public Opinion Quarterly* 36 (1972): 176–87; and Amos Tversky and Daniel Kahnemann, "The Framing of Decisions and the Psychology of Choice," *Science* 211 (1981): 453–58.

24. Markus Prior, "Media and Political Polarization," *Annual Review of Political Science* 16 (2013): 101–27.

25. Kevin Arceneaux et al., "The Influence of News Media on Political Elites: Investigating Strategic Responsiveness in Congress," *American Journal of Political Science* 60:1 (2016): 5–29.

26. Matthew S. Levendusky, "Why Do Partisan Media Polarize Viewers?," *American Journal of Political Science* 57:3 (2013): 611–23.

27. Kevin Arceneaux, Martin Johnson, and Chad Murphy, "Polarized Political Communication, Oppositional Media Hostility, and Selective Exposure," *Journal of Politics* 74:01 (2012): 174–86.

28. See Eric Alterman, *What Liberal Media?* (New York: Basic Books, 2003); and Bernard Goldberg, *Bias* (New York: Regnery, 2001).

29. This description runs on the editorial masthead of every issue of *The Nation*.

30. Tal Kopan, "Carson Slams Reporters over Questions about His Past," November 6, 2015, www.cnn.com/2015/11/06/politics/ben-carson-responds-violent-past-new-day (accessed 11/20/15).

31. Project Censored, "The Top 25 Censored Stories of 2016–2017," http://projectcensored.org/category/the-top-25-censored-stories-of-2016-2017/ (accessed 1/31/18).

32. Carl Bialik, "Scare Headlines Exaggerated the US Crime Wave," September 11, 2015, http://fivethirtyeight.com/features/scare-headlines-exaggerated-the-u-s-crime-wave (accessed 11/20/15).

33. Pew Research Center, "Press Widely Criticized, but Trusted More than Other Information Sources," September 22, 2011, www.people-press.org/2011/09/22/press-widely-criticized-but-trusted-more-than-other-institutions (accessed 9/17/12).

34. Markus Prior, *Post-Broadcast Democracy: How Media Choice Increases Inequality in Political Involvement and Polarizes Elections* (New York: Cambridge University Press, 2007).

35. Pablo Boczkowski, *Imitation in an Age of Information Abundance* (Chicago: University of Chicago Press, 2010).

36. Jonathan Ladd, "Four Approaches to Providing Political News Given That So Many People Don't Want It," August 20, 2015, www.mischiefsoffaction.com/2015/08/four-approaches-to-providing-political.html?m=1 (accessed 11/5/15).

37. Thomas Patterson, "Bad News, Period," *Political Science and Politics* 29 (1996): 17–20.

38. Shanto Iyengar, Helmut Norpoth, and Kyu Hahn, "Consumer Demand for Election News: The Horserace Sells," *Journal of Politics* 66 (2004): 157–75.

39. Steve M. Barkin, *American Television News: The Media Marketplace and the Public Interest: The Media Marketplace and the Public Interest* (New York: Routledge, 2016).

40. Dhrumil Mehta, "The Media Has Really Neglected Puerto Rico," September 28, 2017, https://fivethirtyeight.com/features/the-media-really-has-neglected-puerto-rico/ (accessed 2/5/18).

41. T. E. Patterson, *The Vanishing Voter* (New York: Knopf, 2002); J. N. Cappella and K. H. Jamieson, *Spiral of Cynicism: The Press and the Public Good* (New York: Oxford University Press, 1997).

42. Robert McChesney, *The Problem of the Media: U.S. Communication Politics in the 21st Century* (New York: Monthly Review Press, 2004).

Chapter 8

1. Joseph Schlesinger, *Political Parties and the Winning of Office* (Ann Arbor: University of Michigan Press, 1994).

2. William Nesbit Chambers and Walter Dean Burnham, *The American Party Systems: Stages of Political Development* (Oxford, UK: Oxford University Press, 1966).

3. Donald H. Hickey, "Federalist Party Unity and the War of 1812," *Journal of American Studies* 12 (April 1978): 23–39; William T. Bianco, David B. Spence, and John D. Wilkerson, "The Electoral Connection in the Early Congress: The Case of the Compensation Act of 1816," *American Journal of Political Science* 40 (February 1996): 145–71.

4. John Aldrich, *Why Parties?* (Chicago: University of Chicago Press, 2005).

5. James MacPherson, *Battle Cry of Freedom: The Civil War Era* (New York: Oxford University Press, 1988).

6. Michael F. Holt, *The Rise and Fall of the Whig Party: Jacksonian Politics and the Onset of the Civil War* (New York: Oxford University Press, 1999).

7. Harold W. Stanley, William T. Bianco, and Richard G. Niemi, "Partisanship and Group Support over Time: A Multivariate Analysis," *American Political Science Review* 80 (1986): 969–76.

8. Eric Schickler, *Racial Realignment: The Transformation of American Liberalism, 1932–1965* (Princeton, NJ: Princeton University Press, 2016).

9. Hans Noel, *Political Ideologies and Political Parties in America* (New York: Cambridge University Press, 2014).

10. Aldrich, *Why Parties?*

11. James L. Sundquist, *Dynamics of the Party System*, rev. ed. (Washington, DC: Brookings Institution, 1983).

12. John H. Aldrich and Richard G. Niemi, "The Sixth American Party System: Electoral Change, 1952–1992," in *Broken Contract: Changing Relationships between Americans and Their Governments*, ed. Steven Craig (Boulder, CO: Westview Press, 1993).

13. Charles S. Bullock III, Donna R. Hoffman, and Ronald Keith Gaddie, "Regional Variations in the Realignment of American Politics, 1944–2004," *Social Science Quarterly* 87:3 (2006): 494–518.

14. Jon F. Hale, "The Making of the New Democrats," *Political Science Quarterly* 110:2 (1995): 207–32.

15. James Monroe, *The Political Party Matrix* (Albany: SUNY Press, 2001).

16. Gary Cox and Mathew McCubbins, *Legislative Leviathan* (Berkeley: University of California Press, 1993); James M. Snyder and Michael M. Ting, "An Informational Rationale for Political Parties," *American Journal of Political Science* 46 (2002): 90–110.

17. Jason Roberts and Steven Smith, "Procedural Contexts, Party Strategy, and Conditional Party Government," *American Journal of Political Science* 47:2 (2003): 305–17.

18. Catherine Rampell, "Tax Pledge May Scuttle a Deal on Deficit," *New York Times*, November 18, 2011, p. B1.

19. Donald Green, Bradley Palmquist, and Eric Schickler, *Partisan Hearts and Minds* (New Haven, CT: Yale University Press, 2004); Christopher Achen, "Political Socialization and Rational Party Identification," *Political Behavior* 24:2 (2002): 151–70.

20. Morris Fiorina, *Retrospective Voting in American National Elections* (New Haven, CT: Yale University Press, 1981).

21. Walter Dean Burnham, "The Reagan Heritage," in *The Election of 1988: Reports and Interpretations*, ed. Gerald M. Pomper et al. (Chatham, NJ: Chatham House, 1989).

22. Martin P. Wattenberg, *The Decline of American Political Parties: 1952–1994* (Cambridge, MA: Harvard University Press, 1996).

23. David S. Broder, *The Party's Over: The Failure of Partisan Politics in America* (New York: Harper and Row, 1971).

24. Donald P. Green and Bradley Palmquist, "Of Artifacts and Partisan Instability," *American Journal of Political Science* 34:3 (August 1990): 872–902.

25. Samara Kiar and Yanna Krupnikov, *Independent Politics: How American Disdain for Parties Leads to Political Inaction* (New York: Cambridge University Press, 2016).

26. Larry M. Bartels, "Partisanship and Voting Behavior, 1952–1996," *American Journal of Political Science* 44:1 (2000): 35–50.

27. Daniel Schlotzman, *When Movements Anchor Parties: Electoral Alignments in American History* (Princeton, NJ: Princeton University Press, 2015).

28. Jill Lawrence, "Party Recruiters Lead Charge for '06 Vote; Choice of Candidates to Run in Fall May Decide Who Controls the House," *USA Today*, May 25, 2006, p. A5.

29. Marty Cohen, David Karol, Hans Noel, and John Zaller, *The Party Decides: Presidential Nominations before and after Reform* (Chicago: University of Chicago Press, 2008).

30. Jonathan Bernstein, "Clinton Knows Who's Boss: Her Party," November 18, 2015, www.bloombergview.com/articles/2015-11-18/democratic-party-is-more-important-than-hillary-clinton (accessed 11/20/15).

31. Compiled from information available at www.ballot-access.org (accessed 2/18/18).

32. The Center for Responsive Politics, opensecrets.org (accessed 10/30/18).

33. Heather Caygle, "Anti-abortion Democrat snubbed by party for reelection." *Politico*, February 26, 2018, www.politico.com/story/2018/02/25/lipinski-democrats-abortion-chicago-illinois-423431 (accessed 5/9/18).

34. John Gerring, *Party Ideologies in America, 1828–1996* (New York: Cambridge University Press, 2001).

35. See www.lp.org/elected-officials-2 (accessed 2/19/17).

36. Janet Hook and Peter Wallsten, "GOP Feels Sting of Candidates' Rejection," *Los Angeles Times*, October 10, 2005, p. A1.

37. Gary Cox, *Making Votes Count: Strategic Coordination in the World's Electoral Systems* (Cambridge, UK: Cambridge University Press, 1997).

38. Peter Hanson, *Too Weak to Govern: Majority Party Power and Appropriations in the U.S. Senate* (New York: Cambridge University Press, 2015).

39. Thomas B. Edsall, "GOP Gains Advantage on Key Issues, Polls Say," *Washington Post*, January 27, 2002, p. A4.

Take a Stand

a. Nelson Polsby, *Consequences of Party Reform* (New York: Oxford University Press, 1983).

b. Daniel A. Smith and Caroline J. Tolbert, *Educated by Initiative: The Effects of Direct Democracy on Citizens and Political Organizations in the American States* (Ann Arbor: University of Michigan Press, 2004).

Chapter 9

1. Morris P. Fiorina, *Retrospective Voting in American National Elections* (New Haven, CT: Yale University Press, 1981); V. O. Key, *The Responsible Electorate* (New York: Vintage Books, 1966).

2. David Mayhew, *Congress: The Electoral Connection* (New Haven, CT: Yale University Press, 1973).

3. For details on early voting, see the Early Voting Information Center site at http://earlyvoting.net/resources/ (accessed 5/9/18).

4. Barry C. Burden, David T. Canon, Kenneth R. Meyer, and Donald P. Moynihan, "Election Laws, Mobilization, and Turnout: The Unexpected Consequences of Early Voting," *American Journal of Political Science* 58 (2014): 95–109.

5. United States Government Accountability Office, "Issues Related to State Voter Identification Laws," 2014, www.gao.gov/assets/670/665966.pdf (accessed 3/4/16).

6. Minor-party candidates are typically selected during party conventions.

7. Barbara Norrander, "Presidential Nomination Politics in the Post-reform Era," *Political Research Quarterly* 49 (1996): 875–90.

8. Larry Bartels, *Presidential Primaries and the Dynamics of Public Choice* (Princeton, NJ: Princeton University Press, 1988).

9. William G. Mayer, "Forecasting Presidential Nominations or, My Model Worked Just Fine, Thank You," *Political Science and Politics* 36 (2003): 153–59.

10. Marty Cohen, David Karol, Hans Noel, and John Zaller, "Beating Reform: The Resurgence of Parties in Presidential Nominations, 1980 to 2000" (paper presented at the 2001 American Political Science Association Annual Meeting, San Francisco, CA).

11. Richard Herrera, "Are 'Superdelegates' Super?," *Political Behavior* 16 (1994): 79–93.

12. FairVote, "Maine and Nebraska," www.fairvote.org/maine_nebraska (accessed 5/9/18).

13. Robert Bennett, "The Problem of the Faithless Elector," *Northwestern University Law Review* 100 (2004): 121–30.

14. James Q. Wilson, "Is the Electoral College Worth Saving?," *Slate*, November 3, 2000, www.slate.com/id/92663 (accessed 10/19/12).

15. Robert Erikson and Christopher Wlezien, *The Timeline of Presidential Elections* (Chicago: University of Chicago Press, 2013).

16. Larry M. Bartels and Christopher H. Achen, *Democracy for Realists: Why Elections Do Not Produce Responsive Government* (Princeton, NJ: Princeton University Press, 2016).

17. Linda Fowler and Robert McClure, *Political Ambition: Who Decides to Run for Congress* (Ann Arbor: University of Michigan Press, 1989).

18. Robin Kolodny, *Pursuing Majorities: Congressional Campaign Committees in American Politics* (Norman: University of Oklahoma Press, 1999).

19. Steven Ansolabehere and Alan Gerber, "Incumbency Advantage and the Persistence of Legislative Majorities," *Legislative Studies Quarterly* 22 (1997): 161–80.

20. For a discussion of Johnson's decision, see Robert A. Caro, *The Path to Power* (New York: Knopf, 1983).

21. Thomas Mann and Norman Ornstein, *The Permanent Campaign and Its Future* (Washington, DC: American Enterprise Institute, 2000).

22. Mayhew, *Congress: The Electoral Connection.*

23. Henry Chappell and William Keech, "A New Model of Political Accountability for Economic Performance," *American Political Science Review* 79 (1985): 10–19.

24. Jonathan Krasno and Donald P. Green, "The Dynamics of Campaign Fundraising in House Elections," *Journal of Politics* 56 (1991): 459–74.

25. Michael J. Goff, *The Money Primary: The New Politics of the Early Presidential Nomination Process* (New York: Rowman & Littlefield, 2007).

26. Michael Babaro, "Candidates Stick to Script, If Not the Truth, in the 2016 Race," *New York Times*, November 7, 2015, p. A1.

27. Chris Cillizza, "Consulting Firms Face Conflict in 2008," *Roll Call*, June 20, 2005, p. 1.

28. For details, see the House Ethics Committee guidelines at https://ethics.house.gov/campaign-activity/campaign-work-house-employees (accessed 5/9/18).

29. Cherie Maestas, Walter Stone, and L. Sandy Maisel, "Quality Counts: Extending the Strategic Politician Model of Incumbent Deterrence," *American Journal of Political Science* 48 (2004): 479–90.

30. Matt Bai, "Turnout Wins Elections," *New York Times Magazine*, December 14, 2003, p. 100.

31. Christopher Drew, "New Telemarketing Ploy Steers Voters on Republican Path," *New York Times*, November 6, 2006.

32. The Centre for Responsive Politics, opensecrets.org (accessed 10/30/18).

33. For a history of presidential debates, see the Commission on Presidential Debates site at www.debates.org (accessed 10/19/12).

34. For a video library of presidential campaign ads, see Museum of the Moving Image, "The Living Room Candidate: Presidential Campaign Commercials 1952-2012," http://livingroomcandidate.org (accessed 10/19/12).

35. Museum of the Moving Image, "The Living Room Candidate: 1964: Johnson vs. Goldwater," http://livingroomcandidate.org/commercials/1964/dowager (accessed 10/19/12).

36. Museum of the Moving Image, "The Living Room Candidate: 1964: Johnson vs. Goldwater."

37. For examples of this argument, see Thomas Patterson, *The Vanishing Voter* (New York: Knopf, 2002), and Jules Witcover, *No Way to Pick a President: How Money and Hired Guns Have Debased American Politics* (London: Routledge, 2001).

38. Richard Adams, "US Midterm Elections 2010: The 10 Worst Political Ads," *The Guardian*, November 2, 2010, www.theguardian.com/world/richard-adams-blog/2010/nov/02/us-midterm-elections-2010-top-10-worst-political-ads (10/24/18).

39. Paul Freeman, Michael Franz, and Kenneth Goldstein, "Campaign Advertising and Democratic Citizenship," *American Journal of Political Science* 48 (2004): 723–41.

40. Constantine J. Spilotes and Lynn Vavreck, "Campaign Advertising: Partisan Convergence or Divergence?," *Journal of Politics* 64 (2002): 249–61.

41. Kathleen Hall Jameson, *Packaging the Presidency: A History and Criticism of Presidential Campaign Advertising* (New York: Oxford University Press, 1996).

42. Steven Ansolabehere and Shanto Iyengar, *Going Negative: How Political Advertisements Shrink and Polarize the Electorate* (New York: Free Press, 1997); Richard Lau, Lee Sigelman, Caroline Heldman, and Paul Babbitt, "The Effects of Negative Political Advertisements: A Meta-analytic Analysis," *American Political Science Review* 93 (1999): 851–70.

43. Jonathan Krasno and Frank J. Sorauf, "For the Defense," *Political Science and Politics* 37 (2004): 777–80.

44. Contribution and spending data are available from the Center for Responsive Politics at www.opensecrets.org.

45. Brian Stelter, "The Price of 30 Seconds," *New York Times*, October 1, 2007, http://mediadecoder.blogs.nytimes.com/2007/10/01/the-price-of-30-seconds (accessed 10/19/12).

46. For a review of this literature, see Michael Malbin, *The Election after Reform: Money, Politics, and the Bipartisan Campaign Reform Act* (Washington, DC: Rowman & Littlefield, 2006).

47. Lynda Powell, *The Influence of Campaign Contributions in State Legislatures* (Ann Arbor: University of Michigan Press, 2012).

48. David Karol, "If You Think Super PACS Have Changed Everything about Presidential Primaries, Think Again," 2015, www.washingtonpost.com/blogs/monkey-cage/wp/2015/09/21/if-you-think-super-pacs-have-changed-everything-about-the-presidential-primary-think-again (accessed 9/21/15).

49. For a discussion, see Patterson, *The Vanishing Voter*, especially Chapter 1, "The Incredible Shrinking Electorate," pp. 3–22.

50. William H. Riker and Peter Ordeshook, "A Theory of the Calculus of Voting," *American Political Science Review* 62 (1968): 25–39.

51. Michael McDonald, The United States Elections Project, www.electproject.org (accessed 5/11/18).

52. Pew Research Center, "Regular Voters, Intermittent Voters, and Those Who Don't," October 18, 2006, www.people-press.org/files/legacy-pdf/292.pdf (accessed 7/29/16).

53. For a review of the literature on issue voters, see Jon K. Dalager, "Voters, Issues, and Elections: Are Candidates' Messages Getting Through?," *Journal of Politics* 58 (1996): 486–515.

54. Richard P. Lau and David P. Redlawsk, *How Voters Decide: Information Processing during Electoral Campaigns* (New York: Cambridge University Press, 2006).

55. Samuel Popkin, *The Reasoning Voter* (Chicago: University of Chicago Press, 1991).

56. Richard R. Lau and David P. Redlawsk, "Advantages and Disadvantages of Cognitive Heuristics in Political Decision Making," *American Journal of Political Science* 45 (2001): 951–71.

Chapter 10

1. U.S. Department of Education, "U.S. Department of Education Announces Opportunity for Federal Student Loan Borrowers to be Reconsidered for Public Service Loan Forgiveness," May 23, 2018, www.ed.gov/news/press-releases/us-department-education-announces-opportunity-federal-student-loan-borrowers-be-reconsidered-public-service-loan-forgiveness (accessed 6/5/18).

2. Robert A. Dahl, *A Preface to Democratic Theory* (Chicago: University of Chicago Press, 1951) and *Who Governs? Democracy and Power in an American City* (New Haven, CT: Yale University Press, 1961); David Truman, *The Governmental Process* (New York: Harper and Row, 1951).

3. Theodore Lowi, *The End of Liberalism: The Second Republic of the United States* (New York: W. W. Norton, 1979). E. E. Schattschneider, *The Semisovereign People: A Realist's View of Democracy in America* (Hinsdale, IL: Dryden Press, 1975).

4. Frank R. Baumgartner, Jeffrey M. Berry, Marie Hojnacki, David C. Kimball, and Beth L. Leech, *Lobbying and Policy Change: Who Wins, Who Loses, and Why* (Chicago: University of Chicago Press, 2009).

5. Lobbying regulations are often changed; the discussion here is just a general guide. For a summary of federal law, see "Lobbying Disclosure Act Guidance," Office of the Clerk, U.S. House of Representatives, January 31, 2017, https://lobbyingdisclosure.house.gov/amended_lda_guide.html; for state law, see Lobbying Regulation, National Conference of State Legislatures, www.ncsl.org/research/ethics/lobbyist-regulation.aspx (accessed 6/5/18).

6. Nadja Popovich, Livia Albeck-Ripka, and Kendra Pierre-Louis, "67 Environmental Rules on the Way Out Under Trump," *New York Times*, January 31, 2018, www.nytimes.com/interactive/2017/10/05/climate/trump-environment-rules-reversed.html (accessed 6/5/18).

7. Frank Baumgartner and Beth Leech, *Basic Interests: The Importance of Interest Groups in Politics and in Political Science* (Princeton, NJ: Princeton University Press, 1999), p. 109.

8. Beth L. Leech, Frank R. Baumgartner, Timothy M. La Pira, and Nicholas A. Semanko, "Drawing Lobbyists to Washington: Government Activity and the Demand for Advocacy," *Political Research Quarterly* 58:1 (March 2005): 19–30.

9. Roxana Tiron, "Lockheed Martin Leads Expanded Lobbying by US Defense Industry," *Washington Post*, January 26, 2012, www.washingtonpost.com/business/economy/lockheed-martin-leads-expanded-lobbying-by-us-defense-industry/2012/01/26/gIQAlgQtaQ_story.html (accessed 2/4/14).

10. Tim LaPira, Lee Drutman, and Matthew Grossmann, "The Interest Group Top Tier: More Groups, Concentrated Clout," paper presented at the 2014 American Political Science Association Annual Meeting.

11. Ranked Sectors, Center for Responsive Politics, www.opensecrets.org/lobby/top.php?indexType=c&showYear=2018 (accessed 6/5/18).

12. For more on this argument, see Tim Harford, "There's Not Enough Money in Politics," *Slate*, April 1, 2006, www.slate.com/id/2138874 (accessed 7/29/16); and Stephen Ansolabehere, John M. de Figueiredo, and James M. Snyder, "Why Is There So Little Money in American Politics?," *Journal of Economic Perspectives* 17 (2003): 105–30.

13. Scott Ainsworth, *Analyzing Interest Groups: Group Influence on People and Policies* (New York: W. W. Norton, 2002).

14. Timothy LaPira and Hershel F. Thomas III, "Revolving Door Lobbyists and Interest Representation," *Interest Groups and Advocacy* 3 (2013): 4–29.

15. Sixty-one members retired in January 2017; 26 of those were employed by mid-2018, and 16 of those were in lobbying. Data available at www.opensecrets.org/revolving/departing.php (accessed 10/10/18).

16. Theodoric Meyer, "Has Trump Drained the Swamp in Washington?," *Politico*, October 19, 2017, www.politico.com/story/2017/10/19/trump-drain-swamp-promises-243924 (accessed 12/19/17).

17. Robert H. Salisbury, John P. Heinz, Edward O. Laumann, and Robert L. Nelson, "Who Works with Whom? Interest Group Alliances and Opposition," *American Political Science Review* 81 (1987): 1217–34.

18. Business-Industry Political Action Committee, "About BIPAC," www.bipac.org/about-us (accessed 6/5/18).

19. Becky Peterson, "Citizens Angry over GOP Healthcare Bills Are Overloading the Bot Designed to Help Them Reach Congress," *Business Insider*, September 22, 2017, www.businessinsider.com/resistbot-overloaded-users-fax-congress-about-gop-healthcare-2017-9; Jason Putorti, "Welcome to Resistbot v3," November 9, 2017, https://resistbot.news/welcome-to-resistbot-v3-5fe513aa457a (both accessed 12/19/17).

20. Thomas Holyoke, "Choosing Battlegrounds: Interest Group Lobbying across Multiple Venues," *Political Science Quarterly* 56 (2003): 325–36.

21. AARP, "Policy and Research for Professionals in Aging," www.aarp.org/research/ppi (accessed 4/8/08).

22. James Q. Wilson, *Political Organizations* (New York: Basic Books, 1974).

23. American Automobile Association, Foundation for Traffic Safety, www.aaafoundation.org/home (accessed 7/29/16).

24. Kenneth Kollman, *Outside Lobbying: Public Opinion and Interest Group Strategies* (Princeton, NJ: Princeton University Press, 1998).

25. Jack Walker, *Mobilizing Interest Groups in America* (Ann Arbor: University of Michigan Press, 1991).

26. John P. Heinz, Edward O. Laumann, and Robert Salisbury, *The Hollow Core: Private Interests in National Policymaking* (Cambridge, MA: Harvard University Press, 1993).

27. Richard L. Hall and Alan V. Deardorff, "Lobbying as Legislative Subsidy," *American Political Science Review* 100 (2006): 69–84.

28. Hall and Deardorff, "Lobbying as Legislative Subsidy."

29. David Austen-Smith and John R. Wright, "Counteractive Lobbying," *American Journal of Political Science* 38:1 (1994): 25–44.

30. Key Lehman Schlozman and John T. Tierney, *Organized Interests and American Democracy* (New York: HarperCollins, 1986).

31. Baumgartner and Leech, *Basic Interests*, p. 152.

32. Anthony Madonna and Ian Ostrander, "If Congress Keeps Cutting Its Staff, Who Is Writing Your Laws? You Won't Like the Answer," *Washington Post*, August 20, 2015, www.washingtonpost.com/news/monkey-cage/wp/2015/08/20/if-congress-keeps-cutting-its-staff-who-is-writing-your-laws-you-wont-like-the-answer/?utm_term=.d4773b24c7cf (accessed 12/20/17).

33. Christine A. DeGregorio, *Networks of Champions: Leadership, Access, and Advocacy in the U.S. House of Representatives* (Ann Arbor: University of Michigan Press, 1992).

34. Daniel Carpenter, *The Forging of Bureaucratic Autonomy: Reputations, Networks, and Policy Innovation in Executive Agencies, 1862–1928* (Princeton, NJ: Princeton University Press, 2002).

35. Public Citizen," Our Work," www.citizen.org (accessed 12/20/17).

36. Derived from a search of the NRA Institute for Legislative Action site, www.nraila.org (accessed 9/19/12).

37. Kim Scheppele and Jack L. Walker, "The Litigation Strategies of Interest Groups," in *Mobilizing Interest Groups in America*, ed. Jack Walker (Ann Arbor: University of Michigan Press, 1991).

38. Lauren Cohen Bell, *Warring Factions: Interest Groups, Money, and the New Politics of Senate Confirmation* (Columbus: Ohio State University Press, 2002).

39. Kevin W. Hula, *Lobbying Together: Interest Group Coalitions in Legislative Politics* (Washington, DC: Georgetown University Press, 1999).

40. Jeanne Cummings, "Word Games Could Threaten Climate Bill," *Politico*, June 9, 2009, www.politico.com/news/stories/0609/24059.html (accessed 9/19/12).

41. AARP, "A Guide to Your Elected Officials," https://action.aarp.org/site/SPageServer?pagename=electedOfficials (accessed 6/5/18).

42. Erica Chenoweth and Jeremy Pressman, "This Is What We Learned by Counting the Women's Marches," *Washington Post*, February 7, 2017, www.washingtonpost.com/news/monkey-cage/wp/2017/02/07/this-is-what-we-learned-by-counting-the-womens-marches/?utm_term=.4dd6925ad4a6 (accessed 12/20/17).

43. In addition to Planned Parenthood and the Natural Resources Defense Council, other supporting organizations included the AFL-CIO, Amnesty International USA, the Mothers of the Movement, the National Center for Lesbian Rights, the National Organization for Women, MoveOn.org, Human Rights Watch, Code Pink, Black Girls Rock!, the NAACP, the American Indian Movement, EMILY's List, Oxfam, Greenpeace USA, and the League of Women Voters.

44. Richard Fenno, *Home Style: U.S. House Members in Their Districts* (Boston: Little, Brown, 1978). See also Brandice Caines-Wrone, David W. Brady, and John F. Cogan, "Out of Step, Out of Office: Electoral Accountability and House Members' Voting," *American Political Science Review* 96 (2002): 127–40.

45. Emily Yoffe, "Am I the Next Jack Abramoff?," *Slate*, April 1, 2006, www.slate.com/id/2137886 (accessed 8/28/09).

46. Kollman, *Outside Lobbying*.

47. Gregory Calderia, Marie Hojnacki, and John R. Wright, "The Lobbying Activities of Organized Interests in Federal Judicial Nominations," *Journal of Politics* 62 (2000): 51–69.

48. *Citizens United v. Federal Election Commission*, 558 U.S. 310 (2010).

49. Data from www.opensecrets.org and www.fec.gov (accessed 12/20/17).

50. John G. Matsusaka, "Direct Democracy and Fiscal Gridlock: Have Voter Initiatives Paralyzed the California Budget?," *State Politics and Policy* 5 (2005): 346–62.

51. Thad Kousser, *Term Limits and the Dismantling of State Legislative Professionalism* (New York: Cambridge University Press, 2004).

52. History of Marijuana on the Ballot," Ballotpedia, https://ballotpedia.org/History_of_marijuana_on_the_ballot (accessed 11/12/18).

53. Frederick J. Boehmke, "The Initiative Process and the Dynamics of State Interest Group Populations," *State Politics and Policy Quarterly*, 8:4 (Winter 2008): 362–83.

54. John G. Matsusaka, *For the Many or the Few: The Initiative, Public Policy, and American Democracy* (Chicago: University of Chicago Press, 2004).

55. Elizabeth R. Gerber, *The Populist Paradox: Interest Group Influence and the Promise of Direct Legislation* (Princeton, NJ: Princeton University Press, 1999).

56. Baumgartner and Leech, *Basic Interests*, Chapter 8, pp. 147–67.

57. Lee Drutman, "The Solution to Lobbying Is More Lobbying," *Washington Post*, April 29, 2015, www.washingtonpost.com/blogs/monkey-cage/wp/2015/04/29/the-solution-to-lobbying-is-more-lobbying (accessed 2/16/16).

58. Keith E. Schnakenberg, "Informational Lobbying and Legislative Voting," *American Journal of Political Science*, 61:1 (January 2017): 129–145.

59. Nicholas Fandos, "House Votes to Sharply Expand Concealed-Carry Gun Rights," December 6, 2017, *New York Times*, www.nytimes.com/2017/12/06/us/politics/house-concealed-carry-guns-nra-reciprocity.html (accessed 6/5/18).

60. Emma Leathley, "Net Neutrality," OpenSecrets.org, December 2017, www.opensecrets.org/news/issues/net_neutrality/ (accessed 12/20/17).

61. Eric Bradner, "Alabama Election: Doug Jones Scores Stunning Win, But Moore Won't concede," CNN, December 13, 2017, www.cnn.com/2017/12/12/politics/alabama-senate-election-mainbar/index.html (accessed 6/5/18).

62. David Lowery, "Why Do Organized Interests Lobby? A Multi-Goal, Multi-Context Theory of Lobbying," *Polity* 39 (2007): 29–54.

63. Amy McKay, "Negative Lobbying and Policy Outcomes," *American Politics Review* 40 (2011): 116–46.

64. Jeffrey M. Berry, *The Interest Group Society* (New York: HarperCollins, 1997); Raymond A. Bauer, Ithiel de Sola Pool, and Lewis Dexter, *American Business and Public Policy* (New York: Atherton Press, 1963).

65. Kollman, *Outside Lobbying*.

66. Frank Baumgartner and Beth Leech, "Interest Niches and Policy Bandwagons: Patterns of Interest Group Involvement in National Politics," *Journal of Politics* 63 (2001): 1191–1213.

Take a Stand

a. Jacob Weisberg, "Three Cities, Three Scandals: What Jack Abramoff, Anthony Pellicano, and Jared Paul Stern Have in Common," *Slate*, April 9, 2006, www.slate.com/id/2140238 (accessed 10/25/12).

b. Herschel F. Thomas and Timothy M. LaPira, "How Many Lobbyists Are in Washington? Shadow Lobbying and the Gray Market for Policy Advocacy," *Interest Groups and Advocacy* 6:3 (2017): 199–214.

Chapter 11

1. Katie Reilly, "Here's What President Trump Has Said about DACA in the Past," *Time*, September 5, 2017, http://time.com/4927100/donald-trump-daca-past-statements/ (accessed 2/15/18).

2. Most of the poll questions specified the conditions of the DACA program for becoming a citizen: "To qualify, immigrants had to be under the age of 30 as of 2012, have no criminal record, and be a student, in the military, or have earned a high school diploma." A few only mentioned not having a criminal record. See www.pollingreport.com/immigration.htm for a record of the polls taken early in 2018 (accessed 2/9/18).

3. See Wendy J. Schiller and Charles Stewart III, *Electing the Senate: Indirect Democracy before the Seventeenth Amendment* (Princeton, NJ: Princeton University Press, 2015), for an analysis of Senate elections before the popular vote; see Paul Gronke, *The Electorate, the Campaign, and the Office: A Unified Approach to Senate and House Elections* (Ann Arbor: University of Michigan Press, 2000), for research showing that the House and Senate elections share many similar characteristics. See Richard F. Fenno, *Senators on the Campaign Trail: The Politics of Representation* (Norman: University of Oklahoma Press, 1996), for a good general discussion of Senate elections.

4. The poll data on Congress's general approval is from PollingReport.com (www.pollingreport.com/CongJob.htm [accessed 5/18/18]). The occupations poll was conducted by Gallup in December 2017 (http://news.gallup.com/poll/1654/honesty-ethics-professions.aspx, accessed 2/15/18).

5. "Congress Less Popular than Cockroaches, Traffic Jams," Public Policy Polling, January 8, 2013, www.publicpolicypolling.com/pdf/2011/PPP_Release_Natl_010813_.pdf (accessed 4/11/14).

6. Claudine Gay, "Spirals of Trust? The Effect of Descriptive Representation on the Relationship between Citizens and Their Government," *American Journal of Political Science* 46:4 (October 2002): 717–32.

7. In addition to those mentioned in the text, there were two other African Americans who were elected by state legislatures to serve in the Senate during the Reconstruction period. And in more recent times, there was an African American, Roland Burris (D-IL), who was appointed to serve the remainder of Senator Barack Obama's term.

8. David T. Canon, *Race, Redistricting, and Representation: The Unintended Consequences of Black Majority Districts* (Chicago: University of Chicago Press, 1999); Katherine Tate, *Concordance: Black Lawmaking in the U.S. Congress from Carter to Obama* (Ann Arbor, MI: University of Michigan Press, 2014); Stella M. Rouse, *Latinos in the Legislative Process: Interests and Influence* (New York: Cambridge University Press, 2013); Michele L. Swers, *Women in the Club: Gender and Policy Making in the Senate* (Chicago: University of Chicago Press, 2013); Michele L. Swers, *The Difference Women Make: The Policy Impact of Women in Congress* (Chicago: University of Chicago Press, 2002).

9. R. Douglas Arnold, *The Logic of Congressional Action* (New Haven, CT: Yale University Press, 1990), pp. 60–71.

10. Richard F. Fenno, *Home Style: House Members in Their Districts* (Boston: Little, Brown, 1978).

11. David R. Mayhew, *Congress: The Electoral Connection* (New Haven, CT: Yale University Press, 1974).

12. Mayhew, *Congress*, p. 17.

13. Mayhew, *Congress*, p. 37.

14. Patrick J. Sellers, "Fiscal Consistency and Federal District Spending in Congressional Elections," *American Journal of Political Science* 41:3 (July 1997): 1024–41.

15. David T. Canon, "History in the Making: The 2nd District in Wisconsin," in *The Battle for Congress: Candidates, Consultants, and Voters*, ed. James A. Thurber (Washington, DC: Brookings Institution Press, 2001), pp. 199–238.

16. Gary C. Jacobson, *The Politics of Congressional Elections*, 5th ed. (New York: Longman, 2001), pp. 24–30.

17. Fenno, *Home Style*.

18. Morris Fiorina, *Congress: Keystone of the Washington Establishment*, rev. ed. (New Haven, CT: Yale University Press, 1989).

19. Steve Peoples and Ken Thomas, "Not All GOP Candidates Want Trump to Stump, Associated Press, May 19, 2018, www.yahoo.com/news/trump-plans-aggressive-role-midterms-welcome-044428991--politics.html (accessed 6/7/18).

20. The language used by the Court in 1960 was "one-man, one-vote." The Court ruled in *Baker v. Carr*, 369 U.S. 186 (1962), that state legislative districts that were unequal in population violated the equal protection clause of the Fourteenth Amendment. *Wesberry v. Sanders*, 376 U.S. 1 (1964), applied the same principle to U.S. House districts.

21. *Davis v. Bandemer*, 478 U.S. 109 (1986); *Vieth v. Jubelirer*, 541 U.S. 267 (2004); *League of United Latin American Citizens v. Perry*, 548 U.S. 399 (2006).

22. *Beverly R. Gill, et al. v. William Whitford, et al.*, 585 U.S. ____ (2018); *Benisek v. Lamone*, 585 U.S. ____ (2018).

23. *Shelby County v. Holder*, 570 U.S. (2013).

24. See Kenneth R. Mayer and David T. Canon, *The Dysfunctional Congress: The Individual Roots of an Institutional Dilemma*, 2nd ed. (New York: Columbia University Press, forthcoming), for an extended discussion of this argument.

25. Richard F. Fenno, "If as Ralph Nader Says, Congress Is the 'Broken Branch,' How Come We Love Our Congressman So Much?," in *Congress in Change: Evolution and Reform*, ed. Norman J. Ornstein (New York: Praeger, 1975), pp. 277–87.

26. Russell Berman, "A Major Infrastructure Bill Clears Congress," *The Atlantic*, December 4, 2015, www.theatlantic.com/politics/archive/2015/12/a-major-infrastructure-bill-clears-congress/418827 (accessed 3/19/16).

27. Leo Shane III, "2016 Defense Budget Deal Finally Nailed Down by Congress," *Military Times*, December 18, 2015, www.militarytimes.com/story/military/capitol-hill/2015/12/18/omnibus-passage-partisan-success/77569538 (accessed 3/19/16).

28. An important qualification to the norm was imposed by Republicans in 1995 when they set a six-year term limit for committee and subcommittee chairs.

29. *2016 CQ Almanac*, Washington, D.C.: Congressional Quarterly, 2017, B6.

30. David W. Rohde, *Parties and Leaders in the Post-reform House* (Chicago: University of Chicago Press, 1991).

31. David Rohde and John Aldrich, "The Transition to Republican Rule in the House: Implications for Theories of Congressional Politics," *Political Science Quarterly* 112:4 (Winter 1997–1998): 541–67.

32. Nelson W. Polsby, *Congress and the Presidency*, 4th ed. (Englewood Cliffs, NJ: Prentice Hall, 1986), p. 111.

33. Paul Steinhauser, "Obama 2014 Campaign Role: Fundraiser-in-Chief," CNN Politics, March 20, 2014, http://politicalticker.blogs.cnn.com/2014/03/20/obama-2014-campaign-role-fundraiser-in-chief (accessed 4/16/14).

34. Kathryn Watson, "Trump Addresses Record-setting GOP Fundraiser," CBS News, March 20, 2018, www.cbsnews.com/news/trump-addresses-one-of-the-biggest-gop-fundraisers-of-the-year (accessed 6/7/18).

35. Cristina Marcos, "The Republicans Who Didn't Vote for Ryan," *The Hill*, October 28–29, 2015, http://thehill.com/blogs/floor-action/house/258542-the-republicans-who-didnt-vote-for-ryan (accessed 3/19/16).

36. However, recent research shows that members of Congress do not confine their credit claiming to legislative activity that is rooted in committee work. See Justin Grimmer, Sean J. Westwood, and Solomon Messing, *The Impression of Influence: Legislator Communication, Representation, and Democratic Accountability* (Princeton, NJ: Princeton University Press, 2014).

37. Keith Krehbiel, *Information and Legislative Organization* (Ann Arbor: University of Michigan Press, 1992).

38. Richard F. Fenno, *Congressmen in Committees* (Boston: Little, Brown, 1973).

39. Richard L. Hall, *Participation in Congress* (New Haven, CT: Yale University Press, 1996).

40. Lindsey McPherson, "House Rules Committee Adopts Closed Rule for GOP Tax Bill," *Roll Call*, November 15, 2017, www.rollcall.com/news/policy/house-rules-approves-tax-bill-republicans (accessed 2/20/18).

41. Barbara Sinclair, *Unorthodox Lawmaking* (Washington, DC: CQ Press, 2000), p. xiv.

42. Edward Epstein, "Dusting Off Deliberation," *CQ Weekly*, June 14, 2010, pp. 1434–42.

43. Jennifer Shutt, "Five Continuing Resolutions? Par for the Course on Capitol Hill," *Roll Call*, February 7, 2018, www.rollcall.com/news/politics/five-continuing-resolutions-par-for-the-course-on-capitol-hill (accessed 6/7/18).

44. USA Patriot Act, Hearing before the Subcommittee on the Constitution, Civil Rights and Civil Liberties, Committee on the Judiciary, House of Representatives, September 22, 2009, www.gpo.gov/fdsys/pkg/CHRG-111hhrg52409/html/CHRG-111hhrg52409.htm (accessed 6/7/18).

45. Mike DeBonis, Ed O'Keefe, and Erica Werner, "Here's What Congress is Stuffing into its $1.3 Trillion Spending Bill," *Washington Post*, March 22, 2018 www.washingtonpost.com/news/powerpost/wp/2018/03/22/heres-what-congress-is-stuffing-into-its-1-3-trillion-spending-bill/?utm_term=.cae1f7d276e2 (accessed 6/7/18).

46. Congressional Record, 46th Congress, 2nd session, April 22, 1880, p. 2661.

47. Howard H. Baker Jr., "Leaders Lecture Series Address to the Senate," July 14, 1998, www.senate.gov/artandhistory/history/common/generic/Leaders_Lecture_Series_Baker.htm (accessed 5/7/08).

48. Paul Kane, "Reid, Democrats Trigger 'Nuclear' Option; Eliminate Most Filibusters on Nominees," *Washington Post*, November 21, 2013, www.washingtonpost.com/politics/senate-poised-to-limit-filibusters-in-party-line-vote-that-would-alter-centuries-of-precedent/2013/11/21/d065cfe8-52b6-11e3-9fe0-fd2ca728e67c_story.html (accessed 6/6/14).

49. Matt Flegenheimer, "Senate Republicans Deploy 'Nuclear Option' to Clear Path for Gorsuch," *New York Times*, April 6, 2017, www.nytimes.com/2017/04/06/us/politics/neil-gorsuch-supreme-court-senate.html (accessed 2/20/18).

50. Philip Rucker and Robert Costa, "McCarthy's Comments on Benghazi Probe May Be a Political Gift to Clinton," *Washington Post*, October 1, 2015, www.washingtonpost.com/politics/mccarthys-comments-on-benghazi-probe-may-be-a-political-gift-to-clinton/2015/10/01/6ceb6e88-6857-11e5-9223-70cb36460919_story.html (accessed 3/20/16). House Majority Leader Kevin McCarthy told Fox News host Sean Hannity, "Everybody thought Hillary Clinton was unbeatable, right? But we put together a Benghazi special committee, a select committee. What are her numbers today? Her numbers are dropping. Why? Because she's un-trustable. But no one would have known any of that had happened had we not fought."

51. Catherine Herridge, "Nunes Seeks Transcripts from Carter Page FISA Warrant Hearing," Fox News, February 9, 2018, www.foxnews.com/politics/2018/02/09/nunes-seeks-transcripts-from-carter-page-fisa-warrant-hearing.html (accessed 2/21/18).

52. Mathew McCubbins and Thomas Schwartz, "Congressional Oversight Overlooked: Police Patrol versus Fire Alarm," *American Journal of Political Science* 28:1 (February 1984): 165-77.

53. Richard Simon, Christi Parsons, and Michael A. Memoli, "VA Chief and White House Spokesman Resign, Fueling Unease," *Los Angeles Times*, May 30, 2014, www.latimes.com/nation/la-na-shinseki-20140531-story.html#page=1 (accessed 6/6/14).

Take a Stand

a. The warning against entering the "political thicket" comes from *Colegrove v. Green*, 328 U.S. 549 (1946).

Chapter 12

1. John Aldrich, *Why Parties?* (Chicago: University of Chicago Press, 1995).

2. Ernest R. May, *The Making of the Monroe Doctrine* (Cambridge, MA: Harvard University Press, 1975).

3. Arthur M. Schlesinger Jr., *The Age of Jackson* (Boston: Little, Brown, 1945).

4. David Greenberg, "Lincoln's Crackdown," *Slate*, November 30, 2001, www.slate.com/id/2059132 (accessed 8/8/16).

5. Stephen Skowronek, *Building a New American State: The Expansion of National Administrative Capacities* (New York: Cambridge University Press, 1982).

6. Theda Skocpol, *Protecting Soldiers and Mothers: The Political Origins of Social Policy in the United States* (Cambridge, MA: Harvard University Press, 1995).

7. Kendrick Clements, *The Presidency of Woodrow Wilson* (Lawrence: University Press of Kansas, 1992).

8. Thomas J. Knock, *To End All Wars: Woodrow Wilson and the Quest for a New World Order* (New York: Oxford University Press, 1992).

9. William E. Leuchtenburg, *FDR Years: On Roosevelt and His Legacy* (New York: Columbia University Press, 1995).

10. Chester Pach and Elmo Richardson, *The Presidency of Dwight D. Eisenhower* (Lawrence: University Press of Kansas, 1991).

11. Thomas J. Weko, *The Politicizing Presidency: The White House Personnel Office, 1948-1994* (Lawrence: University Press of Kansas, 1995).

12. Kenneth Mayer, *With the Stroke of a Pen: Executive Orders and Presidential Power* (Princeton, NJ: Princeton University Press, 2001).

13. Brian Hallett, *Declaring War: Congress, the President, and What the Constitution Does Not Say* (New York: Cambridge University Press, 2012).

14. Richard F. Grimmett, "The War Powers Resolution: After Thirty Years," Congressional Research Service Report RL32267, March 11, 2004, www.hsdl.org/?view&did=446200 (accessed 6/2/14).

15. Lewis Fisher and David G. Adler, "The War Powers Resolution: Time to Say Goodbye," *Political Science Quarterly* 113:1 (1998): 1-20.

16. William G. Howell and Jon C. Pevehouse, *While Dangers Gather: Congressional Checks on Presidential War Powers* (Princeton, NJ: Princeton University Press, 2007).

17. Mark A. Peterson, *Legislating Together: The White House and Capitol Hill from Eisenhower to Reagan* (Cambridge, MA: Harvard University Press, 1990).

18. Andrew Rudalevige, *Managing the President's Program: Presidential Leadership and Legislative Policy Formation* (Princeton, NJ: Princeton University Press, 2002).

19. Charles Cameron and Nolan M. McCarty, "Models of Vetoes and Veto Bargaining," *Annual Review of Political Science* 7 (2004): 409-25.

20. Mark J. Rozell, "The Law: Executive Privilege: Definition and Standards of Application," *Presidential Studies Quarterly* 29:4 (1999): 918-30.

21. See Oyez, *United States v. Nixon*, 418 U.S. 683 (1974), www.oyez.org/cases/1973/73-1766, for a summary of the case (accessed 6/5/18).

22. Mark J. Rozell, *Executive Privilege: The Dilemma of Secrecy and Democratic Accountability* (Baltimore, MD: Johns Hopkins University Press, 1994).

23. John Hart, *The Presidential Branch: From Washington to Clinton* (Chatham, NY: Chatham House, 1987).

24. Kelly Chang, David Lewis, and Nolan McCarthy, "The Tenure of Political Appointees" (paper presented at the 2003 Midwest Political Science Association Annual Meeting, Chicago, April 4, 2003).

25. David E. Lewis, "Staffing Alone: Unilateral Action and the Politicization of the Executive Office of the President, 1988-2004," *Presidential Studies Quarterly* 35 (2005): 496-514.

26. For a series of articles detailing Cheney's role, see "Angler: The Cheney Vice Presidency," *Washington Post*, June 24-27, 2007, www.voices.washingtonpost.com/cheney/ (accessed 4/29/08).

27. Richard E. Neustart, *Presidential Power and the Modern Presidents* (New York: Simon and Schuster, 1991).

28. Terry M. Moe and William G. Howell, "The Presidential Power of Unilateral Action," *Journal of Law, Economics, and Organization* 15 (1999): 132-46.

29. These examples appear throughout Moe and Howell, "The Presidential Power of Unilateral Action"; see also William G. Howell, "Unilateral Powers: A Brief Overview," *Presidential Studies Quarterly* 35:3 (2005): 417-39.

30. Andrew Rudalevige, *The New Imperial Presidency: Renewing Presidential Power after Watergate* (Ann Arbor: University of Michigan Press, 2005).

31. Louis Fisher, *Presidential War Power*, 2nd ed. (Lawrence: University Press of Kansas, 2004); James M. Lindsay, "Deference and Defiance: The Shifting Rhythms of Executive-Legislative Relations in Foreign Policy," *Presidential Studies Quarterly* 33:3 (2003): 530-46; Lawrence Margolis, *Executive Agreements and Presidential Power in Foreign Policy* (New York: Praeger, 1985), 209-32.

32. Christopher Deering and Forrest Maltzman, "The Politics of Executive Orders: Legislative Constraints on Presidential Power," *Political Research Quarterly* 52:4 (1999): 767-83.

33. David E. Lewis, *Presidents and the Politics of Agency Design: Political Insulation in the United States Government Bureaucracy, 1946-1997* (Palo Alto, CA: Stanford University Press, 2003).

34. David Epstein and Sharyn O'Halloran, *Delegating Powers* (Cambridge, UK: Cambridge University Press, 1999).

35. William G. Howell, *Thinking about the Presidency: The Primacy of Power* (Princeton, NJ: Princeton University Press, 2015).

36. George C. Edwards III, *The Public Presidency* (New York: St. Martin's Press, 1983); George C. Edwards III, *On Deaf Ears: The Limits of the Bully Pulpit* (New Haven, CT: Yale University Press, 2003).

37. For evidence, see Edwards, *On Deaf Ears*.

38. George C. Edwards III, *Predicting the Presidency: The Potential of Persuasive Leadership* (Princeton, NJ: Princeton University Press, 2015).

39. Stephen Skowronek, *Presidential Leadership in Political Time: Reprise and Reappraisal*, 2nd ed., revised and expanded (Lawrence: University of Kansas Press, 2011).

Chapter 13

1. Dwight Waldo, *The Administrative State: A Study of the Political Theory of American Public Administration* (1948; repr. Piscataway, NJ: Transaction, 2006).

2. For details, see Cornelius Kerwin, *Rulemaking: How Government Agencies Write Law and Make Policy* (Washington, DC: CQ Press, 1999).

3. Enterprise Risk Management Initiative, "Costs Associated with Regulatory Risks," December 31, 2008, www.mgt.ncsu.edu/erm/index.php/articles/entry/regulatory-risk-cost/ (accessed 2/3/10).

4. Andrew Pollack, "New Sense of Caution at FDA," *New York Times*, September 29, 2006, www.nytimes.com/2006/09/29/business/29caution.html?_r=0 (accessed 8/29/16).

5. There are two exceptions. A patient can enroll in a clinical trial for a new drug during the approval process, but there is a good chance that the patient will get a placebo or a previously approved treatment rather than the drug being tested. The FDA does allow companies to provide some experimental drugs to patients who cannot participate in a trial, but only those drugs that have passed early screening trials.

6. Susan Okie, "Access before Approval—a Right to Take Experimental Drugs?," *New England Journal of Medicine* 355 (2004): 437–40.

7. Stephen Skowronek, *Building a New American State: The Expansion of National Administrative Capacities, 1877-1920* (New York: Cambridge University Press, 1982).

8. Terry Moe, "An Assessment of the Positive Theory of Congressional Dominance," *Legislative Studies Quarterly* 4 (1987): 475–98.

9. Leon Neyfakh, "The FCC Just Voted to Reduce the Exorbitant Cost of Prison Phone Calls," *Slate*, October 22, 2015, www.slate.com/blogs/the_slatest/2015/10/22/prison_phone_calls_the_fcc_is_finally_making_them_cheaper.html (accessed 5/6/16).

10. Frances E. Rourke, "Responsiveness and Neutral Competence in American Bureaucracy," *Public Administration Review* 52 (1992): 539–46; Max Weber, *Essays on Sociology* (New York: Oxford University Press, 1958).

11. Samuel Workman, *The Dynamics of Bureaucracy in the U.S. Government* (New York: Cambridge University Press, 2015).

12. Karen Orren and Steven Skowronek, "Regimes and Regime Building in American Government: A Review of the Literature on the 1940s," *Political Science Quarterly* 113 (1998): 689–702.

13. Michael Nelson, "A Short, Ironic History of American National Bureaucracy," *Journal of Politics* 44 (1982): 747–78.

14. Nelson, "A Short, Ironic History of American National Bureaucracy."

15. Nelson, "A Short, Ironic History of American National Bureaucracy."

16. John Aldrich, *Why Parties?* (Chicago: University of Chicago Press, 1995).

17. Nelson, "A Short, Ironic History of American National Bureaucracy."

18. Matthew A. Crenson, *The Federal Machine: Beginnings of Bureaucracy in Jacksonian America* (Baltimore, MD: Johns Hopkins University Press, 1975).

19. James Q. Wilson, "The Rise of the Bureaucratic State," in *The American Commonwealth*, ed. Nathan Glazer and Irving Kristol (New York: Basic Books, 1976).

20. Skowronek, *Building a New American State*.

21. Robert Harrison, *Congress, Progressive Reform, and the New American State* (New York: Cambridge University Press, 2004).

22. Lawrence C. Dodd and Richard L. Schott, *Congress and the Administrative State* (New York: Wiley, 1979).

23. Ira Katznelson and Bruce Pietrykowski, "Rebuilding the American State: Evidence from the 1940s," *Studies in American Political Development* 5:2 (1991): 301–39.

24. David Plotke, *Building a Democratic Political Order: Reshaping American Liberalism in the 1930s and 1940s* (New York: Cambridge University Press, 1996).

25. Theda Skocpol and Kenneth Finegold, "State Capacity and Economic Intervention in the Early New Deal," *Political Science Quarterly* 97 (1999): 255–70.

26. Michael Brown, "State Capacity and Political Choice: Interpreting the Failure of the Third New Deal," *Studies in American Political Development* 9 (1995): 187–212.

27. Ira Katznelson, Kim Geiger, and Daniel Kryder, "Limiting Liberalism: The Southern Veto in Congress, 1933–1950," *Political Science Quarterly* 108 (1993): 283–306.

28. Joseph Califano, "What Was Really Great about the Great Society," *Washington Monthly*, October 1999, https://washingtonmonthly.com/1999/10/01/what-was-really-great-about-the-great-society (accessed 7/16/08).

29. David T. Canon, *Race, Redistricting, and Representation: The Unintended Consequences of Black Majority Districts* (Chicago: University of Chicago Press, 1999).

30. Charles Murray, *Losing Ground: American Social Policy, 1950–1980* (New York: Basic Books, 1984).

31. Henry J. Aaron, *Politics and the Professors: The Great Society in Perspective* (Washington, DC: Brookings Institution Press, 1978).

32. Michael B. Katz, *In the Shadow of the Poorhouse: A Social History of Welfare in America* (New York: Basic Books, 1996).

33. Richard P. Nathan, *The Administrative Presidency* (New York: Wiley, 1983).

34. Andrew Rudalevige, "The Structure of Leadership: Presidents, Hierarchies, and Information Flow," *Presidential Studies Quarterly* 35 (2005): 333–60.

35. David E. Lewis, *Presidents and the Policy of Agency Design* (Palo Alto, CA: Stanford University Press, 2003).

36. Terry M. Moe, "An Assessment of the Positive Theory of Congressional Dominance," *Legislative Studies Quarterly* 4 (1987): 475–98.

37. William A. Niskanen, *Bureaucracy and Public Economics* (Washington, DC: Edward Elgar, 1976); Robert Whaples and Jac C. Heckelman, "Public Choice Economics: Where Is There Consensus?," *American Economist* 49 (2005): 66–78.

38. Alan Schick and Felix LoStracco, *The Federal Budget: Politics, Process, Policy* (Washington, DC: Brookings Institution Press, 2000).

39. Joel D. Aberbach, "The Political Significance of the George W. Bush Administration," *Social Policy and Administration* 39:2 (2005): 130–49.

40. David E. Lewis, "The Politics of Agency Termination: Confronting the Myth of Agency Immortality," *Journal of Politics* 64 (2002): 89–107.

41. Ronald A. Wirtz, "Put It on My . . . Er, His Tab: Opinion Polls Show a Big Gap between the Public's Desire for Services and Its Willingness to Pay for These Services," *Fedgazette*, January 2004, www.minneapolisfed.org/publications/fedgazette/put-it-on-my-er-his-tab (accessed 6/25/18).

42. James L. Perry and Annie Hondeghem, *Motivation in Public Management: The Call of Public Service* (Oxford, UK: Oxford University Press, 2008).

43. Paul Light, *A Government Well-Executed: Public Service and Public Performance* (Washington, DC: Brookings Institution Press, 2003).

44. Dennis Cauchon, "Some Federal Workers More Likely to Die Than Lose Jobs," *USA Today*, July 19, 2011, p. A1.

45. Ronald N. Johnson and Gary D. Liebcap, *The Federal Civil Service System and the Problem of Bureaucracy* (Chicago: University of Chicago Press, 1993).

46. For the details of the Hatch Act, see Daniel Engber, "Can Karl Rove Plot Campaign Strategy on the Government's Dime?," *Slate*, April 21, 2006, www.slate.com/id/2140418 (accessed 8/29/16).

47. Timothy Noah, "Low Morale at Homeland Security," *Slate*, September 14, 2005, www.slate.com/id/2126313 (accessed 8/29/16).

48. For details on the SES, see www.opm.gov/policy-data-oversight/senior-executive-service/ (accessed 5/7/18).

49. "Tracking How Many Key Positions Trump Has Filled So Far," *Washington Post*, www.washingtonpost.com/graphics/politics/trump-administration-appointee-tracker/database/?utm_term=.1b5914b69716 (accessed 5/18/18).

50. Lisa Rein and Juliet Eilperin, "White House Installs Political Aides at Cabinet Agencies to Be Trump's Eyes and Ears," *Washington Post*, March 19, 2017, p. A03

51. Todd Frankel, "Why the CDC Still Isn't Researching Gun Violence, Despite the Ban Being Lifted Two Years Ago," *Washington Post*, January 14, 2015, p. A01.

52. Umair Irfan, "'Climate Change' and 'Global Warming' Are Disappearing from Government Websites," *Vox*, January 11, 2018, www.vox.com/energy-and-environment/2017/11/9/16619120/trump-administration-removing-climate-change-epa-online-website (accessed 5/18/18).

53. John D. Huber and Charles R. Shipan, *Deliberate Discretion? The Institutional Foundations of Bureaucratic Autonomy* (New York: Cambridge University Press, 2002).

54. David Epstein and Sharyn O'Halloran, *Delegating Powers: A Transaction Cost Politics Approach to Policy Making under Separate Powers* (New York: Cambridge University Press, 1999).

55. Mathew D. McCubbins, Roger G. Noll, and Barry R. Weingast, "Structure and Process as Solutions to the Politician's Principal–Agency Problem," *Virginia Law Review* 74 (1989): 431–82.

56. Barry R. Weingast, "Caught in the Middle: The President, Congress, and the Political–Bureaucratic System," in *Institutions of American Democracy: The Executive Branch*, ed. Joel D. Aberbach and Mark A. Peterson (New York: Oxford University Press, 2006).

57. Keith Whittington and Daniel P. Carpenter, "Executive Power in American Institutional Development," *Perspectives on Politics* 1 (2003): 495–513.

58. Roger Noll, Mathew McCubbins, and Barry Weingast, "Administrative Procedures as Instruments of Political Control," *Journal of Law, Economics, and Organization* 3 (1987): 243–77.

59. Mathew McCubbins and Thomas Schwartz, "Congressional Oversight Overlooked: Fire Alarms vs. Police Patrols," *American Journal of Political Science* 28 (1984): 165–79.

60. McCubbins and Schwartz, "Congressional Oversight Overlooked."

61. Steven J. Balla and John R. Wright, "Interest Groups, Advisory Committees, and Congressional Control of the Bureaucracy," *American Journal of Political Science* 45 (2001): 799–812.

62. Daniel P. Carpenter, "The Gatekeeper: Organizational Reputation and Pharmaceutical Regulation at the FDA" (unpublished paper, Harvard University, 2006).

63. Terry M. Moe, "Political Control and the Power of the Agent," *Journal of Law, Economics, and Organization* 22 (2006): 1–29.

64. See David Weil, "OSHA: Beyond the Politics," *Frontline*, January 9, 2003, www.pbs.org/wgbh/pages/frontline/shows/workplace/osha/weil.html (accessed 8/29/16).

Chapter 14

1. Joan Biskupic, "Justice Ruth Bader Ginsburg Calls Trump a 'Faker,' He Says She Should Resign," July 13, 2016, CNN Politics, www.cnn.com/2016/07/12/politics/justice-ruth-bader-ginsburg-donald-trump-faker/index.html (accessed 3/13/18).

2. Editorial Board, "Justice Ginsburg's Inappropriate Comments on Donald Trump," *Washington Post*, July 12, 2016, www.washingtonpost.com/opinions/justice-ginsburgs-inappropriate-comments-on-donald-trump/2016/07/12/981df404-4862-11e6-bdb9-701687974517_story.html?utm_term=.fed5635b0e1a (accessed 3/13/18).

3. Editorial Board, "Donald Trump Is Right about Justice Ruth Bader Ginsburg," *New York Times*, July 13, 2016, www.nytimes.com/2016/07/13/opinion/donald-trump-is-right-about-justice-ruth-bader-ginsburg.html (accessed 3/13/18).

4. Eliza Collins, "Ginsburg on Trump Comments: 'I Regret Making Them,'" *USA Today*, July 14, 2016, www.usatoday.com/story/news/politics/onpolitics/2016/07/14/ginsburg-apologizes-trump-comments/87074576/ (accessed 3/12/18).

5. SCOTUSblog, Stat Pack, October Term 2017, June 29, 2018, www.scotusblog.com/wp-content/uploads/2018/06/SB_votesplit_20180629.pdf (accessed 8/15/18).

6. Ralph Ketcham, *The Anti-Federalist Papers and the Constitutional Convention Debates* (New York: Penguin Putnam, 2003), p. 304.

7. Lester S. Jayson, ed., *The Constitution of the United States of America: Analysis and Interpretation* (Washington, DC: U.S. Government Printing Office, 1973), p. 585.

8. David G. Savage, *Guide to the U.S. Supreme Court*, 4th ed. (Washington, DC: CQ Press, 2004), p. 7.

9. Savage, *Guide to the U.S. Supreme Court*, pp. 5–7.

10. Winfield H. Rose, "*Marbury v. Madison*: How John Marshall Changed History by Misquoting the Constitution," *Political Science and Politics* 36:2 (April 2003): 209–14. Rose argues that in a key quotation in the case Marshall intentionally left out a clause of the Constitution that suggests that Congress *did* have the power to expand the original jurisdiction of the Court. Other constitutional scholars reject this argument.

11. *Marbury v. Madison*, 5 U.S. 1 Cranch 137 (1803).

12. Revisionist historians, legal scholars, and political scientists have challenged the landmark status of *Marbury v. Madison*. For example, Michael Stokes Paulsen's *Michigan Law Review* article points out that *Marbury* was not cited in subsequent Supreme Court cases as a precedent for judicial review until the late nineteenth century. Legal scholars in the early twentieth

century were the first to promote the idea that *Marbury* was a landmark decision. Paulsen also notes that when the opinion was delivered in 1803 it was not controversial. Even the Jeffersonian Democrats, who were at odds with Marshall's Federalists, thought that it was a reasonable decision and not the institutional power grab that is described in modern accounts. Finally, Marshall made a very narrow case for judicial review, arguing that the Supreme Court could declare legislation that was contrary to the Court's interpretation of the Constitution null and void only if it concerned judicial powers. Revisionists argue that what appear to be broad claims of judicial power in *Marbury* (e.g., the Court has the power "to say what the law is") are taken out of the context of a much more narrow claim of power. Michael Stokes Paulsen, "Judging Judicial Review: *Marbury* in the Modern Era: The Irrepressible Myth of *Marbury*," *Michigan Law Review* 101 (August 2003): 2706–43.

13. Bureau of Justice Statistics, Criminal Cases, www.bjs.gov/index.cfm?ty=tp&tid=23 (accessed 3/13/18).

14. *Wal-Mart v. Dukes*, 564 U.S. (2011). However, in 2011 the Court struck down any class-action claim unless there was "convincing proof of a companywide discriminatory pay and promotion policy"—statistical evidence of pay disparities would not suffice. David Savage, "Supreme Court Blocks Huge Class-Action Suit against Wal-Mart," *Los Angeles Times*, June 21, 2011, http://articles.latimes.com/2011/jun/21/nation/la-na-court-walmart-20110621 (accessed 7/13/16).

15. The Internet sales tax case was *South Dakota v. Wayfair, Inc.*, 585 U.S. ___ (2018), and the case that was overturned was *Quill Corp. v. North Dakota*, 504 U.S. 298 (1992).

16. *Lujan v. Defenders of Wildlife*, 504 U.S. 555 (1992).

17. The case concerning the bombing in Libya was *Kucinich v. Obama*, 821 F.Supp. 2d 110 (Dist. of Columbia 2011). The cases limiting taxpayers' standing to challenge laws they disagree with are *Flast v. Cohen*, 392 U.S. 83 (1968), and *Arizona Christian School Tuition Org. v. Winn*, 131 S.Ct. 1436 (2011).

18. United States Courts, Authorized Judgeships, www.uscourts.gov/judges-judgeships/authorized-judgeships (accessed 3/13/18).

19. The official name for each appeals court is the "United States Court of Appeals for the Circuit."

20. United States Courts, Authorized Judgeships.

21. United States Courts, Authorized Judgeships.

22. *Ledbetter v. Goodyear Tire & Rubber Co.*, 550 U.S. 618 (2007).

23. The Eleventh Amendment does not mention lawsuits against a state brought in federal court by citizens of that same state. However, in *Alden v. Maine* (527 U.S. 706 [1999]) the Court extended the logic of sovereign immunity to apply to these cases as well.

24. Savage, *Guide to the U.S. Supreme Court*, p. 1003.

25. Chris Weigant, "Supreme Court's Lack of Religious Diversity," The Blog, *Huffington Post*, December 6, 2017, www.huffingtonpost.com/chris-weigant/supreme-courts-lack-of-re_b_5545989.html (accessed 3/14/18).

26. Adam Liptak and Matt Flegenheimer, "Neil Gorsuch Confirmed by Senate as Supreme Court Justice, *New York Times*, April 7, 2017, www.nytimes.com/2017/04/07/us/politics/neil-gorsuch-supreme-court.html (accessed 3/14/18).

27. "President Bush Discusses Judicial Accomplishments and Philosophy," Cincinnati, Ohio, October 6, 2008, https://georgewbush-whitehouse.archives.gov/news/releases/2008/10/20081006-5.html (accessed 12/14/11).

28. Paul Kane, "Reid, Democrats Trigger 'Nuclear' Option; Eliminate Most Filibusters on Nominees," *Washington Post*, November 21, 2013, www.washingtonpost.com/politics/senate-poised-to-limit-filibusters-in-party-line-vote-that-would-alter-centuries-of-precedent/2013/11/21/d065cfe8-52b6-11e3-9fe0-fd2ca728e67c_story.html (accessed 5/2/14).

29. Alliance for Justice, "Judicial Vacancies without Nominees," March 6, 2018, www.afj.org/wp-content/uploads/2014/11/ReportCurrentAndFutureVacancies.pdf (accessed 3/14/18).

30. John Roberts, "2017 Year-End Report on the Federal Judiciary," U.S. Supreme Court, December 31, 2017, www.supremecourt.gov/publicinfo/year-end/2017year-endreport.pdf (accessed 3/14/18).

31. Supreme Court of the United States *In Re Frederick W. Bauer*, On Motion for Leave to Proceed in forma pauperis, No. 99-5440, Decided October 18, 1999, per curiam, http://supreme.lp.findlaw.com/supreme_court/decisions/99-5440.html (accessed 9/26/16).

32. Roberts, "2017 Year-End Report on the Federal Judiciary."

33. For a critical account of the Supreme Court's reduced caseload, which dates back to the Rehnquist Court, see Philip Allen Lacovara, "The Incredible Shrinking Court," *American Lawyer*, December 1, 2003, pp. 53–58.

34. *New Jersey v. New York*, No. 120 Orig., 118 S.Ct. 1726 (1998), and *Kansas v. Colorado*, No. 105 Orig., 125 S.Ct. 526 (2004).

35. Henry J. Abraham, *The Judiciary: The Supreme Court in the Governmental Process*, 7th ed. (Boston: Allyn and Bacon, 1987), p. 25, says that original jurisdiction has been invoked "about 150 times." A Lexis search revealed an additional 27 original-jurisdiction cases between 1987 and December 2004. A search of the U.S. Supreme Court's website, www.supremecourt.gov, found 13 more original jurisdiction cases from 2005 to 2017.

36. Amanda L. Tyler, "Setting the Supreme Court's Agenda: Is There a Place for Certification?," *George Washington Law Review Arguendo* 78 (May 2010): 101–18.

37. Savage, *Guide to the U.S. Supreme Court*, p. 848.

38. See Thomas G. Walker and Lee Epstein, *The Supreme Court of the United States: An Introduction* (New York: St. Martin's Press, 1993), pp. 80–85, for a more detailed discussion of these concepts and citations to the relevant court cases.

39. *Shaw v. Reno*, 509 U.S. 630 (1993).

40. *Elk Grove Unified School District v. Newdow*, 542 U.S. 1 (2004).

41. Gregory A. Caldeira and John R. Wright, "The Discuss List: Agenda Building in the Supreme Court," *Law and Society Review* 24 (1990): 813.

42. Walker and Epstein, *Supreme Court*, p. 89; Ryan C. Black and Ryan J. Owens, *The Solicitor General and the United States Supreme Court: Executive Branch Influence and Judicial Decisions* (New York: Cambridge University Press, 2012).

43. U.S. Supreme Court, "The Court and Its Procedures," www.supremecourtus.gov/about/procedures.pdf (accessed 5/27/16).

44. Lee Epstein, Jeffrey A. Segal, Harold J. Spaeth, and Thomas G. Walker, *The Supreme Court Compendium: Data, Decisions, and Developments*, 3rd ed. (Washington, DC: CQ Press, 2003), Table 7-25.

45. Gregory A. Caldeira and John R. Wright, "*Amicus Curiae* before the Supreme Court: Who Participates, When, and How Much?," *Journal of Politics* 52 (August 1990): 803.

46. Richard L. Pacelle Jr., John M. Scheb II, Hemant K. Sharma, and David H. Scott, "The Influence of the Solicitor General as Amicus Curiae on the Roberts Court, 2005–2014: A Research Note," *Justice System Journal* 38:2 (2017): 202–8.

47. Andrew Christy, "'Obamacare' Will Rank among the Longest Supreme Court Arguments Ever," National Public Radio, November 15, 2011, www.npr.org/blogs/itsallpolitics/2011/11/15/142363047/obamacare-will-rank-among-the-longest-supreme-court-arguments-ever (accessed 5/2/14).

48. U.S. Supreme Court, *Rules of the U.S. Supreme Court*, adopted April 19, 2013, effective July 1, 2013, Rule 28.7, www.supremecourt.gov/ctrules/2013RulesoftheCourt.pdf (accessed 5/27/16).

49. Savage, *Guide to the U.S. Supreme Court*, p. 852.

50. U.S. Supreme Court, Argument Transcripts, www.supremecourt.gov/oral_arguments/argument_transcript/2017 (accessed 6/8/18).

51. Garrett Epps, "Clarence Thomas Breaks His Silence," *The Atlantic*, February 29, 2016, www.theatlantic.com/politics/archive/2016/02/clarence-thomas-supreme-court/471582/ (accessed 5/27/16).

52. Quoted in Savage, *Guide to the U.S. Supreme Court*, p. 854.

53. Richard J. Lazarus, "Back to 'Business' at the Supreme Court: The 'Administrative Side' of Chief Justice Roberts," *Harvard Law Review Forum* 129:33 (2015): 33–93.

54. Michael A. McCall and Madhavi M. McCall, "Quantifying the Contours of Power: Chief Justice Roberts & Justice Kennedy in Criminal Justice Cases," *Pace Law Review* 37:1 (2016): 115–74.

55. *Smith v. Allwright*, 321 U.S. 649 (1944).

56. Walker and Epstein, *Supreme Court*, p. 110.

57. Linda Greenhouse, "Chief Justice Roberts in His Own Voice: The Chief Justice's Self-Assignment of Majority Opinions," Yale Law School, Public Law Research Paper no. 496, August 15, 2013.

58. Savage, *Guide to the U.S. Supreme Court*, p. 854.

59. Lee Epstein, William M. Landes, and Richard A. Posner, "Are Even Unanimous Decisions in the United States Supreme Court Ideological?," *Northwestern University Law Review* 106:2 (2012), 702.

60. SCOTUSblog, 2018.

61. In cases involving statutory interpretation, the language of the law passed by Congress would be the starting point. The logic of these various perspectives on constitutional interpretation generally applies to statutory interpretation as well.

62. Quoted in Lee Epstein and Thomas G. Walker, *Constitutional Law for a Changing America: Institutional Powers and Constraints*, 5th ed. (Washington, DC: CQ Press, 2004), p. 29.

63. *Maryland v. Craig*, 497 U.S. 836 (1990).

64. Epstein and Walker, *Constitutional Law for a Changing America*, p. 31.

65. Seth Stern and Stephen Wermiel, *Justice Brennan: Liberal Champion* (Boston: Houghton Mifflin Harcourt, 2010).

66. Epstein, Segal, Spaeth, and Walker, *Supreme Court Compendium*, Table 6-2.

67. Forrest Maltzman and Paul J. Wahlbeck, "Strategic Policy Considerations and Vote Fluidity on the Burger Court," *American Journal of Political Science* 90 (1996): 581–92; Forrest Maltzman, James F. Spriggs, and Paul J. Wahlbeck, *Crafting Law on the Supreme Court: The Collegial Game* (New York: Cambridge University Press, 2000), p. 33.

68. Finley Peter Dunne, Paul Green, and Jacques Barzun, *Mr. Dooley in Peace and in War* (1898; repr., Champaign-Urbana: University of Illinois Press, 2001).

69. Robert Dahl, "Decision-Making in a Democracy: The Supreme Court as a National Policy-Maker," *Journal of Public Law* 6 (1957): 279–95, is the classic work on this topic. More recent work has challenged Dahl's methods but largely supports the idea that the Court follows the will of the majority.

70. Jeffrey A. Segal, Richard J. Timpone, and Robert M. Howard, "Buyer Beware? Presidential Success through Supreme Court Appointments," *Political Research Quarterly* 53:3 (September 2000): 557–73; Gregory A. Caldeira and Charles E. Smith Jr., "Campaigning for the Supreme Court: The Dynamics of Public Opinion on the Thomas Nomination," *Political Research Quarterly* 58:3 (August 1996): 655–81.

71. William Mishler and Reginald S. Sheehan, "The Supreme Court as a Countermajoritarian Institution? The Impact of Public Opinion on Supreme Court Decisions," *American Political Science Review* 87:1 (March 1993): 87–101.

72. Thomas R. Marshall, *Public Opinion and the Supreme Court* (Boston: Unwin Hyman, 1989), p. 12; as cited in Epstein and Walker, *Constitutional Law for a Changing America*, p. 92.

73. Matthew E. K. Hall, "The Semiconstrained Court: Public Opinion, the Separation of Powers, and the U.S. Supreme Court's Fear of Nonimplementation," *American Journal of Political Science* 58:2 (April 2014): 352–66; Matthew E. K. Hall, *The Nature of Supreme Court Power* (New York: Cambridge University Press, 2011).

74. *Stanford v. Kentucky*, 492 U.S. 361 (1989); *Roper v. Simmons*, 543 U.S. 551 (2005).

75. David O'Brien, *Storm Center: The Supreme Court in American Politics*, 4th ed. (New York: W. W. Norton, 1996), p. 276.

76. Helmut Norpoth and Jeffrey A. Segal, "Popular Influence in Supreme Court Decisions," *American Political Science Review* 88 (1994): 711–16.

77. Thomas M. Keck, *The Most Activist Supreme Court in History: The Road to Modern Judicial Conservatism* (Chicago: University of Chicago Press, 2004).

78. Marshall, *Public Opinion*, Table 6-8.

79. Jeffrey Rosen, "Has the Supreme Court Gone Too Far?," *Commentary* 116:3 (October 2003), pp. 41–2.

80. *National Federation of Independent Business v. Sebelius*, 567 U.S. (2012).

81. Abby Phillip, Robert Barnes, and Ed O'Keefe, "Supreme Court Nominee Gorsuch Says Trump's Attacks on Judiciary Are 'Demoralizing,'" *Washington Post*, February 9, 2017, www.washingtonpost.com/politics/supreme-court-nominee-gorsuch-says-trumps-attacks-on-judiciary-are-demoralizing/2017/02/08/64e03fe2-ee3f-11e6-9662-6eedf1627882_story.html?utm_term=.ade3f9791d87 (accessed 3/15/18).

82. *Foster v. Neilson*, 27 U.S. 253 (1829).

83. *Charles B. Rangel v. John A. Boehner*, United States District Court for the District of Columbia, Civil Action No. 13-540, December 11, 2013, p. 48, https://ecf.dcd.uscourts.gov/cgi-bin/show_public_doc?2013cv0540-24 (accessed 5/2/14).

84. We thank Dan Smith for raising this point.

Take a Stand

a. Martin Kady, "Justice Alito Mouths 'Not True'," *POLITICO*, January 27, 2010, www.politico.com/blogs/politico-now/2010/01/justice-alito-mouthes-not-true-024608 (accessed 8/24/18).

b. Donald J. Trump, Twitter, https://twitter.com/realdonaldtrump/status/828342202174668800?lang=en (accessed 3/15/18).

Chapter 15

1. "Donald Trump's Speech on Trade," *Time*, June 28, 2016, http://time.com/4386335/donald-trump-trade-speech-transcript/ (accessed 4/26/18).

2. David Choi, "'This Is the Dumbest Possible Way to Do This': Republican Senator Elbows Trump over New $100 Billion Tariff Threat to China," *Business Insider*, April 5, 2018, www.businessinsider.com/ben-sasse-against-trump-on-china-tariff-2018-4 (accessed 4/26/18).

3. Ben White, "Trump and Sanders' Common Cause," *Politico*, April 3, 2016, www.politico.com/story/2016/04/donald-trump-bernie-sanders-trade-221506 (accessed 4/26/18).

4. Benn Steil and Benjamin Della Rocca, "Trump Steel Tariffs Could Kill Up to 40,000 Auto Jobs, Equal to Nearly One-Third of Steel Workforce," Council on Foreign Relations, March 8, 2018, www.cfr.org/blog/trump-steel-tariffs-could-kill-40000-auto-jobs-equal-nearly-one-third-steel-workforce (accessed 4/26/18).

5. Merrit Kennedy, "Trump's Steel, Aluminum Tariffs Could Raise Car, Beer and Candy Prices," National Public Radio, March 2, 2018, www.npr.org/sections/thetwo-way/2018/03/02/590314013/trumps-steel-aluminum-tariffs-could-raise-car-beer-and-candy-prices (accessed 4/26/18).

6. The classic article on deflation is Irving Fisher, "The Debt-Deflation Theory of Great Depressions," *Econometrica*, 1933, https://fraser.stlouisfed.org/docs/meltzer/fisdeb33.pdf (accessed 6/2/16). For articles on recent policies concerning deflation, see www.nytimes.com/topic/subject/deflation-economics (accessed 4/19/18).

7. Daniel Yergin and Joseph Stanislaw, *The Commanding Heights: The Battle for the World Economy* (New York: Free Press, 2002), pp. 60–64.

8. Central Intelligence Agency, "Country Comparison: Distribution of Family Income, Gini Index," *World Factbook*, https://www.cia.gov/library/publications/resources/the-world-factbook/rankorder/2172rank.html (accessed 7/25/18).

9. The phrase comes from environmental economist E. F. Schumacher's influential book, *Small Is Beautiful: Economics as If People Mattered* (New York: Harper and Row, 1973).

10. Jonathan Rowe and Judith Silverstein, "The GDP Myth: Why 'Growth' Isn't Always a Good Thing," *Washington Monthly* 31:3 (March 1999): 17–21.

11. Congressional Budget Office, *The Budget and Economic Outlook: 2018 to 2028*, April 2018, Table 4-1, p. 81, www.cbo.gov/system/files/115th-congress-2017-2018/reports/53651-outlook.pdf (accessed 4/19/18).

12. Shaghil Ahmed, Carol Bertaut, Jessica Liu, and Robert Vigfusson, "Should We Be Concerned Again about U.S. Current Account Sustainability?," IFDP Notes, Board of Governors of the Federal Reserve System, March 9, 2018, https://doi.org/10.17016/2573-2129.42 (accessed 4/19/18).

13. The classic work on the appropriations process in the pre-reform era is Richard F. Fenno's *The Power of the Purse: Appropriations Politics in Congress* (Boston: Little, Brown, 1966). D. Roderick Kiewiet and Mathew D. McCubbins reexamined the appropriations process in the post-reform era and found that the appropriations committees have maintained much of their power; see *The Logic of Delegation: Congressional Parties and the Appropriations Process* (Chicago: University of Chicago Press, 1991).

14. Bill Heniff Jr., "Congressional Budget Resolutions: Historical Information," November 15, 2015, Table 12, p. 29, www.senate.gov/CRSReports/crs-publish.cfm?pid=%270E%2C*PLS2%23%20%20%20%0A (accessed 6/2/16). This study shows the failure to pass a budget resolution in 8 of the past 14 years, but Congress also failed to pass the resolution before April 15 for the 2017 fiscal year.

15. Stan Collender, "GOP-Led Budget Committees Have Just One Job . . . and Are Refusing to Do It," *Forbes*, April 22, 2018, www.forbes.com/sites/stancollender/2018/04/22/gop-led-budget-committees-have-just-one-job-and-are-refusing-to-do-it/#549a29aa5fb1; Stan Collender, "The Federal Budget Process Is Dead and Desperately Needs to Be Buried," *Forbes*, April 24, 2018, www.forbes.com/sites/stancollender/2018/04/24/the-federal-budget-process-is-dead-and-desperately-needs-to-be-buried/#82292162255d (both accessed 4/24/18).

16. The specific provision is paragraph (1)(E) of section 313(b)(1) of the Budget Control Act. James Thurber, "Centralization, Devolution, and Turf Protection in the Congressional Budget Process," in *Congress Reconsidered*, ed. Lawrence C. Dodd and Bruce I. Oppenheimer, 6th ed. (Washington, DC: CQ Press, 1997), pp. 325–46.

17. These figures exclude the Social Security surplus. Including Social Security, the government had a small surplus in 1969. See the CBO's historical budget data, www.cbo.gov/about/products/budget-economic-data#2 (accessed 7/30/18). For data before 1962, see the 1981 *Economic Report of the President* (Washington, DC: Government Printing Office, 1981), p. 316.

18. Robert Keith, "The Statutory Pay-As-You-Go Act of 2010: Summary and Legislative History," Congressional Research Service, April 2, 2010, http://democrats.budget.house.gov/sites/democrats.budget.house.gov/files/documents/CRS-stat-paygo.pdf (accessed 6/2/2016). The programs and activities exempt from sequestration include Social Security and Tier I Railroad Retirement benefits; federal employee retirement and disability programs; veterans' programs; net interest; refundable income tax credits; Medicaid, the Children's Health Insurance Program (CHIP), the Supplemental Nutrition Assistance Program (SNAP), Supplemental Security Income (SSI), Temporary Assistance for Needy Families (TANF), and certain other low-income programs; and unemployment compensation, among others.

19. "H.R. 2, Medicare Access and CHIP Reauthorization Act of 2015," Congressional Budget Office, March 24, 2015, www.cbo.gov/sites/default/files/114th-congress-2015-2016/costestimate/hr22.pdf (accessed 6/2/16).

20. The size of the tax cut was initially estimated at $1.5 trillion over 10 years by the nonpartisan Joint Committee on Taxation. A few months later, the Office of Management and Budget estimated the tax cut at $2.3 trillion, and then in April, the Congressional Budget Office estimated the 10-year cost at $1.9 trillion (www.cbo.gov/publication/53787 [accessed 9/7/18]). For a discussion of the tax cuts' short-term economic impact, see Indradip Ghosh and Shrutee Sarkar, "Tax Cuts to Boost U.S. Economy, But Benefits to Be Short-Lived: Reuters Poll," Reuters Business News, January 22, 2018, www.reuters.com/article/us-economy-usa-poll/tax-cuts-to-boost-u-s-economy-but-benefits-to-be-short-lived-reuters-poll-idUSKBN1FC0FX (accessed 4/24/18).

21. Office of the United States Trade Representative, "About Us," https://ustr.gov/about-us (accessed 7/30/18).

22. National Economic Council, www.whitehouse.gov/administration/eop/nec (accessed 7/28/14).

23. See Charles M. Cameron, *Veto Bargaining: Presidents and the Politics of Negative Power* (New York: Cambridge University Press, 2000), for a general discussion of the strategic elements of issuing veto threats.

24. "The Structure and Functions of the Federal Reserve System," Federal Reserve Education.org, www.federalreserveeducation.org/about-the-fed/structure-and-functions (accessed 6/2/16).

25. William McChesney Martin, who was appointed by Harry Truman, served through the presidencies of Eisenhower,

Kennedy, and Johnson and part of Nixon's first term. Paul Volcker served under Carter and Reagan, while Alan Greenspan's tenure spanned the presidencies of Reagan, Bush, Clinton, and the second Bush. Federal Reserve Board, "Membership of the Board of Governors of the Federal Reserve System, 1914–Present," www.federalreserve.gov/aboutthefed/bios/board/boardmembership.htm (accessed 7/16/14).

26. Federal Reserve Board, *Annual Report, 2017*, June 2018, Table 10, p. 319, and Table 13, p. 324, www.federalreserve.gov/publications/annual-report/files/2017-annual-report.pdf (accessed 7/30/18).

27. Senator Sherrod Brown, Hearing on the Nomination of Jay Powell, Senate Banking Committee, November 28, 2017, www.banking.senate.gov/imo/media/doc/Brown%20Statement%2011-28-17.pdf (accessed 4/24/18).

28. Edward R. Tufte, *Political Control of the Economy* (Princeton, NJ: Princeton University Press, 1978); Douglas Hibbs, "The Partisan Model of Macroeconomic Cycles: More Theory and Evidence for the United States," *Economics and Politics* 6 (1994): 1–23.

29. Jim Granato, "The Effect of Policy-Maker Reputation and Credibility on Public Expectations," *Journal of Theoretical Politics* 8 (1996): 449–70; Peter Conti-Brown, *The Power and Independence of the Federal Reserve* (Princeton, NJ: Princeton University Press, 2016).

30. U.S. Department of the Treasury, "Role of the Treasury," https://home.treasury.gov/about/general-information/role-of-the-treasury (accessed 7/30/18).

31. United States Treasury, Resource Center, www.treasury.gov/resource-center/faqs/Currency/Pages/edu_faq_currency_production.aspx; United States Mint, *2017 Annual Report*, February 2018, www.usmint.gov/wordpress/wp-content/uploads/2018/01/2017-annual-report.pdf (both accessed 4/24/18).

32. Carl Hulse, "Pressure Builds on House after Senate Backs Bailout," *New York Times*, October 1, 2008, p. A1.

33. David M. Herszenhorn, "Bailout Plan Wins Approval; Democrats Vow Tighter Rules," *New York Times*, October 3, 2008, p. A1.

34. U.S. Department of Treasury, "TARP Tracker from November 2008 to June 2018," www.treasury.gov/initiatives/financial-stability/reports/Pages/TARP-Tracker.aspx#All (accessed 7/30/18).

35. The one area of loans that has not turned a profit yet is loans to the auto industry. See U.S. Department of the Treasury, "TARP Tracker from November 2008 to June 2018," www.treasury.gov/initiatives/financial-stability/reports/Pages/TARP-Tracker.aspx#All (accessed 7/30/18).

36. "Recent Balance Sheet Trends," Board of Governors of the Federal Reserve System, July 25, 2018, www.federalreserve.gov/monetarypolicy/bst_recenttrends.htm (accessed 7/30/18).

37. John Maynard Keynes, *The General Theory of Employment, Interest and Money* (1936; repr., New York: Macmillan, 2007).

38. Brian Domitrovic, "Trashing JFK's Tax Cuts, One of the Greatest Policy Successes of All Time," *Forbes*, March 12, 2013, www.forbes.com/sites/briandomitrovic/2013/03/12/trashing-jfks-tax-cuts-one-of-the-greatest-policy-successes-of-all-time/#347c0b863e2f (accessed 7/31/18).

39. In Laffer's original argument, there was only one tax rate. However, to apply the Laffer curve to the real world of tax policy, the theoretical argument must be presented in terms of the top marginal rate, which is the tax rate paid on the last dollars earned (and thus the rate that influences the marginal decision to work more or fewer hours). The end point of zero tax revenue associated with a 100 percent tax rate would be for Laffer's single tax rate, rather than the top marginal rate (because people would still work as long as they could keep some income in the marginal brackets below the top rate).

40. Arthur B. Laffer, "The Laffer Curve: Past, Present, and Future," Heritage Foundation Backgrounder #1765, June 1, 2004, www.heritage.org/research/reports/2004/06/the-laffer-curve-past-present-and-future (accessed 10/3/16).

41. These figures come from the Congressional Budget Office, "Historical Budget Data," www.cbo.gov (accessed 4/18/08). Tax revenue fell from 19.6 percent of GDP in 1981, the last year before the tax cuts went into effect, to 18.1 percent of GDP in 1988, the last year of the Reagan presidency. Individual income tax revenue fell from 9.3 percent to 8 percent of GDP over the same period, so most of the decrease in revenue was due to lower individual income taxes. While overall government spending did increase during the 1982–1983 recession, spending from the beginning of Reagan's term to the end dropped slightly, from 22.2 percent to 21.2 percent of GDP.

42. Congressional Budget Office, "An Analysis of the President's 2019 Budget," May, 2018, Table 1, p. 2, Table 4, p. 8, www.cbo.gov/system/files?file=2018-06/53884-apb2019.pdf (accessed 7/31/18).

43. The "starve the beast" line is usually attributed to David Stockman and his book *The Triumph of Politics: The Inside Story of the Reagan Revolution* (New York: Avon Books, 1986). A Web search for "David Stockman" and "starve the beast" produced 566 hits, including a reference in a *National Review* article: Norman B. Ture, "To Cut and to Please," June 10, 2004, www.nationalreview.com/article/211069/cut-and-please-norman-b-ture (accessed 7/7/16). However, we have been unable to find the phrase "starve the beast" in Stockman's book. More recently, smaller-government proponents such as conservative political advocate Grover Norquist have embraced the concept.

44. The payroll tax figure comes from Congressional Budget Office, "The Distribution of Household Income and Federal Taxes, 2010," December 2013, Table 3, p. 13, http://cbo.gov/sites/default/files/cbofiles/attachments/44604-AverageTaxRates.pdf (accessed 6/30/14), and the income tax figure comes from Scott Greenberg, "Summary of the Latest Federal Income Tax Data, 2016," Tax Foundation, February 2017, Table 1, p. 2, https://files.taxfoundation.org/20170201091804/TaxFoundation-FF540.pdf (accessed 7/31/18).

45. Congressional Budget Office, "The Distribution of Household Income, 2014," March 2018, Figure 7, p. 16, www.cbo.gov/system/files?file=115th-congress-2017-2018/reports/53597-distribution-household-income-2014.pdf (accessed 9/7/18).

46. The details get a bit more complicated, but this is essentially how money is created. Banks must hold a reserve of 10 percent of all "demand deposits" (which is what economists call checking accounts), so only $90,000 would actually be put into the money stream because the $10,000 reserve would have to come from money that someone deposited in the bank. Also, the money supply would contract as you pay back your loan. The overall effect on the money supply has to take into account the "multiplier effect"—that is, the money you spend from your loan will get spent many times over. The computer store will take your $10,000 and deposit it in its bank, which allows that bank to make more loans, and so on.

47. Milton Friedman, "The Quantity Theory of Money: A Restatement," in *The Optimum Quantity of Money and Other Essays* (Chicago: Aldine, 1969), p. 52.

48. These figures are hypothetical. In reality, under the Monetary Control Act (MCA) of 1980, the reserve requirement can range from 8 percent to 14 percent for all demand deposits greater than $25 million. In the original law, banks with demand deposits under $25 million had to have a reserve of only 3 percent. The amount that is subject to the lower reserve requirement is increased every year to reflect overall money supply and currently is about $71 million. See Board of Governors of the Federal Reserve System, "Reserve Requirement," www.federalreserve.gov/monetarypolicy/reservereq.htm#table1 (accessed 2/7/12).

49. In December 2002, the discount rate was effectively discontinued as an active policy tool and was pegged to 1 percent above the targeted FFR (which means that the "discount rate" is oddly named—it really should be called the premium rate). In the economic crisis of 2008–2009, the Fed temporarily dropped the difference between the FFR and the discount rate to .25 percent and then to .50 percent, where it remains today; see *Federal Reserve Bulletin*, December 2002, pp. 482–83. See also "Frequently Asked Questions—Discount Window Lending Programs," Federal Reserve, www.frbdiscountwindow.org/en/Frequently_Asked_Questions.aspx (accessed 6/3/16).

50. Brian W. Cashell, "The Federal Government Debt: Its Size and Economic Significance," Report RL31590 (Washington, DC: Congressional Research Service, March 1, 2005), p. 9.

51. William Greider, *Secrets of the Temple: How the Federal Reserve Runs the Country* (New York: Simon and Schuster, 1987), pp. 295–98.

52. Board of Governors of the Federal Reserve System, Credit and Liquidity Programs and Balance Sheets, Recent Balance Sheet Trends, www.federalreserve.gov/monetarypolicy/bst_recenttrends.htm (accessed 6/3/16).

53. John B. Taylor, *Economics*, 4th ed. (New York: Houghton Mifflin, 2003), Chapter 10. Some economics textbooks also define regulation of externalities, such as pollution, as economic regulation.

54. *United States v. Microsoft*, 87 F. Supp. 2d 30 (D.D.C. 2000). For a detailed discussion of the case, see Alan Reynolds, *Microsoft Antitrust Appeal: Judge Jackson's "Findings of Fact" Revisited* (Washington, DC: Hudson Institute, 2002).

55. Michael Birnbaum and Brian Fung, "E.U. Fines Google a Record $2.7 Billion in Antitrust Case over Search Results," *Washington Post*, June 27, 2017, www.washingtonpost.com/world/eu-announces-record-27-billion-antitrust-fine-on-google-over-search-results/2017/06/27/1f7c475e-5b20-11e7-8e2f-ef443171f6bd_story.html?utm_term=.f433adf6664f (accessed 4/24/18).

56. "U.S. Patent Statistics Chart Calendar Years 1963–2015," U.S. Patent and Trademark Office, www.uspto.gov/web/offices/ac/ido/oeip/taf/us_stat.htm (accessed 6/3/16).

57. Daniel Carpenter and David A. Moss, eds., *Preventing Regulatory Capture: Special Interest Influence and How to Limit It* (New York: Cambridge University Press, 2014).

58. For a running list of changes to environmental regulations, see Michael Greshko, Laura Parker, and Brian Clark Howard, "A Running List of How Trump Is Changing the Environment," *National Geographic*, April 24, 2018, https://news.nationalgeographic.com/2017/03/how-trump-is-changing-science-environment/; also see Nadja Popovich, Livia Albeck-Ripka, and Kendra Pierre-Louis, "76 Environmental Rules on the Way Out under Trump," *New York Times*, January 31, 2018, www.nytimes.com/interactive/2017/10/05/climate/trump-environment-rules-reversed.html. The $1 billion in savings was cited in Juana Summers and Boris Sanchez, "EPA's Pruitt Fulfilling Trump's Anti-regulatory Agenda," CNN, April 3, 2018, www.cnn.com/2018/04/03/politics/scott-pruitt-donald-trump-environment-policy/index.html (all accessed 4/25/18).

59. Michael Hiltzik, "No Longer Termed a 'Failure,' California's Cap-and-Trade Program Faces a New Critique: Is It Too Successful?," *Los Angeles Times*, January 12, 2018, www.latimes.com/business/hiltzik/la-fi-hiltzik-captrade-20180111-story.html (accessed 4/25/18).

60. Bureau of Labor Statistics, "Measuring Green Jobs," www.bls.gov/green/#faqs (accessed 4/25/18).

61. Environmental and Energy Study Institute, "Fact Sheet—Jobs in Renewable Energy and Energy Efficiency (2017)," February 15, 2017, www.eesi.org/papers/view/fact-sheet-jobs-in-renewable-energy-and-energy-efficiency-2017 (accessed 4/25/18).

62. U.S. Department of Commerce, Bureau of Economic Analysis, "International Services and International Investment Position Tables," www.bea.gov/newsreleases/international/intinv/intinvnewsrelease.htm (accessed 11/13/16).

63. Kimberly Amadeo, "Who Owns the U.S. National Debt?" *The Balance*, August 21, 2018, www.thebalance.com/who-owns-the-u-s-national-debt-3306124 (accessed 8/27/18).

64. Kimberly Amadeo, "Who Owns the U.S. National Debt?" *The Balance*, August 21, 2018, www.thebalance.com/who-owns-the-u-s-national-debt-3306124 (accessed 8/27/18).

65. Mark J. Perry, "Trump Is Completely Wrong about the U.S. Trade Deficit," *Los Angeles Times*, March 18, 2016, www.latimes.com/opinion/op-ed/la-oe-0316-perry-trade-benefits-20160316-story.html (accessed 6/4/16).

66. David Ricardo, *The Principles of Political Economy and Taxation* (1817). Robert Torrens actually developed the point first in an 1815 essay on the corn trade, but Ricardo usually gets the credit because he explained it more fully.

67. This argument ignores transportation costs and the costs of shifting labor from one industry to another, but its logic is quite powerful. More intuitive, perhaps, is what happens when one nation has a large *absolute* advantage in the cost of production over another. In these situations, if there is free trade most production of that good will shift to the country that can produce it more cheaply.

68. James McBride and Mohammed Aly Sergie, "NAFTA's Economic Impact," Council on Foreign Relations, October 4, 2017, www.cfr.org/backgrounder/naftas-economic-impact (accessed 4/25/18).

69. Suketu Mehta, "A Passage from India," *New York Times*, July 12, 2005, p. A21.

70. See Ronald Rogowski, *Commerce and Coalitions* (Princeton, NJ: Princeton University Press, 1986), for the constituency view. James Shoch, *Trading Blows: Party Competition and U.S. Trade Policy in a Globalizing Era* (Chapel Hill: University of North Carolina Press, 2001), pp. 13–19, reviews both explanations.

71. Judith Goldstein, *Ideas, Interests, and American Trade* (Ithaca, NY: Cornell University Press, 1993).

Take a Stand

a. The comment was in response to the takeover of a federal wildlife refuge in Oregon. Rubio called for the occupiers to lay down their arms but showed sympathy for their central demand that the federal government cede control over much of the Bureau of Land Management land. "Marco Rubio on Oregon Federal Land Business," *Des Moines Register* editorial board interview, January 6, 2016, www.desmoinesregister.com/videos/news/elections/presidential/caucus/2016/01/06/78384514/ (accessed 6/4/16).

b. John Tierney, "The Sagebrush Solution," *New York Times*, July 26, 2005, p. A19. Additional information was drawn from www.hcn.org (accessed 7/31/18).

c. A very detailed account of this saga may be found in Raymond B. Wrabley Jr., "Managing the Monument: Cows and Conservation in the Grand-Staircase-Escalante National Monument," *Journal of Land, Resources and Environmental Law* 29:2 (2009): 253–80.

Chapter 16

1. Ed O'Keefe, "The House Has Voted 54 Times in Four Years on Obamacare," *Washington Post*, March 21, 2014, www.washingtonpost.com/blogs/the-fix/wp/2014/03/21/the-house-has-voted-54-times-in-four-years-on-obamacare-heres-the-full-list/ (accessed 5/27/14); Steve Benen, "On Groundhog Day, Republicans Vote to Repeal Obamacare," February 2, 2016, MSNBC, www.msnbc.com/rachel-maddow-show/groundhog-day-republicans-vote-repeal-obamacare (accessed 6/7/16).

2. White House, "Impacts and Costs of the Government Shutdown," November 2013, https://obamawhitehouse.archives.gov/blog/2013/11/07/impacts-and-costs-government-shutdown (accessed 5/27/14).

3. Sarah Dutton, Jennifer De Pinto, Anthony Salvanto, and Fred Backus, "Poll: Congress, Tea Party Take Hits from Government Shutdown," CBS News, October 22, 2013, www.cbsnews.com/news/poll-congress-tea-party-take-hits-from-government-shutdown/ (accessed 5/27/14).

4. Joseph P. Williams, "Report: Obamacare Coverage Gains Are Eroding," *US News and World Report*, May 1, 2018, www.usnews.com/news/healthiest-communities/articles/2018-05-01/obamacare-gains-in-insurance-coverage-starting-to-erode-report-says (accessed 7/2/18).

5. Carmen Heredia Rodriguez, "Popular Coverage for Children under 26 May Be Health Law's Achilles' Heel," CNN Money, March 21, 2017, http://money.cnn.com/2017/03/21/news/economy/health-law-coverage-children-26/index.html; Kaiser Family Foundation, "Medicaid Expansion Enrollment," www.kff.org/health-reform/state-indicator/medicaid-expansion-enrollment/?currentTimeframe=0&sortModel=%7B%22colId%22:%22Location%22,%22sort%22:%22asc%22%7D (both accessed 7/2/18).

6. Amy Goldstein, "Nearly 12 Million People Enrolled in 2018 Health Coverage under the ACA," April 3, 2018, *Washington Post*, www.washingtonpost.com/national/health-science/nearly-12-million-people-enrolled-in-2018-health-coverage-under-the-aca/2018/04/03/247d3496-377c-11e8-8fd2-49fe3c675a89_story.html?utm_term=.ff546941414f (accessed 7/2/18).

7. Sara R. Collins, Munira Z. Gunja, Michelle M. Doty, and Herman K. Bhupal, "First Look at Health Insurance Coverage in 2018 Finds ACA Gains Beginning to Reverse," Commonwealth Fund, May 1, 2018, www.commonwealthfund.org/blog/2018/first-look-health-insurance-coverage-2018-finds-aca-gains-beginning-reverse (accessed 7/2/18).

8. Noam N. Levey, "Trump Administration Finalizes Rule to Allow for Skimpier Health Plans," *Los Angeles Times*, June 19, 2018, www.latimes.com/politics/la-na-pol-trump-insurance-deregulation-20180619-story.html (accessed 7/2/18).

9. Theda Skocpol, *Social Policy in the United States: Future Possibilities in Historical Perspective* (Princeton, NJ: Princeton University Press, 1995), p. 37.

10. Franklin Delano Roosevelt's second fireside chat, "Government and Modern Capitalism," Washington, DC, September 30, 1934. For the full text, see John T. Woolley and Gerhard Peters, "The American Presidency Project," University of California, Santa Barbara, www.presidency.ucsb.edu/ws/index.php?pid=14636 (accessed 8/8/08).

11. Skocpol, *Social Policy in the United States*, pp. 145–60.

12. David M. Kennedy, *Freedom from Fear: The American People in Depression and War, 1929–1945* (New York: Oxford University Press, 2001); Byron W. Daynes, William Pederson, and Michael P. Riccards, eds., *The New Deal and Public Policy* (New York: St. Martin's Press, 1998).

13. Robert Dallek, *Flawed Giant: Lyndon Johnson and His Times, 1961–1973* (New York: Oxford University Press, 1998); Irving Bernstein, *Guns or Butter: The Presidency of Lyndon Johnson* (New York: Oxford University Press, 1996).

14. Catherine Boudreau, "House Farm Bill Passes with Controversial Food Stamp Changes," *Politico*, June 21, 2018, www.politico.com/story/2018/06/21/house-passes-farm-bill-663124 (accessed 7/3/18).

15. Kayla Fontenot, Jessica Semega, and Melissa Kollar, "Income and Poverty in the United States: 2017," September 2018, U.S. Census, p. 47 (accessed 10/11/18).

16. Kayla Fontenot, Jessica Semega, and Melissa Kollar, "Income and Poverty in the United States: 2017," September 2018, U.S. Census, Table 3, p. 12 (accessed 10/11/18).

17. This figure includes income from capital gains. Thomas Piketty and Emmanuel Saez, "Income Inequality in the United States, 1913–1998," *Quarterly Journal of Economics* 118:1 (2003): 1–39. (Longer updated version published in A. B. Atkinson and Thomas Piketty, eds., *Top Incomes over the Twentieth Century: A Contrast between European and English-Speaking Countries* [Oxford: Oxford University Press, 2007].) (Tables and figures updated to 2015 in Excel format, June 2016, https://eml.berkeley.edu/~saez/ [accessed 7/3/18].)

18. Kerry A. Dolan, "Inside the 2016 Forbes 400: Facts and Figures about America's Richest People," *Forbes*, October 4, 2016, www.forbes.com/sites/kerryadolan/2016/10/04/inside-the-2016-forbes-400-facts-and-figures-about-americas-richest-people/?ss=forbes400#46e1c08b3973 (accessed 10/23/16).

19. The housing expenditure figures are from the President's 2017 Budget, Housing and Urban Development, "Budget Outlays by Program, Comparative Summary, Fiscal Years 2017–2019," www.hud.gov/sites/dfiles/CFO/documents/3%20-%20FY19CJ%20-%20Dept.%20Summary%20-%20Budget%20Outlays%20-%20Updated.pdf. The top 20 percent figure is from Ilya Somin, "Mortgage Interest Deduction Mostly Benefits the Rich—End It," *The Hill*, November 7, 2017, http://thehill.com/opinion/finance/358922-mortgage-interest-deduction-mostly-benefits-the-rich-end-it. Data on tax expenditures are from Joint Committee on Taxation, "Estimates of Federal Tax Expenditures for Fiscal Years 2017–2021," May 25, 2018, www.jct.gov/publications.html?func=startdown&id=5095 (all accessed 7/3/18).

20. Dean Baker, *The Conservative Nanny State: How the Wealthy Use the Government to Stay Rich and Get Richer*, May 2006, https://deanbaker.net/images/stories/documents/cnswebbook.pdf (accessed 8/8/18).

21. Michael Tanner, "Welfare for the Non-Poor," Cato Institute, August 29, 2013, www.cato.org/publications/commentary/welfare-non-poor (accessed 5/29/14).

22. Congressional Budget Office, "The Distribution of Household Income, 2014," March 2018, www.cbo.gov/publication/53597 (accessed 7/3/18).

23. Charles M. Blow, "Santorum's Gospel of Inequality," *New York Times*, February 17, 2012, www.nytimes.com/2012/02/18/opinion/blow-santorum-exalts-inequality.html (accessed 3/1/12).

24. Jonathan Swan, "Trump: US Needs Rich People to Be Great Again," *The Hill*, March 15, 2016, http://thehill.com/blogs/ballot-box/presidential-races/273180-trump-us-needs-rich-people-to-be-great-again (accessed 6/7/16).

25. Neal Gabler, "The Secret Shame of Middle-Class Americans," *The Atlantic*, May 2016, www.theatlantic.com/magazine/archive/2016/05/my-secret-shame/476415/ (accessed 6/7/16).

26. Larry M. Bartels, *Unequal Democracy: The Political Economy of the New Gilded Age* (Princeton, NJ: Princeton University Press, 2008).

27. Joe Soss, *Unwanted Claims: The Politics of Participation in the U.S. Welfare System* (Ann Arbor: University of Michigan Press, 2000).

28. Greg Jaffe and Ed O'Keefe, "Obama Accepts Resignation of VA Secretary Shinseki," *Washington Post*, May 30, 2014, www.washingtonpost.com/politics/shinseki-apologizes-for-va-health-care-scandal/2014/05/30/e605885a-e7f0-11e3-8f90-73e071f3d637_story.html (accessed 7/23/14).

29. Daniel P. Carpenter, *The Forging of Bureaucratic Autonomy: Reputations, Networks, and Policy Innovation in Executive Agencies, 1862–1928* (Princeton, NJ: Princeton University Press, 2001).

30 Michael Stratfor, "Budget Fleshes Out Trump Higher Ed Agenda," *Politico*, February 13, 2018, www.politico.com/newsletters/morning-education/2018/02/13/budget-fleshes-out-trump-higher-ed-agenda-103874 (accessed 7/3/18).

31. For the current issues on which AARP is lobbying, see AARP, "Politics and Society: Advocacy," www.aarp.org/politics-society/advocacy/ (accessed 7/3/18).

32. See William T. Bianco, *Trust: Representatives and Constituents* (Ann Arbor: University of Michigan Press, 1994), Chapter 6, for a discussion of the repeal of the Catastrophic Coverage Act.

33. Steve Kelman, "'Reinventing Government,' 25 Years Later," December 6, 2017, FCW: The Business of Federal Technology, https://fcw.com/Articles/2017/12/06/Kelman-25-years-of-acquisition-reform.aspx?Page=1 (accessed 7/5/18).

34. James Q. Wilson, *Bureaucracy: What Government Agencies Do and Why They Do It* (New York: Basic Books, 1989).

35. For information on the pre-1994 policy, see U.S. Department of Agriculture, "USDA01: End the Wool and Mohair Subsidy," http://govinfo.library.unt.edu/npr/library/reports/ago1.html; for more on the current law, see U.S. Department of Agriculture, "2002 Farm Bill, Title 1: Commodities Programs," www.ers.usda.gov/webdocs/publications/42660/13771_ap022_6_.pdf (both accessed 8/28/08). For a discussion of mohair and other subsidies, see George Will, "How American Government Became Encrusted with Subsidies," National Review, August 16, 2015, www.nationalreview.com/2015/08/government-growth-subsidies-sclerosis/ (accessed 7/5/18).

36. The stages model was first presented in James E. Anderson, *Public Policy Making* (New York: Praeger, 1974). Also see Thomas R. Dye, *Understanding Public Policy*, 15th ed. (New York: Pearson, 2017).

37. Jessica Glenza, "Opioid Crisis: Overdoses Increased by a Third across US in 14 Months, Says CDC," *Guardian*, March 6, 2018, www.theguardian.com/us-news/2018/mar/06/opioid-crisis-overdoses-increased-by-a-third-across-us-in-14-months-says-cdc (accessed 7/5/18).

38. John Kingdon, *Agendas, Alternatives, and Public Policy* (Boston: Little, Brown, 1984).

39. Frank R. Baumgartner and Bryan D. Jones, *Agendas and Instability in American Politics*, 2nd ed. (Chicago: University of Chicago Press, 2009); Nikolaos Zahariadis, "The Shield of Heracles: Multiple Streams and the Emotional Endowment Effect," *European Journal of Political Research* 54:3 (August 2015): 466–81.

40. Graeme Boushey, *Policy Diffusion Dynamics in America* (New York: Cambridge University Press, 2010).

41. Charles R. Shipan and Craig Volden, "The Mechanisms of Policy Diffusion," *American Journal of Political Science* 52:4 (October 2008): 840–57.

42. Kathleen Romig and Arloc Sherman, "Social Security Keeps 22 Million Americans out of Poverty: A State-by-State Analysis," Center on Budget and Policy Priorities, October 25, 2016, https://www.cbpp.org/research/social-security/social-security-keeps-22-million-americans-out-of-poverty-a-state-by-state (accessed 7/5/18).

43. Social Security Administration, *2018 OASDI Trustees Report*, June 5, 2018, Table V.A3, p. 93, www.ssa.gov/OACT/TR/2018/tr2018.pdf (accessed 7/5/18).

44. Social Security Administration, *2018 OASDI Trustees Report*, Table IV.B3, p. 61.

45. Kayla Fontenot, Jessica Semega, and Melissa Kollar, "Income and Poverty in the United States: 2017," September 2018, U.S. Census, Table 3, p. 12 (accessed 10/11/18).

46. In general, poorer people get back as much as they paid in plus interest much more quickly than wealthier people because of the progressive nature of the benefits. For a study on projected benefits that retirees will receive, see Dean R. Leimer, "Cohort-Specific Measures of Lifetime Social Security Taxes and Benefits," Social Security Administration, Office of Research, Evaluation, and Statistics, December 2007, www.ssa.gov/policy/docs/workingpapers/wp110.pdf (accessed 10/3/16).

47. Social Security Administration, *2018 OASDI Trustees Report*, Table II.B1, p. 7, and Figure II.D5, p. 17.

48. Social Security Administration, *2018 OASDI Trustees Report*, p. 20.

49. For a detailed account of the fiscal impact of the various proposals, see Charles Pineles-Mark "Options for Social Security," Congressional Budget Office, March 8, 2017, www.cbo.gov/publication/52471 (accessed 7/5/18).

50. The life expectancy numbers provided here are for all people. Women have always lived longer than men: in 1940 the difference at age 65 was 1.5 years, and in 2017 the difference was 2.5 years. That is, women's life expectancy at age 65 in 2017 was 85.7 and men's was 83.2. Social Security Administration, *2018 OASDI Trustees Report*, Table V.A4, p. 96.

51. The National Commission on Fiscal Responsibility and Reform, "The Moment of Truth," White House, Washington, D.C., December 2010, www.washingtonpost.com/wp-srv/politics/documents/TheMomentofTruth.pdf (accessed 8/7/18).

52. Organization for Economic Cooperation and Development, "Spending on Health, Latest Trends," June 2018, www.oecd.org/health/health-systems/Health-Spending-Latest-Trends-Brief.pdf; OECD.Stat, "Health Expenditure and Financing," https://stats.oecd.org/index.aspx?DataSetCode=HEALTH_STAT (both accessed 7/5/18).

53. Department of Health and Human Services, Centers for Medicare and Medicaid Services, "Brief Summaries of Medicare and Medicaid," https://www.cms.gov/Research-Statistics-Data-and-Systems/Statistics-Trends-and-Reports/MedicareProgramRatesStats/Downloads/MedicareMedicaidSummaries2017.pdf (accessed 8/7/18).

54. Department of Health and Human Services, *2015 Actuarial Report on the Financial Outlook for Medicaid*, Table 3, p. 14, www.medicaid.gov/medicaid/finance/downloads/medicaid-actuarial-report-2015.pdf (accessed 9/27/16).

55. Alison Mitchell, "Medicaid's Federal Medical Assistance Percentage (FMAP)," Congressional Research Service, April 25, 2018, https://fas.org/sgp/crs/misc/R43847.pdf (accessed 7/5/18).

56. Medicaid.gov, Annual Enrollment Reports, "2017 Unduplicated Number of Children Ever Enrolled in CHIP and Medicaid," data as of May 30, 2018, www.medicaid.gov/chip/downloads/fy-2017-childrens-enrollment-report.pdf (accessed 7/5/18).

57. Michael Hiltzik, "Republicans Fund Children's Health Insurance Program, but Leave Their Local Health Centers in the Lurch," *Los Angeles Times*, January 23, 2018, www.latimes.com/business/hiltzik/la-fi-hiltzik-community-health-20180123-story.html (accessed 7/5/18).

58. *2018 Medicare Trustees Report*, June 5, 2018, Table V.F2, p. 207, www.cms.gov/Research-Statistics-Data-and-Systems/Statistics-Trends-and-Reports/ReportsTrustFunds/Downloads/TR2018.pdf (accessed 7/5/18).

59. *2018 Medicare Trustees Report*, p. 3.

60. Peter Grier, "Health Care Reform Bill 101: Who Must Buy Insurance," *Christian Science Monitor*, March 19, 2010, www.csmonitor.com/USA/Politics/2010/0319/Health-Care-Reform-Bill-101-Who-must-buy-insurance (accessed 5/14/12). This article provides an excellent overview of the essential parts of the bill.

61. Congressional Budget Office, "Cost Estimates for H.R. 4872, Reconciliation Act of 2010 (Final Health Care Legislation)," March 20, 2010, www.cbo.gov/doc.cfm?index=11355 (accessed 5/14/12).

62. David Nather and Susan Levine, "A Brief History of Obamacare Delays," *Politico*, March 25, 2014, www.politico.com/story/2014/03/obamacare-affordable-care-act-105036.html#ixzz33QRP8biR (accessed 6/1/14).

63. Namrata Uberoi, Kenneth Finegold, and Emily Gee, "Health Insurance Coverage and the Affordable Care Act, 2010–2016," March 3, 2016, Health and Human Services, ASPE Issue Brief, https://aspe.hhs.gov/sites/default/files/pdf/187551/ACA2010-2016.pdf (accessed 6/10/16).

64. "Medicaid Enrollment Data Collected through MBES, July–September 2015 Medicaid MBES Enrollment Report," posted March 2016, Medicaid.gov, www.medicaid.gov/medicaid-chip-program-information/program-information/medicaid-and-chip-enrollment-data/medicaid-enrollment-data-collected-through-mbes.html (accessed 6/10/16).

65. Sara R. Collins, Munira Z. Gunja, Michelle M. Doty, and Herman K. Bhupal, "First Look at Health Insurance Coverage in 2018 Finds ACA Gains Beginning to Reverse," The Commonwealth Fund, May 1, 2018, https://www.commonwealthfund.org/blog/2018/first-look-health-insurance-coverage-2018-finds-aca-gains-beginning-reverse (accessed 7/9/18).

66. Eligibility information for food stamps may be found at U.S. Department of Agriculture Food and Nutrition Services, Supplemental Nutrition Assistance Program (SNAP), U.S. Department of Agriculture, "Latest Available Month," www.fns.usda.gov/pd/supplemental-nutrition-assistance-program-snap (accessed 7/9/18).

67. U.S. Department of Labor, "Unemployment Insurance Data Summary, 1st Quarter 2018," http://workforcesecurity.doleta.gov/unemploy/content/data_stats/datasum18/DataSum_2018_1.pdf (accessed 7/9/18).

68. Internal Revenue Service, "2018 EITC Income Limits, Maximum Credit Amounts and Tax Law Updates," April 23, 2018, www.irs.gov/credits-deductions/individuals/earned-income-tax-credit/eitc-income-limits-maximum-credit-amounts-next-year (accessed 7/9/18).

69. Internal Revenue Service, "EITC Fast Facts," January 29, 2018, www.eitc.irs.gov/partner-toolkit/basic-marketing-communication-materials/eitc-fast-facts/eitc-fast-facts (accessed 7/9/18).

70. Maximum benefits are from Social Security Administration, "SSI Federal Payment Amounts for 2018," www.ssa.gov/oact/cola/SSI.html; average benefits and number of recipients are from Social Security Administration, "Fast Facts & Figures about Social Security, 2017," www.ssa.gov/policy/docs/chartbooks/fast_facts/ (both accessed 7/9/18).

71. R. Kent Weaver, *Ending Welfare as We Know It* (Washington, DC: Brookings Institution Press, 2000).

72. Center on Budget and Policy Priorities, "Chart Book: TANF at 20," August 17, 2017, www.cbpp.org/research/family-income-support/chart-book-tanf-at-20 (accessed 7/9/18).

73. U.S. Department of Education, "Department Overview," www.ed.gov/about/landing.jhtml?src=gu (accessed 10/3/16).

74. Trymaine Lee, "Has the world gone crazy over Common Core?" June 2, 2014, http://www.msnbc.com/msnbc/common-core-crazy-reactions-education-teachers (accessed 8/7/18).

75. National Conference of State Legislatures, "College and Career Readiness Standards Legislation," www.ccrslegislation.info/CCR-State-Policy-Resources/common-core-status-map#PleaseNote (accessed 7/9/18).

76. U.S. Department of Education, "Race to the Top Fund," www2.ed.gov/programs/racetothetop/index.html (accessed 2/23/10).

77. Bill and Melinda Gates Foundation, www.gatesfoundation.org/united-states/Pages/program-overview.aspx (accessed 6/17/16).

Take a Stand

a. National Conference of State Legislatures, "School Vouchers," www.ncsl.org/research/education/school-choice-vouchers.aspx#What%20States%20Have%20Done (accessed 7/9/18).

b. John F. Witte, *The Market Approach to Education: An Analysis of America's First Voucher Program* (Princeton, NJ: Princeton University Press, 2001).

c. *Zelman v. Simmons-Harris*, 536 U.S. 639 (2002).

Chapter 17

1. For an example of the isolationist approach, see Patrick J. Buchanan, *A Republic, Not an Empire*, updated ed. (Washington, DC: Regnery, 2002).

2. Robert O. Keohane, *After Hegemony: Cooperation and Discord in the International System* (1984; repr., Princeton, NJ: Princeton University Press, 2005).

3. The distinction was first made in E. H. Carr, *The Twenty Years' Crisis, 1919–1939: An Introduction to the Study of International Relations* (London: Macmillan, 1939). Realism was elaborated as a general theory in Hans Morgenthau, *Politics among Nations: The Struggle for Power and Peace* (New York: Knopf, 1948). For a general overview, see Jonathan Haslam, *No Virtue like Necessity: Realist Thought in International Relations since Machiavelli* (New Haven, CT: Yale University Press, 2002).

4. John Mearsheimer, "America Unhinged," *National Interest*, January–February 2014, http://nationalinterest.org/article/america-unhinged-9639 (accessed 5/5/14).

5. Gilbert Felix, *To the Farewell Address: Ideas in Early American Foreign Policy* (Princeton, NJ: Princeton University Press, 1961).

6. A synoptic account of the United States as a world power, which takes the story up to the 2003 invasion of Iraq, is Niall Ferguson, *Colossus: The Price of America's Empire* (New York: Penguin Press, 2004).

7. Samuel Flagg Bemis, *John Quincy Adams and the Foundations of American Foreign Policy* (New York: Knopf, 1949); Ernest

R. May, *The Making of the Monroe Doctrine* (Cambridge, MA: Harvard University Press, 1975). The latter stresses domestic political considerations and argues that the Monroe Doctrine was "actually the by-product of an election campaign."

8. Daniel M. Smith, *The Great Departure: The United States and World War I, 1914–1920* (New York: Wiley, 1965).

9. Thomas J. Knock, *To End All Wars: Woodrow Wilson and the Quest for a New World Order* (New York: Oxford University Press, 1992).

10. Margaret MacMillan, *Paris 1919: Six Months That Changed the World* (New York: Random House, 2001).

11. John M. Cooper, *Breaking the Heart of the World: Woodrow Wilson and the Fight for the League of Nations* (New York: Cambridge University Press, 2001).

12. John Lewis Gaddis, *Strategies of Containment* (New York: Oxford University Press, 2005).

13. Tony Smith, "Making the World Safe for Democracy in the American Century," *Diplomatic History* 23:2 (1999): 173–88.

14. Winston Churchill, "Sinews of Peace (Iron Curtain)," Westminster College, Fulton, Missouri, March 5, 1946, International Churchill Society at https://winstonchurchill.org/resources/speeches/1946-1963-elder-statesman/the-sinews-of-peace/ (accessed 8/2/18). See also Klaus Larres, *Churchill's Cold War: The Politics of Personal Diplomacy* (New Haven, CT: Yale University Press, 2002).

15. George F. Kennan, "The Sources of Soviet Conduct," *Foreign Affairs* 25:4 (July 1947): 566–82.

16. Robert L. Beisner, *Dean Acheson: A Life in the Cold War* (New York: Oxford University Press, 2006); Dean Acheson, *Present at the Creation* (New York: W. W. Norton, 1969).

17. Michael J. Hogan, *The Marshall Plan: America, Britain, and the Reconstruction of Western Europe* (New York: Cambridge University Press, 1987). See also Martin Schain, ed., *The Marshall Plan: Fifty Years Later* (New York: Palgrave, 2001).

18. Marc Trachtenberg, *A Constructed Peace: The Making of the European Settlement, 1945–1963* (Princeton, NJ: Princeton University Press, 1999).

19. The balance of military power between NATO and the Warsaw Pact throughout the Cold War is traced in David Miller, *The Cold War: A Military History* (New York: St. Martin's Press, 1998).

20. Robert A. Packenham, *Liberal America and the Third World* (Princeton, NJ: Princeton University Press, 1973). For an overview, see David P. Forsythe, "Human Rights in U.S. Foreign Policy: Retrospect and Prospect," *Political Science Quarterly* 105:3 (Autumn 1990): 435–54.

21. Sergei N. Goncharov, John W. Lewis, and Xue Litai, *Uncertain Partners: Stalin, Mao, and the Korean War* (Palo Alto, CA: Stanford University Press, 1999).

22. James A. Bill, *The Eagle and the Lion: The Tragedy of American–Iranian Relations* (New Haven, CT: Yale University Press, 1988).

23. Lawrence Freedman, *Kennedy's Wars: Berlin, Cuba, Laos, and Vietnam* (Oxford, UK: Oxford University Press, 2002).

24. William J. Duiker, *Sacred War: Nationalism and Revolution in a Divided Vietnam* (New York: McGraw-Hill, 1995).

25. Henry Kissinger, *Years of Upheaval* (Boston: Little, Brown, 1982); Jussi Hanhimäki, *The Flawed Architect: Henry Kissinger and American Foreign Policy* (New York: Oxford University Press, 2004).

26. Raymond Garthoff, *Détente and Confrontation: American–Soviet Relations from Nixon to Reagan* (Washington, DC: Brookings Institution Press, 1994).

27. Bill, *The Eagle and the Lion.*

28. Odd Arne Westad, ed., *The Fall of Détente: Soviet-American Relations during the Carter Years* (Oslo, Norway: Scandinavian University Press, 1997).

29. Garthoff, *Détente and Confrontation.*

30. Philip Hanson, *The Rise and Fall of the Soviet Economy* (London: Longman, 2003).

31. Francis Fukuyama, *The End of History and the Last Man*, updated ed. (New York: Free Press, 2006).

32. For a summary of American human rights policy, see John W. Dietrich, "U.S. Human Rights Policy in the Post–Cold War Era," *Political Science Quarterly* 121:2 (Summer 2006): 269–94.

33. Joseph Nye, *Soft Power: The Means to Success in World Politics* (New York: Hachette Book Group, 2009).

34. Samuel P. Huntington, *The Clash of Civilizations and the Remaking of World Order* (New York: Free Press, 2002).

35. Louis Fisher, *Presidential War Power* (Lawrence: University Press of Kansas, 2004).

36. John Mueller and Mark G. Stewart, *Chasing Ghosts: The Policing of Terrorism* (New York: Oxford University Press, 2015).

37. Arthur M. Schlesinger, *The Imperial Presidency* (Boston: Houghton Mifflin, 1973).

38. Terry Moe and William Howell, "Unilateral Action and Presidential Power: A Theory," *Presidential Studies Quarterly* 29:4 (1999): 850–72.

39. David Hoffman and David B. Ottaway, "Panel Drops Covert-Acts Notification; in Compromise, Bush Pledges to Inform Hill in All but Rare Cases," *Washington Post*, October 27, 1989, p. A1.

40. Dahlia Lithwick, "The Enemy Within," *Slate*, June 12, 2008, www.slate.com/id/2193468 (accessed 10/3/16).

41. Somini Sengupta, "As Musharraf's Woes Grow, Enter an Old Rival, Again," *New York Times*, April 6, 2007, p. A3; Leslie Wayne, "Airbus Seeks a Welcome in Alabama," *New York Times*, June 19, 2007, p. C1.

42. Pew Research Center, "U.S. Public Seldom Has Welcomed Refugees into Country," November 19, 2015, www.pewresearch.org/fact-tank/2015/11/19/u-s-public-seldom-has-welcomed-refugees-into-country/ (accessed 5/13/16).

43. Kyle Dropp, Joshua D. Kerzer, and Thomas Zeitoff, "The Less Americans Know about Ukraine's Location, the More They Want U.S. to Intervene," *Washington Post*, www.washingtonpost.com/blogs/monkey-cage/wp/2014/04/07/the-less-americans-know-about-ukraines-location-the-more-they-want-u-s-to-intervene/ (accessed 5/5/14).

44. For details, see Becky Little, "Most Young Americans Can't Pass a Text on Global Affairs—Can You?," *National Geographic*, September 13, 2016, https://news.nationalgeographic.com/2016/09/survey-geography-foreign-relations-americans-students/ (accessed 6/19/2018).

45. Pew Research Center, "Public Opinion Six Months Later," March 7, 2002, www.people-press.org/2002/03/07/public-opinion-six-months-later/ (accessed 8/3/18).

46. A directory of NGOs can be found at the Department of Public Information site, Nongovernmental Organization Section, www.un.org/dpi/ngosection/asp/form.asp (accessed 8/2/08).

47. See Amnesty International, "The Secretive and Illegal U.S. Programme of Rendition," April 5, 2006, www.amnesty.org/en/documents/amr51/056/2006/en/ (accessed 8/3/18).

48. United States International Trade Commission, Official Harmonized Tariff Schedule 2018, www.usitc.gov/tata/hts/index.htm (accessed 6/14/18).

49. Colum Lynch, "U.N. Backs Broader Sanctions on Tehran; Security Council Votes to Freeze Some Assets, Ban Arms Exports," *Washington Post*, March 25, 2007, p. A1.

50. William B. Quandt, *Camp David: Peacemaking and Politics* (Washington, DC: Brookings Institution Press, 1986).

51. U.S. Department of State, *Treaties in Force*, January 1, 2007, www.state.gov/s/l/treaty/treaties/2007/index.htm (accessed 8/12/08).

52. Lisa L. Martin, "The President and International Commitments: Treaties as Signaling Devices," *Presidential Studies Quarterly* 35:3 (2005): 440–65.

53. Johanna Neuman and Megan K. Stack, "Americans' Beirut Exodus Underway; Hundreds Are Evacuated by Ship and Helicopter," *Los Angeles Times*, July 20, 2006, p. A10. The Clinton administration resorted to cruise missile attacks five times: three against Iraq (1993, 1996, 1998), one in 1995 against Bosnian Serb forces in the former Yugoslavia, and one against targets in Afghanistan and Sudan in 1998. James Mann, "Foreign Policy of the Cruise Missile," *Los Angeles Times*, December 23, 1998, p. 5.

54. A comprehensive account of the Afghanistan invasion and its aftermath is in Barnett R. Rubin, "Saving Afghanistan," *Foreign Affairs* 86:1 (January/February 2007): 57–78.

55. For an optimistic review, see Joseph E. Stiglitz, *Making Globalization Work* (New York: W. W. Norton, 2007).

56. Benjamin Applebaum, "Perils of Globalization When Factories Close and Towns Struggle," *New York Times*, May 17, 2015, p. A1.

57. Ellen Nakashima, "China Still Trying to Hack U.S. Firms despite Xi's Vote to Refrain, Analysts Say," *Washington Post*, October 19, 2015, p. A01.

58. John Mueller, "Assessing Measures Designed to Protect the Homeland," *Policy Studies Journal* 38:1 (2010):1–21; John Mueller, *Overblown: How Politicians, the Terrorism Industry and Others Stoke National Security Fears* (New York: Free Press, 2006).

59. Fred Kaplan, "North Korea's Nuclear Test Isn't as Dangerous as Kim Jong-un Wants Us to Believe," *Slate*, January 6, 2016, www.slate.com/articles/news_and_politics/politics/2016/01/north_korea_s_nuclear_test_isn_t_as_dangerous_as_kim_jong_un_wants_us_to.html (accessed 6/20/16).

Study Guide Answer Key

Chapter 1	Chapter 2	Chapter 3	Chapter 4	Chapter 5
1. C	1. B	1. C	1. D	1. A
2. B	2. E	2. B	2. B	2. C
3. C	3. A	3. B	3. A	3. B
4. D	4. C	4. C	4. D	4. E
5. D	5. C	5. C	5. B	5. C
6. C	6. B	6. B	6. C	6. E
7. A	7. D	7. B	7. A	7. B
8. E	8. B	8. B	8. D	8. D
9. A	9. D	9. A	9. A	9. E
10. E	10. B	10. D	10. C	10. A
11. C	11. D	11. B	11. B	11. B
	12. B	12. A	12. C	12. C
	13. A	13. D	13. C	13. C
	14. B	14. A	14. B	14. A
	15. B	15. D	15. C	15. D

Chapter 6	Chapter 7	Chapter 8	Chapter 9	Chapter 10
1. D	1. E	1. C	1. A	1. E
2. B	2. B	2. A	2. B	2. A
3. A	3. D	3. E	3. D	3. C
4. D	4. B	4. B	4. B	4. B
5. C	5. D	5. E	5. B	5. C
6. E	6. C	6. A	6. B	6. E
7. A	7. A	7. E	7. C	7. C
8. D	8. C	8. A	8. E	8. C
9. D	9. A	9. E	9. A	9. A
10. C	10. D	10. C	10. C	10. B
11. B	11. B	11. C	11. B	11. D
12. D	12. E	12. E	12. E	12. D
13. A	13. A	13. C	13. C	13. B
14. C	14. C		14. C	14. A
15. B				

Chapter 11

1. D
2. E
3. B
4. B
5. A
6. D
7. D
8. B
9. D
10. A
11. C
12. E
13. B
14. D
15. B
16. D

Chapter 12

1. A
2. D
3. C
4. D
5. A
6. D
7. E
8. B
9. A
10. B
11. D
12. B
13. A
14. D
15. C

Chapter 13

1. C
2. A
3. D
4. B
5. E
6. B
7. C
8. A
9. B
10. D
11. C
12. A
13. E
14. A
15. B

Chapter 14

1. A
2. D
3. B
4. E
5. A
6. E
7. B
8. C
9. A
10. E
11. B
12. B
13. D
14. C
15. A
16. B

Chapter 15

1. C
2. A
3. C
4. D
5. B
6. C
7. E
8. D
9. B
10. B
11. E
12. E
13. A
14. D

Chapter 16

1. B
2. A
3. E
4. B
5. A
6. C
7. E
8. A
9. C
10. D
11. A
12. B
13. B
14. C
15. B

Chapter 17

1. C
2. A
3. E
4. C
5. D
6. D
7. B
8. C
9. A
10. B
11. C
12. D
13. D
14. B
15. A

Credits

Line Art

Chapter 1, What Do the Facts Say? (p. 16): Map: "2016 Presidential Election, Purple America," by Robert J. Vanderbei, Princeton University. http://www.princeton.edu/~rvdb/JAVA/election2016/. Reprinted by permission of the author.

Figure 5.5 (p. 181): Map: Lifetime Wage Gap for Women Compared with Men, from "The Lifetime Wage Gap, State by State," National Women's Law Center, April 4, 2018. Reprinted by permission.

Figure 6.3 (p. 210): Figure from "Partisans Have Starkly Different Opinions About How the World Views the U.S.," Pew Research Center, Washington DC (November 9, 2017) http://www.people-press.org/2017/11/09/partisans-have-starkly-different-opinions-about-how-the-world-views-the-u-s/. Reprinted with permission.

Figure 6.7 (p. 226): Graph from "Economic Issues Decline Among Public's Policy Priorities," Pew Research Center, Washington, DC (January, 2018) http://www.people-press.org/2018/01/25/economic-issues-decline-among-publics-policy-priorities/. Reprinted with permission.

Figure 8.4 (p. 276): Figure from "A Deep Dive Into Party Affiliation," Pew Research Center, Washington, DC (April, 2015) http://www.people-press.org/2015/04/07/a-deep-dive-into-party-affiliation/. Reprinted with permission.

Figure 8.5 (p. 277): Figure from "Political Polarization in the American Public," Pew Research Center, Washington, DC (June, 2014) http://www.people-press.org/2014/06/12/political-polarization-in-the-american-public/. Reprinted with permission.

Figure 11.6 (p. 400): Graph: Liberal-conservative partisan polarization by chamber, from "Polarization in Congress," March 11, 2018, Jeffrey Lewis, Keith T. Poole, and Howard Rosenthal, voteview.com. Reprinted by permission.

Figure 15.3 (p.550): Chart 1 in "The Crisis Is Over: It Is Time to End Experimental Monetary Policy," Norbert J. Michel, PhD, Backgrounder No. 3265, November 9, 2017, https://www.heritage.org/sites/default/files/2017-11/BG3265.pdf. Reprinted by permission of The Heritage Foundation.

Figure 17.1 (p. 635): Figure: "Where's Ukraine?" by Thomas Zeitzoff / Monkey Cage, from "The Less Americans Know About Ukraine's Location, the More They Want U.S. to Intervene," by Kyle Dropp, Joshua D. Kertzer and Thomas Zeitzoff. The Monkey Cage, April 7, 2014. Reprinted with permission.

Photographs

Front Matter

ii-ii: David Paul Morris/Bloomberg via Getty Images; **vi (top):** Paul B.; **vi (bottom):** Ricardo Galliano Court; **ix (top):** Andrew Harrer/Bloomberg via Getty Images; **ix (bottom):** Kevin Lim/The Straits Times/ZUMA Press/Newscom; **x:** Erik McGregor/Pacific Press/LightRocket via Getty Images; **xi (top):** Mark Peterson/Redux; **xi (bottom):** Michael Matthews - Police Images/Alamy Stock Photo; **xii (top):** David McNew/Getty Images; **xii (bottom):** RJ Sangosti/The Denver Post via Getty Images; **xiii (top):** Jeff J Mitchell/Getty Images; **xiii (bottom):** Bill Clark/CQ Roll Call/Newscom; **xiv (top):** Reuters/REUTERS/Newscom; **xiv (bottom):** Bill Clark/ CQ Roll Call via AP Images; **xv:** AP Photo/J. Scott Applewhite; **xvi (top):** Staff/REUTERS/Newscom; **xvi (bottom):** Chip Somodevilla/Getty Images; **xvii (top):** AP Photo/Evan Vucci; **xvii (bottom):** Angel Valentin/The New York Times/Redux; **xviii:** Saul Loeb/AFP/Getty Images

Chapter 1

3: AP Photo/Andrew Harnik; **5:** Drew Angerer/Getty Images; **7 (left):** US Army Photo/Alamy Stock Photo; **7 (right):** Melvyn Longhurst/Alamy Stock Photo; **10:** Allison Shelley/For The Washington Post via Getty Images; **11:** Olivier Douliery/SIPA/Newscom; **12 (left):** Tom Williams/CQ Roll Call via AP Images; **12 (right):** ZUMA Press, Inc./Alamy Stock Photo; **14 (left):** Patrick Gorski/NurPhoto/Sipa USA/Newscom; **14 (center):** Williams Paul/Icon Sportswire via Getty Images; **14 (right):** AF archive/Alamy Stock Photo; **17 (top):** Chip Somodevilla/Getty Images; **17 (bottom):** © Flip Schulke/CORBIS/Corbis via Getty Images; **19:** AP Photo/J. Scott Applewhite; **23:** Sarah L. Voisin/The Washington Post via Getty Images; **25:** AP Photo/Andrew Harnik

Chapter 2

31: Kevin Lim/The Straits Times/ZUMA Press/Newscom; **33:** North Wind Picture Archives/Alamy Stock Photo; **36:** Bettmann/Getty Images; **37:** Imagno/Getty Images; **38:** © North Wind Picture Archives -- All rights reserved; **41:** Bettmann/Getty Images; **45:** Library of Virginia; **48:** Library of Congress/Getty Images; **49:** Library of Congress; **50:** Francis G. Mayer/Corbis/VCG via Getty Images; **51:** Library of Congress; **53 (top left):** Bob Barket/Stringer/Getty Images; **53 (top center):** Spx Chrome/Getty Images; **53 (top right):** Jewel Samad/Getty Images; **53 (center left):** Spx Chrome/Getty Images; **53 (center):** Jewel Samad/Getty Images; **53 (center right):** Mark Wilson/Getty Images; **53 (bottom left):** JStone/Shutterstock; **53 (bottom right):** Spx Chrome/Getty Images; **54:** AP Photo/Musadeq Sadeq; **55:** The Asahi Shimbun via Getty Images; **56:** World History Archive/Alamy Stock Photo; **58:** AP Photo/Steven Senne; **60:** Porter Gifford/Corbis via Getty Images; **62 (left):** Everett Collection Inc/Alamy Stock Photo; **62 (right):** Everett Collection Inc/Alamy Stock Photo; **64:** AP Photo/Gary Gardiner; **65:** Kevin Lim/The Straits Times/ZUMA Press/Newscom

Chapter 3

71: Erik McGregor/Pacific Press/LightRocket via Getty Images; **73:** Photo by FEMA News Photo - Aug 29, 2017; **76:** AP Photo/Eric Gay; **79 (top):** The Metropolitan Museum of Art, New York, The Edward W. C. Arnold Collection of New York Prints, Maps, and Pictures, Bequest of Edward W. C. Arnold, 1954 (54.90.491); **79 (bottom):** MPI/Getty Images; **81:** Bettmann/Getty Images; **82:** Bettmann/Getty Images; **85 (top left):** J Main/Shutterstock; **85 (top center):** Ivana Star/Getty Images; **85 (top right):** Space Images/Getty Images; **85 (center left):** Food Collection/Getty Images; **85 (center):** Sam Edwards/Getty Images; **85 (center right):** JStone/Shutterstock; **85 (bottom left, top):** Ivana Star/Getty Images; **85 (bottom left, bottom):** Food Collection/Getty Images; **85 (bottom center, left):** Joe Raedle/Getty Images; **85 (bottom center, right):** Sam Edwards/

Getty Images; **85 (bottom right):** Michael Betts/Getty Images; **89:** AP Photo/Maria Danilova; **90:** AP Photo/Martin Meissner; **93:** Joe Raedle/Getty Images; **94:** AP Photo/David Zalubowski; **95:** Justin Sullivan/Getty Images; **96:** Albin Lohr-Jones/Sipa USA/Sipa via AP Images; **98:** Erik McGregor/Pacific Press/LightRocket via Getty Images

Chapter 4

103: Mark Peterson/Redux; **105 (left):** AP Photo/J. Miles Cary, Knoxville News Sentinel; **105 (right):** William Thomas Cain/Getty Images; **107:** David McNew/Getty Images; **111 (top left):** Thinkstock Images/Getty Images; **111 (top center):** Spx Chrome/Getty Images; **111 (top right):** John Parra/Getty Images; **111 (center left):** Spx Chrome/Getty Images; **111 (center):** Heather Ainsworth/Bloomberg via Getty Images; **111 (center right):** Image Navi/Getty Images; **111 (bottom):** Stockbyte/Getty Images; **114:** Eric Reed/ZUMA Press, Inc/Alamy Stock Photo; **116:** Matthew Staver/The New York Times/Redux; **119:** Michael S. Williamson/The Washington Post via Getty Images; **120:** J. Lawler Duggan/For The Washington Post via Getty Images; **122:** Indiana University Campus Art Collection, THB X, *Thomas Hart Benton, Indiana Murals: Parks, the Circus, the Klan, the Press.* Photograph by: Michael Cavanagh and Kevin Montague, Eskenazi Museum of Art at Indiana University. http://www.iuauditorium.com/about-us/thomas-hart-benton-murals; **124:** Sipa USA via AP; **125:** AP Photo/Patrick Semansky; **127:** Boyzell Hosey/ZUMA Press/Newscom; **128:** Anthony Pidgeon/Redferns/Getty Images; **130** (left): John Wingfield/Alamy Stock Photo; **130 (right):** Erin Schaff/The New York Times/Redux; **132:** Chip Somodevilla/Getty Images; **134:** AP Photo; **136:** Jason Reed/Reuters/Newscom; **137:** Bettmann/Getty Images; **139:** Reuters/Newscom; **143 (top):** AP Photo/Michael Stravato; **143 (bottom):** Mark Peterson/Redux

Chapter 5

149: Michael Matthews - Police Images/Alamy Stock Photo; **152 (left):** Library of Congress; **152 (right):** HB Lindsey/Underwood Archives/Getty Images; **153:** Time Life Pictures/Timepix/The LIFE Picture Collection/Getty Images; **155:** Robyn Beck/AFP/Getty Images; **156:** Photo by Library of Congress/Corbis/VCG via Getty Images; **158:** Steven Ferdman/Everett Collection/Alamy Live News; **161:** AP Photo/John Locher; **163 (left):** Feidin Santana via AP Images; **163 (right):** Richard Ellis/Getty Images; **164:** Curtis Compton/Atlanta Journal-Constitution via AP; **168:** Don Cravens/The LIFE Images Collection/Getty Images; **170 (left):** AP Photo/Bill Hudson; **170 (right):** AFP/Getty Images; **171 (left):** Bryan Woolston/REUTERS/Newscom; **171 (right):** Pacific Press/Sipa USA/Newscom; **174:** AP Photo; **179 (left):** David Schaffer/Getty Images; **179 (right):** Tetra Images/Getty Images; **180:** Joe Raedle/Getty Images; **185:** Jim Watson/AFP/Getty Images; **186:** Kristen Zeis/The Virginian-Pilot via AP; **190:** Kevin Lamarque/Reuters/Newscom; **191:** Jose Luis Magana/Reuters/Newscom; **192:** Stephanie Keith/Getty Images; **193:** John Moore/Getty Images; **194:** Michael Matthews - Police Images/Alamy Stock Photo

Chapter 6

199: David McNew/Getty Images; **200 (left):** Fox/Photofest; **200 (right):** Shawn Thew/EPA/Shutterstock; **201:** CALVIN AND HOBBES © 1994 Watterson. Reprinted with permission of ANDREWS MCMEEL SYNDICATION. All rights reserved; **202 (top):** AP Photo/Rogelio V. Solis; **202 (bottom):** Todd Bannor/Alamy Stock Photo; **205 (left):** Ty Wright/Getty Images; **205 (right):** Larry Roberts/Pittsburgh Post-Gazette via AP; **207:** Joe Raedle/Getty Images; **213 (top left):** Tetra Images/Getty Images; **213 (top center):** Daniel Grill/Getty Images; **213 (top right):** Evirgen/Getty Images;

213 (bottom left): John Lamb/Getty Images; **213 (bottom center):** Image Navi/Getty Images; **213 (bottom right):** Hero Images/Getty Images; **219 (left):** Lucy Nicholson/REUTERS/Newscom; **219 (right):** AP Photo/David J. Phillip; **222:** AP Photo; **227 (left):** Jeff Swensen/Stringer/Getty Images; **227 (right):** Tannen Maury/Epa/Shutterstock; **228:** David McNew/Getty Images

Chapter 7

233: RJ Sangosti/The Denver Post via Getty Images; **235:** GRANGER/GRANGER -- All rights reserved; **236 (left):** Randy Holmes via Getty Images; **236 (right):** Evan Agostini/Invision/AP; **238 (left):** Scott Olson/Getty Images; **238 (right):** Carl Court/Getty Images; **239** (top): [NO CREDIT]; **239 (bottom):** Alberto Martinez/Austin American-Statesman via AP; **242:** [NO CREDIT]; **244:** Sean Rayford/Getty Images; **247 (top left):** Frontpage/Shutterstock; **247 (top right):** Klaus Vedfelt/Getty Images; **247 (top center, left):** Photomaster/Shutterstock; **247 (top center, right):** Klaus Vedfelt/Getty Images; **247 (bottom center, left):** Beneda Miroslav/Shutterstock; **247 (bottom center, right):** Justin Sullivan/Getty Images; **247 (bottom):** Photomaster/Shutterstock; **249:** Lou Rocco/ABC via Getty Images; **251:** Robert Cohen/St. Louis Post-Dispatch via AP; **254:** Andrew Harrer/Bloomberg via Getty Images; **256:** Daniel Leal-Olivas/AFP/Getty Images; **257:** RJ Sangosti/The Denver Post via Getty Images

Chapter 8

263: Jeff J Mitchell/Getty Images; **265 (left):** AP Photo/Branden Camp; **265 (center):** Joshua Roberts/Bloomberg via Getty Images; **265 (right):** Pacific Press/Alamy Stock Photo; **266:** © CORBIS/Corbis via Getty Images; **267:** GRANGER/GRANGER -- All rights reserved; **269:** Mark Peterson/Redux; **270:** Andrew Spear for The Washington Post via Getty Images; **274:** Chris Hondros/Getty Images; **280:** Joe Raedle/Getty Images; **283 (left):** Jewel Samad/AFP/Getty Images; **283 (center left):** Jewel Samad/AFP/Getty Images; **283 (center right):** Daniel Acker/Bloomberg via Getty Images; **283 (right):** Gary Coronado/Pool via Bloomberg/Getty Images; **284:** Bill Clark/CQ Roll Call/Getty Images; **285:** Kevin Dietsch/CNP/AdMedia/Newscom; **286:** AP Photo/Charles Dharapak; **288:** AP Photo/Morgan Lee; **291:** Anthony Lanzilote/Bloomberg via Getty Images; **292:** Jeff J Mitchell/Getty Images

Chapter 9

297: Bill Clark/CQ Roll Call/Newscom; **299:** Al Drago/The New York Times/Redux; **300 (top):** AP Photo/Sue Ogrocki; **300 (bottom):** Monica Jorge/NurPhoto via Getty Images; **301 (left):** Ellen F. O'Connell/Hazelton Standard-Speaker via AP; **301 (right):** Marc Serota/Reuters/Newscom; **304:** AP photo/Bob Christie; **305:** AP Photo/Paul Sancya; **312:** Tom Williams/CQ Roll Call via AP Images; **313:** AP Photo/Paul Vernon; **315:** Tom Williams/CQ Roll Call/Getty Images; **316:** Mark Reinstein/Corbis via Getty Images; **319 (left):** Democratic National Committee/LBJ Library; **319 (right):** Democratic National Committee/LBJ Library; **320:** [NO CREDIT]; **322:** [NO CREDIT]; **325:** Drew Angerer/Getty Images; **326:** Brendan Smialowski/AFP/Getty Images; **327:** Scott McIntyre/Bloomberg via Getty Images; **332 (top):** AP Photo/J. Scott Applewhite; **332 (bottom):** Chip Somodevilla/Getty Images; **333:** Bridget Bennett/Bloomberg via Getty Images; **336:** Bill Clark/CQ Roll Call/Newscom

Chapter 10

341: Reuters/REUTERS/Newscom; **348:** Nicole S Glass/Shutterstock; **349:** Tom Williams/Roll Call/Newscom; **350:** Jim West/

age fotostock; **351:** Mike Theiler/AFP/Getty Images; **354:** Business Wire via Getty Images; **357 (top left):** Pressmaster/Shutterstock; **357 (top right):** Yuri Arcurs/Getty Images; **357 (center left):** Image Source/Getty Images; **357 (center):** Tetra Images/Getty Images; **357 (center right):** Greg Bajor/Getty Images; **357 (bottom left):** Mark Wilson/Getty Images; **357 (bottom right):** JStone/Shutterstock; **359:** AP Photo/Elaine Thompson; **360:** TDP Photography/Alamy Stock Photo; **363:** Chris Kleponis/dpa/picture-alliance/Newscom; **365 (left):** Will & Deni McIntyre/Science Source/Getty Images; **365 (right):** AP Photo/Robert F. Bukaty; **368:** AP Photo/Jacquelyn Martin; **369:** Alex Wong/Getty Images; **370:** Reuters/REUTERS/Newscom

Chapter 11

375: Bill Clark/CQ Roll Call via AP Images; **377:** Sarin Images/GRANGER -- All rights reserved; **380:** Lucas Willard/WAMC; **387:** Joshua Roberts; **388:** Jeff Gritchen/Digital First Media Group/Orange County Register via Getty Images; **392 (left):** United States Department of the Interior; **392 (right):** United States Department of the Interior; **394:** Al Drago/Pool via CNP/MEGA/Newscom; **396:** Tom Williams/CQ Roll Call via AP Images; **401 (top):** AP Photo/J. Scott Applewhite; **401 (bottom):** Drew Angerer/Getty Images; **407 (row 1, left):** Mark Wilson/Getty Images; **407 (row 1, right):** Mark Wilson/Getty Images; **407 (row 2, left):** Mark Wilson/Getty Images; **407 (row 2, center):** Beneda Miroslav/Shutterstock; **407 (row 2, right):** Mark Wilson/Getty Images; **407 (row 3, left):** Alex Wong/Getty Images; **407 (row 3, center):** Photomaster/Shutterstock; **407 (row 3, right):** Beneda Miroslav/Shutterstock; **407 (row 4, left):** Mark Wilson/Getty Images; **407 (row 4, right):** Mark Wilson/Getty Images; **407 (row 5, left):** Mark Wilson/Getty Images; **407 (row 5, right):** JStone/Shutterstock; **413:** Gabriella Demczuk/The New York Times/Redux; **414:** Bill Clark/CQ Roll Call via AP Images

Chapter 12

419: AP Photo/J. Scott Applewhite; **421:** Painting/Alamy Stock Photo; **422 (left):** Bettmann/Getty Images; **422 (right):** AP Photo/Bob Daugherty; **425:** Mark Ralston/AFP/Getty Images; **430 (left):** AP Photo/Pablo Martinez Monsivais; **430 (right):** Doug Mills/The New York Times/Redux; **435 (top left):** Jewel Samad/AFP/Getty Images; **435 (top center):** Pete Souza/The White House via Getty Images; **435 (top right):** A Katz/Shutterstock; **435 (center left):** Mark Wilson/Getty Images; **435 (center):** Mark Wilson/Getty Images; **435 (center right):** Nazlisart/Shutterstock; **435 (bottom left):** JStone/Shutterstock; **435 (bottom right):** JStone/Shutterstock; **436:** Al-Mayadeen via AP video; **437:** Ron Sachs/CNP/AdMedia/Newscom; **439 (top):** HO/Jiji Press/Newscom; **439 (bottom left):** Al Drago/The New York Times/Redux; **439 (bottom right):** Jonathan Ernst/REUTERS/Newscom; **442:** Mandel Ngan/AFP/Getty Images; **445 (top):** Mikhail Klimentyev, Sputnik, Kremlin Pool Photo via AP; **445 (bottom):** AP Photo/Andrew Harnik; **448:** AP Photo/Pablo Martinez Monsivais, File; **450:** AP Photo/J. Scott Applewhite

Chapter 13

455: Staff/REUTERS/Newscom; **457:** Luis Sinco/Los Angeles Times via Getty Images; **459 (top left):** J Main/Shutterstock; **459 (top center):** United States Environmental Protection Agency; **459 (top right):** Spx Chrome/Getty Images; **459 (center left):** Jewel Samad/Getty Images; **459 (center):** United States Environmental Protection Agency; **459 (center right):** Jewel Samad/AFP/Getty Images; **459 (bottom left):** United States Environmental Protection Agency; **459 (bottom right):** JStone/Shutterstock; **460:** Andy

Lyons/Getty Images; **464:** AP Photo/Alex Brandon; **465:** CARLSON © 2005 Milwaukee Journal Sentinel. Reprinted with permission of ANDREWS MCMEEL SYNDICATION. All rights reserved.; **466:** Bettmann/Getty Images; **467:** [NO CREDIT]; **468:** Justin Lane/EPA/REX/Shutterstock; **477:** AP Photo/Andrew Harnik; **480:** Andrew Holbrooke/Corbis via Getty Images; **481:** Chip Somodevilla/Getty Images; **482:** AP Photo/Ron Heflin; **484:** Staff/REUTERS/Newscom

Chapter 14

489: Chip Somodevilla/Getty Images; **492:** Terry Ashe/The LIFE Images Collection/Getty Images; **493:** © North Wind Picture Archives -- All rights reserved; **495:** AP Photo/Vince Bucci, Pool, File; **499 (top):** Glow Images/Getty Images; **499 (center left):** Alexsandar Nakic/Getty Images; **499 (center right):** Spx Chrome/Getty Images; **499 (bottom):** Mark Ralston/AFP/Getty Images; **501:** Ken Cedeno/ZUMA Press/Newscom; **504:** Perisha Gates/ZUMA Press/Newscom; **507:** Canva Pty Ltd/Alamy Stock Photo; **509:** David Hume Kennerly/Getty Images; **511:** © Arthur Lien; **513:** Chip Somodevilla/Getty Images; **516:** Bettmann/Getty Images; **521:** John Badman/The Telegraph via AP; **522:** Photograph by Franz Jantzen, Collection of the Supreme Court of the United States; **524:** Alex Wong/Getty Images; **525:** Bettmann/Getty Images; **526:** Chip Somodevilla/Getty Images

Chapter 15

531: AP Photo/Evan Vucci; **532:** Pat Benic/UPI/Newscom; **543 (top left):** PzAxe/Shutterstock; **543 (top right):** J Main/Shutterstock; **543 (bottom left):** Mark Wilson/Getty Images; **543 (bottom center):** PzAxe/Shutterstock; **543 (bottom right):** Photomaster/Shutterstock; **544:** Ronaldo Schemidt/AFP/Getty Images; **546 (top):** Mike Theiler/UPI/Newscom; **546 (bottom):** AP Photo/Richard Drew; **548:** AP Photo/Lauren Victoria Burke; **549:** Andrew Harrer/Bloomberg via Getty Images; **557:** Everett Collection Inc/Alamy Stock Photo; **559:** Bettmann/Getty Images; **560 (left):** David R. Frazier/DanitaDelimont.com "Danita Delimont Photography"/Newscom; **560 (right):** Scott J. Ferrell/Congressional Quarterly/Alamy Stock Photo; **562:** REAL LIFE ADVENTURES © 2010 GarLanco. Reprinted with permission of ANDREWS MCMEEL SYNDICATION. All rights reserved.; **563:** © Alex Webb/Magnum Photos; **567:** AP Photo/Evan Vucci

Chapter 16

573: Angel Valentin/The New York Times/Redux; **574:** Bill Clark/CQ Roll Call/Getty Images; **577:** Everett Collection Inc./Alamy Stock Photo; **585:** ZUMA Press, Inc./Alamy Stock Photo; **589 (top left):** Keystone/Getty Images; **589 (top center):** Omikron/Getty Images; **589 (top right):** FPG/Archive Photos/Getty Images; **589 (center left):** FPG/Archive Photos/Getty Images; **589 (center):** Graphica Artis/Getty Images; **589 (center right):** Tim Sloan/AFP/Getty Images; **589 (bottom):** USA Social Security Administration; **594 (left):** Waring Abbott/Getty Images; **594 (right):** Cultura RM Exclusive/Natalie Faye/Getty Images; **597:** AP Photo/Alex Brandon; **601:** Tom Williams/CQ Roll Call; **607:** Rana Royalty Free/Alamy Stock Photo; **608:** Stephen Crowley/The New York Times/Redux; **609:** Angel Valentin/The New York Times/Redux

Chapter 17

615: Saul Loeb/AFP/Getty Images; **618:** MPI122/MediaPunch/MediaPunch/IPx/AP Images; **619:** Rami Al-Sayed/AFP/Getty Images; **621:** AP Photo; **623:** Stephen Jaffe/Getty Images; **624:** AP Photo/Al Jazeera; **625:** Mohammed Mohammed Xinhua News

Glossary/Index

Akin, David, 24
Alabama
    civil rights movement in, 167, *168*, 168-70, *170*
    immigration policies in, 192
    media coverage of elections in, 247, 255
    prayer in public schools of, 114
    presidential campaign in (2016), 283
    school voucher programs in, 608
    Senate election in (2017), 180, 239, 255, 296-98, 336, 366, 477
    slavery in, 151
    voting rights of African Americans in, *17*, 153
    women's rights in, 177
Alabama, Powell v., 113
Alabama v. Garrett, 91
Alaska, 283
Alexander, Lamar, 340, 342
Alien and Sedition Acts (1798), 118, 235
Alito, Samuel, Jr., 107, 191, 503, 513, 519, 522, 524
alliances in foreign policy, 641-42
Allied Powers in World War II, 620
Al Qaeda, *139*, 617, 624, *624*, 625, 628, 642, 646
aluminum tariffs, 425, 530, 532, 566
Amber Alert system, 591
amendments to Constitution, 61-62, *63*. *See also specific amendment numbers.*
    Civil War amendments, 109, 152-53
    proposal and ratification of, 62, *63*, 76
    proposed and not passed, *64*
American Civil Liberties Union (ACLU), 102, *359*
American Independent Party, 287
American International Group, 549
American-Israel Public Affairs Committee, 357, 631, *631*
American Medical Association, 362
American National Election Study, 214, 215
American Recovery and Reinvestment Act (2009), 552
Americans for Prosperity, 269
Americans with Disabilities Act, 86, 185

amicus curiae, 510, 511, 519 Latin for "friend of the court," referring to an interested group or person who shares relevant information about a case to help the Court reach a decision.

Amish, 105, *105*, 116
Amnesty International, 636
animal cruelty, 129
Annapolis Convention (1786), 35
Annual Economic Report of the President, 544
Anthony, Susan B., 166
Antifederalist Papers, 490

Antifederalists, 38 Those at the Constitutional Convention who favored strong state governments and feared that a strong national government would be a threat to individual rights.
    on civil liberties, 106, 108, 109
    concerns about proposed Constitution, 43, 45, 48-49, 50, 106, 108
    on judiciary, 490
    and pluralism principle, 41
    on presidential powers, 57
    and Second Amendment, 130

appeals courts, 497, 498, 499, 500 The intermediate level of federal courts that hear appeals from district courts. More generally, an appeals court is any court with appellate jurisdiction.

appellate jurisdiction, 491, 491 The authority of a court to hear appeals from lower courts and change or uphold the decision.

Apple, *132*, 345-46, *346*, 362, 381, 645
appointments
    to federal bureaucracy, 456, 477-78
    to Federal Reserve Board, 545, 546, 547
    presidential power in, 55, 63-64, 425-26, 438-39, 440, 466, 477-78, 546

apportionment, 389 The process of assigning the 435 seats in the House to the states based on increases or decreases in state population.

Appropriations Committee, 403, 409, 540
Arab Americans, 159, 192
Arab-Israeli war (1973), 622
Argersinger v. Hamlin, 113

aristocracy, 8
Aristotle, 8
Arizona, 95, 115, 133, 192, 307, 335, 608
Arkansas, 141, 186, 283
Armed Services Committee, 403
arms, right to bear, 130-31
Armstrong, Lance, 135
Arpaio, Joe, 54, 433

Articles of Confederation, 33, 33-35, 36, 37, 41 Sent to the states for ratification in 1777, these were the first attempt at a new American government. It was later decided that the Articles restricted national government too much, and they were replaced by the Constitution.
    compared to Constitution, *39*, 75
    compromises in revision of, 39-48
    confederal form of government in, 74
    tax policies in, 34, *39*, 46

Ashcroft, Gregory v., 91
Asian Americans
    and affirmative action, 189, 191
    civil rights of, 150, 155-56, 194
    composition of U.S. population, *18*
    in Congress, 379
    diversity of, 156
    as federal court judges, 502
    in internment camps, 155-56, *156*
    party identification of, *17*
    presidential appointments of, 186
    voting by, *160*
assembly, freedom of, 110, 123-24, 129
assimilation of immigrants, 18

Astroturf lobbying, 360 Any lobbying method initiated by an interest group that is designed to look like the spontaneous, independent participation of many individuals.

athletes, 135, 154
    kneeling during national anthem, 171-72, 187
AT&T, 135, 136, 366
attack ads, 317-18, 320, 366

attack journalism, 255 A type of increasingly popular media coverage focused on political scandals and controversies, which causes a negative public opinion of political figures.

attitudinalist approach, 517 A way of understanding decisions of the Supreme Court based on the political ideologies of the justices.

Austria, 559
authoritarian governments, 21
authorization process for legislation, 409
al-Awlaki, Anwar, *139*
Axios, 238

baby-boom generation, 593, 594 Americans born between 1946 and 1964, who are retiring in large numbers over the next 20 years.

Baker, Howard, 290, 411
Baker, James, 438
Bakke, Allan, 190

balanced budget, 536, 541, 553 A spending plan in which the government's expenditures are equal to its revenue.

balance of payments, 537, 562-67
Baldwin, Tammy, 384-85, 386
ballots, 301, *301*
Baltimore, Barron v., 78, 109
Bank of America, 159
banks
    and Federal Deposit Insurance Commission, 535
    and Federal Reserve System, 545
    and financial crisis (2008), 548-49
    and monetary policy, 557, 558
    mortgage discrimination by, 159
    national, Supreme Court on, 63, 78
    reserve requirement on, 558
    student loans from, 340, 359
    and Treasury Department, 548
Barrasso, John, *401*
Barron v. Baltimore, 78, 109
Bartels, Larry M., 583
Batali, Mario, 180
Bauer, Frederick W., 505
Baumgartner, Frank, 343, 590
Bear Stearns, 548-49
Beck, Glenn, 607
beer industry, tariffs affecting, 532
Beer Institute, 532
BellSouth, 135
Bennet, Michael, 232, *233*
Benton v. Maryland, 113

Berlin Wall, fall of, *623*
Bernanke, Ben, 546, *548,* 559
bias, 248-50
    in Internet information, 239
    in public opinion polls, 213, 215, 217
    social desirability bias, 217

bicameralism, 377 The system of having two chambers within one legislative body, like the House and Senate in the U.S. Congress.

Bicker, Laura, 30
Biden, Joe, 300

Bill of Rights, 44-45, 49, 50, 62, 80, *108* The first 10 amendments to the Constitution; they protect individual rights and liberties. *See also specific amendments.*
    on civil liberties, 104
    on free press, 244
    on free speech, 325
    on liberty, 21
    origins of, 106-9
    public knowledge of, *200*
    selective incorporation of, 112, *113*

bills, and legislative process, 404-12
bin Laden, Osama, 428, 624, *624,* 625
Bipartisan Campaign Reform Act, 121, 320, 321, 510
Birmingham, Alabama, 169-70, *170*
birth control, 117, 140-41
bisexual people. *See* LGBTQ people
Bismarck, Otto von, 412
Black, Hugo, 125, 141, 515, 517
Blackburn, Marsha, *401*
Black Lives Matter, 164, *171,* 171-72, 188
Blackmun, Harry, 512-13

block grants, 86-88, 90 Federal aid provided to a state government to be spent within a certain policy area, but the state can decide how to spend the money within that area.

"blue states," 15, 16
Blumenthal, Richard, 523
Board of Education, Brown v., 153, 154, 167, 172-73, 520, 521, 525
Board of Education II, Brown v., 154, 173
Board of Education of Ewing Township, Everson v., 113
Boehner, John, 398, 402, 523

Boeing Company, 364
Bollinger, Gratz v., 179
Bollinger, Grutter v., 179
Bond, United States v., 91
Bono, 129
Booker, Cory, *504*
Border Patrol, 628
border wall with Mexico, 57, 374, 376, 410, 626
Bork, Robert, 503
Bosnia, 623
Boston Tea Party, 32
Bowers v. Hardwick, 143, 181, 182
Bowles, Erskine, *597*
Bradley, Joseph, 157
Bradwell, Myra, 156-57
Brady, James and Sarah, 130
Brandeis, Louis, 94
Brandenburg v. Ohio, 119
brand identity of political parties, 270, 313, 398
Braun, Ryan, 135
Brennan, William, 517
Brennan Center for Justice, 160
Brewer, Jan, 192
Breyer, Stephen, 503, 512, *513,* 519, 522, 522
briefs in Supreme Court cases, 510-11, 519

broadcast media, 235-36 Communications technologies, such as television and radio, that transmit information over airwaves.

Brown, Albert G., *377*
Brown, Jerry, *90*
Brown, Michael, *120,* 164
Brown, Sherrod, 546
Brown v. Board of Education, 153, 154, 167, 172-73, 520, 521, 525
Brown v. Board of Education II, 154, 173
Bryan, William Jennings, 557
Buchanan, Patrick, *301*
Budget and Accounting Act (1921), 540
Budget and Impoundment Control Act (1974), 540
Budget Committees, 410, 540, 542

budget deficit, 532, 536, 537, 538, 546 The amount by which a government's spending in a given fiscal year exceeds its revenue.
    and budget-making process, 540-41
    and fiscal policy, 553-54

California
- affirmative action in, 189, 190
- campaign financing in, 321
- cap-and-trade program in, 562
- Chinese immigrants in, 155
- elections in, 279
- electoral votes of, 304–5, 306
- environmental policies in, 90, 94
- gun laws in, 130
- initiatives in, 364
- Latinos in, 154
- marijuana laws in, 95
- and Missouri Compromise, 152
- same-sex marriage in, 182
- shooting incidents in, 131, 132

California, Miller v., 128

California, Robinson v., 113

campaign financing, 121, *281*, 281–84, 312–13, 320–25
- for advertisements, *319*, 324, 325
- in congressional elections, 333, 334, 387, 388, 401–2
- contribution limits in, 121, 321, *321*, 322, 323, 325
- corporations in, 121, 321, 322
- in election cycle, *281*
- 501(c)(3) organizations in, *361*, 361–62
- 501(c)(4) organizations in, 325, *361*, 362
- 527 organizations in, 269, 322, *361*, 362
- and freedom of speech, 121, 325
- hard money in, 322
- interest groups in, 347, 361–63, 366
- political action committees in, 269, *281*, 321, *321*, 322, *322*, *361*, 362
- political parties in, *281*, 281–84, *284*, 290, *321*, 322, 323, 324
- in presidential elections, 284, 303, 322, 323, *323*, 324, 362
- soft money in, 121, 322, 323
- Supreme Court on, 320, 321, 325, 362, 510, 524

campaigns, 309–25
- advertising in, 243, 316, 317, 318–20, *320*, 324, 325, 331, 362, 366
- congressional. *See* congressional campaigns and elections
- debates in, 318
- groups targeted in, 205
- media in, 242–43
- name recognition in, 316, 331
- party organizations in, 284
- positive or negative tone of, 317–18, 320

presidential. *See* presidential campaigns and elections
- push polls in, 216, 317
- spending limits in, 322, 325
- staff in, *313*, 315–16, 317
- voter mobilization in, 316–17, 325, 327
- voting cues in, 327–28

Canada
- foreign aid from, *641*
- health care spending in, 598
- trade with, 530, 564, 566, 638

Cantwell v. Connecticut, 113

Canyon Country Rural Alliance, 563

capital punishment, 60, *64*, 64–65, 139–40, 520

carbon emission regulations, 457, 459, 561, 562

Carpenter, Daniel P., 585

Carson, Ben, 249–50

Carswell, G. Harrold, 503

Carter, Jimmy, 309, *310*, 311, 328, 422–23, *447*, 622

casework, 384, 414 Assistance provided by members of Congress to their constituents in solving problems with the federal bureaucracy or addressing other specific concerns.

Castro, Raúl, *430*

categorical grants, 86, 88–89 Federal aid to state or local governments that is provided for a specific purpose, such as a mass-transit program within the transportation budget or a school lunch program within the education budget.

Cato Institute, 580

caucus, congressional, 271–72, 278, 286, 290, 398 The organization of Democrats within the House and Senate that meets to discuss and debate the party's positions on various issues in order to reach a consensus and to assign leadership positions.

caucus, electoral, 279, 279–81, 282, 283 A local meeting in which party members select a party's nominee for the general election.

in presidential elections, 282, 302–4
- voter turnout for, 327

CBS, 129

cell phone privacy and security, *58*, 132, 134, 381

censorship, 250

Center for Responsive Politics, 238

Centers for Disease Control
- gun-related research, 479

Central American Free Trade Agreement (CAFTA), 566, 638

Central Intelligence Agency, 135, 265, 628, 630

centralized groups, 347, 348 Interest groups that have a headquarters, usually in Washington, D.C., as well as members and field offices throughout the country. In general, these groups' lobbying decisions are made at headquarters by the group leaders.

cert pool, 509 A system initiated in the Supreme Court in the 1970s in which law clerks screen cases that come to the Supreme Court and recommend to the justices which cases should be heard.

Chakrabarti, Samidh, 232

Chamber of Commerce, *346*, 359

Chavez, Cesar, 154

checks and balances, 6, 37, 41, 51–58, 65–66 A system in which each branch of government has some power over the others.
- Antifederalist concerns about, 49
- exclusive powers in, 51–54
- judicial branch in, 6, 52, 57, 492, 493, 525
- negative powers in, 56–58
- in practice, 53
- shared powers in, 54–56
- in War on Terror, 53

chemical weapons
- in Syria, 56, 428, 442, 443, 617, 629, 633
- as weapons of mass destruction, 648

Cheney, Dick, 440

Cher, 129

Commons, John R., 576

Common Sense (Paine), 36

Common Sense Caucus, 376

community, political socialization in, 203

commutations, presidential power in, 433

competitive federalism, 90, 96, 97 A form of federalism in which states compete to attract businesses and jobs through the policies they adopt.

Comprehensive Addiction and Recovery Act (2016), 590

compromise in political conflicts, 11–12
   at Constitutional Convention, 39–48, 50

Compromise of 1850, 421

concurrent powers, 73, 74 Responsibilities for particular policy areas, such as transportation, that are shared by federal, state, and local governments.

concurrent resolution, 405

concurring opinions, *514*

Confederacy, 121, *124*, 152

confederal government, 8, 74 A form of government in which states hold power over a limited national government.

confederations, 347 Interest groups made up of several independent, local organizations that provide much of their funding and hold most of the power.

conference, congressional, 272, 286, 398 The organization of Republicans within the House and Senate that meets to discuss and debate the party's positions on various issues in order to reach a consensus and to assign leadership positions.

conference, of Supreme Court justices, 512

conference committees, 403, 409 Temporary committees created to negotiate differences between

the House and Senate versions of a piece of legislation that has passed through both chambers.

confessions, Miranda rights in, 137

confidentiality, executive privilege for, 433–37

conflicts, political, 5, 8, 9, 10–12, 14
   compromise in, 11–12, 39–48, 50
   and Constitution, 32, 65–66
   critical analysis of political information in, 24–26
   on economic policies, 15, 32, 567–68
   on foreign policy, 643, 650
   gridlock in, 394
   on health care, 12, *19*, 610
   as human nature, 37
   interest group influence in, 368–69
   resolution of, 20–24
   on social policy, 572–75, 610
   sources of, 15–20

Congress, 374–417. *See also* House of Representatives; Senate
   accountability in, 286, 291, 381, 383
   advice and consent role of, 55, 64, 413, 500, 502, 505
   Articles of Confederation on, 33–34, 39
   bipartisan compromise in, 291
   budget process in, 540–41, 542, 543
   campaigns and elections for. *See* congressional campaigns and elections
   casework of, 384, 414
   caucuses and conferences in, 271–72, 286
   checks and balances with other branches, 6, 52, 57–58
   civil rights legislation of, 182–85
   committee system in, 402–3, 404–10, 413, 540, 542, 630
   constituency of, *381*, 381–83, *382*
   constituency service in, 387–88
   Constitutional Convention compromise on, 41–42
   Constitution on, *39*, *40*, 76, 376–77, 404, 539
   credit claiming in, 384, 396
   economic policy role of, 539–41, 542, 543, 545, 549, 567–68
   enumerated powers of, 51–54, 376–77
   exclusive powers of, 51–54
   foreign policy role of, 626, *626*, 629, 630, 650

formal structures in, 396–404

gridlock in, 394

home styles in, 385

ideological polarization in, 272, *273*, *400*, 400–401

impeachment power of, 56–57, 413, 446

informal structures in, 395–96

interest groups lobbying, 340–73

legislative process in, 404–12, 430–33

logrolling in, 395

net worth of members in, 378

oversight role of, 412–13, 481–82, 625

political parties in, 271–72, 284–87, 290–91, 396–402, 403

pork-barrel spending of, 378

power of the purse, 54, 57, 412–13, 630, 632

public opinion on, 378, *382*, 382–83, 394–95

racial and ethnic composition of, 378, 379

regulatory policy role of, 561

relationship with president, 285–86, 377–78, 430, 444–46

representation in, 378–83

and revolving door with interest groups, 348, 349

roll call votes in, 400

seniority in, 396

shared powers of, 55–56

social policy role of, 583–84, 586–89, 604–5, 609–10

specialization in, 396

staff in, 404

testimony at hearings of, 358, 413

typical workday in, 385, 386

and unilateral presidential actions, 444–46

universalism in, 395

war powers of, 55–56, 630, 632

women in, 19, 379, 380, 384–85, *387*, 398, 502

Congress: The Electoral Connection (Mayhew), 383

Congressional Black Caucus, 188

Congressional Budget Office, 540, 542, 543, 580, 600

congressional campaigns and elections, 296–301, *302*, 381, 383–93
   in 1814, 266
   in 1932, 576
   in 1994, 604

consent of the governed, 37 The idea that government gains its legitimacy through regular elections in which the people living under that government participate to elect their leaders.

conservative ideology, 19, 20, 94, 201, 202 The side of the ideological spectrum defined by support for lower taxes, a free market, and a more limited government; generally associated with Republicans.

constitutional authority, 423, 424, 424, 450 Powers derived from the provisions of the Constitution that outline the president's role in government.

constitutional interpretation, 60, 491, 493, 500 The process of determining whether a piece of legislation or governmental action is supported by the Constitution.

constructivism, 617, 618 The idea that foreign policy is shaped by how a state's leaders define the national interest, ideology, and other factors.

defendant, 494–95 The person or party who brings a case to court.
rights of, 132–40

defense attorney, right to counsel from, 138–39

Defense Department, 428, 461, *470*, *472*, *474*, 628

Defense of Marriage Act, 182, 185, 499

Deferred Action for Childhood Arrivals (DACA), 374, *375*, 376, 414

deflation, 534–35 A decrease in the general prices of goods and services.

De Jonge v. Oregon, 113

de jure, 173 Relating to actions or circumstances that occur "by law," such as the legally enforced segregation of schools in the American South before the 1960s.

Delaware, *47*, 304, *305*, 321

delegate, 380–81 A member of Congress who loyally represents constituents' direct interests.

democracy, 21, 23, 24 Government by the people. In most contexts, this means representative democracy in which the people elect leaders to enact policies. Democracies must have fair elections with at least two options.
media in, 253
and nation building, 618, 623
political parties in, 286, 288, 289–91
representative, 21, 41
republican, 36–37

Democratic Congressional Campaign Committee, 272, *281*

Democratic Governors' Association, 269

Democratic Leadership Council, 269, *281*

Democratic National Committee, *265*, 268, 270, 281, *281*

Democratic Party, 264, 292
in bipartisan compromises, 291
in "blue states," *15*, 16
as brand name, 270
in campaign financing, *281*, 281–84, *323*, 324
coalitions in, *276*, 276–77
congressional caucuses of, 271–72, 278, 398
in congressional elections, 247, 268, 291, 296, 298, 299, 329, 331, 333–36, 446
on Constitution as living document, 60
in divided government, 286
economic policies of, 15, 32, 530, 532, 541, 550, 552, 561
in election process, 278–84
on fake news, 4
and federal bureaucracy, 468, 469, 473
on federal government, 267, 532
on health insurance, 572–74, 601
history of, *265*, 265–68
identification with, 203, 205, 272–77, *275*
and ideological polarization, 220, *221*, *400*, 400–401
Latinos in, 17, 155
liberal ideology in, 19, 23
media coverage on, 247
New Deal supported by, 468
organization of, 267, 268–70, *270*
party unity in, *399*, 400
party votes in, *399*, 400
platform of, 284, *314*
policy priorities in, 271, 272, 276, 284, 289–90
in presidential election (2016), 16, 262, *263*
public opinion in, 210–11, 218, 228
racial, gender, and ethnic identity in, *17*, 17
in Reconstruction era, 153
recruiting and nominating candidates from, 278–81, 282, 303, 304
in redistricting, 390, 391, 392
reelection of incumbents in, 329, *330*, 385, 389
on school vouchers, 608
on slavery, 266
social policies of, 576, *583*, 583–84, 585
on Social Security, 595, 596–97
in state and local governments, 45
trade policies of, 566–67
on voter ID laws, 302

Democratic-Republicans, 266, 492

Democratic Senatorial Campaign Committee, 272, *281*

deregulation of media, 236

Derthick, Martha, 98

descriptive representation, 378–80 Representation in which a member of Congress shares the characteristics (such as gender, race, religion, or ethnicity) of his or her constituents.

desegregation
of hotels and restaurants, 174
of military, 443
of public schools, 88, 154, 167, 170, 172–73, 182, 520, 521

Des Moines Independent Community School District, Tinker v., 516

détente, 622 An approach to foreign policy in which cultural exchanges and negotiations are used to reduce tensions between rival nations, such as between the United States and the Soviet Union during the 1970s.

DeVos, Betsy, *89*, 426, 439, 608, 609

dictatorships, 32, 621

Dingell, John, 13

diplomacy, as foreign policy tool, 637–38, *639*

direct incitement test, 119 Established in *Brandenburg v. Ohio*, this test protects threatening speech under the First Amendment unless that speech aims to and is likely to cause imminent "lawless action."

direct lobbying, 355–58, 364 Attempts by interest group staff to influence policy by speaking with elected officials or bureaucrats.

Director of National Intelligence, 628, 630

disabled people, 89, 97, 185
Supplemental Security Income for, 604

disaster response, *73*, 88, 96
Defense Department in, 628
fake news on, 239, *239*

discount rate, 558 The interest rate that a bank must pay on a short-term loan from the Federal Reserve Bank.

without due process of law." Other specific due process rights are found in the Fourth, Fifth, Sixth, and Eighth Amendments, such as protection from self-incrimination and freedom from illegal searches.

Duncan, Arne, 609
Duncan v. Louisiana, 113
Dunne, Finley Peter, 519

Duverger's Law, 288 The principle that in a democracy with single-member districts and plurality voting, only two parties' candidates will have a realistic chance of winning political office, as in the United States.

earmarks, 395–96 Federally funded local projects attached to bills passed through Congress.

Earned Income Tax Credit, 603, 604, *605, 606*
economic conditions
 in business cycle, 552
 in financial crisis (2008), 533, 535, *548,* 548–50, 559
 and fiscal policy, 551–56
 gross domestic product as measure of, 535–36, 638, *638*
 Misery Index on, *534, 535*
 and monetary policies, 558
 and public opinion of president, 208, 210, 218, 223, 541
 as public policy priority, 225, 226, *226*
 and trade policies, 638, *638,* 643–44
 and voting decisions, 309, 310, *310,* 312, 329, 332, 333, *335,* 336

economic depression, 533 A deep, widespread downturn in the economy, like the Great Depression of the 1930s.
 deflation in, 534–35
 in Great Depression. *See* Great Depression

economic equality, 15, 22, 38, 161
economic individualism, 15
economic interests
 at Constitutional Convention, 38, *38,* 41
 political conflicts on, 15, 32

economic policies, 530–71
 balance of payments in, 537, 562–67
 budget deficit in. *See* budget deficit
 as congressional election issue, 329, 331, 333, 336
 congressional role in, 539–41, 542, 543, 545, 549, 567–68
 as Constitutional Convention issue, 38, *38,* 41
 of Democratic Party, 15, 32, 530, 532, 541, 550, 552, 561
 employment in, 533, 535, 539
 Federal Reserve System in, 533, 545–47
 and financial crisis (2008), 533, 535, 548–50, 559
 fiscal, 533, 540, 551–56, 568
 and foreign policy, 638–40
 free market in. *See* free market
 goals of, 533–39
 gross domestic product in, 535–36
 inflation in, 534–35
 Keynesian, 551, 552, 553, 554, 568
 monetary, 312, 533, 540, 545, 557–59
 of Obama, 309, *310,* 312, 541, 549, 552, 562
 political conflicts on, 15, 32, 567–68
 in poverty and income inequality, 579–82
 as presidential election issue (2016), 335, 530, 535, 565
 presidential power in, 540, 541–45, 547, 567–68
 and public opinion of president, 208, 210, 218, 223
 as public policy priority, 225, 226, *226*
 regulatory, 559–62
 of Republican Party, 15, 32, 530, 532, 540, 541, 550, 551–52, 554, 561, 580–82, 586
 on trade. *See* trade policies
 trade-offs between, 539, 561, 562
 Treasury Department in, 547–48
 of Trump, 530, 532, *532,* 541, 543, 550, 552, 556, 561–62

economic sanctions, 640, 649, *649* Penalties applied by one country or group of countries on another, usually in the form of tariffs or other trade barriers.
 on Iran, 640, 649
 on North Korea, 649, *649*
The Economist, 243

education
 affirmative action in, 150, 189, 190, 191, 194
 and civil liberties, 105
 and collective action problems, 7
 controversial speech in, 102–4, 143–44
 desegregation of, 88, 154, 167, 170, 172–73, 520, 521
 drug testing in, 135
 federal government role in, 88, 89, *89,* 585, 606–9
 gender discrimination in, 177, 179, 183–84, *185*
 Great Society programs in, 577, 578
 and group identity, 206
 hate speech in, 102, 122
 for military veterans, 533, 606
 prayer in, 106, 111, 114–15, 521, *521*
 religious schools in, 115
 school choice programs in, 585, 608, 609
 school shootings in, *93, 130,* 131
 school vouchers in, 608, 609
 search policies in, 132–33
 separate but equal doctrine in, 172–73
 social policies on, 577, 578, 585, 606–9
 standardized testing in, 607
 states' rights in, 90, 585, 606
 student activity fees in, 121–22
 student loans for. *See* student loans
 unfunded mandates in, 89
Education Department, 7, *185,* 470, 472, *474,* 606, 627
Edwards, George C., III, 448
Egypt, 104, 640
Eighth Amendment, 64, 64–65, *108, 113,* 139–40, 520
Eisenhower, Dwight D., 186, 422, 446, 501, 521
elastic clause, 54, 59
elderly
 number in population, *593*
 in poverty, 579, *581,* 592

election cycle, 281, 309 The two-year period between general elections.

Election Day, 299, 300
elections, 296–339
 accountability in, 286–87, 291, 299, 381, 383

foreign aid from, *641*
health care spending in, 598
hyperinflation in, *559, 559*
in World War II, 620
Gerring, John, 284
Gerry, Elbridge, 49, 106, 390

gerrymandering, 390, 391, 392 Attempting to use the process of re-drawing district boundaries to benefit a political party, protect incumbents, or change the proportion of minority voters in a district.

get out the vote, 317, 332 A campaign's efforts to "get out the vote" or make sure its supporters vote on Election Day.

Gibbons v. Ogden, 78, 78
GI Bill (1944), 533, 606
Gideon, Clarence, 139
Gideon v. Wainwright, 113, 139
Ginsburg, Ruth Bader, 488, 490, 503, 512, 513, 519, 522, 522, 524, 526
Gitlow, Benjamin, 112
Gitlow v. New York, 112, *113*
glasnost, 622

globalization, 643–46, 644, 645 The increase over the last generation in trade, travel, and the flow of ideas and beliefs between nations.

global warming, 90, 479. *See also* climate change

going public, 448–49 A president's use of speeches and other public communications to appeal directly to citizens about issues the president would like the House and Senate to act on.

gold, as currency standard, 557, *557*
Goldberg, Jonah, 262, 296
Goldman Sachs, *549*
Goldwater, Barry, 318, *319*
Goodyear Tire & Rubber, Ledbetter v., 180, *500*
Goodyear Tire & Rubber Company, 180, *500*
Google, *346,* 362, 366, 560
Gorbachev, Mikhail, *422,* 622

Gore, Al, *301, 304, 308*
Gore, Bush v., 514, 522
Gorsuch, Neil, 23, *55,* 411, 426, *501, 503, 504, 504,* 518, 519, *522, 523*

GOTV (get out the vote), 317, 332 A campaign's efforts to "get out the vote" or make sure its supporters vote on Election Day.

government, 5 The system for implementing decisions made through the political process.
bureaucracy of, 454–87
confederal, 8, 74
divided, 286, 584
federal. *See* federal government
forms of, 8, 33, 44, 73–74
goals of, 5–8
levels of, 73
local. *See* local government
in parliamentary system, 44
president as head of, 424
public opinion on, 222, *222–24, 223, 224*
state. *See* state government
unified, 57, 286, 299, 450
unitary, 8, 74

Government Accountability Office, 136
Government Performance and Results Act (1993), 587
GPS tracking devices, 134
Grand Canyon Trust, 563

grandfather clause, 153 A type of law enacted in several southern states to allow those who were permitted to vote before the Civil War, and their descendants, to bypass literacy tests and other obstacles to voting, thereby exempting whites from these tests while continuing to disenfranchise African Americans and other people of color.

Gratz v. Bollinger, 179
grazing rights, 563
Great Britain
colonial policies of, 32

multilateral actions of, 617
trade with, 566
as UN Security Council member, 637
in World War II, 620

Great Compromise, 42, 43 A compromise between the large and small states, proposed by Connecticut, in which Congress would have two houses: a Senate with two legislators per state and a House of Representatives in which each state's representation would be based on population (also known as the Connecticut Compromise).

Great Depression, 82, *82,* 88, 533, 559
deflation in, 534–35
and New Deal programs, 467, 589
and political parties, 267
and presidential power, 421–22
social policy in, 576, 589
and trade policies, 567

Great Society, 88–89, 225, 468, 577–78, 584 The wide-ranging social agenda promoted by President Lyndon Johnson in the mid-1960s that aimed to improve Americans' quality of life through governmental social programs.

Green, Donald, 204, 274
Green Bay Packers, *94, 98*
green jobs, 562
Green Party, 287, 288
Greensboro, North Carolina, 167–68
Gregory v. Ashcroft, 91

gridlock, 394 An inability to enact legislation because of partisan conflict within Congress or between Congress and the president.

Griswold, Estelle, 140–41
Griswold v. Connecticut, 113, 140–41

gross domestic product, 535–36 The value of a country's economic output taken as a whole.
and budget deficit, 538
and discretionary spending, 553
and health care spending, 600, *600*
and tax rates, 554
and trade, 638, *638*

gross national income, and foreign aid, 640–41, *641*

ground game, 317 A campaign's efforts to "get out the vote" or make sure its supporters vote on Election Day.

group identity, 204–6, *206*
  and descriptive representation, 378–80
  in population of U.S., 18, *18*
Grunwald, Michael, 426
Grutter v. Bollinger, 179
Guajardo, Idelfonso, *544*
Guantánamo Bay detention center, 53, 57
Guardian, 244, 245
Gun Control Act (1968), 130
Gun-Free School Zones Act (1990), 92, *93*
gun laws, *93*, 586
  on bump stocks, 368–69
  and commerce clause, 92
  as congressional election issue (2018), *335*, 336
  interest groups concerned with, 342, 358, 365, 368–69
  and mass shootings, 131, 368
  media coverage of, 250–51, *251*
  party votes on, 402
  as presidential election issue (2016), *314*, 332
  public opinion on, 202, *202*, 211, 220, *226*, 227, 368–69
  research limitations on, 479
  and Second Amendment, 130–31
  "stand your ground," 131
  state differences in, 77, 90, 130, 131
Gutiérrez, Luis, 374, 391

habeas corpus rights, 106
Hague v. CIO, 113
Hamblin, Andrew, 105
Hamdan v. Rumsfeld, 53
Hamilton (musical), 44
Hamilton, Alexander, 35, 37, 50, 77
  at Constitutional Convention, 43
  Federalist Papers of, 235
  on implied powers, 63
  on judicial branch, 54, 490, 492, 521
Hamilton v. Regents of the University of California, 113
Hamlin, Argersinger v., 113
Hancock, John, 39
Hannity, Sean, 248, 249

hard money, 322 Donations that are used to help elect or defeat a specific candidate.

hard news, 255, 257 Media coverage focused on facts and important issues surrounding a campaign.

Hardwick, Bowers v., 143, 181, 182
Harley-Davidson, *532*
Harrison, Benjamin, 308
Harvard University affirmative action policy, 191
Haspel, Gina, 630
Hatch, Orrin, 278, 311, *312*
Hatch Act (1939), 477, *477*
hate crimes, *164*, 164–66, 185

hate speech, 102, 122–23 Expression that is offensive or abusive, particularly in terms of race, gender, or sexual orientation. It is currently protected under the First Amendment.

Hawaii, 56, 620
Hawaiians, Native, *18*
Hayes, Rutherford B., 308
Haynsworth, Clement, 503

head of government, 424 One role of the president, through which he or she has authority over the executive branch.

head of state, 424 One role of the president, through which he or she represents the country symbolically and politically.

Head Start, 577
Health and Human Services Department, *470*, 474, 587
health care
  Affordable Care Act on. *See* Affordable Care Act
  annual spending on, 598, *598*, 600, *600*
  best practices in, 602
  bureaucracy in, 584
  for children, 541, 599, 603
  computerized medical records in, 602
  as congressional election issue (2018), *335*, 335–36
  Great Society programs in, 578
  political conflicts on, 12, *19*, 610

  for preexisting conditions, 601, 603
  as presidential election issue (2016), 313–14, *314*
  public opinion on, 202, 207, *207*, 217–18, 227
  as public policy priority, 225, 226, *226*
  racial disparities in, 162–63
  social policy on, 572–74, 578, 584, *598*, 598–603, 610
  state policies on, 86, 89, 93, 94, 96, 585, 599, 602
  Trump on, 12, 66, 218, 572, 574, 575, 578, 603
  for veterans, 413, 584
hearings, congressional, 358, 361
Hedden, Bill, 563
Heinlein, Robert A., 454
Heller, Dean, *335*
Henry, Patrick, 39, 49
Hibbing, John R., 11
Hibbs, Nevada Department of Human Resources v., 91
Hill, Anita, 502
Hispanics, *18*, 502, *502*. *See also* Latinos
Hobbes, Thomas, 6, 37
Hodges, Obergefell v., 10, 76, 182, 499
Hogan, Hulk, 127, *127*
Hogan, Malloy v., 113

hold, 411 An objection to considering a measure on the Senate floor.

Holder, Eric, 148, 150, 187
Holder, Shelby County v., 91
Hollings, Ernest, 135, 565
Holmes, Oliver Wendell, 60, 118–19
Homeland Security Department, 6, *470*, 474, 553, 628
homicide rates, media coverage on, 251, *251*, 252
homosexuals. *See* LGBTQ people
Hoover, Herbert, 576

horse race, 255 A description of the type of election coverage that focuses more on poll results and speculation about a likely winner than on substantive differences between the candidates.

hostile media effect, 248 The tendency of people to see neutral media coverage of an event as biased against their point of view.

House of Representatives
    Affordable Care Act in, 572–74, 602
    in budget process, 540, 542, 543
    committee system in, 402–3
    compared to Senate, 377, 381
    constituency of, 381, 388
    Constitutional Convention
        compromise on, 42
    descriptive representation in, 378,
        379
    districts represented in, 381
    economic policy role of, 540
    election to. *See* congressional
        campaigns and elections
    foreign policy role of, 630
    Freedom Caucus in, 19, 402
    ideological polarization in, 400
    impeachment process in, 446
    legislative process in, 404–12
    party structure in, 397, 398
    party unity in, 399, 400
    party votes in, 399, 400
    redistricting of, 389–93. *See also*
        redistricting
    term in, 377, 383, 410
    Three-Fifths Compromise on, 46, 47
    typical workday in, 386
    whip system in, 398
    women in, 19, 385, 398
housing
    discrimination in, 159, 183
    government assistance in, 577, 579
    interest rates on loans for, 533
    mortgages on. *See* mortgages
    price of, in financial crisis (2008),
        548, 549
    tax deductions related to, 579
Housing and Urban Development
    Department, 422, 470, 474, 577
Howell, William G., 442
Huawei technology firm, 634
Hughes, Charles, 513
Humane Society, 364
human nature, view of Founders on,
    6, 37
human rights issues, 621, 623, 636
    in antiterrorism efforts, 648
    in globalization of trade, 645
Humphrey, Hubert, 414
Hungary. hyperinflation in, 559, 559
hunting, and right to bear arms, 131
Hurricane Harvey, 73, 88, 96, 239, 239,
    242, 255
Hurricane Irma, 88, 96

Hurricane Katrina, 586
Hurricane Maria, 96, 255, 628
Hurricane Sandy, 578
Hustler magazine, 126
hyperinflation, 559, 559

Idaho, 176, 177

ideological polarization, 220–22, 221
    Sharp differences in Americans'
    overall ideas of the size and scope of
    government.
    of Congress, 272, 273, 400, 400–401
    of political parties, 220, 221, 272, 273,
        277, 400–401
    social media in, 234
    Trump affecting, 187

ideology, 19–20 A cohesive set of ideas
    and beliefs used to organize and
    evaluate the political world.
    conservative, 19, 20, 94, 201, 202
    liberal, 19, 20, 94, 201
    libertarian, 19–20
    and media bias, 249
    and media sources, 240–41
    and public opinion, 201, 202, 202,
        220–22, 221
    of Supreme Court justices, 503, 513,
        517, 518, 519, 521–22, 524, 525

"I Have a Dream" speech of King, 170,
    170
iHeartMedia, 236
Illinois, 123, 131, 251, 252, 391
Immigration and Customs Enforce-
    ment (ICE), 70, 71, 98
immigration policies, 190–93
    by-product theory on knowledge
        about, 240
    on Chinese, 155
    as congressional election issue
        (2018), 335, 336
    and DACA program, 374, 375, 376, 414
    executive orders on, 426–28
    of Obama, 187, 193, 425, 443
    party preferences on, 289–90
    political conflicts on, 4, 5, 17–18, 22
    as presidential election issue (2016),
        314, 314, 332
    public opinion on, 216, 216, 219, 227
    and sanctuary cities, 70, 72, 89, 98
    state and federal power in
        enforcement of, 70–72, 71

of Trump, 66, 70–72, 98, 187, 192,
    193, 285–86, 290, 314, 331, 332,
    374–76, 418, 425, 426–28, 443

impeachment, 56–57, 413, 433, 446 A
    negative or checking power over the
    other branches that allows Congress
    to remove the president, the vice
    president, or other "officers of the
    United States" (including federal
    judges) for abuses of power.

implied powers, 63–64 Powers
    supported by the Constitution that
    are not expressly stated in it.

income inequality, 15, 22, 38, 161, 566
    as congressional election issue
        (2018), 582
    and group identity, 206
    growth in, 579, 580, 582
    international comparison of, 535–36,
        536
    social policies in, 579–84
    in southern states, 38, 152–53
    for women, 18, 180, 180–81, 181, 500

income support, 603–5 Government
    programs that provide support to
    low-income Americans, such as
    welfare, food stamps, unemploy-
    ment compensation, and the EITC.

income taxes, 555, 555, 556
    marginal tax rate in, 551, 551, 556, 556

incumbency advantage, 385–89 The
    relative infrequency with which
    members of Congress are defeated
    in their attempts for reelection.

incumbents, 298–99, 311–12 A politician
    running for reelection to the office
    he or she currently holds.
    accountability of, 299
    advantage of, 385–89
    campaign staff of, 315–16
    constituency service of, 387–88
    credit claiming by, 384
    redistricting affecting, 390
    reelection of, 329–30, 330, 381, 383,
        383–89, 402
    retirement of, 311, 334, 335
    seniority of, 396
    and wave elections, 329

judicial restraint, 519, 521–22, 523 The idea that the Supreme Court should defer to the democratically elected executive and legislative branches of government rather than contradicting existing laws.

judicial review, 58, 491, 492–94, 521, 525 The Supreme Court's power to strike down a law or executive branch action that it finds unconstitutional. activism and restraint in, 176, 519, 521–22, 525–26

Judiciary Act (1789), 491, 493 The law in which Congress laid out the organization of the federal judiciary. The law refined and clarified federal court jurisdiction and set the original number of justices at six. It also created the office of the attorney general and established the lower federal courts.

jurisdiction, 496–97, 498, 507 The sphere of a court's legal authority to hear and decide cases.

jury trials, 49, 109, 139, 157
Justice Department, 470
    and affirmative action, 190
    and civil rights, 183
    discretionary spending on, 553
    and domestic surveillance, 136
    and executive privilege, 437
    and housing discrimination, 159
    and Microsoft, 560
    and Obama, 437, 443
    and police discrimination, 164
    and recreational marijuana, 95
    and redistricting, 176, 390, 391, 393
    and Russia investigation, 413, 418, 454, 472
    and sanctuary cities, 70
    in screening of lower-court judges, 503
    size of, 474
    solicitor general in, 509–10
    and Trump, 54, 72, 98, 125, 413, 418, 443, 454, 472, 484
    and Watergate investigation, 433

Kagan, Elena, 187, 503, 513, 519, 522
Kaibab National Forest, 563

Kansas, 90
Kansas-Nebraska Act, 421
Kaptur, Marcy, 391
Kasich, John, 102, 283
Kavanaugh, Brett, 291, 334–35, 518, 519
Keillor, Garrison, 180
Kelly, John, 438
Kennan, George F., 620
Kennedy, Anthony M., 191, 501, 518, 519, 520, 522, 522
Kennedy, John F., 168, 169, 182, 186, 521, 586
Kennedy, Robert F., 130, 169
Kentucky, 47, 173, 303
Kerry, John, 308, 435
Key, V. O., 198, 228
Keynes, John Maynard, 551

Keynesian economics, 551, 552, 553, 554, 568 The theory that governments should use economic policy, like taxing and spending, to maintain stability in the economy.

Keystone XL pipeline, 345
Kim Jong-un, 30, 31, 32, 430, 430, 617, 638, 649
Kimmel, Jimmy, 236
King, Angus, 278
King, Martin Luther, Jr., 130, 167, 170, 170
King, Rodney, 138
Kingdon, John, 590
Kissinger, Henry, 622
Klobuchar, Amy, 291, 291
Korean War, 135, 621
Kosovo, 623
Kucinich, Dennis, 391
Kuebel, Schilb v., 113
Ku Klux Klan, 119, 122, 124
Kurtzman, Lemon v., 115
Kushner, Jared, 438, 439, 439, 587

labor costs, 564
Labor Department, 470, 474, 604
labor unions, 343, 353–54, 483, 577
Laffer, Arthur, 551
Laffer curve, 551, 552
Lamb, Conor, 309, 311
Land Grant College Act, 606
Las Vegas, Nevada, 128, 131, 368

latent opinion, 201 An opinion formed on the spot, when it is needed (as

distinct from a deeply held opinion that is stable over time).

Latinos
    civil rights of, 154–55
    composition of U.S. population, 18, 379
    in Congress, 378, 379
    discrimination against, 154, 159, 189
    diversity of, 155
    as federal court judges, 502, 502
    party identification of, 17, 155
    police shooting of, 165
    presidential appointments of, 186, 187
    socioeconomic indicators on, 161
    voting by, 160, 332, 333
Lauer, Matt, 180
law enforcement, 521
    discretionary spending on, 553
    as government function, 6, 7
    Miranda rights in, 137
    and police shootings of African Americans, 163, 163–64, 165, 171
    racial profiling in, 148–50, 163, 192, 193, 194
    search and seizure in, 106, 107, 132–36
Lawrence, John Geddes, 143, 181
Lawrence v. Texas, 143, 181, 522
laws. See legislation
lawsuits and litigation strategies of interest groups, 358–59
lawyers
    right to counsel from, 138–39
    women as, 156–57
"layer cake" and "marble cake" models of federalism, 82, 83, 84
lead in water supply, 163, 464
League of Nations, 421, 620

leaking, 125, 243–45, 244 The practice in which someone in government provides nonpublic information to a reporter, with the aim of generating press coverage favorable to the leaker's aims.

Ledbetter, Lilly, 180, 500
Ledbetter v. Goodyear Tire & Rubber, 180, 500
LeFevre, Dell, 563
legal counsel, right to, 138–39

legislation. *See also specific laws.*
  and bureaucracy, 458
  on civil rights, 182–85
  enforcement of. *See* law
    enforcement
  interest groups drafting, 358
  judicial review of, 58, 491, 492–94,
    521, 525
  omnibus, 410, 540, 543
  party influence on, 284–87, 290
  pork barrel, 378, 384, 395, 396, 396,
    410
  on presidential authority, 423, 424,
    424
  presidential interpretation and
    implementation of, 444
  presidential veto of, 57, 409, 430–33,
    442, 545, 630
  signing statements on, 444
  types of, 405
legislative branch, 6, 40, 42–43. *See also*
  Congress
  Articles of Confederation on, 33–34,
    39
  checks and balances with other
    branches, 6, 52, 57–58
  Constitutional Convention compro-
    mise on, 41–42
  Constitution on, 39, 40, 76, 376–77,
    404, 539
  in parliamentary system, 44
  shared powers of, 55–56
legislative process, 404–12
  for Affordable Care Act, 410, 412,
    572–74, 590
  amendments in, 409, 412
  authorization and appropriation in,
    409
  on budget, 540–41, 542, 543, 545
  committee system in, 402–3, 404–10
  conventional, 404–9
  diagrams of, 406, 407
  discharge petition in, 409–10
  earmarks in, 395–96
  filibusters in, 411–12, 610
  logrolling in, 46, 395, 403
  markup in, 408
  president in, 57, 409, 410, 424–25,
    430–33, 442
  reconciliation in, 407, 411–12,
    540–41, 572
  vetoes in, 57, 409, 430–33, 442, 545,
    630
  voting in, 400, 409

Lehman Brothers, 549

Lemon test, 115 The Supreme Court
  uses this test, established in *Lemon
  v. Kurtzman,* to determine whether
  a practice violates the First Amendment's establishment clause.

Lemon v. Kurtzman, 115
Leno, Jay, 66
lesbian people. *See* LGBTQ people
Lessig, Lawrence, 365
"Letter from Birmingham Jail" (King),
  170
Levine, James, 180
Lewinsky, Monica, 413
Lewis, John, 396
LGBTQ people, 143, 151, 157–59
  civil rights of, 143, 150, 157–58,
    181–82, 185, 186, 194
  in Congress, 385
  discrimination against, 97, 143, 150,
    157–58, 159, 181–82, 185, 194
  equal protection of, 93
  hate crimes against, 185
  and interest groups, 362
  liberal policies on, 94
  in military, 66, 157–58, 186, 186, 187,
    193
  as political candidates, 328, 329,
    385
  as presidential election issue (2016),
    158, 314, 322
  privacy rights of, 143
  and same-sex marriage. *See*
    same-sex marriage
  and social movements, 166, 171
  and sodomy laws, 143, 181–82, 522
  and Stonewall uprising, 157, 158

libel, 126–27 Written false statements
  that damage a person's reputation. They can be regulated by the
  government but are often difficult
  to distinguish from permissible
  speech.

liberal ideology, 19, 20, 94, 201 The side
  of the ideological spectrum defined
  by support for stronger government
  programs and more market regulation; generally associated with
  Democrats.
  in domestic policies, 618

  of Supreme Court justices, 503, 513,
    517, 518, 519, 521–22, 524, 525

liberalism, 617, 618, 619, 620 The idea
  that foreign policy decisions reflect
  normative goals such as justice,
  equality, and human rights.

liberal or conservative ideology, 201 A
  way of describing political beliefs in
  terms of a position on the spectrum
  running from liberal to moderate to
  conservative.
  and ideological polarization, 220–22,
    221
  of Supreme Court justices, 503, 513,
    517, 518, 519, 521–22, 524, 525
Libertarian Party, 287, 288, 288

libertarians, 19, 19–20, 287, 288 Those
  who prefer very limited government
  and therefore tend to be conservative on issues such as social welfare
  policy, environmental policy, and
  government funding for education but liberal on issues involving
  personal liberty such as free speech,
  abortion, and the legalization of
  drugs.

liberty, 21–22, 23, 24, 36 Political
  freedom, such as the freedom
  of speech, press, assembly, and
  religion. These and other legal
  and due process rights protecting
  individuals from government
  control are outlined in the Bill of
  Rights of the U.S. Constitution.
  Antifederalist concerns about, 49
  and civil liberties, 102–47
  and conflict resolution, 21–22

Libya, 429, 430, 496, 619, 630, 641, 642
Liccardo, Sam, 70
life expectancy, 162, 596
Lighthizer, Robert, 544
Lilly Ledbetter Fair Pay Act, 180, 500
Limbaugh, Rush, 240, 249

limited government, 33 A political
  system in which the powers of
  the government are restricted to
  prevent tyranny by protecting
  property and individual rights.

multilateral action, 617, 618 Foreign policy carried out by a nation in coordination with other nations or international organizations.

Mulvaney, Michael, 481
murder rate, media coverage on, 251, *251, 252*
Murphy, Walter, 66
Murray, Charles, 102
Muslim countries, travel ban aimed at, 53, 57–58, 192, *192*, 445, *445*, 627

mutually assured destruction, 622 The idea that two nations that possess large stores of nuclear weapons— like the United States and the Soviet Union during the Cold War—would both be annihilated in any nuclear exchange, thus making it unlikely that either country would launch a first attack.

My Story (Parks), 167
NAACP, 160, 172, 188
Nader, Ralph, 288
Nadler, Jerrold, 410
NAFTA, 530, *544, 566,* 623
name recognition in campaigns, 316, 331
NARAL Pro-Choice America, *346,* 362
NASA, 7, 238, 364, 470, 477, 553
NASCAR, 243
Nassar, Lawrence G., 180
The Nation, 249
National Aeronautics and Space Administration (NASA), 7, 238, 364, 470, 477, 553
national anthem, athletes kneeling during, 171–72, 187
National Association for the Advancement of Colored People (NAACP), 160, 172, 188
National Association of Realtors, 345, *346,* 362

national committee, 268 An American political party's principal organization, comprising party representatives from each state.

National Democratic Institute, 636

National Economic Council, 544–45 A group of economic advisers created in 1993 to work with the president to coordinate economic policy.

National Education Association, 609
National Federation of Independent Business v. Sebelius, 91
National Football League, 171–72, 187
 Green Bay Packers in, *94, 98*
 Philadelphia Eagles in, 405, *408*
National Forest Service, 402, *457,* 470, 553
National Governors Association, 607
National Guard, 6, 426, 428
National Highway Traffic Safety Administration, 561
National Independent Automobile Dealers Association, 347
National Instant Criminal Background Check System, 131
National Journal magazine, 12, 257
National Labor Relations Act, 577
National Labor Relations Board v. Jones and Laughlin Steel Corporation, 81–82
National Organization for Women (NOW), 183
National Park Service, 454, 462, 482, 553
National Recovery Administration, 576
National Republican Congressional Committee, 272, *281,* 402
National Republican Senatorial Committee, 272
National Rifle Association, 130, 342, 343, *346, 358,* 365
 as centralized group, *347, 348*
 in opposition to policy change, 366–68, *369*
 public opinion mobilization efforts of, 361
National Science Foundation, 553
national security, 6, 75
 and civil liberties, 104–5
 foreign policy in, 616, 650
National Security Agency, 135–36, 143, 244, *244,* 628

National Security Council, 627, 628 An agency within the EOP that advises the president on matters of foreign policy.

national supremacy clause, 45, 75, 78, 98 Part of Article VI, Section 2, of the Constitution stating that the Constitution and the laws and treaties of the United States are the "supreme Law of the Land," meaning national laws take precedence over state laws if the two conflict.

National Turkey Federation, 346, 368, *368,* 369

nation building, 618, 623 The use of a country's resources, including the military, to help nondemocratic nations transform themselves into democracies.

Nation of Islam, 18, 188
Native Americans, *18,* 151, 620
 affirmative action policies for, 189
 civil rights of, 154, *155*
 presidential appointments of, 186
Nativity displays, 115
NATO (North Atlantic Treaty Organization), 621, 623, 630, 641–42
Natural Resources Defense Council, 360

natural rights, 36, 37 Also known as "unalienable rights," these rights are defined in the Declaration of Independence as "Life, Liberty, and the pursuit of Happiness." The Founders believed that upholding these rights should be the government's central purpose.

Nazi marchers, 123, 144
Near v. Minnesota, 113
Nebraska, 139–40, 305

necessary and proper clause, 54, 59, 75 Part of Article I, Section 8, of the Constitution that grants Congress the power to pass all laws related to its expressed powers; also known as the elastic clause.

Neighborhood Youth Corps, 577
Nelson, Bill, 327
Netflix, 366
net neutrality, 365–66
Nevada
 community standards on obscenity in, 128
 marijuana in, 95

bureaucracy under, 468, 479
campaign strategies of, 205
citizenship of, 198, *199*, 228
as commander in chief, 428, 429
and congressional elections, 389,
    402
DACA program of, 374
and Dakota Access Pipeline, 171
on discriminatory treatment, 159
and divided government, 57, 286
and drone attacks, 436
economy under, 309, *310*, 312, 541,
    549, 552, 562
education policies of, 607, 609
electoral votes for, *308*
environmental policies of, 429, 435,
    459, 562
executive orders of, 64, 331, 427, 443
executive privilege of, 437
fake news on, 239
and Federal Reserve System, 546
and Flint water crisis, 163
foreign policy of, 429, 430, *430*,
    618–19, 624, *629*, 633, 634, 635
on freedom of speech, 102
and gay rights, 158, *158*, 186, 187
on gender pay disparities, 180
going public, 448, 449
and government shutdowns, 402
and Guantánamo Bay detention
    center, 53, 57
and gun laws, 131
on hate crimes, 185
immigration policies of, 187, 193, *425*,
    443
inauguration of, 454, *455*
and marijuana laws, 95
media coverage of, 250
and national debt, 410
pardons by, 125, 433
presidential power of, 423
public opinion on, 198, *199*, 208, *209*,
    210, 218, 223, *225*, 332, *447*
reelection of (2012), 303
and Republican filibusters, 411
social policies of, 578, 584, 585
on Social Security, 596, *597*
spouse of, 440
on student loans, 340
on Supreme Court decisions, 523,
    524
and Syria, 56
trade policies of, 566, 634
and Trump election, 332

unfunded mandates of, 89
unilateral actions of, 443
vetoes from, 432, *432*
voter turnout for, 215–16
Obama, Michelle, 440
Obamacare. *See* Affordable Care Act
Obergefell, Jim, *76*
Obergefell v. Hodges, 10, *76*, 182, 499
obscenity, 128–29
obstruction of justice, 64
Ocasio-Cortez, Alexandria, *265*
Occupational Safety and Health
    Administration (OSHA), 483,
    561
O'Connor, Sandra Day, 92, 138, 143, 182,
    513, 519, 522
Office of American Innovation, 587
Office of Economic Opportunity, 577

Office of Management and Budget, 469,
544, 627 An office within the EOP
that is responsible for creating the
president's annual budget proposal
to Congress, reviewing proposed
rules, and performing other
budget-related tasks.

off the record, 241 Describes comments
a politician makes to the press on the
condition that they can be reported
only if they are not attributed to that
politician.

Ogden, Gibbons v., 78, *78*
Ohio
    presidential election in (2016), 305,
        307
    redistricting in, 389, 391
    school voucher program in, 115
    voter purge in, 161
    voter registration laws in, 511, *511*
Ohio, Brandenburg v., 119
Ohio, Mapp v., *113*, 134
oil
    and foreign policy, 622
    pipeline protests, *155*, 171
Oklahoma, 140, 154, 179, 283
Oliver, John, 238
Olympic Games (1980), 622

omnibus legislation, 410, 540, 543 Large
bills that often cover several topics
and may contain extraneous, or
pork-barrel, projects.

on background, 241 Describes
comments a politician makes to
the press on the condition that they
can be reported only if they are not
attributed to that politician.

O'Neill, Tip, 328
"one-person, one-vote," 390, 523

open market operations, 559 The process
by which the Federal Reserve
System buys and sells securities to
influence the money supply.

open primary, 279, 282, 299 A primary
election in which any registered
voter can participate in the contest,
regardless of party affiliation.

open rules, 412 Conditions placed on
a legislative debate by the House
Rules Committee allowing relevant
amendments to a bill.

open seat, 311 An elected position for
which there is no incumbent.
    in midterm congressional elections
        (2018), 278, 311, *312*, 334, 335

Open Society Foundations, 636
opinion writing by Supreme Court
    justices, 512–14, *514*
opioid overdose and addiction, 590
opportunity, equality of, 22, 188–89

oral arguments, *511*, 511–12 Spoken
presentations made in person by the
lawyers of each party to a judge or an
appellate court outlining the legal
reasons their side should prevail.

order, provision of, 6
Oregon, 95, 116, 131, 300
Oregon, De Jonge v., *113*
O'Reilly, Bill, 180
Organization for Economic Coopera-
    tion and Development, 554
Organization of the Petroleum Export-
    ing Countries (OPEC), 622

original intent, 60, 516, *517* The theory
that justices should surmise the
intentions of the Founders when
the language of the Constitution is
unclear.

presidential systems, compared to parliamentary systems, 8

president pro tempore, 398 A largely symbolic position usually held by the most senior member of the majority party in the Senate.

press. *See also* media
free, 2, 106, 110, 125–26, 129, 244
prior restraint on, 125
price of goods and services
deflation of, 534–35
exchange rate affecting, 564
government regulations on, 559–61
inflation of. *See* inflation
labor costs affecting, 564
in monopolies, 559–61
tariffs affecting, 532, 638, *640*

primary elections, 279, 279–81, **282, 283,** **299–300, 314** A ballot vote in which citizens select a party's nominee for the general election.
campaigns in, 316–18
policy issues in, 314
in presidential elections, 282, 302–4
silent or money primary in, 314
types of, *279,* 299
voter turnout in, 327

priming process, 246–47
Prince (musician), 590

principal–agent game, 462–63, 479, 561 The interaction between a principal (such as the president or Congress), who needs something done, and an agent (such as a bureaucrat), who is responsible for carrying out the principal's orders.

prior restraint, 125 A limit on freedom of the press that allows the government to prohibit the media from publishing certain materials.

Privacy Act (1974), 136

privacy rights, 140–43 Liberties protected by several amendments in the Bill of Rights that shield certain personal aspects of citizens' lives from governmental interference,

such as the Fourth Amendment's protection against unreasonable searches and seizures.
and abortion rights, 141–42
and gay rights, 143
reasonable expectation for, 107
in search and seizures, 132–36

privatization of Social Security, 578, 584, **586, 595, 596–97** The process of transferring the management of a government program (like Social Security) from the public sector to the private sector.

privileges and immunities clause, **76–77** The part of Article IV of the Constitution requiring that states must treat nonstate residents within their borders as they would treat their own residents. This was meant to promote commerce and travel between states.

problem of control, 462–65, 478, 479 A difficulty faced by elected officials in ensuring that when bureaucrats implement policies they follow these officials' intentions but still have enough discretion to use their expertise.

process, political, 8–10, 12–13, 14
citizen involvement in, 12–13, 94–97
in elections, 10, *12*
in social policy, 610
professional associations, *343*
profiling, racial, 148–50, 163–64, 192, 193, 194
Progressive Era, 466–67

progressive taxes, 556 Describes taxes that require upper-income people to pay a higher tax rate than lower-income people, such as income taxes.

Prohibition, repeal of, 62
Project Atmosphere, 136
Project Censored, 250
Project Veritas, 239
property rights, 535
Fifth Amendment on, *108,* 109, 138
Founders on, 36, 37

Fourteenth Amendment on, 109
patents in, 561
and slavery, 79, 152

proportional allocation, 303 During the presidential primaries, the practice of determining the number of convention delegates allotted to each candidate based on the percentage of the popular vote cast for each candidate. All Democratic primaries and caucuses use this system, as do some states' Republican primaries and caucuses.

protectionism, 156–57, 176 The idea under which some people have tried to rationalize discriminatory policies by claiming that some groups, like women or African Americans, should be denied certain rights for their own safety or well-being.

protectionist trade policies, 565, 566, 567, 568
protest movements, 167–72
Black Lives Matter, 164, 171–72
on oil pipeline, *155,* 171
on Vietnam War, 120, 121, 171, *516*
Women's March (2017) in, 19, 171, *171, 360, 360*
Pruitt, Scott, 464, 481, 562
Public Citizen, 343, 358

public goods, 7 Services or actions (such as protecting the environment) that, once provided to one person, become available to everyone. Government is typically needed to provide public goods because they will be under-provided by the free market.

public health, 105

public opinion, 198–231 Citizens' views on politics and government actions.
on abortion, 11, 206, *206,* 210, 301
on Congress, 378, *382, 382–83,* 394–95
considerations in, 207–11, *209, 210*
definition of, 200–201
on federal bureaucracy, 463, *463, 474, 475*

and filtering and framing of news, 250–51
on foreign policy, 634–36
formation process, 203–11, 228
on government and officeholders, 222, 222–24, 223, 224
on gun control, 202, 202, 211, 220, 226, 227, 368–69
on health care, 202, 207, 207, 217–18, 227
and ideology, 201, 202, 202, 220–22, 221
on immigration, 216, 216, 219, 227
importance of, 226–27
influence of, 226–27, 227
intensity of, 202
interest group influence on, 360–61
interpretation of polls on, 24–25
latency of, 201
measurement of, 211–20
media influence on, 245–53
media strategies of politicians on, 241–43
mobilization of, 360–61
policy mood in, 224–26, 225, 226
political influence of, 200–201, 201, 202, 205
on political parties, 262, 264
on presidential performance, 24–25, 208, 209, 210, 210, 218, 222, 223, 420, 446–49
on same-sex marriage, 204, 205
on Social Security, 591–92
on spending cuts, 474, 475
and Supreme Court decisions, 519–20
on terrorism, 200, 204, 208, 635–36, 647
types of, 201–2

public policy, 12, 533 A course of action pursued by government to address a specific problem.
   economic, 533. *See also* economic policies
   social, 575. *See also* social policy

public safety
   balance with civil liberties, 105, 105, 114
   and privacy rights, 133
Public Works Administration, 576
Puerto Rico, Hurricane Maria in, 255, 628

punctuated equilibrium model on policy change, 590
punishment
   capital, 64, 64–65, 139–40, 520
   cruel and unusual, 64, 64–65, 139–40, 520
Pure Food and Drug Act (1906), 467

purposive benefits, 353 Satisfaction derived from the experience of working toward a desired policy goal, even if the goal is not achieved.

push polls, 216, 317
Putin, Vladimir, 445
Puzder, Andrew, 426

Quartet on the Middle East, 617
queer/questioning people. *See* LGBTQ people
quotas in affirmative action programs, 189, 190, 191

race. *See also* African Americans
   and civil rights, 17, 80, 81, 151–54, 159–76, 182–83, 188–90
   composition of U.S. population, 18
   and descriptive representation, 378–80
   discrimination based on, 61, 81, 88, 91–92, 97, 148–50, 153–54, 159, 164, 172–76, 179, 183, 194, 267
   and equality, 22, 151, 159–66
   of federal court judges, 501–2, 502
   and group identity, 206
   and mixed-race marriage, 20
   and party identification, 17, 17, 267, 268–69, 276
   and profiling, 148–50, 163–64, 192, 193, 194, 335
   and redistricting, 390, 391, 393, 508
   and segregation. *See* segregation, racial
   and voter turnout, 159–60, 160, 182, 215–16, 327, 332, 333
race to the bottom, 96, 97, 566
Race to the Top, 607
racism, environmental, 163
radio, 235–36, 240
railroads
   Chinese immigrants in construction of, 155

Interstate Commerce Commission in regulation of, 560
   and Sherman Antitrust Act, 421, 560
Randolph, Edmund, 39, 42

random sample, 212, 214, 215 A subsection of a population chosen to participate in a survey through a selection process in which every member of the population has an equal chance of being chosen. This kind of sampling improves the accuracy of public-opinion data.

Rangel, Charles, 523
Rasmussen Reports polls, 24–25, 213
ratification of Constitution, 39, 48–50, 51, 106–8
   and amendments, 62, 63, 76

rational basis test, 176, 177, 178, 179, 181 The use of evidence to suggest that differences in the behavior of two groups can rationalize unequal treatment of these groups.

Rayburn, Sam, 401
Reagan, Ronald, 225, 328, 460, 468, 594
   approval rating of, 447, 449
   assassination attempt on, 130
   Civil Liberties Act signed by, 155–56
   economic policies of, 551–52, 554
   on federal bureaucracy, 463
   federal court nominations of, 504
   foreign policy of, 622
   interpretation and implementation of laws by, 444
   presidential power of, 422, 423
   social policies of, 578, 584

realignment, 267–68 A change in the size or composition of the party coalitions or in the nature of the issues that divide the parties. Realignments typically occur within an election cycle or two, but they can also occur gradually over the course of a decade or longer.

realism, 617, 618, 619, 620 The idea that a country's foreign policy decisions are motivated by self-interest and the goal of gaining more power.

reserved powers, 44–45, 76, 80, 90, 108
   As defined in the Tenth

reserve requirement, 558 The minimum amount of money that a bank is required to have on hand to back up its assets.

revolving door, 348, 349 The movement of individuals from government positions to jobs with interest groups or lobbying firms, and vice versa.

roll call votes, 400 A recorded vote on legislation; members may vote yes, no, abstain, or present.

runoff elections, 301 Under a majority voting system, a second election is held only if no candidate wins a majority of the votes in the first general election. Only the top two vote-getters in the first election compete in the runoff.

Senior Executive Service, 478

seniority, 396 The informal congressional norm of choosing the member who has served the longest on a particular committee to be the committee chair.

separate but equal doctrine, 153–54, 168, 172–73, 267, 468 The idea that racial segregation was acceptable as long as the separate facilities were of equal quality; supported by *Plessy v. Ferguson* and struck down by *Brown v. Board of Education*.

separation of church and state, 111, 114–15

separation of powers, 6, 8, 37, 41, 51, 58, 65–66 The division of government power across the judicial, executive, and legislative branches.

September 11, 2001, terrorist attacks, 53, 133, 423, 624, *624*, 628
    domestic surveillance after, 135–36, 410
    foreign policy after, 642, 646
    immigration policies after, 192
    public opinions on, 200, 204, 208, 635–36
Servicemen's Readjustment Act (1944), 533
Sessions, Jeff, 70, 247, 298, 366, 440, 472
    executive privilege of, 433, 437
    on free speech, 102
    on leaks to press, 125
    and marijuana laws, 95
Seventeenth Amendment, 62, 377
Seventh Amendment, *108, 113*
sexual harassment, 180
sexual orientation, 157–58, 181–82. *See also* LGBTQ people
Shapiro, Robert Y., 207
shared powers, 54–56
Shaw v. Reno, 175, *393*
Shays, Daniel, 35

Shays's Rebellion, 35 An uprising of about 1,500 men in Massachusetts in 1786 and 1787 to protest oppressive laws and gain payment of war debts. The unrest prompted calls for a new constitution.

Shelby, Richard, 301
Shelby County v. Holder, 91
Shepard, Matthew, 185
Sherman, Roger, 49
Sherman Antitrust Act (1890), 81, 421, 467, 560
Shinseki, Eric, 413, 584
Shulkin, David, 425
Sierra Club, 350, *350*, 351, 352

signing statements, 444 A document issued by the president when signing a bill into law explaining his or her interpretation of the law, which often differs from the interpretation of Congress, in an attempt to influence how the law will be implemented.

Silver, Nate, 215
simple resolution, 405
Simpson, Alan, *597*
Simpson, O. J., *495*
The Simpsons, 200
Sinclair, Barbara, 404
Sindram, Michael, 505
Singapore Summit, *639*

single-member districts, 288, 300 An electoral system in which every elected official represents a geographically defined area, such as a state or congressional district, and each area elects one representative.

Sixteenth Amendment, 62
Sixth Amendment, 60, *108, 113*, 138–39, 516
"size principle," Madison on, 41
Skowronek, Stephen, 449
Slager, Michael, *163, 164*

slander, 126–27 Spoken false statements that damage a person's reputation. They can be regulated by the government but are often difficult to distinguish from permissible speech.

Slants (rock band), 128, *128*
slavery, 22, 151–53, 158
    and Civil War, 48, *48*, 80, 152
    and Civil War amendments, 109, 152–53
    as Constitutional Convention issue, *40, 45*, 45–48

    and *Dred Scott* decision, *78, 79*, 79–80, 152, 493
    as "original sin," *45*, 47
    political party views on, 266
    and presidential power, 421
    state differences in, *40*, 45–48, 79
    Three-Fifths Compromise on, 46, 47
Smoot-Hawley Act (1930), 567
snake handling in religious practice, 105, *105*, 114
Snowden, Edward, 135, 244–45
socialization, political, 203
social media, 232–34
    fake news on, 2–4, 256
    interest group use of, 360–61
    political information on, 234, 237, 238, 239–40, 256, 257–58
    speech restrictions on, 123
social movements on civil rights, 166–72
social networks in political socialization, 203

social policy, 572–613 An area of public policy related to maintaining or enhancing the wellbeing of individuals.
    bureaucracy role in, 584–85, 587
    congressional and presidential role in, 583–84, 586–89, 604–5, 609–10
    contributory programs in, 576
    definition of, 575
    diffusion of, 590–91
    on education, 577, 578, 585, 606–9
    evaluation of, 587, 588–89
    in Great Society, 577–78, 584
    on health care, 572–74, 578, 584, *598*, 598–603, 610
    historical development of, 575–78
    implementation of, 587, 588–89
    on income support and welfare, 603–5
    interest group influence on, 586
    in New Deal, 576–77, 584
    noncontributory programs in, 576
    and ownership society, 578
    policy agenda on, 586–87
    policy-making process for, 586–91
    political conflicts on, 572–75, 610
    in poverty and income inequality, 579–84, 586
    regulatory, 561
    Social Security in, 591–97
    state role in, 585
    types of, *576*

split tickets, 328 A ballot on which a voter selects candidates from more than one political party.

splitting the difference, 46

spoils system, 266, 466, 466 The practice of rewarding party supporters with benefits like federal government positions.

sports
African-American athletes in, 154
kneeling during national anthem in, 171–72, 187
performance-enhancing drugs in, 135
and regional identity, 94, 98
Senate resolution honoring team in, 405, 408
Title IX on sex discrimination in, 183–84, 185
Stalin, Joseph, 2
Stamp Act (1765), 32
standardized testing in schools, 607
Standard Oil, 560

standard operating procedures (SOPs), 464, 466, 483 Rules that lower-level bureaucrats must follow when implementing policies.

standing, 496, 508 Legitimate justification for bringing a civil case to court.

standing committees, 402 Committees that are a permanent part of the House or Senate structure, holding more importance and authority than other committees.

Standing Rock Indian Reservation, 155, 171
"stand your ground" laws, 131
Stanton, Elizabeth Cady, 166
Starbucks, 644, 644

state capacity, 462 The knowledge, personnel, and institutions that the government requires to effectively implement policies.

State Department, 125, 454, 461, 466
evaluation of, 587

in executive branch, 470
foreign policy role of, 627, 637
number of employees in, 474
spending on, 469, 553
state government
Articles of Confederation on, 33, 34–35
autonomy of, 50, 73, 75, 77
balance of power with national government, 6, 8, 38, 44–45, 75–77
Constitution on, 76–77
in daily life, 14
education role of, 90, 585, 606
environmental policies of, 85, 90, 90, 94
federal grants to, 86–88
in federalism, 81–88. See also federalism
forms of, 8
in health care, 86, 89, 93, 94, 96, 585, 599, 602
judicial review on laws of, 493
marijuana policies of, 95
political parties in, 278
reserved powers of, 44–45, 76, 80, 90, 108
responsibilities of, 73, 74
social policy role of, 585
sovereign immunity of, 92
spending trends for, 87, 97
strong role of, 94–97
Supreme Count rulings on, 78, 78–82
Tenth Amendment on, 44–45, 80, 90–91
unfunded mandates for, 86, 89

State of the Union, 430, 448 An annual speech in which the president addresses Congress to report on the condition of the country and to recommend policies.
media coverage of, 237–38, 448
of Obama, 523, 524, 524
of Trump, 237–38, 438, 513

states
at Constitutional Convention, 40, 41–42, 43, 45–48
economic interests of, 38
selective incorporation of civil liberties in, 112, 113

states' rights, 80, 82, 90–93, 94 The idea that states are entitled to a certain amount of self-government, free

of federal government intervention. This became a central issue in the period leading up to the Civil War.

states' sovereign immunity, 92 Based on the Eleventh Amendment, immunity that prevents state governments from being sued by private parties in federal court unless the state consents to the suit.

statutory authority, 423, 424, 424, 450 Powers derived from laws enacted by Congress that add to the powers given to the president in the Constitution.

statutory interpretation, 493–94 The various methods and tests used by the courts for determining the meaning of a law and applying it to specific situations. Congress may overturn the courts' interpretation by writing a new law; thus, it also engages in statutory interpretation.

stealth democracy, 11
steel industry, 425, 530, 532, 566, 640
Stefanik, Elis, 380
Stein, Jill, 262, 263, 287
Stevens, John Paul, 519
Stevenson, Adlai, 310
Stewart, Jon, 198, 228, 255
Stewart, Potter, 128
Stockman, David, 554
Stone, Harlan Fiske, 513
Stonewall uprising, 157, 158
"stop-and-frisk" policy, 148, 149, 163

straight ticket, 328 A ballot on which a voter selects candidates from only one political party.

Strategic Arms Limitation Treaty I (SALT I), 622
strategic model on Supreme Court, 517–19

strict construction, 515–16 A way of interpreting the Constitution based on its language alone.

pardons granted by, 54, 433
as party leader, 447–48
policy agenda of, 45
political party of, 262, 264, 270, 278, 279, 280
presidential campaign and election (2016). *See* presidential campaign and election of 2016
presidential power of, 30–32, 57–58, 418–20, 442, 442, 450
on profiling, 148
progressive movement in response to, 347
public opinion on, 24–25, 207, 208, *209, 210,* 214, 215, 217, 227, 331, 389, 447, 449, *449*
regulations repealed by, 461, 561–62
Republican opposition to, 279, 280, 289, 331, 332, 447
and Russia, 54, 57, 64, 244, 443, 444, *445, 472*
and sanctuary cities, 75, 77, 98
social policies of, 578, 584, 585, 587
spouse of, 440
on student loans, 342
on Supreme Court decisions, 523, 524
Supreme Court nominations of, 23, 55, 291, 426, 488, *489, 501, 503, 504, 504,* 524
tax policies of, 285, 286, 290, 331, 541, *543, 552, 556*
trade policies of, 420, 425, 530, 532, *544, 564–68, 614–16, 626, 634, 639–40, 640, 643–46, 650*
travel ban of, 53, 57–58, 64, 177, 192, 445, 450, 490, 523, 524, 525, 627
unified government of, 450
unilateral actions of, *442, 443, 444, 445, 445, 450*
vetoes from, *432, 433*
and Women's March, 171
Trump, Ivanka, 438, *439*
Trump, Melania, 127, 440
Trump University, 502

trustee, 380, 381 A member of Congress who represents constituents' interests while also taking into account national, collective, and moral concerns that sometimes cause the member to vote against the preference of a majority of constituents.

trust fund for Social Security, 594–95, *595*
Tubman, Harriet, *152*
Turkey, 622

turkey farms, 478 Agencies to which campaign workers and donors can be appointed in reward for their service because it is unlikely that their lack of qualifications will lead to bad policy.

Twain, Mark, 378
Tweed, William "Boss," 266
Twelfth Amendment, 44, 62
Twenty-First Amendment, 62
Twitter, 2, 3, 234
    interest group use of, 360
    Park Service using, 454, 482
    political information on, 237, 238
    Trump use of, 242, 242, 243, 418, 449
Tyler, John, 421

Ukraine, 635, *635,* 636, 642
unalienable rights, 36, 37
Underground Railroad, 152, *152*
unemployment benefits, 116, 541, 575, 576, 603, 604
unemployment rate, 161, 218, 226, 309, 422
    in financial crisis (2008), 550
    in full employment, 533
    globalization affecting, 645, *645*
    in Great Depression, 267, 421, 576
    and inflation rate, *534, 535*
    Misery Index on, *534, 535*
    of Native Americans, 154
    trade-offs between economic goals in, 539
    trade policies affecting, 530, 532, 566, 643–44, 645
Unfunded Mandate Reform Act (1995), 86

unfunded mandates, 86, 89 Federal laws that require the states to do certain things but do not provide state governments with funding to implement these policies.

unified government, 57, 286, 299, 450 A situation in which one party holds a majority of seats in the House

and Senate and the president is a member of that same party.

unilateral actions, national, 617 Independent acts of foreign policy undertaken by a nation without the assistance or coordination of other nations.

unilateral actions, presidential, 442, 442–46, 450, 629 Any policy decision made and acted upon by the president and presidential staff without the explicit approval or consent of Congress.

Union League, 153

unitary executive theory, 443 The idea that the vesting clause of the Constitution gives the president the authority to issue orders and policy directives that cannot be undone by Congress.

unitary government, 8, 74 A system in which the national, centralized government holds ultimate authority. It is the most common form of government in the world.

United Farm Workers Union, 154
United Health, 602
United Kingdom, 8, 74, *536, 641*

United Nations, 422, 617, 618, 621, 630, 633, 636–37 An international organization made up of representatives from nearly every nation, with a mission to promote peace and cooperation, uphold international law, and provide humanitarian aid.
    General Assembly of, 637
    Security Council of, 637, 640

United States, Schenck v., 118
United States International Trade Commission, 638
United States Mexico Canada Agreement (USMCA), 566
United States Mint, 548
United States Patent Office, 561

straight tickets in, 328
by women, 18, 22, 62, 62, 156, 166, *333, 335*

voting cues, 270, 327–28, 330 Pieces of information about a candidate that are readily available, easy to interpret, and lead a citizen to decide to vote for a particular candidate.

voting machines, 301, *301*
voting rights, 65, 159–61, 183, 300, 495
    of African Americans, *17*, 22, 62, 88, 92, 109, 153, 159–61, 183, 513
    grandfather clause on, 153
    of Latinos, 155
    of Native Americans, 154
    Supreme Court on, 511, 513
    of women, 18, 22, 62, 62, 156, 166
Voting Rights Act (1965), *17*, 92, 161, 182, 183, 391, 393, 577
    amendments to, 183
    Supreme Court on, 511
voucher programs for education, 608, 609
Vox, 236

Wade, Roe v., 141, 142, 513, 521, 522
Wainwright, Gideon v., 113, 139
Wallace, George, 287
Wall Street bailout, 380, 549, 549–50
Walmart, 180–81, 362, 495
Ward, Kelli, *304*
War Department, 466
War of 1812, 55–56, 266, 428, 630
War on Poverty, 577, 606
War on Terror, 53, 57, 104–5, 541, 624, 631, 648
war powers, 55–56, 428–29, 442, 632
    of Congress, 55–56, 630, 632
War Powers Resolution (1973), 56, *428*, 428–29, 442, 443, 630
warrants, search, 132–34
Warren, Earl, 173, 501, 503, 517, 522
Warren, Elizabeth, 317, 479, *481*
Warsaw Pact, 621, 622, 623, 641, 642
Washington (state), 95
Washington, D. C., 131, 173
Washington, George, *33*, 34, 51, 55, *56*, 77, 377, 505
    on Congress, 377
    on constitutional amendments, 61
    at Constitutional Convention, 39
    on foreign policy, 619

foreign policy of, 63
justices appointed by, 492
presidential power of, 420, *421*
Washington Mutual, 549
Washington Post, 236, 238, 239, 244, 245, 248, 488
Washington v. Texas, 113
Watergate scandal, *222, 223,* 433, 437
water supply, lead in, 163, 464
wave elections, 329–30, 389
Ways and Means Committee, 403, 540

weapons of mass destruction, 648–50 Weapons that have the potential to cause large-scale loss of life, such as nuclear bombs and chemical or biological weapons.

Weber, Max, 464
Weigel, Dave, 248
Weinstein, Harvey, 180

welfare, 575 Financial or other assistance provided to individuals by the government, usually based on need.
    bureaucracy in, 584, *585*
    corporate, 579–80
    general, promotion of, 7–8
    income support in, 604–5
    state role in, 585

Westboro Baptist Church, *119,* 119–20, 144
West Wing of White House, 438
Whig Party, *265,* 266

whip system, 398 An organization of House leaders who work to disseminate information and promote party unity in voting on legislation.

white population
    composition of U.S., 18, *18*
    flight from cities, 173
    police shooting of, 165
    reverse discrimination against, 150, 189, 190, 191, 194
    socioeconomic indicators on, 161, *162,* 162–63
    voting by, 17, *17,* 159–60, *160,* 182
white primary practice, 153
white supremacists, 121, 124
    hate crimes by, 164, *164*
    and Trump, 66, 187

WikiLeaks, 125, *125,* 245, 433
Wilcox, John A., 377
Wilkie, Robert, 425
Wilson, Darren, *120*
Wilson, James, 39, 587
Wilson, Woodrow, 421, 620
Windsor, United States v., 91
Winner, Reality, 244

winner-take-all, 303, 305, 306 During the presidential primaries, the practice of assigning all of a given state's delegates to the candidate who receives the most popular votes. Some states' Republican primaries and caucuses use this system.

Wired magazine, 245
Wisconsin
    presidential election in (2016), 216, 249, 287, 305, *305,* 307, 309, 332, 530
    redistricting in, 390
    regional identity in, 98
    school vouchers in, 608
    student activity fees in, 121–22
Wisconsin v. Yoder, 105
Witte, Edwin, 576
Witte, John F., 608
Wolf v. Colorado, 113
women, 18–19
    abortion rights of, 141–42
    affirmative action policies for, 180, 189
    civil rights of, 151, 156–57, 166, *166*–67, 176–81, 183–84
    in Congress, 19, 379, 380, 384–85, 387, 398, 502
    discrimination against, 150, 156–57, 159, 176–81, 183–84, *185,* 500
    as federal court judges, 502
    on intercollegiate athletic teams, 460
    as jury members, 157
    party identification of, 17, 269, *335*
    pay gap for, 18, *180,* 180–81, *181,* 500
    presidential appointments of, 186, 187
    sexual harassment of, 180
    on Supreme Court, 187, 380, 503
    voting in 2016 election, *333*
    voting rights of, 18, 22, 62, 62, 156, 166

Voter Registration Information

State	Registration Deadline before Election*	Early Voting Permitted?**	Identification Required to Vote?**	More Information
Alabama	14 days	No	Photo ID requested	alabamavotes.gov
Alaska	30 days	Yes	ID requested; photo not required	elections.alaska.gov
Arizona	29 days	Yes	ID required; photo not required	azsos.gov/elections
Arkansas	30 days	Yes	Photo ID requested	sos.arkansas.gov
California	15 days; election-day registration permitted	Yes	No	sos.ca.gov
Colorado	8 days by mail or online; no in-person deadline	Yes (all voting by mail)	ID requested; photo not required	sos.state.co.us
Connecticut	14 days by mail; 7 days in person; election-day registration permitted	No	ID requested; photo not required	ct.gov
Delaware	24 days	No	ID requested; photo not required	elections.delaware.gov
District of Columbia	30 days by mail or online; no in-person deadline	Yes	No	dcboee.org
Florida	29 days	Yes	Photo ID requested	dos.myflorida.com/elections
Georgia	28 days	Yes	Photo ID required	sos.ga.gov
Hawaii	30 days; no in-person deadline	Yes	Photo ID requested	hawaii.gov/elections
Idaho	25 days; election-day registration permitted	Yes	Photo ID requested	idahovotes.gov
Illinois	27 days; 16 days online	Yes	No	elections.il.gov
Indiana	29 days	Yes	Photo ID required	in.gov/sos/elections
Iowa	10 days; election-day registration permitted	Yes	Photo ID required	sos.iowa.gov
Kansas	21 days	Yes	Photo ID required	kssos.org
Kentucky	27 days	No	ID requested; photo not required	elect.ky.gov
Louisiana	30 days; 20 days online	Yes	Photo ID requested	sos.la.gov
Maine	21 days by mail; no in-person deadline	Yes	No	maine.gov/sos
Maryland	21 days	Yes	No	elections.state.md.us
Massachusetts	20 days	No	No	sec.state.ma.us
Michigan	30 days	No	Photo ID requested	michigan.gov/sos
Minnesota	21 days; election-day registration permitted	Yes	No	mnvotes.org
Mississippi	30 days	No	Photo ID required	sos.ms.gov
Missouri	Fourth Wednesday prior to election	No	ID requested; photo not required	sos.mo.gov
Montana	30 days by mail; no in-person deadline	Yes	ID requested; photo not required	sos.mt.gov

State	Registration Deadline before Election*	Early Voting Permitted?**	Identification Required to Vote?**	More Information
Nebraska	Third Friday prior to election by mail; second Friday prior to election in person	Yes	No	sos.ne.gov
Nevada	31 days by mail; 21 days in person	Yes	No	nvsos.gov
New Hampshire	10 days; election-day registration permitted	No	ID requested; photo not required	sos.nh.gov
New Jersey	21 days	Yes	No	njelections.org
New Mexico	28 days	Yes	No	sos.state.nm.us
New York	25 days	No	No	www.elections.ny.gov
North Carolina	25 days	Yes	No	ncsbe.gov
North Dakota	No voter registration required	Yes	ID required; photo not required	vote.nd.gov
Ohio	30 days	Yes	ID required; photo not required	sos.state.oh.us
Oklahoma	24 days	Yes	ID requested; photo not required	ok.gov/elections
Oregon	21 days	Yes (all voting by mail)	No	sos.oregon.gov
Pennsylvania	30 days	No	No	votespa.com
Rhode Island	30 days; election-day registration permitted	No	Photo ID requested	www.elections.state.ri.us
South Carolina	30 days	No	ID requested; photo not required	scvotes.org
South Dakota	15 days	Yes	Photo ID requested	sdsos.gov
Tennessee	30 days	Yes	Photo ID required	tn.gov/sos/election
Texas	30 days	Yes	Photo ID requested	votetexas.gov
Utah	30 days by mail; 7 days in person; election-day registration permitted	Yes	ID requested; photo not required	elections.utah.gov
Vermont	Wednesday before the election; no in-person deadline	Yes	No	www.sec.state.vt.us/elections
Virginia	22 days	Yes	Photo ID required	elections.virginia.gov
Washington	30 days by mail and online; 8 days in person	Yes (all voting by mail)	ID requested; photo not required	sos.wa.gov/elections/
West Virginia	21 days	Yes	ID requested; photo not required	sos.wv.gov
Wisconsin	20 days by mail; election-day registration permitted	Yes	Photo ID required	sos.state.wi.us
Wyoming	14 days; election-day registration permitted	Yes	No	soswy.state.wy.us

* Information collected from Project Vote Smart, votesmart.org/elections/voter-registration (accessed 11/1/18).

** Information collected from National Conference of State Legislatures, www.ncsl.org (accessed 11/1/18). In states where an ID is "requested," voters who do not bring ID to the polls may be required to sign an affidavit of identity, vote on a provisional ballot, have a poll worker vouch for their identity, or take additional steps after Election Day to make sure their vote is counted.

Note: In November 2018, Arkansas and North Carolina passed ballot measures requiring a photo ID to vote. Michigan passed ballot measures to implement same-day and automatic voter registration.